Bradshaw's Railway Almanack, Directory, Shareholders' Guide, and Manual

George Bradshaw

BRADSHAW'S
RAILWAY MANUAL,
SHAREHOLDERS' GUIDE,
AND
OFFICIAL DIRECTORY for 1885;

CONTAINING THE
HISTORY AND FINANCIAL POSITION OF EVERY BRITISH RAILWAY;
ALSO OF THE
PRINCIPAL CANAL AND ROLLING STOCK COMPANIES;
WITH
STATISTICS, POWERS, AND OTHER DATA TO THE CLOSE OF THE YEAR;
THE RAILWAY INTEREST IN PARLIAMENT, ETC.;
ACCOMPANIED BY AN
ALPHABETICAL ARRANGEMENT OF THE WHOLE ADMINISTRATIVE AND EXECUTIVE STAFFS IN THE THREE KINGDOMS;
TO WHICH IS ADDED
COPIOUS INFORMATION RELATING TO FOREIGN AND COLONIAL LINES;
ILLUSTRATED WITH ELABORATE
STEEL-ENGRAVED RAILWAY MAPS
OF THE
BRITISH ISLES, THE CONTINENT OF EUROPE, INDIA, &c.

VOL. XXXVII.

London:
PUBLISHED BY W. J. ADAMS & SONS,
BRADSHAW'S GENERAL RAILWAY PUBLICATION OFFICES, 59, FLEET STREET, E.C.
AND SOLD BY EFFINGHAM WILSON, 11, ROYAL EXCHANGE, E.C.
Manchester:
HENRY BLACKLOCK & CO., ALBERT SQUARE;
ALSO AT
BRADSHAW'S PUBLICATION OFFICES, 61, DALE STREET, LIVERPOOL;
33, UNION STREET, BIRMINGHAM; FARGATE, SHEFFIELD;
12, HANOVER STREET, EDINBURGH; 144, ARGYLE STREET, GLASGOW;
7, GRAFTON STREET (CORNER OF STEPHEN'S GREEN), DUBLIN,
AND OF ALL BOOKSELLERS.

1885.

PREFACE TO VOLUME XXXVII.

IN the Preface of last year we pointed out that the great depression which then prevailed in the values of the Ordinary Stocks of British Railways did not bear comparison with the slight reduction in net earnings. A continuance of adversity to the respective proprietaries in this respect during 1884, although not quite to so marked an extent as in 1883, induces us to confine our remarks to this subject alone in the limited space at our disposal.

Taken generally, the Dividends for 1884 have not been quite so well maintained as those for 1883, but they should be considered satisfactory, considering the bad trade and financial depression which have continued, and having in view the fact that these influences are not of a permanent, but of a fluctuating character, and may alter for the better at any moment.

Notwithstanding these considerations, out of about twenty Ordinary Stocks of the principal companies only four have improved in value, and those only to a small extent, whilst the fall in prices of the remainder is again very disappointing to holders, as shown below, viz.:—

	End of 1883	End of 1884	Increase	Decrease
Furness	118½	105½	...	13
Glasgow and South Western	116	111	...	5
Great Eastern	64¼	68	3¾	...
Great Northern	115	111½	...	3½
Great Western	144½	134	...	10½
Lancashire and Yorkshire	115¼	116¼	1	...
London, Brighton, and South Coast	120	121	1	...
" " ("A" Stock)	105⅞	104¼	...	1⅝
London, Chatham, and Dover	23½	18¾	...	4¾
London and North Western	173¾	164½	...	9¼
London and South Western	130½	127	...	3½
Manchester, Sheffield, and Lincolnshire	83½	74	...	9½
" " ("A" Stock)	46	36⅛	...	9⅞
Metropolitan	117	112½	...	4½
Midland	134½	130¾	...	3¾
North British	106¾	98⅜	...	8⅜
North Eastern	171⅛	157⅛	...	14
North Stafford	89¼	90	¾	...
South Eastern	124	122	...	2
" ("A" Stock)	110¾	100⅜	...	10⅜
Taff Vale	287⅛	267⅛	...	20

Entertaining what we deem to be a reasonable view of events connected with this subject, and of the fact that the Money Market has been easy for the greater part of the two years, we cannot reconcile ourselves to the opinions of others that the fall in values has been at all justified, coming as it does after the extraordinary depreciation in 1883, which seemed quite to have levelled prices to meet almost any further adverse circumstances, and considering that most companies pay really good Dividends, which give to Investors very handsome returns, compared with the meagre interest yielded by higher class securities.

Under these circumstances, we think it will be considered in strict accordance with the objects of our work if we offer a few comments, for what they are worth, on the subject of those influences which have occasioned the continuance of this abnormally strange depreciation in values, and suggest what we should consider would be the best means of checking, to a greater or lesser extent, their damaging effect upon the interests of those whom we believe it is our duty to protect, namely, the present holders of British Railway Ordinary Stocks.

Whenever market values go against earnings to a greater extent than seems warrantable, the depreciation is, of course, traceable to causes quite apart from the *actual* financial position and earnings of undertakings, such causes being of a varied character, and including political depression, stagnation of trade, scarcity of money, prevalence of strikes, and commercial or financial failures or frauds.

But it is not because these influences exist that fluctuations in values are often so violent and unaccountable, but rather on account of the uses which are made of them to create miscalculations. The plan generally adopted, by syndicates and others interested in producing a fall in prices, is either to flood the country with circulars marked *private* and purporting to expose the worthlessness of this or that undertaking, or by any other available means, to spread broadcast all kinds of pessimist views, and thus frighten holders into a disposal of their property.

As an example, we may mention the misconstruction frequently placed before the uninitiated whenever New Capital is either issued or likely to be issued, a great deal being generally made of what is termed the "Watering of Stocks;" at such times the *real* reasons for such monetary requirements are quite lost sight of, and in the numerous cases where no due examination into the true state of affairs is made the result is often most disastrous.

Forgetting such examples as those of the Great Eastern and many other undertakings, which have raised themselves from bankruptcy by the force of their enterprises, holders *will* persistently swallow the theory that issues of New Capital mean *ruin*, whilst in reality, unless they are required to carry the same traffic, and be therefore unproductive, they are generally beneficial, and not only pay their own way, but in numberless instances have developed undertakings, which otherwise would have remained under a cloud, certainly for years, and perhaps permanently, from a state of adversity to one of prosperity.

We must now try to impress upon the minds of our readers that these written circulars, or otherwise expressed views, are often undertaken by clever men, competent to place matters in such a light as may seem perfectly clear and intelligible at first glance, and therefore, being thus the more dangerous, they should never be taken notice of except when placed side by side and studiously compared with the official reports and other documents issued by the undertaking in question.

Market movements being governed chiefly by the right or wrong interpretation of events, it is impossible to gauge them, whilst if, on the contrary, prices fluctuated merely on calculations of legitimate earnings, their rise or fall would be easily predicted, and regular values maintained; but when holders find their property depreciating from those outside influences which they cannot understand, the result is, only too frequently, nervous sales far under correct valuations, consequent loss to themselves, and further depreciation in value of the respective properties held by others.

For the long period referred to, that which we may perhaps be allowed to term the "luck of circumstance" has been persistently against holders, and thus the disparity between market prices and real values is partly accounted for, but the effect produced in the manner we have endeavoured to describe, especially in panics and semi-panics, is by far the more serious item of regret.

It must be remembered that when holders part with *real stock* it assists in the general depression, by preventing what is termed "backwardations," or charges against persons who have sold stock which they do not possess, and are "cornered" by having to find it; therefore, it follows that holders should be wary of their true interests, and not supply, if they can possibly avoid it, that which feeds the vitality of those who have succeeded in the overthrow of true values.

The means which we advise depend much upon the temperament of holders; to such of them as may deem our advice worthy of consideration, we would suggest that, whenever they have conflicting testimony before them, they should be guided only by facts, and not fancies, in estimating the true value of that which belongs to them.

In order to arrive at this result, they should carefully analyse the Official Reports which are from time to time presented to them, and in doing so they must not base their conclusions upon present results, *but upon those of, say at least seven years*, for it must not by any means be taken for granted that the existing depression will inevitably continue, but rather that prosperity must necessarily, sooner or later, have its turn. Everyone knows how regularly the barometer of values rises and falls, therefore neither good nor bad times can possibly be permanent.

Of course the foregoing arguments may be turned in the opposite direction and applied to the efforts which are made in prosperous times to cause overestimates and induce purchases at prices much beyond true values; but it must be borne in mind that we are writing at a period when the influences referred to have all been against holders, and it is, therefore, that side of the question only with which we have thought proper to deal.

As we have before observed, we abstain from commenting upon topics connected with the fall in values of securities of a speculative character, other than those at home; first, from want of space; secondly, because they are governed by influences at the mercy of foreign combinations; and thirdly, because the market speculations of other countries are difficult to cope with.

Assuring our Subscribers that we continue to be fully alive to their interests, we present our Volume for 1885, which, we trust, may prove as satisfactory to them as undoubted testimony has proved previous editions to have been in past years.

Manchester, Feb. 16th, 1885.

HAWKSLEY'S PATENT TREAD

GREATLY REDUCED IN PRICE.

Proprietor, J. WESTWOOD, Jun.,

LONDON YARD IRON WORKS, ISLE OF DOGS, POPLAR, LONDO

MANUFACTORY:—Hawksley's Patent Staircase Works,

HIGH STREET, BROMLEY-BY-BOW, LONDON, E.

CITY OFFICE:—39, GREAT TOWER STREET, E.C.

For further Particulars and Prices as to Winders and Special Castings, apply at the above Ad

Winders and irregular shaped Treads are measured by the outside dimensions as if sq In ordering please state if any are for top treads or landings, and if so the back flang be left off. There are no flanges to treads for repairing old stone steps. Wood templa paper moulds to be sent full size for winders or irregular shaped Treads, including s or projection past face of riser.

Recommended for d bility, simplicity, footing, elasticity, an perfectly noiseless; excel lead, oak, tea stone; applicable to w and iron staircases, and worn-down s stairs, spiral and c staircases, footpath t to cellars, covers for dr and coal cellars, floo for public buildings aisles of churches, &c.

IN USE AT

Railway Stations.
Accrington
Acton Green
Aldersgate Street
Aldgate
Althorp Park
Altrincham
Aston
Ash Street, Stockport
Banbury
Barnsbury
Barnsley
Batley
Bescot Junction
Birmingham
Bishopsgate
Blackfriars
Blaydon-on-Tyne
Bletchley
Bolton
Bolts Bridge
Bombay, India
Bow
Bowdon Central
Brick Lane
Broadstone, Dublin
Broad Street
Burdett Road
Burscough Junction
Burton
Bury
Canonbury
Camden Road
Chalk Farm
Charing Cross
Cheddington
Cheetham Hill Junction
Clayton
Clifton
Crewe [Crossing
Crooked Billet Level
Cross Lane
Crumpsall
Cullercoates
Dalston
Daybrook
Derby
Droylsden
Drighlington
Dudley
Dudley Port
Dundee
Ealing Common
Ealing Terminus
Earl's Court
Edgware Road
Failsworth
Farington
Farringdon Street
Fenchurch Street
Finchley Road
Forest Gate
Fulham
Gloucester Road
Gower Street
Grantham
Greenwich
Hackney
Haggerston
Hammersmith
Heaton Park
Highbury [send
Highdran Road, Wal-
Hollinwood
Homerton
Holyhead
Hounslow
Keighley
Kemble Junction
Kentish Town
Kensal Green
Kilburn
Kilsby
King's Cross
Lea Bridge
Leamington
Leman Street
Leyland
Leyton
Leytonstone
Lichfield
Limehouse
Little Ealing [chester
Liverpool Road, Man-
Liverpool Street
Llandudno
Long Buckby
Loudoun Road
Manchester
Manchester Road
Mansion House
Mildmay Park
Milverton
Monkwearmouth
Moorgate Street
Newcastle-under-Lyme
New Cross
Newport
Newton Heath
North Brentford
North Bridge [Station)
Northampton (Castle
Nottingham
Oldbury
Old Ford
Paddington
Parsons Green
Patricroft
Penzance
Pickle Bridge
Plaistow
Pleck
Plymouth
Poplar
Portsmouth
Prestwich
Radcliffe
Roade
Salisbury Road
Seedley
Shadwell
Sheffield
Shoreditch
Sloane Square
Snow Hill, Birming
Soho
South Kensington
Spring Grove
Stetchford
Stepney
Stoke
Stourbridge
Stratford
Stretford
Sudbury
Sunderland
Sutton
Temple
Thornton
Torquay
Tower of London
Tring
Tynemouth
Upton Park
Victoria
Victoria Park
Walham Green
Walsall
Waterloo, Liverpool
Weaste
Werneth, Oldham
Westbourne Park
West End Lane
Westminster
Whitchurch
Whitechapel
Whitefield
Whitley
Widnes
Willenhall Bridge
Willesden
Wood Green
Wormwood Scrubbs
Wortley
Wolverhampton
Wolverton

Post and Telegraph Offices.—Belfast Central Post Office, Caledonian Road, Charles Stree Churton Street, Clapham, Dublin General Post Office, High Street, Islington, Norfolk Terrac Notting Hill Gate, Seymour Street, St. James's Street, Waterford, Woolwich. [Lo-

Two or more Bedro
Warmed and
Ventilated by on

MANCHEST

GRATE,

IN EVERY DESI
to suit every sty
Architecture,

Warmin

Two or more Bedrooms Warmed and Ventilated by one

MANCHESTER GRATE,

IN EVERY DESIGN, to suit every style of Architecture, being fixed in ground floor rooms of houses.

THOUSANDS IN USE.

Prospectus & Testimonials on application, Extending over a period of Ten Years.

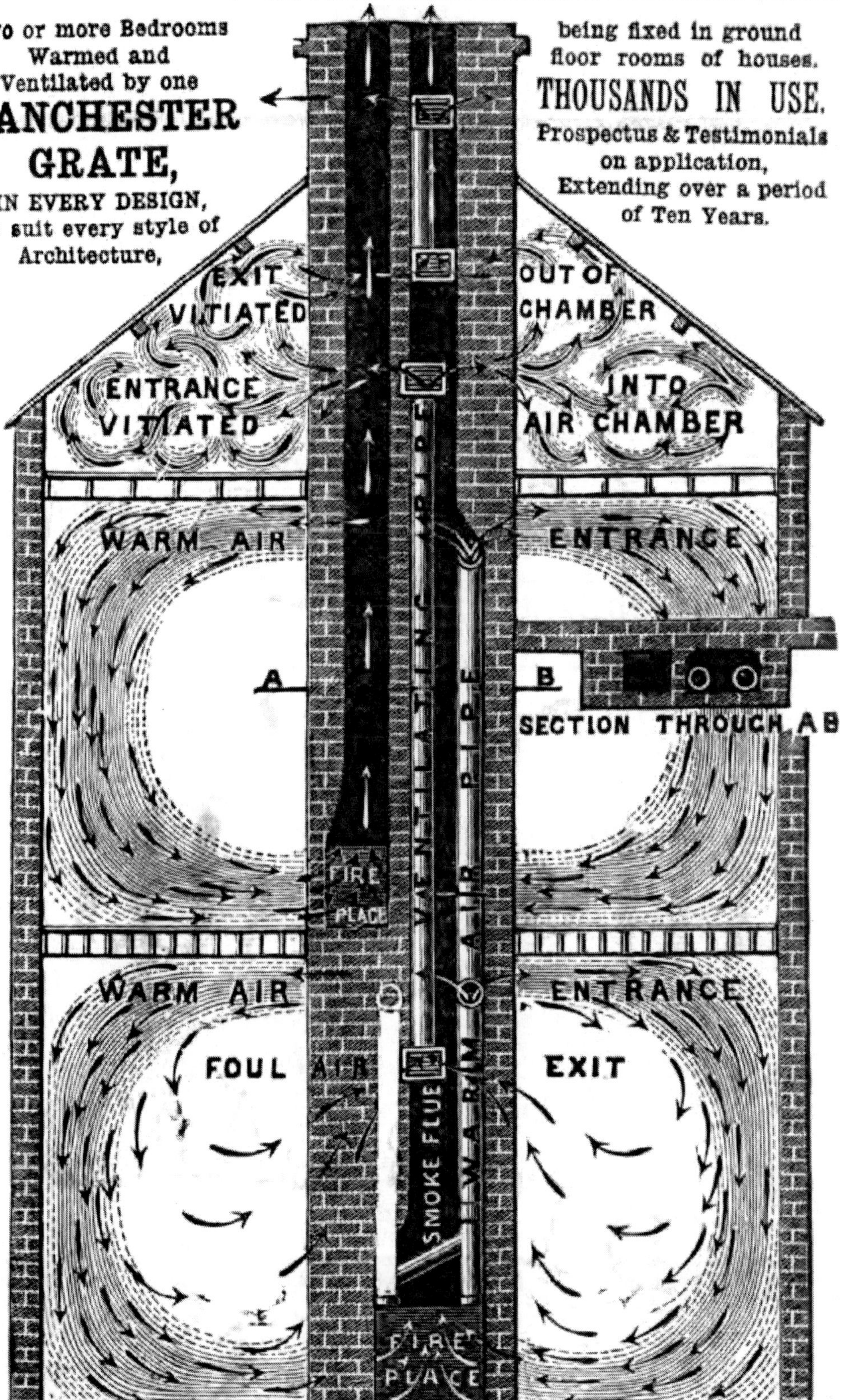

E. H. SHORLAND,

Warming and Ventilating Engineer, St. Gabriel's Works, Erskine St.

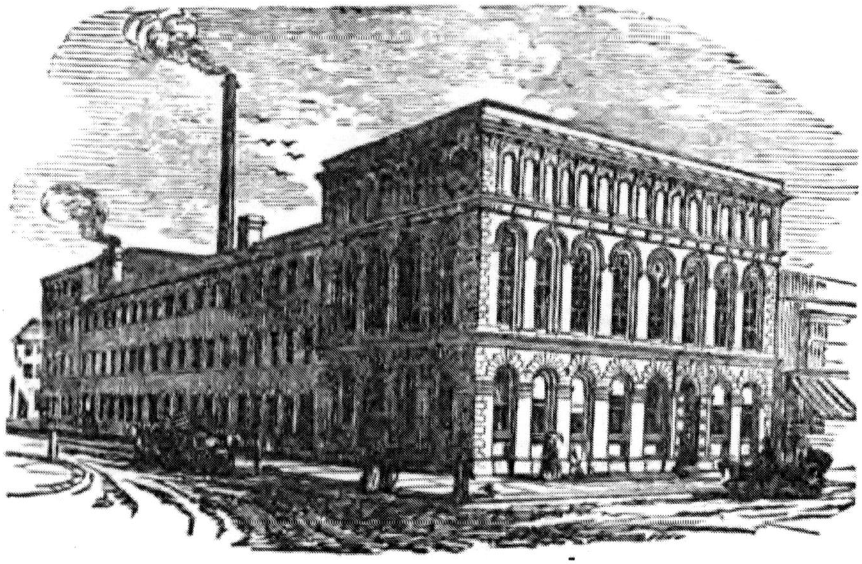

GENERAL INDEX.

*** For Companies Amalgamated, Owned, Leased, or Worked, other than those mentioned below, and for particulars relating to those from whom no recent information has been received, see SUPPLEMENTARY INDEX, page xix.

UNITED KINGDOM.

*CONTINENTAL, &c.

AFRICA.

* See General Notice, page 342.

ASIA.

AUSTRALASIA.

BRITISH NORTH AMERICA.

SOUTHERN AND CENTRAL AMERICA.

UNITED STATES.

WEST INDIES.

CANALS.

AUXILIARY ASSOCIATIONS.

SUPPLEMENTARY INDEX.

NAME.	WITH OR BY WHAT COMPANY AMALGAMATED, OWNED, LEASED, OR WORKED, OR WHERE PARTICULARS MAY OTHERWISE BE FOUND.	PAGE.
Bedford	London and North Western. See MANUAL for 1882, page 194	....
Bedford and Cambridge	London and North Western	189
Belfast and Ballymena	Belfast and Northern Counties	18
Belfast, Holywood, and Bangor	Belfast and County Down	16
Belgian Eastern Junction	No recent information—presumably vested in the Belgian Government. See MANUAL for 1882, page 370	....
Berks and Hants Extension	Great Western	133
Berwickshire	North British	249
Bideford Extension	London and South Western	195
Birkenhead, Chester, and North Wales	Incorporated by act 5th August, 1873; dissolved by act 28th March, 1878	....
Birkenhead, Lancashire, and Cheshire Junc.	Birkenhead	21
Birmingham, Bristol, and Thames Junction	West London	330
Birmingham and Derby	Midland	226
Birmingham and Gloucester	Ditto	226
Birmingham and Lichfield Junction	Incorporated by act 6th August, 1872. See MANUAL for 1881, page 19	....
Birmingham West Suburban	Midland	226
Birmingham, Wolverhampton, & Stour Valley	London and North Western	189
Bishop's Castle	Incorporated by act of 28th June, 1861. In Chancery. Receiver, Mr. Alfred Driver, 23, Leigham Court Road, West Streatham, Surrey, W.	....
Bishop's Stortford, Dunmow, and Braintree	Great Eastern	113
Bishop's Waltham	London and South Western	195
Blackburn	Lancashire and Yorkshire	164
Blackpool and Lytham	London & North Western & Lancashire & Yorkshire (Preston & Wyre)..165	189
Blackwell and Cransley	Midland. See MANUAL for 1881, page 156	....
Blyth and Tyne	North Eastern	257
Bodmin	Incorporated by act of 6th August, 1864. No recent information. See MANUAL for 1881, page 21	....
Bodmin and Wadebridge and Delabole	Incorporated by act 5th August, 1873; abandoned and wound up under act 28th March, 1878	....
Bognor	London, Brighton, and South Coast	178
Bolivar	Vested in the Quebrada Railway, Land, and Copper Company Limited. For other particulars see MANUAL for 1883, page 438	....
Bolton and Preston	North Union	269
Border Counties	North British	249
Boston, Sleaford, and Midland Counties	Great Northern	116
Bourn and Essendine	Ditto	116
Bourton-on-the-Water	Great Western	134
Bradford, Eccleshill, and Idle	Great Northern	116
Bradford and Thornton	Ditto	116
Brading Harbour	Incorporated by act 7th August, 1874. Opened May 27th, 1882	....
Brewood and Wolverhampton	Incorporated by act 16th July, 1874; abandoned by act 23rd May, 1879	....
Bridge of Weir	Glasgow and South Western	103
Brighton	London, Brighton, and South Coast	177
Bristol and Exeter	Great Western	134
Bristol and Gloucester	Midland	226
Bristol Harbour	Great Western	134
Bristol and North Somerset	Ditto	134
Bristol and Portishead	Ditto	134
Bristol and South Wales Union	Ditto	135
Bromley Direct	South Eastern	304
Broxburn	North British	249
Brynmawr and Blaenavon	London and North Western	189
Buckingham and Brackley	London and North Western. See MANUAL for 1882, page 195	....
Buckinghamshire	London and North Western	189
Buenos Ayres and Campana	Buenos Ayres and Rosario	438

NAME.	WITH OR BY WHAT COMPANY AMALGAMATED, OWNED, LEASED, OR WORKED, OR WHERE PARTICULARS MAY OTHERWISE BE FOUND.	PAGE
Cornwall Mineral and Bodmin and Wadebridge Junction	Incorporated by act 5th August, 1873; abandoned by act 28th March, 1878.	....
Corwen and Bala	Incorporated 30th June, 1862, no returns since June 1881, for information to that date see MANUAL for 1884, page 69.	....
Crieff Junction	Caledonian	34
Crieff and Methven Junction	Ditto	32
Croesor and Portmadoc	Portmadoc Croesor and Beddgelert. See MANUAL for 1885, page 280	....
Crofthead and Kilmarnock	Caledonian and Glasgow and South-Western	103
Croydon	London, Brighton, and South Coast.	177
Croydon, Oxted, and East Grinstead	London, Brighton, and South Coast.	178
Crystal Palace and South London Junction	London, Chatham, and Dover	164
Culm Valley Light	Great Western	135
Danube and Black Sea	Incorporated under Limited Liability Act of 1856. Sold to the Roumanian Government in the latter part of 1882. Company in Liquidation. For past information see MANUAL for 1882, page 373	....
Dartmouth and Torbay	Great Western	135
Deeside	Great North of Scotland	127
Denbigh, Ruthin, and Corwen	London and North Western	189
Deeburn Valley	Great North of Scotland and Caledonian 32	127
Denver and Rio Grande Central	This Company is leased to the Denver and Rio Grande at 40 per cent. of the gross receipts	....
Derbyshire, Worcestershire, and Staffordshire Junction	London and North Western (Cannock Mineral). See MANUAL for 1882, page 195	....
Devon and Cornwall Central	Incorporated by Act of 1882. Vested in Plymouth, Devonport, and South Western Junction	....
Devon Valley	North British	249
Dingwall and Skye	Highland	147
Direct Northern	Great Northern	115
Dorset Central	Somerset and Dorset	301
Dover and Deal	London, Chatham, and Dover, and South Eastern	184
Downpatrick, Dundrum, and Newcastle	Belfast and County Down	16
Dublin and Antrim Junction	Great Northern (Ireland)	121
Dublin and Belfast Junction	Ditto ditto	122
Dublin and Drogheda	Ditto ditto	121
Dublin, Dundrum, and Rathfarnham	Dublin, Wicklow, and Wexford	77
Dublin, Rathmines, Rathgar, Roundtown, Rathfarnham, and Rathcoole	Incorporated by act 29th July, 1864. No recent information. See MANUAL for 1881, page 77	....
Dudley and Oldbury Junction	Oldbury	271
Dumfries, Lochmaben, and Lockerbie	Caledonian	33
Dunblane, Doune, and Callander	Ditto	34
Dundalk and Enniskillen	Great Northern (Ireland)	122
Dundalk and Greenore	Dundalk, Newry, and Greenore	79
Dundee and Arbroath	Caledonian and North British	32
Dundee and Newtyle	Caledonian	33
Dundee and Perth and Aberdeen Junction	Ditto	34
Dunfermline and Queensferry	North British	252
Dungannon and Cookstown	Great Northern (Ireland)	122
Dunmanway and Skibbereen	Ilen Valley	152
Dursley and Midland Junction	Midland	226
Dutch Indian	See MANUAL for 1879, page 434. No recent information	....
East Anglian	Great Eastern	110
East Grinstead	London, Brighton, and South Coast.	178
East Kent	London, Chatham, and Dover. See MANUAL for 1881, page 191	....

NAME.	WITH OR BY WHAT COMPANY AMALGAMATED, OWNED, LEASED, OR WORKED, OR WHERE PARTICULARS MAY OTHERWISE BE FOUND.	PAGE.
London and Aylesbury	Incorporated by act of 16th August, 1871. In Chancery. See MANUAL for 1881, page 183	....
London and Birmingham	London and North Western	189
London, Essex, and Kent Coast Junction	Incorporated by act 15th August, 1876; abandoned by act of 1877	....
London and Southampton	London and South Western	195
London and York	Great Northern	115
Londonderry and Coleraine	Belfast and Northern Counties	19
Londonderry and Enniskillen	Great Northern (Ireland)	122
Lostwithiel and Fowey	Incorporated by act 30th June, 1882. Ceased working January, 1880. No recent information. See MANUAL for 1882, page 219	....
Loose Valley	South Eastern	305
Louth and Lincoln	Great Northern	117
Lowestoft and Beccles	Great Eastern (East Suffolk). See MANUAL for 1882, page 112	....
Luton, Dunstable, and Welwyn Junction	Great Northern	117
Lydney and Lydbrook	Severn and Wye	293
Lyme Regis	See MANUAL for 1880. No recent information	....
Lymington	London and South Western	196
Lynn and Dereham	Great Eastern	110
Lynn and Ely	Ditto	110
Lynn and Fakenham	Eastern and Midlands	84
Lynn and Hunstanton	Hunstanton & West Norfolk Junction	151
Lynn and Sutton Bridge	Midland and Eastern	233
Lynn, Yarmouth, and Norwich Section	Eastern and Midlands	85
Macclesfield, Bollington, and Marple	Manchester, Sheffield, and Lincolnshire and North Staffordshire..207,	267
Macclesfield and Knutsford	Manchester, Sheffield, & Lincolnshire	207
Madrid, Saragossa, and Alicante	See MANUAL for 1882, page 378. No recent returns	....
Maenclochog	No recent information. Line privately owned and closed for public traffic December, 1883. See MANUAL for 1883, page 204	....
Maidstone and Ashford	London, Chatham, and Dover	185
Maidstone Extension (part of Sevenoaks, Maidstone, and Tunbridge).	London, Chatham, and Dover. See MANUAL for 1882 page 120	....
Mallow and Fermoy	Great Southern and Western	131
Malmesbury	Great Western	137
Malton and Driffield	North Eastern	257
Manchester and Birmingham	London and North Western	189
Manchester, Bolton, and Bury	Lancashire and Yorkshire	164
Manchester, Buxton, Matlock, and Midlands Junction	Midland	237
Manchester and Leeds	Lancashire and Yorkshire	164
Manchester and Lincoln Union	Manchester, Sheffield, & Lincolnshire	206
Manchester South District	Midland	227
Manchester and Stockport	Sheffield and Midland	295
Marple, New Mills, and Hayfield Junction	Ditto	295
Market Deeping	Incorporated by act of 17th June, 1878. See MANUAL for 1883, page 213. Abandoned by act of 2nd August, 1883	....
Maybole and Girvan	Glasgow and South Western	103
Melbourne and Hobson's Bay United	Transferred to the Victorian Government in July, 1879. For previous information, see the MANUAL for that year, page 413	....
Merrybent and Darlington	Incorporated by act 11th June, 1866. Sold and wound up under act 17th June, 1878	....
Merthyr, Tredegar, and Abergavenny	London and North Western	189
Metropolitan Inner Circle	Incorporated by act of 7th August, 1874. See MANUAL for 1883, page 225. Wound up in 1883	....

APPENDIX.

AGREEMENTS, CONSOLIDATIONS, AMALGAMATIONS, &c.—

GENERAL INFORMATION—

RAILWAY DIRECTORY—

B. FINNIGAN,

PORTMANTEAU & TRAVELLING BAG MANUFACTURER,

115, MARKET STREET, MANCHESTER.

DESPATCH BAGS.
DRESSING CASES.
DRESSING BAGS.
FLASKS (SILVER, &c.)
JEWEL BOXES.
GLADSTONE BAGS
BASKETS.
BONNET BOXES.
FRENCH BOXES.
GUN CASES.
HAT CASES.
KNAPSACKS.
LETTER BAGS.
LUNCHEON BASKETS.
PORTMANTEAUS.
IMPERIALS.
SCHOOL BOXES.
SAMPLE CASES.
&c., &c.

Illustrated Catalogues, containing sizes and prices, sent post free.

B. FINNIGAN, 115, MARKET STREET, MANCHESTER.

CARSON'S PAINT.

PRIZE MEDALS.

VIENNA, 1873.

PARIS, 1875.

MELBOURNE, 1880.

Patronised by

The British, Indian, and Colonial Governments, most of the English Railways, and Canal Companies,

FOR EVERY DESCRIPTION OF

OUT-DOOR WORK,

And for that purpose has been proved, after 80 years' experience, to surpass all other Paints in

Cheapness and Durability.

Experience proves the Anti-Corrosion Paint to be in the end considerably less than half the price of any Paint yet manufactured. and is specially suited to

RAILWAY STATIONS,

SHEDDING, WOOD AND IRON BUILDINGS, TRUCKS, WAGGONS, AND TELEGRAPH POLES.

PATTERNS AND PARTICULARS POST FREE.

The Original Anti-Corrosion Paint can only be obtained of

WALTER CARSON & SONS,

La Belle Sauvage Yard, Ludgate Hill, London, E.C.

Lo-1

INDEX TO ADVERTISEMENTS.

ESTABLISHED 1796.

Prize Medal awarded for Varnishes and Colours, L'Exposition Universelle, Paris, 1867.

Prize Medal awarded for Varnishes, Colours, and Oxidised Oil, International Exhibition, London, 1862.

WILKINSON, HEYWOOD, & CLARK,

PARIS, 1878.

THE ONLY GOLD MEDAL AWARDED

FOR VARNISHES AND COLOURS.

CALEDONIAN VARNISH AND COLOUR WORKS,

Caledonian Road, King's Cross,

Liverpool: 30, SEEL STREET.

LONDON.

Paris: 87, Avenue du Roule, Neuilly.

BOMBAY: 1, Church Lane Fort, Bombay.

Works—West Drayton, Middlesex.

VARNISHES.—Varnishes of all descriptions for Railway Carriage Builders, Coach Builders, Decorators, Ship Builders, Agricultural Implement Makers, Paper Stainers, Floor-Cloth Manufacturers, &c., &c. These Varnishes are all of acknowledged superiority, and will stand the severest tests.

NON-BLOOMING VARNISHES for interior decoration, *guaranteed not to bloom.*

COLOURS, DRY, GROUND AND IN PULP, OF ALL KINDS.—These colours have for many years past been supplied to all the leading Coach Builders, House Painters, Paper Stainers, and Agricultural Implement Makers in the United Kingdom and abroad. They are all of the very finest quality; and for brilliancy, softness, and body are unsurpassed.

NON-POISONOUS COLOURS.—A complete series of original colours, all guaranteed to be non-poisonous.

From these colours an infinite variety of delicate tints can be obtained. Primarily intended for distemper, they can be also used in oil, and supplied in pulp.

COLOURS IN COLLAPSIBLE TUBES.—The advantages of these Tubes are well known. The packages are exceedingly portable; and the exact quantity required can be easily taken out, and the remainder kept in perfect condition for any length of time. Guaranteed absolutely pure; and for brilliancy of colour, strength of staining power, and softness, they are unsurpassed.

PAINTS READY FOR USE IN 1, 2, 3, 4, and 7 lb. TINS.—These Paints are intended for domestic use. The colours are very brilliant and durable. They dry well, and with a good surface.

The demand for these Mixed Paints is rapidly increasing, and large quantities are supplied to all parts of the country, and to the colonies. Tint cards sent on application.

BRUSHES.—Varnish and Paint Brushes of every description always in stock.

All Brushes manufactured by Wilkinson, Heywood, and Clark bear the initials of the firm, have for years past been in great demand, and give the greatest satisfaction. Illustrated Price Lists sent on application.

OILS.—Raw and Boiled Linseed, Colza, Olive, Lubricating, and other Oils, for home and export trades.

WILKINSON, HEYWOOD, & CLARK have long enjoyed a great reputation amongst all the leading Coach Builders, Decorators, House Painters, and Ship Builders, and for years past they have supplied their goods to the Admiralty, to the War Office, to the India Office, to the Colonial Office, to the Board of Trade, and to the largest Shipping Houses and Railway Companies. [Lo-24

BRADSHAW'S
MANUAL AND DIRECTORY.

INTRODUCTION.

THIS MANUAL is divided into four departments, viz., United Kingdom; Continental; Indian, American, and Colonial; and Auxiliary Associations, which may be more or less connected with the railway interest. The Appendix contains Parliamentary Documents, Agreements, &c., and is accompanied by an Alphabetical Arrangement of the whole Administrative and Executive Staff in the Three Kingdoms.

Schemes passed since 1858 have their deposits retained until the line is completed, unless a bond to twice the amount is lodged, or one-half the capital expended on authorised purposes. Companies promoting extensions are debarred paying dividends on ordinary stock when the fixed periods expire, unless the branches are opened under certificate of Board of Trade.

A general clause is also inserted in acts passed since 1856, in these terms:—"That this act, or anything therein, shall not exempt the railway from the provisions of any general act, relating to the recited acts, or this act, or of any general act relating to railways, or to the better or more impartial audit of the accounts of railway companies now in force, or which may hereafter pass during this or any other session of Parliament, or from any future revision or alteration under the authority of Parliament, of the maximum rates of fares and charges by the recited acts, or the maximum rates of small parcels, thereby respectively authorised."

By a clause inserted in the acts passed since 1859, arrears of interest on "preference shares" created on and after that date are not to accumulate. Should the profits in any one year not be sufficient to pay preference dividends, it is expressly stipulated that "no part of the deficiency shall be made good out of the profits of any subsequent year, or out of any other funds of the company."

The subjoined stringent standing order was adopted in the session of 1863:—"In every railway bill in which new works are authorised, the committee shall make provision for insuring the completion of the line by impounding the deposit, or by providing that after the expiration of a period to be limited to such bill, not exceeding five years from the passing of the act in the case of a new bill, and three years in case of the extension of time for completing the line, the company shall be liable to a penalty of not less than 20*l.* and not exceeding 50*l.* per day, to be recoverable as a debt due to the Crown, for every day after the period so limited, until such line shall be completed and open for public traffic; but no penalty shall accrue in respect of any time during which it shall appear, by a certificate to be obtained from the Board of Trade, that the company was prevented from completing or opening such line by unforeseen accident or circumstances beyond their control; but the want of sufficient funds shall not be held to be a circumstance beyond their control."

Another general rule was imported into the legislation of 1864, namely:—"That it shall not be lawful for any company to issue any share, nor shall any share vest in the person accepting the same, unless and until a sum not being less than one-fifth part of the amount of such share shall have been paid up in respect thereof."

The scale of voting is thus regulated by the Consolidation Act (8 Vic., cap. 16, 1845).—"Section 75. At all general meetings every shareholder shall be entitled to vote according to the prescribed mode of voting, and where no scale shall be prescribed every shareholder shall have one vote for every share up to 10, and shall have an additional vote for every five beyond the first 10 shares held by him up to 100, and an additional vote for every 10 shares held by him beyond the first 100 shares; provided always that no shareholder be entitled to vote unless he shall have paid the calls then due upon the shares held by him."

By "The Debenture Stock Act, 1871," 34 and 35 Vic., cap. 27, trustees who are authorised to advance trust moneys on the debentures of a railway company may invest such moneys on the debenture stocks of such company, except where expressly prohibited from so doing.

I.—UNITED KINGDOM.

1.—ABBOTSBURY.

Incorporated by act of 6th August, 1877; length, 6 miles 3 furlongs and 3·18 chains, from Upway to Abbotsbury. Period for completion of works, five years. Working arrangements with Great Western. Capital, 64,000*l*. in 10*l*. shares, with power to divide into "preferred" and "deferred" half-shares. Borrowing powers, 21,300*l*.

By act of 19th May, 1882, the period for completion of works was extended for 3 years from 6th August, 1882, and two deviation lines were authorised in connection with the Wilts, Somerset, and Weymouth Branch of the Great Western. New capital, 10,000*l*.; loans, 3,300*l*.

In 1883 a prospectus was issued inviting applications for 4,600 10*l*. ordinary shares of this company, payable 1*l*. on application, 3*l*. on allotment, and 2*l*. each on 1st November, 1883, and 2*l*. each on 1st February and 1st May, 1884, respectively. The prospectus stated as follows:—"The terms of the agreement entered into with the Great Western are, that that company shall work, equip, manage, and maintain the Abbotsbury in perpetuity for 50 per cent. of the gross receipts, after deduction of the Government duty, and shall pay over to the Abbotsbury, half-yearly on the 30th June and 31st December in each year, the remaining 50 per cent. of such gross receipts, so that be the earnings of the line great or small, the company will be entitled to receive one-half of such earnings. In order, however, to meet the contingency of the dividends falling below the rate of 5 per cent. per annum, the Great Western have further agreed that in the event of the 50 per cent. earnings of the line *per se* not producing sufficient to pay 5 per cent. interest, they—the Great Western—in order to make up the deficiency, will pay or allow to the Abbotsbury, as a rebate, a sum not exceeding 5 per cent. upon the proportion belonging to the Great Western of the receipts arising from all through-booked traffic, carried in trains of the Great Western, to or from the Abbotsbury, over the whole of the Great Western system of railways, thereby virtually making a sound provision against any contingency which might prevent a dividend of 5 per cent."

Works in progress, and the line will shortly be opened.

No. of Directors—4; quorum, 2. *Qualification*, 20 shares.

DIRECTORS:

Chairman—RICHARD PASSMORE EDWARDS, Esq., Clan Villa, Bath.

James Humby, Esq., Widcombe Hill, Bath.

John Walker, Esq., Oxford House, Croydon.

OFFICERS.—Sec., William Manfield, Portesham House, Dorchester; Eng., William Clarke, M.Inst.C.E., 45, Parliament Street, Westminster, S.W; Auditor, L. Robinson, Dorchester; Solicitor, Edwin Burnett, Dorchester; Bankers, Wilts and Dorset Banking Co., Dorchester and Weymouth, and London and Westminster Bank, Lothbury, E.C.

2.—ABINGDON.

Incorporated by act of 15th June, 1855, to make a railway from the Oxford Branch of the Great Western to Abingdon. Length, 2 miles. Capital, 15,000*l*. in 10*l*. shares and 5,000*l*. on loan. Worked by the Great Western, by which the line is rented for 40 per cent. of gross traffic receipts.

By act of 7th August, 1862, the company was authorised to raise additional capital to the extent of 5,000*l*. at 5 per cent., to cancel and re-issue forfeited shares, and to create debenture stock in lieu of loans.

REVENUE.—The dividends on the ordinary capital for the half-years ended 31st December, 1883, and 30th June, 1884, were at the rate of 8 per cent. per annum.

CAPITAL.—The expenditure on this account to 30th June, 1884, amounted to 26,084*l*., whilst the receipts to the same date were as under:—

Ordinary shares	£15,000
Preference shares at 5 per cent.	600
Preference shares at 4 per cent.	450
Loans at 4 per cent.	5,000
Loans from bankers repaid	5,084

Meetings held in March and September.

of Directors—5; minimum, 5; quorum, 3. *Qualification*, 20 shares.

DIRECTORS:

Chairman—JOHN CREEMER CLARKE, Esq., M.P., Abingdon.

John Heber Clarke, Esq., Fitzharris, Abingdon.
Charles Richardson, Esq., Putney, S.W.
James Williams, Esq., Shippon, near Abingdon.
Walter James Sedgefield, Esq., Abingdon.

OFFICERS.—Sec., C. Alfred Pryce, Abingdon; Auditors, E. S. Copeland and Bromley Challenor.

3.—ALEXANDRA (NEWPORT AND SOUTH WALES) DOCKS AND RAILWAY.

Incorporated by act of Parliament, in 1865, as the Alexandra (Newport) Dock Company, and the name was changed, by a further act in 1882, to the above title. In operation, 35 miles.

The company was authorised to construct docks, railways, and other works in connection therewith, which were opened in April, 1875.

They have powers to make arrangements with the London and North Western, Great Western, and other companies.

The total capital is 1,775,000*l*., viz., 1,350,000*l*. shares and stock, and 425,000*l*. loans and debenture stock; of this there has been issued, shares and stock, 853,988*l*., and debentures and debenture stock, 261,000*l*., leaving a total of 660,012*l*. unissued, viz., 406,012*l*. shares and stock, and 164,000*l*. loans and debenture stock.

The share capital issued consists of 200,000*l*. ordinary shares of 20*l*. each, 141,738*l*. Newport Dock stock, and 512,250*l*. first preference consolidated stock "A," all bearing 4½ per cent. interest.

By act of 1882, the company was empowered to make a further dock 30 acres in extent.

Under an act of 16th July, 1874, power was given to the company to lease its dock and other works to the Newport (Alexandra) Dock Company Limited for a term of 28 years. This lease commenced on the 1st January, 1880, the lessee company undertaking to pay as rents in each year the amount of Lord Tredegar's rent-charge, the interest on the debenture stock, 4½ per cent. on the first preference stock, and 4½ per cent. on the ordinary shares and stock of the lessor company.

By an act passed in 1883, the Newport (Mon.) Dock Company was acquired by this company, and was amalgamated with it from and after the 1st January, 1884.

An act has been obtained by the Pontypridd, Caerphilly, and Newport, authorising the construction of an independent line of railway from the Brecon and Merthyr, at Bassaleg, to the Alexandra Dock lines. This railway, when completed, will give a new and direct access from the Aberdare and Rhondda Valleys to the company's docks and railways.

DIRECTORS:

Chairman—The Rt. Hon. Lord TREDEGAR, Tredegar Park, Newport, Mon.

Deputy-Chairman—Sir GEORGE ELLIOT, Bart., M.P., 1, Park Street, S.W., and Houghton Hall, Durham.

Managing Director—J. C. PARKINSON, Esq., 28, Gt. George Street, Westminster.

G. W. Elliot, Esq., M.P., Langton Hall, Northallerton.
E. J. Phillips, Esq., Woodlands, Pontypool, Mon.
Francis Tothill, Esq., The Grove, Stoke Bishop, near Bristol.
E. M. Underdown, Esq., 3, King's Bench Walk, Temple, E.C.
Sir George Walker, Bart., Castleton, near Cardiff.
Colonel Charles Lyne, J.P., Newport, Monmouthshire
John Lawrence, Esq., J.P., Crick House, Chepstow.

OFFICERS.—Sec., J. S. Adam; Chief Eng., W. S. Smyth; Auditors, Turquand, Youngs, and Co. and W. T. Carlisle; Solicitors, Markby, Stewart, and Co., 57 Coleman Street, E.C.

Offices—60, Gracechurch Street, E.C.

4.—ANNAN WATERFOOT DOCK AND RAILWAY.

Incorporated by act of 11th August, 1881, for the construction of a dock (extent about 5½ acres) and railway (length about 1 mile), &c., at Annan; period for completion, 5 years; running powers over Solway Junction. Capital, 66,000*l*., in 10*l*. shares, with power to divide into "preferred" and "deferred" half-shares. Borrowing powers, 22,000*l*. Running powers to Solway Junction, also to Caledonian, but latter only for remainder of period of Solway Junction working agreement.

Works not yet commenced.

No. of Directors.—Maximum, 5; minimum, 3; quorum, 3 and 2. *Qualification*, 30 shares.

FIRST DIRECTORS:

William Eckersley, Esq., M.Inst.C.E., Westminster, S.W.
John Morrison Stobart, Esq., Spring Vale, Ryde, Isle of Wight.
Horace Foster Tahourdin, Esq., 9, Victoria Chambers, Westminster, S.W.

Offices—9, Victoria Chambers, Westminster, S.W.

5.—ANSTRUTHER AND ST. ANDREWS.

Incorporated by act of 26th August, 1880, for the construction and maintenance of a railway from Anstruther to St. Andrews, in the county of Fife. Length, about 15½ miles. Period for completion of works, 5 years. Working agreement with the North British for 10 years at 50 per cent of the gross receipts, after deduction of cartage, &c. Capital, 57,000*l*. in 10*l*. shares, with power to divide into "preferred" and "deferred" half-shares. Borrowing powers, 19,000*l*.

By act of 16th July, 1883, an extension to join the St. Andrew's Branch of the North British was authorised. Period for completion, 5 years. New capital (may be issued as preference), 30,000*l*.; loans, 10,000*l*. An application has been made to the Board of Trade for power to issue other 30,000*l*. of share capital, with further borrowing powers of 10,000*l*.

Line opened on 1st September, 1883, between Anstruther and Boarhills (9 miles); remaining portion in course of construction.

No. of Directors—3; quorum, 2. *Qualification*, 25 shares.

DIRECTORS:

Chairman—JOHN PURVIS, Esq., of Kinaldy, St. Andrews.

Deputy-Chairman—Lieutenant-Colonel JAMES R. BLACKWELL MONYPENNY, of Pitmilly, St. Andrews.

Hugh Cleghorn, Esq., of Stravithie, St. Andrews.

All eligible for re-election.

OFFICERS.—Sec. and Treasurer, J. E. Dovey, C.A., Edinburgh; Eng., John Buchanan, C.E., 24, George Street, Edinburgh; Auditors, George Fortune, Barnsmuir, Fife, and John McGregor, St. Andrews; Solicitors, Stuart Grace and Charles Stuart Grace, W.S., St. Andrews, Oliphant and Jamieson, Anstruther; Bankers, Commercial Bank of Scotland.

Offices—63, Hanover Street, Edinburgh.

6.—ARBROATH AND FORFAR.

Incorporated by act of 17th May, 1836, for construction of a line commencing on the west at Forfar, in conjunction with the Scottish Midland, and terminating on the east at Arbroath Harbour, 15½ miles. Leased in perpetuity to the Caledonian at a yearly rental of 13,500*l*.

CALEDONIAN.—The following clause was inserted in the act by which the Scottish North Eastern is leased to the Caledonian:—Nothing in this act contained shall in any way alter, diminish, prejudice, or affect any right, interest, power, preference, or privilege belonging to or vested in the Arbroath and Forfar, under or by virtue of the Arbroath and Forfar Act, 1846, and the Arbroath and Forfar Act, 1848, or the rent agreed and payable to the Arbroath and Forfar by the Aberdeen, under or in virtue of the same acts, or shall in any way alter, diminish, prejudice, or affect the nature of the rent-charge, real burden, and priority created by such acts in respect of the said rent or the right to levy and recover any such rent under and in terms of such acts; it being hereby expressly provided and declared that all such rights, interest, powers, priority, privileges, rents, rent-charge, and real burden are to remain the same in all respects as if this act had not been passed, with this exception, that where any obligations were conferred or imposed with reference thereto upon the Aberdeen, the same shall, after the passing of this act, be performed by, and may be enforced against, the company, in the same way and manner, and to the same extent and effect as the same, but for the passing of this act ought to be performed by, or might have been enforced against, the Scottish North Eastern under the Scottish North Eastern Act, 1856, and the Scottish North Eastern Act, 1863.

CAPITAL—Year ended 7th March, 1884.—*Received:* Original 25*l*. shares, 70,000*l*.; 12*l*. 10*s*. shares, 50,000*l*.; 6*l*. 5*s*. shares, 40,000*l*.; 5*l*. shares, 29,950*l*.; guaranteed 12*l*. 10*s*. shares, 40,000*l*.; total shares, 229,950*l*. No loan capital. *Expended* on lines and works, 204,248*l*.; working stock, 26,101*l*.; balance to debit of this account, 400*l*

REVENUE—Year ended 7th March, 1884.—*Receipts:* Guaranteed rent from Caledonian, 13,204*l.*; other items, 64*l.*; brought forward from last year's account, 274*l.*; total, 13,542*l.* After payment of 82*l.* for general charges, a dividend at 5 5-6 per cent. per annum was paid on the company's share capital, leaving 340*l.* to be carried forward. Last annual meeting, 31st March, 1884.

Qualification, 4 shares of 25*l.* each.

COMMITTEE OF MANAGEMENT:

Chairman—*ALEXANDER GORDON, Esq., of Ashludie, Arbroath.

*John F. Dickson, Esq., Panbride House, Carnoustie.
George W. Laird, Esq., of Denfield, Arbroath.
Leonard Lyell, Esq., of Kinnordy and Pitmuis.
John Traill, Esq., Arbroath.
James Muir, Esq., Arbroath.

Two rotate, in order required by act, every year, and are eligible for re-election.
* Retiring directors.

OFFICERS.—Sec., W. K. Macdonald; Treasurer, William Rollo, Banker, Arbroath.

Head Offices—Arbroath, N.B.

7.—ATHENRY AND ENNIS JUNCTION.

Incorporated by act of 20th August, 1860, to construct a line from the Midland Great Western, at Athenry, to the Limerick and Ennis, at the latter place. Length, 36 miles. Capital, 200,000*l.* in 10*l.* shares; loans, 66,000*l.*

The following is a list of Acts obtained by this company since its incorporation, with short heads of the objects for which the various powers were sought:—

1863—13TH JULY.—Extension of time for construction. Agreement with Waterford and Limerick.

1865—26TH MAY.—Reconstruction of capital.

1867—17TH JUNE.—Extension of time for completion. Various running powers, and use of terminal station. New arrangements with Waterford and Limerick.

1868—13TH JULY.—Issue of debentures in lieu of preference shares. Lease of Athenry and Tuam. Capital defined at 195,000*l.*; borrowing powers, 91,600*l.*

The line was opened for traffic on 15th September, 1869, and was worked by the directors as an independent system to November, 1872 (the Waterford and Limerick having declined to take up the working and pay over 3,000*l.* subscription to the company, for which it was liable).

The line is now leased to the Waterford and Limerick for 20 years from the date of the opening of the line (September, 1869), under act of 1873, at a clear annual rental of 5,200*l.*, and half of gross receipts over 11,000*l.* a year.

Under the agreement with the Waterford and Limerick to work the traffic, certain accounts have to be kept by that company under the superintendence of a joint committee of the two companies, and all payments have to be made thereout, together with separate accounts for all competitive traffic to and from Ennis, a point common to both lines. As this company has not succeeded in getting the working company to keep such accounts, and having failed to obtain effect to several other conditions of the agreement, such disputed questions have been referred, under warrant of the Board of Trade, to the sole arbitrament of James Allport, Esq., who, after a careful inquiry, made his award in June, 1882, giving this company the substantial amount of 7,000*l.* to December, 1881, in addition to the sums which had been previously apportioned to the company out of the competitive traffic. In addition, the gross receipts arising from such competitive traffic are to be divided equally between the two companies from 1st January last. There are various other conditions in the award in favour of the company. Up to the present time, 8th November, 1883, the Waterford Company have not paid the sum awarded against them, and have declined to meet to carry out the conditions of the award. Legal steps have been taken to compel a compliance, and judgment has been given in this company's favor on every point raised, under which the 7,000*l.* has been paid into court; notwithstanding which the Waterford and Limerick have appealed against the judgment. The appeal came up for hearing on 30th January, before Lord Justice Coleridge, the Master of the Rolls, and Lord Justice Bowen, who, after hearing counsel for the Waterford and Limerick, gave judgment in favour of the Athenry and Ennis in every particular, with costs, without calling on counsel for reply. The sum of 7,000*l.* has since been paid over to the Athenry and Ennis, with 786*l.* for costs.

The conditions of the above award, subsequent to December, 1881, not having been acted upon by the working company, the Athenry and Ennis have again been obliged to appeal to the Board of Trade to reappoint Sir James Allport to adjudicate upon the further questions of the preparation of the competitive traffic receipts and accounts for the years 1882-3-4 and their apportionment. This second arbitration took place in Dublin on the 7th January, 1885.

With regard to the arrears of interest due to the Public Works Loan Commissioners upon the Government loan, an arrangement has been made with that body, under which the commissioners take over, from time to time, all the available revenues of the company in reduction of such claims. On this subject the directors have thought it advisable to treat with the Treasury with the object of obtaining a reduction in the large rate of interest (5 per cent.) charged the company, and the negotiations with that object are still (November, 1884) pending.

CAPITAL.—This consists of 10,000 ordinary 10*l.* shares; 7,500 10*l.* first preference or "A" shares; 2,000 10*l.* second preference or "B" shares; and loan of 91,600*l.* The expenditure on capital account to 30th June, 1884, amounted to 306,370*l.*, whilst the receipts to the same date had been as under, the stocks being placed in order of priority:—

Loans at 5 per cent.	£85,100	
Class "A" preference 10*l.* shares, 5 per cent.	66,590	
Class "B" preference 10*l.* shares, 5 per cent.	20,000	
Ordinary 10*l.* shares (original capital)	99,190	
Interest on calls	359	
Calls on forfeited shares	145	=£271,384
Balance expended in excess of receipts		34,986
		£306,370

TRANSFER DEPARTMENT.—Ordinary form; fee per deed, 2*s.* 6*d.*; if more sellers than one, 2*s.* 6*d.*; certificates must accompany transfers; amounts of stock under 10*l.* not transferable; in acceptances, renunciations, &c., of new stock, proxies, or other forms sent to trustees and others, the signature of the first name required.

Accounts to 31st December and 30th June. Meetings in February and August.

No. of Directors.—Maximum, 9; minimum, 6. *Qualification*, 500*l.* Directors retire and are elected in accordance with the Companies' Clauses Act.

DIRECTORS:

Chairman—2 JAMES FITZGERALD LOMBARD, Esq., J.P., Rathmines, Dublin.

1 L. H. Evans, Esq., Wallbrook, E.C.
1 David Coffey, Esq., J.P., Roebuck, County Dublin.
1 Thomas Greene, Esq., J.P., Ennis.
2 Thomas Redington Roche, Esq., Ryehill, Monivea.
3 William Henry Simpson, Esq., 16, Kent Terrace, Regent's Park, N.W.

1, Retire in February, 1885; 2, in 1886; 3, in 1887.

OFFICERS.—Sec. and Man., John Fowler Nicoll; Auditors, 2 Michael Macnamara and 1 A. Bellew Nolan; Solicitors, Messrs. Renshaw, London.

Offices—Brunswick Chambers, Great Brunswick Street, Dublin.

8.—ATHENRY AND TUAM.

Incorporated by act of 23rd July, 1848, to construct a line from the Midland Great Western, at Athenry, to the town of Tuam. Capital, 90,000*l.* in 10*l.* shares; loans, 30,000*l.* Length, 15½ miles. Single line, opened 27th September, 1860. Under powers of an act passed in 1860, the line was leased to the Midland Great Western for ten years at a clear annual rental of 4,000*l.* This lease expired in October, 1870, and the line was worked as an independent undertaking until 1st November, 1872, from which date it was again leased to the Waterford Company for 20 years, at a clear annual rental of 2,600*l.* per annum, and half of surplus gross receipts over 5,000*l.* per annum. This lease was confirmed by act of 1872.

For details in brief of acts 1860 to 1877, see MANUAL for 1883, and previously.

Arrangements have been completed under which the repayment of the Government loan is commuted into an annuity, which will redeem principal and interest, at 4 per cent., in thirty years from the 2nd June, 1876. The amount of such annuity is 1,734*l.* 18*s.*, payable on 2nd June in each year. These payments have been met out of revenue, and from that source the principal of the loan has been reduced by 5,000*l.* to June 1884.

REVENUE.—The net earnings, which have been accumulating from time to time, and are retained, so far, to cover an over draft of capital account, &c., amounted on the 29th September, 1884, to 11,379*l.* In addition to paying off the loan, a dividend of 1½ per cent. per annum was paid on the ordinary share capital to 29th November, 1884.

CAPITAL.—The expenditure on this account to 29th September, 1884, amounted to 101,360*l.* The receipts to the same date had been as follow:—

Loans at 4 per cent.	£25,071	
Ordinary 10*l.* shares	61,828	
Interest, &c.	616	
Calls on shares forfeited	30	
Transferred from revenue	5,670	=£93,215
Balance expended in excess of receipts		8,145
		£101,360

TRANSFER DEPARTMENT.—Ordinary form; fee per deed, 2*s.* 6*d.*; if more sellers than one, 2*s.* 6*d.*; amounts of stock under 10*l.* not transferable.

Accounts made up to 25th March and 29th September. Meetings in April and October, or in May and November, as may be found most convenient.

No. of Directors.—Maximum, 6; minimum, 3. Directors retire and are elected in accordance with the Companies' Clauses Act. *Qualification*, 50 shares.

DIRECTORS:

Chairman—PERCY BERNARD, Esq., D.L., Castle Hackett, Tuam.

Cecil Robt. Henry, Esq., Tohermore, Tuam
David Rutledge, Esq., Barbersfort, Ballyglunin.
Charles Kelly, Esq., Q.C., Newtown, Ballyglunin.
Colonel James O'Hara, D.L., Lenaboy, Galway.
Colonel John Philip Nolan, M.P., R.A., Tuam.

OFFICERS.—Sec. and Man., John Fowler Nicoll; Auditors, Edward Vaughan and Dennis J. Kirwan.

Offices—Brunswick Chambers, Great Brunswick Street, Dublin.

9.—AYLESBURY AND BUCKINGHAM.

Incorporated by act of 6th August, 1860, to construct a line from the town of Aylesbury to join the Buckinghamshire at Claydon Junction. Length, 12¾ miles. Capital, 98,000*l.* in 25*l.* shares; loans, 32,500*l.* Working arrangements, under usual restrictions, with London and North Western and Buckinghamshire.

By act of 25th July, 1864, the company was authorised to raise additional capital to the extent of 12,000*l.* in shares and 4,000*l.* by loan, and by act of 19th June, 1865, the company was authorised to raise additional capital to the extent of 110,000*l.* in shares and 35,000*l.* on loan. Also to extend the time for completing the undertaking until two years after passing of this act.

AYLESBURY AND RICKMANSWORTH.—See Metropolitan.

REVENUE.—The total receipts during the half-year ended 30th June, 1884, amounted to 1,816*l.*, and the expenses to 1,541*l.*, as against 1,760*l.* and 1,715*l.* respectively for the corresponding period of 1883. The balance against revenue account at 30th June, 1884, amounted to 4,751*l.*, against 4,992*l.* at corresponding period of 1883. In operation, 12¾ miles.

CAPITAL.—The expenditure on this account to 30th June, 1884, amounted to 147,814*l.*, and the receipts to 118,839*l.*, as follow:—

Ordinary shares	£82,089
Ditto, 500*l.*, issued at 50 per cent. discount	250
Loans at 5 per cent	36,500
Balance	28,975
	£147,814

In addition to the capital above received, the sum of 28,920*l.* has been received as temporary loans on security of 30,000*l.* preference shares, authorised by 28 Vic., cap. 93, 1865, and special resolutions of shareholders, at meetings held on the 18th June, 1866, and 26th May, 1868, and 200*l.* on other security.

No. of Directors—Originally 9, but reduced to 5 by special resolution, 27th February, 1882; minimum, 3; quorum, 4; and 2 when reduced to 3. *Qualification*, 250*l.*

DIRECTORS:

Chairman—FRANCIS RUMMENS, Esq., 21, Elgin Road, Maida Vale, W.

Deputy-Chairman—Sir HARRY VERNEY, Bart., M.P., Claydon House, Winslow, Bucks, and 4, South Street, Park Lane, W.

Lieut.-Col. Philip Smith, C.B., The Guards' Club, Pall Mall, S.W., and Wendover, Bucks.
Myles Fenton, Esq., Assoc.Inst.C.E., 22, Ridge Green House, Nutfield, Surrey.
J. W. Williamson, Esq., 4, Stone Buildings, Lincoln's Inn, W.C., and 24, Warwick Road, Maida Hill, W.

OFFICERS.—Sec. and Man., J. G. Rowe; Eng., William Wilson, M.Inst.C.E., 13, Dean's Yard, Westminster, S.W.; Auditor, Alexander Hutt, Railway Clearing House, Euston, N.W.; Solicitors, Jennings, White, and Buckston, Whitehall Place, Westminster, S.W.

Head Offices—Aylesbury.

10.—AYR AND MAYBOLE JUNCTION.

This undertaking is now vested in the Glasgow and South Western (*vide* Glasgow and South Western Act, 1871), but remains incorporated for receiving, and if necessary enforcing, payment of the yearly sum payable under act, and for other purposes. The sum payable yearly is 2,450*l.*, in two equal half-yearly portions, and is equal to a dividend of 7 per cent. on the stock, besides several fixed payments.

Meetings in February or March and in August or September.

No. of Directors.—Maximum, 7; minimum, 4; quorum, 3. *Qualification*, 250*l.*

DIRECTORS:

Chairman—JOHN ROSS, jun., Esq., Merchant, Glasgow.

Deputy-Chairman—WILLIAM B. CUTHBERTSON, Esq., Merchant, Ayr.

David Brown, Esq., Banker, Maybole.
George M'M. T. Bone, Esq., Maybole.
John Cunningham, Esq., Trees, Maybole.

Secretary and Treasurer, John Pollock, Town Clerk, Ayr.

11.—BALA AND FESTINIOG.

Incorporated by act of 28th July, 1873, to construct a line commencing by a junction with the Corwen and Bala at Llangower, and terminating at Festiniog. Length, 22¼ miles; narrow gauge. Capital, 190,000*l.*, and 63,300*l.* on loan. The Great Western may subscribe 150,000*l.*, the Corwen and Bala 24,000*l.*, the Llangollen and Corwen 20,000*l.*, and the Vale of Llangollen 12,000*l.* Power to enter into working and other arrangements with Great Western, Merionethshire, Festiniog, and other companies.

By act of 16th April, 1878, the time for the completion of this railway was extended to 28th July, 1881.

The share capital was increased by 48,000*l.*, and debenture by 16,000*l.*, under authority of Bala and Festiniog Railway Additional Capital Certificate, 1882.

By resolution of shareholders on 11th August, 1882, the share capital of the company is converted into stock, as from 1st September, 1882.

The line was opened for public traffic on the 1st November, 1882.

A further increase of capital was authorised under the powers conferred upon the company by the Bala and Festiniog Railway (Additional Capital) Act, 1884, of 50,000*l.*, and 16,600*l.* on loan.

FESTINIOG AND BLAENAU.—This company became merged in the Bala and Festiniog, under the authority of the Great Western Act, 1880, on the 13th April, 1883. Length, 3½ miles.

No. of Directors.—Maximum, 8; minimum, 3; quorum, 3 and 2. *Qualification*, 500*l.*

DIRECTORS:

Chairman—Sir DANIEL GOOCH, Bart., M.P., 3, Warwick Road, Maida Hill, W.

Captain J. C. Best, Vivod, Llangollen.
J. J. Bibby, Esq., Hardwicke Grange, Shrewsbury.
Samuel Holland, Esq., M.P., Caerdeon, Dolgelley
David MacIver, Esq., M.P., Birkenhead.
C. G. Mott, Esq., Harrow Weald Lodge, Stanmore, Middlesex.
W. E. Oakeley, Esq., Atherstone, Warwickshire.
Owen S. Wynne, Esq., Plas Newydd, Ruabon.

OFFICERS.—Sec., George Boxall; Engs., Robertson and Mackintosh, 7, Westminster Chambers, Victoria Street, S.W.; Solicitors, Longueville, Jones, and Williams, Oswestry; Bankers, Parr's Banking Co., Chester.

Offices – Paddington Terminus, W.

12—BALLYCASTLE.

Incorporated by act of 22nd July, 1878, for the construction and maintenance of a railway from Ballymoney to Ballycastle, in the county of Antrim, Ireland. Length, about 16 miles 1 furlong and 8 chains. Gauge, 3 feet. Period for completion, 5 years. Arrangements with the Belfast and Northern Counties, who may subscribe 18,000*l.* towards the cost of the undertaking, and appoint two directors. Capital, 90,000*l.*, in 10*l.* shares. Borrowing powers, 45,000*l.*

The Belfast and Northern Counties have paid 18,000*l.* towards their subscription.

Opened on the 18th October, 1880. The line is said to be working satisfactorily, the receipts having continued to increase since the opening, but the amount of goods and minerals carried have not been as much as the directors anticipated.

CAPITAL.—The receipts on this account to 30th June, 1884, amounted to 90,723*l.*, viz., 51,575*l.* in ordinary 10*l.* shares, 9,026*l.* in baronial guarantee shares, miscellaneous receipts 121*l.*, and 30,000*l.* on loan—20,000*l.* at 4 per cent., 200*l.* at 4½ per cent., and 9,800*l.* at 5 per cent. per annum. The expenditure to the same date amounted to 101,518*l.*

No. of Directors.—Minimum, 3; maximum, 6; quorum, 2 and 3. *Qualification*, 25 shares. Belfast and Northern Counties appoint two additional, and Grand Jury of County Antrim one additional.

Quorum of meetings—Seven shareholders holding in the aggregate not less than 5,000*l.* in the capital of the company.

Meetings held end of February and August each half-year.

DIRECTORS:

Chairman—1 The Rev. Sir FREDERICK BOYD, Bart., The Mansion, Ballycastle.

Deputy-Chairman—2 JOHN CASEMENT, Esq., J. P., Magherin Temple, Ballycastle.

3 Richard M. Douglas, Esq., J.P., Portballantrae, Coleraine.

1 James M. Knox, Esq., Armoy.

2 William Woodside, Esq., Dunduan House, Coleraine.

* John McGildowney, Esq., J.P., Clare Park, Ballycastle.

3 Thomas McElderry, Esq., Ballymoney.

† Edmund McNeill, Esq., J.P., Craigdun, Craigs, Co. Antrim.

† John Young, Esq., J.P., Galgorm Castle, Ballymena.

1, Retire in 1885; 2, in 1886; 3, in 1887.

* Represents Grand Jury of County Antrim. † Represent Belfast and Northern Counties.

OFFICERS.—Sec. and Gen. Man., Silas Evans; Eng., James F. Mackinnon, Ballycastle; Loco. Supt., George Bradshaw; Auditors, Thomas B. Hamilton, Ballymoney, and Alexander McAlister, Ballycastle; Solicitors, L'Estrange and Brett, 6, Chichester Street, Belfast; Bankers, The Northern Banking Company Limited, Belfast.

Offices—9, Victoria Chambers, Belfast.

13.—BALLYCLARE, LIGONIEL, AND BELFAST JUNCTION.

Incorporated by act of 22nd August, 1881, for the construction of 3 railways in the districts indicated by the title. Length, about 15¾ miles. Period for completion, 5 years. Traffic arrangements with the Belfast Central. Capital, 120,000*l.* in 10*l.* shares, with power to divide into "preferred" and "deferred" half-shares. Borrowing powers, 40,000*l.*

By act of 14th July, 1884, the period for completion of works was extended to 22nd August, 1889.

No. of Directors—Maximum, 6; minimum, 4; quorum, 3. *Qualification*, 25 shares.

FIRST DIRECTORS:

Alexander Young, Esq., 41, Coleman Street, E.C.

Sir Thomas Dakin, 3, Creechurch Lane, Leadenhall Street, E.C.

Three others to be nominated.

OFFICERS.—Sec., James Ray; Solicitors, George Davis, Son, and Co., 80, Coleman Street, E.C.

Offices—41, Coleman Street, E.C.

14.—BALLYMENA AND LARNE.

Incorporated 7th August, 1874, to construct a railway, 17 miles in length, commencing at Ballymena, and terminating by a junction with the authorised Larne and Ballyclare, in the parish of Ballynure; also a railway, 2¾ miles in length (abandoned by act of 1878), commencing by a junction with the aforesaid, in the parish of Ballyclug, and terminating in the parish of Kirkinriola, by a junction with the authorised Ballymena, Cushendall, and Redbay. Gauge, 3 feet. Capital, 136,000*l.* in 10*l.* shares and 45,200*l.* on loan. By this act the powers of the Larne and Ballyclare are transferred to this company.

By act of 8th August, 1878 (Extension Act), the company was empowered to construct three new lines, viz.:—No. 1. Doagh Extension (1 mile 3 furlongs and 4 chains); No. 2. Kilwaughter Branch (1 mile 8 chains); and No. 3, from Ballykeel to Brocklamont (5 furlongs 9 chains), and to abandon the No. 2 line described in the act of 1874. Period for completion of the new lines, 5 years. Mutual facilities with Ballymena, Cushendall, and Redbay. New capital, 40,000*l.*; loans, &c., 20,000*l.*

The line was opened from Larne Harbour to Ballyclare, for goods traffic, on 1st August, 1877, and from Ballyclare Junction to Ballymena on 1st June, 1878. The line from Larne Harbour to Ballyclare and Ballymena (29½ miles) was opened for passenger traffic on 24th August, 1878.

The junction at Ballymena with the Ballymena, Cushendall, and Redbay (½ mile), was opened for goods traffic on 22nd September, 1880.

The extension of the Ballyclare Branch to Doagh was opened for traffic on 1st May, 1884.

Ballymena and Portglenone.—See General Index.

Revenue.—The receipts for the half-year ended 31st December, 1883, after providing for interest on loans, &c., the dividends of 4½ per cent. on the preference share capital, showed a balance remaining of 1,775*l.*, sufficient for the payment of a dividend at the rate of 2½ per cent. per annum on the fully paid up ordinary shares, leaving 422*l.* to be carried forward. For the half-year ended 30th June, 1884, the receipts, after providing for pre-preference and preference charges, showed a balance remaining of 1,553*l.*, out of which a sum of 500*l.* was placed to the credit of reserve fund and 1,053*l.* carried forward.

Capital.—The receipts to 30th June, 1884, amounted to 227,257*l.*, and the expenditure to 238,092*l.*, showing a balance against this account of 10,835*l.* The shares subscribed for amount to 166,832*l.*, and the capital, raised by loans, &c., 60,425*l.*

Quorum of meetings—10 shareholders, holding together not less than 10,000*l.*

No. of Directors.—Maximum, 5; minimum, 3 and 2. *Qualification*, 500*l.*

DIRECTORS:

Chairman—1 JAMES CHAINE, Esq., M.P., Ballycraigie, Muckamore.

Deputy-Chairman—2 OGILVIE B. GRAHAM, Esq., Larchfield, Lisburn.

1 Hugh McCalmont, Esq., 9, Grosvenor Place, S.W.

2 William Eccles, Esq., Larne.

3 Nathaniel Morton, Esq., Ballymena.

1, Retire in February, 1885; 2, in 1886; 3, in 1887.

OFFICERS.—Sec. and Man., F. W. Rew, Larne Harbour, County Antrim; Eng., W. Lewis, C.E., 43, Dame Street, Dublin; Accountant, James Browne, Larne Harbour; Loco. Supt., William Pinkerton, Larne Harbour; Auditors, Alex. Caruth, Ballymena, and W. P. Holmes, Belfast; Solicitors, L'Estrange and Brett, 9, Chichester Street, Belfast; Bankers, The Northern Banking Company, Belfast.

15.—BALLYMENA AND PORTGLENONE.

Incorporated by act of 11th August, 1879, for the construction and maintenance of a railway from Ballymena to Portglenone, both in the County of Antrim. Length, about 10¼ miles. Period for completion, five years. Arrangements with Belfast and Northern Counties and Ballymena and Larne. The latter company may raise capital and subscribe 10,000*l.* towards the capital of the undertaking. Capital, 60,000*l.* in 10*l.* shares, with power to divide into "preferred" and "deferred" half-shares. Borrowing powers, 30,000*l.*

By the company's act of 18th August, 1882, the period granted by the act of 1879 for completion of the railway is extended until the 11th day of August, 1886, and the act of 1879 shall be read and have effect accordingly.

No. of Directors (exclusive of one who may be appointed by the Ballymena and Larne.—Maximum, 5; minimum, 3. Quorum, 3 and 2. *Qualification*, 50 shares.

Quorum of meetings—9 shareholders, holding in the aggregate not less than 3,000*l.* in the capital of the company.

DIRECTORS:

Chairman—ROBERT JACKSON ALEXANDER, Esq., D.L., Portglenone.

William Gihon, Esq., Lisnafillan, Ballymena.

James Chaine, Esq., M.P., Ballycraigie, Muckamore, Co. Antrim.

Nathaniel Morton, Esq., Ballymena.

John McMeekin, Esq., Portglenone.

OFFICERS.—Sec., James Browne, Larne Harbour, Co. Antrim; Engineer, William Lewis, C.E., 43, Dame Street, Dublin; Auditors, John S. Alexander, Portglenone, and Samuel R. Young, Ballymena; Solicitors, L'Estrange and Brett, 9, Chichester Street, Belfast.

Temporary Offices—2, Royal Terrace, Larne Harbour, Co. Antrim.

16.—BANBURY AND CHELTENHAM DIRECT.

Incorporated by act of 21st July, 1873, to construct a line from Banbury to Cheltenham, by way of the Chipping Norton and Bourton-on-the-Water Branches of the Great Western. The line unites two of the principal main lines of the Great Western system, connecting their Birmingham and Oxford Line on the east with their Bristol and Cheltenham Line, and also with their South Wales Line on the west, opening a short and direct route, and bringing Cheltenham, the West of England, and South Wales into closer connection with London and the Midland and Eastern counties. Length of line, 33 miles, of which 16¼ miles (Bourton to Cheltenham, opened 1st June, 1881,) is worked by the Great Western for passenger, minerals, and goods traffic; the remaining 16¾ miles are in great part constructed, and is expected shortly to be opened for traffic.

The line to be worked by the Great Western in perpetuity for 45 per cent. of the gross receipts until they reach 25*l*. per mile per week, and when the receipts exceed that amount this company will receive 50 per cent.

1877 Debenture Stock, &c.—By act of 23rd July, 1877, authority was given to make sundry deviations and new lines (see Manual, 1882), to the working of which the agreement with the Great Western extends, and to issue 400,000*l*. in debenture stock, respecting which clause 32 enacts that the Great Western shall, at the times provided by article 23 of the said agreement, pay the proportion of the gross receipts payable to the company, or so much thereof as may be sufficient to provide for the interest for the preceding half-year on the debenture stock for the time being created and issued under this act to a separate account of the company, to be called the "Banbury and Cheltenham Direct Railway, 1877, Debenture Stock Account." A recent prospectus inviting applications for 100,000*l*. more of this stock states as follows, viz.:—"The 1877 debenture stock is entitled to 4 per cent. annual interest in perpetuity, to be increased to 5 per cent., as authorised by the Company's Act of Parliament of 1881, out of the surplus remaining after 1 per cent. beyond 4 per cent. (making together 5 per cent.) has been paid on the 1873 debenture stock."

By act of 8th August, 1878, further powers were conferred upon the holders of 1877 debenture stock, by which they were entitled to vote and otherwise have the same rights as holders of shares of the company, the holding of every 20*l*. of debenture stock to be equivalent to one share.

1879 Debenture Stock.—By act of 11th August, 1879, 60,000*l*. of debenture stock was authorised to be raised for the completion of the Bourton to Cheltenham Line; this stock is to bear interest at 5 per cent. per annum, to rank in priority to the 1873 and 1877 debenture stocks, and to be a first charge upon the sum payable in respect of debenture interest by the Great Western Railway under the act of 1873.

By act of 6th August, 1880, powers were obtained for a junction at Cheltenham, with provisions for a settlement of the disputes between the company and the Great Western.

1881 Debenture Stock, &c.—(See also paragraphs relating to priorities and voting, &c., powers, on next page). By the act of August, 1881, powers were obtained for raising 250,000*l*. 5 per cent. debenture stock, ranking after the 1873 and 1879, but in priority to the 1877 debenture stocks. Powers to vote and otherwise similar to those conferred on the holders of 1877 stock by the act of 1878 were conferred on the holders of 1873 debenture stock. The period for the completion of the unfinished portion of the line was extended to July, 1884. Authority was given to alter levels, and it is provided by this act that the interest on the debenture debt, which under the act of 1873 was payable by the Great Western direct to the debenture holders, shall be paid to the company, and that the company shall distribute it among the debenture holders. It also provides that in the absence of any other available funds the company may apply a sum not exceeding 5 per cent. on the amount from time to time received from the Great Western in discharging the necessary expenses of administering and carrying on the business of the company.

CAPITAL.—Half-year ended 30th June, 1884, amount expended £1,412,238

Receipts.—Ordinary shares	£41,100	
Ordinary stock	21,300	
Preferred stock (6 per cent.)	268,800	
Deferred stock	268,800	
Debenture stocks (1873, 1877, 1879, and 1881)	861,548	
Rent-charge (capitalised at 20 years' purchase)	9,344	= £1,470,892
Balance		£58,654

MEM.—All interest due up to the 1st November, 1884, on the 1879 debenture stock, was paid on that day, the net traffic receipts from the section open being more than sufficient to cover this.

NEW DEBENTURE CAPITAL.—In October, 1882, the directors invited applications for 250,000*l.* in 5 per cent perpetual debenture stock at par, payable 5*l.* on application, 20*l.* on allotment, and the remainder in three equal instalments, on the 1st January, 1st February, and 1st March, 1883; interest from the respective dates on which the instalments are paid, payable half-yearly, on 30th March and 30th September. This debenture stock ranks, in accordance with the company's acts of Parliament, in priority to 1,000,000*l.* of stocks, viz., 400,000*l.* 1877 debenture stock and 600,000*l* share capital, and immediately after 260,000*l.* of debenture stocks issued and paid up. The whole of this stock has been subscribed for.

By act of 1883 the company was empowered to create 150,000*l.* 1883 5 per cent. debenture stock, ranking after the 1877 debenture stock, and to issue same in payment of arrears of interest on the existing debenture debt, also to create 100,000*l.* 5 per cent. preference stock, ranking after the 1883 debenture stock, and to issue same to creditors in discharge of claims.

PRIORITIES OF STOCKS.—Under act of 11th August, 1881 (clause 9), the priorities of interest on the debenture stocks of the company are thus defined, viz.:—"From and after the passing of this act the revenues of the company, so far as applicable to the payment of interest on the debenture stocks of the company, shall, notwithstanding anything contained in the existing acts of the company, be applied as follow:—1. In payment of interest at the rate of 5*l.* per cent. per annum on the 1879 debenture stock. 2. In payment of interest at the rate of 4*l.* per cent. per annum on the 1873 debenture stock. 3. In payment of interest at the rate of 5*l.* per cent. per annum on the 1881 debenture stock. 4. In payment of interest at the rate of 4*l.* per cent. per annum on the 1877 debenture stock. 5. In payment of further interest at the rate of 1*l.* per cent. per annum on the 1873 debenture stock. 6. In payment of further interest at the rate of 1*l.* per cent. per annum on the 1877 debenture stock. 7. In payment of 5 per cent. on the 1883 debenture stock. 8. In payment of 5 per cent. on the 100,000*l.* preference stock."

VOTING AND OTHER POWERS TO HOLDERS OF DEBENTURE STOCKS.—Clauses 10 and 11 of the act of 11th August, 1881, are as follow:—"The holders of 1873 debenture stock, and of the 1881 debenture stock, shall be entitled to attend, speak, and vote at every general meeting of the company, in the like way, and to the like extent, and in the like proportion with respect to the number of votes as the holders of shares in the company, and shall have the same rights, as such holders, to require the directors of the company to call extraordinary meetings of the company, which rights they may exercise irrespective of, and in addition to, any rights of voting or otherwise to which they may be entitled in respect of any shares in the company, which may be held by them respectively, and the rights by this act conferred upon them may be exercised either jointly with the holders of shares or not. For the purposes of determining the number of votes to which the holders of 1873 debenture stock and of the 1881 debenture stock are entitled, every 20*l.* of that debenture stock shall be deemed to be equivalent to one share. Any holder in his own right of 1873 debenture stock or of 1881 debenture stock, to the amount of 500*l.* or upwards, may be elected and act as a director as fully and effectually as if he were the possessor in his own right of twenty-five shares."

No. of Directors.—Maximum, 6; minimum, 4; quorum, 3 and 2. *Qualification*, 25 shares.

DIRECTORS:

Chairman—General Sir MICHAEL KENNEDY, R.E., K.C.S.I., 102, Gloucester Terrace, Hyde Park, W.

Deputy-Chairman—Col. J. WILKINSON, Southampton Lodge, Highgate, N.

Fred. W. Bond, Esq., 21, Great St. Helens, E.C., and Liverpool.

Charles Kemp Dyer, Esq., J.P., St. Alban's, Herts.

Henry Lovatt, Esq., Assoc.Inst.C.E., Wolverhampton, and Low Hill, Bushbury, Staffordshire.

John Wilson, Esq., Stoke Works, Astwood, Worcestershire.

Two directors retire annually, but are eligible for re-election.

OFFICERS.—Sec., Richard B. Looker; Eng., William Wilson, C.E., 13, Dean's Yard, Westminster, S.W.; Auditors, Arthur Cooper, 14, George Street, Mansion House, E.C., and Roderick Mackay, 8, Lothbury, E.C.; Solicitors, Walter Webb and Co., 23, Queen Victoria Street, E.C., and J. Billingsley Looker, 8, Drapers' Gardens, Throgmorton Street, E.C.; Bankers, The London and Westminster Bank Limited, Bloomsbury Branch, 214, High Holborn, W.C.

Offices—43, Finsbury Square, E.C.

17.—BARNOLDSWICK.

Incorporated by act of 12th August, 1867, to construct a line from Barnoldswick to the Leeds and Bradford Extension of the Midland. Length, 2 miles. Capital, 40,000*l.* in 10*l.* shares and 13,300*l.* on loan.

Arrangements with Midland, which works the line.

No. of Directors—5; minimum, 3; quorum 3. *Qualification*, 250*l.*

DIRECTORS:

William Bracewell, Esq., New Field Edge, Barnoldswick.
Clayton Slater, Esq., Barnoldswick and Canada.
William Hewitt, Esq., Colne.
Henry Slater, Esq., Barnoldswick.

All eligible for re-election.

OFFICERS.—Sec., Henry Waite; Eng., J. I. Mawson, Manchester; Auditor, John Eastwood, Barnoldswick; Solicitors, W. and A. Ascroft, 4, Cannon Street, Preston.

18.—BARRY DOCK AND RAILWAYS.

Incorporated by special Act of Parliament, 47 and 48 Vic., cap. 257, Session 1884. Authorised share capital, 1,050,000*l.* Of this authorised capital 10,000 ordinary shares of 10*l.* each were issued in 1884.

The object of the company is the construction of a dock at Barry Island, 7 miles from Cardiff, and within the port of Cardiff, and the construction of railways of about 26 miles in length from the Dock to the Rhondda Valley, with access by junctions with existing and authorised railways to all the other great mineral-producing districts of the South Wales coalfield.

DIRECTORS:

Chairman—The Right Honourable Lord WINDSOR, St. Fagan's Castle, Cardiff.

Deputy-Chairman—DAVID DAVIES, Esq., M.P., Broneirion, Llandinam, Montgomeryshire.

Crawshay Bailey, Esq., J.P., Maindiff Court, Abergavenny.
John Cory, Esq., J.P., Cardiff and London.
Lewis Davis, Esq., J.P., Ferndale Collieries.
John Fry, Esq., J.P., Shipowner, Cardiff.
Archibald Hood, Esq., J.P., Llwynipia Collieries.
James Walter Insole, Esq., Cymmer Collieries.
John Osborne Riches, Esq., Cardiff.
David Cooper Scott, Esq., 7, Drapers' Gardens, E.C.
Thomas Roe Thompson, Esq., Cardiff.
John Howard Thomas, Esq., Cambrian Collieries.
Edmund Hannay Watts, Esq., London and Cardiff.

OFFICERS.—Sec., G. C. Downing, Vienna Chambers, Cardiff; Engs., Brown and Adams, Cardiff, J. Wolfe Barry and H. M. Brunel, Westminster, and J. W. Szlumper, Westminster; Bankers, The National Provincial Bank of England, Bute Docks Branch, Cardiff.

Offices—Vienna Chambers, Cardiff.

19.—BEDFORD AND NORTHAMPTON.

Incorporated by act of 5th July, 1865, to construct a line from Bedford, on the Midland, to Northampton. Length, between 20 and 21 miles. Capital, 400,000*l.* in 20*l.* shares and 133,000*l.* on loan. Arrangements with Midland. Opened 10th June, 1872.

By act of 23rd July, 1866, the company was authorised to construct several new lines in lieu of others abandoned. Also to divide the shares into "deferred" and "preferred," and by act of 15th July, 1867, the company was authorised to construct several deviations in substitution of lines to be abandoned.

By special agreements, incorporated in the acts of Parliament, the Midland is to maintain, manage, stock, and work the Bedford and Northampton, and to pay over 50 per cent. of the divisible receipts, such receipts being taken in the accounts between the two companies at the minimum of 30*l*. per mile per week.

Amalgamation with Midland.—Subject to the consent of the shareholders an amalgamation with the Midland is announced by the directors, same to be confirmed in the Midland Bill of 1885. The terms are as follow:—"The Midland to take over the debenture stock and rent-charges of the Bedford and Northampton. The Bedford 'preferred' stock to be exchanged for Midland four per cent. preference stock, in the proportion of 112*l*. 10*s*. of Midland preference stock for each 100*l*. of Bedford 'preferred' stock. The 'deferred' stock to be exchanged for Midland four per cent. preference stock, in the proportion of 25*l*. of Midland preference stock for each 100*l*. of Bedford 'deferred' stock, or, at the option of each shareholder, for Midland ordinary stock, in the proportion of 21*l*. of Midland ordinary for each 100*l*. of Bedford 'deferred' stock. Subject to the Bedford satisfying the Midland that all its liabilities on capital and revenue accounts have been or will be discharged, the amalgamation to take effect as from 31st December, 1885."

Revenue.—For the half-years ended 31st December, 1883, and 30th June, 1884, the balances at net revenue sufficed for the payment of a dividend on the "preferred" stock at the rate of 4*l*. 15*s*. per cent. per annum. No dividend has yet been earned on the "deferred" stock.

Capital.—The receipts on this account to 30th June, 1884, amounted to 533,000*l*., the expenditure being the same. The receipts are detailed below:—

Preferred stock (at 5 per cent. over the deferred)	£200,000
Deferred stock	200,000
Rent-charges at 5 per cent.	2,914
Debenture stock at 4 per cent	130,086

Notes.—The dividend on the debenture stock is accumulative, and payable half-yearly on the 1st January and 1st July.

The dividend on the "preferred" stock is contingent upon the profits of each separate year. It is payable immediately after the half-yearly meetings in March and September, the transfer books closing about 14 days before payment.

TRANSFER DEPARTMENT QUERIES AND REPLIES.

Queries.	Replies.
Transfer form—ordinary or special?	Ordinary.
Fee per deed?	2*s*. 6*d*.
Ditto if more sellers than one?	2*s*. 6*d*. each seller, if other than joint holding.
May several classes of stock be transferred on one deed?	Yes.
Are certificates required to accompany transfers?	Yes.
What amounts of stock are transferable, and are parts of 1*l*. sterling allowed to be transferred?	Any amount, except fractions of 1*l*.
To what officer should transfer communications be sent?	Secretary.
In acceptances, renunciations, &c., of allotments of new stock, proxies, or other forms sent to trustees and other joint holders, what signatures are required?	For proxies, signature of first name only; in other cases, signatures of all.

Meetings held in London, half-yearly, in March and September.
***No. of Directors*—7; quorum, 3. *Qualification*, 500*l*.**

DIRECTORS:

Chairman—JAMES HOWARD, Esq., M.P., Clapham Park, Bedfordshire.

Deputy-Chairman—WILLIAM FRANCIS HIGGINS, Esq., Turvey House, Bedfordshire.

Joseph Francis Burke, Esq., C.E., Stratford-on-Avon.
Thomas Jarvis Coombs, Esq., Palace Chambers, St. Stephens, S.W.
Henry Merrick, Esq., Bradford, Wilts.
Joseph Palmer, Esq., Olney, Bucks.
John Morrison Stobart, Esq., Spring Vale, Ryde, Isle of Wight.

OFFICERS.—Sec., H. F. Tahourdin; Auditors, Roderick Mackay and Charles Hobbs; Solicitors, Merrick and Co., 6, Old Jewry, E.C.

Offices—9, Victoria Chambers, S.W.

20.—BELFAST CENTRAL.

Incorporated by act of 25th July, 1864, to connect the several railways in the town of Belfast, and construct a central station therein. Capital, 300,000*l.* in 10*l.* shares; loans, 100,000*l.*

For brief details of subsequent acts, 1865 to 1880, see MANUAL for 1882, and previously.

By act of 19th May, 1884, authority was obtained to deviate part and abandon other parts of their western extensions, and for sundry other purposes.

DEBENTURE STOCKS.—By act of 21st July, 1879, the power to issue the balance of "A" debenture stock under the act of 1872, and to create and issue "B" and "C" debenture stocks, was extinguished, and power given to issue 1st and 2nd debenture stocks of 350,000*l.* and 280,000*l.* respectively, both to be charged upon the undertaking under former acts prior to all shares of the company. The 1st debenture stock, to be issued at par, bears interest at 5 per cent. per annum, to be redeemable at such a premium, not exceeding 5 per cent., and at such times and in such manner as the company may determine at or before the date of issue, and to be allotted to the proprietors of "A" debenture stock in proportion to their holdings, thereby to be extinguished. The 2nd debenture stock to rank next in order of priority to the 1st debenture stock, with interest at 5 per cent. per annum, payable only out of the revenue of the company which would be applicable in each year to the payment of dividends on the shares of the company. The money raised by the issue of the residue of both stocks to be applied to the repayment of mortgages, moneys advanced and interest, Lloyd's bond, &c., and for the completion of the undertaking, purchase of rolling stock, &c.

Length of line in operation, 4 miles 6 chains. Lines of Harbour Commissioners run over, about 5 miles.

ARRANGEMENTS WITH GREAT NORTHERN OF IRELAND.—The arbitration between this company and the Great Northern of Ireland was brought to a close under an award by Mr. Cawkwell, dated 26th January, 1880, which gives directions as to future traffic arrangements between the two companies.

CAPITAL.—The expenditure on this account to 31st December, 1883, amounted to 711,100*l.*, and the receipts were 675,078*l.*, as under:—

Ordinary 10*l.* shares	£150,000
Loans at 4 per cent.	100,000
First debenture stock	249,304
Second debenture stock	175,774
Total	£675,078

Meetings held in London in February and August.

No. of Directors—5; maximum, 8; quorum, 3. *Qualification*, 500*l.*

DIRECTORS:

Chairman—ALEXANDER YOUNG, Esq., 41, Coleman Street, E.C.

M. G. Buchanan, Esq., Hayes, Beckenham, Kent.

R. P. Laurie, Esq., 22, Threadneedle Street, E.C.

Benjamin Piercy, Esq., 8, Drapers' Gardens, E.C.

T. C. Tatham, Esq., Millbrook House, Highgate, N.

OFFICERS.—Sec., James Ray; Gen. Man., J. Bucknall Cooper; Res. Eng., R. J. Calwell; Auditors, H. Bishop and Edward Bellamy; Solicitors, George Davis, Son, and Co., 30, Coleman Street, E.C., and R. D. Bates and Co., Belfast.

Offices—41, Coleman Street, E.C.

21.—BELFAST AND COUNTY DOWN.

Incorporated by act of 20th June, 1846, for a line from Belfast to Downpatrick, with branches to Holywood, Donaghadee, and Bangor; total, 44¾ miles. The branch to Holywood, 4½ miles, was opened on 2nd August, 1848; from Belfast to Newtownards, 12¾ miles, on 6th May. 1850; from Comber to Ballynahinch, on 10th September. 1858, 13 miles; to Downpatrick, 9 miles, on 23rd March, 1859; and the line completed by the opening of the branch from Newtownards to Donaghadee, on 3rd June, 1861, 10 miles. Newcastle, 11½ miles. Belfast, Holywood, and Bangor, 12¼ miles. In operation, 68 miles.

The following is a list of Acts obtained by this company since its incorporation, with short heads of the objects for which the various powers were sought:—

1855—25TH MAY.—Capital fixed at 500,000*l.* Borrowing powers restricted to 166,666*l.* Extension to Ballynahinch, 3¾ miles further.

1857—10TH AUGUST.—Subscription of 15,000*l.* to Portpatrick.

1858—12TH JULY.—Extension of time for the purchase of land.

1860—Extension of time for making Donaghadee Branch.

1861—Abandonment of Bangor Branch.

1861 (Downpatrick and Newry Act).—Subscription of 20,000*l.* to Downpatrick and Newry.

1865—29TH JUNE.—Transfer of Holywood Branch to Belfast, Holywood, and Bangor (see below).

1873—Reduction of rental of Holywood Branch to 4,000*l.* per annum.

1876—11TH AUGUST.—Provisions for the discharge of the company's liabilities and redemption of mortgage debt. Consolidation of stock. New capital, 65,000*l.* in "A" preference stock.

1881—22ND AUGUST.—The Belfast and County Down Railway (Newcastle Transfer) Act, 1881. (See below.)

1884—14TH JULY.—The Belfast and County Down Railway (Bangor Transfer) Act, 1884. (See below.)

BELFAST, HOLYWOOD, AND BANGOR.—During the half-year ended 31st December, 1876, this company discharged a debt due to the Belfast and County Down, and also paid 12,950*l.* on account of the purchase of the Holywood Branch, the terms for which purchase included a charge of 50,000*l.* in cash, with an annual rent of 5,000*l.* in monthly instalments, but redeemable within ten years, by gradual payment of 100*l.* for 4½ of the said rent. By act of 1873 the rental was reduced to 4,000*l.* The purchase was completed during the half-year ended 30th June, 1877, by a further payment of 9,050*l.*, making 22,000*l.* By this purchase the Holywood are relieved of 1,000*l.* per annum of the rent-charge payable by them, thus reducing that charge to 3,000*l.* per annum instead of 4,000*l.* By act of 14th July, 1884, this undertaking was transferred to the Belfast and County Down as from the 1st September, 1884. For particulars as to the position of this company in the past, see MANUAL for 1884, pages 18 and 19.

DOWNPATRICK, DUNDRUM, AND NEWCASTLE.—This railway has now been transferred to the Belfast and County Down, under the provisions of "The Belfast and County Down (Newcastle transfer) Act, 1881," the consideration being the payment of 12,000*l.* in cash and the issue of 38,000*l.* of debentures to the Newcastle Company, and the transfer is subject to certain rent-charges specified in the first schedule annexed to the act. The act received the royal assent on 22nd August, 1881.

The consolidation of the preference shares of the company into one uniform 5 per cent. preference stock was sanctioned by the proprietary on 13th March, 1877, and duly carried into effect.

REVENUE.—The receipts and expenses on this account for the half-years ended 31st December, 1883, and 30th June, 1884, were as under:—

	Dec., 1883.	June, 1884.
Passengers, parcels, mails, &c.	£20,969	£17,859
Goods, minerals, and cattle	11,024	11,018
Rents and transfer fees	210	257
Gross receipts	£32,203	£29,134
Expenditure	16,347	14,871
Net	£15,856	£14,263
Add—Balance from previous half-year	1,213	1,902
Dividend on shares in Portpatrick Railway	319	244
Rent of Holywood Line	1,500	1,500
Interest on current account	145	217
Premium on issue of stocks	...	448
Rebate on Newcastle debentures	1,908	400
Belfast, Holywood, and Bangor.—Received in settlement of account furnished for law costs of Lease Act, 1873.		
Total net revenue	£20,941	£18,974
Interest, &c.	6,104	4,131
	£14,837	£14,843
Dividends on 5 per cent. stock and shares	6,204	6,204
	£8,633	£8,649
Dividends on 4 per cent. stock and shares	832	930
	£7,801	£7,709
Dividends on ordinary stock at 4 per cent. per annum	5,899	4,719
Balance carried forward	£1,902	£2,990

CAPITAL.—The expenditure on this account to 30th June, 1884, amounted to 827,930*l*., as follows:—On lines open for traffic, 658,819*l*.; working stock, 72,461*l*.; subscription to Portpatrick, 15,704*l*.; Belfast, Holywood, and Bangor rent account, less balance of the net revenue account to 31st December, 1876, 21,223*l*.; paid on account of purchase of Downpatrick, Dundrum, and Newcastle, 58,723*l*. The receipts, as given in detail below, amounted to 826,970*l*., the balance against the account being 960*l*.:—

Ordinary 50*l*. shares	£235,950
5 per cent. preference stock	248,141
4½ per cent. "A" preference stock	50,000
4 per cent. preference stock, 1881	50,515
Treasury loan at 3½ per cent.	79,978
Debentures	4,000
Debenture stock at 4 per cent.	64,626
Received from Holywood Company on account of purchase	49,490
Forfeited shares	22,260
Loans paid off under act 1876	22,000
	£826,970

PRIORITIES, DESCRIPTIONS, DIVIDENDS, &c., OF STOCKS AND SHARES.—The following is a list of this company's Securities, numbered in order of priority, with conditions of issue *in brief*, the descriptions of stocks and shares to be observed in transfer deeds and all other legal documents relating thereto, viz.:—

1—FOUR PER CENT. DEBENTURE STOCK.—Issued under act of 1860, for the conversion of mortgages, &c. Interest accumulative, and payable half-yearly, 30th June and 31st December (no arrears). Transfer books close about 7 days before payment.

2—"A" PREFERENCE STOCK.—Issued under act 1876. Dividend at 4½ per cent. per annum, contingent upon profits of each separate half-year, payable 30th June and 31st December (no arrears). Transfer books close about 7 days before payment.

3—FIVE PER CENT. PREFERENCE STOCK.—Issued under acts 1855 and 1876. Dividends accumulative, and payable half-yearly, 1st March and 1st September (no arrears). Transfer books close 14 days before the date of each half-yearly meeting.

4—FOUR PER CENT. PREFERENCE STOCK, 1881.—Issued under act 1881. Dividends payable half-yearly, 1st March and 1st September. Transfer books close 14 days before the date of each half-yearly meeting.

5—ORDINARY SHARES.—Issued under act 1855. These shares are of 50*l*. each.

TRANSFER DEPARTMENT QUERIES AND REPLIES.

QUERIES.	REPLIES.
Transfer form—ordinary or special?	Ordinary.
Fee per deed?	2*s*. 6*d*.
Ditto if more sellers than one?	2*s*. 6*d*.
May several classes of stock be transferred on one deed?	No.
Are certificates required to accompany transfers?	Yes.
What amounts of stock are transferable, and are parts of 1*l*. sterling allowed to be transferred?	4 per cent. debenture, 10*l*.; 4½ per cent. "A" preference, 10*l*.; 5 per cent. preference, 1*l*.; 4 per cent. preference, 1881, 10*l*.
To what officer should transfer communications be sent?	Secretary.
In acceptances, renunciations, &c., of allotments of new stocks, proxies, or other forms sent to trustees, what signatures are required?	The first name.

Meetings held half-yearly, in February and August. Dividends payable 1st March and 1st September.

Scale of Voting.—One vote for every share up to 10; one for every five shares from 10 to 100; and one for every 10 above 100.

No. of Directors.—Maximum, 12; minimum, 8. *Qualification*, 1,000*l*.

C

DIRECTORS:

Chairman—1 RICHARD WOOD KELLY, Esq., 13 and 14, Cope Street, Dublin.

Deputy-Chairman—3 JOSEPH RICHARDSON, Esq., Springfield, Lisburn.

3 James Barbour, Esq., Ardville, Holywood.
1 W. J. Pirrie, Esq., Queen's Island Works, Belfast.
1 John Campbell, Esq., Lennoxvale, Belfast.
2 Henry L. Mulholland, Esq., J.P., Ballywalter Park, County Down.
2 D. L. Coates, Esq., Clonallon, Strandtown, Belfast.
2 Thomas Andrews, Esq., Ardara, Comber.

1, Retire in February, 1885; 2, in 1886; 3, in 1887.

OFFICERS.—Sec., John Milliken, Belfast; Gen. Man., John E. Medley, Belfast; Eng., B. D. Wise, Belfast; Loco. Supt., R. G. Miller; Accountant, Hugh Evans, Belfast; Auditors, W. B. Caughey, Belfast, and H. H. Boyd and Magill, Belfast; Solicitors, Johns, Hewitt, and Johns, Belfast and Dublin.

Head Offices—Queen's Quay, Belfast.

22.—BELFAST AND NORTHERN COUNTIES.

(FORMERLY BELFAST AND BALLYMENA.)

Incorporated by act of 21st July, 1845, for a railway from Belfast to Ballymena, with branches to Carrickfergus and Randalstown.

Under act of 1853, an extension from Randalstown, through Toome, Castle Dawson, Magherafelt, and Moneymore, to Cookstown, was obtained. 27 miles. Single line. Opened 10th November, 1856. The capital for this branch was created on the 30th May, 1856, viz., 192,500*l.* in 25*l.* shares, the whole of which were taken by holders of original stock. By act of 15th May, 1860, the name of the company was changed to "Belfast and Northern Counties," and the capital increased by 70,000*l.* The company was also authorised to purchase the Coleraine Junction from the Ballymena, Ballymoney, and Portrush.

For brief details of Acts 1864, 1874, 1878, and 1881, see MANUAL for 1882, and previously.

1882—3RD JULY.—Construction of railways at Ballylining and Rashee, in substitution for those authorised by act of 1881. Period for completion, 5 years. New capital, 25,000*l.*; loans, 8,000*l.*

1883—16TH JULY.—Company authorised to subscribe a further sum of 5,000*l.* to the Limavady and Dungiven, and powers obtained as to the appointment of directors for the Ballymena, Cushendall, and Redbay. New capital, 10,000*l.*

1884—14TH JULY.—Tramways from Broughshane to Clontrace, and Retreat to Cushendall. Purchase of hotels and sundry agreements. Vesting of Ballymena, Cushendall, and Redbay (see below). New capital, 80,000*l.* in ordinary or preference shares or stock; loans, 25,000*l.*

BALLYCASTLE.—See GENERAL INDEX.

BALLYMENA, BALLYMONEY, COLERAINE, AND PORTRUSH JUNCTION.—Opened 7th November, 1855. Under act of 15th May, 1860, this junction was purchased by the Belfast and Northern Counties, which obtained possession on 1st January, 1861. The purchase money consisted of 160,000*l.* in preference shares, bearing interest at 4 per cent., the Belfast assuming the Portrush bonded debt of 60,000*l.*, making together a total payment of 220,000*l.*—For previous details (in brief), see MANUAL for 1882, page 19.

BALLYMENA, CUSHENDALL, AND REDBAY.—By act of 14th July, 1884, this undertaking was vested in the Northern Counties as from 14th October, 1884.—For particulars as to the position of this company in the past, see MANUAL 1884, page 10.

BALLYMENA AND PORTGLENONE.—See GENERAL INDEX.

CARRICKFERGUS HARBOUR JUNCTION.—See GENERAL INDEX.

CARRICKFERGUS AND LARNE.—A new agreement has been entered into with this company for working the line from 1st January, 1880, to 31st December, 1884, at 40 per cent. after working expenses.

DERRY CENTRAL.—Leased by this company for 21 years from 18th February, 1880, to 18th February, 1901, at 30 per cent. after working expenses (act 1877).—See GENERAL INDEX.

DRAPERSTOWN.—See GENERAL INDEX.

LIMAVADY AND DUNGIVEN.—See GENERAL INDEX.

LONDONDERRY AND COLERAINE.—Incorporated by act of 4th August, 1845, but dissolved and re-incorporated under the same title by an act obtained 23rd May, 1852. Length, 36 miles. By act of 24th July, 1871, the company became vested in the Belfast and Northern Counties. For brief details of the position of this undertaking prior to 1871, see MANUAL for 1882, page 19.

REVENUE.—The gross receipts for the half-year ended 31st December, 1883, amounted to 91,944*l*., and the expenditure to 50,083*l*., leaving a profit of 41,861*l*. The net revenue sufficed for the full interest on all the preferences, and a dividend at the rate of 4 per cent. per annum on the ordinary stock, carrying to reserve fund 1,000*l*., and forward to next half-year 2,422*l*.

The gross receipts for the half-year ended 30th June, 1884, amounted to 82,958*l*., and the expenditure to 49,399*l*., leaving a profit of 33,559*l*. The net revenue sufficed for full dividends on all the preferences, and on the ordinary stock at the rate of 2½ per cent. per annum, carrying forward 613*l*.

The dividends were payable on the 17th February and 17th August last for each half-year respectively.

PRODUCTIVE MILEAGE—30th June, 1884.—Belfast and Northern Counties, 136¼.

CAPITAL.—The statement of stock and share capital created, showing the proportion received to 30th June, 1884, was as follows:—

Description.	Created.	Received.
Ordinary stock	£599,420	£599,320
4 per cent. preference stock	432,500	372,500
4½ " " "	444,600	444,600
	£1,476,520	£1,416,420

The receipts and expenditure to 30th June, 1884, are comprised in the subjoined detail:—

Received.		*Expended.*	
Shares and stock	£1,416,420	Lines opened for traffic	£1,487,032
Loans	60,000	Working stock	285,764
Debenture stock	427,824	Subscriptions to other railways	168,787
	£1,904,244		
Balance	37,339		
	£1,941,583		£1,941,583

Estimate of further expenditure to 31st December, 1884, nil.

Balance of capital		£245,480
Share capital created but not yet issued		60,000
Loan capital authorised but not yet received		21,008
		£326,488
Less balance at debit of capital	£37,339	
" New works in progress, payments on account	33,031=	70,370
		£256,118

PRIORITIES, DESCRIPTIONS, DIVIDENDS, &c.—The following is a list of this company's Stocks and Shares, numbered in order of priority, with conditions of issue *in brief*, the descriptions to be strictly observed in transfer deeds and all other documents relating thereto, viz.:—

1—DEBENTURE STOCK.—Dividend at 4 per cent. per annum, accumulative, and payable half-yearly, on 1st January and 1st July. Transfer books close 10 days before payment.
2—FOUR-AND-A-HALF PER CENT. PREFERENCE STOCK.—Issued under act 1845.
3—FOUR " " " " " 1858.
4—FOUR " " " " " 1860.
5—FOUR-AND-A-HALF PER CENT. " " " " 1860.
6—FOUR-AND-A-HALF PER CENT. " " " " 1864.
7—FOUR-AND-A-HALF PER CENT. PREFERENCE STOCK.—Issued under act 1871.
8—FOUR-AND-A-HALF PER CENT. PREFERENCE 100*l*. STOCK.—Issued under act 1874.
9—FOUR " " " " " 1878.
10—ORDINARY STOCK.—Issued under acts 1845 and 1853.

On all the above-named stocks, except No. 1, the dividends are contingent upon the profits of each separate half-year, and are payable half-yearly, on the 17th February and 17th August, the transfer books closing 21 days before payment.

TRANSFER DEPARTMENT QUERIES AND REPLIES.

Queries.	Replies.
Transfer form—ordinary or special?	Ordinary.
Fee per deed?	2s. 6d.
Ditto if more sellers than one?...	2s. 6d each seller.
May several classes of stock be transferred on one deed?	If from one seller to one buyer.
Are certificates required to accompany transfers?	In all cases.
What amounts of stock are transferable, and are parts of 1l. sterling allowed to be transferred?	Debenture stock 10l. and upwards.
To what officer should transfer communications be addressed?	The Secretary.
In acceptances, renunciations, &c., of allotments of new stock, proxies, or other forms sent to trustees, what signatures are required?	The first-named trustee in proxies; all names in other forms.

Meetings in February and August.

DIRECTORS:

Chairman—1 GEORGE J. CLARKE, Esq., D.L., J.P., The Steeple, Antrim.

Deputy-Chairman—2 Sir CHARLES LANYON, J.P., M.Inst.C.E., The Abbey, Belfast.

3 John B. Gunning-Moore, Esq., J.P., Loymount, Cookstown.

2 John Young, Esq., J.P., D.L., Galgorm Castle, Ballymena.

2 Henry Hugh M'Neile, Esq., J.P., Parkmount, Belfast.

2 Edmund McNeill, Esq., J.P., Craigdunn, Craigs, County Antrim.

2 William Valentine, Esq., J.P., Glenavna, Belfast.

1 George Cather, Esq., J.P., Carrichue, Londonderry.

3 The Right Hon. Viscount Templetown, Castle Upton, Templepatrick.

3 Henry E. Cartwright, Esq., J.P., Manor House, Magherafelt.

3 S. M. Alexander, Esq., D.L., J.P., Roe Park, Limavady.

The figures indicate the order of retirement—No. 1 retiring in August, 1885, when a ballot of shareholders will fill up the vacancies. All eligible for re-election.

OFFICERS.—Sec., Charles Stewart; Gen. Man., Edward J. Cotton; Eng., Robert Collins, C.E.; Loco. Supt., B. Malcolm; Accountant, Francis J. Hopkirk; Treasurer, Belfast Banking Company; Public Accountants, H. H. Boyd and Magill, Belfast; Auditors, John Pim and Henry Archer, Belfast; Solicitors, James Torrens and Sons, Belfast.

Head Offices—Terminus, York Road, Belfast.

23.—BELFAST, STRANDTOWN, AND HIGH HOLYWOOD.

Incorporated by act of 22nd August, 1881, for the construction and maintenance of a railway, commencing by a junction with the Belfast Central, and terminating at Holywood. Length, about 5 miles. Period for completion, 5 years. Traffic arrangements with the Belfast Central. Capital, 72,000l. in 10l. shares, with power to divide into "preferred" and "deferred" half-shares. Borrowing powers, 24,000l.

By act of 28th April, 1884, the period for purchase of lands was extended to 22nd August, 1885.

No. of Directors.—Maximum, 6; minimum, 3; quorum, 3 and 2. *Qualification*, 20 shares.

FIRST DIRECTORS:

Alexander Young, Esq., 41, Coleman Street, E.C.

John Anderson, Esq.

John Harrison, Esq.

Sir Thomas Dakin, Knt., 3, Creechurch Lane, Leadenhall Street, E.C.

John McCance, Esq.

OFFICERS.—Sec., James Ray; Solicitors, George Davis, Son, and Co., 80, Coleman Street, E.C.

Office—41, Coleman Street, E.C.

24.—BILLINGHAY AND METHERINGHAM LIGHT.

Incorporated by act of 16th July, 1883, for the construction of a railway from Billinghay to Metheringham, in the County of Lincoln. Length, about 7¾ miles. Period for completion of works, 5 years. Capital, 42,000*l.* in 10*l.* shares, with power to divide into "preferred" and "deferred" half-shares. Loans, &c., 14,000*l.*

No. of Directors.—Maximum, 5; minimum, 3; quorum, 3 and 2. *Qualification*, 30 shares.

FIRST DIRECTORS:

John Dawson Bowling, Esq.	Hon. Frederick Charles Howard.
George Watson Mutter, Esq.	

25.—BIRKENHEAD.

An amalgamation of a company incorporated under the title of the Birkenhead, Lancashire, and Cheshire Junction, and of the Chester and Birkenhead, under act 11 Vic., cap. 222 (1847). The company assumed its present title under act of 1st August, 1859. Productive, 47 miles.

For brief details of Acts from 1852 to 1871, see Manual for 1882, and previously.

Extension from Grange Lane to Woodside Ferry (Great Western Additional Powers Act, 1881).—The new station at Woodside, in connection with this extension, was opened on the 1st April, 1878.

Arrangement with London and North Western and Great Western.—The terms of this arrangement are as follows:—The two companies, as from 1st January, 1860, assume the Birkenhead debenture stock, mortgage debt, and liabilities on capital account, not exceeding in the whole 512,000*l.* The two companies to pay half-yearly, as from 1st January, 1860, dividends upon Birkenhead ordinary capital of 1,941,505*l.* after the rates following, viz.:—For the years 1860 and 1861, 2½ per cent. per annum; for the years 1862, 1863, 1864, and 1865, 3½ per cent. per annum; and for the year 1866 and thereafter, 4 per cent. per annum. If during the year 1860 the earnings of the Birkenhead, after deduction of interest on debt, and an estimated percentage for working expenses, shall exceed the rate of 2½ per cent. per annum, then the next higher rate of 3½ per cent. per annum shall commence, and be paid in respect of the year 1861, the certificate of the auditors of the two companies on that point being final and conclusive. The two companies to keep the Birkenhead register of stock, and to distribute the dividend, &c. This arrangement was finally completed in August, and the leasing companies took possession on 18th November, 1860.

4½ per cent. preference shares have been issued to the extent of 474,178*l.* 10*s.*, and have since been converted into preference stock.

Capital.—The capital consists of 1,941,505*l.* in ordinary stock, bearing dividend at 4 per cent. per annum, and 474,178*l.* in preference stocks, at 4½ per cent. per annum.

The dividends, computed to 30th June and 31st December, are payable 21st January and 21st July to shareholders registered about the 12th of those months respectively.

Transfer form, common; fee, 2*s.* 6*d.* All communications under this head to be forwarded to S. Reay, Esq., Secretary, Euston Station, London, N.W.

DIRECTORS:

Line managed by a joint committee, representing the Great Western and the London and North Western, viz:—

Great Western.	*London and North Western.*
Sir D. Gooch, Bart., M.P., 3, Warwick Road, Maida Hill, W.	R. Moon, Esq., Copsewood Grange, Coventry.
Sir C. A. Wood, Knt., 11, Elvaston Place, S.W.	W. Cawkwell, Esq., Assoc.Inst.C.E., Euston Station, N.W.
The Right Hon. The Earl of Bessborough, 3, Mount Street, Grosvenor Square, W.	J. Bancroft, Esq., 83, Mosley Street, and Broughton Hall, Manchester.
The Right Hon. Lord Lyttelton, Stourbridge, and 17, Grosvenor Street, W.	O. L. Stephen, Esq., 55, Cadogan Square, S.W.
C. G. Mott, Esq., Harrow Weald Lodge, Stanmore, Middlesex.	J. P. Bickersteth, Esq., Euston Station, N.W.

JOINT OFFICERS.—Sec., J. Wait, Birkenhead; Supt., W. Patchett, Shrewsbury; Eng., R. E. Johnston, M.Inst.C.E., Birkenhead.

Secretary's Offices—Woodside, Birkenhead.

26.—BISHOP'S CASTLE AND MONTGOMERY.

Incorporated by act of 7th August, 1884, for the construction of a railway from the Bishop's Castle Line, at Lydham, to the town of Montgomery. Length, about 11¾ miles. Period for completion of works, 5 years. Capital, 150,000*l.* in 10 shares, with power to divide into "preferred" and "deferred" half-shares; loans, 50,000*l.*

No. of Directors.—Maximum, 6; minimum, 4; quorum, 4 and 2. *Qualification*, 50 shares. Quorum of General Meetings, 10,000*l.* in the capital of the company.

FIRST DIRECTORS:

Sir Offley Wakeman, Bart.	Captain Herbert Morris.
John Corbett, Esq.	
Philip Wright, Esq.	Two others to be nominated.

27.—BLACKPOOL.

Incorporated by act of 7th August, 1884, for the construction of a railway from Preston, by a junction with the West Lancashire, thence through Lytham to Church Street, Blackpool, with extension through Blackpool to the North Shore and Bispham. Total length, about 20 miles. Period for completion, 5 years. Traffic arrangements with Manchester, Sheffield, and Lincolnshire. Capital, 510,000*l.* in 10*l.* shares; loans, 170,000*l.* The lands for the railway are being purchased.

No. of Directors.—Maximum, 6; minimum, 3; quorum, 3 and 2. *Qualification*, 50 shares.

FIRST DIRECTORS:

Sir E. W. Watkin, Bart., M.P., Rose Hill, Northenden, Cheshire, and Charing Cross Hotel, Charing Cross, S.W.	Edward Ross, Esq., London Road Station Manchester.
Nathaniel Eckersley, Esq., M.P., Standish Hall, Wigan.	John Cremer Clarke, Esq., M.P., Abingdon.
	Henry Hall, Esq., Blackpool.
	(One other to be nominated.)

Solicitor, R. W. Perks, 147, Leadenhall Street, E.C.

28.—BLANE VALLEY.

Incorporated by act of 6th August, 1861, to construct a line from Lennoxtown to Strathblane, with a branch to Lettermill, in the county of Stirling. Length, 8½ miles. Capital, 51,000*l.* in 10*l.* shares, and 17,000*l.* on loan. Arrangements with North British, which subscribed 17,000*l.*, and now works the line at 50 per cent. of the gross receipts.

By act of 5th July, 1865, the company was authorised to construct an extension to the Forth and Clyde Junction. Length, 2⅜ miles. Original capital restricted to 33,000*l.* in shares and 11,000*l.* on loan. New capital, 42,000*l.* in shares, with 14,000*l.* on loan.

The earnings on this line have been in the past sufficient to pay part of the dividend on the company's preference stock. For the half-year ended 31st January, 1881, a dividend was earned on this stock at the rate of 4½ per cent. per annum, and the same for the two previous half-years. For the half-year ended 31st January, 1882, a dividend of 1 per cent. was also paid to the ordinary shareholders. For the half-year to 31st January, 1883, 2½ per cent. on preference shares; for the half-year to 31st July, 1883, 4 per cent. on preference shares; and for the half-year ended 31st July, 1884, 4½ per cent.

CAPITAL—31st July, 1884.—*Receipts:* 75,802*l.*, including 33,000*l.* in ordinary 10*l.* shares, 30,210*l.* in preference 10*l.* shares, and 11,000*l.* on loan. *Expenditure* (including subscriptions to other lines, 11,790*l.*), 88,246*l.*; debit balance, 12,444*l.*

Meetings in February or March and August or September.

No. of Directors—6; minimum, 5; quorum, 3. *Qualification*, 250*l.*

DIRECTORS:

Chairman—ROBERT YOUNG, Esq., 4, West Nile Street, Glasgow.

Deputy-Chairman—ROBERT SHARP MUIR, Esq., Glasgow.

Robert Kaye, Esq., of Fountain Bank, Partick.	Henry Grierson, Esq., 8, Park Circus Place, Glasgow.

OFFICERS.—Sec., James Keyden; Auditors, Alexander James Watson and Theodore E. Keyden; Solicitors, Keydens, Strang, and Girvan.

Office—186, West George Street, Glasgow.

29.—BODMIN AND WADEBRIDGE.

Incorporated by 2 and 3 Wm. IV., cap. 47, for the purposes of mineral traffic. Capital, 27,500*l.* in shares and 8,010*l.* on loan. Re-constructed by act of 5th July, 1865. New capital, 75,000*l.* in shares and 25,000*l.* on loan. Length, 15 miles.

REVENUE.—The net revenue for the half-years ended 30th June and 31st December, 1883, amounted to 19*l.* and 86*l.* respectively, and 30th June, 1884, to 191*l.*

CAPITAL.—The receipts on this account to 31st December, 1883, amounted to 35,500*l.*, viz.:—27,500*l.* in ordinary shares (900 of 25*l.* each) and stock (5,000*l.*) and 8,000*l.* on loan. The expenditure to that date amounted to 35,394*l.*, and remained the same at 30th June, 1884.

DIRECTORS:

Chairman—Hon. RALPH HENEAGE DUTTON, 16, Halkin Street West, Belgrave Square, S.W., and Timsbury Manor, Romsey, Hants.

Deputy-Chairman—WYNDHAM SPENCER PORTAL, Esq., Malshanger, Basingstoke, Hants.

William Wither Bramston Beach, Esq., M.P., Oakley Hall, Basingstoke, Hants.

Lieut.-Col. The Hon. Henry Walter Campbell, 44, Charles Street, Berkeley Square, W.

A. E. Guest, Esq., 33, Half-Moon Street, Piccadilly, W.

A. F. Govett, Esq., Sandylands, Virginia Water, and Albert Hall Mansions, S.W.

Capt. James Gilbert Johnston, 39, Hyde Park Square, W.

Major-Gen. F. Marshall, Broadwater, Godalming, and 9, Eaton Place, S.W.

A. Mills, Esq., Bude Haven, Cornwall, and 34, Hyde Park Gardens, W.

Charles Smith Mortimer, Esq., Wigmore House, near Holmwood, Surrey.

William Philip Snell, Esq., Belmont, near Havant, Hants.

OFFICERS.—Sec., F. J. Macaulay, Waterloo Station, S.E.; Supt., Hayes Kyd, Wadebridge; Auditor, C. Harvey, Waterloo Station, S.E.; Bankers, East Cornwall Banking Company, Bodmin.

Offices—Waterloo Station, S.E., and Wadebridge, Cornwall.

30.—BRECON AND MERTHYR TYDFIL JUNCTION.

Incorporated by act of 1st August, 1859, for constructing railways in the district between Brecon and Merthyr Tydfil.

For short heads of Acts obtained during the years 1860 to 1871, see the MANUAL for 1881, and previous editions.

NET REVENUE.—The result of the working for the half-year ended 31st December, 1883, was an available balance of 15,338*l.*, against 12,648*l.* in the corresponding half of last year. Interest and dividends have already been paid on the rent-charges and Rumney preference shares, and the balance sufficed to pay interest for the half-year at the rate of 4 per cent. per annum on the "A" debenture stock, and at the rate of 3 per cent. per annum on the "B" stock. Holders of this latter stock were therefore entitled to receive 1½ per cent. in cash for the half-year, and the balance of ½ per cent. in 1865 preference stock, as provided by the Scheme of Arrangement.

The result of the working for the half-year ended 30th June, 1884, was an available income of 14,793*l.*, against 12,048*l.* in the corresponding half of last year. After deducting the amount paid on the rent-charges and Rumney preference shares, the balance sufficed to pay interest as for the last half-year—viz., at the rate of 4 per cent. per annum on the "A" debenture stock, and at the rate of 3 per cent. per annum on the "B" stock. Holders of this latter stock will therefore be entitled to receive 1½ per cent. in cash for the half-year, and the balance of ½ per cent. in 1865 preference stock, as provided by the Scheme of Arrangement.

TOTAL MILEAGE—30th June, 1884.—Lines owned (including line held jointly with London and North Western), 61½ miles; foreign lines worked over, 6¾ miles; total, 68¼ miles.

CAPITAL.—The statement of stock and share capital, showing the proportion received to 30th June, 1884, furnished the subjoined particulars:—

Description.	Created.	Received.
Preference stock 5 per cent., 1861	£63,000	£62,550
" " 5 per cent., 1862	112,000	111,950
" " 5 per cent., 1863	200,000	200,000
" " 5 per cent., 1863 (Rumney preferences) charged on net receipts of Rumney undertaking	52,900	52,900
" " 5 per cent., 1864	211,000	211,000
" " 5 per cent., 1865	255,000	208,909
Ordinary stock consolidated under act 1865	325,000	264,360
Total	£1,218,900	£1,111,669

In arrear, 140*l.*; unissued, 107,091*l.*

The *Priorities* of the various securities of the company at the 30th June, 1884, were as follow:—

Description of Securities.	Issued.	Unissued or not paid up.	Total capital created.
Rent-charges	£14,075	...	£14,075
Rumney preference shares charged primarily on the Rumney undertaking	52,900	...	52,900
Debenture stock, "A"	301,670	£11,349	313,019
Debenture stock, "B"	497,336	6,339	503,675
5 per cent. preference stock, 1861	62,550	450	63,000
" " 1862	111,950	50	112,000
" " 1863	50,000	...	50,000
" " 1863	150,000	...	150,000
" " 1864	11,000	...	11,000
" " 1864	200,000	...	200,000
" " 1865	208,909	46,091	255,000
Ordinary consolidated stock	264,360	60,640	325,000
	£1,924,750	£124,919	£2,049,669

CONSOLIDATION OF DEBENTURE STOCKS.—For the Scheme of Arrangement, enrolled 19th June, 1882, see MANUAL for 1884, page 24.

CAPITAL.—The receipts and expenditure on this account to 30th June, 1884, were given as follow:—

Received.		*Expended.*	
Shares and stock	£1,111,669	Lines open for traffic	£1,556,803
Debenture stock	930,658	Working stock	106,168
Rent-charges	14,075		£1,662,971
Interest, premiums, forfeited shares, proceeds of telegraph, surplus lands, &c.	4,968	Amount of debenture interest capitalised in A and B stock	234,608
		Amount of debenture interest capitalised in 1865 preference stock	20,849
		Balance of supplemental revenue account, &c.	69,009
		Balance	73,932
	£2,061,370		£2,061,370

TRANSFER DEPARTMENT.—Deed, common; fee, 2*s.* 6*d.* for each seller; stock coupons to accompany deeds; several classes (except debenture stocks) may be transferred on one deed; transfers limited to 1*l.* stock, no fractions transferable; communications under this head to be sent to the Secretary.

Meetings last week in February and August.

No. of Directors—8; quorum, 3. *Qualification*, 500*l.*

DIRECTORS:

Chairman—H. F. SLATTERY, Esq., 13, Old Broad Street, E.C.

William de Winton, Esq., Maesderwen, Brecon.

J. W. Batten, Esq., 15, Airlie Gardens, Campden Hill, W.

James Coates, Esq., 99, Gresham Street, Bank, E.C.

W. Bailey Hawkins, Esq., 39, Lombard Street, E.C.

C. C. Massey, Esq., 1, Albert Mansions, Victoria Street, S.W.

George Pigot, Esq., Pembroke Lodge, Sunningdale, near Staines.

S. G. Sheppard, Esq., 28, Threadneedle Street, E.C.

All eligible for re-election.

OFFICERS.—Sec., Walter Thompson, 132, Palmerston Buildings, E.C.; Gen. Man., Alfred Henshaw, 34, Bridge Street, Newport, Mon.; Eng., C. H. Thomas, Brecon; Loco. Supt., Charles Long, Machen; Audit Clerk and Accountant, F. H. Shepherd, Newport, Mon.; Storekeeper, W. H. Richardson, Brecon; Auditor, Thomas Kennedy, F.C.A., 11, Old Jewry Chambers, E.C.; Solicitors, J. R. Cobb and J. Tudor, Brecon; Bankers, National Provincial Bank of England Limited, Newport, Mon., and London and County Bank, Lombard Street, E.C.

Offices—132, Palmerston Buildings, Old Broad Street, E.C.

31.—BRIDGWATER.

Incorporated by act of 1882. Length about 7 miles, from the Edington Station of the Somerset and Dorset, into Bridgwater. Authorised capital, 135,000*l.* in shares, and 45,000*l.* in debentures.

WORKING AGREEMENT WITH LONDON AND SOUTH WESTERN.—The London and South Western have agreed to work, equip, manage, and maintain the Bridgwater in perpetuity, for 50 per cent. of the gross receipts, and to pay over to the Bridgwater half-yearly, on the 30th June and 31st December in each year, the remaining 50 per cent. of such gross receipts, together with a fixed sum to cover administration expenses. They have further agreed, that in the event of the 50 per cent. of the earnings assigned to the Bridgwater not producing sufficient to pay interest at 4 per cent. per annum upon that company's debentures (45,000*l*.), and dividends 4½ per cent. upon the share capital, they will pay to the Bridgwater a rebate of 3,000*l*. per annum, or so much thereof as may be necessary, out of the receipts of the London and South Western, in respect of traffic conveyed on its railways to and from any station of the Bridgwater. This rebate is supplemented by an additional rebate of 900*l*. per annum (payable under similar conditions), granted by the London and South Western and Midland Companies, out of their receipts on their joint Somerset and Dorset Line, in respect of traffic to and from the Bridgwater.

ORDINARY SHARES.—11,500 of these shares were offered for public subscription in February, 1883, at par. During construction, interest at 4½ per cent. will be paid half-yearly, on 1st June and 1st December.

4 per cent. debenture stock.

Transfer form, common; fee, 2*s*. 6*d*.

No. of Directors.—Maximum, 5; minimum, 3. *Qualification*, 10 shares.

DIRECTORS:

Chairman—JASPER WILSON JOHNS, Esq., 16, Grenville Place, South Kensington, S.W.

R. A. Read, Esq., The Cranes, Surbiton Hill, S.W.

J. Browne Martin, Esq., 2, Westminster Chambers, S.W.

John Parsons, Esq., Bridgwater.

Alfred Peace, Esq., Bridgwater.

OFFICERS.—Sec., E. B. Read; Engs., Wells Owen and Elwes, MM.Inst.C.E., 7, Westminster Chambers, Westminster, S.W.; Auditor, Frank Piggott.

Offices—9, Victoria Chambers, Westminster, S.W.

32.—BRIDPORT.

Incorporated by act of 5th May, 1855, for constructing a railway from Bridport to Maiden Newton, on the Wilts, Somerset, and Weymouth. Altered from broad to narrow gauge. Total length, 11¾ miles. Capital, 65,000*l*. in 10*l*. shares and 21,600*l*. on loan. Worked by Great Western at 47½ per cent. of gross receipts for 21 years from 1st July, 1882.

By act of 18th August, 1859, the company was authorised to lease the line for 21 years from 1st July, 1858, to the Great Western, and to raise additional capital to complete the undertaking, by the creation of 20,000*l*. preference shares, at 6 per cent.

By act of 21st July, 1879, the company was empowered to construct a railway from the Bridport Line to Bridport Harbour; length, 2 miles 1 furlong, which is now completed and opened for traffic. The company was by this act granted running powers over the Great Western Line from Maiden Newton to Dorchester, 7¾ miles, on a second line of rails being laid down. New capital, 42,000*l*. Borrowing powers, 14,000*l*.

The line is now worked by the Great Western, under a lease from 1st July, 1882, for 21 years.

REVENUE.—For the half-year ended 30th June, 1884, the net earnings sufficed for the payment of dividends at the respective rates of 6 per cent., 5 per cent., and 4 per cent. per annum on the preference shares, and 1 per cent. on the ordinary shares, after payment of all prior charges (previous dividends on ordinary shares 1½ per cent. per annum for past 3 years).

CAPITAL.—This account to 30th June, 1884, showed that 139,068*l*. had been received and 137,798*l*. expended, and that the amounts received on shares were as follow:—

£10 ordinary shares	£64,431	
£10 preference shares at 6 per cent.	20,000	
£10 preference shares at 5 per cent.	4,000	
£10 preference shares at 4 per cent.	23,000	=£111,431

NOTE.—The authorised and raised capital having been insufficient for the expenditure on capital account, the deficiency (5,823*l*.) on that account was each half-year gradually reduced, and ultimately extinguished from the revenue account.

New Preference Shares.—23,000*l.* of new capital was issued in 4 per cent. 10*l.* preference shares for the purpose of carrying out the extension of the line to Bridport Harbour. These shares were all taken up at par.

Meetings are held in March and September; all ordinary meetings held in Bridport; quorum of shareholders, 15, representing at least 6,000*l.*

No. of Directors—6; quorum, 3. *Qualification*, 50 shares.

DIRECTORS:

Chairman—1 WILLIAM SWATRIDGE, Esq., Maiden Newton.

Deputy-Chairman—2 JOB LEGG, Esq., Bridport.

3 William Henry Chick, Esq., Bridport.
1 Reginald Douglas Thornton, Esq., Bridport.
3 John Pickard Suttill, Esq., Bridport.
2 Alfred William Hounsell Dammers, Esq., Bridport.

1, Retire in 1885; 2, in 1886; 3, in 1887.

OFFICERS.—Sec., Nicholas Marshall Loggin; Auditors, Stephen Whetham and Henry Good; Solicitors, Loggin and Nantes.

Offices—Bridport.

33.—BRIGHTON AND DYKE.

Incorporated by act of 2nd August, 1877, for making two railways. No. 1, from Aldrington to Hangleton; length, 3 miles 1 furlong 6 chains. No. 2, from Hangleton to Poynings; length, 1 mile 5 furlongs. Period for completion of works, five years. Working arrangements with London, Brighton, and South Coast. Capital, 72,000*l.* in 10*l.* shares, with powers to divide into "preferred" and "deferred" half-shares. Borrowing powers, 24,000*l.*

By act of 18th July, 1881, the powers of the above act were revived, and the period for completion of works extended until the 2nd August, 1885.

Agreement.—In 1882 it was officially stated as follows:—"An agreement has been settled with the London, Brighton, and South Coast to work and maintain the railway in perpetuity, and provide all necessary plant and rolling stock for 55 per cent. of the gross receipts, the net balance of 45 per cent. of the gross receipts to be paid over to the Dyke Company. The Brighton have stipulated that when the Dyke Company's proportion of the receipts under the agreement, after making all the other payments therein provided, amounts to (after payment of the interest on debenture capital) 7 per cent. on its share capital, any surplus shall be divided equally between the two companies."

Capital.—The capital of the company was issued in 1882-3, in 10*l.* shares, interest at 6 per cent. per annum, to be paid half-yearly until the line is completed and opened for traffic.

No. of Directors—5; quorum, 3. *Qualification*, 20 shares. Number may be reduced to 3, with a quorum of 2.

TRUSTEES:

The Hon. Ashley Ponsonby, 9, Prince's Gardens, S.W.

Frederick Edenborough, Esq., 11, Wool Exchange, E.C.

DIRECTORS:

Chairman—The Hon. ASHLEY PONSONBY, 9, Prince's Gardens, S.W.

Major W. F. Gordon.
William Stansfield, Esq.
Sir Humphrey White Jervis, Bart.

OFFICERS.—Sec. *(pro tem.)*, H. Warren; Eng., A. L. Nimmo, M.Inst.C.E., 20, Abingdon Street, Westminster, S.W.; Solicitor, R. Ballard, 2, Clifford's Inn, E.C., and Brighton; Bankers, Glyn, Mills, Currie, and Co., Lombard Street, E.C., and Hall, Bevan, West, and Hall, Union Bank, Brighton.

Brighton Offices—71, Queen's Road.
London Offices—4, Great Winchester Street, E.C.

34.—BRISTOL PORT, RAILWAY, AND PIER.

Incorporated by act of 17th July, 1862, to construct a railway from port of Bristol to the old channel at the mouth of the Avon, with pier, &c. Length, 5¾ miles. Capital, 125,000*l.* in 10*l.* shares and 41,000*l.* on loan.

By act of 29th June, 1865, the mortgage debt was specially defined and consolidated, as well as extended over the whole of the undertaking, instead of portions on each.

By act of 25th May, 1871, the Clifton Extension was transferred to the Midland and the Great Western, and powers conferred on these companies with respect to abandonment of certain junctions and construction of others, the cost being defrayed in equal proportions. Joint committee and standing arbitrator to be appointed. Great Western to provide its subscription out of existing powers, and Midland to raise 153,000*l.* in shares and 51,000*l.* on loan.

The affairs of the company being at present in Chancery, no accounts are published.

No. of Directors—5; quorum, 3. *Qualification*, 500*l.*

DIRECTORS:

Chairman—E. S. ROBINSON, Esq., Bristol.

J. F. Lucas, Esq.
J. Llewellin, Jun., Esq.
W. Smith, Esq.
W. H. Clarke, Esq.
W. H. Harford, Esq., Corn Street, Bristol.

OFFICERS.—Sec., J. W. Barton, 5, Athenæum, Bristol; Gen. Man., R. A. Read; Auditors, T. Gillford and W. H. Stephens.

Offices—5, Athenæum, Bristol.

35.—BUCKFASTLEIGH, TOTNES, AND SOUTH DEVON.

Incorporated by act of 25th July, 1864, to construct a line from the South Devon, at Totnes, to Buckfastleigh, and a branch to Totnes Quays. Broad gauge. Length, 7¾ miles. Capital, 48,000*l.* in 10*l.* shares and 16,000*l.* on loan. Arrangements with Great Western, which works the line at 50 per cent. of the gross receipts.

For brief details of powers under Acts 1865, 1868, and 1869, see MANUAL for 1882, page 28.

By a Scheme of Arrangement enrolled in the Court of Chancery in 1878, the company was empowered to raise 50,000*l.* additional capital, in the shape of "B" debenture stock, to meet the liabilities in respect of Lloyd's bonds, &c., and for the improvement of the undertaking. The scheme also authorised the cancellation of 10,000*l.* preference shares upon the issue of the "B" debenture stock. By an agreement scheduled to the Great Western and South Devon Amalgamation Act of 1878, the Great Western guarantee interest upon the "A" and "B" debenture stocks out of the gross receipts of the Buckfastleigh Railway. The Lloyd's bonds have been exchanged for "B" debenture stock, and the financial position of the company has been much improved.

Opened from Totnes to Ashburton, 1st May, 1872; branch to Quays, 10th November, 1873.

REVENUE.—The report for the half-year ended 30th June, 1884, showed a decrease in the revenue of 50*l.* The net earnings about sufficed for the interest on the debenture stock, &c.

CAPITAL.—The expenditure to 30th June, 1884, amounted to 162,925*l.*, the receipts having been as under:—

Shares	£85,974	
Debenture stock "A."	16,080	
Do. do. "B."	62,071	
Forfeited shares	51	
Subscriptions to Totnes Tramways ...	130	=£164,306

Meetings held at Totnes in April and October.

No. of Directors—6; minimum, 3; quorum, 3 and 2. *Qualification*, 250*l.*

DIRECTORS:

Chairman—3 JEFFREY MICHELMORE, Esq., Berry House, Totnes.

Deputy-Chairman—2 JOHN FURNEAUX, Esq., Hill Crest, Buckfastleigh.

John W. Batten, Esq., 15, Airlie Gardens, Campden Hill, London, W.
Edwin Tucker, Esq., Ashburton.
1 James Hamlyn, Esq., Bossell Park, Buckfastleigh.

1, Retire in 1885; 2, in 1886; 3, in 1887. All eligible for re-election.

OFFICERS.—Sec., Thomas C. Jenkin; Eng., P. J. Margary, M.Inst.C.E., Plymouth; Solicitors, Michelmore and Hacker, Newton Abbot, and J. Brend Batten, 32, Great George Street, Westminster, S.W.; Auditors, Edward Windeatt, Totnes, and John L. Winter, Totnes; Bankers, Devon and Cornwall Bank, Totnes, and Barclay, Bevan, and Co., Lombard Street, E.C.

Offices—Totnes.

36.—BUCKLEY.

Incorporated by act of 14th June, 1860, to construct a line from Buckley to Connah's Quay, Flintshire. Length, 5 miles. Capital, 30,000*l.* in 10*l.* shares; loans, 10,000*l.*

For brief details of powers under Acts 1865 and 1866, see MANUAL for 1882, and previously.

LEASE.—By the Wrexham, Mold, and Connah's Quay Act, 1873, the Buckley was leased to that company for 1,000 years, to take effect from 30th June, 1873, the Wrexham Company paying the interest on mortgages. 5 per cent. per annum on the preference stock, and on the ordinary stock 4½ per cent. per annum, until 1883; afterwards 5 per cent. per annum.

CAPITAL.—The receipts and expenditure on this account to 30th June, 1884, were set out in detail as follow:—

Received.		*Expended.*	
Shares and stock	£66,072	Lines open for traffic	£83,034
Debenture loans	20,000	Working stock	4,938
Sundries	1,931	Balance	31
	£88,003		£88,003

PRIORITIES, DESCRIPTIONS, DIVIDENDS, &c.—The following is a list of this company's Stocks and Shares, numbered in order of priority, with conditions of issue *in brief*, the descriptions to be strictly observed in transfer deeds and all other documents relating thereto, viz.:—

1—DEBENTURES.—Issued under acts 1860 to 1863, in various amounts, with accumulative interest, payable on various dates. The total amounts issued are 6,000*l.* at 4½ per cent.; 8,000*l.* at 4¼ per cent.; 4,000*l.* at 4¾ per cent.; and 2,000*l.* at 5 per cent.

2—PREFERENCE STOCK.—Issued under act 1863. Dividend at 5 per cent. per annum, payable half-yearly, 1st February and 1st August.

3—ORDINARY SHARES.—Issued under act 1860. ORDINARY STOCK.—Issued under act 1863. ORDINARY STOCK.—Issued under act 1866. Dividends at 4½ per cent. per annum until 1883, and 5 per cent. afterwards, guaranteed under the before-mentioned lease, due half-yearly, on the 1st February and 1st August.

MEM.—The transfer books for both preference and ordinary stocks close 14 days before the dates named for the payment of dividend.

TRANSFER DEPARTMENT QUERIES AND REPLIES.

QUERIES.	REPLIES.
Transfer form—ordinary or special?	Ordinary.
Fee per deed?	2*s.* 6*d.*
Ditto if more sellers than one?	2*s.* 6*d.*
May several classes of stock be transferred on one deed?	Yes.
Are certificates required to accompany transfers?	Yes.
What amounts of stocks are transferable, and are parts of 1*l.* sterling allowed to be transferred?	Any amount.
To what officer should transfer communications be sent?	The Secretary.
In acceptances, renunciations, &c., of allotments of new stock, proxies, or other forms sent to trustees, what signatures are required?	All.

Meetings held in Mold in February and August.

No. of Directors.—Maximum, 7; minimum, 5; quorum, 3. *Qualification*, 200*l.*

DIRECTORS:

Chairman—GEORGE MOORE DIXON, Esq., Bradley Hall, near Ashbourne, Derby.

Charles Davison, Esq., Farfield House, Connah's Quay.

J. R. Barnes, Esq., Brookside, Chirk, North Wales.

C. T. Bowring, Esq., 25, Castle Street, Liverpool.

A. T. Roberts, Esq., Coed-dû, Mold.

OFFICERS.—Sec., John Wade; Consulting Eng., G. Bellis, Mold; Auditor, Francis Musgrave; Solicitors, Kelly and Keene, Mold; Bankers, the North and South Wales Bank, Mold.

Offices—Mold.

37.—BURRY PORT AND GWENDREATH VALLEY.

Incorporated by act of 5th July, 1865, to convert the canal into a railway from Burry Port to the Mountain Branch of the Llanelly, with several branches. Length, 18½ miles. Capital, 120,000*l.* in shares and 18,000*l.* on loan. Of the shares, 72,100*l.* represent the old canal property, and 47,900*l.* was required for the conversion.

For subsequent Acts down to 1872, see MANUAL for 1881, and previous editions.

Miles in operation, 19.

CAPITAL—Half-year ended 30th June, 1884.—Amount expended, 246,668*l.* The following amounts have been received, viz.:—

Ordinary shares	£135,400
First preference 5 per cent.	18,000
Second " "	29,600
Third " "	2,220
Loans at 5 per cent.	10,600
" 6 "	31,550
Debenture stock at 5 per cent.	18,700
	£246,070
Balance	598
	£246,668

The affairs of this company are now in Chancery, the secretary (as below) having been appointed Receiver and Manager.

Meetings held in February and August.

No. of Directors—5; minimum, 3; quorum, 3 and 2. *Qualification*, 500*l.*

DIRECTORS:

Chairman—General GEORGE ALEXANDER MALCOLM, C.B., 67, Sloane Street, S.W., and Burry Port, South Wales.

Francis Alexander R. Pemberton, Esq., Newton, Cambridge.

Francis Cancellor, Esq., 7, Tokenhouse Yard, E.C.

OFFICERS.—Receiver and Sec., John Russell; Harbour Master and Supt., Capt. J. P. Luckraft, R.N.; Auditors, Roderick Mackay and William Taylor; Solicitors to the Company, Johnson and Stead, Llanelly; Solicitors to the Receiver, Hopgood, Foster, and Dowson, 17, Whitehall Place, S.W.

Offices—3, Great Winchester Street Buildings, E.C., and Burry Port, South Wales.

38.—BURRY PORT AND NORTH WESTERN JUNCTION.

Incorporated 27th June, 1876, to construct a railway from the Burry Port and Gwendreath Valley, at Llanon, to the Central Wales and Carmarthen Junction, at Llanarthney. Length, 6 miles. Capital, 78,000*l.* in 10*l.* shares; borrowing powers, 26,000*l.* on mortgage or by debenture stock. The company and the London and North Western and Burry Port companies may enter into agreements.

By act of 3rd June, 1881, powers were obtained to construct a junction a little over 2 miles long, from Llanarthney to Llannon. Period for completion, 5 years.

The time for completion of works under act of 1876 is under the same act extended until 27th June, 1884. Additional capital authorised, 25,000*l.* Loans, 8,000*l.*

By act of 28th July, 1884, the time for completion of works was further extended to 3rd June, 1888.

Quorum of general meeting—Ten proprietors holding in the aggregate not less than 4,500*l.* of capital.

No. of Directors—3; maximum, 5; quorum, 2 and 3. *Qualification*, 50 shares.

DIRECTORS:

John Kemp Jacomb-Hood, Esq., Broadwater House, Tunbridge Wells.

Arthur Lionel Woods, Esq., 53, Old Broad Street, E.C.

Douglas Arthur Onslow, Esq., J.P., 14, Waverley Place, St. John's Wood, N.W.

OFFICERS.—Sec., C. H. Ommanney; Solicitors, Sutton and Ommanney, 3 and 4, Great Winchester Street, E.C.

Offices—3 and 4, Great Winchester Street, E.C.

39.—BURY AND TOTTINGTON DISTRICT.

Incorporated by act of 2nd August, 1877, for making two railways, length about 3½ miles, commencing by a junction with the East Lancashire Line of the Lancashire and Yorkshire, near Chamber Hall, Bury, and passing through Woolfold and Tottington, terminating at the village of Holcombe Brook. Works completed. Capital, 57,000*l.* in 10*l.* shares; borrowing powers, 19,000*l.*

By act of 29th June, 1880, the company was authorised to raise the additional sum of 40,000*l.* in ordinary or preference shares, and 13,300*l.* in loans or debenture stock, for general purposes.

By act of 2nd August, 1882, the capital of the company was increased by 40,000*l.* ordinary or preference shares. Borrowing powers, 13,300*l.*

A working agreement has been entered into with the Lancashire and Yorkshire, by which that company undertakes to work the Bury and Tottington District for 54 per cent. of the gross receipts. Opened November 6th, 1882.

Revenue—30th June, 1884.—The balance of net revenue, amounting to 2,510*l.*, is not immediately available for distribution, being composed of the following items, viz.:—

Funds in the hands of the receiver derived from revenue	£320	
Net traffic receipts for half-year ended 30th June, 1884, not yet paid over by the Lancashire and Yorkshire	986	
	£1,306	
Less amount estimated to provide for administration expenses not yet ascertained, and for rent-charges accrued...............	484=	£822
Add amount expended by sanction of the court on capital account, to be replaced by issue of "A" debenture stock ...	£1,653	
Accounts paid out of revenue which were previously charged to capital..	36=	1,688
		£2,510

Capital—30th June, 1884.—*Receipts*:—

Ordinary 10*l.* shares (37,000*l.*)...	£36,980
5 per cent. first preference 10*l.* shares, 1879 (20,000*l.*)...............	20,000
Second do. do. (40,000*l.*, act 1880), not yet issued	...
Third do. do. (40,000*l.*, act 1882), not yet issued	...
Mortgages, &c.:—	
Capitalised value of two rent-charges	5,281
Debenture stock "B"	14,313
Do. do. "C"	237
	£76,811

Amount expended, 149,690*l.*; balance (debtor), 72,879*l.*

The 80,000*l.* created by the acts of 1880 and 1882—by the terms of the Scheme of Arrangement, these powers are not to be exercised.

Balance of mortgage or debenture stock sanctioned under Scheme of Arrangement, 109,762*l.*

No. of Directors.—Maximum, 5; minimum, 3; quorum, 3 and 2. *Qualification*, 50 shares.

DIRECTORS:

Chairman—SAMUEL KNOWLES, Esq., Stormer Hill, Tottington, near Bury, Lancashire.

John Heap, Esq., Nabbs House, Tottington, near Bury, Lancashire.

Hugh Roberts, Esq., Sunny Bower, Tottington, near Bury, Lancashire.

OFFICERS.—Sec., W. Harper, Broad Street, Bury; Engs., Wells, Owen, and Elwes, Westminster, S.W.; Auditors, Charles M. Merchant and Evan Williams.

40.—CALEDONIAN.

Incorporated by 8 and 9 Vic., cap. 162, for a line from Carlisle to Edinburgh and Garriongill, and with a branch from near Gartsherrie to Castlecary, joining the Scottish Central Line at Greenhill. Under powers of various acts this company, at a time of great excitement and much uncertainty as regards the real profits made out of railway undertakings, became involved in engagements which were found to be beyond its resources. After protracted negotiations with the conflicting interests involved in questions arising out of the leases (the position of the preference shares, as to priority, being a particularly difficult point), before the close of the session of 1851, and inquiries in Parliament as to return of capital, &c., giving the early history of the transactions, &c., an agreement was finally arrived at, and the result was the "*Arrangements Act*," 14 and 15 Vic., cap. 134 (1851), of which an ample synopsis was given in the MANUAL for 1854.

PARLIAMENTARY POWERS:—

A list of Acts from 1855 to 1879, with short heads showing the principal objects for which the various powers were sought, will be found on reference to the MANUAL for 1881.

FURTHER POWERS.—The following Acts have since been passed, viz.:—

1880—2ND AUGUST (GUARANTEED ANNUITIES ACT).—Dissolution of Glasgow, Garnkirk, &c., Clydesdale Guaranteed, Greenock Guaranteed, Wishaw Guaranteed, and Glasgow, Barrhead, and Neilston Direct companies respectively.—See particulars under those heads further on.

1880—26TH AUGUST.—New railways and works at Lanark, Renfrew, and Edinburgh; contribution to Alloa; Accident and Life Assurance Fund for Servants; extension of time for completion of works in Lanarkshire, &c., &c.; new capital, shares or stock, 220,000*l.*; borrowing powers, 60,000*l.*

1881—8TH APRIL.—Guaranteed annuities No. 2; dissolution of Lesmahagow, Dundee, Perth, &c., and Forth and Clyde Navigation.—See particulars under those heads respectively, further on.

1881—18TH JULY.—Agreements for working Cathcart District; dissolution and vesting of Busby (see both companies below). New capital, 180,000*l.*

1881—18TH JULY.—New railways to connect the Scottish Central Line at Larbert with Grangemouth Branch, &c., &c. New capital, 100,000*l.*; borrowing powers, 33,300*l.*

1881—18TH JULY.—Lanarkshire Lines Act, being branches to Airdrie and other places in the county of Lanark. New capital, 270,000*l.*; borrowing powers, 90,000*l.*

1881—11TH AUGUST.—Construction of Partick siding. New capital, 4,000*l.*; borrowing powers, 1,300*l.*

1882—19TH MAY.—Additional capital for new lands and works, 1,260,000*l.*; borrowing powers, 400,000*l.*

1882—19TH JUNE.—New lines and works at various places in the vicinity of Glasgow, in the counties of Lanark, Dumfries, Stirling, Perth, and Renfrew, &c. Additional capital, 120,000*l.*; borrowing powers, 40,000*l.*

1883—31ST MAY.—Construction of short lines in the counties of Stirling and Midlothian; abandonment of railway No. 1, act 1875; extension of time for construction of railways authorised by acts 1876, 1878, and 1879; release of Callander and Oban deposit, &c., &c.

1883—18TH JUNE.—Construction of certain works in connection with the Glasgow and Paisley, and Glasgow and Kilmarnock Joint Lines, jointly with the Glasgow and South Western; each company being authorised to issue 60,000*l.* in shares, and 20,000*l.* in loans, &c. Period for completion of works, 5 years.

1884—14TH JULY.—Construction of railways and works in the counties of Renfrew, Forfar, Stirling, and Clackmannan; completion, vesting, and dissolution of Alloa undertaking; agreement with North British as to use of the Stirlingshire, Midland Junction, &c.; and other purposes. New capital, 93,000*l.*; loans, 31,000*l.*

1884 (No. 2.)—28TH JULY.—Railway to Gourock with a quay or pier there, and to connect their railways with the Paisley Canal Line of the Glasgow and South Western, with facilities over that line; extension of time for the sale of certain superfluous lands; and for other purposes

1884 (No. 3.)—Further powers on the Perth General Station Committee; and for other purposes.

BRANCH AND VESTED LINES, LEASES, AGREEMENTS, &c.:—

ALLOA.—Vested in this company under act 14th July, 1884, on payment of the cost of the undertaking.—For other particulars, see MANUAL for 1884, pages 3 and 4.

ALYTH.—Incorporated by act of 14th June, 1868, to make a railway from the Meigle Station of the Scottish North Eastern to the town of Alyth. Length, 5¼ miles. At a meeting held in April, 1874, an agreement was adopted to transfer this undertaking to the Caledonian on the following terms:—"A dividend at the rate of 4½ per cent. per annum for the period from 1st January last to 31st December, 1878, and at the rate of 5 per cent. ever after, payable half-yearly, subject to a power to the Caledonian to redeem the 5 per cent. dividend at 21½ years' purchase at any time before 1st January, 1884, and reserving to the company for behoof of the shareholders all its arrears of calls and debts due, and all its deposited funds. The

Caledonian also pay the company's mortgage debt, and continue to bear the feu duty to Lord Airlie." The line was vested on the foregoing terms under the act of 1875. The preference shares of this section were redeemed on the 1st July, 1880, under the provisions of "The Vesting Act, 1875."

ARBROATH AND FORFAR.—See GENERAL INDEX.

BUSBY.—From the Glasgow, Barrhead, and Neilston Line to Busby, with a branch to the printworks. Length, 4½ miles. Incorporated by act of 11th May, 1863. Vested in the Caledonian under that company's Additional Powers Act, 1881 (clauses 7 and 8), as from 1st February, 1882, the holders of Busby shares receiving an equal amount of 5 per cent. consolidated preference stock of the Caledonian Company.—For particulars relating to the vested company's position prior to amalgamation, see MANUAL for 1882, and previously.

CALLANDER AND OBAN.—See GENERAL INDEX.

CARLISLE CITADEL STATION.—By act of 22nd July, 1861, the Caledonian and London and North Western obtained powers for the better regulation of this station. Its management is placed under the direction of a joint committee, consisting of two representatives from each board, and the agreements respectively made with the Maryport, the Glasgow and South Western, and the North British, were confirmed. New works were also authorised, and further purchase of lands permitted. The Caledonian, under this act, and for its purposes, was authorised to raise new capital to the extent of 25,000*l*., at 5 per cent. preference, and 8,300*l*. on loan. By act of 21st July, 1873, the Caledonian was authorised to subscribe to this undertaking 160,000*l*. New capital to be raised for this purpose, 120,000*l*. in shares or stock and 40,000*l*. on loan.

CATHCART DISTRICT.—See GENERAL INDEX.

DUNDEE AND ARBROATH.—By the North British (Dundee and Arbroath Joint Line) Act, 1879, the Dundee and Arbroath Line and the Carmyllie Branch were transferred to and vested in the Caledonian and the North British jointly, in equal proportions. The North British are bound to pay to the Caledonian a moiety of the half-yearly payments for which this company are liable, in respect of the lines to be converted into joint property, and a capital sum besides, equal to one-half of their value, "subject to the half-yearly payments," as the amount of such value may be determined by agreement or by arbitration.

PERTH, ALMOND VALLEY, AND METHVEN.—Incorporated by act of 29th July, 1856. Length, 6 miles. By act of 23rd June, 1864, this company was leased to the Scottish North Eastern, at 4 per cent., as from 1st January, 1864.

OTHER BRANCH LINES:—

For brief details relating to the following other branch lines, see MANUAL for 1882, and previously, viz.:—

Aberdeen.
Balerno Branch.
Bredisholme and Tannochside.
Carstairs and Dolphinton.
Cleland and Midcalder.
Crieff and Methven Junction.
Denburn Valley.
Dundee and Forfar.
Edinburgh Station.
Forfarshire.
Glasgow and Garnkirk.
Glasgow Harbour.
Lanark.
Lanarkshire and Midlothian Branches.
Leith Branches.
Muirkirk.
Port Carlisle.
Rutherglen and Coatbridge.
Scottish Midland Junction.
Stonehouse.
Wilsontown.

CLELAND AND MORNINGSIDE.—Length, 11 miles. Capital, 160,000*l*. in shares, at 5 per cent., and 53,300*l*. on loan. Certain deviations were authorised by the act of 7th July, 1862.

CLYDESDALE JUNCTION.—This line runs from the South Side Station, Glasgow, to Hamilton, with connecting branch to the Wishaw and Coltness Line at Motherwell, and was amalgamated with the Caledonian in 1846.

CLYDESDALE GUARANTEED.—Under "The Caledonian Guaranteed Annuities Act, 1880," this company was dissolved, and on the 1st August in that year the stock was converted into 4 per cent. guaranteed annuities stock of the Caledonian, of an amount yielding the same rate of interest as the proprietors received during the company's separate existence.—See *Appendix* to the MANUAL for 1881.

CROFTHEAD AND KILMARNOCK.—See Glasgow and South Western.

DALMARNOCK.—By act of 21st May, 1858, the Caledonian was authorised to construct a branch of 1 mile to Dalmarnock. New capital: shares, 37,000*l*.; loans, 12,000*l*.

DUMFRIES, LOCHMABEN, AND LOCKERBIE.—Incorporated by act of 14th June, 1860. Length, 14¼ miles. By act of 5th July, 1865, the line was amalgamated with the Caledonian at 6 per cent. in perpetuity. Running powers to London and North Western between Carlisle, Lockerbie, and Dumfries.

FORTH AND CLYDE NAVIGATION.—By act of 20th June, 1867, the Forth and Clyde Navigation became vested in the Caledonian. Capital, 1,141,333*l.* Annuity, 71,333*l.* —For arrangement with North British, see *Appendix* to the MANUAL for 1868. Under the Caledonian act of 8th April, 1881, this company, as a separate undertaking vested in the Caledonian, was dissolved (as from the 11th November, 1881), and Caledonian 4 per cent. guaranteed annuities stock No. 2 issued in exchange for the 6¼ per cent. stock of the company, at the rate of 156*l.* 5*s.* per cent.

GENERAL TERMINUS AND GLASGOW HARBOUR.—By act of 29th June, 1865, this undertaking was amalgamated with the Caledonian, which issued stock in new and old capital to the extent of 160,000*l.*; guaranteed 4 per cent. till 31st January, 1867; and thereafter, 4½ per cent. The liabilities of the General Terminus are restricted to 54,000*l.*, in addition to 160,000*l.*, the amount of the ordinary stock. The General Terminus connects the Clydesdale Junction with the line to Greenock.

GLASGOW, GARNKIRK, AND COATBRIDGE.—Under "The Caledonian Guaranteed Annuities Act, 1880," this company was dissolved, and on the 1st August in that year the stock was converted into 4 per cent. guaranteed annuities stock of the Caledonian, of an amount yielding the same rate of interest as the proprietors received during the company's separate existence.—See *Appendix* to the MANUAL for 1881.

GLASGOW, BARRHEAD, AND NEILSTON DIRECT.—Under "The Caledonian Guaranteed Annuities Act, 1880," this company was dissolved, and on the 1st August in that year the stock was converted into 4 per cent. guaranteed annuities stock of the Caledonian, of an amount yielding the same rate of interest as the proprietors received during the company's separate existence.—See *Appendix* to the MANUAL for 1881.

GLASGOW AND PAISLEY JOINT.—See GENERAL INDEX.

GLASGOW AND KILMARNOCK JOINT.—See GENERAL INDEX.

GRANTON.—By act of 10th August, 1857, an arrangement is authorised with the promoters of this line, the capital being 60,000*l.*, one-half of which was provided by the Duke of Buccleuch. The loans extend to 20,000*l.* The length of the line is 3¼ miles, and of the branch to Granton western breakwater, 25 chains. By act of 1862, the Granton branches were merged into the Caledonian, and the Duke of Buccleuch bought out.

GREENOCK GUARANTEED (late Glasgow, Paisley, and Greenock).—Under the Caledonian Annuities Act, 1880, this company became vested in the Caledonian as from the 1st August, 1883, the stocks of the Greenock receiving Caledonian 4 per cent. guaranteed annuities stock at the respective rates of 125*l.* for every 100*l.* of Greenock preference stock, and about 71*l.* 7*s* 6*d.* for every 100*l.* Greenock ordinary stock.—For particulars as to the position of this company in the past, see MANUAL for 1883, and previously.

HAMILTON AND STRATHAVEN.—An agreement had been concluded for the acquisition of this railway; the liability of the Caledonian restricted to 36,500*l.*, in addition to the share capital of 70,000*l.* Ratified by act of 25th July, 1864.

KILSYTH AND BONNYBRIDGE.—See GENERAL INDEX.

LESMAHAGOW.—Under the Caledonian act of 8th April, 1881, this company, as a separate undertaking vested in the Caledonian, was dissolved (as from 11th November, 1881), and Caledonian 4 per cent. guaranteed annuities stock No. 2 issued in exchange for the stocks of the company in the following proportions, viz.:—For each 100*l.* of class "A" 6 per cent. stock, 148*l.* 15*s.* of annuities stock; for each 100*l.* of class "B" 5 per cent. stock, 123*l.* 15*s.* of annuities stock.—For brief details of the position of this company prior to the vesting, see MANUAL for 1882, and previously.

SYMINGTON, BIGGAR, AND BROUGHTON.—Length, 8 miles. Incorporated by act of 21st May, 1858. Amalgamated with Caledonian under act of 1st August, 1861.

WISHAW.—Under "The Caledonian Guaranteed Annuities Act, 1880," this company was dissolved, and on the 1st August in that year the stock was converted into 4 per cent. guaranteed annuities stock of the Caledonian, of an amount yielding the same rate of interest as the proprietors received during the company's separate existence.—See *Appendix* to the MANUAL for 1881.

WISHAW AND COLTNESS.—This line, which connects with the main line at Garriongill, was amalgamated by the Wishaw and Coltness Purchase Act, 1849.

SCOTTISH CENTRAL.—Incorporated by act of 31st July, 1845. By act of 28th July, 1863, the Dundee, Perth, and Aberdeen and Dundee and Newtyle were vested in the Scottish Central, the ordinary shareholders receiving dividends as follows:—For the year ended 31st July, 1864, at the rate of 2 per cent.; for the year ended 31st July, 1865, at the rate of 2½ per cent.; and thereafter at the rate of 3 per cent. per annum, with right after 1866 to share the surplus profits on the transferred lines. By act of 5th July, 1865, the Scottish Central was amalgamated with the Caledonian, a full detail of the enactments respecting which being given in the *Appendix* to the MANUAL for 1866.—For sundry other details relating to this company prior to amalgamation, see MANUAL for 1882, and previously.

CALLANDER AND OBAN.—See GENERAL INDEX.

CRIEFF JUNCTION.—Incorporated 15th August, 1853. Length, 9 miles. By act of 29th June, 1865, the Crieff Junction was amalgamated with the Scottish Central as from 1st August, 1864. Capital, 45,000*l*. at par.

DUNBLANE, DOUNE, AND CALLANDER.—Incorporated by act of 21st July, 1856. Length, 10¾ miles. By act of 29th June, 1865, the company was amalgamated with the Scottish Central, and thence transferred to the Caledonian. Substituted stock to ordinary shareholders to be equal to three-fourths of amount paid, and to rank thereafter with Scottish Central stock as guaranteed by the Caledonian. The Dunblane, Doune, and Callander ordinary stock was exchanged for 23,070*l*. of Central stock, being three-fourths of the ordinary share capital issued by the Dunblane.

DUNDEE AND PERTH AND ABERDEEN JUNCTION.—Under the Caledonian Act of 8th April, 1881, this company, as a separate undertaking vested in the Caledonian, was dissolved (as from 11th November, 1881), and Caledonian 4 per cent. guaranteed annuities stock No. 2 issued in exchange for the capital of the company in the following proportions, viz:—

Description.	Amount of Annuities Stock in Exchange.			
Ordinary stock	£106	5	0	per cent.
5 per cent 1st preference	125	0	0	"
Quarter shares	125	0	0	"
New 5 per cent. preference 1862	125	0	0	"
Dundee and Newtyle 5½ per cent. preference	131	5	0	"

SCOTTISH NORTH EASTERN.—For sundry details relating to the position of this company prior to the amalgamation, see MANUAL for 1882, and previously.

AMALGAMATION.—The bill for amalgamation of the Scottish North Eastern with the Caledonian received the royal assent on the 10th August, 1866. The Scottish North Eastern was dissolved on the 31st July, and only existed for payment of dividend for the half-year ending on that day, and winding up the revenue accounts. The following are the principal "Heads of Agreement" between the companies:—"The undertaking of the Scottish North Eastern, and the whole lands, works, plant, property, moneys, estate, and effects of the said company (except the balances due to the said company on revenue account at and prior to the 1st August, 1866, and the revenue stores on hand at that date, which shall be taken over by the Caledonian after being verified and valued) shall be transferred to and vested in the Caledonian, as at the said 1st August, 1866. The Caledonian to undertake all liabilities on capital account of the Scottish North Eastern, including the suspense permanent way renewal account, as at the 1st August, 1866, and the cost of the engines and wagons already contracted for by the Scottish North Eastern, and to relieve the Scottish North Eastern of the same; but the said last mentioned company shall charge to renewal a sum not exceeding 12,000*l*. half-yearly for said renewals and maintenance of permanent way and works. The Scottish North Eastern to have right to all sums due on account of revenue at and prior to 31st July, 1866 (including the value of the revenue stores, including insurance fund as aforesaid), and to free the Caledonian from all liabilities on revenue account at and prior to the said last-mentioned date. The amalgamated company shall pay to the holders of the ordinary Aberdeen capital stock, amounting to 830,000*l*., the following guaranteed minimum dividends, viz.:—From 31st July, 1866, to 31st January, 1867, a dividend at the rate of 3 per cent. per annum. From 31st January to 31st July, 3¼ per cent. per annum. From 31st July, 1867, to 31st January, 1868, 3½ per cent. per annum. From 31st January, 1868, to 31st July, 3¾ per cent. per annum. From 31st July, 1868, to 31st January, 1869, 4 per cent. per annum, and at the same minimum rate in all time thereafter; but in case the Caledonian shall, after 31st January, 1869, in any half-year, pay a dividend on the ordinary capital stock at a rate exceeding 7 per cent. per annum, then the holders of ordinary Aberdeen capital stock shall receive a corresponding increase on their dividends—keeping always 3 per cent. per annum below the dividend payable on the Caledonian ordinary stock for the time. The holders of the Scottish Midland ordinary stock, amounting to 600,000*l.*, and the holders of the Dundee and Arbroath ordinary stock, amounting to 200,000*l.*, shall be entitled to receive the rateable increased dividends which they would have received had the increased dividends before-mentioned been received by the holders of Aberdeen ordinary stock, and the Scottish North Eastern remained, as at present, a separate and independent company; but the holders of other stocks or shares of the Scottish North Eastern shall not participate in or be entitled to receive any increased dividend under this agreement. The Scottish North Eastern shall not be entitled to increase their capital account, or to carry any sums to capital after the date of this agreement, without the consent of the directors of the Caledonian, except only such sums as may be expended on new works, for which they have already obtained statutory powers. The holders of stock in the Scottish North Eastern shall not be entitled to have any future allocations of stock of the amalgamated company, nor to interfere with the mode or conditions on which such future allocations shall be made until 1869, when they shall be entitled to participate in the allocations of stock thereafter raised under powers obtained after August, 1869."

New Lines and Works.—The Lesmahagow and Ferniegair connecting line, 53 chains, opened 18th September, 1876; Clydesdale Junction and Kilmarnock Joint Line, connecting branch at Glasgow, 23 chains, opened 1st February, 1877; Bothwell Branch, 1 mile 10 chains, opened 1st March, 1877; London Road Extension at Glasgow, 66 chains, opened 2nd April, 1877; Uddingston and Holytown Line, about 3¾ miles in length, opened on the 1st October, 1878; and the Kinning Park Branch, Glasgow, about ¼ mile in length, opened on the 7th October, 1878. The hotel, buildings, and other unfinished portions of the works at the Glasgow Central Station, and also the Grangemouth Dock and Harbour are in progress, and the following passenger stations, &c., were opened during the year 1879, viz.:—Bridgeton and London Road Stations, on the 1st of April; Clyde Place, on the 1st of July, when the South Side Station ceased to be used; the remodelled Joint Line Station at Bridge Street, on the 12th of July; the Central Station in Gordon Street, on the 1st of August for the Western, and on the 1st of September for the English and Edinburgh traffic. The Edinburgh, Leith, and Granton Branch was also opened for passenger traffic on the 1st of August. In 1880 the Wishaw Loop Line was opened on the 26th April, and the extension to Oban, of the Callander and Oban, on the 1st July. The line connecting the Hamilton and Strathaven branches, about ¾ of a mile in length, opened 1st May, 1882. The line connecting the Scottish Central and North British railways, near Larbert, about ½ a mile long, opened 3rd June, 1882, and a branch at Grangemouth, about ¾ of a mile long, also opened 3rd June, 1882. The Branch from Poniel Junction to Alton Heights Junction (2 miles), which joins the Muirkirk and Lesmahagow branches, was opened for goods and mineral traffic on 1st April, 1883.

ACCOUNTS:—

Revenue.—The subjoined figures show the result of working for the half-years ended 31st January and 31st July, 1884:—

	Jan. 31.	July 31.
Coaching traffic	£501,601	£481,781
Goods, &c., do.	921,246	892,607
Forth and Clyde Navigation, &c.	47,328	41,718
Rents, transfer fees, &c.	21,286	22,573
Gross receipts	£1,491,461	£1,438,679
Expenditure	729,568	717,679
Net	£761,893	£721,000
Add—Sundry balances and interest	35,137	28,622
Total net revenue	£797,030	£749,622
Interest, rents, preference dividends, &c.	513,419	523,633
Available for ordinary stock	£283,611	£225,989
Dividends at 5 and 4 per cent. per annum respectively	271,440	217,152
Balance carried forward	£12,171	£8,837

Mileage, 31st July, 1884.—Caledonian—*Authorised*, 720 miles; *constructed*, 689 miles; *constructing or in abeyance*, 31 miles. Joint Lines—*Authorised*, 63 miles; *constructed*, 62½ miles. Lines leased—*Authorised and constructed*, 1¾ mile. Lines worked, 155¾ miles. Foreign lines worked over, 49½ miles. Total, 958 miles. Forth and Clyde Canal, 52¼ miles. Productive mileage, 752¾ miles.

Capital.—*Authorised:* Stock and shares, 32,415,111*l.*; loans, 8,508,248*l.*; total, 40,923,359*l.* *Created or sanctioned:* Stock and shares, 31,312,111*l.*; loans, 8,012,588*l.*; total, 39,324,699*l.* Balances available to create stock and shares, 1,103,000*l.*; loans, 495,660*l.*; total, 1,598,660*l.* The subjoined statement of stock and share capital created shows the proportion received to 31st July, 1884:—

Description.	Per cent.	Created.	Received.
Guaranteed capital:—		£	£
Caledonian four per cent. guaranteed annuities stock...	4	2,131,105	2,130,723
Four per cent. consolidated guaranteed stock..............	4	3,667,164	3,666,678
Four per cent. consolidated preference stock, No. 1......	4	3,579,935	3,579,872
Four per cent. consolidated preference stock, No. 2......	4	2,946,342	2,943,828
Guaranteed annuities stock, No. 2	4	2,751,386	2,751,386
Five per cent. consolidated preference stock	5	1,639,890	1,639,715
Caledonian four per cent. preference stock, 1884	4	954,000	386,835
Ordinary stock...	...	10,857,026	10,856,970
Ordinary shares (10*l.* each)	...	570	105
Deferred ordinary stock, No. 1, entitled to participate, *pari passu*, in all Caledonian ordinary dividends above 7 per cent.	...	2,508,027	2,507,316
Deferred ordinary stock, No. 2, entitled to participate, *pari passu*, in all Caledonian ordinary dividends above 9 per cent..	...	276,666	276,343
	...	31,312,111	30,739,771

Mem.—Particulars of the consolidation of guaranteed stocks, under "The Caledonian Guaranteed Annuities Act, 1880," will be found in the *Appendix* to the Manual for 1881, and of a further consolidation of separate companies' stocks, under "The Caledonian Guaranteed Annuities Act of 1881," in the preceding pages under separate heads.

TABLE OF PRIORITIES, DESCRIPTIONS, &c., OF ANNUITIES, MORTGAGES, AND STOCKS (see notes at foot).

No.	Year of Act.	Full Description (to be observed in Transfer Deeds and all other Legal Documents).	Rate ℔ cent ℔ annum.
1	1880	4 per cent. guaranteed annuities stock (see notes).........	4
2	Various	Mortgages	Various
	Various	Debenture stock	4
3	1875	4 per cent. consolidated guaranteed stock......................	4
4	1875	4 per cent. consolidated preference stock, No. 1............	4
5	1875	4 per cent. consolidated preference stock, No. 2............	4
6	1881	4 per cent. guaranteed annuities stock, No. 2 (see notes)	4
7	1878	5 per cent. consolidated preference stock (see notes)......	5
8	Various	4 per cent. preference stock	4
9	Various	Consolidated stock, or consolidated (ordinary) stock ...	...
10	1875	Deferred ordinary stock, No. 1 (see notes)	...
11	1875	Deferred ordinary stock, No. 2 (see notes)	...

Notes.—The annuities, interest, and dividends on all the above descriptions are payable half-yearly, viz., No. 1, 1st February and 1st August; No. 2, mortgages various dates, debenture stock 15th May and 11th November; Nos. 3 to 5 and 7 to 10, 1st April and 1st October; No. 6, 14th May and 10th November.

The transfer books of Nos. 1, 2, and 6 close 14 days before payment of annuities.

The transfer books of Nos. 3 to 5 and 7 to 10 close 21 days before payment of dividends.

On Nos. 1, 2, and 6 the annuities and interest are non-contingent and accumulative.

On Nos. 3, 4, 5, and 7 the dividends are contingent upon the profits of each separate year ending 31st January.

No. 1 was issued for the consolidation of the stocks of the Garnkirk, Clydesdale, Wishaw, and Barrhead companies.

No. 6 was issued for the consolidation of the stocks of the Lesmahagow, Forth and Clyde Navigation, and Dundee, Perth, and Aberdeen Junction companies.

No. 7 was created as 10*l.* 5 per cent. preference shares, on 10th October, 1878, and converted into 5 per cent. consolidated preference stock on 27th September, 1881.

No. 3 was created 25th March, 1884, the proprietors having the option to convert into ordinary stocks, on 1st January and 1st July, in three years, 1886, 1887, and 1888, and on, but not later than, 1st January, 1889, on giving one month's previous notice, the stocks so converted being entitled to such dividends as may be declared on the ordinary stock for the then current half-year.

The stock of the Greenock Guaranteed Company has been consolidated into guaranteed annuities stock.

The deferred No. 1 stock participates in any dividend paid to the ordinary stock over 7 per cent. per annum.

The deferred No. 2 stock participates in any dividend paid to the ordinary stock over 9 per cent. per annum.

The ordinary dividend on the stock is contingent upon the profits of each separate half-year.

TRANSFER DEPARTMENT QUERIES AND REPLIES.

Queries.	Replies.
Transfer form—ordinary or special?	Ordinary.
Fee per deed?	2s. 6d. If more than one class of stock transferred in one deed, 2s. 6d. for each class.
Ditto if more sellers than one?	2s. 6d. each seller.
May several classes of stock be transferred on one deed?	Yes.
Are certificates required to accompany transfers?	Yes.
What amounts of stock are transferable, and are parts of 1l. sterling allowed to be transferred?	Any amount; 10s. in the ordinary stock.
To what officer should transfer communications be sent?	Registrar.
In acceptances, renunciations, &c., of allotments of new stock, proxies, or other forms sent to trustees and others, what signatures are required?	In the case of acceptances and renunciations of allotments of new stock, the general rule is the signature of the first-named trustee for himself and co-trustees. In the case of proxies, the signature of the first-named.

The receipts and expenditure on this account to 31st July, 1884, were detailed as under:—

Received.		*Expended.*	
Shares and stock	£30,739,771	Lines open for traffic	£25,344,806
Loans	1,823,646	Lines, &c., in course of construction	257,730
Debenture stock	5,663,038	Lines authorised, but not yet under construction	67,415
Shares cancelled — unappropriated	23,307	Working stock	5,111,023
Shares abated — Dunblane, Doune, and Callander	7,690	Subscriptions to other railways	565,984
Premium on stock, less discount	348,253	Special items	7,520,205
Telegraph	75,053		
	£38,680,758		
Balance	186,405		
	£38,867,163		£38,867,163

The estimate of further expenditure during the half-year ended 31st January, 1885, and in subsequent half-years, was as under:—

	Half-year ended 31st Jan., 1885.	In subsequent half-years.
Lines open for traffic	£134,680	£159,048
Forth and Clyde Navigation	12,000	13,900
Lines, &c., in course of construction	160,549	359,568
Lines in abeyance	26,500	915,238
Working stock	10,000	...
Subscriptions to other railways	17,500	38,750
Total estimated further expenditure	£361,179	£1,486,504

The capital powers and other assets available to meet this further outlay of 1,847,683*l*. were as follow:—

Share and loan capital authorised but not created or sanctioned	£1,598,660
Stock and share capital created but not received	572,340
Loans and debenture stock—balance of borrowing powers	174,476
Estimated value of land and other property	167,000
	£2,512,476
Deduct—Balance at debit of capital account	186,405
	£2,326,071

NEW CAPITAL.—At the half-yearly meeting held on the 10th October, 1879, the shareholders authorised the creation and issue of 164,000 10*l*. 5 per cent. convertible preference shares, 1878. These shares were allotted to the holders (registered at the date of the meeting) of ordinary and 4 per cent. consolidated guaranteed stocks in the proportion of one new share for every complete 85*l*. of such stocks. The shares are convertible, at the option of the holder, into ordinary stock, at any time within five years from the 22nd October, 1878, but not later than the 1st January and 1st July in any half-year. The price was 11*l*. 10*s*. The first instalment of 2*l*. 10*s*. per share, with 7*s*. 6*d*. premium, was made payable on the 8th November, from which date dividend on such instalment will be calculated. Only a limited number of these shares having been taken up, the directors subsequently issued the remainder at the reduced rate of 12*s*. 6*d*. premium, the deposit being 2*l*. per share, with dividend calculated on 2*l*. 10*s*. per share from the date of payment of the deposit on the first issue, the conditions of conversion, &c., remaining the same. In October, 1882, 600,000*l*. new ordinary stock was allotted at par to the holders of consolidated ordinary and 4 per cent. consolidated guaranteed stocks respectively, ranking for dividend from 1st February, 1883. In April, 1884, 400,000*l*. (part of 954,000*l*.) new 4 per cent. preference stock was allotted at par to holders of ordinary and 4 per cent. guaranteed stock respectively, dividend accruing from 1st May, 1884.

The accounts are made up to 31st January and 31st July in every year, and the statutory meetings held in Glasgow in March or September following.

Scale of Voting.—C. C. C. Act (Scotland), sec. 75.

No. of Directors.—Maximum, 15; minimum, 12. *Qualification*, 2,000*l*. stock.

DIRECTORS:

Chairman—J. C. BOLTON, Esq., M.P., Glasgow, and Carbrook, Stirlingshire.

Deputy-Chairman—THOMAS HILL, Esq., Dean Park House, Edinburgh.

J. C. Bunten, Esq., Glasgow.
Alexander Crum, Esq., M.P., Thornliebank, Glasgow.
John Sharp, Esq., Balmuir, Dundee.
John Cowan, Esq., Stoneleigh, Greenock.
James King, Esq., Campsie, Glasgow.
Major Green Thompson, Bridekirk, Cumberland.
The Rt. Hon. the Earl of Breadalbane, Taymouth Castle, Aberfeldy.
Daniel Ainslie, Esq., The Gart, Callander, and 48, Moray Place, Edinburgh.
Hugh Brown, Esq., Glasgow.
Lieut.-Col. William W. Hozier, Mauldslie Castle, Lanarkshire.
James Taylor, Esq., Starley Hall, Burntisland.
James Badenach Nicolson, Esq., Glenbervie House, Kincardineshire.

Directors retire in the order in which they are placed, and are all eligible for re-election.

OFFICERS.—Sec., Archibald Gibson; Gen. Man., James Thompson; Gen. Goods Man., Arch. Hillhouse; Eng., George Graham, C.E.; Eng. of Northern Division, Thomas M. Barr; Eng. of Southern Division, Robert Dundas; Gen. Supt. of the Line, Irvine Kempt; Loco. Supt., Dugald Drummond; Treasurer, Alexander Fergusson; Accountant, James Drynan; Registrar, William Riddell; Traffic Auditor, James Martin; Store Supt., William Haig; Auditors, John Young, Accountant, London, and John Graham, C.A., Glasgow.

Head Offices—302, Buchanan Street, Glasgow.

41.—CALLANDER AND OBAN.

Incorporated by act of 5th July, 1865, to construct a line from the town of Oban to the Dunblane, Doune, and Callander. Length, 72 miles. The line from Callander to Killin was opened 1st June, 1870, from Killin to Tyndrum on 1st August, 1873, and the Extension to Oban on 1st July, 1880. Arrangements with Caledonian, which, by the act of 1870, is to maintain and work the line at cost price, and in accordance with the decision of a standing arbitrator.

For list of Acts obtained from 1870 to 1878, with short heads showing the objects for which the various powers were sought, see the MANUAL for 1881, page 41.

By act of 19th June, 1882, the company was authorised to raise additional capital to the extent of 100,000*l.*, with borrowing powers 33,300*l.*

By the Caledonian and Callander and Oban Act, 31st May, 1883, the balance deposit made by this company was released.

In operation, 72 miles.

REVENUE.—The report for the half-year ended 31st January, 1884, stated that, after providing for interest on loans, and a dividend at the rate of 4½ per cent. per annum on the 4½ per cent. preference stock, and a further dividend at the rate of ½ per cent. per annum of arrears of dividend on the preference shares for half-year ended 31st July, 1883, left a balance of 19*l.* to be carried to next half-year. For the half-year ended 31st July, 1884, the balance, after providing for interest on loans, amounted to 2,755*l.*, out of which a dividend at the rate of 2 per cent. per annum was paid, and 163*l.* carried forward.

CAPITAL.—The receipts and expenditure on this account to 31st July, 1884, were reported as under:—

Received.		*Expended.*	
Ordinary shares, 10*l.* each	£276,710	Line open for traffic	£746,321
4½ per cent. pref. shares, 10*l.* each	259,200		
Loans at 4 per cent.	48,152		
Do. at 3½ per cent.	128,168		
Shares forfeited	592		
Balance	33,499		
	£746,321		£746,321

The estimate of further expenditure requires 2,000*l.* on line open for traffic for half-year ended 31st January, 1885, and 30,179*l.* in subsequent half-years. The assets amounted to 32,179*l.*

NEW CAPITAL.—By resolution of the shareholders, at a special meeting held on 26th September, 1882, the company was authorised to create 10,000 new shares of 10*l.* each, under the powers of the Callander and Oban Act, 1882, bearing a preferential dividend of 4½ per cent. out of the profits of each year, ending 31st January. 5,420 of these shares have been issued.

By resolution passed at a special meeting of shareholders held on 18th September, 1883, the company was authorised, under the powers of the Callander and Oban Act, 1882, to borrow on mortgage or to create and issue debenture stock to the amount of 33,300*l.*; also, at the same special meeting, authority was given to create and issue, under the Callander and Oban Acts of 1865, 1870, 1874, and 1878, debenture stock to the amount of 161,300*l.*, in lieu of mortgages authorised to be issued under the said acts.

Meetings held in Glasgow in March and September.

No. of Directors—9; quorum, 3. *Qualification*, 500*l.*

DIRECTORS:

Chairman—*J. C. BOLTON, Esq., M.P., West George Street, Glasgow, and Carbrook, near Stirling.

Deputy-Chairman—*DANIEL AINSLIE, Esq., 48, Moray Place, Edinburgh, and The Gart, Callander.

1 John Wingfield Malcolm, Esq., Achnamara, Lochgilphead.

3 John Munro Mackenzie, Esq., of Mornish, Mull.

2 His Grace the Duke of Argyle, Inveraray Castle, Inveraray.

† The Right Hon. the Earl of Breadalbane, Taymouth Castle, Aberfeldy.

* Hugh Brown, Esq., Merchant, Glasgow.

* William Wallace Hozier, Esq., of Mauldslie Castle, Lanarkshire.

* John Cowan, Esq., Stoneleigh, Greenock.

* Represent the Caledonian. † Represents the London and North Western.
1, Retires in 1885; 2, in 1886; 3, in 1887.

OFFICERS.—Sec., John Anderson; Eng., Thomas M. Barr, C.E., Perth; Auditors, John Graham and James Muir, Chartered Accountants, Glasgow; Solicitor, George Jackson.

Offices—58, Bath Street, Glasgow.

42.—CALNE.

Incorporated by act of 15th May, 1860, to construct a line from the Great Western at Chippenham to Calne. Length, 5½ miles. Capital, 35,000*l.* in 10*l.* shares; loans, 11,600*l.* Worked by the Great Western at 52 per cent. of the traffic receipts.

Under the act of 28th April, 1864, and the Scheme of Arrangement enrolled in the Court of Chancery, 16th April, 1864, the debenture capital of the company was increased by 32,000*l.*

REVENUE.—The balance of net revenue for the half-year ended 31st December, 1883, amounted, with 608*l.* brought in from the previous half-year, to 2,048*l.*, which sufficed for the payment of interest on the debentures, and a dividend on the ordinary shares for the half-year at the rate of 4*l.* per cent. per annum, carrying forward 569*l.* The gross receipts for the half-year ended 30th June, 1884, amounted to 3,033*l.*, and the expenditure to 1,717*l.*, leaving, with the balance from previous half-year, a total net revenue of 1,885*l.*, which sufficed for the payment of the half-year's interest charges, and a dividend on the ordinary shares for the half-year at the rate of 3½ per cent. per annum, carrying forward 568*l.*

CAPITAL.—The expenditure on this account to 30th June, 1884, amounted to 69,367*l.*, whilst the receipts to the same date had been as under:—

Ordinary 10*l.* shares	£20,820
Debentures at 4, 4½, and 5 per cent.	42,920
Paid out of revenue	5,597
Lord Lansdowne for Black Dog Siding	30
	£69,367

Meetings in February or March and August or September.

No. of Directors—5; quorum, 3. *Qualification*, 300*l.*

DIRECTORS:

Chairman—W. J. DOWDING, Esq., Thames Bank, Marlow.

West Awdry, Esq., Chippenham.
J. J. Lane, Esq., Calne.
Thomas Harris, Esq., Calne.
Henry Weaver, Esq., Devizes.

Retire by rotation. All eligible for re-election.

OFFICERS.—Sec., Edward R. Henly, Calne; Auditor, Charles F. Hart, Devizes. Offices—Calne.

43.—CAMBRIAN.

Incorporated by act of 25th July, 1864, and formed out of the following undertakings:—OSWESTRY AND NEWTOWN: Incorporated by act of 26th June, 1855; length, 30 miles. LLANIDLOES AND NEWTOWN: Incorporated by act of 4th August, 1853; length, 12¼ miles. NEWTOWN AND MACHYNLLETH: Incorporated by act of 27th July, 1857; length, 23 miles. OSWESTRY, ELLESMERE, AND WHITCHURCH: Incorporated by act of 1st August, 1861; length, 18 miles; and ABERYSTWYTH AND WELSH COAST: Incorporated by act of 22nd July, 1861; length, 86 miles.

Opened from Machynlleth to Borth (12 miles), on 1st July, 1863; from Aberdovey to Llwyngwril (12 miles), in November, 1863; from Borth to Aberystwyth (8¾ miles), on 1st August, 1864; Llwyngwril to Barmouth Junction, 3rd July, 1865; Barmouth to Pwllheli, 10th October, 1867; Glandovey to Aberdovey (deviation), 14th August, 1867; Penmaenpool to Dolgelley, 21st June, 1869.

For sundry other details, including parliamentary powers down to 1867, see MANUAL for 1882, and previously.

1883—29TH JUNE.—Authority to extend pier and works at Aberdovey, purchase land at Abereirch, and to establish hotels, refreshment rooms, and savings banks. New capital, 20,000*l.* Power to sell 30,000*l.* coast No. 5 debenture, 175,000*l.* coast ordinary, and 30,000*l.* inland ordinary stocks respectively, "for such prices as they can get for the same respectively."

AGREEMENTS.—By 27 and 28 Vic., cap. 263, the Cambrian was authorised to enter into agreements with regard to traffic, and rebate with the London and North Western, the Hereford, Hay, and Brecon, and the Brecon and Merthyr Tydfil. Traffic facilities were also authorised with the Mid Wales (see below).

AGREEMENT WITH LONDON AND NORTH WESTERN.—This agreement (confirmed by act 27 and 28 Vic., cap. 163, 25th July, 1864) is for 99 years, from 23rd April, 1864, and afterwards terminable on four years' notice being given by either party, the London and North Western to have running powers over the Oswestry and Newtown, the Llanidloes and Newtown, and the Oswestry, Ellesmere, and Whitchurch, giving "A rebate of 50 per cent. from the mileage receipts of the North Western upon all traffic (except minerals) sent from the lines of the Welsh Companies to the lines of the North Western, when the lines of the Welsh Companies and North Western form the shortest route." The rebate fund is applicable to the payment of working expenses, certain rent and preference charges, and a dividend on Cambrian ordinary stock equal to the London and North Western ordinary dividend, the balance (if any) to be paid to the London and North Western. The report for the half-year ended 30th June, 1878, stated that all questions with the London and North Western had been amicably settled, and the rebate account, so long a subject of dispute, had been adjusted.

ARRANGEMENTS ACT, &c.—By 31 and 32 Vic., cap. 177 (31st July, 1868), it was enacted as from 1st July, 1868, that the revenue from all the undertakings of the company should form one common fund, and that after deduction of working expenses, the surplus should be divided between the Coast and Inland, in proportions to be determined. That a provisional period of ten years should be established for this division, separate accounts of receipts and payments being kept, and the net surplus of each section being carried to a distinct fund. During this provisional period of ten years the Board shall consist of ten directors, four appointed by the Coast Section and four by the Inland Section. Arbitrators and umpire are to be appointed to decide on the proportions of surplus to be assigned to each section, and their award may be revised three times within the provisional period of ten years. From and after the termination of this provisional period, the division of the net surplus shall continue for ever as determined by the arbitrators. By the same act power was given to the company to create debenture stock, and also certain regulations enforced in respect to the raising of the mortgage sums of 100,000*l*. and 47,300*l*. The first amount is to be paid to the landowners on the Coast Section, in payment of lawsuits in respect to the same, in completing the railway and works, and in recouping to income the sums paid therefrom to capital. The 47,300*l*. to be offered in the same manner and for the like purposes on the Inland Section. The right of voting on preference stock was also conferred, subject only to the same conditions as relate to the possession of ordinary stock.

The Inland lines Scheme of Arrangement was duly enrolled on the 10th November, 1871, and in pursuance thereof the arrears of interest on the debenture debt of that section, as well as on the certificates of indebtedness up to 31st December, 1871, have been discharged. The arrears of interest on the Llanidloes and Machynlleth preference stocks to 30th June, 1871, have also been discharged. The entire debenture debt and the amount due on certificates of indebtedness have been converted into debenture stock. The whole of the liabilities of the company in respect of the fixed charges upon its Inland income up to 31st December, 1871, have been discharged, thus extricating the Inland Section of the company's undertaking from the litigation and difficulties with which it had been surrounded. Section 8 of this scheme enacts as follows:—"Any surplus of net revenue accruing to the company in respect of the Inland Sections of its undertakings in any autumn half-year, after providing for all fixed charges affecting the Inland Section, whether under this scheme or otherwise, and accruing due during the same autumn half-year, shall be carried forward to the credit of the succeeding spring half-year, and form part of the assets for divisios therein, until the spring half-year's net revenue shall for two consecutive years be sufficient to meet all fixed charges affecting the Inland Section, whether under this scheme or otherwise, and accruing due during the spring half-year without the assistance from the preceding autumn half-year hereby given."—See also notes to capital account, showing order of priority, &c.

The Coast Line Scheme of Arrangement was enrolled in Chancery on 7th August, 1872, and by it the company was authorised—"To convert the mortgage debt and the certificates of indebtedness into 4 per cent. debenture stock; to capitalise the arrears of interest thereon; to settle accounts between the Inland and Coast Sections for advances made by the former; and to apply the revenues in the following order, viz., in payment of rent-charges, the interest on the pre-preference capital, the mortgage debt, the capitalised arrears of interest thereon, the certificates of indebtedness, the capitalised arrears of interest thereon, the interest on debt due to Inland Section from Coast, and dividends on the preference and ordinary stocks, according to their respective priorities." Effect has been given to the powers thus conferred, and the interest accrued on the debenture debt at 4 per cent. from January, 1871, to 30th June, 1872, was paid on 17th September, 1872. Exchange of the debenture stock for the mortgages, and issue of stock for the capitalised arrears thereon, was made at the same time.—See also notes to capital account, showing order of priority, &c. See also clause 8 of the Inland scheme of arrangement mentioned above, and the note to revenue account given below.

ARBITRATION AWARDS.—The arbitrators first made their award on 5th November, 1869, based upon two half-yearly accounts ending respectively 31st December, 1868, and 30th June, 1869, and awarded that as and from the 1st July, 1868, the net surplus of the common fund mentioned in the act of 1868, should belong to the Coast and Inland Sections respectively in the following proportions—that is to say, 65·43 per cent. to the Inland Section, and 34·57 to the Coast Section; but by act of 11th August, 1875, the provisional period created by the act of 1868 was determined as from the 30th June, 1875, and the recently pending arbitration dispensed with. The existing arbitrators and umpire were constituted the future arbitrators, and were to proceed with all practicable despatch to determine for all time to come the proportions in which the two sections are to divide the net surplus of the common fund from and after the 1st July, 1875, and as regards the accounts for the three half-years ended 30th June, 1875, the percentages payable to each section under the same were to be governed by the final award, and such accounts, if necessary, amended accordingly. The act also provides for a reference of other matters to the arbitrators, if needful. Future capital to be deemed a liability of the company, and the interest or dividend attaching thereto to be divided between the sections in the proportions to be fixed by the final award, which was given on the 23rd November, 1877, and decides that for the provisional period since June 30th, 1875, and in the future, the proportions will be 62 per cent. of such fund to the Inland Section, and 38 per cent. to the Coast Section, against 65·43 per cent. and 34·57 per cent. respectively, which was the award given by the arbitrators in 1869.

APPROPRIATION OF THE BALANCE OF NET REVENUE OF THE COAST SECTION TO 31ST DECEMBER, 1877.—The surplus to be distributed to the holders of Nos. 2 and 3 Coast Debenture Stocks, according to the report for the half-year ended 30th June, 1878, amounted to 36,169*l*., and the debenture stock No. 4, to be issued to the holders of No. 2, entitled to arrears of interest, amounted to 9,221*l*. The distributions were made on the 16th September, 1878, and the amounts actually paid were as follow:—In cash to No. 2, 18,411*l*.; to No. 3, 17,632*l*.; total, 36,043*l*.; and in No. 4 debenture stock to No. 2, 9,032*l*. The rates *per cent.* being on No. 2, in cash, 13*l*. 2*s*. 5*d*. on No. 4, debenture stock, 6*l*. 11*s*. 5*d*.; on No. 3, in cash, 24*l*.

OSWESTRY AND LLANGYNOG.—See GENERAL INDEX.

REVENUE.—The receipts and expenditure on this account for the half-years ended 31st December, 1883, and 30th June, 1884, were as follow:—

	Dec. 31, 1883.	June 30, 1884.
Passengers, parcels, &c.	£53,891	£37,723
Goods, minerals, and cattle	43,183	40,842
Rents, interest, tolls, transfer fees, &c.	3,511	2,581
Gross receipts	£100,585	£81,147
Expenditure	57,582	48,912
Surplus for division (as below)	£43,003	£32,235

According to the arbitrators' award given above, 62 per cent. of the above surpluses goes to the net revenue account of the Inland Section, and 38 per cent. to that of the Coast Section.

In operation, 180¾ miles.

*NET REVENUE—*Inland Section*.—For the half-year ended 31st December, 1883, the debit balance carried forward to the general balance sheet, after payment of interest on debentures and dividends on Llanidloes and Machynlleth preference stocks, amounted to 11,715*l*. For the half-year ended 30th June, 1884, after charging the dividends on the Llanidloes and Machynlleth preference, a debit balance of 18,395*l*. was carried forward.

*NET REVENUE—*Coast Section*.—For the half-year ended 31st December. 1883, the balance was sufficient for the payment of interest on all charges down to debenture

* For the clause under which balances are held over until the spring half-year, see paragraph relating to the Inland Scheme of Arrangements Act. on page 43. A similar power exists under the Coast scheme, for securing regular payment of interest on No. 1 debenture stock.

stock No. 3 (priority to No 2, see below), and left a balance which sufficed for payment of interest on debenture stock No. 2 at 1*l.* 8*s.* 6*d.* per cent., which was paid on the 1st March following, leaving a deficiency to be carried forward of 683*l.* 18*s.* 1*d.*; and for the half-year ended 30th June, 1884, after charging the interest on the preferential Nos. 1 and 2 debenture stocks, a debit balance was carried forward amounting to 2,962*l.*

CAPITAL.—Authorised for the purposes of the Inland lines.—Shares and stock, 1,718,554*l.*; loans, 597,959*l.*; total, 2,316,513*l.* Authorised for the purposes of the Coast lines—Shares and stock, 1,250,000*l.*; loans, 793,861*l.*; total, 2,043,861*l.*; and for the purposes of the joint undertaking, shares or stock, 20,000*l.*; loans, 50,000*l.* The subjoined statement of stock and share capital created shows the proportion received to 30th June, 1884:—

Description.		Created.	Received.
INLAND STOCK:—			
Llanidloes No. 1 Preference	5 per cent.	£104,125	£104,125
Llanidloes No. 2 Preference................	"	73,479	73,479
Machynlleth No. 1 Preference	"	134,750	134,750
Machynlleth No. 2 Preference................	{ 4½ per cent.	80,000	80,000
	{ 5 "	16,200	16,200
Oswestry & Newtown, 1860 "A" Preference	5 per cent.	75,000	75,000
" 1860 "B" "	"	40,860	40,860
" *1861 "	"	165,000	165,000
" 1863 "	"	200,000	200,000
†Oswestry, Ellesmere, & Whitchurch Act, 1864 .... "	"	100,000	100,000
†Oswestry and Newtown Act, 1864.. "	"	100,000	100,000
†Oswestry and Newtown (Aberystwyth and Welsh Coast Act, 1864)................ "	"	100,000	75,000
†Llanidloes and Newtown Act, 1864 "	"	40,000	40,000
†Cambrian (Amalgamation) Act, 1864 "	"	30,000	30,000
No. 1 Ordinary		459,140	446,121
		£1,718,554	£1,650,585
COAST STOCK:—			
Four per cent. Pref., 1863 }	With a contingent increase of 1 per cent. as provided in Scheme of Arrangement (Coast Sec.), 1872	£150,000	£150,000
" " 1864 }		330,000	330,000
" " 1865 }		120,000	120,000
Ordinary................		650,000	386,017
		£1,250,000	£986,017
JOINT STOCK:—			
Pier stock		20,000	2,908
Total		£2,988,554	£2,669,460

In arrears, 200*l.*; unissued, 301,802*l.*

PRIORITIES, DESCRIPTIONS, &c., OF STOCKS.—The following is a list of the Debenture, Preference, and Ordinary Stocks of the Joint, Inland, and Coast Sections respectively, numbered in order of priority for dividend, &c., with conditions of issue *in brief*, the descriptions to be strictly observed in transfer deeds and all other legal documents relating thereto, viz.:—

JOINT UNDERTAKING.

PRE-PREFERENCE DEBENTURE STOCK, 1877.—Issued under act 1877. Amount, 50,000*l.* Dividend at 5 per cent. per annum, accumulative, and payable half-yearly (see note). No arrears. This stock ranks next in order of priority to the pre-preference debenture stock, 1868, of both Sections (numbered 2 in the Inland, and 1 in the Coast list below, respectively).

INLAND SECTION.

1—DEBENTURE STOCK issued in lieu of Inland Certificates of Indebtedness.—Amount, 85,521*l.* Dividend at 5 per cent. per annum, accumulative, and declared to be chargeable as an additional security upon rolling stock, payable half-yearly (see note).

2—PRE-PREFERENCE DEBENTURE STOCK, 1868 (Inland and Coast).—Amount for Joint Sections, 144,510*l.* Dividend at 5 per cent. per annum, accumulative, and payable half-yearly (see note).

* Some of the coupons of this stock are stamped 1862.
† The whole of these stocks form one class.—*Vice-Chancellor's Order*, 7th May, 1870.

3—DEBENTURE STOCK issued in lieu of Inland Mortgages existing at date of "Cambrian Railways Act, 1864."—Amount, 191,635*l*. Dividends accumulative, and payable half-yearly (see note).

4—LLANIDLOES No. 1 FIVE PER CENT. PREFERENCE STOCK (104,125*l*.)
" No. 2 " " " " (73,479*l*.)
MACHYNLLETH No. 1 FIVE " " " (134,750*l*.)
" No. 2 FOUR-AND-A-HALF PER CENT. PREFERENCE STOCK (80,000*l*.)
" No. 2 FIVE " " " (16,200*l*.)

The above stocks were issued under act 1864, and rank as first and second charges upon the receipts of their respective Sections of the Cambrian undertaking, subject to rights of mortgagees. Dividends are made half-yearly (see note), and are accumulative.

5—DEBENTURE STOCK issued in lieu of Mortgages renewed since date of "Cambrian Railway Act, 1864" (171,511*l*.)—Dividend at 5 per cent. per annum, accumulative, and payable half-yearly (see note).

6—DEBENTURE STOCK issued in lieu of Mortgages, authorised by act 1864, (96,102*l*.)—Dividend at 5 per cent. per annum, accumulative, and payable half-yearly (see note).

NOTE.—Interest on pre-preferences 1868 and 1877, and on Inland certificates of indebtedness stock, was announced for payment on October 14th, 1884; on "existing" debenture stock on 15th November, 1884, and on Coast No. 1 debenture stock and Llanidloes and Machynlleth No. 1 and No. 2 preference stocks on 24th December, 1884.

The remaining stocks are described, and rank in the order in which they appear, in the table of stocks, with the respective amounts created and received, as copied from the company's report, and given on a preceding page; the whole of these stocks, commencing with the Oswestry 1860A downwards, being, in regard to dividend, contingent upon the profits of each separate year, the dividends being payable as far as earned, in February or August, the books closing by notice.

NEW ORDINARY STOCK, OR "PIER STOCK."—At a special general meeting, held 30th August, 1883, the following resolution was passed, viz.:—"That in pursuance of the Cambrian Railways Act, 1883, this meeting, specially convened for the purpose, hereby sanctions the raising of the sum of 20,000*l*., authorised by the said act, by the creation and issuing, in the manner therein mentioned, of new ordinary stock for that amount, to form a separate class of stock, to be called "Pier Stock," and to be entitled to dividends only out of the tolls, rates, and charges authorised by the said act, after deducting the cost of maintaining the pier, embankment, and works thereby authorised, and not out of any other receipts or revenues of the company." Of the stock authorised by the above resolution 3,240*l*. is issued, and 2,908*l*. received.

COAST SECTION.

1—PRE-PREFERENCE DEBENTURE STOCK, 1868.—This stock is identical with No. 1 stock in the Inland Section, which see.

The other debenture stocks of the Coast Section are as follow:—

No. 1*	£409,826
" 3*	74,531
" 2*	140,320
" 4	32,710
" 5	30,000
	£687,387

Total debenture stocks, Inland and Coast, 1,426,666*l*.

On Nos. 1 and 2 debenture stocks the dividends are accumulative; but in certain events the money applicable to payment of No. 2 is payable to No. 3. The dividends on Nos. 1 and 3 are payable half-yearly, on 1st January and 1st July. On the remainder, as well as on the preference stocks, which rank for dividend, and are to be described as in the table of the company's capital, inserted herein on a previous page, and before referred to, the dividends are *not* accumulative, but are contingent upon the profits of each separate year.

* By the Scheme of Arrangement the No. 3 stock takes precedence of No. 2. See also Appropriation of the Balance of Net Revenue of the Coast Section, on a preceding page.

TRANSFER DEPARTMENT QUERIES AND REPLIES.

Queries.	Replies.
Transfer form—ordinary or special?	Ordinary.
Fee per deed?	2s. 6d.
Ditto if more sellers than one?	2s. 6d. each transaction.
May several classes of stock be transferred on one deed?	Debenture stock by separate deed; ordinary and preference stock may be included in one deed.
Are certificates required to accompany transfers?	Yes.
What amounts of stock are transferable, and are parts of 1l. sterling allowed to be transferred?	Even pounds, but no fractions.
To what officer should transfer communications be sent?	Secretary.

The receipts and expenditure on capital account to 30th June, 1884, are given in detail below:—

INLAND SECTION.

Receipts.		*Expenditure.*	
Shares and stock	£1,680,535	Lines open for traffic	£1,770,78
Debenture stocks	544,769	Working stock	191,960
Debenture stock—preferential	47,300	Subscriptions to other lines (now amalgamated)	205,000
		Coast debenture stock No. 5, held on behalf of Inland Section, in accordance with scheme of arrangement, 1872	30,000
		Arrears of interest to 30th June, 1870	74,862
	£2,272,604		£2,272,604

COAST SECTION.

Receipts.		*Expenditure.*	
Shares and stock	£986,017	Lines open for traffic	£1,737,075
Debenture stocks	687,387	Arrears of interest to 31st December, 1870, on debentures and Lloyd's bonds, and to 31st December, 1873, on debenture stock No. 2, capitalised in accordance with scheme of arrangement (Coast Section), 1872	36,329
Debenture stock—preferential	97,210		
Rent-charges—created subsequent to the act of 1868	2,790		
	£1,773,404		£1,773,404

JOINT PURPOSES.

Pier stock	£2,908	Lines open for traffic	£51,887
Debenture stock—preferential	50,000	Working stock	19,584
Amount realised by sale of Coast ordinary stock belonging to Inland Section	10,239		
Balance	8,324		
	£71,471		£71,471

Meetings held in February and August.

No. of Directors—8; quorum, 3. *Qualification*, 500l.

DIRECTORS:

Chairman—2 R. D. PRYCE, Esq., Cyfronydd, Welshpool.

Deputy-Chairman—3 JAMES F. BUCKLEY, Esq., Greenfield, Oldham.

3 William Bailey Hawkins, Esq., 39, Lombard Street, E.C.

1 Arthur Charles Humphreys-Owen, Esq., Glansevern, Garthmyl, Montgomeryshire.

Hon. Robert Charles Herbert, Orleton, Wellington, Salop.

2 John William Maclure, Esq., The Home, Whalley Range, Manchester.

1 Henry Francis Slattery, Esq., 18, Old Broad Street, E.C.

Lord Henry Vane-Tempest, Plas Machynlleth, Montgomeryshire.

1, Retire in 1885; 2, in 1886; 3, in 1887.

OFFICERS.—Sec., J. Conacher, Oswestry; Eng., George Owen, M.Inst.C.E., Oswestry; Loco. Supt., Wm. Aston, Oswestry; Accountant, R. Brayne, Oswestry; Audit Clerk, Wm. Finchett, Oswestry; Storekeeper, T. S. Goldsworthy, Oswestry; Auditors, John Young, 41, Coleman Street, E.C., and James Fraser, 2, Tokenhouse Buildings, King's Arms Yard, E.C.; Solicitor, Henry Christian Corfield; Bankers, The National Provincial Bank of England.

Offices—Oswestry, Salop.

44.—CARRICKFERGUS HARBOUR JUNCTION.

Incorporated by act of 3rd July, 1882, for making a railway to connect the Belfast and Northern Counties undertaking with the Harbour of Carrickfergus. Length, about 1½ mile. Period for completion, 5 years. Working and traffic arrangements with the Belfast and Northern Counties. Capital, 7,500*l.* in 10*l.* shares; borrowing powers, 5,000*l.*

No. of Directors—8; quorum, 5. *Qualification*, 10 shares.

FIRST DIRECTORS:

Marriott Robert Dalway, Esq.	Thomas Greer, Esq.
John Jellie, Esq.	Alexander Johns, Esq.
James Taylor Reid, Esq.	William Gorman, Esq.
James Logan, Esq.	David Gray, Esq.

45.—CARRICKFERGUS AND LARNE.

Incorporated by act of 15th May, 1860, for constructing a railway from the Belfast and Northern Counties, at Carrickfergus, to Larne. Length, 14½ miles. Capital, 125,000*l.* in 25*l.* shares; loans, 41,500*l.* The Belfast and Northern Counties subscribed 12,500*l.*, and work the line.

LARNE AND STRANRAER SHORT SEA ROUTE.—At a special meeting, held on the 13th August, 1875, the directors were authorised to lend 6,000*l.* to the Larne and Stranraer Steamboat Company, for the purpose of acquiring another steamer. The company's report for the half-year ended 30th June, 1882, stated that owing to some legal proceedings between the Portpatrick and Girvan companies, this route had been stopped from 7th February, 1882; it was, however, re-opened on the 1st August, 1883.

A new arrangement has been made with the Belfast and Northern Counties for running powers over the piece of line from the junction with their railway near Woodburn to Carrickfergus Station, and the use of that station, the rent payable to this company being now 422*l.* 10*s.* per annum, against 275*l.*, the sum previously received. This arrangement took effect on the 1st January, 1880, the term being fixed at 10 years.

REVENUE.—The gross receipts for the half-year ended 31st December, 1883 (including 4,477*l.* from coaching, and 2,978*l.* from goods traffic), amounted to 7,462*l.*, and the expenditure (including 4,512*l.* paid to the Northern Counties for working the line) to 4,833*l.*, leaving, with the balance of 511*l.* brought in from the previous account, a net income of 3,540*l.*, which was appropriated to the following payments:—Interest on loans and debenture stock, 893*l.*; interest on banking account, 14*l.*; rebate on traffic from steamer, 60*l.*; dividend on 80,400*l.* (25*l.*) ordinary shares at 4½ per cent. per annum, 1,810*l.*; balance to next half-year, 564*l.*

The gross receipts for the half-year ended 30th June, 1884 (including 3,180*l.* from coaching and 2,651*l.* from goods traffic), amounted to 6,239*l.*, and the expenditure (including 3,574*l.* net paid to the Belfast Company for working the line) to 3,998*l.*; net revenue, 2,521*l.* Adding the amount brought in from previous account, and deducting 900*l.* for interest charges, &c., there remained a divisible sum of 1,966*l.* Dividend at the rate of 4 per cent. per annum absorbed 1,612*l.*, and the remaining 354*l.* was carried forward to next half-year. In operation, 14½ miles.

CAPITAL.—The expenditure on this account to 30th June, 1884, amounted to 124,502*l.*, the receipts having been as under:—

Ordinary shares	£80,600	
Received on forfeited shares	2,359	
Debenture stock	41,470	=£124,429

The conversion of the bonded debt into 4 per cent. debenture stock has been fully carried out.

Meetings held in Belfast in February and August.

DIRECTORS:

Chairman—1 The Rt. Hon. Lord TEMPLETOWN, Castle Upton, Templepatrick.

Deputy-Chairman—3 Sir EDWARD COEY, Knt., Merville, Belfast.

3 Thomas S. Dixon, Esq., Belfast.
3 John Crawford, Esq., Larne.
1 Sir Charles Lanyon, Knt., M.Inst.C.E., The Abbey, Belfast.
1 John Macaulay, Esq., Red Hall, Larne.
1 George B. Johnston, Esq., Glynn.
2 William Valentine, Esq., Glenavna, Belfast.
2 James Chaine, Esq., M.P., Antrim.
1 Hugh H. Smiley, Esq., Paisley.
1, Retire in 1885; 2, in 1886; 3, in 1887. All eligible for re-election.

OFFICERS.—Sec., Charles Stewart; Eng., Robert Collins; Auditors, George Smith and Henry Archer; Solicitors, James Torrens and Son, Wellington Place, Belfast.

Offices—York Road, Belfast.

46.—CATHCART DISTRICT.

Incorporated by act of 7th September, 1880, for the construction of three short railways in and near to the district of Cathcart, on the south side of Glasgow. Total length, about 2½ miles. Period for completion of works, 5 years. Power to make working arrangements with Caledonian and Glasgow and South Western. Capital, 175,000*l.* in 10*l.* shares, with power to divide the same into "preferred" and "deferred" half-shares. Borrowing powers, 58,330*l.*

By the Caledonian (Additional Powers) Act of 18th July, 1881, an agreement was authorised for the maintenance, working, and management of this undertaking at 45 per cent. of the gross receipts, and in the event of the remaining 55 per cent. being insufficient to pay a dividend at 4½ percent. per annum upon the share capital of the Cathcart, provision is made for its being made up to that rate by the Caledonian, subject to a certain limitation.

No. of Directors.—Maximum, 4; minimum, 3. *Qualification*, 50 shares. Quorum of general meetings, 10 shareholders, holding in the aggregate not less than 5,000*l.* in the capital of the company.

DIRECTORS:

Provost Browne.
R. G. Somerville, Esq.
T. R. J. Logan, Esq.
James King, Esq., Campsie, Glasgow.

Secretary, John M. Robertson, 120, Bath Street, Glasgow.

47.—CENTRAL WALES AND CARMARTHEN JUNCTION.

Originally portion of the Llanelly, but by act of 1871 incorporated into a separate undertaking as the Swansea and Carmarthen. By act of 28th July, 1873, the name was again changed as above, the share capital being fixed at 537,000*l.*, and the borrowing powers at 178,886½*l.* The company's lines south of Pontardulais have been sold to the London and North Western for 310,000*l.*, and the undertaking now consists of a line from Llandilo to Carmarthen. Length, 18¾ miles. The moneys received from the London and North Western enabled the company to pay off its debenture debt and reduce its subscribed capital to 495,000*l.* The capital powers conferred by the act of 1871 (36,000*l.* share and 12,000*l.* loan) have not yet been exercised.

By act of 28th July, 1873, power was obtained to abandon the Mumbles Extension of the Swansea and Carmarthen, and the time for the purchase of land and completion of railway at Carmarthen extended to 12th July, 1876.

By act of 2nd August, 1883, traffic facilities were granted to this company over the London and North Western, Great Western, Vale of Towy, Llanelly Railway and Dock, Milford, Milford Haven Dock and Railway, and Milford Haven Railway and Estate Companies respectively.

The London and North Western has worked the line since 1st July, 1871, and has exercised the running powers given it by act of Parliament.

It was reported in February, 1876, that the umpire before whom the arbitration with the Llanelly was pending had made his award, the result of which is the payment to this company of 13,461*l.* 15*s.* 1*d.* out of the money retained by the London and North Western to meet the claims of the Llanelly Company.

REVENUE.—The net earnings for the year ended 30th June, 1884, sufficed for the payment of a dividend on the first preference stock at 1½ per cent. per annum, against 1½ per cent. per annum for 1883. The amount carried forward was 133*l.*, against 146*l.*

CAPITAL.—The receipts on this account to 30th June, 1884, amounted to 494,500*l.* and the expenditure to 458,706*l.*, leaving a balance in hand of 35,794*l.*

The meetings are held towards the latter end of February and August.

No. of Directors—5; minimum, 3; quorum, 3 and 2. *Qualification*, 500*l.*

DIRECTORS:

Chairman—JAMES KITSON, Jun., Esq., Headingley, near Leeds.

John Winterbotham Batten, Esq., 15, Airlie Gardens, Campden Hill, W.

Alfred Cromwell White, Esq., Park Villa, St. Ann's, Wandsworth, S.W.

John Watson, Esq., Ethelburga House, E.C.

William Cuthbert Quilter, Esq., 14, King's Arms Yard, E.C.

OFFICERS.—Sec., C. J. Hayter; Gen. Man., Frank Grundy; Auditors, John Newton and David S. Derry; Solicitors, S. F. and H. Noyes, 1, The Sanctuary, Westminster, S.W.

Head Offices—1, Drapers' Gardens, Throgmorton Avenue, E.C.

48.—CHARNWOOD FOREST.

Incorporated by act of 16th July, 1874. The line will commence by a junction with the Leicester and Burton Branch of the Midland at Coalville, and passing through Whitwick, Thringstone, and Sheepshed, will terminate by a junction with the main line of the Midland, near the Loughborough Station, having also a spur line for the purpose of communicating with the joint line of the Midland and London and North Western from Coalville through Shackerstone to Nuneaton, so as to afford a communication at its western terminus with both systems. Length, about 11¼ miles. Capital, 159,000*l.* in 10*l.* shares and 53,000*l.* on loan. Arrangements with London and North Western to work the line in perpetuity at 50 per cent. of the gross receipts, and subscribe 50,000*l.* towards the share capital of the undertaking.

By act of 24th July, 1876, the line was so amended and extended as to form a direct communication with the Midland and London and North Western joint line from Coalville to Nuneaton, thus enabling the company to interchange traffic with these two systems. New capital, 24,000*l.*; borrowing powers, 8,000*l.* Powers were also given to enter into agreements with the London and North Western for working the line.

By act of 16th April, 1878, the company was authorised to construct deviation railways as follow, viz.:—At Hugglescote and Donington (7 furlongs and 2 chains); at Thringstone (3 miles 3 chains and 50 links); and at Loughborough (4 furlongs 2 chains and 50 links). Period for compulsory purchase of lands, three years; and for completion of works, four years. Extension of time limited by act of 1874 until 16th July, 1882, and abandonment of certain portions of the line authorised by the same act; the time limited by the act of 1876 also extended for two years.

By act of 27th June, 1881, a further diversion of the line at Hugglescote was authorised, and the time limited by act of 1878 for the completion of the railway was extended until 16th April, 1884.

In November, 1882, the balance of the ordinary share capital, consisting of 2,685 shares of 10*l.* each, was issued at par, the prospectus stating that interest at 5 per cent. per annum would be paid thereon until 1st January, 1883.

CAPITAL.—The capital of the company consists of 159,000*l.* in 15,900 shares of 10*l.* each, of which the balance (7,689 shares) was issued at par in July, 1882.

The line was opened for traffic on the 16th April, 1883.

No. of Directors.—Maximum, 5; minimum, 3; quorum, 3 and 2.

DIRECTORS:

Chairman—HENRY HUMPHREYS, Esq., Woodhouse, near Loughborough.

Major George Thomas Mowbray, J.P., Grange Wood House, Overseal, near Ashby.

Clement Stretton, Esq., J.P., Leicester.

Charles Burton, Esq., Whitwick, Leicester.

A. H. Holland-Hibbert, Esq., Munden, Watford, Herts.

OFFICERS.—Sec., Joseph Hands; Eng., Chas. Liddell, C.E., 24, Abingdon Street, Westminster, S.W.; Auditors, E. P. White and T. W. Marshall; Solicitors, Bircham and Co., 46, Parliament Street, S.W.; Bankers, Messrs. Pares' Leicestershire Banking Co., Leicester, &c., and Robarts, Lubbock, and Co., 15, Lombard Street, E.C.

Offices—Town Hall, Loughborough.

49.—CHESHIRE LINES.

This committee is formed of representatives of the Manchester, Sheffield, and Lincolnshire, the Great Northern, and the Midland companies; was first authorised by act of 5th July, 1865, and was incorporated as a separate undertaking under the control of the three companies by act of 15th August, 1867.

The following lines have, from time to time, been amalgamated with, and vested in the Committee:—

	Date vested in Committee.	Length.	
	1865.	miles.	
Stockport and Woodley...	5th July	2½	Woodley to Stockport.
Stockport, Timperley, and Altrincham	do.	9	Stockport to Altrincham.
Cheshire Midland	do.	12¾	Altrincham to Northwich.
West Cheshire...............	do.	22¾	Northwich to Helsby, with branches to Winsford and Winnington.
Garston and Liverpool ...	do.	4	Garston to Liverpool (Brunswick).
	1866.		
Liverpool Central Station	30th June	1¼	Junction with Garston and Liverpool, to Liverpool Central Station.
Liverpool Extension	16th July	36½	Cornbrook to Garston, and from Timperley to Glazebrook.
Godley and Woodley......	10th Aug.	2	Junction with Sheffield Line at Godley, to Woodley.
Chester Extension	do.	7¾	Junction with West Cheshire at Mouldsworth, to Chester.
Northwich Salt Branches	...	3¾	
Manchester Central	...	1¼	Manchester to Cornbrook.
Liverpool North Extension...........................	...	15	Hunt's Cross to Huskisson.
Warrington Straight Line	...	2¼	
Total.....................	...	121½	
Foreign lines worked......	...	12	
Total in operation...	...	133½	

By act of 27th June, 1872, various additional powers were conferred on the committee, including construction of a line in Manchester; length, 2 furlongs 6 chains. The three companies each to raise 167,000*l.* in stock and 55,000*l.* on loan. The capital, under the whole of the acts, is raised in joint proportions by the three companies.

By act of 23rd July, 1873, power was obtained to construct a line from the town of Marston to the Victoria Salt Works, at Wincham. Length, 3 furlongs 4 chains. Any money under the control, or at the disposal of the committee, and which is not required for other authorised purposes, may be applied for the purposes of this act.

By act of 29th June, 1875, the committee was empowered to stop up and alter certain streets and road in and near Manchester, to close up certain portions of the Manchester and Salford Canal, and to acquire additional lands. Time for completion of certain railways, authorised by act of 1865, extended to 15th August, 1875, and for compulsory purchase of lands, authorised by the act of 1872, to 27th June, 1875.

By act of 28th June, 1877, powers were obtained to construct a line, 1 mile 8 chains in length, commencing in Kirkdale and terminating in Sandhills Lane, in the parish of Walton-on-the-Hill, to be completed within five years, and to be vested in the committee, the joint companies having separate powers for the raising of additional capital for the purposes of the undertaking.

By act of 18th June, 1883, the committee were authorised to construct short lines, and make certain widenings and other improvements in their lines at Warrington, Knutsford, and sundry other places. Period for completion, 5 years.

Liverpool North Extension.—By act of 30th July, 1874, powers were obtained to construct a line from the Liverpool Extension Line, near Halewood, to Walton-on-the-Hill (length, 14 miles); and also a branch to Messrs. Verdin's Salt Works, at Winsford. The former line was opened December 1st, 1879.

The line from Walton-on-the-Hill to Huskisson Station was opened for traffic on 1st July, 1880. Warrington Straight Line, 2 miles 17½ chains, opened 1st September, 1883.

MANCHESTER CENTRAL.—The line and temporary Central Station were opened for traffic on 9th July, 1877, and an hourly system of express trains between Manchester and Liverpool first established. The Manchester Central Station was opened on 1st July, 1880. An extensive goods station is constructed on the site of the temporary passenger station.

SOUTHPORT AND CHESHIRE LINES EXTENSION—See GENERAL INDEX.

REVENUE.—The gross traffic receipts for the half-year ended 31st December, 1883, amounted to 316,091*l*., and the expenses to 227,392*l*., leaving a balance of 88,699*l*. Interest on bankers' balances and land purchases absorbed a further sum of 2,243*l*., leaving a net profit on the half-year's working of 86,456*l*., which was divided equally between the three companies.

The receipts for the half-year ended 30th June, 1884, amounted to 295,684*l*., and the expenses to 224,055*l*., the half-year's working resulting in a profit of 71,629*l*. The interest charges of the half-year amounted to 2,312*l*., leaving a sum of 69,317*l*. to be divided in equal proportions among the three companies.

CAPITAL.—The capital is authorised to be raised and subscribed by the three owning companies in equal proportions, and is shown in their separate accounts. The loan powers were transferred, by the act of 1871, to the three companies. The receipts and expenditure on capital account to 30th June, 1884, were as follow:—

Received.		*Expended.*	
From Midland	£3,249,992	Lines open for traffic	£9,398,979
From Great Northern	3,249,992	Working stock	303,513
From Manchester, Sheffield, and Lincolnshire	3,249,992		£9,702,492
		Balance	47,484
	£9,749,976		£9,749,976

The estimated further expenditure for the half-year ended 31st December, 1884, and for subsequent periods, furnished the subjoined information:—

	Dec. 31st.	Subsequently.	Total.
Lines open for traffic	£105,000	£100,000	£205,000
Working stock	15,000	20,000	35,000
	£120,000	£120,000	£240,000

No. of Members—9; three to be appointed by each company.

DIRECTORS:

* Sir James Joseph Allport, Knt., Littleover, Derby.

‡ The Right Hon. Lord Auckland, Edenthorpe, Doncaster.

† Laurence Richardson Baily, Esq., Atherton Hall, Woolton, Lancashire.

† The Right Hon. Lord Colville, K.T., 42, Eaton Place, S.W.

* J. W. Cropper, Esq., Dingle Bank, Liverpool.

† Abraham Briggs Foster, Esq., Northowram Hall, Halifax, and Canwell Hall, Tamworth.

* Matthew W. Thompson, Esq., Guiseley Hall, Leeds.

‡ Sir Edward William Watkin, Bart., M.P., Northenden, near Manchester, and Charing Cross Hotel, Charing Cross, S.W.

‡ The Right Hon. the Earl of Wharncliffe, Wortley Hall, near Sheffield.

* Represent Midland; † Great Northern; ‡ M. S. & L.

OFFICERS.—Sec., Edward Ross, London Road Station, Manchester; Man., David Meldrum, Liverpool; Eng., W. G. Scott, M.Inst.C.E., Central Station, Liverpool; Accountant, R. R. Walker, Liverpool; Loco. Supt., Charles Sacré, M.Inst.C.E.; Estate and Rating Agent, Glegge Thomas, Liverpool; Storekeeper, W. H. Legge, Warrington; Auditors, W. Grinling, William Pollitt, and W. H. Hodges; Solicitors, Messrs. Lingard, Manchester; Bankers, Manchester and Salford Bank and Liverpool Commercial Bank.

50.—CITY OF GLASGOW UNION.

Incorporated by act of 1864. Length, 6¾ miles. By act of 12th July, 1869, the company was authorised to construct a deviation, to sanction financial arrangements with the North British and the Glasgow and South Western, and to confirm an agreement with the North British, for which see *Appendix* to the MANUAL for 1870.

For brief details of information relating to Acts 1865, 1867, 1872, 1873, 1874, and 1876, see MANUAL for 1882, and previously.

The Harbour Terminus Railway was opened for traffic on the 5th October, 1874. The Sighthill Extension and Parkhead Branch were opened for goods and mineral traffic on the 16th August, 1875, thus completing the junction between the Glasgow and South Western and North British systems, and thereby affording special facilities for the interchange of through traffic.

REVENUE.—The earnings for the half-years ended 31st January and 31st July, 1884, were sufficient for the payment of the preference dividends, which take about 13,750*l*. to discharge. In the latter half-year a dividend was also earned on the ordinary stock at the rate of 3 per cent. per annum, and 157*l*. was carried forward. The dividends were made payable on the 25th March and 30th September respectively. In operation, 6¾ miles.

CAPITAL.—The stock and share capital of the company at 31st July, 1884, stood as follows:—

Dates of Creation.	Description.	Created.	Received.
27th October, 1864	Ordinary 10*l*. shares	£600,000	£600,000
19th October, 1869	College Station 5 per cent. preference stock	100,000	100,000
Various	"C" 5 per cent. pref. 10*l*. shares...	250,000	250,000
26th June, 1876	"F" 5 per cent. preference shares.	200,000	200,000
		£1,150,000	£1,150,000

The receipts and expenditure on capital account to 31st July, 1884, amounted to 1,224,974*l*., showing a debit balance of 116,186*l*.

PRIORITIES, DESCRIPTIONS, &c.—The stocks rank in order of priority, and should be described in transfer deeds and all other legal documents as above.

The dividend on College Station Stock is secured by the ground annual.

The dividends on stocks "C" and "F," should the companies' revenues be insufficient for payment, are guaranteed by the Glasgow and South Western and North British companies.

On all these stocks of the company the dividends are *non-contingent* and accumulative, and are payable half-yearly, in March and September.

TRANSFER DEPARTMENT QUERIES AND REPLIES.

QUERIES.	REPLIES.
Transfer form—ordinary or special?	Ordinary.
Fee per deed?	2*s*. 6*d*.
Are certificates required to accompany transfers?	Yes.
What amounts of stock are transferable, and are parts of 1*l*. sterling allowed to be transferred?..	From 1*l*. upwards.
To what officer should transfer communications be sent?................................	Secretary.

Meetings in March or April and in September or October.

No. of Directors.—By the Union Act of 1867 the number of directors is declared to be eight, of whom four shall annually be elected by the Glasgow and South Western and four by the North British; 3 a quorum.

DIRECTORS:

Chairman—* ROBERT BARCLAY, Esq., 21, Park Terrace, Glasgow.

*R. W. Cochran-Patrick, Esq., M.P., of Woodside, Beith.
*Benjamin Nicholson, Esq., Annan.
*Peter Clouston, Esq., 1, Park Terrace, Glasgow.
†Sir James Falshaw, Bart., 14, Belgrave Crescent, Edinburgh.
†Henry Grierson, Esq., 8, Park Circus Place, Glasgow.
†Robert Young, Esq., 107, Buchanan Street, Glasgow.

* Represent Glasgow and South Western. † Represent North British.

Appointed annually before the first general meeting each year from the respective boards of the two companies.

OFFICERS.—Sec. and Man., Q. Y. Lawson; Auditors, Walter Mackenzie and L. Robertson, Accountants, Glasgow; Solicitors, M'Grigor, Donald, and Co., 172, St. Vincent Street, Glasgow; Bankers, Union Bank of Scotland, Glasgow.

Offices—98, Dunlop Street, Glasgow.

51.—CLARA AND BANAGHER.

(LATE MIDLAND COUNTIES AND SHANNON JUNCTION).

The Midland Counties and Shannon Junction was incorporated by act of 6th August, 1861, to construct a line from Clara, on the Great Southern and Western, to Meelick, on the Shannon. Length, 19 miles. Capital, 115,000*l.* in 10*l.* shares and 38,300*l.* on loan. Powers are given in the act to make arrangements with the Great Southern and Western "for the use, working, and management of so much of the undertaking as lies to the east of the Shannon." By act of 16th July, 1866, the company was authorised to purchase additional lands, and also to extend the time for purchasing lands to the 16th July, 1868, and for completion of works to 16th July, 1869. Powers are conferred by the same act to cancel 50,000*l.* of original shares, and to issue in lieu thereof an equal amount of preference capital, bearing interest at the rate of 5 per cent. By act of 10th August, 1872, the powers of the company were revived, the time for completion of works being extended to 1875. Preference shares divided into two classes of 25,000*l.* each, "Class A" to take dividend in priority of "Class B."

The latter act having expired without the works being finished, together with a further limit granted by the Board of Trade, the works remained in a derelict condition, when a few gentlemen interested in the line, together with Mr. Nicoll, who had been connected with the company in its early stages, applied for an act to renew the expired powers, and to make such changes in the capital resources of the company as would ensure the completion of the line.

The application was successful, and an act was obtained on the 7th September. 1880, extending the time for purchase of the land and the completion of the works to 1882 and 1883 respectively.

The name of the company was at the same time changed to "The Clara and Banagher," and the following changes were authorised in the capital resources of the company, which now stand thus:—Ordinary shares, 65,000*l.*; preference shares, 20,000*l.*; loans, 68,300*l.*

That section of the county—the Barony of Garrycastle—which is so much interested in the completion of the railway, having passed a resolution under the powers conferred by the "Relief of Distress (Ireland) Bill, 1880," guaranteeing the interest upon certain bonds of the company, amounting to 30,000*l.*, the treasury has agreed to advance that sum, which, with a similar amount obtained through the Public Works Loan Board in Ireland, the directors (July, 1882), have been enabled to enter into a contract with a substantial contractor to have the line completed for public traffic.

The works were completed for traffic and opened on 29th May last, and the line is now being worked under the agreement entered into with the Great Southern and Western. It is intended to run steamers between Banagher, the southern terminus of the railway, and Killaloe, on Loch Derg, from which town a railway connection exists with Limerick and the south, and *via* Cork and Waterford with Milford, which will add materially to the traffic resources of the line and the convenience of that section of the country, and a company is about being formed for placing steamers on the route.

CAPITAL.—30th June, 1884.—2,000 5 per cent. preference shares of 10*l.* each, 6,500 ordinary shares of 10*l.* each, and 63,270*l.* on loan at 5 per cent. per annum. Total receipts, 150,366*l.*; expenditure, 165,295*l.*; debit balance, 14,929*l.*

Accounts are balanced to 30th June and 31st December. Meetings in April or October, at Dublin, or other convenient place.

No. of Directors—6; minimum, 3; quorum, 3 or 2 respectively. *Qualification*, 1,000*l.*

DIRECTORS:

Chairman—JAMES FITZGERALD LOMBARD, Esq., Rathmines, Co. Dublin.

Managing Director—JOHN FOWLER NICOLL, Esq., Monkstown, Co. Dublin.

David Coffey, Esq., Roebuck, Co. Dublin.
John Eyre, Esq., Eyre Court Castle, Eyre Court.
John Hill, Esq., C.E., Ennis.
Thomas Perry, Esq., Belmont, Banagher.

OFFICERS.—Clerk to Board, Alexr. S. Nicoll, Dublin; Eng., John H. Brett, Naas; Solicitor, George Keogh, Dublin.

Principal Offices—Brunswick Chambers, Great Brunswick Street, Dublin.

52.—CLEATOR AND WORKINGTON JUNCTION.

Incorporated 27th June, 1876, to construct a railway (length, 15 miles) from Cleator to Workington, with short connecting lines to Moss Bay, Harrington, &c. Total length, about 15 miles. Capital, 150,000*l.* in 20*l.* shares; borrowing powers, 50,000*l.* Works to be completed within five years.

By act of 4th July, 1878, the company was authorised to extend their line to the Rowrah and Kelton Fell Mineral Railway, from Distington to Rowrah, a distance of 6 miles 3 furlongs and 4 chains; period for completion, 5 years. Power to enter into agreements with the Rowrah, and to increase the number of directors to 8. New capital, 63,000*l.*; loans, &c., 21,000*l.*

By Board of Trade Certificate, 1880, the company was authorised to raise additional capital by shares amounting to 60,000*l.*, and by loans to 20,000*l.*

By act of 3rd June, 1881, the company was authorised to construct a branch from Distington Junction to Distington Iron Works, and to raise additional capital amounting to 40,200*l.* by shares and 13,400*l.* by loans.

By act of 16th July, 1883, seven new extensions were authorised, the chief of which being from Workington to Brayton, on the Maryport and Carlisle (15¾ miles), the remainder between Workington Bridge, Workington, and Harrington. Total length, about 19½ miles. Period for completion, 5 years. New capital, 204,000*l.*; loans, 68,000*l.*

Arrangement with Furness.—Under an agreement dated 6th April, 1877, confirmed by act of 28th June, 1877, the Furness undertake to work this company jointly with the London and North Western from and after the opening of the line for public traffic until determined by mutual agreement, at 33⅓ per cent. of all receipts for traffic other than mineral traffic, and 35 per cent. of all receipts for mineral traffic. Whenever this company shall be desirous of transferring their undertaking by lease or otherwise, the Furness to have the option, in priority to all other parties, of vesting the line in their own undertaking, on their signifying their acceptation of such terms as may be offered to them for that purpose. By act of 21st July, 1879, the Furness was empowered to purchase and hold shares in this undertaking.

Twenty-one and a half miles are now open for traffic, the branch to Rowrah having been opened on the 1st of May, 1882.

Revenue—Half-year ended 31st December, 1883.—*Receipts:* 18,665*l.*; *Expenses:* 11,032*l.*; net revenue, 7,633*l.*; interest on parliamentary deposit. Rowrah Branch, 149*l.*; balance brought forward, 201*l.*; total, 7,983*l.*; interest on mortgages, &c., absorbed 2,396*l.*, dividends at the rate of 4½ per cent. and 4 per cent. on the preference stocks, and 3 per cent. on the ordinary stock respectively, 7,684*l.*, and left a balance to next account of 299*l.*

Half-year ended 30th June, 1884.—*Receipts:* 16,845*l.* *Expenses:* 9,719*l.* Net revenue, 7,125*l.*; balance brought in, 299*l.*; total, 7,424*l.* This sum sufficed for the payment of all mortgage and other interest, and a dividend on the ordinary capital at 2½ per cent. per annum, leaving 252*l.* to be carried forward.

Capital.—Up to the 30th June, 1884, the receipts and expenditure on this account amounted to 417,600*l.* and 446,830*l.* respectively, showing a debit balance of 29,230*l.* The receipts include 213,000*l.* in ordinary stock, 60,000*l.* consolidated 4½ per cent. preference stock, 40,200*l.* consolidated 4 per cent. preference stock, and 104,400*l.* in loans at 4 per cent.

New Capital.—At the meeting held on the 22nd August, 1884, resolutions were passed for the creation and issue of 2,550 "new 10*l.* ordinary shares, 1883," and 2,550 "preference 4 per cent. 10*l.* shares, 1883," bearing interest at 4 per cent. per annum, payable half-yearly, 1st January and 1st July.

PRIORITIES, DESCRIPTIONS. DIVIDENDS, &c., OF STOCKS AND SHARES.—The following is a list of this company's Bonds, Shares, and Stocks, numbered in order of priority, with conditions of issue *in brief.* Descriptions of shares and stocks to be strictly observed in transfer forms and all other legal documents relating thereto, viz.:—

1—Mortgage Bonds.—50,000*l.* issued under act 1876. Interest at 4 per cent. per annum, accumulative, and payable half-yearly, 1st January and 1st July.

2—Mortgage Bonds.—21,000*l* issued under act 1878. Interest same as No. 1.

3—Mortgage Bonds.—20,000*l.* issued in Board of Trade Certificates (1880). Interest same as No. 1.

4—Mortgage Bonds.—13,400*l.* issued under act 1881. Interest same as No. 1.

5—Consolidated Four-and-a-Half per Cent. Preference Stock—60,000*l.* issued under act 1880. Dividends payable half-yearly, 1st January and 1st July.

6—CONSOLIDATED FOUR PER CENT. PREFERENCE STOCK—40,200*l.* issued under act 1881. Dividends payable on 1st January and 1st July.

7—ORDINARY STOCK.—150,000*l.* issued under act 1876, and 63,000*l.* under act 1878, together 213,000*l.* Dividend contingent upon the profits of each half-year ended 30th June and 31st December.

TRANSFER DEPARTMENT QUERIES AND REPLIES.

QUERIES.	REPLIES.
Transfer form—ordinary or special?	Ordinary.
Fee per deed?	2*s.* 6*d.*
Ditto if more sellers than one?...	2*s.* 6*d.*
May several classes of stock be transferred on one deed?	Yes, if stamp covers amount of conversion.
Are certificates required to accompany transfers?	Yes.
What amounts of stock are transferable, and are parts of 1*l.* sterling allowed to be transferred?	1*l*; no fraction less.
To what officer should transfer communications be sent?	Secretary.
In acceptances, renunciations, &c., of allotments of new stock, proxies, or other forms sent to trustees, what signatures are required?	All the parties whose names are registered

Quorum of general meeting—7 shareholders, holding together not less than 5,000*l.* capital.

No. of Directors.—Maximum, 8; minimum, 5; quorum, 3. *Qualification*, 50 shares of 20*l.* each.

DIRECTORS:

Chairman—WILLIAM FLETCHER, Esq., Brigham Hill, Cockermouth.

Deputy-Chairman—ROBERT A. ROBINSON, Esq., South Lodge, Cockermouth.

John S. Ainsworth, Esq., Harecroft, Gosforth.

Major Green-Thompson, Bridekirk, Cockermouth.

Charles J. Valentine, Esq., Workington.

J. R. Bain, Esq., Harrington.

Robert Jefferson, Esq., Rothersyke, Carnforth.

OFFICERS.—Sec. and Gen. Man., T. S. Dodgson, Workington; Accountant, Geo. H. Anyon, Accountant, Workington; Engs., John Wood, Carlisle, and A. H. Strongitharm, Barrow-in-Furness; Auditors, Alfred Peile, Workington, and J. W. Pickard, Leeds; Solicitors, E. and E. L. Waugh, Cockermouth, and Lumb and Howson, Whitehaven.

Offices—Workington.

53.—CLEVELAND EXTENSION MINERAL.

Incorporated by act of 7th July, 1873, for a line, commencing by a junction with the Cleveland Branch of the North Eastern, at Brotton, and terminating by a junction with North Yorkshire and Cleveland, at Lythe. Length, 10¼ miles. Capital, 170,000*l.* in 10*l.* shares and 56,000*l.* on loan. Power to enter into working and other agreements with North Eastern. Works commenced in August, 1882.

By act of 16th April, 1878, the powers granted to this company were revived and extended until 7th July, 1879, for the compulsory purchase of lands, and for the completion of the line until 7th July, 1881.

By act of 8th April, 1881, the company's powers were revived, and the time for completion of works extended until 7th July, 1884.

By act of 28th July, 1884, a short line from Brotton to Skelton was authorised, and the period for completion of works, under act 1881, was further extended to 7th July, 1887.

CAPITAL.—The issued capital of the company is 170,000*l.* in 10*l.* shares. The report to 30th June, 1883, issued in August last, stated that 8,563 10*l.* shares altogether had been taken up, upon which 64,695*l.* had been received under calls. It is stated that interest upon the company's shares at the rate of 5 per cent. per annum (on shares allotted since October, 1881), payable on 1st January and 1st July each half-year, had been secured by an adequate investment in consols, until the completion of the railway on 1st August, 1884.

No. of Directors.—Maximum, 4; minimum, 3; quorum, 3 and 2. *Qualification*, 200*l.*

DIRECTORS:

Chairman—JAMES GOODSON, Esq., Hill House, Mitcham, and 32, Kensington Gardens Square, W.

Joseph C. Wakefield, Esq., 25, Holland Villas Road, Kensington, W.

Walter Graham, Esq., 24, Upper Baker Street, W.

OFFICERS.—Sec., Douglas A. Onslow; Engs., Edward Wilson and Co., 9, Dean's Yard, Westminster, S.W.; Auditors, Lovelock and Whiffin, 19, Coleman Street, E.C.; Solicitors, Sutton and Ommanney, 3 and 4, Great Winchester Street, E.C; Bankers, The Union Bank Limited and The National Provincial Bank of England Limited, Stockton.

Offices—3 and 4, Great Winchester Street, E.C.

54.—CLONAKILTY EXTENSION.

Incorporated by act of 22nd August, 1881, for the construction and maintenance of a railway from Gaggan to Scartagh (Clonakilty), County Cork. Length, about 8¾ miles. Period for completion, 5 years. Working agreements with Cork and Bandon. Capital, 40,000*l.* in 10*l.* shares, divided as follows:—15,000*l.* in baronial guaranteed shares; 25,000*l.* in ordinary shares. Borrowing powers, 20,000*l.*

By the Cork and Bandon and this company's joint act of 14th July, 1884, the period for completion of works was extended to 22nd August, 1887. Powers were also given to the Bandon to subscribe towards this undertaking 7,500*l.*

No. of Directors—4; quorum, 3. *Qualification*, 20 shares.

FIRST DIRECTORS:

Adam Perry, Esq.

William Thorley Stewart, Esq.

John Warren Payne, Esq., Beach House, Bantry, Co. Cork.

One other to be appointed.

55.—COCKERMOUTH, KESWICK, AND PENRITH.

Incorporated by act of 1st August, 1861, to construct a line from the Cockermouth and Workington to Penrith on the Lancaster and Carlisle. Length, 31½ miles. Capital, 200,000*l.* in 20*l.* shares and 66,000*l.* on loan. Arrangements with Cockermouth and Workington and London and North Western for use of stations.

WORKING ARRANGEMENT.—By act of 29th June, 1863, several new works were authorised. Certain shares were cancelled, and a preference issue of 5 per cent. allowed instead. Powers not exercised. The London and North Western and the Stockton and Darlington were permitted to subscribe 25,000*l.* each to the undertaking, and to enter into working agreements, the terms of which, when subsequently fixed, provided for the working of the traffic in perpetuity, in consideration of 33⅓ per cent. of the receipts for passengers and goods and 35 per cent. for minerals.

By Board of Trade Certificate, 1865, the company was authorised to raise 34,000*l.* additional share capital, and to borrow, on mortgage, 11,000*l.*; and by another Certificate of the Board of Trade (1867) the share capital was increased by 25,000*l.*, and the borrowing powers 8,000*l.* In 1876 a further increase of share capital was authorised to the extent of 25,000*l.*, and the borrowing powers increased 8,000*l.*

REVENUE.—The results of working the line during the half-years ended 31st December, 1883, and 30th June, 1884, are detailed below:—

	Dec. 31, 1883.	June 30, 1884.
Gross receipts	£23,038	£20,330
Expenditure	13,398	12,149
Net revenue	£9,640	£8,181
Balance from last half-year	488	427
Add sundry interests	145	148
Total net revenue	£10,272	£8,756
Interest and other prior charges	2,745	2,721
	£7,527	£6,035
Dividend on preference shares	625	625
Available for dividend on ordinary shares	£6,902	£5,410

The dividend on the ordinary stock was, for the half-year ended 31st December, 1883, at the rate of 5 per cent. per annum, with a balance of 427*l.* carried to next account. For the half-year ended 30th June, 1834, a dividend was paid upon the ordinary stock at the rate of 4 per cent. per annum, a balance of 230*l.* being carried forward. In operation, 31½ miles.

CAPITAL.—The expenditure on this account to 30th June, 1884, amounted to 380,061*l.*, the receipts having been as follow:—

Shares and stock	£284,000
Loans	8,700
Debenture stock	75,300
Premiums upon issue of debenture stock	994
Balance	11,067=£380,061

PRIORITIES, DESCRIPTIONS, DIVIDENDS, &c., OF STOCKS AND SHARES.—The following is a list of this company's Bonds, Shares, and Stocks, numbered in order of priority, with conditions of issue *in brief*. Descriptions of shares and stocks to be strictly observed in transfer forms and all other legal documents relating thereto, viz.:—

1—MORTGAGE BONDS.—Total amount, 8,700*l.*, consisting of various bonds issued for different terms under acts and Board of Trade Certificates, 1861, 1865, 1867, and 1876. Interest at 3½ and 4 per cent. per annum respectively, payable 15th January and 15th July. These bonds are convertible or redeemable at the option of the holders on the expiration of the respective terms for which the loans have been severally granted; convertible into 4 per cent. debenture stock, on terms to be agreed upon, or redeemable in cash at *par*.

2—DEBENTURE STOCK.—Amount, 75,300*l.* Created by resolution of the shareholders, February 26th, 1876. Issued for the conversion of loans, &c. Interest at 4 per cent. per annum, payable half-yearly, on 1st January and 1st July.

3—PREFERENCE STOCK.—Issued under Board of Trade Certificate, 1867, in 5,000 shares of 5*l.* each (consolidated into stock in August, 1882). Dividends at 5 per cent. per annum, not accumulative, but contingent upon the profits of each half-year, payable with the dividends on the ordinary stock, usually on 1st March and 1st September, the transfer books closing about 21 days before payment.

4—ORDINARY STOCK (259,000*l.*), originally issued in 20*l.* shares, 200,000*l.*; 4*l.* shares (fifths), 34,000*l.*; and 5*l.* shares (new ¼), 25,000*l.* Consolidated in August, 1882.

The dividends are payable usually on the 1st March and 1st September, the transfer books closing about 21 days before payment.

TRANSFER DEPARTMENT QUERIES AND REPLIES.

QUERIES.	REPLIES.
Transfer form—ordinary or special?	Ordinary.
Fee per deed?	2*s.* 6*d.*
Ditto if more sellers than one?	2*s.* 6*d.* for each seller.
May several classes of stock be transferred on one deed?	Yes; other than debenture.
Are certificates required to accompany transfers?	Yes.
What amounts of stock are transferable, and are parts of 1*l.* sterling allowed to be transferred?	Any amount, but not parts of 1*l.*
To what officer should transfer communications be sent?	Secretary.

Meetings held in February and August.

DIRECTORS:

Chairman—JOHN JAMES SPEDDING, Esq., Greta Bank, Keswick.

Deputy-Chairman—Sir HENRY RALPH VANE, Bart., Hutton-in-the-Forest.

Capt. Henry Gandy, Skirsgill Park.
‡John Pattinson, Esq., Frenchfield, Penrith.
Henry Charles Howard, Esq., Greystoke Castle.
‡Edward Waugh, Esq., M.P., Cockermouth.
‡Thomas Altham, Esq., Penrith.
William McGlasson, Esq., Embleton.
* James Cropper, Esq., M.P., Eller Green, Kendal.
* Miles MacInnes, Esq., Rickerby House, Carlisle.
† Sir Henry M. Meysey-Thompson, Bart., Kirby Hall, York.
† David Dale, Esq., West Lodge, Darlington.

* Nominated by London and North Western. † Nominated by North Eastern.
‡ Retire in 1885; eligible for re-election.

OFFICERS.—Sec. and Gen. Man., Peter Thompson; Eng., John Wood, M.Inst.C.E., 8, Fisher Street, Carlisle; Accountant, Joseph Wales; Auditors, ‡John Fisher Crosthwaite, Keswick, and Joseph Nicholson, Whitehaven; Solicitor, Edward Lamb Waugh, Cockermouth.

Offices—Keswick.

56.—COLCHESTER, STOUR VALLEY, SUDBURY, AND HALSTEAD.

Incorporated in 1846, to construct a line from Marks Tey, in the county of Essex, to Sudbury, in the county of Suffolk, with a branch to the Hythe Bridge, in Colchester. Length, 13 miles. Capital, 250,000*l.* in 25*l.* shares and 83,000*l.* on loan. By act of 1847 the line was leased for 999 years to the Eastern Union, now Great Eastern, at a clear yearly rental of 9,500*l.* By act of 25th May, 1855, the company was authorised to convert the money which they had borrowed into capital, and to attach a preference or priority of dividend thereto, such dividend not to exceed 5 per cent. per annum.

Dividends on ordinary stock are regularly paid, half-yearly, at the rate of 3*l.* 5*s.* to 3*l.* 7*s.* per cent. per annum.

Capital.—The expenditure on this account to 30th June, 1884, amounted to 286,646*l.* The receipts to the same date had been as follow:—Consolidated ordinary stock, 228,675*l.*; guaranteed 5 per cent. preference shares (issued to pay off the bond debt of the company), 30,230*l.*

Meetings held in London in January and July.

DIRECTORS:

Chairman—1 WILLIAM QUILTER, Esq., 3, Moorgate Street, E.C.

3 Fred. Adolphus Philbrick, Esq., Q.C., Lamb Building, Temple, E.C.
2 Walter C. Alers Hankey, Esq., Beaulieu, Hastings, Sussex.

OFFICERS.—Sec., Frederick Blomfield Philbrick, Colchester; Auditors, Charles F. Fenton, 51, High Street, Colchester, and Charles William Coleman, Colchester.

Offices—6, New Broad Street, E.C., and Colchester.

57.—COLEFORD, MONMOUTH, USK, AND PONTYPOOL.

Incorporated by act of 20th August, 1853, for a central line through Monmouthshire, to develope the mineral resources, from Llanfihangel Pontymoyle (junction with the Newport and Hereford) to Coleford, Gloucestershire; branch, Dixton to Monmouth gas works.

The company has created and expended the whole of its share and debenture capital, and is leased to the Great Western for 999 years, from 1st July, 1861, under the Coleford Lease Act, 1861, by which the company is to be worked at a fixed rent of 10,764*l.* per annum, less 2,500*l.* per annum, the debenture interest. The traffic returns appear in those of the Great Western.

This undertaking may be vested in the Great Western upon the terms and conditions and in the manner and subject to the provisions following (that is to say):—The Great Western, with the previous consent of three-fourths of the votes of the shareholders in that company on the one hand, and in the Pontypool on the other hand, present in person or by proxy at some general meeting of the respective companies specially convened for the purpose, may issue to every holder of ordinary shares in the Pontypool, in lieu of, or in exchange for, the shares in that company so held by him, consolidated guaranteed stock of the Great Western, bearing interest at the rate of 5*l.* per cent. per annum to an amount not exceeding 100*l.* per cent. of the amount paid up, upon, or in respect of the shares of the Pontypool held by him.

The dividends paid on the ordinary stock are at the rate of 5 per cent. per annum.

No. of Directors.—Maximum, 12; minimum, 9; quorum, 4. *Qualification*, 25 *sui juris.*

DIRECTORS:

Chairman—THOMAS HOLLAND, Esq., Fern Lodge, Malvern.

Deputy-Chairman—THOMAS GRATREX, Esq., Maindee, near Newport, Monmouthshire.

John Lawrence, Esq., Crick, Chepstow.
Edw. Lawrence, Esq., Newport.
James Lewis, Esq., Plas Draw, Aberdare.
J. H. Matthews Esq., Belsize Park, Hampstead, N.W.
H. A. Smith, Esq., Chepstow.

Secretary and Solicitor, H. Stafford Gustard, Usk.

Offices—Usk.

58.—COLNE VALLEY AND HALSTEAD.

Incorporated by act of 30th June, 1856, to make a railway from the Chappel Station of the Colchester and Stour Valley to the town of Halstead, in the county of Essex. Total authorised capital to 30th June, 1882, 218,000*l.* in 10*l.* shares, and 71,633*l.* in loans, together 289,633*l.* Of this amount 236,333*l.* has been created, viz.:—Ordinary shares, 70,000*l.*; preference shares, 108,000*l.*; loans, 58,333*l.*

Agreement with Colchester and Stour Valley and Great Eastern.

By the Amalgamation Act of 1862, the Great Eastern is bound to take and work the Colne Valley, if the company call upon them to do so, on the terms of paying over 50 per cent. of the earnings. Facilities are also given for transmission and receipt of traffic between the Colne Valley and the Great Eastern, by through booking and through rates, in case the former company should prefer to work its own line.

Powers for extension, &c., were obtained under acts 1859, 1861, 1863, and 1865.

REVENUE.—The gross receipts for the half-year ended 30th June, 1884, amounted to 4,832*l.*, and the expenditure to 5,140*l.* No dividend is being paid at present; the balances in favour of revenue account have been carried forward.

CAPITAL.—The receipts and expenditure on this account to 30th June, 1884, were detailed as follow:—

Received.		*Expended.*	
Ordinary shares	£61,200	Cost of obtaining acts of Parliament	£19,163
Preference shares	84,250	Land and compensation, works, engineering, permanent way, interest, stations, and plant...	270,043
Debentures	58,245	Direction, audit, and office expenses	6,240
Lloyd's bonds *	76,200		
Balance	14,762		
Received on account of arrears of call	789		
	£295,446		£295,446

The affairs of the company have been administered under the order of the Court of Chancery, the secretary of the company being receiver.

In operation, 19 miles.

Meetings in February and August.

No. of Directors—6; minimum, 3; quorum, 3. *Qualification*, 250*l.*

DIRECTORS:

Chairman—WILLIAM CLARKE, Esq., M.Inst.C.E., 45, Parliament Street, S.W.

James Brewster, Esq., Ashford Lodge, Halstead, Essex.

Henry John Tweedy, Esq., 3, New Square, Lincoln's Inn, W.C.

J. R. Vaizey, Esq., Attwoods, Halstead, Essex.

George James Addison Richardson, Esq., Manor House, Burnham, Maldon, Essex.

Robert Walker Childs, Esq., 5, Fetter Lane, Fleet Street, E.C.

OFFICERS.—Sec. and Receiver, William George Bailey, 3, Throgmorton Avenue, E.C.; Gen. Man., George Copus, Halstead, Essex; Auditors, R. B. Rose, 3, Throgmorton Avenue, E.C., and James B. Laurie, A.C.A., 2, Gresham Buildings, E.C.; Solicitors, Baxters and Co., 6, Victoria Street, Westminster, S.W., and Mayhew, Salmon, and Whiting, 30, Great George Street, Westminster, S.W.

Offices—3, Throgmorton Avenue, E.C., and Halstead, Essex.

59.—CORK AND BANDON.

Incorporated by act of July, 1845, for a line from Cork to Bandon. By 11 Vic., cap. 194, a deviation and extension into Cork was authorised. Length, 20 miles. Capital, 240,000*l.* in 50*l.* shares and 80,000*l.* on loan.

By act of 28th May, 1852, this company has been further authorised to raise an additional capital of 48,000*l.*; to issue new shares for the additional capital authorised and in lieu of shares forfeited, cancelled, or surrendered, with guaranteed interest not exceeding 6 per cent. per annum, under sanction of three-fifths of special meeting; also to create "debenture shares" in lieu of loans under first act, with interest not exceeding 5 per cent. per annum.

By act of 1854 the company was entitled to create 6,000 shares of 5*l.* each, at 6 per cent. dividend till 31st December, 1863; 4 per cent. in perpetuity thereafter. These were issued on 7th August, 1854, and 12th February, 1856.

* For position &c., of these bonds, see *Appendix* to thi sVolume.

By the West Cork Railways Act, 1860, the company was authorised to create 20,000*l*. new share capital; by the Cork and Kinsale Act, 1860, the borrowing powers were increased 8,000*l*.; and by the Ilen Valley Railway Act, 1874, the borrowing powers were further increased 20,000*l*.

By act of 24th July, 1879, the company was authorised to purchase the undertakings of the Cork and Kinsale Junction and West Cork, and to acquire certain rights belonging to the Ilen Valley (see below and Ilen Valley). West Cork preference stock and Kinsale preference stock to be created and issued for the acquirement of those undertakings.

By act of 14th July, 1884 (Cork and Bandon and Clonakilty Extension Joint), powers were obtained to convert debenture shares into debenture stock. (See also Clonakilty Extension, page 55.)

BANTRY EXTENSION.—This extension was opened for traffic on 1st July, 1881.

CLONAKILTY EXTENSION.—See GENERAL INDEX.

CORK AND KINSALE JUNCTION.—Incorporated by act of 19th April, 1859, to construct a line from the Cork and Bandon to Kinsale, with a branch or tramway to Kinsale Harbour. Capital, 45,000*l*. in 10*l*. shares; loans, 15,000*l*. The line commences 13¼ miles from Cork, and terminates at the military barracks in Kinsale. Length from junction of line with Cork and Bandon to the deep water in Kinsale Harbour, 11 miles. The railway was completed and opened for traffic on the 27th June, 1863, and has been for a long time worked by the Cork and Bandon. By act of 24th July, 1879, authority was obtained for the purchase of this company by the Cork and Bandon, on terms to be settled by arbitration (see below).

ILEN VALLEY.—See GENERAL INDEX, and below for arbitration award.

WEST CORK.—Incorporated by act of 28th August, 1860. This railway commences at Bandon, and runs through Ballineen to Dunmanway, where the Ilen Valley line joins it, and runs thence through Drimoleague to Skibbereen. Length about 18 miles. Subscribed capital about 380,000*l*., including debenture stock. By act of 24th July, 1879, authority was obtained for the sale of this company to the Cork and Bandon, the amount of purchase money to be settled by arbitration (see below).—For particulars as to the working, &c., of this undertaking in the past, see the MANUAL for 1878, and previous editions.

ARBITRATION AWARDS.—The following information is extracted from the company's report for the half-year ended 31st December, 1879, viz.:—"Mr. Leeman has awarded to the West Cork—17¼ miles in length—the sum of 141,934*l*., including 13,300*l*. for the value of rolling stock handed over to us; and to the Cork and Kinsale—10¾ miles in length—the sum of 48,009*l*. By the same act the Ilen Valley Line —16 miles long—also comes under our management, by virtue of a lease made to the West Cork. Thus it will be observed that the powers which were lately exercised by four different boards are now all brought under one control. This will enable us to work the whole on a uniform system and with greater economy, and at the same time to afford more accommodation to the public. The amalgamated lines have been worked by this company since the 1st January, 1880."

ARRANGEMENT WITH POSTMASTER-GENERAL.—See MANUAL for 1884, page 62.

REVENUE.—The report for half-year ended 30th June, 1884, stated that after providing for debenture interest and dividends on preference stock a balance remained of 8,786*l*., out of which the directors recommended the payment of a dividend on the ordinary stock of the company at the rate of 3 per cent. per annum (less income tax), carrying forward 5,208*l*. to next half-year.

CAPITAL.—This account, to the 30th June, 1884, shewed that 597,056*l*. had been expended. The receipts had been as follow:—

Ordinary 100*l*. stock	£175,241	
No. 1 preference 5½ per cent. stock	48,000	
No. 2 preference 4 per cent. stock	29,593	
West Cork preference 4 per cent. stock	163,586	
Kinsale preference 4 per cent. stock	33,263	
Loans	107,400	
Sundries	16,222=£573,305	
Balance		23,752=£597,057

The accounts are made up to 30th June and 31st December in each year, and the meetings held in Cork in February and August.

In operation—Lines owned, 60 miles; lines worked, 15¾ miles.

No. of Directors.—Maximum, 12; minimum, 6; quorum, 3. *Qualification*, 1,000*l*. stocks, except debenture stock. Committee of directors, 3 to 7; quorum, 3.

DIRECTORS:

Chairman—WILLIAM SHAW Esq., M.P., Beaumont, Cork.

Deputy-Chairman—WM. LUMLEY PERRIER, Esq., J.P., South Mall, Cork.

John Warren Payne, Esq., J.P., Bantry.
Joseph Pike, Esq., J.P., D.L., Dunsland, Dunkettle, Cork.
John H. Sugrue, Esq., J.P., Sidney Place, Cork.
John S. Haines, Esq., J.P., Lakeville, Douglas, Cork.
Theodore F. Carroll, Esq., Afgan House, Cork.
Captain Adam Perry, Kinsale.
Thomas K. Austin, Esq., J.P., Talbot Lodge, Blackrock, Co. Dublin.
William M. Murphy, Esq., Dartry, Upper Rathmines, Dublin.

OFFICERS.—Sec. and Accountant, J. J. Mahony; Man., Alexander Gordon; Consulting Eng., J. W. Dorman; Resident Eng., John R. Kerr; Loco. Eng., Thomas Conran; Auditors, F. Sargent and H. H. Beale; Solicitors, Barrington and Son, Dublin, and Babington and Babington, Cork; Bankers, Bank of Ireland, Cork.

Head Offices—Albert Quay, Cork.

60.—CORK, BLACKROCK, AND PASSAGE.

Incorporated by act of July, 1846, for a line (Cork to Passage West), 6½ miles. In 1847 an extension was granted to Monkstown Baths, 1¼ mile, but the project was subsequently abandoned. Fast steamboats run in connection with trains from Passage to Glenbrook, Monkstown, Ring, Queenstown, Crosshaven, and Curraghbinny.

By act 44 and 45 Vic., 1881, the company obtained certain powers to provide and use steam and other vessels, and for other purposes. New capital, 26,000*l.*; borrowing powers, 8,600*l.*

REVENUE.—The balances of the net revenue accounts for the six months ended 31st December, 1883, and six months ended 30th June, 1884, after payment of all interest and preferential dividends and charges, sufficed for the payment of dividends on the ordinary shares, at the rate of 2½ per cent. per annum and 1½ per cent. per annum respectively.

CAPITAL.—The expenditure on this account to 30th June, 1884, amounted to 176,291*l.*, the receipts having been as under:—

Shares and stock	£128,480	
Loans	13,000	
Debenture stock	25,500	
Bonus on shares re-issued	339	
Forfeited shares	336	
Old materials of abandoned line	1,525	
Temporary loans	2,000	= £171,180

TRANSFER DEPARTMENT QUERIES AND REPLIES.

QUERIES.	REPLIES.
Transfer form—ordinary or special?	Ordinary.
Fee per deed?	2*s.* 6*d.*
Ditto if more sellers than one?	2*s.* 6*d.*
May several classes of stock be transferred on one deed?	No.
Are certificates required to accompany transfers?	Yes.
What amounts of stock are transferable?	Not less than 50*l.*
Are parts of 1*l.* sterling allowed to be transferred?	No.
To what officer should transfer communications be sent?	Secretary.

At the half-yearly meeting held 31st May, 1878, a resolution was passed authorising the conversion of debentures into debenture stock, not exceeding 4½ per cent., which is now being acted upon as the loans fall due.

The accounts are made up to 30th June and 31st December, and the statutory meetings held at Cork in February and August.

Scale of Voting.—1 to 5 shares, 1 vote; 6 to 10 shares, 2 votes; and 1 additional vote for every 10 shares.

No. of Directors.—Maximum, 7; present number, 11, to be reduced, as directors die or resign; quorum, 3. *Qualification*, 20 shares.

DIRECTORS:

Chairman—*JOHN H. SUGRUE, Esq., J.P., Sidney Place, Cork.

William Thomas Barrett, Esq., Silver-spring, Cork.
John Chinnery Armstrong, Esq., B.L., Kenilworth Square, Dublin.
*Timothy Mahony, Esq., J.P., Sidney Place, Cork.
*William Foot, Esq., J.P., 10, Raglan Road, Dublin.
Denny Lane, Esq., Monkstown, and South Mall, Cork.
*Edmund Burke, Esq., J.P., Lota Park, Cork.
W W. Harris, Esq., LL.D., Mountjoy Square, Dublin.
Joseph H. Carroll, Esq., South Mall, Cork.

Those marked thus * retired in rotation in December, 1883, and were re-elected unanimously.

OFFICERS.—Sec., F. K. Parkinson; Supt. and Eng., Thomas Warriner, Cork; Auditors, *Denis M'Carthy Mahony and Thomas Exham; Accountant, J. J. O'Sullivan; Solicitor, H. B. Julian, Cork.

Head Office—Albert Street, Cork.

61.—CORK AND KENMARE.

Incorporated by act of 11th August, 1881, for the construction and maintenance of a railway from Macroom to Kenmare. Length, about 34½ miles. Period for completion, 5 years. Working and traffic arrangements with the Cork and Macroom Direct, which may subscribe up to 40,000*l*. Capital, 220,000*l*., in 10*l*. shares, with power to divide into "preferred" and "deferred" half-shares. Borrowing powers, 110,000*l*.

By act of 2nd August, 1883, the company was authorised to construct certain railways at Coolnacaheragh, Ballyvourney, Dereenacullig, Ardtully, Kenmare, &c., in lieu of portions of those authorised by act of 1881. Total length, about 14½ miles.

By act of 14th July, 1884, powers were obtained for the construction of a branch line from Loo Bridge to Headfort, to be called the Kenmare Junction Line, and to abandon the Macroom and Loo Branch, authorised by act of 1881; also to reduce the capital of the company, authorised under that act, from 220,000*l*. to 120,000*l*., and loans from 110,000*l*. to 60,000*l*.

No. of Directors.—Maximum, 6; minimum, 5; quorum, 3. *Qualification*, 50 shares.

FIRST DIRECTORS:

Sir George St. John Colthurst, Bart.
Patrick Francis Dunn, Esq.
John Henry Sugrue, Esq., Sidney Place, Cork.

Three others to be nominated.

62.—CORK AND MACROOM DIRECT.

Incorporated by act of 1st August, 1861, to construct a line from the Cork and Bandon, near Cork, to the town of Macroom. Length, 24¾ miles. Capital, 120,000*l*. in 10*l*. shares; loans, 50,000*l*.

By act of 31st July, 1868, the company was authorised to convert 50,000*l*. of the *unissued* original shares into preference shares, at 6 per cent., with powers to borrow an additional sum of 10,000*l*. on mortgage.

By act of 11th June, 1877, the company was authorised to construct a railway, a little over six furlongs in length, from Ballyphehane to Capwell. New capital, shares or stock, 21,000*l*.; loans, 7,000*l*.

CORK AND KENMARE.—See above.

REVENUE.—The report for the half-year ended 30th June, 1878, showed that the earnings were sufficient to provide for the payment of a dividend on the company's ordinary stock at the rate of 7½ per cent. per annum. No dividends have since been paid, owing to the general depression in trade and other adverse causes.

CAPITAL.—The expenditure on this account to 30th June, 1881, amounted to 201,107*l*., and the receipts to 194,841*l*., leaving a balance against the account of 6,266*l*. The receipts are given in detail below:—

Ordinary shares	£75,850
Ditto new	18,000
5 per cent. preference shares	44,150
Loans	41,430
Debenture stock at 4 per cent.	15,350
Premium on ditto	36
Sundries—land sold	25
	£194,841

New Works.—The works of the new independent line into Cork were commenced in February, 1878, and opened to Capwell Station, Cork, in October, 1879.

No. of Directors—9; minimum, 5; quorum, 3. *Qualification*, 500*l*.

DIRECTORS:

Chairman—W. HUTCHINSON MASSY, Esq., J.P., Mount Massy, Macroom.

Sir John Arnott, Knt., D.L., Woodlands, Cork.
Capt. Richard Tonson Rye, D.L., Rye Court, County Cork.
Timothy Mahony, Esq., J.P., Sydney Place, Cork.
Charles Raycroft, Esq., J.P., Macroom.
E. Ronayne Mahony, Esq., Dunedin, County Cork.
Denny Lane, Esq., South Mall, Cork.
William Harrington, Esq., J.P., Cork.

OFFICERS.—Sec., George Purcell; Traff. Man., F. L. Lyster; Con. Eng., W. F. Madden; Loco. Supt., Charles Storer; Auditors, Edward Harding and Henry Coppinger.

Offices—Capwell Station, Cork.

63.—CORNWALL.

Incorporated by act of August, 1846, for a line in connection with the South Devon, at Plymouth, to Falmouth. In operation, 65¾ miles.

By the act of incorporation, each of the following companies were authorised to subscribe, viz., the Great Western, for 75,000*l*.; Bristol and Exeter, for 112,000*l*.; and South Devon, for 150,000*l*.; and the line might be leased or sold to those three companies or any of them. By subsequent authority of Board of Trade, the Great Western subscribe 60,000*l*.; Bristol and Exeter, 90,000*l*.; South Devon, 52,000*l*.; instead of the above amounts.

Until 1853 the entire undertaking had been in abeyance. After various financial schemes had been tried, with only partial success, it was at last determined to divide the shares into "A" and "B" stock. An agreement was also ratified between the Cornwall on the one hand, and the Great Western, the Bristol and Exeter, and the South Devon, which, in fixed proportions between themselves, guarantee interest on debenture debt.

For brief details relating to acts 1857, 1858, 1861, and 1871, see Manual for 1882, and previously.

With concurrence of all parties interested it has been agreed that, with regard to locomotives, the South Devon, the Cornwall, and the West Cornwall be worked as one system, and that, after making due allowance for interest on capital, the locomotive expenditure be carried to one account and divided between the three companies in proportion to the number of miles run on each section.

Proposed Sale of the Undertaking.—Negotiations have been on foot for the vesting of the undertaking. The following is the substance of the reports on this subject, viz.:—A committee was appointed to enter into negotiations for the disposal of the line, but without any practical result. The Great Western offered to give 5*l*. of their stock for every 20*l*. of Cornwall stock, with a dividend deferred for five years. This proposal was rejected, and the negotiations fell through, the general feeling, however, being that the line should be got rid of, but on better terms than those offered.

Revenue.—The results of the last two half-years' working is shown by the following figures:—

	Dec. 31, 1883.	June 30, 1884.
Gross receipts	£76,474	£76,017
Expenditure	39,654	39,464
Net revenue	£36,820	£36,553
Interest received from West Cornwall, and on account of extension to Keyham	639	639
Bankers' interest	79	72
Total net revenue	£37,538	£37,264
Interest on loans and all prior charges	15,550	15,575
Available for interest on guaranteed preference shares	£21,988	£21,689
Sum required	17,991	17,991
Credit balance to next half-year	£3,997	£3,698

Capital.—The following is a statement of this company's capital (all of which was authorised under act 1861) to 30th June, 1884, in order of priority, the interest and dividends on the whole of the company's capital, except the ordinary shares, being guaranteed by the Great Western, and accumulative:—

1—Guaranteed Debenture Stock.—Interest at 4½ per cent. per annum, payable half-yearly on the 22nd June and 22nd December, the transfer books closing 7 days before payment.

2—The Share Capital.—In order of guarantee as regards Nos. 1 to 3; all the original shares rank for dividend *pari passu* as follows (see notes):—

Description.		Created.	Received.
1 Guaranteed 4½ per cent. perpetual preference stock		£400,000	£400,000
2 Guaranteed 4½ per cent. perpetual preference shares		250,000	250,000
3 Guaranteed 4½ per cent. perpetual preference stock		149,600	149,600
4 Original £20 shares	£299,820		
5 £10 "A" shares	137,820		
6 £10 "B" shares	137,820=	575,460	575,460
Total		£1,375,060	£1,375,060

Notes.—The descriptions given above must be strictly observed in transfer deeds and all other legal documents relating thereto.

The dividends on No. 1 in the foregoing list are payable half-yearly on the 7th February and 7th August. The transfer books close 7 days before payment.

The dividends on No. 2 are payable half-yearly on the 1st June and 1st December. The transfer books do not close.

The dividends on No. 3 are also payable half-yearly on 15th April and 15th October, the transfer books closing 14 days before payment.

TRANSFER DEPARTMENT QUERIES AND REPLIES.

Queries.	Replies.
Transfer form—ordinary or special?	Ordinary.
Fee per deed?	2*s.* 6*d.*
Ditto if more sellers than one?	2*s.* 6*d.*
May several classes of stock be transferred on one deed?	Each class separately.
Are certificates required to accompany transfers?	Stock certificates are; share certificates are not.
What amounts of stock are transferable, and are parts of 1*l.* sterling allowed to be transferred?	Preference stock 5*l.*, or a multiple; debenture stock 1*l.*, or a multiple.
To what officer should transfer communications be sent?	The Secretary.

The receipts and expenditure on capital account to the 30th June, 1884, were as under:—

Received.		*Expended.*	
Shares and stock	£1,375,060	Lines open for traffic	£1,902,728
Loans and debenture stock	458,000	Extension to Keyham Dockyard	8,760
Received from Great Western, under act 1871	55,000		
Premiums on sale of debenture stock	21,330		
Balance	2,098		
	£1,911,488		£1,911,488

The accounts are made up to 30th June and 31st December, and the statutory meetings held in February or March and August or September in every year.

Scale of Voting.—C. C. C. Act, sec. 75. The subscribing companies have one vote for every two shares.

DIRECTORS:

Chairman—3 ROBERT TWEEDY, Esq., Truro.

Deputy-Chairman—* ALEXANDER HUBBARD, Esq., Derwentwater House, Acton, W.

4 E. D. Anderton, Esq., Falmouth.
4 W. Bolitho, Jun., Esq., Penzance.
2 John Carlyon, Esq., Truro.
2 John Claude Daubuz, Esq., Killiow, Truro.
1 G. W. Edwards, Esq., Bristol.
3 W. L. Martin, Esq., Plymouth.
1 The Rt. Hon. Lord Robartes, Lanhydrock, Cornwall.
* W. A. Bruce, Esq., Ashley, Box, Wilts.
* Michael Castle, Esq., Clifton, Bristol.
* Sir Massey Lopes, Bart., M.P., Marystow, Plymouth.

* Represent Great Western.

1, Retire in February, 1885; 2, in 1886; 3, in 1887; 4, in 1888.

OFFICERS.—Sec. (also to Joint Committee), Frederic S. Fowler; Chief Accountant, James Hender; Traffic Supt., C. E. Compton; Goods Man., W. H. Avery; Eng., P. J. Margary; Auditors, W. W. Deloitte and T. Adams; Solicitors, Smith, Paul, and Archer.

Offices—Plymouth.

64.—CORNWALL MINERALS.

Incorporated 21st July, 1873. The undertaking consists of a system of railways in the county of Cornwall, stretching from Newquay Bay, on the north west, to Par Harbour, and thence to Fowey, on the north east, with branches therefrom. Length, about 47 miles. Capital, 854,918*l*., consisting of 750,000*l*. in 100*l*. shares (375,000*l*. 6 per cent. preference and 375,000*l*. ordinary). Rent-charges, 29,918*l*. Borrowing powers, 380,350*l*.

By act of 19th July, 1875, powers were conferred upon the Fal Valley and Temple Mineral to transfer their undertakings to this company. Powers were granted to this company to work, use, and maintain so much of the Bodmin, Wadebridge, and Delabole as has been transferred to the Bodmin and Wadebridge. New capital, 75,000*l*. by shares or stock, and 25,000*l*. by loans or debenture stock.

Under the powers of this act, 24,589*l*. 6 per cent. rent-charge stock, issued under the act of 1873, has been converted into a 5 per cent. rent-charge stock for the sum of 29,507*l*.

FAL VALLEY.—Incorporated 30th July, 1874, to construct a line from the Ratew Branch of the Cornwall Minerals to Bramwell, with a short branch to St. Enoder. Length, 3 miles. Capital—Shares, 45,000*l*.; loans, 15,000*l*. By act of 28th June, 1877, the powers of this company, except as regards the raising of capital, were transferred to and vested in, the Cornwall Minerals.

By an agreement dated 30th April, 1877 (sanctioned by Act 40 and 41 Vic., cap. 223, 10th August, 1877), the Great Western undertook to work this line for a term of 999 years, dating from the 1st July, 1877; the Great Western having the option, for a period of five years from that date, of converting the agreement into a lease, subject to the payments under the agreement hereafter stated, and a further sum of 4 per cent. and 2½ per cent. per annum on the preference and ordinary capital, not exceeding 450,000*l*. and 375,000*l*. respectively, except such preference capital as may be raised with the consent of the Great Western. The option does not now exist. The company is to be worked at a cost not to exceed the percentage of gross receipts at which the Great Western is from time to time worked, and the Great Western guarantee to the Cornwall Minerals a minimum net income of 15,000*l*., 16,000*l*., and 17,000*l*. per annum for the first three years respectively, increasing each year by 250*l*., until the sum has reached 18,500*l*.; and for each year thereafter, ending the 1st July, 18,800*l*., payable half-yearly, on the 1st March and 1st September. If at any time the per centage of receipts exceeds the sums required, the Great Western may recoup themselves for any previous losses incurred, whenever such per centage has shown a deficiency; it is also agreed that 11,500*l*. shall be placed in the hands of the Great Western, as a further provision against any deficiency they may have to make good. The amounts receivable from the Great Western provide for the payment of interest on the loan capital and a few exceptional and preference charges. This agreement did not come into operation until 1st October, 1877, owing to certain obligations having to be fulfilled before the agreement became binding upon the Great Western.

New 4 per Cent. Perpetual Debenture Stock.—In December, 1877, the directors invited application for 125,000*l.* of this stock, to be secured by the fixed minimum net rent, payable by the Great Western, under the agreement mentioned above, and an investment of 12,000*l.* in 4 per cent. debenture stock of the Great Western in the names of trustees, to provide for a small annual deficiency while the rent is attaining its maximum.

Priorities of Debenture Stocks.—The following paragraph is extracted from the company's report for the half-year ended 30th June, 1881, issued in August following, viz.:—"The judgment of the Court of Appeal relative to the priorities of the several classes of debentures and debenture stocks has been given to the effect that the interest upon the debentures and debenture stock issued prior to the act of 1875, amounting together to 72,255*l.*, is a first charge upon the net revenue; the principal sum of such debentures (31,230*l.*) ranks next; after which the interest on 167,975*l.* of the 5 per cent. debenture stock issued after the passing of that act, and prior to the act of 1877, becomes payable; and, lastly, the interest upon the 4 per cent. debenture and debenture stock (134,770*l.*) subsequently issued."

Notwithstanding the appointment of the receiver, the directors have prepared the usual statements of account, so far as they are applicable in the present position of the company.

Revenue—30th June, 1884.—The accounts received from the Great Western of the traffic for the past six months show an increase of gross receipts over the corresponding six months of 1883 of 66*l.*

The amount of net income accumulated in the hands of the receiver, and deposited in the Bank of England, is 16,195*l.* This sum does not include the accumulated interest, amounting to 1,711*l.*, on the 7,076*l.* of Great Western debenture stock in the hands of the trustees for the debenture stockholders, nor the six months' minimum guaranteed traffic due from the Great Western to the 30th June, and payable in September, 1884.

The report for the half-year ended 30th June, 1884, stated as follows:—"The receiver in the chancery action has paid to the holders of the company's debentures, and of the first issue of 5 per cent. debenture stock, their interest in full to the 30th June, 1883, and has also paid a further half-year's interest to 31st December last on the Cornwall Junction mortgages; he has made a considerable payment in respect of arrears of interest on the Cornwall Junction rent-charge stock. Under a recent order, the receiver has also, since the close of the last half-year, paid the year's interest to 30th June last on the company's debentures and the first issue of 5 per cent. debenture stock. Assents to the Scheme of Arrangement of the company's affairs were given by holders of every class of stock of the company to the full amount necessary to enable the directors to apply to the court for confirmation of the scheme. Application for such confirmation was accordingly made, and came on to be heard on Friday, the 8th August instant; when Mr. Justice Kay, after going through the details of the scheme, which in a general way he spoke of as meritorious, took exception to a portion of it proposing a reservation of preference and ordinary stocks for meeting the Great Western Company's claim for minimum rent advanced in excess of net traffic, and he postponed the further hearing until the courts sit again in November next, for the directors to consider how they shall meet the objection. This may render it necessary to recast a portion of the scheme; in which event particulars thereof as varied will be issued to every stockholder and his assent asked. One holder of 5 per cent. debenture stock of both issues, and one holder of 6 per cent. preference stock, were the only parties who appeared before the court to oppose the present scheme, whilst debenture and debenture stockholders, judgment creditors, and the Lostwithiel and Fowey appeared by counsel to support it."

Capital—30th June, 1884.—*Receipts:* Ordinary shares, 375,000*l.*; 6 per cent. preference shares, 375,000*l.*; New Quay and Cornwall Junction 5 per cent. rent-charge stock, 29,507*l.*; 5 per cent. preference shares, 1877, 75,000*l.*; 5 per cent. loans, 31,230*l.*; 4 per cent. loans, 500*l.*; 5 per cent. debenture stock, 209.000*l.*; 4 per cent. debenture stock, 134,270*l.*; sale of rolling stock, 25,047*l.*; total, 1,254,554*l.* *Expended:* 1,333,104*l.* Debit balance, 78,550*l.*

PRIORITIES, DESCRIPTIONS, DIVIDENDS, &c., OF STOCKS AND SHARES.—The following is a list of this company's Stocks, numbered in order of priority, with conditions of issue *in brief*, the descriptions to be strictly observed in transfer forms and all other legal documents relating thereto, viz.:—

No. in order of priority.	Year of Act Authorising Creation and Issue.	FULL DESCRIPTION (To be observed in Transfers).	DIVIDENDS. Rate per cent. per annum.	Whether non-contingent (or accumulative) or contingent on profits.	If contingent. Whether on profits of year or half-year.
1	1873	Debentures ....(£31,230)	5	accumulative	..
2	1873	5 per cent. debenture stock ....(£41,025)	5	do	..
3	1873	5 per cent. debenture stock........(£167,975)	5	do	..
4	1873	Debentures..........................(£500)	4	do	..
5	1877	4 per cent. debenture stock........(£134,270)	4	do	..
6	1873	6 per cent. preference stock.......(£375,000)	6	contingent	Year.
7	1875	5 per cent. preference stock ......(£75,000)	5	do	do.
8	1873	Ordinary stock ....(£375,000)	—	do	do.

The Cornwall Minerals is also liable to pay the interest on the following stocks of the Newquay and Cornwall Junction, which interest is however provided for by the assignment (under a clause in this company's act of 1877) of one eleventh of the fixed net payments secured to this company under their agreement with the Great Western, and this company has no other liability with reference thereto.

1 2	1873 & 1875	Rent-charge stock ....(£29,506 16s.)	5	accumulative	..
3	1875	Debentures ....(£4,100)	6	do	..
4	1875	Debentures ....(£1,250)	5	do	..

NOTES.—The principals of debentures No. 1 and 2, and also the New Quay and Cornwall Junction Co.'s debentures are redeemable at par, but are overdue.

The ordinary and preference stocks were issued in substitution of shares under the consolidation passed by the proprietary, 29th August, 1878.

TRANSFER DEPARTMENT QUERIES AND REPLIES.

QUERIES.	REPLIES.
Transfer form—ordinary or special?	Ordinary.
Fee per deed?	2s. 6d.
Ditto if more sellers than one?	2s. 6d.
May several classes of stock be transferred on one deed?	Yes, classes of stock of the same description.
Are certificates required to accompany transfers?	Yes.
What amounts of stock are transferable, and are parts of 1*l.* sterling allowed to be transferred?	Any amount not being part of 1*l.*
To what officer should transfer communications be sent?	Secretary.
In acceptances, renunciations, &c., of allotments of new stock, proxies, or other forms sent to trustees and others, what signatures are required?	In joint holdings and for executors the signatures of all the parties are required to transfers, &c., but for proxies the signature of the first-named holder for self and co-proprietors or co-executors is sufficient.

No. of Directors.—Maximum, 7; minimum, 5; quorum, 3. *Qualification*, 1,000*l.*

DIRECTORS:

Chairman—ROBERT JACKSON, Esq., Rochdale.

Deputy-Chairman—GEORGE CHAMBERLAIN, Esq., Helenshome, Southport.

Robert Arthur Read, Esq., The Cranes, Surbiton Hill, S.W.

Josiah Henry Lancashire, Esq., 30, Cross Street, Manchester.

Ernest Taylor Woodward, Esq., 17, Bertram Road, Sefton Park, Liverpool.

Thomas Spooner Soden, Esq., 1, Hare Court, Temple, E.C.

Richard Hurst, Esq., Spring Hill, Rochdale.

OFFICERS.—Sec., H. Gibbs; Auditors, Price, Waterhouse, and Co., 44, Gresham Street, E.C.; Solicitors, Cope and Co., 3, Great George Street, Westminster, S.W.

Offices—9, Victoria Chambers, Westminster, S.W.

65.—CORRIS.

Incorporated for making a railway or tramroad from the Aberllefenny and Corris Slate Quarries, in the parish of Talyllyn, in the County of Merioneth, to Llandyrnog. on the River Dovey, in the parish of Towyn, with branches therefrom, and for other purposes. Length, 11 miles. Capital, 15,000*l*. in shares and 5,000*l*. debentures. Gauge, 2ft. 3in. In operation, 11 miles, single line—5 miles main line, Machynlleth to Corris, 6 miles branches to quarries.

By act of 9th July, 1880, former powers were amended, and new regulations made as to tolls, rates for luggage, &c.

By act of 18th June, 1883, this company was authorised to use their railways for passenger as well as for goods traffic.

Revenue.—The net earnings for the half-years ended 31st December, 1883, and 30th June, 1884, sufficed for the payment of debenture interest, &c., and left a balance from which a dividend at the rate of 5¾ per cent. per annum was announced. In previous years good dividends have been earned upon the ordinary capital.

Capital.—The capital account to 30th June, 1884, showed that 19,950*l*. had been received and 19,800*l*. expended. The capital consists of 15,000*l*. in ordinary consolidated stock, and 4,950*l*. in 5 per cent. debenture stock.

Meetings held in February and August.

DIRECTORS:

Chairman—ALFRED JAMES LAMBERT, Esq., 9, Craven Hill, W.

James Fraser, Esq., 169, Camden Road, N.W.

William Ward, Esq., 13, Milner Square, N.

E. T. Gourley, Esq., M.P., Roker, Sunderland.

OFFICERS.—Sec., John. W. Alison, 4, Copthall Buildings, E.C.; Gen. Traff. Man., J. R. Dix; Auditor, James Fraser, Jun., 2, Tokenhouse Buildings, E.C.; Bankers, National Provincial, Machynlleth; Solicitor, Hugh C. Godfray, 101, Finsbury Pavement, E.C.

Offices—4, Copthall Buildings, E.C.

66.—COWBRIDGE.

Incorporated by act of 29th July, 1862, for making railways from Cowbridge, in the county of Glamorgan, to join the Llantrissant and Taff Vale Junction, and the South Wales at the Llantrissant Station. Length, 6 miles. Capital, 35,000*l*. in 3,500 shares of 10*l*. each; power to borrow on mortgage, 11,600*l*. The line has been leased to the Taff Vale for a term of 999 years, at a rent, commencing from 1st January, 1876, of 1,500*l*., and this rent to be paid for 1877, but for the following and subsequent years the rent is to increase at the rate of 100*l*. per annum, up to a final sum of 2,000*l*. per annum. The maximum rent of 2,000*l*. per annum is now received.

Under the Scheme of Arrangement enrolled in the High Court of Justice (Chancery Division), on the 20th January, 1876, the borrowing powers conferred by the act of 1862 were extinguished, and the debenture capital is now fixed at 56,100*l*., as follows, viz.:—"A" debenture stock at 4½ per cent., interest if not paid out of current half-year to be paid out of next or subsequent half-years. "B" debenture stock to take 2½ per cent., and after payment of 2 per cent. to "C" debenture stock, and 15*s*. per cent. to ordinary shares, to take an extra 10*s*. per cent. if available. "C" debenture stock to take 2 per cent., and ½ per cent. additional, if available after payment of 15*s*. to ordinary shares as above; the interest on the "B" and the "C" debenture stock, if not paid in the half-year, not to be a charge against any subsequent half-year. The amounts issued of the various stocks are here stated:—"A," 11,350*l*. to pay for land purchases, &c.; "B," 28,600*l*. to pay debts referred to specially in the Scheme of Arrangement; "C," 10,101*l*. to pay general debts.

Revenue.—For the half-years ended 31st December, 1883, and 30th June, 1884, the balance of net revenue account admitted of the payment of dividends on the share capital of the company at 1*l*. 14*s*. and 1*l*. 9*s*. 6*d*. per cent. per annum for each half-year respectively.

Capital.—The expenditure to 30th June, 1884, amounted to 69,516*l*., whilst the receipts to the same date had been 69,034*l*. The share capital consists of 2,000 ordinary shares of 10*l*. each=20,000*l*. Debenture stocks: "A," 11,350*l*.; "B," 28,600*l*.; and "C," 10,101*l*.; total debenture stocks, 50,051*l*.

Meetings held at Bristol in February and August.

Director's Qualification, 200*l*. shares, or 1,000*l*. debenture stock.

DIRECTORS:

Chairman—HUBERT CHURCHILL GOULD, Esq., St. Hilary, Cowbridge.
Thomas Gratrex, Esq., Newport, Monmouthshire.
Debenture Stock Director—Thomas Rees, Esq., Cowbridge.

OFFICERS.—Sec., James G. Nicholson, Cardiff; Auditor, James Barnard Baker, Bristol.

Offices—Taff Vale Railway Office, Cardiff.

67.—COWES AND NEWPORT (Isle of Wight).

Incorporated by act of 8th August, 1859, for a railway from West Cowes to Newport, Isle of Wight. Length, 4¼ miles. Capital, 30,000*l.* in 10*l.* shares; loans, 10,000*l.*

By act of August, 1863, the company was authorised to raise new capital to the extent of 20,000*l.* in shares and 6,500*l.* on loan.

By act of 14th June, 1875, the company was authorised to raise 10,000*l.* by the creation of new shares or stock, and to borrow on mortgage a further sum of 3,300*l.*

ARRANGEMENTS WITH RYDE AND NEWPORT.—The two companies are now worked as one system, under a joint committee. A new agreement between the two companies has been confirmed by act of 12th July, 1877, under the terms of which this company is entitled to a priority payment of 2,000*l.* per annum, after which the Ryde and Newport receive 2,600*l.* per annum, any surplus being divisible between the two companies in mileage proportion.—See also Ryde and Newport.

REVENUE.—Half-year ended 30th June, 1884. The gross traffic of the joint lines during this half-year amounted to 7,014*l.*, as against 7,137*l.* in the corresponding period of last year, being a decrease of 123*l.* The working expenses for the same period amounted to 5,803*l.*, as against 5,528*l.*, being an increase of 275*l.*

CAPITAL.—The expenditure on this account to 30th June, 1884, amounted to 120,571*l.* The receipts were as follow, viz.:—

Description.	Created.	Received.
	£	£
Ordinary shares	50	50
Ordinary stock	29,950	29,950
First 5 per cent. Preference stock	20,000	20,000
Second ditto ditto	10,000	10,000
Third ditto ditto	30,000	30,000
Loans, &c.	29,800	29,800
Total	119,800	119,800

Meetings in February and August, in London, or Newport or Cowes, Isle of Wight.

No. of Directors—5; reduced to 4. *Qualification*, 300*l.*

DIRECTORS:

Chairman—The Hon. H. W. PETRE, Springfield, Chelmsford, Essex.

H. J. Castle, Esq., 40, Chancery Lane, W.C.
P. W. Colley, Esq., Chelmsford.
Joseph Bourne, Esq., Sandown, Isle of Wight.

OFFICERS.—Sec., John Crick, 8, Drapers' Gardens, E.C.; Eng., Henry D. Martin, 18, Abingdon Street, Westminster, S.W.; Traffic Supt., H. Simmons; Auditors, James Binfield Bird, West Cowes, Isle of Wight, and Henry Pinnock, Beechwood, Newport, Isle of Wight; Bankers, The National Provincial Bank of England, Newport, Isle of Wight.

Offices—8, Drapers' Gardens, E.C.

68.—CRANBROOK AND PADDOCK WOOD.

Incorporated by act of 2nd August, 1877, from Cranbrook to Paddock Wood, wholly in the county of Kent. Length, 13 miles 5 furlongs 1 chain 25 links. Period for completion, 5 years. Arrangements with South Eastern. Capital, 100,000*l.* in 10*l.* shares, with power to divide into "preferred" and "deferred" shares. South Eastern may subscribe any sum not exceeding 50,000*l.*, and if they elect to subscribe the whole of that sum they may appoint two directors. Borrowing powers, 33,000*l.*

By act of 27th May, 1879, the company obtained powers to divert portions of their authorised line, the deviations to be eight in number, the total mileage being about 6¼ miles. Period for completion of works, 4 years.

By act of 1882 the period for the completion of the line is extended to August, 1884, and power is granted to extend the line 2¼ miles to Hawkhurst, and to raise further capital for that purpose. The line is now under the control of the South Eastern, who have purchased most of the land required for the construction of the railway.

By act of 14th July, 1884, the periods for completion of works under acts 1877 and 1879, were extended until 2nd August, 1887, and 27th May, 1886, respectively.

No. of Directors.—Maximum, 7; minimum, 5; quorum, 3. *Qualification*, 25 shares.

DIRECTORS:

The Right Hon. Lord Brabourne, 3, Queen Anne's Gate, S.W., and Smeeth Paddock, near Ashford, Kent.

The Hon. John Stewart Gathorne Hardy, M.P.

The Hon. J. M. O. Byng.

OFFICERS.—Sec., John Shaw, London Bridge, S.E. Solicitors, Fowler and Perks, 117, Leadenhall Street, E.C.

69.—CROMFORD AND HIGH PEAK.

(LEASED IN PERPETUITY TO LONDON AND NORTH WESTERN.)

This old established canal and tramway (6th Geo. IV., cap. 30) was re-incorporated by act of 26th June, 1855. The undertaking consists of a railway from Peak Forest Canal to the Cromford Canal, and to a junction with the Manchester, Buxton, Matlock, and Midlands Junction.

By act of 28th June, 1858, the company was authorised to issue additional capital to the extent of 60,000*l.* at 6 per cent., on an equality with existing preference shares, and by borrowing to the extent of one-third of additional share capital.

By act of 30th June, 1862, a lease in perpetuity to the London and North Western was authorised and the capital re-arranged. This lease took effect on 25th March, 1861, at a rent of 3,500*l.* for the first year and 4,000*l.* subsequently.

The meetings may be held in Derby twice a-year, or at such times and places as the directors appoint. Quorum of shareholders, 5; qualification, 10,000*l.*

No. of Directors—10; minimum, 5; quorum, 3. *Qualification*, 500*l.*

DIRECTORS:

Chairman—WILLIAM JESSOP, Esq., Royal Victoria Yacht Club, Ryde.

Albert Cantrell Hubbersty, Esq., The Ford, Alfreton.

Albert Frederic Hurt, Esq., Alderwasley Hall, near Derby.

Robert Rippon Duke, Esq., Buxton.

George Marsden, Esq., Wirksworth.

John A. Wheatcroft, Esq., Darley Dale, Matlock.

Charles Wright, Esq., Wirksworth.

OFFICERS.—Sec., Francis Barton, Wirksworth; Auditors, George Staley, Butterley, and Henry Wheatcroft, Cromford.

Office—Wirksworth, near Derby.

70.—DARE VALLEY.

Incorporated by act of 21st July, 1863, to construct a line from certain collieries to the Aberdare, with a branch to Hirwain. Length, 2¾ miles. Capital, 35,000*l.* in 10*l.* shares and 11,500*l.* on mortgage.

By act of 20th June, 1870, the company was authorised to raise additional capital to the extent of 21,000*l.* in shares and 7,000*l.* on loan; to abandon the branch to Hirwain Common, and to lease the undertaking to the Taff Vale for 999 years from 1st January, 1871, at 5 per cent. per annum, on a share capital of 56,000*l.*, with the sum of 250*l.* for directorial and secretarial expenses. Taff Vale to pay interest on debenture debt, as well as interest at 5 per cent. on share capital of 56,000*l.* The half-yearly dividends for 1884 were made payable on the 8th January and 8th July in that year respectively.

CAPITAL.—The expenditure to 30th June, 1884, amounted to 61,382*l.*, the receipts having been—from shares 49,500*l.*; from loans, 11,500*l.*; from premiums, 61*l.*; total, 61,061*l.*

Meetings held at Bristol in February and August.

No. of Directors—6; minimum, 4; quorum, 3. *Qualification*, 300*l.*

DIRECTORS:

Chairman—3 HUBERT CHURCHILL GOULD, Esq., St. Hilary, Cowbridge.

1 Charles Henry Williams, Esq., Roath Court, Cardiff.

1 Ebenezer Lewis, Esq., Maindee Hall, Newport, Monmouthshire.

2 Samuel Jones, Esq., 115, Pembroke Road, Clifton, Bristol.

1, Re-elected in February; 2, for re-election in February, 1886; 3, for re-election in February, 1887. All eligible for re-election.

OFFICERS.—Sec., James G. Nicholson, Cardiff; Auditors, Wilberforce Tribe, Bristol, and Sidney Coleman, Cardiff.

Offices—Cardiff.

71.—DERRY CENTRAL.

Incorporated 11th August, 1875, to construct certain railways between the towns of Magherafelt and Coleraine, in the county of Londonderry. Length, 34 miles. Capital, 220,000*l.* in 10*l.* shares, divided into the following classes, viz.:—85,000*l.* "A" or "preferred" shares; 45,000*l.* "B" of county guaranteed shares; and 90,000*l.* "C" or ordinary shares. Of the 90,000*l.* of "C" or ordinary shares, interest at 5 per cent. on 15,000*l.* is guaranteed by the Worshipful Companies of Mercers and Ironmongers. Borrowing powers, 100,000*l.* Works to be completed in five years. The line was opened for traffic on the 19th February, 1880, and is worked by the Belfast and Northern Counties (which may subscribe 35,000*l.*), at 70 per cent., under an agreement for 21 years, from 18th February, 1880, to 18th February, 1901. This agreement was authorised by act of 1877.

By an act passed in the session of 1877, the Belfast and Northern Counties was authorised to subscribe 10,000*l.* to this undertaking.

REVENUE—Half-year ended 30th June, 1884.—*Gross receipts*, 4,539*l.* *Expenditure*—Northern Counties, for working, at the rate of 70 per cent., 3,224*l.*; general charges, 328*l.* Balance, 987*l.*, to meet the payment of interest on the Government loan.

CAPITAL.—Half-year ended 30th June, 1884. *Expenditure:* 218,344*l.*

Receipts:

"A" or Preferred shares	£35,110	
"B" or County guaranteed shares	45,000	
"C" or Ordinary shares	25,645	
"C" or London companies	15,000=	£120,755
Board of Works loans, 5 per cent.		100,000
		£220,755

No. of Directors.—Maximum, 5; minimum, 3; quorum, 3 and 2. *Qualification*, 50 ordinary or "C" shares. Quorum of a general meeting, seven proprietors, holding in the aggregate not less than one-twentieth part of the nominal capital of the company.

DIRECTORS:

Chairman—2 Sir HENRY HERVEY BRUCE, Bart., M.P., Downhill, Londonderry.

Vice-Chairman—2 Col. H. S. B. BRUCE, D.L., J.P., Ballyscullion House, Castledawson.

* Sir Charles Lanyon, J.P., The Abbey, Whiteabbey, near Belfast.
3 John Huey, Esq., Cloonavin, Coleraine.
3 Joseph Clarke, Esq., M.D., Kilrea.
† B. M. Giveen, Esq., D.L., J.P., Cooldaragh, Coleraine.
1 C. M. Holland, Esq., Bryn-y-Grôg, Wrexham.

1, Retire in February, 1885; 2, in 1886; 3, in 1887.

The Grand Jury of the city and county of Londonderry and the Belfast and Northern Counties Railway may each appoint a director.

* Appointed by the Belfast and Northern Counties.

† Appointed by the Grand Jury of Londonderry.

OFFICERS.—Sec., James Blair Stirling; Eng., James Barton; Auditors, Francis J. Hopkirk and John M. Jack; Solicitor, John Glover.

Offices—Manor House, Coleraine.

72.—DEVON AND CORNWALL.

Incorporated by act of 17th July, 1852, to construct a line from the North Devon, at Colebrook, to Okehampton. Length, 13 miles. Capital, 130,000*l.* in 20*l.* shares; loans, 43,200*l.* Arrangements with South Western, by which the line is worked.

For heads of Acts, 1863 to 1873, see the MANUAL for 1881, page 72.

By the London and South Western (Various Powers) Act, 1876, the Devon and Cornwall was authorised to sell its Holsworthy Branch, or if required its entire undertaking to that company. The Holsworthy Branch was subsequently transferred, the purchase being completed in 1880.

By act of 2nd August, 1880, powers were obtained for the release of the deposit provided for under the Western Extensions Act of 1873, the construction of such extensions having been abandoned.

Meetings in February or March and in August or September.

No. of Directors.—Maximum, 10; quorum, 3. *Qualification*, 500*l.*

DIRECTORS:

Chairman—ALEXANDER YOUNG, Esq., 41, Coleman Street, E.C.

J. W. Batten, Esq., 15, Airlie Gardens, Campden Hill.

Alderman Sir Thomas Dakin, Knt., 2 and 3, Creechurch Lane, E.C.

William McAndrew, Esq., South Hill, Bromley, Kent.

OFFICERS.—Sec., George Readdy, 41, Coleman Street, E.C.; Eng., W. R. Galbraith, M.Inst.C.E., 1, Victoria Street, Westminster, S.W.; Joint Solicitors, James Brend Batten, 32, Great George Street, Westminster, S.W., and George Davis, 80, Coleman Street, E.C.

Offices—41, Coleman Street, E.C.

73.—DEVON AND SOMERSET.

Incorporated by act of 29th July, 1864, to construct a line from the Bristol and Exeter, at Taunton, to Barnstaple. Converted into narrow gauge in May, 1881. Length, 42¾ miles. Capital, 500,000*l*. in 25*l*. shares and 166,000*l*. on loan. Working arrangements with Bristol and Exeter.

By act of 26th May, 1865, an agreement with the Bristol and Exeter was confirmed, by which that company is to work and maintain the Devon and Somerset in perpetuity at 50 per cent., and by "The Great Western and Bristol and Exeter Amalgamation Act, 1876," this agreement was made binding on the Great Western.

By act of 15th July, 1867, the company was authorised to make certain deviations and to construct a junction with the Tiverton and North Devon.

By act of 12th August, 1867, the Devon and Somerset was released from its obligations to contribute to the construction of the Ilfracombe, imposed upon it by the act of 2nd June, 1865.

By the "Scheme" enrolled in the High Court of Chancery, 29th July, 1868, the affairs of the company were re-adjusted, and power given:—1. To create 270,000*l*. 6*l*. per cent. "A" debenture stock, ranking as a first charge. 2. To convert the existing debentures (166,000*l*.), then partly issued, into 5*l*. per cent. "B" debenture stock, ranking as a second charge. 3. To create 12,000*l*. 5*l*. per cent. preference shares, ranking after "B" stock, in lieu of certain ordinary shares to that amount.

The "Scheme" also reduced the ordinary share capital to the amount then issued, viz., 260,700*l*., which, by a resolution of the special meeting of 21st February, 1871, was converted into a general capital stock, to be called ordinary stock.

By act of 27th June, 1872, the company was authorised to issue "A" debenture stock to the extent of 100,000*l*., to rank *pari passu* with the other "A" stock, at 6 per cent. per annum.

By act of 30th July, 1874, the company was authorised to issue further "A" debenture stock to the extent of 60,000*l*., to rank *pari passu* with the existing "A" stock, at 6 per cent. per annum.

The line from Taunton to Wiveliscombe (7¼ miles) was opened for traffic 8th June, 1871, and the remainder (35 miles) on 1st November, 1873.

In operation, 42¾ miles.

REVENUE.—The receipts for the half-year ended 30th June, 1884, showed a decrease of 943*l*. as compared with the corresponding period of 1883; the net earnings were sufficient for the payment of interest at 2¾ per cent. per annum on the "A" debenture stock for the past half-year. For the half-year ended 31st December, 1883, the interest on the "A" debenture stock was at the rate of 3¾ per cent. per annum.

CAPITAL.—The total authorised capital now is—"A" debenture stock, 430,000*l*.; "B" stock, 166,000*l*.; preference shares, 12,000*l*.; ordinary stock, 259,455*l*.; ordinary shares, 1,245*l*.; total, 868,700*l*. The receipts and expenditure to 30th June, 1884, were as under:—

Received.		*Expended.*	
Shares and stock	£271,583	Authorised line of the company	£864,137
Debenture stock	594,835	Subscriptions to Barnstaple and Ilfracombe	6,896
Interest, &c.	4,904		£871,033
		Cash balances	289
	£871,322		£871,322

TRANSFER DEPARTMENT QUERIES AND REPLIES.

Queries.	Replies.
Transfer form—ordinary or special?......	Ordinary.
Fee per deed?	2s. 6d.
Ditto if more sellers than one?..	2s. 6d. per seller.
May several classes of stock be transferred on one deed?	Yes.
Are certificates required to accompany transfers?	Yes.
What amounts of stock are transferable, and are parts of 1l. sterling allowed to be transferred?	No part of 1l. allowed, any other amount.
To what officer should transfer communications be sent?	Secretary.
In acceptances, renunciations, &c., of allotments of new stock, proxies, or other forms sent to trustees, what signatures are required?	All (except proxies, when first name is sufficient).

Estimate of further expenditure, 146l. Assets, debenture stock authorised and created but not yet received, 1,165l., and balance of unexpended capital, 289l.

Meetings held in London in April and October.

DIRECTORS:

Chairman—GEORGE HERRING, Esq., 6, Park Crescent, Portland Place, W.

Deputy-Chairman—WILLIAM BAILEY HAWKINS, Esq., 39, Lombard Street, E.C.

John Arthur Locke, Esq., J.P., North Moor, Dulverton, Somerset.

Montague Bere, Esq., Q.C., Morebath, North Devon, and Grimstone, Horrabridge, South Devon.

Edward Parker Wolstenholme, Esq., 2, Stone Buildings, Lincoln's Inn, W.C.

Arthur Barff, Esq., 16, Ashburn Place, South Kensington, S.W.

OFFICERS.—Receiver and Sec., John Wade; Auditors, S. F. Porter, St. Margaret's, Twickenham, S.W., and Robert Dymant, Great Northern Railway, London; Solicitor, S. F. Taylor, 5, Gray's Inn Square, W.C.

Offices—134, Palmerston Buildings, Bishopsgate Street, E.C.

74.—DIDCOT, NEWBURY, AND SOUTHAMPTON.

(LATE DIDCOT, NEWBURY, AND SOUTHAMPTON JUNCTION).

Incorporated under five separate acts of Parliament, passed 5th August, 1873, 24th July, 1876, 9th July, 1880, 10th August, 1882, and 16th July, 1883. The liability of the shareholders is limited to the amount of their shares.

The acts provide that the undertaking shall be divided into three separate sections, called the "Newbury Section," the "Southern Section," and the "Southampton Section."

The NEWBURY SECTION, which was opened for public traffic in April, 1882, commences at Didcot by a junction with the Great Western (which runs from thence to Oxford and the north, and to Bristol and the west), and proceeds south, with stations at Upton, Compton (for East Ilsley), Hampstead Norris, and Hermitage to Newbury. About 50 villages are thus accommodated. The capital applicable to this section is 300,000l., in preference and ordinary shares, with the usual borrowing powers of 100,000l.

The SOUTHERN SECTION, as now altered by the act of 1882, commences at Newbury, and proceeds south to Burghclere, where it joins the Southampton Section. The capital applicable to this section is also 300,000l., in preference and ordinary shares, and the usual borrowing powers of 100,000l.

The SOUTHAMPTON SECTION joins the Southern Section at Burghclere, passing by Whitchurch, where it effects a junction with the main line of the London and South Western to Salisbury, Exeter, Plymouth, and the west. From Whitchurch the line proceeds south to the city of Winchester, thence by Twyford, Allbrook, Chilworth, and Shirley to Southampton, and, by means of the tramways belonging to the Southampton Harbour Board, will obtain access to the Southampton docks and to the company's new pier, whence the steamers arrive and depart.

The total authorised capital, by the special Act of Parliament for the Southampton Section, is 1,000,000*l*., 500,000*l*. to be issued as 5 per cent. preference shares, and 500,000*l*. in ordinary shares, which will not be entitled to any dividends whatever in any year, unless the preference shares have received for that year their full dividend of 5 per cent. per annum. Borrowing powers, 333,000*l*.

The act authorising the Southampton Section specially provides that it is to form "a separate undertaking, distinct and apart from the rest of the undertaking of the company," separate accounts of capital and revenue being kept as would be the case if it belonged to an independent company. It is not to be liable for the debenture debts for the other sections, or for the interest thereon.

The general expenditure and liabilities for management of the undertaking will be fairly apportioned between the three sections.

The first sod was cut on the 26th August, 1879. The first section, from Didcot to Newbury, was opened in April, 1882; the second, or Southern Section, is now in course of construction, and a special act for the construction of the Southampton Section has passed the Committees of both Houses of Parliament.

By act of 16th July, 1883, the name of the company was changed as above, and the created capitals of the various sections consolidated on equal terms into two stocks as follow:—30,800 ordinary shares of 10*l*. each=308,000*l*.; and 64,300 perpetual 5 per cent. preference shares of 10*l*. each=643,000*l*.; together 951,000*l*. out of a total authorised consolidated sum of 1,600,000*l*., the loan capital being consolidated into one common aggregate sum of 533,000*l*.

Capital.—In the latter part of 1879 the company invited applications for 10,000 shares of 10*l*. each, at par, bearing interest at 5 per cent. per annum, guaranteed by the contractors until 31st December, 1881, or the sooner opening of the line. In July, 1882, there were offered for subscription 50,000 5 per cent. preference shares of 10*l*. each, to be called "Southampton Section 5 per cent. preference shares," bearing a guaranteed interest at 5 per cent. per annum during construction, payable half-yearly, on the 1st February and 1st August.

During the past year it was reported that "considerable progress was made in the construction of the line between Litchfield and Winchester, but it is stated that the construction of the line from Winchester to Southampton has been temporarily suspended, although the requisite land at the latter place has not only been paid for, but taken possession of, some part of the works having already been carried out."

Working Arrangement.—The Great Western report for the half-year ended 30th June, 1882, stated as follows:—"By this memorandum the terms of the existing agreement for working the Didcot, Newbury, and Southampton (a draft of which was approved by the proprietors on the 3rd of March, 1881), are to be so varied that until the revenue of the Didcot Company is sufficient to pay 4 per cent. per annum on their paid-up capital, the Great Western are to retain 51½ per cent. of the gross receipts; when the Didcot Company's revenue suffices to pay 4½ per cent., the Great Western will retain 52 per cent.; and when the Didcot Company's revenue will pay 5 per cent. and upwards, the Great Western will retain 52½ per cent. of the receipts. These altered conditions are to take effect when the new railways have been completed, and the authorised railways have been constructed throughout with a double line.

No. of Directors.—Maximum, 12; minimum, 5; quorum, 5 and 3. *Qualification*, 100 shares.

DIRECTORS:

Chairman—Lieut.-Col. Sir ROBERT JAMES LOYD-LINDSAY, K.C.B., V.C., M.P., Lockinge House, near Wantage, Berkshire.

Deputy-Chairman—JOHN WALTER, Esq., M.P., Bearwood, Wokingham, Berkshire.

Viscount Baring, M.P., Stratton Park, Winchester.

George Palmer, Esq., M.P., The Acacias, Reading.

James Staats Forbes, Esq., 13, Chelsea Embankment, S.W.

Sir Julius Vogel, K.C.M.G., 135, Cromwell Road, South Kensington, S.W.

Henry Lee, Esq., M.P., Sedgeley Park, Prestwich, Manchester.

John Henry Cooksey, Esq., Kingsbridge House, Southampton.

George Thomas Harper, Esq., Brynhfyred, Portswood, Southampton.

William Howley Kingsmill, Esq., Sydmonton Court, Newbury.

William George Mount, Esq., Wasing Place, Reading.

OFFICERS.—Sec., Charles H. Bingham, 6, Westminster Chambers, Victoria Street, S.W.; Eng., John Fowler, C.E., 2, Queen Square Place, Westminster, S.W.; Auditors, J. Henry Schröder, 4, Lincoln Inn's Fields, W.C., and Walter Money, Newbury; Solicitors, Lake, Beaumont, and Lake, 10, New Square, Lincoln's Inn, W.C., and Pearce, Paris, and Smith, Southampton; Bankers, The London and County Bank, 21, Lombard Street, E.C., and its Branches, and Slocock, Matthews, and Southby, Newbury.

Offices—6, Westminster Chambers, Victoria Street, Westminster, S.W.

75.—DORE AND CHINLEY.

Incorporated by act of 28th July, 1884, for the construction of a railway from Dronfield and Dore to Glossop. Length, about 20½ miles. Period for completion, 5 years. Arrangements with Midland. Capital, 1,050,000*l*. in 10*l*. shares, with power to divide into "preferred" and "deferred" half-shares; loans, 350,000*l*.

No. of Directors.—Maximum, 7; minimum, 3; quorum, 3 and 2. *Qualification*, 50 shares.

FIRST DIRECTORS:

Robert How Ashton, Esq.
William Henry Greaves Bagshawe, Esq.
William Henry Brittain, Esq.
George Henry Cammell, Esq.
Arthur Francis Pennell, Esq.
John Spencer Ashton Shuttleworth, Esq.
William George Thorpe, Esq.

76.—DOWNHAM AND STOKE FERRY.

Incorporated by act of 24th July, 1879, for the construction and maintenance of a line from the Ely and Lynn Branch of the Great Eastern to Stoke Ferry. Length, 7 miles 1 furlong 4 chains. Period for completion, 5 years. Capital, 60,000*l*. in 10*l*. shares, with power to divide into "preferred" and "deferred" half-shares. Loans, or debenture stock, 20,000*l*. Opened 1st August, 1882.

The Great Eastern work and maintain the line under an agreement by which the Great Eastern guarantee 4 per cent. on the ordinary capital of the company and 4½ per cent. on the debentures, the agreement to be unconditionally determinable by the Stoke Ferry at the end of 10 years from the passing of the act of incorporation, and unless so determined by the Stoke Ferry, the agreement to be in perpetuity.

By act of 29th June, 1883, the company obtained powers to extend their railway to Gooderstone (3½ miles). Period for completion, 5 years. New capital, 30,000*l*.; loans, 10,000*l*. Great Eastern may subscribe, the working agreement with that company being extended.

No. of Directors.—Maximum, 6; minimum, 3; quorum, 3. *Qualification*, 25 shares.

DIRECTORS:

Chairman—Sir HENRY GEORGE PASTON BEDINGFELD, Bart., Oxboro' Hall, Norfolk.

Deputy-Chairman—Lord CLAUDE JOHN HAMILTON, M.P., 23, Lowndes Square, S.W.

Charles Henry Parkes, Esq., Netherfield, Weybridge.
Major Michael Stocks, Woodhall, Norfolk.
Hugh Aylmer, Esq., West Dereham Abbey, Norfolk.

Secretary, Edward Stephens Copeman, Downham Market, Norfolk.

77.—DRAPERSTOWN.

Incorporated by act of 22nd July, 1878, 41 and 42 Vic., cap. 178, for making railways between Magherafelt and Draperstown, both in the county of Londonderry. Length, about 8 miles. Period for completion, five years. Working arrangements, &c., with the Belfast and Northern Counties, who may raise new capital, subscribe 8,000*l*. (in "B" shares) towards the cost of the undertaking, and appoint a director. Capital, 10,000*l*. in "A" or preference 10*l*. shares, and 30,000*l*. in "B" or ordinary 10*l*. shares; total, 40,000*l*.; borrowing powers, 20,000*l*.

The above-named act gives power to the company to accept from the Worshipful Company of Drapers, the Worshipful Company of Skinners, and the Worshipful Company of Salters, or other landowners, by way of charge on lands or otherwise, and in such form as may be agreed upon, a guaranteed dividend of 5 per cent. per annum upon any of the "B" shares, defining such shares by their numbers, such guarantee to be for 23 years, since extended to 30 years, after the issue of such shares, or from the date of such agreement. All shares issued under a guarantee as aforesaid to be endorsed with the terms and conditions thereof, and the dates when such guarantee will expire.

The net receipts of the undertaking, after payment of expenses of management and working, and satisfying the interest on all debenture stock, mortgages, rent-charges, &c. (if any), are to be applied to the payment of dividends not exceeding 5 per cent. on the "A" and "B" shares, and then in repayment to the guarantors above referred to, *pro rata*, any amount previously paid by them to make up the 5 per cent. dividend on the "B" shares, any surplus then remaining to be divided amongst the "B" or ordinary shareholders.

A new agreement has been entered into under which the Northern Counties are to work the line from the opening at 30 per cent., after working expenses, the owning company to have running powers over 1 mile of the working company's line, and the use of their station at Magherafelt. The line to be constructed is 7 miles; the 1 mile for running over makes 8 miles.

CAPITAL.—30th June, 1884—*Receipts:*—
"A," or preferred capital (10,000*l.*) £380
"B," or ordinary capital (30,000) ....28,918=£29,298
Loan from Board of Works .... 8,000=£37,298
Calls in arrear, 1,222*l.*

Line opened for traffic 20th July, 1883.

No. of Directors.—Not less than 4 or more than 5; quorum, 2 and 3 respectively. *Qualification*, 20 shares (except the director appointed by the Belfast and Northern Counties). Quorum of general meetings, 7 proprietors holding at least 1-20th of the nominal capital.

DIRECTORS:

Chairman—The Hon. ROBERT TORRENS O'NEILL, Shane's Castle, Antrim.

James Henry, Esq., Draperstown.
Col. Sir W. Lennox Conyngham, Moneymore.
*Henry Edmund Cartwright, Esq., J.P., Manor House, Magherafelt.
George L. Young, Esq., Dungiven.

* Representative of the Belfast and Northern Counties.

OFFICERS.—Sec., Charles Stewart; Eng., John Lanyon, C.E.; Auditors, Francis J. Hopkirk and Thomas S. Taylor.

78.—DUBLIN AND KINGSTOWN.

Incorporated by 1 and 2 William IV., cap. 69, for a line from Dublin to Kingstown, open since 17th December, 1834 (6 miles); subsequently an extension of 1¾ mile was made, on the atmospheric system, to Dalkey; altered in 1856 to a locomotive branch, in connection with the Dublin and Wicklow.

In 1846 an act was obtained for an extension to Bray (7½ miles), which, under the act incorporating the Dublin and Wicklow, has been transferred to that company, including the Dalkey Branch.

The line is now leased to the Dublin, Wicklow, and Wexford for 35 years, from 1st July, 1856, with a clause of renewal for a further term of 35 years, at an annual rental of 36,000*l.*, which sum, according to past accounts, is sufficient for the payment of dividends on the ordinary stock at the rate of about 9½ per cent. per annum, that rate of dividend having been declared in the past and for the half-year ended 31st August, 1882. This lease was made perpetual by the Dublin, Wicklow, and Wexford Act of 1865.

The dividends for 1883–84 were made payable on the 1st April and 1st October in the latter year respectively.

CAPITAL—31st August, 1884.—*Receipts:* General capital stock, 350,000*l.*; debentures, at 4 per cent., 70,000*l.* *Expenditure:* 418,553*l.*; balance (credit), 1,447*l.*

Certificates are required to accompany transfer deed. Registration fee, 1*s.* per 100*l.* stock, but not exceeding 5*s.* on any one deed.

No. of Directors—9. *Qualification*, 1,000*l.*

DIRECTORS:

Chairman—WILLIAM JAMES PERRY, Esq., Ardlui, Blackrock.

Deputy-Chairman—WILLIAM HONE, Jun., Esq., Monkstown.

William James Perry, Esq., Blackrock, Dublin.
*William Jameson, Esq., Montrose, Donnybrook.
Robert Culley, Esq., Monkstown.
*Graves S. Warren, Esq., Belfort, Blackrock.
*John Jameson, Esq., Bow Street, Dublin.
Robert Samuel Palmer, Esq., Merrion Square, Dublin.
George Pim, Esq., Brennanstown, Cabinteely.
Richard Pim, Esq., Stradbrook Hall, Blackrock.

* Retire in March next, but re-eligible.

OFFICERS.—Sec., Joseph B. Pim; Solicitor, Frederic R. Pim, LL.D.

Offices—35, Westland Row, Dublin.

79.—DUBLIN AND MEATH.

Incorporated by act of 23rd July, 1858, to construct a line from a junction with the Midland Great Western, at Clonsilla, to a junction at Navan, with the Navan and Kells Branch of the Dublin and Drogheda (over which branch running powers are secured), with a branch from Kilmessan to Trim and Athboy. Length, 23 miles; branch, 12 miles.

By act of 3rd June, 1862, the company was authorised to raise additional capital to the extent of 45,000*l.*, preference interest not to exceed 6 per cent., and 15,000*l.* on loan. Also to cancel and re-issue forfeited shares at like preference.

By act of 23rd May, 1864, the company was authorised to raise new capital to the extent of 75,000*l.* in shares, and not exceeding 6 per cent. preference, and 25,000*l.* on loan.

By act of 13th May, 1869, a working agreement with the Midland Great Western of Ireland (for which see *Appendix* to the MANUAL for 1871) was sanctioned and confirmed. This line has been worked by the Midland Great Western at 52 per cent.

The Dublin and Meath has power to subscribe 40,000*l.* to the Navan and Kingscourt, which see.

MIDLAND GREAT WESTERN.—By act of 19th July, 1875, the company was authorised to lease their undertaking to the Midland Great Western for 99 years, on the following terms:—The Midland Great Western to pay the Dublin and Meath 48 per cent. of the traffic receipts, provided that when the gross receipts in any two consecutive half-years shall exceed the sum of 20,000*l.*, then the Midland shall, so long as the gross receipts shall exceed the sum of 20,000*l.* per annum, pay over to the Meath, as their proportion of and in such gross receipts, 48 per cent. up to 18,000*l.* per annum, and 60 per cent. in respect of all gross receipts exceeding 18,000*l.* per annum.

REVENUE.—For the half-years ended 31st December, 1883, and 30th June, 1884, the earnings sufficed for the payment of dividends at 2 per cent. per annum on the first preference capital, payable 10th April and 10th October, 1884, respectively.

CAPITAL.—*Authorised:* Stocks and shares, 341,000*l.*; loans, 150,000*l.*; total, 491,000*l.* All created. The expenditure on capital account to 30th June, 1884, amounted to 487,435*l.*, whilst the receipts had been as under:—

Ordinary shares (136,600*l.* created)	£133,155	
5 per cent. preference stock (129,400*l.* created)	129,159	
6 per cent. preference stock (75,000*l.* created)	72,710	
Debenture stock at 4 per cent.	35,000	
Debenture stock at 4½ per cent.	114,994	=£485,018
Balance		2,417
		£487,435

Meetings held in February and August.

DIRECTORS:

Chairman—THOMAS R. TIGHE CHAPMAN, Esq., J.P., Southhill, Delvin, Co. Westmeath.

Deputy-Chairman—WILLIAM ACTON, Esq., J.P., Brookville, Raheny.

Edmond Bayley, Esq., D.L., J.P., Rookwood, Athleague, Roscommon.
Frederick B. Falkiner, Esq., Streamville, Ballybrack (Managing Director).
William Findlater, Esq., M.P., 22, Fitzwilliam Square South.
John B. Lane, Esq., J.P., Kilbogget House, Cabinteely.
Henry Guinness, Esq., J.P., Burton Hall, Stillorgan.

OFFICERS.—Sec., Joseph James; Auditors, O. H. Braddell and Brindley Hone.

Offices—10, Hume Street, Stephen's Green, Dublin.

80.—DUBLIN, WICKLOW, AND WEXFORD.

Originally incorporated as the WATERFORD, WEXFORD, WICKLOW, AND DUBLIN, by act of 16th July, 1846, for the construction of a line from Dundrum, near Dublin, to Waterford, and a branch from Kingstown (where it joins the Dublin and Kingstown) to Bray, forming a junction near Bray with the former or main line. Powers also over a line from Dundrum to Dublin, which was afterwards purchased up from the Dublin, Dundrum, and Rathfarnham; the latter company has since been formally dissolved, by act of 3rd July, 1857, and merged with the Dublin and Wicklow. Several acts had been obtained between 1846 and 1857; and by act of 24th July, 1851, the undertaking was re-constructed, the original capital reduced to 500,000*l*., with borrowing powers for 166,666*l*., the portions of the original line beyond Wicklow to Wexford and Waterford abandoned, and the name of the company changed to the Dublin and Wicklow. Additional capital authorised by the above act of 1857, 200,000*l*., which has been raised in 10*l*. shares (since converted into stock) at 6 per cent. perpetual preference, with borrowing powers for 66,666*l*.

FURTHER PARLIAMENTARY POWERS.—A list of acts obtained by this company from 1859 to 1878, with short heads of the objects for which the various powers were sought, will be found on reference to the MANUAL for 1881, page 78.

By act of 19th June, 1882, powers were obtained for certain diversions in the townlands of Shauganagh, Rathdown, Ballynerrin, and Ballygannon. Sundry extension of time for completion of works authorised by acts of 1877 and 1878; and authority to reduce the share capital and increase the borrowing powers of the company.

By act of 28th, July, 1884, powers were obtained for construction of a railway connecting Westland Row Terminus with the railways of the Great Northern of Ireland and the Midland Great Western, on the north side of River Liffey, to be called "The City of Dublin Junction Railways." New capital, 300,000*l*.; loans, 100,000*l*., to be a separate capital called "City of Dublin Junction Railways Capital."

DUBLIN AND KINGSTOWN.—This company is also in the hands of the Dublin and Wicklow under a lease in perpetuity, commencing 1st July, 1856, at a rental of 36,000*l*. a year.—See Dublin and Kingstown.

The London and North Western gives through booking facilities over the whole of the Wicklow system, including portion of Waterford, New Ross, and Wexford Junction Line, purchased under act of 1876.

WATERFORD, NEW ROSS, AND WEXFORD JUNCTION.—For particulars of the incorporation, &c., of this company, see "Great Southern and Western." By act of 13th July, 1876, the Public Works Loan Commissioners were authorised to sell the line (36 miles in length) to the Dublin, Wicklow, and Wexford and Great Southern and Western for 40,000*l*. The portion lying between Ballywilliam and Macmine was taken by the Dublin and Wicklow for 16,000*l*., and the remainder by the Southern and Western for 24,000*l*. Under the sale act the Dublin and Wicklow was authorised to raise 20,000*l*. additional share capital, and to borrow on mortgage 6,800*l*.

In operation—Lines owned. 129½ miles; lines leased, 6 miles; total worked 135½ miles. Foreign lines worked over, 21 miles; total, 156½ miles.

REVENUE.—The gross receipts for the half-year ended 31st December, 1883, amounted to 121,938*l*., and the expenditure to 53,038*l*., giving, with the balance brought forward, a total net revenue of 68,900*l*., which sufficed for the half-years' interest, rents, and preference dividends, and a dividend on the ordinary stock at the rate of 2 per cent. per annum, which absorbed 6,450*l*., and left 5,940*l*. to be carried forward. The gross receipts for the half-year ended 30th June, 1884, were 111,285*l*., and the expenditure 52,758*l*., giving, with the balance (5,940*l*.) from previous half-year, a total net revenue of 64,417*l*., which sufficed for the half-year's interest, rents, and preference dividends, and a dividend on the ordinary stock at the rate of 2 per cent. per annum, and left a balance of 379*l*. to next half-year.

CAPITAL.—30th June, 1884.—*Authorised:* Stocks, 1,835,000*l*.; loans, 677,232*l*.; total, 2,512,232*l*. Stocks—amount created, 1,835,000*l*.; ditto amount received, 1,748,710*l*. Loans—amount received, 556,855*l*.

In April, 1884, 55,150*l*. of new ordinary stock was issued at 40 per cent. discount, participation for dividend as follows:—On 20 per cent. paid on allotment dividend payable on 60 per cent. from 1st January, 1884; on 20 per cent. payable in May, 1885, dividend on 80 per cent. from date of payment; on 20 per cent. payable May, 1886, dividend on par from date of payment.

PRIORITIES, DESCRIPTIONS, DIVIDENDS, &c., OF STOCKS AND SHARES.—The following is a list of this company's Stocks, numbered in order of

priority, with conditions of issue *in brief*, the descriptions to be strictly observed in transfer forms and all other legal documents relating thereto, viz.:—

No. in order of priority.	Year of Act Authorising Creation and Issue.	FULL DESCRIPTION (To be observed in Transfers).		INTEREST AND DIVIDEND.		
				Rate per cent. per annum.	Whether non-contingent (or accumulative) or contingent on profits.	If contingent. Whether on profits of year or half-year.
1	1863 & various others.	Debenture stock............(£94,430)	£556,855)	4½	accumulative	..
2		Do. ....(£257,984)		4½	do.	..
3		Do. ....(£204,441)		4	do.	..
4	1857	6 per cent. preference stock............	(£200,000)	6	accumulative	..
5	1859-60	5 per cent. preference stock............	(£300,000)	5	contingent	Whole year
6	1864	Do. do.	(£150,000)	5	do.	do.
7	1865	Do. do.	(£150,000)	5	do.	do.
8	1875	Do. do.	(£150,000)	4½	do.	do.
9	1877	Do. do.	(£120,000)	4	do.	do.
10	1851 & 1863	Ordinary stock	(£678,710)	2	do.	do.

NOTES.—The Government loan had priority over all; it has since been paid off. Debenture stocks have equal priority over the other stocks. The company is also liable for the Dublin and Kingstown rent-charge or lien, amounting to 36,000*l.* a year, should that company fail in its payment.

TRANSFER DEPARTMENT QUERIES AND REPLIES.

QUERIES.	REPLIES.
Transfer form—ordinary or special?......	Ordinary.
Fee per deed?	2*s.* 6*d.*
Ditto If more sellers than one?...	Not allowed on one deed.
May several classes of stock be transferred on one deed?	The several classes of stock may be included in one deed, but if debenture stocks be included there must be a special stamp for that stock.
Are certificates required to accompany transfers?	Yes.
What amounts of stock are transferable; and are parts of 1*l.* sterling allowed to be transferred?	No part of 1*l.*, but any other amount allowed.
To what officer should transfer communications be sent?	Secretary.
In acceptances, renunciations, &c., or allotments of new stock, proxies, or other forms sent to trustees, what signatures are required?	Each registered proprietor in the account—except proxies, for which first name only has power to vote.

The expenditure on this account to 30th June, 1884, was 2,331,147*l.*, the receipts having been as under:—

Stocks..	£1,748,710	
Debenture stock	556,855	
Balance..	25,582	= £2,331,147

The estimate of further expenditure is set down at 198,790*l.*, the amount of the capital powers and other available assets being 181,685*l.*

Meetings half-yearly, in February and August, in Dublin. Accounts made up to 31st December and 30th June. Transfer books close 14 days before meetings. Proxies, 48 hours at least.

DIRECTORS:

Chairman—RICHARD MARTIN, Esq., D.L., J.P., 81, Merrion Square, Dublin.

William Foot, Esq., J.P., 10, Raglan Road, Dublin.

Lieut-Colonel James Stuart Tighe, D.L., Rossanagh, Ashford, Co. Wicklow.

Michael Murphy, Esq., J.P., 17, Eden Quay, Dublin.

Major Percy Raymond Grace, J.P., D.L., Boley, Monkstown, Co. Dublin

William Watson, Esq., 15, Eden Quay Dublin.

Richard Owen Armstrong, Esq., J.P., Clifton Terrace, Monkstown, Co. Dublin.

Brindley Hone, Esq., Vevay, Ballybrack.

OFFICERS.—Sec., E. William Maunsell, 7, Prince Edward Terrace, Blackrock, County Dublin; Traffic Man., W. L. Payne, Harcourt Street Terminus, Dublin; Eng., John Chaloner Smith, M.Inst.C.E., Bray; Loco. Supt., William Wakefield, Grand Canal Street, Dublin; Auditors, Thomas Graydon, Toomon, Delgany, and Thomas P. Cairnes, J.P., Drogheda; Solicitor, George Keogh, 50, Westland Row, Dublin.

Offices—Westland Row Terminus, Dublin.

81.—DUNDALK, NEWRY, AND GREENORE.

Incorporated by act of 28th July, 1863, as Dundalk and Greenore, to construct a line from the Irish North Western, at Dundalk, to Greenore. Length, 13¾ miles. Capital, 110,000*l.* in shares and 36,600*l.* on loan.

By act of 12th August, 1867, the company obtained an extension of time till 12th August, 1870, for completion of the works, and also to construct an extension to Dundalk, as well as to complete the joint works authorised by the Newry and Greenore Act, 1863. Length, ¾ of a mile. New capital, 50,000*l.* in shares and 16,600*l.* on loan. Also to issue debenture stock at 5 per cent. Arrangements with Irish North Western and London and North Western (which latter subscribes 130,000*l.*), and facilities to Ulster (now Great Northern) and Midland Great Western.

By act of 26th July, 1869, an extension of time for the completion of works was obtained till July, 1871.

By act of 21st July, 1873, the name of company was changed to Dundalk, Newry, and Greenore, and it received powers to make a line 12 miles in length, commencing by a junction with the Albert Basin Extension of Newry and Armagh, in Newry, to a junction with the line near Greenore Point. New capital, 240,000*l.* in shares and 80,000*l.* on loan. Power was given to the London and North Western to subscribe.

By the London and North Western (New Lines) Act, 1876, the company was authorised to raise new capital to the extent of 51,000*l.* in shares and 16,800*l.* on loan.

REVENUE.—In past years the results of the working have shown balances to the debit of net revenue account. The line is worked under arrangements with the London and North Western and Irish North Western (now Great Northern of Ireland). In operation, 26¼ miles.

CAPITAL.—The whole of the share capital of 451,000*l.* has been created in shares of 25*l.* each; debenture stock at 4 per cent., 133,200*l.* The amount received to 30th June, 1884, was 486,700*l.*; the calls in arrear amounted to 900*l.*; and there remained unissued and uncalled 96,600*l.* The receipts and expenditure on capital account to 30th June, 1884, had been as under:—

Received.		*Expended.*	
Ordinary 25*l.* shares	£353,500	Lines open for traffic	£452,931
L. and N. W. 4 per cent. debenture stock	133,200	Working stock	33,830
Balance	61		
	£486,761		£486,761

No. of Directors—10; quorum, 3. *Qualification*, 500*l.*

DIRECTORS:

Chairman—RICHARD MOON, Esq., Copsewood Grange, Coventry.

John Pares Bickersteth, Esq., Grove Mill House, Watford, Herts.

William Cawkwell, Esq., Fernacre, Maresfield Gardens, South Hampstead, N.W.

Alfred Fletcher, Esq., Allerton, Woolton, Liverpool.

A. H. H. Hibbert, Esq., Munden, Watford, Herts.

The Rt. Hon. the Earl of Kilmorey, Gordon House, Isleworth.

Hon. W. Lowther, M.P., Lowther Lodge, Kensington Gore, W.

J. W. Murland, Esq., 25, Fitzwilliam Square, Dublin.

The Rt. Hon. D. R. Plunket, M.P., 37, Merrion Square, Dublin, and 12, Mandeville Place, W.

OFFICERS.—Sec., Stephen Reay, Euston Station, N.W.; Eng., F. Stevenson, M.Inst.C.E., Euston Station, N.W.; Auditors, E. Waterhouse, 44, Gresham Street, E.C., and Robert Benson, 4, Bishopsgate Street Within, E.C.; Solicitors, C. H. Mason, Euston Station, N.W., and R. A. Macrory, Ulster Chambers, Belfast.

82.—DUNDEE SUBURBAN.

Incorporated by act of 28th July, 1884, for making two short lines from Dundee to Liff and Benvie. Total length, about 4½ miles. Period for completion, 5 years. Traffic arrangements with Caledonian and North British. Capital. 250,000*l*. in 10*l*. shares, with power to divide into "preferred and deferred" half-shares; loans, 83,300*l*.

No. of Directors.—Maximum, 5; minimum, 3; quorum, 3. *Qualification*, 40 shares.

FIRST DIRECTORS:

Frank Stewart Sandeman, Esq.
Joseph Grimond, Esq.
James Thomas Harris, Esq.
Charles Stuart Blair, Esq.
Peter Cooper, Esq.

83.—EAST CORNWALL MINERAL.

Originally incorporated by act of 1869 as the CALLINGTON AND CALSTOCK, to construct a line between these places, in the county of Cornwall. Length, 7 miles. Capital, 60,000*l*. in 10*l*. shares and 20,000*l*. on loan.

By act of 25th May, 1871, the company was authorised to divert a junction of the line extending to nearly 2 miles. Preference not exceeding 6 per cent. to be attached to a portion of unissued shares not exceeding 30,000*l*.

The line, about 6¾ miles in length, was opened for traffic on 7th May, 1872.

By act of 15th August, 1876, the company was authorised to extend their line to the South Devon at Tavistock, and to the Morwellham Quay on the River Tamar; and to make certain alterations in the levels and alter the gauge (to 4ft. 8½in.) of their existing railway. Length of new lines, 8¾ miles. The Extension Railway to form a separate undertaking of the company, with a capital (to be called extension capital) of 200,000*l*., and borrowing powers 66,660*l*. Powers to company and London and South Western to enter into working and traffic agreements.

By act of 3rd July, 1879, powers were obtained for the abandonment of the Extension Railway authorised by the act of 1876 mentioned above.

REVENUE—30th June, 1884.—The directors in their report to this date state that the powers conferred by the Devon and Cornwall Central Railway Act, 1882, have become vested in the Plymouth, Devonport, and South Western Junction, and by agreement with this latter company, the following clauses have been inserted in their bill which has passed its third reading in both Houses:—"Within one year after the opening of through communication by the company between Lidford and Devonport, the company shall complete the purchase from the East Cornwall Mineral of their railway, and shall enter into possession of that railway under the provisions of the Devon and Cornwall Central Railway Act, 1882 (as made obligatory by this act upon the company), and if the purchase money shall not then be paid, the company shall pay interest from the date of taking possession or expiry of the said year, whichever shall first happen, on the amount of the said purchase money to the East Cornwall Mineral at the rate of 5 per cent. per annum until payment of such purchase money. And such interest shall be paid by the company (or any other company working the railway of the company, or any part of the same) out of and as a first charge upon the receipts of the company next after the working expenses. The railway of the East Cornwall Mineral shall be duly conveyed to the company, who shall not call upon the East Cornwall Mineral to show any other title to the lands than deeds purporting to be conveyances of the same, and it shall not be competent for the company to investigate or enquire into the title of the respective vendors to the East Cornwall Mineral. The traffic of the line continues satisfactory. The net results have, however, been, so far as the last year is concerned, largely diminished by the legal expenses consequent upon the application to Parliament in connection with the above arrangement."

CAPITAL.—The receipts to 30th June, 1884, consisted of 30,000*l*. in original shares of 10*l*. each, 30,000*l*. in 6 per cent. preference shares of 10*l*. each, and 15,000*l*. on loan, the other 5,000*l*. to make up the loan capital of 20,000*l*. not being issued on account of a land rent-charge of 250*l*. per annum, equal to 5,000*l*. There is also a Lloyd's bond of 21,320*l*. 12*s*. 8*d*. The expenditure was detailed as follows:—

Parliamentary and preliminary, &c.	£9,139
Land, works, &c.	65,202
Salaries	950
Working stock	21,364
	£96,655

The accounts are made up to 31st December and 30th June, and the meetings are held in February and August in each year.

DIRECTORS:

Chairman—JAMES ATKINSON LONGRIDGE, Esq., 15, Great George Street, Westminster, S.W.

Walter J. Cutbill, Esq., 37, Old Jewry, E.C.

Arthur S. Hughes, Esq., 37, Old Jewry, E.C.

Geo. A. Barkley, Esq., 16, Albert Mansions, Victoria Street, S.W.

Walmsley Stanley, Esq., 15, Great George Street, Westminster, S.W.

OFFICERS.—Sec., David Amey, 4, Old Jewry, E.C.; Man., W. Sowden; Auditors, Howard H. Ashworth and F. Wontner, 3, Copthall Buildings, E.C.

Secretary's Office—4, Old Jewry, E.C. Manager's Office—Calstock.

84.—EAST GLOUCESTERSHIRE.

Incorporated by act of 29th July, 1864, to construct lines from Cheltenham to Witney, and to Faringdon. Length, 50 miles; mixed or narrow gauge. Capital, 600,000*l.* in 10*l.* shares and 200,000*l.* on loan. Arrangements with Midland and Great Western, the former company afterwards entering into an arrangement to work the East Gloucestershire, upon terms that would secure payment of 5 per cent. upon 300,000*l.* of "A" or "preferred" stock, and 200,000*l.* of debentures, and the application of the additional earnings (after the payment of the working expenses) to the payment of dividend on the "deferred" capital. The Great Western disputed the right of the Midland to enter into an agreement for that purpose, and the question was accordingly referred to the arbitration of Captain Galton, who decided that the Midland might work the local line with Cheltenham (3 miles), but that it ought not to work the main line (47 miles in length). Subsequently an agreement was entered into with the Great Western, particulars of which will be found further on.

By act of 18th July, 1866, certain deviations were allowed to be completed within three years.

By act of 15th July, 1867, the company obtained till 1st October, 1871, wherein to complete its works, and was also authorised to enter into arrangements with the Great Western.

By act of 13th May, 1872, the capital of the undertaking was reduced to 225,000*l.* in shares and to 75,000*l.* on loan, to be applied solely to such portion of the railway as lies between Witney and Fairford. Arrangements with Witney Railway for joint use of line and stations.

By the Great Western Act of 22nd July, 1878, agreements were authorised relative to the payment of interest on this company's debenture debt, and the exercise by the Great Western of this company's borrowing powers.

Agreement with Great Western.—The Great Western have entered into a working agreement for 20 years, from the 12th November, 1871, with this company, to work the line at 50 per cent. of the gross receipts, the working company guaranteeing that the East Gloucestershire Company's share of such receipts shall equal 5*l.* per mile per week; this mileage receipt is not being realised, and the Great Western have had to make up the deficiency; such deficiency is, however, repayable to the Great Western out of future excess beyond 5*l.* per mile per week in any half-year of the earnings apportioned to the East Gloucestershire. It is stated that the Great Western guarantee the interest on the company's 4½ per cent. first mortgage bonds (75,000*l.*) These bonds have been issued for 5, 7, and 12 years, in multiples of 100*l.*, assignable only by transfer in the company's books.

Agreement with Banbury and Cheltenham.—By an agreement with the Banbury and Cheltenham Direct, the latter pays an annual rent-charge of 4 per cent. per annum on the amount awarded for the East Gloucestershire Company's land and works at Andoversford, viz., 11,855*l.*, which rent-charge accrues from the 22nd February, 1878.

Revenue.—The accounts for the half-year ended 30th June, 1884, showed the company's proportion of traffic receipts to have been 1,647*l.*, which, with 173*l.* received from the Great Western under the above agreement, made a total of 1,820*l.* After payment of general expenses and the half-year's interest on mortgages, a balance of 3,920*l.* in favour of net revenue account was carried forward. In operation, 14 miles.

CAPITAL.—The receipts and expenditure on this account to 30th June, 1884, were as under:—

Received.		*Expended.*	
Stock and shares	£206,500	General expenditure	£88,635
Loans at 4½ per cent. (see agreement with Gt. Western, page 81)	71,400	Purchase of land at Cheltenham	10,638
		Purchase of land and works at Andoversford	31,181
Balance	2,510	Purchase of land and works between Witney and Fairford	149,956
	£280,410		£280,410

Meetings in February or March and August or September.

No. of Directors—5; minimum, 4; quorum, 3. *Qualification*, 2,000*l*.

DIRECTORS:

Chairman—The Right Hon. Sir MICHAEL E. HICKS-BEACH, Bart., M.P., Williamstrip Park, Fairford, Gloucestershire.

J. R. Raymond-Barker, Esq., Fairford Park, Fairford, Gloucestershire.

Hon. and Rev. G. G. C. Talbot, Withington, Cheltenham.

H. C. Barkley, Esq., Northleach.

T. Sebastian Bazley, Esq., Hatherop Castle, Fairford, Gloucestershire.

Hon. R. Henley Shaw Eden, Minety House, Malmesbury.

OFFICERS.—Sec., George Broom, 11, Abchurch Lane, E.C.; Engs., Charles Liddell and E. Richards, 24, Abingdon Street, Westminster, S.W.; Auditors, R. B. Hays, 11, Abchurch Lane, E.C., and Chas. T. Hawkins, Broad Street, Oxford; Solicitor, J. Jordan, 3, Westminster Chambers, S.W., and Sewell and Newmarch, Cirencester, Gloucestershire.

Offices—11, Abchurch Lane, E.C.

85.—EAST LONDON.

Incorporated by act of 26th May, 1865, to connect by means of the Thames Tunnel the railways on the north and south of the Thames. Length, 8 miles. Capital, 1,400,000*l*. in shares and 466,600*l*. on mortgage.

The line was opened from New Cross to Wapping on the 6th December, 1869, and from Wapping to the junction with the Great Eastern on the 11th April, 1876. In operation, 5½ miles.

This line commences by junctions with the Brighton, South London, South Eastern, and North Kent railways, near New Cross, accommodating in its course the Surrey and Commercial Docks, the London Docks, and the East of London, and terminates in the city at a great terminal station in Liverpool Street. The line passes through and accommodates the districts of New Cross, Deptford, Rotherhithe, Wapping, St. George's-in-the-East, Limehouse, Stepney, Whitechapel, Bethnal Green, Bishopsgate, and Shoreditch.

A list of Acts, from 1866 to 1879, with short heads showing the objects for which the various powers were obtained, will be found on reference to the MANUAL for 1881, page 83.

FURTHER PARLIAMENTARY POWERS.—1881—8TH JULY.—Provisions for payment of the debts of the company by the issue of debenture stock at 3½ per cent., guaranteed under certain conditions by the Brighton and South Eastern.

1882—10TH AUGUST.—New line at St. Mary Whitechapel, in connection with the Metropolitan and District (City Lines and Extensions); abandonment of Bethnal Green Junction; lease to the London, Brighton, and South Coast, and other companies (see below); new capital, 125,000*l*., in shares or stock, or debenture stock.

1884—14TH JULY.—Working and rental of Whitechapel Junction undertaking. Cancellation of agreement with Metropolitan dated 19th July, 1883, &c.

AGREEMENT.—The agreement with the Brighton, dated 17th November, 1869, is for a term of 21 years, from 1st January, 1870, that company having the option to continue the working from five years to five years thereafter, for so long as they may choose, on giving to this company six months' prior written notice. The line is to be worked at 53 per cent. of the gross receipts until 1st January, 1875, and thereafter at the same rate, or at such a reduction every fifth year as may be settled by arbitration or otherwise, on the principle that the Brighton shall work at a per centage which shall not exceed the actual cost of working at a fair estimate. The South Eastern and London, Chatham, and Dover may, on six months' notice, participate in the agreement, but so as not to interfere with the control by the Brighton.

The six months' notice under this agreement was given by the South Eastern on the 30th June, 1879, and on the 1st April, 1880, the South Eastern commenced running over the East London system.

The directors being dissatisfied generally with the arrangements made by the Brighton for the working and development of the traffic over the railway, and failing to obtain any relief, appealed to the Railway Commissioners for a settlement of the various important matters in difference. Judgment was delivered in favour of this company on the 16th August, 1876.

Proceedings in Chancery.—In November, 1878, the three classes of debenture holders applied to the Vice-Chancellor for the appointment of a receiver of the company, the interest in arrear due to them having amounted to 158,211*l.* The Vice-Chancellor granted the application, and appointed Sir Edward Watkin receiver, but at the same time ordered that the receiver should pay out of the earnings of the company all expenses necessary for the working and maintenance of their railway.

Lease of the Undertaking.—Under the act of 10th August, 1882, the line is to be leased in perpetuity to the Brighton, South Eastern, District, Metropolitan, and Chatham companies, at a minimum of 30,000*l.* per annum. For the heads of agreement under this proposed lease, see *Appendix* to the Manual for 1882. By section 38 of the act, this lease takes effect from the completion of the Whitechapel Extension, and its connection with the Metropolitan and District railways.

Whitechapel Extension.—In the report for the half-year ended 30th June, 1884, it is stated that this extension was opened on the 3rd March, 1884, and that it had since been worked by the South Eastern on behalf of this company.

Revenue.—The gross receipts for the half-year ended 30th June, 1884, amounted to 26,580*l.* Balance brought forward, 23,609*l.*; total, 50,189*l.* The total expenditure including 12,736*l.* paid to the Brighton Company for working, amounted to 23,434*l* leaving a profit of 26,755*l.* to be carried forward to next half-year.

Six months' interest was paid by the receiver in December, 1879, to the holders of the first-charge debenture stocks and bonds of the company other than the 6 per cent. debenture stock, 1874 (see below), and a further sum, equal to 4 per cent., *pro rata* to the three classes of debenture stocks—6, 5½, and 5 per cent.—was paid on August 10th, 1883, to stockholders registered on the 5th July.

Capital.—The subjoined statement of stock and share capital created shows the proportion received to 30th June, 1884:—

Description.	Created.	Received.
70,000 shares of 20*l.* each, created 1865, since consolidated into stock	£1,400,000	£1,400,000
5 per cent. first preference stock, sanctioned 1872, issued at a discount of 27*l.* 10*s.* per cent.	400,000	400,000
5 per cent preference stock, 1877 (issued at 24*l.*) 2,000*l.* issued since at 34*l.* 15*s.*	900,000	240,405
Total	£2,700,000	£2,040,405

Mem.—A report on the various issues of this company's capital, giving the order of priority, terms of issue, and other details of interest, appeared with the company's report for the half-year ended 31st December, 1878, and a copy of it will be found inserted for future reference in the *Appendix* to the Manual for 1880.

Debenture Stock, 1874.—In July, 1880, the following notice was published, viz.—"Referring to the 400,000*l.* 6 per cent. debenture stock raised by this company under the powers of their act of 1874, complaints having been made of the difficulties attending dealings in the stock by reason of one portion of the issue having received 5¾ months' interest in excess of the other, I am instructed by my directors to acquaint you, for the information of the members of the stock exchange, that they have decided to allow any holder who may desire it to refund the excess interest so paid (equal net to 2*l.* 7*s.* 5*d.* on each 100*l.* stock), and have his stock registered as claiming arrears from the 1st July, 1876, in common with the greater portion of the issue."

The receipts and expenditure on this account to 30th June, 1884, were detailed as follow:—

Received.		*Expended.*	
Shares and stock	£2,040,405	Line in course of construction	£3,785,047
Debenture stock	1,657,570		
Sale of surplus property and premiums on debenture stock	84,898		
Balance	2,174		
	£3,785,047		£3,785,047

The estimate of further expenditure on capital account is 55,000*l*.

Capital powers and other assets available to meet further expenditure:—

Share and loan capital authorised or credited but not yet received............	£693,625
Balance of capital account	2,174
	£691,451

Exclusive of the value of surplus lands and property undisposed of.

Reorganisation of Capital.—A scheme has been proposed under which the 88,410*l*. 5 per cent. debenture stock, the 5,650*l*. 5½ per cent. debenture stock, and the 465,590*l*. 6 per cent. debenture, should be consolidated and converted into a proportionate amount of 4 per cent. debenture stock, to be called "First 4 per cent. debenture stock," with the same rights as the existing stocks from which they were converted. The consolidation and conversion were to take effect from the 30th June, 1885. It was also suggested that the 400,000*l*. 6 per cent. debenture stock of 1874 should be converted into a proportionate amount of 4 per cent. debenture stock, to be called "Second 4 per cent. debenture stock." The ordinary stock it was proposed should remain as at present.

Meetings held in January and July.

No. of Directors—12; quorum, 3. *Qualification*, 50 shares of 20*l*. each.

DIRECTORS:

Chairman—Sir EDWARD WILLIAM WATKIN, Bart., M.P., Charing Cross Hotel, Charing Cross, S.W., and Rose Hill, Northenden, Cheshire.

Deputy-Chairman—Lord ALFRED SPENCER CHURCHILL, 16, Rutland Gate, S.W.

The Right Hon. Lord Brabourne, 3, Queen Anne's Gate, S.W., and The Paddocks, Smeeth, near Ashford, Kent.

Andrew Cassels, Esq., 51, Cleveland Square, W.

James Whatman, Esq., Vinters, near Maidstone.

General J. S. Brownrigg, C.B., 28, Lowndes Street, S.W.

OFFICERS.—Sec., John Shaw; Con. Eng., F. Wilton; Auditor, Henry Dever, 4, Lothbury, E.C.; Surveyor and Valuer, E. N. Clifton; Solicitors, Wilson, Bristows, and Carpmael, 1, Copthall Buildings, E.C.; Bankers, The National Provincial Bank of England.

Offices—London Bridge Station, S.E.

86.—EASTERN AND MIDLANDS.

Incorporated by act of 18th August, 1882, and comprising the Lynn and Fakenham, the Yarmouth and North Norfolk (Light), and the Yarmouth Union undertakings, which were dissolved on and from the 31st December, 1882. By the same act the Midland and Eastern, and Peterborough, Wisbech, and Sutton lines were also incorporated with the above-named undertakings from the 1st July, 1883, the continuous lines between Lynn on the one hand, and Yarmouth and Norwich on the other, having been completed and opened up for traffic on the previous 5th April. Five miles of the Cromer Branch to Holt were opened on the 1st October last.

The agreements by which the Great Northern and Midland companies work the Midland and Eastern, and the Midland the Peterborough, Wisbech, and Sutton sections, remain undisturbed.

By act of 3rd July, 1884, the period limited by the Lynn and Fakenham Act, 1880, for completion of railways was extended to 12th August, 1886. New capital, 100,000*l*.; loans, 33,000*l*.

Length of Amalgamated Lines.—Peterborough, Wisbech, and Sutton section, 26¾ miles; Midland and Eastern section, 34¼ miles; Lynn, Norwich, and Yarmouth section, 125¼ miles; running powers at Lynn, 2½ miles; running powers at Yarmouth, 1¼ mile; total, 190 miles.

Capital.—*Authorised and Created.*

Lynn and Fakenham Act, 1876, ordinary stock	£150,000	
Lynn and Fakenham (Extensions) Act, 1880, ordinary stock	380,000	
*Lynn and Fakenham (Extensions) Act, 1880, 5 per cent. preference stock	100,000	
Lynn and Fakenham Act, 1881, 5 per cent. preference stock	198,000	
†Lynn and Fakenham Act, 1882, 5 per cent. preference stock	150,000	=£978,000
Yarmouth and North Norfolk (Light) Act, 1876, ordinary shares	98,000	
Yarmouth and North Norfolk (Light) Act, 1878, 5 per cent. preference shares	60,000	
‡Yarmouth Union Act, 1880, ordinary shares	20,000	= 178,000
Midland and Eastern and Norwich and Spalding (Amalgamation) Act, 1877, ordinary stock	156,000	
Midland and Eastern and Norwich and Spalding (Amalgamation) Act, 1877, 4 per cent. preference stock	227,000	= 383,000
Peterborough, Wisbech, and Sutton Acts, 5 per cent. "preferred" original shares	150,000	
Peterborough, Wisbech, and Sutton Acts, "deferred" original shares	135,000	= 285,000
Eastern and Midlands (Amalgamation) Act, 1882, 5 per cent. preference		160,000
		£1,984,000

Authorised but not Created.

Eastern and Midlands Act, 1883, ordinary or preference	12,000
	£1,996,000

Loans—*Authorised and Created.*

Lynn and Fakenham Act, 1876, 4½ per cent. debenture stock	£50,000	
Lynn and Fakenham (Extensions) Act, 1880, 4½ per cent. debenture stock	160,000	
Lynn and Fakenham Act, 1881, 4½ per cent. debenture stock	66,000	
Lynn and Fakenham Act, 1882, 4½ per cent. debenture stock	50,000	=£326,000
Yarmouth and North Norfolk (Light) Act, 1876, 5 per cent. rent-charge	7,088	
Yarmouth and North Norfolk (Light) Act, 1876, 4½ per cent. debenture stock	25,512	
Yarmouth and North Norfolk (Light) Act, 1878, 4½ per cent. debenture stock	20,000	
§Yarmouth Union Act, 1880, 5 per cent. debenture bonds	5,500	= 58,100
Midland and Eastern and Norwich and Spalding (Amalgamation) Act, 1877, 4½ per cent. debenture stock		127,000
Peterborough, Wisbech, and Sutton Acts, 4½ per cent. debenture stock		94,999
Eastern and Midlands (Amalgamation) Act, 1882, 5 per cent. rent-charge		2,040
Eastern and Midlands (Amalgamation) Act, 1882, 4½ per cent. debenture stock		50,960
		£659,099

Authorised but not Created.

Eastern and Midlands Act, 1883	4,000
Total	£663,099

For information relating to Peterbro', Wisbech, and Sutton, and Midland and Eastern, up to 31st December, 1882, see General Index.

LYNN, YARMOUTH, AND NORWICH SECTION.

Revenue.—The receipts from traffic of all kinds carried in the half-year ended 30th June, 1884, show an increase of 4,865*l*. over the corresponding period of 1883. The gross receipts amounted to 26,535*l*.

* 1,080*l*. converted into 5 per cent. preference stock, 1882 (amalgamation).
† 30,630*l*. converted into 5 per cent. preference stock, 1882 (amalgamation).
‡ Converted into 5 per cent. preference stock, 1882 (amalgamation).
§ Converted into 4½ per cent. debenture stock, 1882 (amalgamation).

WORKING EXPENSES.—The working expenses still absorb a large portion of the gross receipts, but the directors have reason to believe that material improvement may henceforth be looked for in this respect. With a view to increased efficiency in management and economy in working, they have recently carried out a reorganisation of the staff, which has so far worked well, and from which they anticipate satisfactory results in the future.

The merchandise traffic for the months of July, August, and September, shows an increase of upwards of 40 per cent. over that for the corresponding period of 1883, concurrently with a diminution in train mileage and working expenses.

MIDLAND AND EASTERN SECTION.

The fixed guaranteed rent to the 30th June last has been received from the working companies, and has been duly applied in payment of interest on the debenture stock, and of dividends on the 4 per cent. guaranteed stock of this section.

PETERBOROUGH SECTION.

The accounts received from the Midland (by which company this section is worked) show a gross receipt of 12,243*l.* for the six months, 50 per cent. of which has been paid to this company in accordance with the agreement, and has been applied to the payment of interest on the debenture stock and dividend on the 5 per cent. preferred shares.

NEW WORKS.—Since the last report the line to Holt has been opened for traffic, and additional goods accommodation provided at Norwich, North Walsham, Aylsham, and other stations.

TRANSFER DEPARTMENT.—Ordinary form; fee, 2*s.* 6*d.* per deed; if more sellers than one, 2*s.* 6*d.* Separate deed required for debenture stock. Certificates must accompany transfers. Fractions of 1*l.* not allowed to be transferred. In acceptances, renunciations, &c., of allotments of new stock, proxies, or other forms sent to trustees, the signature of all the trustees is required.

The extension from Lenwade to Norwich (City) was opened on 2nd December, 1882; from Melton Constable to North Walsham for through access to Yarmouth was opened on 5th April, 1883; from Melton Constable to Holt was opened on 1st October, 1884.

For particulars relating to the position of the amalgamated companies in the past, see information under the respective heads in the MANUAL for 1882, and previous editions.

Quorum of general meeting. C. C. C. Act, 1845, sec. 72.

No. of Directors—5; maximum, 6; quorum, 3 and 4. *Qualification*, 400*l.*

DIRECTORS:

Deputy-Chairman and Managing Director—ROBERT A. READ, Esq., 9, Victoria Chambers, Westminster, S.W.

Jocelyn T. F. Otway, Esq., 17, Charles Street, St. James's, S.W.

William Martin Wilkinson, Esq., 44, Lincoln's Inn Fields, W.C

Francis Wm. Slade, Esq., 120, Grosvenor Road, S.W.

OFFICERS.—Sec., E. B. Read, 9, Victoria Chambers, Westminster, S.W.; Traffic Man. and Accountant, Alfred Aslett, King's Lynn; Eng. and Loco. Supt., Wm. Marriott, Melton Constable; Outdoor Supt., G. R. Curson; Auditors, James Fraser and W. S Ogle; Solicitors, F. C. Mathews and Browne, 151, Cannon Street, E.C.; Bankers, The Imperial Bank Limited, Westminster, and London and Provincial Bank, King's Lynn.

Head Offices—King's Lynn.

87.—EAST AND WEST JUNCTION.

Incorporated by act of 23rd June, 1864, to construct a line from Towcester, on the Northampton and Banbury, to Old Stratford, on the Honeybourne Branch of the Great Western. Length, 33 miles. Capital, 300,000*l.* in 20*l.* shares and 100,000*l.* on loan.

FURTHER PARLIAMENTARY POWERS.—See the MANUAL for 1881, page 86.

The line was opened on 1st July, 1873, from Stratford-on-Avon to Blisworth, 33¼ miles, the section between Kineton and the Fenny Compton Station of the Great Western having been opened since June, 1871.

The extension from Stratford-upon-Avon to Broome, on the Midland, completed under the Evesham, Redditch and Stratford-upon-Avon Junction Act, 1873, has been recently opened for traffic, and an extension at the east end of the line, from

Towcester to Olney, on the Bedford and Northampton (Midland System), has been authorised by the "Easton Neston Mineral and Towcester, Roade, and Olney Junction Railway Act," which received the royal assent on the 15th August, 1879. The company who own this extension had their name changed to "The Stratford-upon-Avon, Towcester, and Midland Junction," in the Session of 1882 (when they also obtained an extension of their expiring powers); and in the session of 1883 they obtained further powers from Parliament under which the relaying of the East and West Junction, and its equipment for passenger service, has been proceeded with.

DIRECTORS:

Chairman—Major DICKSON, M.P., Glemham Hall, Wickham Market, Suffolk, and Carlton Club, Pall Mall, S.W.

M. Meredith Brown, Esq., 7, Tokenhouse Yard, E.C.
George Hall, Esq., 2, Church Villas, Merton Road, Wimbledon.
Thomas Hillas Crampton, Esq., Assoc.-Inst.C.E., 4, Victoria Street, Westminster, S.W.
Thomas J. Coombs, Esq., Palace Chambers, Bridge Street, Westminster, S.W.

The affairs of the company are under the supervision of the Court of Chancery. which has appointed the above-mentioned directors, one being a representative of creditors, managers of the undertaking.

OFFICERS.—Sec., Charles Banks; Traffic Man. and Eng., J. F. Burke, Stratford-on-Avon; Bankers, Smith, Payne, and Smiths, 1, Lombard Street, E.C., and The Old Bank, Stratford-upon-Avon; Solicitors, Merrick and Co., 8, Old Jewry, E.C.

Offices—Palace Chambers, Bridge Street, Westminster, S.W.

88.—EAST AND WEST YORKSHIRE UNION.

Incorporated by act of 2nd August, 1883, for making five railways, from East Ardsley, through Rothwell, Drax, and Wakefield, to Leeds. Total length, about 30 miles. Period for completion, 5 years. Traffic arrangements with Hull, Barnsley, and West Riding, &c., undertaking. Capital, 1,200,000*l.* in 10*l.* shares, with power to divide into "preferred" and "deferred" half-shares. Loan capital, 400,000*l.*

No. of Directors.—Maximum, 9; minimum, 5; quorum, 5 and 3. *Qualification*, 50 shares.

FIRST DIRECTORS:

Right Hon. Lord Beaumont, Carlton Towers, Selby.
Joseph Charlesworth, Esq.
Edward Bower, Esq.
Charles Ernest Charlesworth, Esq.
Samson Fox, Esq.
(4 others to be nominated.)

89.—EASTON AND CHURCH HOPE.

Incorporated 25th July, 1867, to construct a railway from Easton, in the Isle of Portland, to Church Hope Cove, with a pier in connection therewith. Length, 1¼ mile. Capital 30,000*l.* in 20*l.* shares and 10,000*l.* on loan, which may be converted into debenture stock. Either broad or narrow gauge.

By act of 14th August, 1884, branch railways in the parish of Portland were authorised. Length, about 3¼ miles. New capital, 50,000*l.*; loans, 16,600*l.*

CAPITAL.—The receipts on this account to 30th June, 1881, were 20,250*l.* The expenditure was:—Legal expenses, 3,433*l.*; engineering, 1,029*l.*; works, 9,631*l.*; purchase of land and compensation, 8,039*l.*; general charges, 741*l.*; total, 22,872*l.*; debit balance, 2,622*l.*

No. of Directors—5; minimum, 3; quorum, 3 and 2. *Qualification*, 200*l.* in shares.

OFFICERS.—Sec., Henry Green; Auditors, F. George Smith and W. L. Hunt.

Office—12, Tokenhouse Yard, E.C.

90.—EDINBURGH AND BATHGATE.

Incorporated by act of 3rd August, 1846, and amended by subsequent acts, for a line from the Edinburgh and Glasgow, near Ratho Station, to Bathgate. Capital, 250,000*l.* in shares and 83,000*l.* on loan. In operation, 10¼ miles. Leased to North British for 999 years at 12,500*l.* per annum, which yields a dividend of 5 per cent. per annum on the company's stock. It is provided that, in lieu of the rents formerly paid to the Bathgate, the North British shall, as from 31st January, 1869, and during the currency of the lease, pay the clear yearly rent of 12,500*l.*, and such rent shall have the same security, lien, and priority as was provided for in regard to the former rents. The mortgages granted by the Bathgate to the extent of 3,224*l.* are declared as between the two companies to be debts of the North British. The Bathgate to pay off the remainder, and the power of re-borrowing their mortgage debt, not exceeding 83,000*l.*, to be exclusively exercised by the North British.

The last two half-yearly dividends, at 5 per cent. per annum (as above), were made payable on the 6th February and 6th August last respectively.

CAPITAL.—This account to 31st July, 1884, showed that 250,000*l.* of stock had been issued, 2,622*l.* remaining in the hands of the company. No debentures have been issued.

The accounts are made up to the 31st January and 31st July, and the meetings held in Edinburgh in February and August.

DIRECTORS:

Chairman—3 FRANCIS BRODIE IMLACH, Esq., F.R.C.S.E., 48, Queen Street, Edinburgh.

2 James Taylor, Esq., Starley Hall, Burntisland.

1 Thomas Hill, Esq., Dean Park House, Edinburgh.

1, Retires in 1885; 2, in 1886; 3, in 1887; eligible for re-election.

OFFICERS.—Sec., Fred. W. Carter, C.A.; Auditors, F. Hayne Carter, C.A., and William Wood, C.A., Edinburgh; Solicitors, Waddell and McIntosh, W.S.

Offices—5, St. Andrew Square, Edinburgh.

91.—EDINBURGH SUBURBAN AND SOUTH SIDE JUNCTION.

Incorporated by act of 26th August, 1880, for the construction and maintenance of railways from St. Cuthbert's to Duddingston, by junctions with the North British. Length, about 9 miles. Period for completion of works, 5 years. The undertaking to be worked by the North British at 50 per cent. of the gross receipts, after deduction of cartage, &c. Capital, 225,000*l.* in 10*l.* shares, with power to divide into "preferred" and "deferred" half-shares. Borrowing powers, 75,000*l.* The report for the half-year ended 30th June, 1884, showed that 229,457*l.* had been received, and 242,151*l.* expended on this account to that date.

By act of 24th July, 1882, the company was authorised to abandon certain portions of their undertaking, and to construct four short lines at Liberton, in connection with the St. Leonards Branch.

This line was opened for traffic on the 1st December, 1884.

No. of Directors—3; quorum, 2. *Qualification*, 50 shares. Quorum of general meetings, 10 shareholders holding in the aggregate not less than 5,000*l.* in the capital of the company.

DIRECTORS:

Chairman—Sir JAMES FALSHAW, Bart., 14, Belgrave Crescent, Edinburgh.

John Weir, Esq. | Thomas Landale, Esq.

OFFICERS.—Sec., G. B. Wieland, 4, Prince's Street, Edinburgh; Engs., Trimble and Peddie; Auditors, Francis A. Bingloe and James J. Dobson.

92.—ELY AND NEWMARKET.

Incorporated 11th August, 1875, to construct a railway from Ely to Newmarket, and a short branch or loop line near the last-mentioned place. Length, 12 miles. Capital, 100,000*l.* in 10*l.* shares and 33,333*l.* on loan. Worked by the Great Eastern on terms which will return 5 per cent. on the capital expended on the line. The line was opened for traffic on the 1st September, 1879, and the interest on the share capital has since been paid.

CAPITAL.—Half-year ended 31st December, 1883.—*Receipts:* Ordinary 10*l.* shares, 100,000*l.*; loans, 33,333*l.*; total, 133,333*l.* *Expenditure:* 152,406*l.* Debit balance, 19,073*l.*

No. of Directors.—Maximum, 5; minimum, 3; quorum, 3 and 2. *Qualification*, 20 shares.

DIRECTORS:

Chairman—JAMES CHARLES, Esq., Kennet House, Harrow, and South Sea House, E.C.

Hon. Richard Denman, Westergate, Arundel.

Ernest Villiers, Esq., 9, Glendower Place, South Kensington, S.W.

OFFICERS.—Sec., Thomas C. Fryer; Eng., George Hopkins, C.E., 30, Parliament Street, Westminster, S.W.; Auditor, Frederick Waddy, Liverpool Street Station, E.C.

Offices—Liverpool Street Station, E.C.

93.—ENNISKILLEN, BUNDORAN, AND SLIGO.

Incorporated by act of 11th July, 1861, to construct a line from the Londonderry and Enniskillen, near Lowtherstown, to Bundoran, County Donegal. Length, 35¼ miles. Capital, 200,000*l.* in 10*l.* shares; loans, 66,600*l.* Arrangements with Irish North Western (now transferred to the Great Northern of Ireland), which works the line at a percentage of the receipts, the Bundoran Company finding all materials for the permanent way and works.

By act of 19th June, 1865, the company was authorised to raise new capital to the extent of 100,000*l.* in preference shares, at not exceeding 5 per cent. for the first ten years, and 5 per cent. in perpetuity thereafter. Also to raise 33,300*l.* on loan. An extension of time for three years was conceded to the Sligo Extension.

By act of 24th June, 1869, the company was authorised to effect an arrangement with respect to its mortgage and other debts. Arrears of interest to 1st January, 1869, were extinguished; 10,000*l.* of 5 per cent. debenture stock created as a first charge on the undertaking; interest at 4 per cent. on 66,000*l.* of debentures to be second; interest at 4 per cent. on 23,000*l.* to be third; and creditors' stock in lieu of Lloyd's bonds, at 3 per cent., to be fourth in priority of preference stocks or shares.

By act of 22nd July, 1878, the bond entered into under an act of 1862, for the construction of the Sligo Extension, was cancelled, no steps having been taken to carry out the making of that railway.

By act of 15th August, 1879, the company was authorised to make a railway from their Castlecaldwell Station to Donegal, to be called the "Fermanagh and Donegal." Length, 14 miles. Period for completion, 5 years. New capital, 50,000*l.* in "A" or preference (extension) shares, and 20,000*l.* in "B" or ordinary (extension) shares. Separate accounts of the working of this line to be kept. Loans or debenture stock, 35,000*l.*

A new agreement with the Great Northern of Ireland was concluded during the half-year ended 31st March, 1877, by which the Great Northern undertake to work this railway for five years, at the rate of 62½ per cent., until the receipts reach 13,099*l.*, when a reduction in the per centage charge will take place as the receipts increase each year.

FERMANAGH AND DONEGAL.—See act of 15th August, 1879, mentioned above.

REVENUE.—The gross receipts for the half-year ended 31st March, 1883, amounted to 3,972*l.*, and the expenditure (including payment of 2,467*l.* to the Great Northern of Ireland for haulage and working of line) to 3,544*l.*, leaving a net profit of 427*l.* The gross receipts for the half-year ended 30th September, 1883, amounted to 7,015*l.*, and the expenditure (including payment of 4,348*l.* to the Great Northern of Ireland for haulage and working of the line) to 5,445*l.*, leaving a net profit of 1,570*l.* The balance carried forward to net revenue account amounted to 17,098*l.* In operation, 35¼ miles.

CAPITAL.—The expenditure to 30th September, 1884, amounted to 432,179*l.*, the receipts having been as under:—

Ordinary shares	£46,848	
Preference 5 per cent. shares	100,000	
Loans at 4 per cent.	88,663	
Loans at 5 per cent.	2,447	
Debenture stock at 5 per cent.	7,553	
Debenture stock at 3 per cent.	153,453	
Sale of iron rails, plant, &c.	8,000	
Miscellaneous receipts	698=£407,662	
Balance		24,517=£432,179

The accounts are made up to 31st March and 30th September, and the meetings usually held in Dublin in April and October.

No. of Directors—9; minimum, 6; quorum, 3. *Qualification*, 1,000*l.*

DIRECTORS:

Chairman—ALBERT BRASSEY, Esq., Great George Street, Westminster, S.W.

John Caldwell Bloomfield, Esq., D.L., Castlecaldwell, County Fermanagh.
Major Francis D'Arcy, Castle Irvine, Irvinestown.
Wm. D'Arcy Irvine, Esq., D.L., Castle Irvine, Irvinestown.
William Aitken, Esq., Aston's Quay, Dublin.
William G. Skipworth, Esq., Rathgar, Dublin.
Samuel Willcox, Esq., Maidehurst, Beckenham, Kent.

OFFICERS.—Sec. and Accountant, James H. Connell; Eng., W. H. Mills; Auditors, Thomas MacBlain and J. B. Wilson; Solicitors, John Collum and Son.

Offices—2, Aston Place, Aston's Quay, Dublin.

94.—EVESHAM, REDDITCH, AND STRATFORD-UPON-AVON JUNCTION.

Incorporated by act of 5th August, 1873, for making a line to connect the Evesham and Redditch (now vested in the Midland) with the East and West Junction. Length, 7¾ miles, with running powers (55 miles 5 furlongs) over the Midland to Evesham and Redditch, and over the East and West Junction. Capital, 90,000*l*. In 4,500 preference half-shares of 5*l*. each, 4,500 "deferred" half-shares of 5*l*. each, and 30,000*l*. on loan. Rebates granted by Evesham and Redditch and East and West Junction for securing a dividend. To be worked, maintained, and managed by the East and West Junction.

By a Certificate of the Board of Trade, dated 21st March, 1878, the company was empowered to construct a deviation railway (2 miles 7 furlongs and 5·6 chains) from Binton to Old Stratford, in substitution of a portion of the railway No. 1, authorised by the act of 1873.

DEBENTURES.—In June, 1879, the directors invited applications for 24,000*l*., part of 30,000*l*. 5 per cent. debentures, and the prospectus stated that, as a guarantee for the due payment of the interest during the 6½ years currency of the debentures, a sufficient sum will be invested in the debenture stock of the Midland in the names of G. Cavendish Taylor, Esq., and the Hon. Robert Henley Eden, as trustees on behalf of the debenture holders for that purpose. In order to give effect to this guarantee, the trustees will collect the interest coupons on the debentures from the company, and will themselves issue in substitution therefor, attached to the debentures, 13 half-yearly warrants, signed by themselves, of 2½*l*. each, payable 1st July and 1st January in each year, on presentation at their bankers, the Union Bank of London.

AGREEMENT.—The railway was, under an agreement scheduled to the act, worked, stocked, and maintained by the East and West Junction at 50 per cent. of the gross receipts. This agreement has expired by effluxion of time, and the line is being worked temporarily, and pending definitive arrangements, by the East and West Junction.

The line has been completed to the satisfaction of the Board of Trade, and it was opened for traffic by the East and West Junction as a part of their system on the 2nd June, 1879.

No. of Directors.—Maximum, 5; minimum, 3; quorum, 3 and 2. *Qualification*, 50 half-shares.

DIRECTORS:

Chairman—WILLIAM D. GARDINER, Esq., Lincoln's Inn, W.C.

M. Meredith Brown, Esq., 7, Tokenhouse Yard, E.C.

T. Coombs, Esq., Palace Chambers, Bridge Street, Westminster, S.W.

John Spencer Longden, Esq., 8, Old Jewry, E.C.

George Cavendish Taylor, Esq., 42, Elvaston Place, South Kensington, S.W.

OFFICERS.—Sec., C. G. Musgrave; Eng., J. F. Burke, Stratford-on-Avon; Solicitors, Merrick and Co., 8, Old Jewry, E.C.; Bankers, Birmingham, Dudley, and District Banking Company, Birmingham.

Offices—8, Old Jewry, E.C.

95.—EXETER, TEIGN VALLEY, AND CHAGFORD.

Incorporated by act of 20th August, 1883, for the construction and maintenance of railways from St. Thomas, through Doddescombsleigh, to Chagford. Length, about 18 miles. Period for completion, 5 years. Great Western to work the line in perpetuity, at 50 per cent. of the gross receipts. Capital, 240,000*l*., in 20*l*. shares, with power to divide into "preferred" and "deferred" half-shares; loans, &c., 80,000*l*.

No. of Directors.—Maximum, 6; minimum, 3; quorum, 3 and 2. *Qualification*, 40 shares.

FIRST DIRECTORS:

Edwin Fox, Esq.

Lieut.-Col. John Walker.

John Norton, Esq.

Three others to be nominated.

96.—FELIXSTOWE RAILWAY AND DOCK.

Incorporated 19th July, 1875, for the purpose of constructing a railway, commencing in the parish of Felixstowe, and terminating by a junction with the Great Eastern, in the parish of Westerfield. Length, 13¼ miles. Also a pier at Felixstowe, in connection with the above. Capital, 130,000*l*. in 10*l*. shares and 43,300*l*. on loan. Arrangements with Great Eastern, which company commenced to work the line on the 1st September, 1879.

By act of 13th July, 1876, the company was authorised to construct a tidal basin, or dock, and other works at Felixstowe. Works to be completed in seven years. New capital, 40,000*l*. by shares or stock and 13,300*l*. by loans.

By act of 21st July, 1879, the name of the company was changed from "Felixstowe Railway and Pier" to "Felixstowe Railway and Dock," and the company obtained authority to abandon the works authorised by the above-mentioned act of 1876, and to construct and maintain other works in lieu thereof. New capital, 150,000*l*. Loans or debenture stock, 50,000*l*.

The line was completed during the half-year ended 30th June, 1877, and was opened for passenger traffic on the 1st May, and for goods traffic during the month of June following.

REVENUE—Half-year ended 31st December, 1883.—The results showed a balance in favour of revenue account of 834*l*., which reduced the balance against net revenue account to 4,899*l*. In operation, 13¾ miles.

CAPITAL.—The share capital of 130,000*l*. has been fully subscribed and paid up. The expenditure to 31st December, 1883, had been 242,762*l*., showing a debit balance against this account of 69,462*l*. 43,300*l*. debenture stock issued.

Quorum of general meeting—7 shareholders, holding together not less than 5,000*l*.

No. of Directors.—Maximum, 8; minimum, 3; quorum, 4 or 2. *Qualification*, 20 shares.

DIRECTORS:

Chairman—3 Colonel GEORGE TOMLINE, Orwell Park, Ipswich, and 1, Carlton House, Terrace, S.W.

Deputy-Chairman—2 ALEXANDER YOUNG, Esq., 41, Coleman Street, E.C.

1 John Watts, Esq., Harwich, Essex.

1, Retires in 1885; 2, in 1886; 3, in 1887. All eligible for re-election.

OFFICERS.—Sec., Frederick Kirtley; Accountant, Eustace Booker; Auditors, George Shelbourn and John B. Geard; Solicitors, Farrer, Ouvry, and Co., 66, Lincoln's Inn Fields, W.C.

Offices—1, Carlton House Terrace, S.W.

97.—FERMOY AND LISMORE.

Incorporated by act of 24th June, 1869, to construct a railway from the Great Southern and Western, at Fermoy, to Lismore. Length, 15¾ miles. Capital, 100,000*l*. in 10*l*. shares, and 33,300*l*. on loan. Working arrangements with Great Southern and Western, which works the line.

It was reported in August, 1871, that the line had been constructed at the expense of the Duke of Devonshire, his sole object being to benefit his numerous tenantry in the district, and to develop the trade and resources of a locality rich in agriculture.

No. of Directors—5; minimum, 3; quorum, 3 and 2. *Qualification*, 200*l*.

DIRECTORS

Chairman—His Grace the Duke of DEVONSHIRE, K.G., Devonshire House, Piccadilly, W.

Frederick John Howard, Esq., Eastbourne.
Francis Edmund Currey, Esq., Lismore.
Sir James Ramsden, Knt., M.Inst.C.E., Barrow-in-Furness, Lancashire.

OFFICERS.—Sec., George Noble; Engs., Purdon and Lewis, MM.Inst.C.E., 8, Victoria Chambers, Westminster, S.W.; Solicitors, Currey, Holland, and Currey, London, and Barrington and Jeffers, 10, Ely Place, Dublin.

Head Office—14, Great George Street, Westminster, S.W.

98.—FESTINIOG.

Originally incorporated in 1832, to construct a railway or tramroad from Portmadoc to certain slate quarries, near Festiniog, in the counties of Merioneth and Carnarvon. Gauge, 1 foot 11½ inches. By act of 26th July, 1869, the company was re-incorporated, and authorised to widen and improve the railway, to construct additional works and two branch junction lines about three furlongs in length. The existing share capital was fixed at 86,186*l*., and the borrowing powers at 12,000*l*. New share capital was, however, authorised to the extent of 90,000*l*., and further borrowing powers of 30,000*l*. conferred. Of the new capital, 40,000*l*. has been issued in 5 per cent. preference shares, and 10,000*l*. in 4½ per cent. preference shares.

REVENUE—Half-year ended 30th December, 1883.—The net earnings this half-year amounted to 3,057*l*., which, with 212*l*. brought in, made up a total of 3,269*l*.; after satisfying all interest and preferential charges there remained a balance of 1,018*l*., which sufficed for a dividend on the ordinary capital at 1 per cent. per annum, and left 587*l*. to be carried forward.

Half-year ended 30th June, 1884.—The net earnings amounted to 3,035*l*.; sundry amounts, including balance from last half-year, 718*l*., made a total of 3,753*l*.; after providing for all interest and preferential charges there remained a balance of 1,463*l*., which sufficed for a dividend on the ordinary capital at the rate of 2 per cent. per annum, and left 598*l*. to next account.

In operation, 16¼ miles.

CAPITAL.—The receipts on this account to 30th June, 1884, amounted to 148,185*l*., and the expenditure to 150,229*l*., showing a debit balance of 2,044*l*. The receipts are given in further detail below:—

Ordinary stock	£86,185
Preference shares at 5 per cent.	40,000
Preference shares at 4½ per cent.	10,000
Debenture stock at 4½ per cent.	12,000
	£148,185

Meetings held in London in February, and company's offices, Portmadoc, in August.

No. of Directors—4; minimum, 3; quorum, 3 and 2. *Qualification*, 500*l*.

DIRECTORS:

Chairman—JOHN GRAVES LIVINGSTON, Esq., Clifton.

Col. George Halpin, 54, Belsize Park, N.W.

T. Plunket Cairnes, Esq., Stameen, Drogheda.

Thomas Kerl, Esq., Marlborough Buildings, Bath.

Retire in rotation; all eligible for re-election.

OFFICERS.—Sec. and Gen. Man., C. E. Spooner; Traff. Man., F. G. Crick; Loco. Supt., W. Williams; Auditors, Thomas Graydon and C. B. Robinson; Solicitors, Sandilands, Humphry, and Armstrong, Fenchurch Avenue, Fenchurch Street, E.C.

Offices—Portmadoc.

99.—FINN VALLEY.

Incorporated by act of 15th May, 1860, to make a railway from Stranorlar, County Donegal, to Strabane, on the Londonderry and Enniskillen—now Great Northern (Ireland). Length, 14 miles. Capital, 60,000*l*. in 10*l*. shares; loans, 20,000*l*. Opened 7th September, 1863.

By Certificate of the Board of Trade, dated 1st April, 1865, the company was empowered to raise additional capital to the extent of 20,000*l*. by redeemable 6 per cent. preference shares.

At a special meeting, held on 30th October, 1871, it was resolved to exercise the powers granted by the Board of Trade Certificate of 1865, to the extent of 20,000*l*.

By act of 13th July, 1871, the company was further authorised to attach a preference of 6 per cent. to ordinary unissued shares, amounting to 15,020*l*., and to enter into agreements with the Irish North Western—now Great Northern (Ireland).

Agreements (sanctioned by extraordinary meetings of shareholders on 9th February and 3rd October, 1881), have been entered into for the working of the West Donegal Railway which was opened for traffic on 25th April, 1882, to the temporary terminus at Druminin (14 miles), and when subsequently opened to the town of Donegal (18 miles, its full length).

AGREEMENT WITH WEST DONEGAL.—At an extraordinary meeting of the West Donegal, on 12th August, 1884, it was resolved—"That this meeting hereby sanctions the proposed agreement between the West Donegal and the Finn Valley, now produced and read to us, whereby it is provided—that on a light railway from Druminin to Donegal being completed by the West Donegal, under the provisions of the Tramways Acts (Ireland), the working and traffic agreement of the 15th March, 1881 (between the Finn Valley and the West Donegal), come into operation, and have the same effect as if the said light railway had been completed by the West Donegal under the provisions of their special act."

WEST DONEGAL.—See GENERAL INDEX.

REVENUE.—The receipts for the half-year ended 31st December, 1883, were 3,352*l*., and the expenditure 1,913*l*. The fixed charges amounted to 1,563*l*., which left a debit balance of 108*l*.

The receipts for the six months ended 30th June, 1884, were 3,353*l.*, and the expenditure 2,150*l.*, leaving a surplus of 1,203*l.* The fixed charges required 1,712*l.*, leaving a debit balance of 509*l.*

CAPITAL.—The expenditure on this account to 30th June, 1884 (including subscription to the West Donegal, 13,560*l.*), amounted to 99,860*l.*, the receipts having been as follow:—

Shares	£62,290
Loans and debenture stock	33,179
Profits on revenue account capitalised by resolution of 1st April, 1869	3,768
	£99,237
Balance	623
	£99,860

WEST DONEGAL SHARES AND STOCK.—Under the West Donegal Act of 1879, the company was authorised to subscribe 15,000*l.* as "B" or ordinary shares in the West Donegal undertaking, and to raise 15,000*l.* in loans or debenture stock; of the latter 15,000*l.* 5 per cent. debenture stock has been issued. This stock ranks equally with debentures and debenture stock issued under "The Finn Valley Act, 1860," and takes priority of the preference and ordinary paid-up share capital of the company, amounting to 62,460*l.* The stock may be transferred in any amount from 10*l.* and upwards. Interest is payable on 1st May and 1st November in each year.

In operation, 14 miles.

Meetings held in February or March, or in August or September.

No. of Directors—8; minimum, 5; quorum, 3. *Qualification*, 300*l.*

DIRECTORS:

Chairman—The Right Hon. Viscount LIFFORD, Meen Glas, Stranorlar, County Donegal, and Cecil House, Wimbledon, S.W.

Vice-Chairman—BARTHOLOMEW M'CORKELL, Esq., Richmond, Londonderry.

James Thompson Macky, Esq., J.P., Belmont, Londonderry.
James Cochrane, Esq., 2, Great Charles Street, Mountjoy Square, Dublin.
Sir S. H. Hayes, Bart., Drumboe, Stranorlar, County Donegal.
John B. Popplewell, Esq., Chellow Dean House, near Bradford, Yorkshire.
John Cooke, Esq., Strand, Londonderry.
Henry J. M'Corkell, Esq., Glengallaugh, Londonderry.

OFFICERS.—Sec. and Gen. Man., James Alex. Ledlie, Stranorlar; Auditors, Archibald M'Corkell, Londonderry, and Edward A. Hamilton, Londonderry; Bankers, Northern Banking Company.

Offices—Stranorlar.

100.—FOREST OF DEAN CENTRAL.

Incorporated by act of 11th July, 1856, to make a railway from the South Wales, near Brimspill, to Howbeach Valley, in the Forest of Dean (broad gauge). Capital, 65,000*l.* in 10*l.* shares; loans, 21,660*l.* The Woods and Forest Commissioners advanced 20,000*l.*, secured by prior claim of 5 per cent. Length of main line, 4¼ miles; of Fox Bridge Branch, 2¼ miles; and of the branch which terminates by a junction with that railway, 4 furlongs 7½ chains.

By act of 20th August, 1860, an extension of time for completion of works was conceded till 14th July, 1862. Agreements were also authorised with the South Wales, and joint committee appointed to be formed. New capital to the extent of 1,000*l.* to be raised in shares; and the Commissioners of Woods and Forests were authorised to grant an extension of time for repayment by the company of sums advanced by them—five years, instead of one twelvemonth, being now allowed.

By act of 22nd July, 1861, the company was authorised to construct some new works for coal traffic, and to increase the capital of the undertaking by 15,000*l.* in shares at 6 per cent., and 5,000*l.* in loans.

No. of Directors—7; minimum, 3; quorum, 4; if at minimum 2. *Qualification*, 500*l.*

DIRECTORS:

Chairman—A. T. PRATT BARLOW, Esq., 47, Norfolk Square, Hyde Park, W.

William Bower, Esq., 96, Tottenham Court Road, W.
Chas. Greenwood, Esq., 61, Nelson Square, Blackfriars Road, S.E.
Edmund Kendall, Esq., 48, Cawley Road, Victoria Park, E.
George Williams Morris, Esq., 15, Southgate Road, Winchester.

OFFICERS.—Sec., J. Wilson Theobald; Solicitor, Francis Venn, 1, Serjeants' Inn, W.C.; Bankers, Ransom, Bouverie, and Co., 1, Pall Mall East, S.W.

Offices—8, Drapers' Gardens, E.C.

101.—FORTH BRIDGE.

Incorporated by act of 5th August, 1873, to construct a line from near Dalmeny, on the Queensferry Branch of the North British, to Inverkeithing and Burntisland. Total length, 14¾ miles. Capital, 1,250,000*l.* in 10*l.* shares and 416,666*l.* on loan.

By act of 12th July, 1882, the company was authorised, in substitution for the railway No. 1, of the act of 1873, to make a railway 4 miles 2 furlongs in length, from the Queensferry Branch of the North British, in the parish of Dalmeny, to the Dumfermline and Queensferry Branch, in the parish of Inverkeithing, and crossing the Firth of Forth by means of a bridge; the works to be completed within 5 years from the passing of the act. The structure of the bridge to be maintained by the Forth Bridge, and the railway to be worked and maintained by the North British. The railway No. 2, from Inverkeithing to Burntisland, of the act of 1873, is transferred to the North British, and the capital under that act is accordingly reduced by 134,000*l.* New capital:—Shares, 634,000*l.*; loans, 211,333*l.* The directors to be 10, two being appointed by each of the North British, Great Northern, North Eastern, Midland, and Forth Bridge companies. In lieu of the conditional guarantee under the previous acts, an absolute and perpetual guarantee of 4 per cent. per annum is provided for as from 30th June, 1882, the four companies being liable therefor in the following proportions:—North British, 30 per cent.; Midland, 32½ per cent.; Great Northern and North Eastern, 18¾ per cent. each; but if the North British shall at any time hereafter for four consecutive years pay a dividend on their ordinary stock equal to an average rate of 5 per cent. per annum, then they shall thereafter relieve the North Eastern, Great Northern, and Midland companies of one-half of their respective guarantees. In consideration of this guarantee the four companies to receive the net revenue of the railway from all sources, and to apply it thus:—(1) In repayment to the four companies of all guarantee moneys, with 5 per cent. interest thereon, which may be paid by them (after the interest fund has been exhausted) prior to the opening of the railway; (2) in repayment to the North Eastern, Great Northern, and Midland companies rateably of all guarantee moneys which may be paid by them after the opening of the railway, and (3), the balance to belong to the North British.

Running powers are given to the guaranteeing companies mentioned below, in accordance with the terms of sections 6 and 7 of the act of 17th June, 1878.

WORKING ARRANGEMENTS WITH THE NORTH BRITISH.—The act of 1882 provides that the North British shall, from and after the opening of the railway, work and maintain the line in perpetuity, in the same manner and with the same powers and obligations as if the railway formed part of the North British system The North British to pay over to the company the mileage proportion of receipts, provided that if the net amount of such proportion shall not amount to 40,000*l.* the North British shall make up the deficiency, that is to say, the North British shall guarantee an income of 40,000*l.* per annum whilst the bridge is available for traffic, and if the traffic be suspended in any year, then at the rate of 40,000*l.* per annum for such period as it may have been available for traffic. The terminals to be deducted before ascertaining the proportion of traffic shall not be those usually allowed by the Railway Clearing House, but at such lesser rates as may either be agreed upon or settled under Arbitration Act, 1859.

GUARANTEE.—The North British, Midland, North Eastern, and Great Northern companies, the first named working the line, and the other three having running powers (as above), jointly and severally guarantee in perpetuity, as from the 30th June, 1882, interest or dividend on the "nominal share capital of the company at present issued as from time to time called up," at the rate of 4 per cent. per annum, payable half-yearly, in the proportions above-mentioned; the four companies also guarantee in perpetuity, and in the same proportion, all interest or dividend which may become payable on the nominal amount of the mortgages or debenture stock from time to time issued, and of any additional share or loan capital which may, with the consent of the four companies, be hereafter raised or issued by the company under the authority of Parliament for completing the railway.

Works in progress.

CAPITAL.—The capital created is 1,116,000*l.*, of which 439,332*l.* had been received up to 30th June, 1884.

Meetings held in January or February and July or August.

No. of Directors.—Maximum, 10; quorum, 5. *Qualification*, 200*l.*

DIRECTORS:

Chairman—The Right Hon. Lord COLVILLE, K.T., 42, Eaton Place, S.W.

Deputy-Chairman—JOHN DENT DENT, Esq., Ribston Hall, Wetherby.

Sir James Falshaw, Bart., 14, Belgrave Crescent, Edinburgh.
Matthew W. Thompson, Esq., Guiseley, near Leeds.
James H. Renton, Esq., 9, Drapers' Gardens, Throgmorton Street, E.C.
Sir Matthew W. Ridley, Bart., M.P., Blagdon, Cramlington, Northumberland, and 10, Carlton House Terrace, S.W.
Wm. U. Heygate, Esq., Roecliffe, Loughborough.
Henry John Trotter, Esq., Langton Grange, Gainford, Darlington, and The Temple, Fleet Street, E.C.
Spencer Brunton, Esq., 18, Finch Lane, E.C.
Samuel Charles Allsopp, Esq., M.P., Doveridge Hall, Derbyshire.

OFFICERS.—Sec., G. B. Wieland; Eng., John Fowler, 2, Queen's Square Place, Westminster, S.W.; Auditors, Walter Mackenzie and J. Wyllie Guild; Solicitors, Millar, Robson, and Innes.

Offices—4A, Princes Street, Edinburgh.

102.—FORTH AND CLYDE JUNCTION.

Incorporated by act of 4th August, 1853, for a railway from Stirling (junction with the Scottish Central) to Alexandria (junction with the Caledonian and Dumbartonshire), near Balloch, foot of Loch Lomond. The line connects the east and west of Scotland and the Rivers Forth and Clyde by the shortest possible route. Length, 30 miles.

By act of 13th July, 1857, the company was authorised to cancel certain forfeited shares, of the nominal value of 43,000*l.*, and to issue the same amount, and also 21,000*l.* additional, at 5 per cent. preference. The act also contained clauses for converting the same share capital and mortgage debt, and the money to be borrowed under the act, into stock, and to authorise the company to attach a preference to the shares for all or any of the additional money to be raised, and to fund the debt of the company, with various provisions in relation thereto.

By act of 1st August, 1861, the company was authorised to raise new capital to the extent of 21,000*l.* in shares, and 7,000*l.* on loan. Also to construct a branch to Dalmonach Print Works. Length, 62 chains.

NORTH BRITISH.—At a special meeting, held on 29th September, 1871, it was resolved to lease the line under an agreement, of which the following is an abstract:—The North British to work and maintain the undertaking, on terms which will secure hereafter a minimum net revenue sufficient to meet the payment of feu duties and other concurrent expenses, interest on debenture loans, dividend in full on all the preference stock and shares, and about 1¼ per cent. per annum on the ordinary stock. The agreement also secures a share *pro ratâ*, in the increase of revenue of the North British undertaking, including the Forth and Clyde, from 31st July, 1871, in the proportion that this company's revenue for the year ending 31st January, 1871, bears to that of the North British for the same period. The North British to purchase the rolling stock, machinery, stores, &c., for which there will be no further need, the proceeds going in liquidation of the fully ascertained debts of the company, payment of deferred dividend warrants, and undeclared arrears of dividend on the first 5 per cent. preference stock, and in payment of dividend in full on the first and second preference stock and shares, leaving a balance of 1,851*l.* at the credit of capital account, to meet certain contingent liabilities not yet fully ascertained.

The line has since been leased to the North British for 50 years, from 1st August 1875. Dividend on the ordinary stock:—6 per cent. for the first year, 6½ per cent. for second year, and 7 per cent. third year; rising *pari passu* with the dividend of the North British ordinary stock after the latter reaches that point. It is stated in the official reports, that the North British are carrying out the terms of the agreement in a satisfactory manner.

REVENUE.—The last two half-yearly dividends (at 7 per cent. per annum) were declared on the 4th March and 26th August, 1884, and made payable on the 11th March and 9th September respectively.

CAPITAL.—31st July, 1884. *Receipts:—*

5 per cent. second preference shares	£21,000	
Less converted into 6 per cent	16,480	
		£4,520
6 per cent. redeemable second preference shares		16,480
5 per cent. first preference stock		64,000
Consolidated stock		106,390
		£191,390
4 per cent. debenture stock		61,595
Premium on debenture stock and forfeited calls		1,605
		£254,590

Expended, 254,235*l.*; balance (credit) 355*l.*

Meetings half-yearly (at Stirling) in August or September and February or March.

No. of Directors—9; quorum, 4; committee of directors, 3 to 5; quorum, the majority. *Qualification*, 50 shares.

DIRECTORS:

Chairman—3 Col. ALEXANDER WILSON, Bannockburn.

Deputy-Chairman—1 ROBERT YOUNG, Esq., 4, West Nile Street, Glasgow.

2 Alexander McDonald, Esq., Comely Bank, Dumbarton.
2 John Anderson, Jun., Esq., Atlantic Mills, Bridgeton, Glasgow.
T. L. Galbraith, Esq., Stirling.
3 M. Pettigrew, Esq., 85, Queen Street, Glasgow.
1 P. Turnbull, Esq., C.A., 31, Princes Street, Edinburgh.

1, Retire in 1885; 2, in 1886; 3, in 1887.

OFFICERS.—Sec., James Hutton, C.A., 179, West George Street, Glasgow; Auditors, John G. Curror, Writer, Stirling, and Patrick Graham Morison, 1, Strathearn Place, Edinburgh; Solicitors, J. and J. Mathie and McLuckie, Writers, Stirling, and Thomas L. Galbraith, Writer, Stirling.

Offices—179, West George Street, Glasgow.

103.—FRESHWATER, YARMOUTH, AND NEWPORT (ISLE OF WIGHT).

Incorporated by act of 26th August, 1880, for the construction and maintenance of a railway from Freshwater Gate to a junction with the Cowes and Newport, at Newport. Length, about 13¼ miles. Period for completion, 5 years. Traffic arrangements with the Isle of Wight, Ryde and Newport, and Cowes and Newport; also with the London and South Western and London, Brighton, and South Coast. Capital, 100,000*l.* in 10*l.* shares, with power to divide into "preferred" and "deferred" half-shares; borrowing powers, 33,300*l.*

By act of 20th August, 1883, the time limited for completion of works was extended to 26th August, 1888. New capital, 42,000*l.* Loans, 14,000*l.* Agreements with London and South Western and Didcot, Newbury, and Southampton, and powers for sundry other purposes.

No. of Directors.—Maximum, 6; minimum, 3; quorum, 3 and 2. *Qualification*, 50 shares.

FIRST DIRECTORS:

Lieut.-Col. John Walker.
Edwin Fox, Esq.
William Charles Harvey, Esq.
John Norton, Esq.
George Gordon Leicester Macpherson, Esq.
One other to be nominated.

104.—FURNESS.

Incorporated by act of 1844, for a line commencing at Barrow and Piel Pier, Morecambe Bay, mainly for the conveyance of minerals from Dalton and Kirkby mines. The line was subsequently extended to Broughton, power being also obtained for an extension eastward from Dalton to Ulverston, where a junction was afterwards (1857) formed by the Ulverston and Lancaster. By the Consolidation Act, 1855, the existing capital was fixed at 460,000*l.*, and the borrowing powers at 140,000*l.* In operation, 170¾ miles, including one-half of the Whitehaven, Cleator, and Egremont.

FURTHER PARLIAMENTARY POWERS:—

For list of Acts from 1862 to 1879, with short heads of the objects for which the various powers were sought, see the MANUAL for 1881, page 97.

1881.—Construction of sundry short lines, sidings, roads, bridges, &c., at Barrow and Ulverston; abandonment of main line between Park Junction and Millwood Junction. Sundry agreements as to supply of water, stopping up roads, &c., &c. New capital, 300,000*l*.; loans, 100,000*l*.

1881—22nd August.—New railways in Barrow-in-Furness and Ulverston, and various other powers. New capital, 300,000*l*.; borrowing powers, 100,000*l*.

1883—May.—New capital authorised by Board of Trade Certificate, 200,000*l*.; loans, 66,600*l*.

AMALGAMATIONS, &c.:—

Cleator and Workington Junction.—See General Index.

Coniston.—Incorporated by act of 10th August, 1857, for making a railway from Broughton (junction with the Furness Line) to Coniston Lake. Length, 9 miles. Capital, 45,000*l*.; loans, 15,000*l*. This undertaking was amalgamated with the Furness, under an act passed on the 7th July, 1862.

Ulverston and Lancaster.—Incorporated by act of 24th July, 1851, for a line from the Furness, at Ulverston, to a junction with the Lancaster and Carlisle, at Carnforth, 7 miles north of Lancaster. Length, 19 miles. Original capital, 220,000*l*.; additional capital, 180,000*l*.; debentures, 123,333*l*., under the powers of the Ulverston and Lancaster Acts, 1858. Transferred to the Furness by the act of 12th July, 1858.

Whitehaven, Cleator, and Egremont.—For joint ownership under the London and North Western Act of 17th June, 1878, see London and North Western.

Whitehaven and Furness Junction.—Incorporated by act of 21st July, 1845, for a railway from Whitehaven to a junction with the Furness, near Dalton; subsequently extended to a junction at Whitehaven with the Whitehaven Junction, and fixing the junction with Furness at Foxfield, near Broughton. By act of 16th July, 1866, the Whitehaven and Furness was amalgamated with the Furness, at 8 per cent. on the ordinary stock.—For brief details of previous legislation, see Manual for 1882, and previously.

New Lines and Works.—The Park Loop Line, &c. (length, 9¼ miles), and the new station at Barrow, were opened for traffic on the 1st June, 1882.

ACCOUNTS:—

Revenue.—The result of working for the half-years ended 31st December, 1883, and 30th June, 1884, was as follows:—

	Dec. 31, 1883.	June 30, 1884.
Gross revenue	£285,701	£250,269
Expenditure	126,192	119,751
Net	£159,509	£130,518
Add balance brought forward	475	700
Interest	1,296	1,901
Total net revenue	£161,280	£133,119
Interest, preference dividends, &c. (net)	94,530	92,515
Available for ordinary stock	£66,750	£40,604
Dividends at 5 and 3 per cent. per annum respectively	66,050	39,630
Balance to next half-year	£700	£974

Capital.—The company's stock and share capital at 30th September, 1884, stood as follows (see notes):—

PRIORITIES, DESCRIPTIONS, DIVIDENDS, &c., OF STOCKS AND SHARES.—The following is a list of this company's Stocks, numbered in order of priority, with conditions of issue *in brief*, the descriptions to be strictly observed in transfer forms and all other legal documents relating thereto, viz.:—

No.	Year of Act.	Full Description (to be observed in Transfer Deeds and all other Legal Documents).	Rate ℔ cent ℔ annum.
1	Various	4 per cent. perpetual debenture stock ....(£1,580,180)	4
2	1879	4 per cent. consolidated guaranteed stock, 1881 (£779,125)	4
3	1879	4 per cent. consolidated preference stock, 1881 (£1,300,750)	4
4	1881	4 per cent. preference stock "A" ....(£350,000)	4
5	1883	4 per cent. preference stock "B"..................(£100,000)	4
6	Various	Consolidated ordinary stock ....(£2,642,000)	...

Notes.—The dividends on Nos 1 and 2 are non-contingent and accumulative, and payable half-yearly on 1st January and 1st July.

The dividends on Nos. 3, 4, and 5, are contingent upon the profits of each separate year, ended 31st December, and payable half-yearly on 1st January and 1st July.

The dividends on the consolidated ordinary stock are always payable on the 1st March and 1st September.

The transfer books of all stocks generally close for 14 days before payment of dividends.

The stocks Nos. 2 and 3 were issued for the consolidation of other stock, (Manual, 1881), as below; date of act, 21st July, 1879; date of scheme, 26th January, 1881.

TRANSFER DEPARTMENT QUERIES AND REPLIES.

QUERIES.	REPLIES.
Transfer form—ordinary or special?	Ordinary.
Fee per deed?	2*s.* 6*d.*
Ditto if more sellers than one?	2*s.* 6*d.*; if more than two sellers, 2*s.* 6*d.* each.
May several classes of stock be transferred on one deed?	Yes.
Are certificates required to accompany transfers?	Yes (if not deposited before).
What amounts of stock are transferable, and are parts of 1*l.* sterling allowed to be transferred?	Any amount not involving fractions of 1*l.*
To what officer should transfer communications be sent?	Secretary.
In acceptances, renunciations, &c., of allotments of new stock, proxies, or other forms sent to trustees and others, what signatures are required?	All joint proprietors should sign.

CONSOLIDATION OF STOCKS.—The guaranteed and preference stocks of the company were consolidated into two classes on the 25th February, 1881; the terms upon which the various stocks were exchanged will be found on reference to MANUAL for 1882, page 100.

The receipts and expenditure on capital account to 30th June, 1884, have been as under:—

Received.		*Expended.*	
Shares and stock	£4,668,500	Lines open for traffic	£2,854,444
Loans	4,300	Lines in course of construction	296,939
Debenture stock	1,543,347	Working stock	923,659
		Docks, steamboats, &c.	2,125,979
	£6,216,147	Windermere Yacht Company's purchase	16,932
Balance	1,806		
	£6,217,953		£6,217,953

The estimate of further expenditure was 32,957*l.* for the half-year ended 31st December, 1884, and 70,692*l.* for subsequent periods.

Capital powers and other assets available to meet further expenditure:—

Share and loan capital authorised but not yet created or sanctioned	£66,600
Share capital uncalled	25,000
Share capital unissued	100,000
Balance of available borrowing powers	22,319
Estimated value of land at Barrow which will not be required for railway purposes	60,000
	£273,919
Balance at debit of capital account	1,806
	£272,113

Scale of Voting.—As per Companies' Clauses Consolidation Act.

No. of Directors.—Maximum, 9; minimum, 4. *Qualification,* 500*l.* capital. Rotate three every February.

DIRECTORS:

Chairman—2 His Grace The Duke of DEVONSHIRE, K.G., Devonshire House, Piccadilly, W.

2 Lord Edward Cavendish, M.P., Devonshire House, Piccadilly.
3 Frederick I. Nicholl, Esq., 1, Howard Street, Strand, W.C.
1 3 Sir Henry M. Meysey-Thompson, Kirby Hall, York, and 42, Albemarle Street, W.
1 3 Sir James Ramsden, Barrow-in-Furness.
2 Sir George Kettilby Rickards, K.C.B., Fyfield House, Oxford.
1 Edward Wadham, Esq., Millwood, Barrow-in-Furness.
1, Retire in 1885; 2, in 1886; 3, in 1887.

OFFICERS.—Sec. and Traffic Man., Henry Cook, Assoc.Inst.C.E.; Assistant Sec., Frederic J. Ramsden; Eng., F. C. Stileman, M.Inst.C.E.; Loco. Supt., Richard Mason; Accountant, Thomas Edge; Auditors, Robert F. Miller and John L. McIlraith, Public Accountants, Barrow-in-Furness.; Solicitors, Currey, Holland, and Currey.

Head Offices—Barrow-in-Furness.

105.—GARSTANG AND KNOT END.

Incorporated by act of 30th June, 1864, to construct a line from the Lancaster and Preston Junction to Knot End. Length, 11¾ miles. Capital, 60,000*l.* in 10*l.* shares and 20,000*l.* on loan.

By act of 3rd May, 1867, the time for completion of these works was extended till 1st July, 1869.

By act of 12th July, 1869, the period for completion of works was further extended till 1871, and power given to the company to raise new capital to the extent of 30,000*l.* in shares and 10,000*l.* on loan; also to create and issue debenture stock.

Open from Garstang and Catterall to Pilling; remainder in progress.

No. of Directors—6; quorum, 3. *Qualification*, 500*l.*

DIRECTORS:

W. Chapman, Esq., J.P., Wyre Bank, Garstang.
Thomas Seed, Esq., St. Stephen's Place, Fleetwood.
William Forrester, Esq., Leyland, Preston.
Jos. Gornall, Esq., Pilling, Fleetwood.
Thomas Pearson, Esq., Manor House, Nateby, Garstang.
John Pearson, Esq., Nateby, Garstang.

OFFICERS.—Sec., John Noble, Church Street, Garstang; Man., J. Noble; Auditors, Hartley and Wardley, Garstang; Solicitor, Richard Finch, Fox Street, Preston.

Offices—Garstang.

106.—GIANTS CAUSEWAY, PORTRUSH, AND BUSH VALLEY.

Incorporated 26th August, 1880, for the construction of a railway and tramways in the County of Antrim, commencing at Derveck by a junction with the Ballycastle, and terminating at Clogher. Length, about 7¼ miles. Capital, 45,000*l.* in 10*l.* shares; borrowing powers, 20,000*l.*

No. of Directors—5; quorum, 3. *Qualification*, 20 shares. Quorum of general meetings 7 shareholders, holding not less than 3,000*l.* of capital.

DIRECTORS:

Anthony Traill, Esq., F.T.C.D.
Charles McDaniel Stuart, Esq.
Charles R. Atkinson, Esq., C.E., Belfast.
Samuel Gray, Esq.
Sir William Thomson, Knt., F.R.S.

OFFICERS.—Sec. and Man., Daniel Fall, Jun.; Eng. of Tramway, W. Traill.

Offices—Portrush.

107.—GIRVAN AND PORTPATRICK JUNCTION.

Incorporated by act of 5th July, 1865, to construct a line from Girvan, on the Maybole, to a junction with the Portpatrick, at East Challoch. Length, 30¾ miles. Capital, 250,000*l.* in 10*l.* shares and 83,300*l.* on loan.

A list of Acts, from 1870 to 1877, with short heads showing the objects for which the various powers were obtained, will be found on reference to the MANUAL for 1881, page 100.

FURTHER POWERS:—

1879—11TH AUGUST.—Powers to borrow such a further amount on mortgage as would enable the company to become joint owners with the Portpatrick Company of the Stranraer section of that company's railway, and of the East Pier of Stranraer, &c., &c.

This line is worked by the Glasgow and South Western under an agreement which was approved of by the Railway Commissioners on 20th July, 1883.

LLOYD'S BONDS.—For particulars relating to the position of these bonds, see *Appendix* to this Volume.

CAPITAL.—The receipts and expenditure on this account to 31st August, 1884, were as under:—

Receipts.		*Expenditure.*	
Shares and stock	£262,645	Line open for traffic	£535,782
Loans	20,000	Interest	5,800
Debenture stock "A" "B" and "C" under Arrangement Act, 1882	302,487	Under Arrangement Act, 1882	54,496
Shares surrendered	13,306		£596,078
		Balance	2,360
	£598,438		£598,438

Rates of interest payable on debenture stocks and division of surplus to shareholders of the Girvan and Portpatrick Junction given in order of priority:—

	First division.	Second division (additional).	Third division (additional).	Fourth division (additional).
	Per cent.	Per cent.	Per cent.	Per cent.
"A" debenture stock	*2½	1	½	...
"B" debenture stock	*2	1	1	...
"C" debenture stock	1	1	1	½
Preference shareholders	...	...	†½	‡
Ordinary shareholders	...	...	†¼	‡

Interest at the rate of 1 per cent. was declared to the holders of "A" debenture stock at the half-yearly meeting held 31st October, 1884. No interest has been paid on any of the other stocks.

The capital powers and other assets available to meet further expenditure amount to 28,677*l*.

Meetings held in Edinburgh in April and October.

DIRECTORS:

Chairman—J. CARMENT, Esq., LL.D., 32, Albany Street, Edinburgh.

Robert Landale, Esq., S.S.C., of Pitmedden, 15, Royal Circus, Edinburgh.

John Campbell, Esq., Slagnaw, Castle Douglas.

Walter Gowans, Esq., 3, Victoria Place, Trinity, Edinburgh.

OFFICERS.—Sec. and Treasurer, William Brown, 10, St. Andrew Square, Edinburgh; Eng., A. Galloway, Glasgow; Auditors, James Martin, C.A., Castle Street, and J. A. Robertson, C.A., North St. David Street, Edinburgh.

Offices—10, St. Andrew Square, Edinburgh.

108.—GLASGOW CITY AND DISTRICT.

Incorporated by act of 10th August, 1882, for making railways from the Stobcross Branch of the North British to the Glasgow and Coatbridge Branch, and the Helensburgh Branch. Length, about 3 miles. Period for completion, 5 years; running powers to the Caledonian; working agreement with the North British. Capital, 550,000*l*. in 10*l*. shares, with powers to divide into "preferred" and "deferred" half-shares. Borrowing powers, 183,300*l*.

No. of Directors.—Maximum, 6; minimum, 4; quorum, 3 and 2. *Qualification*, 50 shares.

Quorum of Meetings.—10 shareholders, holding in the aggregate not less than 10,000*l*. in the capital of the company.

FIRST DIRECTORS:

William Weir, Esq.
James Black, Esq.
James Rodger Thomson, Esq.
James Parker Smith, Esq.
Thomas Reid, Esq.
William Laird, Esq.

* Interest accumulative. † *Pari passu* at above rates. ‡ Surplus divided in proportion of two-thirds to preference shareholders, and one-third to ordinary shareholders.

109.—GLASGOW AND KILMARNOCK JOINT.

By act of 12th July, 1869, the Caledonian and Glasgow and South Western were jointly authorised to improve and complete a direct line of railway between Glasgow and Kilmarnock, *viâ* Crofthead, to be vested in these two companies, who accordingly succeeded on 1st August, 1869, to the Caledonian Company's interest in the Glasgow, Barrhead, and Neilston Direct and Glasgow Southern Terminal railways, to the Crofthead and Kilmarnock Extension, and to part of the Caledonian Company's Glasgow South Side Station. The Kilmarnock Direct Railway of the South Western to be abandoned. The joint undertaking to be managed by a committee of eight directors, four of whom to be appointed by each company, and a standing arbitrator to have the casting vote.

The line begins at Gorbals, on the south side of Glasgow, and terminates at Kilmarnock, having a branch to Beith. The Caledonian and South Western each join it, the former at Langside Junction and Strathbungo, and the latter by means of the City Union at Gorbals.

By act of 13th May, 1872, the time for completing certain portions of the authorised undertaking was extended to June, 1873. Powers to construct a branch in connection with the Joint Line, and to the Glasgow and South Western to acquire additional lands at Kilmarnock.

By act of 25th July, 1872, the two companies were authorised to connect the Hamilton Branch of the Caledonian Line and the Kilmarnock Joint Line with the City of Glasgow Union, and powers were obtained to shut up a portion of South Side Station and certain roads.

By act of 16th July, 1874, the two companies obtained powers to acquire certain lands.

By act of 29th June, 1875, the two companies were authorised to construct several short lines in the counties of Lanark and Ayr in connection with the Kilmarnock Joint Line, and to abandon certain portions of the line authorised by the act of 25th July, 1872. Further extension of time for completion of works to June, 1877.

By act of 27th June, 1876, the two companies were authorised to acquire additional lands, and execute certain works of minor importance.

By act of 18th June, 1883, the two companies were authorised to acquire additional lands, and to widen certain bridges.

The accounts are included in those of the Caledonian and Glasgow and South Western.

DIRECTORS:

Caledonian.	*Glasgow and South Western.*
John Cowan, Esq., Stoneleigh, Greenock.	Robert Barclay, Esq., Glasgow.
Hugh Brown, Esq., Glasgow.	Benjamin Nicholson, Esq., Annan.
James King, Esq., Glasgow.	James Finlayson, Esq., Merchiston, Johnstone.
J. C. Bunten, Esq., Glasgow.	Abram Lyle, Esq., Greenock.

OFFICERS.—Sec. and Man., James Hay; Eng., Thomas J. Nicolls, M.Inst.C.E.; Solicitor, T. R. Mackenzie.

Offices—14, Bridge Street, Glasgow.

110.—GLASGOW AND PAISLEY JOINT.

In 1837 the Glasgow, Paisley, Kilmarnock, and Ayr (now the Glasgow and South Western), and the Glasgow, Paisley, and Greenock (now the Caledonian), were each incorporated. Between Glasgow and Paisley the two lines were laid out in nearly the same route, and the promoters agreed that that part of the latter company's line should be dropped, and that of the former company made a joint line, managed by a committee of eight directors, four from each company. The Glasgow, Paisley, Kilmarnock, and Ayr Acts of 1837 and 1840 regulate the line, while slight amendments of these acts applicable to the line are also contained in that company's acts of 1842 and 1845.

The South Western Additional Powers Act of 1863, authorising a junction of that company's Paisley and Renfrew Railway with the joint line, conferred on the joint line a user of the railway from the junction to Abercorn Station, Paisley, and of that station.

The Joint Line Act of 1864 authorised, among other things, the formation of the Govan Branch, and empowered the two companies to raise 70,000*l.* in shares and 23,200*l.* in loan, in equal proportions.

The Joint Line Act of 1874 authorised the widening of the main line to a point near Paisley passenger station, and also the opening up of Arkleston tunnel. Each company empowered to raise 100,000*l.* in shares, and 33,300*l.* on loans.

The Joint Line Act of 1883 authorised the widening of the main line through Paisley passenger station, and also the enlarging of that station. Each company empowered to raise 60,000*l.* additional capital, and to borrow 20,000*l.*

In Glasgow the South Western Company join the line from St. Enoch's at Shields Road, by means of the City Union, and the Caledonian from the Central at Bridge Street, where there is also a separate joint station, which is the terminus of the line.

The accounts are included in those of the Glasgow and South Western and Caledonian.

DIRECTORS:

Glasgow and South Western.
Robert Barclay, Esq., Glasgow.
Benjamin Nicholson, Esq., Annan.
James Finlayson, Esq., Merchiston, Johnstone.
Abram Lyle, Esq., Greenock.

Caledonian.
John Cowan, Esq., Stoneleigh, Greenock.
Hugh Brown, Esq., Glasgow.
James King, Esq., Glasgow.
J. C. Bunten, Esq., Glasgow.

OFFICERS.—Sec. and Man., James Hay; Eng., Thomas J. Nicolls, M.Inst.C.E.; Solicitor, T. R. Mackenzie.

Offices—14, Bridge Street, Glasgow.

111.—GLASGOW AND SOUTH WESTERN.

An amalgamation of the GLASGOW, PAISLEY, KILMARNOCK, AND AYR, and GLASGOW, DUMFRIES, AND CARLISLE, taking effect from the opening throughout from Cumnock to Gretna, 28th October, 1850. The terms were a reduction of the "G D and C" shares from 25*l.* to 8*l.* 6*s.* 8*d.* each, and distribution of the remaining capital required to complete the line *pro ratâ* amongst the shareholders of both companies. The main line, Glasgow to Ayr, 40 miles, was opened 12th August, 1843; the remainder, ending with completion of Dumfries Line, on 28th October, 1850. The Ayr and Dalmellington was opened in August, 1856.

The Consolidation Act of 26th June, 1855, entirely reconstituted the company. By the same act, a short extension of the Mayfield Branch into the Grouger coalfield, and a branch for connecting the main line with the Ardrossan, near the Eglinton iron works, were approved of.

PARLIAMENTARY POWERS:—

For list of Acts from 1858 to 1876, with short heads of the objects for which the various powers were sought, see the MANUAL for 1881, page 103.

FURTHER POWERS:—

1878—22ND JULY.—Construction of new lines, Nos. 1 and 2, at Glasgow, and Ayr Dock lines, Nos. 1, 2, 3, and 4 (in connection with St. Enoch Station and the northern portion of the City of Glasgow Union Lines). The former to be completed within five years, and the latter within three years from the passing of the act. New capital, 750,000*l.*; loans, &c., 250,000*l.*

1881—18TH JULY.—Extension of West Kilbride Branch to Largs, 2¼ miles; construction of branches to New Docks, at Garvel Park, Greenock, about 1¾ mile; and the conversion of Paisley Canal into a railway, about 9 miles. Capital, 450,000*l.*, and 150,000*l.* by mortgage.

1882—19TH JUNE.—A short branch, about a mile and a half in length, from the company's Paisley Canal Line, between Paisley and Elderslie; for the alteration and enlargement of certain bridges and acquisition of additional land for sidings, and also for the completion of the College Goods Station. Capital, 180,000*l.* in shares and 60,000*l.* by mortgage.

1883—29TH JUNE.—Construction of a railway, about 3 furlongs 4 chains, to join the fork formed by the Paisley Canal Line and the line authorised in 1882. Purchase of land, &c., for completion of College Station. Transfer from City Union Railway Company, and vesting of St. Enoch Station in the company. Creation of rent-charge stock in the company, in lieu of St. Enoch Station stock in the Union Company, and borrowing 250,000*l.* on mortgage.

AMALGAMATION, LEASES, AGREEMENTS, &c.:—

AYR AND MAYBOLE JUNCTION.—Incorporated by act of 1854. Length, 5½ miles. By act of 29th June, 1871, the Ayr and Maybole was vested in the Glasgow and South Western, at 7 per cent., as from 1st February, 1871.—For other particulars, see MANUAL for 1882, and previously.

AYRSHIRE LINES.—By act of 5th July, 1865, the Glasgow and South Western was authorised to construct six different branches of an aggregate length of 24 miles. New capital, 300,000*l.* in shares and 100,000*l.* on loan. Running powers and through booking in favour of the Caledonian. By act of 28th June, 1866, the company was authorised to construct other lines in Ayrshire of about 14 miles in length, with a further capital of 100,000*l.* in shares and 33,000*l.* on loan. Also to create debenture stock.

BRIDGE OF WEIR.—Incorporated by act of 7th July, 1862, to construct a line from Johnstone, on the Glasgow and South Western, to the village of Bridge of Weir. Length, 3¾ miles. Capital, 25,000*l.* in 10*l.* shares and 8,300*l.* on loan.

CASTLE DOUGLAS AND DUMFRIES.—Incorporated by act of 21st July, 1856, for making a railway from Castle Douglas, by Dalbeattie, to Dumfries, by a junction with the Glasgow and South Western, with which traffic arrangements are sanctioned. Capital, 120,000*l.* in 10*l.* shares; loans, 40,000*l.* Length, 19½ miles. By act of 21st July, 1859, the company was authorised to raise 72,000*l.*, at a preference of not exceeding 6 per cent., and 24,000*l.* on mortgage, in addition to capital authorised by original act.

CITY OF GLASGOW UNION.—See GENERAL INDEX.

CROFTHEAD AND KILMARNOCK.—Incorporated by act of 29th June, 1865, to construct a line from Crofthead to Kilmarnock, with a branch to Beith. Length, 20¼ miles. Capital, 240,000*l.* in shares and 80,000*l.* by mortgage. By act of 12th July, 1869, the Crofthead and Kilmarnock, with several deviations, was vested jointly in the Caledonian and Glasgow and South Western, the latter providing one-half of the capital. Completion of works extended to 1872.—See Glasgow and Kilmarnock Joint Line.

GIRVAN AND PORTPATRICK JUNCTION.—See GENERAL INDEX.

GREENOCK AND AYRSHIRE.—Incorporated by act of 5th July, 1865, for making a railway from Greenock, by Bridge of Weir, to Howwood, with a junction with Glasgow and South Western Company's line at both those places (for further particulars, see previous MANUALS). Length, 15 miles. By act of 18th July, 1872, this undertaking was amalgamated with the Glasgow and South Western as from 1st August, 1872.

KIRKCUDBRIGHT.—Incorporated by act of 1st August, 1861, to construct a line from Castle Douglas to Kirkcudbright. Length, 10¼ miles. Capital, 60,000*l.* in 10*l.* shares and 20,000*l.* on loan.

KILMARNOCK JOINT LINE.—By act of 2nd June, 1865, the Glasgow and South Western was authorised to construct new lines between Kilmarnock and Glasgow. Length, 22 miles. Capital, 500,000*l.* in shares and 166,600*l.* on loan. The Glasgow and Kilmarnock Joint Line Act, 1869, authorised the abandonment of the Kilmarnock Direct, and made the line by Crofthead joint property with the Caledonian, and reduced the ordinary 10*l.* shares to 7*l.* 10*s.* per share, and cancelled the remaining call.—See Glasgow and Kilmarnock Joint Line.

MAYBOLE AND GIRVAN.—Incorporated by act of 14th July, 1856, to make a railway from the town of Maybole to the town and harbour of Girvan. Capital, 68,000*l.* in 10*l.* shares; loans, 22,600*l.* Length, 12¾ miles. By act of 21st July, 1859, certain deviations were authorised, as well as new capital to the extent of 45,000*l.*, in 5 per cent. preference shares, and 15,000*l.* on loan.

PAISLEY CANAL.—By act of 24th June, 1869, the Glasgow, Paisley, and Johnstone Canal was vested in the Glasgow and South Western, the annual payment in respect to which is fixed at 3,471*l.* 12*s.* 8*d.*, such sum to be paid in priority of dividend on the ordinary stock of the railway. By act of 29th June, 1871, the Glasgow and South Western was authorised to raise 25,250*l.* in preference or ordinary shares, with 65,000*l.* by borrowing, for the purpose of providing funds for the payment of the canal debts and shares acquired under the act of 1869. By an act of 18th July, 1881, the company obtained powers to shut up the canal and convert the portion lying between Glasgow, Paisley, and Elderslie into a railway.

WEST KILBRIDE TO FAIRLIE.—This extension (3¾ miles) was opened on the 1st June, 1880, and to Fairlie Pier on the 1st July, 1882.

ACCOUNTS:—

The ordinary half-yearly meeting of this company was held on the 18th September, 1884, when the Directors' report and statement of accounts then presented were adopted. The following is an abstract of the accounts for the half-year ended 31st July, 1884, viz.:—

CAPITAL.

Receipts.		*Disbursements.*	
From shares, viz.:—		Lines and works open for traffic	£10,023,016
Ordinary stock	£4,927,920	Lines and works in course of construction	468,188
Preference stocks	4,733,749	Lines authorised but not constructed	8,669
Total stock and share capital	£9,661,669	Working	1,632,749
From loans, viz.:—		Subscriptions to other railways	370,000
Debentures £230,310		Glasgow and Paisley canal	62,163
Debenture stock 2,379,019	= 2,609,329		
	£12,270,998		
Premiums on issue of stocks and shares	126,157		
Balance Dr.	167,630		
	£12,564,785		£12,564,785

CONSOLIDATION SCHEME.—For the nominal addition to capital in the scheme for the consolidation and conversion of the guaranteed and preference stocks, &c., &c., see *Appendix* to the MANUAL for 1882.

SAINT ENOCH STATION RENT-CHARGE STOCK.—In the latter part of 1883 the existing Saint Enoch Station 4 per cent. stock of the City of Glasgow Union Company was converted into a rent-charge stock under the above title (see also City of Glasgow Union).

TABLE OF PRIORITIES, DESCRIPTIONS, DIVIDENDS, &c. (see also notes):—

No.	Year of Act.	FULL DESCRIPTION (to be observed in Transfer Deeds and all other Legal Documents).	Rate ₩ cent ₩ annum.
1	Various	Mortgage	Various
2	Various	4 per cent. funded debt (debenture stock)	4
3	1876	Guaranteed 4 per cent. stock	4
4	1876	Preference 4 per cent. stock	4
5	1878	4½ per cent. (convertible) preference stock	4½
6	1878	10*l.* 5 per cent. preference (convertible) shares	5
7	1881	10*l.* 4 per cent. preference shares, 1882, allotted to holders of ordinary stock on the 18th July, 1882, at the rate of one share for each 80*l.* of stock. Price, par. First call, 2*l.* per share, paid 1st August, 1882. 2nd call, 8*l.* per share, paid 29th September, 1883	4
8	Various	Ordinary consolidated stock	...
9	1876	Deferred stock	...

NOTES.—On No. 1 the interest is accumulative, and payable half-yearly on 15th May and 11th November.

On No. 2 the dividend is accumulative, and payable half-yearly on 2nd February and 2nd August. Transfer books close 14 days before payment.

On No. 3 the dividend is also accumulative.

On Nos. 3 to 8 dividends are payable 31st March and 30th September, the transfer books closing 21 days before the half-yearly meeting.

Nos. 3, 4, and 9 were issued under the consolidation scheme, dated 1st March, 1881, authorised by act of June, 1876.

Nos. 5 and 6 are convertible at the option of the holders into ordinary stock at *par*, as from 31st July, 1885, on notice being given not later than 30th September, 1885.

No. 9 (deferred) participates in any dividend paid to the ordinary stock above 5 per cent. per annum.

TRANSFER DEPARTMENT QUERIES AND REPLIES.

Queries.	Replies.
Transfer form—ordinary or special?	Ordinary.
Fee per deed?	2*s.* 6*d.* each stock.
Ditto if more sellers than one?	2*s.* 6*d.* each.
May several classes of stock be transferred on one deed?	Yes.
Are certificates required to accompany transfers?	Yes.
What amounts of stock are transferable, and are parts of 1*l.* sterling allowed to be transferred?	13*s.* 4*d.* and 6*s.* 8*d.* of ordinary, but no fraction of a 1*l.* of any other stock.
To what officer should transfer communications be sent?	Secretary.
In acceptances, renunciations, &c., of allotments of new stock, proxies, or other forms sent to trustees, what signatures are required?	For proxies first name only; in other cases it depends how the stock is registered.

The estimate of further expenditure on capital account is as given below:—

	During half-year ending 31st Jan., 1885.	In subsequent half-years	Total.	
Lines and works open for traffic—	£	£	£	£
Land and works on Glasgow & Paisley Joint (one-half)..	11,500	50,000	61,500	
Do. do. Glasgow & Kilmarnock Joint (do.)	3,308	26,055	29,363	
Extension and completion of stations and depots, additional sidings, platforms, land and compensation, &c.	78,778	282,181	360,959	
	93,586	358,236		451,822
Lines and works in course of construction—				
Largs Line; Garvel Dock Lines, and arches under road and aqueduct at Greenock; Paisley Canal Line, and branch to Potterhill	165,000	109,120	..	274,120
Working stock, including continuous brake appliances ..	5,350	8,750	..	14,100
Amount of estimated further expenditure....	263,936	476,106	..	740,042
Permissive powers to subscribe to other railways—				
Under Girvan and Portpatrick Junction Railway Company's Acts, 1865 and 1870	..	..	50,000	150,000
Under Solway Junction Railway Company's Act, 1866..	..	..	100,000	
Total	..	..	..	£890,042

The capital powers and other available assets are as under:—

Share capital authorised, but not created or sanctioned		£230,000
Stock and share capital created but not received:—		
Calls in arrear	£21	
Amount uncalled, less paid in advance	253,310	
		253,331
Loans and debenture stock—balance of available borrowing powers	409,471	
Less—capitalised amount of feu duties	85,130 =	324,341
		£807,672
Deduct—balance at debit of capital account		167,630
Total available assets		£640,041

Revenue.

The following is a comparative view of the working of this undertaking for the last three half-years, viz.:—

Receipts.	1883. July 31.	1884. Jan. 31.	1884. July 31.
Passengers, parcels, horses, and mails	£233,328	£235,055	£234,465
Goods, minerals (less cartage), and live stock	319,183	324,230	311,535
Rents, fees, mileage, way-leave, and telegraphs	8,494	17,449	17,172
Dividends on shares in other companies	9,125	5,775	5,475
	£570,130	£582,509	£568,647

Expenses.	1883. July 31.	1884. Jan. 31.	1884. July 31.
Maintenance of way, works, and stations	£59,986	£53,856	£57,500
Locomotive power	70,055	73,147	69,355
Carriage and wagon repairs	35,418	33,110	34,570
Traffic expenses	78,769	80,596	79,901
General charges	11,660	11,919	12,215
Ordinary working charges	£255,888	£252,628	£253,541
Law and Parliamentary	3,337	1,370	10,578
Compensation	2,362	3,155	1,488
Rates, taxes, and Government duty	16,726	25,349	14,138
Total working expenses	£278,313	£282,502	£279,745
Preference charges, viz.:—			
Feu dues and ground rent	2,911	3,086	2,914
Interest on loan capital and general interest account	48,811	54,104	55,602
Rents, annuities, &c.	33,991	33,066	32,689
Dividend on preference capital	76,157	80,168	81,371
	£440,183	£453,521	£452,321
Net balances each half-year	£129,947	£128,988	£116,326
Balances brought from previous half-years	7,492	7,528	6,605
Balances available for dividend on ordinary stock	£137,439	£136,516	£122,931
Dividends declared at 5½, 5½, and 4¾ per cent. respectively	129,911	129,911	117,038
Surplus carried forward	£7,528	£6,605	£5,893

Summary showing the results of the last half-year's working compared with that of the corresponding period of 1883, viz.:—

Net balance 31st July, 1883	£129,947	Thus:—	
„ 31st July, 1884	116,326	Gross receipts—decrease	£1,483
		Working charges—increase £1,432	
		Preference charges—inc. 10,706	
			12,138
Loss in 1884	£13,621	Net loss in 1884	£13,621

Per centage of traffic receipts and expenses per train mile for the last three half-years, viz.:—

31st July, 1883.			31st January, 1884.			31st July, 1884.		
Receipts.	Expenses.	Per cent. of Expenses on Traffic Receipts.	Receipts.	Expenses.	Per cent. of Expenses on Traffic Receipts.	Receipts.	Expenses.	Per cent. of Expenses on Traffic Receipts.
4·94*s.*	2·48*s.*	50·37.	4·88*s.*	2·47*s.*	50·02.	4·90*s.*	2·51*s.*	51·23.

MILEAGE.—*Authorised*, 364½; *constructed*, 349; *constructing, or to be constructed*, 15½; *other lines worked*, 38. Foreign lines worked over, 15¾; total, 402¼. Productive mileage, 329.

No. of Directors—10. *Qualification*, 1,000*l.* stock.

DIRECTORS:

Chairman—1 MATTHEW WILLIAM THOMPSON, Esq., Park Gate, Guiseley, near Leeds.

Deputy-Chairman—2 ROBERT BARCLAY, Esq., 21, Park Terrace, Glasgow.

8 James Finlayson, Esq., of Merchiston, Johnstone.
7 Benjamin Nicholson, Esq., Annan.
9 Abram Lyle, Esq., Greenock.
10 R. W. Cochran-Patrick, Esq., M.P., of Woodside, Beith.
4 Peter Clouston, Esq., 1, Park Terrace, Glasgow.
5 John Campbell White, Esq., Merchant, Glasgow.
3 James Brown, Esq., Viewfield, Bellahouston, Glasgow.
6 W. Renny Watson, Esq., 18, Woodlands Terrace, Glasgow.

Retiring directors eligible without waiting.

OFFICERS.—Sec., John Morton; Gen. Man., W. J. Wainwright; Eng., Andrew Galloway; Supt. of Line, John Mathieson; Man. of Goods Traffic, David Dickie; Supt. of Loco. Dept., Hugh Smellie; Accountant and Cashier, James Thomson; Audit Clerk, William Brown; Auditors, William MacLean and Walter Mackenzie; Solicitor, Thomas Brunton.

Head Offices—St. Enoch Station, Glasgow.

112.—GLASGOW, YOKER, AND CLYDEBANK.

Incorporated by act of 4th July, 1878, for making a railway and branches from the Stobcross Railway to Yoker and Clydebank. Length, about 3¼ miles. Period for completion, 5 years. Arrangements with the North British, which company may subscribe to the extent of 25,000*l.* towards the undertaking, and appoint persons to vote at general meetings. Capital, 85,000*l.* in 10*l.* shares, with power to divide into "preferred" and "deferred" half-shares. Borrowing powers, 28,300*l.*

By act of 29th June, 1883, the company was authorised to make a short line at Govan. New capital, 17,500*l.*; loans, &c., 5,830*l.* Power was also given to enter into agreement with North British.

Opened December, 1882.

Agreement with North British.—In October, 1881, the directors issued a prospectus, inviting applications for the share capital of the company, in which the following was stated to be the arrangement entered into with the North British, viz.:—"An agreement confirmed by an Act of Session, 1880, has been entered into with the North British, to endure for 10 years from the passing of the act of 1878, and for such further period from the expiry of the said period, not exceeding 10 years, as the Board of Trade may, after the lapse of said period, determine. By that agreement the North British engage to work and manage the traffic upon and maintain the railway, and provide all necessary locomotive power, rolling stock, and plant for a remuneration of 50 per cent. of the gross earnings. The agreement also provides that, if the net receipts from the local traffic on the railway do not suffice to yield 5¼ per cent. per annum to the shareholders from the date of the opening of the railway, the North British are to make good any deficiency out of the receipts (after deducting 50 per cent. for working expenses) accruing to them each year from the through traffic passing over their own line to or from the railway. As a large part of the traffic will consist of goods and minerals carried for long distances over the North British, the receipts accruing to them ought to form a sufficient guarantee for the minimum dividend on the comparatively small capital of the Yoker and Clydebank. In addition to this provision for a minimum dividend of 5¼ per cent. per annum, the agreement further stipulates that any surplus revenues of the company over that rate, less any sum advanced by the North British to make good any previous deficiencies, with interest thereon at 4 per cent., are to be divided equally between the company and the North British.

Meetings half-yearly, in March or April and September or October.

No. of Directors.—Minimum, 4; maximum, 6; quorum, 2 and 3 respectively. *Qualification*, 25 shares.

Quorum of meetings—10 shareholders, holding in the aggregate not less than 2,000*l.* in the capital of the company.

DIRECTORS:

James Robert Napier, Esq.
James Rodger Thomson, Esq.
Burnett Harvey, Esq.
Isaac Beardmore, Esq., Parkhead Forge, Glasgow.
Robert Twentyman Napier, Esq.

One other to be appointed.

113.—GLENARIFF RAILWAY AND PIER.

Incorporated by act of 26th August, 1880, for the construction and maintenance of a railway (about 2¾ miles) from Parkmore, by a junction with the Ballymena, Cushendall, and Redbay, to Cloghcor, on the bank of the Lower River, with a Pier, at Glenariff, to be purchased from the Glenariff Iron Ore and Harbour Co. Limited. Period for completion of works, five years. Capital, 70,000*l.* in 10*l.* shares; borrowing powers, 20,000*l.*

No. of Directors.—Maximum, 5; minimum, 3; quorum, 3 and 2. *Qualification*, 30 shares.

FIRST DIRECTORS:

Anthony Traill, Esq.
William McCandlish, Esq.
Thomas Sterling Begbie, Esq.
James Van Homrigh Irwin, Esq., 36, Wallbrook, E.C.
One other to be nominated.

114.—GOLDEN VALLEY.

Incorporated 13th July, 1876, to construct a railway from the Great Western, at Pontrilas, to Dorstone. Length, 10¾ miles. Capital, 60,000*l.* in 10*l.* shares and 20,000*l.* on loan. Power to enter into working agreements with the Great Western. Facilities to London and North Western.

By act of 19th June, 1882, the time for completion of works is extended until the 2nd of August, 1884, and a preference or priority for payment of dividends is attached to 2,400 10*l.* shares, part of the capital of the company. The company are by that act also empowered to borrow 20,000*l.* for payment of debts and liabilities.

By act of 14th August, 1884, powers were obtained for the abandonment of a portion of Railway No. 1, act 1877, and substitute two new lines at Clifford and Cusop. Length, about 6 miles. New capital, 45,000*l.*; loans, 15,000*l.*

Opened September 1st, 1881, and now in operation.

No. of Directors—5; minimum, 3; quorum, 3. *Qualification*, 25 shares.

DIRECTORS:

Thomas F. Lewis, Esq.
Richard D. Green-Price, Esq.
Henry Haywood, Esq.
Edward L. G. Robinson, Esq.

OFFICERS.—Sec., Frederick Bodenham, Hereford; Man., E. A. Taunton, Vowchurch, Herefordshire; Eng., G. Wells Owen, Westminster, S.W.

115.—GORSEDDA JUNCTION AND PORTMADOC.

Incorporated by act of 25th July, 1872, for the purpose of adapting and maintaining an existing railway from the Gorsedda Slate Quarry to Portmadoc, and of making an extension from Blaen-y-Pennant, in the county of Carnarvon, to join the existing line. Lengths, 8½ miles and 5¼ miles. Gauge, 2 feet. Capital, 20,000*l.* in 10*l.* shares; loans, 6,666*l.* in debentures.

By act of 13th July, 1876, the company was authorised to maintain two existing portions of railway diverted from the course authorised by the act of 1872; to construct a siding in the parish of Ynyscynhairn; to use a portion of the Festiniog Railway; and to raise 10,000*l.* additional share capital, and borrow a further sum of 3,333*l.*

At a special meeting held on the 22nd September, 1876, a resolution was passed sanctioning the issue of 1,000 perpetual 5 per cent. first preference shares of 10*l.* each.

Working agreements and traffic facilities with the Cambrian, Festiniog, and the Portmadoc, Croesor, and Beddgelert. The line was opened for slate, mineral, and goods traffic on the 2nd September, 1875. In operation, 11¼ miles.

CAPITAL.—The expenditure on this account to 30th June, 1883, amounted to 31,560*l.*, whilst the receipts to the same date had been as under:—

Ordinary 10*l* shares	£19,995
165 perpetual 5 per cent. first preference 10*l.* shares	2,100
Loans at 6 per cent.	800
Loans at 8 per cent.	5,800

No. of Directors—7; minimum, 3; quorum, 3 and 2. *Qualification*, 200*l.*

DIRECTORS:

James Stewart, Esq., 49, Leadenhall Street, E.C.
Charles Barton, Esq., Holbrook House, Wincanton.
Rev. Logan Logan, Eastcliffe House, Bournemouth.

OFFICERS.—Sec., G. J. Gray; Auditor, Edward Brooks.
Offices—St. Clement's House, Clement's Lane, E.C.

116.—GREAT EASTERN.

Incorporated by act of 7th August, 1862, and comprising the EASTERN COUNTIES, NORFOLK, EASTERN UNION, EAST ANGLIAN, EAST SUFFOLK, and other subsidiary undertakings in connection therewith. Productive, 983 miles, including 116¼ miles of joint lines.

PARLIAMENTARY POWERS:—

For a list of Acts from 1863 to 1879, with short heads of the objects for which the various powers were sought, see the MANUAL for 1881, pages 109 and 110.

FURTHER POWERS:—

1881—3RD JUNE.—Transfer of the East Norfolk undertaking to this company, see particulars under that head further on.

1881—18TH JULY.—Various powers for widening of railways and other alterations and improvements in relation to the Great Eastern itself, and other undertakings. New capital, 700,000*l*.; borrowing powers, 230,300*l*.

1882—24TH JULY.—Additional lines in the counties of Middlesex, Hertford, and Cambridge; improvements on March and Spalding Line; tramways at Wisbeach; diversion of Hertford Branch; and other purposes. New capital, 450,000*l*.; borrowing powers, 41,666*l*.

1883—29TH JUNE.—Vesting of Tendring Hundred and Clacton-on-Sea companies, see further on.

1883—16TH JULY.—New railways and docks, widenings and improvements in the county of Essex, at Shenfield, Wickford, Rayleigh, Prittlewell, Burnham, Southminster, Heybridge, and Walthamstow. Length of new lines, about 48 miles. Period for completion, railways 5 years, graving dock at St. Nicholas, Harwich, 7 years. New capital, 1,500,000*l*. Loans, &c., 500,000*l*. Power to enter into agreements with London, Brighton, and South Coast, and London, Chatham, and Dover undertakings jointly or separately.

AMALGAMATIONS, LEASES, AGREEMENTS, &c.:—

I. EASTERN COUNTIES, which is mainly formed of two arteries—the one to Colchester and the other to Cambridge; the first was incorporated by act of 1836, for a railway from London to Norwich and Yarmouth, by Romford, Chelmsford, Colchester, and Ipswich. Owing, however, to difficulties in raising the requisite funds, the original scheme was not carried beyond Colchester.

NEWMARKET.—By resolutions, 17th April, 1851, this line is worked at the rate of 40 per cent. on gross receipts, under an agreement dated 28th May, 1851 (confirmed by an act obtained 28th May, 1852), whereby the Newmarket proprietors received such a sum as, with their own net earnings, were sufficient to make up a dividend of 3 per cent. per annum on their share capital of 350,000*l*.

NEWMARKET-BURY EXTENSION.—Incorporated by act of 16th July, 1846, as the NEWMARKET AND CHESTERFORD, for a line from Chesterford Junction (Eastern Counties) to Newmarket, with a branch to Cambridge, 23 miles. In 1847 the company obtained power to extend the line to Thetford (junction with Norfolk), and its title was altered; also to make branches to Ely on the one hand and Bury St. Edmunds on the other. The Eastern Counties purchased the original line at 15*l*. per share, payable in debentures at three years' date, bearing 4 per cent. interest in the meantime, and to work the extension at 5 per cent. upon the outlay, not exceeding 145,000*l*.

NORTHERN AND EASTERN.—See GENERAL INDEX.

II. NORFOLK.—An amalgamation of the YARMOUTH AND NORWICH and NORWICH AND BRANDON. The former was incorporated 18th June, 1842, for a line from Norwich to the port of Yarmouth. The latter was incorporated in 1844, for a line in continuation from Norwich to Brandon (where a junction was formed with the Eastern Counties), with a branch to East Dereham, which has since been continued to Fakenham.

EPPING.—Incorporated by act of 13th August, 1859, for connecting Loughton, Epping, and Chipping Ongar. Capital, 100,000*l*. in 10*l*. shares; loans, 33,000*l*. The first line commences by two junctions with the Woodford and Loughton Branch of the Great Eastern and terminates near Epping; the second by a junction with the first near Coopersale, and terminates near Chipping Ongar. By act of 29th July, 1862, the Epping was transferred to the Eastern Counties, and thence became a portion of the Great Eastern.

WELLS AND FAKENHAM.—Incorporated by act of 24th July, 1854. The line (10 miles) was promoted by residents in the districts, who determined to obtain possession of the land at reasonable prices before commencing the works. Capital, 70,000*l*. in 20*l*. shares; power to borrow extends to 23,000*l*. By act of 13th August, 1859, the company was authorised to extend the line along the quay at Wells, to raise additional capital to the extent of 3,800*l*. at 6 per cent. preference, with loans of 1,200*l*., and to convert the debenture debt into stock. By the same act the Norfolk guaranteed interest or dividend on the new capital of 3,800*l*., provided the annual net revenue would so permit.

III. EASTERN UNION.—An amalgamation (under powers obtained in 1867) of the original EASTERN UNION and the IPSWICH AND BURY. The Eastern Union was incorporated in 1844, for a line (18 miles) from Colchester to Ipswich. The Ipswich and Bury was incorporated for a line from Ipswich to Bury St. Edmunds, with an extension from Haughley to Norwich. The Eastern Union leases the Colchester and Stour Valley, which see.

WAVENEY VALLEY.—Incorporated by act of 3rd July, 1851, for a line from the Tivetshall Station of the Eastern Union, and terminating at Bungay, Suffolk. Length, 13 miles.—For brief heads of other legislation, see previous MANUALS.

IV. EAST ANGLIAN.—An amalgamation of three distinct companies, viz., the LYNN AND ELY, a line from a junction with the Eastern Counties, at Ely, to the port of Lynn, with a branch to Wisbech, 36½ miles; the LYNN AND DEREHAM, a line from a junction with a branch of the Norfolk and Dereham, to join the Lynn and Ely, at Lynn, 26½ miles; and ELY AND HUNTINGDON, a line from a junction with the Lynn and Ely, at Ely, to Huntingdon, 22½ miles.—At a special meeting on 22nd September, 1863, it was resolved to divide the East Anglian stock into two classes, one to be called No. 1 stock, amounting to 206,721*l.*, to be entitled to fixed dividends at the rate of 5*l.* per cent., and the other to be called East Anglian No. 2 stock, amounting to 826,885*l.*, to be entitled to a dividend thereon equal to one-half of the amount of dividend exceeding 3*l.* per cent., which shall in any half-year be declared upon the ordinary stock. The practical effect of the arrangement is that every proprietor of 100*l.* stock became entitled to 20*l* of a new 5*l.* per cent. stock, and 80*l.* of a stock bearing a dividend equal to *one-half* of the excess over 3*l.* per cent. paid at any time on Great Eastern ordinary stock, *one-half* of such excess on 80*l.* being the same as *two-fifths* on 100*l.*

V. EAST SUFFOLK.—Incorporated as HALESWORTH, BECCLES, AND HADDISCOE by act of 5th June, 1851, for a line from Halesworth to Beccles, and to join the Lowestoft at Haddiscoe, in Norfolk, with a branch. By act of 1854 the name of the company was changed to "East Suffolk" (for sundry other particulars, see previous MANUALS). By act of 22nd July, 1861, the company was authorised to determine the lease to Sir Morton Peto. The Great Eastern issued to the East Suffolk 340,000*l.* debenture stock, bearing a guaranteed dividend of 4 per cent., and a further sum of 335,000*l.* 4½ per cent. preference stock. Out of this stock the East Suffolk indemnify the Great Eastern against the fixed liabilities of 340,000*l.* debenture stock, 86,488*l.* simple contract debts, and 177,860*l.* East Suffolk stock, convertible into preference stock or redeemable at par. The Great Eastern to issue to the East Suffolk such an amount of ordinary stock, fully paid up, as Captain Galton determined to be the amount of that ordinary stock, which, taking into consideration the probable natural future development of the traffic of the East Suffolk undertaking, ought to be so issued.

VI. SUNDRIES.—BISHOP'S STORTFORD, DUNMOW, AND BRAINTREE.—Incorporated by act of 22nd July, 1861, to construct a line from Bishop's Stortford, on the Great Eastern, through Dunmow to Braintree, with a branch to join the Epping at Dunmow. Length, 19 miles. Capital, 120,000*l.* in 10*l.* shares; loans, 40,000*l.* By act of 29th June, 1865, this line was vested in the Great Eastern, and by act of 31st July, 1868, it was provided that the Great Eastern should pay, in debentures and stock, an ascertained balance due to the contractors, on which the Bishop's Stortford became part of the Great Eastern system.

BLACKWALL.—By act of 12th June, 1865, the Blackwall was leased to the Great Eastern from 1st January, 1866, at a fixed guarantee of 4½ per cent. on its ordinary stock, the London and North Western, the Great Northern, and the Midland obtaining various running powers.

BURY ST. EDMUNDS AND THETFORD.—Incorporated by act of 5th July, 1865, to construct a line from Bury St. Edmunds to Thetford, to and from the Great Eastern, at these places. Opened 1st March, 1876. In operation, 12¾ miles. The report for the half-year ended 30th June, 1878, stated that the line had been sold to the Great Eastern for 33,300*l.* of that company's 4 per cent. debenture stock, and 75,000*l.* of that company's ordinary stock. It was estimated that in addition to the 68,572*l.* received on account of shares, and 21,100*l.* received on account of debentures, it would take 25,000*l.* to discharge all the liabilities of the company, and the cost of winding up its affairs. The sale was effected under the powers contained in the Act 41 and 42 Vic., cap. 175, 22nd July, 1878.

CLACTON-ON-SEA.—Incorporated by act of 7th August, 1877. Length, about 4¼ miles from Great Clacton to Thorpe-le-Soken. Transferred to Great Eastern by act of 29th June, 1883, as from 1st July, 1883.—For other particulars previously, see MANUAL for 1883, page 52.

ELY AND ST. IVES (late Ely, Haddenham, and Sutton).—Incorporated by act of 23rd June, 1864, to construct a line from Ely, through Haddenham, to Sutton. Length, 6¾ miles. Capital, 36,000*l.* in 10*l.* shares and 12,000*l.* on loan. The Great Eastern subscribed 12,000*l.*, and worked the line at 50 per cent. of the traffic receipts. By act of 7th April, 1876, the company was authorised to extend its line to the St. Ives and March Railway of the Great Eastern at Holywell-cum-Needingworth. Length, 8½ miles. New capital, 60,000*l.*; borrowing powers, 20,000*l.* On completion of the extension line the name of the company was changed to "Ely and St. Ives." The extension was opened in the beginning of 1878. Under the powers of a Board of Trade Certificate, the company, in 1882, raised 2,000*l.* additional capital, which is added to the 36,000*l.* raised under the act of 1864. By an agreement scheduled to the company's act of 1876, the Great Eastern take the line for a term of 999 years, paying administration expenses, interest on debentures and debenture stocks, 4 per cent. on the 38,000*l.* stock, and 5 per cent. on the 60,000*l.* stock. By the Great Eastern Act of 21st July, 1879, that company takes power to lease the line on terms based upon the agreement.—Secretary, James B. Bond, 4, Queen Anne's Gate, Great Queen Street, Westminster, S.W.

EAST NORFOLK.—Formerly worked by the Great Eastern at 50 per cent. of the gross receipts; now vested in that company under act of 3rd June, 1881. The following official communication was issued at the time of the amalgamation, viz.:—"This amalgamation having taken place, I have to inform you that the stocks of the former company have now become stocks in this company in the following proportions, viz.:—

East Norfolk Stocks.	*Great Eastern Stocks.*
4 per cent. debenture	Equal amount of 4 per cent. debenture stock.
6 per cent. first preference	125 per cent. of 4 per cent. preference stock, 1881; and 33 per cent. of deferred ordinary stock.
6 per cent. second preference	125 per cent. of 4 per cent. preference stock, 1881.
Aylsham Extension	125 per cent. of 4 per cent. preference stock, 1881.
Ordinary	75 per cent. of deferred ordinary stock.

So soon as the necessary arrangements have been made, the East Norfolk certificates will be called in for exchange. Until this has been done they will be received with any transfers for the equivalent amount of new stock, but the present proportion must be inserted in all deeds sent in for registration. No transfers can be received for fractions of 1*l.* Any such arising out of the exchange will be paid by the company in cash."

RAMSEY.—Incorporated 22nd July, 1861, to construct a line from Holme, on the Great Northern, to Ramsey, in Huntingdonshire. Length, 5¾ miles. Capital, 30,000*l.* in 10*l.* shares and 10,000*l.* on loan; almost the whole of which is held in trust for the Great Eastern. Opened in July, 1863. Worked by the Great Northern. By act of 19th July, 1875, the line was vested in the Great Eastern, by whom it was leased to the Great Northern for 21 years.

SAFFRON WALDEN.—Incorporated by act of 22nd July, 1861, to construct a line from Wenden, on the Great Eastern, to Saffron Walden. Length, 2 miles. Capital, 25,000*l.* in 10*l.* shares and 8,000*l.* on loan. By act of 22nd June, 1863, the company was authorised to construct an extension to Bartlow, on the Great Eastern. Length, 6¼ miles. New capital, 70,000*l.* in 10*l.* shares and 23,000*l.* on loan. The Great Eastern subscribes 28,000*l.* By act of 28th June, 1877, this undertaking became vested in the Great Eastern, who purchased it on the following terms, viz.:—The sale to take effect on the 1st January, 1877, the consideration to be 70,750*l.*, payable as follows, viz.: 12,500*l.* in 5 per cent. preference; 26,800*l.* ordinary and 31,000*l.* in 4 per cent. debenture stocks of the latter company respectively, together with 450*l.* in cash, the whole to be divided amongst the proprietary of the Saffron as follows:—The Saffron preference holders to receive 50 per cent. of Great Eastern preference stock; the debenture stock to be distributed amongst the Saffron debenture holders; the ordinary stock, 450*l.* in cash, and other assets, after payment of debts, to be distributed rateably amongst the Saffron ordinary shareholders.

TENDRING HUNDRED.—Incorporated by act of 13th August, 1859. Length, 2¼ miles, from Hythe to Wivenhoe. Amalgamated with Great Eastern by act of 29th June, 1883, as from 1st July, 1883, the ordinary stock being exchanged for Great Eastern ordinary stock at the rate of 70*l.* of the latter for every 100*l.* of the former; the debenture stock being exchanged for Great Eastern 4 per cent. debenture stock *pro rata*.—For other particulars of the position of this undertaking prior to amalgamation, see MANUAL for 1883, page 323.

THETFORD AND WATTON, AND WATTON AND SWAFFHAM.—*Thetford and Watton.*—Incorporated by act of 16th July, 1866, for a line from Thetford, on the Great Eastern, to Watton. Length, 9 miles. Capital, 45,000*l.* in 10*l.* shares; 15,000*l.* on loan. By act of 7th July, 1873, the company obtained power to extend the line to join the Bury St. Edmunds and Thetford, to use portion of the Great Eastern, to subscribe 10,000*l.* to the Watton and Swaffham, and to enter into working agreements with the Bury St. Edmunds and Thetford. New capital, 16,000*l.* in shares and 5,300*l* on loan. *Watton and Swaffham.*—Incorporated by act of 12th July, 1869, to construct an extension of the Thetford and Watton to the Great Eastern at Swaffham. Length, 9½ miles. Capital, 60,000*l.* in 10*l.* shares and 20,000*l.* on loan. Power in conjunction with the Thetford and Watton to make use of part of Great Eastern, which is to afford facilities. Working arrangements with Thetford and Watton. By act of 18th May, 1872, an extension of time for completion of works was authorised till 1st August, 1875. Opened 15th November, 1875. Under act of 21st July, 1879, these companies are leased to the Great Eastern for 999 years from the 1st March, 1880, at the following rentals, viz.:—

	For Thetford and Watton. £	For Watton and Swaffham. £
For the year 1880	1,500	1,500
„ 1881	1,600	1,600
„ 1882	1,700	1,700
„ 1883	1,800	1,800
„ 1884	1,900	1,900
„ 1885	2,000	2,000
„ 1886	2,100	2,100
For the year 1887	2,200	2,200
„ 1888	2,250	2,250
„ 1889	2,350	2,250
„ 1890	2,450	2,250
„ 1891 and every subsequent year	2,550	2,250

Secretary and Accountant (to both companies), T. C Line, 68, Lincoln's Inn Fields, W.C.

TOTTENHAM AND HAMPSTEAD JUNCTION.—An agreement for working this line received the approval of the proprietors in June, 1862.

WARE, HADHAM, AND BUNTINGFORD.—Incorporated by act of 12th July, 1858, to construct a line from the Eastern Counties at Ware to Buntingford. Capital, 50,000*l.* in 10*l.* shares, and 16,000*l.* by loan. The Great Eastern subscribed 22,000*l.* to this line, and works the traffic.

PROPOSED AMALGAMATION WITH GREAT NORTHERN.—In 1877, negotiations for the amalgamation of this company with the Great Northern took place, but were broken off, and the "Northern Extension" scheme substituted.—For more detailed particulars under this head, see the MANUAL for 1878.

SUBSCRIPTIONS TO OTHER LINES, &C.—The Great Eastern has subscribed to the following railways the sums stated below:—

Lynn and Hunstanton	£20,000
Tottenham and Hampstead Junction	103,300
West Norfolk	30,000
Mistley, Thorpe, and Walton	13,200
Tendring Hundred	28,000
Ely, Haddenham, and Sutton	12,000
Wivenhoe and Brightlingsea	8,330
Downham and Stoke Ferry	33,000
King's Lynn Dock	20,000
	£267,830

ACCOUNTS:—

The 44th ordinary half-yearly meeting of this company was held on the 29th July, 1884, when the reports and accounts then presented were adopted. The following gives an abstract of the respective accounts for the half-year ended 30th June, 1884:—

CAPITAL.—*Authorised:* Shares and stock, 28,814,579*l.*; loans, 12,841,882*l*: total, 41,656,461*l.* *Created or sanctioned:* Shares and stock, 28,245,221*l.*; loans, 12,841,882*l.*

total, 41,087,108*l*. The following statement shows the amounts received and expended on this account to 30th June, 1884:—

Receipts.

Share capital, viz.:—		
Ordinary stock	£12,273,016	
Deferred ordinary stock, 1881	81,531	
		£12,354,547
Preference capital, viz.:—		
5 per cent.	£3,147,817	
4 "	11,256,718	
4½ "	292,281	
		£14,696,766
Total share capital		£26,969,782
Loan capital, viz.:—		
Debentures	£782,684	
Ditto stocks (red.)	2,837,120	
Ditto (irred.)	8,601,890	
		£12,221,694
Total share and loan capital		£39,191,476
Sundries, being mortgages and "B" debenture stock redeemed, premium on debenture, &c., stocks sold not entitled to dividend, telegraphic award, and Colchester and Stour Valley stocks held (16,870*l*.)		520,607
		£39,712,083
Balance		245,931
		£39,958,014

Expenditure.

Lines open for traffic, including working stock	£31,786,218
Lines in course of construction	159,160
Great Northern and Great Eastern Joint Lines	1,317,983
Additional working stock	2,325,900
Subscriptions to other lines	241,830
Railway account	£35,831,081
Wensum Valley abandonment	7,014
Highbeach abandonment	13,744
Docks and steamboats	954,362
Loss on issue of ordinary stock and difference on conversion and redemption of stocks, &c.	3,151,813
	£39,958,014

The estimate of further expenditure on capital account during the half-year ended 31st December, 1884, and in subsequent half-years, is given below:—

	31st Dec., 1884.	Subsequently.	Total.
Lines open for traffic	£275,000	£1,400,000	£1,675,000
Northern Extension	5,000	95,000	100,000
Working stock	100,000	100,000	200,000
Subscriptions to other lines	...	25,000	25,000
Total	£380,000	£1,620,000	£2,000,000

The capital powers and other assets available to meet this estimated further outlay are given in detail below:—

Share capital authorised but not created or sanctioned	£569,358
Stock and share capital created but not received	1,275,439
Loans and debenture stock—balance of available borrowing powers	457,356
	£2,302,153
Deduct—balance at debit of capital account	245,931
	£2,056,222

REVENUE.—Comparative results of the working for the last three half-years, viz.:

Receipts.	1883. 30th June.	1883. 31st Dec.	1884. 30th June.
Passengers, parcels, horses, mails, &c.	£752,028	£963,646	£784,150
Merchandise (net)	507,583	550,030	533,955
Live stock and minerals	221,625	242,364	220,603
Carriage and wagon hire	...	...	105
Steamboats, &c.	84,979	101,209	88,905
Rent of arches, &c., tolls, harbour and pier dues, and fees	45,066	52,319	47,892
Dividends on shares in other lines	4,221	5,225	5,411
	£1,615,502	£1,914,793	£1,681,022

Expenses.	1883. 30th June.	1883. 31st Dec.	1884. 30th June.
Maintenance of way, works, and stations	£140,776	£155,572	£137,309
Locomotive power	246,577	269,337	238,668
Carriage and wagon repairs	68,214	84,661	68,530
Traffic expenses	281,984	308,559	284,191
General charges	35,631	38,994	37,371
Law and Parliamentary	7,428	7,775	6,842
Compensation	15,712	12,290	21,599
Rates, taxes, and Government duty	69,552	69,601	55,690
Steamboats	69,325	81,815	76,399
Ferryboats, harbours, &c	14,115	14,632	11,780
Ordinary working expenses	£949,314	£1,043,167	£938,380
Less amount chargeable to other companies for working their lines	11,405	10,168	9,028
	£937,909	£1,032,999	£929,352
Preference charges, viz.:—			
Interest on loan capital and general interest (net)	270,595	282,439	282,660
Rents on leased lines	112,631	113,141	113,616
Permanent way and rolling stock renewal accounts	...	15,000	...
Dividend on preference capital and interest on rent-charge, Metropolitan, and land security stocks	299,862	302,355	302,362
	£1,620,997	£1,745,934	£1,627,990
Net balances each half-year	*Dr.*£5,495	£168,859	£53,032
Balances brought from previous half-years	7,800	2,305	10,378
Balances available for dividend on ordinary stock	£2,305	£171,164	£63,410
Dividends at nil, 2¼, and ¾ per cent. per annum respectively	...	160,786	46,228
Balances carried forward to next half-year	£2,305	£10,378	£17,182

Summary, showing the results of the last half-year's working as compared with the corresponding period of 1883:—

Net Balance—30th June, 1884	£53,032	Thus:—	
Do. 30th June, 1883	*Dr.* 5,495	Gross traffic—increase	£65,520
		Less:—	
		Working charges—dec. £8,557	
		Preference „ —inc. 15,550	
			6,993
Gain in 1884	£58,527	Net gain in 1884	£58,527

MILEAGE:—*Authorised*, 941¼; *constructed*, 914¾; *constructing or to be constructed*, 26¾; leased or rented, 93¾; total, 1,008¼.

REDEMPTION OF "B" 5 PER CENT. DEBENTURE STOCK, 1867.—On the 1st June, 1882, the company held their first drawing for the redemption of this stock, the scheme being as follows:—The register of the "B" debenture stockholders to be divided into 10 groups, as near as possible of equal amounts. These groups to be lettered "A" to "J" respectively. The letters to be put into a box, and one to be drawn by a stockholder not being an official of the company. All the holders under the drawn letter to be paid off 10 per cent. of their stock at the price of 120*l.* per cent.—fractional parts of 10*l.* of stock drawn to be considered as 10*l.* So soon as the drawing has taken place, notice to be sent to those holders whose stock has been drawn to send in the certificate thereof, such certificate to be marked and returned with a cheque for the amount of the redemption. Interest on the amount drawn will cease from the 1st July, 1882. The half-yearly interest to 30th June to be paid by warrant in the usual way.

CONSOLIDATION AND REDEMPTION OF STOCKS.—During the half-year ended 30th June, 1878, the company, under the provisions of the act of 1876, and with the sanction of the proprietors, converted their East Anglian preference capital into "East Anglian debenture stock," bearing interest at 4 per cent. per annum, and taking the same priority as the stocks so consolidated, the holders receiving such an amount of debenture stock in exchange for their respective holdings as would yield them the same rate of interest they had previously been entitled to. The East Anglian No. 2 stock was at the same time converted into Great Eastern ordinary stock, at the rate of 20*l*. of the latter for every 100*l*. of East Anglian stock. Copies of the scheme and of explanatory circulars will be found in the *Appendix* to the MANUAL for 1878. During the year 1877 various guaranteed stocks were consolidated into one stock, called "Great Eastern Consolidated 4 per cent. Irredeemable Guaranteed Stock" (for scheme see *Appendix* to the MANUAL for 1879), and in May, 1879, the Lowestoft and various other stocks were consolidated, see *Appendix* to the MANUAL for 1880.

NEW CAPITAL.—In February, 1879, a further amount of 5 per cent. preference stock, 1876 (170,000*l*.) was issued, to form part of 1,000,000*l*. authorised, of which 826,430*l*. had already been issued. The whole of this stock is redeemable at 5 per cent. premium on the 1st January, 1888, or on the 1st January in any subsequent year, at the option of the company, on 3 months' notice being given to the proprietors. In February, 1882, ordinary stock, under act 1881, amounting to 1,076,920*l*., was allotted to holders of Great Eastern ordinary stock and Northern and Eastern 5 per cent. stock in the proportion of 10*l*. for each 100*l*. stock registered on the 24th January, 1882, price 65 per cent., payable as follows:—20 per cent. deposit; 15 per cent. each on 5th July and 13th December, 1882, and 11th April, 1883, respectively.

NORTHERN EXTENSION CAPITAL.—This new capital, amounting to 1,500,000*l*., was allotted to the proprietary in August, 1879, at par. It is called "Northern Extension 5 per cent. Preference Stock," and bears a dividend at the rate of 5 per cent. per annum; it is redeemable in 1888, on the same conditions as the "5 per cent. Preference Stock, 1876," mentioned above.

DIRECTORS:

Chairman—CHARLES HENRY PARKES, Esq., Netherfield, Weybridge, Surrey.

Deputy-Chairman—Lord CLAUD JOHN HAMILTON, M.P., 23, Lowndes Square, S.W.

James Charles, Esq., Kennet House, Harrow, and South Sea House, E.C.

George Wodehouse Currie, Esq., 26, Pall Mall, S.W.

The Hon. Richard Denman, Westergate, Arundel.

Horace Walker, Esq., Sherde Manor, Wales, near Sheffield.

John Francis Holcombe Read, Esq., Hoe Street, Walthamstow.

Colonel William Thomas Makins, M.P., 1, Lowther Gardens, Prince's Gate, S.W., and Rotherfield Court, Henley-on-Thames, Oxon.

Howard John Kennard, Esq., 20, Hyde Park Terrace, W.

Henry John Trotter, Esq., Langton Grange, Gainford, near Darlington, and Temple, E.C.

Sir Henry Whatley Tyler, M.P., Pymmes Park, Edmonton.

OFFICERS.—Sec., J. Hadfield; Gen. Man., W. Birt; Supt., J. Robertson; Goods Man., W. Gardner; Eng., John Wilson, M.Inst.C.E.; Loco. Supt., T. W. Worsdell; Auditors, Charles Morgan, Old Jewry, E.C., and Harry Chubb, 6, Prince's Square, Hyde Park, W.; Solicitor, W. F. Fearn.

Head Offices—Liverpool Street Terminus, E.C.

117.—GREAT NORTHERN.

An amalgamation of the LONDON AND YORK and DIRECT NORTHERN. Incorporated by act of 26th June, 1846, for construction of a line from London to York, *viâ* Peterborough, Newark, and Retford, with a loop line from Peterborough, through Boston and Lincoln, rejoining the main line at Retford. Productive, 888 miles.

PARLIAMENTARY POWERS:—

A list of Acts granted to this company from 1854 to 1879, with short heads of the objects for which they were obtained, will be found on reference to the MANUAL for 1881, pages 121 and 122.

FURTHER POWERS:—

1880—6TH AUGUST.—Vesting of the branch to the Midland at Melton Mowbray jointly with London and North Western. Various improvements in connection with the joint undertakings of the company, and the Great Eastern and London and North Western. Agreements with Midland for the use of the station at Leicester, and the undertakings belonging to or leased by the Midland at Keighley, and sundry other purposes.

1881—18TH JULY.—Powers to acquire the Stafford and Uttoxeter undertaking (see particulars under that head, further on) and for sundry other purposes. New capital, 1,100,000*l*.; borrowing powers, 333,000*l*.

1882—10TH AUGUST.—Vesting of Louth and Lincoln.—See Louth and Lincoln.

1883—16TH JULY.—Construction of the following new lines, &c., viz.:—Dudley Hill to Low Moor, 2¼ miles; branch at Laister Dyke, ¾ mile; branch at Dewsbury

¾ mile; Crofton Branch, 1½ mile; Eaton Branch, 3½ miles; railway and road at Stafford, ¼ mile; footpath at Spalding, sundry widenings and deviations, &c. Purchase of Hatfield and St. Alban's (see further on), &c.

1884—19TH MAY.—Sundry branch lines at Eaton, Eastwell, and Stanton, length, about 3 miles; and other general powers appertaining thereto.

AMALGAMATIONS, LEASES, AGREEMENTS, JOINT LINES, SUBSCRIPTIONS, &c.:—

BOSTON, SLEAFORD, AND MIDLAND COUNTIES.—Incorporated by act of 20th August, 1853, for a line from the Great Northern, at Boston, Lincolnshire, to the Great Northern at Barkstone (North of Grantham Junction). The line runs across the country (east to west) from the Great Northern loop to Great Northern main or towns line, and so connects with the Ambergate. Length, 28 miles.

BOURN AND ESSENDINE.—Incorporated by act of 12th August, 1857, to construct a line from the Great Northern Station, at Essendine, to the town of Bourn. Capital, 48,000*l.* in 10*l.* shares; loans, 16,000*l.* Length, 6½ miles. Amalgamation with Great Northern by act of 25th July, 1864.

BRADFORD AND THORNTON.—Incorporated by act of 24th July, 1871, to construct railways in the neighbourhood of Bradford. Length, 7 miles. Capital, 275,000*l.* in 10*l.* shares and 91,600*l.* on loan. Opened October 14th, 1878.

BRADFORD, ECCLESHILL, AND IDLE.—Incorporated by act of 28th June, 1866, to construct a line from Bradford, through Eccleshill, to Idle. Length, 3½ miles. Capital, 65,000*l.* in 10*l.* shares and 21,600*l.* on loan. Vested in Great Northern, which subscribed 30,000*l.*, by act of 24th July, 1871.

CHESHIRE LINES.—By act of 13th July, 1863, the Great Northern obtained power to subscribe to and pay interest on the capital of the Stockport and Woodley Junction, the Cheshire Midland, the Stockport, Timperley, and Altrincham, the West Cheshire, and the Manchester and South Junction, on completion of agreement with the Manchester, Sheffield, and Lincolnshire. New capital, 720,000*l.*, at 5 per cent., and 166,000*l.* on loan. By act of 15th August, 1867, the "Cheshire Lines Committee" was incorporated as one body corporate, with perpetual succession and a common seal.—See GENERAL INDEX.

EAST LINCOLNSHIRE.—Incorporated by act of 26th July, 1846. Commences (in conjunction with the Great Northern Loop) at Boston, and terminates (in conjunction with the Manchester, Sheffield, and Lincolnshire) at Great Grimsby—47½ miles. This company, by act of 1846, and under sanction of the lessees, who are the responsible parties, purchased the unexpired interest of Messrs. F. and G. Chaplin, in the lease held by them for 48 years, commencing from 28th August, 1828, in the Louth Navigation; also of the unexpired lease of a piece of land, known as "Mallard Ings," held by Mr. Thomas Chaplin for 99 years, commencing from 9th April, 1800, the consideration paid being an annuity of 1,500*l.* for the unexpired term, and an assumption of the bond debt of the canal, supposed to be 1,500*l.* per annum. By act of 1847, power was given to make the Great Grimsby Branch and Sheffield Junction half a mile additional length. By act of 1847, this line has been leased in perpetuity to the Great Northern at a fixed rental of 36,000*l.* per annum, equal to 6 per cent. per annum on the share capital (fixed capital of 600,000*l.*), from 1st October, 1848; the Great Northern providing all extra cost of construction and assuming the loan debt. Lease is dated 21st February, 1848, and the terms are repeated in sec. 34 of 13 Vic., cap. 84, which gives this company right to re-possess, on non-payment of the rent for seven months, from 1st April and 1st October. Meantime the Great Northern pay all expenses connected with the registration of transfers, the distribution of dividend, and all other administrative charges attending the same. MEM.—There are certain powers given to the Great Northern to redeem the East Lincolnshire stock at 50 per cent. premium, but this right could only be exercised with the consent of the East Lincolnshire shareholders.

EDGWARE, HIGHGATE, AND LONDON.—Incorporated by act of 3rd June, 1862, to construct a line from the Great Northern, through Highgate, Finchley, and Hendon, to Edgware. By act of 15th July, 1867, the Edgware was transferred to the Great Northern under the subjoined arrangements:—From opening of the main line the shareholders of the Edgware participate in the Great Northern dividend in the following proportions, viz.:—For the first year after the opening of the line, 4/14ths of the Great Northern dividend; for the second year, 6/14ths; for the third year, 8/14ths; for the fourth year, 10/14ths; and for the fifth and all subsequent years, 11/14ths. At the end of the fourth year the Edgware stock merged into and became Great Northern stock; each shareholder in the Edgware Line receiving for every 100*l.* of Edgware stock 11/14ths of 100*l.* in Great Northern stock.

Proposed Amalgamation with Great Eastern.—The negotiations with this company for an amalgamation of the two systems have been broken off. Detailed accounts of such negotiations and the reasons for the abandonment of the project are given in the reports of each company for June, 1877.—The basis of the scheme, &c., will be found on reference to the Manual for 1878, under the head "Great Eastern."

Halifax and Ovenden.—Incorporated by act of 30th June, 1864, to construct a line from the Lancashire and Yorkshire, at Halifax, to Ovenden. Length, 2¾ miles. Capital, 90,000*l.* in 10*l.* shares and 30,000*l.* on loan. By act of 1st August, 1870, the undertaking is vested in the Lancashire and Yorkshire and the Great Northern, the two companies having the option to pay off the shareholders at par at any time previous to 1st January, 1873, either in cash or debenture stock, at 4 per cent.

Halifax, Thornton, and Keighley.—Length, 12 miles. Constructed by the Great Northern at a cost of about 700,000*l.* Thornton to Denholme, 1 mile 35 chains, opened for traffic 1st January, 1884; Denholme to Ingrow, 4¾ miles, 7th April, 1884; Ingrow to Keighley, 1½ miles, 1st November, 1884.

Hatfield and St. Albans.—Incorporated by act of 30th June, 1862. Length, 6 miles. Vested in Great Northern by act of 16th July, 1883, as from 1st November following, for the sum of 51,500*l.*—For other particulars previously to transfer, see Manual for 1883, page 143.

Hertford, Luton, and Dunstable.—An amalgamation by act of 28th June, 1855, of the Hertford and Welwyn Junction and of the Luton, Dunstable, and Welwyn Junction.—See below and next page.

Hertford and Welwyn Junction.—Incorporated by act of 3rd July, 1854. The line joins these two towns, and forms a connection between the Great Northern and Great Eastern, with both of which it may come in alliance. It has also running powers over the Great Eastern from Hertford to Ware. Capital, 65,000*l.* in 20*l.* shares; power to borrow, 21,600*l.* Opened 1st March, 1858, 7½ miles.

Idle and Shipley.—Incorporated by act of 12th August, 1867, to construct a line from the Bradford, Eccleshill, and Idle, to Shipley. Length, 2½ miles. Capital, 55,000*l.* in 10*l.* shares and 18,300*l.* on loan. Vested in Great Northern by act of 24th July, 1871.

Leeds, Bradford, and Halifax Junction.—Incorporated by act of 30th June, 1852, for a line from the Bowling Junction (Lancashire and Yorkshire), Bradford, to Leeds Junction. By act of 5th July, 1865, the Leeds, Bradford, and Halifax was amalgamated on equal terms with the Great Northern, as from 5th September, 1865.

Leicestershire Joint Lines.—These lines are situated between Melton Mowbray and Market Harbro', and complete the connection between the Great Northern and London and North Western. Opened for traffic on the 15th December, 1879.

Louth and East Coast.—See General Index.

Louth and Lincoln.—Incorporated by act of 6th August, 1866. Length, 22 miles, from Louth to Great Northern Loop Line at Lincoln. Amalgamated with Great Northern under powers of act of 10th August, 1882, the purchase being settled on the 30th June, 1883, and the company dissolved from that date, except for the purpose of distributing the purchase money. The debentures are paid off, and the balance was distributed amongst the shareholders.—For full particulars as to the position, &c., of this company in the past, see the Manual for 1883, and previous editions.

Luton, Dunstable, and Welwyn Junction.—Incorporated by act of 16th July, 1855, for constructing a railway from the London and North Western, at Dunstable, to the Great Northern, at Welwyn. Length, 17 miles. By act of 12th June, 1861, the line is amalgamated with the Great Northern, which pays for the Dunstable and Welwyn section a fixed dividend on the original capital amounting to 70,000*l.*, commencing at 3 per cent. for the first year, 4 per cent. for the second and third years, and 4½ per cent. per annum subsequently: for the Welwyn and Hertford section, 1 per cent. per annum until April, 1866, upon 55,000*l.*, and 3½ per cent. per annum thereafter. The Great Northern also pays interest on mortgage and preference capital amounting to 152,500*l.*

Manchester, Sheffield, and Lincolnshire.—By act of 23rd July, 1858, the Great Northern was authorised to enter into financial and traffic arrangements with this company, in accordance with which the Sheffield is entitled to receive, out of the earnings arising from through traffic, such a sum as would, with other receipts, make up the gross sum of 10,000*l.* per week, subject to being repaid when their gross receipts exceed 11,000*l.* per week.

Metropolitan Junction.—By act of 23rd July, 1860, the Great Northern was authorised to construct a communication from near King's Cross to the Metropolitan, to be completed within five years. New capital, 30,000*l.*, at 4½ per cent., in shares, and 10,000*l.* on loan.

NORTHERN EXTENSION.—See Great Eastern.

NOTTINGHAM AND GRANTHAM.—See GENERAL INDEX.

OVENDEN AND QUEENSBURY.—This branch, which forms the new route between Bradford and Halifax, was opened for traffic on the 1st December, 1879.

ROYSTON AND HITCHIN.—See GENERAL INDEX.

SOUTHPORT AND CHESHIRE LINES EXTENSION.—See GENERAL INDEX.

STAFFORD AND UTTOXETER.—Incorporated by act of 29th July, 1862, to construct a line from Stafford, on the London and North Western, to Uttoxeter, on the North Staffordshire, with a branch to the Colwich Station of the latter company. Length, 13¼ miles (for other details see MANUAL for 1882, and previously). The line has been sold to and taken possession of by the Great Northern, on the 1st August, 1881, under their act of 18th July, 1881, the consideration or purchase money being 100,000*l*.; debenture stock "A," "B," and "C" to be paid off at sums not exceeding 90 per cent., 50 per cent., and 30 per cent. of the holding respectively. Preference stock at 20 per cent. (the whole subject to certain rights of receivers and creditors), any balance then remaining to be divided amongst the ordinary shareholders.

WEST RIDING AND GRIMSBY.—On the 1st February, 1866, the Great Northern and Manchester, Sheffield, and Lincolnshire took possession of this line, and since that date the traffic to the West Riding of Yorkshire has passed over that line, and a saving of time of about twenty minutes between Leeds and London has been effected by adoption of this route.

WEST YORKSHIRE.—Incorporated by act of July, 1854, and by act of 5th July, 1865, amalgamated with the Great Northern.

YORK AND NORTH MIDLAND.—An agreement with this company permits the use of 20 miles from Knottingley into the station at York. The use of the intervening link from Askerne to Knottingley (belonging to the Lancashire and Yorkshire) is also permanently secured, and the agreement legalised by act 14 and 15 Vic., cap. 45.

ACCOUNTS:—

The seventy-sixth half-yearly meeting of this company was held on the 11th August last, when the report and accounts then presented were adopted. The following is an abstract of these accounts made up to 30th June, 1884, viz.:—

CAPITAL.—*Authorised:* Stock and shares, 27,323,724*l*.; loans, 9,103,325*l*.; total, 36,427,050*l*. *Created or sanctioned:* Stock and shares, 26,784,724*l*.; loans, 8,595,326*l*.; total, 35,330,050*l*. The receipts and expenses on this account to 30th June, 1884, were detailed as follow:—

Receipts.		*Expenditure.*	
Original "A" and "B" stocks	£12,091,054	Lines and works open for traffic, including lines purchased and amalgamated, and additional expenditure thereon, including also Leeds Hotel	£23,959,569
Preference stocks	13,747,023	Lines and works in course of construction, and to be constructed	852,597
Leeds, Bradford, and Halifax	*575,000	Working stock, machinery, and tools	4,139,708
Total stock and share capital	£26,413,077	Subscriptions to other lines	6,025,300
Debenture stock	8,589,626		£34,977,174
		Balance	25,529
	£35,002,708		£35,002,708

The estimate of further expenditure required for the half-year ended 31st December, 1884, was 300,000*l*., and for subsequent half-years, 1,663,419*l*.; total, 1,963,419*l*. The capital powers and other available assets are given below:—

Share capital authorised but not yet created or sanctioned	£539,000
Loan " " " "	508,000
Share capital created but not yet received	371,648
Loan capital created but not yet received	5,699
Credit balance on capital	25,528
Total available assets	£1,449,875

* This stock is entitled to the full dividend payable on the company's ordinary capital, of which a fixed dividend of 3 per cent. is payable for the half-year ending 30th June, and the remainder for the half-year ending 31st December; provided, nevertheless, that such remainder shall never be less than 3 per cent., thus constituting it virtually a *minimum* 6 per cent. stock.

REVENUE.—The following is a comparative view of the working of this undertaking for the last three half-years:—

Receipts.	1883. June 30.	1883. Dec. 31.	1884. June 30.
Passengers, parcels, horses, mails, &c.	£620,805	£733,492	£642,970
Merchandise (less cartage), live stock, and minerals	940,013	974,465	916,207
Dividends on shares in other companies	3,795	3,925	3,719
Rents, transfer fees, &c.	22,183	24,985	23,053
North Liverpool lines guarantee fund	4,535	2,520	4,766
Canals and navigations	4,686	4,626	4,478
	£1,596,017	£1,744,013	£1,595,193
Joint and worked lines—Great Northern proportion	239,678	257,430	231,934
	£1,835,695	£2,001,443	£1,827,127
Deduct—Amount received for running expenses included in Great Northern receipts	48,216	...	29,173
	£1,787,479	£2,001,443	£1,797,954

Expenses.	1883. June 30.	1883. Dec. 31.	1884. June 30.
Maintenance of way, works, and stations	£130,600	£153,968	£133,784
Locomotive power	246,030	254,471	249,128
Carriage and wagon repairs	81,909	86,516	85,400
Traffic expenses	309,128	328,193	315,199
General charges	45,302	47,742	45,745
Law and Parliamentary	5,222	6,372	5,274
Compensation	30,469	12,654	12,727
Rates, taxes, and Government duty	66,048	68,405	58,789
Mileage and demurrage	9,256	5,349	9,750
Canal expenses	3,485	3,467	3,457
Total Great Northern expenditure	£927,449	£967,137	£919,253
Joint and worked lines expenses	177,859	178,780	164,621
Total expenditure	£1,105,308	£1,145,917	£1,083,874
Deduct running expenses included in Great Northern expenditure	48,216	40,060	29,173
Preference and exceptional charges viz.:—	£1,057,092	£1,105,857	£1,054,101
Interest on mortgages, debenture stock, calls in advance, banking balances, and general interest (net)	164,999	176,117	174,225
Rent of leased lines, &c.	51,470	51,470	51,470
Rent of navigations	5,278	5,272	5,273
Interest on capital expended at Manchester for accommodation of joint traffic	2,187	2,188	2,188
Dividends on preference stock	324,697	324,697	324,700
	£1,605,718	£1,665,601	£1,612,557
Net balances each half-year	£181,761	£335,842	£185,397
Balances brought from previous half-years	2,120	2,099	2,345
Balances available for dividend on ordinary stock	£183,881	£337,941	£187,742
Dividends declared at 3½, 6, and 3½ per cent. per annum respectively	181,781	335,596	181,781
Surplus carried forward	£2,100	2,345	£5,961

The following summary will therefore show the results of the last half-year's working, as compared with those of the corresponding period of 1883, viz.:—

Net balance—30th June, 1884 ...	£185,397	Thus:—	
Ditto 30th June, 1883 ...	181,761	Gross traffic—increase............	£10,475
		Expenses—decrease..............	2,391
			£12,866
		Less:—	
		Preference charges—increase..	9,230
Gain in 1884....................	£3,636	Net gain in 1884................	£3,636

MILEAGE—30TH JUNE, 1884.—LINES OWNED:—*Authorised*, 638¼; *constructed*, 622; *constructing, or to be constructed*, 16¼; *worked*, 622. JOINT LINES, G. N. PROPORTION:—*Authorised*, 157; *constructed*, 156; *constructing, or to be constructed*. 1; *worked*. 122. LINES WORKED:—*Authorised, constructed, and worked*, 165. Total lines worked, 909.

NEW CAPITAL.—In February, 1881, 830,000*l*. "4 per cent. preference stock, 1881," was created and issued. This stock was allotted rateably at par to the proprietors of ordinary and Leeds, Bradford, and Halifax stocks. It ranks immediately before the ordinary capital, and is convertible at the option of the holders into ordinary stocks on the 1st September, 1886 (on or before which date notice must be given by parties desirous of exercising such option). The dividend is contingent upon the profits of each separate year.

At a special meeting held on the 6th January, 1882, 1,200,000*l*. of new 4 per cent. perpetual preference stock, authorised by act of 1881, was created and subsequently allotted. This stock ranks for dividend immediately after the above-named issue and before the ordinary stocks, the dividends being contingent upon the profits of each separate year.

NEW ORDINARY STOCK.—Under resolutions passed at a special meeting held in January, 1884, 1,000,000*l*. of additional capital was created and issued in ordinary stock, with dividend accruing from 1st March, 1885, the stock to be incorporated with the original stock after payment of the dividend for the half-year ended 30th June, 1885.

The accounts are made up to 30th June and 31st December in every year, and the statutory meetings held in February and August.

TRANSFER OF STOCKS.—Fractions of 1*l*.—The Secretary has notified that since the consolidation of stocks transfers of stocks are limited to a pound, and that parts of a pound sterling are not allowed as formerly.

Scale of Voting.—C. C. C. Act, sec. 75. Holders of preference shares under act of 1853 have same votes as if original shares. Holders of debenture stock to have no vote unless three-fifths of a meeting specially notified shall so resolve.

Registration fee, 2s. 6d. each deed transferring stock or bonds.

DIRECTORS:

Chairman—The Rt. Hon. Lord COLVILLE of Culross, K.T., 42, Eaton Place, S.W.

Deputy-Chairman—SAMUEL CHARLES ALLSOPP, Esq., M.P., Burton-on-Trent, and Doveridge Hall, Derby.

John Harvey Astell, Esq., Woodbury Hall, Sandy, Beds.

Laurence Richardson Baily, Esq., Allerton Hall, Woolton, Lancashire.

Sir John Brown, Knt., Assoc.Inst.C.E., Endcliffe Hall, near Sheffield.

Hon. Reginald A. Capel, 21, Chesham Place, S.W., and Watford, Herts.

Sir Andrew Fairbairn, M.P., 15, Portman Square, W., and Askham Richard, near York.

Frederick William Fison, Esq., Eastmoor, Ilkley, and Bradford.

Abraham Briggs Foster, Esq., Queensbury, near Bradford, and Northowram Hall, Halifax.

William Lawies Jackson, Esq., M.P., Allerton Hall, Chapel Allerton, near Leeds.

Lesley Charles Probyn, Esq., 23, Thurloe Square, S.W.

Frank Shuttleworth, Esq., Old Warden Park, Biggleswade, and Lincoln.

W. H. Fellowes, Esq., M.P., 20, Upper Brook Street, W.

One-fourth of the directors retire annually.

OFFICERS.—Gen. Man., Henry Oakley, Assoc.Inst.C.E.; Sec., Arthur Fitch; Assistant Sec., William Latta; Accountant, William Grinling; Supt. of the Line, F. P. Cockshott; Assistant Supt. of the Line, J. Alexander; Chief Goods Man., R. Dymant; Managers of Goods Dept., J. Medcalf, Southern Division, and R. Robinson, Northern Division; Mineral Man., William Newton; Con. Eng., John Fowler, M.Inst.C.E., 2, Queen Square Place, S.W.; Eng., Richard Johnson, M.Inst.C.E.; Assistant Eng., T. W. Horn; Loco. Eng., Patrick Stirling; Auditors, Major John C. Fitzmaurice and Julian Hill; Parliamentary Agents, Dyson and Co., Parliament Street, S.W.; Solicitors, Nelson, Barr, and Nelson, King's Cross Station, N., and Leeds.

Head Offices—King's Cross, N.

118.—GREAT NORTHERN (IRELAND).

An amalgamation of the DUBLIN AND DROGHEDA, DUBLIN AND BELFAST JUNCTION, IRISH NORTH WESTERN, ULSTER, and other companies. Productive, 467 miles.

By the acts of 28th June, 1877, powers were given for the vesting of the Banbridge and Dungannon undertakings, and confirming the amalgamations with Dublin and Drogheda, Dublin and Belfast Junction, Irish North Western, and Ulster companies respectively, particulars of which appear in the following pages; authority was obtained for the raising of new capital for vesting purposes to the extent of 645,000*l*. in shares or stock, and 255,000*l*. in debentures or debenture stock.

By act of 24th July, 1879, powers were obtained to purchase additional lands and execute certain works near the Dundalk and Dungannon stations, &c., &c., and to purchase the Dublin and Antrim Junction and Newry and Armagh undertakings, particulars of which are given in the following pages.

By act of 3rd June, 1881, powers were obtained for extensions to Carrickmacross (6½ miles) and Belturbet (4 miles); period for completion, 5 years.

1883—16TH JULY.—Vesting of Londonderry and Enniskillen (see further on).

BANBRIDGE EXTENSION.—Incorporated under the act of 1861, for making a railway commencing by a junction with the Banbridge and Lisburn at or near the town of Banbridge, and terminating in the townland of Lackan, with a short siding to connect the main line with the Banbridge Junction and a branch to Rathfriland. By act of 28th June, 1877, this railway having never been completed, powers were given to the Great Northern (Ireland) to vest the undertaking in that company, the powers granted under the act of 1861 being revived and transferred to the Great Northern, so far as regards the construction of the extension to the main line from Edenderry to Lackan, a distance of 8 miles 7 furlongs and 8 chains.

BANBRIDGE JUNCTION.—Incorporated by act of 20th August, 1853, for a line from Banbridge to a junction with the Dublin and Belfast Junction, near Scarva, and opening up communication with the ports of Newry, Dublin, and Belfast. Length, 6¾ miles (other details given in MANUAL for 1882, pages 122 and 123). By act of 28th June, 1877, this line became vested in the Great Northern (Ireland), the transfer taking effect on the 23rd March, 1876, and the lease to the Dublin and Belfast Junction ceasing from that date. The purchasing company to cancel certain shares held by them, forfeit certain claims, and pay over to the Banbridge the sum of 3,250*l*., which sum and interest thereon accruing, from the date of transfer, to be applied first to the payment of certain debts, and then to be divided rateably among the shareholders.

BANBRIDGE, LISBURN, AND BELFAST.—Incorporated by act of 4th June, 1858, to construct a line from Banbridge to Lisburn (other details, MANUAL for 1882, page 123). By act of 28th June, 1877, this line was vested in the Great Northern (Ireland), from the 30th June, 1877, and the lease to the Ulster cancelled from that date. The purchase money, amounting to 48,050*l*., free of all claims with respect to moneys advanced or shares held by the Ulster, to be applied first to the payment of all preferential and exceptional charges up to the date of transfer, and secondly in payment to the holders of 1,098 preference shares, 5*l*. for every 10*l*. paid up, the residue to be divided rateably among the ordinary shareholders.

BELFAST CENTRAL.—See GENERAL INDEX.

DUBLIN AND ANTRIM JUNCTION.—Incorporated by act of 11th July, 1861, to construct a line from the Ulster, at Lisburn, to the Belfast and Northern Counties at Antrim. Length, 18¼ miles. Capital, 120,000*l*. in 10*l*. shares; loans, 40,000*l*. Under the Great Northern of Ireland Act of 24th July, 1879, the line was purchased by that company for 70,000*l*.—For particulars relating to the past history of the company, see the MANUAL for 1878, and previous editions.

DUBLIN AND DROGHEDA.—Incorporated 1836, to construct a line from Dublin to Drogheda (31¾ miles), with a branch to Howth, 3½ miles (other details, MANUAL for 1882, page 123). The Dublin to Drogheda Line was opened 26th May, 1844; the

Howth Branch, 30th July, 1846; the Kells to Oldcastle Extension, 17th March, 1863. The productive mileage of the Dublin and Drogheda at the time of the amalgamation was 75 miles.—For terms of amalgamation, see below.

DUBLIN AND BELFAST JUNCTION.—Incorporated 21st July, 1845, to construct a line from Drogheda to Newry, a junction line to the Ulster at Portadown, and a branch line to Navan. By act of 1847 the company was authorised to amalgamate with the Dublin and Drogheda, the Dundalk and Enniskillen, or the Ulster, its productive mileage at the time of the amalgamation (for terms of which see next paragraph) being 63 miles, including the mileage of the Banbridge Junction.

AMALGAMATION.—The amalgamation of the Dublin and Drogheda and Dublin and Belfast was effected on 1st March, 1875, when the name of the united company was changed to "Northern of Ireland." The amalgamation is upon the basis that the Drogheda ordinary capital (705,000*l.*) be taken at par, and the Belfast ordinary capital (873,500*l.*) at 77½*l.* per cent., thus bringing the united company's ordinary capital to 1,381,962*l.*, the preference capital (stocks and debentures) becoming, of course, liabilities of the joint undertaking, at existing rates. Fractional amounts of 1*l.* of ordinary capital not to be transferable, and persons becoming holders of such fractional amounts to have issued to them respectively at par price such amounts of unissued ordinary capital stock of the united company as shall make such fractional amounts respectively equal to entire pounds respectively, the first dividend upon the ordinary capital of the united company to be made upon foot of the accounts for the half-year ended 30th June, 1875, which shall comprise the accounts of the two companies respectively from 31st December, 1874, to 1st March, 1875, and the accounts of the united company from that date to 30th June, 1875. As the interest on the debenture stock of the Dublin and Drogheda was payable 15th January and 15th July, and of the Belfast Company 10th April and 10th October, it was arranged that, in order to adjust this discrepancy, interest for three months ended 30th June, 1875, should be paid on the Belfast debenture stock. In future the interest on all debenture stock will be payable on 15th January and 15th July.

DUBLIN NORTH WALL EXTENSION.—This extension connects the company's line with the London and North Western at North Wall, and is now open for traffic.

DUNGANNON AND COOKSTOWN.—Incorporated 30th July, 1874, to construct a railway from the Portadown, Dungannon, and Omagh Junction, at Dungannon, to the Belfast and Northern Counties, at Cookstown, with a short branch or spur line near the first-mentioned place. Length, 14 miles. By the act of 28th June, 1877, this line was vested in the Great Northern of Ireland, the transfer to take effect on the 1st July, 1876, the purchasing company to fulfil all contracts and engagements with respect to the purchase of land and the completion of the line, and to pay to the Dungannon 15,500*l.* to be applied to the payment of debts and liabilities, and the re-payment of that company's paid up capital. The line was opened for traffic on the 28th July, 1879.

IRISH NORTH WESTERN.—Formerly the *Dundalk and Enniskillen*, the name being changed to Irish North Western under powers conferred by the act of 1864. The undertaking before the amalgamation consisted of a main line from Dundalk, in the east (by way of Clones, Enniskillen, Omagh, and Strabane), to Londonderry, in the north, and branches from Ballybay to Cootehill, from Clones to Cavan, and from Omagh to Fintona. Productive, 146 miles (other details, MANUAL 1882, page 124). On the 1st January, 1876, the Irish North Western was amalgamated with the Northern of Ireland, on the following terms:—The 30*l.* ordinary shares of the Irish North Western (amounting in all to 171,420*l.*) to be exchanged for 5*l.* of Northern ordinary stock (taken at 20 per cent. above par); and each 100*l.* of Irish North Western preference stock (amounting in all to 476,623*l.*) to be exchanged for 50*l.* of Northern ordinary stock.

LONDONDERRY AND ENNISKILLEN.—Incorporated by act of 1845. Length, 60 miles. Amalgamated with Great Northern of Ireland by act of 16th July, 1883, as from the 1st January, 1884, the holders of Londonderry stocks receiving in exchange "Great Northern (Ireland) Londonderry guaranteed stock," bearing a perpetual guaranteed dividend at the rate of 5 per cent. per annum, payable half-yearly, 30th June and 31st December, ranking next after the whole of the debenture capital of the company at the following rates, viz.:—

"A" preference exchanged at par.		
"B" ,,	,,	100*l.* 19*s.* 4 per cent.
"C" ,,	,,	100*l.* 19*s.* 4 ,,
Original stock	,,	137*l.* 11*s.* 5 ,,

Debenture stockholders receiving par of Great Northern debenture stock at same rates of interest as those existing before amalgamation.—For full particulars of the position, &c., of this company before amalgamation, see the MANUAL for 1883, and previous editions.

NEWRY AND ARMAGH.—Incorporated 31st July, 1845, as the Newry and Enniskillen, and amalgamated with the Great Northern of Ireland under that company's act of 24th July, 1879. The amalgamation took effect as from the 30th June, 1879, and the terms of purchase as copied from the act will be found on reference to the MANUAL for 1883, page 125.

It was stated in November, 1880, that the ordinary shareholders had received a return of 20 per cent, and that among them there might be a small amount still to divide.—For particulars relating to the past history of this railway, see the MANUAL for 1878, and previous editions.

ULSTER.—Incorporated by act of 19th May, 1836, for a line from Belfast to Armagh (36 miles), partly opened August, 1839, and to Portadown in 1842 (for other details see MANUAL for 1876, and previously, and MANUAL for 1882, pages 125 and 126). On the 1st April, 1876, the Ulster was amalgamated with the Northern of Ireland, and the name of that company was then changed to the "Great Northern of Ireland." The terms upon which the amalgamation was effected were that the ordinary stock of the Northern should be taken at par, and the ordinary stock of the Ulster at 124*l.* 10*s.*; the debentures and guaranteed and preference stocks preserving their existing priorities.

AGREEMENTS.—The Enniskillen, Bundoran, and Sligo is now worked by the Great Northern; the Finn Valley works its own line, but has arranged with the Great Northern for a supply of engine power for ten years. Working arrangements have been made with the Dundalk, Newry, and Greenore, and with the London and North Western for through traffic.

REVENUE.—The main features of this account for the half-years ended 31st December, 1883, and 30th June, 1884, are given in the subjoined statement:—

	1883. 31st Dec.	1884. 30th June.
Coaching traffic	£182,235	£159,812
Goods traffic	138,532	136,953
Rents, transfer fees, &c.	2,986	3,453
Gross receipts	£323,753	£300,218
Expenditure	164,300	167,644
Net	£159,453	£132,574
Add balance brought in and interest	7,455	16,238
Total net revenue	£166,908	£148,812
Less interest, rents, preference dividends, &c.	78,198	77,916
Available for ordinary stock	£88,710	£70,896
Dividends at 4½ per cent. per annum each half-year	73,261	66,508
Balance to next half-year	£15,449	£4,388

The dividends are payable on the 1st March and 1st September each half-year.

CAPITAL.—*Authorised:* Stock and shares, 5,064,350*l.*; loans, 1,799,368*l.*; total, 6,863,718*l.*, *all created or sanctioned.* The annexed statement of stock and share capital created shows the proportion received to 30th June, 1884:—

ORDER OF PRIORITY AND DESCRIPTION OF STOCKS, subject to rights of holders of debenture bonds (at 4½ per cent.) and debenture stock (at 4, 4¼, 4½, and 5 per cent.), which take rank as first charges. The description to be observed in transfers and all other legal documents relating thereto:—

	Created.	Received.
Londonderry guaranteed 5 per cent. stock	£507,416	£507,416
Guaranteed 4 per cent. stock (dividend accumulative)	100,000	100,000
„ 4½ do. (dividend accumulative)	120,000	120,000
Ulster 4½ per cent. preference stock	200,000	200,000
„ (Dungannon) 4½ per cent preference stock	75,025	75,025
„ „ 3 „ „ until 30th June, 1885, afterwards 3½ per cent.	224,550	224,550
Preference 4 per cent. stock	645,000	645,000
Ordinary stock	3,192,359	3,129,820
Amount unissued, 62,539*l.*	£5,064,350	£5,001,811

NOTE—Interest and dividends are payable half-yearly, as follow:—On debenture bonds, 1st January and 1st July; on debenture stock, 15th January and 15th July; on guaranteed stock, 11th April and 11th October.

TRANSFER DEPARTMENT QUERIES AND REPLIES.

Queries.	Replies.
Transfer form—ordinary or special?	Ordinary.
Fee per deed?	2s. 6d.
Ditto if more sellers than one?...	Only one seller allowed.
May several classes of stock be transferred on one deed?	Yes, the stamp being accurate.
Are certificates required to accompany transfers?	Yes.
What amounts of stocks are transferable, and are parts of 1l. sterling allowed to be transferred?	Any amount, except fractions of 1l.
To what officer should transfer communications be sent?	Secretary.

The receipts and expenditure on capital account to 30th June, 1884, are given in the following statement:—

Receipts.		*Expenditure.*	
Shares and stock	£5,001,811	Lines open for traffic	£6,086,673
Debenture stock	1,710,430	Lines in course of construction	15,479
Loans	4,000	Working stock	734,676
Rent-charge	801		
Forfeited and merged shares, premiums, &c.	103,791		
	£6,820,833		
Balance	15,995		
	£6,836,828		£6,836,828

The estimate of further expenditure on capital account required 40,000l. for the half-year ended 31st December, 1884; for subsequent half-years, 40,000l.; total, 80,000l. The capital powers and other available assets were:—

Share capital created but not yet issued	£62,539	
Loan capital created but not yet received..................................	84,136	
		£146,675
Less debit balance on capital account..		15,995
Amount available, exclusive of value of surplus land............		£130,680

Meetings held in Dublin and Belfast in February and August respectively.

No. of Directors.—To decrease by death or resignation until reduced to 15. *Qualification*, 2,000l. ordinary stock.

DIRECTORS:

Chairman—JAMES WILLIAM MURLAND, Esq., Nutley, Booterstown, Co. Dublin.

Deputy-Chairman—JAMES GRAY, Esq., Hazelbank, Whiteabbey, Belfast.

John Brady, Esq., Johnstown, Clones.
James C. Colvill, Esq., Bachelor's Walk, Dublin.
Sir Edward P. Cowan, D.L., Notting Hill, Belfast.
The Earl of Erne, Crom Castle, Newtownbutler.
Lucius O. Hutton, Esq., 8, Fitzwilliam Place, Dublin.
Thomas P. Cairnes, Esq., Stameen, Drogheda.
Luke John M'Donnell, Esq., 38, Merrion Square East, Dublin.
Joseph F. Meade, Esq., Eastwood, Newtown-Mount-Kennedy, Co. Wicklow.
George Pim, Esq., Brennanstown House, Cabinteely, Co. Dublin.
C. A. W. Stewart, Esq., Carrickfergus.
Henry T. Vickers, Esq., Hermitage, Cross Avenue, Blackrock, Co. Dublin.
J. G. Winder, Esq., Armagh.

OFFICERS.—Sec., Joseph P. Culverwell, Dublin; Asst. Sec., Foster Coates, Belfast; Traffic Mans., Thomas Shaw, Belfast, Henry Plews, Enniskillen, and Thomas Cowan, Dundalk; Engineer-in-Chief, W. H. Mills, Dublin; District Engineers, C. R. Atkinson, Belfast, W. Greenhill, Dundalk, W. Purdon, Enniskillen, and G. A. Armstrong, Dublin; Accountant, W. Thompson; Loco. and Carriage Supt., James C. Park, Dundalk; Auditors, Robert Warren, 40, Rutland Square, Dublin, and Samuel H. Close, Henry Street, Dublin; Solicitors, Crawford and Lockhart, 4, Queen's Square, Belfast.

Offices—Amiens Street, Dublin.

119.—GREAT NORTHERN AND LONDON AND NORTH WESTERN JOINT LINES.

By act of 30th July, 1874, the Great Northern and London and North Western companies were authorised to make railways between Market Harborough and Nottingham, with branches to connect the two companies' lines. Length, about 45 miles, included in which are portions of the Newark and Melton and Melton and Leicester lines also to be vested in the two companies. Reciprocal running powers. Great Northern may raise 250,000*l*. by creation of new shares or stock, and may borrow 83,300*l*. London and North Western may issue 500,000*l*. new shares or stock, and borrow 166,600*l*.

The lines between Bingham and Melton Mowbray were opened for goods traffic on the 1st July, and for passenger traffic on September 1st, 1879. The line was further opened from Bottesford to Harby and Stathern, and from Melton Mowbray to Market Harborough, on 15th December, 1879.

JOINT COMMITTEE:

Represent Great Northern.

The Right Hon. Lord Colville of Culross, K.T., 42, Eaton Place, S.W.
Abraham Briggs Foster, Esq., Northowram Hall, Halifax, and Canwell Hall, Tamworth.
Samuel Charles Allsopp, Esq., M.P., Doveridge Hall, Derbyshire.

Represent L. & N. Western.

William Cawkwell, Esq., Assoc.Inst.C.E., Fernacre, Maresfield Gardens, South Hampstead, N.W.
The Marquis of Stafford, M.P., Stafford House, St. James's, S.W.
Oscar Leslie Stephen, Esq., 55, Cadogan Square, S.W.

Secretary, F. Harley, Euston Station, N.W.

120.—GREAT NORTHERN AND WESTERN.

(LEASED TO MIDLAND GREAT WESTERN.)

Incorporated by act of 27th July, 1857, for making railways from Athlone to Roscommon and Castlerea. Line to Roscommon, 18 miles; that to Castlerea, 16½ miles. In operation, 105 miles, Athlone to Westport and Ballina.

PARLIAMENTARY POWERS.—A list of Acts from 1858 to 1871, with short heads showing the objects for which the various powers were obtained, will be found on reference to the MANUAL for 1881, pages 133 and 134.

LEASE.—By act of 4th July, 1870, the undertaking from Athlone to Westport Quay and Foxford is leased to the Midland Great Western for a term of 999 years, from 1st November, 1870, at a guaranteed net rental of 28,500*l*. per annum, to increase annually until the year 1885, by 350*l*. a year, to a maximum sum of 33,500*l*. per annum during the remainder of the period.

By act of 25th May, 1871, this further portion of the railway from Foxford to Ballina was similarly leased to the Midland Great Western of Ireland upon its completion at an additional rental of 2,737*l*., increasing yearly by about 33*l*. to 1887, when the maximum rental will, of the whole undertaking, be 36,718*l*. This further extension was opened May, 1873. The Midland Great Western of Ireland to pay all outgoings of every description connected with the maintenance and working of the railway, including rates and taxes, except income tax.

ACCOUNTS:—

REVENUE.—For the half-year ended 30th June, 1884, under the above-mentioned lease, the earnings, after payment of all interest, preferential charges, and dividends on the preference stocks, were sufficient to provide for the payment of dividend on the ordinary stock at the rate of 5*l*. 5*s*. per cent. per annum. The dividends are payable, less income tax, on the 1st April and 1st October each half-year.

CAPITAL.—The statement of stock and share capital created, showing the proportion received to 30th June, 1883, furnished the subjoined particulars:—

Priority.	Description.	Created.	Received.
4	Ordinary stock	£387,700	£383,024
	Ditto received on forfeited shares	...	597
1	5 per cent. preference stock	25,400	25,400
2	New 5 per cent. preference stock	25,040	25,040
3	New 6 per cent. ditto	17,020	17,020
	Total	£455,160	£451,081

With 3,979*l*. in arrear, and 100*l*. unissued.

The expenditure on capital account to 30th June, 1884, amounted to 764,541*l.*, the receipts to the same date having been as under:—

Shares and stock	£451,082	
Debenture stock	276,339	
Interest on deposits and calls	3,042	
Transfer fees, 23*l.*; rents, 8*l.*	31	
Dividends on forfeited shares	946	
Premium on debenture stock	6,428=	£737,868
Transferred from revenue		18,231
		£756,099
Balance		10,441
		£766,540

The estimate of further expenditure requires 830*l.*, to meet which the available capital powers are 9,837*l.*

The accounts are made up to 30th June and 31st December, and meetings held in London in the months of February and August.

No. of Directors.—Maximum, 12; minimum, 3; quorum, 3 and 2. *Qualification*, 1,000*l.*

DIRECTORS:

Chairman—General the Right Hon. the Earl of LUCAN, G.C.B., Castlebar, Co. Mayo, and 12, South Street, W.

John Alers Hankey, Esq., 17, Sussex Square, Brighton.

The Right Hon. Viscount Hardinge, South Park, Penshurst, Kent.

*Sir Ralph Smith Cusack, Knight, 24, Rutland Square, Dublin.

*Robert Warren, Esq., D.L., J.P., Rutland Square, Dublin.

*George Woods Maunsell, Esq., 10, Merrion Square South, Dublin.

*Directors of the Midland Great Western.

OFFICERS.—Sec., Benjamin Room; Auditors, James Gildea and George Leeming; Solicitors, Walker and Martineau, 36, Theobald's Road, Gray's Inn, W.C.

Offices—79, Cheapside, E.C.

121.—GREAT NORTH OF SCOTLAND.

Incorporated by act of 1846, for a line from Aberdeen to Inverness, with branches to Banff, Portsoy, Garmouth, and Burghead. Length, 286¼ miles. This and the Aberdeen were to have formed one undertaking when half of the capital of each had been paid up; but an act of 1850 (14 Vic., cap. 78) repealed the Amalgamation Act, 11 Vic., cap. 195.

PARLIAMENTARY POWERS:—

A list of Acts obtained by this company from 1854 to 1877, with short heads for which the various powers were obtained, will be found on reference to the MANUAL for 1881, pages 117 and 118.

1881—11TH AUGUST.—Transfer of the Morayshire undertaking; see particulars under that head further on.

1882—19TH MAY.—Consolidation and conversion of stocks; see further on, and see *Appendix* to the MANUAL for 1883.

1882—19TH MAY.—Sundry extensions of time for completion of works, &c. (short act).

1882—12TH JULY.—Branch line from Portsoy to Elgin. Length, 25¼ miles Period for completion, 5 years. New capital, 165,000*l.*; borrowing powers, 55,000*l*

1884—28TH JULY.—Extension to Rosehearty, in the county of Aberdeen, and othe purposes. New capital, 75,000*l.*; loans, 25,000*l.*

AMALGAMATION, AGREEMENTS, &c. :—

The whole system was consolidated by act of 30th July, 1866, which took effect on 1st August, 1866. The act provided as regards the Alford Valley, the Aberdeen and Turriff, the Banff, Macduff, and Turriff Extension, the Keith and Dufftown, and the Strathspey, that the original share capital be cancelled, and a like amount of new ordinary shares in the amalgamated company created in lieu thereof, to be given off to the original shareholders in the branch lines for like nominal amounts of their shares so cancelled; the shares created in lieu of those subscribed by the Great North of Scotland to be divided rateably among the original shareholders.

Aboyne and Braemar.—Incorporated 5th July, 1865, to construct a line from the Deeside Extension, at Aboyne, to Bridge of Gairn. Length, 11 miles. Capital, 66,000*l.* in 10*l.* shares; loans, 22,000*l.* The Deeside subscribed 10,000*l.* By act of 13th July, 1876, the undertaking was vested in the Great North of Scotland as from 31st January, 1876, Aboyne and Braemar proprietors receiving for every 100*l.* of fully paid-up shares 60*l.* of Great North of Scotland ordinary stock.

Banffshire.—Incorporated by act of 27th July, 1857, to construct a line from the Grange Station of the Great North of Scotland to the harbour of Banff, with a branch to the harbour of Portsoy. Capital, 90,000*l.* in 10*l.* shares; loans, 30,000*l.* By act of 12th August, 1867, the Banffshire was amalgamated with the Great North of Scotland.

Deeside.—Originally incorporated 16th July, 1846, and re-incorporated by act of 28th May, 1852, to construct a line from Aberdeen, along the left bank of the River Dee, to Banchory (for sundry other details, see Manual for 1882, page 120). By act of 13th July, 1876, the Deeside undertaking and the Deeside Extension were amalgamated with the Great North of Scotland, as from 1st August, 1875. For the purposes of the amalgamation, the G. N. of S. creates the following additional capital, viz.:—24,000*l.* Great North of Scotland (Deeside Preference) Stock, to be exchanged for the preference shares in the Deeside Company; 116,250*l.* Great North of Scotland (Deeside Original) Stock, to be exchanged for the original shares of the Deeside; 80,000*l.* Great North of Scotland (Deeside Extension) Stock to be exchanged for the Deeside Extension shares. The dividend on the original stock for the year ended 31st August, 1876, is to be 9¼ per cent.; for 1877, 9½ per cent.; for 1878, 9¾ per cent.; and for 1879, 10 per cent. On the extension stock, the dividend for the year ended 31st August, 1876, is to be 6 per cent.; for 1877, $6\frac{3}{16}$ per cent.; for 1878, $6\frac{4}{16}$ per cent.; and for 1879, 6¾ per cent. After the maximum dividend is reached, the stocks to be exchanged for a 4 per cent. preference stock. In September, 1879, the Deeside "Original" and "Extension" stocks were converted into Deeside "A" and "B" stocks, the holders of Deeside "Original" stock receiving 250*l.* and the holders of Deeside "Extension" 169*l.* of Deeside "A" stock, entitled to a perpetual guaranteed dividend of 4 per cent. per annum, in exchange for each 100*l.* of the old stocks held by them respectively, and in addition 25*l.* of Deeside "B" stock, ranking for dividend *pari passu* with the ordinary stock in any dividend upon that stock which the company may earn in any year ending 31st July, *in excess* of 5 per cent. per annum in right of each 100*l.* of Deeside "A" stock allotted as above. The "B" stock not to carry voting powers.—For provisions of the act under which this conversion was effected see *Appendix* to the Manual for 1880.

Denburn Valley.—Authorised by act of 23rd June, 1864, and consisting of a line through the city of Aberdeen to connect with the Great North of Scotland. Length, 1¾ mile. Through booking and mutual facilities.

Morayshire.—Incorporated by act of 16th July, 1846. Transferred to Great North of Scotland by act of 11th August, 1881, as from the 1st October, 1880. The chief terms of this amalgamation, as affecting holders of the securities of the vested company, are briefly as follow:—Morayshire preference shares (11,740*l.*) to be converted into "Great North of Scotland (Morayshire Lien) 5 per cent. preference stock," at the rate of 15*l.* of stock for every 10*l.* share. Morayshire preference shares (23,080*l.*), created under acts 1860 and 1863, to be converted into an equal nominal amount of the above named "Morayshire Lien" stock of the Great North of Scotland. Morayshire ordinary shares to be exchanged for an equal amount of Great North of Scotland ordinary stock. The existing mortgages or debentures of the Morayshire to become mortgages or debentures of the Great North of Scotland, and also to be a first charge during their subsistence upon the Morayshire undertaking.—For particulars as to past working, &c., see the Manual for 1881, page 270.

Old Meldrum Junction.—This line, formerly leased to the Great North of Scotland, is amalgamated with it, the rent (560*l.*) secured as a fixed charge against the Great North of Scotland, and converted into a dividend of like amount on a preferential stock of 13,810*l.*—to be called "Great North of Scotland (Old Meldrum) Preference Stock."

ACCOUNTS:—

Revenue.—The receipts for the half-year ended 31st January, 1884, amounted to 160,471*l.*, and the expenditure to 85,075*l.*, leaving a balance of 75,396*l.* To this was added 2,450*l.* from previous half-year, 148*l.* on general interest account, making

77,994*l*. From this was deducted 21,094*l*. for interest on debentures and debenture stock, &c., and 53,621*l*. for dividends on guaranteed preference and ordinary stocks; balance carried forward, 3,279*l*.

The receipts for the half-year ended 31st July, 1884, amounted to 156,443*l*., and the expenditure to 81,505*l*., leaving a balance of 74,938*l*. To this was added 3,279*l*. from preceding half-year, and 198*l*. for interest account, making 78,415*l*. From this was deducted 21,486*l*. for interest on loans and debenture stock, &c., and 54,269*l*. for dividends on guaranteed preference and ordinary stocks, leaving a balance of 2,660*l*.

In operation, 290¾ miles. Line doubled from Kintore to Inveramsay (7½ miles) since October, 1881. Total double miles, 23¾.

The line from Portsoy to Tochineal (4¼ miles) was opened 1st April, 1884, and from Elgin to Garmouth (8¼ miles) 12th August, 1884.

It may be mentioned that the holders of "B" preference stock have, since the 1st August, 1877, become re-entitled to the full dividend at 4½ per cent. per annum, which they relinquished for a dividend at 3 per cent. per annum, under the act of 1873.

CAPITAL.—The receipts and expenditure on this account to 31st July, 1884, were as under:—

Received.		*Expended.*	
Shares and stock	£3,870,181	Lines open for traffic	£3,405,580
Loans on debenture	153,734	Working stock	471,125
Debenture stock	891,046	Lines in course of construction	125,989
Premiums on stock and shares	27,276	Nominal addition on consolidation of stocks	1,013,172
	£4,942,237	Arrears of dividend on 5 per cent. preference consolidated stock, &c.	29,715
Balance	103,344		
	£5,045,581		£5,045,581

The estimate of further expenditure required 97,000*l*. for the half-year ending 31st January, 1885, and 137,786*l*. for subsequent periods; total, 234,786*l*. The assets were—share capital authorised but not yet created, *nil*; ditto created but not yet received, 331,068*l*.; loan capital created but not yet received, 33,574*l*.; less balance at debit of capital account, 103,344*l*.; total, 261,297*l*.

The stock and share capital, numbered in order of priority as ranking after loans and debenture stock, at 31st July, 1884, was as follows, viz:—

	Description to be observed in transfer deeds and all other legal documents.	Created.	Received.
1	Old Meldrum 4½ per cent. preference stock, 1866	£13,810	£13,810
2	Aberdeen and Turriff 5 per cent. preference stock 1866	32,900	32,900
2	Formartine and Buchan 5 per cent. preference stock, 1866	203 270	203,270
2	Do. ordinary stock, 1866, 3 per cent.*	133,190	102,822
2	Banffshire 5 per cent. preference stock, 1867	46,010	46,010
2	Deeside preference stock, 1876, 4½ per cent.†	17,040	17,040
2	Do. "A" stock, 1879, 4 per cent.	433,655	432,953
2	Morayshire rent-charge stock	39,274	39,274
3	5 per cent. preference stock, 1859‡	291,090	291,090
4	4½ per cent. "A" preference stock, 1859	482,050	482,050
5	Redeemable 4 per cent. pref. stock, 1873, not exceeding par	30,868	30,868
6	4½ per cent. "B" preference stock, 1862	329,132	325,130
7	5 per cent "C" preference shares, 1880	225,000	90,780
8	Morayshire lien stock	41,000	40,350
9	Ordinary stock, Acts 1859, 1866, 1867, and 1876	937,073	920,133
10	Deeside "B" stock, 1879§	106,456	106,306
	Total	£3,361,818	£3,174,786

* With right to participate in any dividend paid on the Great North of Scotland ordinary stock above 3 per cent. per annum.

† Option to convert into Deeside "A" stock at 112*l*. 10*s*. per cent.

‡ With right to participate in any dividend paid on the ordinary stock above 5 per cent. per annum.

§ Entitled to participate *pari passu* with any dividend paid on the ordinary stock of the company above 5 per cent. per annum.

CONSOLIDATION AND CONVERSION OF STOCKS.—In September, 1882, under the provisions of the act of 19th May, 1882, the above-named preference and other stocks of the company were consolidated as follow, viz.:—

Table of stocks extinguished on the 22nd day of September, 1882, and of the stocks allocated and issued in substitution for the same.

1.—Stocks to be extinguished.	2.—Stocks to be allocated and issued in substitution.		
For every £100 of	There will be allocated in exchange		
	£	s.	
G. N. of S. (Old Meldrum) preference stock	112	10	of Great North of Scotland 4 per cent. Lien stock.
G. N. of S. (Aberbeen and Turriff) do.	125		
G. N. of S. (Formartine and Buchan) do.	125		
G. N. of S. do. do. ordinary do...	75		
G. N. of S. (Banffshire) preference stock............	125		
G. N. of S. (Deeside) do. do.	112	10	
G. N. of S. (Deeside) "A" stock	100		
G. N. of S. (Morayshire) rent-charge do.............	100		
G. N. of S. 5 per cent. preference stock, 1859........	125		of Great North of Scotland 4 per cent. guaranteed stock.
G. N. of S. 4½ per cent. "A" preference stock........	112	10	of Great North of Scotland 4 per cent. "A" pref. stock.
G. N. of S. (Morayshire Lien) 5 per cent. stock......	125		
G. N. of S. 4½ per cent. "B" preference stock........	112	10	of Great North of Scotland 4 per cent. "B" pref. stock.
G. N. of S. (Deeside) "B" stock	100		of Great North of Scotland Deferred ordinary stock No. 2.
Also for every £100 of the above-mentioned	There will be allocated		
G. N. of S. (Formartine & Buchan) ordinary stock..	100		of Great North of Scotland Deferred ordinary stock No. 1.
G. N. of S. 5 per cent. preference stock, 1859........	100		of Great North of Scotland Deferrred odinary stock No. 2.

New stocks will be issued in the same proportions for any greater or smaller amount than 100*l.*

BUCKIE EXTENSION CAPITAL.—This consists of 22,000 shares of 10*l.* each, bearing interest at 4 per cent. per annum in perpetuity (with a lien upon the gross receipts of the separate undertaking). These shares were allotted at par, in November last, to the ordinary stockholders, at the rate of one new share for every 150*l.* stock, no allotment being made on holdings below 300*l.* The calls were made payable as follow, viz.:—2*l.*, 27th November, 1882; 2*l.*, 27th March, 1883; 2*l.*, 27th August, 1883; 2*l.*, 27th February, 1884; and 2*l.*, 28th June, 1884.

TRANSFER DEPARTMENT QUERIES AND REPLIES.

QUERIES.	REPLIES.
Transfer form—ordinary or special?......	Ordinary.
Fee per deed?	2*s.* 6*d.* per deed; but if more than one class of stock transferred on one deed, 2*s.* 6*d.* for each class of stock.
Ditto if more sellers than one?...	2*s.* 6*d.* for each.
Are certificates required to accompany transfers?	Yes.
What amounts are transferable, and are parts of 1*l.* sterling allowed to be transferred?	Any amount; but not parts of 1*l.*
To what officer should transfer communications be sent?	Secretary.
In acceptances, renunciations, &c., of allotments of new stock, proxies, or other forms sent to trustees or other joint holders, what signatures are required?	In the case of acceptances or renunciations of allotments of new stock, the signature of the first-named trustee, for himself and co-trustees, is required; in the case of proxies, that of the first-named holder upon register.

Accounts made up half-yearly to 31st January and 31st July. Meetings held at Aberdeen in March or April and September or October. Dividends payable in April and October; transfer books close 14 days before half-yearly meetings.

New Capital.—In October, 1880, the directors issued 100,000*l.* in 10,000 "Great North of Scotland 'C' Preference Shares" entitled to a preferential dividend at the rate of 5 per cent. per annum, ranking next in order of priority to the 4½ per cent. "B" shares. This new capital is a first issue of that authorised by "The Denburn Valley Act, 1864," and "The Great North of Scotland Act, 1877." The shares were allotted to proprietors of at least 100*l.*, or ordinary stock at the rate of about 12 shares for every 1,000*l.* stock. Price par. Calls payable as follow, viz.:—2*l.* 10*s.* on allotment; 2*l.* 10*s.* on each 1st March, 1st August, and 1st December, 1881, respectively.

Scale of Voting.—One vote for each share held.

Certificates must accompany transfer deed, the fee for registration of which is 2*s.* 6*d.* each stock.

No. of Directors.—Maximum, 13; minimum, 7. *Qualification*, 20 shares.

DIRECTORS:

Chairman—WILLIAM FERGUSON, Esq., of Kinmundy, Mintlaw.

Deputy-Chairman—THOMAS ADAM, Esq., Banker, Aberdeen.

The Right Hon. the Earl of Aberdeen, Haddo House, Aberdeen.

John Crombie, Esq., Balgownie Lodge, Aberdeen.

Alexander Edmond, Esq., Garthdee, Aberdeen.

James Grant, Esq., of Glengrant, Rothes.

Robert Kaye, Esq., Partick Hill, Glasgow.

James Moir, Esq., Banker, Portsoy.

The Right. Hon. the Earl of Kintore, Guthrie Castle, Forfarshire.

James Badenach Nicolson, Esq., Glenbervie House, Kincardineshire.

Colonel John Ramsay, of Barra, Straloch, by Aberdeen.

John G. Smith, Esq., Minmore, Glenlivet, N.B.

Owen Hugh Williams, Esq., 17, Brown's Buildings, Liverpool.

OFFICERS.—Gen. Man. and Sec., William Moffatt; Assistant Man., John S. Stuart; Passenger Supt., A. G. Reid; Supt. of Northern Section, Alex. Watt, Elgin; Goods Man., A. M. Ross; Loco. Supt., James Manson; Eng., Patrick M. Barnett; Accountant and Cashier, Samuel Paterson: Audit Clerk, James Rutherford; Registrar, James Mortimer; Auditors, James Augustus Sinclair, Aberdeen, and William Milne, C.A., Aberdeen; Solicitors, Adam, Thomson, and Ross, 75, Union Street, Aberdeen; Parliamentary Agents, Dyson and Co.; London Bankers, Union Bank, London; Commercial Bank, Liverpool; National Bank of Scotland and branches; North of Scotland Bank, Aberdeen.

Head Offices—Waterloo Station, Aberdeen.

122.—GREAT SOUTHERN AND WESTERN.

Incorporated by acts of 6th August, 1844, and 21st July, 1845, for a line from Dublin to Cork, passing by or near Portarlington, Thurles, Tipperary, and Mallow, with a branch to Carlow. Powers were subsequently obtained for making an extension to the River Lee, a branch from Portarlington to Tullamore, and incorporating the Clonmel and Thurles; also authorising subscriptions to other companies to the following extent, viz.:—Killarney Junction, 100,000*l.*; Mallow and Fermoy, 100,000*l.*; Irish South Eastern, 90,000*l.*

Further Parliamentary Powers:—

A list of Acts from 1851 to 1879, with short heads showing the objects for which the various powers were obtained, will be found on reference to the Manual for 1881, pages 135 and 136.

1881—18th July.—Extension to Baltinglass (24 miles). Junction with the Limerick and Kerry. Period for completion, 5 years.

1884—14th July.—Extension railway to Tullow, in the county of Carlow, from Baltinglass. Length, 10½ miles. New debenture stock, 80,000*l.*

1884—14th July.—Construction of a railway in substitution for a portion of the Cork and Youghal and Great Southern and Western Junction, and other purposes.

AMALGAMATIONS, LEASES, AGREEMENTS, &c.:—

Castleisland and Gortatlea.—Incorporated by act of 13th May, 1872, to construct a line from the market town of Castleisland to Gortatlea, on the Great Southern and Western. Length, 4½ miles. The line was opened 30th August, 1875. The Great Southern and Western Additional Powers Act, 1879, sanctioned the purchase of the line by that company, and the line became vested therein as from 1st May, 1879.

CORK AND LIMERICK DIRECT.—Incorporated by act of 3rd July, 1860, to construct a line from the Great Southern and Western, near Charleville, to the Limerick and Foynes, near Patrick's Well. Also a short line at Limerick. Length, 25 miles. By act of 13th July, 1871, the Cork and Limerick was vested in the Great Southern and Western, 60 per cent. of its ordinary stock being exchanged for 100*l*. of the Cork and Limerick; the debenture debt to be assumed and the preference shares paid off at par.

CORK AND YOUGHAL.—By act of 28th June, 1866, the company was authorised to form a junction with the Cork and Youghal, and to purchase that railway for the sum of 310,000*l*.

FERMOY AND LISMORE.—Worked by the Great Southern and Western.—See GENERAL INDEX.

IRISH SOUTH EASTERN.—Carlow to Kilkenny, 25 miles. Incorporated with the Great Southern and Western on 1st July, 1863, each share in the former being exchanged for 5*l*. stock in the latter company.

KILLARNEY JUNCTION.—Incorporated by act of 1846 for a line from a junction of the Great Southern and Western, near Mallow, to Killarney, 41 miles. The Great Southern and Western had power, under the act of incorporation, to amalgamate with, to lease, or purchase this undertaking; also to subscribe 60,000*l*., and nominate three directors. The line was completed in May, 1854, and incorporated in the Great Southern and Western.

KILLORGLIN.—Incorporated under act of 1871, for making a railway in the county of Kerry from Farranfore Station to Killorglin. Capital, 40,000*l*. in shares. The company being unable to raise the share capital, and the powers under the act of 1871 having expired, the undertaking was revived under act of 12th August, 1880, and certain provisions in the act of 1871 were in that act amended. The act of 1880 authorised the making of the railway mentioned in act of 1871, with certain diversions about 5 miles in length, making a total of about 17 miles. Capital, 60,000*l*., upon which interest at 5 per cent. per annum will be guaranteed by the several baronies and unions of Tralee, Killarney, Cahirciveen, and Dingle. Borrowing powers, 30,000*l*. The railway to be completed before 1st November, 1882. The powers under which the railway was authorised have since been transferred to the Great Southern and Western, under that company's act of 11th August, 1881. It was stated about the middle of 1884, that this line might possibly be opened for traffic before the close of that year.

LIMERICK AND CASTLE CONNELL.—Under the award of the arbitrators, the company had to repay the Great Southern and Western 10,000*l*., being the amount invested in the Castle Connell.

MALLOW AND FERMOY.—Incorporated by act of 3rd July, 1854, for making a line from the Great Southern and Western, near Mallow, to Fermoy. Length, 17 miles. By act of 27th July, 1856, this company was dissolved and its powers transferred to Great Southern and Western.

NORTH WALL EXTENSION.—This extension was opened for passenger traffic on the 2nd September, 1877.

ROSCREA AND PARSONSTOWN.—Incorporated by act of 4th August, 1853, for a line from the Great Southern and Western to Parsonstown. Length, 22½ miles. Capital, 100,000*l*. Scheme vested in Great Southern and Western on 17th November, 1855. Extension—Roscrea to Birdhill, authorised by act of 1861.

TRALEE AND KILLARNEY.—Incorporated by act of 10th July, 1854, in lieu of the act of 1853, for a line from Killarney Junction to Tralee. Length, 22 miles. Since incorporated in the Great Southern and Western.

TULLAMORE TO ATHLONE.—Authorised by Athlone Extension Act, 20 and 21 Vic., 1857.

WATERFORD, NEW ROSS, AND WEXFORD JUNCTION.—Incorporated 10th August, 1866, to construct a line from Waterford to New Ross, Ballywilliam, and Ballyhoge, on the Dublin, Wicklow, and Wexford. Length, 36 miles (other details in MANUAL for 1882, page 134). Eventually the line was sold under powers of an act passed 13th July, 1876, to the Great Southern and Western and Dublin, Wicklow, and Wexford companies for 40,000*l*. The Dublin and Wicklow took that portion of the line lying between Ballywilliam and Macmine for 16,000*l*., and the remainder was taken by the Great Southern and Western for 24,000*l*.

The Clara and Banagher is worked under agreement by the Great Southern and Western.

ACCOUNTS:—

REVENUE.—The gross receipts for the half-year ended 30th June, 1884, amounted to 347,669*l.*, and the expenditure to 199,164*l.*, giving, with the balance from previous account, a total net revenue of 164,014*l.*, which sufficed for the following payments:—Interest on debenture stock (less general interest account), 25,881*l.*; dividend on preference stock, 26,582*l.*; dividend on ordinary stock, at 4¼ per cent. per annum, 105,426*l.*; balance to next account, 6,124*l.*

The gross receipts for the half-year ended 31st December, 1883, amounted to 387,162*l.*, and the working expenses to 203,799*l.*, leaving a profit (including interest in net revenue account) of 185,834*l.*, which, with the balance brought forward, sufficed for the half-year's interest on the debenture stock and 4 per cent. preference stock, and a dividend at the rate of 5 per cent. per annum on the consolidated ordinary stock of the company, leaving a balance of 15,508*l.* for the next account.

MILEAGE—30TH JUNE, 1884.—Lines owned, 462¾ miles; lines rented, 7¼ miles; lines partly owned, 2¾ miles; lines worked, 33 miles; foreign lines worked over, 2 miles.

CAPITAL.—*Authorised:* Shares and stock, 6,309,940*l.*; loans, 1,873,965*l.*; total, 8,183,905*l.*; all created. The following statement shows the receipts and expenditure on this account to 30th June, 1884:—

Receipts.		*Expenditure.*	
Ordinary stock	£4,961,250	Lines open, &c.	£6,331,761
4 per cent. preference stock	1,329,100	Working stock	930,894
4 per cent. debenture stock	1,383,202	Queenstown Deep-Water Quay	15,882
Premium on stock sold	104,370	Baltinglass extension	108,156
Balance	37,315	Killorglin Railway	53,297
		North Wall extension (Nos. 1 & 2)	86,839
		" (Nos. 3 & 4)	288,408
	£7,815,237		£7,815,237

NEW FOUR PER CENT. DEBENTURE STOCK.—In August, 1884, a resolution was passed authorising the creation and issue of 400,000*l.* debenture stock, and of the Great Southern and Western (Tullow Extension) Act, 1884, 80,000*l.* debenture stock, with interest thereon respectively at 4 per cent. per annum.

The estimate of further expenditure was 142,846*l.* for the half-year ended 31st December, 1884, and 73,818*l.* in subsequent half-years; total, 216,664*l.* The capital powers and other available assets amount to 473,038*l.*

The accounts are made up to 30th June and 31st December, and the statutory meetings held in Dublin in February and August.

Scale of Voting.—One vote for every 250*l.* original stock up to 2,500*l.*, and one additional vote for every 500*l.* original stock afterwards.

Certificates must accompany transfer deed. Registration fee, 2*s.* 6*d.* each deed.

No. of Directors—10. *Qualification*, 2,000*l.* stock; allowance, 3,000*l.*

DIRECTORS:

1 Chairman—JAMES C. COLVILL, Esq., Coolock House, Co. Dublin.

1 Deputy-Chairman—JAMES W. MURLAND, Esq., Nutley, Booterstown.

2 Colonel John Bonham, Grangecon, Athy.

3 Samuel H. Close, Esq., Henry Street, Dublin.

2 Chas. Purdon Coote, Esq., Bearforest, Mallow.

1 Luke John M'Donnell, Esq., 38, Merrion Square East, Dublin.

2 Jerome J. Murphy, Esq., Ashton, Cork.

2 Joshua Joseph Pim, Esq., Fortal, Dalkey, Co. Dublin.

3 William Robertson, Esq., 30, Fitzwilliam Square, Dublin.

3 John E. Vernon, Esq., Mount Merrion, Booterstown.

OFFICERS.—Sec., Francis B. Ormsby; Traffic Man., George Edward Ilbery; Eng.-in-Chief, Kennett Bayley; Loco. Eng., John A. F. Aspinall; Accountant, John R. McCready; Auditors, Henry T. Vickers and Lucius O. Hutton; Solicitors, Barrington and Son, Ely Place, Dublin, and Limerick; Bankers, Glyn, Mills, Currie, and Co., Lombard Street, E.C., and Bank of Ireland, Dublin.

Head Offices—Kingsbridge Terminus, Dublin.

123.—GREAT WESTERN.

This undertaking, which was re-modelled by acts of 1867 and 1869, is constituted of the Great Western, the West Midland, the South Wales, the Bristol and Exeter, and the South Devon, with the whole of the subsidiaries of these various incorporations. Productive, 2,301 miles.

By resolutions adopted in 1870, the various ordinary stocks were consolidated at the following prices:—

For each 100*l*.	Consolidated.
Great Western (ordinary)	£100
Oxford "	70
Newport "	60
South Wales "	108

FURTHER PARLIAMENTARY POWERS:—

A list of the various Acts granted to this Company from 1870 to 1878, with short heads of the objects for which the various powers were sought, will be found on reference to the MANUAL for 1881, pages 138 and 139.

1880—2ND AUGUST.—Amalgamation with the Monmouthshire undertaking.—See further on.

1881—6TH AUGUST.—Vesting of Ely and Clydach Valleys, Malmesbury, Micheldean Road and Forest of Dean Junction, and, jointly with the Bala and Festiniog, the Festiniog and Blaenau undertakings. New railways in Buckinghamshire, Monmouthshire, and Glamorganshire. Sundry extensions of time, abandonments, subscriptions to other companies, and various other additional powers. New capital, 200,000*l*. (in addition to that required for vesting purposes); borrowing powers, 66,000*l*.

1881—22ND AUGUST.—Vesting of Coleford, Monmouth, Usk, and Pontypool. Various alterations and improvements. New capital, 300,000*l*.; borrowing powers, 100,000*l*.

1882 (No. 2)—24TH JULY.—New lines and works in the County of Glamorgan, &c. Vesting of the Torbay and Brixham (see further on). New capital (other than that required for vesting purposes), 200,000*l*.; borrowing powers, 66,000*l*.

1882 (No. 1)—10TH AUGUST.—Vesting of Berks and Hants and Swindon and Highworth Light; new lines and works, and various other powers. New capital, 250,000*l*.; borrowing powers, 83,000*l*.

1883.—Acts passed for general purposes, and for amalgamation of Llynvi and Ogmore, and Stratford-on-Avon (see further on).

1884—28TH JULY.—Three short lines at Siddington and Cirencester, in Gloucestershire, and other purposes.

1884—7TH AUGUST.—Vesting of the Coleford and Bristol and North Somerset undertakings (see further on), agreements with other companies, and other general purposes. New capital, 450,000*l*.; loans, 150,000*l*.

1884—14TH AUGUST.—Vesting of Bristol and Portishead (see further on), and other purposes.

AMALGAMATIONS, LEASES, AGREEMENTS, SUBSCRIPTIONS, &c.:—

The following is an alphabetical list of the undertakings in which the Great Western is interested:—

ALCESTER.—Incorporated by act of 6th August, 1872, to construct a railway from the Bearley Station of the Stratford-on-Avon to the Alcester Station of the Evesham and Redditch. Length, 6½ miles. On the 4th September, 1877, the maintenance of the railway was handed over to the Great Western as provided for by an agreement between the two companies, and by the Great Western Act of 22nd July, 1878, authority was given for the vesting of this company in the Great Western and Stratford-on-Avon companies, those companies being proprietors of one half each of the capital of the Alcester. The terms and conditions only affect the companies interested, a joint committee to be appointed for the management of the vested undertaking.

BALA AND DOLGELLEY.—Incorporated by act of 30th June, 1862, to construct a line from Bala to Dolgelley. By act of 23rd July, 1877, this undertaking became vested in the Great Western, the Dolgelley ordinary shareholders receiving 80 per cent. of Great Western consolidated 5 per cent. preference stock in lieu of their holding, the amalgamation to take effect on the 1st August, 1877, the Dolgelley shareholders to pay 15*s*. per cent. on the amount of their holding towards expenses.

BALA AND FESTINIOG.—See GENERAL INDEX.

BERKS AND HANTS EXTENSION.—Incorporated by act of 13th August, 1859, and amalgamated with Great Western by that company's act of 10th August, 1882 (No. 1), as from the 1st July in that year, the holders of each 100*l*. of Berks and Hants ordinary stock receiving 87*l*. 10*s*. of Great Western consolidated ordinary stock, fractions of 1*l*. being paid off. The existing Berks and Hants 5 per cent. preference shares, 1863, are to retain their position as redeemable shares until redeemed.—For particulars relating to the working, &c., of this undertaking in the past, see MANUAL for 1882, and previously.

Birkenhead.—See General Index.

Bourton-on-the-Water.—Incorporated by act of 14th June, 1860, to construct a line from the Great Western (West Midland Section), at the Chipping Norton Junction, to Bourton-on-the-Water. By act of 27th June, 1874, the Bourton-on-the-Water was amalgamated with the Great Western as from 1st February, 1874. Under the terms of amalgamation every holder of 100*l*. of Bourton-on-the-Water ordinary stock (amounting to 29,900*l*.) received 55*l*. of Great Western consolidated preference stock. The debenture debt of the Bourton on-the-Water, amounting to 10,000*l*., has also been adopted by the Great Western.

Bristol and Exeter.—Incorporated 19th May, 1836, to construct a broad gauge line from Bristol, where it joins the Great Western, to Exeter, there joining the South Devon, which runs to Plymouth; the Cornwall and the West Cornwall continuing the broad gauge from Plymouth to Falmouth and Penzance, with branches to Weston-Super-Mare, Clevedon, Tiverton, and other places. By act of 27th June, 1876, the Bristol and Exeter, at the time under lease to the Great Western (at 6 per cent. for six years from 1st January, 1876, and afterwards at 6½ per cent. in perpetuity) was amalgamated with that company as from the 1st August, 1876. The provisions under the more important sections of the act are as follow:—15.—On and after the amalgamation the mortgage debt of the Bristol and Exeter to become the mortgage debt of the Great Western, and the latter company may borrow in lieu of the former. 18.—Bristol and Exeter debenture stockholders to become Great Western debenture stockholders. 19.—Bristol and Exeter proprietors to become holders of Great Western capital in the following proportions:—For every 100*l*. of Bristol and Exeter inconvertible 4 per cent. stock, and for every 100*l*. of Bristol and Exeter perpetual 4 per cent. preference stock, 80*l*. of Great Western 5 per cent. rent-charge stock; for every 100*l*. of Bristol and Exeter perpetual 4½ per cent. preference stock, 90*l*. of Great Western 5 per cent. consolidated preference stock; for every 100*l*. of Bristol and Exeter perpetual 5 per cent. preference stock, 100*l*. of Great Western 5 per cent. consolidated preference stock; for every 100*l*. of Bristol and Exeter ordinary stock, 120*l*. of Great Western 5 per cent. consolidated preference stock, and also a certificate entitling the holder at any time after the 31st December, 1882, to be registered as the owner of such a further sum of Great Western 5 per cent. consolidated preference stock (at the rate of 10*l*. of such stock for every 100*l*. of Bristol and Exeter ordinary stock) bearing dividend as from 1st January, 1883, as shall be registered on such certificate. 20.—The Great Western may, from time to time, issue consolidated preference stock to redeem Bristol and Exeter 4½ per cent. redeemable preference stock; provided that the consolidated stock issued shall in no case exceed 90*l*. for every 100*l*. of the stock redeemed.—For brief heads of further powers, and arrangements with canals and other undertakings, see Manual for 1882, and previously.

Bristol Harbour.—Incorporated 28th June, 1866, to construct a wharf and depôt at Wapping, in Bristol, and a railway to connect the railways of the Great Western and the Bristol and Exeter with the Floating Harbour there. Opened for goods traffic on 11th March, 1872. The undertaking is now merged in the Great Western, under the following terms, viz.:—Bristol Harbour debenture stock to be exchanged for Great Western debenture stock bearing the same interest, and Bristol Harbour stockholders to become holders of Great Western stock in the following proportions:—For every 100*l*. of Bristol Harbour guaranteed 5 per cent. stock, 100*l*. of Great Western 5 per cent. consolidated guaranteed stock; and for every 100*l*. of Bristol Harbour guaranteed 4½ per cent. stock, 90*l*. of Great Western 5 per cent. consolidated guaranteed stock.—For other details, see Manual for 1882, and previously.

Bristol and North Somerset.—Incorporated by act of 21st July, 1863, and vested in the Great Western, under act of 7th August, 1884, as from the 1st July, 1884, the holders of the 110,000*l*. North Somerset 5 per cent. debenture stock receiving Great Western 4 per cent. debenture stock exchanged at par.—For particulars as to the position of this company in the past, see Manual for 1884, pages 27 and 28.

Bristol and Portishead.—Incorporated by act of 29th June, 1863, and vested in the Great Western by act of 14th August, 1884, as from the 1st July, 1884, the consideration being the granting by the Great Western, to the Portishead, of an annual rent-charge in perpetuity, amounting to 11,750*l*., after deduction of the amount of such rent-charges for land granted by the Portishead as may remain unredeemed by that company.—For particulars as to the position of this company in the past, with addresses of Directors and Officers, &c., see Manual for 1884, page 28.

BRISTOL AND SOUTH WALES UNION.—Incorporated by act of 27th July, 1857, to construct railways between the city of Bristol and the South Wales, in the county of Monmouth, with a steam ferry across the River Severn in connection therewith (for short details of further powers, see MANUAL for 1882, and previously). By "The Great Western Act, 1868," the Bristol and South Wales Union was merged into and amalgamated with the Great Western, the latter taking upon itself the following liabilities:—1. The debenture debt of the Union, bearing interest at not exceeding 5 per cent., 98,000*l.* 2. The preference share capital of the Union, bearing interest in perpetuity at 5 per cent. on and from 1st February, 1870; these shares are to be converted into Great Western (South Wales Union) guaranteed 5 per cent. preference stock, 120,450*l.* 3. The ordinary share capital of the Union, on and from 1st February, 1870; these shares are to be converted into and rank with Great Western ordinary stock, 168,225*l.*

CARMARTHEN AND CARDIGAN.—This concern was purchased by the Great Western as and from the 1st July, 1881, and was ordered to be wound up in September of that year, Mr. Henry Spain and Mr. David Cornfoot, 10, Cambridge Gardens, Richmond, Surrey, being appointed liquidators. The principal effect of the arrangement is that the liquidators have been able to distribute about 40*l.* in cash for each 100*l.* of the Carmarthen and Cardigan "A" stock, and a less proportion in respect of the "B" and "C" stocks, the Great Western assuming the liability of the Carmarthen and Cardigan debenture stock.—For particulars as to the working of this undertaking in the past, see the MANUAL for 1881, and previous editions.

COLEFORD.—Incorporated by act of 18th July, 1872, and vested in the Great Western under act of 7th August, 1884, as from the 1st July, 1884, the mortgage debt and other capital liabilities of the Coleford being taken over by the Great Western, and the ordinary shareholders receiving Great Western ordinary stock in exchange for the amount of their holdings, on equal terms.—For particulars as to the position of this company in the past, see MANUAL for 1884, page 59.

COLEFORD, MONMOUTH, USK, AND PONTYPOOL.—See GENERAL INDEX.

CORNWALL.—The Great Western, in addition to subscribing 202,500*l.* to this line, guarantees the debenture debt and preference stocks of that company.—See GENERAL INDEX.

CORNWALL MINERALS.—See GENERAL INDEX.

CULM VALLEY LIGHT.—Incorporated by act of 15th May, 1873, to construct a single line from the Tiverton Junction Station of the Bristol and Exeter to Hemyock. Length, 7¼ miles. Capital, 25,000*l.* in 10*l.* shares, and 8,000*l.* on loan. The line was opened for traffic 29th May, 1876, and was formerly agreed to be worked in perpetuity by the Great Western (which held 4,000*l.* ordinary shares in it) at 50 per cent. of the gross receipts, with a rebate on through traffic. Under the provisions of the Bristol and Exeter Act, 1875, the sale and transfer of this company to the Great Western has been effected. This arrangement was made in April, 1880, when it was agreed that the vesting company should adopt the debenture debt, and issue to the Culm Valley 13,600*l.* of Great Western preference stock, and 1,250*l.* Great Western ordinary stock, in satisfaction of all claims, whether of creditors or shareholders. It was expected that when the accounts were finally closed, the ordinary shareholders would receive about 5 per cent. on their holdings. The final meeting was held in London, on the 3rd November, 1882.—For particulars as to the working of the undertaking in the past, see the MANUAL for 1880, and previous editions.

DARTMOUTH AND TORBAY.—This line having belonged to the South Devon is now part of the Great Western system.—For other particulars, see the South Devon in the MANUAL for 1878, and previous editions.

DIDCOT, NEWBURY, AND SOUTHAMPTON.—See GENERAL INDEX.

EAST SOMERSET.—Incorporated by act of 5th June, 1856, to make a railway from the Wilts, Somerset, and Weymouth, near Frome, to Shepton Mallet. Broad gauge. Capital, 75,000*l.*; loans, 25,000*l.* By the Great Western Company's Act of 1874, the East Somerset was transferred to that company as from 1st August, 1874, the terms of transfer being that each holder of nine ordinary shares in the East Somerset should receive 28*l.* of Great Western consolidated 5 per cent. preference stock, and so in proportion for any less number of shares; and that each holder of nine preference shares in the East Somerset should receive 80*l.* of like Great Western stock. The amount of Great Western preference stock so exchanged would be 67,442*l.*

ELY AND CLYDACH VALLEYS.—Incorporated by act of 5th August, 1873, for a line commencing by a junction with the Ely Valley, near the Pen-y-Graig Colliery, and terminating at or near the Clydach Vale Colliery. Length, 2 miles 5 furlongs. Capital, 33,000*l.* in 10*l.* shares and 11,000*l.* on loan. This line became vested in the Great Western, under that company's Amalgamation Act of 1880, the ordinary stockholders of the vested company receiving an equal amount of Great Western consolidated ordinary stock in exchange for their holdings.—For particulars relating to the working of the undertaking in the past, see the MANUAL for 1880, and previous editions.

ELY VALLEY.—Incorporated by act of 13th July, 1857, to construct a line from the Llantrissant Station of the South Wales to Penrhiwfer, Glamorganshire, with branches to Glanmychydd and Mynydd Gellyrhaidd. Agreement for lease to the Great Western for 999 years, confirmed by act of 29th July, 1862, came into operation as from 1st January, 1861. The Great Western hold 35,000*l.* of Ely Valley stock. and pay Ely Valley a rent of 4,000*l.*, which pays 5½*l.* per cent. on Ely Valley stock and debenture debt.

FESTINIOG AND BLAENAU.—See Bala and Festiniog.

GLOUCESTER AND DEAN FOREST.—Incorporated by act of 27th July, 1846, for a line in connection with the Great Western, at Gloucester, to the Hereford, Ross, and Gloucester, at Westbury, and also to the South Wales, at Awre. Length, 16 miles. The total capital subscribed was 354,000*l.* The South Wales held 4,000 shares (100,000*l.*); subsequently, in lieu thereof, the company took upon itself the construction of 7 miles of the line, from Awre to Grange Court, and the capital became reduced, and the 4,000 shares treated as cancelled. The Great Western subscribed 50,000*l.* In 1847, the Gloucester and Dean Forest was empowered to construct a dock at Gloucester (canal). Powers were given by these acts to either sell or lease the line to the Great Western; and in accordance with these powers, and by virtue of the Great Western Act, 1874, the line is leased to the Great Western for 999 years, from 1st July, 1874. Under the terms of the lease, holders of five shares in the Gloucester and Dean Forest would receive 105*l.* Great Western rent-charge stock, bearing interest at 5 per cent. per annum, and so in proportion for any less number of shares.

GREAT MARLOW.—Incorporated by act of 13th July, 1868, to construct a line from Bourne End Station, on the Wycombe, Thame, and Oxford Branch of the Great Western, to the town of Great Marlow. Length, 2¾ miles. Capital, 18,000*l.* in 10*l.* shares and 6,000*l.* on loan. Arrangements with Great Western, which subscribed 15,000*l.* and works the line. Opened June 27th, 1873. At a meeting, held 26th August, 1872, it was agreed that in future 972 of the 1,800 shares forming the capital of the company should receive a preference dividend up to 5 per cent., after payment of which all surplus profits would be divided on the remaining 828 ordinary shares.—Secretary and Registered Officer, John Rawson, Great Marlow.

GREAT WESTERN AND BRENTFORD.—Incorporated by act of 14th August, 1855, to make a railway from the Great Western, at Southall, to Brentford, with docks, &c. Length, 4½ miles. There is a dock in connection with the railway at the terminus at Brentford. By act of 5th July, 1865, the Great Western and Brentford was authorised to be transferred to the Great Western on such terms as might be agreed upon. The dividends for the half-year ended 31st December, 1870, and 30th June, were respectively at the rate of 2½ per cent. per annum. At a special meeting of the Great Western, held on 29th February, 1872, it was resolved:—"That, for the purposes of the intended vesting in the company of the undertaking of the Great Western and Brentford, and in pursuance of the powers of 'The Great Western Additional Powers Act, 1871,' there be created consolidated preference stock of the company, bearing interest at the rate of 5*l.* per cent. per annum, to an amount not exceeding 47,435*l.*, and that the directors be authorised to issue the said stock to the holders of ordinary shares in the Great Western and Brentford in exchange for the certificates of such shares. And that there be also created consolidated guaranteed stock, bearing interest or dividend at the rate of 5*l.* per cent. per annum, to an amount not exceeding 69,080*l.*, and that the directors be authorised to issue the said stock to the holders of the preference shares in the Great Western and Brentford in exchange for the certificates of such shares."

HAMMERSMITH AND CITY.—Incorporated by act of 22nd July, 1861, to construct a line from the Great Western, at Green Lane Bridge, to Hammersmith, with branch to Kensington, &c. Under "The Great Western Additional Powers Act, 1867," the line is vested jointly in the Great Western and the Metropolitan.

HELSTON.—See GENERAL INDEX.

KINGSBRIDGE AND SALCOMBE.—See GENERAL INDEX.

Launceston and South Devon.—This line, having formerly belonged to the South Devon, is now part of the Great Western system.—For other particulars, see South Devon in the Manual for 1878, and previous editions.

Leominster and Kington.—See General Index.

Limerick and Kerry.—See General Index.

Llanelly—This line is now leased to the Great Western.—See General Index.

Llynvi and Ogmore.—This was an amalgamation of the Llynvi Valley and Ogmore Valley systems, the capitals being kept distinct. Length, 56¼ miles. Amalgamated with Great Western as from the 1st July, 1883, under act of 29th June, 1883, upon the following terms, shareholders to receive Great Western stocks as follow:—

For every 100*l.* of	Great Western Stock in Exchange.
5 per cent. guaranteed 5 per cent., 1855. .	100*l.* of 5 per cent. consd. guarntd. stock
5 per cent. perpetual, 1862 and 1872	" " " " "
Llynvi ordinary stock	120*l.* " " " "
Ogmore " "	120*l.* " " " "
Cardiff " "	120*l.* " " " "
4½ per cent. shares, 1874.......................	90*l.* " " " "

Llangollen.—An agreement is made for working this railway (5¼ miles in length) on terms of a percentage upon receipts as in case of the East Somerset; together with a fixed annual sum of 400*l.*, in consideration of a saving of expense to the Great Western, by dispensing with the Llangollen Road Station.

London and North Western.—By arrangements with this company, Great Western traffic to Manchester is conveyed by the London and North Western from Chester, *viâ* Warrington.

London, Chatham, and Dover.—This company having obtained an act for bringing a railway through the populous districts south of the River Thames into connection with the Metropolitan, in the neighbourhood of Farringdon Market and Victoria Street, powers have been conferred upon the Great Western and the London, Chatham, and Dover to agree with the Victoria Station for joint lease and occupation of a portion of the passenger station in Pimlico.

Malmesbury.—Incorporated by act of 25th July, 1872, to construct a line from Dauntsey, on the Great Western, to Malmesbury. The line was opened for traffic on the 18th December, 1877, and subsequently became vested in the Great Western under that company's Amalgamation Act, 1880, the holders of ordinary stock of the vested company receiving Great Western consolidated ordinary stock exchanged at the rate of 15 per cent. of their holdings.—For particulars as to the working of the undertaking in the past, see the Manual for 1880, and previous editions.

Metropolitan.—The Great Western runs a portion of the trains on this line, carrying the local passengers of the Metropolitan, along with those from Hammersmith, Ealing, &c.

Milford.—See General Index.

Minehead.—Incorporated by act of 29th June, 1871, to construct a line from the West Somerset, at Watchet, to Minehead. Length, 8¼ miles. Capital, 60,000*l.* in 10*l.* shares, "preferred" and "deferred." No provision appears to have been made for exercise of borrowing powers. By special agreement with the Bristol and Exeter (now Great Western) that company is to pay a perpetual rent for the Minehead of not less than 2 000*l.* a year, but at more than 50 per cent. of gross receipts, when this arrangement would provide a higher amount. Out of this rent the "A" shares are to receive 4½ per cent., and the B's 6, with a further 1½ per cent. to the A's, and the remainder to the B's whenever the rent is sufficient for that purpose.

Mitcheldean Road and Forest of Dean Junction.—Incorporated by act of 13th July, 1871, to construct a line from the Hereford, Ross, and Gloucester, at Mitcheldean, to the Whymsey Branch of the Forest of Dean. Length, 4½ miles. The line became vested in the Great Western under the latter company's Amalgamation Act, 1880, the holders of ordinary stock of the vested company receiving Great Western consolidated ordinary stock exchanged at par.

Monmouthshire.—Incorporated by act of 31st July, 1845, for a line from Newport to Pontypool, 12 miles (with several branches and canal). This railway was authorised to be made by the Monmouthshire Canal Navigation (which, as a canal company, had previously been in existence more than 50 years). Productive. 52 miles. As from 1st August, 1880, the line became amalgamated with the Great

Western, under the act of that year, the conditions of the arrangement are that the debenture and preference stocks of the Monmouthshire shall be exchanged for equivalent amounts of debenture stock and guaranteed stock of the Great Western, and that the holder of every 100*l.* paid up Monmouthshire ordinary stock shall receive 130*l.* of Great Western 5 per cent. guaranteed stock—being the equivalent of 6½ per cent. dividend—and also a further amount of 10*l.* of guaranteed stock carrying a dividend of 10*s.* per cent. per annum from the 1st February, 1883, so that in effect the surplus half profits under the existing arrangement will be commuted by a dividend at the rate of 10*s.* per cent. per annum from the 1st February, 1883.—For particulars as to the working of this railway in the past, see the MANUAL for 1880, and previous editions.

MORETONHAMPSTEAD AND SOUTH DEVON.—Incorporated by act of 7th July, 1862, to construct a line from the South Devon, at Wolborough, to Moretonhampstead. Length, 12¼ miles. Capital, 105,000*l.* in 10*l.* shares and 35,000*l.* on loan. By act of 18th July, 1872, the company was amalgamated with the South Devon as from the 1st of that month.—For heads of agreement, see *Appendix* to the MANUAL for 1873. The South Devon having become vested in the Great Western, this line now belongs to the latter company.

NANTWICH AND MARKET DRAYTON.—See GENERAL INDEX.

PLYMOUTH DOCKS.—This undertaking has been absorbed by the Great Western, under the powers of the South Devon Act, 1874, and the subsequent acts for effecting the amalgamation of the Associated Companies.

PONTYPOOL, CAERLEON, AND NEWPORT.—Incorporated by act of 5th July, 1865. Length, 12 miles—from Pontypool Road to Newport, on the Great Western. Opened for goods and mineral traffic on 17th September, and for passengers 21st December, 1874. Up to 31st December, 1874, the line earned a dividend on its ordinary stock of 5 per cent. per annum. By act of 13th July, 1876, this line became vested in the Great Western undertaking, the shareholders receiving an amount of Great Western consolidated guaranteed 5 per cent. stock equal to their respective holdings, and the loan capital being exchanged for debenture stock of the Great Western.

PRINCETOWN.—See GENERAL INDEX.

RADSTOCK, WRINGTON, AND CONGRESBURY JUNCTION.—This line when completed is to be worked by the Great Western.

SEVERN TUNNEL.—Incorporated by act of 27th June, 1872, to construct a tunnel under the Severn from the Bristol and South Wales Union to the South Wales. Length, 8 miles. Capital, 750,000*l.* in 10*l.* shares, which Great Western may subscribe, or guarantee so much as has not been subscribed by it. Loans, 250,000*l.*, or by debenture stock. The powers conferred by this act are exercised by the Great Western, in their own name, under the provisions of the act. The tunnel and railway are now in course of construction.—For other details, see MANUAL for 1882, page 316.

SEVERN VALLEY.—Incorporated by act of 20th August, 1853, for a line from near Hartlebury Station, on Oxford, Worcester, and Wolverhampton, to Shrewsbury; also for a railway or tramway, Benthall to Madeley, supplying Stourport, Bewdley, Coalbrookdale, &c. For other details (in brief), see MANUALS for 1882 and previously. By act of 18th July, 1872, this line became vested in the Great Western, its preference shares being exchanged for consolidated preference stock of that undertaking.

SHREWSBURY AND HEREFORD.—This line is vested—one-half in the London and North Western and the other moiety in the Great Western.—See GENERAL INDEX.

SOUTH DEVON.—By act of 22nd July, 1878, this undertaking, which was incorporated by act of 4th July, 1844, was vested in the Great Western. The amalgamation took effect on the 1st August, 1878, the South Devon debentures, and debenture and preference stocks, becoming securities of the Great Western, and the ordinary stockholders receiving 65*l.* of Great Western consolidated ordinary stock for every 100*l.* of their holding, and in addition a certificate representing 5*l.* of Great Western for every 100*l.* of South Devon ordinary stock, the dividend upon such certificate being deferred until 1st February, 1883, after which date the effect of the exchange will of course be 70*l.* per cent. of Great Western ordinary stock, for every 100*l.* of South Devon ordinary stock. On the winding-up of the concern, the proprietary received a distribution of 2*s.* 6*d.* per cent. in addition to dividend for the first half-year of 1878 (which was equal to 65 per cent. of the 3½ per cent. per annum Great Western dividend for that half-year). The Great Western subsequently offered to the holders of the deferred certificates above mentioned, the option of exchanging such certificates for Great Western consolidated ordinary stock on the following terms, viz:—"That the holders shall pay to the company a sum calculated at the rate of 1*l.* in respect of each 5*l.* of deferred certificates; that such option shall be declared on or before 1st December next, and the money paid by the 10th of that month, that upon such payment the stock shall be registered in the books of the company carrying dividend as from the 1st August, 1878." Copies of the circulars issued to the proprietary giving full particulars relating to the amalgamation, and a table, showing the company's capital account at that time, will be found in the *Appendix* to the MANUAL for 1880; and for the position of the company previously, with its vested undertakings, &c., see the MANUAL for 1878, and previous editions.

SOUTH DEVON AND TAVISTOCK.—Incorporated by act of 24th July, 1854. Length, 13 miles. Opened 22nd June, 1859. By act of 5th July, 1865, the Tavistock was amalgamated with the South Devon, at a perpetual dividend of 3½ per cent. on its ordinary stock. The South Devon having become vested in the Great Western (as above), this line now belongs to the latter company.

STRATFORD-ON-AVON.—Incorporated by act of 10th August, 1857. Stratford-on-Avon to Hatton, 9¼ miles. Amalgamated with Great Western from 1st July, 1883, under an act passed in that year.—"The chief terms of the amalgamation are:—(1) On and after the time of amalgamation the mortgage debt and other capital liabilities of the Stratford will become part of the mortgage debt and liabilities of the Great Western; (2) the 10*l*. 5 per cent. preference shares of the Stratford will be exchanged for the same amount of the Great Western consolidated preference stock; (3) for every 100*l*. of the Stratford ordinary shares 135*l*. of Great Western consolidated ordinary stock will be issued, and a proportionate amount of that stock for every amount of Stratford shares less than 100*l*. The Great Western to issue certificates of their company in exchange for the certificates of the preferential and ordinary shares of the Stratford."—For full particulars as to the position, &c., of this company in the past, see the MANUAL for 1883, and previous editions.

SWANSEA CANAL.—By act of 25th July, 1872, this undertaking was vested in the Great Western, each 100*l*. of canal stock to be exchanged for 202*l*. of Great Western 5 per cent. stock.

SWINDON AND HIGHWORTH LIGHT.—Purchased by Great Western under act (No. 1) 1882.

TEIGN VALLEY.—See GENERAL INDEX.

TENBURY.—Incorporated by act of 21st July, 1859, to construct a railway from the Woofferton Station of the Shrewsbury and Hereford to Tenbury. Length, 5¼ miles. The Shrewsbury and Hereford disposed of part of the Leominster Canal to the company, and agreed to work the Tenbury for seven years, paying out of the first receipts 500*l*. per annum and 40*l*. per cent. of the balance of such receipts, retaining the residue to cover working expenses and maintenance. The Shrewsbury and Hereford having passed into the hands of the London and North Western and the Great Western, the lease of this line became vested in those companies under act of 1866. Dividends at 4½ per cent. from 1st July, 1871.

TENBURY AND BEWDLEY.—Incorporated by act of 3rd July, 1860, to construct a line from the Severn Valley, near Bewdley, to the town of Tenbury. Length, 14 miles. The agreement with the Great Western for a transfer of the undertaking was confirmed by act of 1869.

TIVERTON AND NORTH DEVON.—See GENERAL INDEX.

TORBAY AND BRIXHAM.—Purchased by Great Western under act (No. 2) 1882.

UXBRIDGE AND RICKMANSWORTH.—See GENERAL INDEX.

VALE OF LLANGOLLEN.—See GENERAL INDEX.

WALLINGFORD AND WATLINGTON.—Incorporated by act of 25th July, 1864, to construct a line from the Great Western, at Cholsey, to Wallingford and to Watlington. Length, 9 miles. Vested in Great Western by act of 18th July, 1872.

WATLINGTON AND PRINCES RISBOROUGH.—Incorporated by act of 26th July, 1869 (see the MANUAL for 1883, page 336). Sold to Great Western for 23,000*l*., under act of 1883.

WELLINGTON AND DRAYTON.—Incorporated by act of 7th August, 1862, for a railway from Wellington, on the Great Western, to Drayton, in connection with the Nantwich and Market Drayton. Length, 15¼ miles. By act of 14th July, 1864, the company was authorised to make several deviations, and to transfer the undertaking to the Great Western.

WEST CORNWALL.—This line, formerly worked by the Great Western, Bristol and Exeter, and South Devon, has, since the amalgamation of the three companies, become part of the Great Western system as from the 1st August, 1878.—For other particulars, see the MANUAL for 1878, and previous editions.

WEST LONDON.—A moiety of the lease (30,000*l.*) to the London and North Western is borne by and belongs to the Great Western.—For further arrangements with this company, see West London.

WEYMOUTH AND PORTLAND.—This line is leased to the Great Western and the London and South Western.—See GENERAL INDEX.

WOODSIDE STATION, BIRKENHEAD.—This station, said to be one of the most spacious and convenient erections of the kind in the kingdom, was opened for traffic on the 31st March, 1878.

WREXHAM AND MINERA.—Incorporated by act of 17th May, 1861, to construct a line from the Wrexham to the Minera Station of the Shrewsbury and Chester. The line became vested in the Great Western under act of 31st July, 1871.

WYCOMBE.—Incorporated by act of 26th July, 1847, for a line from Great Western, at Maidenhead, to High Wycombe (for other details, see the MANUAL for 1882, and previous editions). By act of 23rd July, 1866, the line was authorised to be absorbed in the Great Western system, which took place on 1st February, 1867.

ACCOUNTS:--

REVENUE.—The receipts and expenditure on this account, for the half-years ended 31st December, 1883, and 30th June, 1884, are given below:—

	31st Dec., 1883.	30th June, 1884.
Passengers, parcels, &c.	£1,890,630	£1,634,512
Goods, minerals, and cattle	2,203,047	2,120,137
Canal traffic, dock dues, and miscellaneous receipts	76,909	71,294
Gross receipts	£4,170,586	£3,825,943
Expenditure	2,031,929	1,956,175
Net	£2,138,657	£1,869,768
Add sundry balances and div. on shares held	38,637	59,434
Total net revenue	£2,177,294	£1,929,202
Interest, rents, preference dividends, &c.	1,449,705	1,449,853
Available for ordinary stock	£727,589	£479,349
Dividends at 7½ & 5¼ ₿ cent. ₿ ann. respectively	689,404	472,166
Balance carried forward	£38,185	£7,183

The last two half-yearly dividends were made payable on the 16th February and 16th August respectively.

MILEAGE—30TH JUNE, 1884.—*Authorised:* Lines owned, 1,701¼; partly owned, 91⅛; leased or rented, 580; total, 2,372⅜. *Constructed:* Lines owned, 1,621⅓; partly owned, 84⅓; leased or rented, 580; total, 2,286. *Constructing:* Lines owned, 80¾. *Worked by engines:* Lines owned, partly owned, and leased or rented, 2,382¼; foreign lines worked over, 107¾; total, 2,490 miles.

CAPITAL.—The amount authorised to 30th June, 1884, extended to 56,523,322*l.* in stocks or shares, and 19,285,628*l.* on loan or by debenture stock, making a total of 75,808,950*l.* The statement of stock and share capital created, showing the description to be observed in transfer deeds, &c., and the order of priority, also the proportion received to 30th June, entered into the subjoined details:—

	Created.	Received.
5 per cent. rent-charge stock	£7,610,878	£7,609,630
5 per cent. consolidated guaranteed stock	16,142,990	15,646,580
5 per cent. consolidated preference stock	11,663,759	11,364,572
Consolidated ordinary stock	20,315,695	18,886,670
Total	£55,733,322	£53,507,452

Calls in arrear, 8,593*l.*; amount unissued, 2,208,777*l.*

The receipts and expenditure to 30th June, 1884, were detailed as under:—

Received.

Loans	£56,333
Debenture stocks	16,931,124
Rent-charges	36,687
Stratford Canal annuities	63,240
Shares and stock	53,507,452
Premium on shares and stocks issued	2,250,346
	£72,845,182

Expended.

Lines and works open for traffic (including Weston Loop)	£58,976,144
Lines and works in course of construction:—	
Bodmin Branch	2,299
Bolham deviation	21,889
Bristol Loop	11,777
Exe Valley	107,777
Newcastle Emlyn Extension	100
Quaker's Yard to Merthyr Joint	10,303
Severn Tunnel	1,175,639
Working stock	8,324,915
Subscriptions to other companies:—	
Alexandra (Newport) Dock	20,000
Bala and Festiniog	200,000
Bridport	13,000
Bristol and North Somerset	65,000
Calne	31,320
Coleford	66,000
Cornwall	202,500
Corwen and Bala	15,000
Great Marlow	9,720
Limerick and Kerry	10,000
Marlborough	10,000
Newent	105,070
Newport Dock	40,000
Oldbury	45,000
Princetown	30,000
Ross and Ledbury	105,500
Severn Navigation	20,367
Somersetshire Coal Canal	794
Somerset and Dorset	9,393
Staines and West Drayton	48,105
Swindon Waterworks	7,800
Tiverton and North Devon	40,000
Waterford and Central Ireland	10,000
Waterford, Dungarvan, and Lismore	5,500
West London Extension	185,000
Whitland and Cardigan	25,000
Worcester, Bromyard, and Leominster	50,632
Docks—Briton Ferry	102,854
Plymouth	393,639
Porthcawl	126,127
Steamboats	251,885
Leased lines:—	
Coleford, Monmouth, Usk, and Pontypool (debentures paid off)	50,000
Ely Valley	35,000
Wenlock	24,025
Canals:—	
Brecon	61,862
Bridgwater and Taunton	74,012
Grand Western	30,640
Kennet and Avon	217,261
Stourbridge Extension	49,437
Stratford-on-Avon	173,661
Swansea	149,377
Joint lines' debentures paid off and debenture stocks assumed:—	
Birkenhead	300,000
Hammersmith and City	40,000
Shrewsbury and Hereford—Tenbury	117,500
West London Extension	8,933
	£72,207,756
Balance	637,425
	£72,845,181

The estimate of further expenditure on capital account was as follows:—

	Half-year ending 31st Dec., 1884.	In subsequent half-years.	Total.
Lines and works open for traffic........................ ,, ,, in course of construction	£160,000	£174,037	£334,037
Subscriptions to other companies	10,000	108,943	118,943
Working stock	110,000	76,792	186,792
Further works	180,000	1,064,849	1,244,849
Further expenditure under estimates requiring sanction	140,000	140,000	280,000
Total estimated further expenditure.........	£600,000	£1,559,621	£2,159,621

The capital powers and other assets available to meet this outlay were detailed as under:—

Share and loan capital authorised but not created £1,040,000

Stock and share capital created but not received:—

Calls in arrear	£8,593	
Amount unissued	2,208,777=	2,217,370
Available borrowing powers	£1,422,868	
Loan capital sanctioned, not yet exercised	525,377=	1,948,245
Balance at credit of capital account..............................		637,425
Total..		£5,843,040

The accounts are made up to the 30th June and 31st December, and the statutory meetings are held in January or February and July or August.

Scale of Voting.—One vote for every 50*l.* up to 500*l.* one vote for every 250*l.* after first 500*l.* up to 5,000*l.*, and one vote for every 500*l.* after first 5,000*l.*

Certificate must accompany transfer deeds. Registration, 2*s.* 6*d.*

No. of Directors—19. *Qualification*, 2,000*l.* stock.

DIRECTORS:

Chairman—Sir DANIEL GOOCH, Bart., M.P., 3, Warwick Road, Maida Hill, W.

Deputy-Chairman—Sir ALEXANDER WOOD, Knt., 11, Elvaston Place, S.W.

Richard Basset, Esq., Highclere, Newbury.
The Rt. Hon. the Earl of Bessborough, 3, Mount Street, Grosvenor Square, W.
James J. Bibby, Esq., Hardwick Grange, Shrewsbury.
The Right Hon. E. P. Bouverie, 44, Wilton Crescent, S.W.
W. A. Bruce, Esq., Ashley, Box, Wilts.
Michael Castle, Esq., Clifton, Bristol.
Lewis L. Dillwyn, Esq., M.P., 10, King's Bench Walk, E.C., and Hendrefoilan, near Swansea.
Alexander Hubbard, Esq., Derwentwater House, Acton, W.
W. C. King, Esq., Bracknell, Berks.
Sir Massey Lopes, Bart., M.P., Plymouth.
The Rt. Hon. Lord Lyttelton, Stourbridge, and 17, Grosvenor Street, S.W.
David MacIver, Esq., M.P., Woodslee, Spital, near Birkenhead.
Richard Michell, Esq., 3, Kensington Park Gardens, W.
C. G. Mott, Esq., Harrow Weald Lodge, Stanmore, Middlesex.
Walter Robinson, Esq., 20, Gledhow Gardens, S.W.
Christopher R. M. Talbot, Esq., M.P., Port Talbot, and 3, Cavendish Square, W.
Sir Watkin W. Wynn, Bart., M.P., Ruabon, and 18, St. James's Square, S.W.

OFFICERS.—Sec., Fred. G. Saunders; Gen. Man., James Grierson, Assoc.Inst.C.E.; Registrar, John Crier; Loco. Supt., William Dean, Swindon; Chief Eng., W. G. Owen, M.Inst.C.E., Paddington, W.; Chief Accountant, J. H. Matthews, Paddington, W.; Audit Accountant, R. R. Friend; Supt. of Line, G. N. Tyrrell, Paddington, W.; Asst. Supt. of Line, N. J. Burlinson; Chief Goods Manager, Henry Lambert, Paddington, W.; Asst. Goods Man., J. C. Richardson; Storekeeper, H. Dunn, Swindon; Auditors, Edward Harper and James William Bowen; Solicitor, R. R. Nelson, Paddington, W.

Chief Offices—Paddington Terminus, W.

124.—GREENOCK AND WEMYSS BAY.

Incorporated by act of 17th July, 1862, to construct a line from the Greenock Branch of the Caledonian at Port Glasgow to Wemyss Bay. Length, 9¼ miles. Capital, 120,000*l.* in 10*l.* shares; loans, 40,000*l.* Arrangements with Caledonian, which subscribed 30,000*l.*, and works the line at 45 per cent. of the receipts.

By act of June, 1862, the company was authorised to construct an extension (16 chains), and a pier in connection therewith. New capital, 30,000*l.* in shares, at 5 per cent. preference, and 10,000*l.* on loan. In operation, 10 miles 6 chains.

REVENUE.—The net earnings for the half-years ended 31st January, 1884, and 31st July, 1884, after payment of interest on debentures, &c., and the dividend in full on the preference shares, went to reduce the debts of the company to the extent of 1,139*l.*

CAPITAL.—The expenditure on this account to 31st July, 1884, amounted to 200,445*l.*, the receipts to the same date having been 183,327*l.*, as under:—

Ordinary shares	£120,000
Preference shares, 5 per cent	30,000
Loans at 4 per cent	28,264
Premiums	431

Meetings in February or March and in August or September. Accounts to 31st July and 31st January.

No. of Directors—5; minimum, 3; quorum, 2. *Qualification*, 500*l.*

DIRECTORS:

Chairman—JAMES LAMONT, Esq., of Knockdow, Innellan.

Thomas Spark Hadaway, Esq., Merchant, Glasgow.
Robert Maclean, Esq., Banker, Hillhead.
James W. Turner, Esq., Greenock.
Charles Magnay, Esq., London.

OFFICERS.—Sec., James Keyden; Eng., Thomas D. Weir, C.E., Glasgow; Auditors, Walter Mackenzie and George Miller, C.A., Glasgow.

Offices—186, West George Street, Glasgow.

125.—HALESOWEN.

Incorporated by act of 5th July, 1865, to construct several short lines in the county of Worcester, connecting the Midland and the West Midland section of the Great Western. Length, 7½ miles. Capital, 120,000*l.*, in 12,000 10*l.* shares, and 40,000*l.* on mortgage. Arrangements with the Midland and the Great Western companies, the line to be handed over to those companies when completed, to be stocked, maintained, and worked by them in perpetuity, at 50 per cent. of the gross receipts; the two companies have also agreed to allow a liberal rebate upon all traffic brought on to their lines by this company.

By act of 6th August, 1866, the company was authorised to construct two small branches in the county of Worcester. Length, 3¾ miles. New capital, 48,000*l.* in shares and 16,000*l.* on loan; but by act of 1st August, 1870, the company was authorised to abandon one of the lines sanctioned in 1866, and obtained an extension of time for completion of the remainder till 1873. New capital reduced to 27,000*l.* in shares instead of 48,000*l.*, and on loans from 16,000*l.* to 9,000*l.*

By act of 21st July, 1873, the company was authorised to construct certain deviations of their authorised lines, and to abandon as much of their authorised railways and works as may be rendered unnecessary by the construction of the new lines. The time for completion of works was further extended to August, 1876.

By act of 13th July, 1876, the name of the company was changed from "Halesowen and Bromsgrove Branch Railways" to "Halesowen Railway;" the time limited for the compulsory purchase of lands extended to 21st July, 1877; and power given the company to raise 45,000*l.* additional capital and borrow a further sum of 15,000*l.*

By act of 11th August, 1879, powers were obtained to facilitate arrangements with the Great Western for the construction of a junction with the line of the latter company at Halesowen Station.

By act of 26th August, 1880, the company obtained further powers to construct a junction with the Great Western near the Halesowen Station of that company, and for the acquirement of certain lands. New capital, 21,000*l.* in shares or stock, and 7,000*l.* in loan or debenture stock.

By act of 16th July, 1883, the Halesowen and Bromsgrove Branch Act, 1865, was amended so as to enable the company to enter into agreements with the Midland as to the Exchange Station at Northfield, and works for exchange of traffic, &c.

In May, 1882, the works were finally approved by the Board of Trade Inspector, and the line was opened for traffic in September, 1883.

CAPITAL.—This account to 30th June, 1884, showed that 219,861*l.* had been received (viz.: 90,350*l.* in ordinary shares, 66,000*l.* in preference shares, 62,000*l.* in debenture stock, and 1,511*l.* on interest account), and 222,438*l.* expended.

DIRECTORS:

Chairman—A. F. GODSON, Esq., 3, Pump Court, Temple, E.C., and Tenbury, Worcestershire.

M. S. Lynch-Staunton, Esq., Union Club, St. James's, S.W.
G. Cavendish Taylor, Esq., 42, Elvaston Place, South Kensington, S.W.
Reuben Gaunt, Esq., Farsley, near Leeds.

OFFICERS.—Sec., James Fraser; Eng., Edward Richards, 24, Abingdon Street, Westminster, S.W.; Auditor, W. H. Elliot, A.C.A.: Solicitors, Newman, Stretton, and Hilliard, 75 and 76, Cornhill, E.C.; Bankers, The Consolidated Bank Limited, Threadneedle Street, E.C., and Birmingham, Dudley, and District Banking Company, Birmingham.

Offices—2, Tokenhouse Buildings, King's Arms Yard, E.C.

126.—HALIFAX HIGH LEVEL AND NORTH AND SOUTH JUNCTION.

Incorporated by act of 7th August, 1884, for the construction of five short railways at Halifax, through Ovenden, to Holmfield and Holdsworth. Total length, about 5¼ miles. Period for completion, 5 years. Capital, 320,000*l.* in 10*l.* shares, with power to divide into "preferred" and "deferred" half-shares; loans, 106,666*l.*

No. of Directors.—Maximum, 7; minimum, 3; quorum, 3 and 2. *Qualification*, 40 shares.

FIRST DIRECTORS:

William Irving Holdsworth, Esq.
James Booth, Esq.
Frederick Hungerford Bowman, Esq.
Alfred Ramsden, Esq.
Thomas Smith Scarborough, Esq.
George Clegg, Esq.
James Carter, Esq.

127.—HALIFAX AND OVENDEN.

This line is now vested in the Great Northern and the Lancashire and Yorkshire, which see. No separate report or balance sheet is made out.

No. of Directors—8; 4 each by the Great Northern and Lancashire and Yorkshire; quorum, 3.

JOINT COMMITTEE:

Representing Lancashire and Yorkshire.

2 Samuel Fielden, Esq., Todmorden.
1 George John Armytage, Esq., Clifton Woodhead, Brighouse.
3 Edward Green, Esq., Heath Old Hall, Wakefield.
4 John Pearson, Esq., Golborne Park, Newton-le-Willows.

Representing Great Northern.

Abraham Briggs Foster, Esq., Queensbury, near Bradford, and Northowram Hall, Halifax.
Sir Andrew Fairbairn, M.P., 15, Portman Square, W., and Askham Richard, York.
William Lawies Jackson, Esq., M.P., Allerton Hall, Chapel Allerton, near Leeds.

Secretary, William Grinling, Great Northern Railway, King's Cross, London.

128.—HARBORNE.

Incorporated by act of 28th June, 1866, for constructing a line from the Birmingham, Wolverhampton, and Stour Valley section of the London and North Western, in Birmingham, to the town of Harborne, in Staffordshire. Length, 3 miles. Capital, 100,000*l.* in 10*l.* shares and 33,000*l.* on loan, with power to create and issue debenture stock. Arrangements with London and North Western, which works the line in perpetuity at 50 per cent. of the gross receipts. The line was opened for traffic on the 10th August, 1874.

REVENUE.—The company's net receipts for the half-year ended 30th June, 1884, amounted to 1,079*l.*, against 1,041*l.* at the corresponding period of 1883.

CAPITAL.—30th June, 1884.—*Expended:* 99,990*l.* *Receipts:* ordinary shares, 55,990*l.*; debenture stock, 17,700*l.*, total, 73,690*l.*; debit balance, 26,300*l.*

No. of Directors—5; minimum, 3; quorum, 2. *Qualification*, 30 shares.

DIRECTORS:

Chairman—W. BAILEY HAWKINS, Esq., Assoc.Inst.C.E., 39, Lombard Street, E.C.

John Winterbotham Batten, Esq., 15, Airlie Gardens, Campden Hill, W.

Arthur S. Hamand, Esq., M.Inst.C.E., 9, Bridge Street, Westminster, S.W.

OFFICERS.—Sec., Alexander F. Jennings, 114, Gresham House, Old Broad Street, E.C.; Surveyors, J. Mathews and Sons, Birmingham; Auditors, John Wade, 134, Palmerston Buildings, Bishopsgate Street, E.C., and D. S. Derry, 22, Great Winchester Street, E.C.; Solicitors, Wilkins, Blyth, and Dutton, 112, Gresham House, Old Broad Street, E.C.

Offices—114, Gresham House, Old Broad Street, E.C.

129.—HELSTON (Cornwall).

Incorporated by act of 9th July, 1880, for the construction and maintenance of a railway from the Gwinear Road Station of the West Cornwall to Helston. Length, about 8¾ miles. Capital, 70,000*l.* in 20*l.* shares, with powers to divide into "preferred" and "deferred" half-shares. Borrowing powers, 23,333*l.* Period for completion, 5 years.

Under an agreement with the Great Western, the line is to be worked by that company in perpetuity at 50 per cent. of the gross receipts.

CAPITAL.—In the beginning of the year 1882 the balance of the ordinary share capital, consisting of 59,660*l.* in 20*l.* shares, was issued at par, payable by instalments, the final payment being 5*l.* per share on the 1st January, 1883, a sum having been invested to provide for interest at 5 per cent. per annum on such capital until the completion of the undertaking.

The prospectus inviting subscriptions to the capital stated that the construction of the line was in active progress, and expected to be completed by June, 1883.

No. of Directors.—Maximum, 7; minimum, 3; quorum, 3 and 2. *Qualification*, 25 shares.

FIRST DIRECTORS:

Chairman—WILLIAM BICKFORD-SMITH, Esq.

David Wise Bain, Esq.
Wm. Bolitho, Jun., Esq., Penzance.
Richard Skewes Martyn, Esq.

Richard G. Rows, Esq.
Walter Molesworth St. Aubyn, Esq., M.P.

OFFICERS.—Sec., J. R. Daniell; Eng., S. W. Jenkin.

Offices—Camborne.

130.—HEMEL HEMPSTED AND LONDON AND NORTH WESTERN.

Incorporated by act of 1863, to construct a line from Boxmoor, on the London and North Western, to Hemel Hempsted. Length, 9 miles 37 chains. Capital, 20,000*l.* in shares and 6,600*l.* on loan. By act of 1866 the company was authorised to extend the line to the Hertford, Luton, and Dunstable Branch of the Great Northern at Harpenden, and to construct another branch to join the Midland at that place. New capital, 170,000*l.* in shares and 56,600*l.* on loan. By act of 18th July, 1872, the company was further authorised to construct an extension (1 furlong 3 chains) to Boxmoor, and a deviation as well as alteration of the line and levels of the project of 1866. By the same act were also authorised to attach a preference of 6 per cent. to 85,000*l.* of unissued ordinary shares, as well as to create debenture stock. The line was opened for traffic from Harpenden to Hemel Hempsted on 16th July, 1877.

By the Midland (Further Powers) Act of 12th July, 1877, an agreement, dated 1st December, 1876, was confirmed; it provides for the working by the Midland of the new line, authorised by the acts obtained by this company in 1866 and 1872, to extend their railway to join the Midland at Harpenden. This new line is connected with the Midland Main Line, and, therefore, the latter company undertake to work the traffic under the following terms:—The payment by the Midland each half-year, ending 30th June and 31st December respectively, in perpetuity, of a rental equal to 3,750*l.* per annum, payable within one month after such rental becomes due.

REVENUE.—On the 30th June, 1884, the net revenue account showed a debit balance of 8,052*l.*

CAPITAL.—The receipts on this account to 30th June, 1884, amounted to 45,000*l.* (being wholly from shares); the expenditure to same date was 143,134*l.*, showing a debit balance of 98,134*l.*

Total length of line authorised, 10 miles 41 chains.

Meetings held in February and August in each year.

No. of Directors—5; quorum, 3. *Qualification*, 100*l.*

DIRECTORS:

Chairman—JOHN JAMES BARROW, Esq., Holmewood, Tunbridge Wells.

John Burton Barrow, Esq., Ringwood Hall, Chesterfield.

Wm. Felix Poole, Esq., 15, Spilman Street, Carmarthen.

William Wavell, Esq., 54, Oxford Terrace, Hyde Park, W.

C. Stanley Williams, Esq. Shirley, Tunbridge Wells.

OFFICERS.—Sec., Rod. Mackay; Eng., J. W. Grover, M.Inst.C.E.; Auditors, James Fraser and Alfred Powell.

Office—3, Lothbury, E.C.

131.—HENLEY-IN-ARDEN AND GREAT WESTERN JUNCTION.

Incorporated by act of 5th August, 1873, to construct a line from the Birmingham and Oxford Branch of the Great Western, at Rowington, to Henley-in-Arden. Length, 4 miles. Arrangements with Great Western.

By act of 23rd June, 1884, the powers of the act of 1873 were revived, and the time for completion of works extended to 23rd June, 1887.

No. of Directors.—Maximum, 5; minimum 3; quorum, 3 and 2. *Qualification*, 20 shares.

DIRECTORS:

Samuel H. Agar, Esq.
Edward Cooper, Esq.
Robert E. Cooper, Esq.
Edward Harvey, Esq.
Edwin Dixon, Esq.

132.—HEREFORD, HAY, AND BRECON.

Incorporated by act of 8th August, 1859, to construct a line from Brecon, through Hay, to the Shrewsbury and Hereford, at the latter town. Capital, 280,000*l.* in 10*l.* shares; loans, 93,000*l.* Length, 34 miles. By act of 3rd July, 1860, the company was authorised to relinquish the junction with the Shrewsbury and Hereford, and in lieu thereof to form a communication with the Newport, Abergavenny, and Hereford section of the West Midland, at Barton Station. By act of 6th August, 1860, the Hay Railway was vested in the Hereford, Hay, and Brecon, but parts of the line transferred to the Mid Wales, Brecon and Merthyr Tydfil Junction, and a portion disused. By act of 30th June, 1862, various alterations of levels and deviations were authorised; all to be completed by 6th August, 1864. In operation, 26½ miles.

By act of 4th May, 1863, the company was authorised to raise new capital to the extent of 75,000*l.* in shares, at 5 per cent., and 25,000*l.* on loan; and by act of 5th July, 1865, the Hereford, Hay, and Brecon was authorised to amalgamate with the Brecon and Merthyr, on a share capital not exceeding 355,000*l.*

By act of 1869, the company was re-incorporated as a separate undertaking, and authorised to raise the sum of 22,000*l.* by the issue of debenture stock, and also to convert their debentures into 5 per cent. irredeemable debenture stock, and for the appointment of two debenture directors. By the same act running powers were granted to the company over a portion of the Mid Wales and Brecon and Merthyr to Brecon.

By the Midland and Hereford, Hay, and Brecon Act, 1874, the line was leased in perpetuity to the Midland, at a progressive rent, the act (section 6) providing that the rent, after providing thereout for payment of the current interest on the debenture stock of the Hereford Company, shall be applied by the Hereford Company in payment of dividends on the preference and ordinary stocks of that company as follows (that is to say):—At the rate of 2 per cent. per annum for the half-year ended the 31st December, 1874, and thereafter at a rate increasing by ½ per cent. per annum until the dividend shall amount to 4 per cent. per annum on the preference and ordinary stocks respectively, after which period the rent shall be applied in payment of dividends on the preference and ordinary stocks at that rate. The maximum rate of 4 per cent. was reached in 1882, and has been paid on both stocks since that date.

CAPITAL.—This account to 30th June, 1876, showed that 473,860*l*. had been received and 473,049*l*. expended, leaving a balance of 810*l*.

No accounts have been published since 30th June, 1876.

DIRECTORS:

F. A. Fynney, Esq., Queen's Chambers, Manchester.

William Laurence Banks, Esq., F.S.A., Hendrewaelod, near Conway.

OFFICERS.—Sec., James Fraser, 2, Tokenhouse Buildings. King's Arms Yard, E.C.; Solicitors, Godden and Holme, 34, Old Jewry, E.C.; Bankers, London and South Western Bank Limited, 7, Fenchurch Street, E.C.

Offices—2, Tokenhouse Buildings, King's Arms Yard, E.C.

133.—HIGHLAND.

An amalgamation of the INVERNESS AND ABERDEEN JUNCTION and the INVERNESS AND PERTH JUNCTION, authorised by act of 29th June, 1865. Capital, 3,305,000*l*.; borrowing powers, 1,107.780*l*. In operation, 31st August, 1883—Highland, 291¾ miles; lines worked, 110½ miles; foreign lines worked over, 7¼ miles; total, 409½ miles.

By act of 28th July, 1884, the company was authorised to construct new railways from Inverness to Aviemore. Total length, about 37½ miles. Period for completion, 5 years. Facilities to Great North of Scotland. New capital, 400,000*l*.; loans, 133,300*l*.

Act 1884, 28th July.—Amalgamation of the Sutherland undertakings (see below).

INVERNESS AND ABERDEEN JUNCTION.—Incorporated 21st July, 1856, to construct a single line from Nairn to Keith. Length, 40 miles. Capital, 325,000*l*. in 10*l*. shares and 108,300*l*. on loan. Opened for traffic, 18th August, 1858. Branch, Alves Station to Burghead; opened 23rd December, 1862. Extension from Invergordon to Tain and Bonar Bridge. Length, 26¾ miles. Opened in 1864. Inverness to Nairn, with a branch to Inverness Harbour. Length, 15½ miles. Opened 5th November, 1855, and by act of 17th May, 1861, amalgamated with the Inverness and Aberdeen. Inverness to Invergordon. Length, 31¼ miles. Opened to Dingwall, 18 miles, 11th June, 1862; to Invergordon, 23rd May, 1863, and amalgamated with the Inverness and Aberdeen by act of 30th June, 1862.

INVERNESS AND PERTH JUNCTION.—Incorporated 22nd July, 1861, to construct a single line from Forres, on the Inverness and Aberdeen, to Birnam, on the Perth and Dunkeld, with a branch to Aberfeldy. Length, 103¾ miles; branch, 9 miles. Traffic arrangements with the Scottish North Eastern, Scottish Central, and North British. Opened from Dunkeld to Pitlochry, 1st June, 1863; from Forres to Aviemore, 3rd August; and throughout, 9th September, 1863. *Perth and Dunkeld.*—Incorporated 10th July, 1854, to construct a line from the Scottish North Eastern, near Stanley, to Dunkeld. Length, 8¾ miles. Opened 7th April, 1856. By act of 8th June, 1863, the line was amalgamated with the Inverness and Perth.

DINGWALL AND SKYE.—Incorporated by act of 5th July, 1865, to construct a line from Dingwall to Kyle of Loch Alsh, with a pier thereat. Length, 63½ miles. Amalgamated with the Highland by act of 2nd August, 1880.

By the Highland (Additional Capital) Act, 1874 (21st May), the company was authorised to raise 500,000*l*. by the issue of ordinary or preference stock or shares, and to borrow on mortgage or by debenture stock 166,000*l*.

By act of 24th April, 1877, authority was granted to provide and use steam and other vessels.

By the Highland and Dingwall and Skye Amalgamation Act, 1880, the company was authorised to raise 74,000*l*. by the issue of debenture stock, and to restrict the ordinary capital of the Dingwall and Skye by that amount.

KEITH TO BUCKIE.—This branch was authorised by act of 12th July, 1882. Length, about 13¾ miles. Period for completion, 5 years. New capital, 100,000*l*.; borrowing powers, 33,600*l*. Opened 1st August, 1884.

SUTHERLAND AND SUTHERLAND AND CAITHNESS.—These undertakings were vested in the Highland by act of 28th July, 1884, as from the 1st September, 1884, the Highland to assume all liabilities, and to issue to the holders of ordinary stock of the amalgamated companies Highland ordinary stock at the following rate, viz.:—Sutherland exchanged at 60 per cent., Sutherland and Caithness exchanged at 50 per cent., the latter, however, not to receive dividend until after 31st August, 1886.—For particulars relating to the position of these companies in the past, see MANUAL for 1884, pages 311 and 312.

Revenue.—For the half-years ended 28th February and 31st August, 1884, this was as under:—

	Feb. 28, 1884.	Aug. 31, 1884.
Coaching	£88,069	£109,996
Goods, &c.	74,613	72,400
Miscellaneous	2,476	3,008
Gross receipts	£165,158	£185,404
Expenditure	91,668	93,027
Net	£73,490	£92,377
Add—Balance brought in	3,448	511
Total net revenue	£76,938	£92,888
Deduct—interest and preference dividends &c. (net)	46,277	46,458
Available for ordinary stock	£30,661	£46,430
Dividends at 3¼ and 5 per cent. per annum respectively	30,150	43,071
Balance carried forward	£511	£3,359

Capital.—The stock and share capital, as it stood on the 31st August, 1884, is given below, with

DESCRIPTIONS to be observed in transfer deeds and all other legal documents; and order of Priority, subject to debenture stocks, at 4½ and 4 per cent. which rank as a first charge (see notes):—

	Created.	Received.
1—Dunkeld 6 per cent. preference	£76,000	£76,000
2—Nairn 5 " "	45,000	45,000
3—Nairn 6 " " (minimum)	59,080	59,080
4—Class "A" 4½ " "	513,650	513,650
5—Class "B" 5 " "	400,000	400,000
6—Ordinary	1,777,270	1,722,843
	£2,871,000	£2,816,573

Notes.—The debenture stocks rank for dividend *pari passu*, the dividend being accumulative.

The Dunkeld stock has a lien over 7 miles of the company's railway.

The dividends on the whole of the company's-stocks, debenture included, are payable half-yearly, in May and November; the transfer books closing 14 days before payment.

The dividends on all the companies' stocks (Nos. 1 to 6) comprised in the above table are contingent upon the profits of each half-year.

The receipts and expenditure to 31st August, 1884, were as under:—

Received.		*Expended.*	
Shares and stock	£2,816,573	Lines open for traffic	£3,138,742
Debenture stock	1,041,240	Lines in course of construction or to be constructed	118,585
Balance	70,086	Working stock	590,572
		Subscriptions to other railways	80,000
	£3,927,899		£3,927,899

TRANSFER DEPARTMENT QUERIES AND REPLIES.

Queries.	Replies.
Transfer form—ordinary or special?	Ordinary.
Fee per deed?	2*s.* 6*d.*
Ditto if more sellers than one?	2*s.* 6*d.* for each seller.
May several classes of stock be transferred on one deed?	Yes.
Are certificates required to accompany transfers?	Yes.
What amounts of stock are transferable?	1*l.*
Are parts of 1*l.* sterling allowed to be transferred?	No.
To what officer should transfer communications be sent?	The Secretary.
In acceptances, renunciations, &c., of allotments of new stock, proxies, or other forms sent to trustees, and other joint account holdings, what signatures are required?	A majority in all cases except proxies, and for such, the signature of party first named in register.

Meetings in March or April and September or October in Inverness. Quorum, 15 shareholders in person or by proxy, and holding 30,000*l*.

Scale of Voting—2 to 10 shares, one vote; for each 10 additional shares to 100, one vote; and for every 20 shares above 100, one vote.

No. of Directors—18; minimum, 9; quorum, 3. *Qualification*, 2,000*l*.

DIRECTORS:

Chairman—3 Hon. THOS. CHARLES BRUCE, M.P., 42, Hill Street, Berkeley Square, W.

Deputy-Chairman—2 The Right Hon. LORD LOVAT, Beaufort Castle, Beauly, Inverness-shire.

3 Sir Alex. Matheson, Bart., of Lochalsh, Ardross Castle, Ross-shire, and 38, South Street, W.
3 Eneas W. Mackintosh, Esq., of Raigmore, Inverness.
3 William James Tayler, Esq., of Glenbarry, Huntly.
3 Sir Arnold B. Kemball, K. C. B., Uppat House, Sutherlandshire.
3 Alex. Henderson, Esq., of Stemster, Caithness.
1 James Grant-Peterkin, Esq., of Grange, Forres.
1 His Grace the Duke of Athole, Blair Castle, Blair Athole.
1 Sir Geo. Macpherson-Grant, Bart., M.P., Ballindalloch Castle, Ballindalloch.
1 Sir James Falshaw, Bart., Edinburgh.
1 His Grace the Duke of Sutherland, Dunrobin Castle, Sutherlandshire, and Stafford House, St. James's, S.W.
1 The Right Hon. Lord Thurlow, Dunphail House, Morayshire.
2 Ewen Macpherson, of Cluny Macpherson, Cluny Castle, Kingussie.
2 The Right Hon. the Earl of Fife, Mar Lodge, Braemar, and 4, Cavendish Square, W.
2 Colonel Hugh Inglis, of Kingsmills, Inverness.
2 R. B. Æ. Macleod, Esq., of Cadboll, Invergordon Castle, Invergordon.
2 Charles Waterston, Esq., Inverness.

The directors who retire annually have their places supplied by the election of the shareholders in terms of "The Companies' Clauses Consolidation (Scotland) Act, 1845."

OFFICERS.—Sec. and Gen. Man., Andrew Dougall; Assist. Sec. and Accountant, Wm. Gowenlock; Goods Mans., Thomas Mackay and George K. Ellis; Supt. of Line, Thos. Robertson; Resident Eng., Murdoch Paterson, M.Inst.C.E.; Loco. Supt., David Jones; Audit Accountant, C. S. Mc Hardy; Storekeeper, John G. Bulmer; Audit Inspector and Factor, Chas. Lamond; Auditors, A. Penrose Hay and William R. Grant, Inverness; Solicitors, John K. Lindsay, S.S.C., Edinburgh, and Stewart, Rule, and Burns, Inverness; Parliamentary Solicitors, Martin and Leslie, London; Bankers, Commercial Bank of Scotland, British Linen Company Bank, and Caledonian Bank.

Head Offices—Inverness.

134.—HORNCASTLE.

Incorporated by act of 1854, and estimated to cost 45,000*l*. Length, 8 miles. Capital, 48,000*l*. in 10*l*. shares; loans, 13,000*l*. Single line. The line forms a junction with the Great Northern at Kirkstead, about 123 miles from London. Worked by the Great Northern for 50 per cent. of gross receipts. Productive, 7¼ miles.

The Board of Trade, upon the application of this company, and with the concurrence of the Great Northern, have made an order for the continuance of the existing arrangements between the two companies, as prescribed by "The Horncastle Act, 1854," for a further period of ten years from 1875, and the agreement of 11th February, 1855, has likewise been renewed for the same period.

REVENUE.—The sums received from the Great Northern suffice for the payment of dividends at the rate of about 7 per cent. per annum=7*s*. per share on the ordinary share capital of the company.

CAPITAL.—The receipts include 4,800 ordinary shares of 10*l*. each, and 13,000*l*. in debenture stock at 4 per cent. The expenditure amounts to 61,000*l*.

The accounts are made up to the 30th June and 31st December, and the meetings held in Horncastle in March and September.

No. of Directors—8; minimum, 4. *Qualification*, 20 shares.

DIRECTORS:

Chairman—JAMES BANKS STANHOPE, Esq., Revesby Abbey.

The Rev. Thomas Livesey, The Close, Lincoln.
Hugh George, Esq., M.D., Horncastle.
Thomas Blakey, Esq., Horncastle.
James Isle, Esq., Horncastle.
John Burrell, Esq., Horncastle.
Robert C. Isle, Esq., Horncastle.
Thomas Waller, Esq., Raithby Lodge, Spilsby.

The directors retire in rotation, one-third yearly, but are eligible for re-election.

OFFICERS.—Sec. and Solicitor, Fred. W. Tweed, Horncastle; Eng., Richard Johnson, M.Inst.C.E.; Auditors, Robert Clifton Armstrong and Henry Nicholson, Horncastle.

135.—HOUNSLOW AND METROPOLITAN.

Incorporated by act of 26th August, 1880, for the construction and maintenance of a railway from Hounslow to Ealing, in the county of Middlesex, and by act of 29th June, 1883, the company was authorised to extend its railway by a branch to Hounslow Town. The first portion of the line (4 miles, 3 furlongs, 6 chains, 91 links), including the Hounslow Town Branch, was opened May 1st, 1883, the remaining portion (1 mile, 4 furlongs, 1 chain, 94 links), July 21st, 1884. Total length of railway, 5 miles, 7 furlongs, 8 chains, and 85 links. Arrangements with Metropolitan District to work the line at 50 per cent. of the gross receipts. Capital, 270,000*l.* in 10*l.* shares, with power to divide into "preferred" and "deferred" half-shares. Borrowing powers, 90,000*l.*

Capital.—The receipts on this account to 30th June, 1884, were 238,000*l.*, and the expenditure amounted to 244,996*l.* Credit balance, 6,996*l.*

Works completed throughout and opened July 21st, 1884.

No. of Directors.—Maximum, 5; minimum, 3; quorum, 3 and 2. *Qualification*, 25 shares.

DIRECTORS:

Chairman—Major A. G. DICKSON, M.P., 10, Duke Street, St. James's, S.W., and Carlton Club, 124, Pall Mall, S.W.

Deputy-Chairman—THOMAS EYKYN, Esq., 51, Ladbroke Grove, Bayswater, W.

Henry Daniel Davies, Esq., Spring Grove, Isleworth, Middlesex.

Jasper Wilson Johns, Esq., 16, Grenville Place, Cromwell Road, S.W., and 90, Cannon Street, E.C.

OFFICERS.—Sec., Charles Eley; Engs., Wells Owen and Elwes, MM.Inst.C.E., 7, Westminster Chambers, Westminster, S.W.; Auditors, George Browning and W. Tudor Johns.

Offices—201, Mansion House Chambers, Queen Victoria Street, E.C.

136.—HULL, BARNSLEY, AND WEST RIDING JUNCTION.

Incorporated by act of 26th August, 1880, for the construction and maintenance of several railways, amounting in the aggregate to about 66 miles, and a dock and river wall embankment (with lock or entrance to the River Humber), at Drypool and Southcoates, in the town and county of the town of Kingston-upon-Hull. Capital, 3,000,000*l.* in 10*l.* shares, with power to divide into "preferred" and "deferred" half-shares. Borrowing powers, 1,000,000*l.*

By the Hull, Barnsley, and West Riding Junction Railway and Dock Company's Extensions Act, 1882, the company is authorised to construct additional railways connecting their system with the towns of Huddersfield and Halifax; to take further land for the purposes of timber yards, ponds, &c; to construct a new fish dock; to raise 2,400,000*l.* additional capital; further borrowing powers, 800,000*l.*

By the terms of an agreement with the Midland, the Hull and Barnsley obtain running powers into Cudworth, where a joint station is provided for, and the Midland obtain running powers into Huddersfield and Halifax.

By the Various Powers Act, 1883, the company is authorised to construct a deviation railway in the town of Hull, and various other works, and for these purposes to issue 600,000*l.* additional capital; borrowing powers, 200,000*l.*

By act of 23rd June, 1884, the company was authorised to construct two short lines at Kingston-upon-Hull, length, about ¾ mile; and powers were obtained for various purposes in connection therewith.

By the Money Act of 14th August, 1884, the company is authorised to raise 1,500,000*l.* by means of debenture stock, debentures, or mortgage bonds; such capital to be devoted to the completion of the works authorised by the act of 1880, and works in connection therewith.

Capital.—The ordinary share capital of the company is 300,000 shares of 10*l.* each, which are now fully paid. There has also been 960,000*l.* raised on five years' terminable debentures at 4½ per cent. per annum.

The creation and issue of the additional capital has been authorised by the shareholders.

No. of Directors.—Maximum, 14; minimum, 9; quorum, 5 and 4. *Qualification*, 50 shares. Transfer form, ordinary; fee, 2*s.* 6*d.*

DIRECTORS:

Chairman—† Lieut.-Colonel GERARD SMITH, M.P., Tranby Lodge, Hessle.

Deputy-Chairman—† JOHN FISHER, Esq., J.P., Manor House, Willerby.

† William Rayment, Esq., High Street, Hull
† Henry Briggs, Esq., Posterngate, Hull.
The Rt. Hon. Lord Beaumont, Carlton Towers, Selby.
Samuel Swarbrick, Esq., The Cedars, Tottenham, N.
Edward Leetham, Esq., Humber Dock Side, Hull.
Samuel Joshua, Esq., 18, Westbourne Terrace, W.
J. S. Forbes, Esq., Victoria Station, S.W.
James Stuart, Esq., High Street, Hull.
Watson Arton Massey, Esq., 7, Quay Street, Hull.
J. A. M. Cope, Esq., 14, Pembridge Square, W.
*John Leak, Esq., Bowlalley Lane, Hull.
*Thomas Witty, Esq., Wincolmlee, Hull.

* Appointed by the Corporation of Hull.
† Retire in February, 1885; all eligible for re-election.

OFFICERS.—Sec., J. Daniell; Traffic Man., Vincent W. Hill; Accountant, W. H. Wood; Registrar, W. C. Prescott; Engs.—*For the Dock*, Eng.-in-Chief, James Abernethy, F.R.S.E., M.Inst.C.E., Delahay Street, Westminster, S.W.; Acting Engs., Oldham and Bohn, MM.Inst.C.E., Hull; *For the Railway*, William Shelford, M.Inst.C.E., F.G.S., Great George Street, Westminster, S.W., and George Bohn, M.Inst.C.E., Hull; Auditors, John Young and W. P. Burkinshaw; Solicitors, Brooksbank and Galland, 14, Gray's Inn Square, W C., and Lowe, Moss, and Co., Hull; Bankers, Smith, Payne, and Smiths, Lombard Street, E.C., and Samuel Smith, Brothers, and Co., Hull.

Offices—4, Charlotte Street, Hull. London Office—16, Tokenhouse Yard, E.C.

137.—HUNSTANTON AND WEST NORFOLK JUNCTION.

LYNN AND HUNSTANTON.—Incorporated 1st August, 1861, to construct a line from the East Anglian section of the Great Eastern, at Lynn, to the town of Hunstanton. Length, 15 miles. Capital, 60,000*l.* in 10*l.* shares and 20,000*l.* on loan. Working arrangements with the Great Eastern.

WEST NORFOLK JUNCTION.—Incorporated 23rd June, 1864, to construct a line from the Lynn and Hunstanton, at Heacham, to the Great Eastern at Wells. Length, 18¼ miles. Capital, 75,000*l.* in 10*l.* shares and 25,000*l.* on loan. The Great Eastern subscribed 30,000*l.*, and works the line at 50 per cent.

By act of 8th June, 1874, the two companies were amalgamated as the HUNSTANTON and WEST NORFOLK JUNCTION. Capital, 135,000*l.* (60,000*l.* "A" stock and 75,000*l.* "B" stock), with power to increase to 195,000*l.* Debenture capital, 45,000*l.*, which may be increased to 65,000*l.* All previous working agreements between the Lynn and Hunstanton and West Norfolk companies and the Great Eastern are confirmed by this act, and the Great Eastern is authorised to subscribe 20,000*l.*, and to raise money for that purpose. The 60,000*l.* "A" stock has been allotted amongst the stockholders in the Lynn and Hunstanton, and the 75,000*l.* "B" stock amongst the shareholders in the West Norfolk, in the proportion in which the capital of the old companies was held by them.

The profits of the company applicable to the payment of dividends upon the said "A" and "B" stocks will be from time to time apportioned as follows:—Three-fourths thereof shall be apportioned amongst and be paid to the holders of the "A" stock, according to the amount of stock held by them respectively, and the remaining one-fourth shall in like manner be apportioned amongst and be paid to the holders of the "B" stock; provided always that, whenever in any year the profits divisible as aforesaid shall be more than sufficient to pay dividends upon the "A" stock at the rate of 12*l.* per cent. per annum, and upon the "B" stock at the rate of 3*l.* 4*s.* per cent. per annum, the surplus, after providing for those rates of dividend, shall be divisible amongst the holders of the "A" stock and "B" stock in proportion to the amount of stock held by them respectively, and as if the "A" stock and "B" stock were one and the same stock.

REVENUE.—The earnings for the half-years ended 31st December, 1883, and 30th June, 1884, sufficed for the following dividends, viz.:—On the "A" stock, 12 and 8 per cent. per annum; and on the "B" stock, 3¼ and 2 per cent. per annum respectively.

CAPITAL.—The receipts on this account to 30th June, 1884, amounted to 211,331*l.*, being 414*l.* less than the expenditure, which amounted to 211,745*l.* The receipts are detailed below:—

Ordinary stock "A" (Lynn and Hunstanton)	£60,000
Ordinary stock "B" (West Norfolk)	75,000
Preference stock at 4½ per cent. (created under the act of 1874)	16,000
Preference stock at 4 per cent.	12,000
Debenture stock at 4½ per cent.	20,000
Debenture stock at 5 per cent.	25,000
Extra works	3,292
Interest and amounts owing	39
	£211,331

Meetings held in Lynn in February or August.

No. of Directors.—Maximum, 6; minimum, 3; quorum, 3 or 2. *Qualification*, 500*l.*

DIRECTORS:

Chairman—J. S. VALENTINE, Esq., 6, Queen Anne's Gate, S.W.

Edwin Elmer Durrant, Esq., North Runcton, Lynn.

Major H. J. Hare, Broadwater Down, Tunbridge Wells.

Hamon Le Strange, Esq., Hunstanton Hall.

William Henry Simpson, Esq., 16, Kent Terrace, Clarence Gate, N.W.

OFFICERS.—Sec., Thomas Paul Bond, 4, Queen Anue's Gate, Westminster, S.W.; Auditors, George W. Page and John D. Thew; Solicitor, J. T. Valentine, 6, Queen Anne's Gate, Westminster, S.W.

Offices—4, Queen Anne's Gate, Westminster, S.W.

138.—ILEN VALLEY.

(FORMERLY DUNMANWAY AND SKIBBEREEN.)

Incorporated by act of 25th July, 1872, to construct a line in the county of Cork from Dunmanway to Skibbereen. Length, 15¾ miles. Capital, 80,000*l.* Baronial guaranteed 5 per cent. shares, of 10*l.* each, 53,000*l.*; ordinary 10*l.* shares, 27,000*l.*

By act of 8th August, 1878, the company was authorised to make a new railway, to be called the "Bantry Extension," from Drimoleague to Carrignagat. Length, 11 miles 1 furlong 9 chains. Period for completion, five years. The extension to form a separate undertaking. Capital, 40,000*l.* in "A" or baronial guaranteed extension 10*l.* shares, and 30,000*l.* in "B" or ordinary 10*l.* shares; total, 70,000*l.* Borrowing powers, 35,000*l.* The "A" shareholders are guaranteed dividends at 5 per cent. per annum for 35 years. The moneys paid by the baronies (if any) to be a charge on the railway and income until repaid. This railway was eventually constructed by the Cork and Bandon Company, under that company's act of 24th July, 1879.

By the Cork and Kinsale, Cork and Bandon, West Cork, and Ilen Valley Act, of 24th July, 1879, the sale of the West Cork (which works this undertaking) to the Cork and Bandon was authorised, the transfer to take effect as and from the 1st January, 1880. The agreement with this company, dated 28th March, 1876, to remain in force, and not to alter in any respect, except in the substitution of the name of the Cork and Bandon for that of the West Cork. Other arrangements between the Cork and Bandon and this company were also authorised.—See also Cork and Bandon.

Opened from Dunmanway to Skibbereen, July 21st, 1877; formerly worked by the West Cork, but now by the Cork and Bandon, at 52 per cent of the gross receipts.

CAPITAL—Half-year ended 30th June, 1884.—Amount expended, 120,015*l.* *Receipts:* Baronial 5 per cent. guaranteed stock, 53,000*l.*; ordinary stock, 27,000*l.*; loans, 40,000*l.*; total, 120,000*l.* Debit balance, 15*l.*

In February, 1879, the company passed a resolution authorising the consolidation of the whole of the shares of the company into "Baronial Guaranteed Stock," guaranteed by certain Baronies for 35 years, from 21st July, 1877, and "General Capital Stock" respectively; the exchanges were made at par, and all other conditions of issue remain the same as before the consolidation.

TRANSFER DEPARTMENT QUERIES AND REPLIES.

Queries.	Replies.
Transfer form—ordinary or special?	Ordinary.
Fee per deed?	2*s.* 6*d.*
May several classes of stock be transferred on one deed?	No.
Are certificates required to accompany transfers?	Yes.
What amounts of stock are transferable?	Any amount.
Are parts of 1*l.* sterling allowed to be transferred?	No.
To what officer should transfer communications be sent?	Secretary.

No. of Directors—7; quorum, 3. *Qualification*, 200*l.*

DIRECTORS:

2 Chairman—JOHN WARREN PAYNE, Esq., J.P., Beach House, Bantry.

1 Deputy-Chairman—EUGENE COLLINS, Esq., M.P., 38, Porchester Terrace Hyde Park, W.

1 Edward Richard Townsend, Esq., M.D., 14, Patrick's Hill, Cork.

2 John Edward Barrett, Esq., J.P., Carriganass Castle, Bantry.

2 O'Donovan, D.L., Lissard, Skibbereen.

3 Rev. Somers Henry Payne, Upton, Co. Cork.

1, Retire February, 1885; 2, 1886; 3, 1887.

OFFICERS.—Sec., Edward H. Dorman; Eng., William Barrington, 84, George Street, Limerick; Auditors, William Wilson and Patrick O'Brien; Arbitrators, Nathaniel Jackson, C.E., William Norwood, J.P., and Henry R. Marmion; Solicitors, Babington and Babington, 24, Marlborough Street, Cork.

Offices—54, South Mall, Cork.

139.—ISLE OF MAN.

The Isle of Man Railway Company Limited was authorised by the Isle of Man Railway Act, 1872, to construct a line from Douglas to Peel, a distance of 11½ miles; and another line from Douglas to Port Erin, *via* Castletown and Port St. Mary, a distance of 15½ miles. Capital, 200,000*l.* in 5*l.* shares and 66,666*l.* on loan.

The line from Douglas to Peel was opened for public traffic on the 2nd July, 1873, and that from Douglas to Port Erin on 1st August, 1874.

REVENUE.—The gross receipts for the year ended 31st December, 1883 (including 20,771*l.* from passengers, &c., and 3,825*l.* from goods, &c.), amounted to 24,721*l.*, and the expenditure to 12,464*l.*, leaving a profit of 12,257*l.* Adding the balance from previous account and sundries, the total net revenue was 13,288*l.*, which was sufficient, after payment of interest on debentures, &c., and 160*l.* for rent-charges, for full dividends on the preference capital, and dividends at 4 per cent. per annum on the ordinary capital, of which 4 per cent. per annum was paid as an interim dividend and 4 per cent. per annum as a final dividend for the year, after which a balance of 2,115*l.* was carried to the next year's accounts. In operation, 27 miles.

CAPITAL.—This account to 31st December, 1883, showed that the expenditure had been 254,041*l.*, and the receipts 250,881*l.*, viz.:—189,688*l.* by shares and 61,193*l.* on loan.

The last annual ordinary general meeting was held on the 2nd March, 1883.

DIRECTORS:

Chairman—JOHN PENDER, Esq., M.P., 18, Arlington Street, S.W., and Minard Castle, Argyleshire.

Deputy-Chairman—Major J. S. GOLDIE-TAUBMAN, Speaker of the House of Keys, The Nunnery, Isle of Man.

John Thomas Clucas, Esq., M.H.K., Thornhill, Isle of Man.

Richard Penketh, Esq., M.H.K., Hampton Court, Isle of Man.

W. B. Stevenson, Esq., M.H.K., Balladoole, Isle of Man.

Major-General James P. Beadle, R.E., 6, Queen's Gate Gardens, South Kensington, S.W.

Two directors retire annually by rotation, the two who shall have been longest in office, reckoning from the time of their last election, but they are always eligible for re-election.

OFFICERS.—Sec. and Man., G. H. Wood; Eng., H. Greenbank, M.Inst.C.E., 15, Delahay Street, S.W.; Loco. Supt., H. R. Hunt; Auditors, Turquand, Youngs, and Co., Coleman Street, E.C.; Advocates, Sir James Gell, Attorney-General, Castletown, Isle of Man, and G. A. Ring, Douglas; Bankers, Glyn, Mills, Currie, and Co., London, and Dumbell's Banking Co. Limited, Isle of Man.

Offices—St. George's Street, Douglas, Isle of Man.

140.—ISLE OF WIGHT.

Incorporated by act of 23rd July, 1860, to construct a line from Ryde to Ventnor. Length, 12 miles. Capital, 125,000*l.* in 10*l.* shares; loans, 41,600*l.*

By acts of 1863, 1865, and 1867 extensive powers were conferred upon the company, but these have not been exercised. and are now expired. The company's Steamboat Act of 1865 authorised the creation of 20,000*l.* share capital and 5,000*l.* loans.

SCHEME OF ARRANGEMENT, 1869.—Under the scheme of arrangement between the company and its creditors, the directors were authorised to cancel all unissued share and loan capital, and (in order to enable the company to complete the station and other works, and to augment the supply of rolling stock) to create and issue, in lieu of such cancelled share and loan capital, new debenture stock, to rank next after the then existing debenture stock, which, for distinction, was classed "A" debenture stock. Article 3 of the scheme of arrangement provides that the company may grant to the owners of land taken for the purposes of the Eastern Lines annual rent-charges carrying interest at a rate not exceeding 5 per cent., to rank next after the existing rent-charges and mortgages. Under this scheme the capital (exclusive of the steamboat capital which remained unaltered) was fixed as follows:—Ordinary capital, 109,150*l.*; Eastern Lines preference stock, 67,210*l.*; "A" debenture stock, 68,536*l.*; "B" debenture stock, 71,464*l.*—The scheme will be found in full in the *Appendix* to the MANUAL for 1875.

By Board of Trade Certificate, 1876, the capital was increased 50,000*l.* and the borrowing powers 16,600*l.*

REVENUE.—The net earnings for the half-year ended 30th June, 1884, sufficed, after providing for debenture and other fixed charges, for the payment of the full dividend on the preference stock, and 1½ per cent. on ordinary stock, leaving a balance of 555*l.*

CAPITAL.—The expenditure on this account to 30th June, 1884, was 399,095*l.* The receipts, to the same date, were as follow:—

Ordinary stock	£149,572
Preference stock	67,210
Debenture stock	145,984
Premiums on stocks (less discount)	7,857
Rent-charges (capitalised value)	6,056
Miscellaneous	8,813
Revenue balance to 31st December, 1869, transferred to credit of capital	13,575
	£399,067
Balance	28
	£399,095

Meetings in February and August.

No. of Directors—6; minimum, 5; quorum, 3. *Qualification*, 250*l.*

DIRECTORS:

Chairman—HORACE F. TAHOURDIN, Esq., 9, Victoria Chambers, Westminster, S.W.

A. D. De Pass, Esq., Bembridge, Isle of Wight.

F. W. Slade, Esq., 120, Grosvenor Road, S.W.

J. M. Stobart, Esq., Olga House, Spring Vale, Ryde, Isle of Wight.

Capt. H. F. Twynam, 10, Down Street, Piccadilly, W.

Retire as provided by C.C.C. Act; all eligible for re-election.

OFFICERS.—Sec., R. Hicks; Eng. and Traffic Man., James Conner, Sandown, Isle of Wight; Auditors, C. L. Christian, 9, Westminster Chambers, Victoria Street, S.W., and E. Waterhouse, 44, Gresham Street, E.C.; Solicitors, Beale, Marigold, and Co., 28, Great George Street, Westminster, S.W.; Bankers, The National Provincial Bank of England, London, and Ryde Branch.

General Offices—122, Cannon Street, E.C.

141.—ISLE OF WIGHT (NEWPORT JUNCTION).

Incorporated by act of 31st July, 1868, to construct railways to connect Newport and Cowes with Sandown, Ryde, and Ventnor. Length, 9¼ miles. Capital, 84,000*l.* in 10*l.* shares and 28,000*l.* on loan. Joint stations at Newport and Sandown, with running powers over parts of the Isle of Wight and Cowes and Newport.

By act of 6th August, 1872, the company was authorised to extend the line to the Yarmouth and Ventnor; also to construct other new lines and works by revival of powers, &c. Length, 4 miles. New capital, 50,000*l.* in shares and 16,600*l.* on loan or by debenture stock. Joint station with Yarmouth and Ventnor, as well as working agreements, &c. These works have since been abandoned.

By act of 16th April, 1878, the powers under the act of 1872 were revived, and the time for the completion of the unfinished portion of the new joint line extended for one year. New capital, 36,000*l.*; loans, &c., 12,000*l.* (See Scheme of Arrangement further on).

The line from Sandown to Newport was opened on the 1st February, 1875.

Junction with the Cowes and Newport.—This junction was completed and opened for traffic on the 1st June, 1879.

Revenue.—Half-year ended 30th June, 1884.—Net earnings and balance from last half-year, 1,517*l.*; debenture and other interest, rent-charges, &c., 3,492*l.*; balance (debit), 1,975*l.*

Capital.—The expenditure on this account to 30th June, 1884, amounted to 196,702*l.* The receipts were 183,726*l.*, and are detailed below:—

Ordinary shares	£58,100
Preferred shares	50,000
Loans at 4½ per cent.	600
Loans at 5 per cent.	10,160
"A" Debenture stock at 4½ per cent.	36,205
"B" „ 4 „	28,661
	183,726

By a Scheme of Arrangement between the company and its creditors, filed in the Court of Chancery on the 18th December, 1880, the company's affairs were settled on a satisfactory basis. It may be well to point out that the scheme thus defines the priorities for dividend, &c., of the various classes of securities which under that, and the acts of Parliament mentioned above, have from time to time been issued by the company, viz.:—"The net income of the company, after payment of the working expenses of the company, including the performance of all statutory requirements, shall be applied as follows:—(*a*) In payment of annual rent-charges granted to vendors of land to the company. (*b*) In payment to the holders of mortgages remaining unexchanged and the holders of 'A' debenture stock *pari passu*, the several amounts of interest due on the said mortgages and stock respectively. (*c*) In payment to the holders of 'B' debenture stock the interest on that stock *pari passu*. (*d*) In payment to the holders of preferred shares in the said company of interest at the rate of 6*l.* per cent. per annum. (*e*) In payment of the dividend on the ordinary shares of the company. With reference to the debenture stocks hereby authorised to be created and issued, and subject nevertheless and without prejudice to any of the other articles in this scheme contained, and to any rights and privileges conferred by or to arise under such articles or any of them, this scheme shall be deemed to be a Special Act of Parliament authorising the company to raise the said sum of 87,545*l.* by the creation and issue of debenture stock, and incorporating part 3 of the Companies' Clauses Act, 1863, as amended by the Companies' Clauses Act, 1869. The said debenture stocks shall be redeemable by the company at any time at par on six months' notice to the holder thereof for the time being. It shall be lawful for all trustees, executors, administrators, corporations, and married women, holding or being entitled to or interested in any mortgage, debt, debenture, or debenture stock of the company, upon any trust or otherwise, or for the guardians and committees respectively of any infants or lunatics respectively, who may hold or be entitled to or interested in any such mortgage, debt, debenture, or debenture stock, to accept the debenture stocks to be issued under the provisions of this scheme."

The scheme further sets forth that "the company shall not be at liberty to and shall not exercise any of the powers for raising capital or for borrowing on mortgage, or on debenture stocks conferred upon them by any of the hereinbefore recited acts, to any greater extent or amount than such powers respectively have at the date of the filing of this scheme been exercised."

TRANSFER DEPARTMENT QUERIES AND REPLIES.

Queries.	Replies.
Transfer form—ordinary or special?	Ordinary.
Fee per deed?	2s. 6d.
May several classes of stock be transferred on one deed?	One deed.
Are certificates required to accompany transfers?	Yes.
What amounts of stock are transferable, and are parts of 1l. sterling allowed to be transferred?	Any amount, but not fractions of 1l.
To what officer should transfer communications be sent?	Secretary.
In acceptances, renunciations, &c., of allotments of new stock, proxies, or other forms sent to trustees, what signatures are required?	Either of the trustees.

Meetings held in London in February and August.

No. of Directors—5; minimum, 3; quorum, 3 and 2. *Qualification*, 500l.

DIRECTORS:

John Winterbotham Batten, Esq., 15, Airlie Gardens, Campden Hill, W.
Percy Mortimer, Esq., Ricard's Lodge, Wimbledon.
Thomas Dolling Bolton, Esq., 3, Temple Gardens, Temple, E.C.
R. E. Webster, Esq., Q.C., 2 Pump Court, Temple, E.C.

OFFICERS.—Sec., David S. Derry; Gen. Man. and Loco. Supt., H. Simmons; Eng., Charles Douglas Fox, M.Inst.C.E., 2, Victoria Mansions, Westminster, S.W.; Solicitors, Saunders, Hawksford, and Bennett; Bankers, Capital and Counties Bank and their branches in the Isle of Wight; The London Joint Stock Bank, Prince's Street, London.

General Offices—22, Great Winchester Street, E.C.

142.—JERSEY RAILWAYS COMPANY LIMITED.

Incorporated under the Companies' Acts, 1862 to 1880. These railways are constructed under powers granted by special acts of the States of Jersey, confirmed by Her Majesty in Council.

The first section commences at St. Heliers, the capital of Jersey, and extends to St. Aubin's, one of the largest towns in the Island, with four intermediate stations. The gross receipts of the section for the financial year ended 10th July, 1884, amounted to 6,202l., and the expenditure to 3,877l., leaving a profit of 2,325l. The number of passengers carried, exclusive of season tickets, was about 500,000 during the year.

The second section (which was not opened until 23rd August, 1884), commences at St. Aubin's and terminates at La Moye, where extensive and important granite quarries exist; in addition there will be a short branch line to the St Aubin's Harbour Pier. The proprietors of the La Moye Quarries have entered into a contract to send over the Jersey Railways a minimum of 75,000 tons of granite per annum, for three years, from the date of the opening of this section.

Capital.—120,000l., 60,000l. in 6,000 shares of 10l. each, and 60,000l. in 5 per cent. mortgage debenture stock, which is secured as a first charge on the entire undertaking by a deed of mortgage and trust, registered at the Joint Stock Companies' Registration Office, in favour of trustees on behalf of the holders of debenture stock. Owing to certain requirements of the States of Jersey, which were not anticipated on the formation of the company, it has become necessary to raise additional capital, and the Debenture Stockholders have therefore consented to allow the creation of a first mortgage to the extent of 20,000l upon the property in priority to the debenture stock.

TRUSTEES FOR HOLDERS OF DEBENTURE STOCK:

The Right Hon. Viscount Ranelagh, K.C.B.
E. B. de Fonblanque, Esq.
Capt. Francis William Lowther, R.N., 35, Hans Place, Knightsbridge, S.W.

DIRECTORS:

Chairman—T. HAYWARD BUDD, Esq., 33, Bedford Row, W.C.

Arthur Clarence Jones, Esq., Portlett House, Jersey.
The Honourable Dudley O. Murray, Union Club, Trafalgar Square, S.W.
William C. Heaton Armstrong, Esq. F.R.A.S., 34, Old Broad Street, E.C.
Maurice Grant, Esq., 60, Lancaster Gate, W.

OFFICERS.—Sec., George Fraser; Eng., Alfred Rumball, 1, Victoria Street, S.W.; Auditor, Roderick Mackay, Esq., 3, Lothbury, E.C.; Solicitors, Rodgers and Clarkson, 4, Walbrook, E.C.; Bankers, Brown, Janson, & Co., 32, Abchurch Lane, E.C., and The Jersey Banking Company Limited, St. Helier's, Jersey.

Offices—2, Tokenhouse Buildings, E.C.

143.—KELVIN VALLEY.

Incorporated by act of 21st July, 1873, to construct a line from the Glasgow, Dumbarton, and Helensburgh, at Maryhill, to Kilsyth, with a branch to the Campsie Branch of the North British. Length, 11¼ miles. Capital, 90,000*l.* in 10*l.* shares and 30,000*l.* on loan; a minimum dividend of 5¼ per cent. on the ordinary capital is *provisionally* guaranteed by the North British from the opening of the line.

KILSYTH.—Incorporated by act of 13th July, 1876. Length, 2 miles 1 furlong. By act of 40 Vic., cap. 17, 17th May, 1877, this company was vested in the Kelvin Valley; the portion of the Kelvin Valley rendered unnecessary by the construction of the above 2 miles 1 furlong was abandoned, and further financial arrangements were made with the North British. The North British Act (No. 2) of 17th May, 1877, empowers that company to subscribe 30,000*l.* to this undertaking, and to hold shares in this company to the same amount, but without power of sale or transfer. They amounted at 31st July, 1884, to 62,783*l.*

KILSYTH AND BONNYBRIDGE.—See GENERAL INDEX.

Under the Kelvin Valley Act of 1877, the North British was bound to advance the funds necessary for the completion of the railway, such advances by that company to rank for dividend after the authorised share and loan capital.

The railway was completed in 1879. The North British (under agreement), are to work and maintain the line, providing rolling stock, &c., in perpetuity, at 50 per cent. of the gross receipts.

REVENUE.—For the half-years ended 31st January and 31st July, 1884, the company earned dividends upon its ordinary capital at the rate of 3*l.* 15*s.* and 3*l.* 17*s.* 6*d.* per cent. per annum.

CAPITAL.—The receipts to 31st July, 1884, amounted to 120,000*l.* (being 90,000*l.* in 9,000 ordinary shares at 10*l.* each, and 30,000*l.* on loans at 4 per cent. per annum), and the expenditure to 182,015*l.*

TRANSFER DEPARTMENT QUERIES AND REPLIES.

QUERIES.	REPLIES.
Transfer form—ordinary or special?	Ordinary.
Fee per deed?	2*s.* 6*d.*
Ditto if more sellers than one? ...	2*s.* 6*d.*
Are certificates required to accompany transfers?	Yes.
What amounts of stock are transferable?	10*l.*
Are parts of 1*l.* sterling allowed to be transferred?	No.
To what officer should transfer communications be sent?	Secretary.

Meetings held in April and October.

No. of Directors.—Maximum, 6; minimum, 3; quorum, 3 and 2. *Qualification* 25 shares.

DIRECTORS:

Chairman—1 HUGH BARTHOLOMEW, Esq., of Glenorchard, Stirlingshire.

1 Henry Grierson, Esq., 8, Park Circus Place, Glasgow.
2 William Whyte, Esq., Kilsyth.
2 Robert Young, Esq., 4, West Nile Street, Glasgow.
3 A. R. Duncan, Esq., Blairguhosh, Strathblane.

1, Retire in 1885; 2, in 1886; 3, in 1887. All eligible for re-election.

OFFICERS.—Sec., Henry Lamond; Engs., Formans and Mc.Call; Auditors, Alexander Moore, C.A., and James Hutton, C.A.; Solicitors, H. and R. Lamond; Bankers, Union Bank of Scotland Limited and branches.

Offices—93, West Regent Street, Glasgow.

144.—KETTERING, THRAPSTON, AND HUNTINGDON.

Incorporated by acts of 1862 and 1863, and the Midland, under agreement, worked the line in past years for 40 per cent. of the gross receipts for seven years, and afterwards for 50 per cent. The line is now leased to that company in perpetuity.

This railway branches from the Midland at Kettering, passes under the London and North Western at Thrapston, under the Great Northern, with which it communicates, near Huntingdon, and effects a junction with the Great Eastern at Huntingdon. Length, 26 miles. By agreement with the Great Eastern, the Midland had powers of running through trains, passing over the Kettering and Thrapston, from Leeds, Bradford, Sheffield, Nottingham, Derby, Leicester, &c., to Cambridge, thus establishing direct communication between the whole of the Great Eastern system and the northern and midland manufacturing and mineral districts.

MIDLAND.—An agreement has been concluded with the Midland, under which the Kettering, Thrapston, and Huntingdon is guaranteed a minimum income of 17,500*l.* per annum, as from 1st January, 1877. The excess of all gross receipts in 1877 and future years beyond 35,000*l.* a-year to be divided, the Midland receiving 80 per cent. and the Kettering 20 per cent.

The capital of the company now consists of 75,600*l.* debenture stock at 4½ per cent.; 162,500*l.* 4 per cent. guaranteed "A" stock; 180,000*l.* 4 per cent. guaranteed "B" stock; and 100,000*l.* ordinary stock, all of which rank for dividend in the order named, and must be so described in transfer deeds and all other legal documents.

"The interest on both the 'guaranteed A' and 'guaranteed B' stocks is covered by and will be paid out of the annual minimum rent guaranteed by the Midland, and it is provided under their act of 1876, that, after the gross receipts amount to 35,000*l.* per annum, this company shall receive 20*l.* per cent. of the increase beyond that amount." A dividend of ⅙ per cent. on the ordinary stock was paid for the year ended 31st December, 1878, ¾ per cent. 31st December, 1882, and ¾ per cent. 31st December, 1883.

The capital account is irrevocably closed, the Midland having to provide, without interest, for all expenditure required for additional accommodation or extensions of the lines or works of the railway.

NOTE.—The dividends on the whole of the above named stocks, except the ordinary, are accumulative, and payable half-yearly as follows:—Debenture stock 1st January and 1st July, guaranteed stocks, "A" and "B," 15th January and 15th July.

TRANSFER DEPARTMENT QUERIES AND REPLIES.

QUERIES.	REPLIES.
Transfer form—ordinary or special?......	Ordinary.
Fee per deed?	2*s.* 6*d.*
Ditto if more sellers than one?...	2*s.* 6*d.* each seller.
May several classes of stock be transferred on one deed?	Separate deed required for debenture stock.
Are certificates required to accompany transfers?	Yes.
What amounts of stock are transferable, and are parts of 1*l.* sterling allowed to be transferred?	Any amount not fractions of 1*l.*
To what officer should transfer communications be sent?	Secretary.
In acceptances, renunciations, &c., of allotments of new stock, proxies, or other forms sent to trustees, or other joint holders, what signatures are required?	For proxies signature of first name only; in other cases signatures of all.

Meetings held in February or March and August or September.

Director's Qualification, 800*l.*

DIRECTORS:

Chairman—CHARLES WARING, Esq., Assoc.Inst.C.E., Grosvenor Square, W.

Deputy-Chairman—WILLIAM WARING, Esq., 39, Prince's Gardens, S.W., and Taverham Hall, Norwich.

Robert A. Read, Esq., The Cranes, Surbiton Hill, S.W.

Francis William Slade, Esq., Eldon Park, South Norwood.

Henry Waring, Esq., Beenham House, Reading.

OFFICERS.—Sec., E. B. Read, 9, Victoria Chambers, S.W.; Auditors, Henry W. Notman and Mardon and Co.; Solicitor, J. S. Beale, 28, Great George Street, S.W.

Offices—9, Victoria Chambers, S.W.

145.—KILKENNY JUNCTION.

Incorporated by act of 23rd July, 1860, to construct a line from the Waterford and Kilkenny, at the latter town, to Mountrath. Length, 25¼ miles. Capital, 140,000*l.* in 10*l.* shares; loans, 46,000*l.* The Waterford and Kilkenny subscribed 20,000*l.*, and created new shares for that purpose. Traffic arrangements under usual conditions.

For list of other Acts from 1861 to 1877, with short heads relating to the objects for which the various powers were sought, see the MANUAL for 1881, page 165.

In pursuance of the agreement between the company and the Waterford and Central Ireland, approved at the special meeting of the proprietors, held on the 6th of August, 1874, Mr. Grierson, the general manager of the Great Western, made his award on the matters submitted to him by the agreement. He awarded to the Waterford, for working expenses, maintenance, &c., 80 per cent. of the gross receipts for the year ended 1st November, 1874, 77 per cent. of the gross receipts for the year ended 1st November, 1875, and 1 per cent. less for each succeeding year of the ten years for which the agreement was made.

NEW WORKING AGREEMENT.—Terms have been arranged with the Waterford and Central Ireland for a new agreement, to take effect from the 1st November, 1883, on the following terms:—"The working company to work and maintain the railway as in the previous agreement, and to retain out of the receipts 70 per cent. up to the first 12,000*l.*, and 50 per cent. upon all receipts over and above the first 12,000*l.*"

"At the half-yearly meeting of the shareholders, held November, 1883, when the terms of the working agreement between the company and the Waterford and Central Ireland were submitted for approval, it was deemed advisable by a majority of the shareholders present that the agreement should terminate at the end of twelve months, if the Mountmellick Extension were not then opened for traffic, and a proviso to that effect was added to the agreement.

"The directors reported in May, 1884, that they had received an intimation from the Waterford and Central Ireland that the necessary capital to complete this extension had been subscribed conditionally upon the rescission of this proviso. Under these circumstances the directors recommended that the following memorandum be approved and endorsed upon the working agreement, and a formal resolution to this effect was proposed at the special general meeting and agreed to:—

"Memorandum of agreement between the within named Kilkenny Company of the one part and the within named Waterford Company of the other part. Whereas, with stock which the Great Western have agreed to take, under agreement with the Waterford, dated 6th September, 1878, capital sufficient for the completion of the section of the Central Ireland from Maryborough to Mountmellick, mentioned in clause 19 of the within written agreement, has been subscribed by other parties; and the several persons subscribing the same have agreed to pay in full the amounts they have respectively subscribed, on the demand of the Waterford, on or before the 1st day of July next, provided this memorandum of agreement shall have been previously approved by the Railway Commissioners. Now therefore, in consideration of the Waterford immediately after such approval by the Railway Commissioners, demanding payment of such capital in full on or before the 1st day of July next, and immediately appropriating the same when received to the completion of the said section, it is agreed by and between the said two companies for themselves, their successors, and assigns, that the said clause 19 of the within written agreement is hereby rescinded, but that in all other respects the said agreement shall remain and be in full force and operation as if the said clause 19 had never been inserted therein."

REVENUE.—The balance carried to net revenue account for the half-years ended 1st May and 1st November, 1884, provided for the payment of interest at the rate of 4 per cent. per annum on the "A" debenture stock.

CAPITAL.—The expenditure on this account to 1st November, 1883, amounted to 349,269*l.*, the receipts to the same date having been as below, the stocks being properly described and given in order of priority for dividend, viz.:—

Perpetual debenture stock "A," 5 per cent.	£102,011
Perpetual debenture stock "B," 5 per cent.	131,860
Preference 10*l.* shares, 6 per cent.	40,880
Ordinary 10*l.* shares (200,000*l.* issued, but 134,350*l.* cancelled)	60,575
Sundries—Great Western Rebate	1,898
Total	£337,224

NOTE.—The debenture stocks and preference shares were issued under various acts, the dividends being accumulative and payable half-yearly in June and December; there are arrears of dividend due to these stocks to the extent of about 33½ per cent. on the "A" debenture stock, 64 per cent. on the "B" debenture stock, and 138 per cent. on the preference shares. The scheme under which these stocks were issued is dated November, 1872.

TRANSFER DEPARTMENT QUERIES AND REPLIES.

QUERIES.	REPLIES.
Transfer form—ordinary or special?	Ordinary.
Fee per deed?	2*s.* 6*d.*
Ditto if more sellers than one?	2*s.* 6*d.* each seller.
May several classes of stock be transferred on one deed?	Yes.
Are certificates required to accompany transfers?	Yes.
What amounts of stock are transferable?	Any.
Are parts of 1*l.* sterling allowed to be transferred?	No.
To what officer should transfer communications be sent?	Secretary.
In acceptances, renunciations, &c., of allotments of new stock, proxies, or other forms sent to trustees, or other joint holders, what signatures are required?	First name.

Meetings held usually in London in May and November.

No. of Directors—9; minimum, 6. *Qualification*, 500*l.*

DIRECTORS:

Chairman—JOHN WINTERBOTHAM BATTEN, Esq., 15, Airlie Gardens, Campden Hill, W.

Arthur Kavanagh, Esq., Borris House, Borris, County Carlow.

Edwin Henry Galsworthy, Esq., 18, Park Crescent, Portland Place, W.

The Right Hon. The Viscount de Vesci, Abbeyleix, Queen's County.

James Philip Hurst, Esq., 12, Furnival's Inn, E.C.

OFFICERS.—Sec., C. J. Hayter; Auditors, John Newton and Henry Spain, F.C.A.; Solicitors, S. F. and H. Noyes, 1, The Sanctuary, Westminster, S.W.

Offices—1, Drapers' Gardens, Throgmorton Avenue, E.C.

146.—KILSYTH AND BONNYBRIDGE.

Incorporated by act of 10th August, 1882, for making a railway from the Kelvin Valley to the Denny Branch of the Caledonian. Length, 8¼ miles. Period for completion, 5 years. Working and traffic arrangements with Caledonian and North British, and running powers over a portion of the Kelvin Valley. Capital, 130,000*l.* in 10*l.* shares, with power to divide into "preferred" and "deferred" half-shares; borrowing powers, 43,300*l.*

No. of Directors.—Maximum, 5; minimum, 3; quorum, 3 and 2. *Qualification*, 40 shares.

Quorum of general meetings, 10 shareholders, holding in the aggregate not less than 5,000*l.* of capital.

FIRST DIRECTORS:

Robert Balloch, Esq., Glasgow.

Henry Cadell, Esq.

John Lang, Esq., Ingram Street, Glasgow.

Joseph Wilson, Esq.

William Whyte, Esq., Kilsyth.

147.—KINGSBRIDGE AND SALCOMBE.

Incorporated by act of 24th July, 1882, for the construction of a railway from the Brent Station of the Great Western to Kingsbridge and Salcombe, in substitution for the Kingsbridge undertaking, authorised by act of 1864 (see MANUAL for 1880, page 160). Length, about 16 miles. Period for completion, 5 years. Working arrangements with the Great Western. Capital, 160,000*l.* in 10*l.* shares, with power to divide into "preferred" and "deferred" half-shares; borrowing powers, 53,000*l.*

No. of Directors.—Maximum, 7; minimum, 3; quorum, 5 and 2. *Qualification*, 25 shares.

DIRECTORS:

Right Hon. the Earl of Devon, Powderham Castle, Exeter.
W. R. Hilbert. Esq.
Alexander Hubbard, Esq., Derwentwater House, Acton, W.
Richard Basset, Esq., Highclere, near Newbury.
Edwin Fox, Esq.
Benjamin G. Lake, Esq.

Engineer, F. W. Fox, C.E., 8, Queen Anne's Gate, Westminster, S.W.

148.—KING'S LYNN DOCKS (WITH RAILWAYS).

Incorporated by act of 19th June, 1865, to construct a line from Purfleet on the Great Eastern; also to construct docks and other works at King's Lynn. Length, ½ mile. Capital, 66,000*l.* in shares and 22,000*l.* on loan. Powers to Corporation of King's Lynn, and to the Lynn and Sutton Bridge, and the Peterborough, Wisbech, and Sutton to subscribe.

By act of 24th June, 1869, the railway authorised by act of 1865 was abandoned, and a line from the Great Eastern, in the parish of Gaywood, substituted. Length, ¾ mile. New capital, 9,500*l.*; further borrowing powers, 3,160*l.* Arrangements with Great Eastern, Great Northern, and Midland.

By act of 1873, the company was authorised to erect new warehouses and to construct other works. New capital, 60,000*l.*; borrowing powers, 20,000*l.*

By act of 23rd July, 1877, the company obtained powers for the construction of a new dock and works connected therewith, and to raise new capital, viz.:—Shares or stock, 130,000*l.*; loans, 43,200*l.* Of the above newly authorised capital, 30,000*l.* in 6 per cent. preference stock was created and issued in November last.

REVENUE.—The net earnings for the half-years ended 31st December, 1883, and 30th June, 1884, sufficed for the payment of dividends at 5 and 6 per cent. per annum on the preference stocks; and 3 per cent. per annum on the ordinary stock.

CAPITAL.—The expenditure on this account to 30th June, 1884, amounted to 207,239*l.*, and the receipts to 226,825*l.*, as follow:—

Railway ordinary stock	£59,308
Ordinary stock, 1877	80,281
Railway preference stock at 6 per cent.	14,250
Do. do. (1877)	45,000
Warehouse, 6 per cent. preference capital	37,554
Loans at 5 per cent.	74,450
Warehouse loans	14,000

Meetings in February or March and August or September.

No. of Directors—8; minimum, 3; quorum, 3. *Qualification*, 200*l.*

DIRECTORS:

Chairman—Sir LEWIS W. JARVIS, Knt., Lynn.

W. Burkitt, Esq., Lynn.
J. D. Thew, Esq., Lynn.
Wm. Thompson, Esq., Lynn.
Lord Claud John Hamilton, M.P., 23, Lowndes Square, S.W.
Wm. Pattrick, Esq., Lynn.
W. L. Annes, Esq., Lynn.

OFFICERS.—Sec., T. P. Bond, 4, Queen Anne's Gate, Westminster, S.W.; Eng., J. S. Valentine, C.E., 11, Queen Anne's Gate, Westminster, S.W.; Auditors, Septimus Short & Co.; Bankers, Jarvis and Jarvis, Lynn.

149.—KINGSTON AND LONDON.

By the Transfer Act of 1882, this company was dissolved, and the line (Fulham to Kingston) is now under the management of a joint committee of six directors of the London and South Western and the Metropolitan District, viz.:—

JOINT COMMITTEE:

The Hon. R. H. Dutton, 16, Halkin Street West, Belgrave Square, and Timsbury Manor, Romsey.
A. F. Govett, Esq., Sandylands, Virginia Water, Staines, and 18, Albert Hall Mansions, S.W.
W. W. B. Beach, Esq., M.P., Oakley Hall, Basingstoke. Hants.
J. S. Forbes, Esq., 18, Chelsea Embankment, S.W.
G. W. Currie, Esq., 26, Pall Mall, S.W.
J. Murray, Esq., 25, Portman Street, W.

Joint Secretaries, F. J. Macaulay and A. Powell.

Offices—Waterloo Station.

150.—KINGTON AND EARDISLEY.

Incorporated by act of 30th June, 1862, to construct a line from the Leominster and Kington to the Hereford, Hay, and Brecon, at Eardisley. Length, 13 miles. Capital, 100,000*l*. in 10*l*. shares and 33,000*l*. on loans. Arrangements with the Leominster and Kington, the Hereford, Hay, and Brecon, and the Great Western.

By act of 26th May, 1865, the company was empowered to divide the capital into half-shares, "preferred" and "deferred."

For short heads of other Acts from 1868 to 1875, see the MANUAL for 1881, page 167.

The line was opened from Kington to Eardisley (7 miles) on the 3rd August, 1874. The extension line from Kington to New Radnor (6½ miles) was opened on the 25th September, 1875.

This company having worked at a loss, a scheme of arrangement with its creditors was filed on the 28th October, 1876, came into operation on the 5th July, 1877, and is now carried out. The following are the chief provisions of the scheme, viz.:—1st. The debentures of the company, together with the arrears and accumulations of interest thereon up to the 31st December, 1877, are converted into or capitalised as debenture stocks, distinguished as classes "A1," "A2," "A3," and "A4," carrying a first charge on the net annual income for interest at the rate of 4 per cent. per annum, with priorities *inter se* corresponding to the dates of the acts under which the debentures were originally issued. 2nd. Debenture stock, to be distinguished as class "B," is created, with which it is proposed to discharge the liabilities of the company to its common creditors. This debenture stock, for an amount not exceeding, with the classes "A1," "A2," "A3," and "A4," a total of 130,000*l*., will rank for interest at the rate of 4 per cent. per annum upon the net annual income, next after the "A1," "A2," "A3," and "A4" debenture stocks. 3rd. The preference shares of the company are converted into preference stocks, carrying interest at the rate of 4 per cent. per annum payable out of the surplus net annual income, after the annual interest on the debenture stocks shall have been provided for. 4th. The ordinary shares are converted into ordinary stock, carrying similar rights and privileges as those heretofore existing. 5th. Until the 31st day of December, 1877, the net income of the company was applied to the payment of the debts due to landowners, of the costs of the scheme, of the cost of completing the works to be constructed under the agreement with the Great Western, of the common debts under 10*l*., and of the expenses of administering the company. Under this scheme, new "B" debenture stock has been issued to the extent of 40,937*l*.

Worked temporarily by Great Western. On this subject, the company's report for the half-year ended 30th June. 1880, issued in the following October, stated as follows, viz.:—"Your directors have to report that the Great Western, acting on the powers given to them under article 42 of the working agreement of the 3rd August, 1875, gave formal notice in April last of their intention to determine such agreement as and from the 3rd August last. Prolonged negotiations with the Great Western have resulted in the heads of a new agreement for five years from that date. The terms of the new agreement, shortly stated, are as follow:—The Great Western to work the company's line at 50 per cent. of the gross receipts; to allow a rebate of 25 per cent. on their proportion of all through traffic to and from the Eardisley Line, where the traffic passes over the Eardisley Line, and a like rebate on the New Radnor Line traffic, whether it goes over the Eardisley Line or not; to credit a mileage proportion of the traffic to and from Kington and the New Radnor Line where the Eardisley Line would form the shortest route, whether such traffic is carried *via* Eardisley or not, but no rebate to be payable on the Great Western proportion of the earnings of this traffic; to pay the rent of Eardisley Station, and to make no charge for rent in respect of the Kington and Titley stations. The agreement of the 3rd August, 1875, being determined, the Great Western no longer guarantee the payment of a minimum rent-charge."

REVENUE.—For the half-year ended 30th June, 1884, the net income, after providing for the administration expenses, amounted to 986*l*., which, with the balance brought forward, provided for interest at the rate of 4 per cent. per annum on class "A 1" debenture stock, and at the rate of 3½ per cent. per annum on class "A 2" debenture stock.

CAPITAL.—The expenditure on this account to 30th June, 1884, amounted to 272,220*l*., being 482*l*. in excess of the receipts, which were as under:—

Stock	£134,171
Loans	129,827
Miscellaneous	7,740

Productive mileage, 13½ miles.

DIRECTORS:

Chairman—STEPHEN ROBINSON, Esq., Lynhales, Kington, Herefordshire.

Edward Howorth Greenly, Esq., Titley Court, Titley.

Richard Dansey Green Price, Esq., Belle Vue, Shrewsbury.

Charles Chambers, Esq., 3, Westminster Chambers, S.W.

Sir Richard Green Price, Bart., M.P., Norton Manor, Presteign.

OFFICERS.—Sec., George Sneath; Eng., George Wells Owen, M.Inst.C.E., 7, Westminster Chambers, Victoria Street, Westminster, S.W.; Auditors, Wm. Edwards, Jackson, and Browning, 18, King Street, Cheapside, E.C.; Solicitors, Fowler and Co., 3, Victoria Street, Westminster, S.W.; Bankers, Birmingham, Dudley, and District Banking Company Limited, Kington.

Offices—44, Gresham Street, E.C.

151.—LAMBOURN VALLEY.

Incorporated by act of 2nd August, 1883, for making a railway from Lambourn to Newbury. Length, about 12 miles. Period for completion, 5 years. Working arrangements with Great Western and Didcot, Newbury, and Southampton. Capital, 100,000*l*. in 10*l*. shares; loans, &c., 33,000*l*.

No. of Directors.—Maximum, 5; minimum, 3; quorum, 3 and 2. *Qualification*, 50 shares.

FIRST DIRECTORS:

George Branston Eyre, Esq.

Thomas Chaloner Smith, Esq.

Henry Hippisley, Esq.

(Two others to be nominated).

152.—LANARKSHIRE AND AYRSHIRE.

Incorporated by act of 1883. Capital, 375,000*l*. in 10*l*. shares; loans, 124,000*l*. Worked, maintained, and managed in perpetuity by the Caledonian. Of this capital 100,000*l*. has been privately applied for, and the balance of 275,000*l*. was offered to the public in shares of 10*l*. each, payable as follows:—10*s*. per share on application, 10*s*. per share on allotment, and the balance by calls of not more than 1*l*. each, at not less intervals than two months. Subscribers have the option (to a limited extent) of paying in full at any of the above periods; interest being allowed at 5 per cent. on all payments in advance of calls.

This company, by act of parliament passed in 1883, was authorised, under the name of the "Barrmill and Kilwinning Railway Company," to make a line of railway, now in a forward state of construction, from Barrmill to the town of Kilwinning, and has by the act of 1884 been authorised to change its name to the "Lanarkshire and Ayrshire Railway Company," and empowered to construct the following extension lines, the whole to be worked and maintained by the Caledonian:—To the towns of Stevenston, Saltcoats, and Ardrossan, and Ardrossan Harbour; to the Royal Burgh of Irvine; to Glengarnock, Glengarnock Ironworks, and the town of Kilbirnie.

DIRECTORS:

Chairman—The Hon. G. R. VERNON, Auchans House, Kilmarnock.

Deputy-Chairman—J. C. CUNINGHAME, Esq., of Craigends, Renfrewshire.

The Right Hon. the Earl of Eglinton and Winton.

The Right Hon. the Earl of Glasgow.

A. W. R. Cuninghame, Esq., of Auchenharvie, Ayrshire.

R. W. Knox, Esq., of Moorpark, Kilbirnie, Ayrshire.

James Neilson, Esq., of Mossend, Glasgow.

Archibald Russell, Esq., Glasgow.

John Watson, Esq., of Earnock, Glasgow.

John Cuninghame, Esq., Glasgow.

OFFICERS.—Sec., G. Y. Strang-Watkins, Glasgow; Eng., John Strain, M.Inst.C.E., Glasgow; Solicitors, Keydens, Strang, and Girvan, Glasgow; Bankers, The Union Bank of Scotland Limited, Glasgow, Edinburgh, London, and Branches.

Offices—186, West George Street, Glasgow.

153.—LANCASHIRE AND YORKSHIRE.

This company is an amalgamation of the MANCHESTER AND LEEDS, the MANCHESTER, BOLTON, AND BURY, the LIVERPOOL AND BURY, the HUDDERSFIELD AND SHEFFIELD, the WAKEFIELD, PONTEFRACT, AND GOOLE, the WEST RIDING UNION, the EAST LANCASHIRE, and other lines. The present title was conferred by act of 1847. Productive, 493 miles 3 chains.

By East Lancashire and Lancashire and Yorkshire Act of 3rd July, 1854, the companies became joint owners of the lines between Clifton and Manchester and Burscough and Southport, and were authorised to erect an independent station at Southport. Capital under this act, 200,000*l.* in shares and 66,000*l.* in loans.

AMALGAMATION.—By act of 13th August, 1859, the East Lancashire was amalgamated with the Lancashire and Yorkshire, the ordinary stocks of both companies ranking, in all respects, on equal terms, that of the East Lancashire being simply exchange for a like amount of Lancashire and Yorkshire stock, the preference stocks being exchanged in like manner, but preserving their existing rights as to priorities, &c., and from that date ceased to exist as an independent company. By the same act the board of directors may be reduced to 12; the power to create perpetual annuities is repealed; power given to convert mortgage debt into debenture stock; and the through traffic from Penistone and Huddersfield facilitated and regulated; provision is also made for the enlargement of stations; the North Union and Preston and Wyre engagements continued: and the tolls on the united railways revised. These tolls, however, may again be revised and reduced, when the dividend on the paid-up capital stock, upon the average of three years, last preceding, shall equal or exceed 8 per cent. per annum. Power was also given to convert the borrowed capital into debenture stock at a fixed dividend, not exceeding 4 per cent.

FURTHER PARLIAMENTARY POWERS:—

For short heads of other Acts from 1859 to 1879, see the MANUAL for 1881, pages 169 to 171.

1881—18TH JULY.—Certain improvements in the North Union and Preston and Wyre undertakings, and sundry agreements appertaining thereto. Additional capital, 1,500,000*l.*; borrowing powers, 500,000*l.*

1883—2ND AUGUST.—New railway from Pendleton to Hindley, to shorten the distance from Manchester to Southport. Length, about 12¾ miles. About 1¼ mile of short lines at Pendleton, Sandhills, and Bradford, Yorkshire. Widening line at Wakefield. Sundry diversions at Seaforth. Period for completion of railways, five years. Acquirement of lands at sundry places and for other purposes. New capital, 1,860,000*l.*; loans, &c., 620,000*l.*

1884–14TH JULY.—Three short lines at Westhoughton, Bolton, and Wakefield; acquirement of lands in various towns, and other purposes. New capital, 255,000*l.*; loans, 85,000*l.*

1884—14TH JULY (PRESTON AND WYRE).—Alterations of roads and other improvements; acquirement of lands, &c. New capital, 162,000*l.*; loans, 54,000*l.*

OTHER AMALGAMATIONS, LEASES, AGREEMENTS, &c.:—

BLACKBURN.—Under the provisions of the act authorising a purchase of this line (1858), the joint owners are authorised to redeem the preference and ordinary stock of the Blackburn upon terms which make it the interest of the two companies that such redemption should take place.

FLEETWOOD, PRESTON, AND WEST RIDING.—By act of 17th June, 1867, the London and North Western and the Lancashire and Yorkshire were jointly authorised to lease the Fleetwood, Preston, and West Riding.—See London and North Western.

HALIFAX AND OVENDEN.—Incorporated by act of 30th June, 1864, to construct a line from the Lancashire and Yorkshire, at Halifax, to Ovenden. Length, 2¾ miles. Capital, 90,000*l.* in 10*l.* shares and 30,000*l.* on loan. Arrangements with Great

Northern and Lancashire and Yorkshire. By act of 1st August, 1870, the undertaking is vested in the Lancashire and Yorkshire and the Great Northern, the two companies having the option to pay off the shareholders at par at any time previous to 1st January, 1873, either in cash or debenture stock, at 4 per cent.

HULL DOCKS.—The Lancashire and Yorkshire has contributed 100,000*l*. to this undertaking, and appoints one member to the board.

LEEDS AND LIVERPOOL CANAL.—The Lancashire and Yorkshire was at one time interested in a lease of this company, which has expired.—For further information, see Leeds and Liverpool Canal.

LIVERPOOL, CROSBY, AND SOUTHPORT.—Incorporated by act of 2nd July, 1847, for a line joining the Bury Line, at 1¾ mile from Tithebarn Street, Liverpool, over the Lancashire and Yorkshire and East Lancashire to Crosby and Southport, 18½ miles, of which 1¾ mile to the Kirkdale junction belongs to the Lancashire and Yorkshire. At a special meeting of the Liverpool, Crosby, and Southport, on June 14th, 1855, an agreement was entered into on these terms:—"That the Lancashire and Yorkshire become purchasers of the Liverpool, Crosby, and Southport; shall assume its entire engagements and liabilities; and pay to the proprietors upon the share capital a dividend of 2½ per cent. for the year 1855, 3¼ per cent. for the years 1856 and 1857 pespectively, and from and after 31st December, 1857, the same dividend as that payable to holders of Lancashire and Yorkshire ordinary stock.

NORTH UNION.—This company is vested in the Lancashire and Yorkshire and London and North Western, at an annual perpetual rent of 66,066*l*. 18*s*. from 1st January, 1864, and the interest of mortgage debt. The proportion borne by the Lancashire and Yorkshire is 34-94ths of the profit or loss.

PRESTON AND WYRE.—This company, incorporated 1835, capital, 130,000*l*. and loans 40,000*l*.; further, 307,000*l*. and 126,000*l*.; total, 603,000*l*.; leased to Lancashire and Yorkshire under acts of 1846. The London and North Western participate in this lease; the larger proportion, viz., two-thirds, is borne by the Lancashire and Yorkshire. The terms of this lease are a rent of 7*l*. 1*s*. 6*d*. per cent., 35*s*. 4½*d*. per share, till the end of 1854, when it advanced to 7*l*. 17*s*. 2*d*. per cent., 39*s*. 3½*d*. in perpetuity per share, on a total capital of 668,000*l*. By act of 26th May, 1865, the Lancashire and Yorkshire was authorised to raise new capital to the extent of 16,000*l*. in shares and 4,000*l*. on loan, and the London and North Western 8,000*l*. in shares and 2,000*l*. on loan, for widening and otherwise improving the Preston and Wyre. By act of 29th June, 1871, the Blackpool and Lytham was amalgamated with the Preston and Wyre, further powers in connection therewith being conferred on the London and North Western and the Lancashire and Yorkshire. The sum of 33,600*l*. was paid by them on 1st July, 1871, to the ordinary shareholders in the Lytham, the whole of the other obligations being undertaken by the two companies, the London and North Western being authorised to apply its existing funds for the purposes of the act, while the Lancashire and Yorkshire were to raise 60,000*l*. in shares, with 12,000*l*. on loan or by debenture stock.

ROCHDALE CANAL.—For particulars concerning this canal, at one time leased by this company jointly with the North Eastern, London and North Western, and Manchester, Sheffield, and Lincolnshire, the term of lease (21 years) expiring in 1876, see Rochdale Canal.

NORTH LANCASHIRE LOOP LINE.—This new line, 9 miles 4 chains in length, was opened for traffic from Rose Grove to Padiham on the 1st September, 1876, and from Padiham to Blackburn on the 15th October, 1877.

NEW LINES, &c.—The Hoddlesden Branch (2 miles) was opened on the 1st October, 1876; the Docks at Fleetwood on October 8th, 1877; the Astley Bridge Branch (2 miles) on October 15th, 1877; the Kearsley Branch (2 miles) on 24th March, 1878; the Manchester Loop Line (2¼ miles) on 1st August, 1878; the Ripponden Branch (3 miles) on 5th August, 1878; the Chatburn to Gisburn Line (5¾ miles) on 2nd June, 1879; the loop line at Bradley Fold (1¼ mile) on 13th July, 1879; the Clayton West Branch (3¾ miles) on 1st September, 1879 The line from Manchester, through Cheetham Hill and Prestwich, to Whitefield (5 miles) was opened on 1st September, 1879, and from Whitefield to Radcliffe (2½ miles) on 1st December, 1879. The Hollinwood Branch (4 miles) was opened on the 17th May, 1880, and the line from Gisburn to Hellifield (6¾ miles) on the 1st June, 1880. The Pickle Bridge and Brighouse Branch (3 miles and 72 chains) and extension of Ripponden Branch to Rishworth (¾ mile) were opened on the 1st March, 1881, and the

Extension of the Shawforth Line to Bacup was opened on 1st December, 1881. The Bury and Tottington Line (3 miles 30 chains), worked by the Lancashire and Yorkshire, was opened in November, 1882.

ACCOUNTS:—

HALF-YEAR ENDED 30TH JUNE, 1884.

CAPITAL.—*Authorised:* Shares and stock, 32,368,526*l.*; loans, 10,383,633*l.*; total 42,752,159*l.* *Created or sanctioned:* Shares and stock, 32,368,526*l.*; loans, 9,423,870*l.*; total, 41,792,396*l.*; balance, 959,763*l.*

Receipts.		*Expenditure.*	
Share capital, viz.:—		Lines open for traffic	£31,367,727
Ordinary stock	£14,192,995	Working stock	4,309,006
Guaranteed and preference stocks	13,524,483	Lines in course of construction	2,396,281
Total stock and share capital	£27,717,478	Subscriptions to other railways	310,296
Loan capital, viz.:—		Fleetwood & Belfast Steamers	43,733
Debentures £1,053,796		Balance	66,994
Debenture stock ... 8,318,309 =	9,372,105		
Capital entitled to interest and dividend	£37,089,583		
Amount received on forfeited shares and in virtue of arrangement with "fifths," calls in advance, and premium on shares not entitled to dividend	1,259,540		
Telegraph award (balance)	144,914		
	£38,494,037		£38,494,037

PRIORITIES, DESCRIPTIONS, DIVIDENDS, and other conditions of issue of the various Securities of the company, existing on 30th September, 1881 (see notes).

No.	Year of Act.	FULL DESCRIPTION (to be observed in Transfer Deeds and all other Legal Documents).	Rate ℔ cent ℔ annum.
1	Various	4 per cent. debenture stock	4
2	Various	6 per cent. preference stock	6
3	Various	Minimum 6 per cent. preference stock	6
4	Various	Minimum 4½ per cent. preference stock	4½
5	Various	Guaranteed 4 per cent. preference stock	4
6	Various	Preference 4 per cent.	4
7	Various	Convertible stock, 1880, 4 per cent. to January 1st, 1888	4
8	Various	4 per cent. 15*l.* shares, 1882	4
9	Various	4 per cent. 15*l.* shares, 1884	...
10	1877-9	Ordinary stock	4

NOTES.—Convertible Stock.—No. 7 is convertible on the date given above into ordinary stock at par.

Minimum Stocks.—Nos. 3 and 4 participate *pro rata* with the ordinary stock in any dividends earned over 6 and 4½ per cent. per annum respectively.

Consolidations.-Nos 5 and 6 were issued for the consolidation of other stocks under act of 1877, and scheme dated 18th January, 1879.

Dividends Non-Contingent or Contingent.—Nos. 1 to 5 are non-contingent and accumulative, the remainder are contingent upon the profits of each separate year.

Dividends Payable.—All half-yearly and subject to income tax. No. 1, 1st January and 1st July; No. 2, 31st January and 31st July; remainder usually on the day after the half-yearly meetings, in February and August.

VOTING POWERS.—All preference and other stocks, except debenture stocks, carry voting powers.

TRANSFER DEPARTMENT QUERIES AND REPLIES.

Queries.	Replies.
Transfer form—ordinary or special?	Ordinary.
Fee per deed?	5s.
Ditto if more sellers than one? ...	5s.
May several classes of stock be transferred on one deed?	Yes, ordinary and preferences, but not debenture, on same deed.
Are certificates required to accompany transfers?	Yes.
What amounts of stock are transferable, and are parts of 1l. sterling allowed to be transferred?	No fraction of 1l. except as they already exist in the company's books.
To what officer should transfer communications be sent?	Secretary.
In acceptances, renunciations, &c., of allotments of new stock, proxies, or other forms sent to trustees, what signatures are required?	Signature of first proprietor for acceptances and proxies, and of all in other cases.

Consolidation of Stocks.—On the 26th February, 1879, the proprietary sanctioned a scheme for the consolidation of various guaranteed and preference stocks into stocks to be called "Consolidated Guaranteed 4 per cent. Stock," and "Consolidated Preference 4 per cent. Stock" respectively. The scheme will be found in the *Appendix* to the Manual for 1880.

The estimate of further expenditure on capital account for the half-year ended 31st December, 1884, and for subsequent half-years, was as under:—

	31st Dec., 1884	Subsequently.
Lines open for traffic	£567,500	£764,991
Lines in course of construction	282,500	1,748,557
Total...	£850,000	£2,513,548

The capital powers and other assets to meet this further outlay of 3,363,548l. were particularised as follow:—

Balance of capital authorised but not yet sanctioned..............................	£959,763
Capital sanctioned but not received..	2,947,480
Balance of available borrowing powers at June 30th, 1884	51,765
Balance to credit of capital	66,994
	£4,026,002
Less—Moneys in advance	254,853
Total	£3,771,149

Revenue.—The following is a tabular view of the working of this undertaking for the past three half-years. viz.:—

Receipts.	1883. June 30.	1883. Dec. 31.	1884. June 30.
Passengers, parcels, and mails	£682,759	£759,914	£702,254
Merchandise, live stock, and minerals (less cartage)	1,107,694	1,166,753	1,110,384
Fleetwood and Belfast steamers	4,896	1,870	3,375
Rents, Hull docks, mileage, and demurrage, &c. ...	17,040	13,081	14,732
	£1,812,389	£1,941,618	£1,830,745

Expenses.	1883. June 30.	1883. Dec. 31.	1884. June 30.
Maintenance of way, works, and stations	£166,715	£186,729	£159,303
Locomotive power	249,933	257,121	248,766
Carriage and wagon repairs	95,465	100,216	105,990
Traffic expenses	381,638	386,172	381,588
General charges	39,530	40,921	39,093
Law and Parliamentary charges	3,577	7,983	3,195
Compensation	13,961	9,570	9,472
Rates, taxes, and Government duty......................	59,244	73,838	51,555
Working expenses (carried forward)	£1,010,063	£1,062,550	£998,962

Expenses.	1883. June 30.	1883. Dec. 31.	1884. June 30.
Brought forward	£1,010,163	£1,062,550	£998,962
Preference charges, viz.:			
Interest on debenture stock and loan capital, calls in advance, bankers' and general interest (net)	193,643	194,912	194,498
Rents of leased lines	35,755	35,392	36,298
Preference dividends	289,679	303,010	314,245
	£1,529,140	£1,595,864	£1,544,003
Net balances each half-year	£283,249	£345,754	£286,742
Balances brought from previous half-years	11,715	11,104	19,774
Balances available for dividend on ordinary stock	£294,964	£356,858	£306,516
Dividends declared at 4, 4¾, and 4 per cent. per annum respectively	283,860	337,084	283,860
Surplus carried forward	£11,104	£19,774	£22,656

Summary showing the results of the last half-year's working of this line, as compared with that of the corresponding period of 1883:—

Net balance 30th June, 1884......	£286,742	Thus:—	
" 30th June, 1883......	283,249	Gross traffic—increase £18,356	
		Working charges—dec. £11,101 =	£29,457
		Less:—	
		Pref. charges—increase.........	25,964
Gain in 1884	£3,493	Net gain in 1884	£3,493

Mileage—June 30th, 1884.—Lines owned, 454¼; partly owned, 42=496¼. Foreign lines worked over, 29¾. Total, 526.

New Capital.—At an extraordinary meeting, held on the 8th January, 1879, the proprietary sanctioned the issue of 1,200,000*l*., in 8*l*. shares, to be called "8*l*. shares, 1879," entitled to a 4 per cent. dividend until 1st July, 1884, and to become ordinary stock from that date. In October, 1880, 134,800 new 10*l*. shares were issued, to be called "10*l*. shares, 1880," entitled to a dividend at 4 per cent. per annum to 1st January, 1888, and to become ordinary stock from that date. These shares were allotted to the proprietary at the rate of one new share for every 110*l*. of stock, the first call at 2*l*. per share being made payable on the 1st January, 1881; remaining calls at discretion of directors. In August, 1882, there were issued 142,000 15*l*. shares=2,130,000*l*., ranking for dividend in priority to the ordinary stock, out of the profits of each separate year, at 4 per cent. per annum in perpetuity. A call of 3*l*. per share was made payable on the 30th September, 1882; 3*l*., 2nd July, 1883; 3*l*., 1st October, 1883; 3*l*., 1st February, 1884; and 3*l*., 1st July, 1884.

In July, 1884, there were issued 168,000 15*l*. shares=2,520,000*l*., ranking for dividend in priority to the ordinary stock out of the profits of each separate year at 4 per cent. per annum in perpetuity. A call of 3*l*. per share was made payable on the 15th August, 1884, the balance to be called up at the discretion of the directors.

The accounts are made up to 30th June and 31st December in every year, and the meetings held in Manchester in February and August.

Scale of Voting.—One vote for every 100*l*. stock, nominal amount.

Certificates must accompany transfer deed. Registration fee, 5*s*. each deed or bond. Parts of 1*l*. may not be transferred. Several classes of shares or stock may go on one deed. Transfer books close usually 21 days before meetings.

No. of Directors.—Maximum, 16; minimum, 12. *Qualification*, 2,500*l*. stock, nominal value. Allowance, 6,500*l*. Present board, 16.

DIRECTORS:

Chairman—JOHN PEARSON, Esq., Golborne Park, Newton-le-Willows.

Deputy-Chairman—GEORGE JOHN ARMYTAGE, Esq., Clifton Woodhead, Brighouse.

Thomas Barnes, Esq., Farnworth, near Bolton.

Louis John Crossley, Esq., Halifax.

Samuel Fielden, Esq., Todmorden.

Edward Green, Esq., Heath Old Hall, Wakefield.

Theodore Julius Hare, Esq., Crook Hall, Chorley.

William Hinmers, Esq., Cleveland House, Lancaster Road, Eccles, near Manchester

William Henry Hornby, Esq., Blackburn.

Rt. Hon. Lord Houghton, Fryston Hall, Ferrybridge.

S. M. Milne, Esq., Calverley House, near Leeds.

James Pilkington, Esq., Blackburn.

Joshua Radcliffe, Esq., Rochdale.

Henry Yates Thompson, Esq., Thingwall, Liverpool, and 26A, Bryanston Square, W.

William Tunstill, Esq., Reedyford, Nelson, near Burnley.

William Rome, Esq., Liverpool.

OFFICERS.—Sec., J. H. Stafford; Asst. Sec., D. Norman; Chief Traffic Man., William Thorley; Assistant Traffic Man., T. Collin; Eng., William Hunt; Asst. Eng., J. G. Crosbie Dawson; Accountant, William Sloane; Audit Accountant, C. W. Bayley; Loco. Supt., William Barton Wright, M.Inst.C.E., M.I.M.E.; Passenger Supt., John Maddock, Victoria Station; Goods Man., Benjamin Shaw; Solicitor, Christopher Moorhouse, Victoria Buildings, Manchester; Bankers, Cunliffes, Brooks, and Co., Manchester.

Head Offices—Hunt's Bank, Manchester.

154.—LATIMER ROAD AND ACTON.

Incorporated by act of 18th August, 1882, for a line commencing by a junction with the Hammersmith and City (belonging to the Great Western and Metropolitan), near the Latimer Road Station on that railway, and terminating at Acton, adjoining the Acton Station of the Great Western. Length, 2 miles 1 furlong 5·90 chains. Capital, 120,000*l.* in 10*l.* shares, and 40,000*l.* on loan. Arrangements with Great Western and Metropolitan.

No. of Directors—5; quorum, 3. *Qualification*, 500*l.*

DIRECTORS:

Gen. Sir Michael K. Kennedy, R.E., K.C.S.I., 102, Gloucester Terrace, Hyde Park, W.

Sir Charles Craufurd, Bart.

George Wright, Esq.

Richard Lawrence Cosh, Esq.

William George Wilde, Esq.

OFFICERS.—Sec., William Mann, 5, The Sanctuary, Westminster, S.W.; Eng., Edward Wilson, C.E., 9, Victoria Chambers, Westminster, S.W.; Solicitors, Burchell and Co., 5, The Sanctuary, Westminster, S.W.

155.—LEOMINSTER AND BROMYARD.

Incorporated by act of 30th July, 1874, for making a line from the Shrewsbury and Hereford, at Leominster, to join the Worcester, Bromyard, and Leominster, at Bromyard. Length, 12 miles. Capital, 210,000*l.* in 21,000 shares of 10*l.* each, with power to borrow 70,000*l.* on mortgage.

By act of 8th August, 1878, the time for the completion of this railway was extended until 30th July, 1882, and a new railway at Leominster, 5 furlongs and 8 chains in length, was authorised, to be completed in five years. Powers were also obtained for the division of the company's ordinary shares into "preferred" and "deferred" half-shares; to borrow 20,000*l.* when the line is opened to Steen's Bridge, and for other purposes.

By act of 7th August, 1884, the company was authorised to extend their authorised line from Steens Bridge to Bromyard.

The line has been constructed as far as Steen's Bridge, and was inspected and opened at the beginning of 1884. An agreement for working this section has been entered into with the Great Western.

No. of Directors—6; quorum, 3. *Qualification*, 250*l.*

DIRECTORS:

Chairman—Colonel PRESCOTT-DECIE, Bockelton Court, near Tenbury.

James Rankin, Esq., M.P., Bryngwyn, near Hereford.

Thomas Bristow Stallard, Esq., Leominster.

Major Heygate, Buckland, near Leominster.

Major Howarth Ashton, Hatfield Court, near Leominster.

T. Davies Burlton, Esq., North Eaton, Leominster.

OFFICERS.—Engs., William Clarke, M.Inst.C.E., and George Wells Owen, M.Inst.C.E.; Auditor, Edwin Alfred Williams; Solicitors, Fowler and Co., 3, Victoria Street, Westminster, S.W., and E. Lloyd, Leominster.

Offices—Leominster.

156.—LEOMINSTER AND KINGTON.

Incorporated in 1854 to construct a line from the Shrewsbury and Hereford, at Leominster, to Kington, in Herefordshire. Length, 13¾ miles; single line. Capital, 80,000*l.* in 10*l.* shares and 26,000*l.* on loan. By act of 19th April, 1859, the company was authorised to attach a preference of 4½ per cent. to all unissued shares, amounting to 20,990*l.*

By act of 31st July, 1871, the company was authorised to make a branch from Titley to Presteign. Length, 5¼ miles. New capital, 40,000*l.* in 10*l.* shares and 13,000*l.* on loan. This branch was opened on the 10th September, 1875.

By the Great Western Act of 23rd July, 1877, a further agreement with that company was confirmed by which the Leominster Company obtained authority to further extend their railway at Presteign. The arrangement mentioned above to apply to the new extension provided the capital raised for that purpose does not exceed 10,750*l*.

By the Great Western Act, 1880, power was given to that company to adopt the whole of the debenture debt of this company, and power was given to this company to create 2,000*l*. additional capital, which it is estimated will be sufficient to cover the whole expenditure on account of Presteign Branch; this 2,000*l*. has been raised by the issue of 200 shares of 10*l*. each which have been fully paid up.

LEASE.—By act of 13th July, 1863, the company was authorised to enter into working arrangements with the West Midland, and to devise a lease to that company. By provisions of a lease to the Great Western, in accordance with this act, the shareholders receive a minimum of 4 per cent., with a future increase in proportion to increase of traffic. The directors have stipulated for the purchase of the line at 5 per cent. whenever the amount of traffic shall warrant the purchase. The dividends on the ordinary shares have not yet exceeded the 4 per cent. The dividends at 4 per cent. per annum continue to be paid regularly on the 1st March and 1st September each half-year.

In operation, 18¾ miles.

CAPITAL.—The expenditure on this account to 30th June, 1884, amounted to 162,333*l*., and the receipts to 161,000*l*., showing a debit balance of 1,333*l*., as detailed below:—

Ordinary shares	£59,010
4½ per cent. preference shares (20,990*l*. created)	20,990
Presteign Branch shares (42,000*l*. created)	42,000
Loans at 3½ per cent.	1,100
Loans at 4 per cent.	32,900
Loans at 4½ per cent.	5,000
Balance	1,333 = £162,333

TRANSFER DEPARTMENT QUERIES AND REPLIES.

QUERIES.	REPLIES.
Transfer form—ordinary or special?	Ordinary.
Fee per deed?	2*s*. 6*d*.
Ditto if more sellers than one?	2*s*. 6*d*.
May several classes of stock be transferred on one deed?	Yes.
Are certificates required to accompany transfers?	Yes.
What amounts of stock are transferable, and are parts of 1*l*. sterling allowed to be transferred?	The capital is all in 10*l*. shares, and no part of a share is transferable.
To what officer should transfer communications be sent?	Secretary.
In acceptances, renunciations, &c., of allotments of new stock, proxies, or other forms sent to trustees and other joint holders, what signatures are required?	The first on the list.

The accounts are made up to 31st December and 30th June, and the meetings held at Leominster in February or March and August or September. Dividends are made payable half-yearly, 1st March and 1st September, the transfer books closing about 10 days previously.

DIRECTORS:

Chairman—STEPHEN ROBINSON, Esq., Lynhales, near Kington.

Deputy-Chairman—THOMAS BRISTOW STALLARD, Esq., Leominster.

John Percy Severn, Esq., The Hall, Penybont.

Josiah Newman, Esq., Buckfield, Leominster.

Richard William Banks, Esq., Ridgebourne, Kington.

Richard Green, Esq., The Whittern, near Kington.

OFFICERS.—Sec. and Acct., J. A. Daggs; Eng., W. G. Owen, M.Inst.C.E.; Auditors, V. W. Holmes and E. A. Williams; Solicitors, Baxters and Co., 6, Victoria Street, Westminster, S.W.

Offices—Leominster.

157.—LETTERKENNY.

Incorporated by act of 3rd July, 1860, for making a railway from Cuttymanhill in the town of Letterkenny. Length, 16 miles. Capital, 150,000*l.* in 10*l.* shares; loans, 123,000*l.*

For short heads of further powers from 1863 to 1878, see the MANUAL for 1881, page 175.

By act of 29th June, 1880, the company was authorised to change the gauge of their line; an extension of time was also obtained for the completion of works to 30th June, 1883; and authority was granted to enter into working agreements with the Londonderry and Lough Swilly.

Line opened 30th June, 1883 (worked by Londonderry and Lough Swilly).

No of Directors—7; quorum, 3. *Qualification*, 300*l.*

DIRECTORS:

Chairman—JAMES T. MACKY, Esq., Belmont, Londonderry.

Deputy-Chairman—JOSEPH COOKE, Esq., Boomhall, Londonderry.

Robert Hamilton, Esq., Foyle Street, Londonderry.
Major Thos. Patterson, Gortlea, Letterkenny.
Alexander Black, Esq., Londonderry.
Bartholomew M'Corkell, Esq., Richmond, Londonderry, and Glenburnie, Moville.
John M'Farland, Esq, Belfast and Londonderry.

OFFICERS.—Sec., E. A. Hamilton; Consulting Eng., Robert Collins, Belfast; Auditors, Francis J. Hopkirk, Belfast, and Archibald M'Corkell, Londonderry.

Offices—Londonderry.

158.—LIMAVADY AND DUNGIVEN.

Incorporated by act of 4th July, 1878 (41 and 42 Vic., cap. 139), for making a railway, commencing by a junction with the Belfast, at Limavady, to Dungiven. Length, 10 miles 2 furlongs and ½ chain. Running powers over the Belfast and Northern Counties. Period for completion, five years. The Belfast Company may raise money and subscribe 18,000*l.* towards the undertaking, and may appoint two directors. The two companies to have power to enter into working agreements, &c. Capital, 75,000*l.* in 10*l.* shares. Borrowing powers, 25,000*l.*

By this company's act of 19th May, 1882, the Belfast and Northern Counties subscribe 35,000*l.* to the undertaking, and hold corresponding guaranteed or preference shares of the company in respect thereof; further powers are also given confirming an agreement with the Skinners Company to attach a preference to certain shares, and to take additional lands.

By the Belfast and Northern Counties Act, 16th July, 1883, that company was empowered to subscribe a further sum of 5,000*l.* to this undertaking.

Line opened for traffic 4th July, 1883.

No. of Directors.—Maximum, 5; minimum, 3. The Belfast Company may appoint two directors out of the five, who need not be shareholders in the undertaking. Quorum of directors—Maximum, 5; minimum, 3. Quorum of general meetings, seven proprietors holding in the aggregate not less than one-thirtieth of the nominal capital of the company. *Qualification* (other than those appointed by the Belfast and Northern Counties), not less than 30 ordinary shares.

DIRECTORS:

Chairman—2 ARCHIBALD FREDERICK PAULL, Esq., 4, Cullum Street, E.C., and The Paragon, Bath.

Deputy-Chairman—* SAMUEL MAXWELL ALEXANDER, Esq., D.L., Roe Park, Limavady.

* Edmond M'Neill, Esq., J.P., Craigdunn, Craigs, County Antrim.
3 Henry Tyler, Esq., J.P., Limavady.
1 Samuel Martin Macrory, Esq., J.P., Ardmore, Limavady.
1, Retire in 1884; 2, in 1885; 3, in 1886.

* Represent the Belfast and Northern Counties.

OFFICERS.—Sec., David Hamilton, Limavady; Eng., John Lanyon, C.E., Belfast; Auditor, F. J. Hopkirk, Belfast; Solicitor, B. H. Lane, Limavady and Dublin.

159.—LIMERICK AND KERRY.

Incorporated by act of 5th August, 1873, to construct a line between the present station at Newcastle West, in the county of Limerick, and the station of the Great Southern and Western at Tralee, in the county of Kerry. Length, 42¼ miles. Capital, 5 per cent. guaranteed shares, guaranteed for 23 years by the counties of Limerick and Kerry, 150,000*l.*; ordinary shares, 110,000*l.*=260,000*l.*; 130,000*l.* on loan. The Waterford and Limerick has subscribed 25,000*l.*, and the Great Western of England 10,000*l.*, towards the undertaking.

By act of 18th July, 1881, powers were obtained to raise 30,000*l.* as preferable mortgage, 200,000*l.* in new shares or stock, and 100,000*l.* on ordinary loans or debenture stock, and to vest in this company that of the Rathkeale and Newcastle Junction (which see). Agreements with the Waterford and Limerick were by this act confirmed.

By act of 3rd July, 1884, the company was authorised to convert guaranteed shares and debentures into debenture stock.

The line is to be worked by the Waterford and Limerick, the principal provisions being that the Waterford shall receive for working 60 per cent. of the receipts until they exceed 17*l.* per mile per week, when the Waterford would retain 59 per cent., and so on until the traffic exceeds 21*l.* per mile per week, when the Waterford will retain 55 per cent. The Waterford to subscribe 25,000*l.* to the undertaking of the company; the agreement is contingent on the new agreement with the Rathkeale being entered into by the Waterford; the railway is to be constructed by the Limerick and Kerry in accordance with certain plans appended to the agreement, and any further capital expenditure is to be made by the Waterford; and the railway is to be worked in perpetuity by a three-train service and to be managed by a joint committee composed of equal numbers of the directors of each company.

The whole of the capital (280,000*l.*) required for the construction of the line has been subscribed for, and the line has been opened. So far the receipts, considering the political troubles of the country, have been satisfactory, and the line is reported in good working order.

The acts direct that 150,000*l.* guaranteed share capital shall be issued under the following titles:—

£38,000	Limerick and Kerry Guaranteed (Limerick) Shares	To which the guarantee of the county of Limerick specially attaches.
£112,000	Limerick and Kerry Guaranteed (Kerry) Shares ...	To which the guarantee of the county of Kerry specially attaches.
Total...£150,000		

The ordinary share capital amounts to 110,000*l.*

The acts expressly provide that the net receipts of the line during such period of 23 years shall be applied to the payment of the dividend on the 150,000*l.* guaranteed shares "in priority to any other purpose whatsoever," net receipts being defined by the acts to be "receipts arising from the railway after paying the working expenses thereof (the amount of which is determinable by arbitrators), and before the payment of any principal dividends or interest on loans, mortgages, debentures, debenture stock, or other capital or debts of the company." It is also provided that the holders of the above guaranteed shares shall be entitled to the benefit of the guarantees as given by the acts "to the exclusion of all other persons whatsoever, whether shareholders in or creditors of the company."

The holders of the guaranteed shares will, therefore, be entitled for such 23 years to an absolute first charge, both on the net receipts of the company, and also on the contributions from the counties of Limerick and Kerry.

No. of Directors.—Maximum, 9; minimum, 5; quorum, 5 and 3. *Qualification*, 200*l.*

DIRECTORS:

Chairman—The Right Hon. the Earl of DEVON, Powderham Castle, Exeter.

George Hewson, Esq., J.P., Ennismore, Listowel, County Kerry.

Charles Edward Napier Curling, Esq., J.P., The Castle, Newcastle West, Co. Limerick.

Joseph William Hume Williams, Esq., 1, Essex Court, Temple, E.C.

Falkiner S. Collis Sandes, Esq., J.P., Oriental Club, London, and Sallowglen, Tarbert, County Kerry.

*Edmond Ronayne Mahony, Esq., 3, Camden Quay, Cork.

*James Spaight, J.P., 77, George Street, Limerick.

†Edward William O'Brien, Esq., D.L., Cahirmagee, Ardagh, Co. Limerick.

†George Sandes, Esq., J.P., Listowel.

* Represent the Waterford and Limerick.

† Represent the Counties of Limerick and Kerry.

OFFICERS.—Sec., Chas. Henry Bingham; Con. Eng., John Fowler, M.Inst.C.E., 2, Queen's Square Place, Westminster, S.W.; Auditors, J. Henry Schröder and Henry Holmes; Solicitors, Lake, Beaumont, and Lake, Huggard and Denny, Tralee, and Leahy and Son, Newcastle West; Bankers, the National Bank and its branches.

Offices—6, Westminster Chambers, Victoria Street, S.W.

160.—LISKEARD AND CARADON.

Incorporated by act of 27th June, 1843, to construct a railway from Liskeard to Tokenbury, with a branch to Cheesewring. Length then, 8¾ miles.

By act of 15th May, 1860, the capital being by shares 18,825*l*., was to be increased by a sum not exceeding 12,000*l*., and the mortgage debt being 1,000*l*., borrowing powers to 10,000*l*. were given, and company authorised to lease or purchase the Kilmar.

By act of 12th July, 1882, the company was authorised to make 7 short railways for the improvement and extension of their undertaking. Period for completion, 5 years. New capital, 30,800*l*.; borrowing powers, 15,300*l*.

By act of 28th July, 1884, the company was authorised to make a further extension of their present undertaking to form a point of junction with the North Cornwall near Launceston.

The line is now 12 miles in length.

Liskeard and Looe.—This line is leased by the company.

Annual meeting second Tuesday in February.

No. of Directors—8. *Qualification*, 4 shares.

DIRECTORS:

Chairman—RICHARD HAWKE, Esq., Westbourne, Liskeard.

Deputy-Chairman—J. C. ISAAC, Esq., Liskeard.

N. Tregelles, Esq., Liskeard.
J. W. Dingle, Esq., Linkinhorne.
R. Kittow, Esq., Altarnun.
J. P. Milton, Esq., Penzance.
J. C. Trewren, Esq., Liskeard.
J. Elliott, Esq., Tokenbury, Liskeard.

OFFICERS.—Sec., R. Childs; Traffic Supt., J. H. Smythurst; Eng., S. W. Jenkin.

Offices—Liskeard, Cornwall.

161.—LIVERPOOL, SOUTHPORT, AND PRESTON JUNCTION.

Incorporated by act of 7th August, 1884, for the construction and maintenance of two railways, commencing by a junction with the Cheshire Lines Extension at Downholland, and terminating by a junction with the West Lancashire at Southport. Length, about 7½ miles. Period for completion, 5 years. Working arrangements with the West Lancashire. Capital, 200,000*l*. in 10*l*. shares, with power to divide into "preferred" and "deferred" half-shares. Borrowing powers, 66,600*l*.

No. of Directors.—Maximum, 5; minimum, 3; quorum, 3 and 2. *Qualification*, 50 shares.

FIRST DIRECTORS:

Edward Holden, Esq., Laurel Mount, Shipley.
Walter Smith, Esq., Southport.
Thomas Fisher, Esq., Southport.
Thomas Henry Isherwood, Esq., The Albany, Old Hall Street, Liverpool.

One other to be appointed.

162.—LLANELLY.

Incorporated (dock portion) by act of 1828, and (railway) by act of 1835, for a line from Llanelly to Llandilo, with branches to Cwmamman Spitty, Mynydd Mawr, Brynamman, &c. In operation, 36½ miles, with joint working of Vale of Towy, 11 miles.

For short heads of further powers, 1853 to 1869, see the Manual for 1881, page 178.

Vale of Towy.—This line, which is a virtual continuation of the communication to Llandovery, was opened on 1st April, 1858. By an act of 1858 the two lines might be worked under one management The terms were:—Capital of the Vale of Towy not to exceed 50,000*l*. in shares and 18,000*l*. in debentures—together, 68,000*l*. The Llanelly to pay interest not exceeding 5 per cent. on the debenture capital, and on the share capital 2 per cent. for five years; 3 per cent. for next five years; with power to the Llanelly to determine the lease at the end of the fifth year, on giving a year's notice, and paying a penalty of 1,000*l*. to the Vale of Towy. This line has since been jointly leased by the London and North Western and the Llanelly, so as the more efficiently to develope the traffic on the Central Wales, &c.

SWANSEA AND CARMARTHEN.—By act of 1871, these lines were incorporated into a separate company, but continued to be worked by the Llanelly until 1st July, when the Swansea and Carmarthen made arrangements with the London and North Western for that company to work the lines. In 1873 the London and North Western purchased the Swansea Line, and they continue to work the Carmarthen Line also.

GREAT WESTERN.—An agreement has been entered into with the Great Western for the working of the Llanelly upon such terms as would provide a 5 per cent. dividend on the ordinary stock for four years ending June 30th, 1877, and a 5½ per cent. dividend after that period. In addition to the guaranteed dividend, a further dividend of 1 per cent., derived from funds arising out of the realisation of assets, was made on the ordinary and "A" preference stocks for the half-year ended 31st December, 1875; whilst for the half-year ending 30th June, 1876, an additional dividend of 3 per cent., amounting to 7,920*l.*, was paid out of the sum applicable as interest under the Swansea and Carmarthen Act, 1871, and other realised assets of the company. Since then an additional ½ per cent. per annum is derived from interest on invested assets.

NET REVENUE.—The earnings on this account for the half-years ended 31st December, 1883, and 30th June, 1884, sufficed, after the payment of all prior charges, for dividends on the 200,000*l.* ordinary stock and 64,000*l.* "A" preference stock at 6 per cent. per annum. Balance to next half-year, 963*l.*

CAPITAL.—The receipts on this account to 30th June, 1884, amounted to 485,308*l.*, and the expenditure to 434,071*l.*, leaving a credit balance of 51,237*l.*

Scale of Voting.—For every 25*l.* up to 250*l.* nominal value of shares, 1 vote; for every sum of 125*l.* beyond 250*l.* and up to 2,500*l.*, 1 additional vote; and for every sum of 250*l.* beyond 2,500*l.*, 1 additional vote.

Certificates must accompany transfer deeds. Registration fee, 2*s.* 6*d.*

Meetings held usually in London in February and August.

No. of Directors.—Maximum, 9; quorum, 3. *Qualification*, 1,000*l.*, nominal. Committees, 3 and 5; quorum 2.

DIRECTORS:

Chairman—1 CHARLES TOWNSHEND MURDOCH, Esq., 1, Pall Mall East, S.W.

1 Major G. W. Rice Watkins, Llwyn-y-brain, near Llandovery.

3 William Blount, Esq., Orch Hill House, Gerrard's Cross.

2 Sir C. Alexander Wood, Knt., 11, Elvaston Place, S.W.

2 Sir Daniel Gooch, Bart., M.P., Fulthorpe House, Warwick Road, W.

3 The Hon. Robert St. John F. Butler, Rutland Lodge, Knightsbridge, S.W.

1, Retire in January, 1885; 2, in 1886; 3, in 1887.

OFFICERS.—Supt. and Sec., Richard Glascodine, Swansea; Auditors, W. Thomas and E. R. Thomas; Solicitors, Markby, Stewart, and Co., 57, Coleman Street, E.C.; Bankers, Cocks, Biddulph, and Co., 43, Charing Cross, W.

Head Offices—Burrows Lodge, Swansea.

163.—LLANELLY AND MYNYDD MAWR.

Incorporated 19th July, 1875, to construct a line between Llanelly and Mynydd Mawr, in the county of Carmarthen. Length, 12¾ miles. Capital, 60,000*l.* in 10*l.* shares and 20,000*l.* on loan. Arrangements with Great Western.

By act of 29th June, 1880, the time for the completion of works was extended until 19th July, 1883.

No. of Directors.—Maximum, 5; minimum, 3; quorum, 3 and 2. *Qualification*, 20 shares.

DIRECTORS:

Chairman—Sir JOHN J. JENKINS, M.P., Llanelly.

John Randell, Esq.

John Powell, Esq.

Henry Rees, Esq.

Secretary, John Jennings, Llanelly.

Offices—Llanelly, Carmarthenshire.

164.—LLANGAMMARCH AND NEATH AND BRECON JUNCTION.

Incorporated by act of 10th August, 1882, for making a railway from the Central Wales Extension Line of the London and North Western, at Llangammarch, to the Neath and Brecon, at Devynock. Length, about 13¾ miles. Period for completion, 5 years. Working and traffic arrangements with the Neath and Brecon. Capital, 130,000*l.* in 10*l.* shares, with power to divide into "preferred" and "deferred" half-shares. Borrowing powers, 43,300*l.*

No. of Directors.—Maximum, 5; minimum, 3; quorum, 3 and 2. *Qualification*, 50 shares.

FIRST DIRECTORS:

Robert Peter Laurie, Esq., 22, Threadneedle Street, E.C.
Henry Pigeon, Esq.
Sir L. G. Heath, K.C.B.
M. G. Buchanan, Esq., Hayes, Beckenham, Kent.

One other to be nominated.
Secretary, James Ray.

Offices—41, Coleman Street, E.C.

165.—LLANGOLLEN AND CORWEN.

Incorporated by act of 6th August, 1860, to construct a single line from the Vale of Llangollen to Corwen, to join the Denbigh, Ruthin, and Corwen, and thus complete communication from Shrewsbury to the Chester and Holyhead. Length, 10 miles. Capital, 90,000*l.* in 10*l.* shares; 20,000*l.* in 5 per cent. preference shares; loans, 30,000*l.*

Great Western.—An agreement with this company provides for the working, maintenance, and use of the Llangollen and Corwen by the Great Western, at 60 per cent. of the gross receipts after payment of the interest on the debenture debt, with an allowance in lieu of the rebate on traffic passing over the Great Western.

Revenue.—Under the arrangement with the Great Western, the company has, in the past, earned dividends on the ordinary capital at the rate of 3 per cent. per annum. The dividend on the ordinary shares for the half-year ended 30th June, 1884, was at the rate of 1¼ per cent. per annum.

Capital.—The expenditure on lines open for traffic to 30th June, 1884, amounted to 120,040*l.*, and the subscription to the Bala and Festiniog to 20,000*l.*, the total expenditure on capital account being 140,040*l.* The receipts were as follow:—Shares and stocks, 110,000*l.*; loans, 29,820*l.*; calls on forfeited shares, 40*l.*; premium on issue of debenture stock, 1,362*l.*; total, 141,222*l.*, showing a balance to the credit of this account of 1,182*l.*

New Capital.—In the company's report for the half-year ended 30th June, 1884, the following resolution was proposed, viz.:—"That the company under the provisions of the Bala and Festiniog Railway Act, 1873, raise for the purpose of its subscription to the undertaking of the Bala and Festiniog, as thereby authorised, the sum of 15,000*l.* sterling, by the issue at once of 1,500 new shares of the company of 10*l.* each, to be preferential to the ordinary share capital of the company, and to be irredeemable, and to bear in perpetuity dividends at the rate of 4*l.* per cent. per annum, the shares so to be issued to be in lieu of and in substitution for the subscription to the said undertaking already made by the issue of 1,500 5 per cent. redeemable preference shares, Nos. 1 to 1,500 inclusive, and to be applied accordingly in and towards such redemption, and which said last-mentioned shares are, upon such application as aforesaid, to be and shall be thereupon cancelled and extinguished."

No. of Directors—9; minimum, 5; quorum, 3. *Qualification*, 500*l.*

DIRECTORS:

Chairman—HENRY ROBERTSON, Esq., M.P., Palé, Corwen.

Sir Watkin Williams Wynn, Bart., M.P., Wynnstay, Ruabon, and 18, St. James's Square, S.W.
Colonel George Henry Wilson, Bala.
Captain J. C. Best, R.N., Vivod, Llangollen.
James Brend Batten, Esq., 32, Great George Street, Westminster, S.W.
Major Charles Robert Worsley Tottenham, Plas Berwyn, Llangollen.
Samuel Willcox, Esq., Maidehurst, Beckenham.

All eligible for re-election.

OFFICERS.—Sec., Charles Richards; Eng., Henry Robertson, M.Inst.C.E.; Auditors, William Patchett and Joseph Wagstaff Blundell; Solicitors, Longueville, Jones, and Williams, Oswestry, and Charles Richards and Sons, Llangollen.

Offices—Llangollen.

166.—LLANTRISSANT AND TAFF VALE JUNCTION.

Incorporated by act of 7th June, 1861, to construct a line from the Taff Vale, at Llantwit Vartre, to Llantrissant, with a branch to the Ely Valley and another to Llantrissant Common. Length, 5¼ miles. Capital, 40,000*l.* in 10*l.* shares; loans, 13,000*l.* Power was taken to purchase the Llantwit Railway, and to authorise the Taff Vale to subscribe 13,000*l.*, also to lay down the narrow gauge on the Ely Valley.

For short heads of acts, 1866 to 1877, see the Manual for 1881, page 180.

By act of 29th June, 1880, the company obtained a further extension of time for the completion of the railway No. 1, mentioned above, until 1st January, 1882.

The Taff Vale undertakes maintenance of railway and works and entire arrangement of the traffic, and collection of tolls and charges incidental thereto, and pays the Llantrissant 5 per cent. upon its paid up share capital, interest upon debenture debt for the time being, with an additional annual payment of 250*l.* for management. In operation, 7 miles 58¼ chains.

REVENUE.—The debenture interest is paid direct by the Taff Vale, which company also guarantees dividends at the rate of 5 per cent. per annum on the ordinary capital. The last two half-yearly dividends at that rate were made payable on the 8th January and 8th July, 1884, respectively.

CAPITAL.—The expenditure on this account to 30th June, 1884, amounted to 174,907*l.*, of which 73,297*l.* was on lines open for traffic, and 101,610*l.* on lines in course of construction. The receipts to same date amounted to 189,492*l.*, viz., 175,520*l.* by shares, 13,000*l.* by loans, and 972*l.* premiums on shares sold.

Meetings held in February and August.

No. of Directors—6; minimum, 4; quorum, 3. *Qualification*, 300*l.*

DIRECTORS:

Chairman—1 JOSEPH HAYNES NASH, Esq., Clifton Hill, Clifton.

1 Henry Bourchier Osborne Savile, Esq., Clifton.
2 Samuel Jones, Esq., Clifton, Bristol.
3 Charles H. Williams, Esq., Roath Court, Cardiff.

1, Retire in 1885; 2, in 1886; 3, in 1887. All eligible for re-election.

OFFICERS.—Sec., James G. Nicholson; Eng., George Fisher, M.Inst.C.E.; Accountant, Sidney Coleman; Auditors, Wilberforce Tribe and James Barnard Baker, Bristol; Bankers, National Provincial Bank of England, Cardiff.

Offices—Crockherbtown, Cardiff.

167.—LONDON AND BLACKWALL.

Incorporated by 6 and 7 Wm. IV., cap. 123, for a line from the Minories to Blackwall, and subsequently extended from the Minories to Fenchurch Street. In 1849 a branch from Stepney to Bow was constructed to connect the line with the Eastern Counties, now the Great Eastern, in 1872 a branch was constructed from Poplar, through the East and West India and Millwall Dock companies' property, to the Thames at Millwall, opposite Greenwich, and in 1880 a branch was constructed from Limehouse to the Stepney and Bow Branch.

The various further acts obtained by this company for improvements, new capital, and other purposes, are dated as follow:—25th June, 1855; 3rd July, 1860; 16th May, 1862; 25th July, 1864; 19th June, 1865; 13th July, 1868; 20th June, 1870; 21st July, 1873; 27th June, 1876; and 28th June, 1877. More detailed particulars have been given from time to time in past editions of the MANUAL.

By act of 3rd June, 1881, the company obtained an extension of time for the completion of certain works, authorised by act of 1876, from 27th June, 1881, to 27th June, 1884.

The undertaking was leased to the Great Eastern in 1865 for 999 years at a rent equal to 4½ per cent. per annum on its capital stock, the lessees paying also the interest on loan capital.

The last two half-yearly dividends, at 4½ per cent. per annum, were made payable on the 6th February and 6th August, 1884.

CAPITAL.—The capital authorised by the several acts of Parliament is 2,082,180*l.* by stock and shares, and 689,000*l.* by loans. The capital created or sanctioned is 2,082,180*l.* by shares, and 689,000*l.* by loans. The expenditure on this account to 30th June, 1884, amounted to 2,730,976*l.* The receipts were:—

Shares and stock	£2,073,808	
Debenture stock	658,100=£2,731,908	
Add discount		8,372=£2,740,280

PRIORITIES, DESCRIPTIONS, DIVIDENDS, &c., OF STOCKS (see notes).—The Stocks in order of priority, and must be described, are as follow:—

1—4½ per cent. debenture stock.
2—4½ per cent. preference stock.
3—Ordinary stock.

NOTES.—The dividend on debenture stock is accumulative, and payable 1st January and 1st July, the transfer books closing for 15 days before payment.

The dividends on preference and ordinary stocks are contingent upon the profits of each separate year, and also upon the terms of the above-named lease; they are payable half-yearly, in February and August, the transfer books closing for 10 days previously.

TRANSFER DEPARTMENT QUERIES AND REPLIES.

QUERIES.	REPLIES.
Transfer form—ordinary or special?	Ordinary.
Fee per deed?	2s. 6d.
Ditto if more sellers than one?...	2s. 6d. each transferer (not joint accounts).
May several classes of stock be transferred on one deed?	All except debenture stock.
Are certificates required to accompany transfers?	Yes.
What amounts of stock are transferable, and are parts of 1l. sterling allowed to be transferred?	10l., or multiples of 10l., except the preference stock, of which any parts of 1l. may be transferred.
To what officer should transfer communications be sent?	Secretary.
In acceptances, renunciations, &c., of allotments of new stock, proxies, or other forms sent to trustees and other joint holders, what signatures are required?	The first-named in joint account.

The estimate of future expenditure required for the half-year ended 31st December, 1884, was 5,000l., and in subsequent half-years 10,000l., total 15,000l.; the available assets were described as follow:—

Capital authorised		£2,771,180
Shares and stock received	£2,073,808	
Loans and debenture stock received	658,100	
	£2,731,908	
Add discount on issue of consolidated stock............	8,372=	2,740,280
		£30,900
Credit balance on capital account		931=£31,831

The accounts are made up to 30th June and 31st December in every year, and the statutory meetings held in February and August.

DIRECTORS:

Chairman—Alderman Sir CHARLES WHETHAM, Knt., 52, Gordon Square, W.C.

F. W. Haigh, Esq., Bickley, Bromley, Kent.

Thomas Wrake Ratcliff, Esq., 8, St. Mark's Square, N.W.

OFFICERS.—Sec. and Registrar, Samuel Le Cren; Auditors, James Goodson and T. M. Fairclough; Solicitors, Hollingsworth, Tyerman, and Andrewes, 4, East India Avenue, Leadenhall Street, E.C.

Offices—Fenchurch Street Terminus, E.C. (chief entrance, John Street, Crutched Friars).

168.—LONDON, BRIGHTON, AND SOUTH COAST.

An amalgamation of the Croydon and the Brighton, under powers of an act of 27th July, 1846. In operation, 455 miles.

FURTHER PARLIAMENTARY POWERS:—

A list of Acts obtained by this company from 1856 to 1879, with short heads showing the objects for which the various powers were sought, will be found on reference to the MANUAL for 1881, pages 184 to 186.

1880—19TH JULY.—Short extensions to the Lewes and East Grinstead and Chichester and Midhurst Sections, &c.

1882—28TH APRIL.—Power to raise 1,250,000l. additional capital, and to borrow 416,600l. for the general improvement of the undertaking.

1882—3RD JULY.—New lines and works at Keymer, and Old and New Shoreham, in the county of Sussex, with powers for new roads at Portsea, and for other purposes.

1882—3RD JULY.—Amendment of "Newhaven Harbour Improvement Act, 1878." —See further on, under the heading "Newhaven Harbour."

1884—3RD JULY.—For taking over the undertaking of the Oxted and Groombridge, and the raising of the capital, authorised by that company's act; and improvements of railway at Lewes.

AMALGAMATIONS, LEASES, AGREEMENTS, &c.:—

BANSTEAD AND EPSOM DOWNS.—Incorporated by act of 17th July, 1862, to construct a line from the Sutton Station of the Croydon and Epsom Branch of the Brighton to Banstead and Epsom Downs. Length, 4¼ miles. Capital, 85,000*l.* in 10*l.* shares and 28,300*l.* on loan. Amalgamated with Brighton by act of 1864.

BOGNOR.—Incorporated by act of 11th July, 1861, for making a line from Eastergate to Bognor. Length, 3½ miles. Amalgamated with the Brighton by act of 1864, but amalgamation not completed till 1871.

CHICHESTER AND MIDHURST.—Incorporated by act of 23rd June, 1864, to construct a line from the Brighton, at Chichester, to join the Mid Sussex and Midhurst and Petersfield. The undertaking is practically embodied in the London, Brighton, and South Coast, the line being opened by that company on the 11th July, 1881.

CROYDON, OXTED, AND EAST GRINSTEAD.—Construction authorised by act of 17th June, 1878. Period for completion, 4 years. No. 1, Croydon to Oxted, 10 miles 5 chains; No 1a, Junction with the South Eastern between Oxted and Crowhurst, 2 miles 2 furlongs 1·50 chains; No. 2, Oxted to East Grinstead, 6 miles 6 furlongs 25 chains; No 3, Junction Line at Withyham, 7 furlongs 1·50 chains. Lines 1, 1a, and 2 were opened for traffic on the 10th March, 1884. Power to South Eastern, with the consent of its proprietary, to raise 110,000*l.* in stock and shares, and 36,600*l.* on loan, &c., and become joint owners of railways No. 1 and No. 1a, under a joint committee, the revenue to be disposed of as follows:—1st, in payment of a dividend at 4 per cent. per annum upon the capital contributed by the two companies respectively; 2nd, in payment of a dividend at 4½ per cent. per annum on the expenditure (not exceeding 150,000*l.*) already made by the Brighton; and 3rd, to the benefit of the two companies respectively in equal proportions. By the same act the Lewes and East Grinstead was vested in this company, particulars of which will be found below under the head of amalgamations, &c. New capital, 750,000*l.*; loans, &c, 250,000*l.*

EAST GRINSTEAD.—Incorporated by act of 8th July, 1853, for a line from the Brighton at Three Bridges to East Grinstead. Length, 6¾ miles. Capital, 50,000*l.* This line was purchased in January, 1865, for 50,000*l.* 4 per cent. stock, the Brighton taking upon itself the mortgage debt.

EAST LONDON.—See GENERAL INDEX.

HAYLING.—This undertaking is leased to the Brighton, under act of 1874, as from 1st January, 1872, at an annual rental of 2,000*l.* and establishment charges, which suffices to pay the 5 per cent. preference dividend, and dividends of about 2½ per cent. per annum upon the ordinary shares.

HAYLING BRIDGE AND CAUSEWAY.—Powers for the purchase of these works were given to the Brighton by a separate act of 17th June, 1878, and have since been exercised.

HORSHAM, DORKING, AND LEATHERHEAD.—Incorporated by act of 17th July, 1862, to construct a line from Horsham and Dorking. Length, 13¼ miles. Capital, 120,000*l.* in 10*l.* shares and 40,000*l.* on loan. Arrangements with the Brighton, which contributed 75,000*l.*, and guaranteed 4 per cent. on capital, under Amalgamation Act of 1864. Embodied in the Brighton, 4 per cent. preference stock being exchanged for shares in the Horsham.

HORSHAM AND GUILDFORD DIRECT.—Incorporated by act of 6th August, 1860, to construct a line from the Mid-Sussex (Brighton) to the Godalming Branch of the South Western, at Guildford. Length, 14 miles. Capital, 160,000*l.*; loans, 50,000*l.* Amalgamated with Brighton by act of 1864.

LEWES AND EAST GRINSTEAD.—Incorporated by act of 10th August, 1877. Length, 17 miles 13 chains. Under the Brighton Company's Act of 17th June, 1878, the undertaking is amalgamated with the Brighton; the Lewes proprietary having the option of either being paid off or accepting a 4 per cent. preference stock of the Brighton Company, to be created for that purpose, equal to the amount of their holding. The line was opened on the 1st August, 1882. An extension of this line from Horsted Keynes to Hayward's Heath, 4 miles 55 chains, authorised by the Brighton Company's Act of 19th July, 1880, was opened on the 3rd September, 1883. —For past agreement and other details, see the MANUAL for 1882, and previous editions.

LEWES AND UCKFIELD.—Incorporated by act of 27th July, 1857, to make a railway from Lewes to Uckfield. Capital, 59,000*l.* in 50*l.* shares; loans, 16,500*l.* Length, 7½ miles. Its termini are at the one end, a junction with the Keymer Branch of the Brighton, in the parish of Hamsey, and at the other end the town of Uckfield. Purchased by the Brighton on 31st May, 1860, for 33,900*l.* 4 per cent. preference stock, and takes the mortgage debt.

MID-SUSSEX.—Incorporated by act of 10th August, 1857, to construct a line from the Brighton, at Horsham, to Pulborough, with a branch to Petworth. Length, 17 miles. Purchased by the Brighton on 31st May, 1860, for 100,000*l*. 4 per cent. preference stock, the Brighton taking the mortgage debt, 50,000*l*.

MID-SUSSEX AND MIDHURST JUNCTION.—Incorporated by act of 13th August, 1859, for making a railway from the Coultershaw Branch of the Mid Sussex to Midhurst. Capital, 70,000*l*. in 10*l*. shares; loans, 20,000*l*. Length, 5¼ miles. By act of 7th August, 1862, the company obtained till 1863 to complete its works, and also power to sell or lease the undertaking to the Brighton. Purchased by the Brighton in June, 1874, for 69,160*l*. 4 per cent. preference stock, the mortgage debt (20,000*l*.) being also taken over.

NEWHAVEN HARBOUR.—A scheme has been for some time in preparation for the improvement of this harbour to facilitate the working of the Brighton Company's Continental traffic. The proposed work is as follows, viz.:—1. A breakwater extending about 900 yards out to sea. 2. Extension of quay accommodation 570 yards from the railway wharf to the harbour mouth, and extension of the pier. 3. A new sea wall or pier in connection with the above. 4. A tramway (1 mile 2 furlongs 7·30 chains) from near Newhaven Town Station to the Breakwater. 5. A dock on the eastern side of the River Ouse. 6. A sea wall (750 yards long) from the said dock to the existing sea wall of the Tide Mill. 7, 8, and 9. The straightening of Mill Creek and other works and improvements. The capital authorised is 320,000*l*., with borrowing powers to the extent of 106,666*l*. By act of 17th June, 1878, a company was incorporated to carry out the work, and authorising the Brighton to raise money and subscribe all or part of 150,000*l*. towards the capital of the undertaking. This capital has been fully subscribed by the Brighton as authorised. Works in progress. By act of 3rd July, 1882, additional powers were granted for making another tramway; purchase of lands; extending time for completion of first section of works to 17th June, 1888; raising additional capital of 100,000*l*., with borrowing powers to the extent of 33,300*l*.; and Brighton Company may subscribe not exceeding 100,000*l*., or, instead, guarantee interest on share and loan capital, which latter they have done. [NOTE.—An act was passed in 1872 incorporating a company for the purpose of improving the Continental communication between Newhaven and Dieppe, particulars concerning which were fully given in the MANUAL for 1879, and previously, under the head "Continental Communication—Newhaven and Dieppe."]

PORTSMOUTH HARBOUR LINE.—Length, 1 mile 5 chains. Opened 2nd October, 1876.

RYDE NEW PIER AND RAILWAY, AND SERVICE BETWEEN RYDE AND PORTSMOUTH.—See London and South Western.

SURREY AND SUSSEX JUNCTION.—Incorporated by act of 6th July, 1865, to construct a line from the Brighton, at Croydon, to junctions with the East Grinstead and Uckfield and Tunbridge branches of the same system. Length, 24¼ miles. Capital, 705,000*l*. in shares and 235,000*l*. on loan. By act of 25th July, 1867, the company was authorised to make certain alterations in the mode of constructing the line, to acquire additional land, and the share capital reduced from 705,000*l*. to 455,000*l*. By act of 12th July, 1869, the Surrey and Sussex was amalgamated with the Brighton, and has been since abandoned, but the Northern Section of it now forms part of the Croydon, Oxted, and East Grinstead, and the Southern Section is virtually the Oxted and Groombridge.

TOOTING, MERTON, AND WIMBLEDON.—Incorporated by act of 29th July, 1864, for lines from Wimbledon, *viâ* Tooting and Merton, to join the Brighton Line at Streatham. Length, 5¾ miles. Capital, 95,000*l*.; loans, 31,600*l*. By act of 5th July, 1865, this undertaking was vested jointly in the Brighton and South Western, and a further junction of half a mile authorised. New capital, 52,500*l*. in shares and 17,500*l*. on loan.

TUNBRIDGE WELLS AND EASTBOURNE.—Incorporated by act of 5th August, 1873, to construct a line from Tunbridge Wells to Hailsham. Length, 20½ miles. Capital, 115,000*l*. in 10*l*. shares and 38,000*l*. on loan. By act of 27th June, 1876, the powers of the company were vested in the London and Brighton, and the undertaking so modified as to consist of a line 12¾ miles, from Rotherfield to Hailsham, and a short connecting line between the Hailsham and the Eastbourne branches of the company. Powers were also given to the Brighton to raise 200,000*l*. additional capital, and to borrow on mortgage or by debenture stock 66,660*l*. Opened in 1880. The South Eastern report for the half-year ended 31st December, 1877, has the following, viz.:—"Parliament has confirmed the agreement made between this company and the London, Brighton, and South Coast, dated 29th March, 1877, in reference to the London and Eastbourne traffic, and the agreement is scheduled to the South Eastern Act of

1877. Clause 2 of the agreement so scheduled is as follows:—'The gross receipts from all through traffic passing from Eastbourne to or through London, and *vice versa*, whether *via* Tunbridge Wells or *via* Lewes, or *via* any other route of the Brighton, after deduction by the carrying company of 25 per cent. on account of working expenses, shall be divided between the two companies as follows:—One half to the Brighton in respect of the traffic *via* Lewes, or any other route of the Brighton; and as to the other half, viz., in respect of the traffic *via* Tunbridge Wells, the same shall be divided in due mileage proportions between the two companies, the division to commence from 6th July, 1879, whether the Tunbridge Wells and Eastbourne be then completed or not.'"

UCKFIELD AND TUNBRIDGE WELLS.—Incorporated by act of 22nd July, 1861, to construct a line from Uckfield to Tunbridge Wells. Length, 15 miles. Capital, 200,000*l*. in 20*l*. shares; loans, 65,000*l*. Amalgamated with Brighton by act of 1864. Opened in 1868.

VICTORIA STATION.—Opened 1st October, 1860. The Brighton owns half of this station, and the London, Chatham, and Dover and Great Western rent the other portion. The London and North Western use the Brighton portion under a toll arrangement.

WEST LONDON EXTENSION.—The Brighton joined the London and North Western, the Great Western, and South Western, in providing capital for the extension of this line to Pimlico. The estimated outlay is 555,000*l*.; and the proportion contributed by the Brighton is 92,500*l*., and took effect from 1st July, 1859. By the Great Western Act, 1875, the four companies were authorised to assume the mortgage debt of the Extension Company.

WIMBLEDON AND CROYDON.—Incorporated 8th July, 1853, to construct a line from the South Western, at Wimbledon, to the Brighton, at Epsom. By negotiation with the Brighton and the South Western, altered to a line from Wimbledon to Mitcham, and thence to Croydon. Length, 8¼ miles. Parliamentary estimate of cost, 45,000*l*. Opened, 22nd October, 1855. By act of 21st July, 1856, the line was leased to the Brighton, and 15,000*l*. additional capital authorised to lay down a double line of rails when required. Transferred, absolutely, to the Brighton, 1st January, 1866.

WOODSIDE AND SOUTH CROYDON.—Incorporated by act of 6th August, 1880 (see MANUAL for 1882, page 366). Transferred to the South Eastern and London, Brighton, and South Coast, under the South Eastern Act of 10th August, 1882.

NEW LINES.—The first section of the Tunbridge Wells and Eastbourne (from Hailsham to Heathfield) was opened on the 5th April, 1880, and the second section (from Heathfield to Eridge) on the 1st September, 1880. Part of the Ryde Pier was brought into use on the 5th April, 1880, and it was opened throughout on the 12th July, 1880. A branch from the East London to the South Eastern was opened on the 1st April, 1880. The Lewes and East Grinstead was opened 1st August, 1882, and an extension of this line from Horsted Keynes to Hayward's Heath on the 3rd September, 1883. The Croydon, Oxted, and East Grinstead was opened for traffic on the 10th March, 1884.

ACCOUNTS:—

REVENUE.—The subjoined statement shows the comparison of receipts and expenditure for four half-years, ended 30th June, 1884:—

Half-years ending............	31st. Dec., 1882.	30th June, 1883.	31st Dec., 1883.	30th June, 1884.
Miles open	430¾	430¾	435¼	455
Miles run by passenger trains	3,311,702	3,144,130	3,377,321	3,288,512
Ditto by goods trains	698,129	708,310	718,996	705,078
Total miles run by trains	4,009,831	3,852,440	4,096,317	3,993,590
Gross revenue.............................. £	1,126,899	£971,365	1,163,645	£981,997
Maintenance of way, &c........................	£78,320	£83,559	£81,476	£85,459
Locomotive power........................	151,048	143,293	157,982	152,117
Carriage and wagon department	48,433	42,732	47,912	43,959
Traffic charges	150,993	147,349	152,367	149,382
General charges..............................	19,578	19,805	18,828	19,779
Law and Parliamentary charges	7,911	12,518	8,591	13,048
Compensation..............................	12,809	6,337	6,040	3,696
Rates and taxes..............................	41,195	41,277	41,656	42,259
Government duty	24,041	20,721	22,520	14,967
Mileage and demurrage of rolling stock and tolls..............................	*Cr*. 1,883	*Cr*. 1,420	*Cr*. 1,072	42
	£532,465	£516,171	£536,300	£524,708

The net receipts for the four half-years, and the manner in which they were appropriated, are given below:—

	Dec., 1882.	June, 1883.	Dec., 1883.	June, 1884.
Net revenue	£594,435	£455,193	£627,345	£457,289
Add—former balances, &c.	7,735	4,897	10,504	9,064
Total net revenue	£602,170	£460,090	£637,849	£466,353
Deduct interest on debentures, preference stock, &c.	383,054	385,468	383,816	382,622
Balance available for dividend	£219,116	£74,622	£254,033	£83,731
Dividend on ordinary stock	214,219	68,550	248,309	75,000
At per annum	3¼ per cent	2 per cent	3¾ per cent	1 per cent
Balance carried forward	£4,897	£6,072	£5,724	£8,731

The dividends were made payable on the 5th February and 4th August, 1883, and on the 5th February and 5th August, 1884.

CAPITAL.—The statement of stock and share capital created, showing the proportion received up to 30th June, 1884, was as follows:—

Description.	Created.	Received.
Consolidated guaranteed 5 per cent. stock	£1,955,860	£1,955,860
Consolidated preference 5 per cent. stock	6,190,315	6,190,315
Second consolidated preference 5 per cent. stock	2,000,000	1,999,900
Preference 4 per cent. stock	50,000	50,000
Ordinary stock—undivided	3,224,300	7,499,833
Do. preferred	2,137,850	
Do. deferred	2,137,850	
	£17,696,175	£17,695,908

Calls in arrear, 267*l.*

PRIORITIES, DESCRIPTIONS, DIVIDENDS, and other conditions of issue of the various Stocks of the company, on the 30th September, 1882 (see notes):—

No.	Year of Act.	FULL DESCRIPTION (to be observed in Transfer Deeds and all other Legal Documents).	Rate ℔ cent ℔ annum.
1	Various	Perpetual 4 per cent. debenture stock	4
2	Various	Perpetual 4½ per cent. debenture stock	4½
3	29&30 Vic., cap. 281	Consolidated guaranteed 5 per cent. stock	5
4		Consolidated preference 5 per cent. stock	5
5	Various	Second consolidated preference 5 per cent. stock	5
6	45&46 Vic., cap. 219	Preferential 4 per cent. stock	4
7	Various	Ordinary stock	...
8	Regulat'n of Railwys Act, 1868	Preferred ordinary stock	6
9		Deferred ordinary stock	...
10	...	Contingent rights in respect of late 6 per cent. stock No. 1	...

NOTES.—The contingent rights or benefits of No. 10 stocks "are two in number—(1) When the dividend exceeds 6 per cent. for any one year on the ordinary stock, participation rateably and proportionately in the excess, and (2) participation *pro rata* in any allotment of new stock offered to proprietors of ordinary stock."

To ascertain the dividend on stocks Nos. 8 and 9, double the ordinary dividend for any year ending 31st December, deduct therefrom 6 per cent., which first accrues to the "preferred" stock, the "deferred" stock is then entitled to whatever residue there may be. The option of dividing the ordinary stock into "preferred" and "deferred" may be exercised between the time of closing the transfer books of the companies prior to the first half-yearly ordinary meeting in any year, and the time of closing such transfer books prior to the second half-yearly ordinary meeting in the same year.

The dividend on No. 9 is payable annually in February.

The dividends on Nos. 1, 2, and 3 are non-contingent or accumulative, on Nos. 4 and 5 stocks they are contingent upon the profits of each separate year ended 31st December; they are payable, with the exception of No. 9, half-yearly, as follows:—Nos. 1 and 2, 30th June and 31st December; all the remainder in February and August.

The transfer books close as follow:—Of Nos. 1 and 2, 14 days before payment of dividend; the remainder 21 days previous to each half-yearly general meeting.

TRANSFER DEPARTMENT QUERIES AND REPLIES.

Queries.	Replies.
Transfer form—ordinary or special?	Ordinary.
Fee per deed?	*2s. 6d.*
Ditto if more sellers than one?...	*2s. 6d.*
May several classes of stock be transferred on one deed?	Yes.
Are certificates required to accompany transfers?	Yes.
What amounts of stock are transferable, and are parts of *1l.* sterling allowed to be transferred?	8 and 9 in sums of *10l.* or multiples of *10l.*; 3, 4, and 5, no fractions of *1l.* are allowed.
To what officer should transfer communications be sent?	Secretary.
In acceptances, renunciations, &c., of allotments of new stock, proxies, or other forms sent to trustees and other joint holders, what signatures are required?	Signature of first-named proprietor, except authorities for payment of dividends which require the signatures of all the joint holders.

The receipts and expenditure on this account to 30th June, 1884, were detailed as follow:—

Received.		*Expended.*	
Stock and shares	£17,879,733	Lines and works open for traffic	£19,608,045
Deduct—discount and commission, less premiums, and add nominal reduction of capital on consolidation of stocks	466,249	Lines in progress	234,093
		Lines abandoned under act 1868	216,400
	£17,413,484	Surrey and Sussex Junction.	467,925
		West Sussex Junction	10,361
Debenture stock	5,609,161	Working stock, machinery, and tools	2,515,208
Add—premium on sale of 4½ per cent. debenture stock...	209,348	Steamboats and dredgers......	141,869
			£23,193,902
		Balance..........................	38,090
	£23,231,992		£23,231,992

The estimate of further expenditure on capital account was detailed in these terms and figures:—

	Half-year ended 31st Dec., 1884.	In subsequent Half-years.	Total.
Lewes and East Grinstead	£8,440	...	£8,440
Joint Croydon, Oxted, and East Grinstead	10,000	...	10,000
Croydon, Oxted, and East Grinstead No. 2	15,000	£26,300	41,300
Oxted and Groombridge	50,000	250,000	300,000
Joint Woodside and Croydon	10,000	...	10,000
Littlehampton Direct	5,000	6,000	11,000
Enlargement of Stations, additional sidings, works, &c....	32,500	99,400	131,900
New engine sheds at Norwood Junction, Battersea, and Newhaven..	20,000	25,000	45,000
Interlocking points, signals, &c..................................	3,000	12,120	15,120
Two new boats for Portsmouth and Ryde service	18,500	...	18,500
Total estimated further expenditure of capital	£172,440	£418,820	£591,260

The capital powers and other assets to meet this expenditure are as under:—

Share and loan capital authorised but not yet created	£1,018,967	
Share capital created, but not yet issued or received	267	
Balance of loan and debenture stock	279,905=	£1,299,139
Add capital account, balance to credit thereof		38,090
		£1,337,229
Surplus lands and property estimated at		64,225
Total		£1,401,454

NEW CAPITAL.—At the half-yearly meeting, held 29th January, 1879, the proprietors sanctioned the creation and issue of 1,445,000*l.* of capital, as a second consolidated preference 5 per cent. stock (authorised by acts of 1876, 1877, and 1878). The stock was issued to the proprietors of ordinary stock, and of contingent rights of the late 6 per cent., No. 1 stock at the price of 110*l.* per cent. The allotment was at the rate of about 25 per cent.

At the half-yearly meeting, held on 26th January, 1881, the proprietors sanctioned the creation of 350,000*l.* of capital, and it was issued on the 16th November, 1881, to proprietors of ordinary stock and of contingent rights, as second consolidated preference 5 per cent. stock, at the price of 120*l.* per cent. The allotment was at the fate of 5 per cent. on holdings of not less than 100*l.*

At the half-yearly meeting, on the 19th July, the proprietors sanctioned the creation of 205,000*l.* of capital, as second consolidated preference 5 per cent. stock, and it was allotted on the 31st July, 1882, to persons whose tenders were at the rate of 124 per cent. and upwards.

At the half-yearly meeting on the 24th January, 1883, the proprietors sanctioned the creation and issue of 645,000*l.* ordinary stock, which stock was issued to proprietors of ordinary stocks and of contingent rights at the price of 110*l.* per cent. The allotment was at the rate of 9 per cent. on holdings of not less than 100*l.*

NEW WORKS.—The works at Newhaven Harbour are in progress.

The accounts are made up to 30th June and 31st December, and the statutory meetings are held in London within one month of 31st January and 31st July.

Scale of Voting—Ordinary Stockholders.—3 votes for 50*l.* of stock up to 500*l.*, and 3 additional votes for each 250*l.* beyond 500*l.*

Preference Stockholders.—3 votes for 100*l.* of stock up to 1,000*l.*, and 3 additional votes for each 500*l.* beyond 1,000*l.*

Regulated by special acts as well as C. C. C. Act.

Qualification for Directors, 1,000*l.* stock.

DIRECTORS:

Chairman—2 SAMUEL LAING, Esq., M.P., 5, Cambridge Gate, Regent's Park, N.W.

Deputy-Chairman—2 JONAS LEVY, Esq., Kingsgate Castle, Isle of Thanet, Kent.

Deputy and Assistant Chairman—1 RALPH LUDLOW LOPES, Esq., Sandridge Park, near Melksham, Wiltshire.

3 John Pares Bickersteth, Esq., Grove Mill House, near Watford, Hertfordshire.

2 Christopher Baldock Cardew, Esq., East Hill, Liss, near Petersfield, Hants.

1 The Hon. Thomas Francis Fremantle, M.P., 22, Chesham Place, Belgrave Square, S.W.

3 Robert Jacomb-Hood, Esq., 112, Lexham Gardens, Kensington, W.

3 Lord Alexander Gordon Lennox, 21, Pont Street, Belgrave Square, S.W.

1, Retire in 1885; 2, in 1886; 3, in 1887.

OFFICERS.—Sec., Allen Sarle; Assistant Sec., W. J. C. Wain; Gen. Man., John Peake Knight, Assoc.Inst.C.E.; Res. Eng., Fred. D. Banister, M.Inst.C.E.; Loco. and Carriage Supt., W. Stroudley, Assoc.Inst.C.E., Brighton; Goods Man., G. W. Staniforth, London Bridge Terminus; Accountant, George Steer, London Bridge Terminus; Surveyor and Estate Agent, J. Cripps; Registrar, W. Medhurst; Auditors, William Cash and Major John C. Fitzmaurice; Solicitors, Norton, Rose, Norton, & Co., 6, Victoria Street, Westminster, S.W., and London Bridge Terminus, S.E.

Head Offices—Terminus, London Bridge, S.E.

169.—LONDON, CHATHAM, AND DOVER.

Incorporated by act of 4th August, 1853, for a line from Strood to Canterbury, continuing the South Eastern (North Kent); length (originally), 29 miles, with branches to Faversham Quays, ½ mile, and Chilham, 1½ mile.

FURTHER PARLIAMENTARY POWERS:—

A list of Acts obtained by this company from 1855 to 1879, with short heads of the objects for which the various powers were sought, will be found on reference to the MANUAL for 1881, pages 191 and 192.

1881—27TH JUNE.—Powers to construct a railway in Kent, called the Maidstone and Faversham Junction. Length, about 9½ miles. Period for completion, 5 years. New capital, 240,000*l.* Borrowing powers, 80,000*l.*

1881—27TH JUNE.—Another act of this date gives powers for the construction of a railway with a bridge over the River Thames. Period for completion of works, 5 years. New capital, 300,000*l.* Borrowing powers, 100,000*l.*

1881—18TH JULY.—Further general powers to extend the Greenwich Branch from Blackheath Hill into the town of Greenwich; to construct a short line at Kearsney to connect the company's main line, in the direction of London, with the Dover and Deal Joint Line; to extend the Sittingbourne and Sheerness Branch into the town of Sheerness. Period for completion, 5 years. Power to subscribe to Medway Docks Company not exceeding 50,000*l.*, and to appoint three directors. New capital, 270,000*l.* Borrowing powers, 90,000*l.*

1883—29TH JUNE.—Powers to transfer the Maidstone and Ashford undertaking to the company, from date of opening for passenger traffic, which took place on the 1st July, 1884, the Chatham Company paying for the same the actual amount expended by the Maidstone Company. Powers are also given to merge the Gravesend Company in the Chatham undertaking on passing of the act, the latter company being authorised to raise 250,000*l.* by 4 per cent. debenture stock for this purpose. Authority is also given to raise 460,000*l.*, and 150,000*l.* similar debenture stock, for purchase of the Maidstone undertaking. The company is also authorised to raise 450,000*l.* by share capital for general purposes, including improved steam vessels for the Channel Mail Service, with borrowing powers for 150,000*l.* in respect of the same. Extension of time for completion of sundry works.—See further on.

1884—14TH JULY.—Construction of railways and works, and other improvements, in the counties of Surrey and Kent, and in the city of London. New capital, 123,000*l.*; loans, 41,000*l.*

AMALGAMATIONS, LEASES, AGREEMENTS, &c.:—

CHATHAM DOCKYARD LINE.—Opened 16th February, 1877. Length, 1 mile 63½ chains.

CRYSTAL PALACE AND SOUTH LONDON JUNCTION.—Incorporated 17th July, 1862, to construct a line from the Metropolitan Extension of the London, Chatham, and Dover to the Crystal Palace at Sydenham. Length, 6¼ miles. Capital, 675,000*l.* in 10*l.* shares and 225,000*l.* on loan. By act of 23rd June, 1864, the company was authorised to connect the line with the Greenwich Branch of the London, Chatham, and Dover. Length, 1¼ mile. No new capital. By act of 12th July, 1869, the company was authorised to construct the "Loughborough Loop Line," forming a junction with the Chatham and Dover at East Brixton. Length 22 chains. New capital, 75,000*l.* in shares and 25,000*l.* on loan. By act of 27th June, 1872, all actions against the company, on the part of its creditors, were stayed for three years; and in the event of three-fourths of the mortgagees consenting, the following provisions were to take effect, viz.:—Interest on debentures to be reduced to 4½ per cent.; unpaid interest to become principal. An additional sum of 40,000*l.* to be created, and issued at a discount, if necessary, to pay debts to landowners, and in providing additional station accommodation, &c. By act of 19th July, 1875, the undertaking was vested in the London, Chatham, and Dover. The following is an epitome of the agreement for the purchase. The Chatham and Dover to purchase the line on and from the 1st July, 1875. The Loughborough Loop Line to vest in the Dover Company from the same date. The Dover to issue to the Crystal Palace Company, as consideration for the absolute purchase of that line, the following proportions of stock of the London, Chatham, and Dover:—

Arbitration debenture stock	£140,533
Arbitration preference stock	341,650
Arbitration ordinary stock	544,150

The aggregate of these sums being equivalent to the aggregate nominal capital of the Crystal Palace Company. Such stock to rank for dividend from 1st July, 1875, *pari passu* with the existing stocks of the Dover Company of the same denomination. The Crystal Palace Company to waive claims of every kind on the Dover Company, except claims in respect to working for year ended 30th June, 1875. The Dover Company has agreed that the line should be worked for that year at 66 per cent. of the gross receipts. The Crystal Palace Company to give the Dover Company absolute possession of the line on the 1st July, 1875, and to discharge all their liabilities and debts up to that date.

DOVER AND DEAL.—By act of 30th June, 1874, the South Eastern and London, Chatham, and Dover companies were authorised to make this railway. Length, about 8½ miles. Works to be completed within five years. The two companies to have equal rights in respect of the joint undertaking, which will be managed by a committee of six members, three to be appointed by each company. In addition to any moneys they are already authorised to raise, the two companies may, for the purposes of this railway, each issue new preference or ordinary shares or stock, to an amount not exceeding 125,000*l*., and borrow on mortgage 40,000*l*., the capital created to form part of the general capital of the company issuing the same. By act of 22nd July, 1878, the time for compulsory purchase of lands limited by act of 1874, and extended by an act of 1877, was further extended until the 22nd July, 1879. By act of 23rd May, 1879, the time for compulsory purchase of lands was further extended to 23rd May, 1880, and for the completion of works to 23rd May, 1881. The ceremony of cutting the first sod was performed by Earl Granville on the 29th June, 1878, and the line was opened for traffic on the 15th June, 1881.

GRAVESEND.—Incorporated by act of 18th July, 1881. Length, 5 miles. Vested in the Chatham Company by act of 29th June, 1883, by transfer to the former company of all the powers obtained under the Gravesend Acts of 1881 and 1882. The Chatham Company may issue new capital for the acquirement of this undertaking not exceeding 250,000*l*. in 4 per cent. debenture stock.—For particulars prior to vesting, see MANUAL for 1883, page 108.

HOLBORN VIADUCT.—Incorporated by act of 13th July, 1871, to construct a station and a short line (292 yards) to connect the same with the London, Chatham, and Dover. Capital, 300,000*l*. in 10*l*. shares, "preferred" and "deferred," and 100,000*l* on loan or by debenture stock.

HOLBORN VIADUCT TERMINUS HOTEL.—This new and magnificent hotel, leased to Messrs. Spiers and Pond, was opened on the 17th of November, 1877.

KENT COAST.—Incorporated by act of 17th August, 1857, to construct a line between Herne Bay and Faversham (other brief details are given at page 189 of MANUAL for 1882). By act of 31st July, 1871, the Kent Coast was authorised to be amalgamated with the London, Chatham, and Dover, under an agreement sanctioned by the proprietors of both companies in August, 1871, and given *in extenso* in the *Appendix* to the MANUAL for 1872.

MAIDSTONE AND ASHFORD.—Incorporated by act of 12th August, 1880. Length, 19 miles. Vested in Chatham Company by act of 29th June, 1883, from the date of the completion of the line and opening for traffic, for a sum equal to the amount expended on the line, ascertained at the time of such completion and opening. The Chatham Company may issue stock for the above purpose. The line was opened on the 1st July, 1884.—For particulars prior to vesting, see MANUAL for 1883, page 205.

METROPOLITAN.—The London, Chatham, and Dover runs 80 trains per day to and from Moorgate Street, paying the Metropolitan for the use of their railway a mileage proportion of such fares as might be fixed by the Chatham, and for the use of the station at Moorgate Street a rental based upon the traffic actually carried. The company to be at liberty to terminate the agreement at or after ten years on paying 30,000*l*. to the Metropolitan.

METROPOLITAN EXTENSIONS.—See MANUAL for 1882, page 190.

MID KENT (BROMLEY TO ST. MARY CRAY).—By act of 7th August, 1862, this line was leased to the London, Chatham, and Dover for 999 years, at a rent equal to 4 per cent. on the share capital, and such interest as may be payable from time to time on the loan capital.

SEVENOAKS, MAIDSTONE, AND TUNBRIDGE.—Incorporated as the "Sevenoaks Railway Company," 1st August, 1859, to construct a line from Sutton-at-Hone, on the London, Chatham, and Dover, to Sevenoaks. By act of 21st July, 1879, this company became vested in the Chatham, as from 30th June, 1879. 152,000*l*. arbitration preference, 350,000*l*. arbitration ordinary, and 211,000*l*. "B" debenture stocks, respectively, of the latter company to be created and appropriated among the holders of the following Sevenoaks stocks, in such manner as the company may determine, or as may be provided by Parliament, viz., 126,046*l*. debentures and debenture stock, together with arrears of interest. 132,000*l*. preference shares; 120,000*l*. ordinary shares; 211,000*l*. Maidstone Extension 4½ per cent. guaranteed stock; and 100,000*l*. Maidstone Extension ordinary stock.—For further particulars respecting this company, see MANUAL for 1882, and previous editions.

SITTINGBOURNE AND SHEERNESS.—Incorporated 7th July, 1856, to construct a railway from Sittingbourne to Sheerness. Opened 19th July, 1860 (for other brief details, see MANUAL for 1882, and previously). Under an agreement dated the 30th May, 1866 (and confirmed by the Dover Company's act of that year), the line was vested in the London, Chatham, and Dover, as from the 19th July, 1865, for the clear yearly sum of 7,000*l*. The Dover Company to create 155,556*l*. of "Sheerness rent-charge 4½ per cent. stock," and issue the same for the purposes, and in the order of priority following:—In discharge of the landowners' claims, amounting to 17,156*l*.; in discharge of the mortgage debt of 39,000*l*.; in discharge of the company's costs and expenses subsequent to 1863; the surplus to be divided between the preferential shareholders and creditors other than mortgagees. The Dover Company also to create and issue to the ordinary shareholders of the Sheerness to the extent of 4,805*l.* fully paid 10*l.* shares, 50*l.* of Dover ordinary stock for every 100*l.* of Sheerness shares. By act of 13th July, 1876, provision was made for the dissolution of the company, the winding up of its affairs, the payment of their remaining debts, and the distribution of any surplus of assets.

SOUTH EASTERN.—The proportions of division of net profit under the recently proposed agreement for the fusion of the two companies were as follow:—

	To the London, Chatham, and Dover.	To the South Eastern.
1st year of fusion	31 per cent.	69 per cent.
2nd "	31½ "	68½ "
3rd "	32 "	68 "
4th "	32½ "	67½ "
5th and following years of fusion	33 "	67 "

The other heads of the arrangement will be found in the *Appendix* to the MANUAL for 1877. In conformity with the agreement, the necessary notices were given for the introduction of a bill before Parliament in the next session, but the Chatham proprietors, at their meeting in February, 1878, almost unanimously refused to approve the bill containing the proposed terms.

VICTORIA STATION.—An agreement has been made between the Victoria Station and Pimlico, the London, Chatham, and Dover, and the Great Western, for joint use of a certain portion of the Victoria Station, and of the Pimlico Railway, from 1st October, 1860, temporary station accommodation being provided at a reduced rate till 1862, when more permanent station buildings were provided. The cost of the accommodation works is limited to 105,000*l.* The rent for the station accommodation and use of the railway on the mixed gauge is to be 13,250*l.* for the first year, 18,000*l.* for the second year, and so on, increasing for about seven years, until the rent amounts to 32,000*l.* a year.

WEST END AND CRYSTAL PALACE.—An agreement has been entered into with this company. The following article occurs in this agreement:—"The said West End shall provide, or cause to be provided, for the East Kent, such accommodation for engines, carriages, and stores, as well as for goods, materials, and passenger traffic at the Battersea Station of the West End Company, as the said East Kent may require; the extent and nature of such accommodation, and the terms of payment in respect thereof, to be agreed upon between the companies, or in the event of difference to be settled by arbitration." By act of 23rd July, 1860, the Farnborough Branch of the Crystal Palace Line was transferred to the London, Chatham, and Dover, and an extension of time to the 8th August, 1862, conceded.

NEW LINES AND WORKS.—The Kearsney Loop Line, constructed under powers of act 1881, was opened on the 1st July, 1882, the extension into the town of Sheerness on 1st June, 1883, and the extension from Maidstone to Ashford on the 1st of July, 1884.

REVENUE.—For the half-years ended 31st December, 1883, and 30th June, 1884, this was as under:—

	31st Dec.	30th June.
Passengers, parcels, &c.	£467,937	£377,813
Goods, minerals, and cattle	135,515	116,385
Steamboats	63,323	54,012
Rents, tolls, and transfer fees	18,833	19,214
Gross receipts	£685,608	£567,424
Expenditure	338,127	325,176
Net	£347,481	£242,248
Add—Balance from previous account	305	45,838
Bankers' and other interest	*Dr.* 1,240	*Dr.* 1,587
Interest on Chatham Dockyard Extension outlay	1,088	1,088
Total net revenue	£347,634	£287,587
Deduct—Interest, guarantees, &c.	176,071	181,483
Available for preference dividend	£171,563	£106,104
Dividend on arbitration 4½ per cent. preference stock at 4½ and 3¾ per cent. per annum each half-year, payable 27th February and 15th August respectively	125,725	104,771
Balance to next half-year	£45,838	£1,333

Prior to the half-year ended 31st December, 1879, dividends under the arbitration award were distributed annually, but under the act of 1879 the company obtained powers to pay dividends half-yearly, commencing with those declared out of the earnings of that half-year.

CAPITAL.—*Authorised:* Stocks and shares, 18,192,363*l*.; loans, 8,115,696*l*.; total, 26,308,059*l*. *Created:* Stocks and shares, 17,499,713*l*.; loans, 7,885,696*l*.; total, 25,385,409*l*; balance, 922,650*l*. The subjoined statement of stock and share capital created shows the proportion received to 30th June, 1884:—

Description.	Created.	Received.	Unissued.
Sheerness rent-charge stock, 4½ per cent.......	£155,556	£151,556	£4,000
Arbitration preference stock, 4½ per cent. ...	5,587,774	5,587,774	...
Second preference stock, 4½ per cent.	633,332	292,260	341,072
Arbitration ordinary stock	11,123,051	11,123,051	...
	£17,499,713	£17,154,641	£345,072

NEW CAPITAL.—Under powers of the acts of 1881, the sum of 570,000*l*. was authorised to be raised by the issue of a new 4½ per cent. stock in July, 1882, for carrying out various extensions and improvements, including the New City and Suburban Traffic Station. This new capital is called "Second Preference 4½ per cent. Stock," ranking for dividend immediately before the ordinary stock. The price was 90 per cent., 50 per cent. of which was made payable on the 15th September, 1882, and the remainder on the 1st July, 1883. Of this about one-half was subscribed. A further sum has been issued at 70 per cent., and the remainder was offered on the 1st January, 1885, at 55 per cent.

The receipts and expenditure on this account to the same date were detailed as follow:—

Received.		*Expended.*	
Shares and stocks...............	£17,154,641	Lines open for traffic	£22,231,670
Loans	166,666	Lines in course of construction	610,096
Debenture stock	7,009,030	Working stock	1,345,327
Subscriptions by other railways..............................	416,000	Subscriptions to other railways	162,888
	£24,746,337	Docks, steamboats, and other special items	616,818
Balance	220,462		
	£24,966,799		£24,966,799

The estimate of further expenditure on capital account amounted to 1,752,263*l*., the capital powers and other available assets to meet which were set down as under:—

Balance of capital authorised by act of 1876	£33,513
Share and loan capital authorised but not yet created	922,650
Share capital created but not yet received	345,072
Debenture stock created but not yet received	710,000
Estimated value of surplus lands	13,750
	£2,024,985
Less balance at debit of capital account	220,462
Total available assets	£1,804,523

MILEAGE—30th June, 1884.—Lines owned, 166¾ miles; foreign lines worked over, 6¼ miles.

The accounts are made up to the 31st December and 30th June in each year, and the meetings held in London in February and August.

Scale of Voting.—Until the dividend on the arbitration preference stock has been paid in full for two consecutive years, one vote for each complete sum of 100*l*. arbitration debenture stock, 100*l*. arbitration preference stock, and 300*l*. arbitration ordinary stock; thenceforth until a dividend of not less than 2 per cent. per annum has been paid on the arbitration ordinary stock for two consecutive years, one vote for every 300*l*. of arbitration debenture stock, 100*l*. of arbitration preference stock, and 200*l*. of arbitration ordinary stock; thenceforth no vote for any sum of debenture stock, but one vote for every 100*l*. of either preference or ordinary stock.

Registration fee, 2*s*. 6*d*. each deed. Certificates of stock must accompany transfers. 1*l*. lowest sum transferable; several classes of stock may go on one transfer.

No. of Directors—8; quorum, 3. *Qualification*, 100*l*. arbitration debenture, 100*l*. arbitration preference, or 300*l*. arbitration ordinary stocks.

DIRECTORS:

Chairman—JAMES STAATS FORBES, Esq., 18, Chelsea Embankment, S.W.

Deputy-Chairman—Sir SYDNEY HEDLEY WATERLOW, Bart., M.P., 29, Chesham Place, Belgrave Square, W.

James Brand, Esq., 33, Old Broad Street, E.C.

George Wodehouse Currie, Esq., 23, Park Lane, W.

Major A. G. Dickson, M.P., Glemham Hall, Wickham Market, Suffolk, and Carlton Club, S.W.

Gen. Lord Alfred Paget, 56, Queen Anne Street, Cavendish Square, W.

Edward Leigh Pemberton, Esq., M.P., Torry Hill, Sittingbourne, Kent.

G. Cavendish Taylor, Esq., 42, Elvaston Place, South Kensington, W.

OFFICERS.—Sec., John Morgan; Man., Mortimer Harris; Continental Man., A. B. Godbold; Res. Eng., William Mills; Loco. Supt., William Kirtley; Supt. of Line, William Cockburn; Goods Man., C. H. Chapman; Marine Supt., Capt. Morgan, R.N.; Solicitor, John White; Auditors, S. B. Bristowe and R. Mackay.

Offices—Victoria Station, Pimlico, S.W.

170.—LONDON AND GREENWICH.

This line (3¾ miles) is leased to the South Eastern for 45,000*l.* per annum, on a rent-charge on the whole of the lines for 999 years. The guaranteed 5 per cent. interest is on 222,720*l.* capital, payable 1st April and 1st October. The ordinary dividends for the half-years ended 30th June, 1884, and 31st December, 1884, were at the rate of 1*l.* 7*s.* 6*d.* per cent. for each half-year, paid 15th January and 15th July following, clear of income tax.

Capital.—This account gives the subjoined particulars of income and expenditure:—

Received.		*Expended.*	
Shares and stock	£1,084,260	Land and compensation	£252,900
Loans	224,860	Buildings	570,138
Profit on investment account	70	Charges on capital	143,104
		Parliamentary expenses	10,520
	£1,309,190	Engineer	8,307
Balance	7,900	Surveyor	1,692
		Bonus	5,894
		Expenses of lease, proportion of	280
		Difference between nominal amount and price of issue of shares authorised by acts 1839 and 1840	324,260
	£1,317,090		£1,317,090

The share capital*, according to the company's reports, is as follows:—

20,000 shares of 20*l.* each (1832).
7,500 " " " (1837).
3,636 " " " (1839).
23,077 " " " (1840).

Qualification of Directors.—1,000*l.* ordinary or preference stock.

Scale of Voting.—10 shares, one vote; 20 shares, two votes; 35 shares, three votes; 50 shares and upwards, four votes.

Transfer fee, 2*s.* 6*d.* each seller. Ordinary and preference stock may be transferred together on the same deed. Parts of 1*l.* sterling are not allowed to be transferred. Certificates must accompany transfer deed. The books for ordinary stock close about ten days before each half-yearly meeting. The books for preference stock close about ten days before each payment of interest, which payments are made on the 1st April and 1st October in each year.

DIRECTORS:

Chairman—3 HENRY DRAYSON PILCHER, Esq., Morgan's Lane, Tooley Street, S.E.

Deputy-Chairman—2 WILLIAM KNOX WIGRAM, Esq., The Chesnuts, St. Margaret's, Twickenham.

4 William Henry Simpson, Esq., 16, Kent Terrace, Clarence Gate, N.W.

5 Edgar Horne, Esq., 46, Russell Square, W.C.

1 Thomas Eykyn, Esq., 51, Ladbroke Grove, W.

1, 2, 3, &c., order of retirement; all eligible for re-election.

---

* The shares have been converted into stock.

OFFICERS.—Sec., John William Brett; Auditors, Frederick Waddy, of the Great Eastern Railway, Liverpool Street, E.C., and John Theodore Prestige, New Cross, S.E.; Solicitors, Clarke, Rawlins, and Clarke, 66, Gresham House, E.C.

Offices—173, Gresham House, Old Broad Street, E.C.

171.—LONDON AND NORTH WESTERN

The company is formed out of the LONDON AND BIRMINGHAM, GRAND JUNCTION, and MANCHESTER AND BIRMINGHAM, by act of 16th July, 1846.

ADDITIONAL PARLIAMENTARY POWERS:—

A list of Acts obtained by this company from 1855 to 1879, with short heads of the objects for which the various powers were sought, will be found on reference to the MANUAL for 1881, pages 197 to 201.

1880—29TH JUNE.—Construction of Sutton Coldfield and Lichfield, &c. (see further on).

1880—6TH AUGUST.—Power to construct five new railways at Littleworth, West Leigh, Atherton, Bolton, and Bangor. Further joint powers in connection with the lessees of the North and South Western Junction, Great Western, Lancashire and Yorkshire, Manchester, Sheffield, and Lincolnshire, and Furness, in respect of other undertakings in which they are jointly interested; and for other purposes.

1881—3RD JUNE.—Joint powers with the Midland for the Market Harborough Line, and for sundry alterations and diversions in connection therewith. Period for completion of works, 4 years. New capital, 33,000*l*. Borrowing powers, 11,000*l*.

1882—3RD JULY.—New railway at Ordsall Lane Station to connect with the Manchester, South Junction, and Altrincham Line. New capital, 9,000*l*. Borrowing powers, 3,000*l*.

1882—12TH JULY.—Joint powers with the Lancashire and Yorkshire and Great Western for the construction of new lines and works, and other improvements, at various places; agreement with Midland respecting Rugby Station, &c.; and for other purposes. New capital, 700,000*l*. Borrowing powers, 233,000*l*.

1883—16TH JULY.—New railways at Soho, Handsworth, and Perry Barr, and widening from Golborne to Springs Branch; vesting of Lancashire Union (see further on). New capital, 900,000*l*.; borrowing powers, 200,000*l*.

1883—2ND AUGUST.—Widening of railways in Warwickshire, Lancashire, and Yorkshire; new works and additional lands. New capital, 1,000,000*l*.; borrowing powers, 333,000*l*.

1884—14TH JULY (PRESTON AND WYRE).—Widenings and improvements (jointly with Lancashire and Yorkshire). New capital, 81,000*l*.; loans, 27,000*l*.

1884—28TH JULY.—New railways at Nottingham and Edge Hill; widening of railway at Stockport; new works and additional lands; joint powers with the South Staffordshire, the Great Western, the Lancashire and Yorkshire, and the Manchester, Sheffield, and Lincolnshire, to construct new lines and additional works, and to acquire lands; vesting of Vale of Towy; extension of steam vessel powers to 31st December, 1899. New capital, 750,000*l*.; borrowing powers, 250,000*l*. Agreement with Lancashire and Yorkshire respecting North Union.

Railways amalgamated with the London and North Western (for terms and details other than those given below see MANUAL for 1884, and previous editions):—

Anglesea Central, 1876.
Bangor and Carnarvon, 1867.
Bedford and Cambridge, 1865.
Birmingham, Wolverhampton, and Stour Valley, 1867.
Blackpool and Lytham (jointly with Lancashire and Yorkshire), 1871.
Brynmawr and Blaenavon, 1869.
Buckinghamshire, 1879.
Cannock Chase, 1863.
Cannock Mineral, 1869.
Carnarvon and Llanberis, 1870.
Carnarvonshire, 1870.
Central Wales, 1868.
Central Wales Extension, 1868.
Chester and Holyhead, 1879.
Cockermouth and Workington, 1866.
Conway and Llanrwst, 1867.
Denbigh, Ruthin, and Corwen, 1879.
Hampstead Junction, 1867.
Huddersfield and Manchester Railway and Canal, 1847.
Kendal and Windermere, 1879.
Knighton, 1868.
Lancashire Union, 1883.
Lancaster and Carlisle, 1879.
Leeds, Dewsbury, and Manchester, 1847.
Merthyr, Tredegar, and Abergavenny, 1866.
Nerquis, 1868.
Newport Pagnell, 1875.

Preston and Longridge (jointly with Lancashire and Yorkshire), 1856.
St. George's Harbour, 1861.
St. Helens, 1864.
Shrewsbury and Welshpool (jointly with Great Western), 1865.
Sirhowy, 1876.
South Leicestershire, 1867.
South Staffordshire, 1867.
Stockport, Disley, and Whaley Bridge, 1866.
Swansea Lines, 1873.
Vale of Clwyd, 1867.
Vale of Towy, 1884.
Warrington and Stockport, 1867.
Watford and Rickmansworth, 1881.
Whitehaven, Cleator, and Egremont (jointly with Furness), 1878.
Whitehaven Junction, 1866.
Wrexham and Minera (jointly with Great Western), 1866.
West London, 1863.

The London and North Western has engagements with the following companies (for other particulars, see MANUAL for 1882, and previous editions):—

Cromford and High Peak.
Harborne.
Mold and Denbigh.
Shropshire Union.
Birmingham Canal.
Lancaster Canal.
Charnwood Forest.

Jointly with Great Western.

Birkenhead.
Clee Hill.
Shrewsbury and Hereford.
Tenbury.

Jointly with Lancashire and Yorkshire.

North Union.
Preston and Wyre.

Jointly with Midland and North London.

North and South Western Junction.

Jointly with Manchester, Sheffield, and Lincolnshire.

Oldham, Ashton, and Guide Bridge.

Jointly with Great Western, South Western, and London, Brighton, and South Coast.

West London Extension.

LANCASHIRE UNION.—Incorporated by act of 25th July, 1864. Length, 21 miles. Vested in the London and North Western by act of 16th July, 1883, as from 1st July, 1883, subject to the estate and interest which the Lancashire and Yorkshire have acquired in the vested undertaking, the shareholders of which to receive 137*l*. 10*s*. cash for every 100*l*. of ordinary capital.—For particulars prior to transfer, see MANUAL for 1883, page 160.

CONSOLIDATION OF STOCKS.—Under the powers of the act of 1877 the company's guaranteed and preference stocks were consolidated into two classes, viz., "4 per cent. consolidated guaranteed stock," and "4 per cent. consolidated preference stock." The consolidation was effected in December, 1878, and included all the 5 per cent. preference stocks, as well as the stocks of various amalgamated companies. Various stocks, including the Lancaster and Carlisle, were also converted, some into ordinary stock, and others into the above-named stocks. The details will, however, be found in the scheme which is fully given in the *Appendix* to the MANUAL for 1879.

NEW CAPITAL.—In May, 1880, the proprietary sanctioned the issue of new capital to the extent of 5,752,500*l*., of which 4,000,000*l*. was issued as ordinary stock, and allotted at par to the holders of existing ordinary stock, at the rate of about 12 per cent. upon their respective holdings, excluding fractions under 5*l*. The first instalment was made payable on the 1st July, 1880, and the remainder at 10 per cent. each on the 1st January and July respectively in each succeeding year, until the whole amount is paid up, proprietors having the option, on application to the secretary, of receiving fully paid up consolidated stock certificates for the amount of each instalment, as paid. It was then recommended that the balance of stock created (1,752,500*l*.) should be issued at some future time as a 4 per cent. preference stock, forming part of the existing consolidated preference stock of the company. 400,000*l*. of the latter-named stock was allotted to the proprietary in November, 1882, at the rate of 100*l*. of stock for 110*l*. of money. This issue completed the amount authorised as above.

ACCOUNTS:—

The half-yearly meeting of this company was held on the 16th August last, when the report and accounts then presented were adopted. The following is an abstract of those accounts for the half-year ended 30th June, 1884:—

CAPITAL.—*Authorised:* Stocks and shares, 79,876,426*l*.; loans, 27,547,280*l*.; total, 107,423,706*l*. *Created:* Stocks and shares, 75,948,233*l*.; loans, 25,736,133*l*.; total,

101,684,366*l*. The subjoined statement of stock and share capital created shows the proportion received to 30th June, 1884:—

* *Receipts.*		*Disbursements.*	
Consolidated stock (ordinary)	£34,339,613	Lines open for traffic	£78,485,253
Consolidated 4 per cent. stock (guaranteed)	11,776,120	Lines in course of construction	699,530
Consolidated 4 per cent. preference stock	18,961,496	Working stock	8,311,146
		Subscriptions to other lines...	3,359,151
		Steamboats	411,563
Total	£65,077,229	Leased lines (extra cost and debentures converted)	1,558,612
Loan capital, viz.:—			
Debentures £11,600		Total	£92,825,255
Debenture stock... 24,705,879	24,717,479	Balance	1,029,614
Total stock and loan capital (actual)	£89,794,708		
Premiums on issue of stocks and shares	4,060,161		
	£93,854,869		£93,854,869

* For full particulars of nominal additions to capital, amounting to 2,144,764*l*. on consolidated (ordinary), 3,324,286*l*. on guaranteed, and 4,119,124*l*. on consolidated preference stocks respectively, total 9,588,174*l*., under the recent Consolidation Scheme and previous amalgamations, see the extract from the company's report for the half-year ended 31st December, 1878, published for future reference in the *Appendix* to the MANUAL for 1880, page 536.

TABLE OF PRIORITIES, DESCRIPTIONS, DIVIDENDS, and other conditions of issue of the various Stocks of the company on 30th Sept., 1881 (see notes):—

No.	Year of Act.	FULL DESCRIPTION (to be observed in Transfer Deeds and all other Legal Documents).	Rate ℔ cent ℔ annum.
1	Various	Perpetual debenture stock	4
2	1877	Consolidated guaranteed stock	4
3	1877 & 79	Consolidated preference stock	...
4	Various	Consolidated stock	Varies

NOTES.—Nos. 2 and 3 stocks were issued for the consolidation of other stocks, which merged into those stocks under various schemes dated as follows:—General scheme, 15th July, 1878; Buckinghamshire, 19th July, 1878; Chester and Holyhead, 19th July, 1878; Lancaster and Carlisle, 12th December, 1878.

The dividends on Nos. 1 and 2 stocks are non-contingent and accumulative; on No. 3 the dividend is contingent upon the profits of each separate year; on No. 4 the dividend is contingent on the profits of each half-year; they are payable half-yearly as follow:—No. 1, 15th January and 15th July, all the remainder one or two days after the half-yearly meetings, held in February and August.

The transfer books close as follow:—Stocks No. 1 15 days before payment of dividend, remainder 28 days before the half-yearly meetings.

TRANSFER DEPARTMENT QUERIES AND REPLIES.

QUERIES.	REPLIES.
Transfer form—ordinary or special?	Ordinary.
Fee per deed?	2*s*. 6*d*.
Ditto if more sellers than one?	2*s*. 6*d*.
May several classes of stock be transferred on one deed?	Yes, except debenture stock, which should be by separate deed.
Are certificates required to accompany transfers?	Yes.
What amounts of stock are transferable, and are parts of 1*l*. sterling allowed to be transferred?	Any amount not containing the fraction of 1*l*.
To what officer should transfer communications be sent?	Secretary, Euston Station, London, N.W.
In acceptances, renunciations of allotments of new stock and proxies, what signatures are required?	In renunciations of allotments of new stock all the proprietors must sign, and in the case of proxies and acceptances of new stock the first-named in the account.

The estimate of further expenditure on capital account (as sanctioned by the proprietors) for the half-year ended 31st December, 1884, and in subsequent half-years, is given below:—

	Dec., 1884.	Subsequently.	Total.
Lines open for traffic	£400,000	£2,751,124	£3,151,124
Lines constructing	120,000	425,567	545,567
Steam boats	25,000	20,835	45,835
Subscriptions to other lines	5,000	15,715	20,715
Works in abeyance	5,000	527,813	532,813
Total as sanctioned	£555,000	£3,741,054	£4,296,054
Under estimate to be submitted	240,000	723,776	963,776
Total	£795,000	£4,464,830	£5,259,830

The capital powers and other available assets to meet this further outlay, and for the conversion of Shropshire Union and Lancashire Union stock (539,327*l.*), &c., amount to 7,644,292*l.*, leaving a balance of 1,845,135*l.*

Revenue.

Comparative statement of the amounts received on this account for the last three half-years:—

Receipts.	1883. June 30.	1883. Dec. 31.	1884. June 30.
Passengers, parcels, horses, mails, cars, &c.	£1,837,770	£2,186,048	£1,856,980
Merchandise (net), live stock, and minerals	3,083,688	3,185,309	2,982,442
Rents of land and buildings (net)	74,970	84,658	74,208
Transfer fees	724	638	756
Dividends on shares in other companies	79,995	73,984	72,454
	£5,077,147	£5,530,637	£4,986,840

Expenses.	1883. June 30.	1883. Dec. 31.	1884. June 30.
Maintenance of way, works, and stations	£405,365	£521,239	£407,086
Locomotive power	599,742	617,509	613,389
Carriage and wagon repairs	158,967	171,353	185,719
Mileage account with other companies	13,823	11,431	13,979
Traffic expenses	952,194	964,727	941,888
General charges	114,213	127,374	115,337
Law and Parliamentary	26,647	25,498	25,289
Compensation	27,297	40,320	30,857
Rates, taxes, and Government duty	171,258	181,727	132,715
Proportion of expenses of joint lines	40,971	48,240	42,239
Cost of working and depreciation of steamers	44,277	52,189	47,616
Canal expenses	5,018	5,984	5,050
	£2,559,772	£2,762,583	£2,561,164
Preference charges, viz.:—			
Interest on debentures and debenture stocks, chief rents, and general interest (net)	449,217	469,640	460,015
Rent and charges on leased lines and arrangements with other companies (net)	115,410	90,977	116,382
Dividends on guaranteed stock	302,008	302,008	302,008
Dividends on preference stock	461,612	461,612	461,612
	£3,888,019	£4,086,820	£3,901,181
Net balances each half-year	£1,189,128	£1,443,817	£1,085,659
Balances from previous half-years	72,794	27,228	43,790
Balances available for dividend on ordinary stock	£1,261,922	£1,471,045	£1,129,449
Dividends declared at 7, 8, and 7 per cent. per annum respectively	1,234,694	1,427,255	1,087,352
Surplus carried forward	£27,228	£43,790	£42,097

Summary showing the results of the last half-year's working of this line, as compared with that of the corresponding period of 1883:—

Net balance 30th June, 1884...	£1,085,659	Thus:—	
" 30th June, 1883...	1,189,128	Gross traffic—decrease	£90,307
		Add:—	
		Working charges—inc.... £1,392	
		Pref. charges—increase 11,770=	13,162
Loss in 1884	£103,469	Net loss in 1884	£103,469

MILEAGE.—The extent of the company's system at 30th June, 1884, is shown in the following table:—

	Miles Authorised.	Miles Constructed.	Miles worked by engines.
Lines owned by the company....................	1,570¼	1,528¾	1,528¼
Do. partly owned	80¾	79¾	152
Do. leased or rented	146½	142½	213¾
Total	1,797¼	1,751	1,889¼
Lines worked	30¾	30¾	33¾
Foreign lines worked over	...	...	562¾
Total	1,828¼	1,781¾	2,485¾

NEW WORKS, &c.—Engineer's report on progress of works, dated 6th August, 1884:—"At Willesden good progress is being made with the works for the Junction railway to connect the Kensington and Kew lines. Enlargement of Rugby Station; the earthwork and bridges are nearly complete, and progress is being made with the buildings and roofing. Portions of the new joint passenger station at Market Harboro' will be brought into use next month. The widening of the line from Leamington to Kenilworth, and the new railway from Kenilworth to Berkswell, were opened for passenger traffic on the 1st June last. The extension of New Street Station, Birmingham, will be ready for traffic by the end of the year. The Sutton Coldfield and Lichfield Railway will be ready for goods traffic next month. Portions of the new Exchange Station, Manchester, were brought into use on the 1st July; the remainder of the works will be ready for traffic at the end of the year. The two additional lines between Longsight and Heaton Norris, together with the new stations at Heaton Chapel, Levenshulme, and Longsight, were opened in April last. The two additional lines between Speke and Widnes and the new stations at Speke and Halebank, also the widening and deviation of the Bolton and Kenyon Railway, together with the stations at Chequerbent and Daub Hill, will be ready for traffic at the end of the year. The conversion of the tunnel into open cutting, and widening for two additional lines between Lime Street and Edge Hill Stations, are making rapid progress, and I expect that the whole of the works will be completed at the end of the year. Satisfactory progress is being made with the works of the West Leigh branches, in connection with the Bolton and Kenyon and Tyldesley and Wigan lines. On the new railway from Stalybridge to Saddleworth, the viaducts are built, and of the 627 yards of tunnel 500 yards are constructed. The widening of the two viaducts at Slaithwaite has been commenced, and the excavation and masonry for the Springwood and Huddersfield second tunnels are being proceeded with. Fair progress is now being made with the works for the new goods warehouse at Huddersfield Station. The two additional lines between Hill House and Heaton Lodge Junction are finished, and will be brought into use on the 18th instant. The Bangor and Bethesda Railway was opened for passenger traffic on the 1st July, and will be ready for goods traffic next month. About one-third of the work for the tidal dock and wharf at Deganwy is complete."

The accounts are made up to 30th June and 31st December, and the statutory meetings held in London in February and August.

Scale of Voting.—One vote for every 100*l.* stock up to 1,000*l.*; then one for every 500*l.* up to 10,000*l.*; above that, one vote additional for every 1,000*l.*

No. of Directors (consolidated by act, 1846)—30; of whom one is appointed by the Duke of Sutherland. *Qualification*, 1,000*l.* stock.

DIRECTORS:

Chairman—RICHARD MOON, Esq., Copsewood Grange, Coventry.

Deputy-Chairmen—{JOHN PARES BICKERSTETH, Esq., Grove Mill House, near Watford, Herts.
WILLIAM CAWKWELL, Esq., Fernacre, Maresfield Gardens, South Hampstead, N.W.}

James Bancroft, Esq., 83, Mosley Street, and Broughton Hall, Manchester.
John Bateson, Esq., Emsworth, Wavertree, Liverpool.
Ralph Brocklebank, Jun., Esq., Childwall Hall, Childwall, near Liverpool.
William Coare Brocklehurst, Esq., Butley, Prestbury, near Macclesfield, and 33, Milk Street, Cheapside, E.C.
Thomas Brooke, Esq., Armitage Bridge, near Huddersfield.
The Hon. Thomas Charles Bruce, M.P., 42, Hill Street, Berkeley Square, W.
George Crosfield, Esq., 109, Lancaster Gate, Hyde Park, W.
Richard Ryder Dean, Esq., 97, Gloucester Place, Portman Square, W.
Alfred Fletcher, Esq., Allerton, Woolton, Liverpool.
Henry Russell Greg, Esq., Lode Hill, Handforth, Manchester.
The Right Hon. Lord Richard Grosvenor, M.P., Assoc.Inst.C.E., 12, Upper Brook Street, W.
A. H. H. Hibbert, Esq., Munden, Watford, Herts.
Thomas H. Ismay, Esq., Dawpool, Thurstaston, *via* Birkenhead.
John Hick, Esq., M.Inst.C.E., Mytton Hall, near Whalley, Lancashire.
The Hon. C. N. Lawrence, 27, Clement's Lane, E.C.
The Hon. William Lowther, M.P., Lowther Lodge, Kensington Gore, S.W.
Miles MacInnes, Esq., Rickerby, Carlisle.
Rt. Hon. D. R. Plunket, M.P., 12, Mandeville Place, W., and 87, Merrion Square, Dublin.
The Most Honourable the Marquis of Stafford, M.P., Stafford House, St. James's, S.W.
Oscar Leslie Stephen, Esq., 55, Cadogan Square, S.W.
His Grace the Duke of Sutherland, K.G., Dunrobin Castle, Golspie, and Stafford House, St. James's, S.W.
Edmund Howard Sykes, Esq., Edgeley, near Stockport.
William Tipping, Esq., Brasted Park, Sevenoaks, Kent.
Henry Ward, Esq., Rodbaston, Penkridge, Stafford.
Francis S. P. Wolferstan, Esq., Statfold Hall, Tamworth.

OFFICERS.—Auditors: E. Lawrence and E. Waterhouse.—Secretary: Stephen Reay.—Solicitor: C.H.Mason.—General Manager: George Findlay, Assoc.Inst.C.E.—Mechanical Engineer: Francis W. Webb, M.Inst.C.E.—Marine Superintendent: Admiral Dent.—Civil Engineer: Francis Stevenson, M.Inst.C.E.—District Engineers: H. Woodhouse, Stafford; H. Footner, M.Inst.C.E., Crewe; W. Smith, M.Inst.C.E., Bangor; H. M. Bradford, Swansea; S. B. Worthington, M.Inst.C.E., Victoria Station, Manchester; and J. Kellett, Northampton.—Chief Goods Manager: T. Kay, Euston Station, N.W.—Superintendent of the Line: G. P. Neele, Euston Station, N.W.—Assistant Superintendent of the Line: F. Harrison, Euston.—Assistant Goods Manager: T. Houghton, Euston.—Out-door Goods Manager: W. Fewkes, Euston.—District Goods Managers: R. D. Sharpe, Rugby; J. Charnock, Wolverhampton; H. Sheppard, Crewe; S. Singer, Bristol; E. Braide, Warrington; D. Taylor, Waterloo Station, Liverpool; E. Farr, London Road Station, Manchester; G. Hitchens, New Station, Leeds; T. Henshaw, Chester; G. Greenish, Northampton; and W. Murfin, jun., Sheffield.—Goods Superintendents: W. J. Nichols, Birmingham; and W. Bingham, Nottingham.—Cattle Superintendent: F. W. Salmon, Edge Hill.—District Passenger Superintendents: E. M. G. Eddy, Euston; W. Sutton, New Street Station, Birmingham; J. Shaw, Lime Street Station, Liverpool; G. E. Mawby, London Road Station, Manchester; E. Wood, Chester; R. Purssell, Northampton.—District Traffic Superintendents: D. Stevenson, Broad Street Station, Eldon Street, E.C.; J. Entwistle, Shrewsbury; J. Bishop, Abergavenny; A. Entwistle, Bransty Station, Whitehaven; and H. Cattle, Castle Station, Lancaster.—District Traffic Manager: W. G. Skipworth, North Wall Station, Dublin.

Offices—Euston Station, Euston Square, N.W.

172.—LONDON AND SOUTH WESTERN.

Incorporated in 1834, under the title of the LONDON AND SOUTHAMPTON, which it retained until 1839. By act of 14th August, 1855, the whole of the company's acts were consolidated, and other powers conferred. It removed certain irregularities which had in the course of years grown up in the creation of a portion of the ordinary share capital, and settled its amount at 7,354,650*l.*, with borrowing powers at 2,400,416*l.*

FURTHER PARLIAMENTARY POWERS:—

For short heads of Acts from 1852 to 1879, see the MANUAL for 1881, pages 215 to 217.

1880—26TH AUGUST.—Further powers for the acquirement of lands, and construction of roads and other works in various places, arrangements for furure transfer of Mid Hants, management of Seaton and Beer, and consolidation of stocks, &c. New capital, 500,000*l*. Borrowing powers, 166,600*l*.

1881—22ND AUGUST.—New railways in the county of Surrey; extension of Lymington Branch; purchase or lease of Mid Hants undertaking. New capital irrespective of purchase of Mid Hants), 600,000*l*. Borrowing powers, 200,000*l*.

1882—10TH AUGUST.—Sale or lease of Plymouth and Dartmoor (see that company); sundry improvements in lines and works. New capital, 1,000,000*l*.; borrowing powers, 333,000*l*.

1883—20TH AUGUST.—Construction of new lines in Southampton and Dorset; widening of part of the Ringwood, Christchurch, and Bournemouth; and jointly with the Midland to construct the Corfe Mullen Junction Line (2¾ miles), county of Dorset. Period for completion, 5 years. New capital, 510,000*l*.; loans, &c., 170,000*l*.

1883—20TH AUGUST.—Construction of new lines and works in the counties of Southampton, Middlesex, and Surrey, and in connection with the North Cornwall; vesting of Salisbury and Dorset Junction, and lease of Southsea undertakings (see further on), and for various other purposes. New capital, 1,000,000*l*.; loans, &c., 333,000*l*.

1884—7TH AUGUST.—Widenings at Lambeth, Walton, and Winchester; junctions at Wimbledon; works at Bishopstoke, Basingstoke, and other places; traffic arrangements with Wimbledon and West Metropolitan Junction, and other purposes. New capital, 500,000*l*.; loans, 166,666*l*.

AMALGAMATIONS, LEASES, AGREEMENTS, &c.:—

ANDOVER AND REDBRIDGE.—Incorporated by act of 12th July, 1858, to construct a railway between Andover and Redbridge, and to convert the Andover Canal into a railway. Length, 22¼ miles. Purchase of canal, 12,500*l*. in money and 1,250 shares in railway. By act of 29th June, 1863, the Andover was amalgamated with the South Western, the latter taking up the debenture debt and other liabilities, and securing to the shareholders an annuity equal to 3 per cent.

BARNSTAPLE AND ILFRACOMBE.—Incorporated by act of 4th July, 1870, to construct a "light railway" from Barnstaple, on the South Western, to Ilfracombe. Length, 14¾ miles. Opened, 20th July, 1874. At first this line was leased to the London and South Western at 6,000*l*. per annum, which covered the debenture interest and gave 4½ per cent. on the share capital. It has now been formally transferred to the South Western, and its proprietors have become rent-charge stockholders in this company.

BIDEFORD EXTENSION.—Incorporated by act of 4th August, 1853, for a line from North Devon Terminus, at Fremington Pill, to Bideford. By an act of 1854, this undertaking was amalgamated with the South Western as from 1st January, 1855.—For other details, see previous editions.

BISHOP'S WALTHAM.—This line is worked by the London and South Western.

BODMIN AND WADEBRIDGE.—See GENERAL INDEX.

CHARD.—Incorporated by act of 25th May, 1860, to construct a line from the South Western Extension to the town of Chard, with tramroad to canal. Length, 3 miles. Amalgamated with South Western by act of 22nd June, 1863.

EPSOM AND LEATHERHEAD.—Incorporated by act of 14th July, 1856, to construct a line from Epsom, on the Brighton, to Leatherhead. The line was taken over and opened by the South Western on the 1st February, 1859. By act of 23rd July, 1860, the undertaking was transferred solely to the South Western, when it was agreed that the consideration to be given for the railway should be 44,444*l*. of the South Western 4½ per cent. guaranteed stock, giving an income equal to the rent of 2,000*l*. per annum. From this amount of stock the South Western was to deduct 10,000*l*., and take upon itself the debenture debt, amounting to 10,000*l*.

EXETER AND CREDITON.—Incorporated by act of 1st July, 1845, for construction of a line from Cowley Bridge Station of the Bristol and Exeter, and terminating by a junction with the North Devon, at Crediton. Length, 5¾ miles. A lease of this company to the South Western having expired on the 31st January, 1878, under which the company had been paying dividends on the ordinary capital ranging from 3 to 5 per cent. per annum, the South Western have purchased the undertaking under powers conferred upon them by act of 13th July, 1876, and the amalgamation was carried into effect in 1879.

EXETER AND EXMOUTH.—Incorporated by act of 22nd July, 1855, to construct a railway from the South Devon to Exmouth, with a branch to the Exeter Canal. By act of 5th July, 1865, the Exeter and Exmouth was amalgamated, as from 1st January, 1866, with the South Western, on the following terms:—The preference shareholders to accept and receive 4½ per cent. preference South Western stock to the amount of 27,000*l.* at par. The ordinary shareholders to accept and receive 4½ per cent. preference, or, at their option, ordinary South Western stock at par, in the proportion of 50*l.* for every 100*l.*, that is, 18,400*l.* for 36,800*l.*

HOLSWORTHY LINE (Okehampton to Holsworthy).—This is a single line worked under the absolute block system. It was opened for traffic on the 20th January, 1879, and has since been purchased by the South Western.

KINGSTON AND LONDON.—See GENERAL INDEX.

LYMINGTON.—Incorporated by act of 7th July, 1865, to make a railway from Lymington to the South Western, at Brockenhurst, with a landing-place at Lymington. Length, 4 miles. In 1878 this company became vested in the London and South Western. The terms of purchase are in brief—1. The adoption as at 1st July, 1878, of the debenture debt of the Lymington (7,000*l.*). 2. The issue to that company as of the same date—(*a*) 16,011*l.* 4 per cent. preferential stock of this company, in exchange for the Lymington preferential 5½ per cent. stock (11,860*l.*), thus providing to the holders nearly the same aggregate yearly income; and (*b*) 22,140*l.* 4 per cent. preference stock of this company in exchange for the Lymington ordinary shares to the same nominal amount. 3. The absolute transfer to this company of the Lymington undertaking.

MID HANTS.—Vested in London and South Western in 1884. For other particulars, see MANUAL for 1884, page 224.

NORTH CORNWALL.—See GENERAL INDEX.

NORTH DEVON.—Incorporated as TAW VALE, by act of 11th June, 1838, revived 21st July, 1845, for a line from Crediton (Exeter and Crediton) to Barnstaple, with a branch to the Docks at Fremington Pill, and effecting a junction across from the Bristol to the English Channel. At a special meeting on 30th July, 1862, the following terms of lease to the South Western, for 1,000 years, from 1st January, 1863, were agreed to:—The South Western to pay the interest on the North Devon debenture debt, and on the 6 per cent. redeemable preference stock and dividends on the original share capital as follows:—

For seven years, ordinary stock,	2 per cent.	and afterwards	2½ per cent.
" " "A" stock......	1 per cent.	in	1 per cent.
" " "B" stock......	4 per cent.	perpetuity,	5 per cent.

The sanction of South Western proprietors was given at the same time to an agreement, to be obtained at the option and expense of the South Western, for amalgamating the two companies on the following terms:—The debenture debt of the North Devon to become debenture debt of the South Western. The 6 per cent. preference stock to become preferential redeemable stock of the South Western. Ordinary stock of the South Western to be given in exchange for the North Devon stock in the following proportions, viz.:—

50*l.*	South Western stock	for every	100*l.*	North Devon	ordinary	stock.
20*l.*	ditto	ditto	100*l.*	ditto	"A"	stock.
100*l.*	ditto	ditto	100*l.*	ditto	"B"	stock.

This act was obtained in the session of 1864, to take effect from 1st January, 1865.

PETERSFIELD.—Incorporated by act of 23rd July, 1860, to construct a line from the Mid Sussex and Midhurst Junction, at Midhurst, to Petersfield, on the Direct Portsmouth. Length, 10¼ miles. Amalgamated with South Western by act of 22nd June, 1863.

PLYMOUTH AND DARTMOOR.—See GENERAL INDEX.

POOLE AND BOURNEMOUTH.—Incorporated by act of 26th May, 1865. Length, 4 miles. Now vested in the London and South Western.—For other particulars, see MANUAL for 1883, page 279.

PORTSMOUTH.—Incorporated by act of 8th July, 1853, for a line from Godalming Station to Havant, junction with the Brighton, and the Fareham Extension of the South Western, and direct to Portsmouth. By act of 21st July, 1859, the line and works were authorised to be leased to or amalgamated with the South Western, which was completed under the following arrangement:—"Debenture debt, 92,000*l*.; interest at 4¼ per cent. thereon will annually absorb 3,910*l*. of the 18,000*l*., and leave 14,090*l*. to be paid to the Portsmouth. The whole 18,000*l*. a year is divided into 144,000 annuities of 2*s*. 6*d*. per annum each. Of these, 31,280, amounting to 3,910*l*. per annum, is retained to cover debenture interest at the agreed rate; 87,500, amounting to 10,937*l*. 10*s*. per annum, have been issued to Portsmouth proprietors; that is to say, five (or 12*s*. 6*d*. per annum) in respect of each of these 17,500 shares of 20*l*. each, and the rest of the annuities (25,220), amounting to 3,152*l*. 10*s*. per annum (or at 25 years' purchase equal to 78,812*l*. in money), were retained by the South Western until all the liabilities of the Portsmouth had been satisfied."

Ringwood, Christchurch, and Bournemouth.—Amalgamated with the South Western from 1st January, 1874, on the following terms:—The South Western assumed the debenture debt of the Ringwood Company, not exceeding 25,000*l*.; also the nominal amount of ordinary stock of the Ringwood (75,000*l*.); the South Western giving in exchange a like nominal amount of its 5 per cent. preference stock, created for that purpose. The South Western further paid in cash the debt owing to the Ringwood Company's capital account (372*l*.), together with a further sum of 2,000*l*.

Ryde New Pier and Railway, and Portsmouth Steam Packet Service.—The Ryde New Pier and Railway was completed throughout and opened for traffic as a double line from the St. John's Road Station to the Pier Head on the 12th July, 1880. Joint arrangements with London, Brighton, and South Coast.

Salisbury and Dorset Junction.—Incorporated by act of 1861. Length, 18¾ miles. Vested in the London and South Western by act of 20th August, 1883, as from 1st January, 1883. Purchasing company's 4 per cent. debenture stock to be issued to holders of Salisbury "A" debenture stock at par; Purchasing company's 4 per cent. preference to be issued to holders of Salisbury stocks as follows:—"B" and "C" debenture exchanged at 117 per cent. (or ordinary L. & S. W. stock at 92 per cent., option to be exercised before 31st December, 1882). Preference stock exchanged at 111 per cent., ordinary stock exchanged at 65 per cent. (or ordinary L. & S. W. stock at 52½ per cent., or 70*l*. per cent. in cash, options to be exercised as above).—For particulars prior to transfer, see Manual for 1883, page 292.

Salisbury Market House Line.—This line has been worked by the South Western since its completion, and a renewal of the agreement has recently been approved.

Salisbury and Yeovil.—Incorporated by act of 1854, to construct a single line from the South Western, at Salisbury, to the Junction at Yeovil of the Great Western and Bristol and Exeter. Length of main line, 40 miles, and branch to join the Wilts, Somerset, and Weymouth, 3 furlongs. The line has since been doubled throughout its length. Other particulars appear in past editions of the Manual. By the London and South Western Act of 4th July, 1878, that company's act of 1858 was made applicable to the sale or transfer of the undertaking under the powers of the London and South Western Acts of 1865 and 1876. The following are the terms, viz.:—"1. The 4½ per cent. debenture stock of the Salisbury and Yeovil to become debenture stock of the South Western, bearing the same rate of interest, and the latter company to assume the debenture debt of the former as on and from the 1st of January, 1878. 2. The amount paid up on preference shares issued by the Salisbury and Yeovil to be exchanged for an equal nominal amount of 5 per cent. South Western preference stock to be created, the dividends thereon to accrue as from the 1st of January, 1878. 3. The amount paid up on ordinary shares of the company to be exchanged for 5 per. cent. South Western stock to be created, 260*l*. nominal amount of such stock being given in exchange for every 100*l*. nominal amount of this company's ordinary shares, and so in proportion for any lesser amount, with an option to the holders of such ordinary shares to be exercised at the time of exchange of taking South Western ordinary stock, either wholly or in part, at the same rate. Dividends on these respective stocks to accrue as from the 1st of January, 1878. 4. The debt on capital account as on the 31st December last to be agreed upon between the companies, and to be paid in cash by the South Western, together with a further sum of 4,500*l*. 5. The revenue balance as on 31st December, 1877, to belong to the Salisbury and Yeovil, out of which they will pay all liabilities and revenue account, inclusive of dividends and interest applicable to the half-year ended on that date. 6. The Salisbury and Yeovil to discharge its liabilities as soon as possible, and then to be wound up and cease to exist." The last half-yearly meeting was held on the 14th August, 1878.

SEATON AND BEER.—See GENERAL INDEX.

SIDMOUTH.—See GENERAL INDEX.

SOUTHAMPTON AND NETLEY.—Incorporated by act of 1st August, 1861, to construct a line from the South Western, near Southampton, to Netley. Amalgamated with South Western as from 1st January, 1865, by act of 14th July, 1864.

SOUTHSEA.—See GENERAL INDEX.

STAINES AND WOKINGHAM.—Incorporated by act of 8th July, 1853, for a line from Staines Junction, South Western Windsor Line, to Wokingham, junction with Reading, Guildford, and Reigate, and branch over Chobham, to the London and South Western Line at Woking. Length 22¾ miles. Capital, 300,000*l.* in 10*l.* shares and 90,000*l.* on loan. Opened for traffic, 4th June, 1856, as far as Ascot, and 9th July following to Reading. Particulars of subsequent acts and arrangements will be found on reference to the MANUAL for 1878, and previous editions. By the London and South Western Act of 4th July, 1878, the amalgamation of this undertaking with that company was authorised, the terms to be those adopted under an agreement dated 17th September, 1877, of which the following are the leading features, viz.:—"1. Existing lease to be cancelled as from 1st July, 1877, and new lease to be granted under the existing powers of the companies, and to endure until the completion of the purchase, which is to take place as from 1st July, 1878, or so soon thereafter as it shall be authorised by Parliament. 2. Rent, until 1st July, 1878, to be the same as now payable under the existing lease, and, after that day, during the continuance of the lease, to be the same as will be the aggregate of the dividend on the preferential stock agreed to be issued to the Staines and Wokingham proprietors on the completion of the purchase, and of the interest of the debenture debt of that company. 3. The consideration for the purchase to be 445,150*l.* in 4 per cent. preferential stock of this company, and the adoption of the Staines and Wokingham Company's debenture debt of 89,995*l.*, and of certain (comparatively trifling) liabilities of that company." The sale or transfer to be effected on the terms of giving to the proprietors 150*l.* South Western 4 per cent. perpetual preference stock for every five ordinary 20*l.* shares of the Staines and Woking, and 125*l.* of the same stock for every five 20*l.* preference shares of the Staines and Woking. All expenses incurred in the transfer and act of Parliament to be borne by the South Western. The fifty-first, and presumably the last, half-yearly meeting was held on the 9th August, 1878, when a dividend of 6 per cent. per annum was declared, and a balance of 334*l.* was retained by the directors to meet expenses and contingencies in finally winding up the affairs of the company.

STOKES BAY RAILWAY AND PIER.—The undertaking was purchased in 1875, and is now the absolute property of the London and South Western.

SWANAGE.—See GENERAL INDEX.

TOOTING, MERTON, AND WIMBLEDON.—Incorporated by act of 29th July, 1864, for lines from Wimbledon, *via* Tooting and Merton, to join the Brighton at Streatham. Length, 6 miles. By act of 5th July, 1865, this undertaking was vested jointly in the Brighton and South Western, and a further junction of half a mile authorised. New capital 52,500*l.* in shares and 17,000*l.* on loan, to absorb amounts named in the first act.

WEST LONDON EXTENSION.—For the London and South Western interest in this company, see West London Extension.

WIMBLEDON AND DORKING.—Incorporated by act of 27th July, 1857, to construct a line from the South Western, at Wimbledon, to Epsom. Length, 5¾ miles. By 25 Vic., cap. 42, the undertaking was transferred to the South Western, which allotted 4½ per cent. stock to yield 4 per cent. in perpetuity on this company's shares, upon receiving, in cash, the difference between 3½ and 4 per cent. for four years upon the capital.

CONSOLIDATION OF DEBENTURE STOCKS.—The consolidation into one 4 per cent. stock, to be called "New Consolidated Debenture 'B' Stock," of all the company's several debenture stocks (except the "A" debenture stock) was effected on the 1st July, 1878, under the powers of the company's act of 1877. The exchange having been made rateably in proportion to the interest previously received, the annual income of the holders thus remained the same as before the consolidation.

CONSOLIDATION OF GUARANTEED AND PREFERENCE STOCKS.—The scheme for the conversion and consolidation of the above-named stocks, which was issued to the proprietary interested by the directors in November 1880, will be found inserted for future reference in the *Appendix* to the Volume for 1881.

ACCOUNTS:—

REVENUE.—This account for the half-years ended 31st December, 1883, and 30th June, 1884, gave the following particulars:—

	Dec., 1883.	June, 1884.
Coaching traffic	£1,013,220	£896,276
Goods, minerals, and cattle	459,718	429,888
Steamboats—Net receipts	37,184	11,785
Rents, transfer fees, tolls, &c.	29,860	33,076
Gross receipts	£1,539,982	£1,371,025
Expenditure	843,555	798,013
Net...	£696,427	£573,012
Add—Balance brought forward	14,254	13,459
Dividend on shares held	1,637	1,557
Total net revenue	£712,318	£588,028
Less—Interest, rents, preference dividends, &c.	356,458	366,614
Available for ordinary stock	£355,860	£221,414
Dividends at 7 and 4½ per cent. per annum respectively	342,401	207,900
Balance to next half-year	£13,459	£13,514

CAPITAL.—*Authorised:* Shares and stock, 22,820,478*l.*; loans, 8,093,619*l.*; total, 30,914,097*l.* *Created or sanctioned:* Shares and stock, 21,820,478*l.*; loans, 6,935,953*l.*; total, 28,756,431*l.* The statement of stock and share capital, showing the proportion received to 30th June, 1884, furnished the subjoined particulars:—

Description.	Created.	Received.
4 per cent. consolidated guaranteed stock	£797,981	£652,349
4 per cent. consolidated preference stock	8,845,136	7,894,033
4 per cent. perpetual preference stock, 1884	600,000	300,000
Consolidated ordinary stock	11,577,361	10,437,442
Total	£21,820,478	£19,283,824

Nominal additions, 1,096,574*l*; amount uncalled, 346,089*l*; amount unissued, 1,093,991*l.*

NOTES.—The above is the order of priority and true descriptions of the company's existing stocks, other than debenture stocks; they rank for dividends immediately after consolidated debenture stock "B" (5,146,490*l.*), which follows the perpetual debenture stock "A" (1,000,000*l.*)

Dividends on all the company's stocks are payable half-yearly as follow:—On debenture stocks "A" and "B" 10th January and 10th July, on guaranteed, preference, and ordinary stocks, about the 20th February and August.

Transfer books for all stocks close about three weeks before the dates appointed for the payment of the dividends.

TRANSFER DEPARTMENT QUERIES AND REPLIES.

QUERIES.	REPLIES.
Transfer form—ordinary or special?	Ordinary.
Fee per deed?	2*s.* 6*d.*
Ditto if more sellers than one?	2*s.* 6*d.* each sale.
May several classes of stock be transferred on one deed?	Consolidated (ordinary), preferential, and guaranteed may be transferred on one deed.
Are certificates required to accompany transfers?	Yes.
What amounts of stock are transferable, and are parts of 1*l.* sterling allowed to be transferred?	10*l.* and upwards, not fractional parts of 1*l.*
To what officer should transfer communications be sent?	Treasurer.
In acceptances, renunciations, &c., of allotments of new stock, proxies, or other forms sent to trustees, what signatures are required?	Registered proprietors.

The receipts and expenditure on this account to 30th June, 1884, were detailed as under:—

Received.		*Expended.*	
Shares and stock	£19,282,823	Lines open for traffic	£21,608,949
Loans	166,300	Lines constructing	615,523
Debenture stock	6,608,658	Working stock	2,992,444
	£26,058,781	Subscriptions to other companies	420,228
Deduct discount, less premium on stock and shares	88,796	Steamboats	290,271
		Dock telegraph block system, and other special items	126,145
			£26,053,560
		Balance	94,017
	£26,147,577		£26,147,577

The estimate of further expenditure on capital account required for the half-year ended 31st December, 1884, 649,160*l.*, and for subsequent half-years, nil. The capital powers and other assets were given as follow:—Share and loan capital authorised or created but not yet received, 3,691,769*l.*; less sundries not yet allocated, 5,233*l.*: total, 3,686,536*l.*

MILEAGE.—In operation, lines owned, 679½; partly owned, 26½; leased or rented, 29½; total, 735. Foreign lines worked over, 64¼.

The accounts are made up to 30th June and 31st December, and the statutory meetings held in August and February in every year.

Scale of Voting.—One vote for every 50*l.* of stock up to 500*l.*; one additional vote for every 250*l.* of stock above 500*l.* up to 5,000*l.*; and one additional vote for every additional sum of 500*l.* above 5,000*l.*

No. of Directors—12. *Qualification*, 3,000*l.* of ordinary stock.

DIRECTORS:

Chairman—The Hon. RALPH HENEAGE DUTTON, 16, Halkin Street West, Belgrave Square, S.W., and Timsbury Manor, Romsey, Hants.

Deputy-Chairman—WYNDHAM SPENCER PORTAL, Esq., Malshanger, Basingstoke.

W. W. B. Beach, Esq., M.P., Oakley Hall, Basingstoke, Hants.

Lieut.-Colonel The Hon. Henry Walter Campbell, 44, Charles Street, Berkeley Square, W.

A. F. Govett, Esq., Sandylands, Virginia Water, and 18, Albert Hall Mansions, S.W.

Arthur E. Guest, Esq., 33, Half Moon Street, Piccadilly, W.

Captain James Gilbert Johnston, 39, Hyde Park Square, W.

Lieut.-General F. Marshall, Broadwater, Godalming, and 9, Eaton Place, S.W.

A. Mills, Esq., Bude Haven, Cornwall, and 34, Hyde Park Gardens, W.

Charles Smith Mortimer, Esq., Wigmore, near Holmwood, Surrey.

William Philip Snell, Esq., Belmont, Havant, Hants.

OFFICERS.—Sec., F. J. Macaulay; Gen. Man., Archibald Scott; Chief Res. Eng., William Jacomb; Loco. and Car. Supt., W. Adams; Traffic Supt., E. W. Verrinder; Goods Man., J. T. Haddow; Treasurer, C. Harvey; Auditors, James Dickson, Larchmoor, Slough, Bucks., and Peter Henry Rooke, 2, New Square, Lincoln's Inn, W.C.; Solicitors, Bircham & Co., Parliament Street, S.W., and Waterloo Station.

Head Offices—Waterloo Station, S.E.

173.—LONDON, HENDON, AND HARROW.

Incorporated by act of 20th August, 1883, for the construction of railways from Hornsey to Hendon and Harrow. Length, about 10 miles. Period for completion, 5 years. Capital, 300,000*l.* in 10*l.* shares, with power to divide into "preferred" and "deferred" half-shares; loans, 100,000*l.*

No. of Directors.—Maximum, 5; minimum, 3; quorum, 3 and 2. *Qualification*, 50 shares.

FIRST DIRECTORS:

Admiral Sir George Elliot, K.C.B.

Daniel Bayley, Esq.

Richard Jonathan Jenkins, Esq.

Charles Hodgson, Esq.

One other to be nominated.

174.—LONDON, TILBURY, AND SOUTHEND.

This line was originally authorised, by the act of 1852, to be constructed by the Eastern Counties and Blackwall companies jointly, from Forest Gate Junction to Tilbury Fort (opposite Gravesend) and Southend, with the right to convey passengers in steamboats across the river at Gravesend to and from the trains. Capital, 400,000*l.*; borrowing powers, 100,000*l.* By the same act the companies were authorised to raise separate capital for this purpose. A contract was entered into with Messrs. Peto, Brassey, and Betts, under which they agreed to construct the line, and take a lease thereof for 21 years, from 3rd July, 1854, guaranteeing a net rent equal to 6 per cent. on the share capital and half surplus profits earned beyond that guarantee and the payment of the interest for the time being on the debenture capital. Since the expiration of this lease in 1875, the company have worked the line, and have provided locomotive and carriage stock.

For short heads of Acts from 1854 to 1875, see the MANUAL for 1881, page 224.

By act of 19th July, 1880, the company was authorised to improve and extend the West Street Pier at Gravesend, and to construct a wharf at Thames Haven.

By act of 24th July, 1882, the provisions of the act of 1862, empowering the Great Eastern and London and Blackwall to appoint two-thirds of the directors, were repealed, and the number of directors limited to not less than five nor more than seven, all of whom must be shareholders, and be elected by the proprietors in the usual way. Directors' qualification, 1,000*l.* stock. The new board was elected on the 1st August, 1882.

By the said act the company was empowered to construct three new railways, to be named as follow:—No. 1, Barking and Pitsea (19¾ miles); No. 2, Shoeburyness Extension (3¾ miles); No. 3, Whitechapel Goods Branch (½ mile). Period for completion, five years. New capital, 600,000*l.*; borrowing powers, 200,000*l.*

1883—20TH AUGUST.—Construction of railways at Upminster, Grays Thurrock, Romford, East Ham, and Little Ilford. Length, about 9¾ miles. Period for completion, 5 years. Facilities to Great Eastern. New capital, 180,000*l.*; loans, &c., 60,000*l.* Conversion of 4½ per cent. debenture stock into 4 per cent. stock.

1884—14TH JULY.—Purchase of lands, and other purposes. New capital, 150,000*l.*; loans, 50,000*l.*

REVENUE.—The gross receipts for the half-year ended 31st December, 1883, amounted to 80,554*l.*, and the expenditure to 39,206*l.*, giving, with 497*l.* balance from last half-year, and 1,102*l.* bankers' and general interest, a total net revenue of 42,947*l.*, which was appropriated as follows:—Interest on debenture stock and rent of Fenchurch Street Station, 7,208*l.*; placed to insurance and reserve fund, 1,500*l.*; balance, 34,239*l.*, of which sum the dividend on the preference stock at 4½ per cent., and a dividend on the consolidated stock at the rate of 8½ per cent. per annum, absorbed 33,637*l.*, leaving 602*l.* to be carried forward to next half-year.

The gross receipts for the half-year ended 30th June, 1884, amounted to 63,512*l.*, and the expenditure to 37,284*l.*, giving, with 602*l.* balance from last half-year, a total net revenue of 26,830*l.*, which was appropriated as follows:—Interest on debenture stock and rent of Fenchurch Street Station, 8,840*l.*; insurance and reserve fund, 1,000*l.*, bankers' and general interest, 199*l.*; redemption of Thames Haven lease account, 400*l.*; dividend on preference stock, 289*l.*; a dividend on the ordinary stock at the rate of 3¾ per cent. per annum amounting to 13,985*l.*, and 441*l.* for interest on the new ordinary stock, 1884, leaving 1,676*l.* to be carried forward.

In operation, 49 miles 10 chains.

The Shoeburyness Extension was opened 1st February, 1884.

CAPITAL.—The expenditure on this account to 30th June, 1884, amounted to 1,645,181*l.*, whilst the receipts to the same date had been as under:—

Ordinary stock	£799,128	
4½ per cent. convertible preference stock (see below)	12,850	
Debenture stock at 4 per cent. (see below)	371,345	
Consolidated ordinary stock, 1883	252,032	
Consolidated ordinary stock, 1884	65,618	
Premium on stock sold	62,123	=£1,563,096

NEW CAPITAL.—In February, 1879, 65,000*l.* of 4½ per cent. convertible preference stock was created. In February, 1881, 85,000*l.* additional capital was created, and 60,590*l.* issued as consolidated stock, 60,430*l.* at 10 per cent., and 160*l.* at 17 per cent. premium. In February, 1883, 300,000*l.* consolidated ordinary stock was created and issued to the proprietors of ordinary and preference stocks in the proportion of 38 per cent. of their holdings, and at the price of 126*l.* for each 100*l.* stock. The dividend on the stock will commence to accrue from the 1st January, 1886. 25 per cent. of the amount allotted and 25 per cent. of the premium was payable on the 1st March, 1883, and the balance was made payable by three equal instalments of 25 per cent. on the amount allotted, together with 25 per cent. of the premium, on the 2nd July, 1883, 1st January, 1884, and 1st July, 1884. In March, 1884, 220,000*l.* consolidated ordinary stock was created and issued to the proprietors of ordinary and preference stocks, in the proportion of 20 per cent. of their holdings, and at the price of 120*l.* for each 100*l.* stock. 25 per cent. of the amount allotted, and the whole of the premium (making 45 per cent. in all), was payable on the 15th April, 1884, and the balance was made payable by three equal instalments of 25*l.* per cent. of the amount allotted on the following dates, viz.:—1st July, 1st October, 1884, and 1st January, 1885. The stock will bear interest at the rate of 4 per cent. per annum on the amount paid up from time to time (exclusive of the premium), and from the date when it will be paid in full, viz., 1st January 1885, it will rank for dividend with the ordinary stock.

NOTES.—The dividend on the preference stock is contingent upon the profits of each separate year; the dividends upon that stock and the consolidated stock are payable half-yearly, in January and July.

The last two half-yearly dividends were made payable on the 30th January and 30th July, 1884, respectively.

DEBENTURE STOCK.—Under the provisions of the London, Tilbury, and Southend Railway Act, 1883, the 240,000*l.* 4½ per cent. debenture stock was on the 1st March, 1884, converted at the rate of 106*l.* 5*s.* per cent., and increased to 255,000*l.* 4 per cent. stock, since which date 116,345*l.* stock has been issued. The interest is payable half-yearly, on the 1st January and 1st July.

The transfer books close as follows:—For debenture stock 14 days, and the other stocks about 10 days before payment of the dividends respectively.

The preference stock is convertible on any 1st January or 1st July, up to 1st January, 1890, at the option of the holders, into consolidated stock at par, on their giving one month's previous notice to the company.

TRANSFER DEPARTMENT QUERIES AND REPLIES.

QUERIES.	REPLIES
Transfer form—ordinary or special?	Ordinary.
Fee per deed?	2*s.* 6*d.*
Ditto if more sellers than one?	2*s.* 6*d.* each seller, except in case of joint holdings, which are regarded as one transfer.
May several classes of stock be transferred on one deed?	Yes, consolidated and preference.
Are certificates required to accompany transfer?	Yes.
What amounts of stock are transferable, and are parts of 1*l.* sterling allowed to be transferred?	Ordinary and preference stocks, 10*l.*, and multiples of 10*l.* Debenture stock, 1*l.*
To what officer should transfer communications be sent?	Secretary.
In acceptances, renunciations, &c., of allotments of new stock, proxies, or other forms sent to trustees and other joint holders, what signatures are required?	In renunciations of allotments of new stock all the proprietors must sign, and in the case of proxies and acceptances of new stock the first-named in the account.

The estimate of further expenditure required is 135,000*l.* during the half-year ended 31st December, 1884.

The accounts are made up to 30th June and 31st December in each year, and the statutory meetings are held in January and July.

No. of Directors.—Maximum, 7; minimum, 5. *Qualification*, 1,000*l.* stock.

DIRECTORS:

Chairman—HENRY DOUGHTY BROWNE, Esq., West Lodge, 34, Avenue Road, Regent's Park, N.W.

Deputy-Chairman—THOMAS WRAKE RATCLIFF, Esq., 22, Albert Road, Regent's Park, N.W.

Charles Bischoff, Esq., 23, Westbourne Square, W.

William Ford, Esq., 46, Kensington Park Road, Notting Hill, W.

Henry Oxenham, Esq., 4, Chester Terrace, Regent's Park, N.W.

James Hall Renton, Esq., 39, Park Lane, W., and 9, Drapers' Gardens, E.C.

John Turner, Esq., Prospect House, Windmill Lane, Cheshunt, Herts.

OFFICERS.—Sec., H. Cecil Newton; Eng. and Man., Arthur L. Stride; Loco. Supt., Thomas Whitelegg; Auditors, Thomas Adams and John Jackson Gosset; Solicitors, F. C. Mathews and Browne, 151, Cannon Street, E.C.

Offices—Fenchurch Street Terminus, E.C.

175.—LONDONDERRY AND LOUGH SWILLY.

Incorporated by act of 1853, and revised by act of 1st August, 1859, to construct a line from the western shore of Lough Foyle to Carrowan, in the county of Donegal. Length, 14½ miles. Capital, 40,000*l.* in 10*l.* shares and 13,300*l.* on loan.

By act of 22nd July, 1861, the company was authorised to extend the line to Buncrana. Length, 6½ miles. Capital, 20,000*l.* in shares and 6,600*l.* on loan. Arrangements with the Letterkenny and the Finn Valley.

By act of 25th July, 1864, the company was authorised to extend the line towards Londonderry. Length, 5 chains. New capital, 20,000*l.* in shares and 6,600*l.* on loan.

By the Letterkenny Act of 1880, powers were obtained for working agreements with that company.

By act of 3rd July, 1882, the company was empowered to purchase additional lands, to create debenture stock, to raise 50,000*l.* additional capital in preference stock, and to enter into certain working agreements with the Harbour Commissioners.

Letterkenny.—Now worked by this company.

Capital.—The amount expended on this account, from time to time, reaches over 102,000*l.*

Meetings held at Londonderry in February and August.

DIRECTORS:

Chairman—JAMES THOMPSON MACKY, Esq., J.P., Belmont, Londonderry.

Joseph Cooke, Esq., Boomhall, Londonderry.
Alexander Black, Esq., J.P., Strand, Londonderry.
Henry Lecky, Esq., J.P., Londonderry.
David M. Colquhoun, Esq., Fahan.
B. McCorkell, Esq., J.P., Richmond, Londonderry, and Glenburnie, Moville.
David Gillies, Esq., Londonderry.
Thomas Colquhoun, Esq., J.P., Rockfort, Buncrana.
John M'Farland, Esq., Belfast and Londonderry.

OFFICERS.—Sec. and Gen. Man., Frederick Dawson; Eng., C. E. Stewart; Auditors, G. H. Mitchell, St. Helens, Buncrana, and Richard Waller, Londonderry; Solicitor, Alfred M. Munn, Londonderry.

Offices—Londonderry.

176.—LONGTON, ADDERLEY GREEN, AND BUCKNALL.

Incorporated by act of 1866, for making a line from the Uttoxeter Line of the North Staffordshire, at Longton, to the Biddulph Valley Line of the same company, at Bucknall, with two short branches. Capital, 50,000*l.* in shares of 10*l.* each, with power to borrow 16,000*l.* The North Staffordshire to maintain and work the line, furnishing all plant and stock at the same rate of working expenses as their own.

By act of 1872 the time for completion of works was extended to 1875, and one of the branch lines was authorised to be abandoned.

The line was opened for mineral traffic in September, 1875.

Capital.—The receipts on this account to 31st December, 1878, amounted to 62,037*l.*, of which 46,037*l.* was by shares and 16,000*l.* on loan. The expenditure to the same date amounted to 63,172*l.*, leaving a balance of 1,135*l.* against the account.

DIRECTORS:

Chairman—JOSEPH HULSE, Esq., Dresden, Stoke-on-Trent.

Frederic Bishop, Esq., The Laurels, Redhill, Surrey.
John Hackett Goddard, Esq., Longton, Stoke-on-Trent.
John Walker, Esq., Longton, Stoke-on-Trent.

OFFICERS.—Sec., Matthew Follitt Blakiston, Stafford; Eng., Charles J. Homer, Ivy House, Stoke-on-Trent; Auditors, John Wade and John Newton; Solicitors, Hand, Blakiston, Everett, and Hand, Stafford; Bankers, Lloyds, Barnetts, and Bosanquet's Bank Limited, Longton Branch.

Offices—Stafford.

177.—LOUTH AND EAST COAST.

Incorporated by act of 18th July, 1872, to construct several single lines in Lincolnshire (in all about 17 miles in length), the first (12 miles) commencing by a junction with the East Lincolnshire Branch of the Great Northern, at Louth, and terminating at Mablethorpe (post town and bathing place); the second (2¼ miles) by a junction with No. 1, and terminating in the parish of Skidbrook-cum-Saltfleet; the third (2¼ miles) following the termination of No. 2 to North Somercotes; and the fourth (3¼ furlongs) commencing at Skidbrook-cum-Saltfleet, and terminating at Saltfleet Haven. Capital, 96,000*l*. in 10*l*. shares and 32,000*l*. on loan or by debenture stock. Agreement with Great Northern to work the line at 50 per cent. of the gross receipts.

By act of 17th May, 1877, authority was obtained to construct a railway, 2 miles 5 furlongs 9·30 chains, commencing in the parish of Skidbrook-cum-Saltfleet, and terminating in the parish of North Somercotes; to purchase additional lands; to extend the time for completion to 17th May, 1881; to abandon certain portions of Railway No. 2 and the Railway No. 3; and to raise additional capital, viz.:—Shares or stock, 48,000*l*.; loans, 16,000*l*.

The main line was opened from Louth to Mablethorpe (which is stated to be gradually improving as a favourite bathing place), October, 1877. Length, 12 miles.

In March, 1881, the directors made the following statement, when inviting subscriptions for the "A" debenture stock of the company, viz.:—"The directors, acting under the powers of the company's scheme of arrangement, have been for some time past endeavouring to dispose of the 43,000*l*. 4 per cent. "A" debenture stock, thereby authorised to enable them to discharge the 32 000*l*. 5 per cent. mortgage debentures, the principal of which became due on the 8th December last, and for the other purposes mentioned in the scheme, but as yet they have only been able to place the sum of 7,463*l*. 9*s*., as will be seen by the accounts. When those debentures have been paid off, the "A" debenture stock will constitute a first charge on the undertaking of the company. The accounts show that even in these times of agricultural depression the company's income is considerably more than sufficient to pay all the interest in full on that stock. The fact that the line is now in the hands of a receiver (Mr. Cartwright, the chairman of the company) affords a guarantee that the whole of the company's income, by law applicable to the payment of such interest, will be strictly so applied."

NOTE.—Since the above, the company have placed all but about 5,000*l*. of the 43,000*l*. "A" debenture.

Meetings held in Louth in February or March and August or September.

No. of Directors—6; quorum 3. *Qualification*, 20 shares.

DIRECTORS:

Charles Aldin, Esq., 39A, Queen's Gate Gardens, South Kensington, S.W.
J. W. Batten, Esq., 15, Airlie Gardens, Campden Hill, W.
William Robert Emeris, Esq., J.P., Louth.
John Hay, Esq., Louth.
Charles Goodwin Smith, Esq., Louth.

OFFICERS.—Sec., James William Wilson, Louth; Eng., William Shelford, 35A, Great George Street, Westminster, S.W.; Auditors, Charles Wilson and William Walker; Solicitors, Wilson and Son, Louth; Bankers, Garfit, Claypon, Garfits, and Ingoldby, Louth.

Offices--Westgate Place, Louth.

178.—LUDLOW AND CLEE HILL.

Incorporated by act of 22nd July, 1861, to construct a line from Ludlow, on the Shrewsbury and Hereford, to Clee Hill. Length, about 6 miles. Capital, 30,000*l*. in 10*l*. shares; loans, 10,000*l*. Powers for Shrewsbury and Hereford to subscribe 5,000*l*. The line is now worked by the Great Western and London and North Western for 30 years as from the 1st June, 1867, for the first two years for 90 per cent., for the second two years for 80 per cent., for the remaining years for 70 per cent. of the gross receipts from traffic, with option of purchase, on terms to be fixed in case of difference by arbitration.

No report is issued. The Clee Hill Company simply take 40 per cent. of the receipts, which for the two last half years amounted to 4,790*l*.

Meetings in February or March and in August or September.

No. of Directors—6; minimum, 3; quorum, 3. *Qualification*, 200*l*.

DIRECTORS:

Chairman—Sir CHARLES H. ROUSE BOUGHTON, Bart., Downton Hall, Ludlow.

Andrew Johnes Rouse Boughton Knight, Esq., Downton Castle, Ludlow.

William Thomas Carlisle, Esq., 8, New Square, Lincoln's Inn, W.C.

OFFICERS.—Sec., W. Patchett; Auditors, Mr. Bell and Mr. Eberall, Shrewsbury; Solicitor, John Ordell, 8, New Square, Lincoln's Inn, W.C.

Offices—Shrewsbury.

179.—LYDD.

Incorporated by act of 8th April, 1881, for the construction and maintenance of a railway from Appledore to Lydd, in the county of Kent. Length, 10 miles. Period for construction, 5 years. Working arrangements with the South Eastern. Capital, 75,000*l.*, in 10*l.* shares. Borrowing powers, 25,000*l.* The railway was completed and opened on 5th December, 1881. The South Eastern guarantee a dividend of 4½ per cent. upon the ordinary and debenture capital, all of which is issued.

By act passed 24th July, 1882, power was given to extend the line northward from Appledore to Headcorn (15 miles), and to make a lopp line (3 miles) into New Romney. Power was also given to erect a pier at Dungeness The New Romney Extension was completed and opened for traffic on 1st June, 1884. Power to raise 160,000*l.* new capital, and borrow 53,333*l.*

By act of 2nd August, 1883, power was obtained to make a railway (9 miles) from Headcorn to join the Loose Valley Line of the South Eastern at Maidstone The railway from Headcorn to Loose is now being constructed. Working agreements with South Eastern. New capital, 120,000*l.*; loans, &c., 40,000*l.*

No. of Directors—3; quorum, 2. *Qualification*, 40 shares.

DIRECTORS:

A. M. Watkin, Esq., Dunedin Lodge, Folkestone.

Wm. Mewburn, Esq., Wykham Park, Banbury.

Colonel C. F. Surtees, Long Ditton, Surrey.

OFFICERS.—Sec., C. Sheath, London Bridge Station, S.E.; Solicitor, R. W. Perks, 147, Leadenhall Street, E.C.

180.—MANCHESTER AND MILFORD.

Incorporated by act of July, 1860, to construct a line from Llanidloes to Pencader. Capital, 555,000*l.*; loans, 185,000*l.*

By act of July, 1865, the company was authorised to make certain new railways in substitution for part of their authorised railway and Aberystwyth Branch, and to create additional capital, beyond that authorised by the act of 1860, of 15,300*l.*, and further loans, beyond that authorised by the act of 1860, of 5,100*l.* 175,000*l.* of the capital authorised by the act of 1860 cancelled as ordinary shares, and authorised to be issued as preference shares. By the same act running powers were given over the Carmarthen and Cardigan, between Pencader and Carmarthen.

By act of 15th May, 1873, the company was authorised to construct a branch from Devil's Bridge to Aberystwyth, with a station at the latter place, and to raise 40,000*l.* new capital. By act of 27th April, 1876, the time for the completion of these works was extended to 15th May, 1881, and under act of 19th July, 1880, the branch was abandoned.

The undertaking is now in the hands of a receiver appointed by the Court of Chancery.

CAPITAL.—The expenditure to 30th June, 1884, amounted to 752,187*l.*, viz., 736,011*l.* on lines open for traffic, and 16,176*l.* on working stock. The receipts to same date amounted to 701,672*l.* The following is a list in order of priority for dividend:—

Rent-charges capitalised at 20 years purchase	£24,682	
Loans at 5 per cent.	163,240	
Loans at 4½ per cent	500	
Preference shares	190,200	
Ordinary shares	323,050	=£701,672

NOTES.—The interest on rent-charges and debenture bonds is accumulative, and payable half-yearly, viz.:—On rent-charges, 25th March and 29th September; on debenture bonds, 30th June and 31st December. The interest is in arrear in both cases to the extent of 8,877*l.* upon the former, and 135,022*l.* on the latter. The debenture bonds are redeemable at par.

The dividends on preference and ordinary shares are contingent upon the profits of each separate year.

The transfer books for all classes close 14 days before the payment of interest or dividends.

TRANSFER DEPARTMENT QUERIES AND REPLIES.

Queries.	Replies.
Transfer form—ordinary or special?	Ordinary.
Fee per deed?	2*s.* 6*d.*
Ditto if more sellers than one? ...	2*s.* 6d.
May several classes of stock be transferred on one deed?	Yes.
Are certificates required to accompany transfers?	Yes.
What amounts of stock are transferable, and are parts of 1*l.* sterling allowed to be transferred?	Shares and debenture bonds as they are.
To what officer should transfer communications be sent?	Secretary.
In acceptances, renunciations, &c., of allotments of new stock, proxies, or other forms sent to trustees, what signatures are required?	All the trustees.

Meetings usually held in London in February and August.

DIRECTORS:

Chairman—JOHN JAMES BARROW, Esq., Holmewood, Tunbridge Wells.

John Burton Barrow, Esq., Ringwood Hall, Chesterfield.

William Wavell, Esq., 54, Oxford Terrace, Hyde Park, W.

C. Stanley Williams, Esq., Shirley Hall, Langton, Tunbridge Wells.

OFFICERS.—Sec., William Felix Poole; Auditors, James Fraser, 2, Tokenhouse Buildings, King's Arms Yard, E.C., and Roderick Mackay, 3, Lothbury, E.C.

Offices—15, Spilman Street, Carmarthen.

181.—MANCHESTER, SHEFFIELD, AND LINCOLNSHIRE.

An amalgamation of the SHEFFIELD, ASHTON-UNDER-LYNE, AND MANCHESTER, the GREAT GRIMSBY AND SHEFFIELD JUNCTION, the SHEFFIELD AND LINCOLNSHIRE, the SHEFFIELD AND LINCOLNSHIRE EXTENSION, and the GREAT GRIMSBY DOCK companies, by virtue of powers conferred by act of 1846. The act of 1847 authorised amalgamation with the MANCHESTER AND LINCOLN UNION; the whole were dissolved and reincorporated as one company, under this title, by the "Consolidation Act" of 1849.

MILEAGE.—In operation: lines owned, 290 miles; jointly with other companies, 214 miles; total, 504 miles.

Canals and navigations owned by the company, 169 miles.

The first section of the line opened for public traffic was from Manchester to Godley on the 17th November, 1841.

By act of 16th July, 1855, the whole acts of the company were consolidated, for ample abstract of which see *Appendix* to the MANUAL for 1856.

FURTHER PARLIAMENTARY POWERS:—

A list of Acts obtained by this company from 1858 to 1878, with short heads of the objects for which the various powers were sought, will be found on reference to the MANUAL for 1881, pages 231 to 233.

1879—21ST JULY.—Powers to the company to acquire additional lands; to subscribe a further 100,000*l.* to Cheshire Lines Committee; to raise further capital, 500,000*l.* in shares and 166,000*l.* in debentures; to cancel the amount uncalled on the 6 per cent. perpetual shares, and to issue 5 per cent. guaranteed stock in lieu thereof; to consolidate 6 per cent. perpetual shares with 5 per cent. guaranteed stock; to commute contingent dividend on Garston and Liverpool stock, and consolidate that stock with 5 per cent. perpetual preference stock; to consolidate debenture stocks, &c.

1881—8TH APRIL.—Power to company to acquire additional lands; extension of time for various uncompleted works; consolidation of first preference and 4½ per cent. preference stocks.

1881—18TH JULY.—Confirmation of agreement with Wigan Junction as to working and maintenance of Wigan Line. Further subscription to Wigan Company. Branch from Abram to West Leigh. Construction of sea wall at Cleethorpes.

Agreement with London and North Western as to lines in Wigan district. Further capital, 500,000*l*. in shares and 166,560*l*. on loans.

1882—12TH JULY.—Power to company to incorporate the Trent, Ancholme, and Grimsby. Confirmation of agreement with Lancashire and Yorkshire and London and North Western companies granting running powers between Penistone and Huddersfield.

1883—2ND AUGUST.—Power to company to make railways from Wigan to Longton, with a junction with the West Lancashire; to raise further capital, 1,150,000*l*. in shares, and 1,011,500*l*. on loan; to dissolve Peak Forest Canal, Macclesfield Canal, and Ashton Canal companies, and to convert canal annuities into company's 4½ per cent. debenture stock; to subscribe 30,000*l*. to Isle of Axholme and Marshland Steam Tramways Company Limited; to make experimental borings under River Humber; running powers over West Lancashire.

1884—14TH JULY.—Powers to company to make a tunnel under River Humber; reverse curve at Thorne; to acquire additional lands; to raise further capital—350,000*l*. in shares, and 116,000*l*. on loans; extension of time for various uncompleted works and purchase of lands; further subscription to Wigan Company; to purchase Cleethorpes Pier undertaking; to make bye-laws as to docks, &c., at Grimsby.

1884—28TH JULY.—Construction of branch from Cheshire Lines at Chester to Connah's Quay. Length, about 7 miles. New capital, 200,000*l*.; loans, 66,000*l*.

AMALGAMATIONS, LEASES, AGREEMENTS, &c.:—

CANALS.—*Peak Forest, Macclesfield, and Ashton.*—Vested in Manchester, Sheffield, and Lincolnshire by act of 2nd August, 1883; from that date shareholders or annuitants in each company respectively to receive 4½ per cent. debenture stock of the Manchester, Sheffield, and Lincolnshire, bearing interest equivalent to their previous income.—For particulars prior to transfers, see MANUAL for 1883, and previous editions.

CHESHIRE LINES.—The Sheffield is joint owner, along with the Great Northern and Midland companies, of the Cheshire Midland, Stockport and Woodley, Stockport and Timperley, West Cheshire, Garston and Liverpool, and Liverpool Extension lines.—See Cheshire Lines.

GREAT NORTHERN.—By act of 23rd July, 1858, the company was authorised to enter into arrangements with the Great Northern. The act enables the division and apportionment of traffic, the working of the line of one company by the other, the purchase of stock, the provision of capital for common purposes, and the appointment of a joint committee with full powers.

MACCLESFIELD, BOLLINGTON, AND MARPLE.—Incorporated by act of 14th July, 1864, to construct a line from Macclesfield, through Bollington, to Marple. Length, 10½ miles. By act of 25th May, 1871, the line is vested in a joint committee of the Manchester, Sheffield, and Lincolnshire and the North Staffordshire, who each provide half of the capital.

MACCLESFIELD AND KNUTSFORD.—Originally incorporated by act of 16th June 1871, to construct a line from Macclesfield to Knutsford. Length, 11 miles 3 furlongs. By act of 16th July, 1874, the company was dissolved, and the powers vested in the Sheffield.

MANCHESTER, SOUTH JUNCTION, AND ALTRINCHAM.—The Sheffield and London and North Western companies are joint owners of this line.—See GENERAL INDEX.

MANCHESTER AND STOCKPORT.—See Sheffield and Midland Joint Lines.

MARPLE, NEW MILLS, AND HAYFIELD JUNCTION.—See Sheffield and Midland Joint Lines.

OLDHAM, ASHTON, AND GUIDE BRIDGE.—By act of 30th June, 1862, this line is vested in the London and North Western and the Sheffield, the latter being thereby authorised to raise additional capital to complete its share of the purchase of the Oldham.

SOUTHPORT AND CHESHIRE LINES EXTENSION.—See GENERAL INDEX.

SOUTH YORKSHIRE RAILWAY AND RIVER DUN NAVIGATION.—Incorporated as the South Yorkshire, Doncaster, and Goole, by act of 22nd July, 1847, to construct a line from Doncaster to the Midland, at Swinton, and to connect the same with the Sheffield, Rotherham, and Goole, at Barnsley. Length, about 38 miles. The same act authorised the purchase of the River Dun Navigation and the Dearn and Dove Canal Navigation. By act of 1874 the South Yorkshire was vested in the Manchester, Sheffield, and Lincolnshire

TRENT, ANCHOLME, AND GRIMSBY.—Incorporated by act of 22nd July, 1861, to construct a line from the River Trent, near Keadby, to join the Sheffield at Barnetby. Length, 14 miles. By act of 12th July, 1882, this company was dissolved, and powers vested in Manchester, Sheffield, and Lincolnshire.

WIDNES.—See Sheffield and Midland Joint Lines.

WIGAN JUNCTION.—See GENERAL INDEX.

PROPOSED TRANSFER OF THE UNDERTAKING TO THE GREAT NORTHERN AND MIDLAND.—On the 16th October, 1877, negotiations were commenced between the several boards for the vesting of this company in the Great Northern and Midland companies jointly, either by purchase or perpetual lease from 1st July, 1878. The terms proposed at first secured the interest and dividend on the guaranteed and preference stocks, and dividends on the ordinary stock at 2 and 2½ per cent. per annum for the first two half-years respectively, and a gradual increase up to 4 per cent. per annum for the year 1882, and thereafter in perpetuity; these payments to be charged on a fund to be formed of the gross receipts of the two companies from traffic passing over any portion of the Manchester, Sheffield, and Lincolnshire or Cheshire Lines. The objections to this proposal were that the 4 per cent. dividend should take the form of a rent-charge; that the rising dividend commenced at too low a figure; and that until 1882 was too long a term to wait for the 4 per cent. The proposals were afterwards modified so far as the dividends were concerned to 3 per cent. per annum for the first two years, 3½ per cent. per annum for the next two years, and 4 per cent. per annum for each subsequent year; but a split occurred as to the nature of the security, the Sheffield Company insisting on an absolute rent-charge upon the undertakings of the three companies to secure the above dividends, or a perpetual increased dividend at 4½ per cent. per annum from 1882, "secured in the most satisfactory manner that the solicitors can devise and Parliament will approve." The latter terms being refused by the Great Northern and Midland companies the negotiations came to an end.

NEW CAPITAL.—In accordance with resolution passed at a special meeting of proprietors on the 27th July, 1881, new capital to the amount of 1,380,000*l.* was created, in 138,000 shares of 10*l.* each, bearing 5 per cent. preferential dividend, and ranking after existing preference stocks and shares of the company. The holders have the option of converting the same, when fully paid up, into a corresponding amount of ordinary stock at any time previous to 1st January, 1889. If not so converted, the shares to be entitled to 5 per cent. in perpetuity.

ACCOUNTS:—

The ordinary half-yearly meeting of this company was held on the 23rd July last, when the report and accounts then presented were adopted. The following is an abstract of those accounts made up to 30th June, 1884, viz.:—

CAPITAL.—*Authorised:* Stocks and shares, 22,273,489*l.*; loans, 8,607,869*l.*; total, 30,881,358*l.* *Created or sanctioned:* Stocks and shares, 19,571,325*l.*; loans, 7,677,302*l.*; total, 27,248,627*l.*

Receipts.				*Expenditure.*	
From stocks and shares, viz.:—				Lines open for traffic............	£13,968,706
Ordinary............	£1,659,633			Working stock	2,518,628
Preferred	1,916,460			Subscriptions to other lines...	6,300,843
Deferred	1,916,460			Docks, steamboats, and other special items.....................	3,499,793
			£5,492,553		
From preference stocks and shares...	£13,049,881				
,, Dearne & Dove share capital	45,500				
			13,095,381		
Total stock and share capital			£18,587,934		
Loan capital, viz.:—					
Terminable debs.		£23,650			
Debenture stocks:—					
4 per cent.	£79,577				
4½ ,,	7,150,132				
5 ,,	300,000				
		7,529,709			
			£7,553,359		
Advance on account of Great Grimsby fishing docks.........			4,000		
			£26,145,293		
Balance.................			142,677		
			£26,287,970		£26,287,970

PRIORITIES, DESCRIPTIONS, AND DIVIDENDS of the various Securities of the company, existing on the 30th June, 1884 (see notes).

No.	Year of Act.	FULL DESCRIPTION (to be observed in Transfer Deeds and all other Legal Documents).	Rate ℔ cent ℔ annum.
1	...	Debenture loans ....(£16,150)	4
2	...	Ditto ....(£2,500)	4¼
3	...	Ditto ....(£3,000)	4½
4	...	4 per cent. debenture stock ....(£79,577)	4
5	Various	4½ ditto ditto ....(£7,150,132)	4½
6	...	5 ditto ditto ....(£800,000)	5
7	1850	First preference stock ....(£1,066,083)	4½
8	...	3½ ditto ditto ....(£266,698)	3½
9	...	6 ditto ditto ....(£572,000)	6
10	...	5 per cent. guaranteed stock ....(£521,376)	5
11	Various	5 per cent. perpetual preference stock ....(£1,008,000)	5
12	...	4 per cent. guaranteed South Yorkshire rent-charge stock (£448,960)	4
13	...	Irredeemable 5 ℔ cent. South Yorkshire rent-charge stock (£490,000)	5
14	Various	4½ per cent. South Yorkshire rent-charge stock (£1,797,428)	4½
15	Various	4 per cent. preference stock ....(£1,100,000)	4
16	Various	5 per cent. convertible preference stock, 1872 (£1,000,000)	5
17	1873	5 ditto ditto 1874 (£1,080,000)	5
18	Various	5 ditto ditto 1876 (£1,500,000)	5
19	1876	5 ditto ditto 1879 (£1,000,000)	5
20	Various	5 ditto ditto 1881 (£729,316)	5
21	Various	Ordinary stock ....(£1,659,633)	...
22	1867	Preferred ordinary stock ....(£1,916,400)	...
23	1867	Deferred ordinary stock ....(£1,916,400)	...

NOTES.—Nos. 1, 2, and 3 are redeemable at various dates at par.

Nos. 1 to 6 rank for dividend *pari passu*.

Nos. 21 and 22 rank for dividend *pari passu* after No. 20.

Nos. 12, 13, and 14 (South Yorkshire).—"62 per cent. of gross receipts of South Yorkshire undertaking form a primary security for payment of dividends on these stocks."

Nos. 16 and 17.—The option of conversion on these stocks has lapsed.

Nos. 18, 19, and 20.—Option of conversion into ordinary stock at par prior to 1st January, 1884, 1st January, 1888, and 1st January 1889, in the order named respectively.

Nos. 1 to 10 and No. 12 stocks.—Dividends on these stocks are *non-contingent* and accumulative. Dividends on all other stocks are *contingent* upon the profits of each separate year.

Nos. 22 and 23 ("preferred" and "deferred" ordinary).—To ascertain the dividend on these stocks double the ordinary dividend for any year ending 31st December, deduct therefrom 6 per cent., which first accrues to the "preferred" stock; the "deferred" stock is then entitled to whatever residue there may be. The option of dividing the ordinary stock into "preferred" and "deferred" may be exercised between the time of closing the transfer books of the companies prior to the first half-yearly ordinary meetings in any year, and the time of closing such transfer books prior to the second half-yearly ordinary meetings in the same year.

Interest and dividends on Nos. 1 to 6 payable 1st January and 1st July.

Dividends on all stocks from No. 7 downward are payable in February and August.

The transfer books of debenture stocks close 14 days, and of all the other stocks 21 days before the dates appointed for the half-yearly payment of dividends.

TRANSFER DEPARTMENT QUERIES AND REPLIES.

Queries.	Replies.
Transfer form—ordinary or special?	Ordinary.
Fee per deed?	2*s.* 6*d.*
Ditto if more sellers than one?...	2*s.* 6*d.* each seller.
May several classes of stock be transferred on one deed?	Yes, except debenture stock, which must go on separate deeds.
Are certificates required to accompany transfers?	Yes.
What amounts of stock are transferable, and are parts of 1*l.* sterling allowed to be transferred?	Parts of a 1*l.* not transferable; transfers of divided ordinary limited to 10*l.* and multiples of 10*l.*
To what officer should transfer communications be sent?	Secretary.
In acceptances, renunciations, &c., of allotments of new stock, proxies, or other forms sent to trustees and other joint holders, what signatures are required?	In proxies, signature of first registered holder; in other cases, signatures of all registered holders.

Fee for registration of probates of wills or letters of administration, 5*s.* each. Certificates of death and marriage, or declaration as to lost scrip, 2*s.* 6*d.* each.

The estimate of further expenditure required 139,400*l.* during the half-year ended 31st December, 1884, and 776,000*l.* in subsequent half-years. The available assets are detailed as below:—

Share and loan capital authorised but not created	£3,632,431
Share capital created but not yet received, viz.:—	
Amount uncalled	....
Amount unissued	1,028,891
Available borrowing powers	123,943
	£4,785,265
Less—Balance to debit of capital account	142,677
	£4,642,588

Revenue.—Comparative view of the working of this undertaking for the last three half-years, viz.:—

Receipts.	1883. 30th June.	1883. 31st Dec.	1884. 30th June.
Passengers, horses, parcels, &c.	£210,899	£254,656	£221,652
Merchandise (less cartage), live stock, and minerals	618,580	676,579	611,277
Grimsby Dock dues and wharfage........................	14,968	20,787	16,087
Canal receipts (net)	20,247	23,541	17,817
Manchester, South Junction, and Altrincham (net)	10,898	10,719	11,461
West Riding and Grimsby (net)	9,509	11,428	10,988
Sheffield and Midland Joint Lines (net)	5,859	7,361	6,793
Cheshire Lines (net)	20,236	30,564	23,900
Oldham, Ashton, and Guide Bridge (net)...............	*Dr.* 62	200	295
Rents, fees, mileage and demurrage, and sundries...	27,240	25,041	27,246
Interest due by Gt. Northern on commission outlay	2,187	2,187	2,187
Balance of steamship receipts, expenses, and depreciation (net)..	7,260	3,260	1,061
	£947,831	£1,066,828	£960,864

Expenses.	1883. 30th June.	1883. 31st Dec.	1884. 30th June.
Maintenance of way, works, and stations	£56,272	£58,974	£57,066
Locomotive power	95,368	105,828	97,289
Carriage and wagon repairs.................................	39,044	38,859	38,854
Traffic expenses	155,222	166,111	159,411
General charges	25,736	24,870	26,223
Ordinary working expenses (carried forward.)	£371,642	£394,642	£378,843

Expenses.	1883. 30th June.	1883. 31st Dec.	1884. 30th June.
Brought forward	£371,642	£394,642	£378,863
Law and Parliamentary	5,636	8,066	7,205
Compensation	5,467	4,955	8,595
Rates, taxes, and Government duty	25,016	25,157	24,044
Rents and tolls	17,906	19,486	20,199
Ferry boats and Grimsby Docks	14,518	15,006	14,610
Ordinary working and other expenses	£440,185	£467,311	£453,516
Preference charges, viz.:—			
Debenture and general interest (net)	154,959	168,680	172,141
Sheffield Canal annuities	15,023	880	880
Loss on working joint lines	401	83	308
Preferential dividends	303,071	305,519	310,248
	£913,639	£942,473	£937,093
Net balances each half-year	£34,192	£122,850	£12,771
Balances brought from previous half-years	2,684	2,548	2,816
Balances available for dividend on ordinary stock	£36,876	£126,398	£16,587
Dividends declared at 1¼, 4½, and ½ per cent. per annum respectively	34,328	123,582	13,731
Surplus carried forward	£2,548	£2,816	£2,856

The following summary will therefore show the general results of the last half-year's business, compared with that of the corresponding period of 1883, as shown by the above figures, viz.:—

Net balance 30th June, 1884	£13,771	Thus:	
,, 30th June, 1883	34,192	Gross traffic—increase	£3,033
		Less:	
		Working charges—inc.... £13,331	
		Pref. charges—increase.. 10,122	=23,454
Loss in 1884	£20,421	Net loss in 1884	£20,421

New Works, &c.—The Manchester Central Temporary Station was opened on 9th July, 1877. The Manchester Central Station was opened on 1st July, 1880. Liverpool North Extension Line was opened for passenger traffic as far as Walton-on-the-Hill on the 1st December, 1879, and from Walton-on-the-Hill to Huskisson Station on 1st July, 1880. The extension of the Barnsley Coal Railway to the West Riding and Grimsby Line was opened for passenger traffic on 1st September, 1882. Two short reverse curves were also opened in 1882, viz., at Stairfoot and Wath.

Docks and Works at Grimsby.—The Alexandra Dock, connecting the Old and Royal Docks, was completed in June, 1879, and was formally opened by the Prince and Princess of Wales on the 22nd July. The cost of this dock was 258,700*l*. The Great Coates Branch connects the Old Dock with the main line of railway without having to pass through the passenger station and the complicated system of sidings which provide for the traffic of the Royal Dock.

The company now own a water area of 97¼ acres of dock accommodation at Grimsby, as under:—

Royal Dock	25 acres.	
Union Dock	1¼ ,,	
Alexandra Dock	48 ,,	
Old Fish Dock	12 ,,	
New Fish Dock	11 ,,	=97¼ acres,

besides two large graving docks. They propose to construct another dock of 19 acres in extent for the accommodation of the timber trade.

Canals.—The company are the owners or lessees of the following canals and navigations:—Ashton and Oldham, Chesterfield, Dearne and Dove, Macclesfield, Peak Forest, River Dun Navigation, Sheffield, and Stainforth and Keadby; representing a waterway of 169 miles.

REDEMPTION OF STOCKS.—The company have completed the redemption and conversion of the following stocks:—

Stocks Redeemed.	Rate of Redemption.	Stock offered in exchange for each 100*l.* of old stock.	Date.
5 per cent. redeemable South Yorkshire rent-charge stock, 1860	5 prem	105*l.* 4½ per cent. South Yorkshire rent-charge stock	1st March 1878.
5 per cent. redeemable South Yorkskire rent-charge stock, 1863	par.	100*l.* 4½ per cent. South Yorkshire rent-charge stock	1st Sept., 1878.
6 per cent. perpetual 10*l.* shares.	20 prem.	120*l.* 5 per cent. guaranteed stock........	29th Jan., 1880.
Garston and Liverpool preference stock	par.	100*l.* 5 per cent. perpetual preference stock	19th Mar., 1880
5 per cent. redeemable preference stock, 1865	5 prem	110*l.* 4 per cent. preference stock	1st Mar., 1882.

The accounts are made up to the 30th June and 31st December, and the statutory meetings are held in January and July every year.

Scale of Voting.—One vote for each 100*l.* of nominal capital up to 1,000*l.*; beyond that amount, one vote additional for every 300*l.*

No. of Directors.—Maximum, 18; minimum, 9. *Qualification*, 1,000*l.* of stock.

DIRECTORS:

Chairman—Sir EDWARD WILLIAM WATKIN, Bart., M.P., Rose Hill, Northenden, Cheshire, and Charing Cross Hotel, Charing Cross, S.W.

Deputy-Chairman—The Right Hon. Lord AUCKLAND, Edenthorpe, Doncaster.

Edward Chapman, Esq., Hill End, Mottram.

The Right Hon. Sir Richard Assheton Cross, G.C.B., M.P., Eccle Riggs, Broughton-in-Furness, Lancashire.

Charles Henry Firth, Esq., Riverdale, Sheffield.

Sir Gilbert Greenall, Bart., Walton Hall, Warrington.

John William Maclure, Esq., The Home, Whalley Range, Manchester.

George Morland Hutton, Esq., Gate Burton, near Gainsbro'.

Abraham Laverton, Esq., Farleigh Castle, Bath.

Tom Harrop Sidebottom, Esq., Etherow House, Hadfield, near Manchester.

Alfred Mellor Watkin, Esq., Dunedin Lodge, Folkestone, Kent.

The Right Hon. The Earl of Wharncliffe, Wortley Hall, near Sheffield, and 15, Curzon Street, W.

OFFICERS.—Gen. Man., R. G. Underdown, Assoc.Inst.C.E.; Sec., Edward Ross; Eng. and Supt. of Loco. and Stores Dept., Charles Sacré, M.Inst.C.E.; Supt. of Line, W. Bradley; Goods Man., Charles T. Smith; Mineral Man., Alfred Ormerod; Accountant, William Pollitt; Auditors, Adam Murray, Manchester, and Edward Mellor, Bowdon; Solicitor, R. Lingard-Monk; Bankers, Williams, Deacon, and Co., London; Liverpool Commercial Bank; Yorkshire Banking Co., Leeds and Hull; Manchester and Salford Bank, Manchester; Sheffield Banking Company; and Smith, Ellison, and Co., Lincoln.

Head Offices—London Road Station, Manchester.

182.—MANCHESTER SOUTH JUNCTION, AND ALTRINCHAM.

Incorporated by act of 1845. This line is in two divisions—1st, the South Junction (1¼ mile), connecting the lines at London Road, Manchester, with the London and North Western, at Ordsal Lane, Salford. 2nd, the Altrincham Branch, 7¾ miles, from the South Junction to Altrincham and Bowdon.

By act of 23rd July, 1858, the management was so far improved as to authorise the appointment of a standing arbitrator, who shall attend at the meetings of the joint board, and affirm, modify, or negative such resolutions as could only be carried by casting vote of chairman, which is abolished.

By act of 4th July, 1878, the company obtained powers to construct certain works, widening, and improvement at Manchester, &c. The London and North Western and Manchester, Sheffield, and Lincolnshire companies to raise new capital, and contribute towards their cost. The South Junction to raise 60,000*l.* through the contributions of the above-named companies in equal proportions, and those companies to participate in the dividends and profits of the South Junction, in proportion to the amount of capital held by them respectively.

CAPITAL.—*Authorised:* 1st act, 650,000*l.*; act 1872, 50,000*l.*; act 1874, 50,000*l.*; act 1878, 60,000*l.*; total, 810,000*l.*; loans, 216,666*l.* The line being vested in the London and North Western and the Manchester, Sheffield, and Lincolnshire, those companies each subscribe half the authorised capital, which is included in their capitals. Returns of traffic are rendered conjointly to the partner companies, the dividend on which appears in their respective accounts.

The expenditure on the line has been 1,027,275*l.*, with 7,000*l.* of borrowing powers unexercised.

DIRECTORS:

Sir Edward Wm. Watkin, Bart., M.P., Rose Hill, Northenden, Cheshire, and Charing Cross Hotel, Charing Cross, S.W.
A. M. Watkin. Esq., Dunedin Lodge, Folkestone, Kent.
James Bancroft, Esq., 83, Mosley Street, and Broughton Hall, Manchester.
Henry Russell Greg, Esq., Lode Hill, Handforth.
Edmund Howard Sykes, Esq., Edgeley Fold, Stockport.
John William Maclure, Esq., The Home, Whalley Range, Manchester.

OFFICERS.—Sec., R. H. Brown; Eng., Henry Woodhouse.

Offices—Oxford Road Station, Manchester.

183.—MANX NORTHERN LIMITED.

Authorised by the Manx Northern Railway Act, 1878, to construct a line from the town of Ramsey to St. John's Station on the Douglas and Peel Railway, in the Isle of Man (a distance of about 16½ miles), and to lay a tramway from the station to and along the quay at Ramsey.

The line passes through or near the populous villages of Kirk Michael, Ballaugh, and Sulby, and connects the town of Ramsey and the northern parts of the island with Douglas and the other towns of the island. The gauge is the same as the Peel and Port Erin Railways, viz., three feet. The line was opened for public traffic, 23rd September, 1879.

The capital of the company is 90,000*l.* in shares of 5*l.* each, with borrowing powers of 45,000*l.* The share capital is divided into 40,000*l.* ordinary and 50,000*l.* 5 per cent. preference. The Government of the Isle of Man guarantee for 25 years from the date of opening the line a minimum dividend of 4 per cent. upon 25,000*l.* of the preference capital.

In the accounts the preference capital is divided into "A" and "B." This is done merely to distinguish them, and does not indicate a preference of one class over the other. Both "A" and "B" rank equally with each other so far as the company is concerned, but the "B" have attached to them the Government guarantee as above.

REVENUE.—The earnings for the year ended the 31st December, 1883, sufficed for the payment of all prior charges and a dividend at 2½ per cent. on the preference shares.

CAPITAL—31st December, 1883.—*Expended*, 122,480*l.*

Receipts.—Loans at 4½ per cent.	£39,000
Preference "A" shares, 5 per cent.	23,425
Preference "B" shares, 5 per cent., of which 4 per cent. is guaranteed by the Government of the Isle of Man.	25,000
Ordinary shares	30,839
	£118,264

Accounts made up at the end of each year.

DIRECTORS:

Chairman—JOHN THOMAS CLUCAS, Esq., M.H.K., Thornhill.

Government Director—Col. F. H. RICH, R.E., 5, New Street, Spring Gardens, S.W.

W. B. Christian, Esq., M.H.K., Milntown.
J. C. LaMothe, Esq., H.B., Ramsey.
E. C. Farrant, Esq., M.H.K., Ballakillingan.
C. H. E. Cowle, Esq., J.P., Ballaghaue, Andreas.
Wm. Todhunter, Esq., Merchant, Douglas.
J. R. Cowell, Esq., M.H.K., Ramsey.

One third, or if their number is not a multiple of three, then the number nearest one-third retire annually (with the exception of the Government Director), but all are eligible for re-election.

OFFICERS.—Sec. and Man., John Cameron, Ramsey; Chief Clerk and Accountant, Robert W. Langlands; Auditors, Turquand, Youngs, and Co., Coleman Street, E.C.; Standing Counsel, Sir James Gell, H.M. Attorney-General for the Isle of Man; Solicitor, John Frederick Gill, Castletown; Bankers, The Isle of Man Banking Company Limited, Douglas, and the London and Westminster Bank, Lothbury, E.C.

Registered Office—Railway Station, Ramsey.

184.—MARLBOROUGH.

Incorporated by act of 22nd July, 1861, to construct a line from the Berks and Hants Extension to Marlborough. Length, 5½ miles. Capital, 45,000*l.* in 10*l.* shares; loans, 15,000*l.* Arrangements with Great Western. By a Certificate of the Board of Trade, 1868, the share capital was increased 6,000*l.*

REVENUE.—The net balances available for dividend for the half-years ended 31st December, 1883, and 30th June, 1884, being the amounts received for rent, less rent-charges, interest on debentures, &c., and other prior claims and charges (net), amounted to 1,047*l.* and 900*l.* respectively, which sufficed for full dividends on the 6 per cent. preference shares and dividends on the ordinary shares at the rate of 4 and 3 per cent. per annum.

The dividends on the ordinary capital are paid free of income tax.

CAPITAL.—The expenditure to 30th June, 1884, amounted to 51,257*l.* The receipts to the same date were as follow:—Shares, 35,931*l.*; loans, 12,865*l.*; rent-charge, 2,100*l.*; amount transferred from revenue, 661*l.*; total, 51,257*l.*

On the 17th September, 1884, resolutions were passed for the conversion of shares into stock, and empowering the directors to issue debenture stock at 3½ per cent., in place of existing debenture bonds at 4 per cent.

Meetings in February or March and August or September.

No. of Directors—5; maximum, 8; minimum, 3; quorum, 3. *Qualification*, 300*l.*

DIRECTORS:

Chairman—1 The Most Hon. the Marquis of AILESBURY, 6, St. George's Place, Hyde Park Corner, S.W., and Savernake Forest, Marlborough.

Deputy-Chairman—2 RICHARD EDMONDS PRICE, Esq., Broomfield Hall, Bridgwater.

3 Henry Richard Tomkinson, Esq., 13, Stratton Street, Piccadilly, W.

4 The Rev. John Shearme Thomas, Barton Hill, Marlborough.

5 James Blake Maurice, Esq., M.D., Marlborough.

OFFICERS.—Sec., James Leader, Marlborough; Auditors, J. Wilson Theobald and James Morrison; Solicitors, Rose and Johnson, 26, Great George Street, Westminster, S.W., and Merrimans and Gwillim, Marlborough; Bankers, Capital and Counties Bank, Marlborough, and Robarts, Lubbock, and Co., Lombard Street, E.C.

Offices—Marlborough.

185.—MARYPORT AND CARLISLE.

Incorporated by act of 1837. The act of June 26th, 1855, provided for new capital for doubling the rails and other improvements to the extent of 77,712*l.* 10*s.* in 12*l.* 10*s.* shares, making a total of 342,288*l.*, with borrowing powers to the extent of 135,000*l.*

By act of 30th June, 1862, the company was empowered to construct branches to Bolton and Wigton (7½ miles), to purchase additional land, and to raise new capital to the extent of 75,000*l.* in 12*l.* 10*s.* shares and 20,000*l.* on loan. These shares were created at a meeting on 20th August, 1862, and issued to the proprietors as ordinary stock, although the act authorised a preference not exceeding 5 per cent.

By act of 19th June, 1865, the company was authorised to construct the Derwent Branch (6 miles), to enlarge the Bullgill Station, to purchase additional lands, and to raise further capital to the extent of 60,000*l.* in shares and 20,000*l.* by mortgage. By completion of this branch between the Bullgill Station and the junction with the Cockermouth and Workington, at Brigham, a short and direct communication has been opened out between Scotland and Newcastle and the extensive iron ore mines and iron furnaces of West Cumberland. This branch also gives direct connection with the Cockermouth and Workington and Whitehaven, Cleator, and Egremont (both now part of the London and North Western system), and the Cockermouth, Keswick, and Penrith.

By act of 25th May, 1871, the company was authorised to raise 77,712*l.* in ordinary stock, to pay off the 5 per cent. preferences, and to increase the capital to the extent of 37,000*l.* in shares and 15,000*l.* on debenture. It also allows the conversion of 4 and 4½ per cent. minimum stocks, amounting to 175,112*l.*, into ordinary stocks, and the paying off at par on 31st December, 1871, of the 5 per cent. preference.

By Board of Trade Certificate of 1878, 70,500*l.* in shares and 23,500*l.* loans capital was authorised for new works.

1883—16TH JULY.—An act to reduce the maximum tolls and rates chargeable by the company to those authorised by Cleator and Workington Junction Act, 1876.

Productive, 41½ miles.

REVENUE.—The summary given below shows the result of working for the half-years ended 31st December, 1883, and 30th June, 1884:—

	Dec., 1883.	June, 1884.
Gross receipts	£66,757	£59,405
Expenditure	27,719	24,523
Net	£39,038	£34,882
Add—balances brought in, &c.	848	1,525
Total net revenue	£39,886	£36,407
Interest, preference dividends, &c.	1,477	1,412
Balance available for division	£38,409	£34,995
Dividend on ordinary capital at 9½ and 8¾ per cent. per annum respectively	36,945	34,029
Balance carried forward	£1,464	£966

CAPITAL.—The receipts and expenditure on this account to 30th June, 1884, have been as follow:—

Received.		*Expended.*	
Ordinary stock	£775,800	Lines open for traffic	£716,699
4 per cent. minimum stock	2,000	Working stock	133,042
	£777,800		£849,741
Debenture Stock	73,500	Balance	1,559
	£851,300		£851,300

PRIORITIES, DESCRIPTIONS, DIVIDENDS, &c., of the various Securities of the company, existing on the 30th September, 1884 (see notes).

No.	Year of Act.	FULL DESCRIPTION (to be observed in Transfer Deeds and all other Legal Documents).	Rate ₽ cent ₽ annum.
1	1871	4 per cent. irredeemable debenture stock	4
2	1855	4 per cent. minimum	4 min.
3	Various	Ordinary stock	...

NOTES.—The minimum stock (No. 2) is convertible at any time, at the option of the holders, into ordinary stock.

Dividends.—No. 1 is non-contingent on profits, Nos. 2 and 3 are contingent upon profits of each separate half-year; they are payable half-yearly on No. 1, 1st January and 1st July; on Nos. 2 and 3, 1st March and 1st September.

Transfer books close: For No. 1, 14 days before payment of interest; for Nos. 2 and 3, 14 days before each half-yearly meeting.

TRANSFER DEPARTMENT QUERIES AND REPLIES.

QUERIES.	REPLIES.
Transfer form—ordinary or special?	Ordinary.
Fee per deed?	2*s.* 6*d.*
Ditto if more sellers than one?	2*s.* 6*d.* each seller.
May several classes of stock be transferred on one deed?	No.
Are certificates required to accompany transfers?	Yes.
What amounts of stock are transferable, and are parts of 1*l.* sterling allowed to be transferred?	10*s.*
To what officer should transfer communications be sent?	Secretary.
In acceptances, renunciations, &c., of allotments of new stock, proxies, or other forms sent to trustees and other joint accounts, what signatures are required?	The whole of the signatures.

The accounts are made up to the 30th June and 31st December, and the meetings held in February and August.

DIRECTORS:

Chairman—2 Sir WILFRID LAWSON, Bart., M.P., Brayton Hall, Carlisle.

Deputy-Chairman—3 ROBERT RITSON, Esq., Ellen Bank, near Maryport.

2 Major T. C. Thompson, Milton Hall, Carlisle.
3 H. Pocklington Senhouse, Esq., Hames Hall, Cockermouth.
1 Edward Tyson, Esq., Maryport.
3 Joseph Hannah, Esq., Castle View, Carlisle.
2 David Ainsworth, Esq., M.P., The Flosh, Cleator, *via* Carnforth.
1 Thomas Milburn, Esq., Brunswick Street, Carlisle.
1 Thomas Hartley, Esq., Armathwaite Hall, Cockermouth.
2 John Addison, Esq., The Castle Hill, Maryport.

1, Retire in the autumn of 1885; 2, in 1886; 3, in 1887, but eligible for re-election.

OFFICERS.—Sec. and Gen. Man., Hugh Carr; Eng., Joseph Cartmell; Loco. Supt., Robert Campbell; Traffic Supt., John Ellwood; Accountant, Daniel Dixon; Auditors, Joseph Nicholson and William Elliot; Solicitors, Tyson and Hobson.

Head Offices—Maryport.

186.—MAWDDWY.

Incorporated by act of 5th July, 1865, to construct a line from the Cemmes Road Station of the Cambrian to the town of Dinas Mawddwy. Length, 6¾ miles. Capital, 21,000*l.* in shares and 7,000*l.* on loan. Arrangements with Cambrian.

No printed accounts issued, the railway being almost entirely the property of the chairman.

No. of Directors—6; minimum, 3; quorum, 3 and 2. *Qualification*, 300*l.*

Chairman—Sir EDMUND BUCKLEY, Bart., of Plas, Dinas Mawddwy, Merionethshire.

Secretary and Manager, William Williams, Dinas Mawddwy, and Salop Road, Oswestry.

Offices—Salop Road, Oswestry.

187.—MELLIS AND EYE.

Incorporated by act of 5th July, 1865, to construct a line from the Great Eastern, at Mellis, to Eye. Length, 3 miles. Capital, 15,000*l.* in shares and 5,000*l.* on loan. Arrangements with Great Eastern.

NEW AGREEMENT.—The agreement made in 1869, under which the Great Eastern worked the line at 50 per cent. of the gross receipts, was renewed in 1878 for a term of 10 years, subject to the percentage payable to the Great Eastern being increased from 50 to 60 per cent. of the gross receipts.

REVENUE.—The gross receipts for the half-year ended 30th June, 1883, amounted to 788*l.*, and the expenditure to 506*l.*, leaving a balance of 282*l.* No dividend was proposed on the share capital of the company.

In operation, 2¾ miles.

CAPITAL.—The expenditure on this account to 30th June, 1883, amounted to 22,391*l.*, the receipts being distinguished as under:—

Shares and stock	£14,691	
Sale of land, interest, &c.	236	
Balance	7,464	=£22,391

DIRECTORS:

Chairman—Sir EDWARD KERRISON, Bart., Brome Hall, and Oakley Park, Suffolk.

William C. Curties, Esq., Scole.
Walter W. Miller, Esq., Eye.
Henry Wells, Esq., Occold.
The Right Hon. Lord Henniker, Thornham Hall, Suffolk.
Edward Peck, Esq., Eye.

OFFICERS.—Sec., J. C. Warnes, Solicitor, Eye; Auditors, Edward Kemp and Sidney V. Bishop.

188.—MERIONETHSHIRE.

Incorporated by act of 29th June, 1871, to construct a junction between the Cambrian and the Festiniog. Gauge, 2 feet. Length, 10 miles. Capital, 80,000*l.* in 10*l.* shares and 28,000*l.* on loan. By act of 24th June, 1876, the time for completion of works was extended to 29th June, 1879. By act of 3rd July, 1879. a further extension was granted to 29th June, 1882, and by act of 19th May, 1882, the time was further extended to 29th June, 1885.

DIRECTORS:

Chairman—SAMUEL HOLLAND, Esq., M.P., 46, Thurloe Square, S.W.

William Casson, Esq., J.P., Beckton House, Cheshire, and Cynfal, Festiniog.
James Hassall Foulkes, Esq., J.P., Llay Place, Wrexham.
Hugh Owen, Esq., 460, Camden Road, N.
Morgan Lloyd, Esq., M.P., Temple, E.C., and 53, Cornwall Gardens, S.W.
Andrew Augustus Robinson, Esq., 62, Leadenhall Street, E.C.

OFFICERS.—Sec., Mr. Shirreff, Palê, Corwen; Engs., J. W. Grover, Westminster, S.W., and C. M. Holland, Manchester; Auditors, Edward Bellamy, 7, Westminster Chambers, W.C., and James Fraser, 2, Tokenhouse Buildings, King's Arms Yard, E.C.; Solicitor, E. Breese, Portmadoc.

Offices—Palê, Corwen.

189.—MERSEY.

Incorporated by act of 28th June, 1866, to construct a line to connect Birkenhead with Liverpool by a passage beneath the River Mersey. Length, 1¼ mile. Capital, 350,000*l.* in 20*l.* shares, divided, and 116,600*l.* on loan or in debenture stock.

By act of 31st July, 1868, an extension of time for purchase of lands and completion of works was obtained, the latter till 31st July, 1873.

By act of 14th August, 1871, the company was authorised to make certain deviations, as well as to connect the line with those at Liverpool and Birkenhead. New line, 1 mile 8 chains. Extension of time till 1874. Additional capital, 300,000*l.* in shares, "preferred" and "deferred," and 100,000*l.* on loan. Arrangements with Great Western.

By act of 19th July, 1880, the period for completion of works was extended until 14th August, 1883.

By act of 1882 important additional powers were obtained as to the acquisition of property in Liverpool and Birkenhead, and effecting a final settlement with the Corporation of Birkenhead respecting their ferry rights, and for raising additional capital.

By act of 20th August, 1883, the company was authorised to raise, for the furtherance of their undertaking, new capital amounting to 150,000*l.* in shares and 50,000*l.* in loans, &c.

By act of 7th August, 1884, the company was authorised to make a branch railway in Birkenhead. New capital, 300,000*l.*; loans, 100,000*l.*

In July, 1881, the directors invited subscriptions for part of the share capital of the company, authorised under the various acts mentioned above (viz.:—866,600*l.*, consisting of 650,000*l.* in 20*l.* shares and 216,600*l.* in debentures). This issue represented 30,000 shares of 20*l.* each at par, payable 4*l.* on allotment, and the balance as follows, viz.:—4*l.* on 29th September, 1881; 4*l.* on 29th March, 1882; 4*l.* on 29th September, 1882; and 3*l.* on 29th December, 1882. A further portion of the authorised share capital, amounting to 394,980*l.*, in 20*l.* shares, was issued in January, 1884, at par, 7*l.* per share to be paid up by 1st April following.

The prospectus of the 1st issue of capital gave the following information, viz.:—"The railway will be a little over 2½ miles in length. Under an agreement with the London and North Western, it will form a junction at Tranmere with the Birkenhead Joint of the London and North Western and Great Western, and passing through Birkenhead and under the River Mersey will, for the present, terminate in Church Street, Liverpool, near to the Central Station of the Midland, Great Northern, and Manchester, Sheffield, and Lincolnshire. The Great Western, recognising the value and importance of this undertaking, as connecting the railway at Birkenhead with Liverpool, and affording their system of railways a ready access to that city, have nominated two of their directors to represent them on the Mersey Railway

Board, as evidence of the interest which the company take in the successful accomplishment of the object in view.

"The Mersey Railway, running, as it will, in a direct line between the business centres on both sides the river, and with most convenient passenger stations at Tranmere, and in the neighbourhood of Hamilton Square, Birkenhead, and in Lord Street and Church Street, near to the Central Station in Liverpool, will place these centres within ten minutes of each other by commodious and well-lighted trains, running at intervals of a few minutes in each direction. The tunnel will be thoroughly ventilated throughout. It is also intended, by means of stations near Woodside, Birkenhead, and near St. George's Dock, Liverpool, to provide rapid through communication for goods of all kinds between the docks on both sides of the river. The connection with the Joint Railway at Birkenhead will, for the first time, open up a through route for passengers and goods from the whole of the Great Western system to Liverpool, and a much more direct connection between Liverpool, Chester, and the coalfields of North and South Wales, by the Great Western and the London and North Western. It will also considerably shorten the distance by railway between Liverpool and Ireland *via* Holyhead."

The engineers' report, issued 28th January, 1884, states that "The works of this railway continue to progress in a very satisfactory manner, the contractor, Mr. John Waddell, of Edinburgh, having done everything in his power to ensure their early completion, and to carry them out in a thoroughly substantial and efficient manner. The bottom heading of the tunnel is now open throughout from the shaft in Hamilton Street, Birkenhead, passing under the River Mersey to the shaft in Lord Street, opposite North John Street, Liverpool, the last barrier of the new red sandstone rock, which has proved very hard and compact, having been pierced on the 17th instant, in the presence of your chairman, Major Isaac, and the officials of the company. The date of this establishment of through communication accords closely with the anticipations of our last report. Its early completion is largely due to the Beaumont boring machine, which has proved most efficient, having attained a speed of 30 yards per week through the solid sandstone rock, and cutting a circular heading 7 feet in diameter. This heading is connected with the pumping shafts by drainage headings on each side of the river. It is much to the credit of the resident engineers that the lines and levels, laid out under circumstances of rather special difficulty, were found to accord exactly. The main tunnel has been worked at steadily from several faces, so that altogether 1,717 lineal yards are completed and bricked to the full size for the double line of railway. Now that through communication is established, fresh faces will be opened up, and we fully anticipate that the tunnel between Hamilton Square, Birkenhead, and James Street, Liverpool, will be ready for public traffic before the end of the present year. With this view the station buildings at the surface will be at once commenced, the underground arrangements being already in a very forward state. The works of the covered way and the approaches to the junction with the joint railway have been steadily pushed forward, and will shortly be completed. Temporary shafts have been sunk in Hamilton Street, Birkenhead, and Lord Street, Liverpool, and have much facilitated the progress and ventilation of the tunnels. The pumping machinery, with its engines and boilers, is in thorough repair. The quantity of water pumped has not materially increased. The new 40-inch pumping machinery provided as duplicates, to prevent any stoppage of the works during repairs, is fixed and ready for work at Liverpool, and is being rapidly completed at Birkenhead. There are at the present time 1,427 men and 177 horses employed upon the works, the tunnelling being carried forward night and day."

CAPITAL.—30th June, 1883.—*Created:* Ordinary capital, 43,000 shares of 20*l.* each, 920,000*l.*; debenture stock, 116,600*l.* The amount expended to the same date was 360,695*l.* See page 217.

No. of Directors—7; minimum, 3; quorum, 3 and 2. *Qualification*, 500*l.*

DIRECTORS:

Chairman—The Right Hon. HENRY CECIL RAIKES, M.P.

Deputy-Chairman—The Right Hon. EDWARD PLEYDELL BOUVERIE, Manor House, Market Lavington, Wilts.

*Charles Grey Mott, Esq., Harrow Weald Lodge, Stanmore, Middlesex.

*Alexander Hubbard, Esq., Derwentwater House, Acton, W.

Emanuel Boutcher, Esq., London and Liverpool.

George Cavendish Taylor, Esq., 42, Elvaston Place, South Kensington, W.

* Great Western directors.

OFFICERS.—Sec., W. F. Knight; Engs., James Brunlees, past-President, M.Inst. C.E., and Charles Douglas Fox, M.Inst.C.E., 5, Delahay Street, Westminster, S.W.; Resident Eng., A. H. Irvine, C.E.; Auditors, Turquand, Youngs, and Co.; Solicitors, Baxters and Co., 5, Victoria Street, Westminster, S.W., and Gill and Archer, 14, Cook Street, Liverpool; Bankers, Robarts, Lubbock, and Co., Lombard Street, E.C., The Royal Bank of Scotland and its branches, London, Edinburgh, and Glasgow, and Bank of Liverpool (Heywood's Branch).

Offices—9, Victoria Chambers, Victoria Street, Westminster, S.W.

190.—METROPOLITAN.

Re-incorporated by act of 7th August, 1854, being an extension of the North Metropolitan. In operation, 19¼ miles; quadruple lines, 2¼ miles.

FURTHER PARLIAMENTARY POWERS:—

A list of Acts from 1855 to 1881, with short heads showing the objects for which the various powers were sought, will be found on reference to the MANUAL for 1882, pages 236 to 240.

By act of 3rd July, 1882, the company was authorised to purchase certain lands in the parishes of Hammersmith and Kensington; to make further provision with reference to the completion of the Inner Circle; to vest outstanding shares in the Metropolitan and St. John's Wood in the company; to raise additional capital, and for other purposes. New capital, 150,000*l.*; borrowing powers, 50,000*l.*

By act of 18th June, 1883, the company was authorised to raise 400,000*l.* additional capital for repayment of sums expended in excess of their proportion of the capital authorised by the City Lines Act of 1879, in the construction of the railway from Aldgate to Trinity Square (Tower Hill); also 50,000*l.* for payment to Her Majesty's Treasury of alleged passenger duty arrears.

By the (Various Powers) Act of 1884, the company was authorised to deviate parts of the Rickmansworth Extension and Chorley Wood Lane; to purchase additional lands; to extend the time for compulsory purchase of lands and completion of works; to give effect to an arrangement for vesting in them the powers to make and maintain Railway No. 2, authorised by the Metropolitan and District Railways (City Lines and Extensions) Act, 1879; to provide for consolidation of debenture stocks, and for other purposes. New capital, 100,000*l.*

By the East London Act of 1882, powers were conferred upon the two companies, or either of them, to enter into agreements with the East London with reference to the construction and working of that company's Whitechapel Extension.

EAST LONDON RAILWAY WHITECHAPEL JUNCTION ACT, 1884.—This act authorises the company, jointly with the District, to work and rent the East London Whitechapel Junction, and for other purposes.

RICKMANSWORTH EXTENSION.—By act of 6th August, 1880, the company was authorised to construct a railway about 7¾ miles in length, from Harrow-on-the-Hill, by a junction with the Kingsbury and Harrow, to Rickmansworth. Period for completion of works, 5 years. New capital, 200,000*l.*; borrowing powers, 66,600*l.* This railway is now in course of construction.

AYLESBURY AND RICKMANSWORTH.—By act of 18th July, 1881, power was given for the construction and maintenance of a line from the Aylesbury and Buckingham, at Aylesbury, to the Rickmansworth Extension, at Rickmansworth. Length, 21¾ miles. Period for completion of works, 5 years; extended under Metropolitan Act, 1884, to 18th July, 1887. Traffic arrangements with Aylesbury and Buckingham. New capital, 400,000*l.*; borrowing powers, 133,000*l.*

HENDON EXTENSION.—By act of 7th August, 1884, the company was authorised to make a railway, about 3¾ miles in length, commencing by a junction at or near the West Hampstead Station, and terminating in the parish of Hendon. Period for completion of works, 5 years. New capital, 180,000*l.*; borrowing powers, 60,000*l.*

METROPOLITAN AND ST. JOHN'S WOOD.—This company now forms part of the Metropolitan under the powers of the act of 1882 above referred to.

The extensions from Moorgate Street to Bishopsgate (Liverpool Street), from thence to Aldgate (High Street), and from thence to Tower Hill, were opened on the 12th July, 1875, 18th November, 1876, and 25th September, 1882, respectively. Swiss Cottage to Walm Lane (Willesden Green) Extension was opened 1st December, 1879, and from Walm Lane to Harrow-on-the-Hill 2nd August, 1880.

The Inner Circle and Extension to Whitechapel were opened for public traffic on the 6th October, 1884.

ACCOUNTS:—

The half-yearly meeting of this company was held on 17th July, 1884, when the report and accounts for the half-year ended 30th June, 1884, were received and adopted. The following is an abstract of those accounts, viz.:—

CAPITAL.—*Authorised:* Stock and shares, 10,100,408*l.*; loans, 3,656,135*l.*; total, 13,806,543*l.*

Received.

Ordinary stocks, viz.:—		
Original undivided	£5,281,245	
Preferred	83,270	
Deferred	83,270	
		£5,447,785
Preference stocks, viz.:—4 per cent. perpetual preference stock, 1881	£2,502,038	
Do. 1882	83,170	
4 per cent. irredeemable	250,000	
		2,835,208
Total share capital		£8,282,993
Loan capital, viz.:—		
Debentures	£43,975	
Ditto stock	2,940,319	
		2,984,294
		£11,267,287
Deduct:—		
Nominal addition to capital occasioned by consolidation of 5 per cent. preference stocks.................		400,408
		£10,866,879
Deduct:—		
Discount on issue of 3½ per cent. debenture stock		9,721
		£10,857,158
By balance...............		402,818
		£11,259,976

Expended.

Lines open for traffic (less sale of lands to 30th June, 1884), &c.	£9,193,098
Lines in course of construction	695,939
Working stock	335,439
Contribution to Joint Committee (City Lines and Extensions)	995,500
Hammersmith and City Debentures	40,000
	£11,259,976

In July, 1881, the various 5 per cent. preference stocks, and the 4 per cent. preference stock, 1881, were consolidated and converted into an uniform 4 per cent. perpetual preference stock, such an amount of the 4 per cent. being given in exchange for the 5 per cent. as would produce the same dividend prior to the consolidation and conversion.

THE PRIORITIES, DESCRIPTIONS, DIVIDENDS, &c.. of the various Stocks of the company, after the above-named consolidation and conversion, will be as follows (see notes):—

No.	Year of Act.	FULL DESCRIPTION (to be observed in Transfer Deeds and all other Legal Documents).	Rate ℔ cent ℔ annum.
1	...	3½ per cent. debenture stock	3½
	Various	4 per cent. debenture stock	4
	Various	4¼ per cent. debenture stock........................	4¼
	Various	4½ per cent. debenture stock........................	4½
2	1877	4 per cent. perpetual preference stock	4
3	1882	4 per cent. perpetual preference stock (1883 issue)	4
4	1879	4 per cent. irredeemable preference stock	4
5	Various	Consolidated ordinary stock	5
	Various	Preferred ordinary stock	6
	Various	Deferred ordinary stock........................	4

NOTES.—No. 2 stock, issued under the consolidation and conversion scheme (mentioned above), dated July, 1881.

Dividends *non-contingent* and accumulative on No. 1; *contingent* upon profits of each separate half-year on the remainder; all payable half-yearly, as follows:—No. 1, 15th January and 15th July; remainder about the 30th or 31st January and July.

Transfer books close for No. 1 on 30th June and 31st December, and for remaining stocks 10 to 14 days before dates of half-yearly meetings.

To ascertain the dividend on the "preferred" and "deferred" stocks, double the ordinary dividend for the year, deduct therefrom 6 per cent., which first accrues to the "preferred" stock, the "deferred" stock is then entitled to whatever residue there may be. Dividend on the "deferred" stock is paid annually.

TRANSFER DEPARTMENT QUERIES AND REPLIES.

Queries.	Replies.
Transfer form—ordinary or special?	Ordinary.
Fee per deed?	2s. 6d. each stock.
Ditto if more sellers than one?	2s. 6d. each seller.
May several classes of stock be transferred on one deed?	Yes, with the exception of debenture stock, which must be by separate deed.
Are certificates required to accompany transfers?	Yes.
What amounts of stock are transferable, and are parts of 1l. sterling allowed to be transferred?	1l. upwards, not fractions.
To what officer should transfer communications be sent?	Secretary.
In acceptances, renunciations, &c., of allotments of new stock, proxies, or other forms sent to trustees and other joint accounts, what signatures are required?	First name in each account.

The estimate of further expenditure on capital account required 218,300l. for the half-year ended 31st December, 1884, and 537,000l. for subsequent half-years—together, 755,300l. The capital powers and other available assets were:—

Surplus lands, Brompton to Aldgate		£935,881	
Deduct amount to be appropriated out of sales in extinction of debenture capital	£440,000		
Less received on account of sales from 1st October, 1874, to date, and so applied	134,431		
		305,569	
			£630,312
Add—Capital authorised but not yet created		£1,888,430	
" created and issued but not yet received		585	
" created but not yet issued		450,000	
Available borrowing powers		200,241	
		£2,539,256	
Balance to debit of capital account		402,818	
			2,136,438
Total			£2,766,750

REVENUE.

Tabular view of the working of this undertaking for the last three half-years:—

Receipts.	1883. June 30.	1883. Dec. 31.	1884. June 30.
Passengers, parcels, horses, carriages, &c.	£284,273	£289,077	£289,699
Merchandise, live stock, and minerals	13,967	16,450	14,832
Rent of stations, refreshment rooms, &c.	17,826	18,004	17,762
Transfer fees	129	114	139
Estate revenue account	33,582	34,010	34,126
Interest on Hammersmith and City debenture account	800	800	800
	£350,577	£358,455	£357,358

Expenses.	1883. June 30.	1883. Dec. 31.	1884. June 30.
Maintenance of way, works, and stations	£13,633	£13,774	£13,421
Locomotive power	28,393	29,691	30,462
Carriage repairs	9,932	10,986	10,511
Traffic expenses	32,319	34,851	34,382
General charges	13,000	11,956	13,032
Law agency	1,156	3,104	3,576
Compensation	146	157	188
Rates, taxes, and Government duty	21,686	19,672	18,415
Working joint lines	5,093	5,401	5,510
	£125,358	£129,542	£129,437
Less received for working other lines	7,016	7,317	7,178
Ordinary working expenses	£118,342	£122,225	£122,259
Preference charges, viz.:—			
Interest on loans and debenture stock, and bankers' and general interest (net)	59,793	63,513	62,635
Rents, commissions, interest on land purchases, and sundries (net)	2,767	2,763	2,772
Dividend on preference stocks	51,704	51,704	51,704
	£232,606	£240,205	£239,370
Net balances each half-year	£117,971	£118,250	£117,988
Balances brought from previous half-years	717	1,228	2,019
Balances available for dividend on ordinary stock	£118,688	£119,478	£120,007
Dividends declared at 5 per cent. per annum each half-year	117,459	117,459	117,459
Surplus carried forward	£1,229	£2,019	£2,548

Summary showing the results of the last half-year's working as compared with those of the corresponding period of 1883, viz.:—

Net balance—30th June, 1883	£117,971	Thus:—	
„ 30th June, 1884	117,988	Fixed charges—increase...£2,847	
		Working charges—increase 3,917	=£6,764
		Less:—	
		Gross traffic—increase	6,781
Gain in 1884	£17	Net gain in 1884	£17

New Capital.—In September, 1881, 750,000*l.* new ordinary stock was issued and allotted to the proprietors. This stock has now been fully called up, the dividend on which commenced to accrue as from the 1st October, 1884.

No. of Directors—12; minimum, 6; quorum, 3. *Qualification*, 1,000*l.*, one vote for every 10*l.* ordinary stock, and one vote for every 20*l.* preference stock.

DIRECTORS:

Chairman—Sir EDWARD WILLIAM WATKIN, Bart., M.P., Rose Hill, Northenden, Cheshire, and Charing Cross Hotel, Charing Cross, W.C.

Deputy-Chairman—H. D. POCHIN, Esq., 22, Harrington Gardens, S.W.

Andrew Cassels, Esq., 51, Cleveland Square, W.

The Right Hon. Lord Brabourne, Smeeth, near Ashford, Kent, and 3, Queen Anne's Gate, S.W.

George Morphett, Esq., St. Leonards-on-Sea.

Benjamin Whitworth, Esq., M.P., 22, Dalcham Gardens, Hampstead, N.W.

Alfred Mellor Watkin, Esq., Dunedin Lodge, Folkestone, Kent.

OFFICERS.—Sec., John Meredith Eyles; Gen. Man., John Bell; Locomotive Supt. and Res. Eng., J. Tomlinson, jun., M.Inst.C.E., Locomotive Works, Neasden, N.W.; Auditors, Edwin Waterhouse and Francis Pavy, 44, Gresham Street, E.C.; Solicitors, Fowler and Perks, 147, Leadenhall Street, E.C.; Bankers, National Provincial Bank of England Limited, Bishopsgate Street, E.C.

Offices—32, Westbourne Terrace, Paddington, W.

191.—METROPOLITAN DISTRICT.

Incorporated by act of 29th July, 1864, to construct a series of lines to complete an inner circle of railway north of the Thames, extending from Kensington, by Westminster Bridge and the north bank of the Thames, to Tower Hill. Length, 8 miles. Capital, 3,600,000*l.* in shares of 20*l.* each and 1,200,000*l.* on loan. Arrangements with Metropolitan and facilities to London and North Western. Opened between Kensington and Westminster Bridge on 24th December, 1868; to Blackfriars on 30th May, 1870; and to Cannon Street on 1st July, 1871. City Lines and Extensions opened for public traffic 6th October, 1884.

FURTHER POWERS.—For list of Acts, 1865 to 1878, with short heads showing the objects for which the various powers were sought, see the MANUAL for 1881, page 246.

1879—11TH AUGUST.—Metropolitan and District Railways (City Lines and Extensions) Joint Act.—See below.

1880—2ND AUGUST.—Purchase of lands at Fulham; vesting of Eel Brook Common, &c.

1881—3RD JUNE—CITY LINES AND EXTENSIONS.—Period for completion of works extended to 11th August, 1883.

1881—27TH JUNE.—West Brompton Junction. Length, 1 furlong 9 chains and 69 links. Period for completion, 2 years. Provision for conversion of 6 per cent. debenture stock. New capital, 100,000*l.*

1884—7TH AUGUST.—Subway at South Kensington; acquirement of lands, and other general purposes.

CITY LINES AND EXTENSIONS.—By the Metropolitan and District Railways (City Lines and Extensions) Act of 11th August, 1879, powers were conferred upon the two companies jointly to make certain railways, for completing the Inner Circle, and connecting their railways with the East London. The act also gave powers for the two companies to enter into agreements with the Corporation of London, the Metropolitan Board of Works, and the Commissioners of Sewers, for new streets and improvements in the City of London. Capital authorised, 2,500.000*l.*; loans, 800,000*l.*; half to be raised by each company. By act of 24th July, 1882, the period for completion of works was extended to 11th August, 1884. Up to August, 1883, 655,000*l.* of the capital authorised by the act of 1879 was issued at par as "4 per cent. perpetual guarantee stock," when a further issue of 345,000*l.* was offered to shareholders at 94 per cent. The dividends upon this portion of stock offered in August, 1883, began to accrue on 1st September, 1884. The certificates of the new stock will bear the following endorsement:—"The Metropolitan District guaranteed stock, of which this stock is part, is issued on the terms that the same shall be a cumulative charge—firstly, upon the share or proportion of the District Company of the joint undertaking created by the within-mentioned act of 1879, after payment thereout of the expenses of and incident to the working, control, management, maintenance, and repair thereof, including rates and taxes and passenger duty, if any; and secondly, upon the other revenues of the District Company to rank next after the mortgage debt and debenture stocks of the District Company."

EALING EXTENSION.—The bill authorising the construction of this extension as a separate undertaking has been sanctioned by Parliament. The line was opened for traffic on the 1st July, 1879. At a special meeting of the District Company, held 20th August, 1877, the proprietors sanctioned the creation of 250,000*l.* of Ealing Extension Railway Rent-charge Stock, which was accordingly issued in September, and offered first to the District proprietary at the price of 102½ per cent. The stock bears a fixed perpetual dividend of 4½ per cent. per annum, payment of which is, however, deferred until the opening of the new line, upon which it is secured. The line was opened for traffic on the 1st July, 1879.

FULHAM EXTENSION.—The following resolutions were passed at a special meeting held under the act of 4th July, 1878, viz:—Resolved, "That the terms and conditions upon which the Fulham Extension, authorised by the Metropolitan District Act, 1878, shall be worked and managed by the Metropolitan District, and the dividends or annual or other sums to be paid to or upon the shares or stock constituting the separate capital of the said undertaking out of the gross receipts arising from the traffic passing, as well upon the Metropolitan District Fulham Extension as upon such extension and the other railways of the company, and the payments to be made in respect of the use of such Metropolitan District Fulham Extension, for the traffic of the company, shall be as follows:—The separate capital of 300,000*l.* constituting the capital of such separate undertaking shall be raised by the issue of stock to be called 'The Fulham Rent-charge Stock,' which shall be entitled to a perpetual guaranteed rent or dividend at the rate of 4½ per cent. per annum, to be calculated up to and payable on the 15th of April and 15th of October in every year. The first payment to be made on such one of the said days as shall first follow the granting the Certificate by the Board of Trade of the completion and opening of the Fulham Extension, and the dividends of the rent-charge stock, amounting to 13,500*l.* a year, shall be a first charge on the gross receipts arising from all traffic conveyed upon the Fulham Extension, or conveyed upon the District Railway, on to or from the Fulham Extension, and in addition thereto shall, if in arrear, be a charge on the revenues of the District Railway as for rent in arrear." The above-named capital was issued in August, 1878, at 102*l.* 10*s.* per cent., dividend to accrue from 1st October, 1879, previously to which date the line will have been opened for traffic. The extension was opened for traffic on the 1st March, 1880.

HAMMERSMITH EXTENSION.—Incorporated 17th July, 1873, to construct a line from the Metropolitan District, at Fulham, to the Broadway, Hammersmith. Length, 1 mile 7 chains. Capital, 244,444*l.*, guaranteed 4½ per cent. by the District. By act of 30th June, 1874, the line was leased to the Metropolitan District for 999 years, the latter company taking over all the liabilities of the Extension Company. Opened 9th September, 1874.

HAMMERSMITH JUNCTION.—Authorised by the act of 1875 as above. By an agreement with the Midland Company, dated 25th April, 1876, and confirmed by that company's act of 12th July, 1877, it is provided that the District Company shall, with all convenient expedition, construct, complete, and open the line for traffic; the capital expended to be kept separate from the capital of the District Company, so as to form a separate and distinct undertaking, and that on its completion, the Midland Company shall have certain running powers over portions of the District Line connected with the Hammersmith Junction (subject to the payment of tolls) and the use of the Junction Line; the receipts of the Midland over the line and the receipts of the Hammersmith Junction to form a fund, out of which the District Company is to receive the expenses of maintenance and a sum equal to the payment of a dividend of 4½ per cent. per annum on the Hammersmith paid-up capital, the balance of the fund to be paid to the Midland Company. By act of 4th July, 1878, before referred to, provision is made that, instead of the terms contained in the fourth article of the above-named agreement, the Midland shall from 1st July, 1878, pay a rental equal to 4 per cent. per annum on the Hammersmith paid-up capital (350,000*l.*); the "Junction Fund" to be applied as follows:—The District to receive thereout such a proportion of the amount standing to the credit thereof as the gross working expenses of their railway in the previous year bore to the gross receipts for that year, the balance to be handed over to the Midland.

HOUNSLOW AND METROPOLITAN.—See GENERAL INDEX.

KENSINGTON JOINT LINES.—In accordance with the agreement of the 27th June, 1871, the Joint Lines and stations (South Kensington, Gloucester Road, and High Street) were to be worked on common account, the District receiving 40 per cent., and the Metropolitan 60 per cent. of the excess of receipts over expenditure. The agreement provided for a revision of terms at the end of the first seven years. The traffic contributed to the Joint Lines by the District having considerably increased as a consequence of the extensions westward, a new arrangement has been come to by which each company shares equally in the net revenue of these Joint Lines, as from the 1st July, 1879.

KINGSTON AND LONDON.—See GENERAL INDEX.

REVENUE.—The receipts and expenditure for the half-years ended 31st December, 1883, and 30th June, 1884, are given in the subjoined table:—

	Dec., 1883.	June, 1884.
Gross revenue	£202,504	£205,415
Expenditure	85,819	86,196
Net	£116,685	£119,219
Sundry balances, &c.	2,998	2,539
Total net revenue	£119,683	£121,758
Interest, rents, guarantees, &c.	81,656	81,885
Available for division	£38,027	£39,873
Dividends on preference stock, at 5 per cent. per annum each half-year respectively	37,500	37,500
Balance carried forward	£527	£2,373

CAPITAL.—The statement of stock and share capital, showing the proportion received to 30th June, 1884, furnished the subjoined particulars:—

Description.	Created.	Received.
Hammersmith rent-charge stock	£244,444	£244,444
5 per cent. preference stock (discount on issue 548,766*l*. 18*s*.)	1,500,000	1,500,000
Ealing rent-charge stock	250,000	250,000
Fulham rent-charge stock	300,000	300,000
4 per cent. guaranteed stock	1,250,000	1,000,000
Ordinary stock	2,250,000	2,250,000
	£5,794,444	£5,544,444

MEM.—Metropolitan District guaranteed 4 per cent. perpetual preference stock.— See page 223.

The receipts and expenditure on this account to the same date were detailed as under:—

Received.		*Expended.*	
Shares and stock	£5,544,444	Lines open for traffic	£6,329,521
Loans	90,150	Lines in course of construction (City Lines Extension)	1,210,199
Debenture stock	1,781,625	Working stock	236,751
	£7,416,219		£7,776,471
Balance	77,256	Less realisation of surplus lands	282,996
	£7,493,475		£7,493,475

The estimate of expenditure (including lines in course of construction) during the half-year ended 31st December, 1884, required 623,500*l*.; in subsequent half years, 472,000*l*.; total, 1,095,000*l*.; the available assets being 1,180,639*l*.

The accounts are made up to the 30th June and 31st December, and the meeting held in February or March and August or September in each year.

No. of Directors—6. *Qualification*, 1,000*l*.

DIRECTORS:

Chairman—JAMES STAATS FORBES, Esq., 13, Chelsea Embankment, S.W.

Deputy-Chairman—GEORGE WODEHOUSE CURRIE, Esq., 6, Park Lane, W.

The Right Honourable Viscount Gort, 1, Portman Square, W.

Lewis Henry Isaacs, Esq., 3, Pembridge Square, W.

James Murray, Esq., 25, Portman Street, W.

George Wyld, Esq., M.D., 41, Courtfield Road, South Kensington, S.W.

OFFICERS.—Sec., George Hopwood; Gen. Man., Lord Sackville A. Cecil; Con. Eng., John Fowler, M.Inst.C.E.; Accountant, Alfred Powell; Auditors, Benjamin Room and Roderick Mackay; Valuers, Sir Henry Arthur Hunt and Robert Ritchie; Solicitors, Baxters and Co., 6, Victoria Street, Westminster, S.W.; Bankers, Glyn, Mills, Currie, and Co., 67, Lombard Street, E.C.

Offices—Parliament Mansions, Victoria Street, S.W.

192.—MID KENT (BROMLEY TO ST. MARY CRAY).

Incorporated by act of 21st July, 1856, to construct a line from Bromley, at the West End of London and Crystal Palace Line, to St. Mary Cray. Length, 2½ miles Capital, 61,550*l*. stock; loans, 23,000*l*.

By act of 7th August, 1862, the line was leased to the London, Chatham, and Dover, from 1st September, 1863, for 999 years, at a rent equal to 4 per cent. on the share capital.

CAPITAL.—This account is now closed at 84,967*l*., the amount expended on the line. The receipts were 84,550*l*., viz., 61,550*l*. capital stock, and 23,000*l*. debentures. The balance of 417*l*. was paid out of revenue.

Meetings are held in London in February and August.

DIRECTORS:

Chairman—CHARLES HILL, Esq., Rockhurst, West Hoathly, Sussex.

N. W. J. Strode, Esq., Chislehurst.

Frederick Hughes, Esq., 28, Threadneedle Street, E.C.

OFFICERS.—Sec., Fred. W. Smith; Auditors, Thomas B. Hill and Chas. Ros Brown.

Offices—31, Queen Victoria Street, E.C.

193.—MIDLAND.

An amalgamation of the NORTH MIDLAND, MIDLAND COUNTIES, and BIRMINGHAM AND DERBY, since 10th May, 1844. With the company thus amalgamated there have been incorporated, by an issue of Midland guaranteed shares, the following railways, viz.:—Bristol and Gloucester, and Birmingham and Gloucester (95½ miles), Sheffield and Rotherham (9½ miles), Leicester and Swannington (16 miles), and Leeds and Bradford (43 miles). In addition to which the following extensions have been authorised and constructed since the amalgamation, viz.:—Syston and Peterborough (48½ miles), Nottingham and Lincoln and Southwell Branch (36 miles), Leicester and Swannington Extensions (21¼ miles), the Erewash Valley (21½ miles), the Nottingham and Mansfield (12½ miles), and the Mansfield and Pinxton (7½ miles). Other amalgamations and extensions will be found further on.

The Midland had power by act of 1847-48 to make a line from Leicester to Hitchin, but abandoned it on arrangements with Great Northern. In 1853 it obtained an act to make a line from Wigston Station, Leicester, to Hitchin Station, and branch to Wellingbro' Station of London and North Western, 62 miles; branch, 1 mile; also to lay down additional rails on Rugby and Stamford.

FURTHER PARLIAMENTARY POWERS:—

A list of Acts obtained by the company from 1853 to 1879, with short heads showing the objects for which the various powers were sought, will be found on reference to the MANUAL for 1881, pages 253 to 257.

1880—6TH AUGUST.—Various new railways and works in the counties of Middlesex, Lancashire, Gloucestershire, Staffordshire, and Nottinghamshire, all short lines and curves, and other works in connection with the Sharpness New Docks, Birmingham Navigation, and Severn Bridge companies. Sundry extensions of time for sale of lands and completion of works, &c. New capital, 1,350,000*l.*; borrowing powers, 450,000*l.*

1881—3RD JUNE.—Joint powers with the London and North Western for the construction of a railway at Market Harborough, and for sundry alterations and diversions of lines in connection therewith. Period for completion, 4 years. New capital, 90,000*l.* Borrowing powers, 30,000*l.*

1881—18TH JULY.—Various powers; vesting of Keighley and Worth Valley New capital, 1,800,000*l.*; borrowing powers, 600,000*l.*

1882—12TH JULY.—Vesting of Evesham and Redditch (see that company); construction of sundry new lines and works at Wormfield, Featherstone, Normanton, Stroud, Keighley, and Swansea Vale. Period for completion, 5 years. New capital, 1,500,000*l.*; borrowing powers, 500,000*l.*

1883—16TH JULY.—New lines and works at Skipton, Ilkley, Liverpool, Derby, and other places. Confirmation of agreement with Hull, Barnsley, and West Riding Junction and Severn Bridge companies. New capital, 1,350,000*l.*; loans, &c., 450,000*l.*

1884—3RD JULY.—Short lines at Ripley and Heanor, and various other purposes. New capital, 1,200,000*l.*; loans, 400,000*l.*

AMALGAMATIONS, LEASES, AGREEMENTS, &c.:—

BIRMINGHAM WEST SUBURBAN.—Incorporated 31st July, 1871, to make a line from Albion Wharf, Birmingham, to King's Norton, on the Midland. Length, 6¾ miles. Capital, 100,000*l.* in 10*l.* shares and 33,300*l.* on loan. By act of 7th July, 1873, the company was authorised to make certain abandonments, diversions, and alterations, and to extend the time for completion of works to July, 1876. New capital, 65,000*l.* in shares or stock and 21,500*l.* on loan. By the Midland (Additional Powers) Act, 1875, the undertaking was vested in the Midland in its entirety, each holder of preference shares in the Birmingham West Suburban to receive in exchange a like amount of Midland 5 per cent. consolidated preference stock; and of West Suburban ordinary shares, 90 per cent. of Midland 5 per cent. stock.

CHESTERFIELD AND BRAMPTON.—Incorporated by act of 12th May, 1870, to construct a line from the Midland, at Chesterfield, to Brampton, with branches or tramways. Length, 2 miles. Capital, 10,000*l.* in 10*l.* shares and 3,300*l.* on loan. Vested in Midland by act of 1871.

DURSLEY AND MIDLAND JUNCTION.—Incorporated by act of 25th May, 1855, for making a railway from the parish of Cam, in Gloucestershire, by a junction with the Bristol and Birmingham (Midland), to the town of Dursley. Length, 2½ miles. Capital, 12,000*l.* in 20*l.* shares; loans, 4,000*l.* The purchase money amounted to 10,750*l.*, on which the Midland allows 4 per cent.

EVESHAM AND REDDITCH.—Incorporated by act of 13th July, 1863, Evesham to Redditch, with a branch to the West Midland. Length, 17¾ miles. Capital.—Amount expended, 198,600*l.* Receipts as follow:—Ordinary 10*l.* shares, 149,000*l.*; debenture stock at 4½ per cent., 49,600*l.*

Vesting of the Undertaking in that of the Midland.—An agreement has been entered into, dated the 14th day of February, 1882, and confirmed by the Midland Company's Additional Powers Act of 12th July, 1882, which provides that the Evesham and Redditch undertaking do vest in the Midland from the 1st of July, 1882, from which date the Midland assumes the liability to the holders of the debenture stock, and issues to the holders of debenture stock of the Evesham an equivalent amount of Midland 4 per cent. debenture stock. From the vesting period the Midland will pay to the Evesham an annual rent or sum of 5,215*l.*, clear of all deductions, except for property or income tax, by equal half-yearly payments, on the 1st day of January and the 1st day of July in each year, this annual rent to be employed in payment of a dividend at the rate of 3½ per cent. per annum, free from all deductions, except income tax, to the shareholders for the time being of the Evesham and Redditch.

FURNESS AND MIDLAND.—Incorporated by act of 22nd June, 1863, by which the Furness and the Midland are authorised to construct a line from Carnforth to Wennington, connecting the Ulverston and Lancaster and the Little North Western. Length, 9¾ miles. Capital, 150,000*l.* in shares, to be provided in equal proportions by the two companies; borrowing powers, 50,000*l.*

HAMMERSMITH JUNCTION.—See Metropolitan District.

HEMEL HEMPSTEAD.—See GENERAL INDEX.

HEREFORD, HAY, AND BRECON.—Leased to the Midland, as from the 1st July, 1874.—See Hereford, Hay, and Brecon.

KEIGHLEY AND WORTH VALLEY.—Incorporated by act of 30th June, 1862, to construct a line from the Leeds and Bradford Extension of the Midland, at Keighley, to Haworth and Lowertown. Length, 4¾ miles. The line was for some time worked by the Midland at 50 per cent. of the gross receipts, but became vested in the Midland under that company's act of 18th July, 1881, as from the 1st July, 1881, at an annual rental of 4,200*l.*, payable half-yearly on the 15th January and 15th July. The Midland in addition paying 60,000*l.* to the Keighley, for the purpose of discharging the debts and liabilities of the latter company prior to the transfer.

KETTERING AND MANTON.—This line was opened for goods and mineral traffic on the 1st December, 1879, and for passenger traffic early in 1880.

MANCHESTER, BUXTON, MATLOCK, AND MIDLANDS JUNCTION.—Incorporated by act of 16th July, 1846, for a line between Ambergate and Rowsley, near Chatsworth. Length, 11½ miles. Opened 4th June, 1848. By act of 26th June, 1870, this line is incorporated with the Midland, on and from 1st July, 1871, when the registered holders of shares became holders of (Matlock) stock in the capital of the Midland, of an amount equal to the amount held by them in the company, and to be entitled to a dividend thereon at the rate of 5*l.* per cent. per annum in perpetuity, payable half-yearly. Within twelve months after 1st July, 1871, shareholders may, by notice in writing to the secretary of the Midland, elect to accept ordinary stock of the Midland in exchange for the whole amount of their respective holdings in Matlock stock, as from the then next 30th June or 31st December, as the case may be.

MANCHESTER SOUTH DISTRICT.—Incorporated by act of 5th August, 1873, to construct a line from Manchester to Alderley, with branches therefrom. Length, 11¾ miles. Capital, 350,000*l.* in 10*l.* shares and 118,000*l.* on loan. Power to enter into arrangements with Cheshire Lines Committee and Macclesfield, Knutsford, and Warrington. By act of 11th August, 1877, the rights and powers of this company were transferred to the Midland, with the proviso that the Great Northern may elect to become joint owners of the undertaking. Opened from Manchester (Central Station) to Stockport (Tiviot Dale) January 1st, 1880.

MANCHESTER AND STOCKPORT.—See Sheffield and Midland Joint Lines.

MIDLAND AND NORTH EASTERN JOINT (SWINTON AND KNOTTINGLEY).—This line was opened for traffic on the 1st July, 1879.—See GENERAL INDEX.

MIDLAND AND SOUTH WESTERN JUNCTION.—Incorporated by act of 14th July 1864, to construct a line from the North and South Western Junction, at Acton, to the London Extension of the Midland, at Hendon. Length, 4 miles. Capital, 90,000*l.* in 10*l.* shares, 53,000*l.* of which was paid up in September, 1867, and 30,000*l.* on loan. Vested in the Midland at an annual rental of 6,000*l.* per annum.

NEATH AND BRECON.—See GENERAL INDEX.

NORTH AND SOUTH WESTERN JUNCTION.—Joint lease with London and North Western and North London.—See GENERAL INDEX.

NORTH WESTERN.—Originally incorporated by act of 30th June, 1846, for a railway from the Leeds and Bradford, at Skipton, to the Lancaster and Carlisle, at Low Park, Kendal, with a diverging line to Lancaster. Various acts of Parliament reduced the undertaking to a line from Skipton to Ingleton and Poulton, a connection with Lancaster and Carlisle. Length, 47 miles. By act of 23rd June, 1864, the company was authorised to divide its 20*l*. shares into one of 12*l*. and another of 8*l*., the former bearing a perpetual fixed dividend of 5 per cent., and the latter taking the residue of the rent with any contingent advantage that may arise out of the lease to the Midland. This alteration was duly effected on the 11th July, 1864. A new arrangement with the Midland was agreed to in August, 1870, of which the subjoined are the main particulars:—The terms agreed upon in respect to the "A" and "B" stock, as originally united, are—For the year 1871, 3¾ per cent.; 1872, 4; 1873, 4¼; 1874, 4½; 1875, 5; and thenceforward in perpetuity. As the "A" stock already takes a first and preferential dividend over the "B" stock of 5 per cent, its position remains unaltered; and the latter stock, taking all contingent benefit from or in lieu of the fourth rent, will receive the whole of the remaining dividend, and will be entitled to the progressive increase as follows:—For the year 1871, 1*l*. 17*s*. 6*d*. per cent.; 1872, 2*l*. 10*s*.; 1873, 3*l*. 2*s*. 6*d*.; 1874, 3*l*. 15*s*.; 1875, 5*l*.; and thenceforward in perpetuity. The absolute conveyance of the North Western to the Midland took place on the 1st January, 1871.

NOTTINGHAM AND MELTON.—This line was opened for traffic early in 1880.

REDDITCH.—Incorporated by act of 23rd July, 1858, to construct a line from Redditch to the Midland at Barnt Green. Capital, 35,000*l*. in 10*l*. shares; loans, 11,500*l*. Length, 4¾ miles. By act of 7th August, 1862, the company was authorised to raise new capital to the extent of 15,000*l*. in shares, at not exceeding 6 per cent., and 5,000*l*. on loan. Also to create debenture stock in lieu of loans. Leased to Midland at 4 per cent. per annum, and worked by that company.

SETTLE AND CARLISLE.—Opened for goods traffic on the 1st August, 1875, and for passenger traffic on the 1st May, 1876. The Hawes Branch of this line was opened for goods traffic on the 1st August, 1878, and for passenger traffic a little later on.

SOUTHPORT AND CHESHIRE LINES EXTENSION.—See GENERAL INDEX.

STONEHOUSE AND NAILSWORTH.—Incorporated by act of 13th July, 1863, to construct a line from Stonehouse, on the Bristol and Birmingham Line of the Midland, to Nailsworth. In operation, at 30th June, 1875, 5¾ miles. On the 20th December, 1871, a scheme of arrangement was enrolled in the Court of Chancery fixing the share capital at 75,940*l*., and the borrowing powers at 29,000*l*. The line has been in the past leased to the Midland at 50 per cent. of the traffic receipts. By the Midland Company's Act of 17th June, 1878, authority was obtained for the vesting of this company in the Midland, as from the 1st July, 1878, on the following terms:—The existing powers of the Stonehouse Company to be taken over by the Midland. The Midland to pay to the Stonehouse 20,768*l*., to be applied by the latter company to the payment of their debts and liabilities. Debenture stock to be issued by the Midland in substitution of the mortgages of the Stonehouse not paid off, &c. Shares held by the Midland in the undertaking to be cancelled, and the capital thereof thus reduced to 40,940*l*., consisting of 2,047 ordinary shares of 20*l*. each. The Midland to pay to the Stonehouse annual sums as follow:—From the vesting period to 31st December, 1879, 1*s*., and for the year 1880 and for all subsequent years, 1,228*l*. 4*s*., payable by equal half-yearly payments on the 15th January and 15th July in each year. The Stonehouse Company to hold the sums of money so received, and apply them in the same manner as their income as a separate undertaking would be applicable.

SWANSEA VALE.—This was originally a registered company, formed in January, 1850, to acquire the Swansea Valley Railway—a line authorised by act of 2nd July, 1817, from the port of Swansea to Cadoxtan-Juxta-Neath, 19 miles. By act of 15th June, 1855, the company was converted into one acting under the authority of Parliament, with a capital of 147,000*l*. in 35*l*. shares, and a debenture debt of 49,000*l*. (for sundry other details, see MANUAL for 1882, page 249). In operation, 26¼ miles. By act of 11th August, 1876, the undertaking was vested in the Midland on the following terms:—The Midland to create and issue to every holder of shares in the Swansea Vale such an amount of Midland preference stock as will yield to him an annual dividend equal to the amount of rent to which the said holder is entitled under the Lease Act of 1874.

TEWKESBURY AND MALVERN.—Incorporated by act of 25th May, 1860, to construct a line from the Ashchurch and Tewkesbury Branch of the Midland to Great Malvern. Length, 14¼ miles. Opened from the Malvern Junction with the West Midland to Malvern Hill Station on 1st July, 1862, and throughout on 1st May, 1864. By act of 11th August, 1876, the undertaking was vested in the Midland as from the 1st of July, 1877, on the following payments:—To the holders of the first mortgages in the Tewkesbury Company (amounting to 29,400*l.*) the full amount of their holdings, together with arrears of interest; to the holders of the second mortgages (amounting to 59,100*l.*) 50 per cent. of the amount held; to the holders of Lloyd's bonds (amounting to 107,250*l.*) 10 per cent of the amount held; to the holders of shares (amounting to 155,610*l.*) 10 per cent. of the amount held.

WALSALL EXTENSION.—This branch was opened for traffic on the 1st July, 1879.

WOLVERHAMPTON AND WALSALL.—Incorporated 29th June, 1865, to construct a line from Wolverhampton to Walsall. The line was opened throughout on the 1st November, 1872. By the London and North Western (New Lines and Additional Powers) Act, 1875, the Wolverhampton and Walsall was vested in that company as from the 1st July, 1875, on the following terms:—The London and North Western to subscribe for the unissued preference shares, amounting to about 25,000*l.*; to pay 4 per cent. per annum on the preference capital of the Walsall Company, and dividends on the ordinary capital after the following rates:—For the years ending 30th June, 1877, and 30th June, 1878, 2 per cent.; for the years ending 30th June, 1879, and 30th June, 1880, 2½ per cent.; for the year ending 30th June, 1881, 3 per cent.; for the year ending 30th June, 1882, 3½ per cent.; for the year ending 30th June, 1883, and all subsequent years, 4 per cent. The entire mortgage debt of the Walsall Company to be assumed by the London and North Western, which may issue debenture stock in lieu thereof. Provisions are made in the act for the immediate dissolution of the Walsall Company. By act of 1876 the line was sold by the London and North Western to the Midland.

WOLVERHAMPTON, WALSALL, AND MIDLAND JUNCTION.—Incorporated by act of 6th August, 1872, to construct three lines, viz.:—The first (12½ miles) from Walsall, on the Wolverhampton and Walsall, to the Tame Valley Branch of the Midland; the second (3 furlongs) from Rushall, on the foregoing, to a junction with the South Staffordshire at the last lodge level crossing; and third (5 furlongs) from Rushall to the South Staffordshire at North Street. By the Midland (Additional Powers) Act, 1874, the undertaking was dissolved, and vested in the Midland.

WORCESTER AND HEREFORD.—By act of 1858, the Midland subscribed 37,500*l* to this undertaking.

ACCOUNTS:—

The ordinary half-yearly meeting of this company was held on the 15th August last, when the directors' reports and accounts for the half-year ended 30th June, 1884, were presented and adopted. The following is an abstract of those accounts, viz.:—

CAPITAL.—*Authorised:* Stock and shares, 59,585,877*l.*; loans, 18,563,390*l.*; total, 78,149,267*l.* *Created or Sanctioned:* Stock and shares, 58,385,877*l.*; loans, 17,203,390*l.*; total, 75,589,267*l.* The receipts and expenditure on this account to 30th June, 1884, were as follow:—

*Receipts.**—Stocks and shares—		
Ordinary capital		£26,428,079
Preference capital—		
4 per cent. consolidated perpetual rent-charges	£3,205,481	
6 per cent. Sheffield and Rotherham	150,000	
4 per cent. consolidated perpetual guaranteed	5,994,577	
5 per cent. consolidated perpetual	11,158,541	
4½ per cent. perpetual	1,950,000	
4 per cent. perpetual preference stock, 1876	188,309	
Stonehouse and Nailsworth 20*l.* shares	40,940	
4 per cent. perpetual preference shares, 1881	2,089,571	
4 per cent. optional convertible 10*l.* shares	†4,299,415	
11*l.* 4 per cent. perpetual preference shares	1,605,354=	30,682,138
Total stock and share capital		£57,110,217
Loan capital—		
Debentures	£349,678	
Debenture stock	16,835,464=	17,185,142
		£74,295,359
Sundries, being redemption of mortgages, cancelled shares, and premiums on stocks and shares sold		791,455
		£75,086,814

* Including transfers from Swansea Vale, Wolverhampton, and Walsall, and Stonehouse and Nailsworth.

† This amount is convertible into ordinary stock at the option of holders as follows:—2,050,000*l.* not later than 31st August, 1885, and 2,249,415*l.* not later than 31st August, 1887.

DESCRIPTIONS, &c., OF STOCKS AND SHARES.—The following is a list of this company's Stocks and Shares, numbered in order of entry on the company's books, with conditions of issue *in brief*, the descriptions to be strictly observed in transfer deeds and all other legal documents relating thereto, viz.:—

1—FOUR PER CENT. DEBENTURE STOCK.—Issued under various acts. Dividend accumulative, and payable half-yearly, 1st January and 1st July. Transfer books close 14 days before payment.

2—SHEFFIELD AND ROTHERHAM PREFERENTIAL STOCK.—Dividend at 6 per cent. per annum, accumulative, and payable (without deduction of income tax) half-yearly, 14th January and 14th July. Transfer books close 14 days before payment.

3—FOUR PER CENT. CONSOLIDATED PERPETUAL RENT-CHARGE STOCK.—Issued under act 1874, for conversion of other securities. Date of scheme, 11th December, 1874. Dividend accumulative, and payable half-yearly (see notes).

4—FOUR PER CENT. CONSOLIDATED PERPETUAL GUARANTEED PREFERENTIAL STOCK.—Issued under act 1874, for conversion of other securities. Date of scheme, 11th December, 1874. Dividend accumulative, and payable half-yearly (see notes).

5—FIVE PER CENT. CONSOLIDATED PERPETUAL PREFERENCE STOCK.—Issued under act 1874, for conversion of other stocks. Date of scheme, 11th December, 1874. Dividend not accumulative (see notes).

6—FOUR-AND-A-HALF PER CENT. PREFERENCE STOCK.—Issued under act 1875. Dividend not accumulative (see notes).

7—FOUR PER CENT. PREFERENCE STOCK, 1876.—Balance of 17*l.* shares (issued under acts 1876) not converted into ordinary stock. Dividend not accumulative.

8—£10 FOUR PER CENT. PREFERENCE SHARES, 1878.—Issued under acts 1877-8. Convertible at the option of holders, on giving notice not later than 31st August, 1885 (from which date such conversion would be effected), into *par* of ordinary stock. Dividend not accumulative (see notes).

9—£10 FOUR PER CENT. PREFERENCE SHARES, 1880.—Issued under acts 1879-80. Convertible at the option of holders, on giving notice not later than 31st August, 1887 (from which date such conversion would be effected), into *par* of ordinary stock. Dividend not accumulative (see notes).

10—FOUR PER CENT. PERPETUAL PREFERENCE STOCK, 1881.—Created and issued under company's "Additional Powers Act, 1881." Dividends not accumulative (see notes).

11—£11 FOUR PER CENT. PERPETUAL PREFERENCE SHARES, 1883.—Created and issued under company's "Additional Powers Acts, 1882-3," and "South-Western Act, 1882," deposit, 3*l.* per share, 1st January, 1884; second call 3*l.* per share, 1st July, 1884; third call 3*l.* per share, 1st January, 1885; remaining call and payments in advance of calls at discretion of directors. Application to be made to the secretary beforehand. Interest, if such payment allowed, 3½ per cent. per annum. Dividends not accumulative.

12—CONSOLIDATED ORDINARY STOCK.—Issued under various acts (see notes).

NOTES:—The foregoing descriptions must be strictly observed in transfer deeds and all other legal documents. In regard to the ordinary capital, "Consolidated Ordinary Stock" is the correct name, but the company do not object to pass transfers when described as "Consolidated Stock," when in accordance with the description upon the coupons.

The dividends on all stocks, except No. 2, are payable subject to deduction of income tax.

The transfer books of all stocks, except Nos. 1 and 2, close 28 days previous to each half-yearly meeting, generally held in the middle of February and August respectively, the dividends being usually payable at the end of those months.

Upon stocks Nos. 5 to 11 dividends are not accumulative, but contingent upon the profits of each separate year ending 31st December.

The secretary, in supplying information on this subject, states that "the above is the order of the various stocks on the company's books, and does not necessarily imply their legal priority."

TRANSFER DEPARTMENT QUERIES AND REPLIES.

Queries.	Replies.
Transfer form—ordinary or special?	Ordinary.
Fee per deed?	2s. 6d.
Ditto if more sellers than one?	The same, viz., 2s. 6d. per deed.
May several classes of stock be transferred on one deed?	Yes, but debenture stock is subject to a special stamp duty.
Are certificates required to accompany transfers?	Stock securities required, but not certificates of shares, which should be handed over to purchasers with the transfer deeds containing the corresponding numbers.
What amounts of stock are transferable, and are parts of 1l. sterling allowed to be transferred?	No restriction.
To what officer should transfer communications be sent?	James Williams, Secretary, Derby.
In acceptances, renunciations, &c., of allotments of new stock, proxies, or other forms sent to trustees, what signatures are required?	All.

Expenditure.—Lines open for traffic	£56,479,068
Lines and works in course of construction	1,354,101
Lines not commenced and in abeyance	7,612
Working stock	9,746,151
Subscriptions to other railways and contributions to joint lines	7,027,210
Purchase of Ashby Canal	109,900
	£74,724,042
Balance	362,772
	£75,086,814

The estimate of further expenditure on capital account was as follows:—

	Half-year ended 31st Dec., 1884.	In subsequent half-years	Total.
Lines open for traffic, including working stock	£643,000	£1,548,658	£2,191,658
Lines and works constructing, including working stock	315,000	680,343	995,343
Subscriptions to other railways and joint lines	42,000	28,143	70,143
Lines and works not commenced and in abeyance	...	943,537	943,537
Total estimated further expenditure	£1,000,000	£3,200,681	£4,200,681

The capital powers and other assets available to meet this expenditure were stated to amount together to the same sum, viz., 4,200,681l.

REVENUE.—Comparative statement of the amounts received and expended for the last three half-years, viz.:—

Receipts.	1883. 30th June.	1883. 31st Dec.	1884. 30th June.
Passengers, parcels, horses, mails, &c.	£1,086,315	£1,219,998	£1,088,549
Merchandise (less expenses and cartage)	1,346,488	1,418,796	1,374,436
Live stock	29,121	52,557	33,804
Minerals	1,023,749	1,164,985	1,022,739
Canals	2,739	3,006	2,504
Dividends on shares in other lines	1,236	1,992	1,599
Rents and transfer fees	33,621	28,759	30,867
Cheshire Lines proportion of balance on working	19,869	28,218	23,196
Sheffield and Midland ditto ditto	5,718	7,208	6,793
	£3,558,846	£3,915,429	£3,582,307

Expenses.	1883. 30th June.	1883. 31st Dec.	1884. 30th June.
Maintenance of way, works, and stations	£308,667	£347,372	£300,505
Locomotive power	506,649	559,224	514,319
Carriage and wagon repairs	190,570	222,241	252,283
Traffic expenses	618,832	662,724	632,138
General charges	69,574	71,720	70,309
Law and Parliamentary	6,552	10,782	3,992
Compensation and damages to goods	14,032	14,570	14,424
Rates, taxes, and Government duty	117,450	126,822	96,409
Carriage and wagon hire	11,248	15,820	12,688
	£1,843,574	£2,031,275	£1,897,017
Interest on loans and debenture stock, calls in advance, bankers' and general interest, &c. (net)	337,995	336,201	341,496
Rents of leased lines	53,446	50,669	53,121
Dividends on preference and guaranteed stocks	687,609	642,905	658,614
	£2,922,624	£3,061,050	£2,950,248
Net balances each half-year	£616,222	£854,379	£632,059
Balances brought from previous half-years	39,402	13,050	41,552
Balances available for dividend on ordinary stock	£655,624	£867,429	£673,611
Dividends declared at 5¼, 6¼, and 5 per cent. per annum respectively	642,576	825,877	660,702
Surplus carried forward	£13,048	£41,552	£12,909

MILEAGE STATEMENT, 30TH JUNE, 1884.

	Authorised.	Constructed.	Constructing or to be Constructed.	Worked by Engines.
Lines owned by company	1,233	1,168	66	1,162
Do. partly owned	357	352	4	182
Do. leased or rented	47	47	...	47
Total	1,637	1,567	70	1,391
Lines worked	...	...	...	124
Foreign lines worked over	...	...	...	276
Total	...	...	...	1,791

CONSOLIDATION AND CONVERSION OF STOCKS.—The 10*l.* 4½ per cent. preference shares, 1875, were consolidated into 4½ preference stock by resolutions of the proprietors passed at the meetings held 20th February and 14th August, 1877. And of the 16*l.* convertible preference shares, 1872, representing 2,630,000*l.* stock, the option to convert into ordinary stock prior to 31st August, 1877, was exercised by the holders to the extent of 2,057,984*l.*, the balance, representing 572,016*l.*, being consolidated and added to the 5 per cent. consolidated perpetual preference stock.

NEW LINES AND WORKS.—The following is copied from the reports of the engineers and of the directors for the half-year ended 30th June, 1884:—"During the past half-year the lines, sidings, stations, buildings, &c., have been maintained in an efficient state of repair. Thirty-four miles of relaying with steel rails, and forty miles of re-sleepering with creosoted sleepers, have been laid in during that period, and charged to revenue. *Rushton and Bedford Widening* to Sharnbrook is now in use for goods and mineral traffic. *Bootle Goods Branch* is nearly completed, and will be available for traffic in September. *Doe Lea Extension.*—This line will be ready for use by the end of August. *Stroud Branch.*—Most of the bridges and the viaduct are built, and two-thirds of the earthwork done; the station at Stroud and approach thereto are making good progress. *Market Harborough New Line and Works.*—There is about one-sixth of the earthwork to do, and three bridges to finish; the goods station, including the warehouse, is in a forward state, and the works and buildings for the joint passenger station nearly completed. *Snydale Branches, No.* 1.—Most of the bridges are built, and two-thirds of the earthwork done. *Snydale Branches, No.* 2.—The fencing is fixed, and the earthwork and bridges commenced. *Holwell Branch.*—There is only one bridge to finish, the permanent way is nearly laid throughout, and the works on this branch will be completed early in September. *Birmingham West Suburban Extension and Widening.*—The tunnels and covered ways for the extension and widening are finished except the fronts; most of the bridges, viaducts, and retaining walls are in a forward state, and two-thirds of the earthwork done; the new street under the canal, and the goods yard tunnel under the wharf land, are commenced. *St. Pancras, Somers Town.*—Considerable progress has been made with the boundary walls and pillar foundations."

The accounts are made up to 30th June and 31st December, and the statutory meetings held at Derby in February and August in every year.

Scale of Voting.—One vote for every 100*l.* as far as 2,000*l.*, and one vote additional for every 500*l.* above 2,000*l.*

No. of Directors.—Maximum, 20. *Qualification*, 2,000*l.* stock.

DIRECTORS:

Chairman—MATTHEW WILLIAM THOMPSON, Esq., Guiseley, Leeds.

Deputy-Chairman—GEORGE ERNEST PAGET, Esq., Sutton Bonnington, Loughborough.

Michael Biddulph, Esq., M.P., Ledbury, Herefordshire.
Robert Rankin, Esq., 67, South John Street, Liverpool.
William Unwin Heygate, Esq., Roecliffe, Loughborough.
Henry Tylston Hodgson, Esq., Harpenden, Herts.
Henry Wiggin, Esq., M.P., Metchley Grange, Harborne, Birmingham.
Hugh Mason, Esq., M.P., Ashton-under-Lyne.
John Wakefield Cropper, Esq., Dingle Bank, Liverpool.
Frederick Thorpe Mappin, Esq., M.P., Thornbury, Sheffield.
Robert Andrew Allison, Esq., Scaleby Hall, Carlisle.
Charles Thomas, Esq., Woodcote, Stoke Bishop, Bristol.
Lewis Randle Starkey, Esq., Norwood Park, Southwell, Notts.
Sir James Joseph Allport, Knt., Littleover, Derby.
Sir Michael Arthur Bass, Bart., M.P., Rangemore, Burton-on-Trent.

OFFICERS.—Sec., James Williams, Assoc.Inst.C.E.; Gen. Man., John Noble; Assistant Gen. Man., William Harrison; Consulting Eng., William Henry Barlow, M.Inst.C.E., 2, Old Palace Yard, Westminster, S.W.; Res. Eng., Alfred A. Langley; Eng. for New Works, J. Underwood; Supt. of Loco. Dept., S. W. Johnson, M.Inst.C.E., Derby; Supt. of Carriage Dept., T. G. Clayton; Supt. of Passenger Traffic, E. M. Needham, Derby; Man. of Goods Dept., W. L. Newcombe, Derby; Accountant, William H. Hodges; Auditors, Geo. W. Knox, Sheffield, and Geo. B. Kidd, Nottingham.

Head Offices—Derby.

194.—MIDLAND AND CENTRAL WALES JUNCTION.

Incorporated by act of 20th August, 1883, for the construction and maintenance of railways from Stokesay, Shropshire, to Willenhall, Staffordshire. Length, about 38¼ miles. For facilitating communication between the Midland Counties and Milford Haven and Swansea respectively. Period for completion, 5 years. Capital, 1,250,000*l.* in 10*l.* shares, with power to divide into "preferred" and "deferred" half-shares. Loans, &c., 416,660*l.*

No. of Directors.—Maximum, 10; minimum, 6; quorum, 5 and 4. *Qualification*, 50 shares.

FIRST DIRECTORS:

Hon. Richard Thompson Lawley.
Edward Fisher Smith, Esq.
Sidney Hopton Hadley, Esq., Aigburth, Liverpool.
Edwin Dixon, Esq.
Alfred Hickman, Esq.
John William Sparrow, Esq.
Samuel Loveridge, Esq.
Thomas Martin, Esq.
Thomas Martin Southwell, Esq.
Ralph Augustus Benson, Esq., Lutwyche Hall, Much Wenlock.

195.—MIDLAND AND EASTERN.

Incorporated by act of 23rd July, 1866, and being a union of the Lynn and Sutton Bridge and Spalding and Bourn. The united capital consisted of 213,000*l.* in 20*l.* shares and 71,000*l.* on loan. Arrangements with Midland and Great Northern. By the same act the Midland and Eastern was authorised to take a lease of the Norwich and Spalding, also to amalgamate with that company at a future period.

LYNN AND SUTTON BRIDGE.—Incorporated by act of 6th August, 1861, to construct a line from Lynn, on the East Anglian, to Sutton Bridge, on the Norwich and Spalding. Length, 9 miles and 43 chains. Capital, 100,000*l.* in 20*l.* shares; loans, 37,000*l.* By act of 21st July, 1862, the company was relieved from certain onerous obligations in respect to building a new bridge at Sutton; and by act of 25th July, 1864, the use by the company of the Cross Keys Bridge, over the River Nene, was regulated. By act of 29th June, 1865, the company was permitted to execute certain works at Sutton, and to raise additional capital to the extent of 15,000*l.* in shares and 5,000*l.* on mortgage. Also to attach a preference to unissued and cancelled shares.

SPALDING AND BOURN.—Incorporated by act of 28th July, 1862, to construct a line from Spalding, on the Great Northern, to Bourn. Length, 9¼ miles. Capital, 100,000*l.* in 20*l.* shares; loans, 32,500*l.* By act of 12th August, 1867, certain agreements with the Midland and Great Northern were confirmed, by which these two companies work the lines jointly.

NORWICH AND SPALDING.—Incorporated by act of 4th August, 1853, for a line from the Great Northern, at Spalding, to Holbeach. Length, 16 miles. Capital, 170,000*l.*; borrowing powers, 56,000*l.* By act of 13th August, 1859, the company was authorised to extend the line from Holbeach to Sutton Bridge. By an act passed in 1865, this company, or any company working the line, has running powers over the Peterbro', Wisbeach, and Sutton, from Sutton Bridge to Wisbeach. Under an agreement, by which the Great Northern and Midland worked the line, the company was secured a minimum net rent of 7,000*l.* a year, with half surplus profits beyond this sum.

AMALGAMATION WITH NORWICH AND SPALDING.—By the act of 12th July, 1877, this company became amalgamated with the Midland and Eastern. The joint capital now consists of 127,000*l.* debenture stock at 4½ per cent., 227,000*l.* of 4 per cent. perpetual preference stock, and 156,000*l.* ordinary stock. The amalgamation took effect on the 1st July, 1877, and does not prejudice the agreements with the Great Northern and Midland. Under the agreement scheduled to the Midland and Eastern, and Norwich and Spalding Act of 1867, these lines are worked jointly by the Midland and Great Northern, at a minimum rental of 15,000*l.* a year, with half surplus profits when the gross traffic exceeds 30,000*l.* The 15,000*l.* a year covers the interest on the 4½ per cent debenture (127,000*l.*) and 4 per cent. preference (227,000*l.*) stocks of the company. The ordinary stock, upon which no dividend is earned at present, amounts to 156,000*l.*

By the Eastern and Midlands (Amalgamation) Act, 1882, this company, on the 1st July, 1883, was amalgamated with, and became part of, the Eastern and Midlands System (which see). This amalgamation does not affect the agreements with the Great Northern and Midland.

196.—MIDLAND GREAT WESTERN.

Incorporated by act of 21st July, 1845, for a line from Dublin to Mullingar, with a branch to Longford. In 1846 the scheme was extended to Athlone. In 1847 the company obtained power to continue the line to the port of Galway. By act of 1852, further power was obtained to deviate the extension to Longford, and for a branch to Cavan (24 miles). In operation, 425½ miles, including leased lines.

With this undertaking is also incorporated the "Royal Canal," running parallel with the railway from Dublin as far as Mullingar, whence it diverges to Longford. The Royal Canal (said to have cost the original proprietors 1,500,000*l.*) was purchased under the act of incorporation by this company for 298,059*l.*

For list of Acts from 1857 to 1877, with short heads showing the objects for which the various powers were sought, see the MANUAL for 1881, pages 264 and 265.

By act of 27th June, 1881, the company was authorised to construct a branch railway, 6 miles 7 furlongs and 126 yards in length, from a point on their Cavan Line, near Crossdoney Station, to Killeshandra; and also a branch railway, 8 miles 6 furlongs and 15 yards in length, from Attimonmore south to Loughrea, in County Galway. Certain baronies in the County Cavan have guaranteed 600*l.* a year, from opening of line to Killeshandra, for 35 years, and the line is in course of construction; and the provisions of "The Relief of Distress (Ireland) Amendment Act of 1880" was extended to the Loughrea Extension, but the baronies interested not having availed themselves of this concession, the powers to make the line have lapsed. The act also empowers the company to take lands and other premises for ballast pits, &c.; to take water from the Royal Canal at a higher level, and to raise 250,000*l.* additional capital for the above purposes, and for the general purposes of the undertaking by the issue, at the option of the company, of new ordinary shares or stock, or new preference shares or stock, or wholly or partially by any one or more of these modes respectively, and to borrow, on mortgage or debenture stock, 80,000*l.*

SLIGO AND BALLAGHADERREEN.—Incorporated in 1863, to construct a line from near the Boyle Station of the Midland Great Western to the town of Ballaghaderreen, County Mayo. Length, 9¾ miles. Capital, 40,000*l.* in 10*l.* shares and 13,300*l.* on loan. Opened for traffic 1st November, 1874. In 1877, the line became vested, by purchase, in the Midland Great Western —For other information relating to its position prior to the amalgamation, see the MANUAL for 1878, and previous years.

GREAT NORTHERN AND WESTERN.—This line is leased to the Midland Great Western.—For terms, see Great Northern and Western.

GREAT NORTHERN OF IRELAND.—The directors have an arrangement by which the competing lines between Navan and Dublin may be worked so as to avoid undue competition.

THE SPENCER DOCK.—This dock was opened on the 15th April, 1873.

DUBLIN AND MEATH—NAVAN AND KINGSCOURT.—By act of 19th July, 1875, these two companies were leased to the Midland Great Western for 99 years.

REVENUE.—The receipts, expenditure, and net revenue for the half-years ended 31st December, 1883, and 30th June, 1884, were as follow:—

	Dec., 1883.	June, 1884.
Coaching traffic	£92,104	£84,270
Parcels, horses, mails, &c.	19,170	17,844
Goods and cattle	115,847	112,017
Canal and miscellaneous	11,015	12,728
Gross receipts	£238,136	£226,859
Expenditure	131,583	123,527
Net	£106,553	£103,332
Add—sundry balances and dividends	13,549	12,506
Total net revenue	£120,102	£115,838
Interest, preference charges, loss on working Athlone to Galway, rents and per centages to other lines, &c.	54,642	56,702
Balance available for dividends	£65,460	£59,136
Dividends on 300,000*l.* 5 per cent. and 500,000*l.* 4 per cent. preference stocks	17,500	18,157
	£47,960	£40,979
Dividends at 3½ and 3 per cent. per annum, payable 25th March and 25th September respectively	38,512	35,550
Balance carried forward	£9,448	£5,429

CAPITAL.—*Authorised:* Stock and shares, 3,400,000*l.*; loans, 1,807,146*l.*; total, 5,207,146*l.* All created. The subjoined statement of stock and share capital shows the proportion received to 30th June, 1884:—

Description.	Created.	Received.
Ordinary stock	£2,370,000	£2,360,000
Preference stock—5 per cent.	300,000	300,000
Preference stock—4 per cent.	730,000	532,825
	£3,400,000	£3,192,825

The receipts and expenditure on this account to 30th June, 1884, were as under:—

Receipts.		*Expenditure.*	
Shares and stock	£3,192,825	Lines open for traffic	£3,968,024
Debenture stock account No. 3	1,168,208	Lines in course of construction	25,127
Royal canal mortgage	55,800	Working stock	583,066
Athlone to Galway loan £500,000		Subscriptions to other railways	113,350
Less paid off to this date 265,992			
	234,008		
	£4,650,841		
Balance	33,726		
	£4,684,567		£4,684,567

MILEAGE.—Lines owned, 264¾; leased, 160¾; total, 425½.

The accounts are made up to 30th June and 31st December, and the statutory meetings held in Dublin in March and September in every year.

Scale of Voting.—One vote for every 200*l.* stock up to 2,000*l.*; and an additional vote for every 500*l.* after first 2,000*l.* M.G.W.R. Act, 1866.

Certificates must accompany transfer deeds. Registration fee, 2*s.* 6*d.* each deed, 2*s.* 6*d.* for replacement of lost certificate.

No. of Directors—7. *Qualification*, 2,000*l.* consolidated stock.

DIRECTORS:

Chairman—2 Sir RALPH SMITH CUSACK, D.L., J.P., Furry Park, Raheny, Co. Dublin.

2 Right Hon. Viscount Gough, Lough Cutra Castle, Gort, and St. Helen's, Booterstown.

* George Morris, Esq., D.L., Galway, and 48, Lower Leeson Street, Dublin.

George Woods Maunsell, Esq., D.L., J.P., 10, Merrion Square South, Dublin.

1 Captain Thomas James Smyth D.L., J.P., Ballynegall, Mullingar.

1 Richard Owen Armstrong, Esq., J.P., Clifton Terrace, Monkstown, County Dublin.

* Robert Warren, Esq., D.L., J.P., Rutland Square, Dublin.

The figures opposite the names indicate the number of years each party has to serve.

* Re-elected September, 1884.

OFFICERS.—Sec., George Wm. Greene; Assistant Sec., William R. Gill; Chief Eng., G. Newenham Kelly, C.E.; District Eng., A. J. Hamilton-Smythe, Athlone; Assist. Engs., W. P. O'Neill, Longford, and T. J. Myles, Broadstone, Dublin; Loco. Eng., Martin Atock; Storekeeper, M. A. Storen; Traffic Man., J. E. Ward; Assist. Man., John P. Hornsby; Accountant, Thomas Bennett; Cashier, George B. Cleugh; Transfer Officer, R. L. Badham; Audit Supt., M. O'Neill; Auditors, Anthony O'Neill, J.P., Ardbrugh, Dalkey, and George Cree, B.L., Dublin; Solicitor, John Kilkelly, Dublin; Bankers, Royal Bank of Ireland, Dublin, and Williams, Deacon, and Co., London.

Head Offices—Broadstone Terminus, Dublin.

197.—MIDLAND AND NORTH EASTERN JOINT.

OTLEY AND ILKLEY.

By Midland Railway (Otley and Ilkley Extension) Act, and North Eastern Railway Act, both dated 11th July, 1861, the Midland and North Eastern (called "The Otley and Ilkley Joint Line Committee") were authorised to construct, at joint cost, a railway from Otley to Ilkley. Length, 6¼ miles.

Each of the companies is authorised to provide the capital in equal proportions, by the issue of new shares or stock to the extent of 70,000*l.*, and to borrow on mortgage 23,333*l.* There are, therefore, no shareholders.

The line was opened for passenger traffic 1st August, 1865.

Number of the Committee, 6; three to be appointed by each company.

SWINTON AND KNOTTINGLEY.

By act of 16th July, 1874, the "Midland and North Eastern Railway Companies Committee" was incorporated for the construction of a joint railway, commencing by a junction with the Midland, near Swinton, and terminating by a junction with the North Eastern, near Knottingley. Length, 15 miles 5 furlongs. Each of the two companies are authorised to provide the capital in equal proportions by the issue of new shares or stock to the extent of 250,000*l.*, and to borrow on mortgage 83,000*l.* There are, therefore, no shareholders.

By act of 18th May, 1875, the construction of four branch or junction lines was authorised. Length, about 3¼ miles. Each company authorised to raise 50,000*l.* further by shares or stock, and 16,000*l.* further on mortgage.

The Great Northern and Manchester and Sheffield companies have running powers over both the main line and branches.

The line was opened for passenger traffic on the 1st July, 1879.

No. of Members—6; 3 to be appointed by each company.

COMMITTEE:

Appointed by the Midland.

Matthew Wm. Thompson, Esq., Park Gate, Guiseley, Leeds.

F. T. Mappin, Esq., M.P., Thornbury, Sheffield.

Lewis Randle Starkey, Esq., Norwood Park, Southwell, Notts.

Appointed by the North Eastern.

John Lloyd Wharton, Esq., Bramham, Tadcaster, and Dryburn, Durham.

James Kitson, Esq., Elmete Hall, Leeds.

Henry Oxley, Esq., Weetwood, Leeds.

OFFICERS.—Sec., John Sterland Gratton, Railway Station, Derby; Engs., Thomas E. Harrison, York, and Alfred A. Langley, Derby.

198.—MIDLAND AND SOUTH WESTERN JUNCTION.

An amalgamation of the Swindon and Cheltenham Extension and the Swindon, Marlborough, and Andover undertakings, under act of 23rd July, 1884. Total length, about 63 miles. Arrangements with Great Western and Midland.

By act of 23rd June, 1884, powers were given to construct a deviation from Preston (Gloucestershire) to Dowdeswell. Length, 12¾ miles. Period for completion, 5 years. By the same act an agreement with the Great Western was confirmed.

The authorised capital, which was exchanged on equal terms, now consists of 1,185,000*l*. in ordinary shares, and 378,300*l*. on loan, portions of which have been issued by the respective companies at various dates.

For further particulars relating to the capital issued, and acts obtained, by these companies, with other particulars as to the position of both companies in the past, see MANUAL for 1884, pages 313 and 314.

The northern section of the railway, from Swindon to Marlborough, was completed and opened for public traffic on the 26th July, 1881. The line is now open from Andover Junction to Cirencester.

No. of Directors.—Maximum, 11; minimum, 5; quorum, 6 and 4. *Qualification*, 500*l*.

DIRECTORS:

Chairman—The Most Noble the Marquis of AILESBURY, Savernake Forest, Marlborough, and 6, St. George's Place, S.W.

Deputy-Chairman—Lieut.-Col. FRANCIS DOUGLAS GREY, The Angles, East Sheen, S.W.

Ambrose Lethbridge Goddard, Esq., J.P., D.L., The Lawn, Swindon.
Thomas Best, Esq., Red Rice, Andover.
W. E. Nicolson Browne, Esq., Chisledon, Wilts.
Lord Robert Thomas Brudenell Bruce, 21, Eaton Square, S.W.
John Henry Gale, Esq., The Park, Ogbourne, Wilts.
John Blake Maurice, Esq., M.D., Marlborough.
Marcus S. Lynch Staunton, Esq., Union Club, Trafalgar Square, S.W.

OFFICERS.—Sec., Charles L. Brooke, Swindon; Gen. Man., Benjamin L. Fearnley Swindon; Traffic Man., T. Harrison Smith, Swindon; Con. Eng., Chas. Liddell, 24 Abingdon Street, Westminster, S.W.; Res. Eng., J. R. Shopland, Swindon; Auditors, Robert Smith Edmonds, Swindon, and John Morgan, Victoria Station, S.W.; Solicitors, Burchell and Co., 5, The Sanctuary, Westminster, S.W.; Bankers, Capital and Counties Bank Limited, 39, Threadneedle Street, E.C.;

Head Offices—Swindon; London Offices, 5, The Sanctuary, Westminster, S.W.

199.—MID WALES.

Incorporated 1st August, 1859, to construct a line from Llanidloes to Newbridge. Capital, 170,000*l*. in 10*l*. shares; borrowing powers, 56,000*l*. Agreements with London and North Western, Great Western, and Cambrian.

For list of Acts from 1860 to 1866, see the MANUAL for 1881, page 267.

Under a Scheme of Arrangement, enrolled in the High Court of Chancery on the 31st July, 1868, the company was authorised to borrow 32,267*l*.

Under a Scheme of Arrangement, enrolled in the High Court of Chancery on th 6th June, 1873, the company was authorised to borrow a further sum of 20,000*l*.

Under a Scheme of Arrangement, enrolled in the High Court of Chancery on the 14th April, 1880, the company was authorised to borrow 40,000*l*.

REVENUE.—The directors, in their report for the half-year ended 30th June, 1884, published in the middle of August last, stated that there had been "a still further increase in the receipts from most sources of traffic during the half-year. In passengers, 1,988 more have been carried, and 192*l*. further received, and as the markets are all now again open, they anticipate a steady improvement in this respect. Parcels, horses, &c., show an increase of 58*l*., and merchandise of 50*l*., but in minerals there is a decrease of 138*l*., and in live stock of 15*l*.; against this, however, there is an improvement of 135*l*. in tolls received. The expenditure incurred shows an increase of 441*l*., principally resulting from a special outlay for rails, sleepers, &c., as well as for lengthening platforms, new weighing machine, &c., and the extra cost of locomotive coal. The directors intend to renew nine miles of line with steel rails, and to defray the cost by a half-yearly charge to revenue. For this purpose, advantage was taken of the low price of rails, and 1,000 tons were purchased, the cost of which, after debiting the revenue with the proportion for the half-year, and allowing for the proceeds of old rails sold, has been chraged to a 'permanent way renewed suspense account,' as shown in the general balance sheet. When these rails are laid down, 40 miles will have been relaid with steel, out of the total length of 46¼."

MILEAGE—30th June, 1884.—Lines owned, 46½ miles; lines partly owned, 2 miles; foreign lines worked over, 4 miles.

CAPITAL.—*Authorised:* Stock and shares, 812,600*l*.; loans, 315,706*l*.; total, 1,128,306*l*. All created. The subjoined statement of stock and share capital created shows the proportion received to 30th June, 1884:—

Description.	Created.	Received.
Ordinary Shares Act, 1859	£170,000	£167,308
" " Act, 1860	240,000	236,732
Preference " Act, 1863, 5*l*. per cent.	200,000	200,000
" Act, 1864, 5*l*. per cent. ranks after act 1863	90,000	90,000
" Act, 1866, 5*l*. per cent. ranks after acts 1863 and 1864	112,600	112,600
Total	£812,600	£806,640

The expenditure to 30th June, 1884, amounted to 1,050,978*l*. on lines open for traffic, and to 48,272*l*. on working stock; together, 1,099,250*l*. The receipts were thus detailed:—

Shares and stock	£806,640		
Loans	41,050		
Debenture stock "A"	223,872		
Debenture stock "B"	32,267		
Interest on calls in arrear	302	=£1,104,131	
Credit balance		4,881	= £1,104,131

TRANSFER DEPARTMENT QUERIES AND REPLIES.

QUERIES.	REPLIES.
Transfer form—ordinary or special?	Ordinary.
Fee per deed?	All transfer and registration fees abolished
May several classes of stock be transferred on one deed?	Yes.
Are certificates required to accompany transfers?	Yes.
What amounts of stock are transferable, and are parts of 1*l*. sterling allowed to be transferred?	No parts of 1*l*. Any other amount.
To what officer should transfer communications be sent?	Secretary.
In acceptances, renunciations, &c., of allotments of new stock, proxies, or other forms sent to trustees and other joint holders, what signatures are required?	All (except proxies, when first holder's signature is sufficient).

The transfer books for preference and ordinary shares close seven days before the payment of dividends.

No. of Directors—7; minimum, 5; quorum, 3. *Qualification*, 500*l*.

DIRECTORS:

Chairman—SAMUEL GURNEY SHEPPARD, Esq., 28, Threadneedle Street, E.C.

John W. Batten, Esq., 15, Airlie Gardens, Campden Hill, W.

Abel Chapman, Esq., Woodford, Essex.

William Bailey Hawkins, Esq., Assoc.Inst. C.E., 39, Lombard Street, E.C.

Henry Francis Slattery, Esq., 12, Old Broad Street, E.C.

OFFICERS.—Sec., John Wade, 134, Palmerston Buildings, Bishopsgate Street, E.C.; Gen. Man., F. Grundy, Brecon; Auditors, Charles Chandler, Shrewsbury, and William Wilding, Montgomery; Solicitor, S. F. Noyes, 1, The Sanctuary, Westminster, S.W.

Offices—134, Palmerston Buildings, Bishopsgate Street, E.C.

209.—MILFORD.

Incorporated by act of 5th June, 1856, for making a line from Johnston Station of Neyland Extension of the South Wales to the town of Milford. Narrow gauge (originally broad). Capital, 60,000*l*. in 10*l*. shares (since converted into stock); amount of stock (after forfeited shares), 58,420*l*.; loans, 20,000*l*. Length, 4 miles.

By act of 23th July, 1863, an extension of time to 28th July, 1864, was conceded. New capital, 10,000*l.* in shares and 3,000*l.* on loan. The line is worked and rented by the Great Western at 1,466*l.* per annum.

On the 28th August, 1878, a resolution was passed creating debenture stock to be issued in lieu of debentures (14,200*l.*) Arrangements are now in progress for carrying this into effect, and a considerable portion of the stock has already been issued.

REVENUE.—For the half-years ended 31st December, 1883, and 30th June, 1884, the net earnings sufficed for the payment of all interest and fixed charges and dividends on the ordinary capital at the rate of 1*l.* 7*s.* and 1*l.* 7*s.* 6*d.* per cent. per annum respectively.

CAPITAL.—30th June, 1884.—*Received:* Ordinary shares and stock, less discounts &c., net, 57,067*l.*; loans, 14,200*l.*; total, 71,267*l.* *Expended:* 71,255*l.* Credit balance, 12*l.*

TRANSFER DEPARTMENT QUERIES AND REPLIES.

QUERIES.	REPLIES.
Transfer form—ordinary or special?	Ordinary.
Fee per deed?	2*s.* 6*d.*
Ditto if more sellers than one?	2*s.* 6*d.*
Are certificates required to accompany transfers?	Yes.
What amounts of stock are transferable, and are parts of 1*l.* sterling allowed to to be transferred?	Any amount not a fraction of 1*l.*
To what officer should transfer communications be sent?	Secretary.
In acceptances, renunciations, &c., of allotments of new stock, proxies, or other forms sent to trustees and other joint holders, what signatures are required?	First on register.

DIRECTORS:

Chairman—3 RICHARD BASSET, Esq., Highclere, Newbury.

2 Alexander Hubbard, Esq., Derwentwater House, Acton, W.
1 Frederick George Saunders, Esq., Caversham Grove, Reading.
3 Admiral John Lort Stokes, Scotchwell, Haverfordwest.
1 Alderman Sir Charles Whetham, Knt., 52, Gordon Square, W.C.
2 J. W. Williamson, Esq., 24, Warwick Road, Maida Hill, W.

1, Retire in February, 1885; 2, in 1886; 3, in 1887; all eligible for re-election.

OFFICERS.—Sec., A. Currey; Eng., W. G. Owen, M.Inst.C.E.; Auditors, W. R. Barwis and R. G. Marwood; Solicitors, Marriott and Jordan, 3, Westminster Chambers, S.W.

Offices—Paddington Station, W.

201.—MILFORD HAVEN DOCK AND RAILWAY.

Incorporated by act of 23rd July, 1860, to construct a railway, docks, and other works on the north side of Milford Haven. Length, 1¼ mile. Capital, 140,000*l.* in 10*l.* shares; loans, 46,000*l.* Traffic arrangements with Great Western.

By act of 21st July, 1863, an extension of time for completion of works was obtained till 21st July, 1866, and by act of 12th April, 1867, the company obtained another extension of time till 1870 for completion of the works authorised in 1860 and 1863, while by act of 20th June, 1870, an extension of time for ten years was authorised for completion of works.

By act of 3rd June, 1881, the company was empowered to lease their undertaking to Messrs. Samuel Lake & Co., the contractors, for 21 years from the 1st January, 1881, on the following terms, viz.:—"1. A yearly rent, which shall be 250*l.* per annum during the first 7 years of the said term of 21 years, 500*l.* per annum during the second 7 years of the said term, and 1,000*l.* per annum during the last 7 years of the said term. 2. A yearly rent, which shall be a sum in each of the first 5 years of the said term of 21 years equal to 5 per cent. of the gross receipts of the lessees arising from or in respect of the premises hereby demised, or the undertaking and business and transactions at any time carried on by the lessees, or in anywise attributable to such premises, undertaking, and business; and a sum in each of the remaining years of the said term equal to 10 per cent. of such gross receipts as aforesaid." It has since been subleased to the Milford Haven Railway and Estate Company Limited.

The line was opened on the 19th January, 1882.

No. of Directors—6; minimum, 4; quorum, 3. *Qualification*, 200*l*.

DIRECTORS:

Charles W. C. Hutton, Esq.
Henry Constable, Esq.
W. J. Haslam, Esq.
J. W. Williamson, Esq., 24, Warwick Road, Maida Hill, W.

Secretary, Charles C. Hood, 122, Cannon Street, E.C.
Offices—Milford Haven, South Wales; and 48, Gracechurch Street, E.C.

202.—MOFFAT.

Incorporated by act of 27th June, 1881, for the construction and maintenance of a railway from near the Beattock Station of the Caledonian to Moffat. Length, about 1¾ mile. Period for completion, 5 years. Working and traffic arrangements with the Caledonian. By act of 19th June, 1882, powers were obtained for the construction of a branch to the Beattock Station of the Caledonian. Total authorised capital in October, 1883, 19,000*l*. in 10*l*. shares, with power to divide into "preferred" and "deferred" half-shares; of these 1,626 shares had been issued to that date; loans, 6,330*l*. The expenditure amounted to 17,844*l*.

The line has been provisionally leased to the Caledonian for an annual rental of 700*l*.

The line was opened for traffic on the 2nd April, 1883.

No. of Directors.—Maximum, 5; minimum, 3; quorum, 3 and 2. *Qualification*, 500*l*.

DIRECTORS:

Chairman—JOHN JAMES HOPE JOHNSTONE, Esq., of Annandale, Raehills, Lockerbie.

Deputy-Chairman—GEORGE WILLIAMSON, Esq., of Strangcleugh, and Glendouran, Moffat.

John Anderson Johnstone, Esq., of Snar, Archbank, Moffat.
Samuel McMillan, Esq., Moffat.
Robert Ward, Esq., Crosshill Cottage, Baillieston, Glasgow.

OFFICERS.—Sec., Thomas Tait; Eng., John Wood, Carlisle; Auditors, James Grieve, Accountant, Moffat, and H. Kenward Sheils, Accountant, Edinburgh.

Offices—Church Place, Moffat.

203.—MOLD AND DENBIGH JUNCTION.

Incorporated by act of 6th August, 1861, to construct a line from the Mold Branch of the Chester and Holyhead to Denbigh, on the Vale of Clwyd. Length, 14¾ miles. Capital, 125,000*l*. in 20*l*. shares; loans, 41,000*l*.

By act of 29th June, 1865, the company was authorised to make several deviations, and to raise further capital to the extent of 100,000*l*. in shares and 33,000*l*. on loan.

By act of 5th July, 1865, the company was authorised to make certain new lines, and to abandon a portion of the authorised railway. Capital, 100,000*l*. in shares and 33,000*l*. on loan.

By act of 25th July, 1867, the company was authorised to exercise running powers over parts of the Vale of Clwyd and of the Wrexham, Mold, and Connah's Quay; to divide the shares into "deferred" and "preferred;" to create debenture stock; and to pay 6 per cent. to the Vale of Clwyd for outlay on extension of station at Denbigh.

Under a Scheme of Arrangement, enrolled in the High Court of Chancery on the 17th July, 1868, the borrowing powers of the company were increased 140,000*l*.

Working Agreement.—The line is worked by the London and North Western, at 50 per cent. of the gross receipts for one portion, and 75 per cent. for the other portion of the line.

Revenue.—The amounts received from the London and North Western for the half-years ended 31st December, 1883, and 30th June, 1884, less expenses, sufficed for the payment of all interest and fixed charges down to debenture stock "A," and for payments on further account of interest due to debenture stock "B," at the rates of 2¼ and 2½ per cent. per annum, payable 1st May and 1st November respectively.

Capital.—The expenditure on this account to 30th June, 1884, amounted to 573,653*l*.; the receipts to the same amount. The capital account is now closed. The ordinary stock amounts to 73,000*l.*, the "deferred" ordinary to 76,000*l.*, the "preferred" ordinary to 76,000*l.*, and the preference stock to 100,000*l.*; total, 325,000*l.* Amount of debenture stocks "A," 40,000*l.*; "B" (acts 1861-5), 107,000*l.*; "B" (Scheme of Arrangements), 30,000*l.*; "C," 70,000*l.*; total, 247,000*l.* Total capital, 572,000*l.*

TRANSFER DEPARTMENT QUERIES AND REPLIES.

Queries.	Replies.
Transfer form—ordinary or special?	Ordinary.
Fee per deed?	2*s.* 6*d.*
Ditto if more sellers than one?	2*s.* 6*d.*
May several classes of stock be transferred on one deed?	Yes.
Are certificates required to accompany transfers?	Yes.
Are parts of 1*l.* sterling transferable?	Yes.
To what officer should transfer communications be sent?	Secretary.
In acceptances, renunciations, &c., of allotments of new stock, proxies, or other forms sent to trustees and other joint holders, what signatures are required?	All (except proxies, when signature of first-named holder is sufficient).

The last two half-yearly meetings were held on the 24th April and 30th October, 1884, respectively.

No. of Directors—5; minimum, 3; quorum, 3. *Qualification*, 200*l.*

DIRECTORS:

Chairman—PHILIP PENNANT PENNANT, Esq., Bodfari, St Asaph.

George Moore Dixon, Esq., Bradley Hall, Ashbourne, Derby.

A. T. Roberts, Esq., Coed dû, Mold.

F. A. Hamilton, Esq., Founder's Court, Lothbury, E.C.

OFFICERS.—Sec., John Wade; Auditors, John Newton and David S. Derry; Solicitors, S. F. and H. Noyes, 1, The Sanctuary, Westminster, S.W., and Kelly and Keene, Mold.

Offices—134, Palmerston Buildings, Bishopsgate Street, E.C.

204.—MUCH WENLOCK AND SEVERN JUNCTION.

Incorporated by act of 21st July, 1859, to construct a line from Much Wenlock, in Shropshire, to the Severn Valley Railway and the River Severn. Ordinary capital, 33,000*l.* in 10*l.* shares; preference capital, 15,000*l.* in 10*l.* shares; loans, 16,000*l.* Length, 4¼ miles, including communication with the River Severn. Worked by the Great Western under an agreement dated 5th June, 1875. Running powers over part of the Severn Valley Line.

REVENUE.—For the year ended 31st December, 1884, no dividend was earned.

No. of Directors—7; minimum 4; quorum 3. *Qualification*, 250*l.*

DIRECTORS:

Chairman—ANDREW GOOD BROOKES, Esq., Shrewsbury.

Ralph Augustus Benson, Esq., Lutwyche Hall, Much Wenlock.

William Penny Brookes, Esq., Much Wenlock.

Richard Cooper, Esq., Much Wenlock.

Richard T. Davies, Esq., Walton Grange, Much Wenlock.

The Rt. Hon. Lord Forester, 3, Carlton Gardens, S.W., and Willey Park, Shropshire.

OFFICERS.—Sec., Charles J. Cooper, Wenlock; Eng., John Fowler, 2, Queen's Square Place, S.W.; Auditors, Henry Wade, Shrewsbury, and Thomas H. Thursfield, Barrow, Broseley; Bankers, Cooper, Purton, and Sons, Much Wenlock and Bridgnorth.

Offices—Much Wenlock.

205.—NANTWICH AND MARKET DRAYTON.

Incorporated by act of 7th June, 1861, to construct a line from the London and North Western, at Nantwich, to Market Drayton. Length, 10¾ miles. Capital, 60,000*l.* in 20*l.* shares; loans, 20,000*l.* By act of 30th June, 1864, the company obtained an increase of capital to the extent of 60,000*l.* in shares and 20,000*l.* on loan. These shares were created and issued on 31st August, 1865, the whole being guaranteed 4½ per cent. by the Great Western.

The undertaking is now leased to and worked by the Great Western.

CAPITAL.—The expenditure to 30th June, 1883, amounted to 144,890*l.*, the receipts to the same date having been 144,850*l.*, viz., ordinary stock, 120,000*l.*; loans at 4½ per cent., 10,050*l.*, and at 4 per cent., 14,800*l.*

No. of Directors—7; minimum, 4; quorum, 4. *Qualification*, 500*l.*

DIRECTORS:

Chairman—HENRY REGINALD CORBET, Esq., Adderley, Market Drayton.

E. W. Harding, Esq., Old Springs, Market Drayton.
William Rodenhurst, Esq., Market Drayton.
Benjamin S. Gower, Esq., Market Drayton.
George Lewis, Esq., Market Drayton.
Thomas P. Bennion, Esq., Audlem, Nantwich.
Reginald Corbet, jun., Esq., Adderley, Market Drayton.

OFFICERS.—Sec., F. L. Lightfoot, Market Drayton; Eng., John Gardner, M.Inst. C.E., 9, Victoria Chambers, Westminster, S.W.; Auditors, G. J. Whitelaw, Accountant, Paddington Station, and William Welch Deloitte, 5, Lothbury, E.C.; Solicitors, H. P. Cobb, 53, Lincoln's Inn, and J. H. Onions, Market Drayton; Bankers, The Manchester and Liverpool District Bank, Market Drayton.

Offices—Market Drayton.

206.—NAVAN AND KINGSCOURT.

Incorporated by act of 5th July, 1865, to construct a railway from Navan, on the Dublin and Meath, to Kingscourt. Length, 20 miles. Capital, 120,000*l.* in shares and 40,000*l.* on loan. Arrangements with Dublin and Meath, which is authorised to subscribe 40,000*l.*

For list of Acts 1867 to 1878, see the MANUAL for 1881, page 272.

DEBENTURE CAPITAL.—Under a scheme filed on the 17th April, 1874, the debentures authorised by the acts of 1865, 1871, and 1873 were converted into debenture stock, as follow:—"A" debenture stock, 20,000*l.*; Kingscourt "B" debenture stock, 40,000*l.*; Carrickmacross "B" debenture stock, 10,600*l.*; total debenture stock, 70,600*l.*

MIDLAND GREAT WESTERN.—By act of 19th July, 1875, the time for compulsory purchase of lands was extended for two, and for completion of works for three years, and the company authorised to lease the undertaking, so far as completed, to the Midland Great Western, for a period of 99 years. Until the completion to Kingscourt, the Midland Great Western will work the line at 2*s.* 3*d.* per train mile, and after the line is completed to Kingscourt, at 52 per cent. of the traffic receipts. Until the lease comes into force the line will be worked at 1*s.* 9*d.* per train mile.

CAPITAL.—The receipts on this account have amounted to 170,255*l.*, viz., 110,255*l.* by shares and 60,000*l.* by debenture stock. The expenditure on the line amounted to 188,154*l.*, leaving a balance of 17,899*l.* due by capital.

The first 20 miles of railway have been completed.

[No recent returns have been received for publication.—ED.]

Meetings held in February or March and August or September.

No. of Directors—7; quorum, 3. *Qualification*, 500*l.*

DIRECTORS:

William Aitken, Esq., Salem House, Rathmines, Dublin.
Abraham Colles, Esq., J.P., Ballyfallon, Athboy, County Meath.

OFFICERS.—Sec., Henry Charles Hanson; Eng., James Price; Solicitor, Michael Larkin, 51, Dame Street, Dublin; Auditors, James Fraser and W. G. Craig.

Offices—40, Dame Street, Dublin.

207.—NEATH AND BRECON.

Incorporated by act of 29th July, 1862, to construct a line from the Vale of Neath to certain collieries in Breconshire. Length, 9¼ miles. Mixed gauge. By act of 13th July, 1863, certain deviations were authorised, as well as an extension to Brecon. Length, 23¾ miles. The name of the undertaking was also changed to that of the "Neath and Brecon." By act of 29th July, 1864, the company was authorised to extend the line to the Central Wales, and to construct two branches to collieries. Length, 15½ miles. Arrangements with the Central Wales, the Vale of Neath, the Brecon and Merthyr, and the Hereford, Hay, and Brecon.

By act of 27th June, 1872, several additions were authorised to be made to the debenture stocks created by act of 1869, so as to relieve the undertaking from its complicated obligations. The capital of the company was fixed as follows:—"A" debenture stock, 225,000*l.*; "B" debenture stock, 299,870*l.*; "C" debenture stock, 460,000*l.*; "D" debenture stock, 120,000*l.*; preference shares, 122,800*l.*; ordinary shares, 256,230*l.*; total, 1,483,900*l.*

By act of 3rd July, 1879, the company was empowered to effect an arrangement with its creditors, explanations relating to which will be found further on.

SWANSEA VALE AND NEATH AND BRECON JUNCTION.—Incorporated by act of 29th July, 1864, to construct a line from the Swansea Vale to the Neath and Brecon. By act of 26th July, 1869, this company was dissolved, and amalgamated with the Neath and Brecon, which obtained the privilege of suspending for a period of 5 years the whole of the legal proceedings to which it had become subjected, and to convert its mortgage and other debts into debenture stock.

By an agreement dated 30th June, 1877, and approved and confirmed in August, 1877, the line from Brecon to Ynisygenion Junction, 29 miles, was worked by the Midland for five years from the 1st July, 1877, at 70 per cent. of the gross receipts. This agreement was prolonged for one year from the 30th June, 1882, and a further prolongation for five years from 30th June, 1883, has been arranged. This arrangement leaves 11½ miles of the system to be worked by this company.

In January, 1878, a special meeting was held, at which a resolution was passed approving a scheme filed in the High Court of Justice, under the Railway Companies' Act, 1867, between the company and its creditors. The scheme, which was confirmed on the 15th March, 1878, provides for a reduction of the interest on the "A," "B," "C," and "D" debenture stocks, and of the dividend on the "preferred" shares from the rate fixed by the act of 1869, namely, 5 per cent. per annum to 1½ per cent. per annum.

The directors, in their report for the half-year ended 30th June, 1879, stated as follows:—"The whole of the revenue for the past year has, as usual, been collected and retained by the receiver, and will continue to be so until his advances have been entirely repaid, and his accounts finally closed. To the extent of 85,000*l.* his advances were reduced on the 14th January, 1879, by the issue of the like amount of the new first debenture stock, and the directors will endeavour before the end of the current year to close his account, and all matters connected therewith. [MEM.—This First Debenture Stock was issued at par on the 14th January, 1879.] The bill promoted in the last session of Parliament received the royal assent on the 3rd July, 1879, and thereby the stocks and shares held by the different classes of proprietors have received a final Parliamentary title; a small sum beyond that contemplated in the Scheme of Arrangement sanctioned by the High Court of Justice has been made available for the outlay necessary to put the branch line in thorough order; and the company is protected against litigation for a period of five years. It may, therefore, now be hoped that before long the large sums which the company has hitherto had to expend for legal and Parliamentary expenses will disappear from the company's accounts, and that the railway having passed out of the hands of the receiver, the land and works having been acquired and completed, and the whole line put in good order, the gross revenue will appear subject to no other deductions than are caused by working the line and carrying on the current administrations of the company in the most economical manner consistent with efficiency. By the above issue, on the 14th January, 1879, of 85,000*l.* of "First" debenture stock, the interest on that amount, formerly payable at the rate of 6 per cent. per annum, was reduced to 4 per cent.; and the provisions of the scheme for the reduction of the interest on the remaining debenture stocks and preference shares of the company came into operation on that day, the rate of interest on the 'A' debenture stock being reduced from 6 per cent. to 4 per cent. The holders of 'A' stock will remember that by the scheme power was given to issue 'A' debenture stock to the amount of the seven half-yearly interest warrants unpaid at the end of 1877, and by the act it is further provided as follows:—The 'A' debenture stock authorised by this act in addition to the 'A' debenture stock authorised by the said scheme shall be issued at par, and applied in satisfaction *pari passu* of the following claims (that is to say): The arrears of interest on the 'A' debenture stock since the 31st December, 1877, and which may accrue due from time to time after the passing of this act during the continuance of the suspense period, and which the company may at such times be unable to discharge out of the moneys applicable thereto, under the provisions of the said scheme or this act."

EXCHANGE OF CERTIFICATES.—The following official notification was issued in December, 1879, viz.:—"To the debenture stockholders and the preference shareholders.—Notice is hereby given, pursuant to the provisions of 'Neath and Brecon Railway Act, 1879,' the company hereby call in the existing certificates of debenture stocks and preference shares to be cancelled, and that in further pursuance of the said act the company will issue in exchange for the said certificates new certificates, stating the amount of debenture stocks or preference shares to which the holders are entitled, and the interest payable in respect thereof under the provisions of the said act. No interest or dividend upon any debenture stock or preference share of the company issued before the passing of the above act can be paid to any holder of the same until the existing certificates are cancelled and exchanged, as above mentioned."

CAPITAL.—The receipts and expenditure on this account to 30th June, 1884, were as follow:—

Received.		*Expended.*	
Shares	£379,030	Lines open	£1,553,270
Debenture stocks	1,211,938	Working stock	34,818
		Balance	2,880
	£1,590,968		£1,590,968

PRIORITIES, DESCRIPTIONS, DIVIDENDS, &c., OF STOCKS AND SHARES.—The following is a list of this company's Stocks, numbered in order of priority. (See notes.)

No.	Year of Act.	FULL DESCRIPTION (to be observed in Transfer Deeds and all other Legal Documents).	Rate ₩ cent ₩ annum.
1	1879	"First debenture stock" (£109,100)	4
2	1869 1872 & 79	"A" ditto (£267,913)	4
3	1869	"B" ditto class 1 (£151,250)	3
4	1869	"B" ditto class 2 (£24,970)	2
5	1869	"B" ditto class 3 (£73,750)	3
6	1869	"B" ditto class 4 (£49,900)	3
7	1869 & 72	"C" ditto (£430,650)	3
8	1869 & 72	"D" ditto (£104,405)	1½
9	1869	Preference shares (£122,800)	1½
10	1869	Ordinary shares (£256,230)	...

NOTES.—The amounts shown in the Table of Priorities, &c., do not represent the authorised capital, but merely the amounts issued and received upon each class of stock respectively up to 30th June, 1884. The deficiency of the interest on the "First" and "A" stocks in the income of any one year to be made good out of the income of any subsequent year or years. Under the act of 1879 interest on the "A" debenture stock, which the company may be unable to discharge out of profits during the suspense period of five years from the passing of the act (3rd July, 1879), to be satisfied by the issue at par of "A" debenture stock.

The act of 1869 was an "Amalgamation and Arrangement Act."

TRANSFER DEPARTMENT QUERIES AND REPLIES.

QUERIES.	REPLIES.
Transfer form—ordinary or special?	Ordinary.
Fee per deed?	2*s.* 6*d.*
Ditto if more sellers than one?	2*s.* 6*d.* each transaction.
May several classes of stock be transferred on one deed?	Yes, all classes of debenture stock; but separate deeds must be used for the preference shares and the ordinary shares.
Are certificates required to accompany transfers?	Yes.
What amounts of stock are transferable, and are parts of 1*l.* sterling allowed to be transferred?	Any amounts, but no parts of 1*l.*
To what officer should transfer communications be sent?	Secretary.
In acceptances, renunciations, &c., of allotments of new stock, proxies, or other forms sent to trustees and other joint holders, what signatures are required?	For proxies, the signatures of first registered holders; for other cases, the signatures of all the registered holders.

No. of Directors—5; quorum, 3. *Qualification*, 1,000*l*.

DIRECTORS:

Chairman—ALEXANDER YOUNG, Esq., 41, Coleman Street, E.C.

Deputy-Chairman—THOMAS C. SANDARS, Esq., 46, Cleveland Square, Hyde Park, W.

S. B. Bristowe, Esq., Q.C., 2, Paper Buildings, Temple, E.C.

R. P. Laurie, Esq., 22, Threadneedle Street, E.C.

Benjamin Piercy, Esq., 8, Draper's Gardens, E.C.

OFFICERS.—Sec., J. E. Griffith; Gen. Man., F. Kirtley; Auditors, Thomas C. Tatham and James Glegg; Solicitors, Dean and Taylor, 24, Theobald's Road, W.C.; Bankers, The Glamorganshire Banking Company, Neath, and Lloyds, Barnetts, and Bosanquet's Bank Limited, 60 and 62, Lombard Street, E.C.

Offices—41, Coleman Street, E.C., and Neath.

208.—NEWENT.

Incorporated by act of 5th August, 1873, to construct a line from Gloucester to Dymock. Length, 13¼ miles. Capital, 160,000*l*. in 10*l*. shares and 53,300*l*. on loan. Powers to make arrangements with Great Western, which company is authorised to subscribe 130,000*l*.

By act of 21st May, 1874, an abandonment was authorised of a portion of the railway, and a deviation authorised in lieu of the abandoned portion.

By act of 16th April, 1878, the time for the completion of this railway as deviated was extended until 21st May, 1881, and by "Great Western Act of 1881" was extended for a further period of 3 years.

CAPITAL—30th June, 1884.—*Received:* From 16,000 ordinary 10*l*. shares, 105,070*l*. *Expended:* 97,489*l*. Credit balance, 7,581*l*. It is estimated that the further expenditure required to complete the line will amount to 115,811*l*.

Meetings held half-yearly in February and August.

No. of Directors.—Maximum, 5; minimum, 3; quorum, 3 and 2. *Qualification*, 30 shares.

DIRECTORS:

Chairman—Sir DANIEL GOOCH, Bart., M.P., 3, Warwick Road, Maida Hill, W.

Sir Charles Alexander Wood, Knt., 11, Elvaston Place, S.W.

Richard Basset, Esq., Highclere, Newbury.

Walter Robinson, Esq., 20, Gledhow Gardens, S.W.

OFFICERS.—Sec., A. E. Bolter, Paddington Station, W.; Auditors, J. H. Matthews and J. D. Higgins; Solicitors, Godden, Holme, and Co., 34, Old Jewry, E.C.

Offices—Paddington Station, W.

209.—NEWPORT.

Incorporated by act of 6th August, 1866, to construct a railway from the North British, at Ferry-port-on-Craig, to Newport, in the county of Fife. Length, 4¼ miles. Capital, 46,000*l*. in 10*l*. shares and 15,300*l*. on loan. Worked by the North British, under the above act, in perpetuity from the 12th May, 1879, at 45 per cent. of local traffic and 75 per cent. of through traffic, to the North British, in payment for working and maintenance.

For short heads of Acts 1867, 1870, and 1873, see the MANUAL for 1881, page 275.

By the North British Act of 12th August, 1880, the company was authorised to raise new capital by the issue of shares or stock to the extent of 20,000*l*.

REVENUE.—This account to 30th June, 1884, showed net earnings sufficient only to pay the interest on debentures.

CAPITAL.—The report for the half-year ended 30th June, 1884, showed that 61,425*l*. had been received, and 87,219*l*. expended on this account to that date. The receipts include the company's shares issued under acts 1866, 1867, and 1870, all of which are ordinary 10*l*. shares, fully paid. Dividends would be payable half-yearly, in February and August, the transfer books closing for about a week previously.

TRANSFER DEPARTMENT QUERIES AND REPLIES.

Queries.	Replies.
Transfer form—ordinary or special?	Ordinary.
Fee per deed?	2s. 6d.
Ditto if more sellers than one?...	2s. 6d. each seller.
Are certificates required to accompany transfers?	Yes.
To what officer should transfer communications be sent?	Secretary.
In acceptances, renunciations, &c., of allotments of new stock, proxies, or other forms sent to trustees and other joint holders, what signatures are required?	First-named trustee only.

No. of Directors—5; minimum, 4; quorum, 3. *Qualification*, 200*l*.

DIRECTORS:

Chairman—Admiral MAITLAND DOUGALL, R.N., Scotscraig, Tayport.

Harry Walker, Esq., Newport, Fife.
James Calder, Esq., Forgandenny, Perthshire.
Peter Christie, Esq., Scotscraig Mains, Tayport.
Jas. Henderson, Esq., Accountant, Dundee.

OFFICERS.—Sec., G. B. Wieland, Edinburgh; Auditors, Thomas S. Lindsay and James Ireland; Solicitor, Thomas Thornton, Dundee.

Offices—4, Princes Street, Edinburgh.

210.—NEWQUAY AND CORNWALL JUNCTION.

Incorporated by act of 4th July, 1864, to construct a line from the Cornwall, near Burngullow, to the St. Dennis Branch of the Newquay. Length, 5¼ miles. Capital, 27,000*l*. in 20*l*. shares and 9,000*l*. on loan. Arrangements with Cornwall.

By act of 29th May, 1868, the company was authorised to make a deviation in the line, and to extend the time for completion of works till 1871. Also, to cancel unissued shares, and assign a preferential dividend not exceeding 6 per cent. on 7,000*l*., and to raise additional capital to the extent of 3,000*l*., and to borrow thereon by instalments.

Cornwall Minerals.—This company guarantee a dividend to the original shareholders in the Newquay and Cornwall Junction, commencing from 1st July, 1873, to gradually increase till a maximum of 4 per cent. has been reached. The Great Western has taken over the traffic. Only the 1st year's rent had been paid up to the end of 1884.

At the half-yearly meeting, held February 28th, 1878, the chairman stated that the Minerals Company had disputed their liability to pay the guaranteed dividend. It was a question of law, and it had been agreed that it should be decided upon a special case. This special case was ageeed to; the trial took place in May, 1879, and resulted in favour of the Cornwall Minerals, on the ground that no right of action could accrue so long as the receipts of the latter company were insufficient to satisfy the mortgages and preferences of the act of 1873.

Capital.—The receipts and expenditure on this account to 30th June, 1884, amounted to 18,085*l*.

Meetings held at St. Austell in February and August.

No. of Directors—6; minimum, 3. *Qualification*, 200*l*.

DIRECTORS:

Chairman—E. BRYDGES WILLYAMS, Esq., M.P., Carnanton, St. Columb.

John Carlisle, Esq., Richmond Lodge, Putney, S.W.
Edgar Swinton Holland, Esq., 45, Drury Buildings, Water Street, Liverpool.

Two directors retire annually, but are eligible for re-election.

OFFICERS.—Sec., Wm. Polkinghorne, Windsor Villa, Liskeard; Eng., Silvanus Wm. Jenkin, M.Inst.C.E., Liskeard; Auditor, John H. Botterell, Par Station; Bankers, Clymo, Treffry, West, Polkinghorne, and Co., Liskeard, Cornwall.

Office—Liskeard, Cornwall.

211.—NEWRY, WARRENPOINT, AND ROSTREVOR.

Incorporated by act of 27th July, 1846, for a line from Newry to Warrenpoint (6 miles).

By act of 27th July, 1857, the company was authorised to extend its line at Newry and at Warrenpoint (length, ¾ mile), and to enter into arrangements with the Newry and Armagh. New capital, 20,000*l*. by shares and 6,000*l*. by loan.

By act of 14th June, 1860, the company was authorised to regulate its 6 per cent. preference capital, and to create new shares at 5¼ per cent.; to define its borrowing powers as extending to 39,900*l*. The Newry and Armagh was authorised to subscribe 12,500*l*., and agreements between the companies legalised. New works were also permitted, principally connected with water conveyance.

The Newry and Armagh has since become vested in the Great Northern of Ireland, and arrangements are, therefore, being made with the latter company for the regulation of through traffic.

Revenue.—The gross receipts for the half-year ended 31st December, 1883, amounted to 4,101*l*., and the expenditure to 3,392*l*., leaving, with balance of 1,025*l*. from previous account, and 48*l*. increase in value of stores, a total net revenue of 1,775*l*., which was applied to the following payments, viz.—interest on debentures 962*l*., and interest to bankers 5*l*.; total, 967*l*.; leaving a credit balance of 808*l*.

The gross receipts for the half-year ended 30th June, 1884, amounted to 2,727*l*., and the expenses to 2,769*l*. The balance brought in to net revenue, together with an amount credited as increase in value of stores, was applied to the payment of interest on debentures and Government loan, &c.

Capital.—The expenditure to 30th June, 1884, amounted to 157,166*l*. The receipts were described to have been as under:—

Shares and stock	£119,925	
Loans	39,000	
	£158,925	
Less loss on re-issue of forfeited shares	8,586	=£150,339
Balance of expenditure over receipts		6,827
		£157,166

The accounts are made up to the 30th June and 31st December, and the meetings held in Liverpool in February or March, and in Newry in August or September.

Scale of Voting.—One vote for every five shares; no proprietor can have more than 20 votes.

No. of Directors.—Maximum, 13; minimum, 5; under act, 1853. *Qualification*, 20 shares; allowance, nil.

DIRECTORS:

Chairman—J. T. FITZADAM, Esq., London.

Deputy-Chairman—*JOSEPH LUPTON, Esq., Newry.

John Q. Henry, Esq., J.P., Kilkeel.
Peter Quinn, Esq., J.P., Newry.
*James Kennedy, Esq., Liverpool.
Thomas Whitney, Esq., Liverpool.

Retire by rotation, but are eligible for re-election. * Retire in February, 1885.

OFFICERS.—Sec., Robert Cochran, Liverpool; Supt., Thomas Smith; Auditors, L. D. Brooke and W. Bennet.

Secretary's Office, 71, Tower Buildings, Liverpool.

212.—NORTHAMPTON AND BANBURY JUNCTION.

Incorporated by act of 28th July, 1863, to construct a line from Blisworth to Farthinghoe. Capital, 140,000*l*. in 10*l*. shares; loans, 46,000*l*. Opened 1st June, 1872.

For list of Acts and Board of Trade Certificates from 1865 to 1877, see the Manual for 1881, page 277.

An arrangement has been made with the London and North Western for the supply of rolling stock and locomotive power at a fixed charge per train mile; the agreement, having been approved by the Railway Commissioners, came into operation on the 1st November, 1876.

Revenue.—The receipts for the half-year ended 30th June, 1883, were 3,918*l*., and the expenses 3,631*l*., leaving a profit of 287*l*., which was carried to net revenue account. For the half-year ended 30th June, 1884, the receipts were 3,738*l*., and the expenses 3,512*l*., showing a profit of 226*l*. carried to net revenue account; the balance against which account to that date amounted to 95,397*l*.

In operation, 20 miles 47 chains.

CAPITAL.—The expenditure on the line to the 30th June, 1884, amounted to 619,788*l.*; the receipts to the same date having been as follow:—

Stock	£329,790
Capitalised rent-charges	4,070
Debenture stock "A"	115,920
Debenture stock "B"	170,958
	£619,788

Meetings in February and August.

No. of Directors (as settled by act of 1870), 6, viz.:—2 elected by "A" debenture stockholders; 2 by "B" debenture stockholders; and 2 by shareholders; quorum, 3. *Qualification*, 500*l.* of the respective stocks.

DIRECTORS:

Chairman—The Most Hon. the Marquis of AILESBURY, 6, St. George's Place, S.W.

Managing Director—J. WILSON THEOBALD, Esq., 8, Drapers' Gardens, E.C.

J. Alexander, Esq.
Walter Amos Michael, Esq., 12, Tokenhouse Yard, Lothbury, E.C.
W. L. Hunt, Esq.
Henry James Sheldon, Esq., Brailes House, Shipston-on-Stour, Warwickshire.

OFFICERS.—Sec., John Crick, 8, Drapers' Gardens, E.C.; Traffic Supt., Edmund Stanton, Blisworth; Engs., Charles Liddell, C.E., and Edward Richards, C.E., 24, Abingdon Street, Westminster, S.W.; Auditors, Albert D. Michael, Cadogan Mansions, Sloane Square, S.W., and Alfred T. Bowser, 58, Moorgate Street, E.C.; Solicitors, Bircham and Co., 46, Parliament Street, Westminster, S.W., and 26, Austin Friars, E.C.

Offices—8, Drapers' Gardens, E.C.

213.—NORTH BRITISH.

An incorporation by act of 29th July, 1862, of the original North British, the Edinburgh, Perth, and Dundee, the West of Fife, and their several subsidiary connections; and by act of 5th July, 1865, the Monkland was amalgamated with the Edinburgh and Glasgow, which was by act of the same session amalgamated with the North British as from 31st July, 1865. The original North British was incorporated by act of 19th July, 1844, for a line from Edinburgh to Berwick, with a branch to Haddington (62 miles). In 1845 powers were given to purchase the Edinburgh and Dalkeith (14 miles), and to construct a small branch (2 miles) to connect it. The powers of the Edinburgh and Hawick (43½ miles) were transferred in the same year. In 1846 the company obtained power to construct branches to Selkirk, Jedburgh, Kelso, Tranent, Cockenzie, North Berwick, and Dunse (42 miles).

FURTHER PARLIAMENTARY POWERS:—

For list of Acts obtained by this company from 1858 to 1879, with short heads showing the objects for which the various powers were sought, see the MANUAL for 1881, pages 278 to 282.

By act of 6th August, 1880, an agreement between the North British and Yoker companies as to the working of the undertaking of the latter was confirmed.

By act of 12th August, 1880, the Port Carlisle Dock and Railway, the Carlisle and Silloth Bay Railway and Dock, and the North British, Arbroath, and Montrose Railway companies were amalgamated with the North British as at 1st August, 1880; the company was authorised to make a dock at Silloth; agreements with the Corporation of Edinburgh and the Governor and Company of the Bank of Scotland were confirmed; the company was empowered to guarantee interest on Bo'ness loans for principal sums not exceeding 185,000*l.*; to advance 100,000*l.* to the Forth Bridge Company; to raise new capital to the extent of 167,000*l.* in shares and 22,300*l.* on mortgage.

By act of 27th June, 1881, the harbour of Burntisland was vested in eight commissioners, four of whom to be appointed by the Burntisland Town Council and four by the directors of the North British.

By act of 18th July, 1881, the Montrose and Bervie was amalgamated with the North British as from 1st August, 1881.—See particulars under that head further on.

By act of 18th July, 1881, the company was authorised to erect a new viaduct across the Tay, at Dundee, and to raise new capital to the amount of 600,000*l.* in shares, or by redeemable debenture stock.

By act of 11th August, 1881, the company was authorised to make a short railway in the parish of St. Mary, Carlisle; to abandon and disuse a part of the Glasgow, Dumbarton, and Helensburgh, and to raise new capital to the extent of 153,000*l.* in shares and 39,300*l.* on mortgage.

By act of 3rd July, 1882, the company was authorised to make certain railways in Fife, Perth, and Kinross, for improving the route from the proposed Forth Bridge to the north, and to take over railway No. 2 of the Forth Bridge Railway Act of 1873. New capital: shares, 615,000*l.*; loans, 205,000*l.*

By act of 29th June, 1883, the company was authorised to make a short railway in Alloa parish; an agreement as to the traffic on the said railway, entered into between the North British, the Caledonian, and the Alloa companies, was confirmed. The obligation upon the company to tow freighted ships under the Tay Bridge was extended to ships not freighted; and the time for the sale of superfluous lands was extended. New capital, 12,000*l.* in shares and 4,000*l.* on loan.

OTHER AMALGAMATIONS, LEASES, AGREEMENTS, &c.:—

BERWICKSHIRE.—Incorporated by act of 7th July, 1862, to construct a line from the St. Boswell's Station of the North British to Dunse. Length, 20½ miles. By act of 13th July, 1876, the undertaking was vested in the North British as from the 1st August, 1876, Berwickshire proprietors receiving 83*l.* 11*s.* of North British ordinary stock for every 100*l.* of shares held. Berwickshire mortgages became mortgages of the North British.

BLANE VALLEY.—See GENERAL INDEX.

BORDER COUNTIES.—Incorporated by act of July, 1854, for a line from Hexham, on the North Eastern (Newcastle and Carlisle), by the Valley of North Tyne, to Wark, Reedsmouth, Hareshaw Iron Works, Bellingham, Falstone, and Kielder. Length, 26 miles. The Liddesdale Section (15 miles) commences by a junction with the Border Counties, and terminates on the Border Union (Hawick to Carlisle) near Riccarton. By act of 13th August, 1860, amalgamated with North British. Running powers obtained over the portion of the Newcastle and Carlisle between the junction of the Border Counties therewith and Newcastle, and the use of stations on such portion, and security for free passage of traffic between the two railways.

BROXBURN.—Incorporated by act of 12th August, 1867. Length, 1¼ mile. From the Edinburgh and Glasgow, at Broomhouse, to Broxburn. Amalgamated with the North British by act of 28th July, 1873, the latter company guaranteeing 5 per cent. on the amount of purchase (6,100*l.*)

CARLISLE AND SILLOTH BAY.—Incorporated by act of 16th July, 1855, and amalgamated with North British as at 1st August, 1880, by act of 12th August, 1880.—For particulars as to the working, &c., of this company in the past, see the MANUAL for 1880, and previous editions.

DEVON VALLEY.—Incorporated by act of 1858. Amalgamated with North British, as from 1st January, 1875, each 100*l.* of Devon Valley ordinary capital being exchanged for 62*l.* 10*s.* of North British ordinary stock.

DUNDEE AND ARBROATH.—See Caledonian, page 82.

DUNFERMLINE AND QUEENSFERRY.—See St. Andrews.

EDINBURGH AND BATHGATE.—See GENERAL INDEX.

EDINBURGH AND GLASGOW.—Incorporated, originally, by act of 4th July, 1838, for a railway from Edinburgh to Glasgow, with a branch to Falkirk. Capital, 900,000*l.* in shares and 300,000*l.* on loan. The Union Canal became vested in the company in 1848. Amalgamated with North British by act of 5th July, 1865, under which the ordinary stock is to receive a preference dividend of 4½ per cent., and rateably to increase with dividends on North British ordinary stock after the latter receives 3 per cent. Under act of 1876 the Edinburgh and Glasgow preference (ordinary) stock was converted and divided into Edinburgh and Glasgow preference stock and Edinburgh and Glasgow ordinary stock, the former bearing a fixed dividend at 4½ per cent. per annum, and the latter representing the contingent rights of the old stock, the dividend being deferred until the North British ordinary stock receives 3 per cent. per annum and up to 4 per cent. per annum, when the Edinburgh and Glasgow ordinary will take ½ per cent. per annum, and the dividend thereon will increase from that point rateably with the North British. Powers are given in the act of 28th June, 1877, to consolidate the Edinburgh and Glasgow preference stock into a North British No. 3 preference stock to be created for that purpose. —For other details as to Parliamentary powers, arrangements with other companies, &c., prior to the amalgamation, see MANUAL for 1882, page 271, and refer to previous editions.

EDINBURGH, LOANHEAD, AND ROSLIN.—See St. Andrews.

EDINBURGH, PERTH, AND DUNDEE.—This company, under an act of 1847, is an amalgamation of the Edinburgh, Leith, and Granton and the Edinburgh and Northern. These two lines are connected by steam ferry across the Frith of Forth. The above companies were dissolved and re-incorporated under this title, by act of 1849, and again dissolved and re-incorporated by act of 1851, the undertaking being defined to be a line from Edinburgh, in connection with the North British and Edinburgh and Glasgow, to Leith Harbour, Granton Pier, Burntisland (on the opposite shore), and Ladybank; a junction with the Scottish Central, near Perth, to Cupar and Ferry-Port-on-Craig, opposite Broughty Ferry, to join the Dundee and Arbroath to Dundee and the North; branches from Thornton to Dunfermline, to join the Stirling and Dunfermline, and to Kirkcaldy Harbour. Length of railways and ferries, 78 miles. Amalgamated with the North British by act of 29th July, 1862. On the 1st February, 1876, the Edinburgh, Perth, and Dundee ordinary stock was converted into North British ordinary stock, at the rate of 62*l*. 10*s*. per cent. of the latter in exchange for the former.

ESK VALLEY.—Incorporated by act of 21st July, 1863, to construct a line from the Hawick Branch of the North British, at Eskbank Station, to Springfield. Length, 2¼ miles. Capital, 27,000*l*. in 10*l*. shares and 9,000*l*. on loan. Leased to North British by act of 16th July, 1866, and by act of 13th July, 1871, is now amalgamated with that company.

FORTH AND CLYDE JUNCTION.—See GENERAL INDEX.

GLASGOW, BOTHWELL, HAMILTON, AND COATBRIDGE.—Incorporated 16th July, 1874, to make a line from the town of Hamilton to the Coatbridge Railway at Shettleston, and one diverging from the foregoing near Bothwell, and joining the North British system at Coatbridge (Whifflet Branch), and several short branches into neighbouring coalfields. The main lines to be about 12½ miles in length, and to be double; the other lines, about 3 miles in length, to be single. The incorporating act confers certain running powers by which continuous communication may be obtained with the College Station, Glasgow, and other stations and depôts on the North British system. Capital, 500,000*l*. in shares and 166,000*l* on mortgage. The railway was commenced in October, 1874. The portion of line extending from College Station, Glasgow, to Hamilton, was formally opened on the 30th March, 1878, and the Whifflet Branch has since been opened. Under act of 21st July, 1879, this undertaking was amalgamated with the North British, as from 2nd August, 1878, with the following scale of guaranteed dividends secured by a lien, viz.:— For period to 31st January, 1879, 5 per cent.; for the year ending 31st January, 1880, 5½ per cent.; 1881, 6 per cent.; 1882, 6½ per cent; 1883, 7 per cent.; 1884, 7 per cent.; 1885, 7½ per cent.; and thereafter in perpetuity, 8 per cent.

GLASGOW CITY AND DISTRICT.—See GENERAL INDEX.

GLASGOW AND MILNGAVIE JUNCTION.—Incorporated by act of 1st August, 1861, to construct a line from the Glasgow, Dumbarton, and Helensburgh to Milngavie. Length 3 miles 16 chains. Capital, 30,000*l*. in 10*l*. shares; loans, 10,000*l*. By act of 28th July, 1873, the company was amalgamated with the North British; shares, &c., of the Milngavie being exchanged for those of the North British.

JEDBURGH.—Incorporated by act of 25th May, 1855, to construct a line (7¼ miles) from Jedburgh to the Roxburgh Station of the North British. Capital, 35,000*l*. in 10*l*. shares, with power to borrow 11,500*l*. By act of 3rd July, 1860, the line was amalgamated with the North British at 4 per cent.

KELVIN VALLEY.—See GENERAL INDEX.

LEADBURN, LINTON, AND DOLPHINTON.—Incorporated by act of 3rd June, 1862, to construct a line from the Peebles, at its Leadburn Station, to Linton. Length, 10 miles. Capital, 40,000*l*. in 10*l*. shares; loans, 13,300*l*. By act of 16th July, 1866, the Leadburn, Linton, and Dolphinton was amalgamated with the North British, the dividend of the latter in one half-year becoming a preference charge for the next ensuing for the Leadburn.

LESLIE.—Incorporated by act of 7th July, 1857, to construct a line from Markinch to Leslie, with three small branches. Length, 6¼ miles. Capital, 35,000*l*. in 10*l*. shares and 11,500*l*. on loan. Amalgamated with North British by act of 1872. The preference shares to take same rank in North British, and the ordinary capital to become preference at 3 per cent. for 1873, 4 per cent. for 1874, and 4½ per cent. thereafter in perpetuity.

LEVEN AND EAST OF FIFE.—See St. Andrews.

MONKLAND.—An amalgamation of the *Monkland and Kirkintilloch*, the *Ballochney*, and the *Slamannan*, under act of 14th August, 1848. These lines were constructed chiefly as mineral from Kirkintilloch, Coatbridge, Airdrie, Bathgate, and Bo'ness on the Forth (for details respecting sundry extensions prior to the amalgamation mentioned below, see MANUAL for 1882, page 273). By act of 5th July, 1865, amalgamated with Edinburgh and Glasgow on a guaranteed dividend of 6 per cent. on ordinary stock. By act of 28th June, 1877, powers have been obtained to convert the Monkland preference stock along with the Edinburgh and Glasgow preference stock and the North British preference, 1865, into a North British preference No. 3 stock to be created for that purpose.

MONTROSE AND BERVIE.—Incorporated by act of July, 1860. Amalgamated with North British as from the 1st August, 1881, under that company's act, dated 18th July, 1881. The mortgages of the Bervie Company (18,000*l*.) to become mortgages of the North British, but during their continuance, to be a first charge upon the Bervie undertaking. The North British to pay to the shareholders of the Bervie 6*l*. per share for every 10*l*. share held by them respectively. For these and other purposes of the amalgamation, the North British to have power to raise stock amounting to 42,000*l*. either in ordinary stock or stock to be called Bervie lien stock, at their option.—For particulars relating to the working of this company in the past, see the MANUAL for 1881, page 269, and previous editions.

NEWPORT.—See GENERAL INDEX.

NORTH BRITISH, ARBROATH, AND MONTROSE.—Incorporated by act of 13th July, 1871, to construct lines—No. 1, 15 miles 5 furlongs 9·42 chains, from the Caledonian at Arbroath to a point north of Montrose; and No. 2, 4 furlongs 5½ chains, commencing by a junction with No 1 near Montrose and terminating at Dryley's Brickwork. Total, 17⅝ miles (for other details, see MANUAL for 1882, page 273.) Amalgamated with North British as at 1st August, 1880, by act of 12th August, 1880, the shares of the company becoming "North British Montrose Lien Stock" from the former date, and entitled to a dividend at 5 per cent. per annum.

NORTH MONKLAND.—See GENERAL INDEX.

NORTHUMBERLAND CENTRAL.—Incorporated by act of 28th July, 1863, to construct a line from Scot's Gap, by a junction with the North British, to Cornhill, on the Kelso and Berwick Branch of the North Eastern. Amalgamated with North British by act of 18th July, 1872. The preference stock, 1,625*l*., to receive 3 per cent. for the first five years, and 4 per cent. in perpetuity thereafter; and the ordinary stock, 71,985*l*., to receive a preference dividend at the rate of 1 per cent. from 1st February, 1877, and to increase after 1st February, 1878, with any increase in the dividend paid on North British ordinary stock over that paid in the corresponding half of the previous year. The North British to pay 9,600*l*. to discharge the Northumberland Central liabilities, and the mortgage debt of 21,706*l*. to be converted into North British 4 per cent. debenture stock in 1877.

PEEBLES.—Incorporated 8th July, 1853, for a line from the Hawick Branch of the North British (Eskbank Station) to Peebles (single line). Shares, 70,000*l*.; loans, 23,000*l*. Length, 18¾ miles. Sidings, &c., 2¼ miles. Total, 21 miles. By act of 13th July, 1876, the undertaking was vested in the North British, the mortgages of the Peebles (32,000*l*.) becoming mortgages of the North British; the preference shares (27,000*l*.) of the Peebles becoming 5 per cent. lien of the North British; and the ordinary shares (70,000*l*.) of the Peebles becoming 8 per cent. lien stock of the North British. The amalgamation came into force on the 1st August, 1876.

PENICUIK.—Incorporated by act of 20th June, 1870, to construct a line from the Hawthornden Station of the Peebles to Penicuik. Length, 4½ miles. Capital, 54,000*l*. in 10*l*. shares and 18,000*l*. on loan. Opened for goods 9th May, and for passenger traffic 2nd September, 1872. The line was leased in perpetuity to the North British, and worked by that company at 45 per cent. of the gross receipts. By act of 13th July, 1876, the undertaking was vested in the North British as from 1st August, 1876, Penicuik proprietors receiving par price in cash for their shares.

Port Carlisle.—Incorporated by act of 4th August, 1853, for converting a canal into a railway. By 29 Geo. III., cap. 13, the canal was authorised from Carlisle to Solway Firth (Fisher's Cross), Bowness, Cumberland ("Port Carlisle"), and "Carlisle Canal Company." By act of 12th August, 1880, this company was amalgamated with the North British as from the 1st August, 1880, the ordinary stock being exchanged for "North British Port Carlisle Lien Stock," entitled to a dividend at the rate of 1*l*. 5*s*. per cent. per annum.—For other details as to the position, &c., of the undertaking prior to the amalgamation, see Manual for 1882, page 274.

St. Andrews, Dunfermline and Queensferry, Edinburgh, Loanhead, and Roslin, and Leven and East of Fife.—*St. Andrews.*—Incorporated by act of 3rd July, 1851, for a line from Milton Junction, on Edinburgh, Perth, and Dundee, to St. Andrews. Length, 4¾ miles. The last half-yearly meeting of this company as a separate undertaking was held on 29th October, 1877; the accounts showed a profit equal to a dividend of 10 per cent. per annum on the ordinary capital, and a small payment was divisible to the shareholders out of the sinking fund in addition to the dividend. *Dunfermline and Queensferry.*—Incorporated by act of 21st July, 1873, to construct a line from the town of Dunfermline to North Queensferry, and a pier in connection therewith. Length, 5¼ miles. Capital, 105,000*l*. in 10*l*. shares and 35,000*l*. on loan; reduced by the North British Act, 1876, to 75,000*l*. and 25,000*l*. *Edinburgh, Loanhead, and Roslin.*—Incorporated by act of 20th June, 1870, to construct a line from the North British, near Millerhill Station, to Roslin. Length, 6½ miles. Capital, 48,000*l*. in 10*l*. shares, "preferred" and "deferred," with 16,000*l*. on loan or by debenture stock. By act of 5th August, 1873, the company was authorised to make a line of 2 miles in length to Glencross, and one of about 5 furlongs to Penicuik. *Leven and East of Fife.*—The Leven was incorporated by act of 17th June, 1852, to construct a line from the Edinburgh, Perth, and Dundee, at Thornton Junction, Markinch, Fife, to Burnmill, in Scoonie, with branches to Kirklann Works and Leven Harbour. Length, 6 miles. Capital, 23,000*l*. in shares and 5,000*l*. on loan. Opened August, 1854. The East of Fife was incorporated 23rd July, 1855, to construct a line commencing by a junction with the Leven, at the town of that name, and terminating at Kilconquhar, in the county of Fife. Length, 7 miles. Capital, 32,000*l*. in shares and 10,600*l*. on loan. Opened 18th August, 1857. The two companies were amalgamated by act of 22nd July, 1861, under the title of the Leven and East of Fife. The same act also authorises the issue of 17,000*l*. new capital, viz., 14,000*l*. Leven and 3,000*l*. East of Fife. By act of 22nd July, 1861, the Leven and East of Fife was authorised to make an extension from Kilconquhar to Anstruther. Length, 6 miles. New capital, 40,000*l*. at 4½ per cent.; borrowing powers, 13,200*l*. By the act of 28th June, 1877, 40 and 41 Vic., cap. 61, the above-mentioned four companies respectively became vested in the North British undertaking, the amalgamations taking effect on the 1st August, 1877. The mortgages of the vested companies, amounting in the aggregate to 97,750*l*., during their continuance, to be charges upon the respective undertakings upon which they were originally secured, the North British, however, to be liable for all interest which may accrue from the date of the amalgamations, and to have power to raise additional loan capital of their own, undertaking to pay off such mortgages respectively as they fall due. The stock and shares of the respective undertakings were exchanged for equal amounts of lien stocks, called in the act, and bearing *fixed* preferential dividends, as follow, viz.:—

Originally.	Amounting to.	Exchanged for.	Rate per cent. per annum.
St. Andrews shares	£21,000	St. Andrews lien stock	10½
Fife preference stock	62,910	Fife No. 1 lien stock	4½
Leven ordinary stock	37,000	,, No. 2 ,,	10½
East of Fife ordinary stock	35,000	,, No. 3 ,,	5
Loanhead shares	84,000	Loanhead lien stock	4½ for year ending 31st July, 1878, and 5 thereafter.
Queensferry shares	75,000	Queensferry lien stock	3*

Selkirk and Galashiels.—Incorporated by act of 31st July, 1854, for a line between these towns. Capital, 24,000*l*. in 10*l*. shares; loans, 8,000*l*. Length, 6¼ miles. By act of 4th June, 1858, the company was authorised to raise additional capital, 6,000*l*. in shares at 5 per cent., and 2,000*l*. on mortgage. By act of 21st July, 1859,

* Accruing from 1st February, 1878.

the company was amalgamated with North British, the ordinary stock of the latter being exchanged for that of the former.

Tay Bridge.—By act of 1st August, 1870, the company was authorised to construct a bridge over the River Tay, and lines of railway, in connection therewith, commencing by a junction with the main line at Leuchars, and proceeding in a north-westerly direction to near Newport, in the parish of Forgan, in Fifeshire, thence by bridge across the River Tay, with a line through Dundee to join the Dundee and Arbroath Railway at the east end of the town. Total length, 9 miles 3 furlongs 6 chains 60 links. Capital: shares, 350,000*l*.; loans, 116,600*l*. The bridge and relative lines will form a separate undertaking. The undertaking is not chargeable with any debts, engagements, or liabilities, or with any money or interest due on mortgage, of the North British, except such as the said separate undertaking may be specially liable for under any agreement entered into between the company and the subscribers to the separate undertaking. The dividend assigned to the share capital was 5½ per cent., with a lien over the receipts of the undertaking. The bridge and connecting lines were opened for traffic on 1st June, 1878. In 1878 the capital of the Tay Bridge was taken over by the North British at 130 per cent.; some of the proprietary receiving cash at that rate, and others 4 per cent. consolidated lien stock at the rate of 131¼ per cent. This bridge fell on the evening of 28th December, 1879, but the company has obtained Parliamentary power to erect a new viaduct.

Wansbeck.—Incorporated by act of 8th August, 1859, to construct lines from Morpeth to the Border Counties, the Blyth and Tyne, and the North Eastern. Capital, 120,000*l*. in 10*l*. shares; loans, 40,000*l*. Length of main line, 26 miles, to commence at Morpeth, and terminate at Chollerton, by junction with North Tyne Section of Border Counties; branch to Blyth and Tyne, 6¾ furlongs; branch to North Eastern, 2½ furlongs. By act of 21st July, 1863, the company was authorised to create new capital to the extent of 10,000*l*. in shares and 3,300*l*. on loan, and also to amalgamate with the North British.

Wemyss and Buckhaven.—This is a private undertaking, worked by the North British, under authority of a Board of Trade Certificate, at 50 per cent. of the gross receipts, for 90 years from the 15th May, 1881.

West of Fife.—Incorporated by act of 14th July, 1856, for making a line from Dunfermline to Killairnie, 6¾ miles, with a branch to Kingseat, 1 furlong. By act of 27th July, 1857, the company was authorised to construct a branch to Roscobie, 2½ miles. By act of 23rd July, 1860, the company was authorised to extend the Kingseat Branch to Beath, where it unites with the Kinross-shire. Length, 8¼ miles. Amalgamated with North British by act of 29th July, 1862.—For other details of information prior to the amalgamation, see Manual for 1882, page 276.

ACCOUNTS:—

Revenue.—The revenue results, as shown by the accounts for half-years ended 31st January and 31st July, 1884, were as under:—

	1884 January.	1884 July.
Passengers, parcels, &c.	£489,697	£486,262
Goods, minerals, and cattle	835,802	766,997
Canal receipts, rents, &c.	20,640	21,535
Gross receipts	£1,346,139	£1,274,794
Expenditure	634,824	626,413
Net	£711,315	£648,381
Add—Interest and other balances	24,618	24,171
Total net revenue	£735,933	£672,552
Deduct—Interest, rents, feu duties, &c.	200,155	200,956
Available for dividend	£535,778	£471,596

For the half-year ended 31st January the balance was sufficient to pay the preference dividends in full, 5¼ per cent. per annum on the North British ordinary stock, and 2 per cent. per annum on Edinburgh and Glasgow ordinary stock, carrying forward a balance of 5,400*l*. For the half-year ended 31st July, the balance was sufficient to pay the preference dividends in full, 3½ per cent. per annum on the ordinary stock, and ½ per cent. per annum on Edinburgh and Glasgow ordinary stock, carrying forward a balance of 4,423*l*.

CAPITAL—31st July, 1884.—*Authorised:* Stock and shares, 26,406,525*l.*; loans, 8,491,286*l.*; total, 34,897,811*l.* *Created or sanctioned:* Stock and shares, 25,686,525*l*; loans, 7,889,686*l.*; total, 33,576,211*l.* The following statement of stock and share capital created shows the proportion received to 31st July, 1884:—

Description.	Created.	Received.
North British ordinary stock	£4,625,868	£4,625,868
Edinburgh and Glasgow ordinary stock	2,422,485	2,422,485
Consolidated lien 4 per cent.	2,719,471	2,719,471
Bothwell lien stock	500,000	500,000
Montrose lien stock	185,580	185,485
Port Carlisle lien stock	70,600	70,600
Silloth lien stock	75,000	75,000
Consolidated 4 per cent. preference stock, No. 1	2,444,129	2,444,129
Consolidated 4 per cent. preference stock, No. 2	3,850,198	3,850 198
Monkland 6 per cent. preference stock (ordinary)	563,379	563,379
Edinburgh and Glasgow preference stock 4½ per cent.	2,422,485	2,422,485
North British 5 per cent. preference stock (1865)	387,370	387,370
Share capital of the Stobcross undertaking	150,000	150,000
Northumberland Central preference stock, No. 2	11,070	11,070
Convertible 5 per cent. preference stock (1874)	418,890	418,890
North British 4½ per cent. preference stock (1875)	2,290,889	2,290,889
Convertible stock (1875)	709,111	709,111
Convertible 5 per cent. preference stock (1879)	610,000	610,000
Convertible stock (1884)	1,230,000	...
	£25,686,525	£24,456,525

DESCRIPTIONS, DIVIDENDS, and other conditions of issue of the various Securities of the company, existing on the 31st July, 1884 (see notes).

No.	Year of Act.	FULL DESCRIPTION (to be observed in Transfer Deeds and all other Legal Documents).	Rate ℔ cent ℔ annum.
1	Various	Consolidated lien stock	4
2	1879	Bothwell lien stock	7½ to 8
3	1880	Montrose lien stock	5
4	1880	Port Carlisle lien stock	1¼
5	1880	Silloth lien stock	4½
7	Various	4 per cent. debenture stock	4
8	Various	4¼ per cent. debenture stock	4¼
9	Various	4½ per cent. debenture stock	4½
10	Various	Edinburgh, Perth, and Dundee debenture stock B.	5
11	1880	Port Carlisle debenture stock	3
12	1880	Silloth debenture stock	4
13	Various	Mortgage—various	Open.
14	Various	Consolidated preference, No. 1 stock	4
15	Various	Consolidated preference, No. 2 stock	4
16	1865	Monkland preference (ordinary) stock	6
17	1865	Edinburgh and Glasgow preference stock	4½
18	1865 and various	Preference stock, 1865	5
19	1867 & later	Share capital—Stobcross undertaking	4
20	1872	Northumberland Central preference stock, No. 2	Open.
21	1867-72-73	Convertible preference stock (1874)	5
22	1869 & 1875	Preference stock (1875)	4½
23	1869 & 1875	Convertible preference stock (1875)	4½
24	1877-8	Convertible preference stock (1879)	5
25	...	Convertible preference stock (1884)	4
26	Various	North British ordinary stock	Open.
27	1876	Edinburgh and Glasgow ordinary stock	Open.

NOTES.—Dividends Accumulative: Nos 1 to 5, 7 to 14, and 19.

Dividends contingent upon the profits of each separate *half-year:* Nos. 16, 17, 18, 26, and 27.

Dividends contingent upon the profits of each separate *year* ended 31st January: Nos. 15, and 21 to 25.

Exceptions to the above: No. 20, to which the question does not seem to apply.

Deferred Stocks: No. 26 (Edinburgh and Glasgow Ordinary) receives dividend on the following scale, viz.:—When the North British Ordinary dividend is 3 to 3½ per cent., the Edinburgh and Glasgow Ordinary receives a corresponding dividend above 3 per cent.; above 3½ to 4 per cent., ½ per cent., and afterwards ranks *pari passu* for dividend in excess of 4 per cent.; the North British dividends from that figure being always in excess of the Edinburgh and Glasgow by 3½ per cent. per annum.

Stocks with variable Dividends: Nos. 2, 20, 26, and 27. No. 2 stock (Bothwell lien) takes dividend as follows:—7½ per cent. to 31st January, 1885, and 8 per cent. thereafter.

Convertible Stocks: Nos. 21, 23, 24, and 25 are convertible into North British ordinary stock at par at any time.

Northumberland Central Preference Stock, No. 2 (No. 20): This stock shares in dividend on North British ordinary stock to the extent of any increase paid on that stock in any half-year over the corresponding period. It is called a 1 per cent. minimum stock.

Dividends payable at fixed dates (half-yearly): Nos. 1 to 5, and Nos. 10 and 11, 1st February and 1st August; Nos. 7, 8, 9, 12, and 13, 15th May and 11th November. (Dividends on all other stocks are payable in March and September.)

Transfer Books close—how many days before payment of dividends: Nos. 1 to 5, and Nos. 7 to 12, 14 days. (No fixed dates for any of the other securities.)

TRANSFER DEPARTMENT QUERIES AND REPLIES.

Queries.	Replies.
Transfer form—ordinary or special?	Ordinary.
Fee per deed?	2*s.* 6*d.*
Ditto if more sellers than one?	2*s.* 6*d.* each seller.
May several classes of stock be transferred on one deed?	Yes.
Are certificates required to accompany transfers?	Yes.
What amounts of stock are transferable, and are parts of 1*l.* sterling allowed to be transferred?	Any sum. In stocks numbered above, 2 to 12, 16, 18, 19, 20, 21, 23, and 24, fractions of 1*l.* are not allowed to be transferred.
To what officer should transfer communications be sent?	Secretary.
In acceptances, renunciations, &c., of allotments of new stock, proxies, or other forms sent to trustees and other joint holders, what signatures are required?	First-named trustee alone.

The receipts and expenditure on capital account to 31st July, 1884, were as detailed below:—

Receipts.		*Expenditure.*	
Shares and stock	£24,456,525	Lines and works open	£27,270,848
Debenture stocks	6,261,590	Lines constructing or to be constructed	174,892
Loans	1,627,711	Working stock	4,325,218
Premiums on stock and forfeited shares, &c.	244,062	Steamboats and ferry stock	151,699
Balance	332,153	Subscriptions to other lines	859,655
		Special	139,734
	£32,922,041		£32,922,041

The subjoined was the estimate of further expenditure on capital account during the half-year ended 31st January, 1885, and in subsequent half-years:—

Lines open for traffic	£77,593	£114,889	£191,982
Lines, &c., constructing or to be constructed	188,251	977,948	1,166,199
Working stock	15,000	...	15,000
Subscriptions to other railways	7,000	...	7,000
Total	£287,844	£1,092,837	£1,380,181

The capital powers and other assets available to meet the further expenditure were as under:—

Share and loan capital authorised but not created or sanctioned ...	£1,321,600
Stock and share capital created but not received, viz.:—	
Amount unissued	1,230,000
Loans and debenture stock—Balance of available borrowing powers	384
	£2,551,984
Deduct balance at debit of capital account	332,152
	£2,219,832

MILEAGE.—*Miles authorised:* Owned, 918½; partly owned, 23; leased or rented, 40¾. *Constructed:* Owned, 898¾; partly owned, 23; leased or rented, 40¾. *Constructing or to be constructed:* Owned, 19¾. *Worked:* Owned, 895¼; partly owned, 23; leased or rented, 40¾ Lines worked, 57¼. Foreign lines worked over, 122½. Total lines worked by engines, 1,138¾ Union Canal, 32.

Scale of Voting.—One vote for 50*l.* up to 500*l.*; then one vote additional for every 200*l.* up to 10,000*l.*; then one vote additional thereafter for every 500*l.* No voting in respect of debenture stock, or E. and G. ordinary stock.

No. of Directors.—Maximum, 15; minimum, 6. *Qualification*, 3,000*l.* stock. Allowance, 4,100*l.*

DIRECTORS:

Chairman—3 Sir JAMES FALSHAW, Bart., 14, Belgrave Crescent, Edinburgh.

Deputy-Chairman—1 JOHN BEAUMONT, Esq., Ravensknowle, Huddersfield.

3 James Cox, Esq., Clement Park, Dundee.
2 Peter Garnett, Esq., South Woods Hall, Thirsk, and Cleckheaton, Normanton, Yorkshire.
2 The Right Hon. Sir George Harrison, LL.D., Lord Provost of Edinburgh.
3 Sir William Miller, Bart., of Manderston, Berwickshire, and 1, Park Lane, W.
3 George Robertson, Esq., W.S., Edinburgh.
1 Robert Young, Esq., 4, West Nile Street, Glasgow.
2 H. J. Trotter, Esq., Bishop Auckland, and Langton Grange, Gainford, near Darlington.
1 Henry Grierson, Esq., 8, Park Circus Place, Glasgow.
3 Adam Johnstone, Esq., Burntisland.
1 The Marquis of Tweeddale, Yester House, Haddington.

1, Retire in 1885; 2, in 1886; 3, in 1887.

OFFICERS.—Sec., G. B. Wieland. Gen. Man., John Walker. Solicitor, W. W. Millar, Edinburgh. Loco. Supt., M. Holmes, Cowlairs, Glasgow. Gen. Goods Man., D. McDougall, George Square, Glasgow. Accountant, George Simpson. Cashier, J. Macdonald. Audit Accountant, David Anderson. Res. Eng.-in-Chief, James Carswell. District Res. Eng., Charles Boyd, Carlisle. Registrar, A. B. Scott. District Goods Mans., Alexander Rutherford, Edinburgh; D. Deuchars, Dundee; and James Bruce, Coatbridge. Gen. Pass. Supt., James M'Laren. District Supt., George Cunningham, Glasgow. Auditors, Walter Mackenzie and J. Wyllie Guild, Accountants, Glasgow.

Head Offices—Princes Street, Edinburgh.

214.—NORTH CORNWALL.

Incorporated by act of Parliament, passed 18th August, 1882, to construct a railway from Padstow, in the county of Cornwall, to a junction with the Holsworthy Line of the London and South Western at Halwell, in Devon, with powers to deviate, alter, and improve the Bodmin and Wadebridge. Length, including deviations, 52½ miles. Power to agree with the London and South Western for working and management. Capital, 660,000*l.* in shares; 220,000*l.* borrowing powers.

By act of 1884, the company was authorised to constitute a portion of the railway a separate undertaking, with a separate capital of 150,000*l.* Borrowing powers, 50,000*l.* Length, 14 miles, extending from Halwell to Launceston.

Agreements have been entered into with the London and South Western for working the line for 55 per cent. of gross receipts; the South Western pay annual rebate of 10 per cent. of its receipts for through traffic up to a maximum of 12,000*l.*, which rebate is guaranteed at 3,000*l.* for the Halwell and Launceston section, subject to reduction as the traffic of the line earns certain specific dividends. The South Western also purchase the debentures at a premium.

The capital for first section has been raised, and the line is in course of construction.

DIRECTORS:

Chairman—3 JOHN TREMAYNE, Esq., M.P., Heligan, Cornwall, and Sydenham, Devon.

Deputy-Chairman—1 The Right Hon. the Earl of WHARNCLIFFE, Wortley Hall, Sheffield.

* Arthur Mills, Esq., 34, Hyde Park Gardens, W., and Efford Down, Bude, Cornwall.

2 Sir W. W. R. Onslow, Bart., Hengar, Bodmin.

1 Charles Glynn Prideaux Brune, Esq., Prideaux Place, Padstow.

3 Lewis Charles Foster, Esq., The Coombe, Liskeard.

2 Charles Gurney, Esq., Trebursye, Launceston.

2 Thomas Martyn, Esq., Gonvena, Wadebridge.

3 James Oag, Esq., Thorndon, Lifton, Devon.

1 Charles Bainbridge Rendle, Esq., Liskeard.

2 William Teague, Esq., Treliske, Truro.

1 Retire in 1885; 2, in 1886; 3, in 1887.

* Nominated by the London and South Western.

OFFICERS.—Sec., Edward Bellamy; Engs., Galbraith and Church, Victoria Street, Westminster; Land Agents, J. and H. Drew, 15, Queen Street, Exeter; Solicitors, Burchell and Co., 5, The Sanctuary, Westminster, Coode, Shilson, and Co., St. Austell, and Venning and Goldsmith, 26, Ker Street, Devonport.

Offices—57, Moorgate Street, E.C.

215.—NORTH EASTERN.

The company originally comprised the York, Newcastle, and Berwick, the York and North Midland, the Leeds Northern, and the Malton and Driffield, amalgamated in 1854, but other companies have been amalgamated with it at different times since that date, more particularly the Newcastle and Carlisle in 1862, the Stockton and Darlington in 1863, the West Hartlepool and the Cleveland in 1865. Length of line, 1,535¾ miles.

By act of 12th May, 1870, the various ordinary stocks were consolidated in the scale subjoined:—

For every 100*l*. of Berwick	100*l*.	of new stock.
,, ,, 100*l* of York	98*l*.	,, ,,
,, ,, 100*l*. of Leeds	65*l*.	,, ,,
,, ,, 100*l*. of Carlisle	183*l*.	,, ,,
,, ,, 100*l*. of Darlington	136*l*.	,, ,,
,, ,, 100*l*. of Malton and Driffield	10*l*.	,, ,,

FURTHER PARLIAMENTARY POWERS.—For list of Acts from 1857 to 1878, with short heads showing the objects for which the various powers were sought, see the MANUAL for 1881, pages 291 and 292.

1882—19TH MAY—CONSTRUCTION OF ALNWICK BRANCH.—See Amalgamations, Leases, &c., further on.

1882—19TH JUNE—VESTING OF THE TEES VALLEY.—New lines and works in connection with the Blyth and Tyne, Newcastle and Berwick, Pontop and South Shields, Stockton and Darlington Branches, and the Main Line from York to Newcastle. New capital, 1,000,000*l*.; borrowing powers, 332,000*l*.

1883—29TH JUNE.—New lines and works at Darlington (Durham), Romanby, Tadcaster, and other places in the East and West Ridings of Yorkshire. Total length, about 6½ miles. Vesting of Scotswood, Newburn, and Wylam, and Hylton, Southwick, and Monkwearmouth undertakings respectively (see further on), and for other and general purposes. New capital, 250,000*l*.; loans, &c., 83,000*l*.

1884—23RD JUNE.—Short line from Laxton to Eastrington.; additional lands at various places, and other purposes. New capital, 300,000*l*.; loans, 100,000*l*.

AMALGAMATIONS, LEASES, AGREEMENTS, SUBSCRIPTIONS, &c.:—

BLYTH AND TYNE.—Incorporated July, 1852. By various acts passed in 1853, 1857, 1861, 1864, 1867, and 1872, the powers of the company were extended. Length, about 42 miles. By act of 7th August, 1874, the company was amalgamated with the North Eastern. According to the arrangements come to, every 100*l*. of ordinary stock, and every 100*l*. of 10 per cent. preference stock, of the Blyth and Tyne, was exchanged for 250*l*. of "Blyth and Tyne 4 per cent. preference stock" in the North Eastern, and every 100*l*. of 5 per cent. preference stock of the Blyth and Tyne was exchanged for 125*l*. of "Blyth and Tyne 4 per cent. preference stock" in the North Eastern.

FORCETT.—Incorporated by act of 2nd June, 1865, to construct a line from the Darlington and Barnard Castle to Forcett. Length, 5½ miles. Capital, 30,000*l.* in 20*l.* shares and 10,000*l.* on mortgage. Arrangements with North Eastern. By Certificate of the Board of Trade, issued on the 25th March, 1873, the company was authorised to issue 4,200*l.* new share capital, and to borrow on mortgage a further sum of 1,400*l.* In past years this company has earned dividends on the ordinary 20*l.* shares at the rate of 6 per cent. per annum.—For other particulars see past Editions of the MANUAL (General Index). Secretary, T. Richardson. Offices—Barnard Castle.

GREAT NORTH OF ENGLAND, CLARENCE, AND HARTLEPOOL JUNCTION.—This line is leased to the North Eastern, under the York, Newcastle, and Berwick (Hartlepool Dock and Railway, &c., Leasing) Act, 1848.

HEXHAM AND ALLENDALE.—Incorporated by act of 19th June, 1865, to construct lines from the Newcastle and Carlisle, near Hexham, to Allendale Town—length, 12¼ miles; and from Allendale Town to Allenheads—length, 7 miles. In operation, 12¼ miles. By act of 13th July, 1876, the undertaking became vested in the North Eastern, on payment of 6*l.* cash for every fully paid 10*l.* share; and powers were given to North Eastern to borrow in lieu of Hexham Company. Existing mortgages of Hexham Company to have priority.

HULL AND HORNSEA.—Incorporated by act of 30th June, 1862, to construct a line from the North Eastern, near Hull, to Hornsea. Length, 13 miles. By act of 16th July, 1866, the Hull and Hornsea was amalgamated with the North Eastern.

HULL AND SELBY.-Incorporated by act of 1836, for a line connecting those towns, subsequently extended (acts 1843 and 1845) by a branch from Hull to Bridlington. Length, 61 miles. The lease to the North Midland provided for 10 per cent. in perpetuity on 700,000*l.* The lessees had the option, any time after the expiration of five years from date of the lease (30th June, 1845), to pay off the whole of the capital at the rate of 112½*l.* per 50*l.*, of 56¼*l.* per 25*l.*, 28⅛*l.* per 12½*l.* share, on giving six months' notice of such intention. The purchase of the Hull and Selby was completed on 1st March, 1872. The whole of the Hull and Selby purchase stock has been issued and fully paid up.

HYLTON, SOUTHWICK, AND MONKWEARMOUTH.—Vested in North Eastern by act of 29th June, 1883, holders of Hylton shares receiving in exchange 51*l.* 6*s.* 10*d.* of "Hylton preference stock" of the North Eastern for every 100*l.* of their holdings respectively, such preference stock bearing fixed dividends (payable half-yearly, at same times as North Eastern ordinary dividends), from 1st July, 1883, as follow:—2½ per cent. per annum for three years ending 30th June, 1886, and 3½ per cent. per annum thenceforth in perpetuity.

LEEDS, CASTLEFORD, AND PONTEFRACT JUNCTION.—Incorporated by act of 21st July, 1873, to construct a line from the Garforth Station of the North Eastern to Castleford, with a branch to the Lancashire and Yorkshire, near Pontefract. Length, 7 miles. Capital, 120,000*l.* in 10*l.* shares and 40,000*l.* on loan. By act of 30th June, 1874, the company was authorised to make a short line near Castleford (about ½ mile), and to abandon portion of the line authorised by the act of 1873. No new capital. By act of 13th July, 1876, the powers of the company were transferred to the North Eastern; each 100*l.* of ordinary stock receiving in exchange 75*l.* of North Eastern consols.

SCOTSWOOD, NEWBURN, AND WYLAM.—Incorporated by act of 16th June, 1871. Length, 6½ miles. Vested in North Eastern by act of 29th June, 1883, the holders of ordinary shares receiving in exchange at par "Scotswood preference stock" of the North Eastern, bearing a fixed dividend from 1st July, 1883, payable half-yearly, at the same respective times as the dividends are paid on North Eastern ordinary stock, as follows, viz.:—1 per cent. per annum for 2 years ending 30th June, 1885; 2 per cent. per annum for the next two years ending 30th June, 1887; 3 per cent. per annum for the next two years ending 30th June, 1889; and thereafter 3½ per cent. per annum in perpetuity.—For particulars prior to transfer, see the MANUAL for 1883, page 294.

SWINTON AND KNOTTINGLEY JOINT.—Opened for traffic July 1st, 1879.—See "Midland and North Eastern Joint."

TEES VALLEY.—Incorporated by act of 19th June, 1865. Length, 6 miles. The line joins the North Eastern, near Barnard Castle, and terminates at Middleton-in-Teesdale. Under the North Eastern Act of 19th June, 1882, the undertaking became vested in that company from that date in perpetuity, the latter providing for all loans and liabilities (amounting to 22,000*l.*), and subscribing towards the construction of the line 31,000*l.*; also paying in respect of the share capital the sum of 25,188*l*., to be divided as follows, viz.:— To the preference shareholders (other than the North Eastern) 6,839*l*. 17*s*. 6*d*., being equal to 6*l*. 16*s*. 9*d*. per share. To the ordinary shareholders (other than the North Eastern) 18,348*l*. 2*s*. 6*d*., being equal to 19*l*. 7*s*. 6*d*. per share. Any amount by which the liabilities of the company may fall short of 22,000*l*. to be applied—1st, in making up to 7*l*. per share the amount payable to the preference shareholders; and 2nd, in paying the balance to the ordinary shareholders.—For detailed information as to the working of this company in the past, &c., see MANUAL for 1882, page 341, and previous editions.

WEST DURHAM.—A local line, 7 miles in length, connecting the West Hartlepool and the Stockton and Darlington, chiefly employed in the carriage of minerals. Vested in the North Eastern by act of 4th July, 1870.

WHITBY, REDCAR, AND MIDDLESBROUGH UNION.—This company is leased to the North Eastern under the Whitby Company's Act of 1875.—See GENERAL INDEX.

For other information relating to the opening of new lines and works, see previous MANUALS.

ACCOUNTS:—

The half-yearly meeting of this company was held on the 8th August last, when the directors' report and statement of accounts then presented were adopted. The following is an abstract of those accounts made to the 30th June, 1884, viz.:—

CAPITAL.—*Authorised:* Shares and stock, 46,583,075*l*.; loans, 15,242,046*l*.; total, 65,825,121*l*. *Created:* Shares and stock, 43,386,849*l*.; loans, 14,264,046*l*.; total, 57,650,895*l*.; balance, 4,174,226*l*.

Receipts.		*Expenditure.*	
Ordinary (consols)	£22,807,835	Lines and works open for traffic	£49,011,687
Preference stock	20,559,131	Lines in course of construction	159,898
Loan capital	13,625,439	Working stock	9,205,375
	£56,992,405	Subscriptions to other lines	228,450
Balance	298,103		£58,605,410
		Less premiums received on issue of stocks and shares	1,314,902
	£57,290,508		£57,290,508

Amount uncalled, 19,883*l*.

DESCRIPTIONS, DIVIDENDS, and other conditions of issue of the various Ordinary, Preference, and Debenture Stock existing on 30th June, 1883 (see notes).

No.	FULL DESCRIPTION (to be observed in Transfer Deeds and all other Legal Documents).	Rate ℔cent ℔annum.
1	Irredeemable 4 per cent. debenture stock (£12,287,175)	4
2	4½ per cent. debenture stock } (£1,138,119)	4½
3	Stockton and Darlington ditto }	
4	North Eastern consols (ordinary stock) (£22,807,704)	Variable
5	Great North of England purchase stock and shares (£176,045)	4
6	Leeds preference shares, quarters, & extensions, Nos. 1, 2, & 3 (£19,179)	6
7	Leeds preference shares, fifths (£33,540)	5
8	Carlisle 4 per cent. preferential stock (£13,667)	4
9	Carlisle 4½ per cent. preferential stock (£155,000)	4½
10	Darlington "A" preferential 5 per cent. stock (£450,000)	5
11	Darlington "B" and "C" preferential 6 per cent. stock (£1,050,000)	6
12	Darlington "D" preferential 5½ per cent. stock (£595,000)	5½
13	Consolidated preferential 4 per cent. stock (£2,[illegible]00,412)	4
14	6 per cent. guaranteed preference stock (£286,297)	6
15	West Hartlepool preference stock (£3,162,747)	4
16	Hull and Hornsea stock (£62,760)	4
17	Blyth and Tyne 4 per cent. stock (£1,181,250)	4
18	Preference stock, 1876 (£10,727,080)	4½
19	Scotswood preference stock (£85,000)	...
20	Hylton preference stock (£150,000)	...

NOTES.—The priorities, &c., for dividends of the various descriptions of stocks are not, by the above table, defined. The stocks are numbered in the order in which the information relating thereto has been supplied.

Convertible Stocks.—Nos. 5, 6, and 8: No. 5 is convertible at any time into North Eastern consols at par; No. 6 is convertible at any time into 6 per cent. stock at par; No. 8 is convertible at any time into North Eastern consols at 133 per cent., and, until so converted, bears dividend at 4 per cent., with participation in dividend paid on 133*l.* consols in excess of that rate.

Changes in Dividends.—No. 18 (preference stock, 1876) now receives 4 per cent. in perpetuity (dividend reduced from 4½ per cent. to 4 per cent. from 1st January, 1883). No. 19 (Scotswood preference stock), dividend at 1 per cent. for two years from 1st July, 1883, 2 per cent. for next two years, and 3 per cent. for next two years, thenceforth 3½ per cent. in perpetuity. No. 20 (Hylton preference stock), dividend at 2½ per cent. for three years from 1st July, 1883, thenceforth 3½ per cent. in perpetuity.

Dividends Payable.—Nos. 1, 2, and 3 are payable half-yearly, on 1st January and 1st July; Nos. 4 to 20 are payable in Feb. and Aug., after the half-yearly meetings.

Transfer Books Close.—Nos. 1, 2, and 3, for 28 days before payment of dividend; Nos. 4 to 20, for 28 days before the dates of the half-yearly meetings.

TRANSFER DEPARTMENT QUERIES AND REPLIES.

Queries.	Replies.
Transfer form—ordinary or special?	Ordinary.
Fee per deed?	2*s.* 6*d.*
Ditto if more sellers than one?	2*s.* 6*d.* per deed.
May several classes of stock be transferred on one deed?	Yes, to one transferee.
Are certificates required to accompany transfers?	Yes.
What amounts of stock are transferable, and are parts of 1*l.* sterling allowed to be transferred?	Any amount which does not contain a fraction of 1*l.*
To what officer should transfer communications be sent?	The Secretary, York.
In acceptances, renunciations, &c., of allotments of new stock, proxies, or other forms sent to trustees or other joint holders, what signatures are required?	Renunciations of allotments of new stock require the signatures of all the allottees; as a rule this applies to the other cases. As regards proxies of joint holders these are regulated by 8 Vic., c. 16, sec. 78.

The estimate of further expenditure required for the half-year ended 31st December, 1884, and for subsequent periods, was as follows:—

	Dec. 31st, 1884.	Subsequent half-years.	Total.
Lines and works open for traffic	£154,552	£90,192	£244,744
Lines, &c., in course of construction	185,450	592,851	778,301
Works not yet commenced, or in abeyance	3,650	66,418	70 063
Additional rolling stock	50,370	...	50,370
Total	£394,022	£749,456	£1,143,478

To meet which, the available assets were detailed as under, viz.:—

Share and loan capital authorised but not yet created or sanctioned	£4,174,226	
Share capital created but not yet received	19,882	
Borrowing powers unexercised	793,207=	£4,987,315
Deduct—West Hartlepool primary charges	154,600	
" Balance of capital account	298,102=	452,702
		£4,534,613

Revenue.—The following is a statement of the several amounts received and expended on this account for the last three half-years, showing the comparative results, under their respective heads, viz:—

Receipts.	1883. June 30.	1883. Dec. 31.	1884. June 30.
Passengers, parcels, horses, &c.	£811,750	£1,055,470	£827,167
Merchandise (less collection and delivery)	1,058,974	1,093,243	1,018,962
Live stock	46,286	48,133	45,315
Minerals	1,275,624	1,305,250	1,168,318
Rents, fees, dock dues, mileage, and demurrage	75,388	81,949	77.741
Dividends on shares in other companies	4,965	4,715	4,090
	£3,272,982	£3,588,760	£3,141,583

Expenditure.	1883. June 30.	1883. Dec. 31.	1884. June 30.
Maintenance of way, works, and stations	£287,928	£377,399	£282,165
Locomotive power	505,971	552,726	520,687
Carriage and wagon repairs	236,552	248,784	284,618
Traffic expenses	449,896	471,068	458,251
General charges	58,292	58,746	55,241
Stationary engines and inclines	12,701	12,199	11,864
Law and Parliamentary	10,000	11,253	5,390
Compensation	17,360	10,184	11,611
Rates, taxes, and Government duty	96,302	103,930	91,679
Ordinary and working charges	£1,673,002	£1,846,274	£1,666,506
Interest on loan and debenture stock, capital, calls in advance, bankers' and general interest (net)	270,886	270,045	273,805
Way-leave rents	19,783	19,267	19,815
Leased lines rental	3,645	3,290	2,213
Dividends on preference stock	437,046	439,831	429,580
	£2,404,361	£2,578,707	£2,391,419
Net balances each half-year	£868,571	£1,010,053	£750,174
Balances brought from previous half-years	37,847	31,072	43,336
Balances available for dividend on ordinary stock	£906,418	£1,041,125	£793,510
Dividends declared at 7¾, 8¾, and 6¾ per cent. per annum respectively	875,346	997,789	769,835
Balances carried forward	£31,072	£43,336	£23,675

Summary showing the general results of the last half-year's traffic, as compared with that of the corresponding period of 1883, viz.:—

Net balance—June 30, 1884 ...... £750,174
" June 30, 1883 868,571

Loss in 1884 .... £118,397

Thus:—
Gross traffic—decrease £131,339
Less:—
Working charges—dec.... £6,496
Pref. charges—decrease.. 6,446
12,942

Net loss in 1884 .... £118,397

MILEAGE.—*Lines owned:* Authorised, 1,546¾ miles; constructed, 1,495½ miles; constructing or to be constructed, 51¼ miles; worked, 1,495½ miles. *Lines partly owned:* Authorised, 15 miles; constructed, 15 miles; worked, 15 miles. *Lines leased or rented:* Authorised, 25¼ miles; constructed, 25¼ miles; worked, 25¼ miles. Total worked, 1,535¾ miles; foreign lines worked over, 148¾ miles.

No. of Directors.—Maximum, 22; minimum, 12. *Qualification*, 1,000*l.* in stock or shares.

DIRECTORS:

Chairman—JOHN DENT DENT, Esq., Ribston Hall, Wetherby.

Deputy-Chairman—The Right Hon. LORD DERWENT, Hackness Hall, near Scarborough, and 34, Belgrave Square, S.W.

Isaac Lowthian Bell, Esq., Rounton Grange, Northallerton.
John Cleghorn, Esq., 3, Spring Gardens, S.W.
William Charles Copperthwaite, Esq., Beech Grove, Malton.
David Dale, Esq., West Lodge, Darlington.
The Hon Cecil Duncombe, Nawton Grange, York.
James Hartley, Esq., Assoc.Inst.C.E., Ashbrooke, Sunderland.
James Kitson, Esq., M.Inst.C.E., Elmete Hall, Leeds.
Sir Henry M. Meysey-Thompson, Bart., Kirby Hall, York, and 42, Albemarle Street, W.
Henry Thomas Morton, Esq., Biddick Hall, Fencehouses.
Henry Oxley, Esq., Westwood, Leeds.
John William Pease, Esq., Pendower, Newcastle-on-Tyne.
Sir Joseph Whitwell Pease, Bart., M.P., Assoc.Inst.C.E., Hutton Hall, Guisbro', and 24, Kensington Palace Gardens, W.
William Benson Richardson, Esq., Elm Bank, York.
Sir Matthew W. Ridley, Bart., M.P., Blagdon, Cramlington, Northumberland, and 10, Carlton House Terrace, S.W.
John Straker, Esq., Stagshaw House, Corbridge-on-Tyne.
John Lloyd Wharton, Esq., Bramham, Tadcaster, and Dryburn, Durham.
David Wilson, Esq., Park House, Cottingham, near Hull.
William Joseph Young, Esq., Wolviston Hall, Stockton-on-Tees.

OFFICERS.—Sec., C. N. Wilkinson, York. Gen. Man., Henry Tennant, York. Eng.-in-Chief, Thomas E. Harrison, M.Inst.C.E., Newcastle-on-Tyne. Assist. Eng. for New Works, Chas. A. Harrison, Newcastle-on-Tyne. Res. Engs., A. R. C. Harrison, M.Inst.C.E., Newcastle-on-Tyne; H. Copperthwaite, Assoc.Inst.C.E., York; Joseph Cabry, Darlington. Gen. Passenger Supt., Alexander Christison, York. Gen. Goods Man., Robert Pauling, York. Supt. of Goods and Passenger Departments, Darlington Division, William Smith, Darlington. Mineral Traffic Managers, R. W. Bailey, York; William Smith, Darlington; Thomas Audus, Newcastle-on-Tyne. Accountant, William Tidswell, Newcastle-on-Tyne. Treasurer, Edward Towns, Newcastle-on-Tyne. Audit Accountant, Thomas Waddington, Newcastle-on-Tyne. Auditors, G. B. Monkhouse, Newcastle-on-Tyne, and Roderick Mackay, London. Solicitor, George N. Gibb. York.

Head Offices—York; Accountant's Offices, Newcastle-on-Tyne.

216.—NORTHERN AND EASTERN.

Incorporated by act of 4th July, 1836, for construction of a line commencing from a junction with the Great Eastern, at Stratford, 4 miles from London, and terminating at Newport, with a branch to Hertford. Total, 44 miles.

The line is leased to the Great Eastern for 999 years, under Parliamentary powers obtained in 1844, at 5, and a portion at 6 per cent., with half profits when Great Eastern reaches the former amount. Dividends on shares, guaranteed 5 per cent. per annum, 1*l*. 5*s*. each half-year; on shares of 50*l*. guaranteed 6 per cent. per annum, 1*l*. 10*s*. each half-year, less property tax, payable about six days after receipt of rent from Great Eastern, due middle of February and August. These terms have been secured by the Amalgamation Act, and the capital is constituted and confirmed by an act passed in 1847, a first claim on the net revenue of the Great Eastern, before any other classes of shares. The company also receives 1,000*l*. per annum to cover the expenses of management.

CAPITAL.—The receipts and expenditure on this account to 31st December, 1884, were stated as follow:—

Received.		*Expended.*	
Shares	£959,850	Lines open for traffic	£963.594
Capitalised items	3,594	Ditto, Newport extension	219,380
Shares	219,400		£1,182,974
Call received on forfeited shares	190	Balance	60
	£1,183,034		£1,183,034

The accounts are made up to 30th June and 31st December, and the half-yearly meetings (for the declaration of the dividend) are held in London in February and August in every year; the transfer books close a fortnight previously. Dividends for the half-years ended 31st December, 1883, and 30th June, 1884, were made payable on the 21st February and 21st August last respectively.

TRANSFER DEPARTMENT QUERIES AND REPLIES.

QUERIES.	REPLIES.
Transfer form—ordinary or special?	Ordinary.
Fee per deed?	2*s*. 6*d*.
Ditto if more sellers than one?	2*s*. 6*d*.
Are certificates required to accompany transfers?	No.
To what officer should transfer communications be sent?	Secretary.

Scale of Voting.—One vote for each share up to 20; then one for every 5.

No. of Directors.—Maximum, 12; minimum, 12. *Qualification*, 1,000*l*.

DIRECTORS:

Chairman—The Hon. RICHARD DENMAN, Westergate House, Arundel.

Deputy-Chairman—MATTHEW FLOWER, Esq., 14, Norfolk Crescent, Hyde Park, W.

Lord Eustace G. Cecil, M.P., 32, Eccleston Square, S.W.

William Stanley Dent, Esq., Streatham Hill, Surrey.

Robert Thornhagh Gurdon, Esq., M.P., Letton Hall, Norfolk.

Stonhewer Edward Illingworth, Esq., Borough Court, Winchfield, Hampshire.

Howard John Kennard, Esq., 20, Hyde Park Terrace, W.

William Fuller Maitland, Esq., M.P., Stanstead Park, Bishop's Stortford.

Joseph Trueman Mills, Esq., Clermont, Watton, Norfolk.

Percy Ricardo, Esq., Bramley Park, Guildford, Surrey.

Thomas Thornhill, Esq., M.P., 55, Eaton Square, S.W.

John Vigne, Esq., Tokenhouse Yard, E.C.

One-sixth of the directors retire annually, and are eligible for re-election. August meeting fills up vacancies.

OFFICERS.—Sec., Charles Barrett; Solicitors, Markby, Stewart, and Co., 57, Coleman Street, E.C.

Offices—Liverpool Street Station, E.C.

217.—NORTH LONDON.

Incorporated by act of 26th August, 1846, for making a railway from the London and North Western goods station, at Camden Town, to West India Docks, at Blackwall; and authorised by act of 1850 to make a branch to Blackwall Extension, near Bow. Traverses the northern and eastern suburbs of London, and has junctions with the London and North Western, Midland, Great Northern, Great Eastern, London, Tilbury, and Southend, and Blackwall, and access to the steam packet wharf at Blackwall; also junctions (*via* Hampstead Junction and North and South Western Junction) with the Great Western, Midland, and London and South Western lines. In operation, 12 miles.

For list of Acts from 1853 to 1874, with short heads showing the objects for which the various powers were sought, see the MANUAL for 1881, pages 297 and 298.

By act of 18th June, 1883, further powers were conferred upon the company for the acquisition of additional lands in Middlesex, and for other purposes. New capital, 250,000*l.*; loans, &c., 83,800*l.* By this act the London and North Western was empowered to raise 168,193*l.* for the purposes of subscription to this undertaking.

NORTH AND SOUTH WESTERN JUNCTION.—Joint lease with London and North Western and Midland.—See GENERAL INDEX.

REVENUE.—For the half-years ended 31st December, 1883, and 30th June, 1884, this was as under:—

	Dec., 1883.	June, 1884.
Passengers, parcels, &c.	£150,417	£147,113
Goods, minerals, and cattle	80,282	76,247
Miscellaneous	13,455	13,996
Gross receipts	£244,154	£237,356
Expenditure (net)	121,361	113,305
Net revenue	£122,793	£124,051
Sundry balances	1,845	1,259
Total net revenue	£124,638	£125,310
Interest, preference dividends, &c.	49,316	*49,165
Available for ordinary stock	£75,322	£76,145
Dividends at 7½ per cent. per annum each half-year respectively, payable 16th Feb. and 16th August	74,063	74,062
Balance carried forward	£1,259	£2,083

CAPITAL.—The statement of stock and share capital created (in order of priority next after the debenture stocks), showing the proportion received to 30th June, 1884, was as follows:—

Description.	Created.	Called up.
Preference stock (4½ to 5 per cent—see below), 1866	£700,000	£700,000
Second Preference stock (4½ per cent.), 1875	250,000	250,000
Ordinary consolidated stock	1,975,000	1,975,000
Ditto ditto 16th August, 1883	250,000	...
Debenture stock, 970,866*l.*		
	£3,175,000	£2,925,000

NOTES.—The dividends on debenture stocks are accumulative and payable half-yearly, on the 10th January and 10th July, the transfer books closing 10 days before payment.

The dividends on the preference stocks are contingent upon the profits of each separate year, and are payable half-yearly in February and August, the transfer books closing 16 days before payment.

The dividend upon the ordinary stock is contingent upon the profits of each half-year. Dates of payment and closing of transfer books same as preference stocks.

* Includes 3,000*l.* reserve fund.

The first preference capital was, in 1861, issued in 20*l*. shares, which were consolidated and converted into stock in 1866. This is a perpetual preference stock bearing a dividend at the rate of 4½ per cent. per annum, with a contingent right of ½ per cent. per annum.

The second preference capital was, in 1871, issued in 10*l*. shares, which were consolidated and converted into stock in 1875.

The ordinary capital was issued from time to time as ordinary shares, converted and consolidated on the several share capitals being fully paid up.

TRANSFER DEPARTMENT QUERIES AND REPLIES.

Queries.	Replies.
Transfer form—ordinary or special?	Ordinary.
Fee per deed?	2*s*. 6*d*.
Ditto if more sellers than one?	2*s*. 6*d*.
May several classes of stock be transferred on one deed, and with one stamp for the whole?	Ordinary and preference may be transferred on one deed, but debenture stock must be on a separate transfer.
Are certificates required to accompany transfers?	Yes.
What amounts of stock are transferable?	1*l*. and any multiple thereof.
Are parts of 1*l*. sterling allowed to be transferred?	No.
To what officer should transfer communications be sent?	Secretary.
In acceptances, renunciations of allotments of new stock, proxies, or other forms sent to trustees and other joint holders, what signatures are required?	Company do not recognise trust accounts, but in cases of joint accounts the signatures of all the holders are required, excepting the case of proxies, where the signature of the first-named in the holding is sufficient.

The receipts and expenditure on this account to the same date were particularised as under:—

Received.		*Expended.*	
Stock	£2,925,000	Lines open for traffic	£3,540,571
Debenture stocks	970,866	Working stock	375,709
Balance	42,947	North and South Western Junction Railway	22,533
	£3,938,813		£3,938,813

The estimate of further capital expenditure for the half-year ended 31st December, 1884, was 25,350*l*., and in subsequent half-years, 4,300*l*. The overdrawn capital amounted to 42,947*l*., less available assets, 337,364*l*. = 294,417*l*.

The accounts are made up to 30th June and 31st December, and the statutory meetings are held in London in February and August of each year.

DIRECTORS:

Chairman—JAMES BANCROFT, Esq., 83, Mosley Street, and Broughton Hall, Manchester.

Sir William J. W. Baynes, Bart., Forest Lodge, Putney Heath, S.W.
John Pares Bickersteth, Esq., Grove Mill House, Watford, Herts.
Harry Chubb, Esq., 6, Prince's Square, Hyde Park, W.
George Crosfield, Esq., 1c9, Lancaster Gate, W.
Richard Ryder Dean, Esq., 97, Gloucester Place, Portman Square, W.
The Hon. Sidney Carr Glyn, M.P., 6, Hyde Park Street, W.
George Pownall, Esq., 29, Parliament Street, Westminster, S.W.
James R. Robertson, Esq., 11, Oak Hill Park, Hampstead, N.W.
Oscar Leslie Stephen, Esq., 55, Cadogan Square, S.W.
Alexander Stewart, Esq., 2, Talbot Road, Westbourne Park, W.
William Tipping, Esq., Brasted Park, Sevenoaks, Kent.
Charles H. Wigram, Esq., 7, Leadenhall Street, E.C.

OFFICERS.—Gen. Man. and Sec., G. Bolland Newton, Assoc.Inst.C.E., Euston Station, N.W., and Broad Street Station, E.C.; Traffic Supt., F. J. Dunn, Broad Street Station, E.C.; Goods Supt., Thomas Day, Poplar, E.; Loco. Supt., John C. Park, Bow Works, E.; Res. Eng., Thomas Matthews, Broad Street Station, E.C.; Accountant, G. E. Mainland, Broad Street Station, E.C.; Auditors, Francis E. Greenaway, 75, Elgin Crescent, Kensington Park, W., and Edward Lawrence, Beechmount, Aigburth, Liverpool; Solicitors, Paine and Co., 47, Gresham House, E.C.; Bankers, Glyn and Co.

Head Offices—Euston Station, N.W.

218.—NORTH MONKLAND.

Incorporated by act of 18th July, 1872, to construct three short railways in the counties of Lanark and Stirling. Length, 10 miles. Capital, 60,000*l.* in 10*l.* shares and 20,000*l.* on loan.

Arrangements with North British, which works the line in perpetuity at 50 per cent. when the receipts are under 20*l.* per mile per week, and at 47½ per cent. when above that sum.

The line was opened on the 18th February, 1878. Productive, 8 miles 65 chains.

REVENUE.—For the half-year ended 31st January, 1884, the earnings sufficed for the payment of a dividend on the ordinary capital at the rate of 2¼ per cent., and for the half-year ended 31st July, 1884, 1¾ per cent., free of income tax.

CAPITAL.—The receipts on this account to 31st July, 1884, amounted to 80,000*l.* (60,000*l.* from 6,000 ordinary shares of 10*l.* each, allotted at par, 20,000*l.* on loan, and an item of 814*l.* for sundries), and the expenditure to 81,991*l.*, leaving a balance against the account of 1,177*l.*

The accounts are made up to the 31st January and 31st July, and the half-yearly meetings are held at the end of March and September in each year.

No. of Directors—6; minimum, 4; quorum, 3. *Qualification*, 500*l.*

DIRECTORS:

Chairman—2 Colonel D. C. R. CARRICK BUCHANAN, C.B., of Drumpellier, Coatbridge.

4 Allan Kirkwood, Esq., 175, West George Street, Glasgow.

3 James Young, Esq., Skelmorlie.

5 Robert Forrester, Esq., 75, West Nile Street, Glasgow.

1 J. R. Forman, C.E., 160, Hope Street, Glasgow.

Retire in numerical order according to Consolidation Clauses Act (Scotland), 1845.

OFFICERS.—Sec., G. B. Motherwell, Airdrie; Auditors, J. McQueen Barr, C.A. Queen Street, Glasgow, and James Affleck, C.A., Hope Street, Glasgow; Solicitors, Rankin and Motherwell, Airdrie.

Offices—8, East High Street, Airdrie.

219.—NORTH PEMBROKESHIRE AND FISHGUARD.

(LATE ROSEBUSH AND FISHGUARD).

Incorporated by act of 8th August, 1878 (41 and 42 Vic., cap. 218), for the construction and maintenance of a railway, commencing by a junction with the Narberth Road and Maenclochog, near Rosebush Station, and terminating at Goodwick, near Fishguard, all in the county of Pembroke. Length, 13 miles 7 furlongs and 2·80 chains. Period for completion, 5 years. Traffic arrangements with the Great Western and the owners of the Narberth Road and Maenclochog. Capital, 90,000*l.*, in 10*l.* shares, with power to divide into "preferred" and "deferred" half-shares. Borrowing powers, 30,000*l.* The contract for the first section of the railway to Letterston (8 miles) was let to Messrs. Appleby and Lawton, and the works were commenced in August, 1879, and are still in progress.

By act of 11th August, 1878, powers were obtained for a certain deviation of the company's line, and for the sale or lease of the Narberth Road and Maenclochog undertaking to the Rosebush. New capital, 50,000*l.*

By act of 7th August, 1884, the name of the company was changed as above, and the time for completion of parts of the railways authorised under act of 1881 was extended until 8th August, 1887. New capital, 72,000*l.*; loans, 24,000*l.*

No. of Directors.—Maximum, 6; minimum, 3; quorum, 3 and 2 respectively. *Qualification*, 30 shares.

DIRECTORS:

Sir Hugh Owen Owen, Bart., United University Club, S.W.

Joseph Babington Macaulay, Esq., St. Stephen's Club, S.W., and Clynderwen, R.S.O., South Wales.

Col. John Owen, Rosebush, Pembrokeshire.

Frederick Lee, Esq., Fairfield, Leigham Court Road, Streatham, S.W.

OFFICERS.—Sec., Henry E Warren, 57, Fenchurch Street, E.C.; Eng., James B. Walton, 6, Great College Street, Westminster, S.W.

Offices—6, Great College Street, Westminster, S.W.

220.—NORTH AND SOUTH WESTERN JUNCTION.

Incorporated 24th July, 1851, for a line of about 4 miles (since extended) from the London and North Western Willesden Station to Windsor Branch of London and South Western, near Kew, under an agreement to allow toll of 6 miles for minerals and 4 miles for passengers, and to secure to it a *minimum* of traffic sufficient to yield the shareholders at least 3 per cent. net on their paid-up share capital. All profits beyond 6 per cent., and interest on debts, to be divided, one-half to the shareholders, and the remainder to the two contracting companies.

By act of 28th June, 1853, this company was authorised to make a branch to Hammersmith—1¼ mile.

By act of 10th July, 1854, the company was authorised to raise additional capital to the extent of 15,000*l.* in shares and 4,934*l.* in loans.

By act of 23rd June, 1864, the company was authorised to purchase additional land, and to raise new capital to the extent of 10,000*l.* in shares and 3,000*l.* on loan; and by act of 25th June, 1868, the company was authorised to make a deviation in the main line, and to raise further capital to the extent of 15,000*l.* in shares and 5,000*l.* on mortgage.

LEASE.—By act of 14th August, 1871, the North and South Western Junction was leased in perpetuity from 1st January, 1871, to the London and North Western, the Midland, and the North London jointly, at a rental of 9,502*l.*, equal to 7 per cent. on the ordinary capital. Payable half-yearly on 30th June and 31st December, without any deduction except income tax.

A junction with the Midland by a branch from Acton was completed and opened in 1871.

The junction with the Great Western at Acton Wells was completed towards the latter end of 1878.

In operation, 5 miles.

Extra dividends of 2*s.* 6*d.* per cent. were paid for the half-years ended 31st December, 1875, 30th June, 1877, 30th June, 1878, 31st December, 1879, 31st December, 1880, 31st December, 1881, 31st December, 1882, and 30th June, 1884, out of the small annual sum received for interest on the invested reserve fund.

CAPITAL.—The total stock and share capital amounts to 128,600*l.*, of which 125,595*l.* had been expended to 30th June, 1884, leaving a balance on hand of 3,005*l.*

TRANSFER DEPARTMENT QUERIES AND REPLIES.

QUERIES.	REPLIES.
Transfer form—ordinary or special?	Ordinary.
Fee per deed?	2*s.* 6*d.*
Ditto if more sellers than one? ...	2*s* 6*d.* each.
Are certificates required to accompany transfers?	Yes.
What amounts of stock are transferable?	Not less than 1*l.*
Are parts of 1*l.* sterling allowed to be transferred?	No.
To what officer should transfer communications be sent?	Secretary.

The meetings are held at 148, Gresham House, Old Broad Street, E.C., in January and July.

No. of Directors.—Maximum, 7; minimum, 3. *Qualification*, 30 shares.

DIRECTORS:

Chairman—HARRY CHUBB, Esq., 6, Prince's Square, Hyde Park, W.

Philip Debell Tuckett, Esq., 10A, Old Broad Street, E.C.

George Bolland Newton, Esq., 53, Victoria Road, Kensington, W.

Retire by rotation annually in January.

OFFICERS.—Sec., Ferrand Davies; Auditor, Samuel M. Fox, Southwood Lawn Highgate, N.; Bankers, Glyn, Mills, Currie, and Co., Lombard Street, E.C.

Offices—148, Gresham House, Old Broad Street, E.C.

221.—NORTH STAFFORDSHIRE.

Incorporated by three separate acts in 1846, but now acting under Consolidation Act of 1847 (10 and 11 Vic., cap. 108). Authorised capital, 6,001,000*l.*; borrowing powers, 1,992,833*l.* In operation, on 30th June, 1882, 188¼ miles of railway and 118 of canal. Owned by company, half share of Macclesfield, Bollington, and Marple=11 miles, and 4 miles of leased lines. Foreign lines worked over, 121 miles.

FURTHER PARLIAMENTARY POWERS:—

For list of Acts, &c., from 1859 to 1879, with short heads showing the objects for which the various powers were sought, see the MANUAL for 1881, pages 300 and 301.

1880—26TH AUGUST.—Power to make a railway at Uttoxeter, to connect the Churnet Valley Line with the Stoke Branch. Length, about ¾ a-mile. Alteration of provisions of existing acts with respect to rates and charges, and for other purposes.

SUBSIDIARY LINES, LEASES, &c.:—

MACCLESFIELD, BOLLINGTON, AND MARPLE.—Incorporated by act of 14th July, 1864, to construct a line from Macclesfield, through Bollington, to Marple. Length, 11 miles. Capital, 200,000*l.* in 10*l.* shares and 66,000*l.* on loan. By act of 25th May, 1871, the line is vested in a joint committee of the Manchester, Sheffield, and Lincolnshire and the North Staffordshire, who each provide half of the capital. The act also authorises the raising of 36,650*l.* new capital by each company.

NEWCASTLE-UNDER-LYME CANAL.—This canal, and the canal extensions belonging thereto, were leased to the North Staffordshire by act of 23rd June, 1864, on payment by the latter of a rent of 520*l.* per annum, and liquidation of mortgage debt.

POTTERIES, BIDDULPH, AND CONGLETON.—Incorporated by act of 24th July, 1854. The line is in six sections. The first commences on the main line, at Stoke-upon-Trent, and terminates at Congleton (opened August 3rd, 1859); the second diverges from the new branch near the junction with the main line, and terminates in a field in the parish of Stoke; the third leaves the branch at Astbury, and proceeds until it again meets the main line; the fourth also leaves the branch at Astbury, and joins the main line at Congleton Station; the fifth likewise diverges from the first branch, running between the parishes of Bucknall and Caverswell; the next leaves the first at Burslem, and terminates in same parish at Stonybank.

The Potteries Loop Line was opened for traffic from Hanley to Tunstall, &c., in December, 1873; from Tunstall to Goldenhill, 1¾ mile, on the 1st October, 1874; and from Goldenhill to Kidsgrove, in December, 1875.

ACCOUNTS:—

The ordinary half-yearly meeting of this company was held on the 8th August last, when the directors' report and accounts for the half-year ended 30th June, 1884, were presented and adopted. The following is an abstract of those accounts, viz.:—

CAPITAL.

Receipts.

161,507 shares, on which 19*l.* 16*s.* 4*d.* only was paid, but which were converted into stock at the rate of 20*l.* per share		£3,200,000
Preference shares and stocks:—		
1st preference canal shares	£1,170,000	
Preference stock	1,610,901	=2,780,901
Ordinary and preference stocks total		£5,980,901
Loan capital, viz.:—		
Debentures	£400	
Debenture stocks, 4¼ and 4½ per cent	1,856,251	=1,856,651
Premium on debenture and preference stocks		55,669
		£7,893,221

Expenditure.

Lines open for traffic	£5,496,482
Working stock	758,357
Subscriptions to other lines	214,529
For railway purpose	£6,469,368
Canal purchase, and subsequent expenditure thereon	1,404,564
Canal and carting stock	9,362
Total actual expenditure	£7,883 294
Balance (credit)	9,927
	£7,893,221

The estimate of further expenditure on capital account required for the half-year ended 31st December, 1884, 9,000*l.*, and for subsequent half-years 13,000*l.*—together, 22,000*l.*, the available assets to meet which were:—

Share and loan capital authorised or created but not yet received	£20,099
Balance to raise on loans sanctioned	100,612
	£120,711
Balance to credit of capital account	9,928
	£130,639

REVENUE.—The following is a statement showing the comparative results of the working of this line and canal for the last three half-years, viz.:—

Receipts.	1883. 30th June.	1883. 31st Dec.	1884. 30th June.
Passengers, parcels, horses, &c.	£89,502	£98,512	£91,225
Merchandise and live stock (net)	99,008	101,449	102,903
Minerals	103,582	104,570	96,159
Rents, fees, &c.	3,988	4,513	3,944
Railway account	£296,080	£309,044	£294,231
Canal account	45,604	41,669	41,388
	£341,684	£350,713	£335,619

Expenditure.	1883. 30th June.	1883. 31st Dec.	1884. 30th June.
Maintenance of way, works, and stations	£42,671	£44,292	£40,829
Locomotive power	34,772	34,922	36,264
Carriage and wagon repairs	9,517	8,041	8,187
Traffic expenses	42,301	41,913	42,225
General charges	6,744	7,419	7,606
Law and Parliamentary	934	1,264	1,056
Compensation	2,991	1,451	1,340
Rates, taxes, and Government duty	6,378	6,496	5,765
Rents	328	242	305
Burton and Derby goods stations	2,005	2,100	2,320
Railway expenses account	£148,641	£148,056	£145,897
Canal	21,891	20,652	21,991
	£170,531	£168,708	£167,888
Interest on loans and general interest (net)	38,923	39,066	39,259
Rent of sundry branches, land, and sundries	1,685	1,664	1,664
Loss on working Macclesfield, Bollington, and Marple Branch	347	424	231
Rent and expenses at Burton, Derby &c.	2,476	2,684	1,999
Canal shares dividend	29,250	29,250	29,250
Preference stock dividends	38,673	38,673	38,673
	£281,885	£280,411	£279,014
Net balances each half-year	£59,799	£70,302	£56,605
Balances from previous half-years	1,045	4,317	1,941
Balances available for dividend	£47,091	£74,629	£58,546
Dividends declared at 3½, 4½, and 3½ per cent. per annum respectively	56,527	72,678	56,527
Surplus carried forward	£4,317	£1,941	£2,019

Summary showing the result of the last half-year's working, as compared with that of the corresponding period of 1883, viz.:—

Net balance—30th June, 1884 ...	£56,605	Thus:—	
„ 30th June, 1883 ...	59,799	Railway traffic—Decrease..........	£1,849
		„ working—Decrease £2,744	
		Pref. &c., charges—Decrease 228 =	2,972
		Less:—	£1,123
		Canal traffic—Decrease... £4,216	
		„ working—Increase.. 101 =	4,317
Loss in 1884	£3,194	Net loss in 1884	£3,194

The accounts are made up to 30th June and 31st December, and the statutory meetings held in February and August in each year.

Scale of Voting.—C. C. C. Act, sec. 75.

Certificates must accompany transfer deed. Registration fee charged since 1st January, 1861. 2*s.* 6*d.* each transfer.

No. of Directors.—Reduced to 9 by meeting of 17th February, 1875, of whom 3 must be elected from amongst the canal preference shareholders. *Qualification*, 2,000*l.* ordinary stock (the ordinary shares having been converted into stock); the directors representing the canal proprietors, 100 preference shares of 20*l.* each.

DIRECTORS:

Chairman—1 * THOMAS SALT, Esq., M.P., Weeping Cross, Stafford, and United University Club, S.W.

Deputy-Chairman—1 JOHN BRAMLEY-MOORE, Esq., Liverpool, and Gerrard's Cross, Bucks.

3*Francis Stanier, Esq., Peplow Hall, Market Drayton.

2 Arthur Mills, Esq., 34, Hyde Park Gardens, Hyde Park, W., and Bude Haven, Cornwall.

3*Samuel Morley, Esq., The Ashe, near Derby.

2 Colonel Josiah Wilkinson, Southampton Lodge, Highgate, N.

3 William Francis Gordon, Esq., Lichfield.

* Represent the canal preference shareholders.

1, Retire in 1885; 2, in 1886; 3, in 1887. Eligible for re-election.

OFFICERS.—Sec., Percy Morris; Traff. Man., W. D. Phillipps; Res. Eng. and Eng. for Canal Dept., W. H. Stubbs; Loco. Supt., L. Longbottom; Accountant, W. H. Newman; Auditors, J. G. Griffiths and Robert Freeman; Solicitor, William Burchell, 5, The Sanctuary, Westminster, S.W.; Bankers, Glyn, Mills, Currie, and Co., 67, Lombard Street, E.C., and Lloyds, Barnetts, and Bosanquet's Bank Limited, 62 and 73, Lombard Street, E.C.

Head Offices—Stoke-upon-Trent, Staffordshire Potteries.

222.—NORTH UNION.

An amalgamation of the Wigan and Preston and Wigan Branch, under the name of the North Union, by virtue of 4 Wm. IV., cap. 25, with which was afterwards incorporated the Bolton and Preston, by 7 and 8 Vic., cap. 2, established for lines from Parkside Junction with the L. and N. W. to Preston; and from Preston to Bolton. Productive mileage, 39 miles 60 chains.

By the terms of amalgamation the respective capitals of the North Union and Bolton and Preston were classified as follow:—The North Union as "A" stock, 477,327*l.*; the Bolton and Preston as "B" stock, 261,875*l.* The dividend on "A" stock to be always entitled to double the amount of dividend payable on "B" stock until the same amount to 6 per cent. per annum on "A," and 3 per cent. per annum on "B" respectively, when both classes of stock participate equally in all further dividends beyond those per centages. The respective stocks were exchanged as follow:—The holders of North Union shares received 75*l.* 6*s.* of North Union consolidated stock "A," and the holders of Bolton and Preston shares 39*l.* 12*s.* of North Union consolidated stock "B," for each share held by them respectively.

The undertaking is vested for ever jointly in the L. and N. W. and the L. and Y. under powers of act of 27th July, 1846, for a fixed annuity of 66,063*l.* 18*s.* from 1st January, 1846, payable in net moneys, free of deductions, except income tax, half-yearly, 15th February and 15th August, whereof 60-94ths are to be paid by the L. and N. W. and 34-94ths by L. and Y. This annuity is divided, 47,782*l.* 14*s.* 4½*d.* amongst holders of "A" stock, and 18,331*l.* 14*s.* 8½*d.* to "B" stock, equal to 10 per cent. and 7 per cent. respectively.

By act of 19th July, 1875, the companies were authorised to construct a second line between Euxton and Preston. Length, about 5¼ miles. Powers to Mr. Thomas Dicconson to make branch railways; London and North Western to raise 84,000*l.* by new shares or stock and 28,000*l.* on loan; and to Lancashire and Yorkshire to raise 48,000*l.* by shares or stock and 16,000*l.* on loan.

The books are generally closed about a fortnight previous to the date when the dividend warrants are payable, viz., 15th February and 15th August. Certificates must accompany transfer deed. Registration fee, 2*s.* 6*d.* each seller, and for each new certificate or coupon. Both classes may go on one deed. Transfer department conducted by Stephen Reay, Esq., Euston Station, London.

DIRECTORS:

Chairman—1 WILLIAM BIRLEY, Esq., Preston.

2 Samuel Henry Thompson, Esq., Thingwall Hall, Knotty Ash, near Liverpool.

3 James Glover, Esq., Southport.

4 Richard Heywood Thompson, Esq., 7, East Beach, Lytham.

Numbered according to seniority—all at present re-eligible.

OFFICERS.—Sec., Thomas H. Carr; Engs.-in-Chief, same as London and North Western and Lancashire and Yorkshire Companies; Eng., S. B. Worthington.

Joint Lessees' Office—Fleetwood.

223.—NORTH WALES NARROW GAUGE.

Incorporated by act of 6th August, 1872, to construct a railway (23 miles), called the "General Undertaking," from the Croesor and Portmadoc Railway to Bettws-y-Coed; and a railway called the "Moel Tryfan Undertaking," consisting of a line (5¼ miles) from Llanwnda, Carnarvonshire, to Bryngwyn in Llandwrog, and a line (7¾ miles) to Rhyd-ddu, in the parish of Beddgelert. Capital, 150,000*l.* in 10*l.* shares for the General Undertaking and 66,000*l.* for that of the Moel Tryfan. Shares to be distinctively separated. Borrowing powers, 50,000*l.* for the General Undertaking and 22,000*l.* for Moel Tryfan. Gauge, 1 foot 11½ inches. Agreements with the Festiniog, and Croesor and Portmadoc.

By act of 16th June, 1873, the company was empowered to lease to Mr. Hugh Beaver Roberts, of Bangor, its Moel Tryfan undertaking, for 21 years, at a fixed minimum rent of 6 per cent. per annum on the share capital, with extra rent by participation in profits over 6 per cent. from time to time in proportion to the traffic.

By act of 13th July, 1876, the company was authorised to abandon the "General Undertaking," and to raise 40,000*l.* additional capital for the purposes of the Moel Tryfan Line. Further borrowing powers, 13,300*l.*

At a meeting held in August, 1874, Mr. Beaver Roberts, the lessee of the line under the act of 1873, repudiated the lease. No steps were taken to enforce it, as from the financial embarrassment of the company, and the uncompleted state of the line, litigation was unadvisable.

Part of the line, from Dinas to Bryngwyn and Quellyn, was opened for mineral and goods traffic in June, and for passenger traffic on the 15th August, 1877; from Quellyn to Snowdon Ranger, three-quarters of a mile, on 1st June, 1878; and from Snowdon Ranger to Rhyd-ddu, 1¼ mile, 14th May, 1881, bringing up the length of line in working order to 12¼ miles.

CAPITAL.—The receipts on this account to 30th June, 1884, amounted to 122,488*l.*, of which 83,365*l.* was by shares and stock, 6,000*l.* by loans, 30,000*l.* by "B" debenture stock, and 3,123*l.* by "C" debenture stock. The expenditure to the same date amounted to 124,790*l.*, leaving a balance of 2,302*l.*

REVENUE.—The net revenue for the year 1883 amounted to 210*l.*, against 159*l.* for 1882. For the half-year to 30th June, 1884, the net receipts were 132*l.*, against 87*l.* for the corresponding half-year of 1883. The balance against revenue account at 30th June, 1884, was 933*l.*

No. of Directors—7; minimum, 4; quorum, 3 and 2. *Qualification*, 250*l.*

DIRECTORS:

Chairman—*J. CHOLMELEY RUSSELL, Esq., 86, Queen's Gate, S.W.

Chaloner W. Chute, Esq., 23, Old Square, Lincoln's Inn, W.C.

*Abraham FitzGibbon, Esq., Moorside, Bushey Heath, Herts.

Richard Seymour Guinness, Esq., 87, St. George's Square, S.W.

Sir Llewelyn Turner, Knt., Parkia, Carnarvon.

* Retire in 1884, but are eligible for re-election.

OFFICERS.—Sec., Gen. Man., and Eng., R. H. Livesey; Auditors, John Gane and Herbert Jackson, 53, Coleman Street, E.C.

Offices—Dinas, near Carnarvon.

224.—NOTTINGHAM AND GRANTHAM.

(LEASED TO GREAT NORTHERN.)

Incorporated by 9 and 10 Vic., cap. 155, for construction of a line commencing as projected, in conjunction with the Midland, and in continuation thence of the Manchester, Buxton, Matlock, and Midlands Junction, at Ambergate, and terminating in conjunction with the Great Northern, at Spalding, with branches to Sleaford and Boston (90 miles); but, by resolution of general meetings, it was determined to confine all operations to a line from Grantham (where a junction is formed with the Great Northern). The portion in operation is 23 miles, viz., from Grantham to Nottingham. Under act of incorporation, this company had agreed to purchase the Nottingham Canal for 225*l.* in cash, or nine railway shares of 25*l.* each, paid up; and the Grantham Canal for 100*l.* in cash, or five railway paid-up 25*l.* shares for each canal share.

By act of 15th May, 1860, the name of the undertaking was changed to "Nottingham and Grantham," the capital reduced to 1,014,000*l.* in lieu of 1,056,250*l.*, and the borrowing powers from 358,333*l.* to 265,000*l.*; various provisions for consolidation of shares into stock, and for regulating the transfer thereof, were also made.

ORIGINAL WORKING ARRANGEMENT AND SUBSEQUENT LEASE.—In 1855 an arrangement was entered into as follows:—"The Nottingham to complete line into the station at Nottingham. The Great Northern to work the line, exclusive of the Grantham and Nottingham Canals, at 30 per cent. of gross earnings, if the traffic be less than 37,000*l*. a year, or at 35 per cent. if it exceed that sum. The agreement for ten years, with power to the Great Northern to take the whole undertaking at a fixed annual rental of 4 per cent. within four years, or 4½ per cent. within nine years; or to amalgamate the two companies at par." A new arrangement has since been effected, as follows:—To lease the line for 999 years on and from the 1st August, 1861, on the terms of paying a dividend at the rate of 4*l*. 2*s*. 6*d*. per cent. per annum on the capital of 1,014,000*l*., with right to purchase the whole property on repayment of the capital at par value. The rent is regularly paid, and the dividends, equal to about 4*l*. 1*s*. per cent. per annum, declared half-yearly, and paid, less income tax, about the 26th February and August each half-year respectively.

No. of Directors.—Maximum, 9; minimum, 5. *Qualification*, 1,000*l*. Present board, 5, receiving 300*l*. a year.

DIRECTORS:

Chairman—RICHARD SEPTIMUS WILKINSON, Esq., 9, St. Mildred's Court, Poultry, E.C.

Deputy-Chairman—EDWIN HENRY LAURENCE, Esq., 11, Angel Court, Throgmorton Street, E.C.

Thomas Henry Staples, Esq., 10, Argyll Place, Regent Street, W.

Henry Armstrong Esq., Gilnockie, Wick Hill, Bracknell, Berks.

Capt. John Fowler Burbidge, Hursley, Bournemouth.

OFFICERS.—Sec., Henry Lasalle, Nottingham; Auditors, Henry Howe and John Rain Wild; Solicitor, John Thompson Brewster, Nottingham; Bankers, Hardy, Johnstone, and Hardy, Grantham.

Head Offices—London Road Station, Nottingham.

225.—OLDBURY.

Incorporated by act of 21st July, 1873, to form a junction between the London and North Western, at Oldbury, and the South Staffordshire, at Dudley. Length, 3¾ miles. Capital, 100,000*l*. in 10*l*. shares and 33,000*l*. on loan. Arrangements with Birmingham Canal Company and London and North Western.

By act of 11th August, 1876, the company was authorised to construct a new or deviation railway (7¼ furlongs in length), and to abandon certain portions of the railway authorised under the former act. All works to be completed within four years. Powers to company and Great Western to enter into traffic and working agreements.

By act of 4th July, 1878, further powers were obtained extending the time for compulsory purchase of land until 21st July, 1880, and for completion of works until 21st July, 1881. New capital, 70,000*l*.; loans, &c., 23,000*l*.

By act of 11th August, 1881, the name of the company was changed from Dudley and Oldbury Junction to "Oldbury." Time for compulsory purchase of land extended to 21st July, 1883, and for completion of works to 21st July, 1884. Power to abandon a portion of the railway authorised by former acts. Capital reduced to 70,000*l*., borrowing powers to 23,000*l*. Provisions in former acts giving power to Birmingham Canal to appoint directors and control rates repealed. Powers to Great Western to contribute not exceeding 50,000*l*. to the share capital and to appoint directors are given by the new act.

The line was completed and opened for traffic on 7th November, 1884.

DIRECTORS:

Chairman—Sir DANIEL GOOCH, Bart., M.P., 3, Warwick Road, Maida Hill, W.

Deputy-Chairman—ARTHUR ALBRIGHT, Esq., Edgbaston, Birmingham.

Lord Lyttelton, Hagley Park, Stourbridge, and 17, Grosvenor Street, S.W.

Walter Robinson, Esq., 20, Gledhow Gardens, S.W.

B. T. Sadler, Esq., Oldbury.

OFFICERS.—Sec., Alfred E. Wenham; Engs., Edward Wilson and Co., 9, Dean's Yard, Westminster, S.W.; Auditors, J. H. Matthews and P. Spencer; Solicitors, Mathews, Smith, and James, Waterloo Street, Birmingham.

Offices—114, Colmore Row, Birmingham.

226.—OLDHAM, ASHTON-UNDER-LYNE, AND GUIDE BRIDGE.

Incorporated by act of 10th August, 1857, for the construction of railways to supply direct communication between these places. Capital, 140,000*l*. in 10*l*. shares; loans, 46,600*l*. The length of first railway is 4 miles and 7 yards, commencing by a junction of the Oldham Branch of the London and North Western, at or near the Oldham Station, and terminating by a junction with the Ashton and Stalybridge Branch of Lancashire and Yorkshire; length of the second is 1 mile 3 furlongs and 17 yards, commencing by a junction with the Ashton and Stalybridge Branch of Lancashire and Yorkshire, at Peocatties, and terminating by a junction with Manchester, Sheffield, and Lincolnshire, at Guide Bridge; the length of the third is 2 furlongs 6 chains and 17 yards, commencing by a junction with the first railway, in the parish of Ashton, and terminating near the service reservoir of the Ashton Waterworks; the length of the fourth is 5 furlongs 8 chains and 11 yards, commencing by a junction with the first railway near Wood Lane, and terminating at or near Moss Coalpit; and the length of the fifth is 2 furlongs 6 chains and 8 yards, commencing by a junction with the first railway near Lower Althill, terminating in Rochervale. The Manchester, Sheffield, and Lincolnshire and London and North Western subscribe 50,000*l*. each, and appoint the directors. In operation, 6 miles.

By act of 30th June, 1862, the line is vested mutually in the London and North Western and Manchester and Sheffield, who guarantee a dividend on the 40,000*l*. capital held by the local shareholders at the rate of 4½ per cent. per annum.

By the Manchester, Sheffield, and Lincolnshire and London and North Western Acts of 1873 and 1876, the two companies were authorised to subscribe a further 75,000*l*. each to the Oldham undertaking.

By act of 24th July, 1876, the loan powers are transferred to the Sheffield and London and North Western in equal proportions.

By London and North Western Act of 1881, the two companies were authorised to subscribe a further sum of 25,000*l*. each to the undertaking.

CAPITAL.—The expenditure on this account to 30th June, 1884, amounted to 359,982*l*., the receipts having been as follow:—

Shares	£311,300
Sundry receipts	1,400
Received from leasing companies in redemption of loans	46,600
Balance	682=£359,982

TRANSFER DEPARTMENT QUERIES AND REPLIES.

QUERIES.	REPLIES.
Transfer form—ordinary or special?	Ordinary.
Fee per deed?	2*s*. 6*d*.
Ditto if more sellers than one?	2*s*. 6*d*. each seller.
Are certificates required to accompany transfers?	Yes.
What amounts of stock are transferable, and are parts of 1*l*. sterling allowed to be transferred?	10*l*.
To what officer should transfer communications be sent?	Secretary.
In acceptances, renunciations, &c., of allotments of new stock, proxies, or other forms sent to trustees and other joint holders, what signatures are required?	All signatures of registered holders.

Meetings held in the second week of February and August.

No. of Directors—9; minimum, 6; quorum, 3.

DIRECTORS:

James Bancroft, Esq., 33a, Mosley Street, and Broughton Hall, Manchester.

Thomas Brooke, Esq., Armitage Bridge, near Huddersfield.

John William Maclure, Esq., Cross Street, Manchester.

Sir Edward W. Watkin, Bart., M.P., Rose Hill, Northenden, near Manchester, and Charing Cross Hotel, Charing Cross, S.W.

Henry Russell Greg, Esq., Lode Hill, Handforth, near Manchester.

A. M. Watkin, Esq., Dunedin Lodge, Folkestone.

OFFICERS.—Joint Secs., Edward Ross, Manchester, and S. Reay, Euston; Eng., Charles Sacré, M.Inst.C.E., Manchester; Auditors, Robert G. Underdown, Assoc.Inst.C.E., Manchester, and Frederick Whittle, Euston; Solicitor, C. H. Mason, Euston; Bankers, Manchester and Liverpool District Bank, Manchester.

Offices—London Road Station, Manchester.

227.—OSWESTRY AND LLANGYNOG.

Incorporated by act of 10th August, 1882, for the construction of three railways from Llanyblodwell to Llangynog. Total length, about 14½ miles. Period for completion, 4 years. Traffic and other arrangements with the Cambrian and Potteries, Shrewsbury, and North Wales undertakings. Capital, 150,000*l.* in 10*l.* shares, with powers to divide into "preferred" and "deferred" half-shares; borrowing powers 50.000*l.*

No. of Directors.—Maximum, 5; minimum, 3; quorum, 3 and 2. *Qualification*, 50 shares.

FIRST DIRECTORS:

Thomas Dyne Steel, Esq.
John Beattie, Esq.
John Devereux Pugh, Esq.
Two others to be nominated.

228.—OXFORD, AYLESBURY, AND METROPOLITAN JUNCTION.

Incorporated by act of 20th August, 1883, for the construction and maintenance of a railway from Oxford to Quainton, by a junction with the Aylesbury and Buckingham. Length, 17½ miles. Period for completion, 5 years. Working arrangements with Aylesbury and Buckingham and Metropolitan. Capital, 300,000*l.* in 10*l.* shares, with power to divide into "preferred" and "deferred" half-shares; loans, &c., 100,000*l.*

No. of Directors.—Maximum, 7; minimum, 3; quorum, 3 and 2. *Qualification*, 30 shares.

FIRST DIRECTORS:

His Grace the Duke of Buckingham and Chandos.
Sir Harry Verney, Bart., M.P., Claydon House, Winslow, Bucks, and 4, South Street, Park Lane, W.
Henry Arthur Herbert, Esq. J.P., D.L., Muckross Abbey, Killarney, Co. Kerry.

229.—OXTED AND GROOMBRIDGE.

Incorporated by act of 11th August, 1881, for the construction and maintenance of a railway in the districts indicated by the title. Length, about 13 miles. Period for completion, 5 years. Working agreements with London, Brighton, and South Coast and South Eastern. Capital, 330,000*l.* in 10*l.* shares, with power to divide into "preferred" and "deferred" half-shares. Borrowing powers, 110,000*l.*

No. of Directors.—Maximum, 5; minimum, 3; quorum, 3 and 2. *Qualification*, 40 shares.

FIRST DIRECTORS:

J. S. Gainsford, Esq.
W. R. Glasier, Esq.
Robert Arthur Read, Esq., The Cranes, Surbiton Hill, S.W

Solicitors, Cope and Co., 3, Great George Street, Westminster, S.W.

230.—PEMBROKE AND TENBY.

Incorporated by act of 21st July, 1859, to make railways from Pembroke Dock to Tenby, and from the former place to Hobb's Point. Capital, 80,000*l.* in 10*l.* shares; loans, 26,600*l.*

By act of 14th July, 1864, the company was authorised to construct several short lines, including an extension to Whitland. Length, 18 miles. Capital, 200,000*l.* in shares and 66,000*l.* on loan.

By act of 6th August, 1866, the company was authorised to extend the line to Carmarthen and to Milford Haven. Length, 15¾ miles. Capital, 115,000*l.* in shares and 38,000*l.* on loan. Arrangements with Great Western, Cambrian, Central Wales, Llanelly, and Manchester and Milford.

By act of 14th July, 1870, the company was authorised to extend the line to Pembroke Dock, and to make arrangements with the Admiralty. Length, half a mile. New capital, 26,000*l.* in dockyard guaranteed stock. Also to use part of the Carmarthen and Cardigan.

In operation, 42¼ miles.

REVENUE.—The receipts for the half-year ended 30th June, 1884, were 12,568*l.*, and the working expenses 7,351*l.* After providing for interest on mortgage and debenture loans, rent-charges, &c., there remained an available balance of 2,216*l.* A dividend at the rate of 2 per cent. per annum on 205,530*l.* preference shares absorbed 2,055*l.*, leaving a balance of 161*l.*

CAPITAL.—The capital of the company to 30th June, 1884, was as follows:—

No.	Description.	Created.	Received.
1	Rent-charges capitalised at 20 years' purchase	£3,160	£3,160
2	Debenture bonds at 5 per cent.	5,300	5,300
3	Do. do. at 4½ per cent.	13,200	13,200
4	Do. do. at 4 per cent.	2,000	2,000
5	Debenture stock at 5 per cent.	19,900	19,900
6	Do. do. at 4½ per cent.	28,350	28,350
7	Do. do at 4 per cent.	41,290	41,290
8	5 per cent. preference shares (act 1864)	200,000	200,000
9	Do. do. (act 1866)	115,000	27,530
10	Ordinary shares (act 1859)	80,000	79,876
11	Government guaranteed dockyard stock	26,000	23,385

NOTES.—Priorities—No. 1 is a first charge; Nos. 2 to 7 rank *pari passu*; the rest follow in their order, except No. 11, which is a separate security from the other securities of the company.

Dividends non-contingent and accumulative—Nos. 1 to 7.

Dividends contingent upon profits of each separate year—Nos. 8, 9, and 10.

Dividends payable half-yearly.—No. 1, 25th March and 29th September; Nos. 2 to 7 and No. 11, 30th June and 31st December; Nos. 8, 9, and 10, variable.

Transfer books close in all cases 14 days before payment of interest and dividends.

The whole of the debenture bond capital is redeemable at par.

TRANSFER DEPARTMENT QUERIES AND REPLIES.

QUERIES.	REPLIES.
Transfer form—ordinary or special?	Ordinary.
Fee per deed?	2*s.* 6*d.*
Ditto if more sellers than one?	2*s.* 6*d.*
May several classes of stock be transferred on one deed?	Yes.
Are certificates required to accompany transfers?	Yes.
What amounts of stock are transferable, and are parts of 1*l.* sterling allowed to be transferred?	Shares as they are. Debenture stock, 100*l.* Debenture bonds as they are.
To what officer should transfer communications be sent?	The Secretary.
In acceptances, renunciations, &c., of allotments of new stock, proxies, or other forms sent to trustees and other joint holders, what signatures are required?	Of all the trustees.

The receipts and expenditure on capital account to the 30th June, 1884, were as follow:—

Received.		*Expended.*	
Shares and stock	£330,741	Lines open for traffic, &c. *	£384,246
Loans	20,500	Dockyard extension	23,385
Debenture stock	89,540	Working stock	35,857
Rent-charges capitalised at 20 years' purchase	3,160		£443,438
		Balance	503
	£443,941		£443,941

The estimate of further expenditure is limited to 15,000*l.*, the assets for which comprise shares and loans to the extent of 108,638*l.*

Meetings in February and August.

No. of Directors—6; minimum, 5; quorum, 3. *Qualification*, 300*l.*

DIRECTORS:

Chairman—JOHN JAMES BARROW, Esq., Holmewood, Tunbridge Wells.

John Burton Barrow, Esq., Ringwood Hall, Chesterfield.

Wm. Wavell, Esq., 54, Oxford Terrace, Hyde Park, W.

C. Stanley Williams, Esq., Shirley Hall, Langton, Tunbridge Wells.

* Including 20,000*l.* paid to Great Western for converting 14 miles of their broad gauge line between Whitland and Carmarthen into narrow gauge.

OFFICERS.—Sec., W. F. Poole, 15, Spilman Street, Carmarthen; Gen. Man., Isaac Smedley, Pembroke Dock; Eng., Lionel R. Wood, Carmarthen; Auditors, R. Mackay, 3, Lothbury, E.C., and J. Fraser, 2, Tokenhouse Buildings, King's Arms Yard, E.C.

Offices—15, Spilman Street, Carmarthen.

231.—PENARTH EXTENSION.

Incorporated 11th August, 1876, to construct a line from the existing Penarth Railway to Penarth. Length, 1¼ mile. Capital, 15,000*l.* in 100*l.* shares; borrowing powers, 5,000*l.* on mortgage or debenture stock. Works to be completed within two years. Power to enter into working and traffic arrangements with Taff Vale and Great Western.

No. of Directors—3; quorum, 2. *Qualification*, 10 shares.

DIRECTORS:

Chairman—The Right Hon. Lord WINDSOR, St. Fagans Castle, Cardiff.

Lieut.-Col. Hon. G. Windsor Clive, M.P., 12, Stratford Place, W.

Robert Forrest, Esq.

Secretary, E. Bernard Reece, Cardiff.

232.—PENARTH HARBOUR, DOCK, AND RAILWAY.

(LEASED TO TAFF VALE.)

Incorporated as the ELY TIDAL HARBOUR AND RAILWAY, by act of 21st July, 1856, to construct a line from the Taff Vale, 5¼ miles from Cardiff, to the River Ely, County Glamorgan, and for converting part of that river into a tidal harbour. Capital, 130,000*l.* in 100*l.* shares; loans, 43,000*l.* Length, 6¼ miles. Board of Trade may appoint auditor to examine accounts. In operation on 30th June, 1877, 9¼ miles; sidings, single road, 21¼ miles; total, 30¼ miles.

By act of 27th July, 1857, the name of the company was changed to the "PENARTH HARBOUR, DOCK, AND RAILWAY." Various deviations and improvements were sanctioned, and the period of extension extended to five years from date of act, and of others to ten years. New capital authorised to the extent of 192,000*l.* in 100*l.* shares. Power to borrow extended to sum of 107,000*l.*

By act of 11th July, 1851, the company was authorised to raise further capital to the extent of 300,000*l.* in shares and 100,000*l.* on loan, for the purpose of completing the works, the purchase of steamers, &c.

At a special meeting of the Taff Vale, and of the Penarth, on 12th August, 1862, a lease of the Penarth for 10 years was agreed to, in the following terms:—At a rent, till the dock works are open for traffic, that will pay the Penarth interest upon 73,000*l.* of existing debentures, and 4½ per cent. upon 137,000*l.* share capital, with one-half divisible profits. After the dock is open for traffic, the rent will be the interest upon all the debentures, and 4½ per cent. upon all the share capital expended, with one-half divisible profits. Parliament, by act of 22nd June, 1863, sanctioned a lease for 999 years upon the above terms.

NEW CAPITAL, &c.—In 1881 the company obtained an act, dated 3rd June, to extend the existing dock, and to raise for that purpose capital to the extent of 150,000*l.* in shares and 50,000*l.* in loans. The share capital has been created in 12*l.* shares, bearing dividend at 5¼ per cent. per annum, guaranteed by the Taff Vale, and accruing as called up from 1st July, 1881, which have been offered to the holders of 100*l.* shares proportionately to their holding. The whole of this capital is called up to 31st December, 1883. The works for extending the dock have been completed The whole of the 50,000*l.* loan capital has been subscribed in the shape of debenture stock issued at par, bearing interest at 3½ per cent. per annum.

A further arrangement has been made with the Taff Vale, the lessees of the Penarth, whereby the "half profits" have been commuted for an additional fixed charge of ¾ per cent. per annum. The Penarth will now receive 5¼ per cent. per annum on the old share capital of 632,000*l.*, and also on the 150,000*l.* new capital as the latter shall be called up. This arrangement commenced on the 1st July, 1881.

The dividends for the half-years ended 31st December, 1876, and 30th June, 1877, were at the rate of 4¾ and 4½ per cent. per annum. The dividends for subsequent half-years up to 31st December, 1880, have been at the latter rate, 4½ per cent. per annum, payable about the same dates each half-year. The dividend for the half-year ended 30th June, 1881, and subsequently, were at the rate of 5¼ per cent. per annum, and will continue at that rate, and become payable on or about the 6th March and 6th September each half-year.

CAPITAL.—No. 1.—The expenditure to 30th June, 1884, amounted to 880,590*l.*, the receipts to the same period having been as under:—

Original shares	£322,000	
Shares Act, 1861	300.000=	£622,000
Forfeited shares	£170	
Premium on shares	830=	1,000
Balance of 5,000*l.* deposited by order of court towards defraying the company's law costs		3,878
First instalment of amount received from Smith and Knight's surety (with interest)		526
Second instalment		590
Loans on debentures and debenture stock		207,000
Interest on exchequer bills		1,703
Discounts		455
Transfer fees		3
Interest on calls		4,008
Amount transferred from revenue account		39,504
		£880.667

CAPITAL.—No. 2 (Dock Extension).—The expenditure to 30th June, 1884, amounted to 167,427*l.*, the receipts to the same period having been as under:—

Amount received on 12,500 shares	£150,000	
Less arrears	164=	£149,836
Issue of 3½ per cent. debenture stock		50,000
Premium on 190 shares at 3*l.* 7*s.* 6*d.* per share		648
Transfer fees		6
Interest on calls	£46	
Bank interest	438=	484
		£200,974

Meetings held in February and August.

No. of Directors—9; minimum, 7; quorum, 5. *Qualification*, 2,500*l.*

DIRECTORS:

Chairman—1 Lieut.-Col. The Hon. G. H. W. WINDSOR-CLIVE, M.P., 12. Stratford Place, W.

2 Crawshay Bailey, Esq., Maindiff Court, Abergavenny.

3 James H. Insole, Esq., Ely Court, Llandaff.

3 Henry Jones Evans, Esq., Banker, Cardiff.

1 John Nixon, Esq., 117, Westbourne Terrace, Hyde Park, W.

3 Lieut.-Colonel Edmond D'Arcy Hunt, Army and Navy Club, 36, Pall Mall, S.W.

3 George William Griffiths Thomas, Esq., The Heath, near Cardiff.

1, Retire in 1885; 2, in 1886; 3, in 1887.

OFFICERS.—Sec., John E. Bacon; Auditors, David Roberts and William P. Stephenson; Eng., Sir John Hawkshaw, Knt., M. Inst. C.E., London; Solicitors, B. Matthews and Son, Cardiff; Bankers, Wilkins and Co., Cardiff.

Offices—Cardiff.

233.—PEWSEY AND SALISBURY.

Incorporated by act of 16th July, 1883, for making a railway from Pewsey to Salisbury, in Wiltshire. Length, 20¼ miles. Period for completion, 5 years. Traffic arrangements with Great Western. Capital, 350,000*l.* in 10*l.* shares; loans, &c., 116,000*l.*

No. of Directors.—Maximum, 5; minimum, 3; quorum, 3 and 2. *Qualification*, 50 shares.

FIRST DIRECTORS:

Ambrose Denis Hussey-Freke, Esq.

Edgar Figgiss, Esq.

Arthur Pratt Barlow, Esq., 47, Norfolk Square, Hyde Park, W.

234.—PLYMOUTH AND DARTMOOR.

Incorporated by 59 Geo. III., cap. 115, to make a tramroad from Crabtree to the prison in the Forest of Dartmoor. Capital, 35,000*l.* Remodelled by act of 19th June, 1865. New capital, 75,000*l.* in shares and 25,000*l.* on loan.

By act of 19th July, 1875, the company was authorised to construct extension works to connect the harbour of Cattewater with the London and South Western and South Devon. Length, about 1 mile. New capital, 25,000*l.* in shares and 8,300*l.* on loan. Provision is also made for laying down broad gauge to accommodate the South Devon, and powers to make arrangements with the London and South Western and South Devon for use and maintenance of the line.

By act of 10th August, 1882, powers were obtained for the construction of two new lines, and a quay embankment and two piers at Plymouth, and for other purposes. New capital, 60,000*l.*; borrowing powers, 20,000*l.*

By act of 2nd August, 1883, the company was authorised to construct two short lines from Laira Green to Turenchapel and Clovelly Bay. Length, about 2¼ miles. Period for completion, 5 years. Arrangements with London and South Western. New capital, 66,000*l.*; loans, &c., 22,000*l.*

In August, 1878, a working agreement with the London and South Western, at a rental based upon expenditure, "for the working of the authorised railways of this company for communicating with the Cattewater (Plymouth), and the quays and manufactories thereat," was approved.

PRINCETOWN.—See GENERAL INDEX.

VESTING OF A PORTION OF THE UNDERTAKING.—By the London and South Western Act of 10th August, 1882, powers were obtained for the vesting of that portion of the undertaking known as the "Plymouth Extensions Acts, 1873 and 1875," which have hitherto been worked by the London and South Western. The terms of purchase are "so much preferential stock of the South Western as will yield to the Plymouth and Dartmoor the same annual income as the annual amount now payable;" these arrangements have received the approval of both proprietaries.

REVENUE.—This account for the half-year ended 30th June, 1884, showed the receipts to have been 387*l.*, and the expenditure 41*l.*, leaving a profit of 346*l.*; the sum at the credit of net revenue account, after payment of debenture interest, amounted on the same date to 108*l.*, which was appropriated to the payment of dividends on the Plymouth Extension shares, 1875, at ½ per cent., and on Plymouth and Dartmoor preference shares at 2*s.* per cent. per annum, carrying forward 8*l.*

CAPITAL.—The expenditure on this account to 30th June, 1884, amounted to 145,354*l.*, the receipts to the same date having been 145,144*l.*, as under:—

5 per cent. loans	£4,400
4 and 4½ per cent. loans	5,744
5 per cent. Plymouth Extension shares (act 1875)	25,000
5 per cent. preference shares	75,000
Ordinary shares	35,000
	£145,144
Balance	210

NOTES.—Plymouth Extension Loans and Shares.—Interest thereon payable out of an agreed rent, 1,350*l.*, from the London and South Western, and any other traffic receipts on this extension up to 5 per cent.; beyond this the 1,865 preference shares take receipts.

The interest on all the debenture capital is accumulative, and payable half-yearly on the 1st January and 1st July, the transfer books closing seven days before payment. The principal is redeemable at par, on six months' notice being given.

The dividends on the share capital are contingent upon the profits of each separate half-year.

TRANSFER DEPARTMENT QUERIES AND REPLIES.

QUERIES.	REPLIES.
Transfer form—ordinary or special?	Ordinary.
Fee per deed?	2*s.* 6*d.*
Are certificates required to accompany transfers?	Yes.
To what officer should transfer communications be sent?	Secretary.
In acceptances, renunciations, &c., of allotments of new stock, proxies, or other forms sent to trustees or other joint holders, what signatures are required?	One of either of the trustees.

In operation, 12 miles.

No. of Directors—5; minimum, 3; quorum, 3. *Qualification*, 300*l.*

DIRECTORS:

Chairman—J. WINTERBOTHAM BATTEN, Esq., 15, Airlie Gardens, Campden Hill, W.

Deputy-Chairman—JAMES BREND BATTEN, Esq., 32, Great George Street, Westminster, S.W.

The Rt. Hon. Lord Graves, Thanckes, Torpoint, Devon.
Chas. Harrison, Esq., 3, Lancaster Gate, W.
A. Cromwell White, Esq., 3, Harcourt Buildings, Temple, E.C.

OFFICERS.—Sec., David S. Derry, 22, Great Winchester Street, E.C.; Auditors, John Crick and George Mountier; Bankers, Naval Bank, Plymouth.

Offices—22, Great Winchester Street, E.C.

235.—PLYMOUTH, DEVONPORT, AND SOUTH WESTERN JUNCTION.

Incorporated by act of 25th August, 1883, for the construction and maintenance of railways at Plymouth, Devonport, Stoke Damerel, Beer Ferris, Tavistock, Brentnor, and district, Devonshire. Total length, about 28¾ miles. Period for completion, 5 years. Arrangements with London and South Western. Capital, 750,000*l.* in 10*l.* shares, with power to divide into "preferred" and "deferred" half-shares; loans, &c., 249,000*l.*

Devon and Cornwall Central.—Under act of 7th August, 1884, this company was dissolved and its works abandoned, all its powers becoming vested in the Plymouth, Devonport, and South Western Junction.

No. of Directors.—Maximum, 7; minimum, 5; quorum, 4 and 3. *Qualification*, 50 shares.

FIRST DIRECTORS:

His Grace the Duke of Bedford, K.G.
Sir John St. Aubyn, Bart.
John Carpenter Garnier, Esq.
Reginald Butler Edgcumbe Gill, Esq.
Joseph May, Esq.
George Theodotus Rolston, Esq.

One other to be nominated.

236.—PONTYPRIDD, CAERPHILLY, AND NEWPORT.

Incorporated by act of 8th August, 1878 (41 and 42 Vic., cap. 215), for the construction and maintenance of railways (Nos. 1 and 2) in the county of Glamorgan, commencing by a junction with the Taff Vale, near Pontypridd Station, and terminating in the parish of Bedwas by a junction with the Caerphilly Branch of the Brecon and Merthyr Tydfil Junction. Length, about 7 miles. Period for completion, 5 years. Arrangements with the Rhymney, Brecon and Merthyr Tydfil, and Taff Vale. Capital, 105,000*l.* in 10*l.* shares; loans, &c., 35,000*l.*

By act of 12th August, 1880, the company was empowered to construct a deviation line in Glamorganshire, from Llantwit Vardre to Eglwysilan. Length, about five furlongs.

By act of 10th August, 1882, certain agreements with the above-named Rhymney and Brecon Company were confirmed, and an extension of time for completion of railway (No. 1) was authorised to 8th August, 1884. Powers were also obtained for the construction of a short line at Machen, and for other purposes. New capital, 45,000*l.*; borrowing powers, 15,000*l.*

By act of 2nd August, 1883, the company was authorised to construct a new line from Bassaleg to Alexandra Docks. Length, about 2¼ miles. New capital, 45,000*l.*; loans, &c., 15,000*l.*

No. of Directors—5; quorum, 2. *Qualification*, 30 shares.

Secretary, E. R. Creed, 23, Great George Street, Westminster, S.W.

237.—PORTHDINLLEYN.

Incorporated by act of 7th August, 1884, for making a railway from Pwllheli to Porthdinlleyn, Carnarvonshire. Length, 9¼ miles. Period for completion, 5 years. Capital, 120,000*l.* in 10*l.* shares, with power to divide into "preferred" and "deferred." Loans, 40,000*l.*

No. of Directors.—Maximum, 5; minimum, 3; quorum, 3 and 2. *Qualification*, 30 shares.

FIRST DIRECTORS:

Robert Pughe Jones, Esq.
Edmund Bowen Bernard, Esq.

Three others to be nominated.

238.—PORTPATRICK.

Incorporated by act of 10th August, 1857, to construct a line from Castle Douglas to Portpatrick. Capital, 460,000*l.* in 10*l.* shares; loans, 150,000*l.* Length of main line, 61 miles; Stranraer Branch, 7 furlongs and 37 yards; branch to Portpatrick Harbour, 4 furlongs and 32 yards; total, 62½ miles. Main line commences by a junction with the Castle Douglas and Dumfries, at Castle Douglas, and terminates near Portpatrick; the Stranraer Branch diverges from the main line in the parish of Inch, and terminates near Stranraer Harbour; and the other branch diverges from the main line at Portpatrick, and terminates at the north pier of that harbour. Worked by Caledonian.

By act of 29th July, 1864, the company obtained power to alter certain works, to increase the capital, and to arrange with the London and North Western and the Caledonian as to working the line. New capital, 20,000*l.* in shares and 10,000*l.* on loan. Facilities to Glasgow and South Western.

By act of 29th July, 1864, the company was authorised to establish steam communication between Portpatrick and Donaghadee, and between Stranraer and Belfast and Larne. New capital, 72,000*l.* in shares and 24,000*l.* on loan. London and North Western, Glasgow and South Western, Caledonian, and Belfast and County Down subscribe.

By act of 28th June, 1877, the company obtained certain powers for the acquirement of the East Pier at the harbour of Stranraer. New capital: Shares or stock, 30,000*l.*; loans, 10,000*l.*

The Treasury, under authority of an act of Parliament, paid the sum of 20,000*l.* in satisfaction of the claims of the company upon the Government, which sum was applied in payment of debentures. Under the arrangement with the Treasury the whole of the borrowed money as it falls due will be replaced by a loan from the Exchequer at a lower rate of interest than is current in the general market.

REVENUE.—The net receipts for the half-years ended 31st January and 31st July, 1883, after providing for debenture interest, &c., sufficed for the payment of dividends on the ordinary stock at the rates of 3½ and 4½ per cent. per annum each half-year respectively. The dividend for the half-year ended 31st July, 1884, was announced at the rate of 3¾ per cent. per annum.

CAPITAL.—The expenditure to 31st July, 1884, had reached 611,144*l.*, while the receipts were as follow:—

Ordinary stock		£434,790
Loans at 3½ per cent.		92,241
Loans at 4 per cent.		56,202
Sundries, viz., compensation from Government, in terms of act ...	£20,000	
Calls paid on forfeited shares	1,412=	21,412
Balance		6,499
		£611,144

Meetings may be held in Stranraer, Carlisle, or such other places as the directors may appoint.

No. of Directors.—In addition to those to be appointed by the Caledonian, the Lancaster and Carlisle, Glasgow and South Western, and the Belfast and County Down, 10; quorum, 4. *Qualification*, 500*l.*

DIRECTORS:

Chairman—2 The Right Hon. the Earl of STAIR, K.T., Lochinch Castle, Stranraer.

Deputy-Chairman—2 Sir WILLIAM DUNBAR, Bart., Mochrum Park, Kirkcowan, and Somerset House, Strand, W.C.

3 The Earl of Galloway, Cumloden, Newton Stewart, and 17, Upper Grosvenor Street, W.

2 Sir Andrew Agnew, Bart., of Lochnaw, Wigtownshire.

3 T. C. Greig, Esq., Rephad, Stranraer.

3 Mark J. Stewart, Esq., of Southwick and Blairderry, Ardwell House, by Stranraer.

1 Edward J. Stopford Blair, Esq., of Penninghame, Newton Stewart.

1 Admiral The Right Hon. Sir J. C. D. Hay, Bart., M.P., Craigenveoch, Glenluce, and 108, St. George's Square, S.W.

1 Colonel Hathorn, Castlewigg, Whithorn.

* The Hon. T. C. Bruce, M.P., 42, Hill Street, Berkeley Square, W.

† Benjamin Nicholson, Esq., Annan.

† Matthew William Thompson, Esq., Park Gate, Guiseley, near Leeds.

‡ W. J. Pirrie, Esq., Queen's Island Works, Belfast.

* Miles MacInnes, Esq., Rickerby, Carlisle.

§ Major Green Thompson, Bridekirk, Cumberland.

§ Hugh Brown, Esq., Glasgow.

* Appointed by the Lancaster and Carlisle. † Appointed by the Glasgow and South Western. ‡ Appointed by the Belfast and County Down. § Appointed by the Caledonian.

The Portpatrick directors (9) retire by three at the first general meeting of the company in each year, and are eligible for re-election. The order in which they retire is marked above.

OFFICERS.—Sec., James M'Kenzie, Solicitor, Stranraer; Auditors, George Agnew Main, Banker, Carlisle, and John Graham, 212, West George Street, Glasgow.

Head Office—Stranraer.

239.—POTTERIES, SHREWSBURY, AND NORTH WALES.

An amalgamation by 29 and 30 Vic., cap. 201 (16th July, 1866), of the undermentioned undertakings:—

1. SHREWSBURY AND NORTH WALES.—Incorporated by act of 29th July, 1862, to construct a line from Westbury, on the Shrewsbury and Welshpool, to Llanymynech, on the Oswestry and Newtown. Length, 13¾ miles. Capital, 90,000*l.* in 10*l.* shares; loans, 30,000*l.* By act of 13th July, 1863, the company was authorised to make certain deviations in branches, and to enter into arrangements with the London and North Western, Great Western, Shrewsbury and Welshpool, and the Oswestry and Newtown. Length, 8¼ miles. Capital, 60,000*l.* and 20,000*l.* on loan. By act of 30th June, 1864, the company was authorised to construct seven new lines, and to use a portion of the Oswestry and Newtown. Length, 20 miles. Capital, 200,000*l.* in shares and 66,000*l.* on loan. By act of 30th June, 1864, the company obtained power to change its name to that of the "Shrewsbury and North Wales," to construct several smaller branches (18¾ miles), and to raise new capital to the extent of 100,000*l.* in shares and 33,000*l.* on loan. London and North Western and Cambrian to use the railway. By act of 1865 the company was authorised to make certain deviations, and to raise certain capital to the extent of 100,000*l.* in shares or half-shares and 33,000*l.* on loan; and by act of 10th July, 1866, the Shrewsbury and North Wales obtained power to make certain deviations, and also to construct a line to Bryn Tanat. Length, ½ mile. New capital, 80,000*l.* in shares and 26,000*l.* on loan. Arrangements with Cambrian and Drayton Junction.

2. SHREWSBURY AND POTTERIES JUNCTION.—Incorporated by act of 5th July, 1855, to construct various lines to Market Drayton, on the Wellington and Drayton, and connecting with the Shrewsbury and Crewe, the Welshpool and Severn Valley, and the Shrewsbury and Hereford. Length, 23½ miles. Capital, 400,000*l.* in shares and 133,300*l.* on loan. By act of 16th July, 1866, the Shrewsbury and Potteries obtained power to make certain deviations, and also to participate in the ownership of the Wellington and Drayton. New capital, 80,000*l.* in shares and 26,600*l.* on loan.

OSWESTRY AND LLANGYNOG—See GENERAL INDEX.

By act of 25th June, 1868, the company was authorised to make a "substituted" line, and also to abandon portions of the railway.

Lines constructed, 28 miles.

CAPITAL.—The receipts on this account to 30th June, 1875, amounted to 1,388,151*l.*, of which 858,200*l.* was for shares, and 529,952*l.* on debenture stock. The expenditure to the same date amounted to 1,388,800*l.*, viz.:—1,379,433*l.* on line open for traffic, and 9,367*l.* working stock. Balance at debit of account, 648*l.*

No report has been issued since August, 1875.

WINDING-UP AND SALE OF THE UNDERTAKING.—An act authorising the sale of the undertaking was passed on the 18th July, 1881, such sale being made subject to a resolution of the proprietary, whenever a purchaser shall be found. The purchase money to be applied as follows, viz.:—In payment of all costs, &c., of the act and of the sale, and afterwards 60 per cent. to the holders of debenture stock "A;" 40 per cent. to holders of debenture stock "B;" 25 per cent. to debenture stock "C;" 20 per cent. to the creditors of the company; and 7 per cent. to the holders of shares and stock, upon the nominal amounts held by or due to all of them respectively. Any balance to be divided amongst the proprietors of stock and shares rateably, in addition to the 7 per cent. of their holdings mentioned above.

No. of Directors—8; minimum, 5; quorum, 3. *Qualification*, 500*l.*

This undertaking has been closed by order of the Board of Trade, and is now in liquidation. Official Liquidator, Alexander Young, Esq., 41, Coleman Street, E.C.

240.—PRINCETOWN.

Incorporated by act of 13th August, 1878 (41 and 42 Vic., cap. 229), for the construction and maintenance of a railway commencing at Buckland Monachorum, by a junction with the South Devon and Tavistock, near Yelverton Siding, and terminating at Princetown. Length, 10 miles 2 furlongs 2 chains and 80 links. Period for completion, 5 years. Working arrangements with the Great Western, and agreements with the Plymouth and Dartmoor, which two companies may subscribe towards the undertaking. Capital, 60,000*l*., in 3,000 "Princetown Railway 'A' shares," 800 "Princetown Railway 'B' shares," and 2,200 "Princetown Railway 'C' shares," the dividend earned to be applied—first to the payment of 4 per cent. per annum on the "A" shares, next 4 per cent. per annum on the "B" shares, and the remainder (if any) in payment of dividend on the "C" shares; the respective dividends to be contingent upon the profits of each separate year. Borrowing powers, 20,000*l*., at not exceeding 4½ per cent. per annum.

The shares have been authorised to be converted into stock "A" "B" and "C" respectively.

The Great Western subscription is at present 30,000*l*. in preference stock "A" of the Princetown Company.

WORKING AGREEMENT.—By the terms of this agreement the Princetown is to be worked in perpetuity by the Great Western, at a per centage of the gross receipts, varying with the amount of the receipts; such per centage is not, however, to exceed 70 per cent., nor to be less than the proportion which the expenses on the Great Western system bear to the gross receipts.

REVENUE.—This account for the half-year ended 30th June, 1884, showed receipts to have been 695*l*., of which sum 486*l*. was due to the Great Western for working expenses at 70 per cent., leaving 209*l*. Interest on debentures 708*l*., and sundries 44*l*., left a deficit balance of 543*l*., which, with previous deficit of 118*l*. to 31st December, 1883, will be a charge against future earnings.

CAPITAL.—The receipts on this account to 30th June, 1884, amounted to 78,760*l*., of which 59,960*l*. was for shares and stocks, and 18,800*l*. by loans. The expenditure to the same date amounted to 89,209*l*.

The line was opened for traffic on the 11th August, 1883.

No. of Directors—7; quorum, 4. *Qualification*, 20 shares.

DIRECTORS:

Chairman—*Sir DANIEL GOOCH, Bart., M.P., 3, Warwick Road, Maida Hill, W.

*Sir Charles Alexander Wood, Knt., 11, Elvaston Place, S.W.
John Winterbotham Batten, Esq., 3, Harcourt Buildings, Temple, E.C., and Airlie Gardens, Campden Hill, W.
*Michael Castle, Esq., Clifton, Bristol.
*Alexander Hubbard, Esq., Derwentwater House, Acton, W.
Sir Massey Lopes, Bart., M.P., Maristow, near Plymouth, and 28, Grosvenor Gardens, S.W.
Charles Harrison, Esq., 9, Bedford Row, W.C.

* Represent the Great Western.

OFFICERS.—Sec., A. L. Jenkins; Auditors, J. B. Marwood and G. J. Whitelaw. Offices—Paddington, W.

241.—RAMSEY AND SOMERSHAM JUNCTION.

Incorporated 13th August, 1875, to make a railway from the Holme and Ramsey Line, at Ramsey, to the Great Eastern Line, near Somersham. Length, 7½ miles.

By act of 4th July, 1878, the times for purchase of land and completion of works were extended until 13th August, 1880, and 13th August, 1881, respectively.

By act of 8th April, 1881, the time for completion of works was further extended to 13th August, 1884.

By act of 2nd August, 1883, an extension of time for completion of works until 13th August, 1886, was granted, with power to enter into working agreements with the Great Eastern.

CAPITAL.—50,000*l*. in 10*l*. shares and 16,666*l*. on loan. Running powers over the Holme and Ramsey and the St. Ives and March portion of the Great Eastern, and arrangements with that company.

No. of Directors—3; quorum, 2. *Qualification*, 50 shares.

Chairman—ALFRED FULLER, Esq.

OFFICERS.—Sec. Fred. R. Serjeant, Ramsey; Solicitors, Serjeant and Sons, Ramsey, Hunts.

242.—RATHKEALE AND NEWCASTLE JUNCTION.

Incorporated by act of 22nd July, 1861, to construct a line from the Limerick and Foynes, near Rathkeale, to Newcastle, Co. Limerick. Length, 10 miles. Capital, 50,000*l*. in 10*l*. shares; loans, 16,600*l*. Arrangements with Waterford and Limerick, which subscribed 5,000*l*., the Waterford and Limerick having also agreed to work the line.

By act of 25th July, 1864, 20,000*l.* of original shares were cancelled, and preference shares authorised to be issued in lieu thereof.

By act of 12th August, 1867, the company was authorised to issue preference shares, at 5 per cent., to the extent of 11,870*l.*, in lieu of unissued ordinary capital, and also to raise new preference share capital to the extent of 13,000*l.*, also at 5 per cent., and 15,000*l.* on mortgage.

By act of 31st July, 1868, the Public Works Loan Commissioners have power to lend to this company, should they think fit, all or any part of the money it was then authorised to borrow on mortgage, viz., 31,600*l.*

By act of 23rd May, 1879, the company was empowered to create and issue 61,400*l.* of debenture stock, to be called "Rathkeale and Newcastle Junction Railway Company Postponed Debenture Stock," bearing accumulative interest at 5 per cent. per annum, and ranking next after all previous issues of loans or debenture stocks. The unissued ordinary and preference capital to be cancelled (11,870*l.* ordinary and 9,950*l.* preference), and the Earl of Devon to accept an equivalent amount of such debenture stock to cover the amount of his claim, and the claims of unsecured creditors.

By the Limerick and Kerry Act of 1881 powers were given for the transfer of this undertaking to that company, and for subsequent winding up and dissolution if such transfer be agreed to and effected. An agreement with the Waterford and Limerick relating to working this line was also confirmed.

Arrangement with Waterford and Limerick.—By act of 25th July, 1864, the Waterford and Limerick was authorised to work the Rathkeale and Newcastle, to contribute 5,000*l.* to that undertaking, as well as to raise 35,000*l.*, with 7,000*l.* on loan, to provide rolling stock for the same and for their own general purposes. At a special meeting of the Waterford and Limerick, held on the 18th November, 1878, the directors were authorised to purchase the Rathkeale and Newcastle Junction, for a price not exceeding 60,000*l.*, and to create and issue 5 per cent. preference shares for that purpose.

Revenue—31st December, 1883.—Gross traffic receipts, 3,501*l.*; working expenses, 1,817*l.*; credit balance, 1,683*l.* Net revenue balance at debit thereof, 4,725*l.* 30th June, 1884.—Gross traffic receipts, 3,054*l.*; working expenses, 1,649*l.*; credit balance, 1,404*l.* Net revenue balance at debit thereof, 5,597*l.*

Capital.—The expenditure on this account to 30th June, 1884, amounted to 125,735*l.* The receipts to the same date had been as follow:—

Ordinary 10*l.* shares	£16,514
Five per cent. preference shares	10,050
Loans at 5 per cent.	16,600
Perpetual debenture stock	15,000
Postponed debenture stock	61,400
Balance	6,171
	£125,735

Meetings held half-yearly in February and August.

Scale of Voting.—One vote for each share held.

No. of Directors—7; minimum, 3; quorum, 3.

DIRECTORS:

Chairman—The Right Hon. the Earl of DEVON, Powderham Castle, Exeter.

Henry Arthur Herbert, Esq., Muckross, Killarney, Co. Kerry.

George Hewson, Esq., Ennismore, Listowel, Co. Kerry.

Charles Edward Curling, Esq., Newcastle West, Co. Limerick.

William Malcomson, Esq., Portlaw, Co. Waterford.

Joseph William Hume Williams, Esq., 1, Essex Court, Temple, E.C.

OFFICERS.—Sec., Henry Holmes, 6, Westminster Chambers, Victoria Street, S.W.; Eng., William Barrington, M.Inst.C.E., 84, George Street, Limerick; Auditors, Robert Tidey and J. Henry Schroder, F.C.A.; Solicitors, Lake, Beaumont, and Lake, 10, Lincoln's Inn, W.C.; Bankers, London and County Bank, Knightsbridge Branch.

Offices—6, Westminster Chambers, Victoria Street, S.W.

243.—RAVENGLASS AND ESKDALE.

Incorporated by act of 26th May, 1873, to make a "light" railway from the Ravenglass Station of the Whitehaven and Furness Junction to the village of Boot, in Eskdale, near Scawfell, with a branch from the Ravenglass Station to the sea-shore. Total length, 7¾ miles. Gauge, 3 feet. Capital, 24,000*l.* in 10*l.* shares and 8,000*l.* on loan. Arrangements with Furness. Opened for goods traffic 24th May, 1875, and for passenger traffic 20th November, 1876.

CAPITAL.—The receipts on this account have amounted to 29,805*l*., viz., by shares. 21,805*l*.; by loans, 8,000*l*., and the expenditure has been 28,278*l*., of which 27,027*l*. was on lines open for traffic, and 1,251*l*. on working stock. Balance on hand, 1,527*l*,

[No recent returns have been received for publication.—ED.]

The accounts are made up to the 31st December and 30th June in each year, and the meetings held in March or April and September or October.

No. of Directors.—Maximum, 6; minimum, 3; quorum, 3 and 2. *Qualification*, 200*l*.

DIRECTORS:

Chairman—The Right Hon. the Earl of DEVON, Powderham Castle, Exeter, and 32, Lowndes Square, S.W.

Deputy-Chairman—HENRY COPLAND, Esq., Chelmsford, Essex.

Charles Kemp Dyer, Esq., J.P., St. Albans.
James Jennings, Esq., Middlesboro'-on-Tees.
Dr. Henry E. Trewhella.
Thomas B. Hall, Esq., Reading, Berks.

OFFICERS—Sec., J. W. Marshall, 4, Lime Street, E.C.; Gen. Man., Wilson Harrison, Ravenglass; Eng., George Gordon Page, C.E., 4, Great James Street, Bedford Row, W.C.; Auditors, David S. Derry, Hyde Side, Edmonton, N., and Henry M. Leslie; Solicitors, Green, Allin, and Greenop, 75, Peter's Alley, Cornhill, E.C.

Offices—4, Lime Street, E.C., and Ravenglass, by Carnforth.

244.—REGENT'S CANAL CITY AND DOCKS RAILWAY.

Incorporated 18th August, 1882, for the purchase and transfer to the company of the undertaking of the Regent's Canal Company; for authorising the construction of railways from the Great Western Railway at Paddington to the City, and to the Royal Albert Dock of the London and St. Katharine Docks Company, with lines to connect with the systems of the Midland and Great Northern companies at St. Pancras and King's Cross; for the carrying out of certain street improvements and canal works; and for other purposes. Capital, 8,100,000*l*., in 810,000 shares of 10*l*. each, and 2,390,000*l*. on mortgage.

By act of 2nd August, 1883, the canal undertaking was constituted a separate undertaking, with a separate capital of 1,500,000*l*. shares or stock, and 190,000*l*. on mortgage (part of the capital authorised by the act of 1882), in addition to 310,000*l*. which the company are empowered to borrow under the Canal Company's Acts.

By act of 20th August, 1883, the company was authorised to constitute the railways between the Midland and Great Northern systems and the City (Barbican) a separate undertaking (to be called the "City Lines Undertaking"), with a separate capital (part of the capital authorised by the act of 1882), not exceeding in the whole 2,500,000*l*. shares or stock, and 833,300*l*. on mortgage.

REVENUE.—The gross receipts of the canal (including the rent payable by the general undertaking) amounted, for the half-year ended 30th June, 1884, to 44,086*l*., and the expenditure to 13,174*l*. The total net revenue was 31,033*l*., sufficient to meet the interest on the canal debenture stock, and also the full interest on the canal capital stock.

CAPITAL.—Of the canal capital 1,275,000*l*. stock, entitled to accumulative interest at 4 per cent. per annum to 31st March, 1888, and 4½ per cent. per annum thereafter, has been issued and fully paid up; and on the 31st March, 1883, the entire undertaking of the Regent's Canal, with all rights and liabilities (including 260,685*l*. debenture stock, part of 310,000*l*. authorised to be raised under the Canal Company's acts), was conveyed to the company.

Meetings in February or March, and August or September.

No. of Directors.—Minimum, 9; maximum, 12; quorum, if 9 directors, 5; if less than 9 directors, 3.

DIRECTORS:

Chairman—JAMES STAATS FORBES, Esq., Garden Corner, Chelsea Embankment, S.W.

Deputy-Chairman—JAMES BRAND, Esq., 33, Old Broad Street, E.C.

Sir George Henry Chambers, 4, Mincing Lane, E.C.
William Rushton Adamson, Esq., Rushton Park, Battle.
Henry William Carter, Esq., 21, Billiter Street, E.C.
Albert George Sandeman, Esq., 20, St. Swithin's Lane, E.C.
Charles Gassiot, Esq., 37, Mark Lane, E.C.

Secretary (*pro tem.*), Frederick Coole.

Offices—138, Leadenhall Street, E.C.

245.—RHONDDA AND SWANSEA BAY.

Incorporated by act of 10th August, 1882, to connect the Rhondda Valley coal-fields with the Swansea Bay ports.

The line commences by a junction with the Taff Vale, in the Rhondda Valley, at Treherbert, running through the new coal-field in the Avon Valley, and terminating at Briton Ferry, with a branch line from Pontrhydyfen, at the foot of the Avon Valley, to Cwm Avon, Aberavon, and Port Talbot.

By act of 2nd August, 1883, the company obtained further Parliamentary powers to extend their line from Briton Ferry direct to the Prince of Wales Dock at Swansea, and have thus gained what was originally intended, a short, direct, and independent line from the Rhondda. This extension lessens the distance to Swansea a further six miles. The last act also enables the company to make valuable junctions at Briton Ferry with the Great Western, and with the docks there. The line will now serve four different shipping ports, viz., Port Talbot. Briton Ferry, Neath, and Swansea. Mileage, 25½ miles.

The work of construction is being rapidly pushed forward. The branch line from Pontrhydyfen to Port Talbot is open for traffic, and other sections will be opened at an early date. The whole is to be completed within two years.

Capital.—This consists of 585,000*l*. in 10*l*. shares, 6*l*. paid; and 195,000*l*. on loan. The latter has not yet been issued.

Applications for the original share capital were invited in November, 1882. and in October, 1883, 1*l*. being payable on application, 1*l*. on allotment, and 2*l*. on 1st January, 1883, and 1st January, 1884, respectively, and 2*l*. on 5th August, 1884. The balance is to be called up in sums not exceeding 2*l*., at intervals of not less than three months. Interest at 5 per cent. per annum is paid on the uncalled capital paid in advance.

Transfer deeds: common fee, 2*s*. 6*d*. per deed.

Voting under Companies' Clauses Act, 1845, section 75.

No. of Directors.—Maximum, 9; minimum, 5; quorum, 5 and 3. *Qualification*, 100 shares.

DIRECTORS:

Chairman—The Right Hon. the Earl of JERSEY.

Deputy-Chairman—Sir JOHN JONES JENKINS, Knt., M.P., The Grange, Swansea.

Sir Henry Hussey Vivian, Bart., M.P., Parkwern, Swansea.
Charles Bath, Esq., Ffynone, Swansea.
Thomas Cory, Esq., Sketty, Swansea.
Thomas Davies Daniel, Esq., Coed Park, Cwm-Avon.
John Richardson Francis, Esq., Gwydyr Gardens, Swansea.
Morgan Bransby Williams, Esq., Killay House, Swansea.

OFFICERS.—Sec., H. S. Ludlow; Engs., S. H. Yockney and Son, MM.Inst.C.E., 46, Queen Anne's Gate, Westminster, S.W.; Auditors, R. G. Cawker and George Allen; Solicitors, Stricks and Bellingham, Swansea; Bankers, Barclay, Bevan, and Co., Lombard Street, E.C., and the Glamorganshire Banking Company, Swansea.

Offices—8, Fisher Street, Swansea, and 110, Cannon Street, London, E.C.

246.—RHONDDA VALLEY AND HIRWAIN JUNCTION.

Incorporated by act of 12th August, 1867, to construct four short lines in the county of Glamorgan, connecting the Taff Vale and the Vale of Neath. Length, 7 miles. Capital, 135,000*l*. in 10*l*. shares and 45,000*l*. on loan. In operation, 1½ mile. Worked by Taff Vale.

By act of 13th May, 1872, the company was authorised to construct two extensions (2½ miles and 7 chains respectively), to divide the share capital into "deferred" and "preferred," to abandon certain portions of original line, the remainder to be completed within three years, and the new works within five years.

By act of 17th June, 1878, the company, having completed and opened for mineral traffic the railway No. 1, from the Rhondda Fawr Branch of the Taff Vale to a point marked on the plans deposited for and referred to in the act of 1867 (a distance of 1 mile and 4 furlongs), obtained authority to abandon the remainder, and lease the constructed portion to the Taff Vale for 999 years, on terms to be agreed upon between the two companies, the powers, &c., of the company to be exercised by the lessees. The number of directors to be reduced to three with a quorum of two, and the capital to be reduced to 11,900*l*. in 10*l*. shares, with power to issue 5 per cent. debenture stock to the extent of 12,000*l.*, as a first charge upon the undertaking to be applied to the payment of various costs and charges, &c., payment of purchase and compensation money for lands, &c., and in satisfaction of Lloyd's bonds, and the general debts and liabilities of the company.

REVENUE—30th June, 1884.—The balance of net revenue account this half-year sufficed for the payment of a dividend at the rate of 2½ per cent. per annum; and left a small balance carried forward.

CAPITAL—30th June, 1884.—*Receipts:* From 1,190 ordinary shares of 10*l.* each, 11,900*l.*; debenture stock at 4 per cent. per annum, 11,400*l.*; total, 23,300*l.* *Expenditure:* 23,172*l.* Balance, 128*l.*

The accounts are made up to 30th June and 31st December, and the meetings held in January and July.

No. of Directors—3; quorum, 2. *Qualification*, 300*l.*

DIRECTORS:

Chairman—FREDERICK WILLIAM HARRIS, Esq., 81, Gracechurch Street, E.C.

Rees Jones, Esq., Cardiff.

James Dixon, Esq., 81, Gracechurch Street, E.C.

OFFICERS.—Sec., James G. Nicholson; Auditor, Arthur E. Morgan; Bankers, National Provincial Bank of England, Cardiff Docks.

Offices—Cardiff.

247.—RHYMNEY.

Incorporated by act of 24th July, 1854. Capital, 100,000*l.* in 10*l.* shares; borrowing powers, 30,000*l.* The main line extends from Rhymney to a junction with the Great Western (Newport, Abergavenny, and Hereford Line) at the Hengoed (called by the G. W. the Rhymney) Junction, the distance being over 9 miles. By act of 2nd July, 1855, the company was authorised to raise 100,000*l.* additional capital in shares and 30,000*l.* on loan, and to extend their main line from the Hengoed Junction to a junction with the Taff Vale at Walnut Tree Bridge (about 18 miles from Rhymney), to run over 6 miles of the Taff Vale on to Cardiff, and to make the Caerphilly Branch, and branches to the Bute East Dock and Tidal Harbour at Cardiff, leading from and out of the Taff Vale, which terminates at the Bute West Dock. Thus, by the main line, a through communication is opened between Rhymney and Cardiff, the distance being from Rhymney to Cardiff Station 24½, and to the Docks 26 miles. Also by the junction with the Great Western system at Hengoed, through routes are established from Cardiff and Rhymney to all parts of the west and north of England, through Pontypool Road and Hereford, and to Merthyr, Aberdare, and the Vale of Neath, in South Wales. Through the Bargoed Branch, now completed, access is also given to Dowlais, and to the Brecon and Merthyr, Mid Wales, and other Welsh systems.

For list of Acts from 1857 to 1873, see the MANUAL for 1881, page 315.

By act of 18th August, 1882, the company was authorised to construct lines from Quaker's Yard, on the Newport, Abergavenny, and Hereford section of the Great Western, to the Vale of Neath section of the said company, at two points near Merthyr Tydfil, and a branch to connect with Nixon's Merthyr Vale Colliery. Running powers over the Vale of Neath between the western point of junction of the company's authorised lines and Merthyr Tydfil were obtained. Length of lines, about 6½ miles. New capital, 300,000*l.* in shares or stock, and 100,000*l.* by debentures or debenture stock. Provision is made for the Great Western becoming joint owners of the lines.

LONDON AND NORTH WESTERN.—In 1867 the London and North Western obtained an act whereby about a mile and a-half of the company's extension north of Rhymney was made and worked by the two companies jointly. The construction of a short line about 3 miles in length, with running powers over a portion of the London and North Western, enabled the company to convey to Cardiff the produce of some of the principal works in Monmouthshire. It also enabled the two companies to interchange north of Rhymney a considerable traffic formerly exchanged at Hengoed. The result of this alteration in the point of interchange is that traffic passes over 27 miles of the company's railway instead of over about 16 miles. By the London and North Western Company's Act of 12th July, 1877, an agreement, bearing date the 12th November, 1875, was confirmed, by which that company obtained permission to make, maintain, use, and work a junction with the Rhymney Company's Bute Dock "Low Level Line," subject to the payment to the latter company of a yearly rental of 50*l.*, the agreement to be in force for 99 years, from the 29th September, 1875. Mutual running powers were also provided for.

BARGOED BRANCH.—This line, constructed jointly by the Great Western and the Rhymney, was opened for goods and mineral traffic on the 20th December, 1875, and for passengers 1st February, 1876. The line is 9 miles in length, and consists of a double track of rails. It runs out of the Great Western Taff Vale Extension Line at Llancaiach, through the Bargoed Taff Valley, to the Dowlais Iron Works. Several large collieries are now opened in the district traversed by the new railway, and other pits are now being sunk, from which a heavy mineral traffic will probably be derived in the course of a few years.

PONTYPRIDD, CAERPHILLY, AND NEWPORT.—See GENERAL INDEX.

REVENUE.—This account for the half-years ended 31st December, 1883, and 30th June, 1884, showed the following results:—

	Dec., 1883.	June, 1884.
Passengers, parcels, &c.	£8,251	£7,790
Goods, minerals, and cattle	73,333	76,683
Rents, transfer fees, &c.	1,330	1,378
Gross receipts	£82,914	£85,851
Expenditure	39,243	38,934
Net	£43,671	£46,917
Add—Balance brought forward	1,082	580
Total net revenue	£44,753	£47,497
Deduct—Interest, rents, &c.	7,302	7,911
Available for dividend	£37,451	£39,586

The available balance for the half-year ended 31st December, 1883, enabled the dividends to be paid in full for the half-year on the guaranteed and preference stocks, and a dividend at the rate of 10 per cent. per annum on the ordinary stock and shares (14,606*l.*), carrying forward 580*l.*, exclusive of 1,000*l.* carried to a reserve fund. For the half-year ended 30th June, 1884, the available balance sufficed for the full guaranteed and preference dividends and a dividend on the ordinary stock and shares at 10 per cent. per annum (15,249*l.*), carrying forward 3,171*l.*, exclusive of 1,500*l.* carried to a reserve fund.

CAPITAL.—*Authorised:* Shares and stock, 1,312,000*l.*; loans, 437,300*l.*; total, 1,749,300*l.* The subjoined statement of share capital created shows the proportion received to 30th June, 1884:—

PRIORITIES, DESCRIPTIONS, DIVIDENDS, and other conditions of issue of the various Securities of the company, with the amounts received on each.

No.	Year of Act.	FULL DESCRIPTION (to be observed in Transfer Deeds and all other Legal Documents).	Amount received.
1	Various	Debenture bonds, 4 per cent.	£1,300
2	Various	4 per cent. perpetual debenture stock	300,067
3	1857	Consolidated 5 per cent. guaranteed capital stock	90,900
4	1861	Consolidated 6 per cent. preferential capital stock	40,000
5	1861	Consolidated 5 per cent. preferential capital stock	74,000
6	1864	Consolidated 5 per cent. preference capital stock	42,000
7	1864	Consolidated 6 per cent. preference capital stock	213,000
8	1861	Consolidated 5 per cent. preferential capital stock (Capital created 22nd February, 1870)	27,000
9	1867	Consolidated 5 per cent. preference capital stock of 1867	100,000
10	1873	Consolidated 5 per cent. preference capital stock of 1873	149,621
11	Various	Consolidated ordinary capital stock	237,480
	1882	10*l.* ordinary shares	48,136
		Total £	*1,322,604

NOTES.—Dividends accumulative, Nos. 1 to 3; dividends contingent upon profits of each separate year ended 31st December, Nos. 4 to 11.

Dividends Payable.—No. 1, 25th March, 24th June, 29th September, and 24th December; No. 2, 1st January and 1st July; Nos. 3 to 11, 28th February and 31st August.

Transfer Books.—The transfer books close 14 days before each half-yearly meeting, which takes place about the 20th February and 20th August respectively. The dates vary. The books re-open the day after the meeting.

Special Conditions.—No. 4 stock participates with the ordinary stock in any dividend beyond 6 per cent. per annum.

* To which must be added 1,146*l.* received on forfeited shares.

TRANSFER DEPARTMENT QUERIES AND REPLIES.

Queries.	Replies.
Transfer form—ordinary or special?......	Ordinary.
Fee per deed?	2s. 6d.
Ditto if more sellers than one?...	2s. 6d.
May several classes of stock be transferred on one deed?	Yes.
Are certificates required to accompany transfers?	Yes.
What amounts of stock are transferable, and are parts of 1*l.* sterling allowed to be transferred?	1*l.*, or a multiple of 1*l.*
To what officer should transfer communications be sent?	Secretary.
In acceptances, renunciations, &c., of allotments of new stock, proxies, or other forms sent to trustees and other joint holders, what signatures are required?	Signature of first proprietor for proxies, and of all in other cases.

The receipts and expenditure on capital account to 30th June, 1884, were as under:—

Received.		*Expended.*	
Shares and stock	£1,022,383	Lines open for traffic	£1,166,258
Loans	1,300	New lines under act of 1882......	27,865
Debenture stock	300,067	Working stock	165,188
Premium on debenture stock ...	6,953		
	£1,330,703		
Balance........................	28,608		
	£1,359,311		£1,359,311

The estimate of further expenditure on capital account amounted to 31,900*l.* for the half-year ended 31st December, 1884, that for subsequent half-years being pronounced "uncertain." The capital powers available amount to 259,189*l.*

Productive mileage, 42½; foreign miles worked over, 13¼; total, 55¾.

Meetings held in February and August.

DIRECTORS:

Chairman—2 JOHN BOYLE, Esq., Sylvanhay, Bournemouth.

Deputy-Chairman—3 WILLIAM AUSTIN, Esq., Ellernmede, Totteridge, Herts.

2 Alderman Sir Thomas Dakin, Knt., 2 and 3, Creechurch Lane, E.C.

1 Daniel Rees, Esq., Glandare, Aberdare.

3 John Hudson Smith, Esq., The Exchange, Bristol.

1 Franklen G. Evans, Esq., Tynant House, near Cardiff.

1, Retire in 1885; 2, in 1886; 3, in 1887. All eligible for re-election.

OFFICERS.—Sec., William Mein; Traffic Man. and Eng., Cornelius Lundie; Auditors, Wm. P. Stephenson and Ambrose Ford; Accountant, T. Farrance; Solicitor, George Cox Bompas, 4, Great Winchester Street, E.C.

Offices—Cardiff.

248.—ROSS AND LEDBURY

Incorporated by act of 28th July, 1873, for the construction and maintenance of a railway from Ross to Ledbury, in the counties of Gloucester and Hereford. Constructed in three sections. Total length, about 12¼ miles. Period for completion, 5 years. Power to enter into working agreements with the Great Western (which is authorised to subscribe 140,000*l.*) and Ross and Monmouth. Capital, 180,000*l.* in 10*l.* shares, with power to divide into "preferred" and "deferred" halves. Borrowing power 60,000*l.*

By act of 16th April, 1878, the period for completion of the railway called No. 3 in the act of 1873 was extended to 28th July, 1881, and by Great Western Act, 1881, was extended for a futher period of three years.

Capital—30th June, 1884.—Received on account of issue of 18,000 ordinary shares of 10*l.* each, 105,500*l.* Expenditure, 95,486*l.* Estimate of further expenditure for the completion of the lines, 144,514*l.*

Accounts made up to 30th June and 31st December, and meetings held in February and August each half-year respectively.

No. of Directors.—Maximum, 5; minimum, 3; quorum, 3 and 2 respectively. *Qualification*, 30 shares. Quorum of ordinary or special meetings, 7 shareholders, holding not less than 10,000*l.* in the capital of the company.

DIRECTORS:

Chairman—Sir DANIEL GOOCH, Bart., M.P., 3, Warwick Road, Maida Hill, W.

Sir Charles Alexander Wood, Knt., 11, Elvaston Place, S.W.

Richard Basset, Esq., Highclere, Newbury.

Walter Robinson, Esq., 20, Gledhow Gardens, S.W.

OFFICERS.—Sec., A. E. Bolter, Paddington Station, W.; Auditors, J. H. Matthews and J. D. Higgins.

249.—ROSS AND MONMOUTH.

Incorporated by act of 5th July, 1865, to construct a line from Ross, on the Hereford, Ross, and Gloucester, to Monmouth, on the Coleford, Monmouth, Usk, and Pontypool. Capital, 120,000*l.* in shares of 20*l.* each and 40,000*l.* on loan.

By act of 1867, the company was authorised to divert portion of authorised line; extension of time for purchase of lands and completion of works; additional directors. New capital, 40,000*l.* in 20*l.* shares and 13,000*l.* on loan.

By act of 16th June, 1871, the company was authorised to attach a preferential dividend of 6 per cent. on 80,000*l.* of ordinary unissued stock.

By act of 1872, the company was authorised to make traffic and other arrangements with the Great Western.

REVENUE.—The net receipts for the half-year ended 31st December, 1883, after providing for the interest on mortgage loans and rent-charges, sufficed for a dividend on the preference shares of 11*s.* 6*d.* per share, leaving a balance to next half-year of 47*l.*, and for the half-year ended 30th June, 1884, a dividend of 11*s.* 8*d.* per share on preference was declared; balance to debit of next half-year, 3*l.*

CAPITAL.—The receipts, &c., on this account to 30th June, 1884, were as follow, viz.:—

Loans at 4 per cent.	£47,100
6 per cent. preference shares of 20*l.* each	80,000
Ordinary shares of 20*l.* each	80,000
Forfeited shares	35
Sale of surplus lands	1,242
	£208,377
Expenditure	208,172
Balance	205

On 30th June, 1882, the debenture loans, 47,100*l.* at 4½ per cent., were paid off, and re-issued at 4 per cent.

NOTES.—The interest on debenture loans is accumulative and payable half-yearly, on the 1st January and 1st July.

The dividend on the preference shares is contingent upon the profits of each separate year, and is payable half-yearly, in February and August.

In operation, 12 miles 40 chains. Line opened 3rd August, 1873.

TRANSFER DEPARTMENT.—Ordinary form; fee, 2s. 6d. per deed. Several classes of stock cannot be transferred on one deed with one stamp for the whole. Certificates not required to accompany transfers. In acceptances, renunciations, &c., of allotments of new stock, proxies, or other forms sent to trustees and other joint holders, first name on register only required.

No. of Directors—5; quorum, 3. *Qualification*, 500*l.*

DIRECTORS:

Chairman—The Hon. ROBERT HENLEY EDEN, Minety House, near Malmesbury.

George Andrew Barkley, Esq., 16, Albert Mansions, Victoria Street, S.W.

William Partridge, Esq., Wyelands, near Ross, and 49, Gloucester Place, Hyde Park, W.

Charles Liddell, Esq., 24, Abingdon Street, S.W.

Francis Baynham Vaughan, Esq., Courtfield, near Ross, and 17, Cromwell Place, South Kensington.

OFFICERS.—Sec., John Edward Stower Hewett, Ross; Auditor, Thomas Blake, Ross.

Offices—Ross.

250.—ROTHERHAM AND BAWTRY.

Incorporated by act of 22nd August, 1881, for the construction of a railway about 18¼ miles in length, situated in the districts indicated by the title. Period for completion of works, 5 years. Junctions with the Great Northern. Capital, 360,000*l.* in 10*l.* shares, with power to divide into "preferred" and "deferred" half-shares; borrowing powers, 120,000*l.*

By act of 10th August, 1882, the company was authorised to abandon part of their railway No. 1, and to construct new lines at Rotherham in lieu thereof. Junctions with Midland and Manchester, Sheffield, and Lincolnshire. New capital, 50,000*l.*; borrowing powers, 16,600*l.*

By act of 7th August, 1884, the company was authorised to raise additional capital, 75,000*l.*, with borrowing powers, 25,000*l.*

No. of Directors.—Maximum, 5; minimum, 3, quorum, 3 and 2. *Qualification*, 50 shares.

FIRST DIRECTORS

The Rt. Hon. Viscount Lumley.
Rev. Henry Gladwyn Jebb.
George Chambers Revill, Esq.
Henry Vivian Tippett, Esq.
One other to be nominated.

OFFICERS.—Sec., Mr. Sawle; Eng., Mr. Wilson; Solicitors, Bircham and Co., 46, Parliament Street, Westminster, S.W.

251.—ROWRAH AND KELTON FELL MINERAL.

Incorporated by act of 16th July, 1874, for the construction of a line from the Rowrah Station of the Whitehaven, Cleator, and Egremont to Kelton Fell. Length, 4 miles. Capital, 30,000*l.*, in 300 shares of 10*l.* each, and 9,000*l.* ordered to be raised under the authority of "The Rowrah and Kelton Fell Mineral (Additional Capital) Certificate, 1882," by issue of new ordinary shares of 10*l.* each (623 new ordinary shares issued at par, 36,230*l.*) The line is worked by Messrs. Wm. Baird and Co., under an agreement.

In operation, 4 miles.

REVENUE.—The earnings for the half-year ended 31st December, 1883, and for the half-year ended 30th June, 1884, sufficed for the payment of a dividend on the ordinary shares at the rate of 6 and 3 per cent. per annum respectively.

CAPITAL—30th June, 1884.—*Receipts:* On 3,623 ordinary shares of 10*l.* each, 36,230*l.*; loans, 10,000*l.*; sundries, 70*l.*; total, 46,300*l.* *Expenditure:* 44,810*l.* Credit balance, 1,490*l.*

Meetings held at Whitehaven half-yearly, during each February and August. The accounts are made up to 30th June and 31st December each year.

No. of Directors—6; quorum, 3. *Qualification*, 300*l.*

DIRECTORS:

Chairman—1 WILLIAM WEIR, Esq., 168, West George Street, Glasgow.

Deputy-Chairman—2 ANDREW K. M'COSH, Esq., Gartsherrie, Coatbridge.

3 R. A. Robinson, Esq., South Lodge, Cockermouth.
3 John Alexander, Esq., Gartsherrie.
1 William Weir, Esq., Crookedholm, Kilmarnock.

1, Retire in August, 1885; 2, in 1886; 3, in 1887; all eligible for re-election.

OFFICERS.—Sec., Thomas Howson, Whitehaven; Man., William Rankine; Eng., A. H. Strongitharm, Whitehaven and Barrow-in-Furness; Auditors, William Laird and Edward Wadham; Solicitors, Lumb and Howson, Whitehaven; Bankers, The Clydesdale Bank.

252.—ROYSTON AND HITCHIN.

Incorporated by act of 16th July, 1846, for a line commencing from a junction with the Great Northern, at Hitchin, and terminating at Royston. The capital in that act was fixed at 800,000*l.*, but reduced by act of 22nd July, 1847, to 266,666*l.* 13*s.* 4*d.*, with borrowing powers of 88,800*l.* In 1848 powers were given to extend the line from Royston to a point of junction with the Great Eastern Cambridge and Bedford Branch, near Shepreth, with a view of giving the company access to Cambridge, the capital being 80,000*l.*, and borrowing powers 26,666*l.* In 1851 another act was obtained, reducing the nominal value of the original shares to 6*l.* 5*s.* and the total amount of share capital is now 266,675*l.*

A conveyance of the railway from Royston to Hitchin to the Great Northern, under a lease, took effect on the 1st August, 1850, and a conveyance of the Shepreth Extension to the Great Northern in like manner, from the 24th January, 1853.

By act of 23rd June, 1864, the Great Northern and the Great Eastern were authorised to enter upon arrangements with regard to the future occupation of the Royston and Hitchin, and on the 1st April, 1866, the line, which had been leased to the Great Eastern for 14 years, reverted to the Great Northern. The rental is equal to 6 per cent. per annum, the stock having been converted into "Royston, Hitchin, and Shepreth Consolidated Stock." The dividends are computed to 1st February and 1st August each half-year, and are payable about the middle of those months respectively. A deduction of 1*s.* 4*d.* per 100*l.* stock is made from each half-year's dividend, to cover expenses of management.

The accounts are made up to the 30th June and 31st December, and meetings held in February and August. Registration fee, 2*s.* 6*d.* Stock certificates must accompany transfer deed, and a part of a pound allowed. Transfer books close a few days before half-yearly meetings.

DIRECTORS:

Chairman—Sir ROBERT WALTER CARDEN, Knt., M.P., 3, Threadneedle Street, E.C.

John Harvey Astell, Esq., Woodbury Hall, Sandy.
The Right Hon. Lord Colville, of Culross, K.T., 42, Eaton Place, S.W.
Sir Andrew Fairbairn, Knt., M.P., 15, Portman Square, W., and Askham Richard, near York.
Henry Fordham, Esq., Royston.
Francis John Fordham, Esq., Royston.
Alexander Peckover, Esq., Wisbeach.
Frederic Seebohm, Esq., Hitchin.

OFFICERS.—Sec., Arthur Fitch; Registrar, J. A. Colchester; Auditor, Major John C. Fitzmaurice; Bankers, City Bank.

Offices—King's Cross Station, N.

253.—RYDE AND NEWPORT (Isle of Wight).

Incorporated by act of 25th July, 1872, to construct a line between these places. Length, about 8 miles. Capital, 65,000*l.* in 10*l.* shares and 21,600*l.* on loan or by debenture stock. Opened 20th December, 1875.

By act of 14th June, 1875, the company was authorised to raise 30,000*l.* by the creation of preference capital, and to borrow on mortgage a further sum of 10,000*l.* Reciprocal running powers over parts of Isle of Wight and Cowes and Newport. Traffic arrangements with these companies and with Ryde Pier, and also with South Western and Brighton.

By Board of Trade Certificate, 1876, the company was authorised to raise 30,000*l.* additional capital by shares or stock, and to borrow a further sum of 10,000*l.* on mortgage or by debenture stock.

By Ryde and Newport Act, 1877, the company was authorised to raise 30,000*l.* in shares, and 10,000*l.* in debentures.

By Board of Trade Certificate, 1881, the company was authorised to raise 30,000*l.* additional capital by shares or stock, and to borrow a further sum of 10,000*l.* on mortgage or by debenture stock.

An arrangement has been made with the Cowes and Newport for working both the lines as one system under a joint committee appointed by the two companies. The traffic and other receipts to be carried to a joint account and applied as follows, viz.:—After deducting the expenses of the joint account, 2,000*l.* per annum to be paid to the Cowes and Newport for the use of their line, payable half-yearly, on the 30th June and 31st December; and, after payment of all working and other expenses, the residue to be applied in payment to the Ryde Company of a sum not exceeding 2,600*l.* per annum, the balance (if any) to be divided between the two companies in mileage proportion. The agreement is dated March 19th, 1877, and is confirmed by the act of 12th July, 1877, under which the company obtained powers for sundry enlargements, extensions, and other improvements, and to raise additional capital to the extent of 30,000*l.* in shares or stock, and 10,000*l.* in loans or debenture stock; the same amount of new capital being authorised to be raised by the Cowes and Newport.

In operation, 7 miles 76 chains.

REVENUE.—The profit on the two lines for the half-year ended 30th June, 1884, amounted to 1,210*l.*

CAPITAL.—The expenditure on this account to 30th June, 1884, amounted to 226,184*l*., whilst the receipts to the same date were 225,340*l*., viz.:—

Ordinary shares	£65,000
5 per cent. first preference shares	30,000
5 per cent. second preference shares	30,000
5 per cent. third preference shares	30,000
5 per cent. fourth preference shares	15,460
Loans at 5 per cent	51,800
Rent-charges capitalised	3,080

The capital powers and other available assets amounted to 9,800*l*., subject to reduction for any rent-charge granted by the company.

Meetings in February and August.

No. of Directors—4. *Qualification*, 500*l*.

DIRECTORS:

Chairman—GEORGE YOUNG, Esq., 7, The Terrace, Ryde, Isle of Wight.

J. P. Benwell, Esq., 26, Nicholas Lane, E.C.

Rod. Mackay, Esq., 3, Lothbury, E.C.

Henry Pinnock, Esq., Beechwood, Newport, Isle of Wight.

OFFICERS.—Sec., F. L. Beard, 3, Lothbury, E.C.; Eng., Frank C. Stileman, M.Inst.C.E., 23, Great George Street, Westminster, S.W.; Surveyor, J. Binfield Bird, West Cowes, Isle of Wight; Bankers, National Provincial Bank of England, Newport, Isle of Wight.

Offices—3, Lothbury, E.C.

254.—SCARBOROUGH AND WHITBY.

Incorporated by act of 29th June, 1871, to construct a line between these watering places. Length, 20 miles. Capital, 120,000*l*. in shares and 40,000*l*. on loan.

This line extends from Scarborough in a northerly direction through or near Scalby, Burniston, Cloughton Newlands, the romantic glen of Hayburn Wyke, Stainton Dale, Raven Hill, Fylingdales, Thorpe, Robin Hood's Bay, Hawsker, and Stainsacre, to Whitby, and is to a considerable extent a surface line.

By act of 26th May, 1873, the company was authorised to extend their line to join the North Eastern, at Scarborough, and the Middlesbrough Union, near Whitby, and to alter the levels of their authorised lines near Whitby. New works to be completed within five years, and the alteration of levels within three years. New capital, 50,000*l*. in shares or stock and 16,000*l*. on loan.

By act of 12th August, 1880, the company obtained powers for the extension of the periods for compulsory purchase of lands, and completion of the railways authorised by acts 1871 and 1873, until 12th August, 1885, and for other purposes.

By act of 3rd July, 1884, new capital was authorised to the extent of 160,000*l*. in "C" or new preference shares, and 53,333*l*. on loan.

CAPITAL.—The total authorised capital of the company is as follows, viz.:—

Loans	£80,000
"C" preference 5 per cent. 10*l*. shares	145,000
"B" stock	54,740
"A" shares	40,260
	£320,000

The amounts created and received up to 30th June, 1884, were as follow:—

Description.	Created.	Received.
"A" shares	40,260	32,981
"B" stock	54,740	53,686
"C" 5 per cent. preference shares	145,000	75,310
Loans	80,000	63,600
Total	£320,000	£225,577

Up to the same date there had been expended 244,723*l*.

Under the Scarborough and Whitby Act of 1880 the net yearly revenue is to be applied as follows:—First, in payment of interest on debenture stock. Second, in payment of dividend on the "C" 5 per cent. preference shares. After the above payments, the "B" stock and "A" shares are entitled to maximum dividends of 5 and 4 per cent. respectively, after which all surplus profits belong to the "C" preference shares.

Works in satisfactory progress.

Meetings held usually in Scarborough in February and August.

DIRECTORS:

Robt. Foster, Esq., Mayor of Scarborough.
John Corner, Esq., 18, Albert Road, Regent's Park, N.W., and Whitby.
Arthur Marshall, Esq., 7, East India Avenue, E.C., and Highgate, Middlesex.

OFFICERS.—Sec., W. Cash; Engs., Sir C. Fox and Sons, 5, Delahay Street, S.W.; Auditors, J. Petch and H. M. Cockerill, Scarborough; Solicitors, Turnbull, Graham, and Moody, Scarborough.

Offices—90, Cannon Street, London E.C.

255.—SEACOMBE, HOYLAKE, AND DEESIDE.

Incorporated by act of 18th July, 1872, for the purchase and acquiring of the Hoylake Railway, and to enable the Hoylake and Birkenhead Tramway Company to construct tramways from the Docks Station of the Hoylake Railway to Woodside Ferry, Birkenhead. Capital, 70,000*l.* in 10*l.* shares and 23,330*l.* on loan.

By act of 5th August, 1873, the company was authorised to construct new lines. Length, about 1¼ mile. New capital, 24,000*l.* in shares or stock and 8,000*l.* on loan. The works authorised by this act are now completed.

By act of 18th July, 1881, authority was given to extend the railway to Seacombe, to change the name of the company, and for other purposes. New capital in shares and stocks—for new works, 100,000*l.*; for purposes of existing undertaking, 24,000*l.*; and by loans, 41,300*l.*

By act of 12th July, 1882, the company was empowered to extend their line to New Brighton and Liscard. Period for completion, 5 years. New capital, 60,000*l.*; borrowing powers, 20,000*l.*

CAPITAL.—The expenditure on this account to 30th June, 1884, amounted to 87,932*l.*, and the receipts to 90,000*l.* in ordinary shares.

No. of Directors—5; maximum, 9; minimum, 4; quorum, 3. *Qualification*, 200*l.*

DIRECTORS:

Chairman—HENRY ROBERTSON, Esq., M.P., Palé, Corwen.

C. P. Douglas, Esq., Chester.
James Harrison, Esq., Dornden, Tunbridge Wells.
Benjamin Piercy, Esq., 8, Drapers' Gardens, E.C.
R. C. De Grey Vyner, Esq., Newby Hall, Ripon.

OFFICERS.—Sec., W. D. Haswell; Gen. Man., Frederick Kirtley; Solicitors, Birch, Cullimore, and Douglas, Chester.

Head Office—84, Foregate Street, Chester.

256.—SEATON AND BEER.

Incorporated by act of 13th July, 1863, to construct a line from the Colyton Station of the South Western to Seaton. Length, 4¼ miles. Capital, 36,000*l.* in 10*l.* ordinary shares; 12,000*l.* on loan. Arrangements with South Western.

Additional capital to that authorised by Parliament has been raised under Certificate from Board of Trade, to the extent of 12,000*l.* in 5 per cent. preference and 4,000*l.* on loan.

The London and South Western, under an agreement scheduled to their Various Powers Act, 1880, work the line, and have the option to acquire an absolute transfer of the railway, at a rental increasing 100*l.* a year, until it reaches the maximum of 1,510*l.* in 1886. The rent to 30th June, 1884, was sufficient to pay 4*l.* per cent. on the mortgages and 1½ per cent. on the preference stock of 12,000*l.* for the half year, and a dividend of 8*d.* per share on the 3,600 ordinary shares.

AXMOUTH BRIDGE UNDERTAKING.—The new bridge over the River Axe at Seaton has been completed, and has been transferred to Sir A. W. Trevelyan absolutely, by virtue of the London and South Western (Various Powers) Act, 1880.

Meetings held in Seaton in February and August.

No. of Directors—5; minimum, 3; quorum, 3. *Qualification*, 200*l.*

DIRECTORS:

Chairman—GEORGE EVANS, Esq., Seaton, Axminster.

Sir A. W. Trevelyan, Bart., Nettlecombe Court, Somerset.
James Babbage, Esq., Washford.
Arthur Lee Ellis, Esq., 3, Stone Buildings, Lincoln's Inn, W.C.
George Beloe Ellis, Esq., 67, Ladbroke Grove Road, North Kensington, W.

OFFICERS.—Sec., Edwin Hellard, Stogumber, Somerset; Auditors, G. W. Mitchell and John White; Solicitors, Radcliffe, Cator, and Martineau, 20, Craven Street, Strand, W.C.

Offices—Stogumber, Somerset.

257.—SELBY AND MID YORKSHIRE UNION.

(LATE CHURCH FENTON, CAWOOD, AND WISTOW).

Incorporated by act of 21st July, 1879, for the construction and maintenance of a line from Church Fenton to Wistow, both in the West Riding of Yorkshire. Length, 5 miles 4 furlongs and 6·60 chains. Period for completion, 5 years. Capital, 30,000*l.* in 10*l.* shares, with power to divide into "preferred" and "deferred" half-shares. Loans or debenture stock, 10,000*l.*

By act of 16th July, 1883, the name of this company was changed as above, and authority was given to construct a short line to connect the existing railway with the North Eastern. Period for completion, 5 years.

No. of Directors—3; quorum, 2. *Qualification*, 20 shares.

FIRST DIRECTORS:

Charles England, Esq.
William Henry Nicholson, Esq.
Thomas Whiteley, Esq.

OFFICERS.—Sec., T. G. Mann, 1, New Street, York; Solicitors, Mann and Son, 1, New Street, York.

258.—SEVERN AND WYE AND SEVERN BRIDGE.

An amalgamation of the "Severn and Wye" and "Severn Bridge" undertakings, the former incorporated as the "Lydney and Lydbrook" by act of 1809, and the latter by act of 18th July, 1872. The amalgamation was carried out under act of 21st July, 1879. The respective amounts received on capital account from shares and loans and debenture stocks are as follow:—*Severn and Wye*—shares, 317,841*l.*; loans, &c., 185,073*l.*; total, 502,914*l.* *Severn Bridge*—shares, 325,000*l.*; loans, &c., 89,800*l.*; total, 414,800*l.* Joint loans, 18,500*l.*

The productive mileage of the Severn and Wye was 28 miles, and of the Severn Bridge 5½ miles. Total, 33½ miles. The amalgamation took effect from the opening of the Severn Bridge Line, on the 17th October, 1879. Arrangements with the Midland and Sharpness Docks undertakings, both of which subscribe to the Severn Bridge.—For other particulars relating to the past history of these companies, independently, see the MANUAL for 1879, and previous editions.

The Amalgamation Act provides that the respective capitals of the two companies shall remain separate and distinct as at present, and that the net receipts of the amalgamated company be apportioned as follows, viz:—For the 1st and 2nd years, 70 per cent. to Severn and Wye and 30 per cent. to Severn Bridge; for the 3rd year, 55 per cent. to Severn and Wye and 45 per cent. to Severn Bridge; for the 4th year and thence forward, 50 per cent. to Severn and Wye and 50 per cent. to Severn Bridge.

REVENUE.—The joint companies are not earning a dividend at present, the trade in the Forest of Dean having been very depressed.

The following information is copied from the report issued in August, 1884, viz.:—The directors are glad to state that the gross receipts are 3,000*l.* in excess of the corresponding period of last year, when there was a strike in the Forest of Dean, and, notwithstanding the necessary increased expenditure, the net receipts are 1,000*l.* more. The receipts from traffic carried over the two sections are estimated as follow, viz.:—Severn and Wye, 80¾ per cent; Severn Bridge, 19¼ per cent. The directors, after much consideration, have applied to the Court of Chancery that the sum of 1,500*l.* be expended during the present year in relaying with steel rails, in addition to the ordinary outlay, which the Court has sanctioned. With reference to the resolution of the shareholders at their last meeting, "That the directors be requested to consider the desirability of re-arranging the capital of the company so that the two sections may be completely fused into one undertaking," much discussion has taken place upon the subject at the board, and with the view of facilitating the consideration of this important question, the Bridge Section of the directors have made a proposition as to re-arrangement of terms under the Amalgamation Act to the Wye Section directors, which is under their consideration. The receivers' accounts to 31st December, 1883, have been passed by the court, and a sum of 4,000*l.* paid into Chancery; the accounts to 30th June, 1884, showing a cash balance of 8,491*l.*, have been lodged in court for examination, and since the 30th of June a sum of 6,000*l.* paid on account of this balance, making a total of 10,000*l.* now awaiting distribution. The Woods and Forests department of the crown introduced a bill into Parliament this session for the purpose of facilitating the opening of the deep coals in the Forest of Dean, and your directors, believing that it would materially conduce to the prosperity of the district and of your railway, petitioned in its favour. The bill has been referred to a commission of enquiry, which the directors hope will lead to a reconciliation of conflicting interests, and is withdrawn for the present session. The shipment of Welsh coal at Sharpness Docks is still of a limited character, owing to the need of a new tip for loading in deep water.

CAPITAL—30th June, 1884.—Expended: *Wye Section*, 530,459*l.*; *Bridge Section*, 411,905*l.*; *Joint*, 21,108*l.* The share capital is as follows, viz.:—

Description.	Amount created.	Amount received.
Wye Section—		
Ordinary shares of 50*l.* each—acts 1809, 1811, 1814	£188,100	
1,122 shares paid in full	...	£56,100
759 „ issued at a discount of 20*l.* per share	...	22,770
1,881 „ issued at a discount of 39*l.* per share	...	20,691
Guaranteed new shares of 20*l.* each—act 1853:—		
1,500 shares, paid up	30,000	30,000
Preference shares of 10*l.* each. Board of Trade Certificate, 1868:—		
2,000 shares, created in 1868, 5½ per cent. per annum	20,000	20,000
Preference shares of 10*l.* each—ditto 1,800 shares created in 1869, 5 per cent. per annum	18,000	18,000
Preference shares, act 1870. 3,600 shares of 10*l.* each, created in 1871, 5 per cent. per annum	36,000	36,000
Preference shares, act 1872. 6,000 shares of 10*l.* each, created in 1873, 5 per cent. per annum	60,000	60,000
Preference shares, Board of Trade Certificate, 1874:—		
5,000 preference shares of 10*l.* each	50,000	50,000
Preference shares, Board of Trade Certificate, 1876:—		
3,000 preference shares of 10*l.* each	(4,280)	4,280
Total	£406,380	£317,841
MEM.—Amount created £406,380		
Less discount on 2,640 ordinary shares...... 88,539		
Amount received £317,841		
Bridge Section—		
Ordinary shares (22,500 of 10*l.* each)	£225,000	£225,000
Five per cent. preference shares (10,000 of 10*l.* each)	100,000	100,000
Total	£325,000	£325,000

Loans and debenture stock—30th June, 1884:—

Wye Section	5 per cent. loans	£70,355	
„	4¾ per cent. loans	10,900	
„	4½ per cent. loans	14,255	
„	5 per cent. debenture stock	1,620	
„	4½ per cent. debenture stock	62,943	
Severn Bridge subscription	5 per cent. debenture stock	8,180	
„ „ „	4½ per cent. debenture stock	16,020	
„ „ „	5 per cent. loans	800	£185,073
Bridge Section	5 per cent. loans	5,270	
„ „	4¾ per cent. loans	300	
„ „	4 per cent. stock	75,000	
„ „	5 per cent. debenture stock	9,230	89,800
Joint	5 per cent. loans	18,500	18,500

The joint revenue is made up half-yearly to the 30th June and 31st December respectively in each year. Meetings to be held each February and August.

MILEAGE.—Authorised, 41¼; constructed, 37; worked by engines, 33¼. Severn and Wye Original Line (Tramway) opened in 1813; new lines (locomotive) opened in 1872, 1874, and 1875; Severn Bridge Railway opened October 17th, 1879.

TRANSFER DEPARTMENT.—Ordinary form of transfer; shares, mortgages, or debenture stock, each seller 2s. 6d.; certificates of shares are not required to accompany transfers; several classes of shares may be transferred on the same deed; certificates to accompany each transfer of debenture stock; no fractional portion of 1l. transferred.

The company is in chancery, the directors being appointed managers, and the secretary and the manager receivers.

DIRECTORS.—The board consists of 14 directors, one appointed by the Midland, one by the Sharpness Docks, seven by the Severn and Wye, and five by the Severn Bridge undertakings respectively. *Qualification*, 250l. of ordinary capital.

DIRECTORS:

Representing Wye Section:

Deputy-Chairman—JOHN A. GRAHAM-CLARKE, Esq., Frocester, near Stonehouse.

Steuart Fripp, Esq., 6, Cambridge Park, Redland, Bristol.
John Hewitt, Esq., Stapleton, Bristol.
G. B. Keeling Esq., Lydney.
Colonel E. A. Noel, Elston Hall, Newark-on-Trent.
S. J. Sayce, Esq., 21, Ellenborough Crescent, Weston-Super-Mare.
H. Wethered, Esq., Ferncliff, Tyndall's Park, Clifton.

Representing Bridge Section:

Chairman—W. C. LUCY, Esq., Brookthorpe, Gloucester.

W. B. Clegram, Esq., C.E., Saul Lodge, Stonehouse, Gloucestershire.
T. Nelson Foster, Esq., Allt Dinas, Bayshill, Cheltenham.
Sir W. H. Marling, Bart., Stanley House, Stonehouse.
Richard Potter, Esq., York House, Kensington, W.

Representing Midland Railway:
H. T. Hodgson, Esq., Harpenden, Herts.

Representing Sharpness Docks Company:
Major W. E. Price, Hillfield House, Gloucester.

OFFICERS.—Sec., G. R. Richards; Eng. and Gen. Man., G. W. Keeling; Auditors, Fred. A. Jenkins, F.C.A., Bristol, and W. Green, Gloucester; Solicitors, Wintle and Son, Newnham, and Wiltons and Riddiford, Gloucester.

Offices—Lydney, Gloucestershire.

259.—SHEFFIELD AND MIDLAND JOINT LINES.

By act of 24th June, 1869, the Midland and Manchester, Sheffield, and Lincolnshire were jointly authorised to take over the Manchester and Stockport, and to make a short branch from the Stockport and Woodley Junction Line. The Midland to acquire a joint ownership of the Newton and Compstall and the Marple, New Mills, and Hayfield Junction, which had previously belonged solely to the Sheffield. Powers were also given to the Midland to run over certain portions of the Sheffield Company's line, near Manchester. Works to be under the direction of a committee appointed by the two companies.

By the Sheffield Company's Act of 6th August, 1872, the committee appointed under the previous act was incorporated a body corporate, with perpetual succession and a common seal, and powers given to the committee to construct a line from the Manchester and Stockport to the Stockport and Woodley Junction. Length, ⅜ mile.

By act of 26th May, 1873, the committee was authorised to alter the levels of part of the Manchester and Stockport. Power to each company to raise 55,000l. by new shares or stock, and 18,000l. on loan.

MANCHESTER AND STOCKPORT.—Incorporated by act of 16th July, 1866, to construct a line from Manchester, on the Sheffield and Lincolnshire, to the Stockport and Woodley Junction, with branch to the Newton and Compstall Branch of the Sheffield. Length, 7¼ miles. By act of 24th June, 1869, the undertaking of the Manchester and Stockport was dissolved and transferred to the Midland and the Manchester and Sheffield. The line was opened 1st August, 1875.

MARPLE, NEW MILLS, AND HAYFIELD JUNCTION.—Incorporated by act of 15th May, 1860, to construct a line from the Newton and Compstall Branch of the Manchester, Sheffield, and Lincolnshire, at Marple, to New Mills and Hayfield. Junction with Disley and Hayfield. Length, 6 miles. By act of 24th April, 1864, some alterations were authorised, and an extension of time for two years conceded By act of 5th July, 1865, this company was amalgamated with the Manchester and Sheffield.

WIDNES.—By act of 7th July, 1873, the Board of Trade Provisional Certificate was confirmed, and the company incorporated to construct a line from Prescot by way of Cuerdley to Widnes. Length, 3 miles. By Manchester, Sheffield, and Lincolnshire Act, 1874, the undertaking was dissolved, and its powers transferred to the Sheffield. Opened for goods traffic 3rd April, 1877. By act of 29th June, 1875. the Midland became joint owners of the line on refunding the Sheffield half the amount expended. By the same act the committee was authorised to construct two short branches near Prescot. The Widnes Station and lines were opened for passenger traffic on 1st August, 1879.

CAPITAL.—The amount expended on capital up to 30th June, 1884, was 1,650,944*l*., which was provided in equal moieties by the two owning companies.

In operation, 27¾ miles.

DIRECTORS:

*Sir James J. Allport, Littleover, Derby.
†The Rt. Hon. Lord Auckland, Edenthorpe, Doncaster.
*J. W. Cropper, Esq., Dingle Bank, Liverpool.
*Matthew W. Thompson, Esq., Guiseley Hall, Leeds.
†Sir Edward William Watkin, Bart., M.P., Rose Hill, Northenden, Cheshire. and Charing Cross Hotel, Charing Cross, S.W.
†The Rt. Hon. the Earl of Wharncliffe, Wortley Hall, near Sheffield.

* Midland representatives. † Manchester, Sheffield, and Lincolnshire representatives.

OFFICERS.—Sec., Edward Ross, London Road Station, Manchester; Bankers. Manchester and Salford Bank.

260.—SHREWSBURY AND HEREFORD.

Incorporated by act of 3rd August, 1846, for a line commencing at Hereford (in conjunction with the Newport, Abergavenny, and Hereford), and terminating at the joint station at Shrewsbury. 51 miles double line.

An act was obtained in 1850 reconstructing the share capital. It is provided therein that the original 40,000 shares of 20*l*. each, reduced by forfeiture to 29,710, shall be hereinafter considered as 29,710 shares of 10*l*. each, on which the 5*l*. then called, if paid, should be credited. In addition to the above 29,710 original shares—the forfeited (4,943), the unissued (5,201), and the unclaimed (146) shares under 1st act—10,290 shares were re-created, and a further creation of 5,000 shares was sanctioned; thus 15,290 new shares were authorised to be issued and distributed, in the first instance, among the original holders, at 1*l*. discount, or 9*l*. per share, and entitled to the same privileges as the original shares. By act of 23rd June, 1856, the company was enabled to raise a further additional capital beyond that sanctioned in 1850, of 300,000*l*., namely, 225,000*l*. by the creation of shares at 5 per cent. preference, and 75,000*l*. by borrowing on mortgage of bonds. The act also contains a power to convert any borrowed money into a fixed and irredeemable stock, at any rate not exceeding 4½ per cent. By act of 29th July, 1862, the Shrewsbury and Hereford was leased to the London and North Western and Great Western at 6*l*. per cent. on consolidated stock, and on so much of the ordinary share capital as shall from time to time be called up. The same act authorised the Shrewsbury and Hereford or the London and North Western to subscribe 30,000*l*. to the Knighton or Central Wales.

By an act passed in the session of 1870 this undertaking was vested in the London and North Western and Great Western, subject to the payment of the interest on the consolidated stock, the 10*l*. shares at 6 per cent., the preference shares at 4½ per cent., and debentures and other debts.

The consolidated stock and new shares above-mentioned have, under the provisions of the same act, been converted into 625,000*l*. stock, called "Shrewsbury and Hereford Railway 6 per cent. Rent-charge Stock," and the preference shares into 50,000*l*. stock, called "Shrewsbury and Hereford Railway 4½ per cent. Rent-charge Stock."

The dividends on these stocks are calculated to the 30th June and 31st December. and payable to the proprietors registered at these dates. The dividends are payable on the 1st August and 1st February.

The registration business is conducted by Mr. John Crier, Great Western Station, Paddington, W.

261.—SHROPSHIRE UNION.

Incorporating the Newtown and Crewe, 1846, share capital, 1,500,000*l.*; the Chester and Wolverhampton, 1846, share capital, 1,000,000*l.*; Shrewsbury and Stafford, 1846, share capital, 800,000*l.*; total, 3,300,000*l.*, and 1,099,999*l.* on loans. 154 miles, besides Ellesmere and Chester and Shrewsbury and Montgomery Canals, purchased for 482,920*l.*, and loans about 814,207*l.* London and North Western subscribed 101,732*l.*, and under act of 1847 the London and North Western agreed to lease and guarantee dividend on 600,000*l.* (cost of line), and canal capital (now called up, 1,552,564*l.*), equal to one-half of the dividend on London and North Western ordinary consolidated stock.

This company is an amalgamation of railways and canals, with a view originally of converting the latter into the former. This object it was found impracticable to carry out, especially after an arrangement had been entered into with the London and North Western, which was itself invalid until sanctioned by Parliament. The supervening difficulties were got rid of by act of 24th July, 1854, which may be regarded as the incorporating of the company. Length of railway, 23½ miles.

By lease to the London and North Western, under the powers of "The Shropshire Union Leasing Act, 1847," the proprietors of Shropshire Union stock are secured half London and North Western dividend in perpetuity, with right to all surplus profits up to 6 per cent., and half surplus profits above that amount, such surplus profits being taken upon an average of six half-years.

A supplemental agreement between the two companies of even date with the lease (25th March, 1857), as confirmed by Parliament, authorising the two companies to agree upon a composition in lieu of the surplus profits to which the Shropshire Union is entitled, over and above the half London and North Western dividend, and also empowering individual Shropshire Union shareholders to exchange their Shropshire Union stock into stock of the London and North Western, at the rate of 50*l.* London and North Western for 100*l.* Shropshire Union stock, which option is being gradually exercised. Under this agreement a "lease capital account" has been raised, in which both companies are interested, and to which the proceeds of all carrying stock, &c., sold are to be carried. The balance to the credit of this account to the 30th June, 1884, amounted to 410*l.*

The dividends upon the shares and stock under the lease are always one half the amount of dividend paid upon the London and North Western ordinary stock, they are contingent upon the profits of each half-year, and are payable about 3 weeks after the London and North Western dividends are paid, the transfer books closing 7 days before the half-yearly meeting, or about 10 days before payment.

Capital.—The expenditure on this account has amounted to 2,444,015*l.*, of which 1,626,125*l.* was on the canal, and 817,890*l.* on the railway. The receipts have been as under:—

Shares and stock	£1,541,231
Loans	814,207
Interest account	4,711
Sale of tug boats, &c.	357
Surplus land balance	256
Liverpool land sold to Mersey Dock Board	32,113
Sale of land and plant at Ellesmere Port, &c.	3,223
Compensation in respect of telegraphs	2,000
Telegraphs	2,109=£2,400,307

TRANSFER DEPARTMENT QUERIES AND REPLIES.

Queries.	Replies.
Transfer form—ordinary or special?	Ordinary.
Fee per deed?	2*s.* 6*d.*
Ditto if more sellers than one?	2*s.* 6*d.*
Are certificates required to accompany transfers?	Yes.
What amounts of stock are transferable, and are parts of 1*l.* sterling allowed to be transferred?	Any amount not containing the fraction of 1*l.*
To what officer should transfer communications be sent?	Secretary, Euston Station, London.
In acceptances, &c., renunciations of allotments of new stock or proxies, what signatures are required?	In renunciations of allotments of new stock all the proprietors must sign, and in the case of acceptances of new stock and proxies the first-named in the account.

The accounts are made up to 30th June and 31st December, and the statutory meetings are held in Shrewsbury in March and September of each year.

DIRECTORS:

Chairman—The Right Hon. the Earl of POWIS, Powis Castle, Welshpool, and 45, Berkeley Square, W.

Richard Moon, Esq., Copsewood Grange, Coventry.
Hon. Wm. Lowther, M.P., Lowther Lodge, Kensington Gore, W.
J. Pares Bickersteth, Esq., Grove Mill House, near Watford Herts.
John Bateson, Esq., Emsworth, Wavertree, Liverpool.
George Stanton, Esq., Coton Hill, Shrewsbury.
Ralph Brocklebank, junr., Esq., Childwall Hall, Childwall, near Liverpool.
His Grace the Duke of Sutherland, K.G., Dunrobin Castle, Golspie, and Stafford House, St. James's, S.W.
Lord Richard Grosvenor, M.P., Assoc.-Inst.C.E., 12, Upper Brook Street, W.

OFFICERS.—Sec., S. Reay, Euston Station, N.W.; Gen. Traffic Man., Thomas Hales, Chester; Eng., G. R. Jebb, M.Inst.C.E., Shrewsbury; Auditors, Charles Townshend and E. Waterhouse; Public Accountants, Price, Waterhouse, and Co., Gresham Street, E.C.; Solicitors, Potts and Roberts, Chester; Bankers, National Provincial Bank of England, Chester.

262.—SIDMOUTH.

Incorporated by act of 29th June, 1871, to construct a "light railway" from the South Western, at Feniton, to Sidmouth. Length, 8¼ miles, with an approach road of 1¼ mile. Capital, 66,000*l.* in 10*l.* shares and 22,000*l.* on loan or by debenture stock.

By act of 11th August, 1876, the company was authorised to extend their line to Budleigh Salterton and Exmouth (11 miles); to raise 130,000*l.* additional capital (with a preference attached to 65,000*l.* if thought desirable); to borrow on mortgage, or by debenture stock, a further sum of 43,300*l.* Various powers under this act were repealed by act of 23rd May, 1879, and the new extension has, therefore, been abandoned.

Arrangements with the London and South Western, which works the line at 45 per cent. when gross receipts under 4,000*l.* a year, and 50 per cent. when over 4,000*l.* a year. Opened for traffic 6th July, 1874.

REVENUE.—The gross receipts to 31st December, 1883, including balance from previous half-year, amounted to 2,209*l.* The general charges, &c., amounted to 75*l.*, Government duty, 27*l.*, and there was paid to the working company 955*l.*, leaving a profit of 1,151*l.* Interest on debentures absorbed 550*l.*, and a dividend on 58,506*l.* ordinary capital, at 2 per cent. per annum, 585*l.*, leaving 16*l.* to be carried forward.

The net earnings for the half-year ended 30th June, 1884, sufficed for a dividend on ordinary capital at 1¼ per cent. per annum.

CAPITAL.—The receipts on this account to 30th June, 1884, amounted to 80,526*l.*, namely, 58,526*l.* in ordinary 10*l.* shares and 22,000*l.* in debenture stock at 5 per cent. per annum. The expenditure to the same date was 79,726*l.*, leaving on hand 1,259*l.*

Meetings held in February and August.

No. of Directors—5; minimum, 3; quorum, 3 and 2. *Qualification*, 300*l.*

DIRECTORS:

Chairman—Sir JOHN H. KENNAWAY, Bart., M.P., Escot, Ottery St. Mary.

John Fulford Vicary, Esq., North Tawton, Devon.
Neil Bannatyne, Esq., 15, Earl's Court Square, South Kensington, S.W.
Captain Walter G. Barttelot, Coates Castle, Pulborough.

OFFICERS.—Sec., James Sutherland; Auditors, J. W. Collins and Richard Searle. Offices—110, Cannon Street, E.C.

263.—SKIPTON AND KETTLEWELL.

Incorporated by act of 26th August, 1880, for the construction and maintenance of a railway from Skipton, by a junction with the Midland, to Threshfield, in the parish of Linton. Length, about 9¼ miles. Period for completion of works, 5 years. Traffic arrangements with the Midland. Capital, 72,000*l.* in 10*l.* shares; borrowing powers, 24,000*l.*

No. of Directors—3; quorum, 2. *Qualification*, 40 shares.

FIRST DIRECTORS:

Robert Tennant, Esq., Scarcroft Lodge, near Leeds.
James Balfour Wemyss, Esq.
Percy Kelham Langdale, Esq.

264.—SLIGO, LEITRIM, AND NORTHERN COUNTIES.

Incorporated 11th August, 1875, for making a railway from the Midland Great Western, at Ballysadare, to the Irish North Western, at Enniskillen, passing through the counties of Leitrim and Cavan. Length, 42¼ miles. Capital, 200,000*l.* in 10*l.* shares, divided into the following classes, viz.:—50,000*l.* "A" or "preferred" shares; 39,300*l.* (or less) "B" and "C," or landowners' guaranteed shares; and 110,700*l.* ordinary shares, with power to guarantee a further sum out of the ordinary capital, not exceeding 20,700*l.* Borrowing powers, 100,000*l.* Time allowed for completion of works, five years. Provision for doubling part of the Irish North Western and enlarging the Enniskillen Station. Running powers over, and working and traffic arrangements with, the Irish North Western and Midland Great Western.

By act of 29th June, 1880, the time for completion of works was extended to 11th August, 1883, and powers were obtained to raise additional capital to the extent of 40,000*l.*, with borrowing powers not exceeding 20,000*l.*

The first and part of the second section of the line, from Enniskillen to Glenfarne, a distance of 18 miles, is open for traffic, and the second section, from Glenfarne to Manorhamilton, was opened 1st December, 1880. A further portion, from Manorhamilton to Collooney, 17 miles, was opened on the 1st September, 1881, and the remaining or last section was opened for traffic on the 1st November, 1882.

No. of Directors.—Maximum, 5; minimum, 3; quorum, 3 and 2. *Qualification,* 50 shares.

DIRECTORS:

Chairman—Sir HENRY GORE BOOTH, Bart., Lissadell, Sligo.

Deputy-Chairman—FRANCIS LA-TOUCHE, Esq., Dromahair, County Leitrim.

Owen Wynne, Esq., Hazlewood, County Sligo.

John W. Batten, Esq., 15, Airlie Gardens, Campden Hill, W.

Christopher L'Estrange, Esq., Kevinsfoot, Sligo.

OFFICERS.—Sec., R. E. Davis; Traffic Man., S. B. Humphreys; Loco. Supt. and Permanent Way Eng., Henry Tottenham; Solicitors, Stannell and Son, 5, Dawson Street, Dublin.

Offices—Lurganboy, Manorhamilton, County Leitrim.

265.—SOLWAY JUNCTION.

Incorporated by act of 30th June, 1864, to construct a line from the Caledonian, near Kirtlebridge, to the Brayton Station of the Maryport and Carlisle, and branches in connection therewith. Length, 17¾ miles, including 4 miles run over the Carlisle and Silloth Bay Line. Capital, 320,000*l.* in 10*l.* shares and 106,600*l.* on loan.

By act of 29th June, 1865, certain deviations were authorised, power given to use part of the Glasgow and South Western, to make use of the Maryport and Carlisle Station, and an agreement with the North British confirmed.

By act of 23rd July, 1866, the company was authorised to raise additional capital to the extent of 60,000*l.* in shares and 20,000*l.* on loan. Powers were also given to the North British and the Glasgow and South Western to subscribe 100,000*l.* each to the Solway Junction, neither of which have been exercised.

By act of 15th July, 1867, the company was authorised to construct a junction with the Carlisle and Silloth Bay (length, 13 chains), and to divide the capital into "deferred" and "preferred" shares. The Caledonian was also authorised to guarantee the debenture debt of the Solway Junction, as well as to subscribe a sum not exceeding 100,000*l.* towards the share capital of the undertaking. An extension of time of three years for completion of works was also obtained, and traffic facilities were given to the Furness and London and North Western.

By act of 21st July, 1873, the agreement with the Caledonian for the purchase of the northern portion of the line was confirmed. The price paid for the Annan and Kirtlebridge Line (86,439*l.*) was to be applied in payment for land taken for portions of the undertaking other than the Annan and Kirtlebridge, law, Parliamentary, and other debts incurred since 1870 (not exceeding 5,000*l.*), and to payment of arrears of interest due to mortgagees to 31st December, 1872. All powers to raise money by mortgage under former acts are cancelled. The company was authorised to issue 110,000*l.* debenture stock, to pay off mortgages, and to reduce the rate of interest on the 60,000*l.* preference shares to 4 per cent. per annum, but after 4 per cent. has been paid to the ordinary shareholders, the surplus will be divided equally among the two classes. The debenture stock is entitled to 3½ per cent. interest, with the proviso that if in any half-year it is not earned, the balance shall only be a debt against the company for the next succeeding eight half-years, over what is sufficient to pay the interest in each half-year.

By act of 10th August, 1882, the company was authorised to construct a new line (1¾ mile) from their existing railway at Bowness to the North British at Port Carlisle. New capital, 18,000*l.* in shares and 6,000*l.* by borrowing. Power was also given to the company to run over the North British from Abbey Holme Junction to Carlisle, and to the North British to run over the company's line from Abbey Holme Junction to Brayton. Power was also given to the company to raise 30,000*l.* by first debenture stock, with a preference over all existing stocks for repair of viaduct, and new powers to issue 68,608*l.* of surrendered shares as new preference or new ordinary shares. The Caledonian may subscribe the above 30,000*l.*, bearing interest at 4 per cent., if authorised by a meeting of that company.

In operation, 12½ miles; and running powers over 3¾ miles of North British. Worked by the Caledonian at 40 per cent., the Solway Company maintaining the line.

In 1883 the company promoted a bill for the extension of their line from Brayton to Bassenthwaite, with running powers to Keswick, but the bill was rejected by the House of Commons Committee.

In January, 1881, after a frost of exceptional intensity, the viaduct across the Solway Firth, between Dumfries and Cumberland, was carried away by the ice, resulting in the destruction of a part of the viaduct and the stoppage of through traffic. The reconstruction of the viaduct was completed and the line re-opened on 1st May, 1884.

REVENUE.—The revenue for the half-year ended 31st December, 1883, amounted to 2,019*l.*, and admitted of a payment at the rate of 1 per cent. per annum on the debenture stock. The revenue for the half-year ended 30th June, 1884, amounted to 2,408*l.*, and admitted of a payment at the rate of ⅞ per cent. on the debenture stock.

CAPITAL.—The expenditure on lines open for traffic to 30th June, 1884, amounted to 445,730*l.* The receipts, in order of priority, were as under:—

Debenture stock (at 3½ per cent.)	£100,183
4 per cent. preference shares	60,000
Ordinary shares	251,338
	£411,521

The debenture and preference capital is convertible at the option of the holders into ordinary stock at par, at any time on three months' notice, under act 21st July, 1873. On the former dividends are accumulative for 8 half-year's only, and on the latter they are contingent upon the profits of each separate year. The transfer books close about 14 days before the half-yearly meetings.

TRANSFER DEPARTMENT QUERIES AND REPLIES.

QUERIES.	REPLIES.
Transfer form—ordinary or special?	Ordinary.
Fee per deed?	2*s.* 6*d.*
Ditto if more sellers than one?	2*s.* 6*d.* for each seller if other than a joint holding.
May several classes of stock be transferred on one deed?	Separate deed required for debenture stock.
Are certificates required to accompany transfers?	Yes.
What amounts of stock are transferable, and are parts of 1*l.* sterling allowed to be transferred?	Any amount except fractions of 1*l.*
To what officer should transfer communications be sent?	The secretary.
In acceptances, renunciations, &c., of allotments of new stock, proxies, or other forms sent to trustees and other joint holders, what signatures are required?	For proxies signature of first name only in other cases signatures of all.

Meetings held in London, Carlisle, or Whitehaven, in March and September.

No. of Directors—6; quorum, 3. *Qualification*, 200*l.*

DIRECTORS:

Chairman—JOHN MUSGRAVE, Esq., Wasdale Hall, Gosforth, near Whitehaven.

James Gibson Dees, Esq., Whitehaven and Bellingham.

William Eckersley, Esq., M.Inst.C.E., Westminster, S.W.

Robert Alleyne Robinson, Esq., South Lodge, Cockermouth.

Directors go out of office one-third at first meeting each year; eligible for re-election.

OFFICERS.—Sec. and Gen. Man., Horace F. Tahourdin; Engs., Brunlees and McKerrow, 5, Victoria Street, Westminster, S.W.; Res. Eng., J. Brown, Annan; Auditors, James Moffat, jun., Annan, and John Cameron, Whitehaven; Solicitors, Tahourdins and Hargreaves, 1, Victoria Street, Westminster, S.W., J. R. Musgrave, Whitehaven, and Alexander Downie, Town Clerk, Annan.

Offices—9, Victoria Chambers, Westminster, S.W.

266.—SOMERSET AND DORSET.

[LEASED TO THE MIDLAND AND LONDON AND SOUTH WESTERN, FROM NOV. 1, 1875.]

An incorporation by act of 7th August, 1862, of the Somerset Central and Dorset Central, the combination of interests taking place from 1st September, 1862.

For heads of Acts from 1864 to 1878, see the MANUAL for 1881, page 330.

SOMERSET CENTRAL.—Incorporated by act of 17th June, 1852, for construction of a railway commencing at the harbour of Highbridge, north side of the River Brue, and thence crossing the Bristol and Exeter, and forming a junction therewith, near Highbridge Station, and terminating at Glastonbury. Length, 13½ miles. The Bristol and Exeter, former owners of the Glastonbury Canal, sold that property to this company for 8,000*l*., and became shareholders to the extent of 10,000*l*., of which sum 8,000*l*. is deemed the purchase money of the canal. By act of 30th July, 1855, extensions to Wells and Burnham (and pier at latter place) were authorised. Length of new lines: Glastonbury to Wells, 5½ miles; Highbridge to Burnham, 1½ mile; branch to pier, 1 furlong; total, 7 miles. By act of 24th July, 1856, the company was authorised to construct a line from Glastonbury to Bruton. Additional capital, 100,000*l*. and 33,000*l*. on loan. Length, 12 miles. By act of 1st August, 1859, the company was empowered to lay down narrow gauge rails to work in connection with the South Western system, and to raise additional capital by shares and borrowing for that purpose. New capital, 75,000*l*. in shares at 6 per cent.; loans, 24,000*l*. Debentures converted into stock at 5 per cent. By act of 1st August, 1861, an extension of time, till August, 1862, was obtained, in which to construct the line from Glastonbury to Bruton, to be provided with rails for both gauges. The company was also authorised to raise new capital to the extent of 85,000*l*. in shares and 29,300*l*. on loan.

DORSET CENTRAL.—Incorporated by act of 29th July, 1856, to construct a line from Wimborne, on the Southampton and Dorchester Branch of the South Western, to Blandford. Capital, 100,000*l*. in 20*l*. shares; loans, 33,000*l*. Length, 10¼ miles. By act of 10th August, 1857, the line was extended from Blandford along the Vale of Blackmore, a distance of 24 miles, to the Somerset Central, at Bruton. Capital, 300,000*l*. in 20*l*. shares; loans, 100,000*l*. Length, No. 1, 16½ miles; No. 2, 3 furlongs 1 chain; No. 3, 8¼ miles; No. 4, 2 furlongs 2·25 chains; No. 5, 3 furlongs 2·80 chains. By act of 3rd July, 1860, an extension of time for completion of works was obtained for three years.

AMALGAMATION.—The capitals of the two companies are amalgamated on equal terms. The Somerset and Dorset is thus 66 miles in length, commencing at Burnham, on the Bristol Channel, and extending to Wimborne, on the South Western; and, by virtue of an arrangement with that company, the trains of the Somerset and Dorset run into Poole and Bournemouth, thus forming a through connection between the English and Bristol Channels.

The extension line from Evercreech to Bath (26 miles) was opened for traffic on the 20th July, 1874. The Poole and Bournemouth, over which the Somerset and Dorset has running powers, was opened on the 15th June, 1874.

LEASING ARRANGEMENT.—The lease is for 999 years, commencing 1st November, 1875. The rent in the first year is fixed at 43,056*l*., and, increasing gradually until the fourth year, will for that year, and throughout the duration of the lease, stand at 57,408*l*. per annum, with an addition of 1-10th of any amount by which in any year the gross receipts in respect of the leased undertakings shall exceed 114,816*l*. As between the two leasing companies, the relations are to be of complete equality, with entire absence of priority of either company over the other. The lease was confirmed by act of 13th July, 1876, which also authorised the raising of 100,000*l*. new share capital and 33,333*l*. on mortgage by each company for the acquisition of rolling stock, the alteration from broad to narrow gauge, and other purposes connected with the leased undertaking. Traffic facilities to be afforded the Great Western.

REVENUE.—The following is copied from the directors' report for the half-year ended 30th June, 1884:—"The fixed minimum rent of the line for the six months to the 30th April last has been duly received, and applied in payment of interest on the debenture stocks and of the dividend on the extension consolidated stock, in accordance with the act of Parliament. The statement of the gross traffic receipts for the six months to the 30th of April last has been received from the lessees, from which it appears that the earnings for that period amount to the sum of 64,346*l*., as against 62,777*l*. for the corresponding period of last year, showing an increase of 1,569*l*. for the six months."

CAPITAL.—*Authorised:* Shares and stock, 1,867,000*l*.; loans, 1,289,513*l*.; total, 3,156,513*l*. The following statement of stock and share capital created shows the proportion received to 30th June, 1884:—

Description.	Created.	Received.	In arrear.	Unissued.
1. Ordinary stock issued............£550,192				
Ditto "A" 16,460				
Ditto "B" 95,660				
662,312	£1,045,680	£652,294	£10,018	£383,368
2. First 5 per cent. preference stock	100,000	85,000	...	15,000
3. First 4½ ditto ditto	99,960	35,655	...	64,305
4. Second 5 ditto ditto	261,360	90,880	...	170,480
5. Extension ordinary stock..................	360,000	360,000	...	...
Total................................	£1,867,000	£1,223,829	£10,018	£633,153

The expenditure to 30th June, 1884, including 12,000*l*. subscribed to the Burnham Tidal Harbour, amounted to 2,507,756*l*.; whilst the receipts to the same date had been 2,456,209*l*., viz.:—1,223,829*l*. from shares and stock, and 1,232,380*l*. from loans.

DESCRIPTIONS, DIVIDENDS, and other conditions of issue of the various Securities of the company, existing on the 30th June, 1884 (see notes):—

No.	Year of Act.	FULL DESCRIPTION (to be observed in Transfer Deeds and all other Legal Documents).	Rate ⅌ cent ⅌ annum.
1	...	No. 1 debenture stock £160,000	5
2	...	No. 2 debenture stock "Somerset Central" ... 104,824	5
3	...	No. 2 debenture stock "Dorset Central" 148,554	5
4	...	No. 2 debenture stock "Somerset and Dorset" 221,002	2½
5	...	No. 3 debenture stock .... £168,000 (with a further 1 per cent. contingent on increase of traffic).	4
6	1871	Extension ordinary stock £360,000	3½
7	1871	Extension debenture stock, 1871 120,000	5
8	1874	Extension debenture stock, 1874 110,000	5
9	...	No. 4 debenture stock 200,000	5
		Issued. Unissued.	
10	...	First 5 per cent. preference stock... £85,000 ... £15,000	5
11	...	First 4½ per cent. preference stock... 35,655 ... 64,305	4½
12	...	Second 5 per cent. preference stock 90,880 ... 170,480	5
13	...	Ordinary stock .... 550,192 ... 383,368	...
14	...	Ditto "A" 16,460	...
15	...	Ditto "B" 95,660	...

NOTES.—Priorities.—The priorities of the above-mentioned stocks have not been defined; they are numbered in their supposed order of priority, but only for the purposes of these notes.

Dividends.—Nos. 9 to 15 are contingent upon the profits of each separate year, but as yet no dividends have been paid. No. 15 ("B") receives no dividend until 5 per cent. has been paid to No. 14 ("A"). On Nos. 1 to 8 the interest is payable half-yearly, on 30th April and 31st October, but warrants are not issued until the last weeks in May and November, the transfer books closing from 1st to 7th of each May and November respectively.

Guarantees.—On Nos. 1 to 8 the interest and dividends are covered by the fixed minimum rent payable by the lessees of the line (the London and South Western and Midland).

Minimum Dividend.—No. 6 is entitled to increased dividend, without limit as to amount, contingent upon any increase of traffic above that which would secure the guaranteed minimum rent.

Mem.—See also terms of lease, page 301.

TRANSFER DEPARTMENT QUERIES AND REPLIES.

Queries.	Replies.
Transfer form—ordinary or special?	Ordinary, except for ordinary stock "A" and "B," for which special forms may be obtained at the company's office.
Fee per deed?	2s. 6d.
Ditto if more sellers than one?...	2s. 6d.
May several classes of stock be transferred on one deed?	Yes, classes of stock of the same description.
Are certificates required to accompany transfers?	Yes.
What amounts of stock are transferable, and are parts of 1l. sterling allowed to be transferred?	Any amount not being part of 1l.
To what officer should transfer communications be sent?	Secretary.

Meetings held in February and August in each year.

No. of Directors.—Maximum, 8; minimum, 5. *Qualification*, 500l. Bristol and Exeter directors, two, whilst subscribing 13,000l.; if the subscription is reduced below 13,000l., one director only; if the subscription is below 7,000l., then power to appoint any director will cease.

DIRECTORS:

Chairman—CHARLES WARING, Esq., Assoc.Inst.C.E., 2, Grosvenor Square, S.W.

John Clavell Mansel-Pleydell, Esq., Whatcombe, Blandford.

William Waring, Esq., 39, Prince's Gardens, Hyde Park, S.W., and Taverham Hall, Norwich.

James Clark, Esq., Street, Somerset.

Thomas Gibson Bowles, Esq., Cleeve Lodge, Hyde Park Gate, S.W.

George Deedes Warry, Esq., 46, Norfolk Square, Paddington, W., and Shapwick House, Bridgwater.

OFFICERS.—Gen. Man. & Sec., Robert A. Read; Auditor, Sydney Smith, Ethelburga House, Bishopsgate Street, E.C.; Solicitors, W. Toogood, 16, Parliament Street, Westminster, S.W., and W. T. Swayne, Glastonbury; Bankers, The Imperial Bank, Westminster Branch, London.

London Office—9, Victoria Chambers, Westminster, S.W.

267.—SOUTH EASTERN.

Incorporated by act of 21st June, 1836. The original scheme commenced at Reigate and terminated near Dover. In 1839 the company obtained power to run over the Croydon on payment of tolls; from Croydon to Reigate (12 miles) was constructed in the first instance by the Brighton; this company afterwards purchased for 340,000l. (with interest on the cost up to the date of purchase) one-half of that length from the Brighton, and to contribute a share of the expense of erecting a joint station at London Bridge. In 1843 the company obtained power to extend the main line into Dover (88 miles), to make a branch to Maidstone, to build the station at Bricklayers' Arms, and to make a branch thereto. In 1844 extensions were obtained to Canterbury, Ramsgate, and Margate, the Folkestone Branch and Harbour. In 1845 the Tunbridge Wells Branch was authorised; also the widening of the Greenwich; to make the Minster and Deal, and the Ashford and Hastings branches. In 1846 power was also obtained to construct branches from Rye to Rye Harbour; Tunbridge Wells to Hastings; to enlarge the Ashford Station, and to construct the "North Kent," being a line from a junction with the Greenwich Line, and terminating at Gravesend; also to extend that line to Rochester, by purchase of the Gravesend and Rochester Canal. The North Kent is extended to Maidstone. In 1852 the company obtained possession of the Reading, Guildford, and Reigate system, and in 1853 of the Whitstable Line and the Continental Steam Packets. The company are proprietors of the Pavilion Hotel, at Folkestone, and of the Lord Warden Hotel, at

Dover; also of the Folkestone Harbour, &c., under act of 27th June, 1843; the dues arising therefrom being entered to credit of revenue.

FURTHER PARLIAMENTARY POWERS:—

For list of Acts from 1855 to 1879, with short heads of the objects for which the various powers were sought, see the MANUAL for 1881, pages 332 and 333.

By act of 26th August, 1880, powers were obtained for the construction of the Godstone Village Extension Line (about ⅜ mile) and for extensions of time for the completion of sundry lines and works, &c., &c. New capital, 234,000*l*; borrowing powers, 78,000*l*.

By act of 11th August, 1881, powers were obtained for the construction of two new railways in the county of Kent, viz.:—The "Northfleet and Snodland Loop" (about 9¾ miles) and the "Rochester and Chatham Extension" (about 1 mile); for various other works and improvements; for the transfer of the Westerham, Hundred of Hoo, West Wickham, and Loose Valley undertakings; and for various other purposes. New capital, 399,000*l*.; borrowing powers, 133,000*l*.

1882—10th AUGUST.—Sundry extensions of time for completion of works; various alterations, new lines, widenings, improvements, and other purposes; transfer of Greenwich Dock Railway (act 1881) and Woodside undertakings. New capital, 380,000*l*.; borrowing powers, 126,000*l*.

1883—31st MAY.—Construction of Hundred of Hoo Pier, and for sundry other purposes.

1884—28th JULY.—Transfer to company of rights and powers of Elham Valley; extension of time for completion of various works; purchase of additional lands at sundry places, and other general purposes. New capital, 325,000*l*.; loans, 105,000*l*.

AMALGAMATIONS, LEASES, AGREEMENTS, &c.:—

BLACKFRIARS BRANCH.—This branch, which forms a junction with the Chatham Company's Line at Blackfriars, was opened for passenger traffic on the 1st June, 1878.

BROMLEY DIRECT.—Incorporated 16th July, 1874, for making a line from Bromley, Kent, and terminating by a junction with the South Eastern at Grove Park. Length, 1 mile 5 furlongs. Capital, 55,000*l*. in shares, which has all been called up at 10*l*. per share; in addition, 18,300*l*. on mortgage. The line was completed and opened for traffic on the 1st January, 1878, and after being worked at 50 per cent. of the gross receipts, which yielded dividends at about 4 per cent. per annum, the undertaking became vested in the South Eastern under act of 21st July, 1879, the purchase to take effect from that date, and the holders of Bromley stock to receive South Eastern 4½ per cent. preference stock in lieu of their holdings, exchanged at par.

CATERHAM.—Incorporated by 17 and 18 Vic., cap. 68 (1854). The lines run from the town of Caterham to the Brighton Line. Length, 4 miles 5 furlongs 1¼ chain. Opened on 5th August, 1856. By act of 21st July, 1859, this line was sold to the South Eastern for 15,200*l*., having cost 40,000*l*.

CHARING CROSS.—By act of 8th August, 1859, the South Eastern was authorised to subscribe 300,000*l*. to this undertaking, to participate in its management, and to work the line when opened. The amount was voted by meeting of 1st September, 1859, to be raised in 4½ per cent. preference shares. An extension to Cannon Street, with a bridge over the Thames, was authorised by act of 28th June, 1861, to which the South Eastern subscribed the further sum of 250,000*l*. By act of 17th May, 1861, the company was authorised to add to its contributions to the original Charing Cross scheme the sum of 350,000*l*., making in all 900,000*l*., to the lines from Charing Cross to Cannon Street, and to London Bridge. By act of 1863 the South Eastern was authorised to amalgamate the Charing Cross on terms to be agreed upon, which arrangement was carried into effect by resolutions adopted on the 25th August, 1864. By act of 4th July, 1864, the Charing Cross was authorised to raise new capital to the extent of 90,000*l*. in shares and 30,000*l*. on loan. Opened from London Bridge to Charing Cross in August, 1864; to Cannon Street on 1st September, 1866.

CRANBROOK AND PADDOCK WOOD.—See GENERAL INDEX.

DOVER AND DEAL.—This railway is the joint property of the South Eastern and London, Chatham, and Dover companies, and is under the management of a joint committee.

ELHAM VALLEY.—By act of 28th July, 1884, the rights and powers of this company were transferred to the South Eastern.—For other particulars, see MANUAL for 1884, page 90.

GREENWICH DOCK RAILWAY.—Incorporated by act of 11th August, 1881; vested in South Eastern by act of 10th August, 1882.

GREENWICH AND MAZE HILL EXTENSION.—This line was opened for local traffic on the 1st February, and through traffic on the 1st March, 1878.

Hundred of Hoo.—Incorporated by act of 21st July, 1879, for the construction of a line situate wholly in the county of Kent, from Shorne, by a junction with the North Kent Line of the South Eastern, to Stoke. Length, 9 miles 4 chains and 16 yards. Period for completion of works, five years. Agreements with South Eastern. Capital, 80,000*l.* in 10*l.* shares. with power to divide into "preferred" and "deferred" half-shares. Loans or debenture stock, 26,600*l.* By act of 2nd August, 1880, the company obtained powers to extend their line to St. James, Isle of Grain (about 3½ miles). Period for completion of works, 5 years New capital, 200,000*l.*, in ordinary or preference stock. Additional borrowing powers, 65,000*l.* *Medway Extension Capital.*—Under the powers of the acts mentioned above, the South Eastern issued the requisite new capital in 10*l.* minimum 4 per cent. shares, convertible, after further powers have been obtained for that purpose, into South Eastern 4 per cent. rent-charge stock; this new capital was allotted rateably to holders of not less than 1,500*l.* of South Eastern ordinary stock, in September last. The undertaking became vested in the South Eastern, under the latter company's act of 11th August, 1881, the shares of the vested company being exchanged for equivalent amounts of "South Eastern 4 per cent. Hundred of Hoo Company Stock," having a charge upon the receipts of the Hundred of Hoo undertaking, subject to any interest which may be due upon mortgages or debenture stocks.

London, Chatham, and Dover.—With a view to the avoidance of injurious competition, and the economising of working expenses in the conduct of the continental traffic, *viâ* Dover and Folkestone, an arrangement was concluded with this company in 1863, under Parliamentary sanction. The recent heads of agreement, for the fusion of the two companies (since abandoned), will be found in the *Appendix* to the Manual for 1877.—For further particulars, see London, Chatham, and Dover.

London and Greenwich.—See General Index.

Loose Valley.—Incorporated by act of 2nd August, 1877, for making three railways:—No. 1, wholly in Maidstone, Kent. Length, 3 furlongs 2·5 chains. No. 2, also wholly in Maidstone, with a junction with the South Eastern. Length, 9 chains. No. 3, from Maidstone to Loose. Length, 1 mile 4 chains. Period for completion of works, four years. Working arrangements with South Eastern. Capital, 36,000*l.* in 10*l.* shares, with powers to divide into "preferred" and "deferred" half-shares. Borrowing powers, 12,000*l.* By act of 9th July, 1880, the period for compulsory purchase of lands for the purposes of this undertaking was extended for one year from the period limited by the act of 1877. Under provisions of the South Eastern Company's Act, Session 1881, this undertaking has been transferred to, and now forms a portion of, the undertaking of that company.

Mid Kent.—Incorporated by act of 28th July, 1855, to construct a railway from near Beckenham, on the Farnborough Extension of the West London and Crystal Palace, to the North Kent Branch of the South Eastern, at Lewisham. Length, 4¼ miles. By act of 17th July, 1862, the company was authorised to make an extension to Addiscombe. Length, 3¼ miles. Capital, 40,000*l.* in shares and 15,000*l.* on loan. By 13th July, 1863, the company was authorised to raise additional capital to the extent of 15,000*l.*, at 5 per cent., and 5,000*l.* on loan. By act of 29th July, 1864, this company was amalgamated with the South Eastern, by purchase, at a premium of 60,000*l.*

Rye and Dungeness.—Incorporated 5th August, 1873, to construct a railway from the Rye Station of the South Eastern to Dungeness, with a pier at the latter place. Length, 10¾ miles. Capital, 130,000*l.* in 10*l.* shares and 43,333*l.* on loan. By act of 2nd August, 1875, the powers were transferred to the South Eastern, and the company dissolved.

Tunbridge Wells and Eastbourne.—See London, Brighton, and South Coast.

Westerham Valley.—Incorporated 24th July, 1876, to construct a line from the South Eastern, at Dunton Green, to Westerham. Length, about 5 miles. Capital, 66,000*l.* in 10*l.* shares; borrowing powers, 22,000*l.*, on mortgage or by debenture stock. Power to company and to South Eastern to enter into working agreements. The estimated cost of construction is 65,000*l.*; the South Eastern is to provide plant and work the line at 50 per cent. of its gross receipts, guaranteeing also that the share of net profits accruing to the Westerham Valley shall not be less than 2,750*l.* per annum; any excess profit to be divided between the two companies, the working company to have the right of purchasing the line at a moderate premium should they find it advantageous to do so. By South Eastern Act of 1881 this company was amalgamated with the South Eastern.

West Wickham and Hayes.—Incorporated by act of 9th July, 1880, for the construction and maintenance of a railway in the parishes of Beckenham, West Wickham, and Hayes, in the county of Kent. Length, 3¼ miles. Period for completion of works, 5 years. Working agreement with the South Eastern. Capital,

85,000*l.* in 10*l.* shares; borrowing powers, 28,380*l.* By the South Eastern Act of 11th August, 1881, this undertaking was transferred to that company as from the above date.

Woodside and South Croydon.—Incorporated by act of 6th August, 1880 (see Manual for 1882, page 366). Transferred to the South Eastern and London, Brighton, and South Coast, under the South Eastern Act of 10th August, 1882.

Division of Traffic with the London, Brighton, and South Coast.—The agreement for the division of competitive traffic, which commenced on the 1st February, 1869, and was sanctioned by Parliament, would have expired on the 1st February, 1879, but it has been renewed for a period of 10 years.

ACCOUNTS:—

The ordinary half-yearly meeting of this company was held on the 24th July, 1884, when the report and accounts then presented were adopted. The following is an abstract of these accounts made up to the 30th June, 1884, viz.:—

Capital.—*Authorised:* Shares and stock, 19,557,580*l.*; loans, 6,669,375*l.*; total, 26,226,955*l.* *Created or sanctioned:* Shares and stock, 16,520,080*l.*; loans, 5,395,744*l.*; total, 21,915,824*l.*

Receipts.

Stocks and shares, viz.:		
Ord. undivided ...	£3,186,370	
Preferred	2,861,920	
Deferred	2,861,920	
Ord. stock (1876)...	28	
Do. (1882)............	445,260	£
Do. (Charing Cross)	[illegible]9	= 9,355,557
Preference:—		
4½ per cent. stocks	£3,155,170	
5 per cent. stocks	2,640,435	
5½ pr cnt. annuiti	800,000	= 6,595,605
		£15,951,162
4 per cent. stock.—		
Preferential.........	£48,000	
Westerham	66,000	
Hundred of Hoo...	280,000	
West Wickham ...	85,000	= 479,000
Total stock and share capital		£16,430,162
Loan capital:—		
Debentures............	£299,000	
Debenture stock...	5,088,510	= 5,387,510
		£21,817,672
Balance		439,672
		£22,257,344

Expenditure.

Lines open for traffic, including the purchase of the Reading, Guildford, and Reigate, in payment of which annuities referred to per contra were issued	£19,279,429
Working stock	1,831,214
Steam Packets......................	297,760
Subscription to other railways	302,255
Charing Cross Hotel Purchase	447,340
Lines not yet commenced......	99,346
	£22,257,344

Estimated further expenditure on capital account:—

	Half-year ended 31st Dec., 1884.	In subsequent half-years.	Total.
Lines open for traffic	£100,000	£2,735,408	£586,951
Lines in course of construction.			21,134
Working stock			10,200
Steam vessels			...
Subscriptions to other railways			5,000
Works not yet commenced and in abeyance			2,212,123
			£2,835,408

To meet this prospective expenditure, the company's capital powers and other assets are as follow:—

Share and loan capital created but not yet received:—

Shares and loans...	£98,152
Share and loan capital authorised but not yet created	4,311,131
	£4,409,283
Less balance of capital overpaid	439,672
	£3,969,611

REVENUE.—Comparative view of the working of this undertaking for the last three half-years:—

Receipts.	1883. 30th June.	1883. 31st Dec.	1884. 30th June.
Passengers, parcels, horses, mails, &c.	£653,615	£791,568	£663,229
Merchandise, cattle, minerals, tolls, &c.	252,568	309,176	262,290
Steam packet service	31,703	37,338	33,210
Rents and hotel accounts (net)	51,053	48,449	49,946
Transfer fees	230	188	203
Lydd Company—interest on shares and stock	1,168	1,168	1,168
Submarine continental company—return of share capital	...	2,000	...
	£990,337	£1,189,887	£1,010,046
Expenses.	1883. 30th June.	1883. 31st Dec.	1884. 30th June
Maintenance of way, works, and stations	£73,159	£69,464	£66,372
Locomotive power	119,305	119,045	118,968
Carriage and wagon repairs	34,619	37,380	39,226
Traffic expenses	146,002	151,602	148,044
General charges	38,492	41,419	37,851
Law and Parliamentary	10,220	11,000	16,327
Compensation	4,621	6,123	5,548
Rates, taxes, Government duty, haulage, & tolls (net)	69,092	69,270	58,646
Steam packets	21,648	27,372	26,165
Canals, harbours, &c. (net)	2,882	3,095	5,600
Ordinary working expenses	£520,040	£535,770	£522,742
Preference charges, viz.:—			
Interest on loan capital and other interest (net)	135,394	130,386	133,369
Rent of leased lines	25,254	25,248	25,207
Reserve fund—transfer	5,000	...	...
Other amounts, preference dividends, and S. E. annuities	165,162	165,253	165,931
	£850,850	£856,657	£847,249
Net balances each half-year	£139,487	£333,230	£162,797
Balances brought from previous half-years	1,783	869	3,310
Balances available for dividend on ordinary stock.	£141,270	£334,099	£166,107
Dividends declared at 3, 7½, and 3½ per cent. per annum respectively	140,401	330,790	163,721
Surplus to next half-year's account	£869	£3,309	£2,386

Summary showing the comparative results of the last half-year's working as compared with that of 1883, viz.:—

Net balance 30th June, 1884...... £162,797	Thus:
„ 30th June, 1883...... 139,487	Gross traffic—increase £19,709
	Less:
	Working charges—inc... £2,702
	Pref. charges—decrease 6,303 = 3,601
Gain in 1884 .... £23,310	Net gain in 1884.............. £23,310

MILEAGE—*Authorised:* Lines owned, 370½; partly owned, 23¾; leased or rented, 14½; total, 408. *Constructed:* Lines owned, 350¾; partly owned, 20¾; leased or rented, 14½; total, 386. Foreign lines worked over, 22 miles. Total worked by engines, 408 miles.

The accounts are made up to 30th June and 31st December, and the meetings held in London in January and July in each year.

Scale of Voting.—One vote for 30*l.* stock up to 600*l.*; and one vote additional for every 150*l.* beyond the first 600*l.*

In transfers, Reading annuities may be described as so many "Perpetual annuities of 20*s.* 6*d.*, 15 Vic., cap. 103, of and in the undertaking called the S. E. R. Co.," &c.

No. of Directors—14. *Qualification*, 2,000*l.* of stock, held three months previous to their nomination.

DIRECTORS:

Chairman—Sir EDWARD WILLIAM WATKIN, Bart., M.P., Rose Hill, Northenden, Cheshire, and Charing Cross Hotel, Charing Cross, S W.

Deputy-Chairman—The Right Hon. Lord BRABOURNE, Smeeth, Kent.

Mons. Achille Adam, Boulogne-sur-Mer, France.

Alexander Beattie, Esq., Parkfield, Kingston Hill, Surrey.

The Hon. James Byng, Great Culverden, Tunbridge Wells, Kent.

Jonathan Mellor, Esq., Polefield, Prestwich, near Manchester.

James Whatman, Esq., Vinters, near Maidstone.

Col. Charles F. Surtees, Chalcott House, Long Ditton, Surrey.

William Mewburn, Esq., Wykham Park, Banbury, Oxon.

The Right Hon Lord Hothfield, Hothfields, Ashford, Kent, and 2, Chesterfield Gardens, Mayfair, W.

Adolphus W. Young, Esq., Hare Hatch House, Twyford, Berks, and 55A, Davies Street, Berkeley Square, W.

A M. Watkin, Esq., Dunedin Lodge, Folkestone, Kent.

The Hon. Alfred E. Gathorne Hardy, 22, Charles Street, Berkeley Square, W.

Sir George Russell, Bart., 19, Clifton Crescent, Folkestone, and Swallowfield Park, Reading, Berks.

OFFICERS.—Sec., John Shaw; Gen. Man., Myles Fenton; Assistant Sec., Robert Hudson; Deputy-Man., M. D. Tyrwhitt; Goods Man., J. Light, Bricklayers' Arms Station; Chief Res. Eng., Francis Brady, M.Inst.C.E.; Loco. Supt., James Stirling; Carriage and Wagon Supt., William Wainwright; Chief Acct., George Whateley; Acct., John H. Skelton; Store Keeper, Joseph Barnes; Auditors, William Cunliffe Pickersgill, Blendon Hall, Bexley, Kent; and John Thomson Pagan, Oak Lodge, London Road, Guildford, Surrey.

Head Offices—London Bridge Station, S.E.

268.—SOUTHERN OF IRELAND.

Incorporated by act of 5th July, 1865, to construct a line from the Great Southern and Western, at Thurles, to Clonmel, on the Waterford and Limerick. Length, 24¼ miles. Capital, 171,000*l.* in shares and 57,000*l.* on loan. Arrangements with Great Southern and Western and Waterford and Limerick.

By act of 23rd July, 1866, the company obtained power to make several deviations, and also to construct three branches. Length, 9½ miles. Capital, 60,000*l.* in shares and 20,000*l.* on loan. By Certificate of the Board of Trade, an extension of time for completion of works was obtained in 1869.

By act of 21st August, 1871, the company obtained another extension of time till 1874 in which to complete the works, and by act of 16th August, 1876, the time for completion of works was further extended as follows:—For the works authorised by the act of 1865 till 5th August, 1877; for the works authorised by act of 1866 till 5th August, 1879; and for the works authorised by the act of 1873 till 5th August, 1879.

By act of 1873 the company was authorised to make a branch railway to Cashel, to be called the "Cashel Extension."

By act of 1874 the company was authorised to raise further capital, consisting of 20,000*l.* in 10*l.* shares, to form part of the "Main Line Share Capital," and to be applied to the general purposes of the undertaking.

By act of 1876 the time limited for the completion of the main line, the colliery extension, and the Cashel Extension, were respectively extended; the main line until 5th August, 1877, and the two extensions until 5th August, 1879.

By act of 4th July, 1878, the time for completion of the "colliery" and "Cashel" extensions was extended until the 5th August, 1882, and the company was authorised to raise new capital for main line purposes to the extent of 10,000*l.*: borrowing powers, 3,300*l.*

By act of 9th July, 1880, powers were obtained for the abandonment of the Cashel Extension.

WATERFORD AND LIMERICK.—At a special meeting of the Waterford and Limerick, held on the 18th November, 1874, the directors were authorised to subscribe 50,000*l.* to the Southern of Ireland, and to issue 5 per cent. 50*l.* preference shares for that purpose.

Eight miles, from Clonmel to Fethard, was opened for traffic 23rd June, 1879. The remainder of main line, from Fethard to Thurles, was opened in June, 1880.

No. of Directors—12; quorum 3. *Qualification*, 250*l.*

DIRECTORS:

Chairman—W. FORBES, Esq., Grafton Club, Grafton Street, W.
Deputy-Chairman—General J. S. BROWNRIGG, C.B., 28, Lowndes Street, S.W.

John Graham, Esq., 7, Westminster Chambers, S.W.
D. P. Mc.Ewen, Esq., 97, Cannon Street, E.C.
Reginald F. Williams, Esq., J.P., 9, Cheniston Gardens, W.
Jerome J. Guiry, Esq., J.P., Peppardstown, Fethard, Tipperary.
John Riall, Esq., Heywood, Clonmel.

Directors nominated by the Waterford and Limerick Company:—

A. O'Connor, Esq., 86, Merrion Square, Dublin.
T. McMahon, Esq., Domiuick Street, Cork.
W. Henry, Esq. 15, Fitzwilliam Square, Dublin.

OFFICERS.—Sec., George F. Quinton; Engs., Sir Charles Fox and Sons, M.Inst.C.E.; Auditors, Sir Henry M. Brownrigg, Bart., and James Hutt.

Offices—13, Little Queen Street, Westminster, S.W.

269.—SOUTHPORT AND CHESHIRE LINES EXTENSION.

Incorporated by act of 11th August, 1881, for the construction and maintenance of a railway from Aintree Junction to Birkdale, Southport. Length, 13 miles 7 chains. Working agreements with Cheshire Lines Committee, Midland, Great Northern, and Manchester, Sheffield, and Lincolnshire.

By act of 1882 an extension was authorised from Birkdale to Southport. Length, about 1 mile. The line was opened for passenger traffic on the 1st September, 1884.

CAPITAL.—*Authorised:* Shares, 370,000*l.*; loans, 123,000*l.*; total, 493,000*l.* The following statement of share capital created shows the proportion received to 31st December, 1884:—

DESCRIPTION.	Created.	Received.
Ordinary shares, 26,500 of 10*l.* each	£265,000	£265,000
5 per cent. perpetual preference shares, 1882, 10,500 of 10*l.* each	105.000	105,000
	£370,000	£370,000

No. of Directors.—Maximum, 5; minimum, 3; quorum, 3 and 2. *Qualification*, 50 shares.

DIRECTORS:

Chairman—THOMAS WELD-BLUNDELL, Esq., J.P., Ince Blundell, near Liverpool.

Deputy-Chairman—DAVID RADCLIFFE, Esq., J.P., Formby Hall, Formby, near Liverpool.

Samuel Boothroyd, Esq., J.P., Southport.
George Chamberlain, Esq., J.P., Liverpool and Southport.
George C. Dobell, Esq., Grove Mount, Wavertree, Liverpool.

All eligible for re-election.

OFFICERS.—Sec., Alfred Williams; Engs., James Brunlees, M.Inst.C.E., Westminster, S.W., and Charles Douglas Fox, M.Inst.C.E., Westminster, S.W.; Solicitors, Sharman, Ayrton, and Radcliffe, 9, Cook Street, Liverpool; Bankers, North and South Wales Bank Limited, Liverpool, and branches.

Station and Offices—Lord Street, Southport.

270.—SOUTHSEA.

Incorporated by act of 26th August, 1880, for the construction and maintenance of a railway at Southsea for purposes of interchange of traffic between the London and South Western and London, Brighton, and South Coast (length, about 1¼ mile), and for an additional terminal station at Southsea, which has a population of over 30,000. Period for completion, 3 years. Capital, 50,000*l.* in 10*l.* shares. Borrowing powers, 16,600*l.* 4 per cent. on cost guaranteed by the South Western.

By act of 2nd August, 1883, the company was authorised to abandon certain portions of the railway authorised by their previous act, and to construct another junction curve in lieu thereof, and the agreement mentioned below was confirmed.

By the London and South Western Act, 20th August, 1883, the line is to be worked by that company in perpetuity (under certain conditions with the Brighton Company); the lessees to pay, on completion of the line, an annual rental equal to 4 per cent. per annum on the amount expended on the undertaking.

No. of Directors—3; quorum, 2. *Qualification*, 30 shares.

FIRST DIRECTORS:

Edwin Galt, Esq.
Joseph Lush, Esq.
Charles James Mew, Esq.

Solicitors, R. W. Ford and Son, Portsmouth.

271.—SOUTH WALES MINERAL.

Incorporated by act of 15th August, 1853, for a line from Briton Ferry Station of the South Wales to Glyncorrwg, Glamorganshire, and a branch from Baglan to Mitchelstone-super-Avon and Forcedwn Colliery. Length, 12½ miles. Capital, 85,000*l.* in 10*l.* shares and 28,000*l.* on loan.

By act of 25th May, 1855, the line was leased to the Glyncorrwg Coal Company, for 30 years, at 5 per cent. for two years; 5½ per cent. for the next 14 years; and 6 per cent. for remaining 14 years of lease; but a subsequent agreement has been entered into, for which, see below.

By act of 1st August, 1861, the company was authorised to construct an extension to Briton Ferry Docks. Length, 1½ mile. New capital, 30,000*l.* in shares and 10,000*l.* on loan.

By act of 29th July, 1864, the company obtained power to extend the undertaking from Glyncorrwg to Blaen Afon and other places. Length, 4½ miles. New capital, 30,000*l.* in shares and 10,000*l.* on loan.

By act of 16th July, 1874, the arrears of dividend on preference shares are capitalised, and future arrears are to be surrendered. Power to raise 22,210*l.* by shares or stock and 35,000*l.* by the creation of debenture stock, at a rate of interest not exceeding 5 per cent. per annum.

The railway is now worked by a new company, called the Glyncorrwg Colliery Company Limited, 1880, under a temporary agreement, and the Court of Chancery has appointed a receiver.

CAPITAL.—The receipts to 30th September, 1882, were—from shares and stock, including rent-charges capitalised (1,000*l.*), 158,960*l.*, and from loans, 48,000*l.*; together, 206,960*l.* The expenditure of 230,839*l.* left a balance against the account of 23,879*l.*

No. of Directors.—Maximum, 9; minimum, 6; quorum, 3. *Qualification*, 50 shares.

DIRECTORS:

Chairman—EDWARD JAMES PHILLIPS, Esq., Woodlands, Pontypool, Monmouthshire.

Arthur T. Pratt Barlow, Esq., 47, Norfolk Square, Hyde Park, W.
Wollaston Frank Pym, Esq., Stoneleigh, Ewell, Epsom.
Thomas Walker, Esq., The Grove, Tettenhall, Wolverhampton, Staffordshire.
F. C. Norton, Esq., 2, New Square, Lincoln's Inn, W.C.
H. G. Rawson, Esq., 23, Old Square, Lincoln's Inn, W.C.

OFFICERS.—Sec. and Receiver, Thomas John Woods, 6, Victoria Street, Westminster, S.W.; Solicitors, Campbell, Reeves, and Hooper, 17, Warwick Street, Regent Street, W.; Bankers, Glyn, Mills, and Co., Lombard Street, E.C.

Offices—6, Victoria Street, Westminster, S.W.

272.—SOUTHWOLD.

Incorporated 24th July, 1876, to construct a line from the Great Eastern, at Halesworth, to Southwold. Length, 8¾ miles. Gauge, 3ft. Capital, 40,000*l.* in 10*l.* shares; borrowing powers, 13,000*l.* on mortgage or by debenture stock.

The capital was increased under the (additional capital) certificate, 1880, by 9,000*l.* of preference share and 3,000*l.* of debentures. These have been issued, bearing interest at 5 per cent.

The line was opened for passenger and goods traffic on the 24th September, 1879.

REVENUE.—The receipts for the six months ended June, 1884, show an increase in passenger and parcels traffic, and a slight falling off in goods and minerals, owing to the mild weather during the half-year. The working expenses show a slight increase, incurred by additional material for maintenance of way, &c. The traffic, during the six months ended 31st December, exhibited a very satisfactory increase under all heads.

No. of Directors—6; minimum, 3; quorum, 4, 3, and 2. *Qualification*, 25 shares.

DIRECTORS:

Chairman—RICHARD C. RAPIER, Esq., 5, Westminster Chambers, S.W.

Managing Director—ARTHUR C. PAIN, Esq., 5, Victoria Street, S.W.

J. P. Cooper, Esq., B.A., Howden, Yorkshire.
G. Wells Owen, Esq., 7, Westminster Chambers, S.W.
R. A. Withall, Esq., 29, Great George Street, Westminster, S.W.

OFFICERS.—Sec., H. Carne; Bankers, Lacon, Youell, and Co., Southwold.

Offices—5, Victoria Street, S.W.

273.—SPILSBY AND FIRSBY.

Incorporated by act of 7th July, 1865, to construct a line from Spilsby to a junction with the East Lincolnshire at Firsby. Length, 4 miles. Capital, 25,000*l.* in shares and 8,333*l.* on loan. Arrangements with Great Northern, which works the line for 60 per cent. of the traffic receipts.

Revenue.—The company has in the past earned dividends upon its ordinary capital at the rate of 2 per cent. per annum, but for the half-years ended 31st January and 31st July, 1883, dividends were earned at the rate of 4 per cent. per annum.

Capital.—The expenditure on this account to 31st July, 1883, amounted to 46,501*l.*, the receipts to the same date having been as under:—

Ordinary 10*l.* shares	£25,000
Loans at 4½ per cent.	8,333
Receipts as per published accounts	13,168

No. of Directors—5; quorum, 3. *Qualification*, 200*l.*

DIRECTORS.

Chairman—The Rev. EDWARD RAWNSLEY, Raithby Hall.

Lieut.-Col. Henry Valentine Grantham, West Keal Hall.
Harwood Mackinder, Esq., Langton Grange.
Major John Wilby Preston, Dalby Park.
Benjamin Robinson, Esq., Spilsby.

OFFICERS.—Sec., George Walker; Auditor, T. J. Wood.

Offices—Spilsby, Lincolnshire.

274.—STAINES AND WEST DRAYTON.

Incorporated by act of 7th July, 1873, to construct a line from the London and South Western, at Staines, to the Great Western, at West Drayton. Length, 5¼ miles. Capital, 48,000*l.* in 10*l.* shares and 16,000*l.* on loan. Working arrangements authorised with Great Western and London and South Western.

By act of 17th June, 1878, a revival of the powers conferred upon the company was authorised, and the period for completion of works was extended until 7th July, 1881. By act of 1881, mentioned below, the time was further extended for 3 years.

By act of 11th August, 1881, a diversion of this railway was authorised from Iver to Hillingdon; length, about ¼ mile. Period for completion of works, 3 years. New capital, 27,000*l.*; borrowing powers, 9,000*l.*

By act of 2nd August, 1883, a deviation was authorised, about 1 mile in length, into the town of Staines. Additional capital, 45,000*l.*; borrowing powers, 15,000*l.*

Opened from West Drayton to Colnbrook 9th August, 1884.

No. of Directors—3; quorum, 2. *Qualification*, 200*l.*

DIRECTORS:

Chairman—Alderman W. J. R. COTTON, M.P., 47, St. Mary Axe, E.C.

Richard Michell, Esq., 3, Kensington Park Gardens, W.
George Mortimer, Esq.

OFFICERS.—Sec., A. E. Bolter; Solicitors, Le Brasseur and Oakley, 12, New Court, Lincoln's Inn, W.C.

Offices—Paddington Station, W.

275.—STOCKSBRIDGE.

Incorporated by act of 30th June, 1874, for making a line from the Manchester, Sheffield, and Lincolnshire, at Deepcar, to Stocksbridge. Length, 1 mile 7 furlongs. Original capital, 33,000*l.* in 3,300 shares of 10*l.* each, and 11,000*l.* on loan. By a certificate of the Board of Trade, dated 1st May, 1877, the company was authorised to raise 36,000*l.* by the issue of 5 per cent. preference shares, and to borrow a further sum of 12,000*l.* on mortgage. The whole of the share capital of 33,000*l.* and 36,000*l.* has been issued and 15,000*l.* borrowed on mortgage. The Manchester, Sheffield, and Lincolnshire has power to subscribe.

Capital.—Received to 30th June, 1883:—

Ordinary 10*l.* shares	£33,000
100*l.* 5 per cent. preference shares, guaranteed by S. Fox and Co. Limited.	36,000
Loans at 5 per cent.	15,000
	£84,000
Amount expended	83,450

No. of Directors—3; quorum, 2. *Qualification*, 200*l.*

DIRECTORS:

Chairman—SAMUEL FOX, Esq., Townend House, Deepcar, near Sheffield.

Frederick Bardwell, Esq., J.P., Worksop. | Horace Walker, Esq., Rutledge, Sheffield.

OFFICERS.—Sec., Joshua G. Jeffery, Stocksbridge, Deepcar, near Sheffield; Eng., Frederick Fowler, C.E., Sheffield; Auditors, James Halliday, Manchester, and Stanley Pearson, Manchester; Solicitors, Burdekin and Co., 41, Norfolk Street, Sheffield.

Offices—Stocksbridge Works, Deepcar, near Sheffield.

276.—STRATFORD-UPON-AVON, TOWCESTER, AND MIDLAND JUNC.

(LATE EASTON NESTON MINERAL AND TOWCESTER, ROADE, AND OLNEY JUNCTION).

Incorporated by act of 15th August, 1879, for the construction and maintenance of eight short lines, situate in the counties of Northampton and Buckingham, with junctions at various places in connection with the East and West Junction, Northampton and Banbury Junction, Bedford and Northampton, and London and North Western (at Roade) lines. Length, about 12 miles; period for completion, 5 years. Capital, 220,000*l.* in 10*l.* shares, with power to divide into "preferred" and "deferred" half-shares. Loans or debenture stock, 70,300*l.*

By act of 10th August, 1882, the name of the company was changed from Easton Neston, &c., to its present title, the period for completion of works was extended until 15th August, 1886, and the capital was reduced to 200,000*l.*, with borrowing powers restricted to 66,600*l.*

By act of 25th August, 1883, powers were obtained for the working of the East and West Junction by this company under a joint committee, and for the issue of new capital, 120,000*l.*, and loans, &c., 40,000*l.*

No. of Directors.—Maximum, 6; minimum, 4; quorum, 3. *Qualification*, 20 shares.

TRUSTEES:

Samuel Lloyd, Esq., J.P., Sparkbrook, Birmingham.

Henry Merrick, Esq., Bradford-upon-Avon.

DIRECTORS:

Chairman—Sir THOMAS GEORGE FERMOR-HESKETH, Bart., Easton Neston Hall, Towcester.

R. W. Abbotts, Esq., Burton-on-Trent.

Alfred Barratt, Esq., M.D., Great Hampton Row, Birmingham.

Henry Downing, Esq., The Elms, Stratford-upon-Avon.

Thomas Coombs, Esq., 9, Bridge Street, Westminster, S.W.

George Hall, Esq., Merton Road, Wimbledon.

OFFICERS.—Sec., T. Hunt; Eng., Charles Liddell, 24, Abingdon Street, S.W.; Solicitors, Newman, Stretton, and Hilliard, 75 and 76, Cornhill, E.C.; Bankers, Lloyds, Barnetts, and Bosanquet's Bank Limited, 60, Lombard Street, E.C., and Stratford-upon-Avon.

Offices—21, Great Winchester Street, E C., and Corn Exchange, Stratford-upon-Avon.

277.—STRATHENDRICK AND ABERFOYLE.

Incorporated by act of 12th August, 1880, for making railways from the Blane Valley to the Forth and Clyde Junction at Gartness, and from the Forth and Clyde Junction to Aberfoyle. Length, about 8¼ miles. Period for completion, 5 years. Working arrangements with the Blane Valley, North British, and Forth and Clyde Junction. Capital, 50,000*l.* in 10*l.* shares; borrowing powers, 16,666*l.*

Meetings half-yearly, in March and September; quorum, six shareholders present in person or by proxy, holding in the aggregate not less than 2,000*l.* in the capital of the company. Accounts made up to 31st January and 31st July in each year.

No. of Directors.—Maximum, 7; minimum, 3; quorum, 4 and 2 respectively.

DIRECTORS:

Chairman—JAMES MURRAY, Esq., Catter House, Drymen.

James Blackburn, Esq., Killearn House.

John Coubrough, Esq., Blanefield, Strathblane.

James Provan, Esq., 69, St. Vincent Street, Glasgow.

Gilbert Beith, Esq., 19, West Nile Street, Glasgow.

Robert Young, Esq., 4, West Nile Street, Glasgow.

Hugh Kennedy, Esq., Contra Tor, Partick.

OFFICERS.—Sec., James Keyden; Auditors, Alex. Moore and J. Gibson-Fleming.

Office—186, West George Street, Glasgow.

278.—SUTTON AND WILLOUGHBY.

Incorporated by act of 28th July, 1884, for the construction of railways from Sutton-le-Marsh to Willoughby, Lincolnshire. Length, 7¼ miles. Period for completion, 5 years. Capital, 60,000*l.* in 20*l.* shares; loans, 20,000*l.*

No. of Directors—3; quorum, 2. *Qualification*, 15 shares.

FIRST DIRECTORS:

Charles Brenton Basden, Esq.
Richard Brooks, Esq.
Edmund Davy, Esq.

279.—SWANAGE.

Incorporated by act of 18th July, 1881, for the construction of a railway from Swanage to the parish of Lady Saint Mary, Wareham, by a junction with the Southampton and Dorchester Branch of the London and South Western. Length, about 10¼ miles. Period for completion, 5 years. Working agreements with the London and South Western. Capital, 90,000*l.* in 10*l.* shares, with powers for division into "preferred" and "deferred" half-shares; borrowing powers, 30,000*l.*

In accordance with the terms upon which the shares were issued, interest at the rate of 4 per cent. per annum was paid on the 30th August last on amounts paid up.

No. of Directors.—Maximum, 5; minimum, 3; quorum, 3 and 2. *Qualification*, 40 shares.

DIRECTORS:

Chairman—GEORGE BURT, Esq., Purbeck House, Swanage, Dorset, and Westminster, S.W.

William Lansdowne Beale, Esq., Waltham St. Lawrence, Twyford, Berks.
Charles S. Mortimer, Esq., Wigmore, Holmwood, Surrey.
John Charles Robinson, Esq., Newton Manor, Swanage, Dorset, and 10, York Place, Portman Square, W.
Stephen Soames, Esq., Cranford Hall, Kettering.

OFFICERS.—Sec., David S. Derry; Engs., Galbraith and Church, 1, Victoria Street, Westminster, S.W.; Auditors, Percy Mortimer and N. Tapp; Solicitors, Beale, Marigold, Beale, and Groves, 28, Great George Street, Westminster, S.W., and J. J. Freeman, 2, Poet's Corner, Westminster, S.W.; Bankers, Williams, Deacon, and Co., 20, Birchin Lane, E.C.

Offices—22, Great Winchester Street, E.C.

280.—TAFF VALE.

Incorporated 21st June, 1836, to construct a railway from Merthyr Tydfil, in Glamorganshire, to the new docks at Cardiff, with two short branches. Length, 31¾ miles. Capital, 300,000*l.* in 100*l.* shares and 100,000*l.* on loan.

FURTHER PARLIAMENTARY POWERS.—For list of Acts from 1840 to 1879, with short heads showing the objects for which the various powers were obtained, see the MANUAL for 1881, page 344.

By act of 12th July, 1882, the company was authorised to make three small branches at Merthyr Tydvil; acquire certain additional lands; to extend time for completion of railway authorised by act of 1879; to merge the irredeemable stock with the debenture stock; and to raise new capital, 60,000*l.* in shares and 20,000*l.* in loans.

By act of 2nd August, 1883, the company was authorised to make a new railway at Merthyr. New capital, 100,000*l.*; loans, 33,000*l.*

By act of 28th July, 1884, the company was authorised to make a short branch at Cardiff; acquire additional lands; and an agreement with the Bute trustees as to storage, sidings, and working of traffic, was confirmed. New capital, 100,000*l.* in shares and 33,000*l.* by loans.

LEASES:—

ABERDARE.—Incorporated by act of 31st July, 1845, for construction of a line at Aberdare, and terminating by a junction with the Taff Vale, near Ynis Meyric, with branch to Cwmbach Colliery. Length, 8¾ miles. Leased in perpetuity to the Taff Vale, at 10 per cent. per annum.

COWBRIDGE.—This line is leased to the Taff Vale for 999 years, commencing 1st January, 1876. For the first two years, 1876 and 1877, the rental was 1,500*l*., after which it increased 100*l*. per annum up to 2,000*l*., at which it will remain for the rest of the term.—See GENERAL INDEX.

DARE VALLEY.—Leased to Taff Vale on same terms as Llantrissant and Taff Vale.—See GENERAL INDEX.

LLANTRISSANT AND TAFF VALE.—Leased to the Taff Vale for 999 years, the Taff Vale undertaking to pay the Llantrissant 5 per cent. upon share capital, interest upon debenture debt for the time being, with an additional annual payment of 250*l*. for management.—See GENERAL INDEX.

PENARTH HARBOUR.—This undertaking is leased to the Taff Vale for 999 years at 5*l*. 5*s*. per cent. in perpetuity.—See GENERAL INDEX.

PENARTH EXTENSION.—See GENERAL INDEX.

RHONDDA VALLEY AND HIRWAIN JUNCTION.—See GENERAL INDEX.

TREFERIG VALLEY.—Leased to Taff Vale for 999 years from 30th June, 1883, the Taff Vale undertaking to pay debenture interest, 4 per cent. upon share capital, and 50*l*. per annum for management expenses.

ACCOUNTS:—

REVENUE.—The receipts and expenditure on this account for the half-years ended 31st December, 1883, and 30th June, 1884, were as under:—

	Dec. 31, 1883.	June 30, 1884.
Gross receipts	£383,207	£388,145
Expenditure	196.578	196,928
Net revenue	£186,629	£191,217
Sundry credits, including balance brought in	7,856	7,331
Total net revenue	£194.485	£198,548
Less interest on debentures and fixed charges	48,586	49,751
Balance available for dividend	£145,899	£148,797
Preference dividends	27,729	27,729
	£118,170	£121,068
Ordinary dividend at 10 per cent. per annum, payable, less income tax, on 28th February and 31st August respectively	67,184	70,165
	£50,986	£50,903
Bonus of 7 and 8 per cent. per annum each half-year respectively on ordinary stock and preference stock No. 1	45,260	47,049
Balance carried forward	£5,726	£3,854

The preference No. 1 dividends are accumulative and payable on the 8th April and 8th October, and the ordinary dividends on the 22nd February and 22nd August respectively; the bonus distributions at the same times, all subject to the income tax.

CAPITAL.—The following statement of stock and share capital in order of priority shows the proportion created and received to 30th June, 1884:—

Description.		Created.	Received.
Preference stock No. 1 (act 1840), 5 per cent. minimum		£165,000	£165,000
4½ per cent. perpetual preference stock (acts 1844 and 1862)		58.225	58,225
5 " " " (act 1844)		66,775	66,775
5 " preferential stock (act 1873)		300,000	300,000
6 " preference stock (1877)		300,000	300,000
Ordinary stock		1,403,300	1,403,300
		£2,293,300	£2,293,300
Deduct—Capitalised interest	£78,000		
Discount on issue of preference stock No. 1	30,000		
	£108,000		
Less premiums on shares sold	77,154	...	30,846
		£2,293,300	£2,262,454

The receipts and expenditure on this account to 30th June, 1884, have been as under:—

Received.		Expended.	
Stock and shares	£2,262,454	Lines open for traffic	£2,458,824
Debenture stocks	482,275	Lines in course of construction	85,904
	£2,744,729	Working stock	350,300
Balance	155,299	Subscription to Cowbridge Co.	5,000
	£2,900,028		£2,900,028

The estimate of further expenditure required 124,950*l.* for the half-year ended 31st December, 1884, that for subsequent periods being pronounced "uncertain." The capital powers, &c., showed an available balance to meet this expenditure of 52,426*l.*

MILEAGE.—The following statement shows the mileage of the undertaking, as existing at 30th June, 1884:—

	Authorised.		Constructed.		Worked.	
	Miles.	Ch.	Miles.	Ch.	Miles.	Ch.
Lines owned by company	57	20¼	53	8¼	51	48
Lines partly owned	...	...	...	...	0	35½
Lines leased or rented	42	25½	37	42	37	20½
	99	45¾	90	50¼	89	23¾

Constructing or to be constructed, 9 miles 56¾ chains. Foreign lines worked over, 6 miles 46¾ chains.

DOCKS.—Area of docks leased by company, 23 acres.

BUTE DOCKS.—Negotiations are in progress for the acquisition by the company of the Bute Docks. The purchase money payable to the Marquis of Bute's trustees, if the bill deposited receive Parliamentary sanction, will be 862,500*l.* ordinary stock, and 750,000*l.* 4 per cent. preference stock of the Taff Vale. The company to also pay the amount expended on the new Roath Dock now in course of construction, and certain royalties.

NEW CAPITAL.—On the 26th August, 1879, the proprietary sanctioned the issue of new capital to the extent of 300,000*l.* This capital was issued in 11*l.* 10*s.* shares, bearing preferential interest at 6 per cent. per annum, payable out of the profits of each year, and allotted to the holders of ordinary and preference No. 1 stocks at the rate of one new share for every 50*l.* of their holdings. In October, 1881, 10,000 new ordinary shares were allotted at par to the holders of ordinary and preference stock No. 1, the rate of allotment being 1 new share for every 127*l.* 10*s.* of stock held. These 10*l.* shares were converted into ordinary stock at the half-yearly meeting on the 22nd August, 1882.

On 7th December, 1882, 19,330 new ordinary 10*l.* shares were created and alloted to the holders of ordinary and preference stock No. 1, in the ratio of one new share for about every 70*l.* stock held. These shares were converted into ordinary stock at the half-yearly meeting on 12th February, 1884.

On 11th September, 1884, 27,470 new ordinary 10*l.* shares were created and allotted to the holders of ordinary and preference stock No. 1, in the ratio of one new share for about every 57*l.* stock held.

The accounts are made up to 30th June and 31st December, and the statutory meetings are held in February and August in every year.

TRANSFER DEPARTMENT QUERIES AND REPLIES.

QUERIES.	REPLIES.
Transfer form—ordinary or special?	Ordinary.
Fee per deed?	2*s.* 6*d.*
Ditto if more sellers than one?	2*s.* 6*d.* per deed.
May several classes of stock be transferred on one deed?	Yes.
Are certificates required to accompany transfers?	Yes.
What amounts of stock are transferable, and are parts of 1*l.* sterling allowed to be transferred?	Any amount, but not fractions of 1*l.*
To what officer should transfer communications be sent?	The Secretary.
In acceptances, renunciations, &c., of allotments of new stock, proxies, or other forms sent to holders in a joint account, what signatures are required?	All parties interested.

Scale of Voting.—20 votes for first 20 shares, and then one vote for every 5 shares.
No. of Directors—10. *Qualification*, 1,000*l*. in ordinary stock.

DIRECTORS:

Chairman—4 JAMES INSKIP, Esq., Bristol.
Deputy-Chairman—4 GEORGE FISHER, Esq., Cardiff.

2 Reginald Wyndham Butterworth, Esq., Henbury, near Bristol.
Hubert Churchill Gould, Esq., St. Hilliary, Cowbridge.
3 Joseph Haynes Nash, Esq., Rodney Place, Clifton, Bristol.
2 Steuart Fripp, Esq., Cambridge Park, Bristol.
1 Samuel Jones, Esq., Pembroke Road, Clifton, Bristol.
1 Henry Bourchier Osborne Savile, Esq., Rodney Place, Clifton, Bristol.
2 Francis Edmund Stacey, Esq., Llandough Castle, Cowbridge.
3 Charles Henry Williams, Esq., Roath Court, Cardiff.

1, Retire in 1885; 2, 1886; 3, 1887; 4, 1888; all eligible for re-election.

OFFICERS.—Res. Director, George Fisher; Sec., James G. Nicholson; Eng. and Carriage and Wagon Supt., H. O. Fisher; Traffic Manager, James Hurman; Goods Supt., John Jones; Accountant, Sidney Coleman; Loco. Supt., T. Hurry Riches; Storekeeper, William Bevan; Auditors, Wilberforce Tribe and John Curtis, Bristol; Solicitor, J. P. Ingledew; Bankers, National Provincial Bank of England Limited, Cardiff, Bristol, and London.

Head Offices—Cardiff.

281.—TAL-Y-LLYN.

Incorporated by act of 5th July, 1865, to construct a line from the Aberystwyth and Welsh Coast, at Towyn, towards Tal-y-llyn. Length, 6¾ miles. Gauge, 2ft. 3in. Capital, 15,000*l*. in shares and 5,000*l*. on loan.

No. of Directors—6; minimum, 3; quorum, 3 and 2. *Qualification*, 300*l*.

Managing Director—WILLIAM McCONNEL, Esq., Prestwich, and Ancoats, Manchester.

OFFICERS.—Sec. and Man., W. H. McConnel; Solicitors, Howell and Morgan, Machynlleth.

Offices—Towyn, Merioneth.

282.—TEIGN VALLEY.

Originally incorporated in 1863, and revived by act of 10th August, 1872, to construct a line from the Moretonhampstead and South Devon, near Bovey Tracey, to Chudleigh and Doddiscombsleigh, with two short branch lines therefrom. Length, about 10 miles. Capital, 72,000*l*. in shares, "preferred" and "deferred," and 24,000*l*. on loan or by debenture stock. Broad gauge.

By act of 2nd August, 1875, the company was authorised to extend their line to the London and South Western at Crediton. Length, 9¼ miles. New capital, 150,000*l*. in extension shares and 50,000*l*. on loan or by debenture stock; extension capital not to participate in general profits. Power to enter into working agreements with the London and South Western and South Devon, or either of them.

By act of 8th August, 1878, the company was authorised to make certain alterations, &c., in the original line, and the time for completion of works, authorised by act of 1875, was extended until 2nd August, 1883. Powers were also obtained for sundry other purposes.

By act of 26th August, 1880, the company was authorised to abandon a portion of the line situate at Crediton, and to enter into traffic arrangements with the Great Western. New capital, 40,000*l*.; borrowing powers, 13,300*l*.

By act of 11th August, 1881, the company obtained powers to create 24,000*l*. in "A" debenture stock (to be a first charge upon the undertaking), 15,000*l*. in "B" debenture stock, and 20,000*l*. in "C" debenture stock; the proceeds of issue to be applied to the general purposes of the company.

By act of 19th May, 1882, part of the extension railway, from Ready Bridge to Doddiscombsleigh, authorised by act of 1875, was abandoned, and the existing railway defined as from Bovey Tracey to Doddiscombsleigh.

By act of 14th July, 1884, the company was authorised to issue new capital to the extent of 6,000*l*. in "A" debenture stock.

AGREEMENT WITH GREAT WESTERN.—The following is copied from the Great Western report for the half-year ended 31st December, 1881, viz.:—"By this agreement provision is made for the working of the Teign Valley by this company at 55 per cent. of the receipts, the interest on the debenture debt of that company, not exceeding 1,200*l*. a year, being a charge on the gross receipts. The railway, which is nearly completed, extends from the Chudleigh Road Station, on the Moretonhampstead Branch of the South Devon, to Doddiscombsleigh, a distance of about 4 miles."

No. of Directors—6; maximum, 7; quorum, 3. *Qualification*, 500*l*.

DIRECTORS:

Chairman—Sir LAWRENCE PALK, Bart., Haldon House, Exeter, and Grosvenor Gardens, S.W.

Sir George Bowyer, Bart., D.C.L., Radley Park, Berkshire.
Edward Gulson, Esq., Teignmouth.
William Kitson, Esq., Torquay.
Thomas Eales Rogers, Esq., Waye, Ashburton, Devon.
Isaac Baruch Toogood, Esq., Torquay.
R. J. Jenkins, Esq.

OFFICERS.—Eng., Thomas Myers, London; Solicitor, W. Toogood, 16, Parliament Street, Westminster, S.W.

283.—TILBURY AND GRAVESEND TUNNEL JUNCTION.

Incorporated by act of 10th August, 1882, for the construction and maintenance of three new lines at and near Gravesend. Period for completion, 5 years. Running powers to the London, Tilbury, and Southend. Capital, 450,000*l*. in 10*l*. shares, with powers to divide into "preferred" and "deferred" half-shares; borrowing powers, 150,000*l*. A bill has been deposited with Parliament for the abandonment of the company's undertaking.

No. of Directors—5; quorum, 3. *Qualification*, 100 shares.

DIRECTORS:

Chairman—HUME WILLIAMS, Esq., 1, Essex Court, Temple, E.C.

Alexander Beazeley, Esq., New Thornton Heath.
Henry Michell Millett, Esq., The Grove, Holt, Norfolk.

OFFICERS.—Sec., Edgar J. Ford; Engs., A. L. Nimmo, M.Inst.C.E., and Charles Minns, M.Inst.C.E., 29, Abingdon Street, Westminster, S.W.; Solicitors, Hargrove and Co., 3, Victoria Street, Westminster, S.W.

Offices—3, Victoria Street, Westminster, S.W.

284.—TIVERTON AND NORTH DEVON.

Incorporated 19th July, 1875, to construct a railway from the Devon and Somerset, near Morebath, to Tiverton. Length, 8½ miles. Narrow gauge. Capital, 65,000*l*. in 20*l*. shares and 21,166*l*. on loan or by debenture stock. Power to Bristol and Exeter to subscribe 15,000*l*., to guarantee interest on debentures, to appoint a director, to vote at meetings, and to raise new capital for their subscription. Working agreements with Bristol and Exeter, prior to the amalgamation of that company with the Great Western.

AGREEMENTS, &c., WITH THE GREAT WESTERN.—By the Great Western Act of 23rd July, 1877, that company was authorised to subscribe to this undertaking, or take shares to any extent not exceeding 40,000*l*., but not to have power to sell or transfer any shares so held, and the following agreement was confirmed, viz.:—Subject to 25,000*l*. of *bona fide* capital of the Tiverton being subscribed for and taken up on or before January 1st, 1878, the Great Western to find the remainder of the capital, the undertaking to be governed by two directors of the subscribing company, against one of the Tiverton. These arrangements were entered into in consequence of the Tiverton not having previously been able to raise the whole of the necessary capital for the construction of the line.

The line was opened in August, 1884.

CAPITAL—30th June, 1884.—*Received:* On account of 3,250 ordinary shares of 20*l*. each, 64,640*l*.; loans, 19,500*l*.; total, 84,140*l*. *Expended:* 80,544*l*. Credit balance, 3,596*l*.

Meetings to be held in February and August.

No. of Directors.—Maximum, 7; minimum, 3; quorum, 4 and 2. *Qualification*, 15 shares.

DIRECTORS:

Chairman—Sir JOHN HEATHCOAT HEATHCOAT-AMORY, Bart., M.P., Knightshayes Court, Tiverton.

Deputy-Chairman—Sir DANIEL GOOCH, Bart., M.P., 3, Warwick Road, Maida Hill, W.

Michael Castle, Esq., Bristol.
George Woodbury Cockram, Esq., Tiverton.
Alexander Hubbard, Esq., Derwentwater House, Acton, W.
Sir Charles Alexander Wood, Knt., 11, Elvaston Place, S.W.

OFFICERS.—Sec., J. H. Matthews, Paddington, W.; Eng., Francis Fox, Bristol; Auditors, J. Barnes and William Chapple.

285.—TOTTENHAM AND HAMPSTEAD JUNCTION.

Incorporated by act of 28th July, 1862, to construct a railway from the main line of the Hampstead Junction to join the Great Eastern at Tottenham; and a line from the Hampstead Junction to the Great Northern at Hornsey. Length, 5¾ miles.; in operation, 4¾ miles. Capital, 160,000*l.* in 10*l.* shares and 53,300*l.* on loan.

For list of Acts from 1863 to 1868, see the MANUAL for 1881, page 350.

REVENUE.—For the half-years ended 31st December, 1883, and 30th June, 1884, the net revenue sufficed for the payment of dividends on Nos. 1 and 2 preference shares, at the rate of 5 per cent. per annum each half-year, and in addition, dividends on the ordinary shares at the rate of 2¼ and 1¾ per cent. per annum respectively; the balance carried forward from the June half year being 292*l.*

CAPITAL.—The receipts on this account to 30th June, 1884, amounted to 539,331*l.*, and the expenditure to 547,537*l.*, leaving a debit balance of 8,206*l.* The receipts are given in full below:—

Ordinary shares	£273,170
No. 1 preference shares	36,830
No. 2 preference shares	100,000
Midland Railway Company	127,183
Interest	2,148=£539,331

The borrowing powers of the company were vested in the Midland, under their Additional Powers Act, 1874. As the debentures matured they were absorbed by the Midland, and are now all paid off.

The dividends on the ordinary and preference shares are contingent upon the profits of each separate year; they are payable half-yearly in March and September, the transfer books closing 10 to 12 days before payment.

TRANSFER DEPARTMENT.—Ordinary form; fee, 2*s.* 6*d.* per deed; if more sellers than one, 2*s.* 6*d.* each seller; several classes of stock may be transferred on one deed, with one stamp for the whole; certificates must accompany transfers; one share may be transferred; fractional parts of 1*l.* not allowed to be transferred; in acceptances, renunciations, &c., of allotments of new stock, proxies, or other forms sent to trustees, the signatures of all are required.

Meetings held in March or April and September or October.

No. of Directors—9; minimum, 5; quorum, 5. *Qualification*, 500*l.*

DIRECTORS:

* Matthew William Thompson, Esq., Park Gate, Guiseley.

3 Sir James Joseph Allport, Knt., Littleover, near Derby.

† Lord Claud John Hamilton, M.P., 23, Lowndes Square, S.W.

* Henry Tylston Hodgson, Esq., Harpenden, Herts.

† John Francis Holcombe Read, Esq., Hoe Street, Walthamstow.

1 Samuel Swarbrick, Esq., Assoc.Inst. C.E., The Cedars, Tottenham Green, N.

3 Charles Henry Parkes, Esq., Netherfield, Weybridge, Surrey.

2 William Mc.Andrew, Esq., South Hill, Bromley, Kent.

1, Retire in 1885; 2, in 1886; 3, in 1887. All eligible for re-election.

* Nominated by Midland; † nominated by Great Eastern; do not retire.

OFFICERS.—Sec., James Williams: Auditors, W. H. Hodges, Derby, and F. Waddy, London; Solicitors, J. S. Beale and C. A. Curwood.

Offices—Derby.

286.—TRALEE AND FENIT.

Incorporated by act of 26th August, 1880, for the construction and maintenance of a railway from Tralee to Fenit. Length, about 6½ miles. Period for completion, 5 years. Arrangements with the Waterford and Limerick and Limerick and Kerry companies. Capital, 45,000*l.* in 10*l.* shares, with power to divide into "preferred" and "deferred" half-shares; borrowing powers, 15,000*l.* Dividends at the rate of 5 per cent. per annum are to be guaranteed by the county of Kerry on 30,000*l.*, part of the original capital, for 35 years after the opening of the railway for traffic.

The works are about to be commenced, certain baronies of the county of Kerry having given a guarantee to secure the repayment to the Treasury of a sum of 95,000*l.*, which the Treasury has consented to advance for the purpose of forming a pier and harbour at Fenit, a place about 7 miles distant from Tralee. The harbour commissioners believe that the dues to be derived from the proposed works will largely exceed the sum required for the annual repayments to the Treasury. The capital has been subscribed, and a contract for the works completed.

Line in course of construction.

No. of Directors—5; quorum, 3. *Qualification*, 20 shares. Quorum of a general meeting 10 proprietors, holding in the aggregate not less than one-twentieth part of the capital of the company.

DIRECTORS:

Chairman—The Right Hon. the Earl of DEVON, Powderham Castle, Exeter.

Sir Henry Donovan, Knt.
Robert McCowen, Esq.
Samuel Murray Hussey, Esq.
Richard Latchford, Esq.

OFFICERS.—Sec., Robert Fitzgerald, Tralee; Solicitor, Richard Huggard, LL.D., Tralee; Bankers, The National Bank.

287.—TREFERIG VALLEY.

Incorporated by act of 21st July, 1879, for the construction and maintenance of 3 railways, No. 1 and 2 about ½ mile, and No. 3 about 2¼ miles in length respectively. Situate in and about the parish of Llantrissant, in the county of Glamorgan, and connected with the Llantrissant and Taff Vale Junction and Ely Valley lines. Period for completion, 5 years. Arrangements with the Great Western and Taff Vale companies. Capital, 15,000*l.* in 10*l.* shares, with power to divide into "preferred" and "deferred" half-shares; loans or debenture stock, 5,000*l.*

LEASE.—By act of 14th July, 1884, this undertaking is leased to the Taff Vale for 999 years from the 30th June, 1888, the lessors to pay all debenture and other interest, and 4 per cent. per annum on the ordinary capital.

No. of Directors.—Maximum, 5; minimum, 3; quorum, 3 and 2. *Qualification* 30 shares.

DIRECTORS:

Chairman—TUDOR CRAWSHAY, Esq.

John Crockett, Esq.
William Thomas, Esq.

Secretary, W. H. Morgan, Solicitor, Pontypridd.

288.—USK AND TOWY.

Incorporated by act of 24th July, 1871, to construct a line from the Neath and Brecon, at Devynock, to the Central Wales Extension, at Llandovery. Length, 12¾ miles. Capital, 130,000*l.* in 10*l.* shares and 43,300*l.* on loan.

Company may use parts of the Neath and Brecon, Central Wales Extension, and Vale of Towy. Working arrangements with the Brecon and Merthyr Tydfil Junction, the Mid Wales, and the Hereford, Hay, and Brecon, or either of them. Traffic arrangements with the Llanelly.

In January, 1880, it was stated that the company had obtained a grant for extension of time, but that no further progress had been made.

Application is being made to Parliament, this Session, for renewal and extension of powers.

No. of Directors—7; minimum, 3; quorum, 3 and 2. *Qualification*, 300*l.*

DIRECTORS:

Wm. De Winton, Esq., Banker, Brecon.
David Evans, Esq.
Edward Jones, Esq.

Secretary, John Williams, Lion Street, Brecon.

289.—UXBRIDGE AND RICKMANSWORTH.

Incorporated by act of 11th August, 1881, for making a railway from Uxbridge to Rickmansworth. Length, about 8 miles. Period for completion, 5 years. Capital, 144,000*l.* in 10*l.* shares. Borrowing powers, 48,000*l.*

By act of 28th July, 1884, the time for compulsory purchase of lands was extended until 11th August, 1885.

No. of Directors.—Maximum, 5; minimum, 3; quorum, 3 and 2. *Qualification*, 50 shares.

FIRST DIRECTORS:

William Fox Hawes, Esq.
S. L. Mason, Esq.
Stephen Fuller, Esq.
Two others to be nominated.

Secretary, Edward Wickham, 5, Arthur Street East, E.C.

290.—VALE OF LLANGOLLEN.

Incorporated by act of 1st August, 1859, to construct a line from Ruabon, on the Shrewsbury and Chester, to the town of Llangollen. Capital, 45,000*l.* in 10*l.* shares; loans, 15,000*l.* Length, 6 miles. Traffic arrangements, under usual restrictions, with Great Western, by which that company works the line, and practically adopt it as part of their system. The agreement with the Great Western has been renewed for ten years, from 1881.

By act of 11th May, 1863, the company was authorised to raise new capital to the extent of 24,000*l.*, at 5 per cent., and 8,000*l.* by loan. Also to agree with Llangollen and Corwen as to the joint station at Llangollen.

By Certificate of the Board of Trade, dated 17th May, 1870, the company was authorised to issue 5,000*l.* new share capital.

By the Corwen and Bala Act, 1862, the company was authorised to raise 10,000*l.* in shares, but it was not raised.

By the Bala and Festiniog Act, 1873, the company was authorised to subscribe 12,000*l.* to that undertaking, and to raise 12,000*l.* additional capital for that purpose, which was raised.

REVENUE.—The net revenue for the half-year ended 30th June, 1884, after payment of all interest, prior charges, and preference dividends, sufficed for dividend upon the ordinary shares at the rate of 3¼ per cent. per annum, carrying forward 88*l.*

CAPITAL.—The expenditure to 30th June, 1884 (including 12,000*l.* subscribed to the Bala and Festiniog), amounted to 111,787*l.*, the receipts being as under:

Shares and stock	£83,200
Debenture stock	22,447
On forfeited shares	120
Surplus lands	4,190
Transfer from revenue, 31st December, 1869	673
Premium on issue of debenture stock	1,103=£111,733

Meetings in February or March and in August or September, at Llangollen.

No. of Directors—7; minimum, 5; quorum, 3. *Qualification*, 500*l.*

DIRECTORS:

Chairman—HENRY ROBERTSON, Esq., M.P., Palé, Corwen.

Capt. Best, R.N., Vivod, Llangollen.
Owen Slaney Wynn, Esq., Ruabon.
John William Dean, Esq., Palé, Corwen.
Sir Theodore Martin, K.C.B., Onslow Square, S.W.
Henry Beyer Robertson, Esq., Palé, Corwen.

Three go out of office each year; eligible for re-election.

OFFICERS.—Sec., Charles Richards, Llangollen; Eng., Henry Robertson, M.P., M.Inst.C.E.; Auditors, W. Patchett and Joseph Wagstaff Blundell; Solicitors, Longueville, Jones, and Williams, Oswestry, and Charles Richards and Sons, Llangollen.

Offices—Bank Buildings, Llangollen.

291.—VAN.

Constructed under the "Railways Construction Facilities Act, 1864." A Certificate of the Board of Trade was obtained and published in the *London Gazette* 3rd June, 1873.

This line is constructed to connect the Van Lead Mines, Montgomeryshire, with the Cambrian system, the junction being at Caersws. The total length in operation is 6 miles 5 furlongs 2¼ chains.

The line was opened for mineral traffic 14th August, 1871, and for passengers 1st December, 1873.

REVENUE.—The balance at the credit of net revenue account, for the half-year ended 30th June, 1884, after payment of all prior charges, amounted to 68*l.*, which the directors decided should be carried forward to the next year.

CAPITAL.—The receipts on this account to 30th June, 1884, amounted to 23,000*l.*, whilst the expenditure to the same date was 22,897*l.*

The capital consists of 16,000 shares of 1*l.* 5*s.* each, all paid up, and 3,000*l.* in 6 per cent. debenture stock.

Meetings held at the offices of the company in London, in January and July each half-year.

No. of Directors.—Maximum, 10; minimum, 5. *Qualification*, 150 shares of 1*l.* 5*s.*

DIRECTORS:

Deputy-Chairman—ANDREW ROUSE BOUGHTON-KNIGHT, Esq., Downton Castle, Ludlow.

Julius Alington, Esq., Little Barford, St. Neots, Hunts.
David Davies, Esq., M.P., Broneirion, Llandinam, Montgomeryshire.
Charles Clark, Esq., Windsor Chambers, Great St. Helens, E.C.

OFFICERS.—Sec., W. J. Lavington, Dashwood House, New Broad Street, E.C.; Man., J. C. Hughes, Caersws, Montgomeryshire; Eng., W. N. Swettenham, M.Inst.C.E., Newtown, Montgomeryshire; Auditors, Frederick Hunt and Stephen Catterson; Solicitors, Howell and Morgan, Machynlleth.

Offices—95, Dashwood House, New Broad Street, E.C.

292.—VICTORIA STATION AND PIMLICO.

Incorporated by act of 23rd July, 1858, to construct a general station near Victoria Street, Pimlico, and a line to be connected with the West End and Crystal Palace at Battersea. Capital, 675,000*l.* in 10*l.* shares and 225,000*l.* on loan. Length, 1¼ mile, including bridge over the Thames.

By act of 13th August, 1859, the company was empowered to raise additional capital to the extent of 75,000*l.* in 10*l.* shares and 25,000*l.* on loan, the whole of which sums are to be devoted exclusively to the purposes of the undertaking. By the same act authority was given to arrange with Great Western, so as to provide broad gauge rails to accommodate that company to and from the station.

By act of 28th June, 1861, a lease was sanctioned to the Great Western and Chatham and Dover, for the use of one-half of the station for 999 years, at an increasing rental in lieu of tolls; further powers were also conceded to the company in reference to division and apportionment of its capital; also to raise a portion thereof by preference at 5 per cent.

The dividends are now securely placed at 9 per cent. per annum, with an occasional bonus.

CAPITAL.—The expenditure on this account has amounted to 481,855*l.*, and the receipts from stocks and shares (in order of priority) have been as follow:—

4½ per cent. debenture stock	£132,322
4½ per cent. preference stock	130,000
Consolidated ordinary stock	225,000=£487,322

The interest on the debenture stock is accumulative; on the other stocks dividends are contingent upon the profits of each separate year; dividends are payable half-yearly on the 1st January and 1st July, the transfer books closing about 14 days before payment.

TRANSFER DEPARTMENT.—Ordinary form; fee, 2*s.* 6*d.* per deed; if more sellers than one, 2*s.* 6*d.*, but if more separate accounts than one on any deed, then 2*s.* 6*d.* for each account. Several classes of stock may be transferred on one deed, with one stamp for the whole, but in that case the fee is 2*s.* 6*d.* each stock. Certificates must accompany transfers. Any multiple of 1*l.* may be transferred, but no fractional parts of 1*l.*

Meetings in February and August, or such other month as the company may determine.

No. of Directors.—Maximum, 7; minimum, 3. *Qualification*, 500*l.*

DIRECTORS:

Chairman—Sir HENRY ARTHUR HUNT, C.B., 45, Parliament Street, S.W.

Philip Thomas Blyth, Esq., 17, Gracechurch Street, E.C.
John Elger, Esq., 63, Queen's Gate, S.W., and Lewes Crescent, Brighton.
W. H. Roberts, Esq., Birling, near Maidstone, Kent.

OFFICERS.—Sec., Edward Bellamy; Auditors, E. Brooks and J. C. Fitzmaurice; Solicitors, Fladgate and Fladgate, Craven Street, Strand, W.C.; Bankers, Sir Samuel Scott and Co., Cavendish Square, W.

Offices—57, Moorgate Street, E.C.

293.—WAINFLEET AND FIRSBY.

Incorporated by act of 13th May, 1869, to construct a railway from the East Lincolnshire, at Firsby, to Wainfleet. Length, 4¼ miles. Capital, 18,000*l.* in 10*l.* shares and 6,000*l.* on loan. Power to divide shares into "preferred" and "deferred," and to create and issue debenture stock. Opened November, 1871, and worked by Great Northern at 50 per cent. of the traffic receipts.

REVENUE—Half-years ended 31st December, 1883, and 30th June, 1884.—The net earnings, after deducting all prior charges, sufficed for the payment of dividends at 7 and 5 per cent. per annum, payable on the 20th March and 1st October each half-year respectively.

CAPITAL.—On this account the receipts to 30th June, 1884, had been 30,048*l.*, including the whole of the share and loan capital, and 6,048*l.* transferred from revenue. The expenditure to the same date amounted to 30,501*l.*

The accounts are made up to the 30th June and 31st December, and the meetings held in Wainfleet in March and at Skegness in September.

No. of Directors—5; minimum, 3; quorum, 3 and 2. *Qualification*, 200*l.*

DIRECTORS:

Chairman—JAMES MARTIN, Esq., Wainfleet.

Isaac Gunson, Esq., Wainfleet.
James Bradford, Esq., Brighton.
George Roberts Cowen, Esq., Nottingham.
Robert James Harwood, Esq., Boston.

OFFICERS.—Sec., William Hall, Accountant, Skegness, Lincolnshire; Auditors, Thomas James Wood, Boston, and George Booth Walker, Wainfleet; Solicitor, George Walker, Spilsby.

Offices—Skegness, Lincolnshire.

294.—WAINFLEET AND FIRSBY (EXTENSION TO SKEGNESS).

By act of 18th July, 1872, this company was authorised to extend the Wainfleet and Firsby Line from Wainfleet to Skegness. Length, 5 miles. Capital, 27,000*l.* in 10*l.* shares, "preferred" and "deferred," but not to participate in general profits. Loans, 9,000*l.*, or by debenture stock. Opened 28th July, 1873, and worked by Great Northern at 50 per cent. of the traffic receipts.

REVENUE—Half-years ended 31st December, 1883, and 30th June, 1884.—The net earnings, after deducting all prior charges, sufficed for the payment of dividends at 7 and 6 per cent. per annum, payable on the 20th March and 1st October each half-year respectively.

CAPITAL.—The receipts on this account to 30th June, 1884, including all the share and loan capital, and 6,373*l.* transferred from revenue, amounted to 42,373*l.*, and the expenditure to the same date amounted to 44,724*l.*

The accounts are made up to the 31st December and 30th June, and the meetings held in Wainfleet in March and Skegness in September.

No. of Directors—5 minimum, 3; quorum, 3 and 2. *Qualification*, 200*l.*

DIRECTORS:

Chairman—JAMES MARTIN, Esq., Wainfleet.

Isaac Gunson, Esq., Wainfleet.
James Bradford, Esq., Brighton.
George Roberts Cowen, Esq., Nottingham.
Robert James Harwood, Esq., Boston.

OFFICERS.—Sec., William Hall, Accountant, Skegness, Lincolnshire; Auditors, Thomas James Wood, Boston, and George Booth Walker, Wainfleet; Solicitor, George Walker, Spilsby.

Offices—Skegness, Lincolnshire.

295.—WATERFORD AND CENTRAL IRELAND.

Incorporated as the Waterford and Kilkenny, by act of 21st July, 1845, to construct a line between the two places mentioned, and a branch to Kells (6 miles). Capital, 250,000*l.* in shares or stock and 83,000*l.* on mortgage or by debenture stock.

By act of 1850 the company was authorised to raise 200,000*l.* more capital, to enable them to complete the line into Waterford, and for other purposes, and to borrow a further sum of 66,000*l.*

By act of 13th July, 1868, the name of the company was changed to Waterford and Central Ireland, and powers conferred to borrow on mortgage 10,000*l.*, to enable the company to substitute stone or iron viaducts for those already made of wood.

By act of 27th June, 1872, the Waterford and Central Ireland and the Kilkenny Junction were authorised to take additional lands, and this company was authorised to raise 30,000*l.* on mortgage or by debenture stock.

By act of 4th July, 1878, the powers of the Central Ireland Acts, mentioned under that head below, were revived and authorised to continue in force until the 18th July, 1880; the period for the completion of the Central Ireland was also extended until the 18th July, 1882.

CENTRAL OF IRELAND.—By act of 23rd July, 1866, the Waterford and Kilkenny and the Kilkenny Junction were authorised to construct the "Central of Ireland," for which purpose each company was authorised to raise 110,000*l.* by shares and 36,600*l.* on loan. By act of 7th July, 1873, the share capital authorised by the act of 1866 was reduced to 60,000*l*., and the borrowing powers to 20,000*l*. The line commences by a junction with the Kilkenny Junction, near Knockmay, Queen's County, and terminates by a junction with the Great Southern and Western, at Geashill, King's County. Length, 13½ miles. Works to be completed by 18th July, 1882. By act of 19th July, 1875, the Great Western (England) was authorised to subscribe 40,000*l*. to the Central of Ireland undertaking. Lines to be managed by a joint committee. By act of 12th July, 1877, the "Central Ireland Joint-undertaking Committee" was dissolved, and the Kilkenny Company released from its participation in the responsibilities of that undertaking, all powers under various acts, by authority of which the construction of the "Central Ireland" was undertaken, becoming vested in the Waterford Company, the company to continue to be a separate undertaking apart from all other undertakings of the Waterford Company, with a separate and distinct capital, and separate and distinct accounts of the Central Company to be kept by the Waterford Company. The dividend on the "New Central Ireland Stock," at the rate of 5 per cent. per annum, is secured by the appropriation of the Great Western rebates of 2,200*l*. a year up to 1890. A sum of 19,125*l*. was raised on Central Ireland stock during the half-year ending the 29th September, 1884, which enabled the directors to complete the Extension Line from Maryborough to Mountmellick, a distance of 7 miles, and was opened for traffic on the 1st February, 1885.

KILKENNY JUNCTION.—For terms of agreement with this company, see Kilkenny Junction.

In operation, 31 miles.

REVENUE.—The net revenue account for the half-years ended 25th March and 29th September, 1883, after payment of interest and fixed charges, sufficed for a dividend on the preference stock, 1850, at 5 per cent. per annum, each half-year respectively, leaving a balance of 231*l*. to next account.

CAPITAL.—The receipts on this account to 29th September, 1883, amounted to 632,380*l*., and the expenditure to 634,547*l*., showing a debit balance of 2,167*l*.

The accounts are made up to 25th March and 29th September of every year, and the statutory meetings held in London in May and November.

Scale of Voting.—One vote for every 20*l*. stock up to 200*l*.; then one vote for every 100*l*. up to 2,000*l*. stock; then one vote for every 200*l*. stock beyond.

Certificates required to accompany transfer deed. No fee for registration.

No. of Directors.—Maximum, 12; minimum, 8. *Qualification*, 400*l*. stock.

DIRECTORS:

Thomas Adams, Esq., 6, Sydney Terrace, Lewisham, Kent.
John Nugent Cahill, Esq., J.P., Ballycomra House, Co. Kilkenny.
Robert Dobbyn, Esq., Colbeck Street, Waterford.
Charles Evan Thomas, Esq., Gnoll, Neath.
James J. Phelan, Esq., Waterford.
Walter Charles Venning, Esq., 80, Gresham House, Old Broad Street, E.C.
Joseph Strangman, Esq., Waterford.
Sir Charles Whetham, Knt., 52, Gordon Square, W.C.

OFFICERS.—Sec., William Williams; Loco. Supt., Daniel McDowell; Eng., Charles R. Galwey; Auditors, M. R. Stephenson, Waterford, and Charles H. Robinson, London; Solicitors, Radcliffe and Co., London, and A. S. McCoy, Waterford; Bankers, The Bank of Ireland, Waterford.

Head Offices—The Terminus, Waterford.

296.—WATERFORD, DUNGARVAN, AND LISMORE.

Incorporated by act of 18th July, 1872, to construct a line from Waterford, and by way of Dungarvan to Lismore, where it will form a junction with the Fermoy and Lismore. Length, 43 miles. Capital, 280,000*l*. in 10*l*. shares and 93,333*l*. on loan or by debenture stock. Baronies and city to contribute to make dividend equal to 5 per cent.

By act of 7th July, 1873, power was obtained to make deviations from, and abandon portions of, the authorised railways, and the time for completion of works extended to July, 1878. The several baronies and city to guarantee interest on capital during construction, and for 35 years after opening of line.

By act of 22nd July, 1878, the company was authorised to make an extension from their terminus at Waterford into the city of Waterford (3 furlongs 9 chains 50 links). Period for completion, five years. The extension railway to form a separate undertaking, and all accounts relating thereto to be kept separate and distinct from all other accounts of the company. Capital, 35,000*l*.; loans, &c., 11,600*l*.

By act of 18th August, 1882, the period limited by act of 1878 for the completion of the extension railway was extended to the 22nd July, 1885, and working agreements with the Fermoy and Lismore undertaking were authorised.

The line was opened on the 12th August, 1878.

CAPITAL.—This account to the 30th June, 1884, showed that 372,078*l*. had been received and 478,325*l*. expended; debit balance, 106,247*l*. The ordinary 10*l*. shares are entitled to a dividend of 5 per cent. per annum for 5 years, granted for the construction of the railway, and for 35 years after its opening for public traffic payable by presentment to be levied off the rateable property of the county of Waterford, and of the county of the city of Waterford.

No. of Directors—12; minimum, 6; quorum, 4 or 3. *Qualification*, 500*l*.

DIRECTORS:

Chairman—ABRAHAM DENNY, Esq., D.L., Waterford.

Deputy-Chairman—FRANCIS E. CURREY, Esq., Lismore Castle, Lismore.

Sir James Ramsden, Furness Abbey, Barrow-in-Furness.

Henry White, Esq., Harbour View, Waterford.

Wm. Goff Davis Goff, Esq., Glenville, Waterford.

Sir Richard F. Keane, Bart., Cappoquin House, County Waterford.

OFFICERS.—Sec. and Man., Thomas O'Malley; Eng. and Loco. Supt., James Otway; Acct., Robert T. Mortimer; Auditors, William Gallwey and T. D. Smith.

Offices—New Quay, Waterford.

297.—WATERFORD AND LIMERICK.

Incorporated 21st July, 1845, for the construction of a line from Waterford to Limerick, with branches therefrom. Further powers were conferred by acts of 1847 and 1850; the capital authorised to be raised under these three acts being 750,000*l*., and the borrowing powers 250,000*l*. The line was completed between Tipperary and Waterford by the aid of a government loan of 120,000*l*., now nearly paid off.

FURTHER PARLIAMENTARY POWERS.—For list of Acts from 1853 to 1878, see the MANUAL for 1881, page 357.

By act of 29th June, 1883, the company was authorised to raise additional capital, 75,000*l*., loans, &c., 25,000*l*., and certain agreements with the Waterford and Central Ireland, as to making an extension railway and for other purposes, were by the same act confirmed.

AMALGAMATIONS, LEASES, AGREEMENTS, &c.:—

ATHENRY AND ENNIS AND ATHENRY AND TUAM.—These lines have been leased jointly with the Great Western, and are now being worked by the Waterford.—See GENERAL INDEX.

GREAT WESTERN.—For agreement with this company, see *Appendix* to the MANUAL for 1873. There having been some dispute as to the construction of this agreement, the directors, in their report issued in August, 1881, stated as follows:—"The question of the construction of the agreement of April, 1872, with the Great Western, and the liability of the latter company to the Waterford and Limerick, has been submitted to arbitration, and the award, for the years ending 30th June, 1879 and 1880, has been received. The claim of this company for the period referred to has been awarded at a sum of 5,200*l*."

LIMERICK, CASTLE CONNELL, AND KILLALOE.—Incorporated by act of 26th June, 1855, to construct a railway from the Waterford and Limerick, at Killonan, to Castle Connell. Length, 9¾ miles. By act of 2nd August, 1858, the company was authorised to extend the line from Castle Connell to Killaloe, at an outlay of 37,000*l*. in 10*l*. shares and 12,333*l*. on loan. Length, 7¼ miles. By act of 6th August, 1866, the company was authorised to extend the line to the River Shannon. Length, ¾ mile. Capital, 7,500*l*. in shares and 2,500*l*. on loan. Vested in Waterford and Limerick by act of 6th August, 1872, which authorised the Waterford and Limerick to create 69,280*l*. new share capital, and to borrow a further sum of 34,000*l*.

LIMERICK AND ENNIS.—By act of 4th August, 1853, the company was incorporated by this new title; empowered to abandon the branches to Killaloe, the Great Southern and Western, and near Limerick. Reduced length, 24¾ miles, single line. Worked by Waterford and Limerick, under an act of 1862, at 45 per cent. By act of 25th May, 1860, the company was authorised to maintain the line over certain roads on a level, to purchase lands, and to make alterations in respect to meetings, &c. By act of 20th June, 1870, the Limerick and Ennis was authorised to cancel certain unissued shares, to borrow on mortgage in lieu thereof, and to issue debenture stock to the extent of 100,000*l*; of this amount 20,000*l*. have been issued at 4½ per cent. This line was amalgamated with the

Waterford and Limerick on 1st January, 1874, under powers conferred by an act of the previous year, which also authorised the Waterford and Limerick to create 98,000*l.* new share capital and to borrow 100,000*l.*

LIMERICK AND FOYNES.—Incorporated by act of 4th August, 1853, for a line from Limerick to Foynes, Island Quay, Limerick, and the Lower Shannon. Length, 26¼ miles. By act of 26th June, 1855, the company was permitted to borrow one-third of its share capital when one-half thereof should have been paid up, but whether or not the whole of such capital had been subscribed. By act of 12th July, 1858, the company was afforded new powers to raise the funds requisite to complete the undertaking. Unissued shares may be converted into preference, at 5½ per cent., to the extent of 31,975*l.* Cancelled shares also to be issued as preference if within the above amount. By act of 28th June, 1861, the company was authorised to raise new capital to the extent of 40,000*l.* at 5 per cent. By act of 20th June, 1870, the Limerick and Foynes was authorised to cancel certain unissued preference shares, and to borrow on mortgage in lieu thereof, and to issue debenture stock to the extent of 25,000*l.* Amalgamated with the Waterford and Limerick under powers conferred by act of 1873. The Waterford and Limerick to create 126,250*l.* new share capital, and borrow on mortgage 68,300*l.*

LIMERICK AND KERRY.—See GENERAL INDEX.

RATHKEALE AND NEWCASTLE JUNCTION.—See GENERAL INDEX.

SOUTHERN OF IRELAND.—By act of 1873 this company was authorised to subscribe 50,000*l.* to the Southern, and to create and issue for that purpose 50,000*l.* of 5 per cent. preference shares. Preference shares of the Southern, bearing a like dividend, to be received by this company in return.—See GENERAL INDEX.

NEW LINES AND WORKS.—The extension works to deep water below the bridge at Waterford were opened on 1st January, 1884.

ACCOUNTS:—

REVENUE.—The receipts and expenditure on this account for the half-years ended 31st December, 1883, and 30th June, 1884, are shown in the subjoined statement:—

	31st Dec.	30th June.
Coaching traffic	£35,856	£30,412
Goods, minerals, and cattle	43,895	34,856
	£79,751	£65,268
Special and miscellaneous	1,972	1,983
Gross receipts	£81,723	£67,251
Expenditure	43,049	41,953
Net	£38,674	£25,298
Add—Sundry balances and interest, Great Western subsidy, &c. (net)	4,005	16,423
Total net revenue	£42,679	£41,721
Deduct—Interest, rents, preference dividend, &c.	36,670	39,487
Available for ordinary stock	£6,009	£2,234
Dividends	Nil.	Nil.
Balance to next account	£6,009	£2,234

CAPITAL.—Authorised stock and shares, 1,603,530*l.*; loans, 621,600*l.*; total, 2,225,130*l.* The subjoined statement of stock and share capital created shows the proportion received to 30th June, 1884:—

Description.	Created.	Received.
Ordinary 50*l.* shares	£597,600	£597,550
12½*l.* „	1,512½	
	£599,112½	£597,550
4 per cent. consolidated preference 50*l.* stock... 1873 Act	318,950	318,950
4½ per cent. „ preferential 100*l.* „ 1860 „	337,950	337,900
5 per cent. preference 50*l.* shares ... 1872 „	10,080	10,000
5 per cent. „ 50*l.* „ ... 1873 „	49,800	49,800
5½ per cent „ 25*l.* „ (Foynes Amalgam.) 1873 „	29,150	29,150
5 per cent. „ 25*l.* „ (Ennis Amalgam.) 1873 „	8,450	7,675
5 per cent. „ 50*l.* „ (Southern) 1873 „	50,000	50,000
4½ per cent. „ 100*l.* „ (Limerick & Kerry) 1873 „	25,000	25,000
5 per cent. „ 100*l.* „ ... 1878 „	100,000	100,000
5 per cent. „ 100*l.* „ ... 1883 „	75,000	31,800
Total	£1,603,492½	£1,557,825

The above stock and shares were issued at a discount of 28,687*l.*, and charged off, from time to time, against forfeited shares; gain of 44,269*l.*

The receipts and expenditure on capital account to 30th June, 1884, were as under:—

Received.		*Expended.*	
Shares and stock	£1,557,825	Lines open for traffic	£1,701,760
Loans	35,070	Working stock	257,420
Debenture stock	557,201	Subscriptions to other railways	117,562
Forfeited shares gain, less discount on issuing shares, &c.	2,516	Waterford Extension	80,925
	£2,152,612		
Balance	5,055		
	£2,157,667		£2,157,667

The estimate of further expenditure required 13,266*l.* for the half-year ended 31st December, 1884, and 39,344*l.* for subsequent periods; total, 52,610*l.* The assets to meet this amounted to 69,978*l.*

New Capital.—In March, 1879, the directors issued a small portion of the capital authorised by act 1878, in 5 per cent. preference shares of 100*l.* each, three years to run from the date of issue, redeemable then or thereafter at par, on six months' notice being given by the company. In the following September 25,000*l.* of capital, authorised by act of 1873, was issued as a perpetual first preference stock, bearing interest at 4 per cent. per annum. This stock was offered to the proprietors in certificates of 50*l.* each, at the price of 95 per cent., and was intended to pay off a previous issue of 5 per cent. shares. In September, 1880, the balance of 4 per cent. perpetual 1st preference stock (9,000*l.*) was issued in certificates of 50*l.* each, at 98*l.* for each 100*l.* stock, free of stamp duty and all expense to purchasers. In December, 1880, the 25,000*l.* 4½ per cent. redeemable preference shares under Limerick and Kerry Act, 1873, were issued at par in certificates of 100*l.* each, redeemable any time after 1st January, 1886, on six months' notice being given by the company. In May, 1881, the 40,000*l.* 5 per cent. preference shares (act, 1878) were issued at par in certificates of 100*l.* each, redeemable at par on 1st July, 1884, or at any time thereafter on six months' notice being given by the company. In April, 1884, 81,800*l.* 5 per cent. redeemable preference shares, under Waterford and Limerick Act, 1883, were issued at par in certificates of 100*l.* each, redeemable any time after 1st July, 1889, on six months' notice being given by the company.

Mileage.—In operation, 30th June, 1884: Lines owned, 141¾; leased or rented, 129; foreign lines worked over, 1½; total, 271¾ miles. On the 1st July, 1880, the Southern Line was opened throughout to Thurles, and on December 20th, 1880, the Limerick and Kerry (43 miles) was opened through.

The accounts are made up to 30th June and 31st December in every year, and the statutory meetings held in February and August.

Scale of Voting.—5 shares of 50*l.* each, one vote; 10 shares, two votes; 15 shares, three votes; 20 shares, four votes; 40 shares, five votes; then one vote for every 10 shares to 90; ten votes maximum.

Certificates must accompany transfer deed. Registration fee, 2*s.* 6*d.* each deed. Registration of death or marriage, 5*s.*

No. of Directors.—Maximum, 18; minimum, 6. *Qualification*, 1,000*l.* capital.

DIRECTORS:

Chairman—JAMES SPAIGHT, Esq., J.P., Limerick.

Deputy-Chairman—E. RONAYNE MAHONY, Esq., J.P., Camden Quay, Cork, and Dunedin, County Cork.

Abraham Stephens Esq., J.P., Duncannon, County Wexford.
Sir Francis Wm. Brady, Bart., Upper Pembroke Street, Dublin.
Samuel Burke, Esq., Cahir.
Patrick Martin, Esq., Q.C., M.P., 23, Upper Fitzwilliam Street, Dublin.
Terence McMahon, Esq., Dominick Street, Cork.
Anthony O'Connor, Esq., 86, Merrion Square, Dublin.
William Henry, Esq., Fitzwilliam Square, Dublin.
The Rt. Hon. Earl of Bessborough, Bessborough Park, Piltown, Co. Kilkenny.
Percy B. Bernard, Esq., D.L., Castle Hackett, Tuam.
Alexander Bannatyne, Esq., J.P., Limerick

OFFICERS.—Sec. and Acct., John J. Murphy, Waterford; Traffic Man., John Roberts, Limerick; Eng., J. Tighe, Waterford; Loco. Supt., Henry Appleby, Limerick; Auditors, George Gibson and Anthony Cadogan; Solicitor, John O'Connor, Dublin; Bankers, The National Bank Limited, Waterford.

Head Offices—The Terminus, Waterford.

298.—WATERFORD AND TRAMORE.

Incorporated by act of 24th July, 1851, for a railway commencing in the city of Waterford and terminating at Tramore, on the coast. Length, 7½ miles. Capital, 48,000*l*. in 10*l*. shares and 16,000*l*. on loan.

By act of 3rd July, 1857, the company was authorised to raise additional capital of 10,000*l*. in shares, at 5 per cent. preference, and 3,350*l*. in loans, in aid of "new works," station accommodation, &c.; but an extension was refused. This capital was created on 29th September, 1857, at 5 per cent.

REVENUE.—Half-year ended 31st December, 1883, the balance available for dividend, after providing for outstanding accounts and interest on loans, was 2,029*l*., which was appropriated as follows:—Dividend on 5 per cent. preference shares for current half-year, 250*l*.; dividend on original shares of 6*s*. per share, 1,440*l*.; balance to next half-year, 339*l*.; total, 2,029*l*.

Half-year ended 30th June, 1884, the balance available for dividend, after providing for outstanding accounts and interest on loans, is 678*l*., which sufficed for a dividend on the preference shares at the rate of 5 per cent. per annum, carrying forward a balance of 428*l*.

CAPITAL.—The receipts and expenditure on this account to 30th June, 1883, are given in detail below:—

Received.		*Expended.*	
Shares	£58,000	Acts of incorporation	£5,174
Loans	19,350	Law, general, and incidental	3,708
		Land purchase and compensation	5,985
		Permanent way, rails, &c.	35,812
		Miscellaneous works, engine shed, &c.	5,139
		Stations and buildings, machinery, &c.	9,148
		Locomotive and rolling stock	12,019
		Commission and discount	365
	£77,350		£77,350

Meetings held in Waterford in March and September.

DIRECTORS:

Chairman—ABRAHAM DENNY, Esq., J.P., D.L., Waterford, and Rockfield, Tramore.

Deputy-Chairman—CORNELIUS MORLEY, Esq., Springfield, Portlaw.

Charles E. Denny, Esq., Tramore House, Tramore.

John N. White, Esq., King Street, and Rocklands, Waterford.

John L. Blood, Esq, Mountjoy Square, Dublin.

OFFICERS.—Sec. and Traffic Man., William Rea; Eng., James Otway, M.Inst.C.E., Waterford; Auditors, George W. Maunsell, Tramore, and Isaac Thornton, Waterford.

Offices—The Terminus, Waterford.

299.—WELLINGTON AND SEVERN JUNCTION.

Incorporated by act of 28th August, 1853, for a line by a junction with Shrewsbury and Birmingham, at Wellington, and extension to Coalbrookdale. Length, 5¼ miles. Capital, 6,000 shares of 10*l*.; loans, 10,000*l*.

By act of 1st August, 1861, the line is leased to the Great Western for a term of 999 years. The dividend for the first three years was at the rate of 4*l*. 10*s*. per cent., and 5 per cent. for remainder of the term.

Meetings in January or February and in August or September.

DIRECTORS:

Chairman—W. G. NORRIS, Esq., Coalbrookdale.

John Slaney, Esq., Wellington.

William Bullock, Esq., Wellington.

F. W. Yates, Esq., Codsall Wood, Wolverhampton.

Eligible for re-election.

OFFICERS.—Sec. and Solicitor, R. D. Newill, Wellington, Salop; Eng., Henry Robertson, M.P., M.Inst.C.E., Shrewsbury; Auditors, John Hiatt Slaney and R. J. Barber, Wellington; Bankers, Lloyd's Banking Company Limited, Wellington.

Offices—Wellington, Salop.

300.—WENLOCK.

Incorporated by act of 22nd July, 1861, to construct a railway, No. 2, from the Buildwas Station of the Much Wenlock and Severn Junction and Severn Valley companies, across the River Severn, to the Coalbrookdale Iron Works; also to construct a railway, No. 1, commencing by a junction with the Much Wenlock and Severn Junction, at the town of Much Wenlock, and terminating by a junction with the Shrewsbury and Hereford, in the parish of Wistanstow, near Craven Arms. Length of railway No. 2, 1 mile. Length No. 1, 14 miles. Ordinary capital, 100,000*l.* in 10*l.* shares; preference capital, 25,000*l.*; loans, 41,500*l.* Running powers over Great Westernto Ketley Ironworks; over Shrewsbury and Hereford to Craven Arms Station; over the Much Wenlock and Severn Junction Line; and a part of Severn Valley. Worked by the Great Western, which pays a fixed rent-charge of 5,000*l.* per annum.

REVENUE.—For the half-years ended 31st December, 1883, and 30th June, 1884, the net revenue sufficed for the payment of dividends on the preference shares at 5 per cent. and on the ordinary shares at 3 per cent. per annum respectively.

CAPITAL.—The receipts on this account to 30th June, 1884, amounted to 168,988*l.*, and the expenditure was given at the same amount.

Meetings in March and September.

No. of Directors—7; minimum, 5; quorum, 3. *Qualification*, 250*l.*

DIRECTORS:

Chairman—WILLIAM PENNY BROOKES, Esq., Much Wenlock.

Sir Thomas Brassey, K.C.B., M.P., Assoc.-Inst.C.E., Normanhurst Court, Hastings, and 3, St. George's Place, Hyde Park, W.

Frederick Murton, Esq., 85, Addison Road, Kensington, W.

Ralph Augustus Benson, Esq., Lutwyche Hall, Much Wenlock.

Richard Butcher, Esq., Eardington, Bridgnorth.

OFFICERS.—Sec., Chas. J. Cooper; Eng., John Fowler, M.Inst.C.E., 2, Queen's Square Place, Westminster, S.W.; Auditors, Henry Wade, Shrewsbury, and Thomas H. Thursfield, Barrow, Broseley; Bankers, Cooper, Purton, and Sons, Much Wenlock, and Bridgnorth.

Offices—Much Wenlock.

301.—WEST DONEGAL.

Incorporated by act of 21st July, 1879, for the construction of a line from the terminus of the Finn Valley, at Stranorlar, to the town of Donegal. Length, 18 miles (14 miles of which were opened in April, 1882, and it is expected that the remaining 4 miles will be constructed and opened before the end of 1885). Gauge, 3 feet. Finn Valley may subscribe to the extent of 15,000*l.* (of which 13,560*l.* has been paid), and enter into working and traffic arrangements. Capital, 30,000*l.* in 3,000 "A" or preference shares; 70,000*l.* in 7,000 "B" or ordinary shares; and 50,000*l.* on loan or in debenture stock.

Agreements (sanctioned by extraordinary meetings of shareholders on 9th February, 1881, and 3rd October, 1881) have been entered into with the Finn Valley for the working of the West Donegal Line when opened to the temporary terminus at Druminin, and when subsequently opened to the town of Donegal.

In July, 1884, there was issued 7,260*l.* in shares guaranteed by rent-charge on landowners' estates.

At the half-yearly meeting of shareholders, on 31st August, 1883, the directors reported as follows:—"The deputation from the general committee of Irish railway companies who waited upon the Chancellor of the Exchequer in May last has been so far successful that the Treasury has consented to reduce the rate of interest on loans from the Government from 5 to 4 per cent. This concession, which took effect on 1st July last, relieves you of a charge of 390*l.* a year in respect of the 39,000*l.* which your directors have already obtained from the Board of Works.

FINN VALLEY.—At an extraordinary meeting of the company on 12th August, 1884, it was resolved:—"That this meeting hereby sanctions the proposed agreement between the West Donegal and the Finn Valley now produced and read to us, whereby it is provided—That on a light railway from Druminin to Donegal being completed by the West Donegal under the provisions of the Tramways Acts

(Ireland), the working and traffic agreement of the 15th March, 1881 (between the Finn Valley and the West Donegal), come into operation, and have the same effect as if the said light railway had been completed by the West Donegal under the provisions of their special act."

Capital.—The receipts on this account to 30th June, 1884, amounted to 75,887*l*., and the expenditure to 80,474*l*. The estimate of further expenditure on capital account for construction of 4 miles of railway from the temporary terminus at Druminin to the town of Donegal is estimated at 23,000*l*., including expense of order of council.

No. of Directors.—Maximum, 7; minimum, 5 (including a director to be appointed by the Finn Valley on completing their subscription as above; quorum, 3. *Qualification*, 20 shares.

DIRECTORS:

Chairman—The Rt. Hon. Viscount LIFFORD, Meen Glas, Stranorlar, Co. Donegal, and Cecil House, Wimbledon, S.W.

Deputy-Chairman—JAMES MUSGRAVE, Esq., J.P., The Lodge, Carrick, Co. Donegal. and Drumglass House, Belfast.

Bartholomew McCorkell, Esq., J.P., Richmond, Londonderry.

William Sinclair, Esq., D.L., J.P., Drumbeg, Inver, County Donegal.

Joseph Cooke, Esq., Lisahally, Londonderry.

Robert William Newton, Esq., J.P., Bellevue, Londonderry.

OFFICERS.—Sec., James Alex. Ledlie; Eng., James Barton, M.Inst.C.E., Dundalk; Auditors, Archibald M'Corkell, Londonderry, and Edward A. Hamilton, Londonderry; Solicitors, Dane and Todd, Donegal.

Offices—Stranorlar.

302.—WEST LANCASHIRE.

Incorporated by act of 14th August, 1871, to construct a series of lines from Southport to Preston. Length, 16 miles 4 chains. Capital, 155,000*l*. in 20*l*. shares, and 51,666*l*. on loan or by debenture stock.

For particulars relating to acts 1872 to 1878, see the Manual for 1881, page 364.

By act of 3rd July, 1879, the respective periods for completion of works, limited by the act of 1875, were extended as follows:—Original lines until 14th August, 1882, and additional lines until the 6th August, 1883.

By act of 3rd June, 1881, the company was authorised to purchase certain lands in the county of Lancaster, and a branch railway or siding known as the "Tarleton Branch Railway." New capital, 200,000*l*. in ordinary or preference shares; 66,660*l*. on loan or debenture stock.

By act of 19th May, 1884, the company was authorised to raise 250,000*l*., in 5 per cent. debenture stock, for the payment of the debts and liabilities of the company incurred in completing the undertaking.

By act of 7th August, 1884, the company was authorised to extend its railway to the Preston Docks, with powers for other purposes. New capital. 90,000*l*., to be a separate capital called "Preston Docks Extension Capital," with borrowing powers for the purposes of the act not exceeding 30,000*l*.

The line was opened from Hesketh Park Station to Hesketh Bank and Tarleton on the 19th February, 1878; from Windsor Road Station to Hesketh Park on the 10th June, 1878; from Hesketh Bank to Longton on the 18th May, 1882; and from Central Station, Southport, to Windsor Road, and Longton to Preston on the 4th September, 1882; and from Preston to Whitehouse Junction (from which point the company exercises its running powers over the Lancashire and Yorkshire system to Blackburn) on the 16th April, 1883.

By act of 3rd July, 1882, the period for completion of works was extended until 14th August, 1883.

Revenue.—The gross receipts for the half-year ended 30th June, 1884, amounted to 9,200*l*., and the expenditure to 9,186*l*.

Capital.—The receipts from shares to 30th June, 1884, amounted to 685,483*l*. (ordinary capital, 153,267*l*.; preference share capital, 532,216*l*.) The receipts from debenture stock amounted to 259,967*l*., whilst the expenditure to the same date had been 1,092,788*l*.; debit balance, 147,337*l*.

PRIORITIES, DESCRIPTIONS, DIVIDENDS, and other conditions of issue on the Stocks of the company, existing on the 30th September, 1882 (see notes):—

No.	Year of Act.	FULL DESCRIPTION (to be observed in Transfer Deeds and all other Legal Documents).		Rate ℔ cent ℔ annum.
1	1871, 1872, 1875, 1878, 1881	5 per cent. permanent debenture stock	£229,126	5
2	1884	5 per cent. debenture stock	£250,000	5
	1872, 1875	First 5 per cent. perpetual preference shares ...	232,500	5
4	1878, 1881	Second 5 per cent. perpetual preference shares.	300,000	5
5	1871	Ordinary shares	155,000	...

NOTES.—Dividend on debenture stock is payable half-yearly on the 1st January and 1st July, and is accumulative; dividend on 1884 5 per cent. debenture stock is payable quarterly on the 1st March, 1st June, 1st September, and 1st December in each year, and is accumulative; but on the other stocks it is contingent upon the profits of each separate half-year.

NEW DEBENTURE STOCK, 1884.—In June, 1884, 250,000*l.* of new debenture stock. was issued, to be called "5 per cent. 1884 Debenture Stock," ranking after the existing debenture stock, with interest payable quarterly on the 1st March, 1st June, 1st September, and 1st December.

Total length of line, 17 miles.

TRANSFER DEPARTMENT.—Ordinary form; fee, 2*s.* 6*d.* per deed; if more sellers than one, 2*s.* 6*d.* each seller of stock in different lots. Separate deeds required for each class of stock. Certificates must accompany transfers. Any amount of stock may be transferred except fractional parts of 1*l.* In acceptances, renunciations, &c., of allotments of new stock, proxies, or other forms sent to trustees and other joint holders, the signature of all the parties concerned is required.

No. of Directors—7; minimum, 5; quorum, 4 and 3. *Qualification*, 500*l.*

DIRECTORS:

Chairman—EDWARD HOLDEN, Esq., Laurel Mount, Shipley.

Thomas Fisher, Esq., Southport.

Sir Thomas G. Fermor-Hesketh, Bart., Easton Neston Hall, Towcester.

Thomas Henry Isherwood, Esq., The Albany, Old Hall Street, Liverpool.

Albert Ricardo, Esq., 11, Angel Court, E.C.

OFFICERS.—Gen. Man. and Sec., Thomas Gilbert; Con. Engs., James Brunlees, M.Inst.C.E., and Charles Douglas Fox, M.Inst.C.E., London; Accountant, C. J. Maples; Audit Accountant, Chas. Boyle; Auditors, James B. Reay, A.C.A. (J. B. Hughes and Reay, Liverpool), and W. Twist, Southport; Solicitors, Walton and Smith, Southport; Bankers, The Manchester and Liverpool District Banking Co. Limited, Southport Branch.

General Offices—Central Station, Southport, Lancashire.

308.—WEST LONDON.

Incorporated by act of 21st June, 1836, under the title of "THE BIRMINGHAM, BRISTOL, AND THAMES JUNCTION," the object being to unite the London and North Western and Great Western with the western districts of the metropolis, and communicate with the River Thames, through the medium of the Kensington Canal. The canal was purchased for 36,000*l.* The title of the railway was altered by 3 and 4 Vic., cap. 105. Total mileage authorised, 9¼.

By act of 1844, the railway was leased to the London and North Western and Great Western conjointly, for 999 years, commencing 11th March, 1845, at a rent of 1,800*l.* per annum.

By act of 13th August, 1850, the Kensington Canal and all other properties of the West London were absolutely transferred to the London and North Western and Great Western. These companies, in conjunction with the Brighton and South Western, secure the following guarantees to the different classes of properties in West London, viz.: 14*s.* per 20*l.* share, first class preference, which were issued at 10*l.* per cent. discount; 24*s.* per 20*l.* share, second class preference, all paid up; 4*s.* per share to original shareholders after opening of new line, which took place on 2nd March, 1863; 6*s.* per share three years after opening of line; 8*s.* per share six years after opening of line. The company is to dissolve under provisions of the act of 28th July, 1863, so soon as an agreement with the West London Extension is finally resolved upon.

DIRECTORS:

Great Western.

Sir D. Gooch, Bart., M.P., 3, Warwick Road, Maida Hill, W.
Sir C. A. Wood, Knight, 25, Chesham Place, S.W.
The Right Hon. the Earl of Bessborough, 3, Mount Street, Grosvenor Square, W.
The Rt. Hon. Lord Lyttelton, Stourbridge, and 17, Grosvenor Street, W.
C. G. Mott, Esq., Harrow Weald Lodge, Stanmore, Middlesex.

London and North Western.

Richard Moon, Esq., Copsewood Grange, Coventry.
W. Cawkwell, Esq., Euston Station, N.W.
James Bancroft, Esq., 83, Mosley Street, and Broughton Hall, Manchester.
O. L. Stephen, Esq., 5, Whitehall Yard, S.W.
J. P. Bickersteth, Esq., Euston Station, N.W.

JOINT OFFICERS.—Sec., J. Wait, Birkenhead; Supt., K. Neele, Kensington, S.W.

394.—WEST LONDON EXTENSION.

Incorporated by act of 13th August, 1859, to construct the undermentioned lines and works, by the London and North Western, the Great Western, the London, Brighton, and South Coast, and the London and South Western jointly, viz.:—

1. A railway, length 4 miles 6 chains, from a junction with the West London at Kensington, crossing the Thames by a bridge, to a junction with the authorised line of the Victoria Station and Pimlico, at Battersea. This bridge is 340 yards in length, with six arches of 120 feet span each, seven arches of 25 feet span each, and with a headway under each arch of 20 feet above Trinity high water mark.

2 and 3. Branches of the respective lengths of 63 chains and 35 chains, to connect (1) with the West End of London and Crystal Palace, near its Clapham Station, and (2) with the South Western, near the junction of its Richmond Branch with the main line.

4 A branch from Battersea to the South Western.

5. A branch, length 27 chains, from the main line, near the basin of the Imperial Gas Company, to the Thames, near the mouth of the Kensington Canal.

6. A dock in the parish of Fulham.

7. A diversion of a part of the Kensington Canal, belonging to the West London, who are authorised to discontinue the use of the part of the canal north of King's Road, Chelsea.

These lines and branches (except the junction with the South Western) were constructed on the mixed gauge, but the broad gauge has since been taken up.

WEST LONDON.—The absorption of this company by the new company is regulated by the following scheme of compensation:—Holders of first class preferred "A" 20*l.* shares receive per annum 14*s.* per share; holders of second class preferred "B" 20*l.* shares receive per annum 1*l.* 4*s.* per share; holders of original "C" 20*l.* shares, per annum 8*s.* per share. The West London capital consisted of 185,960*l.* in the following shares, there being no mortgage or bond debt:—5,338 ordinary shares of 20*l.* each, 106,760*l.*; 3,200 first class preference shares, 64,000*l.*; 760 second class preference shares, 15,200*l.* The yearly rent of 1,800*l.*, formerly payable to the West London by the London and North Western and the Great Western, is now paid to the company constituted by this act, which, also, by agreement, disburses the annuities due half-yearly to the original and preference shareholders in the West London.

By the Great Western Act, 1875, the debenture debt of the West London Extension is assumed by the four companies interested.

No. of Directors—12; quorum, 5. Appointed as under by the four contributing companies.

SPECIAL CHAIRMAN.—The directors, when they think fit, may select a special chairman, not being one of themselves, to act for any period; but no such appointment to be made except by unanimous resolution of a meeting at which at least one director from each of the four companies is present. In the event of the assembled directors failing to agree in the appointment of a special chairman, then the Board of Trade, on the application of any two or more of the companies, may appoint any person, not being one of the directors, to act as a special chairman for as long a period as it may think fit.

DIRECTORS:

Chairman—JOHN PARES BICKERSTETH, Esq., Grove Mill House, Watford, Herts.—*L. & N. W.*

London and North Western.

Richard Ryder Dean, Esq., 97, Gloucester Place, Portman Square, W.
A. H. Holland Hibbert, Esq., Munden, near Watford, Herts.
Oscar Leslie Stephen, Esq., Bardon Hall, Leicester, and 55, Cadogan Square, S.W.

Great Western.

Richard Basset, Esq., Highclere, near Newbury.

L. L. Dillwyn, Esq., M.P., 10, King's Bench Walk, E.C., and Hendrefoilan, near Swansea.

Richard Michell, Esq., Kensington Park Gardens, W.

Walter Robinson, Esq., 20, Gledhow Gardens, S.W.

London and South Western.

Captain J. G. Johnston, 39, Hyde Park Square, W.

William P. Snell, Esq., Belmont Park, near Havant, Hants.

London, Brighton, and South Coast.

Hon. Thomas F. Fremantle, M.P., 22, Chesham Place, S.W.

R. Jacomb-Hood, Esq., 112, Lexham Gardens, Kensington, W.

OFFICERS.—Sec., Edward Bellamy; Supt., Kingston Neele, Kensington Station, Addison Road. W.; Engs., Francis Stevenson (L. & N. W.), and Lancaster Owen (G. W.); Surveyor, J. Marr, 8, Adam Street, Adelphi, W.C.; Auditor, W. W. Deloitte, 4, Lothbury, E.C.; Solicitor, W. Heggerty, 36, Great George Street, Westminster, S.W.

Offices—57, Moorgate Street, E.C.

305.—WEST RIDING AND GRIMSBY.

Incorporated by act of 6th August, 1862, to construct a line from the Bradford, Wakefield, and Leeds, at Wakefield, to the South Yorkshire, at Barnby-upon-Don. with a branch to Doncaster, and several minor branches. Length, 28¾ miles. Capital, 360,000*l.* in 10*l.* shares and 120,000*l.* on loan. South Yorkshire and Sheffield appoint four directors, and guarantee interest on debentures, and a minimum dividend of 4½ per cent. on share capital. Opened 1st January, 1866.

By act of 23rd June, 1864, the company was authorised to construct a station at Wakefield. Length of new line, ½ mile. Capital (to be kept separate), 80,000*l.* in shares and 26,600*l.* on loan. West Yorkshire may contribute 15,000*l.* of this amount. Arrangements for the use of stations by Midland, West Yorkshire, and Manchester and Sheffield.

By act of 5th July, 1865, the company was authorised to construct a line from Keadby, on the South Yorkshire, to Lincoln, on the Great Northern. Length, 29½ miles. Capital, 400,000*l.* in shares and 133,000*l.* on loan. This act was repealed by act of 25th June, 1868. By another act of the same year, the West Riding and Grimsby was authorised to raise additional capital to the extent of 60,000*l.* in shares and 20,000*l.* on loan.

By act of 28th June, 1866, the West Riding and Grimsby was transferred jointly to the Great Northern and the Manchester, Sheffield, and Lincolnshire, the company to become extinct within one year from the passing of the act.

By act of 31st May, 1867, power was given to the Great Northern and the Sheffield, each to raise additional capital for the purposes of the Wakefield Station, to the extent of 20,000*l.*, with 6,600*l.* on mortgage. Arrangements with Midland for use of Wakefield Station.

VESTING OF THE UNDERTAKING.—By another act of 1867 the line became vested in the Great Northern and the Sheffield, ceasing to exist as an independent undertaking on 28th June, 1867. The West Riding and Grimsby is now worked jointly, and is managed by a committee of three directors from each of the two leasing companies.

By the Great Northern Act of 2nd August, 1883, the joint committee was authorised to construct the Crofton Branch, commencing in the township of Walton, in the parish of Sandal, and terminating by a junction with the Lancashire and Yorkshire, in the parish of Crofton. Length of branch, 1¼ mile.

DIRECTORS:

Great Northern.

Sir John Brown, Knt., Endcliff Hall, Sheffield.

Sir Andrew Fairbairn, Knt., M.P., 15, Portman Square, W., and Askham Richard, York.

William Lawies Jackson, Esq., M.P., Allerton Hall, Chapel Allerton, near Leeds.

Manchester, Sheffield, and Lincolnshire.

The Right Hon. the Earl of Wharncliffe, Wortley Hall, Sheffield.

The Right Hon. Lord Auckland, Edenthorpe, Doncaster.

George Morland Hutton, Esq., Gate Burton, Gainsborough.

Secretary to the Committee, William Grinling.

Offices—King's Cross Station, N.

306.—WEST SOMERSET.

Incorporated by act of 17th August, 1857, to construct a railway from the Bristol and Exeter, at Taunton, to the Harbour, at Watchet. Capital, 120,000*l.* in 10*l.* shares; loans, 40,000*l.* Length, 14½ miles. Broad gauge.

By act of 15th May, 1860, certain new works were authorised. Forfeited shares to be cancelled, and re-issued at 5 per cent. preference.

By Certificate of the Board of Trade, granted in 1866 and 1868, the company was authorised to issue 24,000*l.* new preference share capital. No further borrowing powers.

By arrangement, the Great Western grants to the West Somerset an annuity or clear yearly rent-charge of the following amounts, viz:—For the year ended 31st December, 1871, 5,100*l.*; 1872, 5,400*l.*; 1873, 5,700*l.*; 1874, 6,000*l.*; 1875, 6,300*l.*; 1876, 6,600*l.*; and for every year for ever thereafter the amount to be 6,600*l.*

REVENUE.—For the half-years ended 31st December, 1883, and 30th June, 1884, full dividends were paid on all the preference shares, and dividends of 1*s.* 6*d.* per share each half-year, equal to 1½ per cent. per annum on the ordinary capital.

CAPITAL.—The expenditure to 30th June, 1884, amounted to 183,821*l.*, the receipts having been as under:—

Ordinary 10*l.* shares	£67,796
5 per cent. preference shares, redeemable after 1st December, 1872, at 10 per cent. premium	52,200
5 per cent. supplemental preference shares, redeemable after 1st December, 1872, at 10 per cent. premium	21,540
5 per cent. supplemental preference shares of 10*l.* each, issued at 80 per cent. discount, redeemable at 10 per cent. premium after 1st December, 1872...	1,214
Debenture stock at 4 per cent.	40,000
Gift of Sir T. D. Acland, Bart.	500
Sale of lands, &c.	180
Transferred from revenue	391
	£183,821

The accounts are made up to the 30th June and 31st December, and the meetings held at Taunton in February and August.

No. of Directors—8; minimum, 3; quorum, 3 and 2. *Qualification*, 300*l.*

DIRECTORS:

Chairman—Sir ALEXANDER ACLAND HOOD, Bart., St. Audries, Bridgwater.

Deputy-Chairman—JOHN PHILIP MARTINEAU, Esq., 36, Theobald's Road, Gray's Inn, W.C.

John Halliday, Esq., Chapel Cleeve, Old Cleeve, Somerset.

Henry Sweet, Esq., Taunton, Somerset.

William Stoate, Esq., Watchet, Somerset.

OFFICERS.—Sec., John Wilson Theobald; Auditors, W. B. Hellard, Taunton, and Henry Charles Sweet, Taunton; Solicitors, Radcliffes, Cator, and Martineau, 20, Craven Street, Strand, W.C.; Bankers, Stuckey's Banking Company, Taunton.

Offices—8, Drapers' Gardens, E.C.

307.—WEST SOMERSET MINERAL.

Incorporated by act of 27th July, 1857, for making a railway from the Quay, at Watchet, to the parish of Exton, with a branch therefrom. Share capital under this act, 65,000*l.*, divided equally into "A" and "B" shares. Loan capital, 21,500*l.*, in substitution for which debenture stock was created and confirmed by act of 1869, and by the same act 8,500*l.* due on bond was also authorised to be issued in debenture stock, making a total of 30,000*l.* By "The Watchet Harbour Act, 1860," the company was authorised to create, and they have created, 10,000*l.* of additional class "B" shares.

This line is worked by the Ebbw Vale Steel, Iron, and Coal Company Limited, for 55½ years, from 24th June, 1864. That company guarantees interest on the mortgage debenture stock, as well as 6 per cent. on the 32,500*l.* "A" shares, and 5 per cent. on the 42,500*l.* "B" shares. This agreement was sanctioned by act of 24th June, 1869. In operation, 10½ miles. The dividends are being regularly paid.

CAPITAL.—The expenditure, including loan of 10,000*l.* to Watchet Harbour, has amounted, to 111,774*l.*, and the receipts, amounting to the same sum, included 32,500*l.* in class "A" shares, 42,500*l.* in class "B" shares, 15,600*l.* on loan, and 14,400*l.* in debenture stock.

Meetings held in February or March and in August or September in each year.

No. of Directors—5; minimum, 3; quorum, 3. *Qualification*, 500*l*.

DIRECTORS:

Francis Tothill, Esq., The Grove, Stoke Bishop, Bristol.

William Gregory Norris, Esq., Coalbrookdale, Salop.

Edward Coward, Esq., Heaton Mersey, near Manchester.

OFFICERS.—Sec. and Solicitor, Edwin Hellard, Stogumber, Taunton; Eng., Albert V. Horne; Auditors, Edwin Grove and Joseph Coventry.

308.—WEYMOUTH AND PORTLAND.

Incorporated by act of 30th June, 1862, to construct a line from Weymouth to the Isle of Portland, and an extension of the Wilts, Somerset, and Weymouth to the Harbour. Mixed gauge. Length, 5½ miles. Capital, 75,000*l*. in 10*l*. shares and 25,000*l*. on loan. Opened 9th October, 1865. Leased to Great Western and South Western, which conjointly work the line, at a rental of 4,500*l*. per annum, being equivalent to 4½ per cent. on the share and debenture capital; and this sum, after payment of the interest on debenture stocks (14,250*l*. at 4 per cent., and 10,750*l*. at 4½ per cent.) and expenses of management, is divided among the shareholders.

CAPITAL.—The receipts and expenditure on this account have been as under:—

Received.		*Expended.*	
Ordinary 10*l*. shares	£75,000	Parliamentary expenses, &c.	£3,280
Debenture stock at 4½ per cent.	10,750	Land, works, law, &c.	96,120
Debenture stock at 4 per cent.	14,250	Direction, office expenses, &c.	600
	£100,000		£100,000

Meetings in February or March and August or September.

No. of Directors.—Maximum, 5; minimum, 3; quorum, 2. *Qualification*, 250*l*.

DIRECTORS:

Chairman—A. T. P. BARLOW, Esq., 47, Norfolk Square, W.

Deputy-Chairman—ALEXANDER PEARSON FLETCHER, Esq., 1, Moorgate Street, E.C.

William Henry Homfray, Esq., 6, Storey's Gate, Westminster, S.W.

OFFICERS.—Sec., William Fraser, 26, Great George Street, Westminster, S.W.; Eng., John Fowler, M.Inst.C.E., 2, Queen's Place, Westminster, S.W.; Auditors, J. W. Weldon, 12, Stanley Gardens, W., and Roderick Mackay, 2, Lothbury, E.C.; Solicitors, Rose and Johnson, 26, Great George Street, Westminster, S.W.

Offices—26, Great George Street, Westminster, S.W.

309.—WHITBY, REDCAR, AND MIDDLESBROUGH UNION.

Incorporated by act of 16th July, 1866, to construct a line in the North Riding of York, from the Whitby Branch of the North Eastern to the Cleveland Branch of the same railway. Length, 16 miles. Capital, 250,000*l*. in 10*l*. shares and 83,300*l*. on loan.

The act of 7th July, 1873, empowered the company to alter the line and levels near Whitby, and to abandon portions of authorised railway. Time for completion of works extended to July, 1877.

By act of 30th June, 1874, the company was authorised to raise 100,000*l*. new capital, by the creation of ordinary or preference shares, and to borrow on mortgage or by debenture stock a further sum of 33,000*l*.

LEASE, &c.—By act of 19th July, 1875, the line is leased in perpetuity to the North Eastern, at a minimum rent of 4,500*l*. per annum, with the option of purchase by the latter company after the expiration of 10 years from the opening of the through line to Whitby. By the same act the time limited for completion of works was further extended to 7th July, 1878.

The line was completed and opened for traffic on the 5th December, 1883.

CAPITAL.—This account to 30th June, 1884, showed the expenditure to have been 352,208*l*.; and the receipts as under:—

Ordinary stock	£250,000	
Loans	72,485	
Interest, &c.	547	
Transfer fees	7	=£323,039

Meetings held in February or March and August or September.

DIRECTORS:

Chairman—EDWARD CORNER, Esq., Esk Hall, Whitby.

Adolphus Frederick Govett, Esq., Sandylands, Virginia Water, Staines.

Alfred Joyce Keen, Esq., Buckland Lodge, Betchworth, Surrey.

OFFICERS.—Sec., James Fraser; Auditors, Joseph Wagstaff Blundell and George T. Rait; Solicitors, Godden and Holme, 34, Old Jewry, E.C.; Bankers, North Eastern Banking Company Limited, Middlesbrough.

Offices—2, Tokenhouse Buildings, King's Arms Yard, E.C.

310.—WHITLAND AND CARDIGAN.

Incorporated by act of 12th July, 1869, to construct a railway from the South Wales Section of the Great Western, near Whitland, to Crymmych-Arms, Pembrokeshire, for Cardigan and Newport. Length, 16¼ miles. Capital, 37,000*l*. in 10*l*. shares and 12,300*l*. on loan. Act 1874, additional capital, 10,000*l*., with 3,300*l*. on loan. Great Western to provide a narrow gauge communication to Whitland, and to afford facilities.

By act of 1877, powers were obtained for extension to Cardigan, and for alteration of name from "Whitland and Taf Vale" to "Whitland and Cardigan," with further capital of 6,000*l*. in 10*l*. hares and 2,000*l*. in loans.

By act of 11th August, 1881, a diversion of the line from Llanfihangel-Pembedw to Cilgerran (about 3¼ miles) was authorised; period for completion, 4 years. New capital, 30,000*l*.; borrowing powers, 10,000*l*. for extension line, and 14,000*l*. on loans for original undertaking.

Extension to Cardigan (11 miles) is being pushed on with all speed, and expected to be completed by June, 1885.

Revenue.—The line is not at present working to a profit sufficient for the payment of dividends, there being a small balance to the credit of net revenue account on the 30th June, 1884.

Capital.—Receipts, 31st December 1883—*Original undertaking.*—From ordinary 10*l*. shares, 37,000*l*.; from 6,000 preference 10*l*. shares, 10,000*l*.; loans at 5 per cent., 4,700*l*.; debenture stock at 4½ per cent., 6,962*l*.; other loans, &c., interest not yet fixed, 14,000*l*. Amount expended, 63,544*l*. *Cardigan Extension.*—From ordinary 10*l*. shares, 41,000*l*.; from preference, 30,0000*l*.; loans, 23,600*l*.

No. of Directors—9; minimum, 3; quorum, 3. *Qualification*, 200*l*.

DIRECTORS:

Chairman—JOHN OWEN, Esq., Glogue, Whitland.

L. L. Dillwyn, Esq., M.P., Hendrefoilan, Swansea.

J. W. Bowen, Esq., Q.C., 2, Paper Buildings, Temple, E.C.

Colonel Lewis, Clinfiew, Boncath, South Wales.

Thomas Davies, Esq., Cardigan.

Richard Bassett, Esq., Highclere, Newbury.

Thomas Colby, Esq., Pantyderi.

Captain Gower, Cilgerren, South Wales, R. S. O.

Edward James, Esq., Aberelwyn, Hebron, R. S. O.

OFFICERS.—Sec. and Gen. Man., G. Howell, Whitland; Eng., James B. Walton, Westminster, S.W.; Auditors, J. R. Atcherley, 20, Porteus Road, Paddington, W., and James Fraser, 9, King's Arms Yard, E.C.; Solicitors, Jones and Forrester, Malmesbury, and W. Picton Evans, Cardigan.

Offices—Whitland.

311.—WHITLAND, CRONWARE, AND PENDINE.

Incorporated by act of 2nd August, 1877, for the construction of a railway (No. 1), commencing in the parish of Llanboidy, by a junction with the Great Western near Whitland Station, and terminating in the parish of Cyffig or Kiffig, near Castle Ely Mill. Length, 5 miles and 6·20 chains. And a railway (No. 2), commencing by a junction at the termination of railway No. 1, and terminating in the parish of Eglwyscymmyn. Length, 2 miles and 5 chains. Period for completion of works, five years from the passing of the act. Power to enter into agreements with the Great Western. Capital, 4,500 shares of 10*l*. each (which may be divided into "preferred" and "deferred"), and 15,000*l*. on loan or in debenture stock.

By act of 10th August, 1882, the period for completion of works was extended until 2nd August, 1885, the railway to be constructed as a "light" railway, and the capital to be reduced to 24,000*l*., with borrowing powers, 8,000*l*.

No. of Directors.—Maximum, 5; minimum, 3; quorum, 3 and 2. *Qualification*, 20 shares.

DIRECTORS:

Morgan Jones, Esq.
Samuel Kay, Esq.
Frederick John Padley, Esq.

OFFICERS.—Sec., H. W. Stickland, 28, Bedford Row, W.C.; Solicitors, Gadsden and Treherne, 28, Bedford Row, W.C.

312.—WIGAN JUNCTION.

Incorporated by act of 16th July, 1874. The main line, about 11¼ miles in length, commences by a junction with the Liverpool Extension of the Cheshire Lines Committee, at Glazebrook Station, between Warrington and Manchester, and terminates near the Market Place, in the town of Wigan, with branch to Westleigh, and forming connections with the Lancashire Union and London and North Western. Capital, 210,000*l*. in 10*l*. shares and 70,000*l*. on loan.

MILEAGE.—In operation, 11¼ miles.

By act of 2nd August, 1875, the company was authorised to make alterations and diversions in their authorised railways, and to construct new lines; to acquire additional lands; to raise 240,000*l*. additional capital; and to borrow a further sum of 80,000*l*.

By act of 17th June, 1878, the company was empowered to construct a railway (called in the act altered railway E) from Abram to West Leigh (both near Wigan). Length, 2 miles 2 furlongs 4 chains, and to abandon the railway E authorised by act of 1875. Period for completion of alterations, five years. The time for completion of railways and works, authorised by acts of 1874 and 1875, was extended until 16th July, 1882, and powers were obtained for the Manchester, Sheffield, and Lincolnshire to subscribe to the extent of 200,000*l*. towards the general purposes of the undertaking.

By Manchester, Sheffield, and Lincolnshire (New Works) Act, 1881, the Sheffield Company was authorised to subscribe to the undertaking a further sum of 200,000*l*. in addition to 130,000*l*. already subscribed, to enable the completion of the line up to Darlington Street, Wigan, and to have issued to them preference shares bearing 3½ per cent. in respect of such 200,000*l*. The Sheffield Company to work and maintain the railway and to pay over to the Wigan Company, half-yearly, one half of gross traffic receipts, less the usual terminal and cartage charges and Government duty.

By Manchester, Sheffield, and Lincolnshire (Additional Powers) Act, 1884, the Sheffield Company was authorised to subscribe to the undertaking a further sum of 100,000*l*.

The ceremony of turning the first sod was performed on the 27th October, 1876, by the Right Hon. R. A. Cross, M.P., the Home Secretary, and the works have since been in progress, the line from Glazebrook Junction to the Lancashire Union having been completed and opened for goods traffic on the 16th October, 1879, and for passenger traffic on the 1st April, 1884.

REVENUE.—The gross traffic receipts for the half-year ended 31st December, 1883, were 1,584*l*., and the chief-rents, interest, and working charges, amounted to 5,248*l*. In the half-year to 30th June, 1884, the traffic receipts were 2,504*l*., and the chief-rents, interest, and working charges, 5,677*l*., leaving a debit balance of 3,173*l*. to be carried forward to the next half-year.

CAPITAL.—The amount expended on this account to 30th June, 1884, was 460,645*l*. *Receipts:* Ordinary 10*l*. shares, 209,160*l*.; 5 per cent. preference 10*l*. shares, 25,000*l*.; 3½ per cent. preference 10*l*. shares, 200,000*l*.; loan by Manchester, Sheffield, and Lincolnshire, 19,220*l*.; total, 453,380*l*. Debit balance, 7,265*l*.

TRANSFER DEPARTMENT.—Ordinary form; fee, 2*s*. 6*d*. per deed; if more sellers than one, 2*s*. 6*d*. each seller. Several classes of stock may be transferred on one deed, with one stamp for the whole. Certificates must accompany transfers. In acceptances, renunciations, &c., of allotments of new stock, proxies, or other forms sent to trustees and other joint holders, all signatures of registered holders are required.

No. of Directors—4; quorum, 3. *Qualification*, 300*l*.

DIRECTORS:

Chairman—NATHANIEL ECKERSLEY, Esq., M.P., Standish Hall, Wigan.

Sir Edward Wm. Watkin, Bart., M.P., Northenden, Cheshire, and Charing Cross Hotel, Charing Cross, W.C.
James Henry Johnson, Esq., Southport.
John William Maclure, Esq., The Home, Whalley Range, Manchester.
Edward Chapman, Esq., Hill End, Mottram.

OFFICERS.—Sec., Edward Ross; Eng., Charles Sacré, M.Inst.C.E.; Auditor, Thomas Smith, Wigan; Solicitors, Darlington and Sons, Wigan.

Offices—London Road Station, Manchester.

313.—WIGTOWNSHIRE.

Incorporated by act of 18th July, 1872, to construct a line from Newton-Stewart, on the Portpatrick, to Whithorn, 19¼ miles, and a tramway, 1¾ mile, to Garliestown. Capital, 96,000*l.* in 10*l.* shares, to which the Town Council of Wigtown may subscribe. Loans, 32,000*l.*, or by debenture stock. Agreements with Portpatrick and Caledonian.

The line was opened from Newton-Stewart to Wigtown, 7 miles, on 3rd April, 1875; from Wigtown to Millisle, 8 miles, on 2nd August, 1875; branch from Millisle to Garliestown on 3rd April, 1876; and the remainder of the line from Millisle to Whithorn, 4 miles, on the 9th July, 1877.

By act of 28th June, 1877, the company was authorised to construct a branch to the harbour of Garliestown—length, 1 mile 1 furlong 3 chains and 18 yards; to make certain alterations in their authorised line; to abandon the tramway to the above-named harbour, and to enter into working agreements with Caledonian, Portpatrick, Glasgow and South Western, and London and North Western companies. New capital—shares or stock, 24,000*l.*; loans, 8,000*l.*

Revenue.—The accounts to 31st July, 1884, showed a debit to net revenue of 938*l.* to be carried forward. In operation, 20½ miles, all opened prior to October, 1881.

Capital.—The expenditure on this account to 31st July, 1884, amounted to 156,898*l.*, the receipts to the same date having been as under:—

Ordinary stock	£114,339	
Loans at 4 per cent.	38,000	
Deposit on forfeited shares	48	
Interest on bank account, &c.	579	
Interest on calls	868	
Sundries and transfer fees	25=£153,859	
Debit balance		3,039=£156,898

The estimate of further expenditure on capital account required a total of 315*l.*, the capital powers and other available assets being 4,622*l.*

No. of Directors—7; minimum, 5; quorum, 3. *Qualification*, 300*l.*

DIRECTORS:

Chairman—3 The Rt. Hon. the Earl of GALLOWAY, Cumloden, Newton-Stewart, and 17, Upper Grosvenor Street, W.

Deputy-Chairman—2 ROBERT HATHORN JOHNSTON STEWART, Esq., of Physgill.

3 The Rt. Hon. Lord Borthwick, Ravenstone, Whithorn.
2 Robert Vans Agnew, Esq., of Sheuchan and Barnbarroch.
1 Colonel J. Fletcher Hathorn, of Castlewigg.
1 James M'Lean, Esq., Wigtown.
1 James Drew, Esq., of Craigencallie.

1, Retire in 1885; 2, in 1886; 3, in 1887; are eligible for re-election

OFFICERS.—Sec. and Solicitor, William Mc.Clure, Wigtown, N.B.; Res. Man. and Eng., W. T. Wheatley, C.E., Wigtown; Traffic Supt., William Grafton, Stranraer; Auditors, William Hawthorn, Town Clerk, Wigtown, and A. B. Matthews, Solicitor, Newton-Stewart.

Offices—Wigtown, N.B.

314.—WIRRAL LIMITED.

Capital, 600,000*l.*, in 60,000 shares of 10*l.* each, with borrowing powers. First issue 30,000 shares of 10*l.* each. The price of issue will be 10*l.* per share, payable 1*l* on application, 1*l.* on allotment, and the balance in calls of not more than 2*l.* each, with an interval of not less than two months between each call.

This company was incorporated to effect the following objects:—1. To acquire the shares and exercise the powers of the Seacombe, Hoylake, and Deeside, which has paid for the last three years an average dividend of over 6 per cent. per annum on its issued capital of 90,000*l.*, which is nearly equivalent to 5 per cent. on the sum for which the railway has been purchased. 2. To acquire and exercise the parliamentary powers of the Wirral which was incorporated under Board of Trade Certificate of

1883, and of the act just obtained for extending the railway to Birkenhead Park, and to make the railways. 3. To obtain parliamentary powers for the making of a railway from the Wirral to join the proposed railway and bridge over the River Dee near Connah's Quay, for which powers have lately been granted. 4. To obtain an act of parliament to amalgamate these undertakings into one parliamentary company by the name of the Wirral Railway Company. The existing Hoylake Line is 6½ miles long, the other lines already authorised are 13 miles, the projected line to Connah's Quay 10¾ miles, and the loop towards Chester 1½ mile. By means of the Mersey Railway, which will connect both sides of the Mersey by a tunnel carrying a double line of railway, and will join the proposed railways, the Wirral will in the most direct and convenient manner afford access from Liverpool and Birkenhead to the populous districts of Bidston, Wallasey, New Brighton, Hoylake, and West Kirby, and to the whole Cheshire coast of the Dee estuary.

By act of 14th August, 1884, the Wirral Company was authorised to construct a branch to Birkenhead, length 2½ miles, and to raise additional capital, 165,000*l.*, with borrowing powers, 55,000*l.*

Capital.—In 1884 a first issue of 30,000 shares of 10*l.* each took place, to be applied—1. In the purchase and improvement of the Hoylake Railway; 2, its extension to the Park Station in Birkenhead to meet the Mersey Railway; 3, the extension to New Brighton; 4, the general purposes of the undertaking.

DIRECTORS:

Chairman—HENRY ROBERTSON, Esq., M.P., Palé, Corwen, and 13, Lancaster Gate, W.

William Henry Gladstone, Esq., M.P., Hawarden Castle, Flintshire, and 41, Berkeley Square, W.

Robert Charles De Grey Vyner, Esq., Newby Hall, Ripon, and Bidston Hall, Cheshire.

John Henry Darby, Esq., Brymbo, Wrexham.

Thomas Hughes Jackson, Esq., Manor House, Birkenhead.

Harold Littledale, Esq., Liscard Hall, Cheshire.

Frederic North, Esq., New Brighton, Cheshire.

James Tomkinson, Esq., Willington Hall, Tarporley.

OFFICERS.—Engs., James Brunlees, M.Inst.C.E., and Charles Douglas Fox, M.Inst.C.E., 5, Delahay Street, Westminster, S.W., and Asahel Pilkington Bell, C.E., Manchester; Auditors, Tapp and Bird, 4, Great George Street, Westminster, S.W.; Solicitors, Gill and Archer, 14, Cook Street, Liverpool, and Birch, Cullimore, and Douglas, Friars, Chester; Bankers, Williams & Co. (Old Bank), Chester; Manchester and Liverpool District Bank, Liverpool, and Branches; Lancashire and Yorkshire Bank, King Street, Manchester, and Branches; and Robarts, Lubbock, and Co., 15, Lombard Street, E.C.

Offices—14, Cook Street, Liverpool.

315.—WITNEY.

Incorporated by act of 1st August, 1859, to construct a line from the Great Western (Oxford, Worcester, and Wolverhampton section), at Yarnton, to the town of Witney. Capital, 50,000*l.* in 10*l.* shares; loans, 16,000*l.*

By act of 17th May, 1861, the company was authorised to cancel shares, and to re-issue others at 5 per cent.; and at a special meeting on 8th June, 1861, 1,215 preference shares, at 5 per cent. in perpetuity, were created, representing 12,150*l.* of capital, in lieu of unissued ordinary shares. Agreement in respect to working, maintenance, management, &c., with Great Western.

By act of 18th July, 1872, the company was authorised to borrow 17,000*l.* by additional loans, and to create a sinking fund for its redemption. The Great Western also obtained powers to guarantee the borrowed capital, and to enter into working agreements with the Witney.

By the Great Western Act of 22nd July, 1878, agreements were authorised relative to the payment of interest on this company's debenture debt, and the exercise by the Great Western of this company's borrowing powers.

In operation, 8 miles.

Revenue.—The net revenue account for the half-year ended 30th June, 1884, sufficed, after payment of fixed and preferential charges, and after setting aside to the mortgage sinking fund one-fourth of the amount divisible amongst the ordinary shareholders, for dividend on the ordinary shares at the rate of 4¼ per cent. per annum.

CAPITAL.—The expenditure on this account to 30th June, 1884, amounted to 82,479*l*., the receipts to the same date having been 78,471*l*., as under:—

Ordinary stock	£37,321
Preference stock at 5 per cent.	12,150
Loans at 4 per cent.	29,000

4,000*l*. 4½ per cent. loans paid off out of sinking fund.

Meetings held in March and September.

No. of Directors—6; minimum, 6; quorum, 3. *Qualification*, 200*l*., or 20 shares.

DIRECTORS:

Chairman—C. E. THORNHILL, Esq., Norham Gardens, Oxford.

Deputy-Chairman—LOCOCK WEBB, Esq., Q.C., 5, Elm Court, Temple, W.C.

Joseph Druce, Esq., Eynsham, Oxon.
Charles Early, Esq., Witney, Oxon.
S. B. L. Druce, Esq., Lincoln's Inn, W.C.
Henry Akers, Esq., Black Bourton, Faringdon, Berks.

OFFICERS.—Sec., George Broom, 11, Abchurch Lane, E.C.; Eng., Charles Douglas Fox, M.Inst.C.E., 8, Delahay Street, S.W.; Auditors, William Clinch, Banker, Witney, and Charles Titian Hawkins, Accountant, Oxford; Solicitor, John Jordan, 3, Westminster Chambers, Victoria Street, S.W.; Bankers, The Union Bank of London (Chancery Lane Branch), E.C., and Gilletts and Clinch, Witney.

Offices—11, Abchurch Lane, E.C.

316.—WORCESTER, BROMYARD, AND LEOMINSTER.

Incorporated by act of 11th August, 1861, to construct a line from the West Midland, at Bransford, to the Shrewsbury and Hereford, near Leominster. Length, 24½ miles. Capital, 200,000*l*. in 10*l*. shares; loans, 66,500*l*.

For list of Acts from 1864 to 1878, see the MANUAL for 1881, page 373.

The Great Western maintains and works the line in perpetuity at 52½ per cent. of the gross receipts. The interest on the debenture stock is charged, not on the net earnings, as is usually the case, but is a "first charge on the gross tolls, fares, rates, and charges." Productive mileage, 10¾ miles.

REVENUE.—The report and accounts for the half-year ended 30th June, 1884, showed the traffic receipts to be 2,678*l*., against 2,596*l*. at the corresponding period of 1883.

CAPITAL.—The expenditure on this account to 30th June, 1884, was as follows:—On lines constructed, 116,968*l*.; on 2nd section, 129,601*l*. The receipts were as follow:—On shares (including "shares repudiated"), 111,004*l*.; preference stock, 5,095*l*.; debenture stock, 93,000*l*.; total, 209,099*l*. The balances of expenditure over receipts amounted to 37,469*l*.

Meetings in March and September.

No. of Directors—12; minimum, 5; quorum, 3. *Qualification*, 500*l*.

DIRECTORS:

Chairman—*EDWARD BICKERTON EVANS, Esq., Whitbourne Hall, near Worcester.

*Thomas Rowley Hill, Esq., M.P., Worcester.
*George Woodyatt Hastings, Esq., M.P., Barnard's Green, Malvern.
Captain Francis Sutherland, Caverleigh, Maple Road, Surbiton, S.W.
W. C. King, Esq., Warfield Hall, Bracknell, Berks.
*Thomas Bristow Stallard, Esq., Leominster.
Richard Michell, Esq., Kensington Park Gardens, W.
Thomas Davies Thomas, Esq., Stourbridge.
Wm. Henry Barneby, Esq., Bredenbury Court, Bromyard.
John H. B. Lutley, Esq., Brockhampton, Bromyard.
James W. Williams, Esq., Bromyard.

* Retire in March, 1885. All eligible for re-election.

OFFICERS.—Sec., John Jones; Eng., W. B. Lewis, M.Inst.C.E., 8, Victoria Chambers, Westminster, S.W.; Auditors, Joseph Hall and Richard West, Worcester; Solicitors, Pidcock and Sons, Worcester.

Offices—40, Foregate Street, Worcester.

317.—WREXHAM, MOLD, AND CONNAH'S QUAY.

Incorporated by act of 7th August, 1862, to construct a line from Wrexham to Buckley, with certain branches. Length, 12¼ miles. Capital, 150,000*l*. in 10*l*. shares and 50,000*l*. on loan. Mutual facilities with the London and North Western, the Great Western, and the Wrexham and Minera. In operation, 16½ miles.

By act of 25th July, 1864, the company obtained power to construct an extension to Whitchurch and Brymbo. Length, 20 miles. Capital, 200,000*l*. in shares and 66,600*l*. on loan.

By act of 5th July, 1865, the company was authorised to construct an extension to Connah's Quay. Length, 18 miles. Additional capital, 75,000*l*.; no further borrowing powers.

By act of 9th August, 1869, the company obtained an arrangement with its creditors, and was authorised to raise 162,000*l*. debenture capital.—For details of this arrangement, see Volume for 1870.

By act of 1873 further powers were conferred on the company, which was authorised to raise 6,000*l*. more debenture capital.

By act of 1882, powers were obtained for the construction of sundry branches, by which the railway will be extended into the town of Wrexham, and connected with the principal collieries in the district. Powers were likewise obtained for increasing the dock accommodation at Connah's Quay, and improving the facilities for the interchange of traffic with the London and North Western on their Holyhead Line. New capital authorised, 270,000*l*., to be raised as separate capital, and borrowing powers, 90,000*l*.

By act of 29th June, 1883, the company was authorised to construct a new railway at Hawarden, Flintshire. Length, 4¼ miles. New capital (to be joined to that authorised by act of 1882, and kept separate from other capital), 75,000*l*.; loans, &c., 25,000*l*.

By act of 16th July, 1883 (Capital Arrangements), the company's capital was consolidated (see below).

CONSOLIDATION OF STOCKS.—By act of 16th July, 1883, the whole of the capital, and certain arrears of interest, were consolidated into three classes, as follows, viz:—

Old Stock, &c.	Exchanged for.
100*l*. "A" debenture 6 per cent.	135*l*. New 4 per cent. "A" deb. stock.
100*l*. Arrears interest on do.	80*l*. " " "
100*l*. "A" debenture 5 per cent.	112*l*. 10*s*. " " "
100*l*. Arrears interest on do.	80*l*. " " "
100*l*. Buckley, all classes debenture and shares (optional)	{Debentures at 112*l*. 10*s*. {Shares at 125*l*.
100*l*. "B" debenture 5 per cent.	80*l*. New 4 per cent. "B" deb. stock.
100*l*. "C" " "	60*l*. " " "
100*l*. "D" " "	40*l*. " " "
100*l*. Arrears on "B" debenture	60*l*. " " "
100*l*. " "C" "	40*l*. " " "
100*l*. " "D" "	20*l*. " " "
100*l*. General debts due by company	40*l*. " " "
100*l*. Preference stock	125*l*. New consolidated stock.
Existing ordinary shares	Equal nominal value in do.

BUCKLEY.—See GENERAL INDEX.

REVENUE.—The gross receipts for the half-year ended 30th June, 1884, amounted to 16,151*l*., and the expenditure to 8,582*l*., leaving a profit of 7,569*l*., and after providing for the Buckley Railway rent and the interest on the debenture stocks, there remained a credit balance of 56*l*. to be carried forward.

CAPITAL.—*Authorised*: Shares and stock, 732,750*l*.; loans, 465,000*l*.; total, 1,197,750*l*. *Created*: Shares and stock, 657,750*l*.; debenture stock, 350,000*l*. The receipts and expenditure to 30th June, 1884, were as under:—

Received.		*Expended.*	
Shares and stock	£387,669	Lines open for traffic	£636,580
Debenture stock	288,195	Working stock	36,277
Rent-charges	436		
			£672,857
		Balance	3,443
	£676,300		£676,300

Meetings held at Wrexham in February and August.

No. of Directors—6; minimum, 5; quorum, 3. *Qualification*, 500*l*.

DIRECTORS:

Chairman—THOMAS BARNES, Esq., Farnworth, near Bolton, and The Quinta, Chirk, Denbighshire.

Edmund Bowen Bernard, Esq., 51, Courtfield Gardens, South Kensington, S.W.

Charles Hughes, Esq., Brynhyfryd, Wrexham.

Thomas Henry Jones, Esq., Stansty Lodge, Wrexham.

Richard Venables Kyrke, Esq., Penywern, Hope, Mold.

OFFICERS.—Sec., James Fraser, 2, Tokenhouse Buildings, King's Arms Yard, E.C.; Gen. Man., T. Cartwright; Loco. Supt., F. Willans; Eng., William Davies, C.E., Wrexham: Auditors, John Allmand, Wrexham, and William Snape, Wrexham; Solicitor, Evan Morris, Wrexham; Bankers, The North and South Wales Bank Limited, Wrexham.

Offices—Railway Station, Wrexham. Secretary's Office—2, Tokenhouse Buildings, King's Arms Yard, E.C.

318.—WYE VALLEY.

Incorporated by act of 10th August, 1866, to construct a line from Chepstow to Monmouth. Length, 15¼ miles. Capital, 230,000*l.* in 20*l.* shares and 76,600*l.* on loan. Arrangements with Great Western, which is to work and maintain the line for 55 per cent. of the gross receipts for the first five years after the opening for traffic, and for 50 per cent. for all subsequent years. The arrangement to be convertible into a lease in perpetuity on further Parliamentary sanction being obtained.

By act of 16th June, 1871, the time for completion of works was extended to 1st July, 1874. Powers were conferred on the company by an act passed on the 14th June, 1875, to make railways from the South Wales Line of the Great Western to the Coleford, Monmouth, Usk, and Pontypool Railway.

By act of 11th August, 1876, the company was authorised to construct three short lines (length, 84 chains) in the parish of Chepstow; a river wall or wharf and three piers or jetties on the western bank of the River Wye, at Chepstow; two short lines (length, 40 chains) in the parish of Newland; and a line (length, 29 chains) in the parish of Dixton. New capital, 105,000*l.*, and 34,800*l.* on loan or by debenture stock.

The line was opened for traffic on 1st November, 1876.

REVENUE.—The line is not at present working profitably. The report issued in September, 1884, showed that the gross receipts for the past half-year were 2,517*l.*, against 2,200*l.* in the corresponding period of 1883.

CAPITAL—30th June, 1884.—*Expended:* 400,192*l.* *Receipts:* Ordinary shares, 230,000*l.*; preference stock, 69,650*l.*; loans, 88,000*l.* (upon 76,600*l.* of which the 5 per cent. interest is payable by the Great Western out of the gross receipts); sale of plant, 3,746*l.*; premium and discount (net), 7,643*l.*; lease of Chepstow Wharves, 365*l.*; received to 30th June 1884, in action against late directors (net), 12,347*l.*; total, 411,752*l.*

DIRECTORS:

Chairman—C. C. FERARD, Esq., J.P., Ascot Place, near Windsor.

A. B. Joyner, Esq., 126, Bishopsgate Street Within, E.C.

F. W. Raikes, Esq., 7, King's Bench Walk, Temple, E.C.

E. Teevey, Esq., 27, Ovington Square, South Kensington, S.W.

A. Gallenga, Esq., The Falls, Llandogo, Coleford.

OFFICERS.—Sec., George Sneath; Auditors, James Ford and Wm. Edwards; Solicitors, Newman, Stretton, and Hilliard, 75, Cornhill, E.C; Bankers, The Consolidated Bank, 52, Threadneedle Street, E.C.

Offices—44, Gresham Street, E.C.

II.—CONTINENTAL, &c.

In the MANUAL for 1877, and in former editions, much useful Statistical information will be found relating to the various Railway Networks, &c., of the principal Foreign countries, compiled from Official Returns, but, owing to the constant accumulation of new matter relating to the railways of this country, and the dimensions which the MANUAL has now reached, it has been found absolutely necessary that, in order to prevent the Work from becoming unwieldy, this kind of information should be dispensed with, especially as its omission is of much less importance to British capitalists than the curtailing of that which relates to the formation and working of *separate* companies, and which is more in keeping with the character of the Work.

So far, however, as is practicable, the Foreign portion includes, and will in future include, all the *principal* Foreign companies which have either been floated with British capital, or in which the British investor is most interested.

In order to render this division of the Work more perfect, it is necessary that Officers should forward to the publishers in England (or to the care of M. J. Bil, 6 and 8, Passage des Postes, Boulevard Anspach, Brussels, their Agent for "Guides," &c.) copies of official documents, reports, &c.

Latest information as to Miles Opened, &c., will be found in each current number of "BRADSHAW'S CONTINENTAL GUIDE."

319.—BALTIC.

(BALTISCHE EISENBAHN GESELLSCHAFT.)

The main line of this company (the shares of which are held to some extent in this country) extends from St. Petersburg to Baltischport (392 verstes). At Ligovo, a station on the main line, 13 miles from St. Petersburg, there is a branch to Oranienbaum (length, 26 verstes); and at Gatchino, another station on the main line, 44 miles from St. Petersburg, there is a branch to Tosno (length, 46 verstes). The total length of line operated is thus 464 verstes. It is proposed to extend the Oranienbaum Branch westward to Narva, where it will again join the main line at a distance of 151 verstes from St. Petersburg.

For other particulars respecting revenue, &c., in the past, see MANUAL for 1883, pages 350 and 351, no more recent returns having been received from the company.

DIRECTORS:

President—BARON DE PAHLEN, St. Petersburg.

C. Winbourg. | A. Poleschajeff.
G. Helmersen. | F. Opolsky.

OFFICERS.—Sec., G. Mayer; Eng., Schtschepetoff; Traffic Manager, Wendrick; Loco. Supt., Kolshorn.

Offices—43, Rue Galernia, St. Petersburg.

London Bankers—J. Henry Schröder and Co., 145, Leadenhall Street, E.C.

320.—BUCHAREST AND GIURGEVO.

This State railway extends from Bucharest, in the principality of Roumania, to Giurgevo, and is worked by the Public Works Department. Length, 67 kilomètres. Opened 1st November, 1869.

Agents and Bankers in London—Messrs. C. Devaux and Co., 62, King William Street, E.C.

321.—DUNABURG AND WITEPSK.

Incorporated under the Limited Liability Act of 1862, to construct a line from Dunaburg (the terminus of the Riga and Dunaburg Railway) to Witepsk, under a concession from the Emperor of Russia, dated 19th March (o. s.), 1863. Length, 161 English miles. Nominal capital (fixed by the concession), 2,600,000*l*., on which the Russian Government guaranteed an annual interest of 5*l*. per cent., amounting to 130.000*l*. in sterling money, for 85 years, and an additional 1-12th per cent. to redeem the capital at par in 85 years, by annual drawings, commencing the first year after the opening of the line. By a resolution passed at an extraordinary general meeting of shareholders on the 21st June, 1869, and confirmed on the 12th July, 1869, the company was empowered to borrow 500,000*l*. in relief of its share capital.

REVENUE.—The gross receipts for the year ended 31st December, 1883, amounted to 2,823,796 roubles, and the expenses to 1,809,370 roubles. The net profit amounted to 1,014,426 roubles, against 973,006 roubles in 1882, showing an increase of 41,420 roubles. The directors considered the result of the year's working to be satisfactory as showing progressive improvement, inasmuch as the net results of 1882 were 141,491 roubles in excess of the previous year, and it is further stated that the increase of net profits in 1883 would have been considerably larger except for the extensive repairs and alterations in the carriages and goods wagons, at an outlay of over 153,000 roubles, as against 68,000 roubles expended under the same head in 1882, which accounts for the small increase in the rate of working expenses in 1883. The working expenses in 1883 were 64·07 per cent., against 62·57 per cent. in 1882.

CAPITAL.—The balance sheet to 31st December, 1883, exhibited the receipts and expenditure as follow:—

Receipts.—130,000 shares at 16*l*. per share		£2,080,000
Sundry creditors:—In London	£11,094	
In Russia	35,129=	46,223
Russian Government:—		
Advances on guarantee account	£137,192	
On account of extensions	500,000=	637,192
Sinking fund		56,850
Reserve fund		106,809
Contingent liabilities	£1,308,791	
Less profit in excess of 5 1-12th per cent. applied in reduction	79,403	
	£1,229,387	
		£2,927,074
Expenditure.—As per last account		£2,080,000
Extension account:—For increase of rolling stock and works in Russia...		500,000
Assets in London:—Cash in hand and at bankers	£4,257	
Bills receivable	45,063	
Investments in sundry securities (on account of reserve fund)...	106,809	
Debtors	3,268=	159,397
Assets in Russia:—Cash in hand and at bankers	16,929	
Stores	51,509	
Debtors	62,439=	130,877
Share redemption account (2,840 shares redeemed at 20*l*. each)		56,800
		£2,927,074

The accounts are made up to 31st December, and submitted to the shareholders in the following May. Dividends are paid on the 5th April and 5th October.

DIRECTORS IN LONDON:

Deputy-Chairman—W. R. MOBERLY, Esq. (Messrs. Mitchell, Yeames, and Co.), 4, Fenchurch Avenue, E.C.

H. L. Bischoffsheim, Esq., 31, Throgmorton Street, E.C.

Alexander H. Göschen, Esq. (Messrs. Frühling and Göschen), 12, Austin Friars, E.C.

Loftus Fitz-Wygram, Esq., 89, Eccleston Square, S.W.

Sir William Miller, Bart., 1, Park Lane, W.

Morgan B. Williams, Esq., M.Inst.C.E., Swansea.

DIRECTORS IN RUSSIA:

Chairman—His Excellency J. DE CUBE.

John William Armitstead, Esq.

Hugh Carlile, Esq.

James Henry Hill, Esq.

Charles Rudnitzky, Esq.

OFFICERS.—Sec., S. H. Godefroi; Auditors, William Turquand and Alexander B Sim; Solicitors, Freshfields and Williams, 5, Bank Buildings, E.C.; Bankers, Smith, Payne, and Smiths, 1, Lombard Street, E.C.

Offices—15, Angel Court, Throgmorton Street, E.C.

322.—DUTCH RHENISH.

Incorporated by a decree of the Dutch Government for the purpose of connecting by railway the towns of Amsterdam, Rotterdam, Utrecht, Arnheim, and Emmerich. A branch line from Gouda to the Hague, and tramway to Scheveningen has since been constructed. In operation, 141 miles. Capital authorised—3,000,000*l*., viz.: 2,000,000*l*. original 20*l*. shares; 500,000*l*. new 20*l*. shares (created 6th May. 1867), and 500,000*l*. new 20*l*. shares (created June, 1872, and ranking *pari passu* with the original shares). Loans, 1,100,000*l*. of 4 per cent. in 10 series of 100,000*l*. each, "A" to "K"; 500,000*l*. of 5 per cent. in 5 series of 100,000*l*. each, "A" to "E"; 250,000*l*. of 6 per cent. (not in series), all redeemable at the end of the concession—viz., 31st December, 1898.

REVENUE.—The net profit for the book-year ended 30th April, 1884, sufficed for dividends on the ordinary share capital as follow, viz.:—*Provisional dividends: 20l.* (paid up) shares, 15*s*.; 8*l*. paid shares, 6*s*.; and 3*l*. paid shares, 2*s*. 3*d*. per share respectively. *Balance dividends:* 9*s*., 3*s*. 7*d*., and 1*s*. 4*d*. per share respectively, the total dividend on the 20*l*. shares for the year being 1*l*. 4*s*. per share, equal to 6*l*. per cent. per annum. Provisional dividends on account of the current book-year, 1884-5, were declared in December last, at the respective rates of 10*s*. per 20*l*. paid up share, 4*s*. per 8*l*. paid share, and 1*s*. 6*d*. per 3*l*. paid share.

CAPITAL.—The receipts on this account to 30th April, 1884, were as under:—

Original capital—100,000 fully paid shares at 20*l*.	£2,000,000
First increase of 25,000—22,000 shares at 20*l*. fully paid	440,000
3,000 do. at 8*l*. paid	24,000
Second increase of 25,000 shares—3*l*. per share paid	75,000
	£2,539,000
4 per cent. loan, series "A" to "K"	1,100,000
5 per cent. " "A" to "E"	500,000
6 per cent. loan, 250,000*l*. @ ƒl1·85	246,875
	£4,385,875

The accounts are made up to the end of April in each year, and submitted to the annual meeting at Utrecht in the following June. Any dividend then declared is payable to the English shareholders in July, but interim dividends are paid in the month of January.

DIRECTORS:

President—H. AMESHOFF, Esq., Utrecht.

James S. Forbes, Esq., London.
F. C. Zillesen, Esq., Amsterdam.
J. C. S'Jacob, Esq., Utrecht.
J. J. Uijtwerf Sterling, Esq., Utrecht.

ENGLISH COMMISSARIES:

Sir Thomas Brassey, K.C.B., M.P., Assoc. Inst.C.E., Normanhurst Court, Battle, Sussex, and 3, St. George's Place, Hyde Park, W.
Sir T. Edwards-Moss, Bart., Otterspool, Liverpool.
Ernest Chaplin, Esq., Brooksby Hall, Leicester.
Richard Potter, Esq., York House, Kensington, W.
Alfred Fletcher, Esq., Allerton, Liverpool.
T. Cottingham Edwards-Moss, Otterspool, Liverpool.

Secretary—L. P. J. A. van Hoogstraten, Utrecht.
London Agent—Josiah White, 40, Gracechurch Street, E.C.

323.—DUTCH SOUTH EASTERN.

Incorporated to carry out a concession from the Dutch Government for the construction of a railway from Tilburg to Nymegen, in central Holland.

The capital of the company is as follows:—166,000*l*. "preferred" ordinary or "A" shares, of 20*l*. each, entitled to a preferential dividend of 5 per cent., and a participation in profits after the "B" shares have received 5 per cent.; 166,000*l*. "deferred" ordinary or "B" shares, of 20*l*. each; 181,000*l*. of 5 per cent. debenture bonds. Interest payable 1st January and 1st July; redeemable at par, by annual drawings, within 50 years from 1876.

Arrangements have been in progress with the Dutch Government for a State guarantee of 4½ per cent. on 250,000*l.* as a first charge.

DIRECTORS:

Chairman—J. P. DE BORDES, Esq.

J. B. A. J. M. Verheyen. | J. H. Graadt van Roggen.

COMMISSARIES:

F. A. Müller, Esq.
Baron Sloet van der Beele.
J. A. Diepen, Esq.
Dr. D. van Weel.
Lieut.-Col. F. E. B. Beaumont.
Archibald F. Paull, Esq.

Offices—21, Queen Anne's Gate, Westminster, S.W.

324.—JEREZ TO ALGECIRAS—GIBRALTAR DIRECT.

Established in Madrid by Public Act dated 4th June, 1880, with a Government subvention equivalent to 300,000*l.* Share capital, 415,000*l.*; Government subvention (as above), 300,000*l.*=715,000*l.*

The line, about 78 miles in length, starting from the Jerez Station of the Seville and Cadiz, will have stations at the towns of Arcos, Jimena, Castelar, and San Roque, traverse the wine district of Jerez and a rich agricultural country, and pass within about 4 miles of the lines of Gibraltar before reaching the terminus at Algeciras.

By this railway communication with the coal mines of Belmez, on the Cordova Line, will be established, while timber, oil, corn, and other produce of the district will be brought to the sea, with which no communication, except by mule and cart traffic, at present exists.

A sub-contract for the construction and equipment of the railway has been entered into with Messrs. Eckersley, Bayliss, and Gripper, 4, Westminster Chambers, S.W. The plans, estimates, and specifications have been submitted to the independent examination of Mr. James Livesey, C.E., from whose report it appears that the proposed works present no unusual engineering difficulties.

The railway is, under this contract, to be finished and open for traffic within a period of 4 years, but it is contemplated to open and work it by sections.

In May, 1882, a prospectus was issued inviting subscriptions for 312,500*l.* in 6 per cent. debentures, 1st moiety of the total amount authorised, say 625,000*l.*, secured by a first charge upon the railway and its revenues, after payment of the ordinary working expenses, and bearing 6 per cent. interest, payable half-yearly in London, on the 15th November and 15th May, and redeemable at par by annual drawings, extending over 49 years from the date of the completion of the line, the duration of the concession being 99 years. The price of issue was 97½ per cent.

The debentures (to bearer) will be issued for sums of 500 pesetas, or 20*l.*, or in consolidated debentures of 2,500 pesetas, or 100*l.*

During construction the trustees will retain in their hands funds sufficient for the payment of interest at the rate of 6*l.* per cent. per annum on the amounts paid from time to time on the debentures.

The trustees will hold the proceeds of the debentures, and will apply them under the terms of the Trust Deed, first, in payment of the expenses of and incident to the issue; and, secondly, subject to the retention for interest above mentioned, in payment to the contractors for their outlays upon plans, surveys, concessions, and other expenses incurred by them, as set forth in the contracts, and further in payment for works executed and materials supplied under the certificates of Mr. W. Wilson, C.E., acting as engineer under the contracts of construction.

TRUSTEES:

F. M. Huth, Esq., 12, Tokenhouse Yard, E.C.
Joaquim de Mancha, Esq., 116, Gresham House, E.C.
Sir James Ramsden, Knt., M.Inst.C.E., Barrow-in-Furness.
Joseph Herbert Tritton, Esq., 54, Lombard Street, E.C.

BOARD OF DIRECTION DURING CONSTRUCTION:

President—Exmo. Señor DON ROMERO ROBLEDO.

Vice-Presidents—Exmo. Señor DON EMILIO CASTELAR and Exmo. Señor DON JOSE DE REINA.

DIRECTORS:

Exmo. Señor Marques de Fuentefiel.
Exmo. Señor Don Saturnino Esteban-Collantes.
Exmo. Señor Don Federico Villalva.
Exmo. Señor Don Juan Perez Sanmillan.
Exmo. Señor Don José de Carvajal.
Exmo. Señor Baron de Covadonga.

OFFICERS.—Sec. in London, J. H. Duncan, 41, Coleman Street, E.C.; Eng., W. Wilson, C.E., 13, Dean's Yard, Westminster, S.W.; Solicitors, Freshfields and Williams, 5, Bank Buildings, E.C.; Bankers, Barclay, Bevan, Tritton, and Co., 54, Lombard Street, E.C.

Offices—5, Conde de Aranda, Madrid, and 41, Coleman Street, E.C.

325.—LAKE VALLEY OF SWITZERLAND LIMITED.

Incorporated under the Companies' Acts, 1862 to 1880, for making a railway in Switzerland, from Lenzburg to Emmenbrucke, thus connecting by a through and shorter route the important towns of Lucerne and Lenzburg, for which a concession has been granted by the Federal Government and the Governments of Lucerne and Argovie. The length of railway is about 24 miles. The want of this railway in the above district has been long felt, and now the St. Gothard is completed to Lucerne, the line has become an absolute necessity, forming, as it were, a link in the connection between Italy and Germany.

St. Gothard.—See General Index.

Capital, 150,000*l.*, in 30,000 shares of 5*l.* each, and 60,000*l.* 6 per cent. debentures The line was opened on 15th October, 1883.

DIRECTORS:

Chairman—Lieut.-Col. F. D. GREY, The Angles, East Sheen.

Frederick Edenborough, Esq., 11, Wool Exchange, Coleman Street, E.C.

J. Percy Leith, Esq., 8, Dorset Square, N.W.

Luke Bishop, Esq., 14, Belgrave Road, St. John's Wood, N.W.

Dr. Henry Bartling.

OFFICERS.—Sec., W. C. Twitchett; Eng., Henry Vignoles, M.Inst.C.E., 14, Delahay Street, Westminster, S.W.; Bankers, Brown, Janson, and Co., 32, Abchurch Lane, E.C.

Offices—110, Cannon Street, E.C., and at Hochdorf, Switzerland.

326.—MALTA LIMITED.

Incorporated under the Companies' Acts of 1862 to 1880. Capital, 60,000*l.* in 6,000 shares of 10*l.* each, bearing a guaranteed interest of 5 per cent. during construction, with borrowing powers.

With the approval of the Home Government, a concession for the construction of a line of railway from Valetta to Notabile was granted for 99 years by the Government of Malta to the company.

The line commences in the centre of the city, opposite the Grand Opera House, and passes underneath the fortifications by a tunnel 1,000 yards long. It continues 6 miles and 5 furlongs across the island, through or near the towns of Misida, Curmi, Birchicara, Balzan, Lia, Attard, Zebbug, Musta, Nasciar, terminating at the city of Notabile (or Citta Vecchia). the ancient capital of Malta, near which are the Palace and Gardens of Boschetto, and other attractions, which constitute Notabile the great pleasure resort of the Maltese.

The railway passes through a district containing a population of 100,000 inhabitants, to accommodate which two terminal and seven intermediate stations have been erected. It closely resembles a Metropolitan tramway, and is worked by trains running at frequent intervals, carrying passengers at low fares.

The railway, 6⅝ miles in length, runs across the centre of the island, and serves 100,000 inhabitants, or 15,094 per mile of line. The cost of the railway, equipped and delivered to the company in complete working order, has amounted to about 10,000*l.* per mile.

The line was opened throughout on the 1st March, 1883.

The Malta Government have reserved the right at any time after 15 years from the date of opening, and upon giving six months' notice, to acquire the railway, &c., at a price equal to 17 years' purchase of the net receipts of the company upon an average of the three years next preceding the giving of such notice, with 10 per cent added for compulsory purchase, with a provision that if the average market value of the capital of the company during the said period of three years shall exceed the price to be ascertained as aforesaid, the Government shall pay a sum equal to the amount of such excess by way of addition to that price.

DIRECTORS:

Chairman—GEORGE CAVENDISH TAYLOR, Esq., 42, Elvaston Place, South Kensington, S.W.

Major P. G. Craigie, 6, Lyndhurst Road, Hampstead, N.W.

William Roebuck, Esq., West Lodge, Acton, W.

OFFICERS.—Sec., F. R. Woods; Engs., Wells Owen and Elwes, MM.Inst.C.E., 7, Westminster Chambers, Westminster, S.W.; Auditors, Cooper Brothers and Co., 14, George Street, Mansion House, E.C.; Solicitors, Lane, Monro, and Soutler, 31, Queen Victoria Street, E.C.; Agents and Bankers in Malta, James Bell and Co., Valletta.

Offices—31, Queen Victoria Street, E.C.

327.—METAURENSE VALLEY.

This company has been formed, with a concession for 90 years under royal decree of his Majesty the King of Italy, for the purpose of constructing and working a railway, 23 miles in length, from the Fano Station on the main Brindisi Line, to Santa Barbara, situate in close proximity to Urbino. The railway will traverse the valley of the Metauro and connect the three important cities of Fano, Fossombrone, and Urbino. The total cost of the railway fully equipped, with rolling stock, &c., including all the benefits of the concession, is 93,000*l.* in cash, 30,000*l.* in debentures, and 20,000*l.* in ordinary shares. This is at the low rate of a little over 6,000*l.* a mile. The construction of this line is authorised by the Parliament of Italy and by royal decree. A subsidy is payable of 40,000*l.* in cash, by monthly instalments, as the works proceed, which sum will be invested in Italian Government 5 per cent. rentes. in trust, to apply the same with its accruing interest exclusively to the payment of dividends on the 6 per cent. preference shares, thus securing their due payment for a period of about 10 years without consideration of traffic receipts. Fano has a station on the main Brindisi Line, on the coast of the Adriatic. At a short distance north and south are the ports of Pesaro and Ancona, at the latter of which all the mail steamers stop. Fossombrone is about 15 miles from Fano; it is a market town, and the centre of a large manufacturing and commercial district. Urbino, the capital of the province, is a large military centre, an assize town, and the seat of a large university.

A contract has been entered into, dated 15th August, 1884, between Christopher Firbank, the Italian Railways Syndicate Limited, Henry Kendrick, and the Metaurense Valley Limited.

CAPITAL.—120,000*l.*, viz., 100,000*l.* in 5,000 shares of 20*l.* each, bearing a cumulative preferential dividend of 6*l.* per cent. per annum, and 20,000*l.* in 1,000 ordinary shares of 20*l.* each. The dividends on the 100,000*l.* preference shares will date from the payment of the various instalments from time to time falling due, commencing with the moneys paid on allotment.

TRUSTEES:

(On behalf of the preference shareholders for the administration of the funds set apart for the payment of the 6 per cent. on the preference shares.)

The Right Hon. Lord Brabourne, Smeeth, Kent.

The Right Hon. Lord Thurlow, Dunphail House, Morayshire.

DIRECTORS:

Chairman—The Right Hon. Lord BRABOURNE, Smeeth, Kent.

The Right Hon. Lord Thurlow, Dunphail House, Morayshire.

Harry F. Giles, Esq., Almorah Lodge, Oak Hill Road, Surbiton.

J. Dick-Peddie, Esq., M.P.

A. Curzon Tompson, Esq.

OFFICERS.—Sec. (pro tem.), Henry Stoneman; Chief Eng., Robert Elliott Cooper, M.Inst.C.E., The Sanctuary, Westminster, S.W.; Solicitors, Wild, Bowne, and Wild, Ironmonger Lane, E.C.; Bankers, Herries, Farquhar, and Co., St. James's Street, S.W.

London Offices—10, Pancras Lane, E.C.

328.—METROPOLITAN OF CONSTANTINOPLE.

Established under "The Companies' Acts, 1862 and 1867," with the Articles of Association approved by the Imperial Ottoman Government. Capital, 250,000*l.* sterling, divided into 12,500 shares of 20*l.* each (of which 6,250 shares were offered for subscription in August, 1872, 1,250 shares being reserved to be issued as fully paid up under the contract for works, and 5,000 for subscribers in Turkey). Interest at the rate of 5 per cent. during construction.

The concession from the Imperial Ottoman Government, granted to M. Gavand, is for the term of 42 years from the period fixed for completion of the works (2nd January, 1874), and the line to be constructed and worked by the concessionaire, under the supervision of the Ottoman Government. The concession gives a preferential right to the concessionaire for the construction of any other similar railways which the Government may wish to authorise between Galata and Pera, within a distance of 2 kilomètres (about a mile and a quarter) on either side of the line, or in the city of Stamboul. The concession authorises a maximum tariff of fares for first class passengers of two piastres (about 4*d.*), and for second class passengers one piastre (about 2*d.*) A tariff for animals and goods traffic is also fixed. The concession does not require a third class. The Ottoman Government is to receive 1½ per cent. of the net profits. After 15 years the Government is entitled to purchase the undertaking, paying the concessionaire an annuity for the remainder of the term, calculated upon the average of the net income of the five best of the preceding seven years, but not less than the amount of that received in the last preceding year, and paying also the value of the rolling stock and moveable materials. The Government is also bound to buy the rolling stock, &c., at the end of the concession, if not purchased previously.

This is a very short underground railway. The total length of the tunnel is 634 yards, that of the rails being 672 yards. The difference of level between the two extremities is 200 feet, and the average grade 1 in 10. The speed is 10 miles an hour, and the fares are first class 2d. and second class 1d. The line is double, and worked on the rope system, the descending carriages aiding the ascent of those going up the incline. The excess load allowed for the ascending train being 4½ tons. The motive power is supplied by a pair of winding engines. The engine driver is furnished with a small model, arranged vertically, and worked by the engine, from which he can tell the position of the trains at any moment. The rails are of Bessemer steel, Vignole's type. The greatest depth of the tunnel beneath the surface is 80 feet. The line connects Galata, the shipping and commercial quarter, at the bottom, with Pera, the residential quarter, at the top of the tunnel. The projector, a Frenchman, intended its prolongation from Galata under the Golden Horn, to Stamboul, and the construction of a new port on the Sea of Marmora. It is believed that the realisation of this project would greatly improve the commercial position of Constantinople.

The line was opened for traffic on the 17th January, 1875.

REVENUE.—The gross receipts for the year ended 31st December, 1883, amounted to 13,135*l.* (including rents 625*l.* and interest 612*l.*) The working expenses amounted to 8,716*l.*, and the London office expenses to 705*l.*, leaving a net profit of 3,713*l.*, to which 486*l.* balance from last year was carried, making 4,199*l.* From this amount a dividend of 1 per cent. was declared, payable on 30th April, 1884, 500*l.* was added to reserve account, making it 8,852*l.*, 500*l.* balance of preliminary expenses account was written off, and 699*l.* was carried forward. The revenue has been diminished by the competition of a tramway company.

CAPITAL.—The receipts on this account amounted to 249,986*l.* (including 12,500 shares, 20*l.* each), and there had been expended 247,742*l.* up to 31st December, 1883. The general balance sheet to 31st December, 1883, showed cash at bankers in London and at Constantinople, 1,491*l.* Invested in loans against securities. 13,455*l.*

The annual meeting is held in London in the month of March.

Transfer form, ordinary; fee, 2*s.* 6*d.* per deed. Certificates are required to accompany transfers. All communications to be addressed to the Secretary.

DIRECTORS:

Chairman—THOMAS HUGHES, Esq., Q.C., 11, Stanley Place, Chester.

Charles Schiff, Esq., 43, Lothbury, E.C.

John Graham Stewart, Esq., 13, Curzon Street, Mayfair, W.

Charles Helbig, Esq., Constantinople.

Walter N. Senior, Esq., 98, Cheyne Walk, Chelsea, S.W.

OFFICERS.—Sec., J. Paterson; Auditor, T. S. Lindsay; Solicitors, Bompas, Bischoff, and Dodgson, 4, Great Winchester Street Buildings, E.C.; Bankers, Glyn, Mills, Currie, and Co., 67, Lombard Street, E.C.; General Manager in Constantinople, William Albert.

Offices—35, Walbrook, E.C., and Constantinople.

329.—NORTHERN OF EUROPE LIMITED.

Share capital, 1,500,000*l.*, in 150,000 preference shares of 5*l.* each, and 150,000 ordinary shares of 5*l.* each. 5 per cent. debenture stock, 1,500,000*l.*

Registered 14th July, 1883. This company has been constituted to construct a railway from Lulea, at the north end of the Gulf of Bothnia, to the ice-free Ofoten. Fjord, in Norway. It will enable the vast iron mountains of Gellivara, Kirunavara, and Luosavara to be worked, as well as the great forests on its route, and create a great fish traffic from the Lofodens to the Gulf of Bothnia and Finland. The iron ores on the line contain on an average 70 per cent. of metallic iron. The line is about 280 miles in length.

The works have been commenced at Lulea. Concessions to construct and work the line have been obtained from the governments of Sweden and Norway.

The company have arranged with the owners of the Gellivara iron mountain to work the iron ore which will be quarried. The owner of the Luosavara iron mountain has guaranteed a minimum tonnage of about 500,000 tons of ore per annum.

The issue price of the 5 per cent. debenture stock is 90*l.* per 100*l.*, and 3 years' interest will be deposited. The issue price of the 5 per cent. preference shares is 70*l.* per cent., and 7 years' interest will be deposited. The debenture stock and preference shares are quoted at these prices in Christiania.

Transfer form, common; fee, 2*s.* 6*d.* per deed. No amounts of less than 10*l.* of debenture stock transferred.

TRUSTEES FOR THE DEBENTURE HOLDERS:

Major-General Boileau, R.E., F.R.S.
Rev. Canon Brereton.

DIRECTORS:

Lord Brownlow Cecil, Junior Carlton Club, S.W.
Hume Williams, Esq., 1, Essex Court, Temple, E.C.
Alexander Beazeley, Esq., New Thornton Heath.
William Stronach Lockhart, Esq., Lyndale House, The Bank, Highgate, N.
The Right Hon. Pehr Jakob von Ehrenheim (formerly Minister of State), Stockholm.
Captain Carl Gustaf Hierta, Stockholm.
Lieutenant Ole Lund, Christiania.

OFFICERS.—Sec., Edgar John Ford; Bankers, Smith, Payne, and Smiths, 1, Lombard Street, E.C., and Tho. Joh. Heftye and Son, Christiania; Auditor, H. M. Leslie; Solicitors, Ashurst, Morris, Crisp, and Co., 6, Old Jewry, E.C.
Offices—3, Victoria Street, Westminster, S.W.

330.—NORTHERN OF FRANCE.

The original concession was for 38 years; but in consideration of new lines agreed to be made, by a decree of 19th February, 1852, the concession was extended to 99 years, and will expire on both sections 10th September, 1947. The sum to be placed aside each year for the reduction of the social capital has been reduced from 2,236,384*fr.* to 168,250*fr.*

The shares and obligations of the Northern of France are held to some extent in this country. The obligations are for 500*fr.* (20*l.*) each, and carry interest at 3 per cent. per annum, payable half-yearly, in January and July. They are redeemable at par, by annual drawings, within 75 years.

COUNCIL OF ADMINISTRATION:

President—Baron ALPHONSE DE ROTHSCHILD.

Vice-President—Baron DE SAINT-DIDIER.

M. Alexandre Adam.
Baron Gustave de Rothschild.
M. Joseph Hottinguer.
Duc de Mouchy.
M. Charles Burton.
M. Léon Say.
Baron de Soubeyran.
M. Adolphe Vernes.
M. Gabriel Dehaynin.
Comte A. de Germiny.
Vicomte de Saint-Pierre.
Comte Pillet-Will.
M. Gaston Griolet.
M. Frédéric Moreau.
M. André de Waru.
M. E. Baudelot.
M. Omer Vallon.
M. Edouard Agache.
Baron Arthur de Rothschild.
Martelle Pinguet.

DIRECTORS IN LONDON:

Sir Nathaniel de Rothschild, Bart., M.P., 148, Piccadilly, W.
Baron Alfred de Rothschild, 148, Piccadilly, W.

OFFICERS.—Paris: Emile Castel, Secrétaire de la Cie.; Ramond de la Croisette, Chef du Contentieux et du Domaine; Graffin, Chef de la Comptabilité générale; Binay, Caissier Central; Gateau, Chef du Service des Titres; Felix Mathias, Ingénieur, Chef de l'Exploitation; Sartiaux, Ingénieur, Sous Chef de l'Exploitation; Ed. Delebecque, Ingénieur, Chef du Matériel et de la Traction; Boucher, Ingénieur en Chef des Travaux et de la Surveillance; Vainet, Ingénieur en Chef de l'Entretien.

London Offices—South Eastern Railway, London Bridge Station, S.E.
Agent Résident—A. Sire.

331.—NORTHERN OF SPAIN.

In 1870 subscriptions were invited by Messrs. Bischoffsheim and Goldschmidt for part of 13,277,660*l.* 3 per cent. priority obligations of this company. These obligations for 20*l.* each are to be repaid at par within 81 years from the 1st April, 1878, by annual drawings. Interest coupons are attached, payable in London on the 1st April and 1st October in each year. If the coupons are presented not later than the 15th of either of these months, the payment will be at the rate of 25·20*fr.* to the £ sterling, but if presented later than the 15th of the month, the payment will be made at the exchange of the day.

The main line of the company commences at Madrid, and proceeds in a northerly direction to Avila, Valladolid, Venta de Baños, Burgos, Vittoria, Beasain, San Sebastian, and Irun, where it joins the French railway system; the length of this line is 638 kils. At Venta de Baños, 286 kils. north of Madrid, the line branches off to Cabanas, Quintanilla de las Torres, Santa Cruz, and Santander; the distance from Venta de Baños to Santander being 230 kils. At Quintanilla, there is a branch to Baruello, length 14 kils. Including 10 kils. of railway in Madrid, the company altogether possesses 892 kils.

Bilbao Tudela.—This line is also amalgamated with the Northern of Spain.

Pampeluna, Saragossa, and Barcelona.—This line is now amalgamated with the Northern of Spain, the exchange of obligations of the former for those of the latter company having taken place in the first half-year of 1878.

Variable Revenue Obligations.—In July, 1878, it was stated that the great majority of the holders of the "A" and "B" coupons had, in the past, accepted the alienation of those coupons, in consideration of 15*s.* per coupon paid by the company, but on account of the dividend on the share capital for 1877 reaching 4 per cent., and the original agreement being that the full amount of those coupons should be paid if the dividend reached 3 per cent., a group of holders who kept their coupons on the strength of that agreement had required its execution, and had appealed to the Tribunal of Commerce to support their views.

COUNCIL OF ADMINISTRATION:

President—DUC DE LA TORRE.

Vice-Presidents—M. A. MARTINEZ and J. PEREIRE.

Director—Mons. EDR. GUILLAUME.

OFFICERS.—Sec., P. M. Vigo; Traffic Man., E. Barthelemy; Loco. Eng., E Plainemaison; Consulting Eng., C. Collet, Paris; M. Guerin De Littau, Sec. at Paris.

Offices—9, Paseo de Recoletos, Madrid.
London Agents—Crédit Lyonnais, Lombard Street, E.C.
Paris—25, Boulevard Haussmann.

332.—OTTOMAN—SMYRNA TO AIDIN.

Established by concession from the Turkish Government, who guarantee the company 112,000*l.* per annum. The following is an outline of the principal clauses of the concession:—1. It is perpetual, subject to the right of purchase by the Ottoman Government upon agreed and equitable terms, at the end of 50, 75, 95, and every subsequent 20 years. 2. A guarantee as above-mentioned for 42 years. The line to be opened in sections, and the guarantee to come into operation as each section is opened. Profits over 8 per cent. to be divided with Government. 3. Government lands and materials to be taken and made use of by the company gratuitously. 4. Materials for constructing, working, and renewing the railway, to be imported duty free. 5. Power of working all coal mines within 30 miles of any part of the lines on payment of a fixed royalty. 6. The privileges of erecting warehouses, with a custom-house attached, on company's premises at Smyrna. 7. Government not to grant a concession to any competing line. 8. Unrestricted power of management.

The railway, 80¾ miles in length, connects Smyrna, the most important seaport in the Levant, with Guzel, Hissar, or Aidin, the grand *entrepôt* of the internal trade of Asia Minor. The works were commenced on 24th September, 1858, and 27 miles were opened on 24th December, 1860; 10 on 9th September, 1861; and 3 (completing the first section) on 14th November, 1861. The extension to Ephesus (7½ miles) was opened on 15th September, 1862, the line being opened to Aidin on 1st July, 1866, when the guarantee of 112,000*l.* a-year, by the Turkish Government, came into operation. Productive, 84½ miles.

AIDIN TO SERAIKEUY EXTENSION AND BRANCH FROM TURBALLI TO THYRA.—A Government concession for the construction and working of this extension and branch was approved by a resolution of the proprietors at a special meeting, held 4th June, 1878, the concession to come to an end at the same time as the original concession for the line from Smyrna to Aidin, viz., on the 15th October. N.S., 1910 A.D. The total length of the new lines will be about 139 kilometres, or 87 English miles. Period for completion, forty months from the date of the concession. The new and old lines to be worked by the company at 55 per cent. of the gross receipts for one half the period of concession, and 50 per cent. for the remaining half of the same period so far as concerns the calculations for guarantee. For the full text of the concession see *Appendix* to the MANUAL for 1879. The concession was fully ratified by the firman of the Sultan. In October, 1880, the company made an issue of 350,000*l.* 5 per cent. debentures, at 75*l.* per cent., for the purpose of the extension from Aidin to Kuyujak, a distance of 35 miles, secured by a first charge upon over 65·43 per cent of the net traffic earnings of the existing line, and by a first charge upon the entire undertaking of the extension to be constructed from Aidin to Kuyujak. The works were commenced in October, 1880, and the entire line to Kuyujak opened for traffic in August, 1881, since which time the traffic returns have shown considerable increase.

In February, 1882, the company made a further issue of 100,000*l.* 5 per cent. debentures, at 82*l.* 10*s.* per cent., for the purpose of the extension from Kuyujak to Seraikeuy, secured by a first charge upon 16·08 per cent. of the net traffic earnings of the original line from Smyrna to Aidin, and by a first charge upon the extension to Seraikeuy, from a point at or near to Ortakchi. The extension to Seraikeuy was opened for traffic on 1st July, 1882. The Council of Administration, in their report of September, announced that they would give their earnest consideration to the best means of providing the capital for the line to Bainder and Thyra.

PROPOSED AGREEMENT WITH OTTOMAN GOVERNMENT FOR LEASE OF THE CASSABA AND SMYRNA TO ALESHER LINES (1883).—For full text of this agreement see *Appendix* to the MANUAL for 1884, page 513.

REVENUE.—The gross receipts for the half-year ended 30th June, 1884, were 100.188*l.*, against 62,736*l.* for the corresponding period of 1883, and the expenses 57,230*l.*, as compared with 35,844*l.*, and the net profits amounted to 42,959*l.*, against 26,892*l.* in 1883.

The bonds drawn 1st January, 1884, were paid immediately, and the debenture interest due 1st May, 1881, was paid by the Council of Administration in November, 1884. The coupons for 1st November, 1881, and those which have since fallen due, are now, therefore, in arrear.

CAPITAL.—The expenditure on this account to 30th June, 1884, including interest on shares and debentures, and discount, amounted to 2,676,608*l.*, whilst the receipts to the same date had been as under:—

Shares, 20*l.* each	£891,940
Debentures, 6 per cent. and 5 per cent.	1,345,700
Interest, &c.	54,165
Net revenue applied to redemption of debentures	232,335
Net revenue applied to capital expenditure	195,000

The debentures rank as a first charge, and are divided into 5 classes in order of priority, as follow:—6 per cent. debentures "non-assenting;" 5 per cent. debentures (Kuyujak Extension), and 5 per cent. debentures (Seraikeuy Extension); 6 per cent. debentures "assenting" (Kuyujak Extension), and 6 per cent. debentures (Seraikeuy Extension). The interest is payable on the 6 per cent. debentures (3 years in arrear) on 1st May and 1st November, and on the 5 per cent. debentures 1st March and 1st September. The 6 per cent. debentures are redeemable at par on the 1st November, 1907, and the 5 per cent. debentures on the 1st September, 1910. Sinking funds are provided for, the 6 per cent. being redeemable by annual drawings, and the 5 per cent. by purchase in the markets.

Half-yearly meetings held in London in March and September.

DIRECTORS:

President—Sir GEO. K. RICKARDS, K.C.B., Fyfield House, Oxford.

Sir Algernon Borthwick, Knt., 139, Piccadilly, W.
Charles K. Freshfield, Esq., M.P., Upper Gatton, Surrey.
Eric Carrington Smith, Esq., 1, Lombard Street, E.C.
Sir Arthur Otway, Bart., M.P., 13, Eaton Place, S.W.
Joseph Henry Trewby, Esq., 1, Bryanston Square, W.

All eligible for re-election.

OFFICERS.—Sec., Thos. H. Cooke, 13, Moorgate Street, E.C.; Gen. Man. and Eng., Edward Purser, C.E., Smyrna; Agent, J. S. Dalessio, Constantinople; Auditors, Geo. T. Rait, F.C.A., 70, Bishopgate Street Within, E.C., and Henry Swaffield, 5, Queen Street Place, E.C.; Solicitor, George Hooper, 17, Lincoln's Inn Fields, W.C.; Bankers in London, Smith, Payne, and Smiths, 1, Lombard Street, E.C.; Bankers in Turkey, the Imperial Ottoman Bank.

Offices—13, Moorgate Street, E.C.

333.—PARIS, LYONS, AND MEDITERRANEAN.

A confederation under Imperial decree, dated 19th June, 1857, of the Paris and Lyons, the Lyons and Mediterranean, the Lyons and Geneva, and all the subsidiaries of these companies. The concession is for 99 years from the 1st January, 1860.

In 1874 the London agency of the Credit Lyonnais offered for subscription 600,000 debenture bonds (obligations fusion 1866) issued by this company for the purpose of completing its new lines. These bonds are for 500 francs nominal each, and bear interest at the rate of 3 per cent. per annum, payable in London on the 1st April and 1st October of each year. The principal is repayable at par in October of each year by means of annual drawings extending over a period of 85 years. The coupons must be left at the London Agency, 29, Lombard Street, E.C., two clear days for examination, and the certificates of registered bonds ten clear days.

The company's 5 per cent. obligations are held to a considerable extent in this country. They are for 20*l.* each, and are redeemable at 20 per cent. premium by annual drawings within 99 years from the date of issue. Coupons are attached payable in London on the 1st January and 1st July in each year.

At a special meeting held in December, 1875, the Council of Administration was authorised to issue two new series of 600,000 obligations; these obligations bear interest at the rate of 3 per cent. per annum, and are to be redeemed at 20*l.* each. The nominal addition to the obligation capital of the company is thus 12,000,000*l.*

ALGERIA.—The network in Algeria—consisting of a line from Algiers to Oran (about 286½ miles), and a line from Phillippeville to Oran (about 54⅝ miles)—was conceded to the Paris, Lyons, and Mediterranean Company under Imperial decree dated 11th June, 1863.

The share capital of the company amounts to 16,000,000*l.* in 20*l.* shares. It is the custom with this company to pay 25 francs per share, on account of the current year's income, on the 1st November, and the balance on the 1st May in the following year.

The dividends earned by this company have in the past exceeded 10 per cent. per annum.

The dividends on the ordinary share capital have been as follow, viz.:—

1876—*fr.*55 per 20*l.* share.	1879—*fr.*55 per 20*l.* share.
1877—*fr.*52 ,,	1880—*fr.*70 ,,
1878—*fr.*55 ,,	1881—*fr.*75 ,,

London Agency—The Credit Lyonnais, 40, Lombard Street, E.C.

Offices—17, Rue Lafitte, Paris.

334.—RIGA AND DUNABURG.

Provisionally registered, 7th and 8th Vic., cap. 110. Established by special decree of His Imperial Majesty the Emperor of Russia, dated the 18th May, 1853, granting a guarantee of a minimum interest of 4 per cent. on the sum of 12,000,000 roubles of capital, which is equal to a guarantee of 5 per cent. on the sum required for the construction of the railway, with other valuable privileges. An additional ½ per cent. is also guaranteed on the above sum, to form a sinking fund to redeem the shares at par within 56 years. Length, 140 miles.

Capital (authorised by the Imperial Government), 1,632,000*l.* in 81,600 shares of 20*l.* each, bearing a guaranteed minimum interest of 4 per cent.

Several modifications in the concession were announced in March, 1857. The more prominent were as follows:—"The term of the concession has been extended from

56 to 75 years, dated from the opening of the whole line, during which period the company will enjoy the profits. The Imperial Government has not reserved to itself the right to purchase the line during the term of concession. The terms as now arranged enable the directors to substantiate the original representation of a *minimum interest of 5 per cent.* upon the required capital; and the terms of the contract for the construction of the line, as approved by the Engineer-in-Chief, leave such a margin as to justify the directors in anticipating an increase on that per centage. The company is not required to account to the Imperial Government for its expenditure, but the guarantee applies to the fixed capital for 75 years; hence, any saving in the cost of the works enhances the value of the guarantee."

REVENUE.—The following notice was issued in September 1882, viz.:—"The 49th ordinary general meeting of the shareholders was held on the 6th (18th) of September, 1882. After reading the business report of the company, the auditors certified that they had examined the books, cash accounts, and the appertaining documents, and found them correct. The meeting then resolved to abandon the intended contract for a loan of 2,000,000 roubles, as the Government required conditions which would necessitate a change in the statutes of the company, such change being for formal reasons impracticable. The general meeting then passed the budget for 1883, viz.: Receipts, 3,075,000 roubles; outgoings, 2,432,800 roubles."

DIRECTORS:

Chairman—The Councillor of State, G. VON CUBE, Riga.

Deputy-Chairman—Coll. Ass., A. FALTIN, Riga.

A. Hollander, Esq., Riga.
Councillor Dolmatow.
Henry Robinson, Esq., Riga.

OFFICERS.—Sec., E. Merteus, Riga; Chief Eng., — Bocker; Loco. Supt., — Hentschel; Auditors, Senator Bergengrün and H. Alex. Kroeger.

335.—ROYAL SARDINIAN.

Guaranteed by the Italian Government by a convention, particulars of which will be found below. A *Société Anonyme:* the liability of shareholders limited to the amount of their shares.

The objects of this company are to connect the three ports of Sardinia, Cagliari in the south, Terranova in the north-east, and Porto Torres in the north, and also to construct a branch into the mineral districts, of which the town of Iglesias is the chief centre; these are to be the trunk lines of the island. Branches may subsequently be made in such directions as may be advisable, subject to satisfactory arrangements with the Italian Government.

By the convention, which became law in 1877, the company receive, from the 1st July in that year, a fixed allowance of 6,000*fr.* per kil. for working expenses, and 14,800*fr.* net per kil. on all the lines, old and new, and on the completion of the new lines the fixed sum of 6,000*fr.* for working expenses increased to 7,000*fr.* per kil.

MILEAGE.—Length of lines open and working, first period, 197 kil.; second period, 190 kil.; total length of lines, including Aranci Extension, 413½ kil. (or about 259 miles). The total guarantee per annum on the mileage amounts to about 6,122,000*fr.*

During the year 1882 the Italian Government ordered the extension of the line from Terranova to the Golfo degli Aranci. The Government guarantee was increased to provide the interest upon the further capital issued for this extension. This extension line, about 23 kil., was opened for traffic on the 1st July, 1883.

CAPITAL.

90,000 3 per cent. obligations, series "A" and "B," of 20*l.* each, redeemable at par by annual drawings within 90 years after date of issue.
2,478 Obligations already redeemed.

87,245 Obligations outstanding 1st January, 1884.
191,165—160,000 3 per cent. obligations of 500*fr.* each, issued in 1879, and 10,000 3 per cent. obligations of 500*fr.* each, issued in 1882, for the construction of the lines of the second period, and redeemable at par by annual drawings within 95 years from dates of issue; 21,165 also issued in 1882, for the construction of the extension to the Golfo degli Aranci.
Already redeemed, 1,002.
60,000 5 per cent. preference shares of 10*l.* each.
40,000 Ordinary shares of 10*l.* each.

MEM.—It is stated that the guarantee practically ensures minimum net dividends of 5 per cent per annum on both preference and ordinary shares.

After payment of 5 per cent. per annum on both the preference and ordinary shares, all further dividends are divided between them *pro rata*.

The obligations are redeemable by annual drawings, at par, by means of an accumulative sinking fund, of 1 lire per obligation (10*d*.). The interest on these is payable half-yearly, the "A" and "C" obligations on 1st April and 1st October, and "B" 1st January and 1st July.

The "A," "B," and "C" bonds constitute the first charge on the company's receipts after payment of working expenses; while the preference shares are the second charge.

Article 39 of the new statutes adopted in 1877 provides as follows:—"The net profits remaining after deducting the amount required for the payment of the interest and amortisation of the obligations, as well as all the working expenses, and the expenses of the administration, shall be applied and divided in the following order:—(*a*) 5 per cent. shall be put to a reserve fund until it reaches 2,000,000 lire (about 80,000*l*.) (*b*) To the payment of interest at 5 per cent. upon the preference shares (class 'A'). (*c*) To the payment of interest also at 5 per cent. on the ordinary shares (class 'B')."

The directors in their last report make the following statement with regard to the company's income for the year 1884:—

The estimate for 1884, which may be considered as the normal estimate of our company, and more subject to improvement than otherwise, presents the following results:—

Income	Lire 8,342,900
Expenditure	7,017,200
Leaving a net surplus of	Lire 1,325,700

which, after deducting 5 per cent. for the reserve fund, allows a payment of 5 per cent., free of taxes, to both the preference and ordinary shares.

The full dividend, 5 per cent., on all the 60,000 preference shares, and 10*s*. per share on all the 40,000 ordinary shares, has been paid for the years 1882, 1883, and 1884.

In June, 1882, the following official notice was published, viz.:—"We beg to inform you that the dividend on the preference shares in this company will in future be payable half-yearly instead of yearly; and that the next dividend, maturing on the 30th June, 1882, will be payable on the 1st July, 1882, at the rate of 5 per cent. per annum, free of Italian taxes."

On the 19th of December, 1884, it was announced that the dividend on the ordinary shares will in future be paid half-yearly, instead of yearly, and the next dividend, maturing on the 30th of June, 1885, will be paid on the 1st July, 1885, at the rate of 5 per cent. per annum, like the dividend on the preference shares.—See *Times* and other dailies of the 19th December, 1884.

Accounts made up once a year and submitted to annual meeting in Rome, in March, the dividend on the ordinary shares for the whole of the preceding year being paid early in April.

COUNCIL OF ADMINISTRATION:

Managing Director—Commander EPAMINONDA SEGRÉ, Rome.

Cavalier Francesco Calvi, Cagliari.
Marquis Stefano di Villahermosa e Nissa, Resident Director at Cagliari, Sardinia.
Thomas Barnes, Esq., Manchester.
John Young, Esq., London.
Advocate Carlo Mari, Rome.

OFFICERS.—Sec., Signor B. Besso, Rome; Eng.-in-Chief, Benj. Piercy, C.E.; General Traffic Manager, Cavalier L. Martinoli, Cagliari; Chief Accountant, G. Sica; Auditors, F. Wallop and Cavalier I. De Benedetti, Rome.

Offices—In Rome, 374, Via del Corso.

London Agents—C. de Tivoli and F. G. Whitwham, 8, Drapers' Gardens, Throgmorton Avenue, E.C.

336.—ROYAL SWEDISH.

Originally established under royal charter for the construction of a railway from Köping to Hult. Constructed from Örebro to Köping. Opened in March, 1856, 10 miles; in August, 1857, 25 miles; in 1867, 10 miles, from Arboga to Köping. The ascertained nominal capital is as follows:—92,000 original shares of 5*l*. each; 38,000 preference shares of 4*l*. each; 3,335 new consolidated obligations of 55*l*. each; and 1,200 single obligations of 6*l*. 17*s*. 6*d*. each. In operation at 31st December, 1875, 45 miles.

A line has been constructed by an independent company from Uttersburg to Köping, a distance of 15 English miles north of the latter town, for the accommodation of a mineral district, from whence is brought a considerable supply of rough ore and also manufactured iron. The port of Köping, on the Malar Lake, however, is closed by ice during several months of the year; and a necessity has arisen for securing communication all the year round with the southern ports of Sweden (and especially Gothenburg) over the Government State railways.

In September, 1880, a meeting was held in London to consider the financial arrangements of the company, and to appoint a committee to confer with the directors on the subject, when the following scheme was approved as the basis of future arrangements, viz.:—"That all the outstanding obligations of the Royal Swedish, then amounting to 208,450*l*., should be paid off or converted into debenture stock as soon as possible, in order to liberate any surplus profits for division amongst the shareholders."

Subsequently the following notice was issued, viz.:—"At a meeting of shareholders, held on the 17th September, 1880, resolutions were unanimously passed recommending the creating of a 5 per cent. debenture stock in lieu of the existing obligations, by means of which surplus net revenue would become available for division amongst the shareholders.

To further the objects contained in the two preceding paragraphs, and in order to carry out an arrangement between the preference and the ordinary shareholders, under which the net income of the concern would be divided in the proportion of ⅞th to the preference and ⅛th to the ordinary shareholders respectively, a new company has been formed called "The Associated Proprietors in the Royal Swedish Railway Company Limited," and upon these subjects the directors, in their report issued in July, 1884, stated as follows:—

"Ninety-six of the consolidated obligations, amounting to 5,280*l*. were drawn and paid off on 1st May, 1883, and in the autumn a further sum of 4,277*l*. was set aside to pay off, when presented, 611 of the old obligations of 5*l*. each (with ten years' interest thereon) which have been called in.

"The calling in of these old obligations may be looked upon as an anticipatory drawing of an equivalent amount of existing obligations, and in place of the drawing which would otherwise have taken place in March last, and the obligation debt has been reduced by that amount.

"The sum which would have been available for dividend, if not otherwise applied, is 5,755*l*.

"As regards the important subject of the 'Associated Company' for the purpose of carrying out the arrangement between the two classes of shareholders, together with the conversion of the obligation debt, and the consequent release of the net income for dividend, the directors have to report that about 13,000 preference and 30,000 ordinary shares have been sent in and exchanged for shares of the new company. These shares represent about one-third of the supposed total number of each class respectively; but as the number of shares of which the names and addresses of the holders are known to the directors only amount to about 23,000 preference and 38,000 ordinary, it is thought possible, and even probable, that a large number of ordinary and a proportion of preference shares are not in existence, or may never be presented to claim dividend.

"The directors wish to point out that they have no power to carry out the conversion, except in the manner already sanctioned, without a further appeal to the shareholders, which they do not consider advisable, as it would tend to re-open the whole question, and create an antagonism between the two classes of shareholders, resulting probably in a deadlock as before.

"On the other hand, the new company, besides being the direct means of carrying out the objects for which it is formed, offers other very important advantages, the consideration of which the directors wish to impress upon the attention of the shareholders The whole of the share capital, with the exception of a very few shares, being held in England, the new company brings together the shareholders in a compact body, with identical interests, and enables them to exercise a salutary control over the management of their property, as well as obviates the difficulty which the directors have always experienced in communicating with the shareholders in consequence of the shares being to bearer; and, in addition, reverting to the probable non-existence of shares, would facilitate the possible reconstruction, either by a nominal or virtual sale of the company, so as to be able to deal with this matter for the benefit of the shareholders.

"The question now for consideration is—have a sufficient number of shares come into the new company to render it advisable for the directors to enter into the agreement with the 'Associated Company' for the conversion of the obligations? The opinion of the directors is that more preference shares should first be sent in. They think that at least half the total number should be represented in the new company. This will leave about 6,000 more to be sent in, and the directors hope that at least that number will have been exchanged before the end of the year, when they should make preparations for the conversion of the obligations in the spring. If they are not sent in by that time the directors will consider the propriety of taking the sense of the shareholders upon the subject, and in the meantime herewith is appended a tabular statement, of which the proprietors can judge for themselves, which shows the probable rate of dividend to shareholders, preference and ordinary, in the Royal Swedish Company, and to those who exchange into the Associated Company, under certain conditions as to rate of interest upon Associated Company's debentures or debenture stock, and as to the number of preference shares which may have been exchanged into the new company."

Estimate of relative rates of dividend per cent. upon preference and ordinary share capital of Royal Swedish Company, and upon such preference and ordinary capital which may be exchanged into the Associated Company.

If the rate of interest on Associated Company's Debentures or Debenture Stock be	And the number of Preference Shares exchanged be	And the rate of dividend paid on Preference Shares is			The rate of dividend to Preference Shareholders who have exchanged will be			Rate of dividend to Ordinary Shareholders who may have exchanged. If one-third of total number of Ordinary Shares have been exchanged.			If one-half of total number of Ordinary Shares have been exchanged.		
		Per cent.			Per cent.			Per cent.		Per share.	Per cent.		Per share.
		£	s.	d.	£	s.	d.	s.	d.	d.	s.	d.	d.
5 per cent.—saving of interest £[illegible]	One-third of total number	4	0	0	5	0	0	4	9	2¾	3	1	1¾
		5	0	0	5	17	6	5	6	3¼	3	8	2¼
Ditto	One-half	4	0	0	4	9	11	6	4	3¾	4	3	2½
		5	0	0	5	7	5	7	7	4½	5	1	3
Ditto	Three-quarters	4	0	0	4	3	4	8	10	5¼	5	10	3½
		5	0	0	5	0	9	10	8	6¼	7	1	4¼
4½ per cent.—saving of interest £1,342	One-third	4	0	0	5	16	5	5	6	3¼	3	7	2¼
		5	0	0	6	14	6	6	3	3¾	4	2	2½
Ditto	One-half	4	0	0	5	0	10	7	2	4¼	4	9	2¾
		5	0	0	5	18	4	8	4	5	5	7	3¼
Ditto	Three-quarters	4	0	0	4	10	7	9	7	5¾	6	5	3¾
		5	0	0	5	9	1	11	5	6¾	7	8	4½

The rate of dividend on ordinary shareholders will be nil.

The dividend to shareholders who may have come into the Associated Company is calculated upon the gross receipts, without any deduction on account of expenses, it being intended that the two companies (the Royal Swedish and Associated Companies) shall be under the same management and direction as soon as the obligation debt is arranged, and such expenses will be but small.

Revenue.—The accounts for 1883 showed a balance of 16,734*l.*, out of which the directors paid the half-yearly interest due on the company's "consolidated obligations" in May and November.

The directors' report for the year ended 31st December, 1883, stated that "the traffic for the last year had been satisfactory, considering the depressed state of trade generally, and, as the accounts showed, the gross receipts from all sources amounted to 38,444*l.*, being 1,077*l.* in excess of those of the previous year. The working expenses, however, amounted to 21,710*l.*, being an increase of 1,370*l.*, leaving the net revenue 16,734*l.*, or 293*l.* below that of 1882. As regards the increase in the working expenses it was attributable to three causes. (1) Extra cost in conversion of wagons which have been in use since the opening of the line. (2) To an undercharge for fuel in 1882. (3) To increased compensation for mileage run by foreign wagons. But for these items, the two first of which may be considered exceptional, the working expenses of 1883 would have been 234*l.* less than in 1882."

Coupon No. 19 of the company's consolidated obligations, due 1st May, 1883, was duly paid, and coupon No. 20, due on 1st November, 1883, was paid on that date.

DIRECTORS IN SWEDEN:

Chairman—G. F. WŒRN, Esq.

Managing Director—MARCUS AGRELIUS.

Count A. E. Von Rosen.

P. A. Bergstrom, Governor of the Province of Örebro (ex-officio).

DIRECTORS IN LONDON

Chairman—EDMUND AYRES, Esq., 31, Hyde Park Place, W.

R. J. H. Douglas, Esq., Mayford House, Barnes.
C. G. Hale, Esq., 26, Austin Friars, E.C.
W. H. Gramshaw, Esq., Shorter's Court, E.C.
Henry Kimber, Esq., 79, Lombard Street, E.C.

Secretary, G. A. Hillier.

Offices—136, Gresham House, Old Broad Street, E.C.

337.—RUSSIA.

From an official return, made in the beginning of 1876, it would appear that the construction and equipment of the railways of Russia had involved a total outlay of capital of 190,773,011*l.* The debt of various lines to the State attained an aggregate of 10,289,825*l.* There were at work upon the 12,144 miles of line 2,829 locomotives, 5,112 carriages, and 48,614 trucks. Of the capital embarked in the Russian lines, about 80,000,000*l.* appears to have been raised by shares, and the balance by obligations. Some of the Russian lines have developed a lucrative traffic; the Moscow and Riazan earns 18 per cent. per annum upon its capital, and the Riazan and Kosloff 15 per cent. per annum. The railway guarantees of interest given by the Government involve an annual charge to the Russian Treasury of about 28 per cent. of the whole amount guaranteed.

In the early part of 1878, a writer well informed on this subject stated that:—The fifty-three railways comprising the Russian network have produced during the first half-year of 1877 81,338,487 roubles 26 kopecks, on a length of 18,753 versts. In the corresponding period of 1876 there were only 47 lines, with a total length of 17,378 versts. The receipts amounted to 67,437,790 roubles 16 kopecks. The average receipts per verst in 1876 were 3,811 roubles 33 kopecks, and in 1877 4,345 roubles 23 kopecks, showing an increase of 14 per cent. We are unable to give all the sums guaranteed by the Government to the shareholders of the various companies; the omissions, however, are insignificant, and we believe the following return is complete as far as concerns the *shares* of the companies—

Government Guarantee. Roubles.	Railways.	Per verst. Roubles.		In comparison with 1876. Per cent.
410,083	Rostof Vladikavkaz	1,450	increase	79·30
	Libau Romenskaia	3,240	„	77·46
	Odessa	4,369	„	75·45
	Brest-Graerskaia	3,490	„	75·21
	Kiev-Brest	5,497	„	72·08
976,003	Dunaburg Vitepsk	6,059	„	63·26
459,000	Riga Dunaburg	6,114	„	54·79
2,252,308	Orel Vitepsk	5,780	„	52·58
	Libau-Romenskaia (Libau section)	1,309	„	53·03
	Charkoff Nicolaievsk	2,731	„	47·49
492,161	Lozof-Sebastopol	1,751	„	66·40
1,063,532	Poti Tiflis	3,052	„	21·30
	Koursk Kiev	5,128	„	25·91
222,255	Reajsk-Viazemskaia	1,535	„	24·65
	Livno	1,943	„	24·61
	Finland	7,405	„	23·33
622,443	Varsaw Terespol	5,497	„	23·01
159,283	Mitau	2,176	„	22·69
	Novotorjsk	1,699	„	20·97
	Petersburg Varsaw	4,833	„	18·47
1,426,631	Moscow-Brest	3,279	„	14·55
	Moscow-Koursk	8,204	„	11·54
989,346	Orel-Griaz	3,757	„	11·30
	Sestrorietzkaia	1,138	„	8·60
	Nikolaiersk	18,828	„	7·84
	Tambof Kozlof	5,582	„	7·00
3,116,232	Koursk Charkof Azof	4,026	„	4·16
	Constantinof	799	„	6·86
	Kozlof Voroneje-Rostof	3,095	„	2·27
	Varsaw-Vienna	6,904	„	1·47
	Tambof Saratof	2,932	„	1·18
	Novgorod	1,586	„	0·97
	Moscow Nijni-Gorod	7,556	„	0·19

Government Guarantee. Roubles.	Railways.	Per verst. Roubles.	In comparison with 1876. Per cent
288,000	Volga-Don	2,158	decrease 12·52
	Riga Bolderaskaia	2,242	" 8·87
935,424	Baltic	2,834	" 7·20
75,264	Fabrijno-Lodzinskaia	3,440	" 6·79
279,015	Varsaw Bromberg	3,354	" 4·53
421,743	Riaz-Morchausk	4,261	" 4·44
	Moscow Jaroslaf	4,843	" 4·35
	Riazan Koslof	11,451	" 4·05
	Moscow Riazan	11,925	" 3·63
	Grias Tsaritzin	2,078	" 2·58
	Jaroslaf-Vologodskaia	1,208	" 2·45
285,249	Chowiska-Ivanof	1,836	" 1·42
338,339	Morchausk Sizeransk	1,798	" 1·25
	Ribinsk Vologodskaia	6,527	" 1·18
	Tsarkoe-Tselo	8,813	" 0·40
327,611	Orenburg	1,532	Were not open for traffic prior to 1879.
221,390	Faslof	1,328	
264,562	Vistula	521	
	Borovifskaia	196	
	Riga Toukum	192	

A considerable amount of capital has been subscribed in England in aid of various Russian railway projects, the interest on the greater part of this capital being guaranteed by the Russian Government. The following information has been extracted from time to time from the various prospectuses, as the bonds referred to have been issued:—

Charkoff-Azoff.—In 1868, R. Raphael and Sons offered for subscription in this country 2,600,000*l.* (part of 4,349,280*l.*) of 5 per cent. bonds of this company, at the price of 80*l.* per cent., the interest being guaranteed by the Russian Government. The bonds are repayable at par previous to 1954, by annual drawings held in the month of December. Interest coupons are attached, payable 1st March and 1st September. This company's line commences at Charkoff and extends to Taganrog and Rostow; length, 767 versts. The administration is at St. Petersburg (4, Quai Anglais), the president of the council being S. Poliakoff. The general offices are at Charkoff, the manager there being W. Iwanow. London Agents—Raphael and Sons, 25, Throgmorton Street, E.C.

Charkoff-Krementschug.—Bonds of this railway to the amount of 1,716,000*l.* were offered for subscription by J. Henry Schröder and Co. in 1868, at the price of 80*l.* per cent. Interest at the rate of 5 per cent. per annum is guaranteed by the Russian Government, and the principal is repayable by annual drawings in the month of July, prior to 1950. This line forms part of the Charkoff-Nicolaiew Railway, and is 257 versts long. The administration is at St. Petersburg (88, Perspective de Nevsky). The manager at Krementschug is K. K. Huber. The coupons are payable on the 1st March and 1st September. London Agents—J. Henry Schröder and Co., Leadenhall Street, E.C.

Hango.—Incorporated by decree of the 10th November, 1869. The railway connects at Hyvinje, the port and harbour of Hango, in Finland, with the State Line to St. Petersburg and the interior of Russia. Length, 93 miles. Opened 8th October, 1873. Capital, 1,120,000*l.* The amount authorised to be raised by debentures is 800,000*l.*, of which 100,000*l.* was taken up in Russia, and the remaining 700,000*l.* offered for subscription in London in December, 1873. The debenture loan has since been withdrawn and the line sold to the Government of Finland.

Koursk-Charkoff-Azoff.—This is a continuation of the Moscow-Koursk Railway to Charkoff, where it joins the Charkoff-Azoff and the Charkoff-Krementschug. Length, 763 versts. The company's 5 per cent. bonds (guaranteed by the Russian Government) were offered for subscription in this country in January, 1872, and subscribed to the amount of 1,760,000*l.*, at the price of 87*l.* 10*s.* per cent. The bonds are for 1,000*l.*, 500*l.*, and 100*l.* each, and are repayable at par by annual drawings of 1-12th per cent. accumulative; the first drawing was held in December, 1872. The company reserves to itself the right to pay off the outstanding bonds at a month's notice, or to increase the sinking fund at any time after ten years from 1872. Coupons are attached, payable 1st January and 1st July. Against these bonds the company deposits with the Imperial Russian State Bank at St. Petersburg, as security for the payment of interest and sinking fund, 11,000,000 roubles metallique five per cent

Kursk-Charkow-Azoff shares, bearing the guarantee of the Imperial Russian Government for interest and sinking fund, which guarantee will continue until entire repayment. The management, direction, and general offices are the same as of the Charkoff-Azoff. London Agents—C. J. Hambro and Son, 70, Old Broad Street, E.C.

KOURSK-KIEW.—The shares of this company, carrying interest at the rate of 5 per cent. per annum, and participating in surplus profits, are held to a considerable extent in this country. Extra dividends: 2*l* 10*s*. in 1875; 10*s*. in 1876; 3*l*. in 1878. The coupons are payable 1st February and 1st August, and on the latter date is paid the extra dividend. The length of this company's line is 442 versts. The administration is at Moscow, the president of the council being J. V. Dervis. The engineer is A. Paskin, of Kiew. London Agents—Baring Brothers and Co., 8, Bishopsgate Street Within, E.C.

LOWZOWAIA SEVASTOPOL.—A few of the bonds of this company are held in this country, and the payment of the coupons due 1st April and 1st October is regularly announced by Messrs. R. Raphael and Sons, 25, Throgmorton Street, E.C. The line extends from Lowzowaia, a station on the Koursk-Charkoff-Azoff Railway, to Sineluikovo, Alexandrovsk, and thence in a southernly direction to Sevastopol, in the Crimea; length, 575 versts. At Sineluikovo there is a branch to Jékaterinoslaw (length, 42 versts), and at Alexandrovsk, a short branch to the River Dniéper (3½ versts). The administration is at St. Petersburg, the president of the council being A. Struve. Engineer and Manager, — Prohoroff. General offices at Simféropol, in the Crimea.

MORCHANSK-SYZRAN.—The length of this railway is 479 versts, which will be increased about 109 versts when the line is extended to Samara. The shares of the company are held in small numbers in this country, and the coupons on these shares are paid by Messrs. C. J. Hambro and Son, 70, Old Broad Street, E.C. The administration is at St. Petersburg (11, Wasily Ostrov, Ligne No. 16), the president of the council being D. Grimm. Manager, W. Lachtin, Penza.

MOSCOW-JAROSLAVL.—In 1860 this company obtained in London a loan of 1,920,000*l*. at 5 per cent. interest, which is guaranteed by the Russian Government. The bonds are for 100*l*. each (issued at 78*l*.), and are redeemable at par by annual drawings of ½ per cent. before 1945. Coupons are attached, payable 1st June and 1st December in each year, and the drawings are held in the month of February, and the drawn bonds payable 1st of June following. Originally this reached only from Moscow to Jaroslavl (261 versts), but it has recently been extended to Vologda, a further distance of 191 versts. At Alexandrov (105 versts north of Moscow) there is a branch to Karabanovka, length 10 versts. The administration is at Moscow (Gare de Jaroslavl), the president of the council being — Ischischow, and the manager W. Schmidt. Agents and Bankers in London—Baring Brothers and Co., 8, Bishopsgate Street Within, E.C.

MOSCOW-KOURSK.—100*l*. bonds of this railway were issued in November, 1871, to the amount of 1,700,000*l*., at the price of 92*l*. per bond. They have no Government guarantee, and are redeemable at par by half-yearly drawings, in February and August, within 18 years from the date of issue. Interest at the rate of 6 per cent. per annum is payable by coupon on the 1st May and 1st November. This is a direct line (*via* Tula and Orel) from Moscow to Koursk, at which latter place it joins the Koursk-Charkoff-Azoff Railway; length, 502 versts. The president of the council of administration is — Ischischow, and the managing director P. Klevetsky. Offices—Rue Nikolskaia, Moscow. London Agents—Baring Brothers and Co., 8, Bishopsgate Street Within, E.C.

OREL-JELETZ-GRIAZI.—The length of this line is 287 versts. The administration is at St. Petersburg (4. Rue Galernaia), the president of the council being S. Poliakoff. General Manager, R. V. Desen, Orel. A few of the obligations of this company are held in England, but nothing transpires of its affairs beyond the payment of the coupons on the 5 per cent. bonds, due 1st May and 1st November, by Baring Brothers and Co., 8, Bishopsgate Street Within, E.C.

OREL-VITEPSK.—The capital of this company consists of 4,500,000*l*. in bonds of 100*l*. each, and 1,500,000*l*. in 20*l*. shares, both of which are guaranteed 5 per cent. by the Russian Government. The bonds were issued in 1867, by I. Thomson, T. Bonar, and Co., at the price of 77*l*. 10*s*. per bond. Interest coupons are attached, payable 16th April and 16th October in London, Frankfort, Berlin, or Amsterdam, at the option of the holder. The bonds are redeemable by annual drawings of 1-12th per cent. in the month of October, previous to 1954. The shares of this company are also held, to a considerable extent, in England. This is a direct line from Orel to

Brlansk, Roslavl, and Vitepsk; length, 490 versts. President of the Council of Administration, N. Gerngross, 4, Quai Anglais, St. Petersburg. Managing Director, N. Chludenew, Orel. London Agents—I. Thomson, T. Bonar, and Co., 57½, Old Broad Street, E.C.

RYBINSK-BOLOGOE.—This line extends from Bologoé, on the St. Petersburg and Moscow Railway, to Rybinsk, a distance of 280 versts. A considerable number of the shares and bonds are held in this country, the coupons and drawn bonds of the obligations second issue are paid by the Russian Bank for Foreign Trade. President of the Council of Administration, A. Warschavsky, St. Petersburg. Managing Director, N. Brunner, Rybinsk. Offices—No. 1, Demidoff Péréoulok, St. Petersburg. London Agency—The Russian Bank for Foreign Trade, 32, Lombard Street, E.C.

ST. PETERSBURG AND ZARKOE-ZELO.—The length of this line is 25 versts. The obligations of the company are for 20*l.* each, and carry interest at 5 per cent. per annum; they are redeemable at par by means of annual drawings. The coupons are payable 13th January and 13th July, and bonds drawn for redemption are paid in the month of July. The directors in 1875 issued obligations for 1,800,000 roubles, to enable the company to lay down a second rail, and to redeem the floating debt. President of the Council of Administration, W. Jefremoff. Managing Director, N. Peters. Offices—St. Petersburg. London Agents—The Russian Bank for Foreign Trade, 32, Lombard Street, E.C.

TAMBOFF-KOSLOFF.—This company was established some years ago, for the purpose of completing the railway between Saratoo and Kosloff, a station on the Moscow and Griazi Railway. Length of line, 67 versts. In July, 1868, subscriptions were invited in this country for an issue of 320,000*l.* of the company's 100*l.* bonds, at the price of 72*l.* 15*s.* per bond. Interest at the rate of 5 per cent. per annum (payable by coupon 14th January and 14th July) is guaranteed by the Municipalities of Tamboff and Kosloff, with the sanction of the Imperial Russian Government. Principal redeemable within 88 years by means of an annual sinking fund of 1-12th per cent. The bonds drawn for redemption in the month of December are payable 14th January following. Agents in London—I. Thomson, T. Bonar, and Co., 57½, Old Broad Street, E.C.

TAMBOFF-SARATOV.—A small part of the share capital of this company is held in this country. The dividend warrants falling due 13th January and 13th July are paid at the counting-house of Baring Bros. and Co., 8, Bishopsgate Street Within, E.C. The line commences by a junction with the Tamboff-Kosloff Railway at Tamboff, and is really a continuation of that line to Saratov; length, 353 versts. At Sosnovka, 153 versts west of Tamboff, is a branch to Bekovo; length, 13 versts. The administration is at St. Petersburg (Rue Petite Morskaïa), the president of the council being P. Kowalewsky. Manager, A. Bunge, Saratov.

338.—ST. GOTHARD.

This company, as it has hitherto existed, was formed December 6th, 1871, on the basis of an international treaty of October 15th, 1869, between Switzerland and Italy, the adhesion of Germany to the arrangements being formally secured by a supplementary treaty of October 28th, 1871.

The struggle for the establishment of a Swiss Alpine Railway had lasted over forty years.

After the Gothard Union, composed of deputies from fifteen cantons, and of the greatest railway companies of Switzerland, had worked indefatigably for the construction of the Gothard Line from 1863-1871, and had won over to their cause Germany and Italy, a treaty was concluded at Berne on 15th October, 1869, between Switzerland and Italy, and to which the German Empire acceded in 1871.

The Convention of the States secured the enterprise.

The net to be built according to the treaty mentioned fixed upon the following lines, viz.:—Lucerne, Kussnacht, Immensee, Goldau, and Zoug, St. Adrian, Goldau; further Goldau, Fluelen, Goeschenen, Biasca, Bellinzona; further Bellinzona, Lugano, Lugano-Chiasso, and Bellinzona-Magadino, the Italian frontier, with a branch line from Cadenazzo to Locarno.

Italy obliges herself to join this net at Chiasso and Dirinella with one of the points lying on the direct line to Genoa. The total expenditure of the Gothard line was computed at 187,000,000*fr.*

The Gothard Tunnel cuts the mountain between Goeschenen and Airolo on a length of 14·9 kilometres. It runs almost on a level.

To secure the success of the enterprise the three contracting States engaged themselves to pay a subvention of 85,000,000*fr.*

Towards this sum Switzerland contributed 20,000,000*fr.*, Italy 45,000,000*fr.*, and the German Empire 20,000,000*fr.*

After a sum total of 85,000,000*fr.* had thus been secured, another 102,000,000*fr.* were to be contributed by individual enterprise, divided into 68,000,000*fr.* in bonds, and 34,000,000*fr.* in shares. These sums were forthcoming and paid in full.

The State subvention of Switzerland was not assumed by the Confederation, but partly by the Gothard cantons, Lucerne, Uri, Schwyz, Zoug, Obwalden, Nidwalden, Tessin, Berne, Argovia, Zurich, Bale (town), Bale (country), Soleure, Turgovia, Schaffhouse, and partly by the two railway companies, the North East and the Central.

On the 6th and 20th of December, 1874, the Tessin Valley lines, or the two lines Biasca-Locarno and Lugano-Chiasso, 66 kilometres, separated by Mount Ceneri, whilst the perforating of the Great Gothard Tunnel was being continued.

Partly in consequence of the result of the construction of the Tessin lines, partly by new computations of the lines that had not yet been constructed, the primitive sum of 187,000,000*fr.* was found to be inadequate for the finishing of the whole Gothard Line.

On the 12th of March, 1878, a new treaty was concluded between Switzerland, Germany, and Italy, by which the construction of the three branch lines Lucerne-Kussnacht, Immensee, Zoug, Arth, and Bellinzona-Lugano was deferred till better conditions should allow of their being taken up, and the building capital raised to the sum of 227,000,000*fr.*

To this increase of 40,000,000*fr.*, Switzerland was to contribute 8,000,000*fr.*, Germany and Italy each 10,000,000*fr.*, and individual enterprise 12,000,000*fr.* more.

These new subventions were guaranteed by Germany and Italy. Individual enterprise also proved favourable after all the subventions, which, according to this new treaty made up half of the sum required for the construction of the line, had been secured.

The voting of the Swiss subvention met with great obstacles, as the Gothard cantons had already, with their first contributions, gone almost beyond their means.

The assistance of the confederation was therefore applied for, and after long debates in the Federal Assembly, the bill concerning the grant of subventions towards Alpine railways of the 22nd of August, 1878, was passed.

The chief resolutions of this bill are, that not only the Gothard cantons, but also those cantons which participate with subventions in the construction of Alpine railways in the east and west of Switzerland, shall be assisted by the confederation with a subvention of 4,500,000*fr.* each. The Swiss subvention of 8,000,000*fr.* was got up by the following contributions, viz.:—The confederacy gave 4,500,000*fr.*, the Gothard cantons together 2,000,000*fr.*, the railway companies (the North East and Central) together 1,500,000*fr.* The Federal subvention of 4,500,000*fr.* was to be paid out to the cantons, and not directly to the Gothard Company.

After various preliminaries, including arrangements with the Federal Councils, the construction of the line was proceeded with, and its opening took place on the 1st of June, 1882.

The length of the whole network opened as above is 240 kilometres, in which are comprised the 66 kilometres of the Tessin Valley lines that had, as aforesaid, already been opened since December, 1874.

The remainder, finished completely at the end of April, 1882, comprised the lots:—

Immensee-Fluelen	32·30	kilometres
Fluelen-Goeschenen	38·17	,,
Goeschenen-Airolo	15·74	,,
Airolo-Biasca	45·59	,,
Cadenazzo-Pino	16·39	,,
Ginbiasco-Lugano	26·41	,,
	174·60	kilometres

Or, in a round sum, 175 kilometres.

The lot Goeschenen-Airolo, viz., the Gothard Tunnel, had been opened on the 1st January; and the lot Ginbiasco-Lugano (Ceneri Line) on the 10th of April, 1882.

The two lots, Immensee-Goeschenen and Biasca-Airolo, go by the name of lines of access to the great tunnel.

The mountain lines are:—

Erstfeld-Goeschenen	28·87 kilometres
Airolo-Biasca	45·59 „
Ginbiasco-Lugano	26·41 „
Sum total	100·87 kilometres

The greatest rising on these lots are 25, 26, and 27 °/₀₀; the radius of the smallest curve is 300 metres, and by exception only 280 metres.

The greatest risings of the other parts of the main line are at the utmost 10 °/₀₀

The lines over the mountain (provisionally single) can be doubled without interrupting the traffic.

In consequence, all the tunnels which had required to be walled had received a double track; in solid rocks profiles were broken in such forms as to admit of laying of the double track without any interruption of the traffic.

The great tunnel has the double track throughout. The valley lines are definitely single, with the exception of some parts (tunnels) of the Tessin Valley lines, which have double tracks.

The great Gothard Tunnel forms, with the exception of the curve at the entrance on the south side, a straight line, 14,920 metres in length; the northern entrance at Goeschenen is 1,109, the southern 1,145 metres above the sea; almost in the middle of it the line reaches its highest point at 1,154 metres above the sea.

The number of workmen employed on each side of the tunnel (most of them Italians) was between 400 and 2,000 men. During the time of construction there were 631 casualties, of which 177 resulted in death. The axis of the tunnel was calculated and fixed by trigonometry. The piercing of the horizontal stulm was achieved on the 29th of February, 1880, after seven years and five months, at a distance of 7,795 metres from the north entrance of the prolonged tunnel.

The tunnel was finished at the end of December, 1881, 15 months later than had been stipulated. Though the tunnel was provided with the double track, only one line of rails was laid at the beginning. The total cost of the tunnel line, and other constructions comprised, amounted to 60,000,000*fr*. The final settling of the account has however, not yet taken place.

The safety of the traffic is insured by semaphores, instead of revolving signal points, by bell signals, by contrivances for safely directing the trains at the stations, and for measuring and controlling the swiftness of the motion of the trains, and so on, on the most extensive scale.

The working material of the Gothard Railway consisted, at the opening of the line, of 81 locomotives, 195 carriages, and 714 luggage and goods vans. Of the locomotives there are 23 eight-couple engines, 35 six-couple engines for goods trains on the valley line and passenger trains on the mountain line; 14 four-couple engines for passenger trains for the valley line; 7 four-couple tender engines for ranging or changing service; and 2 small engines for the secondary traffic of the branch line Bellinzona-Locarno. 52 of the engines have peculiar tenders, the other 29 pieces are tender-locomotives.

The carriages are lighted by gas. The express trains are provided with continuous brakes, Hardy system.

Since the opening of the lines two expresses run daily between Milan and Lucerne.

The morning express leaves Lucerne at 10-0 a.m., and reaches Milan at 7-41 p.m.

The evening express leaves Milan at 7-50 p.m., and arrives at Lucerne at 5-42 a.m.

During the summer of 1883 a provisional express ran between Lucerne and Milan, leaving Lucerne at 9-0 a.m., doing the whole journey in 8 hours 30 minutes.

The journey from Lucerne to Milan required 27 hours before the opening of the Gothard Line.

DIRECTORS:

President—J. ZINGG.
Vice-President—Dr. STOFFEL.
Member—H. DIETLER.

OFFICERS.—First Secretary, F. Schweizer, Lucerne; Chief Engineer, R. Bechtle, Lucerne; Archivist, — Wanner, Lucerne; Chief Accountant, A. Furrer, Lucerne; Chief of Traction, T. Stocker; Chief Inspector of Traffic, Siegfried, Lucerne.

Offices—Council of Administration, Lucerne; General Offices and Board of Directors, Lucerne.

339.—SAMBRE AND MEUSE.

This Anglo-Belgian Company was formed in 1844 to construct a line from the coal basin at Charleroi, on the Sambre, to Vireux, on the Meuse. The length of the trunk line from Marchiennes to terminus on the Meuse is 38½ miles; the branch to Morialmé, 8½ miles; and to Llaneffe, 3¾ miles. The branches have a net income of 8,000*l*. per annum for 50 years, guaranteed by the Belgian Government, by whom the deficit is to be made up. Trunk and branches, 68 miles, which are worked by the Great Central of Belgium.

The dividends for the half-years ended 31st December, 1883, and 30th June, 1884, were at the rate of 4*s*. and 4*s*. 6*d*. per share, payable 2nd April and 3rd November respectively.

CAPITAL.—This account to 30th June, 1884, shows the expenditure, including shares in company's hands (22,860*l*.), and discount and investments (55,580*l*.), to have been 1,197,532*l*., while the receipts were as follow:—

Original 20*l*. shares	£420,000
Preference 10*l*. shares, 5½ per cent	200,000
4 per cent. loan guaranteed by the Belgian Government	200,000
4½ per cent. debentures	155,600
Accounts in course of payment and revenue balance (11,000*l*.)	27,984
Amount re-transferred to the credit of capital account in accordance with resolution of general meeting of 10th April, 1874	16,898
	£1,197,532

The bonds and debentures are redeemable at par in 1914. A sinking fund for this purpose is provided, the rate of which increases every year.

The interest on the bonds, debentures, and preference shares is payable half-yearly on 1st January and 1st July.

Meetings are held usually half-yearly in London and Brussels, in March and April, and August, respectively.

In transferring shares no transfer form is required, but merely a written order; for 20*l*. shares 6*d*. per share, for 10*l*. shares 3*d*. per share registering; 6*d*. per share is charged for "unregistering." Certificates required to accompany orders for converting registered shares into shares "to bearer."

DIRECTORS:

Chairman—WILLIAM AUSTIN, Esq., Elleramede, Totteridge, N.

James Brend Batten, Esq., 32, Great George Street, Westminster, S.W.

Mons. Adolph Stoclet, Brussels.

Henry Parkinson Sharp, Esq., 57, Old Broad Street, E.C.

Arnold de Beer, Esq., 29, Elm Park Gardens, S.W.

All eligible for re-election.

OFFICERS.—Sec., A. Snellgrove; Auditors, Kemp, Ford, and Co., 8, Walbrook, E.C.; London Bankers, Consolidated Bank, Threadneedle Street, E.C.

Offices—10, Moorgate Street, E.C.

340.—SMYRNA AND CASSABA.

Incorporated with limited liability for the purpose of acquiring the concession of a line from the city of Smyrna, in the Levant, to the town of Cassaba, with a branch to Bournabat. Length originally 61 miles (at present 108 miles, including the extension mentioned below). Capital, 800,000*l*., viz., 414,160*l*. ordinary shares; 150,000*l*. preference shares (entitled to 7 per cent. interest and one-fifth of net profits after the ordinary receive 7 per cent.); and 235,840*l*. debenture bonds, issued in June, 1872, for five years at 7 per cent., to redeem a like amount of 8 per cent. bonds. This last issue matured 1st August, 1877, and were replaced by bonds to the extent of 230,000*l*. only, which issue expired 1st August, 1882, and having been reduced by half-yearly drawings, it was found necessary only to borrow 80,000*l*. anew, as the outstanding balance of debenture debt, and this was effected at 6 instead of 7 per cent. interest. On the 2nd February, 1884, the whole of the outstanding debentures were paid off.

CONCESSION.—The following are the most important features of the original concession, which was for 99 years from 1st September, 1863:—1. The free grant of Government lands required for the purposes of the railway. 2. A State guarantee of a minimum of 40,000*l*. per annum. 3. The privilege of importing, free of customs and other duties, all materials, rolling stock, and machinery, necessary for establishing the railway. 4. The exemption of the company's property of whatever nature from every kind of taxation. 5. The privilege of fixing its own tariff of charges for passengers, merchandise, &c. 6. A preference of concession for all future extensions connected with this railway. 7. The exclusive privilege of working all mines, forests, quarries, &c., within a range of 33⅓ English miles on either side of the main line. This concession was superseded by a new agreement dated 6th and 18th December 1872, the terms being summarised as follows, viz:—"The original guarantee principal was superseded, and an extension from Cassaba to Alaschier (about 47 miles), built entirely and equipped by the Ottoman Government, was added to the main line. The Government then undertook to purchase the company's line for future delivery, viz., in 16 years from 1st March, 1875 (when the extension line was opened), for 1,280,000*l*., the company having the right of using the whole line from Smyrna to Alaschier during such term, upon payment to the Government of a rental of 40,000*l*. each half-year, such payments to coincide with the due dates of Government mandats given to represent the 1,280,000*l*. purchase money, viz., 32 half-yearly payments of 40,000*l*. each. At the end of the 16 years, say in March, 1891, the purchase and rental accounts will, of course, exactly balance, and the entire undertaking will become the property of the Government, subject to the settlement of the company's claims on the Government." In April, 1881, the shareholders formally approved of two conventions with the Turkish Government, by which the period of the concession for the line to Alaschier is extended, and a right given to the company to prolong the line through Ouschak to Afium Karahissar. These conventions, however, have not yet received the Imperial irade.

At an extraordinary general meeting, held on the 9th July, 1883, and confirmed 25th July, 1883, resolutions were passed by which (after the debenture debt has been redeemed) the net profits of the company will be divided as follows:—7 per cent. to the preference shareholders, 7 per cent. to the ordinary shareholders, and the balance in the proportion of one-fifth to the preference, and four-fifths to the ordinary shareholders. Any priority of redemption in favour of the preference shares out of the net profits after the payment of the dividend on the existing share capital will consequently cease. This resolution has not yet been acted on, and is the subject of an action in the Court of Chancery. Claims on the Ottoman Government, with interest added, 1,611,874*l*., less 746,667*l*. due to Government for rental of railway.

In April, 1877, the directors obtained powers to declare dividends at any time, without waiting for a general meeting in April or October, it being found inconvenient to defer paying the ordinary dividend due on 30th June until October, when money has been in hand for the payment of such dividend at the proper time.

Revenue.—For the half-year ended 30th June, 1884, the directors' report stated as follows:—

The revenue of the company for the half-year ended 30th June, 1884, shows an increase over the corresponding period of 1883 of 28,993*l*. in the gross and 23,811*l*. in the net receipts, the figures being:—

	Gross Receipts.	Net Receipts.
Half-year to 30th June, 1884	£81.920	£47,476
Ditto ditto 1883	52,927	23,665
Increase	£28,993	£23,811

The net revenue is equal to 18·304 per cent. per annum on the total capital of the company.

The dividends, amounting to 9,297*l*., were paid on the 1st July, 1884, and the balance of net revenue, 36,317*l*., will be available for distribution as soon as a decision is given in the suit of Ashbury *v*. The Company, now pending in the Court of Chancery.

The relations of the company with the Imperial Ottoman Government are satisfactory, and negotiations of a mutually friendly nature are proceeding, both as regards a settlement of the company's claim on the Government and the extension of its system.

Capital.—The outstanding capital of the company was, on 30th June, 1884, as follows:—7 per cent. preference shares, 20*l*. fully paid, 125,000*l*.; ordinary 20*l*. shares, 393,740*l*.; total, 518,740*l*.

Preference and Ordinary Shares.—These are a first and second charge respectively upon the whole of the undertaking, and have been redeemable after the debentures, and in a similar manner; but pending the decision of the Court of Chancery redemption is suspended.

TRANSFER DEPARTMENT.—Ordinary form; fee per deed, 2*s.* 6*d.*; both classes of shares can be transferred on one deed, with one stamp for the whole, provided the stamp covers the *ad valorem* duty on the whole; certificates must accompany transfers; in acceptances, renunciations, &c., of new stock, proxies, or other forms sent to trustees and other joint holders, the signature of the first-named trustee, or executor, or joint holders of debentures or shares, only required.

Half-yearly meetings held in London usually in April and October, the transfer books closing for 20 days previously.

DIRECTORS:

Chairman—JOHN STEWART, Esq., 26, Throgmorton Street, E.C.

William Clarence Watson, Esq., 7, Great Winchester Street, E.C.

James Hemmerde, Esq., 26, Throgmorton Street, E.C.

C. A. Winter, Esq., 7, Great Winchester Street, E.C.

T. H. Cowie, Esq., Q.C., 2, Plowden Buildings, E.C.

OFFICERS.—Sec., Richard Pearce; Gen. Man., Henry Kemp, M.Inst.C.E., Smyrna; Auditor, Thomas A. Welton; Solicitors, Bircham and Co.; Bankers, The Alliance Bank Limited.

Offices—7, Great Winchester Street, E.C.

341.—SOUTH AUSTRIAN.

(LATE SOUTH AUSTRIAN, LOMBARDO-VENETIAN, AND CENTRAL ITALIAN).

LINES IN OPERATION.—*Vienna to Trieste*, with branches and connections, 1,287 kilometres; *Hungarian Lines*, 647 kilometres; *Tyrol Lines*, 306 kilometres; total, 2,240; to which are added 367 kilometres, belonging to private companies, but worked by this company.

This important undertaking until lately has been designated as the South Austrian and Upper Italian Railway; but as the Italian portion has been sold to the Italian Government the title is reduced to the above heading, though it is still popularly, though incorrectly, called the "Lombardo-Venetian." The term of concession by the Austrian Government is for 99 years from 1st January, 1870—that is, until 1st January, 1969. It was originally guaranteed a net revenue of 5½ per cent.; but when Venetia became united to the kingdom of Italy it was thought necessary to enter into a new agreement, and a convention was executed at Vienna on the 13th April, 1867, under which the guarantee (unfortunately for the original shareholders) was exchanged for a guarantee by the government, for the whole term of the concession of a gross traffic return, at the present time and hereafter during the concession, of 100,000 florins per mile; (an Austrian mile is equal to 7 kil., 586 metres, or 4 5-7ths English miles). And further, the railway became exempt from income tax and all direct taxes until 1st January, 1880; and then in case the company becomes chargeable with the income tax it will only be imposed on the excess traffic over and above the 100,000 florins per mile guaranteed, and even so only on 3-5ths of such excess.

The Italian portion was sold to the government of that kingdom for the gross sum of *fr*.752,375,648, besides other minor items now in course of settlement. The way in which the payment of the purchase money has been arranged is as follows, viz.:—*fr*.613,252,749 by a fixed annuity of *fr*.33,160,211 (less *fr*.3,590,324 for income-tax) for 78 years, from 1st July, 1876, to 31st December, 1954; and an annuity of *fr*.13,321,008 (less *fr*.546,252 for income-tax) from 1st January, 1955, until 31st December, 1968. These annuities are payable in gold, free from all future taxation or deduction whatever. Of the remaining *fr*.139,123,140 to make up the purchase money, the Government took upon itself the railway debt to the Milan Savings Bank of *fr*.20,000,000 and gave *fr*.119,123,140, in 5 per cent. Italian rentes, payable in gold at the medium rate current on the Paris Exchange during the six months from 1st January to 30th June, 1876. To summarise the above mode of payment there will be payable—

fr.613,252,479	=	£24,530,099	in annuities.
20,000,000	=	800,000	savings bank debt.
119,123,140	=	4,764,925	in rentes.
fr.752,375,619		£30,095,024	

ADJUSTMENT OF ACCOUNTS WITH THE ITALIAN GOVERNMENT.—See MANUAL for 1884, pages 363 and 364, and previous editions.

Capital.—The receipts and expenditure on this account to 31st December, 1883 (irrespective of various small adjustments), were as under:—

Receipts.		*Expenditure.*	
4,238,699 obligations, 500*fr.* each, at 3 per cent., long dates	*fr.*1,038,882,952	South Austrian lines	*fr.*862,885,404
250,000 obligations, 500*fr.* each, at 5 per cent., long dates	107,078,304	Upper Italian lines	700,800,192
	*fr.*1,145,961,256		
750,000 shares of 500*fr.* (about 20*l.* each)	375,000,000		
	*fr.*1,520,961,256		
Balance Dr.	42,724,340		
	*fr.*1,563,685,596		*fr.*1,563,685,596

N.B.—With respect to the above mentioned 3 per cent. obligations (which are divided into sixteen series issued at various periods), they now form one unified debt, inscribed without distinction of priority, and the holders have an hypothecated right over the whole of the property of the company, including the amounts receivable from the Italian Government. The coupons of the obligations, distinguished as series A, C, O, K, H, I, D, S, T, P, Z, F, V, M, U (the series were issued in 1879 and the proceeds were applied in reducing the company's floating debt), are payable on 1st January and 1st July, whilst the coupons of series X are payable on 1st April and 1st October in each year.

Taxation upon Revenue and upon the "Obligations" of the Company.—On the subject of taxation upon revenue the directors have reported as follows, viz:—"By the original act of concession our company was free from taxes upon its revenue. By the convention of the 13th of April, 1867, this exemption was extended to January, 1880. In consideration of the new charges imposed upon our enterprise, these charges have far exceeded the expectations of the contracting parties. We have, therefore, thought it our duty to apply to the two Governments of Austria and Hungary, and to ask them to indemnify the company for the sacrifices made by them without sufficient compensation, by postponing the date at which the tax on their revenues shall be imposed." With regard to the tax on the "obligations" mentioned above, the *Times* published the following extract from the *Semaine Financière*, which periodical is understood to "have access to the best sources of news on the South Austrian railways," viz.:—"The question of the tax imposed on the Lombard obligations is not yet solved. Delayed by the ministerial crisis in Austria, the negotiations the company has engaged to enter into with the Government, in order to obtain either a prolongation of exemption or an equitable compensation, have been resumed with a new cabinet, we believe, and are proceeding at this moment. There is only need of hurry in procuring a solution in case of the tax having to be levied on the January coupon of a series of these obligations. But this coupon represents the interest of the second half of 1879. It will therefore be paid, come what may, on the ordinary conditions. We remind our readers that the enforcement of the tax would absorb at most 1*fr.* per bond per annum."

The negotiations with the Italian Government, which had been suspended in the month of April, 1881, by a ministerial crisis, were resumed in the month of July following; and in the conferences held at Rome all the questions still pending between the Government and the company have been finally settled. The Italian State and the company have reciprocally reduced their claims, and in virtue of an agreement the State is recognised as debtor to the society in the sum of 6,500,000 lires, which was paid in the month of September, 1881.

Train Mileage to 31st December, 1883:—

	Per Kilometre Worked.		Per Kilometre of Distance Run.	
	1882.	1883.	1882.	1883.
Administrative Services	1·112	1·111	0·19	0·18
Maintenance and Superintendence	4·378	4·630	0·76	0·73
Traffic	6·253	6·472	1·09	1·02
Material and Cartage	4·759	5·033	0·83	0·79
Total	16·502	17·246	2·87	2·72

Revenue.—The following were the principal items of this account for the year ended 31st December, 1883:—

The gross receipts of the lines belonging to the company amounted in 1883 to the sum of			*fr.*98,634,686
From which must be deducted—			
The working expenses		*fr.*42,479,091	
General expenses		1,981,460	
Income tax		5,332,407 =	49,792,958
Remainder			*fr.*48,841,728
To be added—			
The company's share in the profits derived from working the railway round Vienna		*fr.*107,069	
Profits on the working of the local line from Liesing to Kaltenleutgeben		479	
Profits on the State account of the Unterdrauburg-Wolfsberg Line		1,310	
Profits on the State account of the Murzzuschlag-Neuberg Line		629	
Receipts from the Gratz-Köflach Line		88,026	
Profits on the working of the Vienna-Pottendorf-Neustadt Line*		14,839	
Profits on the working of the Leoben-Vordenberg Line		2,775	
		*fr.*215,127	
From which deduct—			
Loss on the passenger service on the railway round Vienna	*fr.*53,001		
Loss on the working of the local line between Mödling and Vonderbrühl	1,845		
Loss on the working of the line from Güns to Steinamanger	2,784		
Loss on the working of the lines serving the port of Trieste	88,510 =	146,140 =	68.987
Credit balance of interest on current account, profits and losses, &c.			462,909
Total			*fr.*49,373,624
Amount due by the Hungarian Government in virtue of Article 8 of the treaty of 11th March, 1880			600,000
Annuity received from the Italian Government in accordance with the terms of Article 8 of the Convention of Bâle	*fr.*33,160,211		
From which is to be deducted the tax on personal property		3,590,324 =	29,569,887
Grand total of receipts			*fr.*79,543,511
The yearly charges are as follow—			
Interest and sinking fund of loans †		*fr.*74,146,143	
Less tax of 1*fr.* per year on 3 per cent. obligations		8,328,692	
Remainder		*fr.*65,817,451	
To be added—			
The sinking fund of shares		*fr.*285,000	
Duties and taxes paid upon the obligations ‡		1,396,411	
Losses on exchange		7,557,088 =	75,055,950
Disposable balance for the year 1883			*fr.*4,487,561

The above balance sufficed for a dividend for the year of 6*fr.* per share, carrying forward a balance of 1,957,984*fr.*

---

* Gross receipts, 2,377,091*fr.*; expenses, 987,252*fr.*; together, 1,389,839*fr.* Deduct cost of lease 1,375,000*fr.*; total, 14,839*fr.*

† This sum is thus made up—Interest on 3 per cent. obligations, 62,465,186*fr.*; reimbursement of ditto, 7,235,500*fr.*; interest and reimbursement of 5 per cent. obligations, after deduction Government charges, 4,445,457*fr.*; total, 74,146,143*fr.*

‡ Thus made up—Duties paid in France upon the obligations for admission to the Paris quotation:—Stamp duty, 250,072*fr.*; transit dues, 472,389*fr.*; income tax, 375,103*fr.*; tax on reimbursement, 21,795*fr.*; stamp duty paid in Austria upon the bond coupon, 277,048*fr.*; total, 1,396,411*fr.*

N.B.—The dividends on the ordinary shares ceased in 1874, when a dividend was declared at the rate of 7·50*fr.* per share, represented by coupon No. 31. No dividends were paid for years 1875, 1876, 1877, 1878, 1879, and 1880. In 1882 the payment of dividends was resumed, and on the 1st June in that year a dividend of 4*fr.* per share was paid for the year ended 31st December, 1881, the dividend for the year 1882 being at the rate of 5*fr.* per share.

The 3 per cent. dividend on the obligations=15*fr.* per annum, has been reduced by agreement to 14*fr.* per annum, representing a deduction of 80*c.* for the Italian tax, and 20c. for the French Bourse tax. An additional reduction of 1*fr.* per coupon is now being made to meet the Austrian tax above referred to.

RUDOLPH RAILWAY.—It is stated that a convention with this railway came into force on the 1st January, 1881, under which much benefit is expected to accrue to both companies, as by it the competition previously existing in regard to the Italian freights will cease, and the companies will share alike the profits to be derived therefrom.

The accounts are made up to 31st December, and the statutory meetings held in Vienna not later than May in the following year. The affairs of the company are administered by a board of directors at Vienna, and a committee at Paris. To vote at the company's meetings proprietors must hold at least 40 shares, which must be deposited at least fourteen days before the meeting. Holders of 40 shares have one vote. No single proprietor has more than 10 votes, nor conjointly, as proxy for others, more than 20 votes altogether.

COUNCIL OF ADMINISTRATION AT VIENNA:

President—Baron F. V. DE HOPFEN.

Vice-President—Baron TINTI.

OFFICERS.—AT VIENNA.—Sec., A. V. Schrsiner; Gen. Man., Frederic Schüler; Financial Controller, L. Cavallier; Loco. Supt., A. Gottschalk; Inspector of Way, C. Prenninger.

COMMITTEE AT PARIS:

President—Baron ALPHONSE DE ROTHSCHILD.

DIRECTOR FOR LONDON:

Sir NATHANIEL DE ROTHSCHILD, Bart., M.P.

London Agents—N. M. Rothschild and Sons, New Court, St. Swithin's Lane, E.C.

342.—SWEDISH CENTRAL LIMITED.

Incorporated under "The Limited Liability Act, 1862," for the purpose of acquiring a concession for a line of railway from Frovi to Ludvika, a distance of 60¾ miles, being a portion of the line which is ultimately intended to connect the Köping Hult and State railways with the Gefle Fahlun Line, at Fahlun. The first portion of the line, viz., from Frovi to Linde, a length of 13 miles, was opened in September, 1871; a further portion up to Kopperberg, making 34 miles in the whole, was opened in December, 1872. The line was opened throughout to Ludvika on 1st October, 1873. The capital consists of 165,000*l.* in 10*l.* shares, 300,000*l.* in first mortgage debentures at 5 per cent., of which 13,000*l.* have been paid off by half-yearly drawings, and 195,000*l.* in second mortgage debentures at 5½ per cent.

The concession, which contains all necessary powers of expropriation of lands, was purchased for the sum of 28,300*l.*

On the 24th March, 1879, a petition was presented in Chancery by the representatives of the debenture holders on the board for the liquidation of the company, the directors being of opinion that it was for the interest of all concerned that the company should be wound up voluntarily. A resolution having been passed for that purpose at a meeting of the company, Mr. Roderick Mackay, of 3, Lothbury, E.C., was appointed the liquidator.

On the 1st November, 1881, the Sodra Dalarnes was opened throughout for traffic, from Borlange, on the Bergslag Line, to Krylbo, on the States Line, shortening the distance between Ludvika and Stockholm, as compared with the existing route *via* Frövi, by 3 Swedish miles, or about 21 English miles, and forming a competition route.

REVENUE.—The gross receipts for the year ended 31st December, 1883 amounted to 29,048*l.*, and the expenditure to 17,744*l.*, leaving a profit of 11,304*l.*, which sufficed for the payment of the ½ coupon of first mortgage debentures, due 1st March, 1881, the coupon due 1st September, 1881.

CAPITAL.—The expenditure on this account to 31st December, 1883, amounted to 649,645*l.*, and the receipts to the same date were as under:—

Ordinary shares	£165,000
5 per cent. first mortgage debentures	287,000
5½ per cent. second mortgage debentures	195,000=£647,000
Balance	2,645
	£649,645

Transfer form, ordinary; fee, 2*s.* 6*d.* per deed; share certificates are required to accompany transfers; transfer communications to be sent to the liquidator.

Annual meeting of shareholders held in London in the month of April.

COMMITTEE:

Chairman—H. L. BISCHOFFSHEIM, Esq., 31, Throgmorton Street, E.C.

Arthur Eden, Esq., 57½, Old Broad Street, E.C.
George Goslett, Esq., Eksjö, Sweden.
F. E. Warburg, Esq., 5, Dowgate Hill, E.C.
Chas. Morrison, Esq., 53, Coleman Street, E.C.

OFFICERS.—Liquidator, Roderick Mackay, 3, Lothbury, E.C.; Managing Director, George Goslett; Traffic Chief and Permanent Way Eng. and Loco. Supt., John Johnson; Solicitors, Norton, Rose, Norton, and Co., 24, Coleman Street, E.C.

Offices—3, Lothbury, E.C.

343.—TOURNAY TO JURBISE—LANDEN TO HASSELT.

These railways unite those in Belgium on the west and south; and the former, in accordance with a convention with the Northern of France, is to be placed on the same footing as the Belgian State lines. The Tournay to Jurbise Line is worked by the Belgian Government; the Landen to Hasselt by the Grand Central Company, and both on the same footing, viz., 50 per cent. of the gross receipts. Length of Tournay and Jurbise portion, 30 miles; the Landen and Hasselt, 17½ miles; total, 47½ miles, constructed at a cost of 10,638*l.* per mile, including 4 per cent. interest paid during construction. The terms of the concession are peculiar. Term, 99 years, redeemable by Government at the end of 45 years, upon payment of an annuity for the remainder of the term, equal to the net average income of the preceding five years, with 25 per cent. added. On completion of the line Government took possession, finding working stock, and being at the charge of maintaining and working it, handing over, monthly, to proprietors 50 per cent. of gross receipts. This 50 per cent. is divided:—1st, 5 per cent. on amounts paid up to shareholders, and ½ per cent. in lieu of sinking fund; 2nd, 3-20ths of surplus to Foundateurs; and 17-20ths as addition to dividend. Capital, 500,000*l.* in 25,000 shares of 20*l.* each. New shares have been issued (half in preference at 3 per cent. and half in ordinary stock) in lieu of original shares.

The sinking fund of the preferential shares, which up to 1864 had been limited to ½ per cent., was fixed in that year at 45,000*fr.* per annum. The preferential shares are reimbursed at par by an annual drawing. The dividend shares have also a sinking fund of 25,000*fr.* per annum. This sum is employed in the re-purchase of the shares at the market price of the day, in order to make it coincident with the duration of the concession, which, starting from the year 1864, has but 75 years to run.

COMPROMISE WITH THE TRUSTEES OF THE "BASSINS HOUILLERS."—The company's report for the two half-years of 1877 stated as follows:—Since the year 1871, the past year is the first in which we have had to depend exclusively on the receipts of the lines, and have received nothing on account of the guarantee due to us from the "Bassins Houillers" Company. In our last report we called your attention to the fact that in consequence of the failure of the "Bassins Houillers" Company, we had brought an action against the trustees of the bankruptcy, demanding the dissolution of our contract, with damages, and that we had brought before the competent court a formal declaration of our claims on the bankruptcy for the sums due to us. A judgment of the "Tribunal de Commerce" of Brussels, under date 19th May, 1877, pronounced that the contract entered into between our company and that of the "Bassins Houillers" had become null and void, and that our company, in consequence, was entirely liberated from the stipulations of the contract in question. As regarded the damages the judgment made reserve respecting the rights of both parties. On our side these claims consisted of payment demanded of the guarantee due, and charges resulting from the non-execution of various clauses of the contract. On the other side, the trustees of the bankruptcy pretended that our company was bound to reimburse to the "Bassins Houillers" all sums that might be received by virtue of the judgment given by the court the 1st February, 1876, *versus* the Belgian Government, on the score of indemnity due for the illegal application of the "Wasseige" tariff, from the 1st November, 1871, to the 1st November, 1876. The trustees pretended also that if there were reason for deciding by valuation the damages due to the Tournay and Jurbise Company, there would also be reason for taking into account the fact that in consequence of the contract of 26th April, 1870, the "Bassins Houillers" Company was to profit by the increase of receipts, and so diminish the minimum guarantee in the past as well as during the future, and they pretended in consequence that they would have the means of proving that, *de facto*, no damages were really due to the Tournay and Jurbise. In this state of things, and bearing in mind the protracted nature of legal proceedings, and the uncertainty of our getting possession of the sums that might eventually be adjudged to us, and on the other hand, not losing sight of the pressing necessity that existed of obtaining our liberation from the bonds in which we were held by the "Bassins Houillers" Company, especially with respect to our claims on the Belgian Government, through the illegal tariff aforesaid, we considered it our duty to accept a compromise, which put a stop to all claims and disputes existing, or likely to exist, between us. This compromise was signed on the 13th November, 1877, approved by the official commissary of the bankruptcy, and declared legal by the "Tribunal de Commerce" by judgment of the 24th November, 1877.

REVENUE.—For the half-years ended 31st December, 1883, and 30th June, 1884, dividends were earned at 8*s*. 1¼*d*. and 6*s*. 2*d*. per share respectively on the dividend shares, and 6*s*. per share each half-year on the preference shares.

The accounts are made up to 30th June and 31st December, and the meetings held in Brussels in March and September. The dividends are payable in London on the 1st April and October, at the counting house of I. Thomson, T. Bonar, and Co., 57½, Old Broad Street, E.C., and at the company's office, Brussels.

DIRECTORS:

Chairman—A. B. BRUNEAU, Esq., Brussels.

F. Jamar, Esq., Brussels.
F. Masquelin, Esq., Brussels.
J. Errera-Oppenheim, Esq., Brussels.
Thomas Westwood, Esq., Brussels.

OFFICERS.—Brussels Sec., Thomas Westwood; London Sec., John Cross.

Offices—68, Rue de la Loi, Brussels; and 57½, Old Broad Street, London, E.C.

344.—VARNA.

Constituted in 1863 by statutes under the law of Turkey. Concession, 99 years. Share capital, 900,000*l*., in 45,000 shares to bearer of 20*l*. each. The shares to be redeemed by a sinking fund:—12,500 shares during the first 33 years: 20,000 during the second 33 years; 12,500 during the third 33 years; total, 45,000.

This railway connects Rustchuk, on the banks of the Danube, with Varna, the principal port in the Black Sea.

In March, 1875, an agreement to lease the company to a general company at 3,500*l*. per annum was approved, the Varna to be debarred from any loss and to be connected with the general system of railways. The details of this agreement have not as yet been published. Subsequently the working company made claims of a very large amount, with the view of placing the line in the condition in which they said it ought to have been, but they ultimately agreed to accept 70,000*l*. in settlement of their claims.

In their report to the proprietors, presented at the general meeting of the company, held on the 28th September, 1883, the directors stated as follows:—

"The Bulgarian Government have bound themselves, under a treaty lately concluded, to provide their portion of the International Railway system; but it appears to the Council to be wholly inconsistent with their obligations to the Varna Company for that Government to enter upon the construction of new railways without first settling the claims of the only railway at present existing in their country.

"In reference to the payment by the Porte of the debt to this company, for the guaranteed interest for the year ending the 30th June, 1875, the Turkish Government have, as usual, raised various difficulties to avoid handing to the company's representative at Constantinople the promised haveles. This debt was incurred before the Russian war, was then admitted as due, and recognized since the peace. The Porte undertook to pay the amount to the company by monthly instalments in a Vizierial letter, and subsequently promised Her Majesty's ambassadors, Mr.

Goschen and Lord Dufferin, that the same should be at once settled by haveles; notwithstanding this, they have lately raised two pleas, one that it should be placed in the category of the floating debt of Turkey, the other that it ought to be considered as coming under the 'anterior debts' mentioned in the Treaty of Berlin. The Board represented, both personally and by letter, to the Foreign Office the fallacy and inadmissibility of such pretensions; and are glad to say that Lord Granville has recognised the force of the arguments set forth, and that a letter has been lately received stating that his lordship 'has instructed her Majesty's Chargé d'Affaires at Constantinople to lay before the Porte the considerations urged in the board's letter, and that Mr. Wyndham had been informed that the Ottoman Government having acknowledged their liability to pay this particular debt since the signature of the treaty of Berlin, and having proposed arrangements for doing so, her Majesty's Government hold themselves entitled to claim the execution of this undertaking, pending the settlement by arbitration of the questions connected with the other payments due to the company, and also to support the board's protest against the sum in question being classed with the floating debt of Turkey.'"

At a special general meeting, held in the latter part of 1884, the following resolution was passed, viz.:—"That Messrs. Mavrogordato and Sechiari be requested to proceed to Sofia to continue the negotiations with the view to a speedy settlement of the Varna Company's claims on the basis of the instructions given to the delegates."

CAPITAL.—The expenditure on this account to 30th June, 1883, had been 2,100,477*l*., and the receipts as under:—

Ordinary 20*l*. shares, 44,687 issued	£891,110	
Debentures	1,309,699	=£2,200,809
Less 4,391 3 per cent., 1,180 6 per cent. obligations, and 42 shares purchased for redemption		49,498
		£2,151,311

Meetings held in March and September.

DIRECTORS:

Henry Wollaston Blake, Esq., 8, Devonshire Place, W.
The Hon. Robert W. Grosvenor.
Emanuel Antonio Mavrogordato, Esq.
Henry Parkinson Sharp, Esq.
The Hon. Philip Stanhope.
George Cavendish Taylor, Esq., 42, Elvaston Place, South Kensington, S.W.
Charles Tottenham, Esq.

OFFICERS.—Sec., Robert Pasco; Auditors, Turquand, Youngs, and Co.; Bankers, Robarts, Lubbock, and Co., 15, Lombard Street, E.C.

Offices—56, New Broad Street, E.C.

345.—WEST FLANDERS.

A line from Bruges to Courtrai-Ypres, and from thence to Poperinghe, with branch line from Ingelmunster to Deynze, Roulers to Ypres, and Poperinghe to Hazebrouck. The fixed liabilities consist of 7,700*l*. per annum, interest on preference shares; 26,736*l*. interest and redemption on first and second issue of bonds. Length, 102 miles.

The concession granted to this company under the Belgian Act of May, 1864, is for 90 years from 1st July, 1856.

In 1852 an agreement was entered into with the Belgian Government, and in 1865 the line, subject to such agreement, was leased to the Sociètè Anonyme de Tubise and Sociètè d'Exploitation, at a rental of 36,000*l*. Subsequently these two companies became amalgamated and were afterwards absorbed by a fusion with a company called the "Bassins Houillers," who continued the lease. This latter company became bankrupt in 1877, and the West Flanders re-took possession of their lines on the 1st August in that year. Negotiations have since been on foot for the purchase of the line by the Belgian Government, but up to October, 1883, no advance had been made in furtherance of this project.

DIVIDENDS ON PREFERENCE SHARES.—The dividend on the preference share is accumulative, and payable half-yearly on 15th May and 15th November. In September, 1878, it was officially announced that:—"The Arbitrators in Belgium having decided that the preference shareholders are entitled to receive their arrears of interest before the original shareholders can participate in the profits of the company, and as there is no appeal against this decision, the directors paid on the 19th of that month coupons Nos. 48, 49, and 50, due respectively on 15th November, 1876, 15th May, 1877, and 15th November, 1877, at the rate of 5s. 6d., or 6fr. 87½c. per share. The following coupons on the preference shares due up to the 15th November, 1880, were paid at the rates mentioned above on the following dates, viz.:—No. 51 on 17th December, 1878, Nos. 52 and 53 on 15th May, 1879, No. 54 on the 15th November, 1879, and Nos. 55 and 56 on the due dates, viz., 15th May and 15th November, 1880, respectively. These payments were made at the offices of the company, in London and Bruges, and at Monsieur Brugmann-Fils', banker, in Brussels." There are, therefore, now no arrears to provide, for the coupons on the preference shares having since been regularly paid, the last one (No. 62) was paid on the due date, viz., 15th November, 1883.

Revenue.—For the half-year ended 31st December, 1882, a dividend at the rate of 6s. 1d. per share was paid on the ordinary shares (coupon No. 68) on the 15th May following; for the half-year ended 30th June, 1883, a dividend of 5s. 6d. per share was paid on the ordinary shares (coupon No. 69). This dividend was made payable on the 15th November last. For dividends on the preference shares, see above.

Capital.—The receipts and expenditure on this account to 30th June, 1883, were as under:—

Receipts.—Primitive capital		£324,873
Preference capital		140,000
3 per cent. loan—1st issue	£200,000	
Less rate of issue	100,000=	100,000
3 per cent. loan—2nd issue	600,000	
Less rate of issue	300,000=	300,000
Sundry receipts		19,330
Amount received from traffic in part payment of interest		15,340
		£899,543

The expenditure amounted to 897,135*l*., thus showing a credit balance of 2,408*l*.

Bonds, 1st and 2nd Issue.—These are redeemable by yearly drawings, a sinking fund being provided for that purpose; the interest (at 3 per cent.) is accumulative, and payable half-yearly on the 1st January and 1st July.

Ordinary Shares.—These shares rank as 12*l*. 3*s*., although only 8*l*. 15*s*. was paid, the balance being share of forfeited capital for non-payment of calls to 1848.

Authority forms for the exchange of registered shares into shares to bearer must be applied for to the secretary, fee for the exchange of both ordinary and preference shares, 6*d*. per share.

DIRECTORS:

President—ROBERT TEMPLE FRERE, Esq.

C. W. Williams Wynn, Esq.,
Edward Vaughan Richards, Esq., Q.C.
Thomas Robert Tufnell, Esq.
John Alexander Radcliffe, Esq.

OFFICERS.—Sec., R. N. Collier; London Bankers, Glyn, Mills, Currie, and Co., 67, Lombard Street, E.C.; Gen. Man., Augustus W. Chantrell.

Offices—10, Moorgate Street, E.C., and Marché du Vendredi, Bruges, Belgique.

III.—COLONIAL, INDIAN, AMERICAN, &c.

AFRICA.

346.—GOVERNMENT RAILWAYS (CAPE OF GOOD HOPE).

WESTERN SYSTEM.

Cape Town, Wynberg, Malmesbury, Stellenbosch, Worcester, Wellington, and Beaufort West Lines. Length open, 391½ miles, single, 3ft. 6in. gauge; 8¼ (Wynberg) double gauge. Average monthly earnings, about 30,414*l*.

OFFICERS.—Traff. Man., A. Difford; Res. Eng., H. J. Pauling; Loco. Supt., M. Stephens; Accountant, John Steytler.

Chief Offices—Cape Town.

MIDLAND SYSTEM.

Port Elizabeth, Uitenhage, Graaf Reinet, Grahamstown, and Cradock Lines. Length open, 387 miles, single, 3ft. 6in. gauge; 7¼ double gauge. Average monthly earnings, about 24,615*l*.

OFFICERS.—Traff. Man., A. W. Howell; Res. Eng., T. P. Watson; Loco. Supt., H. R. Thornton; Accountant, P. Conor.

Chief Offices—Port Elizabeth.

EASTERN SYSTEM.

East London, King Williamstown, and Queenstown. Length open, 166 miles, single, 3ft. 6in. gauge. Average monthly earnings, about 16,108*l*.

OFFICERS.—Traff. Man., T. R. Price; Res. Eng., R. W. H. Heenan; Loco. Supt., J. D. Tilney; Accountant, Clarke Thwaits.

Chief Offices—East London.

For particulars relating to the railway enterprises of the Cape Government in the past, see the MANUAL for 1881, pages 411 to 413.

347.—GRAHAM'S TOWN AND PORT ALFRED LIMITED (CAPE OF GOOD HOPE).

Incorporated by the Companies' Acts 1862 to 1880, for the purpose of constructing and working a railway in the colony of the Cape of Good Hope, from Graham's Town to Port Alfred.

The company was incorporated in December, 1880. The construction of the line (which, together with the equipment, has been contracted for at the price of 319,506*l*.) was commenced in the October following, and has since proceeded without interruption.

The line which runs from Graham's Town, the principal inland city of the Eastern Province of the Cape of Good Hope, to Port Alfred, at the mouth of the Kowie River, comprises a length of 44 miles. The first train with passengers was run over the finished section in September, 1882, and the entire line was opened for passenger and goods traffic in October, 1884.

The Government of Cape Colony have reserved power to purchase the railway after the expiration of 20 years on arbitration terms.

At Graham's Town the line connects with the railway to Cradock, from whence an extension to Hope Town has just been completed, and a further extension to the Kimberley Diamond Fields is in contemplation by the Cape Government.

DIRECTORS:

Chairman—The Right Hon. Lord BRABOURNE, 3, Queen Anne's Gate, S.W., and Smeeth, Kent.

Samuel Abbott, Esq., C.E., St. Winifred's, Lincoln.

Harry F. Giles, Esq., Almorah Lodge, Oak Hill Road, Surbiton.

Sir Alfred F. A. Slade, Bart., 48, Grosvenor Gardens, S.W.

G. H. Turner, Esq., Langley Mills, Notts.

Ernest Villiers, Esq., 9, Glendower Place, South Kensington, S.W.

OFFICERS.—Sec., J. Burns Brown; Eng., R. Elliott Cooper, M.Inst.C.E., 8, The Sanctuary, Westminster, S.W.; Auditors, William Edwards, Jackson, and Browning, 18, King Street, Cheapside, E.C.; Solicitors, Ashurst, Morris, Crisp, & Co., 6, Old Jewry, E.C.; Bankers, National Provincial Bank of England Limited, and Branches; Standard Bank of South Africa Limited.

London Office—Parliament Mansions, Victoria Street, Westminster.

348.—NATAL.

There were 116 miles of railway open for general traffic in this Colony on 31st December, 1884, all being the property of and worked by the Colonial Government. The railways were constructed under contract, the first 98¼ miles by Messrs. Wythes and Jackson, and the extensions (now in progress) by Mr. James Perry, of London. The railways are all laid as single lines on a gauge of 3 feet 6 inches, and they connect the Port with the towns of Durban, Verulam (on the north coast), Isipingo (on the south coast), and Pietermaritzburg, the capital, a distance of 71 miles from Durban, whilst the Ladysmith Extension, now partially open beyond Pietermaritzburg, carries the railway to Howick, 88 miles from Durban. The funds for the construction of these railways were raised in England by the Crown Agents for the Colonies, and bear a fixed rate of interest. The gradients and curves on the Natal lines are exceptionally severe. Out of the present total mileage no less than 30 miles are upon grades of 1 in 30 and 1 in 35, and curves of 300 to 350 feet radius; whilst over 60 miles are either on gradients of less than 1 in 60, or on curves of less than 450 feet radius. The main line reaches a height of 3,054 feet above sea level at a distance of 58 miles from Durban, and after falling 1,000 feet in its further progress to Pietermaritzburg, it again rises, 12 miles after passing Pietermaritzburg, to a height of 3,700 feet above the level of the sea. The summit of the extension line to Ladysmith beyond Pietermaritzburg is 5,152 feet above sea level at a point 132 miles from Durban.

Revenue and Expenditure.—The total revenue of the department for the year 1883 amounted to 155,771*l.*, and the gross working expenditure (excluding capital expenditure defrayed from ordinary and special votes) amounted to 151,823*l.*, leaving a balance of 3,949*l.* available towards payment of interest, but there was charged against the working expenditure of the year, as has also been the case in smaller degree in former years, the total cost of renewing with steel rails 14 miles of permanent way, 5¾ miles with new sleepers, and a large proportion of new ballast, at an expense of not less than 15,000*l.* The financial results of the working of the railways during the three years the present system of lines has been in operation are as follows:—

Year.	Gross Revenue.	Gross Expenditure.	Amount of capital expenditure included in gross expenditure and to be deducted therefrom.	Balance available after payment of all working expenditure towards interest on loan.
	£	£	£	£
1881	173,108	129,590	16,002	59,520
1882	163,842	159,718	19,554	23,678
1883	155,771	166,808	14,986	3,949

The average net earnings, after payment of all working expenditure proper, have thus been 2*l.* 8*s.* 5*d.* per cent. per annum.

Extensions.—The extension of the main line from Howick to Ladysmith, a distance of 100 miles, is being proceeded with, under a contract entered into between Mr. James Perry, of London, and the Crown Agents for the Colonies, acting on behalf of the Colonial Government. It is expected that a further portion of the extensions will be opened for traffic to Estcourt (about 60 miles) early in 1885.

Surveys.—Surveys for further extensions beyond Ladysmith have been completed and laid before the Legislative Council, as follows:—From Ladysmith to Biggarsberg summit (37½ miles), and from Ladysmith to the Orange Free State border, at an elevation of 5,500 feet above the sea (34½ miles). Legislative action for the construction of these two lines has, however, been delayed for the present in consequence of financial depression.

OFFICERS.—Gen. Man., David Hunter; Res. Eng., M. W. Carr, M.Inst.C.E.; Con. Eng. (England), George Berkley, C.E., 56, Charing Cross, E.C.

Head Offices—Durban, Natal.

349.—TUNISIAN.

In 1872 the Tunis Railways Company Limited was established to acquire the concession granted by the Bey of Tunis for a term of 99 years, of a railway from Tunis to its seaport, Goletta, with branch lines from Tunis to the Bardo, and to the Holy City of Sidi Boussaid and the Marsa. Length, 22 miles. Capital: ordinary 20*l*. shares, 250,000*l*.; first mortgage bonds, 225,000*l*.; second mortgage bonds, 10,000*l*. In 1873, however, the debenture interest was not paid, and at a meeting, held in January of the following year, it was resolved that the company should be reconstructed and the capital reduced. Accordingly, and with the sanction of the Court of Chancery, this was done. The original share capital was wiped out, and, as an equivalent for the former mortgage debt, there was created 180,000*l*. of ordinary 20*l*. shares and 45,000*l*. of 7 per cent. preference shares. To enable the company to complete the works there was also created a debenture debt of 10,000*l*., and power was given by the Articles of Association to issue debentures up to a total amount of not exceeding 50,000*l*. The railway was subsequently sold to the Societa Rubattino, Rome.

350.—WASSAW LIGHT LIMITED.

This company was registered in 1882, for the purpose of surveying and exploiting a line of railway from Axim to the Wassaw District of the Gold Coast. Authorised capital, 5,000*l*., in 470 10*l*. shares and 30 founders' shares of 10*l*. each, issued under an agreement filed with the registrar of joint stock companies.

DIRECTORS:

Chairman—JAMES IRVINE, Esq.

Deputy-Chairman—JASPER WILSON JOHNS, Esq., 90, Cannon Street, E.C.

T. W. Cairns, Esq.
F. Fitzgerald, Esq.
Dr. J. A. B. Horton.
Emile Bassot, Esq.
J. G. Watson, Esq.

Secretary, W. Tudor Johns.

Offices—15, Walbrook, E.C.

ASIA.

351.—JAPAN GOVERNMENT RAILWAYS.

In May, 1870, the surveys for two sections of railway were commenced under the direction of the late Mr. E. Morel, viz.:—From Tokio (Yedo) to Yokohama, 18 miles. and from Kobé (Hiogo) to Osaka, 20 miles. Both have been completed and opened for public traffic, a portion of the former on the 12th June, 1872, as far as Sinagawa, a suburb of Tokio, and the whole, with a state ceremonial, by his Imperial Majesty the Mikado, on the 14th October, in the same year.

The following is a list of the various lines in operation and in course of progress:—*Government Railway Lines Complete and now Working*.—Tokio to Yokohama, double line, 18 miles; Kobé to Otsu (Lake Bewa*), single line, 58¼ miles; Tsuruga (North Coast) to Nagahama, single line, 26¾ miles; Nagahama (Lake Bewa Side) to Ogaki, (*via* Tarui), single line, 22¾ miles; Island of Hokkaido, single line, about 30 miles. *Government Railway Lines under Construction*.—Ogaki to Takasaki, single line, about 220 miles; Tarui to Yokaichi (South Coast), single line, about 64 miles. *Nippon Railway Company's Lines*.—Complete: Tokio to Maibashi (*via* Takasaki), single line, 68¼ miles. Under Construction: Shinagawa to Kawaguchi, single line, 15 miles. Under Survey: Tokio and Awomori Line.

The traffic receipts for the year ending June, 1883, were $1,792,551. The operating expenses were placed at £759,382. The net receipts were $1,033,169, or something over 8½ per cent. on the capital invested.

OFFICERS.—Sec., A. S. Aldrich; Principal Engs., C. A. W. Pownall, M.Inst.C.E., Kobé; Traffic Man., W. F. Page; Loco. Supt., B. F. Wright, Assoc.Inst.C.E.; Con. Eng. in England, T. R. Shervinton, C.E.; Agents in London, Malcolm, Brunker, and Co.

* The traffic on Lake Bewa is carried on by a regular line of steamers in connection with the railway.

INDIA.

GOVERNMENT STATISTICS.

Colonel F. S. Stanton, R.E., Director General of the Indian Railways, in his report for the year 1883-4, stated as follows:—

I have the honour to submit the second annual report prepared in India for presentation to the Houses of Parliament relating to the administration of railways in India during the year 1883-4. It will be observed that the net receipts for the year 1883 have exceeded those for the previous year by *Rs.*73,47,316, and were equivalent to a dividend of 5·68 per cent. on the capital expended, excluding steamboat services and suspense items, the net profits earned on lines open for traffic returned 5·91 per cent. of their cost. Considering that the average age of 20 per cent. of the length open for traffic is less than five years, this result will, I think be considered satisfactory, as tending to establish the financial success of the existing railway system of India as a whole. It has been said that the public is apt to be misled by general statements of this nature, because, as a fact, the good lines pay for the bad ones; but I may observe that what may be called the "bad lines" were never expected to pay a good dividend. They were constructed for other purposes; and if these are included in the general average, the case of the "good lines" is understated. The financial results of each line can be found in the report; and I have no doubt that any one really interested in the matter will look beyond any statement of generalities and averages.

Between the 31st March, 1884, and the present date, 193¼ miles have been added to the open mileage, consisting of the following lines:—Bengal and North Western, from Bahraich to Gogra Ferry, 73 miles, opened on 2nd April; Cawnpore and Farukhabad, from Farukhabad to Khasgunj, 67 miles, opened on 14th April; Bengal Central, from Goburdunga to Bongong, 11¾ miles, opened on 22nd April; Assam, from Makum Junction to Margherita and Dum-Duma, 31¼ miles, opened on 2nd May; Northern Bengal, from Chiribunder to Dinagepore, 10½ miles, opened on 16th May. Orders have been received for the construction of an extension of the Frontier Railway from Sibi as far as Quetta, thus increasing the totals given in the report to 11,025¾ miles open for traffic, and 14,450 miles sanctioned.

Capital.—Excluding the Assisted Companies, for which complete accounts are not received, the total capital expenditure on Indian railways up to the 31st December, 1883, including lines under construction, amounted to 142,606,911*l*., which may be allocated as follows:—

Guaranteed lines	£66,059,592
East Indian	34,908.390
State lines	38,321,549*
Lines in Native States	3,317,380
	£142,606,911

The Indian expenditure on the Guaranteed lines is converted into sterling at the contract rates of exchange; that on the East Indian and other State lines at 2s. the rupee. The expenditure on the East Indian has been arrived at by taking the outlay on construction, as given in the accounts for the half-year ended 31st December, 1879, and adding thereto the expenditure shown in the accounts of subsequent half-years.

It will be seen that the average cost per mile of all open lines, excluding steam boat service and suspense accounts, is *Rs.*1,36,108, the 5 feet 6 inches and the metre gauge lines having cost respectively *Rs.*1,67,725 and *Rs.*68,758 per mile. The capital expenditure on the East Indian is now exhibited in the financial accounts under the head N. Expenditure on productive public works—capital account—50 State railways. And after the 1st July, 1884, the capital expenditure on the Eastern Bengal, including the liabilities incurred by the State on taking over that line, will be

* Includes State outlay on Patri Branch, *Rs.*8,08,408.

at

and Delhi.

§ Excluding Warora colliery.

C
rep

I
pre
way
the
equ
ste
traf
20 p
this
the
is a
goo
"ba
for
the
in t
will

B
to t
from
Far
Ben
Ass
on
o n
the
in t

C
rec
188
allo

T
cont
rup
out
Dec
sub

It
serv
line
ditu
--B
And
incl

* Includes State outlay on Patri Branch, Rs.8,08,405.

similarly dealt with. The budget allotments for the year 1884-85 for State railways classed as productive public works are as follow:—

	Rs.	*Rs.*
East Indian	54,00,000	
Eastern Bengal	*1,12,37,000=	1,66,37,000
Other State Railways:—		
India:—	*Rs.*	*Rs.*
Rajputana-Malwa	31,72,000	
Rajputana-Holkar Section	1,00,000	
Sindia	50,000	
Reserve	2,00,000	
Stores and miscellaneous	42,02,000=	77,24,000
Central Provinces:—		
Wardha Coal	75,000	
Nagpur-Chhattisgarh	2,50,000=	3,25,000
British Burma:—		
Rangoon and Irrawaddy Valley	3,90,000	
Rangoon and Sittang Valley	20,31,000=	24,21,000
Bengal:—		
Northern Bengal	3,94,000	
Tirhoot and Extensions	7,20,000	
Patna-Gya	95,000	
Nalhati	—7,000	
Calcutta and South Eastern	1,50,000	
Dacca-Mymensingh	25,18,000	
Behar-Assam	27,00,000=	65,70,000
North Western Provinces and Oudh:—		
Ghazipore-Dildarnagar	3,000	
Cawnpore-Achnera	9,92,000	
Bareilly-Pilibhit	3,05,000=	13,00,000
Punjab:—		
Indus Valley	16,51,000	
Punjab Northern	4,78,000	
Amritsar-Pathankote	9,50,000=	30,79,000
Bombay:—		
Dhond and Manmad		1,00,000
Total (excluding East Indian and Eastern Bengal lines)		2,15,19,000

The following statement gives the total cost of each railway and the average cost per mile:—

Railway.	Length of Line open on 31st December, 1883.	Total Capital Outlay to 31st December, 1883.	Average Cost per Mile.
	Miles.	*Rs.*	*Rs.*
East Indian	1,509¼	33,94,67,364	2,24,893
GUARANTEED.			
Madras	861	11,17,22,586	1,29,780
South Indian	654	4,32,72,177	66,165
Great Indian Peninsula	1,288¼	25,34,93,202	1,96,773
†Bombay, Baroda, and Central India	461	8,67,97,460	1,88,322
Eastern Bengal	159¾	3,34,12,450	2,09,299
‡Sind, Punjab, and Delhi	693	11,37,26,651	1,64,131
Oudh and Rohilkhand	546¾	5,89,01,465	1,07,710
IMPERIAL STATE.			
Punjab Northern	420¾	7,12,66,290	1,69,480
Indus Valley and Kandahar	652¼	8,06,24,083	1,23,566
Rajputana-Malwa	1,117½	9,03,51,433	80,869
Sindia	74½	89,54,482	1,20,324
§Wardha Coal	45	52,94,597	1,17,658
Dhond and Manmad	145¾	1,00,45,315	68,922
Rewari-Ferozepore	88¾	40,60,357	45,756
Carried forward	8,717	1,31,13,90,412	...

* Of this amount, *Rs.*1,02,37,000 have been provided to meet the debentures and debenture stock of the company.

† Includes the Patri Branch mileage and capital outlay.

‡ Exclusive of the Rupar Branch, which is being worked experimentally by the Sind, Punjab, and Delhi.

§ Excluding Warora colliery.

Railway.	Length of Line open on 31st December, 1883.	Total Capital Outlay to 31st December, 1883.	Average Cost per Mile.
	Miles.	*Rs.*	*Rs.*
Brought forward	8,717	1,31,13,90,412	...
PROVINCIAL STATE.			
Calcutta and South Eastern	56	90,44,419	1,61,507
Nalhati	27¼	3,15,110	11,564
Northern Bengal	256	2,06,98,887	80,855
Kaunia-Dhurla	32¼	7,66,158	23,735
Tirhoot	193	1,11,85,714	57.990
Patna-Gya	57¼	37,13,703	64,925
Cawnpore-Achnera	138¼	53,50,962	38,705
Dildarnagar-Ghazipur	12	6,93,469	58.206
Nagpur and Chhattisgarh	149	93,27,495	62,601
Rangoon and Irrawaddy Valley	161	1,31,87,905	81.912
NATIVE STATES.			
Bhopal	11½	6,08,822	52,941
Bhavnagar-Gondal	193¼	87,82,250	45,454
Gaekwar of Baroda's	58¾	12,49,239	21,228
Khamgaon	8	4,82,570	60,321
Amraoti	6	4,34,666	72,444
Nizam's	117	1,22,11,715	1,04,285
Mysore	87	40,52,528	46,554
Jodhpore	19	4,99,866	26,309
ASSISTED COMPANIES.			
Darjeeling-Himalayan	50	26,04,304	52,086
Bengal Central	52	28,30,516	54,433
Deoghur	6½	2,73,331	42,051
Assam	39	22,22,258	56,980
Total	10,447	1,42,19,31,294	1,36,108

The total amount available for capital expenditure on State lines classed as productive public works, other than the East Indian and Eastern Bengal, is made up as follows:—

	Rs.
Railway portion of the annual fixed grant of 2,500,000*l.*	1,80,00,000
Estimated saving on the grant of 1883-4	20,46,215
Contribution by the Government of the North Western Provinces and Oudh from surplus Provincial balances to cover the probable outlay on railways in those Provinces, classed as Productive Public Works	13,23,000
Transfer from irrigation grant	1,50,000
Total	2,15,19,215

or, in round numbers, *Rs.*2,15,19,000.

In addition to the above the following expenditure has been sanctioned on works in connection with railways not classed as productive:—

		Rs.
Imperial—		
Establishment, reserve and miscellaneous		7,16,500
Survey in Central Provinces (Wardha Coal Extension)		5,000
Surveys in Assam		96,500
Benares-Cuttack survey (Bengal)		2,85,000
Survey in Madras (Tinnevelly *viâ* Tenkasi and the Arienkaru Pass to Quilon)		2,000
Godra-Rutlam survey (Bombay)		5,000
Total Imperial		11.10,000
Provincial—		
Survey in Assam (Kokilamukh)		2,00,000
Bengal—	*Rs.*	
Construction	1,20,000	
Surveys	50,000	
Establishment and reserve	1,00,000=	2,70,000
Carried forward		4,70,000

	Rs.
Brought forward	4,70,000
North Western Provinces and Oudh—	
Surveys	48,000
Madras—	
Surveys	11,500
Bombay—	
Surveys	27,500
Total Provincial	5,57,000
Total Imperial and Provincial	16,67,000

Under Protective Works the following allotments have been made:—

		Rs.
Bilaspur-Etawah survey (Central Provinces)		68,000
Jhansi-Manikpur construction (North Western Provinces and Oudh)		32,00,000
Rewari-Ferozepore construction (Punjab)		30,60.000
Vizagapatam-Raipur survey (Madras)	Rs.1,68,000	
Cuddapah-Nellore construction ,,	10,30,000	
Bellary-Kistna ,, ,,	31,25,000	= 43,23,000
Reserve for English stores		7,35,000
Total		1,13,86,000
Frontier:—		
Kandahar		—4,15,000
Punjab Northern—Northern Section		—1,56,000
Stores and reserve		—1,59,000
Total		—7,30,000*

The total amount of capital raised by the various Guaranteed and Assisted railway companies amounted on the 31st December, 1883, to 70,233,668*l*., as follows:—

GUARANTEED.

£56,658,110	consists of share capital raised at	5	per cent.
1,196,834	,, ,, ,, ,,	4½	,,
500,000	,, ,, ,, ,,	4¼	,,
3,780,850	,, debentures ,,	4	,,
1,501,900	,, ,, ,,	3½	,,
425,000	,, debenture stock ,,	4½	,,
3,497,458	,, ,, ,,	4	,,
†142,016	capital not bearing interest.		
Total £67,697,168			

ASSISTED.

Bengal Central	£650,000
Rohilkhand-Kumaon	160,000
Southern Mahratta	1,726,500
Total share capital at 4 per cent.	£2,536,500

* This large credit is due to orders issued directing the transfer of all the Frontier Railway stores balances on the 1st April, 1884, to Productive Public Works.

† The capital not bearing interest is made up thus:—

Premium on share capital and debentures, &c.			£444,473
Discount on debenture stock:—			
Stock represented as shown above		£3,922,458	
Cash received		3,629,878	
		£292,580	
Discount on debentures:—			
Amount as shown above	£5,282,750		
Cash received	5,272,873		
		9,877	
			302,457
			£142,016

State of Debenture Loans on the 31st December, 1883.

Railway.	Amount.		Rate of Interest.	Date at which Loan expires.
Bombay, Baroda, and Central India	£375,000		4	1st August, 1884.
" " "	100 000		3½	Not known
		£475,000		
Eastern Bengal	£150,000		4	19th May, 1884.
"	52,650		4	1st November, 1884.
"	409,700		4	12th July, 1886.
		612,350		
Great Indian Peninsula	£4,100		3½	Not known.
" " "	102,200		4	1st January, 1884.
" " "	568,800		4	1st July, 1885.
" " "	39,500		4	1st January, 1886.
		714,600		
Madras	... }	245,500	{ 4 }	Not known.
"	... }		{ 3½ }	
Oudh and Rohilkhand	£60,000		3½	1st August, 1884.
" "	200,000		4	16th August, 1884.
" "	300 000		4	1st May, 1885.
" "	615,300		4	4th June, 1887.
" "	200,000		4	1st October, 1887.
" "	740,000		3½	1st August, 1888.
" "	500,000		3½	Not known.
		2,615,300		
South Indian		620,000	4	1st July, 1884.
		£5,282,750		

REVENUE.—The net revenue derived from railways during the year 1883 amounted to *Rs.*8,41,89,517 as compared with *Rs.*7,68,42,201 in 1882.

The total capital cost of lines open to traffic, on the 31st December, 1883, was *Rs.*1,48,30,56,455, and the percentage of the net earnings on this outlay amounted to 5·68, as compared with a similar percentage of 5·37 in 1882 on a capital outlay of *Rs.*1,43,17,18,565.

The general results of railway working compare as follows for the last three years:—

	1881.	1882.	1883.
Miles open at end of year	9,858·25	10,069	†10,447·09
Capital outlay at end of year	*Rs.*1,34,79,90,895	*Rs.*1,37,84,16,644	*Rs.*1,42,19,31,294
Cost per mile open	1,36,827	1,36,896	1,36,108
Gross earnings during the year	14,32,30,801	*15,23,12,619	16,27,97,525
Working expenses during the year	7,07,12,465	*7,58,05,494	7,87,81,945
Net profits of year	7,25,18,336	*7,65,07,125	8,40,15,580
Percentage of net profits on capital cost	5·38	*5·55	5·91
Gross earnings per mile per week (calculated on mean mileage worked)	*Rs.*285	*Rs.*294	*Rs.*301

The net revenue earned by all State lines during the past year amounted to *Rs.*1,40,94,843‡. being a return of 3·75 per cent. on a total capital expenditure of *Rs.*37,54,45,959‡. Excluding the Punjab Northern and Kandahar Frontier, the net earnings of the State lines were at the rate of 4·68 per cent. on the capital expended.

The net revenue of the East Indian, including the branch State lines worked by it, amounted to *Rs.*3,17,29,543, being at the rate of 8·77 per cent. on a total capital expenditure of *Rs.*36,17,81,299. The surplus profits on this line during the past year, after payment of annuity and interest charges, were *Rs.*1,05,38,609, of which sum ⅘ths, or *Rs.*84,30,887, accrued to Government.

The following statements, relating to Guaranteed railway transactions, are similar to those given in previous reports. Conversions from the Indian currency into sterling have been made at the contract rates of exchange.

It will be seen that the Guaranteed lines returned a net revenue of 3,542,973*l*., being at the rate of 5·25 per cent. on a total capital expenditure of 67,431,448*l*. The guaranteed interest for the year amounted to 3,289,439*l*. So that the net earnings exceeded the guaranteed interest by 253,534*l*.

From the commencement of operations up to the 31st December, 1883, a gross sum of 61,067,964*l*. has been advanced as interest by the State to the Guaranteed

* Excluding Dildarnagar-Ghazipur and Jodhpore.
† Excluding the Rupar Branch, 48 miles.
‡ Excluding Sindia, Patna-Gya, and Dildarnagar-Ghazipur.

railway companies, excluding the East Indian, and up to the 30th June, 1883, the total net earnings of these railways, exclusive of half of any surplus profits realised, amounted to 35,439,120*l*., leaving a net amount of 25,628,844*l*., which has been paid by the State.

The surplus profits realised on Guaranteed railways during the year 1883 amounted to 911,382*l*., as compared with 917,312*l*. in 1882, and 652,196*l*. in 1881.

The following table shows the net earnings and percentages on capital expenditure finally charged off (excluding suspense account) for the principal railways during the last five years, 1879 to 1883:—

Railway.	1883. Net Earnings.	1883. Percentage of Net Earnings per annum on Capital Expenditure.	1882. Net Earnings.	1882. Percentage of Net Earnings per annum on Capital Expenditure.	1881. Net Earnings.	1881. Percentage of Net Earnings per annum on Capital Expenditure.
BROAD GAUGE.	*Rs.*		*Rs.*		*Rs.*	
East Indian	*3,17,29,543	*8·99	2,97,12,511	8·80	3,09,48,310	9·30
Guaranteed:						
Madras	25,26,549	2·26	25,70,841	2·30	20,75,856	1·87
Great Indian Peninsula	1,76,59,653	†6·96	‡1,83,89,856	§7·29	1,62,19,488	6·46
Bombay, Baroda, & Cen. India	67,83,906	7·82	50,10,872	5·91	57,45,702	6·86
Eastern Bengal	26,84,611	7·72	36,38,438	10·52	33,69,281	9·72
Sind, Punjab, and Delhi	49,07,898	4·18	34,10,880	2·94	30,76,660	2·65
Oudh and Rohilkhand	24,80,362	4·21	18,01,371	3·07	19,75,698	3·28
Imperial State:						
Punjab Northern	5,93,018	0·83	5,09,018	0·83	3,59,598	0·58
Indus Valley and Kandahar	32,18,635	3·97	15,76,113	2·01	11,77,288	1·58
Provincial State:						
Patna-Gya	¶	¶	2,15,705	5·68	1,79,145	5·11
Native States:						
Nizam's	2,37,332	1·95	3,75,090	3·06	2,92,775	2·40
METRE GAUGE.						
Guaranteed:						
South Indian	13,22,333	3·05	14,02,329	3·26	12,37,726	2·89
Imperial State:						
Rajputana-Malwa... Rajputana	‖61,31,742	6·49	51,29,252	5·87	28,67,041	5·51
Rajputana-Malwa... Holkar & Sindia-Neemuch					6,02,399	1·90
Provincial State:						
Northern Bengal	11,65,371	5·92	10,93,863	5·38	8,99,316	4·41
Tirhoot	2,59,705	2·22	2,54,047	3·94	2,36,200	3·70
Cawnpore-Achnera	2,07,466	3·88	*a*1,17,110	*a*3·74	*a*84,238	*a*2·70
Nagpur and Chhattisgarh	6,83,860	7·83	1,89,171	2·15	66,056	0·95
Rangoon & Irrawaddy Valley	5,52,266	4·19	6,30,431	4·97	6,45,077	5·16
Native States:						
Bhavnagar-Gondal	3,26,613	3·72	3,54,647	4·24	2,65,294	3·05

Railway.	1880. Net Earnings.	1880. Percentage.	1879. Net Earnings.	1879. Percentage.
BROAD GAUGE.	*Rs.*		*Rs.*	
East Indian	2,87,54,418	8·70	2,90,80,929	8·83
Guaranteed:—Madras	19,57,136	1·77	20,75,170	1·88
Great Indian Peninsula	1,11,05,551	4·44	1,01,90,601	4·10
Bombay, Baroda, and Central India	47,34,653	5·77	37,92,898	4·61
Eastern Bengal	27,24,310	7·88	24,33,530	7·10
Sind, Punjab, and Delhi	54,70,862	4·75	45,40,520	3·99
Oudh and Rohilkhand	19,04,410	3·28	18,19,936	3·24
Imperial State:—Punjab Northern	5,64,171	1·40	3,78,889	1·54
Indus Valley and Kandahar	19,22,399	2·77	6,17,459	1·06
Provincial State:—Patna-Gya	2,11,266	6·56	1,01,787	3·56
Native States:—Nizam's	2,24,309	1·86	89,925	0·77
METRE GAUGE.				
Guaranteed:—South Indian	9,20,018	2·23	10,63,232	2·60
Imperial State:				
Rajputana-Malwa: Rajputana	12,33,305	3·62	11,79,167	3·81
Rajputana-Malwa: Holkar and Sindia-Neemuch	3,53,991	1·40	2,91,898	1·46
Provincial State:				
Northern Bengal	6,43,569	3·20	1,25,120	0·66
Tirhoot	2,40,272	4·49	1,07,818	2·10
Cawnpore-Achnera	..	..	..	..
Nagpur and Chhattisgarh	21,271	0·70	..	..
Rangoon and Irrawaddy Valley	5,21,084	4·23	1,41,743	1·19
Native States:				
Bhavnagar-Gondal	..	..	..	..

* Includes State branch lines worked by the undertaking. † 6·84 deducting amount paid to Government as above. ‡ Includes *Rs.*2,40,023 on account of rent of leased lines. § 7·20 deducting amount paid to Government as above. ‖ Includes Rawari-Ferozepore. ¶ Included with East Indian. *a* Figures for Cawnpore-Farukhabad only.

Guaranteed Interest.—Indian Railways.

Statement of the total amount of interest advanced to each of the under-mentioned railway companies to the 31st December, 1883.

Railway.	Interest advanced to 31st December, 1882.	Interest advanced during 1883. England.	India.	Interest charg'd on o'erdrawn Capital.	Total.	Total.
Bombay, Baroda, & C. India	£7,467,444	£395,716	£299	£1,652	£397,667	£7,865,111
Eastern Bengal	2,647,713	153,297	427	935	154,659	2,802,372
Great Indian Peninsula......	21,539,582	1,141,869	3,341	1,799	1,147,009	22,686,591
Madras	10,507,089	521,030	...	...	521,030	11,028,119
Oudh and Rohilkhand	3,196,711	312,795	704	...	313,500	3,510,211
Sind, Punjab, and Delhi ...	9,699,117	553,114	650	215	553,979	10,253,097
South Indian	2,716,749	203,995	...	1,719	205,714	2,922,463
Total....................£	57,774,405	3,281,816	5,421	*6,320	3,293,558	61,067,964

A statement showing approximately the amounts advanced on account of guaranteed interest to the under-mentioned railway companies to the 30th June, 1883.

Railway.	Total amount advanced to 31st December, 1883.†	Aggregate of Net Revenue Balances for the several half-years to 30th June, 1883, inclusive.	Net amount advanced.
Bombay, Baroda, and Central India	£7,865,111	£4,758,981	£3,106,130
Eastern Bengal	2,802,372	2,642,352	160,020
Great Indian Peninsula..........................	22,686,591	16,595,431	6,091,160
Madras	11,028,119	4,778,221	6,249,898
Oudh and Rohilkhand	3,510,211	1,630,710	1,879,501
Sind, Punjab, and Delhi	10,253,097	3,746,804	6,506,293
South Indian..	2,922,463	1,286,621	1,635,842
Total	£61,067,964	£35,439,120	£25,628,844

Statement showing the Amount of Surplus Profits earned by Guaranteed Railways to 31st December, 1883, inclusive.

Railway.	To end of 1877.	Half-year to 30th June, 1878	Half-year to 31st Dec., 1878	Half-year to 30th June, 1879	Half-year to 31st Dec., 1879	Half-year to 30th June, 1880	Half-year to 31st Dec., 1880
	£	£	£	£	£	£	£
Bombay, Baroda, & Central India......	36,929	...‡	...	...‡	...	...‡	...
Eastern Bengal......	174,229	26,158	64,981	317	63,257	...	99,197
East Indian	3,861,756	539,047	305,834	679,823	468,967	...§	...§
Gt.Indian Peninsula	775,785	364,944	...	112,569	...	101,576	...
Sind, Punjab, & Delhi	...	...	...	...	...	3,872	...
Total...............	4,848,699	930,149	370,815	792,709	532,224	105,448	99,197

Railway.	Half-year to 30th June, 1881	Half-year to 31st Dec., 1881	Half-year to 30th June, 1882	Half-year to 31st Dec., 1882	Half-year to 30th June, 1883	Half-year to 31st Dec., 1883	Total.
	£	£	£	£	£	£	£
Bombay, Baroda, & Central India......	158,450	...	147,830	...	201,974	7,903	553,086
Eastern Bengal......	4,414	149,764	15,304	164,054	45,426	46,276	853,377
East Indian	...§	...§	...§	...§	...§	...§	5,855,427
Gt.Indian Peninsula	338,319	1,248	590,124	...	609,803	...	2,894,368
Sind, Punjab' & Delhi	...	...	...	...	...	...	3,872
Total...............	501,183	151,012	753,258	164,054	857,203	54,179	10,160,130

* The interest on overdrawn capital is for the year 1883, being charged in that year by transfer entry.

† The interest for the half-year to 30th June, 1883, not being paid until the succeeding half-year.

‡ Surplus profits were earned by the Bombay, Baroda, and Central India during these half-years, but no division took place, owing to the special agreement that all surplus profits should be applied to the construction of the Nerbudda Bridge.

§ Surplus profits of the East Indian, after it had been acquired by the State, are omitted in this statement.

Guaranteed Railways.

Year.	Capital expended to 31st March.	Net Revenue for year to 31st December.	Guaranteed Interest for year to 31st December	Interest in excess of Revenue.	Revenue in excess of Interest.
1870.........	£83,910,587	£2,846,600	£4,344,113	£1,497,513	...
1871.........	87,686,857	2,686,260	4,544,764	1,858,504	...
1872.........	90,183,585	2,869,223	4,603,853	1,734,630	...
1873.........	90,660,830	3,185,069	4,613,573	1,428,504	...
1874.........	91,353,883	3,956,071	4,651,088	695,017	...
1875.........	92,441,794	3,576,514	4,641,979	1,065,465	...
1876.........	93,392,600	4,442,430	4,658,947	216,517	...
1877.........	94,108,059	6,117,226	4,662,635	...	£1,454,591
1878.........	95,430,863	5,002,028	4,708,134	...	293,894
1879.........	96,444,666	5,062,188	4,748,233	...	313,955
*1880.........	65,907,288	2,662,213	3,263,179	600,966	...
*1881.........	66,319,320	3,110,824	3,272,651	161,827	...
*1882.........	67,021,755	3,319,439	3,279,407	...	40,032
*1883.........	67,431,448	3,542,973	3,289,429	...	253,634

Results of working the Guaranteed Railways for the year ended 31st December, 1883.

Railway.	Net Revenue.	Guaranteed Interest.	Revenue in excess of Interest.	Interest in excess of Revenue.	Extra Dividend.§ Rate per cent. Dec. 1882	June '83.
GUARANTEED.	£	£	£	£	£ s. d.	£ s. d.
Bombay, Baroda, & C.I.	621,858	396,015	225,848	...	...	1 3 6
Eastern Bengal	246,090	153,720	92,370	...	‡3 0 0	‡0 18 0
Great Indian Peninsula	1,618,802	1,145,210	473,592	...	...	1 7 4
Madras	231,610	523,234	...	291,624	...	...
Oudh and Rohilkand { Main Line, N Extnsion }	248,036	313,500	...	65,464	...	...
Sind, Punjab, and Delhi	449,863	553,765	...	103,902	...	...
South Indian...............	126,724	203,995	...	77,271	...	...
Total	3,542,973	†3,289,439	791,805	538,271	...	...

RATES AND FARES.—The reduction of the lowest class fares on the East Indian Line from three to two and half pies, which was strenuously opposed by the company's officers in India, came into force on the Jubbulpore Branch and on the main line North-West of Allahabad on the 1st January, 1882, and on the remaining portion of the undertaking on the 1st July, 1882. The effect of this measure which was enforced by the Government of India, under the power reserved in the company's contract, may now be fairly judged from actual results.

The numbers travelling and the receipts from the lowest class of passengers, exclusive of season ticket holders, on this line are given below for the last eight half-years.

	Numbers.	Receipts.
First half of 1880	3,802,743	*Rs.*42,51,966
Second half of 1880.....................................	3,497,621	43,40,205
First half of 1881	3,905,665	45,86,759
Second half of 1881	3,672,028	43,50,680
First half of 1882	‖4,645,468	55,76,367
Second half of 1882	4,407,108	43,61,734
First half of 1883	5,649,737	51,55,678
Second half of 1883	4,790,528	46,30,831

On submitting the report and accounts for the 1st half of 1883 to the meeting o the shareholders, the chairman's address contained the following remarks:—"With regard to the diminution of our rates for third class passengers from 3 pies to 2½ pies, the principle of that reduction has been dealt with by me on a former occasion, and we now arrive at the result. The result is that whilst we have lost one-sixth of the fare charged, we have recovered very nearly equal to that in the number of passengers carried, so that we have practically earned the same amount as was

* East Indian excluded.
† This is the interest payable for 1883, and not the amount paid in that year.
‡ Less income tax.
§ Extra dividend (in excess of guaranteed interest) received by the companies as surplus profits.
‖ Part of this increase, estimated at 536,000 passengers, is due to the Kumbh mela, at Allahabad in February, 1882.

asserted would be the case when it was suggested that this reduction should be carried out; in other words, the view which the Government took of the matter at that time has been borne out, and the community of India who use our railway are enjoying the benefit of it."

In the course of the year, the manager of the Indus Valley was authorised to reduce the rate for coal upwards from Karachi to $\frac{1}{10}$ pie per maund per mile. The introduction of this low rate was suggested with the view to utilise the wagons which would otherwise return empty from Karachi, and on account of the East Indian not being prepared to reduce their coal rates to the extent desired by Government. Under the existing contract with that company, the Government cannot enforce the adoption of a rate for minerals and food-grains below $\frac{1}{6}$ pie per maund per mile. There has been much correspondence on this subject, and at present the question of these coal rates on the East Indian is under the consideration of the board of directors.

As an experimental measure, the rate for grain on the Punjab Northern was reduced with effect from May, 1883, to $\frac{1}{8}$ pie per maund per mile. Subsequently the manager reported that this low rate had been advantageous, and that traffic had sprung up at stations which would not otherwise have exported grain. It is as yet too early to say whether the experiment will prove a financial success. But it is of the first importance to foster the traffic on this line.

The fares for first, second, and third class passengers respectively on the South Indian were reduced on the 1st January, 1883, to 12 pies, 4 pies, and 2 pies per mile with satisfactory results.

The following were the most important alterations during the year in respect to the carriage of goods on the Rajputana-Malwa.

From the 1st January the following reduced rates, approximating to those current on the East Indian, were introduced on the Rajputana-Malwa, with the concurrence of the Government of India, in substitution of the existing ordinary class rates and special classes "A," "B," "C," and "D," in local and through booking:—

	Pie per maund per mile.		Pie per maund per mile.
First class	·35	Fourth class	·84
Second "	·525	Fifth "	1·0
Third "	·7		

	Pie per maund per mile.				
	1st 100 miles.	2nd 100 miles.	3rd 100 miles.	4th 100 miles.	Over 400 miles.
Special class "A"	·35	·25	·15	·15	·10
" " "B"	·525	·525	·30	·20	·10

The new special class "A" was made applicable to the following staples of traffic when tendered for despatch in consignments of 270 maunds and over:—

- Cement (masonry)
- Coal
- Firewood
- Grains, edible
- Iron, ore and slag
- Iron, pig
- Kunkur
- Limestone
- Marble, rough
- Oil cake
- Pulses
- Salt
- Saltpetre
- Seeds, common
- Slates, rough, in tiles or slabs, for building purposes
- Stone, unwrought

and tobacco (native, raw) re-classified from the old special class "D" to the new special class "B." Sugar and jagree, hitherto under the old special class "C," were re-classified as 1st class. All special rates were abolished, except those hitherto quoted for piece-goods (pressed, or in boxes) from Bombay to Delhi, Agra and Achnera, or *via* those junctions, and from Ahmedabad to Agra, or *via* Achnera; and for cotton.

Consequent on competitive low rates being quoted by the Sind, Punjab, and Delhi and Indus Valley State lines for the booking from Karachi of iron and steel, a similar reduction of rates was deemed necessary over this and the Bombay, Baroda, and Central Indian lines; with this object a special class "C" rate, on the following basis, was adopted for certain descriptions of iron and steel traffic which were injuriously affected by the competition: the Bombay, Baroda, and Central India uniting in a corresponding reduction in rate. Fibrous materials, destined for the manufacture of paper and gunny bags, were also classified under the new special class "C." These changes in classification occurred with effect from the 1st April in local and through booking.

	Pie per maund per mile.				
	1st 100 miles.	2nd 100 miles.	3rd 100 miles.	4th 100 miles.	Over 400 miles.
Special class	·35	·35	·52	·25	·15

Owing to reductions on the East Indian in booking from Howrah, the following reductions in rates occurred in concert with the Bombay, Baroda, and Central India for the carriage of kerosine oil, flashing at and above 75° Fahrenheit, Abel's test, from Bombay *via* Sabarmati:—

From 1st March	at owner's risk	2nd class.
	at railway's risk	3rd „
From 1st May	at owner's risk	1st „
	at railway's risk	2nd „

With the introduction of the new special "A" class rate from 1st January, the rates per maund for edible grains and common seeds from Delhi and Agra, and *via* those junctions to Bombay (Carnac Bridge), stood as follows:—

	R. M. R.	B.B.&C.I.R.	Total.
From Delhi and *via* Delhi ...	0 9 0	0 4 6	0 13 6
From Agra and *via* Agra ...	0 8 8	0 4 6	0 13 2

Under the orders of the Government of India, a reduction of the through rates per maund from the 1st May was made in booking from Delhi to Bombay to *Rs.*0-11-0 for wheat, and *Rs.*0-11-6 for other grains and common seeds, irrespective of the quantity tendered for despatch. The rates from other Rajputana-Malwa stations to Bombay being reduced proportionately, the Rajputana-Malwa special class "A" rate being applied over both as one line (the rates of *Rs.*0-11-0 and *Rs.*0-11-6 from Delhi being considered as maxima), and the proceeds divided according to mileage. From the 1st June the rates per maund for edible grain and common seeds, booked to Bombay, *via* Khandwa, from stations Neemuch to Rutlam (both stations included), were reduced to—

R. M. R.	G. I. P. R.	Total.
0 4 4	0 6 6	0 10 10

Ordinary tariff rates continuing to apply in booking to Bombay, *via* Khandwa, from Nauganwan and stations south of it.

Traffic and Working.—The main results are summarised below for all railways, and compared with the similar figures for 1882 and 1881:—

	1883.	1882.	1881.
Mean mileage open for traffic	10,408·90	9,985·30	9,637·60
Number of passengers carried	65,098,958	58,875,918‡	54,763,683
Number of tons of goods moved	16,999,264	14,833,243§	13,214,074
Number of tons of general merchandise	10,983,265	9,275,065§	8,503,861
Number of passenger miles	3,018,897,918	2,898,289,587‡	2,620,363,895
Ton mileage of goods	2,970,703,599	2,465,049,623‡	2,309,177 012
Number of train miles	40,182,527	36,751,857‖	34,798,517
Gross receipts	*Rs*16,27,97,525*	*Rs.*15,23,12,619†	*Rs.*14,32,30,801
Working expenses	7,87,81,945*	7,58,05,494†	7,07,12,465
Net receipts	8,40,15,580*	7,65,07,125†	7,25,18,336

In round numbers, the average length open during the year 1883 was 10,409 miles, upon which the traffic work performed was equivalent to 3,019 millions of passengers and 2,971 millions of tons of goods carried one mile.

The total number of passengers carried shows an increase of 10·57 per cent. over the number carried in 1882. The passenger mileage has increased 4·16 per cent., and the receipts from passenger traffic 0·18 per cent. The number of passengers per open mile was 6,254 in 1883, as compared with 5,992 in 1882, and 5,682 in 1881. Of the total number carried in 1883, the lower class passengers constituted 97·45 per cent., the second class 2·08, and the first class passengers only 0·47 per cent.

The distances travelled by each class of passenger were, on an average, first class 84 miles, second class 69 miles, and lower classes 46 miles; and for these journeys the first class passenger paid *Rs.*5 13*a.* 5*p.*, the second class passenger *Rs.*1 14*a.* 1*p.*, and the third class passenger 9*a.* 3*p.*

* Excluding steamboat service.
† Excluding Dildarnagar-Ghazipur line and steamboat service on all lines.
‡ Excluding Sindia, Dildarnagar-Ghazipur, Muttra-Achnera, and Darjeeling lines.
§ Excluding Sindia, Dildarnagar-Ghazipur, Muttra-Achnera, Kaunia-Dhurla, Bhopal, and Darjeeling lines.
‖ Excluding Muttra-Achnera and Darjeeling lines.

The average receipts per coaching train mile were *Rs.*3·15, the highest among the principal railways being *Rs.*4·53 on the Eastern Bengal, the lowest *Rs.*2·29 on the Nizam's and on the Rajputana-Malwa.

The largest average number of passengers carried in a passenger train was 270·68 on the Oudh and Rohilkhand, the smallest 123 on the Wardha Coal Line.

The lowest average cost of hauling one passenger unit one mile was 0·84 pie on the East Indian, on which line the average sum received for this work was 2·72 pies.

The total tonnage of goods lifted during the year shows an increase of 14·80 per cent. as compared with that in 1882; but the total ton mileage shows an increase of 20·51 per cent. over that of the previous year, while the receipts from goods traffic were larger in 1883 than in 1882 by 11·11 per cent. The number of tons of goods carried per mile open was 1,683 in 1883, as compared with 1,516 in 1882, and 1,371 in 1881.

The average receipts per goods train mile were *Rs.*4·42, the highest being *Rs.*7·28 on the Eastern Bengal, and, among the principal railways, the lowest *Rs.*1·69 on the Tirhoot.

The lowest average cost of hauling one ton of goods one mile was 2·27 pies on the East Indian, and the average sum received on that line for doing this work was 6·04 pies.

Including the steam boat service, the gross receipts during the year amounted to *Rs.*16,38,93,812, of which *Rs.*5,63,32,497 were obtained on the East Indian (including the State branches worked by it), *Rs.*7,96,16,415 on the Guaranteed lines, *Rs.*3,10,12,464 on State, *Rs.*23,34,679 on lines in Native States, and *Rs.*5,97,757 on the Darjeeling-Himalayan, and other assisted companies' lines.

Of the total earnings, *Rs.*4,60,69,054 were due to passengers, *Rs.*11,28,88,606 to goods, and *Rs.*49,36,152 to steam boat service and miscellaneous sources.

Compared with the previous year's returns, the traffic receipts (coaching and goods) show an increase of 7·38 per cent. The total receipts per mile open were *Rs.*15,640 in 1883, *Rs.*15,275 in 1882, and *Rs.*14,862 in 1881.

The receipts per train mile in 1883 were *Rs.*4·05, as compared with *Rs.*4·14 in 1882, and *Rs.*4·12 in 1881.

Excluding steamboat expenditure, the total working expenses during 1883 amounted to *Rs.*7,87,81,945, the percentage on gross receipts being 46·39 as compared with a similar percentage of 49·77 in 1882, and of 49·37 in 1881.

The lowest percentages in 1883 were 36·96 on the East Indian, 43·19 on the Bombay, Baroda, and Central India, and 46·19 on the Nagpur and Chhattisgarh.

The expenses per train mile for all lines average *Rs.*1·96, and were, excluding the Calcutta and South-Eastern and Jodhpur lines, lowest on the Rajputana-Malwa *Rs.*1·51, and on the South Indian *Rs.*1.60. On the East Indian the expenses per train mile were *Rs.*1·75, and on the other lines they varied within a maximum of *Rs.*3·31 on the Eastern Bengal.

The aggregate traffic of all railways in grain, pulses, and seeds has been during the last two years—1882, 3,989,969 tons, *Rs* 3,29,57,056; 1883, 5,214,070 tons, *Rs*4,21,14,314.

The wheat traffic was exceedingly brisk during the first half of 1883, the quantities carried by the principal railways for local consumption and in connection with the ports of shipment were for two corresponding half-years—

	Tons.	
	1st half 1882.	1st half 1883.
East Indian	126,053	255,357
Great Indian Peninsula	241,572	274,395
Bombay, Baroda, and Central India	*	51,347
Sind, Punjab, and Delhi (Sind Section)	53,514	172,765

The export from the three chief ports during the same period were:—

	Tons.		
	1st half 1883.	1st half 1882.	
Calcutta	178,124	98,589	Increase 80 per cent.
Bombay	281,746	291,239	Decrease 3·3 per cent.
Karachi	90,463	40,694	Increase 122 per cent.

These figures will not agree with the quantities actually carried by rail during the same periods owing to storage and the shipments of wheat brought down at the end of June being made in a subsequent month.

* The tonnage from wheat was included under the head of grain in 1882.

The statements given below, which are taken from the accounts relating to the trade and navigation of British India for the month of March, 1884, are interesting as showing the quantity and value of Indian wheat exported to the several countries, and the share of each Indian Province in the total quantity of wheat exported.

Principal Countries to which Wheat was Exported.	During the Twelve Months from 1st April to 31st March. Quantity. 1881-82.	1882-83.	1883-84.	Value. 1881-82.	1882-83.	1883-84.
	Cwt.	Cwt.	Cwt.	*Rs.*	*Rs.*	*Rs.*
United Kingdom	9,379,236	6,575,160	10,508,159	3,96,56,431	2,74,31,823	4,33,58,818
Belgium	2,625,227	1,458,894	2,563,861	1,17,64,323	66,09,285	1,09,18,976
France	5,308,073	3,567,712	3,402,596	2,38,88,858	1,58,82,288	1,50,10,788
Holland	712,390	578,246	192,750	26,84,211	24,25,664	8,13,961
Italy	359,318	176,063	445,522	16,77,135	7,27,800	17,88,076
Egypt	919,036	799,550	3,335,909	38,57,878	35,76,624	1,47,11,900
Other countries	560,240	988,778	512,529	25,11,979	40,35,847	21,96,803
Total	19,863,520	14,144,407	20,961,416	8,60,40,815	6,06,89,341	8,87,98,317

Share of each Province and Port in the total quantity of Wheat Exported.	During the Twelve Months from 1st April to 31st March. Quantity. 1881-2.	1882-3.	1883-4.	Value. 1881-2.	1882-3.	1883-4.
	Cwt.	Cwt.	Cwt.	Rs.	Rs.	Rs.
Bengal (Calcutta)	6,668,047	4,439,405	7,611,535	2,52,07,566	1,79,35,567	3,04,27,657
Bombay	11,328,585	6,967,752	8,970,603	5,13,03,583	2,98,95,916	3,88,15,002
Sindh (Karachi)	1,852,334	2,732,275	4,377,753	94,82,433	1,28,12,379	1,95,49,177
Madras	10,996	6,599	1,525	36,178	22,232	6,481
British Burma	3,558	8,376	Nil.	11,065	23,257	Nil.
Total	19,868,520	14,144,407	20,961,416	8,60,40,815	6,06,89,341	8,87,98,317

It will be seen that the export during the year 1883-4 is 48 per cent. in excess of that for 1882-3, and larger than that in any previous year.

The exports from Calcutta have increased in quantity by 71½ per cent., those from Bombay by 29 per cent., and those from Karachi show an increase of 60 per cent. in 1883-4 as compared with 1882-3.

The foreign export of rice shows a decrease in 1883-4. That during the twelve months from the 1st April to the 31st March compares as follows for the last four years.

	Quantity in Cwts. 1880-1.	1881-2.	1882-3.	1883-4.
Bengal	6,731,454	7,684,878	7,855,151	7,422,296
Bombay	927,019	615,639	562,537	521,201
Sind	31,848	48,764	71,473	79,742
Madras	2,755,443	1,776,684	1,448,540	1,994,788
British Burma	16,820,276	18,769,456	21,380,587	17,022,303
Total	27,266,040	28,888,421	31,258,288	27,040,330

Of the total amount exported in 1883-4, in round numbers, 8,660,000 cwt. were sent to the United Kingdom, and 10,300,000 cwt. to Malta, Mauritius, the West Indies, Ceylon, and the Straits Settlement.

Summary.—The total extent of railways opened for traffic in India on the 31st March, 1884, is 10,832¼ miles, of which 6,406 miles are in the hands of companies, 3,922½ miles are State lines, either Imperial or Provincial, and 503¾ miles belong to Native States. On the same date the extent of railway mileage under construction was 3,457¾ miles, of which 1,549½ miles are in the hands of companies, 1,311¾ miles are under construction by the State, and 596½ miles by Native States. The whole capital outlay on the railways and connected steamer services amounted on the 31st December, 1883, to 148,305,646*l.* (at the conventional exchange of 2*s.* to the rupee), of which 108,609,682*l.* has been expended by Guaranteed companies (inclusive of the cost of the East Indian, which stands at 34,824,452*l.*), 36,002,952*l.* on the State lines, 2,895,322*l.* on Native State lines, and 797,690*l.* on Assisted Companies lines. The gross receipts during the calendar year 1883 amounted to 16,389,381*l.*, as compared with 15,352,320*l.* in 1882; the working expenses have been 7,970,430*l.*, as compared with 7,668,100*l.* in 1882. The net revenue amounted during 1883 to 8,418,951*l.*, of which the East Indian, including the State branches worked by the company, contributed *3,164,296*l.*, the Guaranteed lines 3,836,501*l.*, the Assisted Companies 8,720*l.*, the State lines 1,331,071*l.*, and the lines in Native States 78,363*l.* The total net earnings on all lines in 1883 yielded a return of 5*l.* 13*s.* 6*d.* per cent. per annum, as compared with 5*l.* 7*s.* 3*d.* in 1882, or excluding steam-boat services and suspense

* After deducting State expenditure and share of net earnings payable to the East Indian

items, of 5*l*. 18*s*. 2*d*., as compared with 5*l*. 11*s*. The East Indian Line and branches produced 8*l*. 14*s*. 11*d*. per cent., the rest of the Guaranteed lines paid 5*l*. 4*s*. per cent., and the State lines yielded 3*l*. 16*s*. 10*d*. per cent. The total number of passengers carried was 65,098,953, as compared with 58,875,918 in 1882, and the receipts from the coaching traffic have amounted to 4,606,905*l*., as compared with 4,644,085*l*. in 1882. The aggregate tonnage of goods moved has amounted to 16,999,264 tons, as compared with 14,833,243 tons in 1882, and the receipts from goods traffic have amounted to 11,288,861*l*., as compared with 10,159,674*l*. in 1882. The above results may be taken as indicating very healthy progress in the way of direct returns on railway progress in India. The indirect returns cannot be measured in figures, but the expansion of trade indicates advancing prosperity in the country, and every addition to the railway system is an additional safeguard against the devastations caused by recurring famines.

The following table shows the dividends paid from time to time in excess of the guaranteed rate of 5 per cent.:—

	Half-year ending	Per £100 Stock. s. d.	Payable.
Bombay, Baroda, and Central India	June 30th, 1872	0 10	Jan., 1873
" "	" 1874	0 7	" 1875
" "	" 1875	0 10	" 1876
" "	" 1876	2 6	" 1877
" "	" 1877	2 6	" 1878
" "	" 1878	Nil.	... ...
" "	" 1879	Nil.	... ...
" "	" 1880	Nil.	... ...
" "	Dec. 31st, 1880	Nil.	... ...
" "	June 30th, 1881	17 6	Jan., 1882
" "	Dec. 31st, 1881	Nil.	... ...
" "	June 30th, 1882	17 6	Jan., 1882
" "	Dec. 31st, 1882	Nil.	... ...
" "	June 30th, 1883	23 6	Jan., 1884
" "	Dec. 31st, 1883	2 1	July, 1884
" "	June 30th, 1884	27 6	Jan., 1885
Eastern Bengal	Dec. 31st, 1873	3 6	July, 1874
"	June 30th, 1874	3 6	Jan., 1875
"	Dec. 31st, 1874	4 0	July, 1875
"	" 1876	15 0	" 1877
"	June 30th, 1877	5 0	Jan., 1878
"	Dec. 31st, 1877	40 0	July, 1878
"	June 30th, 1878	10 0	Jan., 1879
"	Dec. 31st, 1878	25 0	July, 1879
"	June 30th, 1879	Nil.	... ...
"	Dec. 31st, 1879	25 0	Jan., 1880
"	June 30th, 1880	Nil.	... ...
"	Dec. 31st, 1880	30 6	July, 1881
"	June 30th, 1881	2 0	Jan., 1882
"	Dec. 31st, 1881	52 0	June, 1882
"	June 30th, 1882	2 0	Dec., 1882
"	Dec. 31st, 1882	110 0	June, 1883
"	June 30th, 1883	68 0	Dec., 1883
"	Dec. 31st, 1883	10 0	July, 1884
(Since purchased by the	Secretary of State	for India).	
East Indian	June 30th, 1869	5 0	Dec., 1870
"	" 1870	5 9	" 1871
"	" 1871	4 4	" 1872
"	" 1872	6 0	" 1873
"	" 1873	6 3	" 1874
"	Dec. 31st, 1873	4 3	July, 1874
"	June 30th, 1874	25 0	Jan., 1875
"	Dec. 31st, 1874	2 6	July, 1875
"	June 30th, 1875	5 7	Jan., 1876
"	Dec. 31st, 1875	1 4	July, 1876
"	June 30th, 1876	13 0	Jan., 1877
"	Dec. 31st, 1876	10 0	July, 1877
"	June 30th, 1877	25 0	Jan., 1878
"	Dec. 31st, 1877	19 0	July, 1878

	Half-year ending	Per £100 Stock. s. d.	Payable.
East Indian	June 30th, 1878	17 6	Jan., 1879
"	Dec. 31st, 1878	10 0	July, 1879
"	June 30th, 1879	23 9	Jan., 1880
" (Deferred Annuities)	" *1880	27 0	" 1881
"	Dec. 31st, 1880	17 6	July, 1881
"	June 30th, 1881	29 0	Jan., 1882
"	Dec. 31st, 1881	23 4	July, 1882
"	June 30th, 1882	31 0	Jan., 1883
"	Dec. 31st, 1882	13 6	July, 1883
"	June 30th, 1883	32 6	Jan., 1884
"	Dec. 31st, 1883	20 0	July, 1884
"	June 30th, 1884	21 8	Jan., 1885
Great Indian Peninsula	" 1866	5 0	" 1867
"	" 1875	8 0	" 1876
"	" 1876	6 0	" 1877
"	" 1877	20 0	" 1878
"	" 1878	16 0	" 1879
"	" 1879	6 0	" 1880
"	" 1880	4 6	" 1881
"	Dec. 31st, 1880	Nil.	... ...
"	June 30th, 1881	15 0	Jan., 1882
"	Dec. 31st, 1881	Nil.	... ...
"	June 30th, 1882	26 6	Jan., 1883
"	Dec. 31st, 1882	Nil.	... ...
"	June 30th, 1883	27 4	Jan., 1884
"	Dec. 31st, 1883	Nil.	... ...
"	June 30th, 1884	19 10	Jan., 1885

PURCHASE OF INDIAN RAILWAYS BY THE GOVERNMENT.—The following terms on which the option to purchase may be exercised are copied for future reference from the report of the South Indian issued in June, 1879, viz.:—"Under the terms of clause 31 of the contract of 16th December, 1873, the first date at which notice can be given by the Secretary of State of his intention to purchase the railway is during the first six months after the 1st day of March, 1890; the second during the same period in 1905; and thereafter in any succeeding tenth year. If the purchase be effected previous to 1995, the Secretary of State is bound to pay a sum equal to the mean market value, during the three years immediately preceding, of all the shares and stock of the company.

"Clause 34 of the same contract provides that, in lieu of paying cash, the Secretary of State may transfer to the company such an amount of 5 per cent. Government of India Stock, redeemable at par at the option of such Government, as shall, taking such stock at par, amount to the sum which the Secretary of State would have had to pay if he had chosen to make the payment in cash. There is no power to pay in annuities."

WORKING AGREEMENTS WITH OTHER RAILWAYS AND TELEGRAPHS.—Under Viscount Cranbrook's Act, which received the royal assent on the 11th August, 1879, the following guaranteed companies, viz., Bombay, Baroda, and Central India; Eastern Bengal; Great Indian Peninsula; Madras; Oudh and Rohilkund; Sind, Punjab, and Delhi; and South Indian, may exercise all or any of the following powers, viz.: –

A guaranteed company may from time to time make with the Secretary of State for India in Council, and carry into effect, or, with the sanction of the Secretary of State for India in Council, make with any railway company, and carry into effect, any agreement with respect to any of the following purposes, namely:—

(a) The working, use, management, and maintenance of any railway or part of a railway:

(b) The supply of rolling stock and machinery necessary for any of the purposes hereinbefore mentioned, and of officers and servants for the conduct of the traffic of any such railway or part:

(c) The payments to be made and the conditions to be performed with respect to such working, use, management, and maintenance:

* On the closed Register of 1st November, 1879 (after purchase by Government), an excess dividend of 17s. 4d. per cent. was declared, as a final distribution to the old proprietors.

(*d*) The interchange, accommodation, and conveyance of traffic on, coming from, or destined for the respective railways of the contracting parties, and the fixing, collecting, apportionment, and appropriation of the revenues arising from that traffic:

(*e*) Generally the giving effect to any such provisions or stipulations with respect to any of the purposes hereinbefore mentioned as the contracting parties may think fit and mutually agree on.

A guaranteed company may from time to time make with the Secretary of State for India in Council, and carry into effect, any agreement with respect to any of the following purposes, namely:—

(*a*) The surrendering, selling, or letting by the company to the Secretary of State of all or any part of the telegraphs belonging to the company:

(*b*) The doing of anything connected with the working, use, management, or maintenance of or otherwise relating to any telegraphs in India which belong to the Secretary of State in Council or a guaranteed company, or in which the Secretary of State in Council or any such company is for the time being interested, including the application of the revenue to arise from any such telegraphs:

(*c*) Generally the giving effect to any such provisions or stipulations with respect to any such telegraphs as the Secretary of State in Council and any such company may think fit and mutually agree on.

A guaranteed company may from time to time, with the sanction of the Secretary State for India in Council, exercise all or any of the following powers:—

(*a*) They may use, maintain, farm, or work and take tolls in respect of any bridge or ferry used in connection with their railway:

(*b*) They may construct, use, maintain, and take tolls in respect of any road in connection with a railway bridge:

(*c*) They may provide any means of transport which may be required for the reasonable convenience of persons or goods carried or to be carried on their railway, but not between any places between which any company shall for the time being be carrying on the business of carriers by water:

Provided always, that the capital outlay on the works mentioned in the three preceding sub-sections shall not in the case of any guaranteed company exceed in all ten lacs of rupees:

(*d*) They may make and carry into effect agreements with the Secretary of State for India in Council for the construction of rolling stock, plant, or machinery used on or in connection with railways, or for leasing or taking on lease any rolling stock, plant, machinery, or equipments required for use on a railway.

A guaranteed company shall have, for the purpose of recovering any tolls which they are authorised to take under this section, such powers as may be conferred upon them by laws and regulations made by the Governor-General of India in Council.

The Secretary of State for India in Council may from time to time, with respect to any case or class of cases, delegate to the Governor-General of India in Council the power to give any sanction required under this act.

The powers conferred by this act shall be in addition to and not in derogation of any powers existing independantly of this act.

Any agreement made before the passing of this act by a guaranteed company for any of the purposes specified in this act shall be as valid as if it had been made after the passing of this act.

352.—ASSAM RAILWAYS AND TRADING COMPANY LIMITED.

This company was incorporated in 1881, under the Companies' Acts, for the purpose of constructing and working railways, opening out and developing collieries and petroleum wells, felling timber, and making the same merchantable, and carrying on and promoting other industries in Assam and elsewhere, and also to establish a service of steamers upon the Brahmapootra river.

With the view of effecting the above objects the company has agreed to acquire the following concessions which have been executed on behalf of the Secretary of State for India in Council, namely:—

1st. The right to construct and work a railway, of 1 metre gauge, from the terminus of the steamer lines on the bank of the Brahmapootra, near Dibrugarh, along the Government road towards Sadiya to the 51st mile, and a branch line, about

24 miles in length, to the Makum coal-fields, near the Debing river, under two several indentures dated respectively the 26th May, 1880, and 25th July, 1881, made between the Secretary of State for India in Council and Messrs. Shaw, Finlayson, and Co.

2nd. The right to open and work coal and iron mines within an area of 30 square miles in the Makum coal-fields, under an indenture dated the 30th July, 1881, and made between the Secretary of State for India in Council and Messrs. Shaw, Finlayson, and Co.

3rd. The right to cut, use, and export timber within a distance of 1½ mile on either side of the Makum Branch Railway, under an indenture dated the 28th July, 1881, and made between the Secretary of State for India in Council and Messrs. Shaw, Finlayson, and Co.

The above-mentioned concessions have been duly signed, and the particulars of them may be stated shortly as follow:—

The railway concession is in perpetuity.

By the above concession, dated the 26th May, 1880, executed on behalf of the Secretary of State for India in Council, a guarantee is given for twenty years from the opening of the railway and branch line respectively, of an amount not exceeding in the whole 100,000 rupees per annum. In the event of the net earnings yielding a minimum return of 5 per cent. per annum upon the cost of construction, the Government guarantee will not come into operation. Should the net earnings not give a minimum return of 5 per cent. per annum, the Government guarantee will then be available to an extent not exceeding in the whole 100,000 rupees per annum. Upon the opening of any section of the railways, the Government guarantee will accrue in respect thereof *pro rata*.

By the same concession is likewise granted, free of cost, the use of the Government lands and roads required as the site of the railways, and also the right, until five years after the lines are opened for traffic, to cut and use timber for the purpose of the railways, either in the original construction or subsequent maintenance, and for fuel, without payment of royalty.

The right is reserved to the Secretary of State for India in Council to regulate the rates and fares, but not in such a way as to lead to a diminution of the net profits of the railways below 12 per cent. per annum.

It is also stipulated that the Government is to have the option of purchasing the railway at the expiration of the first five years from the date of opening, and at subsequent intervals of five years, by paying the company 20 per cent. in excess of the value of the lines as a dividend-paying investment; the price to be ascertained in case of difference by arbitration.

The coal concession includes the right to work iron ore, and is for a term of 20 years within an area of 30 square miles, and for a further term of 30 years within an area of at least four square miles, at a dead rent of 50 rupees (about 4*l.* 3*s.* 4*d.*) per square mile per annum, merged in a royalty of 8 annas (3¾*d.*) per ton of coal and 2 annas (2½*d.*) per ton of iron ore.

The license to cut timber is for a term of 20 years, at royalties varying from 2 rupees to 6 rupees per tree, according to the kind of tree.

The terms upon which the above-mentioned concessions are acquired by the company are as follows:—

For the railway concession, coal lease, and timber grant, the company is to pay 13,033*l.* in cash, the vendors not being entitled to any further benefit until after payment of interest on debentures and the sinking fund for their redemption, and until after payment of accumulative dividend of 8 per cent. per annum upon the 35,000 preferred shares; the vendors are then to be entitled to one-fifth of the surplus profits, represented by 8,750 deferred shares of 1*l.* each, to be issued as fully paid-up.

CAPITAL.—500,000*l.* in 50,000 preferred shares of 10*l.* each, entitled to preference in capital, and to accumulative preferential dividend of 8 per cent. per annum (accruing from the date of payment of each call), before the deferred shares, and payable off at 20 per cent. premium, as provided by the articles of association; and 43,750*l.* in 43,750 deferred shares of 1*l.* each, entitled to the surplus profits. Of the deferred shares 8,750 have been allotted, credited as fully paid, to the vendors under the agreement, and the remaining 35,000, also credited as fully paid, have been issued to the holders for the time being of the original 35,000 preferred shares, share for share, as soon as 3*l.* per share had been paid upon the same.

The deferred shareholders take all profits after payment of 8 per cent. cumulative dividend to the preferred shareholders.

NEW CAPITAL.—On the 4th July, 1884, the following resolutions were passed, viz.:—"1. That the capital of the company be increased by the issue of 15,000 new 'A' shares of 10*l*. each, being entitled to all arrears of dividends already accrued, and ranking in all respects with and subject to all the same regulations as the original 'A' shares. 2. That 7,875 of such new 'A' shares shall be issued in accordance with the Articles of Association, at the price of 8*l*. per share (2*l*. being deemed to have been paid up on such shares previously to the issue thereof), and that 125 of such new shares shall be issued (at the price aforesaid) in such manner as the directors shall think fit, and that the remaining 7,000 new 'A' shares shall be reserved for issue hereafter, at such price and in such manner as to the directors may, from time to time, appear desirable."

The directors have the power to raise not exceeding 250,000*l*. on debentures.

The above terms are comprised in an agreement dated the 2nd August, 1881, and made between Messrs. Shaw, Finlayson, and Co., of the one part, and the Assam Railways and Trading Company Limited, of the other part.

The following other agreements have also been entered into, viz.:—An agreement dated the 2nd August, 1881, between the Assam Railways and Trading Company Limited and Benjamin Piercy; and an agreement dated 2nd August, 1881, between Messrs. Shaw, Finlayson, and Co. and Jasper Wilson Johns.

The above particulars are from a prospectus inviting subscriptions for the "preferred" shares, issued August, 1881.

35,000 "preferred" shares (now fully paid) and 43,750 fully paid "deferred" shares have been issued.

79 miles in all now opened for traffic, thus completing the railways.

DIRECTORS:

Chairman—JAMES STAATS FORBES, Esq., 13, Chelsea Embankment, S.W.

Deputy-Chairman—PATRICK COMRIE LECKIE, Esq., 15, Ashburn Place, W.

Thomas Barnes, Esq., The Quinta, Chirk, near Ruabon.
Philip Gosset, Esq., Jersey.
Evan A. Jack, Esq., Cossipore, Upper Norwood, S.E.
J. Berry White, Esq., 36, Bury Street, St. James's, S.W.
Charles Sanderson, Esq., 46, Queen Victoria Street, E.C.

[Two additional directors may be nominated by the Secretary of State for India during the period of 20 years over which the Government guarantee extends.]

OFFICERS.—Sec., William Hill; Eng., Benjamin Piercy, M.Inst.C.E.; Auditors, Price, Waterhouse, and Co.; Solicitors, R. S. Taylor, Son, and Humbert; Bankers, Agra Bank Limited, London and Calcutta; Agents in India, Barry and Co., Calcutta.

Offices—1, Tokenhouse Buildings, Lothbury, E.C.

353.—BENGAL CENTRAL.

Incorporated under the Companies' Acts of 1862-80, with the primary object of carrying into effect a contract with the Secretary of State for India in Council for the construction and working of a single-track railway on the standard 5ft. 6in. gauge from Calcutta to Bongong, Jessore, and Koolna, with a branch from Bongong to Ranaghat on the Eastern Bengal, a total length (exclusive of sidings) of about 130 miles.

Until the 30th June, 1886, or the sooner opening of the line for traffic throughout,* the Secretary of State agreed to pay to the company, out of the revenues of India, half-yearly, on 1st January and 1st July, interest at 4 per cent. per annum.

The net earnings of each year over and above 5 per cent. are to be equally divided, one-half to belong to the company and the other half to be applied in repayment—with simple interest of 4 per cent. per annum—to the Secretary of State of the interest received from him. Only in the case of earnings over 5 per cent. is the Secretary of State entitled to any repayment, and when this has been effected the net earnings will belong exclusively to the company.

The Secretary of State provided, free of cost to the company, on a 99 years lease, all the land required for the line and stations, reserving the right at the end of 30 or 50 years from 1st January, 1882, of purchasing the whole undertaking by a

* The line, extending to 125½ miles (the Government having elected to provide the company with access from Dum-Dum to Calcutta, 4½ miles, and terminal accommodation at the latter place), was opened for through traffic in April, 1884. By special arrangement the Government guarantee was extended to cover up to the end of 1884, notwithstanding such earlier opening for through traffic.

payment to the company of the capital expenditure sanctioned by the Secretary of State, together with a bonus of 25 per cent. thereon, subject to the limitations specified in the contract as to the maximum amounts payable.

The railway is being worked under a temporary agreement by the Eastern Bengal State Railway.

CAPITAL.—In 1881 subscriptions were invited for share capital of the company, viz., 1,000,000*l*. in 10*l*. shares at par. Only 5*l*. per share has been called up. A special general meeting of shareholders authorised the creation of 4 per cent. mortgage debentures to the extent of 250,000*l*., with a view to providing the further capital estimated. All these debentures have been placed by the company at par.

DIRECTORS:

Chairman—Lieut.-Gen. C. H. DICKENS, C.S.I., 75, Lexham Gardens, Kensington, W.

Deputy-Chairman—E. F. HARRISON, Esq., C.S.I.

Colonel Robert Baring.
J. N. Bullen, Esq.
Francis S. Chapman, Esq., 36, Stanhope Gardens, South Kensington, S.W.
David Trail Robertson, Esq., 41, Onslow Gardens, S.W.
George Christian, Esq.
Colonel Arthur Ellis, C.S.I.

OFFICERS.—Sec., D. A. Traill Christie; Consulting Eng., A. M. Rendel. M.Inst.C.E., 8, Great George Street, Westminster, S.W.; Auditors, Turquand, Youngs, and Co., and Gérard van de Linde, F.C.A.; Solicitors, Clarke, Rawlins, and Co., 66, Gresham House, E.C.; Bankers, Smith, Payne, and Smiths, 1, Lombard Street, E.C.; Agent and Chief Engineer in India, S. B. Cary, C.E.

Offices—199, Gresham House, Old Broad Street, E.C.

354.—BENGAL AND NORTH WESTERN LIMITED.

Incorporated under the Companies' Acts of 1862-80. Under contract with the Secretary of State for India in Council. Capital, 2,200,000*l*. sterling, in 220,000 shares of 10*l*. each (which cannot be increased without the sanction of the Secretary of State for India).

This company is formed for the purpose of carrying out a contract with the Secretary of State for India in Council for the construction and working of a single-track system of railways on the metre-gauge, aggregating 446 miles in length, in Northern India, between the rivers Gunduk and Gogra, and between the Gogra and Ganges, in the neighbourhood of Ghazeepore and Benares. The main line will start in the Lieutenant-Governorship of Bengal, from Sonpore, on the Ganges, opposite Patna (which is in direct communication with the Port of Calcutta, both by the river and the East Indian), and pass through the towns of Chupra, Revelgunj, Sewan, Goruckpore, and Gonda, to Baraich, near the Nepal frontier of the Province of Oude. A branch from the main line will run to the north bank of the Gogra to a suitable point for the interchange of traffic with the city of Fyzabad, on the Oude and Rohilkund. Another branch will run from Goruckpore, crossing the Gogra by a bridge, through Ghazeepore, to the city of Benares, where it will be connected with the railway system of India by means of the bridge now being built by the Oude and Rohilkund.

The contract with the Secretary of State is for 99 years, and includes the following terms:—1. The Secretary of State supplies the land free of cost to the company for the term of the contract. 2. The Secretary of State reserves the right of acquiring the undertaking at the end of 30 or 50 years on payment of 25 years' purchase of the company's average net earnings for the preceding five years. 3. During the construction of the railway, but not later than the 31st December, 1887, the company is authorised to pay to the shareholders out of capital such sums as with interim net earnings will amount to 4 per cent. per annum on the paid-up capital, and powers having been taken in the memorandum and articles of association, these payments will be made accordingly on the 1st January and 1st July of each year. The capital has been fixed so as to provide for this charge.

Baraich to Nawabgunj, 73 miles, was opened for traffic 2nd April, 1884, and the main line was opened on the 15th January, 1885.

CAPITAL.—The whole of the share capital has been issued in 10*l*. shares at par, upon which interest is allowed during construction at 4 per cent. per annum, payable half-yearly. Up to October last, 6*l*. per share had been paid, the remainder to be called up in sums of not more than 2*l*. per share at intervals of not less than three months.

DIRECTORS:

Lieut.-Gen. Craven Hildesley Dickens, R.A., C.S.I., 75, Lexham Gardens, Kensington, W.
David Trail Robertson, Esq., 41, Onslow Gardens, S.W.
George Christian, Esq.
Major-Gen. J. S. Trevor, R.E., C.S.I., 75, Ladbroke Road, Notting Hill, W.
Robert Barclay Chapman, Esq., C.S.I.
Col. Arthur Ellis, C.S.I.
George William Allan, Esq., C.I.E.
Gerard Norman, Esq.

OFFICERS.—Sec., E. L. Marryat; Con. Engs., A. M. Rendel, M.Inst.C.E., 8, Great George Street, Westminster, S.W., and Henry Prince, M.Inst.C.E., 262, Gresham House, E.C.; Auditors, Cooper Brothers and Co. and Gérard Van de Linde; Solicitors, Clarke, Rawlins, and Co., 66, Gresham House, E.C.; Bankers in London, Glyn, Mills, Currie, and Co., 67, Lombard Street, E.C.; in India, The Bank of Bengal.

Offices—237, Gresham House, Old Broad Street, E.C.

355.—BOMBAY, BARODA, AND CENTRAL INDIA.

Formed for a trunk line to connect Bombay with Agra, Delhi, and Central India by way of Surat and Baroda, and thus to form a junction between the Trunk Line of the East Indian and the Presidency of Bombay, with branches. Of this project, however, the portion from Bombay to Ahmedabad, with the additions of the Kattiawar Extension and Dakor Branch lines, in all 461 miles, have only been carried out by the company, Government having decided that the line from Ahmedabad to Agra and Delhi should be constructed as a State railway.

Incorporated by act of 2nd July, 1855, by which the company is authorised to enter into contracts with the East India Company, to regulate and increase its capital, to issue debentures, and to register shares and transfers in India. A further concession, dated 2nd November, 1857, was made of an extension from Surat to Bombay, 163 miles.

By act of 13th August, 1859, the company was authorised to convert shares into stock, and otherwise to regulate and define the capital, and raise any additional capital that might be necessary from time to time, for the purposes of any undertaking of the company as may be authorised by the Secretary of State for India in Council.

KATTIAWAR EXTENSION.—This line, 77 miles in length, having been offered to the company by the Indian Government, it was resolved, at a special meeting held on 22nd November, 1869, that the company accept the offer of the Secretary of State for India to construct the extension under a 5 per cent. guarantee; that, when the extension is completed, it shall form part and parcel of the existing undertaking; that the clause in the existing contract as to the division of surplus profits be revised, such profits (over 5 per cent. per annum) being divided equally between the Government and the company during the whole period of the contract, and the Secretary of State cancelling the existing debt due for guaranteed interest, taking no account as against the company of future advances; and giving the Government, in respect of the extension during its construction, the power of supervision and possession as a remedy.

For the purposes of this extension, the sanction of the Secretary of State in Council was received in December, 1869, to the raising of 600,000*l.* in 20*l.* shares, bearing a guaranteed interest of 5 per cent. per annum, at a premium of 3 per cent.

This extension of 77 miles, to Veerumgaum and Wudwan, was constructed on the standard gauge of 5 feet 6 inches, and with rails of 60lb. to the yard, at a cost of under 5,500*l.* per mile, and within a little more than one year from the date of commencement.

The length of main and branch lines open and worked by the company is 461 miles, of which 17 miles, from Pali to Godra, on the Dakor Branch, were opened for traffic in February 1882.

TELEGRAPHS.—Government being desirous to acquire the telegraphs of the railway companies in India, the board concluded an arrangement with the Secretary of State, under which this company's telegraph lines (exclusive of the instruments and offices, which remain the property of the company) have been transferred to Government, who let to the company at a fair rent such telegraph wires as are required for railway purposes, and repaid to the company the capital cost of the railway telegraph line and stores in hand, amounting to about 22,800*l.*

REVENUE—30th June, 1884.—The gross revenue receipts, the expenses charged to revenue, and the net earnings for the half-year, compare as under with the corresponding figures of 1883:—

Half-year ended with	Receipts.	Expenses.	Net Earnings.	Percentage of Expenses to Receipts.
June, 1884	£688,364	£239,634	£448,730	34·81
„ 1883	656,115	247,748	408,367	37·76
Increase in 1884	£32,249	...	£40,363	...
Decrease „	...	£8,114	...	2·95

The net profit of the half-year was equal to the payment of a surplus dividend at 1*l*. 7*s*. 6*d*. per cent., in addition to the guaranteed 5 per cent. per annum.

In operation, 30th June, 1884:—Lines owned, 438 miles; worked, 81 miles; total, 519 miles. Sidings, 97 miles.

CAPITAL.—The total authorised capital of the company is 8,875,000*l*., viz., 6,250,000*l*. of share capital, and 2,625,000*l*. of loans. The expenditure on capital account to 30th June, 1884, amounted to 7,950,419*l*., whilst the receipts to the same date had been as under:—

Consolidated 5 per cent. stock	£7,550,200
375,000 4 per cent. debentures; 100,000 3½ per cent. debentures	475,000
Capital not bearing interest, deposited with Secretary of State	31,699
	£8,056,999

The guaranteed interest on the consolidated stock is payable half-yearly, on 5th January and 5th July, the transfer books closing 14 days before payment.

The above-named debentures consist of two classes, viz., "Debentures 1877," with interest payable 1st February and 1st August, and "Debentures 1882," with interest payable 5th May and 5th November.

TRANSFER DEPARTMENT.—Ordinary form; fee per deed, 2*s*. 6*d*.; if more sellers than one, 2*s*. 6*d*. for each account sold from; certificates must accompany transfers; any amount of stock can be transferred; in acceptances, renunciations, &c., of allotments of new stock, proxies, or other forms sent to trustees or other joint holders, the signature of all the allottees or registered proprietors is required.

GOVERNMENT OPTION OF PURCHASE.—Under the 21st clause of the new contract, dated the 17th November, 1871, the Secretary of State for India has given up the option of purchasing the line at the end of the first period of 25 years, and the earliest date at which such option can now be exercised by Government is the 1st May, 1905.—See also page 889 for terms under which Indian Railways may be purchased in the future, and for copy of the clauses of the act authorising working agreements, &c.

DIRECTORS:

Chairman—3 Lieut.-Col. P. T. FRENCH, 8, Duke Street, St. James's, S.W.

Government Director—JULAND DANVERS, Esq., India Office, Westminster, S.W.

1 Thomas Hicks, Esq., Holmewood, Streatham Hill, S.W.

2 Samuel J. Wilde, Esq., 11, Vicarage Gate, Kensington, W.

2 Major-Gen. J. S. Trevor, R.E., C.S.I., 75, Ladbroke Road, Notting Hill, W.

3 James Mitchell, Esq., 33, Ennismore Gardens, S.W.

1 Lieut.-Gen. Craven Hildesley Dickens, R.A., C.S.I., 75, Lexham Gardens, Kensington, W.

Major-Gen. R. H. Keatinge, V.C., C.S.I., 62, Lexham Gardens, Kensington, W.

1, Retire in 1885; 2, in 1886; 3, in 1887.

OFFICERS.—In LONDON.—Sec., T. W. Wood; Con. Eng., Francis Mathew, M.Inst.C.E.; Auditors, Francis Cooper, 14, George Street, Mansion House, E.C., and George Henry Harris, 25, Bucklersbury, E.C.; Solicitors, Dollman and Pritchard, 3, Lawrence Pountney Hill, Cannon Street, E.C.; Bankers, Union Bank of London, 2, Prince's Street, E.C.

Offices—45, Finsbury Circus, E.C.

356.—EAST INDIAN.

Incorporated for a line from Calcutta to the Northern Provinces. By act of 25th May, 1855, the company was enabled to register shares, transfers, and securities in India, and by act of 21st July, 1856, to convert paid-up capital into stock, as well as issue shares at various rates of interest.

By act of 30th June, 1864, the acts of the company were amended, and power given to raise further capital to the extent of 7,000,000*l.*

By act of 22nd August, 1881, powers were given to the Secretary of State to create India stock at 3½ per cent., or any other rate of interest not higher than 4 per cent., for the purpose of reducing the liabilities of India, and redeeming the annuities created under the East Indian Purchase Act of 1879. The act provides that purchases of the annuities may be made by agreement, "at such a rate of exchange that the annual interest on the stock given in exchange for any annuity shall not exceed eight-ninths of the annuity."

In reply to inquiries on the subject the secretary has written officially to the London Stock Exchange as follows, viz.:—"The Secretary of State for India in Council has recently sanctioned the issue of 321,000*l.* India 3½ per cent. stock in exchange for 12,840*l.* East Indian Railway Annuity Class "A," being at the rate of 25*l.* of stock for each 1*l.* of annuity, and for the present he is willing to comply with applications from holders of East Indian Railway Annuity Class "A," for conversion into 3½ per cent. India stock, on the same terms; the cost of the stamp on the requisite transfers to be borne by the holders of the annuity desirous of effecting an exchange into stock."

The Government had the option to purchase the line from Calcutta to Delhi in February, 1879, and the Jubbulpore Line in April, 1883, but in November 1878, an arrangement for the purchase by Government of both lines was approved, and a bill has been deposited in Parliament for authority to carry out such arrangement. The following is a copy of the official "Memorandum of Terms," viz.:—

1. That the purchase be made by means of an annuity, terminable on the 14th of February, 1953, calculated on a rate of interest of 4*l.* 6*s.* per cent. on a commuted price of 125*l.* per 100*l.* of capital stock, which gives, including 4*s.* for redemption of capital, an annuity of 5*l.* 12*s.* 6*d.* for each 100*l.* of capital stock so commuted at 125*l.* But that the shareholders be allowed an option of leaving in the hands of the Government, for the purposes hereafter mentioned, a proportion not exceeding one-fifth of the commuted value of the capital stock of the company.

2. The existing contracts to cease and determine on 31st December, 1879, and the annuity to accrue from 1st January, 1880.

3. The Secretary of State to enter into a new contract with the company for the future working and management of the line, for a term of fifty years, subject to termination at the end of the 20th, 25th, 30th, 35th, 40th, and 45th years, on two years' previous notice being given by either party.

4. In order to provide the company with a constituent body for the purposes hereafter mentioned, and with a capital in respect of which a share in future surplus profits may be assessed, it is proposed that, out of the capital sum payable to the company, payment of one-fifth part be suspended for such term as may be agreed upon for the duration of such new contract—that is to say, the holders of such capital shall be paid a minimum rate of interest per annum, and shall participate in the profits of the line, reverting, whenever the contract is terminated, to the annuity described in clause 1, and receiving the same for the remainder of the term for which the annuity is granted—viz., till the 14th February, 1953.

5. The Secretary of State in Council shall pay, on the amount of the stock of the company thus commuted, an annual interest of 4 per cent. in London.

6. In addition to the interest, the company will be entitled to one-fifth of the surplus profits as hereinafter defined, payable in India, the same to be declared half-yearly.

7. The amount of net working profits having been ascertained and declared there will be deducted—1. Interest on the debenture bond debt; 2. Interest on the debenture stock; 3. The charge in respect of the annuity; 4. The interest on the company's capital; 5. Contributions to provident fund; 6. The interest on the value of stores in hand at the end of each half-year. The balance then remaining to be the surplus profits divisible between the Government and the company, in the proportion stated, viz.:—⅘ths to be the share of the Government, and ⅕th the share of the company.

8. Application to be made to Parliament for an act declaring the capital of the company, and for other purposes necessary for carrying out the arrangement.

9. The company will be contractors for the management and working of the line.

10. The company shall also be empowered to raise by the issue of debentures, or debenture stock, guaranteed by the Government, any further sums which, in the opinion of Government, may be required for any purposes connected with the line, on terms which may be agreed upon with the Secretary of State in Council.

11. The details of the future relations of the Secretary of State in Council and the company in this country, and between the Government of India and the executive of the company in India, which will be founded mainly on the arrangements made under the existing contracts, will be determined when the contract is under consideration.

The act for the vesting of the undertaking, under the "Memorandum of Terms" before-mentioned, received the royal assent on the 11th August, 1879, after the following amendments had been inserted, viz.:—

"Provision has been made for enabling a stockholder to take all his holding in any one or more of the classes of annuity, or the India 4 per cent. stock.

"The powers to the Government and the company, to enter into contracts, have been extended to making new branches or auxiliary lines and maintaining them.

"The provisions which were originally inserted in section 22 of the bill, relative to the raising money by the issue of stock, or by the exercise of borrowing powers, have been struck out by the committee.

"The section which dealt with the voting power of the deferred annuitants is altered. As originally drawn, it was based on the deed of settlement and on the subsequent acts of Parliament regulating the East Indian, and gave one vote for 1*l*. of deferred annuity; two votes for 20*l*. of deferred annuity; and one extra vote for every complete sum of 10*l*. of deferred annuity over and above the first 20*l*.

"The section as altered by the committee now gives one vote for every 1*l*. of deferred annuity.

"Section 37, which gave the proprietors of stock of the company, on the register on the 1st December, 1879, power to hold meetings after the 1st January, 1880, has been struck out at the instance of, and in its place two new sections have been introduced by, the Government.

"The effect of these sections is to make the separate assets of the company liable for such of their obligations as the Secretary of State is not responsible for, nor bound to indemnify the company.

"After providing for such obligations, the sections give the annuitants of the company, of all classes, for the time being, power to dispose of any surplus of the separate assets. The sections as thus altered were submitted to, and approved by, the committee.

"The schedule to the act defines the separate assets of the company. They are—

"1. Half the value of the plant, &c., at the Kurhurballe and Serampore Coal Fields

"2. The company's contributions to the insurance fund.

"3. All unclaimed interest and dividends, and any sums realised by their investment."

In their report, issued in December, 1879, the directors thus explain the present position of the undertaking, viz.:—

"A contract, to continue in force for a period not exceeding fifty years and not less than twenty years from 1st January, 1880, has been entered into with the Secretary of State for India in Council, embodying the conditions on which the management of the undertaking is continued in the hands of the company."

"As soon as possible after the passing of the company's bill, a circular was sent to each proprietor, requesting him to signify, on or before the 15th November, whether he desired to avail himself of the provision of the act for deferring the payment of a portion of the annuity; for accepting his annuity in class "A" or in class "B"; or for exchanging his annuity for Government of India 4 per cent. stock."

These options may be thus briefly summarised, viz.:—

Deferred Annuity.—An annuity of 4*l*. 10*s*. per cent. per annum, leaving the balance of 1*l*. 2*s*. 6*d*. (part of 5*l*. 12*s*. 6*d*.) deferred for a term of not less than 20 or more than 50 years; the former represents 100*l*. of capital running at 4½ per cent. interest, and the latter the balance of 25*l*. capital or "Deferred Annuity," on which is paid 4 per cent. interest, with a share in the profits of the undertaking to the extent of the one-fifth of the 125*l*., the price paid in the purchase of the undertaking.

Class "A."—An absolute annuity of 5*l*. 12*s*. 6*d*. per annum for every 100*l*. of stock held, to continue for 73 years, and cease to be paid on the 14th of February, 1953.

Class "B."—An annuity of 5*l*. 5*s*., instead of 5*l*. 12*s*. 6*d*., the remaining 7*s*. 6*d*. being left in the hands of trustees, so as to produce by accumulation of interest the capital sum of 125*l*. at the end of the 73 years above-mentioned; this appears to mean practically a 5¼ per cent. stock, redeemable in 73 years at 25 per cent. premium.

[Copies of a communication sent to the London Stock Exchange by the secretary of the company, and of circulars fully explaining the nature of the various options, &c., and offering India 4 per cent. stock in exchange for the annuity of 5*l*. 12*s*. 6*d*. per annum, will be found inserted for future reference in the *Appendix* to the MANUAL for 1880.]

The provisions of the act in this matter have been strictly adhered to, and the decisions of the proprietors ascertained as follows:—

In Annuity class "A"	have been placed	£7,194,392
" Deferred annuity, with share of profits	"	6,550,000
" Annuity class "B" with sinking fund	"	12,873,004
" Government of India 4 per cent. stock, &c.	"	5,132,604
		£32,750,000

On the 1st January, 1880, the new contract before referred to came into operation.

In accordance with the before-mentioned conditions, the books for the registration of stocks finally closed in Calcutta and London on the 1st October and 1st November, 1879, respectively, and were opened for the registration of "A," "B," and deferred annuities on the 1st January, 1880. The stamp duty on transfer of the three classes of annuities will be "at the rate of 10*s*. per cent. on the consideration money indicated in the deed of transfer," being, according to legal opinion, "chargeable in all three cases with *ad valorem* stamp duty, under the heading 'conveyance' or 'transfer on sale' in the schedule to the Stamp Act, 1870."

PRIORITIES, DESCRIPTIONS, DIVIDENDS, and other conditions of issue of the various Securities as existing on the 30th September, 1883 (see notes).

FULL DESCRIPTION (to be observed in Transfer Deeds and all other Legal Documents).		Interest & Dividend. Rate ℔cent ℔ annum.	Date when paid each half-year.
Annuity class "A"	£272,203	...	1st April & 1st Oct.
Do. "B"	£624,900	...	
Deferred annuity capital	£6,550,000	4	January and July.
Debenture stock	£1,500,000	4½	April and October.

NOTES.—The annuities class "A" expire absolutely in 1953.

The annuities class "B" are redeemable in 1953, a sinking fund being provided for that purpose of 1*s*. 4*d*. per annum for every 1*l*. of annuity.

The deferred annuity capital is entitled to participate in surplus profits over 4 per cent. to the extent of one-fifth after all charges referred to on page 14 of Purchase Act have been met.

The debenture stock is irredeemable.

See also a summary of "options" on the preceding page.

REDEMPTION OF ANNUITIES.—See particulars relating to act of 22nd August, 1881, on page 396.

REVENUE.—The gross receipts, the working expenses, and the net earnings for the half-years ended 30th June, 1884 and 1883, are shown in the following statement:—

Half-year ended	Gross Receipts.	Working Expenses.	Net Earnings.
30th June, 1884	£2,246,707	£866,919	£1,379,788
" 1883	2,398,415	848,769	1,549,646

The company's share of the surplus profits, calculated in accordance with the terms of the Purchase Act and the Contract, is *Rs*.9,26,890, inclusive of *Rs*.64,214 in respect of the working of the State lines. This amount has been brought home at the rate of exchange of 1*s*. 7½*d*. the rupee, and has produced the sum of 74,298*l*., which enables the Board to recommend the payment of a dividend for the half-year at the rate of 1*l*. 2*s*. 8*d*. per cent. on the deferred annuity capital, in addition to the guaranteed interest of 2*l*. per cent., leaving a small balance in hand. A resolution authorising this distribution will be submitted to the meeting.

The company's share of profit from the working of the State lines, including an adjustment in respect of the earnings of the Barh Branch between 1st January, 1880, and 31st December, 1882, was 5,217*l*. for the half-year under notice.

The total length of railway opened for traffic to 30th June, 1884, was stated to be 1,509½ miles, of which 469½ miles are double, and 1,040 miles are single. The total length, including sidings, is equal to 2,333 miles of single road.

TRANSFER DEPARTMENT QUERIES AND REPLIES.

Queries.	Replies.
Transfer form—ordinary or special?	Special.
Fee per deed?	2s. 6d.
Ditto if more sellers than one? ...	2s. 6d. for each transaction.
May several classes of stock be transferred on one deed?	No.
Are certificates required to accompany transfers?	Yes.
What amounts of stock are transferable, and are parts of 1l. sterling allowed to be transferred?	Annuities, 1l.; deferred annuity capital, 10l.; no fractional parts thereof.
To what officer should transfer communications be sent?	Secretary.
In acceptances, renunciations, &c., of allotments of new stock, proxies, or other forms sent to trustees, what signatures are required?	All persons in whose names the annuities, &c., stand.

The transfer books for the annuity stocks close about one month before payment of annuity or interest.

DIRECTORS:

Chairman—ROBERT WIGRAM CRAWFORD, Esq., 11, Warwick Square, S.W.

Deputy Chairman—Sir R. MACDONALD STEPHENSON, Assoc.Inst.C.E., Holmfield, Busthall, Tunbridge Wells.

Government Director—JULAND DANVERS, Esq., India Office, Westminster, S.W.

Richard Ryder Dean, Esq., 97, Gloucester Place, Portman Square, W.
Sir T. Douglas Forsyth, C.B., K.C.S.I., 76, Onslow Gardens, W.
Charles Kaye Freshfield, Esq., M.P., Upper Gatton, Surrey.
S. Steuart Gladstone, Esq.
Joseph Silvester Godfrey, Esq.

OFFICERS.—Sec., Arthur P. Dunstan; Con. Eng., A. M. Rendel, M.Inst.C.E.; Agent in Calcutta, Bradford Leslie; Chief Eng., C. H. Denham; Auditors, Edward Bullock, Frederick Simms, and Marcus N. Adler; Chief Auditor in Calcutta, R. C. S. Mackenzie; Solicitors, Freshfields and Williams, 5, Bank Buildings, E.C.; Bankers, The Bank of England, and Glyn, Mills, Currie, and Co., 67, Lombard Street, E.C.

Offices—Nicholas Lane, E.C.

357.—EASTERN BENGAL.

Incorporated by act of 25th August, 1857, to construct a line from Calcutta to Dacca, viâ Pubna, with a branch to Jessore. 112 miles to Koostea, opened on 15th November, 1862; extension to Goalundo, 45 miles, opened 31st December, 1870; branch to Chitpore, 2 miles, opened 25th August, 1873.

The Government, under the contract of 30th July, 1858, guaranteed 5 per cent. on the ordinary capital for a term of 99 years, but determinable at the end of 25 or 50 years by purchase of the railway.

Purchase of Railway by Government.—The first period of twenty-five years expired on the 30th July, 1883, and on the 31st of that month the Secretary of State gave notice of his intention to exercise the power reserved in that contract, to purchase the railway on the 30th June, 1884. Since the completion of the purchase the railway has been worked as a State railway. The purchase money was equal to the value of the share capital calculated according to the mean market value during the three years next preceding the 30th July, 1883, which worked out at a trifle over 150l. per 100l. stock.

The Secretary of State, however, instead of paying the purchase money in a gross sum, has availed himself of his power under the contract to pay an annuity. The contract provides that this annuity shall continue during the residue of the term of 99 years, and that the rate of interest to be used in calculating it should be determined by the average rate of interest during the preceding two years received in London upon public obligations of the Indian Government, and which should be ascertained by reference to the Governor and Deputy-Governor of the Bank of England.

In accordance with the "Eastern Bengal Railway Company Purchase Act, 1884," the annuity paid for the purchase is payable at and managed by the Bank of England, where transfers are made. It commenced from the 1st July, 1884, and will terminate on the 30th July, 1957. It is payable half-yearly on the 1st April and 1st October in each year; the first payment on the 1st October, 1884, being for a period of three months, and the final payment on the 30th July, 1957, for a period of four months. The total amount of the annuity is 139,162*l*. The act provides for the division of the annuitants into two classes, "A" and "B." Annuitants under class "A" receive their share of the annuity, less the deductions (amounting to a little under 4*d*. in the £) for expenses and pensions authorised by the act Annuitants under class "B" receive their share of the annuity, less the deductions mentioned above, and less a further deduction amounting to a little under 1*s*. 8*d*. in the £, which is to be retained and invested as a sinking fund, divisible among the annuitants of this class on expiration of the annuity in 1957.

REVENUE.—The revenue during the half-years ending December is generally larger than during those ending June. The amounts during the last four half-years have been—

Half-year ended	Gross earnings.	Working expenses.	Net earnings.	Surplus over guaranteed interest.	Payment per 100*l*. to the shareholders, including 2*l*. 10*s*. guaranteed.
June 30th, 1882	£194,106	£101,729	£92,377	£4,306	£2 12 0
December 31st, 1882 ...	367,419	126,273	241,146	159,837	5 10 0
June 30th, 1883	252,840	130,390	122,450	44,771	3 8 0
December 31st, 1883 ...	240,731	117,092	123,639	43,783	3 0 0
June 30th, 1884	204,942	136,185	68,757	Nil.	Nil.

At the meeting of the shareholders, held on the 22nd December, 1884, at which the accounts for the half-year ended 30th June, 1884, were presented, a resolution was passed declaring a dividend of 9*s*. 11-16*d*. per cent., but owing to a question being raised by the Government at the last moment, the payment is delayed.

The directors remain in office merely for the purpose of distributing a final dividend from reserved funds, &c., and of winding up the company's affairs, and it was expected that this would be completed by the 31st December, 1884, or shortly afterwards.

DIRECTORS:

Chairman—JOHN FARLEY LEITH, Esq., Q.C., 8, Dorset Square, N.W., and St. Mary's Priory, Puttlewell, Essex.

Government Director—JULAND DANVERS, Esq., India Office, Westminster, S.W.

Salisbury Baxendale, Esq., Bonningtons, Ware.

Major-General James Pattle Beadle, R.E., 6, Queen's Gate Gardens, S.W.

Charles Hallyburton Campbell, Esq., 64, Cromwell Road, S.W.

James Percy Leith, Esq., 8, Dorset Square, N.W.

Charles Sanderson, Esq., 12, Roland Gardens, S.W.

The directors are eligible for re-election.

OFFICERS.—Sec., E. H. Smith; Auditors, Edward Cheshire and Joseph de Castro; Solicitors, Johnson, Budd, and Johnson; Bankers, Smith, Payne, and Smiths, 1, Lombard Street, E.C.

Offices—44, Gresham Street, E.C.

358.—GREAT INDIAN PENINSULA.

Incorporated by acts in 1849 and 1854, and acting under contracts and agreements with the East India Government. The connection of the Great Indian Peninsula with the East Indian at Jubbulpore was effected on 7th March, 1870.

FUTURE PURCHASE BY GOVERNMENT, POWER TO ENTER INTO WORKING AGREEMENTS, &C.—See page 389.

The company having arranged satisfactory terms with Government (under the powers of the act 42 and 43 Vic., cap. 41, of 1879) for working the Berar State lines, viz., the Khamgaon Line, 7¾ miles, and the Oomrawuttee Line, 6 miles, they have been worked since November, 1880, as part of the company's system. The Dhond and Munmar State Line (146 miles) has, under a similar arrangement made with Government, been also worked by this company since the 1st January, 1881.

REVENUE.—The receipts on revenue account amounted to 1,165,133*l*. and the expenditure to 731,325*l*., or 62·77 of the receipts, leaving as net profit (after payment to Government on account of leased lines of 8,749*l*.) 425,059*l*. Compared with 1882 there was a reduction of 67,346*l*. in the net receipts of the half-year.

As regards the coaching traffic, the decrease of 33,155*l.* is due entirely to the special movement of troops in 1882, occasioned by the Egyptian expedition. Apart from the troop traffic there is an increase in ordinary traffic of 28,454*l.*, or over 11 per cent.

The gross revenue receipts of the half-year ended 30th June, 1884, amounted to 1,884,432*l.*, and the expenditure (including 13,547*l.* on account of leased lines) to 839,593*l.*, leaving as net profit 1,044,839*l.* The net earnings sufficed for a dividend at the rate of 19*s.* 10*d.* per cent. in excess of the Government guarantee, making 3*l.* 9*s.* 10*d.* per cent. for the half-year.

CAPITAL—30th June, 1884.—*Authorised:* Shares and stock, 20,000,000*l.*; debenture bonds and stock, 6,666,666*l.*; total, 26,666,666*l.* The expenditure on capital account had been 23,364,023*l.*, whilst the receipts had been as follow:—

Stock and shares created	£20,000,000
Loans on debenture bonds at 4 per cent.	608,300
Loans on debenture bonds at 3½ per cent.	820,500
Debenture stock at 4 per cent., with discount on issue	2,475,559
Premiums on stock and shares deposited with Government as "capital not bearing interest"	297,305
Total receipts	£24,201,664

The interest on the capital stock and debenture stock is payable half-yearly, on the 1st January and 1st July, and on the bonds, 3rd January and 3rd July, the transfer books closing for about one month previously.

TRANSFER DEPARTMENT QUERIES AND REPLIES.

QUERIES.	REPLIES.
Transfer form—ordinary or special?	Ordinary.
Fee per deed?	2*s.* 6*d.*
Ditto if more sellers than one?	2*s.* 6*d.* each deed.
May several classes of stock be transferred on one deed?	Yes.
Are certificates required to accompany transfers?	Yes.
What amounts of stock are transferable, and are parts of 1*l.* sterling allowed to be transferred?	10*l.* and multiples.
To what officer should transfer communications be sent?	The Registrar.

MILEAGE STATEMENT.—Lines owned and worked, 1,288. Sidings, 213. Foreign lines worked, 169½. Sidings, 15¼.

DIRECTORS:

Chairman—Colonel JAMES HOLLAND, Southside, The Park, Upper Norwood, S.E.

Government Director—JULAND DANVERS, Esq., India Office, Westminster, S.W.

Managing Director—THOMAS ROSSITER WATT, Esq.

Henry Wollaston Blake, Esq., 8, Devonshire Place, W.

Alexander H. Campbell, Esq., 62, Cornhill Chambers, E.C.

Francis S. Chapman, Esq., 36, Stanhope Gardens, South Kensington, S.W.

Major-Gen. Harry Rivers, R.E., 31, Arundel Gardens, Notting Hill, W.

Andrew R. Scoble, Esq., Q.C., 21, Kensington Gardens Terrace, W.

OFFICERS.—Agent in India, George A. Barnett, Bombay; Con. Eng., George Berkley, M.Inst.C.E., 57, Charing Cross, S.W.; Auditors, George Smith, West Bank, Lewisham, S.E., and Charles J. L. Nicholson, 20, Threadneedle Street, E.C.; Solicitors, White, Borrett, and Co., 6, Whitehall Place, S.W.; Bankers, London and County Banking Company Limited, 21, Lombard Street, E.C.

Offices—3, New Broad Street, E.C.

359.—MADRAS.

Incorporated by act of 1853. The contracts with Government comprehend about 861 miles, consisting of a main line running south-west from Madras to Beypoor on the Malabar coast, with its branches to Bangalore and the Neilgherry Hills, making together about 520 miles. The north-west line, extending from the Arconum Station, at 42 miles from Madras, on main line, by Cuddapah and Goondacul (with branch to Bellary from the latter), to Raichore, &c., where it forms a junction with the Great

Indian Peninsula coming from Bombay. In operation, 861 miles, the Madras system being completed by the opening of the following lines:—Pothanoor to Coimbatore, 4 miles, 1st February, 1873; Coimbatore to Mettapollium, 22 miles, 31st August, 1873.

For a period of 99 years the Government guarantees 5 per cent. upon the capital stock, and all profits in excess of that rate are to be divided equally between the Government and the company, no account being kept of the arrear interest. The Government has the option of acquiring the line in April, 1907, upon terms based upon the mean market value in London of the shares or stock during the three years immediately preceding the purchase.

Future Purchase by Government, Power to enter into Working Agreements, &c.—See page 389.

Revenue.—The gross receipts for the half-year ended 31st December, 1883, were 299,384*l.*, and the expenses 182,384*l.*, the net profit being 117,000*l.* The ratio of working expenses to gross earnings was 60·92 per cent., in comparison with 61·49 per cent. in the corresponding half of 1882. The train mileage was 939,030, in comparison with 955,579. The receipts were equal to 6*s.* 4½*d.*, and the expenses to 3*s.* 10½*d.* per train mile, in comparison respectively with 6*s.* 6½*d.* and 4*s.* 0½*d.* in the corresponding half of 1882.

The gross receipts for the half-year ended 30th June, 1884, amounted to 337,957*l.*, and the expenses to 193,097*l.*, leaving a profit of 144,860*l.* The ratio of working expenses to traffic receipts was 57·14 per cent., in comparison with 62·86 for the corresponding half of 1883. The number of train miles run was 1,078,469, as against 941,719. The gross earnings were equal to 6*s.* 3*d.*, and the total expenses to 3*s.* 6¾*d.* per train mile, in comparison respectively with 6*s.* 6½*d.* and 4*s.* 1½*d.* for the corresponding half of 1883.

Capital—Half-year ended 30th June, 1884.—*Expenditure*; 10,251,572*l.* *Receipts:* 10,669,632*l.*, viz., 10,257,630*l.* by shares, 400,000*l.* by loans, and 12,002*l.* by capital not bearing interest. Credit balance, 418,060*l.*

The debenture capital is now as follows: 102,200*l* 4 per cent., due 1st January, 1886; 140,000*l.* 3½ per cent., due 1st January, 1887; 97,800*l.* 3½ per cent., due 1st July, 1887; 60,000*l.* 3½ per cent., due 1st January, 1889; total, 400,000*l.* Of these debenture bonds 207,800*l.* are registered bonds, and 192,200*l.* bonds to bearer. The interest to be paid by coupon half-yearly, on the 1st January and 1st July, at the Union Bank of London. Principal and interest guaranteed by the Secretary of State for India in Council.

DESCRIPTIONS, DIVIDENDS, &c., of the Securities of the company, existing on the 31st December, 1883.

Full Description (to be observed in Transfer Deeds and all other Legal Documents).	Interest & Dividend. Rate ₱ cent ₱ annum.	Date when paid each half-year.
4½ per cent. capital stock	4½	1 Jan. and 1 July.
4¾ per cent. capital stock	4¾	"
5 per cent. capital stock	5	"
4 per cent. debenture bonds and 3½ per cent.	4 and 3½	"

TRANSFER DEPARTMENT QUERIES AND REPLIES.

Queries.	Replies.
Transfer form—ordinary or special?	Ordinary.
Fee per deed?	2*s.* 6*d.*
Ditto if more sellers than one?	2*s.* 6*d.* each transfer.
May several classes of stock be transferred on one deed?	Yes.
Are certificates required to accompany transfers?	Yes.
What amounts of stock are transferable, and are parts of 1*l.* sterling allowed to be transferred?	The stock is divisible and transferable in amounts of not less than 10*l.*
To what officer should transfer communications be sent?	Secretary.

The transfer books close about three weeks before the payment of interest on the stocks of the company.

DIRECTORS:

Chairman—G. NOBLE TAYLOR, Esq.

Deputy-Chairman—Sir THOMAS PYCROFT, K.C.S.I.

Government Director—JULAND DANVERS, Esq., India Office, Westminster, S.W.

Arthur Hall, Esq.	Colonel George C. Collyer.
Alexander Forrester Brown, Esq.	General J. Mullins, R.E.

OFFICERS.—Sec., Julian Byrne; Con. Eng., Sir John Hawkshaw, Knt., F.R.S., M.Inst.C.E.; Auditors, George Banbury and Thomas Henry Allan; Solicitors, Freshfields and Williams, 5, Bank Buildings, E.C.; Bankers, The Union Bank of London, 2, Prince's Street, E.C. INDIAN ESTABLISHMENT:—Agent and Man., A. M. Saunders; Chief Eng., W. R. Robinson; Traffic Man., H. E. Church; Loco. Supt., F. H. Trevithick.

Offices—61, New Broad Street, E.C.

360.—OUDE AND ROHILKUND LIMITED.

Incorporated under "The Limited Liability Act." Capital, 4,000,000*l.* in shares of 10*l.* each and 3,000,000*l.* in debentures. The object of this undertaking is to supply a system of railways to the provinces of Oude and Rohilkund. Government gives a guarantee of 5 per cent. on the share capital and 4 or 3½ per cent. on the debenture capital, and also undertakes to deliver, free to the company, the land required for the way and works for a period of 999 years. The lines comprised in this system, and which are now open, are the main line from Benares, through Fyzabad, Nawabgunge, Lucknow, Chundowsee, and Mooradabad to Nagina, 466 miles; from Lucknow to Cawnpore, 46 miles; from Nawabgunge to Byramghat, 22 miles; from Chundowsee to Allyghur, 60 miles, giving a total length of 594 miles. Works of construction are in progress on the remainder of the Northern Extension of the company's system, from Nagina, to join the Scinde, Punjab, and Delhi, at Saharanpore; a length (with branches) of about 93 miles.

FUTURE PURCHASE BY GOVERNMENT, POWER TO ENTER INTO WORKING AGREEMENTS, &c.—See page 389.

REVENUE.—The following table shows the gross receipts, working expenses, and net earnings during each of the last four years ended 31st December respectively:—

	1880.	1881.	1882.	1883.
Mean mileage open	546·85	546·85	546·85	546·85
Earnings	£445,515	£492,873	£526,284	£545,626
Expenses	255,074	295,303	346,147	297,589
Profits	£190,441	£197,570	£180,137	£248,037

CAPITAL—31st December, 1884.—*Authorised:* Stock and shares, 4,000,000*l.*; loans, 3,800,000*l.*; total, 7,800,000*l.* All created. The expenditure had been 6,978,098*l.*, and the receipts as follow:—

Capital stock and shares, guaranteed 5 per cent.	£4,000,000
Debentures (1878) at 4 per cent.	300,000
Debentures (1880) at 4 per cent.	200,000
Debentures (1880) at 4 per cent.	615,300
Debentures (1881) at 3½ per cent	740,000
Debentures (1882) at 3½ per cent.	500,000
Debentures (1884) at 3½ per cent	1,060,000
Debenture stock at 4 per cent. (redeemable 6th May, 1898, at par)	384,700
Capital not bearing interest	19,654
	£7,819,654

DEBENTURE BONDS.—In the first half-year of 1878, 4 per cent. debentures were issued to the extent of 300,000*l.* in bonds of 1,000*l.*, terminable in seven years from the 1st May, 1878. Interest payable half-yearly, by coupon, on the 1st April and 1st October in each year. In September, 1880, a further issue of 200,000*l.* of these bonds took place (being part of 500,000*l.* authorised since June, 1880), the principal and interest being, as before, "guaranteed by the Secretary of State for India in

Council, whose endorsement to that effect the bonds will bear. The debenture bonds, in common with 2,000,000*l*. debenture capital already issued (including the issues mentioned above), are a charge upon the undertaking of the company prior to all other stock or shares, but without any priority among the holders. The bonds will be to bearer, and will run for a period of seven years from the 1st October, 1880. In the event of the railway passing into the possession of the Government, under any of the provisions of the company's contracts, the Government will then assume and stand in the position of the company towards the debenture bondholders. The bonds are, therefore, practically secured on the revenues of India."

On 1st August, 1881, the 500,000*l*. debentures falling due were replaced by 500,000*l*. debentures at 3½ per cent. for the following periods, 60,000*l*. for three years, and 440,000*l*. for seven years from that date. A further issue was made on the same date of 300,000*l*. 3½ debentures for seven years, being the balance of 500,000*l*. authorised since June, 1880.

On 16th May, 1882, a further issue of debentures was made of 500,000*l*., bearing interest at 3½ per cent., of which 345,000*l*. were for three years and the remainder for five years.

On 24th January, 1884, a further issue of debentures took place, the amount being 500,000*l*. at 3½ per cent for three years, and on the 16th August, 1884, the capital was further increased by an issue of 560,000*l*. debentures at 3½ per cent., of which sum 260,000*l*. was required to pay off debentures falling due. Of the 560,000*l*., 529,000*l*. were for three years, and the remainder for five years.

TRANSFER DEPARTMENT QUERIES AND REPLIES.

Queries.	Replies.
Transfer form—ordinary or special?	Ordinary.
Fee per deed?	2*s*. 6*d*.
Ditto if more sellers than one?	2*s*. 6*d*. each seller.
May several classes of stock be transferred on one deed?	No.
Are certificates required to accompany transfers?	Yes.
What amounts of stock are transferable, and are parts of 1*l*. sterling allowed to be transferred?	Consolidated stock, any amount, except parts of 1*l*.; debenture stock, multiples of 10*l*. only.
To what officer should transfer communications be sent?	The Managing Director.

The transfer books of the consolidated guaranteed stock close from 3 to 4 weeks, and of the debenture stock about one week, respectively, before payment of interest.

DIRECTORS:

Chairman—JOHN PENDER, Esq., M.P., 18, Arlington Street, S.W.

Government Director—JULAND DANVERS, Esq., India Office, Westminster, S.W.

Managing Director—Major-General C. C. JOHNSTON, R.E., 74, Gloucester Terrace, Hyde Park, W.

Major-General J. P. Beadle, R.E., 6, Queen's Gate Gardens, S.W.

J. A. Tobin, Esq., Liverpool.

W. G. Probyn, Esq., 5, Collingham Road, S.W.

One-third of the directors retire annually, but are eligible for re-election.

OFFICERS.—Con. Eng., W. Fothergill Batho, M.Inst.C.E., M.Inst.M.E.; Auditors, Turquand, Youngs, and Co., Coleman Street, E.C.; Solicitors, Markby, Stewart, and Co.; Bankers, Bank of England, and Smith, Payne, and Smiths, 1, Lombard Street, E.C.; Brokers, Hill, Fawcett, and Hill, 29, Threadneedle Street, E.C. India.—Agent, Lieut.-Col. John Hadow Jenkins; Eng.-in-Chief, H. B. Hederstedt, M.Inst.C.E.

Offices—29, Martin's Lane, Cannon Street, E.C.

361.—ROHILKUND AND KUMAON LIMITED.

Incorporated under the Companies' Acts of 1862-80. This company has been formed with the primary object of carrying out a contract with the Secretary of State for India in Council for the construction and working of a line of single-track railway, on the metre gauge, to connect the province of Kumaon with the railway system of India. Starting from Katgodam, at the base of the Kumaon Hills, as the upper terminus, the line runs almost in a direct course to the town of Bareilly, on the Oude and Rohilkund, a distance of 66 miles, of which the 12 miles nearest Bareilly have been constructed by Government as part of the State Line to Pilibhit. The contract is for 99 years, and embraces the following important concessions:—

"After the line is opened, the net earnings over 5 per cent. in each year are to be equally divided—one half to belong to the company, and the other half to be applied in repayment of the Secretary of State's interest payments during construction, together with simple interest thereon at 4 per cent. per annum. Only out of earnings over 5 per cent. is the Secretary of State entitled to any repayment after cessation of the guarantee, and when such repayment has been effected in full, the subsequent net earnings will belong exclusively to the company until the end of 1897, when the Government will become entitled to share equally with the company in net earnings over 6 per cent."

SUBSIDIES.—For ten years from the opening of the line for traffic throughout (but not later than 31st December, 1894), the Secretary of State will pay to the company an annual subsidy of *Rs.*40,000, and will also grant an annual sum of *Rs.*10,000, throughout the term of the contract, for carriage of mails by the ordinary train service.

WORKS TO BE UNDERTAKEN BY GOVERNMENT.—The Secretary of State engages that prior to the expiration of one month after opening of the line throughout, he will have constructed, and that he will afterwards maintain a road for wheeled traffic from the upper terminus of the railway at Katgodam to a point on the limits of the important head-quarters station of Naini Tal (over which road the company will provide a transport service, in connection with the traffic of the line). The Secretary of State will also, by the 31st December, 1883, construct the terminal station at Bareilly (with all needful connections with the station of the Oude and Rohilkund Railway), as well as the twelve-mile length of line linking the company's own line with Bareilly, and will give to the company the right to use such link and terminus for its traffic in consideration of an annual rent (to commence on 1st January, 1885, or on the sooner opening of the line for traffic throughout) equal to 4½ per cent. on the cost, but in no case to exceed *Rs.*11,250, and to be subject to reduction proportional to any future joint use of same with the Government.

PURCHASE BY GOVERNMENT.—In case the Secretary of State should exercise the option reserved to him of acquiring the undertaking of the company at the end of 30 or 50 years, the price is agreed to be 25 years' purchase of the company's average annual share of profits during the preceding five years. Similar terms will apply in case of the contract terminating by efflux of time.

At this first ordinary annual general meeting, held on the 30th April, 1883, the following resolution was passed, viz.:—"That this meeting sanctions and approves of the proposal for fixing Bhojupur as the point of junction of the company's line of railway with the Pilibhit State Railway, in lieu of that originally contemplated, leaving the line from Bareilly to Bhojupur to be completed and constructed by the Government as a part of the Pilibhit State Railway, as also the proposal for this company undertaking under agreement with the Secretary of State in Council of India the working of the Pilibhit State Railway, and that the directors be, and they are hereby authorised, on behalf of the company, to contract with the Secretary of State in Council of India for the carrying out of the said proposals on such terms, and in all respects, as to the directors shall seem fit."

The line was opened throughout for traffic on 12th October, and the Pilibhit State Railway on 15th November, 1884.

CAPITAL.—400,000*l.* sterling in 80,000 shares of 5*l.* each; one half of which were issued in October, 1882, at par. The shares are 4*l.* 10*s.*, paid.

DIRECTORS:

Major-General J. S. Trevor, R.E., C.S.I., 75, Ladbroke Road, Notting Hill, W.

David Trail Robertson, Esq., 41, Onslow Gardens, S.W.

Lieut.-Gen. Alexander Fraser, R.E., C.B., Caryll, Faygate, Sussex.

R. Russell Carew, Esq., Carpenders Park, Watford.

George William Allen, Esq., C.I.E. (in India).

Two retire from office this year and are eligible for re-election.

OFFICERS.—Sec., J. Somervail Clerk; Con. Engs., A. M. Rendel, M.Inst.C.E., 8, Great George Street, Westminster, S.W., and Henry Prince, M.Inst.C.E., 262, Gresham House, E.C.; Auditors, Gèrard Van de Linde, C.A., 12, Laurence Pountney Lane, E.C., and Fox and Greig, 17, Austin Friars, E.C.; Solicitors, Clarke, Rawlins, and Co., 66, Gresham House, E.C.; Bankers, Smith, Payne, and Smiths, 1, Lombard Street, E.C.

Offices—206, Gresham House, Old Broad Street, E.C.

362.—SCINDE, PUNJAB, AND DELHI.

Incorporated by act of 2nd July, 1855, by which the company regulates and increases its capital, issues debentures, and registers shares and transfers in India.

SCINDE.—From Kurrachee to Kotree, on the Indus, 109 miles. Opened 13th May, 1861.

PUNJAB.—From Mooltan to Lahore (222 miles) and Umritsur (32 miles). The line is connected with the Scinde by the Indus Valley State Railway, and places Lahore, Umritsur, and other important towns in communication with Kurrachee, the Port of Scinde, the Punjab, and neighbouring territories.

DELHI.—An extension of the Punjab from Umritsur to the East Indian terminus at Delhi completes a continuous line of railway, excepting a bridge at Sukhur, from Calcutta to Kurrachee. Length, 314 miles. Capital, 5,000,000*l.* in 20*l.* shares, upon which the Secretary of State for India in Council guarantees 5 per cent. interest.

The Indus Valley State Line, connecting Kotree with Mooltan, is now open, and there is a mail service between Delhi and Kurrachee the entire distance by rail.

AMALGAMATION.—By act of 12th July, 1869, the company was authorised to amalgamate these undertakings into one body corporate, and to make further agreements with the Secretary of State for India. The amalgamation was carried into effect from the 1st July, 1870. The Government guarantees a return of 5 per cent. on the capital stock for a term of 99 years, from 1st January, 1860, and has the option to purchase the line in 1885. All net earnings in excess of 5 per cent. are divided equally between the Government and the company, and no account is kept of the arrears of interest.

The fares on the two sections are now the same, with the exception of the third class by the Delhi mail train, viz.:—12 pies per mile first class, 8 pies per mile second class, 4½ pies per mile intermediate class, 2½ pies per mile third class mail, and 2¼ pies per mile for mixed trains.

FUTURE PURCHASE BY GOVERNMENT, POWER TO ENTER INTO WORKING AGREEMENTS, &c.—See page 389.

REVENUE.—In the following table is given a summary of the traffic of each half-year from 1st July, 1870, when the amalgamation of the several undertakings of the company took effect, to 30th June, 1884:—

	Receipts from Passengers, &c.	Receipts from Goods, &c.	Gross Receipts	Working Expenses.	Net Revenue	Working Expenses per cent. of Gross Receipts	Net Revenue per cent. of Gross Receipts
	£	£	£	£	£		
Average of 4 Dec. ½-years ended 1873.	90,625	155,426	246,051	205,678	40,372	83·59	16·41
" 4 June ½-years ended 1874.	105,779	184,776	290,555	209,053	81,502	71·95	28·05
" 4 Dec. ½-years ended 1877.	106,779	225,640	332,427	223,069	109,358	67·10	32·90
" 4 June ½-years ended 1878.	125,535	266,092	391,627	237,056	154,571	60·53	39·47
Half-yearly 31 Dec., 1878	163,530	222,265	385,794	254,523	131,271	65·97	34·03
" 30 June, 1879	192,198	313,426	505,624	314,618	191,006	62·22	37·78
" 31 Dec., 1879	163,920	340,556	504,477	279,268	225,209	55·36	44·64
" 30 June, 1880	183,641	390,079	573,720	292,967	280,753	51·06	48·94
" 31 Dec., 1880	219,142	298,975	518,116	297,373	220,743	57·40	42·60
" 30 June, 1881	188,879	297,936	486,815	311,688	175,128	64·03	35·97
" 31 Dec., 1881	145,852	265,806	411,658	304,758	106,900	74·03	25·97
" 30 June, 1882	175,249	286,906	462,155	310,342	151,813	67·15	32·85
" 31 Dec., 1882	155,530	270,995	426,525	265,675	160,851	62·29	37·71
" 30 June, 1883	159,817	395,769	555,587	309,114	246,473	55·64	44·36
" 31 Dec., 1883	155,193	319,332	474,525	271,136	203,390	57·14	42·16
" 30 June, 1884	171,766	332,178	503,944	302,325	201,619	59·99	40·01

CAPITAL—31st December, 1883.—*Authorised:* Stock and shares, 11,418,900*l.*; loans (subject to sanction of the Secretary of State), 3,806,300*l.*; total, 15,225,200*l.* *Created:* Stock and shares, all; loans, none. The expenditure had been 10,811,594*l.*, and the receipts 11,079,653*l.* Shares and stock, guaranteed 5 per cent., 11,075,290*l.*; capital not bearing interest, 4,363*l.*

DIRECTORS:

Chairman—Sir WILLIAM PATRICK ANDREW, C.I.E., Knt., 29, Bryanston Square, W.

Government Director—JULAND DANVERS, Esq., India Office, Westminster, S.W.

Major-General Saunders A. Abbott, 2, Petersham Terrace, S.W.

Sir Thomas Douglas Forsyth, C.B., K.C.S.I., 76, Onslow Gardens, W.

Lieut.-Gen. Craven Hildesley Dickens, R.A., C.S.I., 75, Lexham Gardens, Kensington, W.

OFFICERS.—Sec., J. H. Norman; Con. Eng., W. J. Kingsbury; Auditors, W. G. Goodliffe and R. Minton; Solicitors, Hollams, Son, and Coward; Bankers, Smith, Payne, and Smiths, 1, Lombard Street, E.C. INDIAN ESTABLISHMENT:—Agent, Roscoe Bocquet, C.I.E.; Chief Eng., Ernest Benedict; Traffic Man., David Ross, C.I.E.; Auditor, Jabez Lightfoot.

Offices—Gresham House, Old Broad Street, E.C.

363.—SOUTHERN MAHRATTA LIMITED.

Incorporated under the Companies' Acts, 1862–80, for the purpose of constructing, under a contract with the Secretary of State for India in Council, a system of railways in the Southern Mahratta country, about 450 miles in length, of which portions have already been commenced by the Government.

An agreement has been entered into between the Secretary of State in Council of India and Sir Douglas Forsyth, dated 19th May, 1882, approving a contract intended to be entered into between the Secretary of State and the company, the main features of which are as follow:—

a. The company are to construct and maintain and work for a period of 50 years, expiring 1st June, 1932, determinable as hereinafter mentioned, the following system of railways, viz.:—1. A line from the terminus of the West of India Portuguese Guaranteed Railway on the British Frontier, *via* Gadak, to Bellary, about 202 miles; 2. A line from Gadak to Sholapur, 180 miles; 3. A branch to Bankapur, 36 miles; 4. A branch to Belgaum, 32 miles; total, 450 miles; with certain extensions, if required by the Secretary of State. *b.* The first issue (3,000,000*l.*) of capital, as raised, shall be paid by the company to the Secretary of State for India, to be afterwards drawn by the company, with his sanction, for the purposes of the undertaking. *c.* Should the present capital be insufficient for the objects of the company, any new capital required is to be supplied by the company, or the Secretary of State, on terms to be agreed upon between them at the time of issue. *d.* The Secretary of State shall, during the continuance of the contract, pay to the company, out of the revenues of India, half-yearly, on 1st July and 1st January, interest at 3¼ per cent. per annum on all sums which shall have been so paid to his account under clause "*b*" above. *e.* The Secretary of State shall also, during the first seven years of the contract, in like manner pay to the company an additional ¼ per cent. on all sums mentioned in clause "*b*" above. *f.* Should the gross receipts of the company for any half-year be insufficient to meet the working expenses, the deficit shall be a charge on the profits of succeeding half-years. *g.* In addition to the guaranteed interest of 3¼ per cent., one-fourth of the net earnings of the railways shall be taken by the company, less during the first seven years any amount paid by the Secretary of State in respect of the additional ¼ per cent. *h.* The Secretary of State, at the end of the 25th, 35th, and 45th year of the contract, by a two years' previous notice, and also by a six months' notice should the railways, after completion, have been worked at a loss for the three half-years immediately preceding the notice, and the company at any time, after the expiration of the first five years, by a one year's previous notice, may determine the contract, and on any such determination, or at the expiration of the contract, the Secretary of State shall repay to the company the amount of its paid-up capital without any deduction whatsoever, the company making over the undertaking to the Secretary of State. *i.* The company agrees not to alter its articles of association without the consent of the Secretary of State. *j.* The Secretary of State may appoint a director, to be styled the Government Director.

CAPITAL.—*Authorised:* 5,000,000*l.* *Created and issued:* 3,000,000*l.*, in 150,000 shares of 20*l.* each, at par, upon 74,322 of which 5*l.* per share has been paid, the remaining 75,678 being fully paid up (for guaranteed interest, see above), and 1,700,000*l.* in 3¼ per cent. debentures, interest and principal of which is guaranteed by the Secretary of State for India in Council.

DIRECTORS:

Chairman—Sir DOUGLAS FORSYTH, K.C.S.I., C.B., Upton Court, Slough.

Major-Gen. Sir Henry Green, K.C.S.I., C.B.
Major-Gen. Sir Richard Pollock, K.C.S.I.
F. S. Chapman, Esq., 36, Stanhope Gardens, South Kensington, S.W.
Edwyn Sandys Dawes, Esq.
Major-General J. S. Trevor, R.E., C.S.I., 75, Ladbroke Road, Notting Hill, W.
Frederick Francis, Esq.
Gerard Norman, Esq.

OFFICERS.—Sec., Colonel E. Z. Thornton; Con. Eng., A. M. Rendel, M.Inst.C.E.; Solicitors, Ashurst, Morris, Crisp, and Co.; Bankers, The London and County Banking Co. Limited.

Offices—31, Lombard Street, E.C.

364.—SOUTH INDIAN.

By act of 16th July, 1874, the GREAT SOUTHERN OF INDIA and the CARNATIC were amalgamated under the above title. The terms are that each proprietor of 5 per cent. stock of the Great Southern and the Carnatic shall receive a corresponding amount of stock of the amalgamated company, and each proprietor of stock of the Great Southern which carries the right to interest at the rate of 4½ per cent. shall be entitled either to a corresponding amount of stock of the amalgamated company carrying interest at the like rate, or, at his option, instead of such last-mentioned stock, to an amount of stock of the amalgamated company carrying interest at the rate of 5 per cent., in the proportion of 95 of the latter stock to 100 of the former stock, and that each proprietor of shares in the Great Southern or in the Carnatic shall be entitled to corresponding shares in the amalgamated company, credited with the like amount as shall have been paid upon his existing shares. Capital, 3,800,000*l*. Qualification, 1,000*l*. The directors of both companies are the first directors of the amalgamated company, and directors retiring by rotation shall be qualified for re-election, but no vacancy in the number of the present directors caused by death, resignation, or disqualification, or incompetency to act as a director, or ceasing to be a director from any other cause than that of retiring by rotation, shall be filled up until the whole number of the directors (exclusive of the Government director) shall be reduced below five, after which time the number of directors shall never exceed five.

The Government has the power to purchase the line at certain stated periods, the first being in 1890, and in that event they have the option, instead of paying a gross sum, of transferring to the company such an amount of 5 per cent. Government of India stock (redeemable at par at the option of the Government) as shall, taking such stock at par, amount to the sum which they would have had to pay if the payment had been made in cash. There is no power in the Government to pay by means of annuities terminable or otherwise. See also act of 1879, &c., page 389.

MILES IN OPERATION.—The length of line in operation on 31st December, 1876, was 478 miles. During the years 1877 and 1878, 133 miles in addition were opened for traffic, and on the 1st July, 1879, the six miles between Chidambaram and Anaikarai Chattram, including the bridge (of fourteen 150 feet spans) over the Coleroon River—the most important work of its class on the line—were brought into operation, thus completing through communication between the Northern and the Southern portions of the railway. The works on the extension to connect Conjeveram with the main line at Chingleput are now also completed, the portion between Chingleput and Walajabad having been opened on 1st August, 1880, and the remaining 8 miles on 1st January, 1881.

PONDICHERI LINE, &c.—The railway in French territory from the Gingi River to the town of Pondicheri (8 miles in length) has been constructed by an independent company, under a concession from the French Colonial Government, and was opened for traffic on 15th December, 1879, simultaneously with the connecting branch of 17 miles from the South Indian main line at Villupuram. An agreement, the terms of which have been approved by the Secretary of State for India, has been entered into for the working of the Pondicheri Line by the South Indian, for 10 years from the 15th December, 1879, as an integral part of the system, and at the same rate as the main line is from time to time worked at.

Including the Pondicheri Line, the total length now in actual working is 662 miles, all of which are on the narrow or metre (3ft. 3⅜in.) gauge.

REVENUE—31st December, 1883.—The earnings for the twelve months amounted to 370,843*l*., and the expenditure to 244,119*l*., or 65·83 per cent. of the receipts, leaving a net profit of 126,724*l*., representing a return of 3*l*. 1*s*. 1*d*. per cent. on the total capital expended (4,146,917*l*.) at 31st December, 1883. The revenue for the half-year to 30th June, 1884, amounted to 208,287*l*., and the expenditure to 121,525*l*., leaving a balance of 86,762*l*., equal to a return of 4 per cent. per annum on the capital.

CAPITAL.—*Authorised:* Stocks, 3,800,000*l*.; loans, unlimited. *Created:* Stocks, at 30th June, 1884, 3,210,378*l*.; loans, 1,145,000*l*.; total, 4,355,378*l*. The expenditure amounted, at 30th June, 1884, to 4,358,271*l*., whilst the receipts, including capital not bearing interest, had been as under:—

Stock, guaranteed 5 per cent. / " 4½ "	£3,210,378
Loans, 3½ per cent.	720,000
Debenture stock, 4½ per cent.	425,000
Capital not bearing interest	61,027
	£4,416,405

PRIORITIES, DESCRIPTIONS, DIVIDENDS, &c., of the various Securities of the company, existing on the 31st December, 1888 (see notes).

No.	Year of Act.	Full Description (to be observed in Transfer Deeds and all other Legal Documents).	Rate ℔cent ℔ annum.
1	1874	Debenture bonds	3½
2	1874	Debenture stock	4½
3	1874	4¾ per cent. guaranteed consolidated stock	4¾
		5 per cent. guaranteed consolidated stock	5

NOTES.—The debenture bonds are redeemable at par on the 1st July, 1887, 1889, 1891.

The 4¾ per cent. consolidated stock is convertible into 5 per cent. consolidated stock on application at 95 per cent.

Interest on all classes is payable half-yearly, on the 1st January and 1st July, the transfer books closing about 3 weeks before payment.

In the contract scheduled to the act the Secretary of State for India has the power of purchasing the railway in 1890, again in 1905, and then after the expiration of any succeeding tenth year, by paying a sum equal to the amount of the value of all the shares and ordinary stock of the company, calculated according to the mean market value of such stock during the 3 years immediately preceding the purchase.

TRANSFER DEPARTMENT QUERIES AND REPLIES.

Queries.	Replies.
Transfer form—ordinary or special?	Ordinary.
Fee per deed?	2s. 6d.
Ditto if more sellers than one?	2s. 6d. each seller.
May several classes of stock be transferred on one deed?	Yes, 4¾ and 5 per cent.
Are certificates required to accompany transfers?	Yes.
What amounts of stock are transferable, and are parts of 1l. sterling allowed to be transferred?	Any amount, except fractional parts of 1l., and in the case of the debenture stock, 10l. or multiples thereof.
To what officer should transfer communications be sent?	The Managing Director.
In acceptances, renunciations, &c., of allotments of new stock, proxies, or other forms sent to trustees or other joint holders, what signatures are required?	The company does not acknowledge trusts. The signatures of joint holders required, except for voting, when the person named first in the account is deemed the sole proprietor (*Vide* C. C. C. Act, 1845, sec. 78).

The annual meeting is held in London in June.

DIRECTORS:

Chairman—JOHN CHAPMAN, Esq., 55, Gracechurch Street, E.C.

Deputy-Chairman—Sir R. MACDONALD STEPHENSON, Holmfield, Rusthall, Tunbridge Wells.

Government Director—JULAND DANVERS, Esq., India Office, Westminster, S.W.

Managing Director—HENRY W. NOTMAN, Esq., Assoc.Inst.C.E., 55, Gracechurch Street, E.C.

General Sir James Alexander, K.C.B., 35, Bedford Place, W.C.

Capt. James Gilbert Johnston, Union Club, Trafalgar Square, S.W.

Henry Kimber, Esq., 79, Lombard Street, E.C.

Henry Brockett, Esq., Heath Lodge, Iver, Bucks.

Major-General Charles James Green, R.E., United Service Club.

T. B. Roupell, Esq., Loddon Court, Reading.

OFFICERS.—Con. Engs., George B. Bruce, M.Inst.C.E., and Charles Douglas Fox, M.Inst.C.E.; Auditors, Henry Whitworth and Charles Frewer; Solicitors, Freshfields and Williams; Registrar, M. R. Scott; Bankers, Union Bank of London Limited. INDIAN ESTABLISHMENT:—Agent, William S. Betts; Eng.-in-Chief, David Logan, M.Inst.C.E.; Traffic Manager, Alfred Stanton; Loco. Supt., Charles E. Crighton.

Offices—55, Gracechurch Street, E.C.

AUSTRALASIA.

365.—NEW SOUTH WALES.

The report of the Commissioner of Railways for New South Wales for the year 1882 states that the total amount of capital now invested in New South Wales railways is 26,702,661*l.*, producing an average interest of 4·26*l.* This closely corresponds with the 4·32*l.* earned by our lines. At the close of 1882, 15,848,494*l.* was expended in lines open for traffic, and of this 1,896,178*l.* was expended during the year. Out of 2,210 miles sanctioned, 1,321 have been opened for traffic, leaving 889 to be finished, and with these satisfactory progress is being made. Of miles open 38 are laid with steel rails. In future, extensions and new constructions will only be made on land being given gratis. Gross earnings in 1882 were 1,698,863*l.*, or 254,637*l.* more than in 1881; working expenses were 934,635*l.*, or 196,301*l.* in excess of 1881.

The receipts show an increase of 36,668*l.* in merchandise, 47,717*l.* in minerals, 5,315*l.* in wool, and 60,753*l.* in live stock. The proportion of expenditure to gross receipts has been 55·02 against 51·12 in 1881. The increase has been mainly in southern and western lines. The line from Junee to Hay has been worked at a loss of 9.831*l.*—*Herapath.*

366.—NEW ZEALAND.

The following interesting particulars are taken from the statement presented in June, 1884, by the General Manager of New Zealand Railways, to the House of Representatives, viz.:—

Kawakawa Section.—The department has taken over the Kawakawa Railway, which will be opened for traffic in a few days.

Whangarei Section.—This line has only just paid its working expenses. The increase in the expenditure is due to the additional length of line worked throughout the year. The coal-mining industry has not developed as expected; should it do so, better results may be expected. The line is in good order.

Auckland Section.—An increase of 25 per cent. on goods traffic has taken place and an improved revenue has resulted; the passenger traffic, from special causes, does not show an increase. The condition of the line has been improved by relaying, refishing, and ballasting. Necessary improvements have been made at several country stations by reconstructing sidings, and by giving better water services, leading to greater regularity in the running of trains. The new shops at Newmarket are not yet available, nor is improved station accommodation at Auckland. Until the present shops are removed, the goods yard completed, and a proper passenger station is carried out, the traffic at the Auckland station will be troublesome to deal with and unsatisfactory to the public, and until the new shops are available it will be difficult to keep the stock in proper running order. Six new tender-engines of greater power have been erected, which improve the means of working. Eighty-four new wagons have been built, and 36 more are in hand. The want of shop room has prevented the erection of the carriages needed from being proceeded with. Although large improvements have been made, much remains to be done yet before the line has its equipments equal to those on the other chief lines in the colony. Large expense has been incurred in improving and maintaining Onehunga Wharf. Proposals have been made to vest this wharf in a local body. Owing to the peculiar conditions of competition here, it would be very detrimental to the railway interests to do so.

Napier Section.—The growth of traffic has been satisfactory, and the net revenue has increased. The line and stock are in good order. Hitherto heavy renewals have not been necessary; the time is now at hand when renewals will increase, and expenses under this head will grow more rapidly. The line has been well maintained; 45 wagons have been added to the stock; more carriages and wagons are in hand.

Wellington Section.—The increase of goods traffic has been over 25 per cent. The passenger traffic does not show an increase, owing to special causes. The growth of traffic has been chiefly in those classes of goods the rates for which are very low, as minerals, grain, sheep, and firewood; hence the goods revenue has not increased in proportion to the goods traffic, and the passenger revenue is less. On the other hand, the unavoidable expense upon rails and sleepers, and upon materials for bridge and stock repairs, has been heavy. The net profit is, therefore, less than during the preceding year. Twenty-three wagons have been added to the stock, and five bogie carriages are being built at Petone workshops.

WANGANUI SECTION.—The line has been extended to Manutahi, 16 miles 46 chains. The traffic has been indifferent, and the revenue is slightly below that of the previous year. The expenditure is swelled by the charge of 1,999*l.* due for reconstructing Rangitikei Bridge, and, while an additional mileage has been worked, there has not been a corresponding increase of traffic. There are, however, indications of improvement in business in the future, and the connection of the line with New Plymouth will, no doubt, be an advantage to both lines. Additional accommodation is badly wanted for repairs to stock, and, if not provided at an early date, the needful repairs will fall into arrear.

NEW PLYMOUTH SECTION.—The traffic in both goods and passengers has been depressed; the renewals of bridges, structures, and sleepers have increased. Rimu timber has been largely used both in bridges and sleepers on this line, and, as its decay is very rapid, some heavy expenses will occur during the ensuing two years on this account. Connection with the Wanganui line, when effected, will tend to improve the traffic.

GREYMOUTH SECTION.—A very large increase has occurred both in passenger and goods traffic, amounting to nearly 33 per cent. in both cases. The revenue has also increased largely. The direct steam service has led to a much larger traffic in coal. The expenditure has been large, owing to heavy renewals of rails. Further expenditure must be incurred under this head The results of working have, however, been very favourable, and the increasing demand for coals makes it likely that they will continue to be so. It is desirable to provide greater facilities for shipping coal, if funds are available. Fifty wagons have been added to the stock.

WESTPORT SECTION.—The results of working on this line have shown great improvement. The traffic has largely increased from the same causes which have affected Greymouth. The Buller bar is stated to have been bad during the latter part of the year, and but for this cause the traffic probably would have been still better. Expenses on renewals of the road and structures are not yet heavy on this line, but they will shortly be felt. The cost of repairing the wagon stock is excessive, owing to the use of the wagons on the coal incline, for which they are not adapted. Success in working this line will depend upon the demand for coal, and upon the Buller bar being sufficiently improved to admit larger steamers. Fifty wagons have been added to the stock.

NELSON SECTION.—The passenger traffic has improved; the goods traffic has remained about stationary, while the revenue has declined slightly. An increased expenditure has occurred, due to heavier renewals, which must be expected to increase.

PICTON SECTION.—The traffic in passengers has increased; that in goods has fallen off. The expenses have been lower than in the previous year. The results of working have been less satisfactory than during the previous year, owing to the wool having been carried by sea from Blenheim. On this line the expenses on account of renewals will increase.

HURUNUI-BLUFF SECTION.—The passenger traffic has remained nearly stationary, owing to special circumstances. The goods traffic has increased largely. The chief traffic in local products during the last five years has been as follows:—

Year.	Wool.	Timber.	Grain.	Minerals.	Horses and Cattle.	Sheep and Pigs.
	Tons.	Tons.	Tons.	Tons.	No.	No.
1879–80	35,663	94,037	227,770	220,459	14,159	182,529
1880–81	35,631	104,585	405,283	277,421	13,578	195,855
1881–82	37,917	113,446	353,675	288,424	18,623	219,471
1882–83	43,970	111,444	343,398	308,787	21,421	280,524
1883–84	49,519	89,467	407,623	331,878	20,192	446,426

The diminished timber traffic is no doubt due to slackness in the building trade. While the traffic in the low-rate goods—grain, minerals, and sheep—has increased largely, that in the goods at the higher rates, with the exception of wool, has fallen off, and with diminished rates the revenue has not tended to keep pace with the traffic. Thus, while the live stock has increased from 302,000 to 466,000 head, and the tonnage goods have increased from 1,180,000 to 1,199,000 tons, the revenue for these items has only increased from 403,000*l*. to 416,000*l*. Three causes have tended to make the passenger traffic for the year look unfavourable compared with that of the previous year; first, two Easters fell in the preceding year, and none during 1883–84; secondly, the Christchurch Exhibition largely swelled the passenger traffic in the former; and, thirdly, the weather has been unfavourable for holiday traffic in the latter, and, as all these holiday excursion fares, though low, are much larger fares than the average, being to a great extent long-distance fares, the revenue has suffered. The greater part of the diminution in passenger revenue is traceable to these causes, and the rest to lower fares. Having regard to these special disadvantages, the progress of the passenger traffic must be considered satisfactory. Fourteen miles of line have been opened during the year. Twelve miles of additional sidings have been laid. The line is improved by the relaying with heavier rails when repairing, and by the large amount of ballasting which has been done during the last four years. Forty-nine miles of rails have been relaid, against 36 miles in the previous year. Only 293 miles out of 863 are now laid with rails below the standards, taken at 53lb. for the main line and 40lb. for the branches. The consumption of sleepers has risen since 1879–80 from 50,000 to 100,000. The bridging is heavy, and expensive to maintain, being chiefly of timber. In the Christchurch district there are 8 miles 76 chains; in the Dunedin district there are 3 miles 69 chains; in the Invercargill district there are 1 mile 42 chains: a total of 14 miles 27 chains. The cost of maintaining this will increase annually. During the year 60 miles of fences have been planted, 20 miles of ground have been prepared, 66 acres of plantations of trees have been made, and 50 acres of ground have been prepared. Extensive additions have been made to station accommodation and appliances at Invercargill, Addington, Darfield, Chaney's, Valetta, Maheno, Palmerston, Burke's, Burnside, Henley, Mataura, Bluff, Winton, Gore, Waipahi, Stirling, Milburn, Waikouaiti, and Edendale. Numerous cranes, weighbridges, and improvements to water services have been added. The expenditure by the maintenance department has been—For maintenance, 159,477*l*.; public works department, 31,104*l*.; general public, 6,914*l*.; total, 197,495*l*. Six new private sidings have been granted, and 99 leases. The revenue from leases now amounts to 5,352*l*. per annum. In the locomotive department five new tender-engines have been added to the stock. The wagon stock has been increased by 402, the carriage stock by 13, and the tarpaulins by 458. The expenditure on wagon renewals has been heavy. Brown coal has been chiefly used, giving good economical results. The workshop accommodation has been largely improved, and is now, with some exceptions, fairly equal to the present requirements. The engine shed accommodation is insufficient for the stock; this is a serious defect. Additional water and coal accommodation is needed.

General.—The mileage of line worked by the department on the 31st March was 1,446 miles, inclusive of private lines worked at the expense of the owners. During the year the Waimea Plains Railway Company has cancelled its agreement with the Government for interchange of traffic on its line, 37 miles; and the Shag Point Railway, two miles, has been closed, owing to the stoppage of the coal mine. The net earnings amount to 2*l*. 10*s*. 2*d*. per cent. on the gross capital expenditure on railways opened and unopened. The highest rate is paid by the Napier line, 3*l*. 16*s*. 9*d*. per cent., and the next highest by the Hurunui-Bluff, 3*l*. 3*s*. 11*d*. per cent. The ratio of expenses to revenue is 68·24 per cent., against 62·18 during the previous year. The causes giving rise to these results are various, and have been predicted in the reports of previous years as tending to produce them. On the revenue side the passenger receipts have tended downwards, chiefly through the absence of the special traffic induced by the Christchurch Exhibition, and by the absence of Easter holiday traffic, and by lower fares; and the goods revenue has not risen proportionately to the traffic, owing to diminished timber traffic and lower grain rates. On the other side the expenses have increased from the large aggregate increase in heavy traffic, and the increased cost of renewals of the line and stock. Following is a statement of the principal traffic in local products for the past five years:—

Year.	Wool.	Timber.	Grain.	Minerals.	Horses and Cattle.	Sheep and Pigs.
	Tons.	Tons.	Tons.	Tons.	No.	No.
1879–80	41,895	149,428	240,144	321,060	30,893	260,816
1880–81	42,387	169,695	421,142	406,266	27,230	280,683
1881–82	44,681	192,905	375,725	433,659	22,511	319,837
1882–83	51,703	197,231	367,428	510,088	37,455	449,470
1883–84	62,066	183,449	432,223	574,312	35,948	656,612

It is desirable to make more than a passing remark on the subject of rates. A year or two ago the public seemed in favour of differential rates, and, assuming that the railways were all worked with uniform rates, to some extent found fault. The rates, however, have always been far from uniform. Auckland, Wellington, Picton, Greymouth, and Westport have generally been worked under different rates, and a large number of local and special rates have been and are in force all over New Zealand. Latterly the disposition has been to decry differential rates. It is found that, where a rate is lowered on one part of the railways to secure traffic, persons in other parts not participating are dissatisfied. Amongst railway managers of large experience there is no hesitancy as to the desirability of differential rates: they are essentials for financial success in the railways, and for the development of the trade of the country. The most successful railways in the world—the English railways—are worked wholly on this principle. The German Government, after ten years' enforcement of uniform rates, has abandoned uniformity as a failure. In one of the American States, Illinois, uniformity has been forced on the railway companies by the Government, but has been strenuously resisted by the former. The legislation of that State on this point seems to be of a rigid and inelastic nature, and could not be adopted here without great dissatisfaction. The system of rating differantially in this colony is not carried far enough, and the difficulty which stands in the way is the impatience of the public to submit to different treatment in different cases, and the reluctance to place in the hands of the railway officers the power which would be necessary for carrying out the principle extensively. While retaining publicity by gazetting each rate, were such a principle more widely introduced, the public would not be able to do what it now to some extent essays to do—read and interpret the rates generally; but the practice followed elsewhere would be necessary—the customer would appeal to the station each time he required a rate quoted; and, whether the railways were managed by a minister or board, more power and freedom in respect to rating would have to be placed in the officers' hands. The sensitiveness of the public, then, is the chief difficulty; but this is not allowed to intervene in cases where many millions of revenue are concerned, and can be no doubt overcome here by patience and time, provided that the colony recognizes that the principle is desirable, and gives the proper power to administer it. Maximum rates might be fixed by law, and a suitable court of appeal be constituted to prevent abuse of the powers given.

The improvement in the recent additions to the carriage stock has led to demands from the public for more improved accommodation. To convert the whole carriage stock would cost not under 200,000*l*., and that is an expense which can scarcely be immediately necessary in the interests of the colony. It would seem best to bring about the conversion by degrees, spreading the cost over a few years, rather than to wastefully abandon the present stock, which has cost a large sum of money. The cost of working the traffic has been lower than in preceding years, having regard to the quantities and distances of the traffic. The Auckland line stands first as the cheapest worked, Napier next, and Hurunui-Bluff the third. The total increase in expenditure does not arise from increased cost of working, but, to a large extent, from the fact that more work has been done. The expenditure under the different heads is roughly shown in the following table, in which the cost of stores and wages is approximately separately stated, and the estimated expenditure for 1884–85 is indicated:—

Wages.

Year.	Maintenance.	Locomotive and Stock.	Traffic.	General Charges and Sundries.	Totals.	Miles.	Total per Mile.
	£	£	£	£	£		£
1880–81	145,517	109,477	125,782	31,926	412,701	1,277	323
1881–82	132,520	106,204	126,739	28,428	393,891	1,319	298
1882–83	158,203	118,689	140,840	31,032	448,764	1,358	330
1883–84	165,303	134,125	151,319	33,635	483,382	1,407	346
Estimate 1884–85	187,926	138,476	161,036	32,000	519,438	1,520	341

Stores.

Year.	Maintenance.	Locomotive and Stock.	Traffic.	General Charges and Sundries.	Totals.	Miles.	Total per Mile.
1880–81	35,931	58,117	14,266	942	109,256	1,277	85
1881–82	47,602	65,928	14,205	1,071	129,208	1,319	97
1882–83	51,620	73,805	15,494	3,139	144,058	1,358	106
1883–84	68,633	79,736	15,529	8,710	172,608	1,407	123
Estimate 1884–85	89,340	91,591	16,828	6,292	204,051	1,520	134

The chief items under which expenses have increased are rails and sleepers, wagon stock, bridges, and fencing. The average age of the lines is now six years, and it is probable that the cost of renewals will not rise so rapidly in the future as it has been doing, and that in future years we shall show better financial results as the lines have been greatly improved as a rule, and those of later construction have been more substantially built than the earlier constructed lines were. The only point where the railways are now liable to a serious expense, so far as can be judged, is on the Taieri plain, where a heavy flood might cause a loss of many thousands of pounds. It would be advisable to take precautionary measures to prevent such an accident.

When, as is sometimes stated, the cost of working the railways may appear high, it should be remembered that the original intention expressed in the financial statement of 1870 was that the style of construction should be cheap, in order to limit the capital. Cheap construction entails a comparatively high cost of working. If another 5,000,000*l.* had been expended on the existing lines, a superior result would have been attained in some respects; higher speed and luxurious accommodation for passenger traffic might have been attained, while masonry and iron used instead of timber would have lessened the cost of maintenance. On the other hand, the loss of interest would have been many times greater than the amount which could have been saved in working. There is no reason to doubt that the most economical course has been followed. Too many stations lead to excessive cost in working. The adoption of so many sidings on the main lines, which cannot be placed under control of officers owing to the excessive cost of doing so, is an element of danger, and is one which will prove very embarrassing in future. While it is very easy to create these bad features, it is very difficult afterwards to remove them. If it is essential that general interests should be subordinate to local interests in this respect, it should be recognized that a greater expense in working has to be incurred.

The experience gained in building carriages in the colony tends to show that the department can now turn out nearly the whole of the work at a cheaper rate than it can be imported. We, however, still have to import wheels and axles.

367.—TASMANIAN MAIN LINE.

Incorporated under "The Companies' Acts, 1862 and 1867," and the "Tasmanian Main Line Railway Act, 1877," for the purpose of constructing a railway from Hobart, through the centre of the colony, to Launceston. Length, 133 miles. Power is given to the company to connect its line with the Launceston and Western, with running powers over the same. The period allowed for the construction of this railway terminated in March, 1876. The gauge being 3ft. 6in., the limit of curves 4 chains radius, and the maximum gradient 1 in 40. The principal conditions being that the company run two trains each way per day over the entire length of the line, one at the rate of 23 miles an hour, and the other at the rate of 10 miles an hour. The railway was opened for traffic throughout on 15th March, 1876, and has since been working satisfactorily up to the date of the latest advices, fulfilling all the conditions of the contract with the Government. The Government of Tasmania guarantees, for 30 years after the opening of the railway, 5 per cent. interest on a sum of 650,000*l.* The Government reserves the right to purchase the line upon giving twelve months' notice, at a price, failing agreement, to be decided by a majority of five valuers.

The Government of Tasmania have paid the guarantee as from the 1st November, 1876, at the rate of 32,500*l.* per annum.

By the act of 12th July, 1877, the company is empowered to attach a first preference to a further amount of debenture bonds, not exceeding 100,000*l.*, to be raised for doing certain works on the railway, and discharging certain liabilities; to delay the payment of the interest now overdue on the debenture bonds and stock, and that which shall become due during a certain period, and to waive the coming due of the principal, caused by the non-payment of interest; to empower the holders of debenture and debenture stock to vote as shareholders, and be eligible as directors, and to reduce the interest on the existing 650,000*l.* debenture bonds to the extent of 1 per cent. per annum, or such portion thereof as may be deemed expedient. The whole of the foregoing being subject to the consent of three-fourths of the holders of bonds or stock affected by the arrangement at meetings to be called for the purpose. Certain powers are also given for the sale of railway and distribution of the proceeds thereof, if thought desirable.

An agreement, of which the following is the substance, has been approved and signed in manner prescribed by the "Tasmanian Main Line Railway Act, 1877," viz:—"Nothing is to be done with respect to the issue of new debentures till after the election of directors by the debenture-holders, but as soon as they are elected the company may issue up to 100,000*l.* of new debentures, on such terms as they think fit, providing that the total amount of interest and sinking-fund, if any, shall not exceed 6,500*l.* per annum, which is equal to 1 per cent. upon the 5 per cent. debentures. These new debentures will be secured by a first mortgage or charge upon the company's railway, &c., in priority to all existing debentures. The coupons and interest, now due and to become due on the existing 5 per cent. debentures, down to and inclusive of October 1st, 1878, and the interest on the 5 per cent. debentures down to and inclusive of December 31st, 1878 (being all the interest on both the classes which becomes due before the end of 1878), are not to become payable until the 31st of December, 1878, and are in the meantime to be represented by the certificates of trustees appointed by the agreement; but if the company shall have any surplus funds in its hands of sufficient amount before December 31st, 1878, they are to be applied towards redemption of these certificates. The falling due of the principal of the existing debentures, which was caused by the non-payment of the interest, is suspended; and they will not again become due unless some further default should take place after the 31st December, 1878. The act gives the power to reduce the interest upon the 5 per cent. debentures by any amount not exceeding 1 per cent. The agreement limits the reduction to such amount, not exceeding 1 per cent., as may be required for the service of the 100,000*l.* of new debentures. As the interest and sinking-fund upon the new debentures require the full sum of 1 per cent. upon the old 5 per cent. debentures, the interest to which the holders of these old 5 per cent. debentures are entitled will, for the future, be reduced to 4 per cent.

The agreement under the above act has since been carried into effect, and the 100,000*l.* 1st mortgage 5 per cent. debentures therein mentioned were issued in 1878 at the price of 95 per cent.

REVENUE.—Year ended 31st December, 1883.—*Receipts:* 101,510*l.*, including Government guarantee of 32,500*l.* *Expenses*, 68,973*l.*; net profit, 32,537*l.*, against 32,553*l.* for the year 1882. The interest on debentures and debenture stock, &c., amounted to 35,654*l.* net, the balance standing at the debit of net revenue account being increased to 54,836*l.*

CAPITAL.—31st December, 1883.—Expended to this date, 1,188,316*l.* The receipts have been as follow:—

Ordinary shares	£205,085
6 per cent. preference stock	243,350
Forfeited shares	2,913
5 per cent. 1st mortgage debentures	100,000
5 per cent. debentures reduced to 4 per cent.	650,000
6 per cent. debenture stock	32,125
	£1,233,473
Credit balance	45,157
	£1,188,316

The interest on the 5 per cent. perpetual debenture bonds, reduced to 4 per cent. under the agreement of 25th October, 1877, is payable quarterly on the 1st January, April, July, and October respectively, and up to the 1st January, 1885, this interest seems to have been regularly paid.

The accounts are made up to the 31st December, and the meetings held in London in March, or at such other time as the directors may determine.

DIRECTORS:

Chairman—Colonel FRANCIS D. GREY, The Angles, East Sheen, S.W.

George Scott Freeman, Esq.
William Irving Hare, Esq.
F. C. im Thurn, Esq.
William Wyllys Mackeson, Esq., Q.C.
Telford Macneill, Esq., C.E.
Albert Ricardo, Esq., 11, Angel Court, E.C.
Charles W. Earle, Esq.

OFFICERS.—Sec., William Davison; Eng. and Gen. Man., C. H. Grant; Loco. Supt., William Cundy; Auditor, Fred. Maynard, F.C.A.; Bankers, Consolidated Bank, Threadneedle Street, E.C., and Commercial Bank, Hobart.

Offices—79½, Gracechurch Street, E.C.

BRITISH NORTH AMERICA.

For Government Statistics extracted from the report to 30th June, 1877, of Mr. C. J. Brydges, the General Superintendent of Government Railways, to the Secretary of the Department of Public Works, see the MANUAL for 1881, pages 447 to 450.

368.—BUFFALO AND LAKE HURON.

(LEASED IN PERPETUITY TO THE GRAND TRUNK OF CANADA AT £70,000 PER ANNUM.)

This line extends from Fort Erie, on the Niagara River, to Goderich, on Lake Huron, and was completed 28th June, 1858. Length, 162½ miles.

It is connected with Buffalo by the International Bridge, and communicates with the Erie and New York Central at that city, and with the Great Western of Canada at the town of Paris, and the Grand Trunk at Stratford.

Under the agreement between this company and the Grand Trunk of Canada, made in February, 1870, and ratified by an act of the Parliament of Canada, it is provided "That the Buffalo and Lake Huron may, from time to time, issue mortgage bonds, debentures, or debenture stock, in renewal of, or in substitution for, existing mortgage bonds or debentures; but not to a greater amount nor at a higher rate of interest, including the bonds issued by the Buffalo, Brantford, and Goderich, and including the capitalised coupon bonds issued by the Buffalo in 1865, and all such mortgage bonds, debentures, or debenture stock may extend over the whole of the undertaking of the Buffalo vested in the Grand Trunk, and this, although the securities for which they are substituted may extend over a part only."—See Grand Trunk.

An act of the Canadian Parliament (23rd May, 1873) provides that the bonds which fell due in 1872, and those falling due in August, 1873, shall be converted into a charge, bearing 6 per cent. interest, and secured by a first mortgage on the entire line of railway, the whole sum, or any part thereof, redeemable from time to time at the option of the company at par on six months' notice. The remaining bonds of the company to be converted into a permanent charge, bearing 5½ per cent. interest, and secured by a second mortgage on the whole of the line. The powers under the act were exercised by the directors in April, 1879, the bonds not paid off being substituted for bonds of a similar mortgage in perpetuity, bearing interest at the rate of 5½ per cent. per annum, from 1st March, 1880. Up to the July following holders of 179,500*l.* old bonds had sent in their adhesion to the scheme and assented to the exchange of bonds, and the residue was allocated to the general public.

REVENUE.—The net earnings for the half-years ended 31st December, 1883, and 30th June, 1884, after providing interest on the bonded debt, sufficed for dividends on the ordinary shares at 5*s.* 3*d.* per share each half-year respectively.

CAPITAL.—This consists of 297,600*l.* first mortgage 5½ per cent. bonds (issued to replace the 6 per cent. first mortgage bonds redeemed as above); 466,158*l.* second mortgage 5½ per cent. bonds; and 525,513*l.* in ordinary 10*l.* shares.

The whole of the company's capital is secured on the payment of a rental of 70,000*l.* per annum by the Grand Trunk of Canada.

Share transfer form, special; no stamp; fee, 2*s.* 6*d.* per deed; certificates must accompany transfer deeds; bonds pass from hand to hand without transfer. All communications must be sent to the Secretary.

The accounts are made up to the 30th June and 31st December, and the meetings held in Liverpool in March and September.

DIRECTORS:

Chairman—ARTHUR ASHTON, Esq., John Street, Berkeley Square, W.

Laurence R. Baily, Esq., Liverpool. | Maxwell H. Maxwell, Esq., Liverpool.

Directors re-elected in September each year.

Secretary, Thomas Short, 1, Great Winchester Street, E.C.

369.—CHICAGO AND GRAND TRUNK.

The Chicago and Grand Trunk is a company incorporated under the laws of the United States, and passes through the States of Illinois, Indiana, and Michigan. The total length of line is 335 miles from Chicago to Port Huron.

The various sections of this line were consolidated into one undertaking, and previous to the consolidation a prospectus of the Chicago and Grand Trunk Limited (see the MANUAL for 1881, pages 453 and 454) was issued, offering to the public 500,000*l*. of the debentures of the limited company, to be afterwards exchanged for bonds of this line. The exchange has been made, and in addition, in March, 1881, a further issue of 160,000*l*. of first mortgage bonds was made.

The first mortgage bond capital of this line amounts to 1,240,000*l*., and includes the bonds issued in exchange for the debentures of the limited company, 500,000*l*.; issued in March, 1881, 160,000*l*.; issued to the Grand Trunk, for the proceeds of the sale of the Rivière du Loup Line invested in this company, 340,000*l*., and sold by that company in November last; and the balance consists of sectional bonds, exchanged or to be exchanged for first mortgage bonds.

SECOND MORTGAGE 5 PER CENT. COUPON BONDS.—The total amount authorised is $6,000,000 (1,239,600*l*.), and of this amount $5,868,000 has been issued. An agreement has been entered into by which the second mortgage income bonds (entitled to 7 per cent. interest out of the profits of each year) have been converted into second mortgage bonds carrying 5 per cent. interest, secured by a rebate on the gross sum earned by the Grand Trunk on the traffic exchanged between the two companies. Under the agreement the holders of the old income bonds issued, amounting to $2,500,000 (500,000*l*.), agreed to subscribe at par for an amount of these bonds equal to 50 per cent. of their holdings, absorbing $3,750,000 (750,000*l*.), and there has been issued to the Grand Trunk, in respect of the proceeds of the sale of 340,000*l*. first mortgage bonds above referred to, $2,044,000 (420,000*l*.) The bonds issued are in United States currency, and are for forty years from the 1st January, 1882. The interest on the bonds issued is payable half-yearly, on the 1st January and the 1st July, at the office of the company in New York.

The company have power to issue sterling bonds, with the interest payable in London.

REVENUE.—There are no printed reports; the published accounts are made up yearly. In their report for the year ended 31st December, 1883, the directors of the Grand Trunk stated as follows, viz.:—The gross receipts of the Chicago and Grand Trunk for the year 1883 were 611,622*l*., and the working expenses were 464,401*l*., leaving the net revenue 147,221*l*., to which has to be added the balance brought from the year 1882 of 129*l*., making a total of 147,350*l*. Against this there has been charged the rentals payable to the Grand Trunk Junction (less sums received in respect of the property), 10,479*l*., the interest on the first and second mortgage bonds, 126,489*l*., leaving a balance of 10,382*l*. Out of this sum 10,274*l*. ($50,000) has been repaid to the Grand Trunk in respect of advances made previous to the 30th June, 1882, to meet the interest on bonds, leaving a balance of 108*l*. to be carried forward. This payment of 10,274*l*. is credited to the Grand Trunk in the net revenue account, the amount received from the Chicago Line being 24,266*l*., against 13,958*l* in the corresponding half-year.

LONDON COMMITTEE

(Consisting of Directors of the Grand Trunk of Canada):

President—Sir HENRY W. TYLER, M.P., Assoc. Inst. C.E., Pymmes Park, Edmonton.

Vice-President—Sir CHARLES LAWRENCE YOUNG, Bart, 5, Ashburn Place, Cromwell Road, S.W.

Lord Claud John Hamilton, M.P., 23, Lowndes Square, S.W.
William Unwin Heygate, Esq., Roecliffe, Loughborough.
Right Hon. David Robert Plunket, Q.C., M.P., 12, Mandeville Place, W.
Robert Young, Esq., 4, West Nile Street, Glasgow.

OFFICERS.—Sec., John Brinsden Renton; Solicitors, J. B. Batten and Co., 32, Great George Street, S.W.; Bankers, Glyn, Mills, Currie, and Co., 67, Lombard Street, E.C.

Offices—Dashwood House, 9, New Broad Street, E.C.

370.—GRAND TRUNK JUNCTION.

This company is incorporated under the laws of the State of Illinois, with powers to build branch lines and secure terminal accommodation in Chicago for the passenger and freight business of the Chicago and Grand Trunk. A prospectus was issued in February, 1881, through the agency of the Chicago and Grand Trunk Limited, offering 225,000*l.* of the debentures of the Limited Company, to be afterwards exchanged for first mortgage 5 per cent. coupons of this company. That exchange has now been made. A further amount of 50,000*l.* of bonds was issued in May, 1882. The balance, 75,000*l.*, has now been issued.

The Chicago and Grand Trunk have entered into an agreement to lease the property of the Grand Trunk Junction, and to pay a sufficient rental to secure 5 per cent. on the total authorised amount of the first mortgage bonds, the amount of which is limited to 350,000*l.* It is agreed that the payment of such rental shall form part of the working expenses of the Chicago and Grand Trunk.

In April, 1884, the directors of the Grand Trunk of Canada issued 220,000*l.* of the 5 per cent. mortgage bonds of this company at 97½ per cent., the whole amount being subscribed.

The bonds are for fifty years, maturing on the 1st July, 1934; are redeemable at par; and bear half-yearly coupons for interest payable in London on the 1st January and 1st July, at the offices of the Grand Trunk—the first coupon being payable on 1st January, 1885. The bonds are in sums of 100*l.*, 500*l.*, and 1,000*l.*, and can be registered, if desired, in London.

The bonds form a portion of a total mortgage of 800,000*l.* on all the property and rights acquired, or to be acquired, by the Grand Trunk Junction, subject to the application of 350,000*l.* out of the above amount, which are to be retained for exchange for the existing 5 per cent. bonds of the Grand Trunk Junction, or to be held in trust to meet these bonds at maturity on the 1st January, 1901; but it is believed that as the bonds of the present issue do not mature till 1934, the holders of the existing issue, the bonds of which mature in 1901, will consider it an advantage at once to make the exchange.

The committee of the Chicago and Grand Trunk form a London Committee for this company (see Chicago and Grand Trunk).

371.—GRAND TRUNK OF CANADA.

The act of incorporation of this vast undertaking, which passed the Canadian Legislature in 1852, amalgamated seven incorporated lines, viz.:—The QUEBEC AND RICHMOND, the ST. LAWRENCE AND ATLANTIC, the OLD GRAND TRUNK, the GRAND JUNCTION, the TORONTO, GUELPH, AND SARNIA, and the MAIN TRUNK.

AMALGAMATION WITH THE GREAT WESTERN OF CANADA.—This important amalgamation took effect on the 12th August, 1882, under an agreement dated 25th May, 1882, the full text of which is given in the *Appendix* to the MANUAL for 1883, page 513, and the terms of agreement may also be found on reference to the MANUAL for 1884, page 415.

For the official notices, &c., issued subsequently to the approval of the agreement, as above, see MANUAL for 1883, page 423.

Information as to the respective positions of the Grand Trunk and Great Western companies prior to amalgamation will be found on reference to the MANUAL for 1882, and previously.

ATLANTIC AND ST. LAWRENCE.—This company is leased to the Grand Trunk, and the rent payable in respect of it ranks among the working expenses of the entire undertaking. For exchange of bonds of the leased line, see the MANUAL for 1880, and previously.

BUFFALO AND LAKE HURON.—The agreement with this company, ratified by the Canadian Legislature, provides for a rent-charge, payable by the Grand Trunk to the Buffalo and Lake Huron in perpetuity, by half-yearly instalments, within two months after 1st January and 1st July in each year, say—

For year ended 1st July, 1869	£42,500	For year ended 1st July, 1875	£66,000
,, ,, 1870	45,000	,, ,, 1876	67,000
,, ,, 1871	50,000	,, ,, 1877	68,000
,, ,, 1872	55,000	,, ,, 1878	69,000
,, ,, 1873	60,000	and for every subsequent year ...	70,000
,, ,, 1874	65,000		

2,500*l.* per annum of the rent-charge is to rank next before the first equipment bonds of the Grand Trunk, and the balance will rank next after the second equipment bonds.

CHICAGO AND GRAND TRUNK.—See GENERAL INDEX.

GRAND TRUNK JUNCTION.—See GENERAL INDEX.

GREAT WESTERN OF CANADA.—See page 418.

INTERNATIONAL BRIDGE.—In pursuance of the powers conferred by a clause inserted in the Canadian Act of Parliament for confirming the agreement with the Buffalo, the directors entered into an agreement with the International Bridge for the lease for 999 years of their bridge and all its appurtenances, as well as for the assignment of all the tolls, rights, powers, and franchises of the bridge, upon payment by the Grand Trunk of an annual sum of 20,000*l.*, about 16,000*l.* of which constituted rent, and the remaining 4,000*l.*, along with the tolls from other companies using the bridge, forming a sinking fund for redemption of the capital by yearly drawings on the 1st July. The bridge was opened 3rd November, 1873.

LEWISTON AND AUBURN, 5½ miles.—A lease of this line, dated 25th March, 1874, was ratified and approved on the 29th April, 1879.

MICHIGAN AIR LINE.—Agreements have been entered into whereby the Grand Trunk undertakes for a period of 20 years from the 1st January, 1882, to work the said Michigan Air Line; and agrees to pay out of the gross traffic receipts semi-annually, in London, the sum of 3,255*l.* per annum in respect of the portion of railway, 35 miles long, already completed and in operation from Ridgeway to Pontiac; and similarly to pay in respect of the remaining portion of the line (proportionately as and when every 10 miles is completed) a sum of 12,245*l.* per annum for the 70 miles from Pontiac to Jackson. An issue of 310,000*l.* first mortgage 5 per cent. bonds was made in November, 1882.

MIDLAND OF CANADA.—See GENERAL INDEX.

MONTREAL AND CHAMPLAIN JUNCTION.—An agreement has been entered into whereby the Grand Trunk of Canada undertakes to work the Montreal and Champlain Junction for the whole distance from Brosseaus Junction to Dundee, 62 miles, for 21 years, from the 1st January, 1881, and to pay, by way of tolls for the use of the said railway, an amount equal to 5 per cent. upon the 172,600*l.* first mortgage bonds, issued in November, 1882. The Montreal and Champlain 7 per cent. third mortgage bonds of 1872, were redeemed in 1880.—See MANUAL for 1882, page 441.

RIVIÈRE DU LOUP.—For particulars of arrangements relating to this section, see MANUAL for 1884, page 417.

TORONTO, GREY, AND BRUCE.—See GENERAL INDEX.

WELLAND.—The "Welland Railway Act, 1884," authorised the transfer of the Welland, 25 miles long, to the Grand Trunk. This act practically carries out the agreement with the Welland, submitted to and approved by the shareholders at the general meeting on the 25th October, 1883. It was agreed to issue Grand Trunk 4 per cent debenture stock for 166,952*l.*, instead of securing the interest on the debenture stock of the Welland for a similar amount. Of this stock 25,685*l.* is to be retained by the Grand Trunk in repayment of expenditure previously made. The line passes finally into possession of the Grand Trunk at the expiration of two years from the 30th April, 1884.—For other particulars, see MANUAL for 1884, page 425.

AGREEMENTS WITH NORTH SHORE, MIDLAND OF CANADA, AND WELLAND.—See *Appendix* to Volume for 1884.

MILEAGE.—30th June, 1883. Grand Trunk Section—Portland to Detroit, 854; Lewiston Branch, 5½; Norway Branch, 1½; Quebec and Richmond, 89¾; Arthabaska Branch, 35½; Champlain Division, 73½; Montreal and Champlain Junction, 62½; Extension to Wharves, Montreal, 3; Kingston Branch, 2½; Galt Branch, 14½; London Branch, 22; Buffalo and Goderich, 162; Grand Trunk, Georgian Bay, and Lake Erie, 171½; Michigan Air Line, 106½; branch to Great Western Line, Sarnia, 2½; total, 1,605 miles. Great Western Section—Main Lines, 514½; Wellington, Grey, and Bruce, 168½; Welland, 25; London and Port Stanley, 23¾; London, Huron, and Bruce, 68¾; Brantford, Norfolk, and Port Burwell, 34½=835; total, 2,440 miles

Mileage Table, Corrected to 30th June, 1884.

Lines Owned and Leased.	30th June, 1883.		30th June, 1884.	
	Miles constructed.	Miles worked by Engines.	Miles constructed.	Miles worked by Engines
Lines owned by the company	1,380¼	1,380¼	1,426⅛	1,426⅛
Lines leased or rented	1,425	1,431	1,486	1,492
Total	2,805¼	2,811¼	2,912⅛	2,918⅛

The following is copied from the company's report for the half-year ended 30th June, 1884, viz.:—"The length of lines operated was increased during the half-year from 2,321¼ miles to 2,918¼ miles, or by 597 miles. The Midland, 473¼ miles, was worked by the Grand Trunk from the 1st January, 1884, and the receipts and working expenses are included in the accounts of this half-year; and for purposes of comparison, the corresponding receipts and expenses have been added to the accounts for the half-year ended June, 1883. The Michigan Air Line has been extended to Jackson, 70¼ miles. The Montreal and Champlain Junction has been extended 26¾ miles, to Fort Covington. The Welland, 25 miles, was acquired on the 1st May last; and a loop line near Hamilton, 1¼ mile, is now included."

REVENUE.—The gross receipts of the united system for the half-year ended 31st December, 1883, amounted to 1,898,066*l*., and the working expenses to 1,315,887*l*., leaving a profit of 582,179*l*., which, with interest, &c., 100,945*l*., made up a total net revenue of 683,124*l*., against which 321,501*l*. was deducted for interest on debenture stocks and other prior charges, leaving 361,623*l*. for distribution. This sufficed for dividends as follow:—Great Western 5 per cent. preference stock, at 5 per cent. per annum; Great Western share capital, 3 per cent. per annum; Grand Trunk 1st and 2nd preference, 5 per cent. per annum; Grand Trunk 3rd preference, 3¼ per cent. per annum. The Grand Trunk 70 per cent. share of net receipts amounted to 253,136*l*., and the Great Western 30 per cent. share to 108,487*l*.

The net revenue, less debenture and other interest, for the half-year ended 30th June, 1884, amounted to 114,192*l*.; the Grand Trunk share being 79,934*l*., and the Great Western 34,258*l*., out of which the Grand Trunk first preference, and the Canada 5 per cent. preferences were paid in full; but the payment of the guaranteed dividend at 3 per cent. per annum on Great Western share capital caused a net debit balance to be carried forward, amounting to 70,138*l*.

CAPITAL—30th June, 1884.—*Authorised and created:*—

Stock and shares	£32,865,815	
Loans, &c.	12,869,664	
Canadian Government debentures	3,111,500=	£48,846,979
Amount issued:—		
Great Western share capital—5 per cent. preference stock	£505,754	
Great Western ordinary shares	6,116,802	
Grand Trunk capital:—		
5 per cent. 1st preference	3,218,149	
5 per cent. 2nd preference	2,827,795	
4 per cent. 3rd preference	7,168,055	
Ordinary stock	13,415,203=	£32,751,758
Loans at 6 per cent.	£1,472,700	
Great Western 5 per cent. debenture stock	2,773,900	
Grand Trunk 5 per cent. debenture stock	4,270,575	
Consolidated companies' 4 per cent. debenture stock	1,297,446	
Canadian Government debentures	3,111,500=	12,926,121
Total		£45,677,879

The accounts are made up to the 30th June and 31st December, and the meetings are held half-yearly in London in April and October. By an act passed by the Canadian Parliament in 1881, the company have power to alter the dates fixed for the half-yearly meetings to March and September, should the directors deem it expedient at any time to do so.

CONSOLIDATION SCHEME.—Under "The Grand Trunk Railway Act, 1884," the capital of the United Company, as represented by the above figures to 30th June, 1884, was reconstructed as from the 1st July, 1884, the debenture stocks of both sections to be exchanged for "Grand Trunk consolidated 4 per cent. debenture stock," at rates equivalent to the interest previously received by the holders. A new 4 per cent. guaranteed stock, ranking immediately after the above-named debenture stock, to absorb the ordinary and preference shares of the Great Western of Canada section, and new ordinary stock to be issued in extinguishment of the rights to additional dividend held by the proprietors of Great Western of Canada ordinary and preference shares and Grand Trunk preference stock, thus raising the amount of ordinary stock from 13,417,526*l*. to 20,160,000*l*.

The following paragraphs, copied from the company's report for the half-year ended 31st December, 1883, show the effect of the consolidation, viz.:—

Every holder of 100*l*. of Great Western 5 per cent. preference stock will receive 125*l*. of 4 per cent. guaranteed stock, ranking immediately after the consolidated debenture stock, and entitling him to the same dividend as before, and 20*l*. of the ordinary stock of the United Company.

Every holder of 100*l.* of Great Western ordinary shares will receive 75*l.* of 4 per cent. guaranteed stock, ranking immediately after the consolidated debenture stock, and producing a dividend equivalent to the 3 per cent. minimum dividend secured under the Deed of Union, and 100*l.* of the ordinary stock of the United Company.

The Grand Trunk first preference stock will retain the same relative position as at present, the dividends on the guaranteed 4 per cent stock, which will now rank before it, being the same in amount as the dividends which were secured to the Great Western share capital in priority to it under the Deed of Union; but every holder of 100*l.* of stock will receive 6*l.* of the ordinary stock of the United Company in extinguishment of his existing contingent right to 1 per cent. additional dividend.

The Grand Trunk second preference stock will also retain the same relative position as at present, but every holder of 100*l.* of stock will receive 5*l.* of the ordinary stock of the United Company in extinguishment of his existing contingent right to additional dividend.

The same remarks apply to the Grand Trunk third preference stock, of which every holder of 100*l.* will receive 3*l.* of the ordinary stock of the United Company.

On the subject of the increase of ordinary capital the directors gave the following explanation, viz.:—

The ordinary stock of the United Company will combine in one stock all the reversionary rights of the Great Western share capital, represented by 30 per cent. of the net revenue, as well as all the reversionary rights of the Grand Trunk preference and ordinary stocks. The principal issue of 6,116,802*l.* ordinary stock of the United Company equitably represents the reversionary rights accruing from 30 per cent. of the net revenue available for dividend arising from all sources appropriated under the Deed of Union to the Great Western share capital, and this issue bears a nearly similar proportion of 30¼ per cent. to the total reversionary stock under the act of 20,160,000*l.*

The practical effect of the Consolidation Act will be to entitle the 20,160,000*l.* of ordinary stock of the United Company to receive a dividend earlier than the existing 13,415,202*l.* of the Grand Trunk ordinary stock would receive a dividend under the conditions of the Deed of Union, as the following statement illustrates, viz.: —

On the basis of a net revenue available for dividend of 805,741*l.*, it would require under the act of 1884, a sum as above of 772,811*l.* to meet all the preference dividends in full, leaving the difference of 32,930*l.* available as a dividend, or sufficient to pay 3*s.* 3*d* per cent. per annum on the 20,160,000*l.* of ordinary stock of the United Company; whereas, under the Deed of Union, the 70 per cent. accruing to the Grand Trunk share capital would only be sufficient to pay the dividend on the third preference stock in full, without leaving any dividend for the ordinary stock.

This comparative advantage with respect to dividends on the ordinary stock would continue, though to a diminishing extent, to the period when, under the Deed of Union, the Grand Trunk preference stock would be entitled to receive an extra dividend of 1 per cent.; but as the contingent rights of those stocks will be extinguished by the act of 1884, the ordinary stock will be entitled to the whole reversion.

It should also be remembered that, whilst previous to the union with the Great Western the Grand Trunk ordinary stock represented the reversionary right in 1,474 miles of railway only, the ordinary stock of the United Company will now be entitled to the total reversionary right in 2,429 miles of railway of the United Company, besides 189 miles of the Detroit, Grand Haven, and Milwaukee, making a total of 2,618 miles of railway; without taking into account the reversionary rights in respect of the Chicago and Grand Trunk of 335 miles, and of the Midland of 472 miles.

DIRECTORS IN LONDON:

Chairman—Sir HENRY W. TYLER, M.P., Assoc.Inst.C.E., Pymmes Park, Edmonton.

Deputy-Chairman—Sir CHARLES LAWRENCE YOUNG, Bart., 5, Ashburn Place, Cromwell Road, S.W.

James Charles, Esq., Kennet House, Harrow.

Major Alexander George Dickson, M.P., 10, Duke Street, St. James's, S.W.

Robert Gillespie, Esq., 81, Onslow Gardens, S.W.

Lord Claud John Hamilton, M.P., 23, Lowndes Square, S.W.

William Unwin Heygate, Esq., Roecliffe, Loughborough.

John Marnham, Esq., Boxmoor, Hemel Hempsted.

Right Hon. David Robert Plunket, M.P., Q.C., 12, Mandeville Place, W.

Robert Young, Esq., 4, West Nile Street, Glasgow.

OFFICERS.—Sec. in London, J. B. Renton, Dashwood House, 9, New Broad Street, E.C.; Assistant Sec., Walter Lindley; Gen. Man. in Canada, Joseph Hickson, Montreal; Traffic Man. in Canada, L. J. Seargeant, Montreal; Solicitors in London, Batten, Proffitt, and Scott, 32, Great George Street, S.W.; Auditors, Angus C. Hooper, Montreal, Canada, W. M. Ramsey, Montreal, Harry Chubb, Prince's Square, W., and Thomas Adams, 6, Sydney Terrace, Lewisham, S.E.

Offices—Dashwood House, 9, New Broad Street, E.C.

372.—GREAT WESTERN OF CANADA.

Empowered by various acts of the Canadian Legislature, between 1834 and 1858, for a line in the interior (or western) district of Canada, commencing at Niagara Falls and passing through Hamilton, at the west end of Lake Ontario (whence a branch to Toronto), and terminating at Windsor, Canada West (opposite Detroit, and on the straits connecting Lakes Erie and Huron), being the remaining link of communication from New York to the Far West of America, and joining at Detroit the Michigan Central, the Michigan Southern, the Detroit, Grand Haven, and Milwaukee, and the Wabash, St. Louis, and Pacific. In August, 1882, the Great Western was united to the Grand Trunk (see Grand Trunk).

373.—MIDLAND OF CANADA.

The Midland of Canada, as consolidated by act of the Ontario Legislature, 10th March, 1882, comprises the undertakings and properties of the six following companies, the first five of which previous to the passing of the act were worked separately, and to some extent in competition, viz.:—

Midland—extending from Port Hope to Peterborough, and the Georgian Bay at Midland	142	miles.
Grand Junction—Belleville to Peterborough and Madoc	90	,,
Toronto and Nipissing—Scarborough to Coboconk	80	,,
Whitby, Port Perry, and Lindsay—Whitby to Lindsay	46	,,
Victoria—Lindsay to Haliburton	55	,,
	413	
And Toronto and Ottawa—of which 30 miles are completed	30 = 443	

The consolidated company also work the Lake Simcoe Branch, 27 miles, and, under agreement, use 9 miles of the Grand Trunk between Scarborough and Toronto.

Corrected mileage account to 31st December, 1882:—

District.	Steel Rails. Miles.	Iron Rails. Miles.	Total Miles.
Port Hope to Midland	103·86	15·17	119·03
Millbrook to Lakefield	13·09	10·97	24·06
Scarboro' to Lornville	55·82	...	55·82
Lorneville to Coboconk (40lb. iron)	...	22·27	22·27
Whitby to Haliburton	21·42	78·42	99·84
Belleville to Peterborough	61·86	4·24	66·10
North Hastings Junction to Madoc	11·75	9·75	21·50
Toronto and Ottawa Lines	28·42	0·77	29·18
Total miles owned	296·22	141·59	437·80
Lake Simcoe Branch, leased	...	26·46	26·46
Toronto to Scarboro' over Grand Trunk	9·00	...	9·00
Total miles leased	9·00	26·46	35·46
Total miles	305·22	168·05	473·26

The act above referred to authorised the issue of a consolidated 1st mortgage security for the purpose of—(1), taking up and redeeming outstanding bonds of the above companies, amounting altogether to 1,521,300*l*.; (2), making provision, at the rate of 5,137*l*. ($25,000) per mile, for the construction and equipment of the Toronto and

Ottawa; (3), providing 60,000*l.* for improvements now in progress on the Grand Junction section; and (4), 351,000*l.* to be issued as required for enlargements and extensions of the consolidated company's works, if and when authorised by a general meeting of the shareholders.

Of this security an issue was made in London in July, 1882, for 610,800*l.*, the proceeds to be applied in taking up the bonds on the following sections:—

Grand Junction	£226,000
Whitby, Port Perry, and Lindsay	141,700
Victoria	68,400
Toronto and Ottawa	20,600
	£456,700
And the remainder to be expended on the Toronto and Ottawa	154,100
Total	£610,800

And a further amount has since been sold as follows:—

Bonds on the Midland Section	£180,000	
" Toronto and Nipissing	71,600	
	£251,600	
Improvements on the Grand Junction Section	60,000	
Enlargements and extensions upon the whole system	200,000	=£511,600
		£1,122,400

These bonds, bearing interest at 5 per cent. per annum, payable half-yearly in London 1st January and 1st July, redeemable as to principal at par on 1st January, 1912, are now quoted in the Stock Exchange list. The bonds can be registered at the London office at the option of the holders.

In addition to the above	£1,122,000
There are in existence bonds on the Toronto and Nipissing Section...	288,000
Midland Section	*525,000
Unissued	151,000
Making a total 5 per cent. mortgage of	£2,086,000

The total authorised share capital of the consolidated company is $6,600,000, of which $4,100,000 represent stocks fully paid up of the several companies forming the consolidation.

A traffic agreement was made between this company and the Grand Trunk of Canada, dated the 10th May, 1882, under which the six railways comprising the existing Midland system were consolidated into one undertaking; and these railways have since been worked under a President and Board, having separate control, though in connection with and in the interest of the Grand Trunk system. With the view of promoting still greater unity of action, and greater economy of working, by operating the Grand Trunk and Midland as one system, an agreement has been entered into by which the Midland shall, from the 1st January, 1884, be taken over and worked as part of the Grand Trunk system, the Grand Trunk undertaking to supplement the net receipts of the Midland, if necessary, by payment out of the gross receipts from traffic carried upon the said railway, an amount sufficient to secure the interest on all the bonds of the Midland, as specified above.

For full text of the agreement with the Grand Trunk, see *Appendix* to the MANUAL for 1884, page 511.

REVENUE.—The gross receipts for the year ended 31st December, 1883, amounted to 227,410*l.*, and the expenses to 146,535*l.*; balance, 80,875*l.*; which, added to 4,748*l.*, balance from 1882, made up a net revenue of 85,622*l.*, which provided for interest on bonds, loans, and advances, and left 121*l.*, which was carried to the general balance sheet.

CAPITAL.—The receipts and expenditure on capital account to 31st December, 1883, were as follow:—

Receipts.	$	£
Share capital	6,600,000	1,356,164
Consolidated mortgage bonds	5,462,347	1,122,400
Bonds—Midland section	2,555,000	525,000
Bonds—Nipissing section	1,400,627	287,800
	16,017,974	3,291,364

* These 5 per cent. bonds for 525,000*l.* are quoted in the official list, and the coupons are due on 1st May and 1st November.

Expenditure.	$	$	£
Capital expenditure to 31st December, 1882	...	15,283,391	3,140,423
Do. during year 1883:—			
Improvements of Line—			
Loop line deviation, and iron bridge at Lindsay	67,387	...	...
General works, sidings, telegraph line, new machinery, &c.	29,995	...	...
	97,382		
Less credit for old material sold	16,541	80,841	16,611
New Lines—			
Omemee and Peterborough; Manilla and Wick; Madoc and Bridgewater	...	250,125	51,396
Rolling Stock—			
New engines and cars	32,816	...	...
On further account of engines and cars purchased on deferred payments	64,784	97,600	20,055
Expenditure in connection with consolidation, including preparation of new bonds and stock certificates	...	4,798	986
Discount and expenses on bonds sold, including cost of sterling exchange	...	140,548	28,880
		15,857,303	3,258,350
Balance carried to general balances No. 4		160,671	33,014
		16,017,974	3,291,364

DIRECTORS:

IN CANADA.

President—JOSEPH HICKSON, Esq., Montreal.

Vice-President—WILLIAM GOODERHAM, Esq., Toronto.

J. R. Dundas, Esq., M.P.P., Lindsay, Ontario.
H. P. Dwight, Esq., Toronto.
J. D. Edgar, Esq., Toronto.
James M. Ferris, Esq., M.P.P., Campbellford, Ontario.
F. W. Henshaw, Esq., Montreal.
Robert Jaffray, Esq., Toronto.
Thomas Kelso, Esq., Belleville, Ontario.
E. S. Vindin, Esq., Port Hope, Ontario.

Office in Canada—Peterborough, Ontario.

OFFICERS.—Secretary and Treasurer, H. Read; Superintendent, James Stephenson, Montreal; District Traffic Manager, Arthur White; Engineer, J. G. Macklin; Auditors, H. W. Walker and John Burton; Bankers, The Bank of Montreal, in Canada.

London Office—Grand Trunk Railway Company, Dashwood House, 9, New Broad Street, E.C.

London Bankers—Glyn, Mills, Currie, and Co., 67, Lombard Street, E.C.

374.—NORTHERN OF CANADA.

Incorporated by act of 29th August, 1849, as Toronto, Sarnia, and Lake Huron, with a capital of 500,000*l.* in 5*l.* shares. In 1851 the name was changed to Ontario, Simcoe, and Huron, and in 1858 the name was again changed as above. By act of 21st July, 1853, the company was authorised to increase its capital to 750,000*l.*, and to borrow a further sum of 300,000*l.* By act of 1858 authority was given to call in all the outstanding bonds (excepting those granted to the Government), and to issue to the holders new bonds in lieu thereof; also to issue 200,000*l.* 6 per cent. sterling bonds, for the purpose of funding the floating debt, to extend the works, and to put the road into efficient working order. In operation, 97 miles.

Northern Extension.—The authorised lines of the Northern Extension Railways Company, incorporated by act 25 Vic., cap. 32, of the Ontario Legislature, join and are a continuation of the Northern of Canada, and extend from Collingwood to Owen Sound, and from Barrie to the Georgian Bay, about 109 miles in length. The various municipalities, towns, and cities situated along the lines have granted and paid by bonus or free gift, in aid of their construction, the sum of $242,500. The Government of Ontario have also made an absolute grant of $202,000, being together equal to about 85,200*l.* sterling. The extension railways recently amalgamated continue the communication from Collingwood westward to Meaford (22 miles), and from Barrie eastward to Gravenhurst on Lake Muskoka (50 miles); making a total of 168 miles of the amalgamated undertakings. The Northern and Northern Extension companies were amalgamated by act of 23rd March, 1875. The paid-up capital of the Northern Extension Company at the time of the amalgamation was 295,559*l.* The bonds now form a first charge for interest upon the earnings of the entire undertaking.

Hamilton and North Western.—A working agreement has been concluded with this company, which came into operation on the 1st July, 1879. "The agreement provides for the joint working of both lines under one management for 21 years. The net revenue to be divided between the companies as follows:—Up to 80,000*l.*, in the proportion of 53,000*l.* to the Northern and 27,000*l.* to the Hamilton and North Western; the next 10,000*l.* goes entirely to the Northern. The net revenue between 90,000*l.* and 100,000*l.* is divided in the proportion of 70 per cent. to the Northern and 30 per cent. to the Hamilton and North Western. Over 100,000*l.* the revenue is to be equally divided. The proportion of net revenue due to the Northern for the year ended 31st December, 1883, was 64,560*l.*, which, after payment of interest on the bonded debts of the company, and on the loans on joint working and equipment bonds, left no balance with which to pay dividend on preference or common stocks.

The directors refer to a clause of the report of the executive committee announcing the granting by the Parliament of Canada of a bonus of $12,000 per mile for the construction of the line from Gravenhurst to Callander in connection with the Northern and North Western companies.

Capital.—6 per cent. 1st mortgage bonds	£450,000
6 per cent. preference stock	170,000
Ordinary stock, $1,000,000, say	200,000

The Hamilton and North Western runs from Port Dover, on Lake Erie, to Hamilton, on Lake Ontario, and thence to Collingwood, Georgian Bay, and Barrie, on Lake Simcoe. The total length of the railway is 177 miles, all of which is constructed and in operation, and fully equipped, and 108 miles are laid with steel rails.

North Simcoe.—This line is leased to the Northern of Canada for 999 year, the lease being dated 14th January, 1878.

Capital.—The several classes of capital were, until 1877, as follow:—250,000*l.* 6 per cent. first preference bonds of 100*l.*, with coupons payable 1st January and July, and redeemable August, 1879. 283,900*l.* 6 per cent. second preference bonds of 100*l.*, with coupons payable 1st February and August, and redeemable 1st July, 1884. 150,000*l.* third preference bonds of 100*l.* (irredeemable), ranking for 6 per cent., with coupons payable 1st April and October. 133,200*l.* 6 per cent. extension first mortgage bonds of 100*l.*, issued in 1873, at 93*l.*, with coupons payable 1st January and July, and repayable 1st July, 1893; 44,400*l.* 6 per cent. extension improvement mortgage bonds of 100*l.*, issued in 1874, at 95*l.*, with coupons and principal payments precisely as in the case of the foregoing—(these two classes of "extension" bonds are secured on the extension lines, and the interest guaranteed by the Northern of Canada). 169,276*l.* ordinary stock.

Under an act of the Canadian Parliament (1877), subject to the assent of the bondholders of the company, which was unanimously given, a re-adjustment and extension of the capital account was made by the creation of 850,000*l.* of 5 per cent. first mortgage bonds, secured on the amalgamated lines comprised in the whole undertaking, and taking rank before all previous and existing issues. The purposes for which this new issue was authorised are for acquiring the extension lines under amalgamation; for extinguishing a lien of 475,000*l.* upon the main line, and 50,000*l.* of third preference bonds, both held by the Dominion of Canada; for consolidating the first preference and extension bonds into the new rank by conversion or exchange; and other purposes. Under this act an issue was made in July, 1877, in bonds of 500*l.* and 100*l.*, with coupons payable 1st January and July, and principal repayable in 1902. Since then the holding of the Government of Canada in lien and bonds has been paid off, and the conversion of the first preference bonds has been proceeded with. When the conversion authorised by the act shall have been completed the capital account will be as follows:—

5 per cent. first mortgage bonds	£850,000
4 per cent. perpetual debenture stock	415,650
6 per cent. third preference bonds	100,000
6 per cent. preference stock	150,000
Ordinary stock	162,040

The engagements of the bonds known in this market have been regularly kept.

BALANCE SHEET FOR THE YEAR 1883.

Debtor.		*Creditor.*	
Consolidated capital account...	$6,123,839	5 per cent. first mortgage bonds	$3,281,106
Northern Extension capital account	1,621,515	Northern Extension bonds......	755,798
*London & Westminster Bank	22,795	Second preference bonds.........	1,381,647
*London agents	87,720	Third preference bonds "A" ...	243,833
Northern and North Western deferred account under agreement of 6th June, 1879	631,912	Third preference bonds "B" ...	229,247
All other accounts	87,066	First preference stock	730,000
		Ordinary stock	815,200
		North Grey townships	8,500
		Interest on first mortgage 5 per cent. bonds	81,160
		Interest on Northern Extension bonds	24,277
		Interest on second preference bonds	40,753
		Interest on third preference bonds "A"	17,894
		Interest on third preference bonds "B"	9,038
		Northern and North Western advance account	48,359
		Joint working and equipment bonds appropriation for separate use	100,000
		Moveable property under agreement of 6th June, 1879.	604,671
		All other accounts	215,778
	$8,585,877		$8,585,877

DIRECTORS:

Chairman—Hon. FRANK SMITH, Senator, Toronto.

Deputy-Chairman—WILLIAM LETHBRIDGE, Esq. (Chairman of the London Board), 71, Portland Place, W.

Samuel Barker, Esq., Toronto.
C. J. Campbell, Esq., Toronto.
William Thomson, Esq., Toronto.
John L. Blaikie, Esq., Toronto.
Sir H. M. Jackson, Bart., 61, Portland Place, W.
William Ford, Esq., 46, Kensington Park Road, Notting Hill, W.
John Fisken, Esq., Toronto.
John Rigby, Esq., Q.C., 11, New Square, Lincoln's Inn Fields, W.C.
William Ince, Esq., Toronto.
David Dunn, Esq., *ex-officio*, Warden, County of Simcoe.
Mr. Alderman Adamson, *ex-officio*, for Corporation of Toronto.

OFFICERS.—Gen. Man., Samuel Barker; Sec. and Treasurer, Walter Townsend; Mechanical Supt., Peter Clarke; General Freight and Passenger Agent, Robert Quinn; Transport Supt., James Webster; Auditor, John Langton; Solicitor, George D'Arcy Boulton, Q.C.; Bankers, The Canadian Bank of Commerce, Toronto, and London and Westminster Bank, London.

London Agency—Cutbill, Son, and De Lungo, 37, Old Jewry, E.C.
Offices—Brock Street, Toronto, Ontario.

375.—ST. LAWRENCE AND OTTAWA.

Incorporated by Act of Parliament of the Dominion of Canada, 21st December, 1867. Capital, $1,500,000 in $100 shares, with power to borrow $250,000 on loan, at 8 per cent. By the act of incorporation, this company acquired a railway extending from Prescott, on the River St. Lawrence, connecting with the Grand Trunk, 2 miles north thereof, and running thence direct to the city of

* Cash in London for January dividend.

Ottawa, the capital of the Dominion. Length, 54 miles. Power was also given to extend the line to the important manufacturing establishments at Chaudiere Falls, by a branch of 5 miles in length, which has its terminus in the heart of the great lumber mills of Ottawa. A second mortgage of 50,000*l.* was created in April, 1872, to provide for the cost of the Chaudiere Branch, additional rolling stock, &c.

An act of 14th June, 1872, authorised the extension of the line to the town of Pembroke, in the county of Renfrew, and thence to any point on Lake Nipissing, or French River, or upon the Georgian Bay, and thence again to Sault Ste. Marie, or some point on Lake Superior. The company was also authorised to construct a line from some point on the Chaudiere or Pembroke extensions to the village of Aylmer. New capital, $2,000,000, making the share capital $3,590,000, of which $789,909, being the amount paid up at the passing of the act, is constituted preference capital. The security of the first and second mortgages of 50,000*l.* each not to be interfered with.

An act of 12th April, 1876, empowered the company to raise 200,000*l.* on mortgage, the money so raised, to the extent of 100,000*l.*, to be applied exclusively in paying off the first and second mortgages of 50,000*l.*, authority being given to the company (subject to certain consents since obtained) to pay off the same after thirty days' notice, with interest to the time fixed for payment, and no longer.

The first issue of bonds under the said act was for the sum of 150,000*l.*, in bonds to bearer, at 6 per cent. interest, dated 15th December, 1876, and maturing 15th June, 1910. The issue price was 90 per cent. The whole of the issue was placed, and the old bonds have been paid off. There is a stipulation for a sinking fund of 1 per cent., to be applied in purchase of the new bonds, so long as they can be obtained at not exceeding par, as per endorsement on the bonds. The sum of 1,500*l.* being applicable in purchase of bonds in June, 1878, 1,700*l.* bonds were bought for the sinking fund, costing 1,492*l.* 10*s.* The directors have issued the remaining 50,000*l.* of the 200,000*l.* authorised by resolution of 7th November, 1876. The agents for the first issue were Messrs. Morton, Rose, and Co.

BALANCE SHEET, DECEMBER 31ST, 1881:—

Assets.

Shareholders' capital (paid up stock)		£162,310	
First mortgage 6 per cent. bonds		200,000	
Balance carried down		33,964=	£396,274
Sundry creditors	£6,487		
Interest warrant, 15th December	6,000=	£12,487	
Net revenue to 31st December, 1875	£35,960		
Less balance of capital expended as per contra...	33,964=	1,996	
Sinking fund account—			
Principal	£1,500		
Interest to 15th June, 1881	306=	1,806=	£16,288

Liabilities.

Capital expenditure as on 31st December, 1880	£374,055	
Since expended	22,219=	£396,274
Balance, being excess of expenditure on capital account brought down (placed against net revenue to 31st Dec., 1875, as per contra)	£33,964	
Net revenue, No. 2 account deficiency		£7,116
Stocks of materials, fuel, &c., as per valuation		5,628
Debts due to the company		1,655
Cash in hand		397
Sinking fund investment 1,700*l.* bonds, cost		1,492
		£16,288

In accordance with the arrangement made when the new bonds were issued, the sum of $175,004, or 35,960*l.* sterling, earned in the period ended 31st December, 1875, and applied to equipment purposes, is placed to a separate account.

The coupon due 15th June, 1882, on the bonds has not been paid.

A recent meeting of bondholders appointed a committee to look after their interests.

The directors' report issued in January, 1884, and presented to the first mortgage bondholders at a meeting held on the 8th February, 1884, stated as follows, viz.:—"The Canadian Pacific had now made another proposal which the committee recommended the bondholders to accept. It was that the Canadian Pacific would take a lease of the St. Lawrence and Ottawa on the same terms as to the payment of interest as the former proposal. But for the granting of a legally valid lease by the St. Lawrence and Ottawa it was necessary either that a sufficient amount of its shares should be purchased to carry the requisite proportion of voting power, or that an act of the Canadian Parliament should be obtained giving voting power to the bondholders. In moving the adoption of the report the chairman stated that the resolution to grant a lease must be carried by a majority of two-thirds of the shareholders. The Canadian Pacific held 51 per cent. of the shares, and the Grand Trunk held a greater portion of the remainder. It would be necessary to purchase such shares, which might involve contribution by the bondholders of one year's arrear of interest—4*l*. In case the Grand Trunk refused to sell, or in case the bondholders, as a body, refused to contribute their quota, the only alternative was to get legislature power from the Canadian Parliament for the bondholders to vote. The preliminary steps had already been taken for the introduction of a bill into the Dominion Parliament in the coming session."

Transfer communications to be sent to the secretary; form, special; no fee; certificates are required to accompany transfer deeds; stock may be transferred in any sum in dollars and cents.

Scale of Voting.—One vote for every fully paid up $100 share.

No. of Directors.—Maximum, 7; minimum, 5; quorum, 3. *Qualification*, $5,000 stock.

DIRECTORS:

Cha'rman—CHARLES D. ROSE, Esq., Bartholomew Lane, E.C.

Henry Carter, Esq., 3, Clements Lane, E.C.

Duncan McIntyre, Esq., Montreal.

H. S. Northcote, Esq., M.P., 17, Rutland Gate, S.W.

George Stephen, Esq., Montreal.

All retire annually, but are eligible for re-election.

OFFICERS.—Gen. Supt., Archer Baker; Sec. to the London Board, Thomas A. Welton, 5, Moorgate Street, E.C.

London Office—5, Moorgate Street, E.C.

Chief Offices—Ottawa, Ontario, Canada.

376.—TORONTO, GREY, AND BRUCE.

Incorporated by act of the Ontario Legislature to construct a line from the Grand Trunk at Weston Junction to Orangeville, with branches to Owen Sound, on the Georgian Bay, and to Kincardine, on Lake Huron; total length, 159 miles. The company has running powers over the Grand Trunk, from Toronto to Weston, a distance of 9 miles, and working arrangements have been concluded between the two companies. The authorised capital stock is $3,000,000 in $1,000 shares, with power to increase; the company will receive about $795,000 in bonuses as follows:—$300,000 from the County of Grey, $250,000 from the City of Toronto, and $215,000 from various towns and villages along the line.

The first section, from Weston Junction to Mount Forest, was opened in October, 1872, and the Grey Extension, from Orangeville to Owen Sound, in July, 1873. A junction has been formed with the Wellington, Grey, and Bruce, by the opening of the branch from Mount Forest to Harriston, in November, 1873.

AGREEMENT WITH THE GRAND TRUNK.—In June, 1881, an agreement with the Grand Trunk, upon the following basis, was approved, viz:—

"The first agreement provides for a lease of the Toronto, Grey, and Bruce (191 miles in length) from the 1st July, 1881, to the 1st January, 1882, and for 20 years thereafter, to the Grand Trunk. Under this lease the Grand Trunk undertakes to work the Toronto, Grey, and Bruce, paying to the Toronto, Grey, and Bruce 27½ per cent. of the gross receipts until they reach $400,000, with a minimum rental of $100,000 per annum. As the gross receipts increase beyond $400,000, and up to $500,000, the rental is to be 25 per cent. of the additional gross receipts; and when the gross receipts increase to $500,000 or more, the rental is to be 12½ per cent of the increased gross receipts. The second agreement provides for the probable construction of a short branch to the town of Wingham, for which bonuses have been voted. This branch will, when constructed, be worked by the Grand Trunk as part of the system of the Toronto, Grey, and Bruce."

CAPITAL.—The receipts on this account have been as follow:—

Calls on stock	$275,240
Government and municipal bonuses	1,340,368
Bonded debt ($7,720 per mile owned)	1,322,533
Total ($16,545 per mile)	$2,938,141

There has been also a floating debt (bills payable) of $730,596, which was partly offset by $271,500 bonds unsold.

In December, 1882, payment was announced of 1*l*. 5*s*. per 100*l*. six per cent. sterling bonds in respect of interest accruing during the half-year ended 31st December, 1882; payment to be made on and after 1st January, 1883, at the offices of Messrs, Morton, Rose, and Co., as below.

Meetings held annually in Toronto.

No. of Directors—9. *Qualification*, $10,000.

DIRECTORS:

Chairman—JOHN GORDON, Esq., Toronto.

Deputy-Chairman—WILLIAM RAMSAY, Esq., Toronto.

John Baxter, Esq., Toronto.
William B. Hamilton, Esq., Toronto.
M. Staunton, Esq.
S. J. Lane, Esq.
William M. Clark, Esq., Toronto.
Thomas H. Lee, Esq., Toronto.
B. H. Dixon, Esq., Toronto.

OFFICERS.—Sec. and Treasurer, W. S. Taylor; Gen. Man. and Chief Eng., Edmund Wragge, M.Inst.C.E.; Traffic Supt., William Orr; Gen. Supt., N. Weatherston; Road Master, John Gordon; Master Mechanic, George Dixon; Solicitor, W. H. Beatty; Auditors, James Graham and Samuel Spreull.

Offices—Front Street, Toronto, Ontario.

Agents for the company in England—Morton, Rose, and Co., Bartholomew Lane, E.C.

377.—WELLINGTON, GREY, AND BRUCE.

This line extends from Guelph to Southampton, 102¼ miles. At Palmerston, there is a branch to Kincardine, 66 miles. Through its entire length it traverses a country rich in agricultural produce and timber. The various municipalities through which the line passes have granted free gifts or bonuses in aid of its construction to the amount of $525,000, or, say, 105,000*l*. sterling.

By agreements confirmed by the Legislatures of Canada and the Province of Ontario, the Great Western of Canada (now united to the Grand Trunk of Canada) have undertaken:—

1st. To work the line in perpetuity.

2nd. To provide locomotive engines and rolling stock.

3rd. To repair and maintain the line.

4th. To pay over 30 per cent. of the gross traffic receipts to the Wellington, Grey, and Bruce.

5th. To set aside 20 per cent. of the gross traffic receipts interchanged with the Wellington, Grey, and Bruce—that is, new traffic which did not previously exist—for the acquisition at par of the mortgage bonds by semi-annual drawings, until the whole are acquired by the Great Western, now the Grand Trunk of Canada.

The issue of 1st mortgage bonds is under an act of the Province of Ontario of the 21st December, 1874, limited to a total of 532,000*l*. In operation, 168¼ miles.

REVENUE.—In June, 1884, the company advertised "that the estimated earnings of the railway for the half-year ended 30th June, 1884, applicable to meet interest on the company's bonds, will admit of the payment of 1*l*. 16*s*. on each 100*l*. bond, and that of this amount 1*l*. 7*s*. 6*d*. will be applied in full payment of the coupon No. 20, due July, 1880, and 8*s*. 6*d*. in part payment of the coupon No. 21, due January, 1881." It has also been announced that a further payment of 2*l*. 2*s*. 6*d*., in respect of coupon No. 21, would be made on the 1st January, 1885. The numbers were also published of bonds drawn for payment on the 1st July, 1884, and on the 1st January, 1885.

The bonds are due 1st July, 1891, but it is stipulated on the face of the bonds that the payment and liquidation thereof in respect of both principal and interest is limited, and confined to the fund derived from 30 per cent. of the gross receipts under the agreements above-mentioned. The interest, at 7 per cent. per annum, is "cumulative," and made payable half-yearly on the 1st January and 1st July. The revenue not having been sufficient to pay the full interest, half-yearly payments on account of back interest are made on the 1st January and 1st July in each year.

The option is being offered to the holders of these bonds to exchange them, and all unpaid interest coupons, for perpetual 4 per cent. consolidated debenture stock of the Grand Trunk, particulars of which can be obtained at the London offices of the company. It is officially stated that bonds amounting to 185,000*l*. have already been so exchanged.

President—JOSEPH HICKSON.

London Agent—Walter Lindley, 203, Dashwood House, New Broad Street, E.C.

378.—WINDSOR AND ANNAPOLIS (Nova Scotia).

Incorporated in Nova Scotia by Act of Legislature, passed 1867, and in England under "The Companies' Acts, 1862 and 1867."

The company work 130 miles, viz.:—Company's own line, Windsor to Annapolis, 84 miles; the company lease, and have exclusive use, under agreement with the Dominion Government, of the line Windsor to Windsor Junction, 32 miles; running powers, Windsor Junction to Halifax, 14=130 miles. Connection is made at Annapolis with steamers for St. John, New Brunswick, and Boston, forming direct through communication from Halifax to Canada and the United States. The company commenced to work the line themselves on 1st July, 1870, till which time it was in the hands of the contractors. Capital, 321,000*l*. in shares, and 275,000*l*. in debenture stock.

Debenture Interest.—In 1878 an act was passed by the Legislature of Nova Scotia authorising the absolute guarantee by the province to be extended to the interest on the whole 75,000*l*. of the company's 6 per cent. "A" debenture stock. Notice was given in September, 1884, of the payment, on 1st October, of interest due on this stock to the latter date, as well as on the company's "B" debenture stock.

Particulars in reference to the scheme of arrangement will be found in the Manual for 1883, page 518.

Revenue and Expenditure.—The directors reported in December, 1884, that the traffic had assumed a healthy character. The permanent way and works were certified to have been maintained during the year in good working order and condition, and the rolling stock to be in a highly effective and improved condition. A balance of 2,642*l*., remaining at credit of net revenue account after providing the "A" and "B" debenture stock interest, was carried forward to next year.

Capital.—The receipts and expenditure on this account to 30th September, 1884, were as follow:—

Receipts.		*Expenditure.*	
Preference share capital issued	£219,172	Construction, rolling stock, &c., to 30th September, 1884	£798,361
Ordinary share capital issued...	100,500		
"A" debenture stock issued ...	37,724		
"B" debenture stock issued ...	198,724		
Mortgages	600		
Government subvention, &c. ...	228,906		
	£762,626		
Balance...........................	17,735		
	£798,361		£798,361

The annual meeting is held in London.

DIRECTORS:

Francis Tothill, Esq., Pomfret House, Sunbury-on-Thames.
C. Fitch Kemp, Esq., 8, Walbrook, E.C.
A. D. Leonino, Esq., Middle Wallop, near Stockbridge.

OFFICERS.—Sec., W. R. Campbell; Man., P. Innes, Kentville, Nova Scotia; Solicitors, Bircham, Drake, Burt, and Co., 26, Austin Friars, E.C., and Henry and Weston, Halifax, Nova Scotia; Auditor, W. H. Elliot, 11, Queen Victoria Street, E.C.; Bankers, Roberts, Lubbock, and Co., 15, Lombard Street, E.C., and Bank of Nova Scotia.

Offices—4, Great Winchester Street, E.C., and Kentville, Nova Scotia.

SOUTHERN AND CENTRAL AMERICA.

379.—ALAGOAS LIMITED.

Incorporated in May, 1881, under the Companies' Acts, 1862-80, for making a railway about 55 miles long, to connect the port of Maceio, in the province of Alagoas, with the town of Imperatriz, in the interior of that province.

The railway, which was opened on the 2nd December, 1884, runs along the valley of the River Mundahu, and traverses rich districts of the province, and reaches some of its most productive central parts.

The total population of the province is returned at 340,000, is well distributed, and chiefly employed in agriculture.

The chief foreign exports of the province are sugar and cotton. There is also rice, mandioca, and Indian corn for home use and export to the neighbouring provinces.

Maceio is a port of call for the steamers of the Royal Mail Steam Packet Company, as well as of the Brazil and River Plate Mail Line (Lampert and Holt). It is also visited weekly by steamers which run along the coast of the empire from Rio Grande do Sul to Pará. The value of the import and export trade of the port averaged during the years 1877, 1878, and 1879, 740,000*l.* per annum.

The Brazilian Imperial Government concede, amongst others, the following important favours:—1. Privilege for 90 years from the incorporation of the company, during which no competing railway is to be sanctioned within 20 kilometres of either side of the railway without the consent of the company. 2. Guarantee of 7 per cent. on the maximum capital of *Rs.*4,553,000$000 (512,212*l.* 10*s.*) for 30 years, payable half-yearly, from the date of payments to the company's bankers on the terms appearing in the decrees.

The Government reserve the following rights:—1. Right to purchase the railway at or at any time after 30 years from the completion of the line, at a price, failing agreement, to be based on the average net receipts of the previous five years: such price in no case to be less than the guaranteed capital, and to be payable in Imperial Government obligations of the public debt, bearing 6 per cent. interest per annum. 2. Right to receive one-half of the excess of dividends over and above 8 per cent. per annum, to reimburse any sums paid by the Government as guaranteed interest, until wholly repaid, after which such participation will cease, and the whole revenue will revert to the company. 3. Right to reduce fares when the dividends for two consecutive years exceed 12 per cent. per annum.

By decree, No. 2,450, of 24th September, 1873, a general law authorising subventions to railways, the Imperial Brazilian Government, before granting a guarantee of interest, required to be satisfied that a proposed line would give a net revenue of 4 per cent., and this railway is one of those for which a guarantee of interest has been conceded under the above general law.

The works were carried on under the superintendence and control of the company's engineer, Mr. D. M. Fox, M.Inst.C.E., late superintendent and engineer, and now consulting engineer of the Sao Paulo.

CAPITAL.—*Authorised:* 512,212*l.* *Created and issued:* 300,000*l.* in 15,000 shares of 20*l.* each, all paid (for guaranteed interest see above), and 212,200*l.* in 6 per cent. debentures, redeemable in 30 years.

For the year ended 30th June, 1884, the dividend at 7 per cent., or 28*s.* per share, was paid by two instalments in March and September.

DIRECTORS:

Chairman—JOHN BEATON, Esq., 13, Palace Gardens Terrace, W.

James D. Alexander, Esq., 2, St. Helen's Place, E.C.

Charles A. Cater, Esq., 39, Lombard Street, E.C.

Paget Peploe Mosley, Esq., Lloyd's, and 81, Warwick Road, Earl's Court, S.W.

OFFICERS.—Sec., Henry R. Briggs; Eng., D. M. Fox, M.Inst.C.E.; Auditors, Gerard Van de Linde and William Milward; Solicitors, Bompas, Bischoff, Dodgson, and Coxe, 4, Great Winchester Street, E.C.; Bankers, the New London and Brazilian Bank Limited.

Offices—20, Great Winchester Street, E.C.

380.—ARICA AND TACNA (Peru).

Established in 1853, for the purpose of constructing a railway from the port of Arica to the city of Tacna, in Peru. Length, 40 miles. Capital, 450,000*l*. The dividends are paid in June and December in each year at the Consolidated Bank, 52, Threadneedle Street, E.C.

The whole line is completed and in operation.

DIVIDENDS.—The dividends for 1881, 1882, and 1883 were in each year 5 per cent., and 2½ per cent. in 1884.

DIRECTORS:

Chairman—JAMES HAINSWORTH, Esq., 57, Moorgate Street, E.C.

Coleridge J. Kennard, Esq., M.P., Consolidated Bank, E.C.
Adam S. Kennard, Esq., Crawley Court, Winchester.
J. E. Pollock, Esq., M.D., 52, Upper Brook Street, W.
C. J. Hegan, Esq., 69, Palmerston Buildings, E.C.

OFFICERS.—Corresponding Director, Charles J. Hegan; Auditors, William Smith, Fore Street, and H. R. Sperling, 14, Cornhill, E.C.; Solicitors, Parker and Co., St. Michael's Alley, Cornhill, E.C.; Bankers, The Consolidated Bank Limited, 52, Threadneedle Street, E.C.

Offices—68 and 69, Palmerston Buildings, Old Broad Street, E.C.

381.—BAHIA AND SAN FRANCISCO.

Incorporated in 1858 (with limited liability) under decree of the Emperor of Brazil and laws of the Brazilian and Bahian Provincial Legislatures. The line at present extends from Bahia to Alagoinhas, 77 miles. Capital, 1,800,000*l*. in 20*l*. shares. The grant of the railway is in perpetuity with a guaranteed interest of 7 per cent. per annum on the fixed capital for 90 years, viz., 5 per cent. by the Imperial Government of Brazil, and 2 per cent. by the Provincial Government of Bahia. The traffic is chiefly in sugar and tobacco.

The gross receipts for the half-year ended 30th June, 1884, amounted to 102,352*l*. (including 63,000*l*., the guarantee), and the expenditure in Bahia and London to 36,138*l*., leaving a profit of 66,214*l*., which was applied to the payment of a dividend at the rate of 7 per cent. per annum, or 14*s*. per share.

CAPITAL.—The receipts on this account to 30th June, 1884, amounted to 1,800,000*l*., and the expenditure to 1,799,532*l*., leaving a balance of 468*l*.

The company have an accumulative balance of cash (working capital) of 49,936*l*. belonging to the shareholders; and some warehouses, lighters, mel-tanks, and other adjuncts to the line paid for by the shareholders' cash, pay well.

TRANSFER DEPARTMENT.—Ordinary form; fee per deed, 2*s*. 6*d*.; if more sellers than one, 2*s*. 6*d*. each; certificates must accompany transfers.

Meetings held in London in April and October.

DIRECTORS:

Chairman—T. M. WEGUELIN, Esq., 57½, Old Broad Street, E.C.

Ex-officio Director—His Excellency the Baron DE PENEDO, Brazilian Minister, Granville Place, W.

The Hon. Hallyburton G. Campbell, 61, Ennismore Gardens, Prince's Gate, W.
Sir Daniel Adolphus Lange, Knt., of Lanehurst, Albourne, Hurstpierpoint, Sussex.
Charles Seymour Grenfell, Esq., 27, Upper Thames Street, E.C.
Francis Dawe Wickham, Esq., 36, Brock Street, Bath.

OFFICERS.—Sec., Leonard Micklem; Supt. and Res. Eng. in Bahia, Richard Tiplady, Assoc.Inst.C.E.; Auditors, Joseph de Castro and Dudley C. Stuart; Bankers, N. M. Rothschild and Sons.

Offices—38, New Broad Street, E.C.

382.—BRAZIL GREAT SOUTHERN LIMITED.

Incorporated under the Limited Liability Acts, 1862 to 1880. Length, 114 miles. This company is formed for the purpose of acquiring the concession and rights granted by the Imperial Government of Brazil for the construction and working of a railway in the province of Rio Grande do Sul, from the Quarahim River to the town of Itaqui, a naval depôt and arsenal on the Uruguay River.

The line forms an important part of the railway system laid down by the Brasilian Government for the province of Rio Grande do Sul. At the town of Uruguayana it will form a junction with the system of lines partly open, partly under construction, and the remainder conceded, laid down by the Brazilian Government to serve the whole breadth of this province from the Uruguay River on the west to Porto Alegre, the capital city, and the port of San Pedro do Rio Grande on the east.

The following provisions are, among others, contained in the Imperial Decree of concession:—1. Privilege for 90 years from the date of incorporation of the company, during which no competing line is to be sanctioned within a zone of 20 kilometres on either side of this railway. 2 Guarantee by the Imperial Government of Brazil of 6 per cent. per annum on the capital of 675,000*l.* for 30 years, payable half-yearly from the date of payments to the company's bankers, on the conditions appearing in the decree. 3. After 30 years from the grant of the concession, the Government may purchase the line by agreement with the company, or, failing such agreement, at a price to be determined by the average net income of the 5 preceding years, having regard to the then value of the works. After the expiration of 90 years, the Government may purchase the property on paying the value of the works in their then condition at an amount not exceeding the sum actually expended on them. The purchase money in such case may be paid in Government 6 per cent. internal stock. 4. The Government have the right to one-half of net earnings in excess of 8 per cent. per annum, to reimburse any sums paid by them for guaranteed interest until repaid, after which the whole revenue will belong to the company. 5. The Government have the right to approve the tariff of fares and to reduce the same when the dividends shall have exceeded 12 per cent. per annum for two consecutive years.

By decree No. 2,450 of 24th September, 1873, a general law authorising subventions or guarantees of interest to railways, the Imperial Brazilian Government, before granting a guarantee of interest upon any proposed line, requires to be satisfied that it would yield a net revenue of 4 per cent., and this railway is one of those to which a guarantee of interest has been conceded under the above general law.

The registered share capital of the company was 675,000*l.*, divided as follows 225,000*l.* in 11,250 preference shares of 20*l.* each, entitled to 7 per cent. cumulative dividend; 125,000*l.* in 6,250 deferred shares of 20*l.* each (which are accepted as cash by the contractors), entitled to 6 per cent. like dividend after the 7 per cent. dividend has been paid on the preference shares. This share capital was reduced by special resolution to 350,000*l.*, divided into 11,250 preference shares of 20*l.* each, and 6,250 "A" shares of 20*l.* each. It is intended to raise the remaining capital required for the purposes of the company by the issue of debentures or debenture stock at a lower rate of interest, for which the balance of guaranteed interest, viz., 24,748*l.*, is reserved.

All surplus profits, after the preference shares have received 7 per cent. per annum dividend, and the deferred shares have received 6 per cent. dividend, are to be divided rateably between the holders of the preference shares and deferred shares.

The works of construction will be carried on under the control and superintendence of Mr. Alfred Rumball, M.Inst.C.E., formerly Chief Engineer of the Buenos Ayres Great Southern, who has recently returned from Brazil, after having secured the approval of the Imperial Government of Brazil to the plans and sections of the railway, and the authorisation to the company to carry on its operations in the Empire.

[Mem.—The above particulars are extracted from a prospectus inviting applications for the preference capital.—Ed.]

DIRECTORS:

Chairman—Major-General J. P. BEADLE, R.E., 6, Queen's Gate Gardens, S.W.

Deputy-Chairman—D. M. FOX, Esq., M.Inst.C.E., 5, Westminster Chambers, Victoria Street, S.W.

H. A. Cowper, Esq., F.R.G.S., 34, Elgin Crescent, W.

Charles Neate, Esq., M.Inst.C.E., 4, Victoria Street, Westminster, S.W.

Charles Sanderson, Esq., 12, Roland Gardens, S.W.

OFFICERS.—Sec., William Leighton Jordan; Consulting Eng., Alfred Rumball, M.Inst.C.E., 1, Victoria Street, Westminster, S.W.; Auditors, Price, Waterhouse, and Co., 44, Gresham Street, E.C.; Solicitors, Cope and Co., 3, Great George Street, Westminster, S.W.; Bankers, Glyn, Mills, Currie, and Co., 67 Lombard Street, E.C.

Offices—14, Queen Victoria Street E.C.

383.—BRAZILIAN IMPERIAL CENTRAL BAHIA LIMITED.

Incorporated in England under the Joint-Stock Companies' Act, 1862, and authorised to carry on business in Brazil by the Imperial Decree of the 12th January, 1876, No. 6,094. Minimum net income of 7 per cent. on its capital of Rs.13,000,000, or 1,462,500*l.* (being at the rate of 7,785*l.* per mile on 187¾ miles), guaranteed by the Imperial Government for thirty years, on the terms appearing in the Imperial Decree of the 31st July, 1877, No. 6,637. The guaranteed capital consists of—share capital, 737,500*l.*, of which 320,000*l.* has been subscribed, and 64,000*l.* paid up; debentures, 725,000*l.*

A contract has been entered into for the construction and equipment of the whole line from Cachoeira, on the Bay of Bahia, to the Chapada Diamantina, with a branch to the city of Feira de Santa Anna, for the amount of the authorised capital; and the company will, under the terms of this contract, retain such an amount from each payment to the contractor as will provide a substantial guarantee for the fulfilment of his contract.

In August, 1878, subscriptions were invited for 412,000*l.* in six per cent. debentures of 100*l.* sterling, redeemable at par by annual drawings within thirty years. Interest (free of all taxes of the Empire of Brazil) payable half-yearly by coupons, on the 1st February and 1st August, in sterling, in London. First coupon payable 1st February, 1879. Issue price, 95½ per cent.

In July, 1880, the balance of the share capital, viz., 417,500*l.* in 20,875 shares of 20*l.* each, was issued by the London agents at par, the final call of 5*l.* per share being due on the 31st March, 1881.

In October, 1881, subscriptions were invited for 313,000*l.* (balance of 725,000*l.*, 412,000*l.* having been previously issued) in 6 per cent. debentures of 100*l.* sterling, maturing 1st February, 1912, redeemable by annual drawings, by the operation of an accumulative sinking fund of 1 per cent. Interest, free from all taxes of the Empire of Brazil, payable half-yearly by coupons, on the 1st February and 1st August, in sterling, in London. Special coupon for 1*l.* interest, payable on the 1st February, 1882. Issue price—par, payable 5*l.* per cent. on application, 95*l.* per cent. on 10th November, 1881—100*l.* The principal is redeemable at par by annual drawings, which will take place at the office of Morton, Rose, and Co., in July of each year, in accordance with the redemption table printed on the back of the debentures, and the bonds so drawn will be payable on the 1st August following, on which day all interest thereon will cease. The first drawing will take place on 1st July, 1882.

[No recent returns have been received.—Ed.]

London Agents—Morton, Rose, and Co., Bartholomew House, Bartholomew Lane, E.C.

384.—BRAZILIAN STREET LIMITED.

Incorporated under "The Companies' Acts, 1862 and 1867," for the purpose of constructing railways in the chief towns throughout the Brazilian Empire. Capital, originally 125,000*l.* in 2*l.* shares, of which 100,000*l.* is ordinary and 25,000*l.* preference capital. The only line at present open is one in Pernambuco, 11¾ miles long.

Revenue.—At the annual meeting, held 28th March, 1883, a dividend on the ordinary shares at 1*s.* 2*d.* per share was declared, payable on the 25th April, making 5 per cent. for the year. The usual dividend on the 10 per cent. preference shares for the half-year ended 30th June, and an interim dividend on ordinary shares at 10*d.* per share, was made payable on the 29th October following.

Capital.—The receipts on this account to 31st December, 1883, included 99,200*l.* in fully paid shares of 2*l.* each, and 12,930*l.* in preference shares, of which 430 are fully paid, and 12,070 have only 1*l.* per share paid up.

The accounts are made up to the 31st December, and the meeting held in March.

DIRECTORS:

Chairman—JOSIAH ATWOOL, Esq., Sydney Lodge, Worthing.

Capt. John Charles Pitman, R.N., Hillside, Guildford, Surrey.
Samuel J. Wilde, Esq., 10, Serjeant's Inn, E.C.
William Martineau, Esq., M.Inst.C.E., 6, Great Winchester Street, E.C.
Dr. Jose Bernardo Galvão Alcoforado, Pernambuco, Brazil.
Edward Paton, Esq., Pernambuco.
Philip F. Needham, Esq., Pernambuco.

OFFICERS.—Sec., J. Butt; Gen. Man. in Brazil, W. W. Ostler, Pernambuco; Solicitors, Harries, Wilkinson, and Raikes, 24, Coleman Street, E.C.; Bankers, The Imperial Bank Limited, Lothbury.

Offices—65, Moorgate Street, E.C.

385.—BUENOS AYRES AND ENSENADA PORT.

Incorporated under "The Companies' Acts, 1862 and 1867," with a capital of 700,000*l*. in 10*l*. shares, of which 35,000 are ordinary or deferred shares, and 35,000 are preference shares, on which a minimum dividend of 7 per cent. per annum was guaranteed by the contractors until 31st December, 1875. The company is registered as a *Sociédad Anonima* in Buenos Ayres, under the Argentine law. The railway commences at the Central Station, Buenos Ayres, which is also the terminus of the Northern Line, and extends by way of Boca, Barracas, and Quilmes, to the port of Ensenada. Length, 35 miles. At Ensenada the company has constructed a pier and incidental works at which ships can load and unload into the railway trucks. The sum payable to the contractors, Ogilvie, Wythes, and Wheelwright, for the concessions, railway, and equipment, was 680,000*l*., viz., 330,000*l*. in cash and 350,000*l*. in ordinary or deferred shares of the company.

The entire line was completed and opened for public traffic 1st January, 1873.

By the Articles of Association the preference dividend of 7 per cent. per annum was made a permanent cumulative charge on the profits of the company, to which was added the right to one-half of any divisible net profits, after payment of 7 per cent. on the ordinary shares.

Buenos Ayres and Ensenada Port.—Extinguishment of Arrears of Dividend on Preference Shares:—By act of Parliament of 3rd July, 1884, the preference shareholders were authorised to agree with the company for the relinquishment of the arrears of interest accumulated during the three years ended the 31st December, 1883, in consideration of an increase of the preference dividend from 7 to 8 per cent. per annum.

Revenue.—In May, 1884, a dividend was declared of 7*s*. per share on the preference shares, making, with the interim dividend of the same amount previously paid, the full rate of 7 per cent. per annum, leaving 8,511*l*. to be carried forward.

Capital.—31st December, 1883.—*Authorised:* Ordinary shares, 350,000*l*.; preference 7 per cent. shares, 350,000*l*., since converted under the act mentioned above into 339,600*l*. 8 per cent. preference shares, leaving 10,400*l*. of 7 per cent. preference shares not converted (by the terms of issue these shares carry arrears); total, 700,000*l*., all created, issued, and paid up. Under authority of general meetings of 14th December, 1883, and 4th January, 1884, mortgage debenture stock, bearing interest at the rate of 5 per cent. per annum had been issued to the amount of 40,700*l*. The expenditure had been 733,969*l*., leaving a balance at credit of capital account of 6,730*l*.

The accounts are made up to the end of each year, and presented to the shareholders in April or May. Transfers to be made on common forms; fee, 2*s*. 6*d*. per deed.

DIRECTORS:

Chairman—JOHN W. BATTEN, Esq., 15, Airlie Gardens, Campden Hill, W.

Charles Buchanan Ker, Esq., M.Inst.C.E., 12, Eastcombe Villas, Blackheath, S.E.

Arthur March Tapp, Esq., 4, Great George Street, Westminster, S.W.

William P. Sutherland, Esq., Beckenham.

Representatives in Buenos Ayres—D. C. Gowland, Esq., and Dr. Lucas Gonzales.

OFFICERS.—Sec., John Wilson Theobald; Gen. Man., Arthur E. Shaw, Buenos Ayres; Eng., Edward Woods, M.Inst.C.E., 6B, Victoria Street, S.W.; Solicitors, Bircham, Dalrymple, Drake, and Co., 46, Parliament Street, S.W., and 26, Austin Friars, E.C.; Bankers in London, The London and Westminster Bank Limited, Lothbury, E.C.; Bankers in Buenos Ayres, The London and River Plate Bank Limited.

Offices—8, Drapers' Gardens, E.C.

386.—BUENOS AYRES GREAT SOUTHERN.

Incorporated under "The Companies' Act, 1862," for the purpose of constructing several lines of railway in the city and province of Buenos Ayres. Capital, 5,000,000*l*. in ordinary stock and shares, and 2,000,000*l*. 5 per cent. debenture stock. The Provincial Government of Buenos Ayres originally guaranteed interest at 7 per cent. per annum upon a fixed sum of 700,000*l*., but this guarantee has been commuted by a money payment. The concession is in perpetuity. The original line, Buenos Ayres to Chascomas, 71 miles, was opened on the 14th August, 1865; the Salado Extension, 35 miles, on the 19th May, 1871; the Las Flores Extension, 40 miles, on the 1st

July, 1872; the Dolores Extension, 56 miles, on the 10th November, 1874; the Azul Extension, 68 miles, on the 8th September, 1876; the Ayacucho Extension, 80 miles, on the 7th December, 1880; the Tandil Extension, 39 miles, on the 19th August, 1883; the Bahia Blanca Extension, 247 miles, on 26th April, 1884; making a productive total of 636 miles.

At extraordinary general meetings of the company, held on the 2nd November, 1883, and 31st October, 1884, further extensions were sanctioned, and the capital was increased for the purpose, viz., from Tandil to Juarez, 53 miles; from Juarez to Tres Arroyos, 58 miles; from Maipu to Mar del Plata, 80 miles; and from Barracas al Sud to the river Riachuelo, 3 miles. These prolongations are being proceeded with, and it is expected that the Tandil to Juarez Line will be completed in March of the present year (1885), and the Tres Arroyos and Mar del Plata lines early in the year 1886.

REVENUE.—The company's fiscal year ends on the 30th June of each year. The following is for the year ended 30th June, 1884 :—Gross receipts, 697,629*l.*; working expenses, 371,761*l.*; net receipts, 325,868*l.*; interim dividend of 4 per cent. and bonus of 1 per cent. to 31st December, 1883, 100,000*l.*; interest on debenture stock, 46,215*l.*; proportion of interest on new capital chargeable to revenue, 19,919*l.*; alterations to London premises, 322*l.*; leaving 159,412*l.*, to which add balance from 1882-3, interest on reserve fund and general interest, 31,142*l.*, making a disposable balance of 190,555*l.*, out of which was paid on the ordinary stock a dividend of 4 per cent. and bonus of 2 per cent. for half-year ended 30th June, 1884, both free of income tax. Balance carried forward, 30,104*l.*; reserve fund (at 31st December, 1884), 269,208*l.*; maintenance fund, 43,511*l.*; fire insurance, 10,000*l.*

CAPITAL.—The receipts on capital account to 30th June, 1884, were as detailed below:—

Ordinary stock			£2,000,000
*Permanent debenture stock at 5 per cent.			1,524,296
Bahia, Blanca, and Tandil Extension—			
1st issue	£1,000,000		
2nd issue	600,000		
	£1,600,000		
Less calls unpaid, since received	78,358		
		1,521,642	
			£5,045,938

The interest on the debenture stock is payable half-yearly, on 1st January and 1st July. The dividends on the ordinary stock are contingent upon profits, and payable on the 1st May and 1st November. The transfer books close ten days before payment.

TRANSFER DEPARTMENT QUERIES AND REPLIES.

QUERIES.	REPLIES.
Transfer form—ordinary or special?	Ordinary.
Fee per deed?	Nil.
May several classes of stock and shares be transferred on one deed?	Yes, other than debenture.
Are certificates required to accompany transfers?	Yes.
What amounts of stock are transferable, and are parts of 1*l.* sterling allowed to be transferred?	Any amount not fractions of 1*l.*
To what officer should transfer communications be sent?	Secretary.
In acceptances, renunciations, &c., of allotments of new stock, proxies, or other forms sent to joint holders, what signatures are required?	First name, except in cases of renunciation of new stock, then all names in joint account.

CONVERSION OF SHARES INTO STOCK, AMOUNTS TRANSFERABLE, RIGHTS OF VOTING, &c.—At the general meeting, held on the 23rd May, 1878, resolutions were passed consolidating the shares, Nos. 5,001 to 166,000, both inclusive, into stock, and making the following provisions, viz.:—"That no capital sum of stock less than 1*l.*, and none containing a fractional part of a pound shall be transferred; and that no transfer of less than 10*l.* shall be made to any persons who shall not at the time

* In July, 1882, the whole of the debentures of the company were converted into 5 per cent. stock.

of the said transfer be holders of stock; and that no transfer of less than 10*l.* shall be made to any particular number of persons jointly, unless the same persons shall already jointly hold stock; but that, with the exceptions in this resolution, any amount of stock may be transferred. That any number of persons not exceeding seven, but no more, may be joint transferees. That the holding of stock shall confer the same qualification for being elected as a director, and the same right of voting and other rights under the regulations of the company as the holding of a corresponding nominal amount of shares. Provided always, that, except for the purposes of dividend, or of any return of capital, the holding of a less amount of stock than 10*l.*, and the holding of so much of any larger sum as shall exceed the greatest multiple of 10*l.* therein contained, shall not confer any rights at all. That the certificates of stock shall not constitute the title thereto, but the said title shall consist exclusively of the registration in the books of the company; and the assignment or deposit of the certificates shall, as against the company, confer no title whatever to the stock mentioned therein, which shall be conveyed only in accordance with the regulations of the company for the time being."

Under resolutions passed 10th February and 19th May, 1882, the board were empowered to constitute superannuation and fire insurance funds, and under resolutions passed 16th October, and confirmed 31st October, 1884, the board were empowered to increase the reserve fund from time to time as they shall think fit, and to construct the Tres Arroyos and Mar del Plata Extensions, and to raise 1,000,000*l.* for that purpose in shares of 10*l.* each, to be called "Extension Shares, 1890."

The accounts are now made up to 30th June, and presented to the shareholders in the following October. Interim reports are issued for the half-year ending 31st December, and presented to the meeting in April.

DIRECTORS:

Chairman—FRANK PARISH, Esq., 5, Gloucester Square, Hyde Park, W.

Deputy-Chairman—JOHN FAIR, Esq., 50, Hamilton Terrace, St. John's Wood, N.W.

Edward Ashworth, Esq., Staghills, Waterfoot, Manchester.

George W. Drabble, Esq., 1, Pembridge Square, W.

The Rt. Hon. Lord Hawke, Wighill Park, Tadcaster, Yorkshire.

Joseph Pulley, Esq., M.P., Lower Eaton, Hereford.

John Edward Taylor, Esq., 12, Queen's Gate Gardens, South Kensington, W.

OFFICERS.—Sec., Charles O. Barker; Manager in Buenos Ayres, George Cooper; Con. Eng., James Livesey, C.E., 2, Victoria Mansions, Victoria Street, S.W.; Auditors, William Quilter and William Cash; Solicitor, G. M. Clements, Gresham House, E.C.

Offices—7, Finsbury Circus, E.C.

387—BUENOS AYRES AND PACIFIC LIMITED.

Incorporated under the Companies' Acts, 1862-82, to carry out a concession granted by the National Argentine Government, for a railway which will connect the eastern and western portions of the province of Buenos Ayres, commencing at the town of Mercedes (already in railway communication with the Atlantic seaboard by the Western of Buenos Ayres), and ending at the town of Villa Mercedes, in the Province of San Luis, a point forming a junction with the Argentine system of railways.

A line constructed by the Argentine Government from Villa Mercedes to Mendoza, and which is already completed and opened for traffic, is intended to be connected with the Chilian system. These continuations will bring Buenos Ayres and Valparaiso in direct communication with each other by railway. This international route from the Atlantic to the Pacific will not only open up new and important territories, but will afford direct access by railway (the total length of which will only be about 870 miles) between the two seaboards in lieu of the present route by sea (about 2,700 miles).

The principal provisions of the Government Concession, dated 19th March, 1878, are the following:—"The nation guarantees for the term of twenty years interest at the rate of 7 per cent. per annum on the shares or bonds representing the kilometrical value of each section." This is fixed at 3,995*l.* 18*s.* per kilometre, which on 578 kilos, 650 metres, makes the total amount on which the guarantee is payable 2,312,347*l.* The guarantee is payable in gold or its equivalent in national funds at the price current in London. The guarantee commences from the opening of each of the 23 sections for public service, and the interest is made payable half-yearly. (The interest during construction is payable half-yearly by the contractors on the amounts from time to time paid up.) Subject to the provision in Article 8 as to working expenses, one-half the net receipts over and above the amount required to cover the 7 per cent. are to be applied in formation of a reserve fund, until it amounts to 500,000 dollars; the other half, and, after the reserve fund amounts to 500,000 dollars, the whole of the net receipts, go to the Government, until repayment of its advances under the guarantee, and thereafter the net receipts belong to the company.

The line was commenced in July, 1882, and five years are allowed for its completion, but no lines were opened for traffic up to the latter part of 1884, though it was expected that 90 miles might be opened at the end of that year, it being uncertain as to further completions in 1885.

The capital and income are free from national and provincial taxes for 20 years.

CAPITAL.—The share capital of the company consists of 1,000,000*l.* in 50,000 "preferred" shares of 20*l.* each, and 300,000*l.* in 15,000 "deferred" shares of 20*l.* each. The "preferred" shares are entitled to a cumulative dividend of 7 per cent. per annum, payable half-yearly, and to one-half of the surplus net profits of each year remaining after meeting the obligations of the concessions; the other half of any such surplus will belong to the "deferred" shares. The "preferred" shares were issued in October, 1882; and 12*l.* per share has been paid up. A first and second issue of 400,000*l.* each respectively of 7 per cent. debentures have been made, and were fully subscribed.

Length of line, 358 miles, divided into 23 sections.

DIRECTORS:

Chairman—Sir GABRIEL GOLDNEY, Bart., M.P., Beechfield, Chippenham, and 27, South Street, Park Lane, W.

Deputy-Chairman—M. H. MOSES, Esq., 128, Westbourne Terrace, W.

Paget Mosley, Esq., 81, Warwick Road, S.W.
E. Norman, Esq., 68, Lombard Street, E C.
W. J. Stride, Esq., 3, Queen Street, E.C.
W. Rodger, Jun., Esq., Messrs. Rodger, Best, and Co., Liverpool.
Robert Ryrie, Esq., 34, Park Street, W.

LOCAL BOARD:

Dr. Don Lucas Gonzales, Buenos Ayres.
Senor Don Eduardo B. Madero.
J. G. Cruickshank, Esq.

OFFICERS.—Sec., F. O Smithers; Eng.-in-Chief, James Cleminson, M.Inst.C.E., 7, Westminster Chambers, Westminster, S.W.; Auditors, Turquand, Youngs, and Co., 41, Coleman Street, E.C.; Solicitors, Ashurst, Morris, Crisp, and Co., 6, Old Jewry E.C.; Bankers, Martin and Co., 68, Lombard Street, E.C.

Offices—Dashwood House, New Broad Street, E.C.

388.—BUENOS AYRES AND ROSARIO.

(LATE BUENOS AYRES AND CAMPANA.)

Incorporated under "The Companies' Acts" in 1873, under the title of "The Buenos Ayres and Campana Railway Company Limited," for acquiring the concession for constructing a railway from the city of Buenos Ayres to the port of Campana. Length, 50 miles.

The company was reconstructed in 1884, and the name changed to "The Buenos Ayres and Rosario Railway Company Limited," and the capital increased to provide for the construction of an extension of the railway from Campana to Rosario, under a concession granted by the Argentine Government in October, 1883.

A concession for a further extension from Rosario to the Colonies of Santa Fé (Sunchales), a distance of 150 miles, was granted by the Argentine Government to this company in October, 1884.

The line was opened to Campana, 50 miles, on the 22nd April, 1876, and the first section of the extension to Rosario, 8 miles, was opened for traffic on the 1st January, 1885, leaving 130 miles in course of construction.

A net revenue of 28,000*l.* per annum was guaranteed on the original line, the working expenses for the purpose of the guarantee being fixed at the rate of 50 per cent. of the gross receipts, but this guarantee was surrendered under the terms of the concession for the Rosario Extension, by which a subvention of nearly 70,000*l*. was granted to the company as a set off against the amounts advanced by the Government on account of the original guarantee, thus leaving the future net earnings free for division amongst the proprietors.

CAPITAL.—The expenditure on this account to the 31st December, 1883, amounted to 870,416*l*., and the capital now issued under the terms of the reconstruction scheme, stands as follows:—

Ordinary stock	£500,000
7 per cent. preference shares of 10*l*. each	600,000
5 per cent. debenture stock	733,000
Total (all issued)	£1,833,000

TRANSFER DEPARTMENT.—Ordinary form; no fees; certificates must accompany transfers; any amount not being the fraction of 1*l*. of stock transferable.

Yearly meeting held in London in May. Half-yearly reports.

DIRECTORS:

Chairman—FRANK PARISH, Esq., 5, Gloucester Square, Hyde Park, W.

George Wilkinson Drabble, Esq., 1, Pembridge Square, W.

William Rodger Gilmour, Esq., Argentine Consul, Liverpool.

Joseph Pulley, Esq., M.P., Lower Eaton, Hereford.

Russell Shaw, Esq., 26, Sackville Street. W.

John Coghlan, Esq., C.E., Buenos Ayres.

OFFICERS.—Sec., J. B. Davison; Gen. Man. and Eng., Thomas C. Clarke, Buenos Ayres; Solicitors, Norton, Rose, Norton, and Co., 24, Coleman Street, E.C.; Bankers, Glyn, Mills, Currie, and Co., 67, Lombard Street, E.C., and the London and River Plate Bank, Buenos Ayres.

Offices—2, Coleman Street, E.C.

389.—CAMPOS AND CARANGOLA LIMITED.

Incorporated under statutes approved by the Brazilian Government for constructing and making a railway from Campos, on the banks of the Parahyba, in the province of Rio de Janeiro, to Santo Antonio dos Tombos, on the boundary of the province of Minas Geraes, with branches to the Itabapoana and San Paulo de Muriahé, under concessions by which the Provincial Government of Rio de Janeiro gauranteed interest at 7 per cent. per annum, on a capital of 5,000 contos for 20 years, and that the Imperial Government also guaranteed the due payment of this sum. By a subsequent decree the Imperial Government extended their guarantee of interest to a further 1,000 contos, thus increasing the total guaranteed capital to 6,000 contos (equal at 27*d*. to 675,000*l*.), and prolonged the term of guarantee to 30 years, terminating on the 20th March, 1905. The amount payable by the Government on the capital expended has been punctually paid to the company.

The first section of the main line (from Campos to the Muriahé Falls), and the branch to the Itabapoana (together 127 kilometres), are completed and opened for traffic.

REVENUE.—The revenue of the line for the second half of 1880 almost sufficed to cover the guaranteed interest of 7 per cent. on the capital then raised, the Imperial Government having to pay the company only 17 contos on account of the guaranteed interest for that half-year.

CAPITAL.—The company has a share capital of 2,328 contos of reis (261,900*l*.) fully paid up.

In July, 1881, Messrs. Louis Cohen and Sons, of 31, Throgmorton Street, London, E.C., invited applications (price 99 per cent.) for 398,700*l*. 5½ per cent. debentures to bearer of 100*l*. sterling, with interest at 5½ per cent. per annum, from 1st July, 1881, payable half-yearly by coupons on the 1st January and 1st July. The principal will be redeemable at par, in 24 years, by annual drawings (in accordance with the redemption table printed on the back of the debentures), to take place at the office of Messrs. Louis Cohen and Sons, in the month of April in each year, the first drawing to take place in April, 1882. The numbers drawn will be advertised, and the drawn debentures paid on presentation on the 1st July following each drawing, on which day all interest thereon will cease.

The principal and interest will be payable in London, free of all Brazilian taxes.

By the terms of the decrees the interest guaranteed by the Government is payable at the exchange of 27*d*. per milreis on all the capital of the company raised out of

Brazil. The amount of the guaranteed interest on the whole authorised capital is 420 contos of reis, which would be equal at the above rate of exchange to 47,250*l.* per annum; whilst the amount required for the annual interest and sinking fund of the present loan is only 245 contos, or 27,550*l.*

The principal, interest, and sinking fund of the loan are by the debentures secured as a first charge upon the whole of the guaranteed income and the other revenues of the company.

The debentures were to be fully paid up by November, 1881, in which month it was announced that the definition bonds were ready for delivery in exchange for fully paid scrip.

Agents—Louis Cohen and Sons, 31, Throgmorton Street, E.C.

390.—CARRIZAL AND CERRO BLANCO.

The CARRIZAL RAILWAY was established in 1866, to supersede the tramway then existing between the Port of Carrizal, in Chili, to Canto del Agua, and thence was extended to the rich copper mining district of Carrizal Alto—a distance of 26 miles. An amalgamation was arranged with the Cerro Blanco, taking effect from the 1st July, 1880, the new company taking over the latter line on par terms, say by increasing the joint share capital by $500,000. The capital is now therefore increased to $1,500,000 in shares of $500. Total length, 70 miles.

The CERRO BLANCO, which runs from Canto del Agua to Yerba Buena, a distance of 44 miles, was opened in 1868, and has paid dividends regularly since, varying from 3 per cent. to 9½ per cent., the average for the last five years being 7 per cent. Gauge of line, 4 feet 2 inches.

REVENUE.—Half-year ended 30th June, 1884:—

Profit and loss account shows a surplus of	$58,932
And adding balance from previous half-year	5,372
There is formed a total of	$64,304
This amount was recommended for distribution as under:—	
Dividend at rate of 8 per cent. on capital, $1,500,000	$60,000
Pass to reserve fund 1 per cent. of profit	589
And leave in profit and loss account the balance of	3,714
	$64,303

Dividends on Carrizal system ranged from 10 to 16 per cent. up to 1876, for 1877 9 per cent. was paid, for 1878 6½ per cent., for 1879 8½ per cent., and for first half-year of 1880 at rate of 9 per cent.

Since the amalgamation the following dividends have been declared:—The second half of 1880, at the rate of 10 per cent.; 1881, 8½ per cent.; 1882, 8½ per cent.; 1883, 9 per cent; first half of 1884 at the rate of 8 per cent.

The traffics are published every quarter, and appear in the Liverpool Share List.

Transfer form, special; shares transferable by endorsement; no fee; certificates are required to accompany transfer deeds; transfer communications to be addressed to the secretaries as below.

LOCAL DIRECTORS:

D. Duncan, Esq. | E. W. Davidson, Esq. | James Rose, Esq.

Secretaries, G. A. Tinley and Co.

Office—H10, Exchange Buildings, Liverpool.

391.—CENTRAL ARGENTINE.

Incorporated under "The Companies' Act, 1862," for the purpose of constructing a railway from the port of Rosario to the city of Cordova, in the Argentine Republic. Length, 246½ miles. Authorised stock and debenture stock, 2,000,000*l.*, viz., 1,300,000*l.* in stock, and 700,000*l.* on loan. The Government of the Argentine Republic guarantees for 40 years, reckoned from the date of the railway first beginning to run, a net revenue of 7 per cent. per annum in sterling on a fixed outlay of 6,400*l.* per mile, and at the end of that time all obligations on the part of Government will cease, the railway and all its appurtenances remaining the property of the company in perpetuity.

On October 10th, 1876, the Argentine Congress passed a decree extending the Government guarantee as follows, viz.:—1st. The amount proved to have been expended by the said company in changing the site and widening the station of the Central Railway in the city of Cordoba. The sum guaranteed must not exceed

27,000*l*. 2nd. The amount of the other indispensable works for the junction of the Central Argentine with the Central Northern Line and the working service thereof. This sum must not exceed 16,000*l*.

It was stated in July, 1879, that with a view to improving the existing defective and costly means of transport between the company's terminal station and the Port of Rosario, an arrangement was under consideration for extending the mole and connecting it with the railway, so as to permit the loading and unloading of vessels direct into the company's wagons, the want of which is urgently felt, and it is obvious that when effected it will materially promote the interests of the company and its customers.

The following paragraph appeared in the company's report for the year ended 31st December, 1882, viz.:—"The increase of passenger and goods traffic is all the more satisfactory as arising from the development of the interior provinces, and the additional facilities of communication afforded by the prolongation of the railways constructed by the National Government. The port of Rosario is rapidly acquiring importance as the natural port of shipment for the interior, which must add greatly to the value of the Central Argentine Railway. Rosario is already the terminus of no less than 800 miles of railway in operation, and further extensions are now being made by the Government—(1) from Tucuman towards the Bolivian frontier, and (2) in extending the Andine Line to Mendoza."

The conditional agreement made with the company by the Government of the Argentine Republic, and announced at the ordinary general meeting of the company in July of 1884, has been very recently approved by the Chambers. It is intended to take powers to increase the capital of the company, inclusive of 700,000*l*. borrowed capital, to 2,500,000*l*.

DEBENTURE STOCK.—In July, 1880, the following resolutions relating to the debenture stock debt were passed, viz :—"1. That the directors may, in exercise of the borrowing powers already conferred on them by the articles and resolutions of the company, at any time hereafter, and from time to time, issue certificates (to be called 'Debenture Stock Certificates'), and representing principal money (to be called 'The Debenture Stock Debt'), to bear interest at the rate of not exceeding 6 per cent. per annum, and on the terms that the principal of the debenture stock debt shall not be repayable until the expiration of 99 years, or other long term to be fixed by the directors, or an order for the winding up of the company by or under the supervision of the court; and shall be secured on the undertaking and property of the company, subject only to such of the existing debentures as shall from time to time remain outstanding: Provided that such principal moneys shall not exceed the amount of the present authorised debt of seven hundred thousand pounds (700,000*l*.) in the whole, and shall not be applied to any purpose other than the redemption by exchange for, or payment off of, the existing debentures of the company, and (subject thereto) the carrying into effect of any of the objects for which the existing authorised debenture debt was authorised. 2. That the directors may make provision for the transfer of any portions of the debenture stock debt in the same manner as debenture stock is transferable, or in such other manner as they may think fit and all details in reference to the debenture stock debt and the form and terms of any deeds for securing the debenture stock debt, the regulations for the transfer thereof, and the issue of debenture stock certificates, shall be in the absolute discretion of the directors."

The conversion of the share capital of 1,300,000*l*. into stock was made on the 16th January, 1882, and the stock has been duly issued conformably to the Articles of Association and the resolution of the proprietors authorising the conversion.

REVENUE.—The net revenue for the year ended 31st December, 1883, amounted to 273,096*l*., or after deducting interest charges, &c., of 35,804*l*. to about 240,000*l*. Dividends on the ordinary stock have been paid, free of income tax, for last five years, 1879, 5½ per cent.; 1880 to 1883, 6 per cent.

CAPITAL.—This account, to 31st December, 1883, remained as before, and showed the receipts to have been 1,849,400*l*., and the expenditure 1,775,964*l*., leaving a balance of 73,436*l*. A sum of 90,278*l*. had been carried to a suspense account, pending a settlement of the accounts with the Argentine Government. In January, 1885, power was taken to increase the ordinary capital to 2,000,000*l*., and an allotment of 325,000*l*. was, therefore, subsequently made to the proprietary, at par, in proportion to their holdings.

In the beginning of 1885, it was officially announced that the company had given up the Government concession, in order to free its action in the conduct and development of its business, and securing the full benefit of its earnings.

Annual meeting held in London in the month of July.

DIRECTORS:

Chairman—HENRY BROCKETT, Esq., Heath Lodge, Iver, Bucks.

Henry A. Brassey, Esq., M.P., 6, Cromwell Houses, South Kensington, and Preston Hall, Aylesford.

Lawrence Heyworth, Esq., Wain Vawr, Newport.

Walter Morrison, Esq., Malham Tarn, Bell Busk, near Leeds, and 77, Cromwell Road, S.W.

Alexander Ogilvie, Esq., Assoc.Inst.C.E., 4, Great George Street, Westminster, S.W.

Frank Parish, Esq., 5, Gloucester Square, Hyde Park, W.

Russell Shaw, Esq., Assoc.Inst.C.E., 26, Sackville Street, Piccadilly, W.

Representative in the Argentine Republic—William Thompson, Esq., Buenos Ayres.

OFFICERS.—Sec., George Woolcott, Assoc.Inst.C.E.; Con. Eng., C. D. Fox, M.Inst.C.E.; Gen. Man., Henry Fisher, Rosario; Auditors, W. Hurlbatt and W. T. Linford; Solicitors, Travers Smith and Braithwaite, 25, Throgmorton Street, E.C.; Bankers, The London and Westminster Bank, London.

Head Office—85, Palmerston Buildings, Bishopsgate Street, E.C.

392.—CENTRAL URUGUAY OF MONTEVIDEO LIMITED.

This was originally a *Société Anonyme* for carrying out a concession granted by the Government of Uruguay for a line of railway from Montevideo to Durazno, the chief town of the interior. The concession is perpetual, with a Government guarantee of 700*l.* per mile per annum for 40 years, attaching as each separate section of the line was opened for traffic.

The nominal capital of the company was $6,580,000 (1,400,000*l.* sterling), divided into 28,000 shares of $235 (50*l.* sterling) each. The issued shares being divided into 18,841 preference (of which 17,440 were held in England) and 5,181 ordinary shares (of which 5,180 only were issued, and all of which were held in Montevideo). The preference shares had a first charge upon the revenue and guarantee of the company up to 7 per cent. per annum on their nominal value (subject to the rights of the mortgage bondholders on the Santa Lucia Section of the line); the ordinary shares were then entitled to dividend up to 7 per cent., after which preference and ordinary ranked *pari passu*.

The first section of the line, extending from Montevideo to Santa Lucia (40 miles), was opened for traffic in 1872, and the remaining 87½ miles on the 11th July, 1874. A further section of 2½ miles, embracing a bridge across the River Yi, was opened in November, 1879. Total length of line now open, 130 miles.

A re-construction of the undertaking having been recently carried out, the company is now an English limited company, formed under the "Companies' Acts of 1862 and 1867," with a capital of 1,000,000*l.*, in shares of 10*l.* each. The debenture capital is 550,000*l.* in 6 per cent. permanent debenture stock, of which 490,000*l.* has been issued.

By virtue of a contract with the Government, dated 25th Feburary, 1878, the original concession was so modified as to compensate the shareholders for the losses and injuries they had sustained, the superior Government paying the arrears of guarantee, agreed at $1,600,000, by an issue of bonds of that amount, bearing interest at 4 per cent. per annum, and a cumulative sinking fund of 2 per cent. per annum, both payable quarterly, and undertaking for ten years, from the 1st January, 1879, to assist the new company by means of an annual subvention of $25,000=5,319*l.*, payable in half-yearly instalments. Resolutions approving the reconstruction scheme were published in the *Appendix* to the MANUAL for 1877.

WORKING AGREEMENT WITH HYGUERITAS COMPANY.—An agreement for the working of the Hygueritas Line by this company was made on the 4th March, 1876, under which the Central Company take the entire management, receiving for doing so a proportion of the gross receipts varying from 65 to 45 per cent., as the traffic ranges from 200*l.* to 600*l.* and upwards per week. The net profits accruing to the Hygueritas Company are to be paid over by this company quarterly. This agreement, which has been sanctioned by the Government *vis-à-vis* their guarantee, is for twelve months certain, and is determinable thereafter by either party on six months' notice.

REVENUE.—For the year ended 30th June, 1884, the net earnings, after providing for interest on debenture stock and all other prior charges, sufficed for the payment of a balance dividend of 6*s.* per share=6 per cent. per annum, free of income tax, payable 16th October, 1884, carrying forward a balance of 7,229*l.*

For the half-year ended 31st December, 1883, an interim dividend at 6s. per share=6 per cent. per annum, free of tax, was paid, payable on the 29th April, following, carrying forward a balance of 7,611*l*.

CAPITAL—30th June, 1884.—Amount expended (as adjusted by the reconstruction scheme above-mentioned), 1,525,667*l*. The receipts to this date were as follow:—

100,000 ordinary shares of 10*l*. each	£1,000,000
Permanent 6 per cent. debenture stock	490,000
	£1,490,000
Showing a credit balance of	35,666

NEW CAPITAL.—In May, 1881, 5,438 new shares were issued at 7*l*. 5*s*. per 10*l*. share. These shares rank for dividend *pari passu* with the existing shares; the applications for these shares were largely in excess of the number available for issue.

By special resolutions passed at the ordinary general meeting of the company, held on the 8th October, 1884, and confirmed at an extraordinary general meeting held on the 29th October, 1884, the Board were authorised to increase the nominal share capital of the company to 1,250,000*l*., by the issue of 25,000 10*l*. shares, for the extension of the existing line to the north bank of the Rio Negro. The said shares to bear interest to the 30th June, 1886, at the rate of 6 per cent. per annum, and on and after the 30th June, 1886, such interest to cease, and the shares which shall have borne the same to be merged into and thenceforth form part of the ordinary share capital of the company.

The Board, being of opinion that dividends should be paid half-yearly, commenced to pay interim dividends for the first six months of the year, as from the year ended 31st December, 1880.

DIRECTORS:

Chairman—GEORGE WILKINSON DRABBLE, Esq., 1, Pembridge Square, W.

John Fair, Esq., 50, Hamilton Terrace, St. John's Wood, N.W.

Loftus Fitzwygram, Esq., 89, Eccleston Square, S.W.

Frank Parish, Esq., 5, Gloucester Square, Hyde Park, W.

D. Cooper Scott, Esq., 7, Drapers' Gardens, E.C.

OFFICERS.—Sec., Charles Oxtoby Barker; Consulting Eng., James Livesey, 2, Victoria Mansions, Westminster, S.W.; Auditors, William Cash, 90, Cannon Street, E.C., and T. A. Welton, 5, Moorgate Street, E.C.

Offices—7, Finsbury Circus, E.C.

393.—CONDE D'EU LIMITED.

(PROVINCE OF PARAHYBA, BRAZIL.)

This company was incorporated in 1875, under "The Companies' Acts, 1862 and 1867," in Great Britain, and under the Imperial Decree, No. 6,718, of 13th October, 1877, in Brazil, to carry out a concession granted by the Imperial Government of Brazil for constructing and working a railway from the city of Parahyba, the capital and seaport of the province of that name, to the town of Independencia, including a branch to the town of Pilar, a total distance of about 75 miles. The company has also the exclusive right, on terms to be hereafter agreed, to construct one branch from Pilar to Ingá, and another from Mulungú to Alagôa Grande.

The following are the leading provisions of the concession:—The Imperial Government of Brazil guarantees for a period of 30 years the annual payment of a sum equal to interest at 7 per cent. per annum upon a capital not exceeding in the whole 675,000*l*., to be expended, with the sanction of the Government, in the formation and administration of the company, and in the completion and equipment of the railway. The capital is to be issued in such portions as may from time to time be authorised by the Government. The portion now issued—425,000*l*.—has been so sanctioned, as shown by a letter from the Brazilian Minister. By the consolidation decree of the 12th September, 1877 (No. 6,681, clause XV.), a "reserve fund" to meet any extraordinary expenditure for new works, for complete renewals, for increase of rolling stock, &c., is to be created as follows:—After the line, or any section of it, has been opened for traffic, the net earnings up to 7 per cent are to be applied in payment of dividends on the guaranteed capital; when the net earnings exceed 7 per cent., any difference between that and 7½ per cent. is to be carried to the reserve fund, and if they do not amount to 7 per cent. the Government will, in addition to the guaranteed interest, contribute to the reserve fund an amount equal to a ½ per cent. on the expended capital. Between 7½ and 8 per cent. no further addition to the reserve fund is required, and as soon as the dividends are more than 8 per cent., one moiety of the excess will be paid to the Government for reimbursement of any interest which it may have advanced, such payment ceasing as soon as the interest so advanced has been repaid. When the dividends shall exceed 12 per cent. for two consecutive years, the Government will have a right to require a reduction of the tariffs. The concession or exclusive privilege is for 90 years; but the Government have the right at any time after 30 years, reckoned from the date of the completion of the railway, to purchase the same at a valuation based on the net revenue of the five previous years; the purchase money, however, in no case being less than the guaranteed capital. The railway, unless so purchased by the Government, remains the property of the company in perpetuity.

In May, 1880, an issue of 425,000*l*., in 21,250 shares of 20*l*. each, was made, being the portion of the guaranteed capital sanctioned for the completion and equipment of the line as far as Mulungú. 1*l*. per share was made payable on application, 4*l*. on allotment, and the remainder in calls of not more than 5*l*. per share, at intervals of not less than three months. Payment in full can be made upon allotment or at the respective dates of calls, and interest at the full rate of 7 per cent. will at once accrue. Interest payable half-yearly in London, including period of construction of works, and free of all taxes in Brazil. The prospectus of this issue contained the particulars given above.

The report of the directors for the year ended 30th June, 1884, issued in November last, that the net balance due from the Brazilian Government, after deducting profit on working (2,365*l*.) and interest (2,667*l*.), amounted to 42,290*l*., which provided for interest at 7 per cent. per annum on the share capital, and 5 per cent. per annum to the bondholders. The directors further stated as follows, viz.:—

The inaugural opening of the first division of the line (from Parahyba to Mulungú 74½ kiloms.) took place on the 7th September, 1883, and the running of trains commenced on the 18th of that month. On the third division, or Pilar Branch (from Cobé Junction to Pilar, 24½ kiloms.), trains began running on the 28th November, 1883. The second division (from Mulungú to Independencia, 22½ kiloms.) was opened for traffic on the 4th June, 1884, thus completing the opening of the whole line.

The receipts of the line, up to 30th June last, show an excess of earnings over expenditure amounting to 2,365*l*.; but it must be added that this excess represents in great part the carriage of certain materials chargeable to the contractors, the exact amount of which is not yet agreed.

Cabedello Extension.—The guarantee of the Brazilian Government upon this extension, amounting to 6 per cent. upon 91,000*l*., has been included in the ministerial budget for the present year, but as yet no directions have been received from the Government for proceeding with the estimates. The length of such extension is estimated at 19 kiloms.

Interest and Dividends.—During the construction of the line, the Brazilian Government has paid, each half year, with its accustomed punctuality, the 7 per cent. interest guaranteed upon the capital of the company.

The line being now completed and in traffic, the half-yearly accounts are subject to audit by the Government, for which purpose a period of three months is allotted by the general railway law of Brazil.

Henceforward, therefore, the dates for the payment of dividends will be the 1st May and the 1st November in each year.

DIRECTORS:

Chairman—A. H. PHILLPOTTS, Esq., Carshalton, Surrey.

Deputy-Chairman—Major-General J. P. BEADLE, R.E., 6, Queen's Gate Gardens, S.W.

Charles Samuel Hawkes, Esq., Stoneleigh, Beckenham.
Alfred Phillips Youle, Esq., Croydon.
Edward Keir Hett, Esq., 16, Mark Lane. E.C.

OFFICERS.—Sec., G. Gladstone Turner; Consulting Eng., Charles Neate, M.Inst.C.E., 4, Victoria Street, Westminster, S.W.; Auditors, G. A. Hillier, Gresham House, Old Broad Street, E.C., and Henry Dever, 4, Lothbury, E.C.; Solicitors, Messrs. Burchell, 5, The Sanctuary, Westminster, S.W.; Bankers, London and County Banking Company Limited, 21, Lombard Street, E.C.

Offices—27, Clement's Lane, Lombard Street, E.C.

394.—COPIAPO (Chili).

Concession from the Chilian Congress, dated 20th November, 1849.

	Miles.
This company was formed in October, 1849, to construct a line from the port of Caldera to Copiapo, which was completed and opened in January, 1852	50¾
During 1854 an extension was constructed to Pabellon, and opened for traffic 1st January, 1855	22¾
And during 1865 and 1866, a further extension to San Antonio was constructed, and opened 1st February, 1867	20½
	94
On the 7th November, 1868, at the general meeting of the shareholders, held at Copiapo, it was agreed to purchase the line from Pabellon to Chanarcillo*...	26
	120
On the 7th July, 1869, at the general meeting of the shareholders, held at Copiapo, it was resolved to extend the railway from Paipote, on the main line, to Puquios, which was opened January, 1871†, length about	32
Total length of traffic line........	152

The lines are single, and gauge 4 feet 8½ inches.

The original capital subscribed for the line from Caldera to Copiapo was	$1,300,000
Increased by subscription for extension from Copiapo to Pabellon.........	500,000
" " " Pabellon to San Antonio...	750,000
" bonus shares distributed between years 1851 and 1867......	1,650,000
Making present capital stock 8,400 shares at $500 each..............	$4,200,000

The dividends paid in cash since the opening of the line have been as under:—

Year		Per cent.	Year		Per cent.
1854	Four dividends, amounting to	16	1870	Four dividends, amounting to	8
1855	" " "	12½	1871	" " "	9
1856	" " "	15	1872	" " "	8
1857	" " "	13½	1873	" " "	7
1858	" " "	16	1874	" " "	8
1859	Three " "	12	1875	" " "	8
1860	Four " "	16	1876	" " "	8
1861	" " "	13	1877	" " "	8
1862	" " "	8	1878	" " "	6
1863	" " "	10½	1879	" " "	6
1864	" " "	12½	1880	" " "	6
1865	Three " "	9½	1881	" " "	6
1866	Five " "	11	1882	" " "	6½
1867	Four " "	9½	1883	" " "	7
1868	Three " "	7	1884	First half-year at rate of	5½
1869	Four " "	8			

REVENUE.—The receipts and expenditure on this account were given in the report for the year ended 31st December, 1883.

Receipts.		*Expenses.*	
Passengers	$84,813	General management	$41,465
Freight traffic	477,671	Locomotion and traffic........	146,982
From other sources	40,908	Maintenance and renewal	130,178
Total	$603,392	Total	$318,625

Showing a net result of $284,767 or equal to 6·78 per cent. Dividends have been paid for this year amounting to 7 per cent. The sum of $234,139 now stands at the credit of revenue account undivided.

The receipts for the first six months of 1884 amounted to $259,284, against $299,887 for the corresponding period of 1883. The working expenses amounted to $151,654, against $144,090. Dividends have been paid for this period at the rate of 5½ per cent. per annum.

* The *Chanarcillo Branch*, which cost in construction about $1,000,000, was purchased for $128,000, which amount has been paid for out of revenue. There has not yet been any distribution of capital to the shareholders to represent this amount.

† The *Puquios Branch* was constructed for $380,000, under a guarantee from Don A. Soto and Don Felip S. Matta, who work the line for a period of 10 years, and pay the Copiapo interest on the above sum, and 10 per cent. to a sinking fund, whereby this branch became the property of the Copiapo in 1881 without any outlay whatever.

Transfer form, special; shares transferable by endorsement; no fee; certificates required to accompany transfers; transfer communications to be sent to the Secretaries, as below.

The traffics are published monthly, and appear in the Liverpool Share List.

LOCAL DIRECTORS:

James Cox, Esq., Liverpool.
Francis Thornely, Esq., Liverpool.
Charles G. Rowe, Esq., Liverpool.

SUBSTITUTES
(As required by Chilian Law):

Stephen Williamson, Esq., M.P., Liverpool.
Edward W. Rayner, Esq., Liverpool.
Thomas Brocklebank, jun., Esq., Liverpool.

Secretaries, G. A. Tinley and Co.

Offices—Exchange Buildings East, Liverpool.

395.—COQUIMBO (Chili).

This company was established in November, 1860, with the immediate object of constructing a railway with single lines (for which a concession with exclusive privilege had been obtained), extending from the port of Coquimbo by two branches; the first branch proceeding in a northerly direction, 8 miles, to the city of Serena, and the smelting works of La Compania, 2 miles beyond—in all 10 miles; the second branch in a southerly direction, penetrating into one of the richest copper mining districts in the world, to the foot of the mountain pass of Las Cardas, with a branch of 2 miles to the port and smelting works of Guayacan—in all 30 miles; total, 40 miles: the idea being to extend the line, should circumstances require, to join the Valparaiso and Santiago Railway, and form part of the Grand Trunk Line of the Republic.

The construction of the 40 miles alluded to was commenced in January, 1861, and opened for traffic August, 1862.

In 1864 the company succeeded in obtaining a concession for an extension of the southern branch to La Higuerita, 15 miles south of Las Cardas, with a branch of 4 miles to Panulcillo. The former was completed October, 1866 (and includes one of the most remarkable mountain ascents), and the latter a year afterwards.

At the general meeting, held at Valparaiso, 5th May, 1868, it was resolved to extend the line from Higuerita, south, to the town of Ovalle, 16 miles. The first section, about 8 miles, to Angostura, was opened October, 1870, but various causes prevented the completion to the terminus, Rio Grande, which was only finished July, 1873.

The whole cost of the line has been....................................$3,635,657
Less amount transferred from revenue account .... 221,678*=$3,413,979

In 1882 it was resolved to extend the line from Guamalata to Puntilla (about 1½ mile), and this new section was opened for general traffic in 1883.‡

Gauge of line, 5 feet 6 inches.

The capital, consisting of ordinary shares, $100 each, $2,747,500; and $780,000 debenture bonds, bearing 8 per cent. interest, payable half-yearly, redeemable by a sinking fund of 2 per cent. per annum, out of which $201,000 have been redeemed.

The dividends declared since the opening of the line have been as follow:—To 31st December, 1862, at the rate of 5 per cent. per annum; 1863, 6; 1864, 8; 1865, 7½; 1866, 8¼; 1867, 8¾; 1868, 7¾; 1869, 5¼; 1870, 5¾; 1871, 2; 1872, 1½; 1873, nil*; 1874, nil*; 1875, 3½; 1876, 4; 1877, 2; 1878, 2½; 1879, 3; 1880, 2½†; 1881, 1½†; 1882, 4¾†; 1883, 5; first half of 1884 at the rate of 3½ per cent.

The traffics are published monthly, and appear in the Liverpool Share List.

Transfer form, special; bonds and shares transferable by endorsement; no fee; certificates are required to accompany transfers; transfer communications to be addressed to the secretaries, as below.

---

* The revenue of these years was not divided, but allowed to accumulate, and in 1874 $221,678 was transferred to capital account towards reduction of cost of the line, and $150,000 was appropriated towards a reserve fund.

† During these years 1880, 1881, and first half of 1882) a total sum of $127,528 was paid out of revenue for repairs to the line, in consequence of damage sustained by floods in 1880. These repairs are now completed.

‡ To meet the estimated cost of this extension, new station, &c., the sum of $45,000 was drawn from the reserve fund, reducing that fund from $150,000 to $105,000.

DIRECTORS IN VALPARAISO:

Augustin R. Edwards, Esq.
J. A. Valdez Munizaga, Esq.
Thomas G. Mc.Laughlin, Esq.
José Macandrew, Esq.
Jorge Edwards, Esq.
M. L. Keogh, Esq.

OFFICERS.—Secs., Sothers and Co.; Supt. and Eng., Enrique A. Vivian; Inspectors, R. A. Claude and D. Thomas—all of Valparaiso.

LIVERPOOL LOCAL BOARD:

David Duncan, Esq.
Francis Thornely, Esq., Liverpool.
Edward W. Rayner, Esq., Liverpool.
James Rose, Esq.

Secretaries, G. A. Tinley and Co.

Offices—Exchange Buildings East, Liverpool.

396.—DEMERARA.

Incorporated in 1845, for the purpose of constructing lines in the colony of Demerara, including one from Georgetown to Mahaica. Length, 20 miles. Capital, 280,000*l*., viz:—115,000*l*. 7 per cent. preference, and 165,000*l*. ordinary stock.

REVENUE.—The net earnings for the half-years ended 31st December, 1883, and 30th June, 1884, after payment of all fixed charges and the preference dividend, enabled the directors to announce dividends on the ordinary stock at 6 per cent. per annum. To December, 1882, and June, 1883, the dividends were 6 and 7 per cent. per annum.

CAPITAL.—*Received:* Ordinary stock, 165,000*l*.; 7 per cent. perpetual preference stock, 115,000*l*.; total, 280,000*l*. Expended on construction, 275,000*l*.

Transfer form, ordinary; fee 2*s*. 6*d*. per deed; several classes may be transferred on one deed, with one stamp for the whole; certificates are required to accompany transfers; not less than 5*l*. of stock is transferable; in documents sent to joint holders the signature of the first name on the register only is required. Transfer communications must be addressed to the secretary as below.

The meetings are held in London in April and October. Dividends payable half-yearly, 30th April and 31st October.

DIRECTORS:

Chairman—Sir GEORGE H. CHAMBERS, Knt., 4, Mincing Lane, E.C.
Deputy-Chairman—GEORGE H. LOXDALE, Esq., Liverpool.

Quintin Hogg, Esq., 23, Rood Lane, E.C.
John McConnell, Esq., 9, Gracechurch Street, E.C.
Sir Thomas Edwards-Moss, Bart., Otterspool, near Liverpool.

DIRECTORS IN DEMERARA:

John J. Dare, Esq.
Mewburn Garnett, Esq.
Fredk. A. Mason, Esq., Manager.
Augustus J. Pitman, Esq.
William Henry Sherlock, Esq.

OFFICERS.—Sec., V. Perronet Sells; Auditors, Samuel S. Bankart and Richard C. Coles.

London Offices—4, Mincing Lane, E.C.

397.—EAST ARGENTINE.

Incorporated with limited liability, and since constituted a *Sociédad Anonima*, in accordance with the Argentine law, for the purpose of constructing a railway from the city of Concordia, in the province of Entre Rios, to Monte Caseros, in the province of Corrientes. Length, 96 miles. The line was opened from Concordia to Federacion (34 miles) on the 29th March, 1874, and from Federacion to Monte Caseros (62 miles) on the 20th April, 1875.

The capital consists of 668,000*l*. of fully paid up 20*l*. shares, and 317,000*l*. 6 per cent. debenture stock, replacing the old 7 and 8 per cent. debentures for a like total, which matured and were paid off 1st June, 1884 - together 985,000*l*., upon 960,000*l*. of which sum the Government of the Argentine Republic guarantees for 40 years, from the date of opening of each section of the line, a net revenue of 7 per cent. per annum (less profit on working, if any) in sterling on a sum of 10,000*l*. per mile, which, on the 96 miles of railway, amounts to 67,200*l*. per annum, the railway and all its appurtenances remaining the property of the company in perpetuity. The railway is exempt from all duties and taxes during the term of the guarantee. Payments by the Government, under the guarantee, to be refunded out of surplus profits above 7 per cent., but without interest.

In June, 1878, an extension line from Monte Caseros to the Ceibo Creek (about 3 miles), and also the purchase of a steamer to ply between the Ceibo Creek and the Brazilian Port of Uraguayana, was authorised, the directors being empowered to retain the necessary amount for these works (about 20,000*l.*) out of the Government guaranteed interest before payment of a dividend to the shareholders. A great improvement in the traffic has resulted from this extension, which is now open for traffic, and the steamer has been running since 23rd November, 1880.

REVENUE.—Gross receipts for the years ended 31st December respectively:—

	1883.	1882.
Receipts	£40,205	£40,864
Less, working expenses	31,705	31,001
Profit	£8,500	£9,863

The accounts with the Government have been adjusted to 31st December, 1883, and when the treasury bills received in payment of this guarantee mature a further dividend may be expected.

CAPITAL.—The expenditure on this account to 31st December, 1883, amounted to 986,681*l.*, whilst the receipts to the same date were 985,000*l.*, viz., by ordinary 20*l.* shares 668,000*l.*, and 317,000*l.* 6 per cent. debenture stock.

The accounts are now made up to 31st December in each year, and presented at the annual meeting in the following June. The interest on the 6 per cent. debenture stock is payable on the 1st June and 1st December in each year. Transfers made on common forms, both for shares and debenture stocks; fee, 2*s.* 6*d.* per deed.

DIRECTORS:

Chairman—LAWRENCE J. BAKER, Esq., 3, Copthall Court, E.C.

John Bramley-Moore, Esq., Gerrard's Cross, Bucks.

Robert Wilfred Graham, Esq., Oriental Club, Hanover Square, W.

Wilson Noble, Esq., 1, Queensberry Place, S.W.

RESIDENT DIRECTOR IN BUENOS AYRES:

William Thompson, Esq.

General Manager—Oliver Budge, Concordia.

OFFICERS.—Sec., H. B. Templer Powell; Registrar, W. H. Ollivier; Auditors, John G. Griffiths, 4, Lothbury, E.C., and William Cash, 90, Cannon Street, E.C.; Solicitors, Bircham, Dalrymple, Drake, and Co., 26, Austin Friars, E.C.; Bankers, Glyn, Mills, Currie, and Co., 67, Lombard Street, E.C.

Offices—43, Lothbury, E.C.

398.—GREAT WESTERN OF BRAZIL LIMITED.

Incorporated in 1872, with limited liability in Great Britain, under "The Companies' Acts, 1862 and 1867," and in Brazil by Imperial Decree, No. 5,295, for constructing a railway from the seaport of Pernambuco (Recife) to Limoeiro, with a branch line to Nazareth, in the province of Pernambuco, in the empire of Brazil.

The Brazilian Government have granted a concession for 90 years, and interest at 7 per cent. per annum, payable half-yearly in London, free of all Brazilian taxes, accruing from the date of payment of the respective calls, is guaranteed to the company for 30 years by the Imperial Government, on a kilometric expenditure amounting to a maximum of 562,500*l.*

The Imperial Government have a right to half the surplus profits above 8 per cent., until reimbursed the full amount of interest paid by it under the guarantee, after which the company will be entitled to all profits.

The Government have also the right to purchase the railway on equitable terms defined by the decrees, after the expiration of 30 years.

The railway is now opened throughout.

CAPITAL—30th June, 1884:—

6 per cent. debenture stock	£306,250	
per cent. preference shares of 20*l.* each	300,000	=£606,250

The amount expended on the line to the same date was 585,149*l.*

The interest on the debenture stock is payable half-yearly, on 1st February and 1st August, and on the shares on the 30th April and 31st October, the transfer books of the preference stock closing about 10 days previously each half-year respectively.

In the event of the Brazilian Government exercising their right at the expiration of the first 30 years to purchase the line, this debenture stock will be redeemed at par, otherwise this stock is irredeemable.

TRANSFER DEPARTMENT.—Ordinary form; no fee; several classes of stock can be transferred on one deed, with one stamp for the whole; certificates must accompany transfers; whole shares and sums of 1*l.* are transferable; in acceptances, renunciations, &c., of allotments of new stock, proxies, or other forms sent to trustees and other joint holders, the signature of first-named in joint accounts required.

DIRECTORS:

Chairman—FRANK PARISH, Esq., 5, Gloucester Square, Hyde Park, W.

Major-General James Pattle Beadle, R.E., 6, Queen's Gate Gardens, W.
How Dalrymple Hamilton Fergusson, Esq., 35, Elm Park Gardens, S.W.
William Cotesworth, Esq., Abbotsworthy House, Kingsworthy, Winchester.
Alfred Phillips Youle, Esq., Olinda, Croydon.
Edward Keir Hett, Esq., Mottisfont, Eltham, Kent.

OFFICERS.—Sec., Frederick Wood; Resident Engineer in Pernambuco, Ailsa Janson, M.Inst.C.E.; Consulting Eng., Charles Neate, M.Inst.C.E., 4, Victoria Street, Westminster, S.W.; Auditors, George Alfred Hillier, Gresham House, E.C., and Henry Dever, F.C.A., 4, Lothbury, E.C.; Solicitor, C. Burt, 26, Austin Friars, E.C.; Bankers, Union Bank of London, Prince's Street, Mansion House, E.C.

Offices—6, Great Winchester Street, E.C.

399.—LIMA.

Incorporated under "The Companies' Act, 1862," for the purpose of acquiring two lines of railway in Peru: the first from Lima to Callao (8½ miles), the second from Lima to Chorrillos (9 miles). Capital, 800,000*l.* in 20*l.* shares. The Lima and Callao Line is held under a concession from the Government of Peru of 99 years, with the exclusive privilege of the transport of goods, passengers, &c., for 25 years, expiring April, 1876. The Lima and Chorrillos Line is held under a concession and grant from the Government, in perpetuity, with the exclusive privilege of the transport of passengers, goods, &c., for 20 years, expiring November, 1878.

REVENUE.—During the year 1884 it was reported as follows, viz.:—The report for 1883 shows that the passenger traffic has increased by 212,000. The actual net profit on the year's working is 9,769*l.*, against 5,877*l.* in 1882. This proved sufficient to cover all charges, to pay 1 per cent. on the paid up capital, and allow 2,500*l.* to be applied to the redemption of debentures. The traffic for the first three months of this year, it is stated, shows an increase of 6,000*l.*, whilst the returns to the end of October show an aggregate increase of 17,248*l.* With the rebuilding of Chorrillos, Miraflores, Barranco, and other towns, a considerable influx of traffic is expected. Some disappointment has been felt at the increase in expenditure, but this has solely arisen from the increased rate of wages prevalent in the country since the cessation of hostilities.

CAPITAL.—The expenditure on this account to 31st December, 1883, amounted to 846,340*l.*, and the receipts to 846,331*l.*, including 800,000*l.* in 40,000 shares of 20*l.* each, fully paid, and 30,000*l.* by debentures.

Annual meeting held about May or June.

DIRECTORS:

Chairman—DAVID SYKES, Esq., J.P.

James Hainsworth, Esq., 57, Moorgate Street, E.C.
E. Wickstead Lane, Esq., M.A., M.D.
Lawrence Heyworth, Esq., Wain Vawr, Newport.
Telford Macneill, Esq., C.E.

OFFICERS.—Sec., George T. Curtis; Auditors, Cash and Stone; Solicitor Frederick Heritage, 28, Nicholas Lane, E.C.; Bankers, The Consolidated Bank Threadneedle Street, E.C.

Offices—1, Great Winchester Street, E.C.

400.—MEXICAN.

Incorporated under the limited liability acts, for the purpose of acquiring the concession for a railway from the city of Mexico to the seaport of Vera Cruz (263½ miles), with a branch to Puebla (29¾ miles). Capital, 2,700,000*l.* in 20*l.* shares; borrowing powers, 2,700,000*l.* Of the share capital, 700,000*l.* was allotted to the vendors as fully paid up; 800,000*l.* was subscribed by the Government of Mexico, who have paid thereon 726,620*l.*; and of the remaining 1,200,000*l.* there has been issued 828,100*l.*, all paid up. The section from Mexico to Puebla was opened for traffic on the 16th September, 1869, and the main line was completed and open for traffic on the 23rd January, 1873. The total mileage in operation to 30th June, 1882, was 293 miles of main line and 15 miles of sidings.

Under an agreement with the Government of Mexico, dated 15th March, 1873, and subsequently sanctioned by the shareholders, and ratified by the Mexican Congress, the company obtained a concession for the construction of a loop line (denominated the "Jalapa Section") from Vera Cruz, *viâ* Jalapa, to San Marcos, a station on the main line, 150¼ miles from Vera Cruz. Instead, however, of starting from Vera Cruz, it was subsequently decided that the line should start from Tejeria, a station about 9 miles from Vera Cruz. Article 13 of the agreement authorises the company to raise debenture capital for the amount of its unissued and forfeited shares, and Articles 14 and 18 further sums of 662,169*l.* and 450,000*l.* respectively. The total length of the Jalapa Loop Line is about 146 miles. The section from Vera Cruz to the city of Jalapa, 70¾ miles, was opened throughout on 17th June, 1875. The remainder is not yet under construction. The company was also empowered to construct a pier at Vera Cruz, and provide lighters, &c. which it has since done, and the Government of Mexico has ordered that the pier shall be open for goods for export and for some classes of imported goods.

CONVERSION OF THE BONDED DEBT, &c.—At an extraordinary meeting, held on the 16th December, 1879, the following resolutions were passed, and confirmed at a second extraordinary general meeting held on the 31st of same month, viz.:—

"1. That the directors be authorised to issue perpetual debenture stock bearing interest at 6 per cent., and constituting a first charge on the undertaking, to an amount sufficient to pay off all outstanding bonds of the company, the stock to be issued or the proceeds thereof to be applied by the directors in the redemption of the bonds by exchange or payment off as may be found necessary, and that the directors be further authorised to apply to the purchase in the market of the said perpetual debenture stock, for the purpose of cancelling the same, such sums as may from time to time be received on account of the Government subvention, this application of sums so received being, however, subject to the appropriation by the company in general meeting of any part of such sums to the improvement of the undertaking and the development of the traffic of the railway, by the fulfilment of any object contemplated by the company's memorandum of association.

"2. That, in issuing the perpetual debenture stock mentioned in the foregoing resolution, the directors be authorised to make such provision as they may think fit for the registration or inscription of the said debenture stock, and for the delivery of certificates thereof, and for the transfer or assignment of debenture stock, and for the issue of debenture stock warrants to bearer transferable by delivery, and for the issue from time to time of interest coupons attached to such warrants or otherwise, and for the conversion of warrants to bearer into inscribed or registered debenture stock, and of inscribed or registered debenture stock into warrants to bearer, and generally as to the form and incidents of all documents relating to the said debenture stock, but so that no such provision shall be inconsistent with the last foregoing resolution."

At the time these resolutions were passed the capital of the company, including all outstanding bonds, was stated to be as follows:—

1st preference shares		£2,554,100
2nd do. do.		1,011,960
Ordinary do.		2,254,720
Total shares		£5,820,780
Outstanding of the four issues of bonds:—		
Class "A"	£370,000	
Class "B"	979,100	
Class "C," 1874	237,200	
*Class "D," 1879	400,000 =	1,986,300
Total capital		£7,807,080

The total annual amount required for the interest and redemption of the bonds of these several issues amounted to 219,776*l.* The directors had the power of at any

* These bonds were issued early in 1879 to pay-off certain secured creditors and a small sum due to contractors, and to terminate an arrangement by which rolling stock was temporarily furnished to the company on terms of repayment by instalments. The price of issue was 86*l.* per cent. The loan was specially secured by a mortgage on the Mexican Railway from Vera Cruz to Mexico and Puebla, subject to the mortgages already existing for the "A," "B," and the 1874 ("C") bonds. The bonds bore interest from 15th May, 1879, payable in London half-yearly on 15th May and 15th November in each year, and were redeemable at par by means of a cumulative sinking fund of 4 per cent. per annum, to be applied in yearly drawings on the 1st May in each year, commencing on 1st May, 1880. The drawn bonds to be paid on the 15th May succeeding each drawing.

time paying off the bonds of all the above issues, by giving three months' notice by advertisement. It was also stated that if the conversions under the resolutions were successfully carried out the annual charges to which the net receipts are now subject would be reduced from about 220,000*l*. to about 120,000*l*. Subsequently 2,000,000*l*. 6 per cent. perpetual debenture stock was issued, to be applied in paying off the outstanding bonds of the company mentioned above. The new stock is "specially secured by a first mortgage on the Mexican Railway from Vera Cruz to Mexico and Puebla, bearing interest from 1st April, 1880, payable in London half-yearly on 1st January and 1st July."

The prospectus gave the following further particulars, viz.:—"Scrip certificates to bearer will be issued as soon as possible against allotment letters and bankers' receipts. When paid up in full, the scrip certificates will be exchanged for registered perpetual debenture stock. Transfers of stock must be in sums of not less than 10*l*. or multiples thereof. The holders of the existing bonds who desire to convert the same will secure the allotment of an equal amount of the present issue by depositing their bonds at the offices of the company before the closing of the subscription list, together with an application on the accompanying form marked 'B.' No cash payment will be required with the bonds so deposited. The coupons on the 'A' bonds, due 1st February, will be retained by the holders for payment in due course, but with this exception, all bonds deposited must have the unmatured coupons attached to them. Depositors of bonds will receive a receipt for the same entitling them to an equivalent amount of paid-up scrip; also, as soon as practicable, a separate certificate for the accruing interest, which will become due on the said bonds at the date which may be fixed for paying them off. After the allotment is completed, or earlier if possible, the directors will exercise their right of giving three months' notice by advertisement to pay off all the outstanding bonds which have not been deposited for conversion; but no allotment will be made, and the cash deposit, as well as the deposited bonds, will be returned, should the present issue not be fully subscribed and allotted."

The following formal notice was given by the directors in the latter part of January, 1880, viz.:—"The principal sums secured by

Class "A" mortgage	7 per cent. mortgage 1874 ("C")
Class "B" do. 1871	8 per cent. do. 1879

will be paid by the company to the respective holders on presentment and against delivery of the said bonds with all undue coupons, at the offices of the company, No. 45, New Broad Street, in the City of London, on the 22nd day of April, 1880, after which day the said bonds will not carry interest. If all undue coupons are not given up with any bond, the amount of such coupons not given up will be deducted from the principal."

Revenue.—The net earnings for the half-years ended 31st December, 1883, and 30th June, 1884, after satisfying all prior charges, including dividends on debenture and preference stocks, sufficed for payments of dividends on the ordinary stock at the rate of 2 per cent. (equal 4 per cent. per annum) and 10 per cent (equal 1 per cent. per annum) each half-year respectively, payable 17th June and 15th December. These dividends compare with 14 and 8 per cent. per annum respectively for the half-years ended 31st December, 1882, and 30th June, 1883.

In operation, main line, 293 miles; Jalapa Line, 70¾ miles. Total, 363¾ miles. Sidings, 15 miles.

Capital—30th June, 1884.—*Authorised:* Shares, 5,820,780*l*.; perpetual debenture stock, 2,000,000*l*.; 2nd mortgage debenture stock, 266,500*l*.; total, 8,087,280*l*., all created. *Receipts:*—

Shares (see below)	£5,820,780
Debenture stock (see below)	2,000,000
Second mortgage debenture stock (see below)	266,500
Subvention separate account	298,530
	£8,385,810
Amount expended	8,093,423
Balance	£292,387

In 1880 the Government of Mexico paid 108,673*l*. on account of the 112,000*l*. due for subvention, and in 1881 a portion of the arrears of subvention was paid off. On subvention receipts about one-half only are the absolute property of the company.

PRIORITIES, DESCRIPTIONS, &c., of the Stocks of the company, existing on the 30th September, 1884.

No.	Full Description (to be observed in Transfer Deeds and all other Legal Documents).	Rate ℔ cent ℔ annum.
1	6 per cent. perpetual debenture stock	6
2	2nd mortgage debenture stock	6
3	1st preference 8 per cent. share capital stock	8
4	2nd preference 6 per cent. share capital stock	6
5	Ordinary share capital stock	...

Notes.—The company's stocks rank for dividend in order of priority, as above.

The debenture stock dividend is accumulative, and payable half-yearly on the 1st January and 1st July; the dividends upon both classes of preference stock, and upon the ordinary stock, are contingent upon the profits of each separate half-year.

TRANSFER DEPARTMENT QUERIES AND REPLIES.

Queries.	Replies.
Transfer form—ordinary or special?	Ordinary.
Fee per deed?	2*s.* 6*d.*
Ditto if more sellers than one?	2*s.* 6*d.* each seller.
May several classes of stock be transferred on one deed?	All; *share capital* stocks can be transferred on one deed, provided the stamp is sufficient to properly cover the *consideration* money on which the duty is charged.*
Are certificates required to accompany transfers?	Yes, unless deeds are already certified.
What amounts of stock are transferable?	10*l.* or multiples of 10*l.*
To what officer should transfer communications be sent?	The Registrar, Z. Parker, Esq.

DIRECTORS:

Chairman—THOMAS COLLETT SANDARS, Esq., 46, Cleveland Square, Hyde Park, W.

Henry Hucks Gibbs, Esq., 15, Bishopsgate Street Within, E.C.
Joseph H. Gibbs, Esq., 39, Lombard Street, E.C.
Henry Göschen, Esq., 12, Austin Friars, E.C.
William Newbold, Esq., 7, Broadwater Down, Tunbridge Wells.
George William Campbell, Esq., 3, White Lion Court, Cornhill, E.C.
William Barron, Esq., Mexico.
Thomas Braniff, Esq., Mexico.
Señor Don Felix Cuevas, Mexico.

APPOINTED BY THE MEXICAN GOVERNMENT.

TO ACT IN MEXICO:

Señor Don Justo Benitez.
Señor Don Casimiro Pacheco.

TO ACT IN LONDON:

Señor Don Juan N. Adorno.
Señor Don Ygnacio de Ybarrondo, 74, Oxford Gardens, Notting Hill, W.

OFFICERS.—Sec., W. W. Ritchie; Gen. Traffic Man. in Mexico, Edward W. Jackson; Con. Eng. in England, A. M. Rendel, M.Inst.C.E., 8, Great George Street, Westminster, S.W; Chief Eng. in Mexico, George Foot; Auditors, S. H. Adams, Torrington Square, W.C., George Woolcott, 78, Palace Gardens Terrace, Kensington, W., and Edward Penney, Mexico; Solicitors, Freshfields and Williams, 5, Bank Buildings, E.C.; Bankers, Glyn, Mills, Currie, and Co., 67, Lombard Street, E.C.

Offices—45, New Broad Street, E.C., and Buena Vista Station, Mexico.

401.—MEXICAN CENTRAL.

The following is copied from the report of President Nickerson, dated 7th April, 1884, for the year 1883:—"Two hundred and ninety-six kilometers of track have been constructed on the main line, southern division, during the year. Six hundred kilometers of track have been constructed on the main line, Chihuahua division, during the year. The board have considered it expedient to concentrate our force upon the main line during the past year, and only moderate progress has been

* For *debenture* stock the stamp is 2*s.* 6*d.* per cent. on the nominal amount transferred; it is, therefore, to be transferred by itself, and not classed with any other stock.

made on the Tampico division. Forty-two kilometers of track have been laid, and about 93 kilometers of grading completed. The iron bridge over the Tamesi River, consisting of two fixed spans of 150 feet, and a draw span of 200 feet, has been completed. Superintendent Whorf writes he expects to resume track-laying this month (April). Work on the Pacific division has been greatly delayed by the fatal sickness which prevailed here from June to January 1, 1884, and which, at one time, reduced our force at San Blas to Superintendent Payne and two men. Twenty-five kilometers of grading have been completed, and 1½ kilometer of track finished at the end of the year. That 400 kilometers in the aggregate of all the lines must be completed by 12th April, 1893. As more than 800 kilometers have been built since 13th April, 1883, no further construction is required by our contracts with the National Government until after 12th April, 1887, except upon the Pacific Line, as above stated."

The following is a summarised statement of the earnings and expenses for the year 1883:—

Earnings.

Southern Division:	
Passenger	$567 669
Freight	992,062
Baggage	16,061
Express	27,765
Telegraph	1,744
Miscellaneous	22.828
Total commercial earnings	$1,628,129
Company's material	424,712
Total earnings Southern Division	$2,052,841
Northern Division:	
Passenger	$146,081
Freight	148,846
Baggage	4,503
Express	20,976
Telegraph	7,555
Miscellaneous	3,177
Total commercial earnings	$331,138
Company's material	1,199,436
Total earnings Northern Division	$1,530,574
Total gross earnings, 1883	$3,583,415
Operating Expenses.	
Southern Division	$1,207,085
Northern Division	780,963
Total operating expenses	$1,988,048
Net earnings	$1,595,367

Equivalent in United States currency to $1,416,904.

General Manager, D. B. Robinson.

402.—MINAS CENTRAL OF BRAZIL LIMITED.

This company was constituted on the 25th day of April, 1883, for the purpose of acquiring concessions, rights and subventions, granted in respect of a railway from the most convenient point of the Dom Pedro Segundo State Railway to the city of Pitanguy, thus carrying out an important object of the Imperial Government of Brazil, namely, to create railway communication between Rio de Janeiro, the capital of the empire, and the San Francisco River.

By a decree of the Imperial Government of Brazil, dated the 29th September, 1883, and signed by H.M. the Emperor of Brazil, the statutes of the Minas Central of Brazil were approved, and a further imperial decree, of 6th October, 1883, empowered the company to transact business in the empire, and conceded to the same authority to take certain national lands, without payment, in addition to the advantages already conferred by the concessions of 18th November, 1881; 22nd June, 1882; and 6th October, 1882.

The concessions empowering the construction of the line are respectively dated the 18th November, 1881, the 22nd June, 1882, and the 6th October, 1882. By virtue of the same an annual sum amounting to 6 per cent. in gold on a sum of 1,012,500*l*., or equal to 60,750*l*. in gold, is guaranteed for 30 years; of this guarantee an annual sum of 21,875*l*. will be set aside for the service of interest on the present issue, leaving the company an annual net balance of 38,875*l*. to deal with.

Terms of Concessions.—The Government concede (*inter alia*) the following important privileges:—(*a*) A monopoly for 50 years, during which term no competing railway will be allowed to be constructed within 30 kilometres on either side of the railway. The monopoly will, however, continue in perpetuity, if the company repays to the Government, within one year from the date of the termination of the concession, the amount of interest paid in respect of its guarantee, together with interest thereon at 6 per cent. per annum, together with the amount of any payments made by the Government on account of the company. (*b*) Guarantee of 60,750*l*. per annum in gold for 30 years from the construction of the line (being calculated at the rate of 6 per cent. on $9,000,000) at the fixed rate of exchange of 2*s*. 3*d*. per milreis. (*c*) Guarantee of interest during construction on the amounts expended in each year. (*d*) Powers to create ordinary share capital in excess of the capital of 9,000 contos or 1,012,500*l*.

Share Capital.—732,500*l*., divided into 21,000 ordinary shares of 20*l*. each, and 15,625 7 per cent. preference shares of 20*l*. each. Issue of 210,520*l*. in 10,526 preference shares of 20*l*. each, bearing 7 per cent. interest, payable half yearly in gold in London. These shares, after payment of 7 per cent. dividend on the ordinary shares, will rank equally for further dividend with the ordinary shares. The interest on the preference share capital amounts to 21,875*l*. (or less than 40 per cent. of the said annual Government guarantee), and it forms a charge on the annual payment of 60,750*l*. covered by the above guarantee, which is more than sufficient for the service of interest at the above rate of 7 per cent. per annum on the preference shares, and for the service of the total debenture capital of the company, which is fixed at 600,000*l*.

DIRECTORS:

Chairman—MORGAN LLOYD, Esq., Q.C., M.P., 53, Cornwall Gardens, S.W.

Septimus F. Porter, Esq.
John Bennett, Esq.
Major W. Fletcher Gordon.
James Goodson, Esq., J.P., 32, Kensington Gardens Square, W.
James Doyle, Esq.

OFFICERS.—Sec., Charles Glanvill; Engs., George Manders, Assoc.Inst.C.E., Engineer in Brazil, and William Martineau, M.Inst.C.E., 6, Great Winchester Street Buildings, E.C.; Auditors, Tribe, Clarke, and Co., 2, Moorgate Street Buildings, E.C., and Bristol, Cardiff, and Swansea; Solicitors, Quick and Co., 13, George Street, Mansion House, E.C.; Bankers, Smith, Payne, and Smiths, 1, Lombard Street, E.C.

Offices—11 and 12, Clement's Lane, E.C.

403.—NORTHERN OF BUENOS AYRES.

Incorporated under "The Joint Stock Companies' Acts, 1856 and 1857," for the purpose of constructing a railway from the city of Buenos Ayres to San Fernando. Length, 20 miles. The Provincial Government of Buenos Ayres guaranteed to the company, for 20 years from the opening of the line, a dividend of 7 per cent. per annum on a fixed sum of 150,000*l*., and at the expiration of the said 20 years all obligation on the part of the Government ceased, the railway and its appurtenances remaining the property of the company in perpetuity, free from taxation. The capital of the company consists of 4,500 ordinary shares of 10*l*. each, 5,383 deferred 7 per cent. preference shares of 10*l*. each, and 13,617 guaranteed 7 per cent. preference shares of 10*l*. each; total, 235,000*l*. The borrowing powers amounted to 250,000*l*.

The 79th clause of the Articles of Association provides that—"At the end of each and every year the surplus profits remaining after the payment of the dividends as aforesaid shall be ascertained, and shall be divided into portions of 10*l*. each, and so many preference shares of both classes as shall be equal in number to such portions shall be drawn by lot, and, in respect of each share so drawn, the holder shall receive one portion as a bonus until the whole surplus shall be distributed, and the shares so drawn shall thenceforward cease to be preference shares, and shall thereafter rank as ordinary shares, and as such only shall participate in all subsequent profits."

Revenue.—The net earnings for the year ended 31st December, 1883, sufficed for a dividend at 7 per cent. per annum on the guaranteed preference shares, with 214*l*. carried forward.

CAPITAL.—The expenditure on this account to 31st December, 1883, amounted to 466,709*l.*, the receipts to the same date being as under:—

Guaranteed preference shares	£136,170	
Deferred " "	53,880	
Ordinary shares	45,000=	£235,000
Debenture bonds at 5½, 6, and 7 per cent.	£18,650	
Debenture stock at 5, 6, and 7 per cent	219,370=	238,020
		£473,020

The annual meeting is held in London in the month of May.

DIRECTORS:

Chairman—CHARLES SEALE HAYNE, Esq., 3, Eaton Square, S.W.

Henry D. Browne, Esq., West Lodge, 34, Avenue Road, Regent's Park, N.W.

Simpson Rostron, Esq., Beddington Lane, near Mitcham.

George Nelson Strawbridge, Esq., 11, Blandford Square, N.W.

Frederick Nettlefold, Esq., 54, High Holborn, W.C.

All eligible for re-election.

OFFICERS.—Sec., John Wilson Theobald; Gen. Man. and Eng., Arthur E. Shaw, M.Inst.C.E., Buenos Ayres; Auditors, James Hutt and Francis P. Cockshott; Solicitors, Ashhurst, Morris, and Co., 6, Old Jewry, E.C.; Bankers, The Imperial Bank Limited, Lothbury, E.C., and London and River Plate Bank Limited, Buenos Ayres.

Offices—8, Drapers' Gardens, Throgmorton Avenue, E.C.; and Buenos Ayres, South America.

404.—RECIFE AND SAO FRANCISCO (PERNAMBUCO) LIMITED.

Incorporated under decree of the Emperor of Brazil, and by acts of the Imperial Brazilian Government and Provincial Legislature of Pernambuco, and incorporated in England, under act 7 and 8 Vic., cap. 110. The line of this company extends from the city and port of Pernambuco to the River Una, in the interior. Length, 77¼ miles. The grant of the railway is in perpetuity, with a guaranteed interest of 7 per cent. per annum, on a fixed capital for 90 years, viz., 5 per cent. by the Imperial Government of Brazil, 2 per cent. by the Provincial Government of Pernambuco, and 5 per cent by the Imperial Government on 485,660*l.* additional for 30 years from August, 1870. Capital, 1,200,000*l.* in 20*l.* shares (converted in 1873 into stock), 400,000*l.* advanced by the Government, and 275,000*l.* debentures, at 5 and 5½ per cent. interest (which are being replaced at 4½ per cent. as they mature). Present net income guaranteed to the company is 80,283*l.* per annum.

REVENUE.—The receipts for the half-year ended 31st December, 1883, amounted to 66,644*l.*, and the expenses to 44,502*l.* The amount required from the Government to make up the full guaranteed revenue was 18,000*l.* The available balance of net revenue amounted to 34,007*l.*, and sufficed, after payment of interest and prior charges, for the usual dividend at the rate of 5½ per cent. per annum, leaving a balance of 1,007*l.* to carry forward to next account.

The gross receipts for the half-year ended 30th June, 1884 (including the balance claimed in respect of the Government guarantee), amounted to 88,542*l.*, and the expenses to 48,400*l.* After providing for debenture interest and other special miscellaneous charges, there remained an available balance of 34,398*l.* The usual dividend on the ordinary stock, at the rate of 5½ per cent. per annum, absorbed 33,000*l.*, and left 1,398*l.* to be carried forward.

CAPITAL.—The expenditure on this account to 30th June, 1884, amounted to 1,842,185*l.*, viz.:—Lines open for traffic, 1,787,357*l.*; working stock, 54,828*l.* The receipts to the same date were as under:—

Capital stock		£1,200,000	
Imperial Government		400,000	
Debentures, at 5½ per cent.	£116,020		
" at 5 per cent.	73,660		
" at 4½ per cent.	56,520 =	246,200	
Advance from revenue		16,000=	£1,862,200

The following are officially stated to be the amounts of debentures now running (1st November, 1884) at their respective rates of interest:—

Debentures at 4½ per cent.	£101,970	
" at 5 per cent.	73,060	
" at 5½ per cent.	71,060 =	£246,090

The company's debentures, as they fall due, are to be replaced by others at 4½ per cent. per annum.

TRANSFER DEPARTMENT.—Ordinary form; fee per deed, 2*s.* 6*d.*; if more sellers than one, 2*s.* 6*d.* each seller; certificates must accompany transfers; multiples of 1*l.* can be transferred; in acceptances, renunciations, &c., of allotments of new stock, proxies, or other forms sent to trustees and other joint holders—for proxies one signature is required, other documents, all.

In operation, 77½ miles.

Meetings held in London in April and October.

DIRECTORS:

Chairman—Viscount GORT, 1, Portman Square, W.

Ex-Officio—His Excellency the Baron DE PENEDO, Brazilian Minister, Granville Place, W.

Major-General G. B. Tremenheere, Assoc. Inst.C.E., Spring Grove, Isleworth, W.

W. B. Greenfield, Esq., 35, Gloucester Square, W.

Major-General S. A. Abbott, 2, Petersham Terrace, S.W.

G. O. Mann, Esq., Belfield, St. Leonards-on-Sea.

OFFICERS.—Sec., Underwood P. Harris; Con. Eng., Sir Charles H. Gregory, K.C.M.G., M.Inst.C.E., Delahay Street, S.W.; Auditors, George D. Longstaff, Upper Thames Street, E.C., and Edward Cheshire, 26, Old Broad Street, E.C.; Bankers, Robarts, Lubbock, and Co., 15, Lombard Street, E.C.

Offices—15, Old Jewry Chambers, E.C.

405.--SAN PAULO.

Formed under decree of the Emperor of Brazil and laws of the Imperial Brazilian and San Paulo Provincial Legislatures, and incorporated under "The Joint Stock Companies' Acts, 1856 and 1857," to construct and work a railway from Santos to Jundiahy, in the province of San Paulo. Length, 86½ English miles. Capital, 2,000,000*l.* in 20*l.* shares and 750,000*l.* in debenture stock.

The Imperial Government of Brazil guarantees for 90 years, from 26th April, 1858, an annual interest of 7 per cent. on a fixed sum of 2,650,000*l.* When the net profits exceed 8 per cent., one-half the surplus shall be paid to the Government, the other half remaining the property of the company. When the profits shall have exceeded 12 per cent. per annum for two consecutive years, the tariff rates may be revised by the Government, so as to limit the dividend to 12 per cent. per annum. The Government has the option of purchasing the railway at the end of 30 years from the date of opening of the entire line, on payment to the company of such an amount of Brazilian Government stock as will give an income equal to the average dividends of the previous five years, provided such revenue be not less than 7 per cent. The company may from time to time alter the tariff rates so as to ensure a net profit of 7 per cent. per annum. The grant of the railway is in perpetuity, with a guarantee against competing lines within 20 miles on either side of the railway (with a right to all minerals within the same limits), during the term of 90 years, and the right to import, free of duty, all coke, coal, and other fuel required for the purposes of the railway, for a period of 33 years.

REVENUE.—The net earnings for the half-year ended 30th June, 1884, after payment of all prior charges, sufficed for a dividend upon the ordinary 20*l.* shares at the rate of 5 per cent., making, with interim dividend paid in April previous, 10 per cent. for the year; also a bonus of 1 per cent. or 4*s.* per share, both free of income tax, and after adding 20,000*l.* to the reserve fund, carrying forward a balance of 5,733*l.* The dividends are made payable half-yearly in April and October.

CAPITAL.—The expenditure on this account to 30th June, 1884, amounted to 2,750,000*l.*, the receipts to the same date having been as under:—

Ordinary 20*l.* shares	2,000,000	
Debenture stock at 5½ per cent.	750,000	=£2,750,000

Meetings held in London in April and October, to receive the accounts to 31st December and 30th June respectively.

Scale of Voting.—One vote for five shares, and one additional vote for every additional five shares.

DIRECTORS:

Chairman—MARTIN R. SMITH, Esq., 1, Lombard Street, E.C.

Ex-Officio—His Excellency Baron DE PENEDO, Brazilian Minister, Granville Chambers, Granville Place, W.

J. Harvey Astell, Esq., Woodbury Hall, Sandy, Bedfordshire.

Hon. R. R. Leslie Melville, 75, Lombard Street, E.C.

Frederick Youle, Esq., 4, Montague Street, Russell Square, W.C.

William Bevan, Esq., 12, Bolton Gardens, S.W.

One-third retire in April of each year. All eligible for re-election.

OFFICERS.—Sec., G. A. Hillier; Supt., Wm. Speers; Eng. and Loco. Supt., John Barker; Auditors, Alderman Sir T. Dakin, Knt.. and Edwin H. Galsworthy; Solicitors, Bircham, Dalrymple, Drake, and Co., 46, Parliament Street, S.W., and Gresham House, Old Broad Street, E.C.; Bankers, N. M. Rothschild and Sons, New Court, St. Swithin's Lane, E.C.

Offices—111, Gresham House, Old Broad Street, E.C.

406.—TONGOY.

The company was established in 1865, for formation of railway from the port of Tongoy, in Chili, to Cerrilos (distance, 30 miles), and thence to the copper mines of Tamaya (8½ miles). Total length, 38½ miles. Opened in 1867.

Gauge of line, 3 feet 6 inches.

Capital, $1,100,000, in shares of $500.

Dividend for 1874, 2½ per cent.; 1875, 6 per cent.; 1876, 8½ per cent.; 1877. 5 per cent.; 1878, 1 per cent.; 1879, 4 per cent.; 1880, 2 per cent.; 1881, nil; 1882, nil; 1883, nil.

The net receipts for the first half of 1884 were $23,166. After payment of the usual amount for interest and sinking fund, amount passed for extraordinary renewals, Government tax, &c., and including the debit balance of $861 brought forward from previous half-year, the accounts showed a total debit balance of $11,469.

Special transfer form; shares transferable by endorsement; no fee; certificates required to accompany transfers; all communications to be addressed to the secretaries as below.

The traffics are published quarterly, and appear in the Liverpool Share List.

LOCAL DIRECTORS:

E. Edmondson, Esq. | F. Harrington, Esq. | Jas. Rose, Esq.

Secretaries, G. A. Tinley and Co.

Office—H10, Exchange Buildings, Liverpool.

407.—URUGUAY CENTRAL AND HYGUERITAS.

Incorporated, with limited liability, for the purpose of acquiring from Messrs. Waring Brothers a concession for a line of railway from the Central Uruguay, at Santa Lucia, to Hygueritas. Length, 146 miles. The capital originally consisted of 1,200,000*l*. 7 per cent first mortgage bonds, 300,000*l*. 7 per cent. preference shares, and 300,000*l*. ordinary shares of 20*l*. each. 300,000*l*. of the first mortgage bonds were issued in December, 1873, in bonds to bearer of 100*l*. each, with interest coupons attached, payable on 30th June and 31st December in each year. The bonds to be redeemed by annual drawings, at par, in 40 years, through the operation of a sinking fund. The drawings to take place yearly, on the 1st November, in London, in the presence of the trustees, commencing on the 1st November, 1876, and the bonds so drawn to be paid off on the 31st December following.

The sum required to meet the first two years' interest, during the construction of the works, was placed in the hands of the trustees for the bondholders. The bonds were issued at 85*l*. per cent. With each 100*l*. bond the subscriber received a fully paid-up 20*l*. share, by way of bonus, out of the 300,000*l*. of ordinary share capital, which is entitled to dividend after payment of interest and sinking fund on the bonds, and the interest on the preference shares.

The Government of Uruguay guaranteed to the company, for 40 years from the date of opening of each section of the line, a net revenue of 7 per cent. per annum on a sum of 10,000*l*. per mile, which, on the 146 miles of railway, amounts to 102,200*l*. per annum, the railway and all its appurtenances remaining the property of the company in perpetuity.

The first 20 miles from the Central Uruguay at Juan Chaso to the town of San José was opened on the 20th May, 1876, and is worked by the Central Uruguay at a per centage of the gross receipts, varying according to the traffic carried. This is at present the only productive mileage.

REVENUE.—For the year ended 31st December, 1883, the net profits amounted to 4,554*l*., leaving the Government liable, under their guarantee, for 9,446*l*. The report stated as follows, viz: —

The funds in hand, representing the net profits of the railway to the 31st March, 1884, will admit of a payment of 2*l*. per bond in final settlement of coupon No. 8, and the London and River Plate Bank, 52, Moorgate Street, E.C., have been instructed to pay these amounts on and after the 29th May, 1884. The board regret that they are still unable to deal with the bonds drawn under the operation of the sinking fund.

CAPITAL.—This account, to 31st December, 1883, was as follows:—

Receipts.			*Expenditure.*	
Share capital—			Construction account—	
Preference	£41,100		To 31st December, 1882	£253,052
Ordinary	41,100=	£82,200	Expenditure in Montevideo, 1883	3
Mortgage bonds—				
1644, at 100*l*. each	164,400			
Less 8 drawn, but not yet paid	800=	163,600		
Sinking Fund		800		
Balance expended in excess of capital		6,455		
		£253,055		£253,055

TRUSTEES:

George W. Drabble, Esq., 1, Pembridge Square, W.
Loftus Fitzwygram, Esq., 89, Eccleston Square, S.W.
The Rt. Hon. Lord Henry Charles George Gordon Lennox, M.P., 19, Grosvenor Gardens, S.W.

DIRECTORS:

Granville R. Ryder, Esq., 1, Great George Street, Westminster, S.W.
Alexander Henderson, Esq.
Francis William Slade, Esq., 120, Grosvenor Road, S.W.

OFFICERS.—Sec., Charles O. Barker; Auditor, William Cash, 90, Cannon Street, E.C.; Solicitors, Cope and Co., 4, Victoria Street, Westminster, S.W.; Bankers, Glyn, Mills, Currie, and Co., 67, Lombard Street, E.C.

Offices—7, Finsbury Circus, E.C.

408.—WESTERN OF BUENOS AYRES.

This railway, which extends from the city of Buenos Ayres (the capital of the Argentine Republic), bears the same relation to the western part of the province as the Great Southern does to the southern part, and occupies a well-settled and fertile section of country. It was commenced in 1853, and has been in working operation for more than a quarter of a century, and now connects Buenos Ayres with the important towns of San Nicholas, Junin, Pergamino, La Plata, &c.

The railway and its branches are of uniform gauge, the same as the Great Southern, Central Argentine, &c. It is estimated that the amount expended on the property to the present time amounts to above 3,500,000*l*. sterling.

REVENUE.—It is officially stated that the net receipts show almost continuous yearly increases; the accounts for 1884 were not completed at the time of going to press, but it is estimated that they will show a net return of about 240,000*l*., and that, so soon as the extensions which have been constructed out of the proceeds of the loan of 1882 are fairly developed, the receipts will be further augmented.

The existing charge for interest and sinking fund on the 2,049,180*l*. 6 per cent. debentures, issued in 1882, amounts to 140,000*l*. The net receipts for 1882 amounted to 170,000*l*.

In January, 1885, there were issued 496,000*l*. 5 per cent. sterling mortgage debentures, part of an amount of 10,000,000 national dollars, authorised by law 14th November, 1884, secured by a first mortgage upon the works to be constructed out of the proceeds of this loan, and a second mortgage upon the existing railway, its branches, and rolling stock. Principal repayable 1915, unless previously redeemed by the sinking fund. A sinking fund, not less than 1 per cent. per annum, is directed by the law to be applied half-yearly towards the redemption of the loan by purchases when the price is below par or by drawings at par. Power is reserved at any time to increase the sinking fund. Interest payable in London at the counting-house of Messrs. Morton, Rose, & Co., half-yearly, on the 15th March and 15th September. First coupon for six months' interest payable 15th September, 1885.

TRUSTEES FOR THE DEBENTURE HOLDERS:

Sir John Rose, Bart., G.C.M.G.
Frank Parish, Esq., 5 Gloucester-square, Hyde Park, W.
George W. Drabble, Esq., 1, Pembridge Square, W.

London Agents—Morton, Rose, and Co., Bartholomew Lane, E.C.

409.—WESTERN OF SAN PAULO.

(COMPANHIA PAULISTA DE ESTRADAS DE FERRO DO OESTE.)

Formerly the Companhia Paulista da Estrada de Ferro de Jundiahy a Campinas, Empire of Brasil. Incorporated by imperial decrees; authorised capital, 20,000,000 milreis, at 24*d.* per milreis, 2,000,000*l.*; capital realised, 12,937,000 milreis, at 24*d.* per milreis, 1,293,700*l.*

The line of the Companhia Paulista de Estradas de Ferro do Oeste, which extends from Jundiahy to Descalvado, and branches at Cordeiro towards the River Mogy Guassu, is one of the few important railways in Brazil that have been constructed and successfully worked without the assistance of foreign capital; it runs through the heart of the coffee producing districts of the fertile and flourishing Province of San Paulo—it is of the same gauge throughout as that of the San Paulo Railway Company Limited; and, commencing from the terminus of that company—Jundiahy—it is a virtual extension of it, and its principal feeder; it has, moreover, a through working arrangement with that company to the port of Santos. The present net revenue of the Companhia Paulista considerably exceeds 7 per cent. on the paid-up capital, and there is every prospect of a steady increase of traffic; but, in case it should at any time be necessary, the company has the privilege accorded to it by the Provincial Government to raise the tariff, so as to yield the shareholders a minimum dividend of 7 per cent. on the paid-up capital.

Present extent of line, 151 miles.

In November, 1878, there were issued 150,000*l.* in 1,500 debenture bonds, of 100*l.* each, at par, payable to bearer. Amount subscribed, 139,400*l.* These bonds are redeemable, by annual amortisation, in 1898, and bear interest at 7 per cent. per annum, payable half-yearly by coupons, in London, on the 1st April and 1st October. Both principal and interest constitute, as set forth in the bonds, a first charge on the net revenues of the company, after placing an amount equal to 6-10ths per cent. per annum of the paid-up capital to the reserve fund, which now amounts to 673,579 milreis, at 24*d.* per milreis = 67,358*l.*

REVENUE.—The net revenue for the year ended 31st December, 1883, amounted to 1,620,716 milreis, at 24*d.* per milreis, 162,071*l.* Dividend for the year 1883, 10 per cent.

DIRECTORS:

Dr. Fidencio Nepomuceno Prates, San Paulo.
Colonel José Egydio de Souza Arauha, San Paulo.
Dr. Lins de Vasconcellos.
Dr. Nicholas Queiroz, San Paulo.
Dr. Elias Chaves, San Paulo.

Agents for the purposes of the Loan—The English Bank of Rio de Janeiro Limited, 13, St. Helens Place, E.C.

UNITED STATES.

In consequence of the information relating to the railways of Great Britain (which will not admit of being curtailed) increasing in bulk every year, we are compelled to confine ourselves to insert in this and future editions only that relating to the *leading* American undertakings, such as are brought most prominently before the notice of British investors.

The progress of railroad construction in the United States, from the opening of the Granite Railroad, at Quincy, Massachusetts, in 1827, to 1883, yearly, is shown in the following table:—

Year.	Miles open.	Yearly Increase.	Year.	Miles open.	Yearly Increase.
1827	3	—	1856	19,251	1,853
1828	3	—	1857	22,625	3,374
1829	28	25	1858	25,090	2,465
1830	41	13	1859	26,755	1,665
1831	54	13	1860	28,771	2,016
1832	131	77	1861	30,593	1,822
1833	576	445	1862	31,769	1,176
1834	762	186	1863	32,471	702
1835	918	156	1864	33,860	1,389
1836	1,102	184	1865	34,442	582
1837	1,431	329	1866	35,351	909
1838	1,843	412	1867	36,896	1,545
1839	2,220	477	1868	38,822	1,926
1840	2,797	577	1869	42,272	3,450
1841	3,319	522	1870	48,860	6,588
1842	3,877	558	1871	55,535	6,675
1843	4,174	297	1872	62,647	7,112
1844	4,311	137	1873	69,158	6,511
1845	4,522	211	1874	74,403	5,245
1846	4,870	348	1875	76,206	1,803
1847	5,336	466	1876	77,470	1,264
1848	5,682	346	1877	79,669	2,199
1849	6,350	668	1878	81,776	2,107
1850	7,475	1,125	1879	86,497	4,721
1851	8,589	1,114	1880	93,671	7,174
1852	11,027	2,438	1881	104,813	11,142
1853	13,497	2,470	1882	113,329	8,516
1854	15,672	2,175	1883	121,592	8,263
1855	17,398	1,726			

It will be perceived that, from 1st January, 1856, to 1st January, 1857, the increase in railroad construction was 3,374 miles. This was the largest mileage constructed in any one year up to date. The financial difficulties of 1857-58 suddenly arrested the extravagant expenditures in this special direction. In the 10 years ending 1st January, 1858, there were built 19,418 miles; in the 10 years succeeding that date only 13,732 miles. In the 10 years closing with 1st January, 1875, there were built about 40,000 miles. The great acceleration in construction during this period was the result of the redundant currency issued for war purposes, which found an outlet in the demand for railroads. In this period the great Pacific railroads were mainly constructed, and a large number of other roads were carried into the far interior. In the meantime, the older trunk roads were materially rebuilt and double tracked,

and the rolling stock adequately enlarged. The internal commerce of the country quadrupled, immigration filled up the great interior, and production increased at a rapid rate. No country in the world was apparently more prosperous and wealthy than the United States up to the harvest of 1873. In September of that year the great money panic ensued, and from the same cause as that which overwhelmed the business of the country in 1857—the expenditure of too much money in a single direction. The result was identical—railroad construction ceased, and thousands of men were turned away from their occupation and means of living. In the 10 years antecedent, the average of construction was about 4,100 miles a year, and in one year (1871) 7,379 miles were built. In 1874-5, after the panic of 1873, only 3,817 miles were built; in 1876, 2,712 miles; and in 1877, 2,281 miles. In 1878 the mileage opened was as great as any since 1873, and in 1879 the large figure of 4,721 miles was reached, nearly 20 per cent. of the total mileage being narrow gauge. The greatest amount of track-laying was done in Kansas, where 500 miles of new roads were laid. Minnesota follows with 394, Iowa with 371, Young Dakota with 220, and Old Ohio with 213¼ miles respectively. The 7,174 miles of new track laid during the year 1880 were connected with about 235 different lines; Dakota leads the country with 680 miles; Texas, 659 miles; Ohio, 525 miles; New Mexico, 519 miles; Iowa, 445 miles; Colorado, 401 miles; Nebraska, 385 miles; and Illinois and Kansas over 240 miles each. It will be seen that the mileage constructed in 1881 was greater than for any previous year. For 1880 and 1881 the average mileage constructed was 7,699, against an average for the previous eight years of 3,342 miles per annum. The average mileage in operation for the year 1882 was stated to be 107,158, whilst that for 1883 amounted to 110,414.

410.—ATCHISON, TOPEKA, AND SANTA FÉ.

(MEXICAN CENTRAL, ATLANTIC AND PACIFIC RAILWAYS, &C., AUXILIARY LINES.)

Thirteen years ago the Atchison, Topeka, and Santa Fé consisted of 50 miles of road, viz., between Atchison and Topeka, in the State of Kansas; to-day that company own and operate 2,705 miles of line, distributed continuously (with branches) through the following states, territories, and foreign countries:—In Kansas, 1,441; Missouri, 20; Colorado, 282; New Mexico, 589; Texas, 20; Arizona, 88; and Mexico, 265 miles.

The share capital and bonds (4 and 6 per cent.) of this company (Atchison, Topeka, and Santa Fé proper, without auxiliary or connecting lines), are as follow:—Ordinary shares, 11,382,650*l.*; bonded debt, 5,177,400*l.*; total, 16,560,050*l.* Six per cent. dividend has for some years past been declared on the ordinary shares, which, however, are not allowed to be dealt in on either the New York or London Stock Exchanges, being chiefly held by a number of small investors in the New England States.

The following is a brief description of this railway:—

The main line, Kansas City to Albuquerque and Deming, is of steel, and the bridges of iron or stone. With the Southern Pacific it is joint owner of the Atlantic and Pacific from Albuquerque, New Mexico, to Mojave, California, and with running powers to San Francisco.

The Atchison, Topeka, and Santa Fé offers the shortest and cheapest connection to the 1,200 miles of mountain narrow gauge—Denver and Rio Grande—a very picturesque route to Salt Lake City and Ogden.

The Mexican Central, to the City of Mexico, over 1,200 miles, is practically an Atchison, Topeka, and Santa Fé Southern Extension, from El Paso, and it is chiefly owned by Atchison, Topeka, and Santa Fé shareholders, but the Atchison, Topeka, and Santa Fé have not assumed any obligations on the part either of the Mexican Central or of the Denver and Rio Grande. The company has no floating debt, and never paid any dividend until it completed its construction.

From its nearest point on the Pacific Ocean, Guaymas, on the Gulf of California, it runs its own steamers up and down the Pacific coast. Its line to San Francisco is 33 miles longer from New York than that of the Union and Central Pacific, but as it runs south of the Rocky Mountains, and thus avoids snow, it makes schedule time same as Union Pacific through line, and in all weathers.

DIRECTORS:

President—WILLIAM B. STRONG.

Vice-President—A. E. TOUZALIN.

J. T. Burr.	C. J. Paine.
R. P. Cheyney.	C. W. Pierce.
C. K. Holliday.	L. Severy.
S. A. Kent.	A. Speare.
T. Nickerson.	General Stringfellow.
A. W. Nickerson.	

OFFICERS.—Gen. Man., A. A. Robinson; Traff. Man., J. F. Goddard; Chief Supt. Pass. Dept., W. F. White; Land Commissioner, Colonel Johnson.

English Financial Agents—Baring Brothers and Co.

Agent for the United Kingdom—S. N. Townshend, Esq., J.P., F.R.G.S.

Offices—Topeka, Kansas; 95, Milk Street, Boston, U.S.; and 62, Holborn Viaduct, London, E.C.

411.—ATLANTIC FIRST LEASED LINES RENTAL TRUST LIMITED.

This company was registered on the 12th January, 1880, to take over the existing securities of the Leased Lines (1872) Trust, which were issued in that year to the amount of $3,800,000 in bonds of $1,000 (or 200*l.*) each. Interest at 7 per cent. per annum, payable 1st January and 1st July in New York, in gold, and in London in sterling at 4*s.* per dollar. Principal re-payable by 1908. This issue was part of an authorised total of $5,500,000, wherewith it was intended to acquire the Cleveland and Mahoning, the Niles and New Lisbon, and the Liberty and Vienna railways. The coupons were regularly and fully paid until January, 1875, but only at intervals since that period, the last payment made in January, 1878, completed the partly paid coupon of January, 1876. The management of these lines is vested in the New York, Pennsylvania, and Ohio, who pay a monthly rental to the directors of the Cleveland and Mahoning Valley, equal to a distribution of 3½ per cent. on these bonds.

The following particulars are extracted from the reorganisation scheme, viz.:—The business of the company to be especially limited to the receipt and division of dividends received on the share capital of the Cleveland and Mahoning Valley, the directors of the company having to elect and guide the policy of the board of the Cleveland and Mahoning Valley; also arrange for the new lease, and see from time to time that such lease is properly carried out and adhered to. They also have to investigate and check the accounts of the said company. The $1,000 bonds of the Old Trust to be exchanged for 150*l.* debentures bearing a fixed rate of interest at 4 per cent.; and 150*l.* of the capital stock of the company, thus dividing as dividend on the stock all the surplus receipts over and above the 32,220*l.* required for the interest on the debentures. Every holder of a $1,000 (200*l.*) bond therefore received for each bond paid-up 4 per cent. debentures for 150*l.*, and paid-up shares or stock for 150*l.*, which may be dealt with separately. The interest on the debentures to be absolutely secured, and will be payable on the 31st January and 31st July each half-year. The share capital of the company to be 805,500*l.*, three-fourths the amount of the existing bonds, and to be converted into stock as issued.

Debenture debt	£805,500
Share capital	805,500
	£1,611,000*

or 50 per cent. in addition to the present amount of bonds.

The new debentures have been issued in bonds to bearer of 50*l.* and 100*l.* each the ordinary stock is transferable in amounts of 5*l.* and upwards.

For one purpose only, power will be reserved to raise further capital (with the consent of a general meeting) not exceeding 250,000*l.* in all, viz., to redeem or

*At the present time the amount of capital actually issued is as follows:—Debentures, 805,200*l.* stock, 805 200*l.*

purchase, from time to time, the mortgage debt of the Cleveland and Mahoning, which bears the heavy rate of 7 per cent. interest, and which, therefore, if redeemed by money raised at 4 or even 5 per cent., would leave great profit to the company, to be felt in the shape of increased dividends. Under the form of the late trust no such arrangements were legally possible.

New Lease.—A new lease of the Cleveland and Mahoning has been effected, which provides for an increase of rent to the amount of 11,000*l*. per annum at the beginning of 1885. The company has furnished us with the following information:—The Cleveland and Mahoning Valley Railroad Company are the owners of the valuable line of railroad running from Cleveland to Youngstown and Hubbard, in the State of Ohio, about 80 miles in length, and of two smaller lines, called the Niles and New Lisbon and the Liberty and Vienna, respectively 35 miles and 8 miles in length, all of which are leased for 102 years, from the 1st July, 1880, to the New York, Pennsylvania, and Ohio Railroad Company (formerly the Atlantic and Great Western Railroad Company) at the rent of $357,180 up to the end of December, 1884, and thereafter at the rent of $412,180. There is a mortgage debt of $141,000 due by the Cleveland and Mahoning Company, bearing 7 per cent. interest, which can be paid off as to part in 9 years time, and as to the other part in 12 years time, and could be readily renewed at 5 or 6 per cent. After paying the interest and expenses of management of the company, there remains about $270,000 a year applicable for dividend out of the present rental, but increasing after 1884 to $325,000. The entire share capital of the Cleveland and Mahoning Valley Railroad Company, excepting 19 shares out of 55,184, was placed in trust to secure bonds now amounting to 1,074,000*l*., issued by the Atlantic Company. The whole of these bonds, excepting 2 (which it is conjectured are lost or destroyed), or 400*l*., are the property of this company, and, therefore, when the Cleveland Company pays to the trustees (Messrs. Blake and Lewis), under the trust deed of 1872, the dividend on the shares in trust, such trustees pay the whole amount to this company. The debenture issue of the company, requiring 32,208*l*. per annum, is a first charge upon its revenues, and is, therefore, most amply secured, while a large balance remains for division amongst the stockholders.

The ordinary capital is called "Atlantic First Leased Lines Rental Trust Limited Stock." Dividend, 4 per cent. per annum, payable half-yearly, 31st January and 30th July, transfer books closing for about 14 days previously each half-year.

Revenue.—The following particulars are extracted from the directors' report for the year ended 31st January, 1884:—"The full interest on the debenture issue at 4*l*. per cent. per annum having been provided for, and an interim dividend of 2*l*. per cent. on the stock having been paid in August last, it is proposed to declare a dividend of 2*l*. per cent., making 4*l*. per cent. for the year. This will require 16,104*l*. out of the balance carried forward. The increased rental payable to the Cleveland and Mahoning Valley will commence from 1st January, 1885, which it is expected will enable the dividend on the stock to be permanently maintained at 4*l*. per cent. per annum."

For previous dividends, &c., see Manual for 1883, page 466.

Transfer Department.—Form, ordinary; fee, 2*s*. 6*d*. per deed; certificates must accompany transfers; stock not transferable below 5*l*., and no fraction of 1*l*. registered; in forms to be filled up by joint holders all signatures are required. All communications respecting stock or transfers must be addressed to Charles J. Ford, Registrar, 8, Old Jewry, E.C.

The management of the company is vested in the stockholders, who will possess the reversionary interest in the whole property after the termination of the lease; the debenture holders, therefore, have no vote. The present trustees are permanent *ex-officio* directors, liable to removal by a vote of the stockholders.

DIRECTORS:

Chairman—C. E. LEWIS, Esq., M.P., 29, Norfolk Street, Park Lane, W.

H. W. Blake, Esq., 8, Devonshire Place, W.

Rev. J. L. Bates, M.A., Iden Parsonage, Rye, Sussex.

George Clarkson, Esq., 38, Great James Street, Bedford Row, W.C.

Robert Monckton, Esq., Oak Lodge, Sevenoaks.

OFFICERS.—Sec., R. A. March; Registrar, C. J. Ford; Auditor, Fred W. Smith, F.C.A., 20, Bucklersbury, E.C.; Solicitors, Munns and Longden, 8, Old Jewry, E.C.

Offices—8, Old Jewry, E.C.

412.—BALTIMORE AND OHIO.

The main line of the Baltimore and Ohio extends from Baltimore, Maryland, to Wheeling, Virginia, a distance of 379 miles. The company owns or leases the following lines:—Valley Branch, Harper's Ferry to Harrisonburg, 100 miles; Washington City and Point Look Out, Alexandria Junction to Shepherd, 12 miles; Parkersburg Branch, Grafton to Parkersburg, 103¾ miles; Washington Branch, Relay House to Washington, 31 miles; Washington County Branch, Hagerstown Junction to Hagerstown, 24 miles; Strasburg Branch, Harper's Ferry to Strasburg, 51 miles; Metropolitan Branch, Point of Rocks to Washington, 42 miles; Central Ohio Division, Bellaire to Columbus, 137 miles; Lake Erie Division, Newark to Sandusky, 116 miles; Wheeling, Pittsburg, and Baltimore, Wheeling to Washington, 32 miles; Newark, Somerset, and Straitsville, Newark to Shawnee, 43 miles; Chicago Division, Chicago Junction, Ohio to Chicago, 268 miles; Pittsburg Division, 174 miles. The aggregate length of the company's lines is thus 1,462 miles; 606 miles of track are laid with steel. The cost of the road, rolling power, real estate, two iron bridges over Ohio River, and the Metropolitan Branch Railroad, has been $50,125,477. This sum is exclusive of cost of the Chicago Division (263 miles), which was built for $11,055,071 cash, furnished entirely by the Baltimore and Ohio.

The Pittsburg Division is what formerly comprised the Pittsburg and Connelsville Railway, and consists of a main line from Cumberland to Pittsburg, 149¾ miles; the Hickman's Run Branch, 2 miles; the Fayette County Branch, Connelsville to Uniontown, 13 miles; and the Mount Pleasant Branch, Broad Ford to Mount Pleasant, 10 miles.

The total length of all lines owned, leased, and operated is about 1,450 miles.

REVENUE.—Dividends upon the main stem or ordinary stock have been for many years distributed at the rate of 10 per cent. per annum, whilst the net annual earnings available for dividends have been very largely in excess. In consequence, however, of the revenue of the main line having been reduced through the depression of trade in 1877 and 1878, lower dividends have been declared by the directors as a measure of precaution, and the latest have ranged from 5 to 8 per cent. per annum. Semi-annual dividends at the former rate were paid on the 1st November, 1880, and the 16th May, 1881.

The receipts of the road and branches for the year ended September 30, 1882, amounted to $18,383,876. This company, in addition to investing $4,120,610 in the sinking funds for the reduction of its sterling mortgage debts to September 30, 1882, has heretofore paid from its earnings $10,170,667 of its mortgage obligations, which were incurred for the construction of its various lines. The appropriations for the sinking funds for the redemption of its sterling loans are £58,000 sterling per year, exclusive of the accumulation of interest upon the investments held by the said sinking funds. The entire mortgage debt of the company, in currency and sterling, is $24,695,890, and the surplus fund of the company on the 30th day of September, 1882, was $43,907,659. You will therefore observe that the surplus fund exceeds the entire amount of the mortgage indebtedness by $19,211,769. This fund represents invested capital not represented by stock or bonds, derived from the net surplus earnings of past years, after the payment of all interest upon the indebtedness and dividends upon the stock. The common stock, or ordinary share capital of the company, is $14,792,566, the par of which is $100 per share, and the current market price is $200 per share; and its preferred stock, with dividends fixed and limited at 6 per cent., is $5,000,000, which is in demand at upwards of 20 per cent. premium upon the par value, $100 per share. The cash dividends for years past upon the common stock have been 10 per cent. per annum, paid semi-annually, the earnings each year available for dividends continuing to be very largely in excess of the amount distributed; this remainder of the net annual earnings, beyond the payment of dividends, being represented in its surplus fund.

CAPITAL—30th September, 1881.—The following is a complete statement of the company's capital stock, preferred stock, &c., loan capital, and other liabilities, viz.:—

Stock	$14,783,300	
Stock scrip not funded	9,266	
Preferred stock, dividends fixed and limited at 6 per cent.	5,000,000	
Surplus fund—which represents invested capital derived from net earnings, and which is not represented by either stock or bonds	42,258,681 =	$62,051,247
Loan extended at 4 per cent., interest payable January and July	...	579,506
Loan redeemable in 1885, with coupons payable in April and October, originally	2,500,000	
Less payment on account	790,000 —	1,710,000
City Loan, originally	5,000,000	
Less sinking fund in charge of the City of Baltimore	2,396,220 —	2,603,780
Sterling loan redeemable in 1895. Coupons payable in March and September. 800,000*l*., at $4.84	3,872,000	
Less for sinking fund, 262,351*l*., at $4.84	1,269,780 —	2,602,220
Sterling loan redeemable in 1902. Coupons payable in March and September, 2,000,000*l*., at $4.84	9,680,000	
Less for sinking fund, 322,133*l*., at $4.84	1,553,122 —	8,126,878
Sterling loan redeemable in 1910. Coupons payable in May and November, 2,000,000*l*., at $4.84	9,680,000	
Less for sinking fund, 170,114*l*., at $4.84	823,350 —	8,856,650
Sterling 5 per cent. loan, redeemable in 1927. Coupons payable in June and December. For account of Baltimore and Ohio and Chicago Railroads, 1,600,000*l*., at $4.84	7,744,000	
Secured by bonds Baltimore and Ohio and Chicago Railroads, held by trustees, 1,600,000*l*., at $4.84	7,744,000	
Loan redeemable in 1919. For Parkersburg Branch Railroad	$3,000,000	
Secured by mortgage bonds of the Parkersburg Branch Railroad, held by trustees	3,000,000	
Bond for purchase of the interest of the City of Baltimore in the Pittsburgh and Connellsville Railroad	$1,000,000	
Less, six annual payments on account, of $40,000 each	240,000 —	760,000
Bills payable	...	1,584,496
Bonds to State of Maryland, due July 1st, 1888. Coupons January and July, in settlement under Act of 1878, chapter 155, section 4	...	300,000
Bonds of the North Western Virginia Railroad, of which the payment, principal and interest, has been assumed by the Baltimore and Ohio Railroad, under contract of July 18th, 1864, viz.:—		
Third mortgage endorsed bonds, originally $500,000, reduced to	...	140,000
Loans and obligations	3,189,684	
Less cash obligations secured by collaterals	2,979,217 —	210,467
Unclaimed dues	...	105,324
Washington Branch Road	...	190,557
		$89,831,119

The expenditure to the same date was as follows:—

Cost of road, &c.	$52,891,315
Investments in other companies, materials on hand, &c., &c.	36,801,436
Balance in the treasury	138,368
[No recent returns have been received.—ED.]	$89,831,119

President—JOHN W. GARRETT, Baltimore.
First Vice-President—ROBERT GARRETT.
Second Vice-President—SAMUEL SPENCER.
Third Vice-President—ORLAND SMITH.

OFFICERS.—Sec. and Treasurer, W. H. Ijams; Chief Eng., J. L. Randolph, Baltimore; Gen. Supt., Pittsburgh Division, Thomas M. King; Road Master, S. R. Johnson; Transportation Master, W. M. Clements; Auditor, W. T. Thelin.

Offices—Baltimore, Maryland.

413.—BALTIMORE AND POTOMAC.

This line extends from Baltimore to Popes Creek, with a branch to Washington. Length, 92½ miles. Opened 2nd July, 1872.

The tunnel at Baltimore, through which connection is made with the Northern Central, was commenced 1st June, 1871, and was opened for traffic 29th June, 1873. The length of the tunnel is 6,969 feet, of which 1,057 feet were constructed by drifting, the remainder being built by excavating an open cut, constructing the arch, and then filling in. The entire length of the tunnel is arched with brick, backed up with rubble masonry, and in many places, where quicksands and springs were met with, an inverted arch had to be constructed to protect the road-bed. The tunnel is built for a double track, and is 27 feet wide, the arch being 22 feet high. The tunnel is not continuous, the two sections being separated by an open cutting 200 feet long, at which point a local passenger depôt is to be built. The work is stated to have cost about $2,300,000.

An issue of $1,500,000 Baltimore tunnel first mortgage bonds was advertised in London in 1872, by Messrs. Speyer Brothers, 1, Angel Court, E.C., at the price of 79½ per cent., or 159*l.* per bond of $1,000 (200*l.*) The bonds carry interest at 6 per cent. per annum, payable by coupons on the 1st January and 1st July, in Baltimore in gold, and in London in sterling, at 4*s.* per dollar. The principal is repayable by means of an accumulative sinking fund of 1 per cent. per annum in 1911. These bonds are specially secured upon a mortgage of the tunnel undertaking; and, further, are guaranteed both principal and interest by the Pennsylvania and Northern Central companies.

In 1872 Messrs. Jay Cooke, Mc.Culloch, and Co. offered for subscription in this country $3,500,0000 of 6 per cent. main line mortgage bonds, at price of 183*l.* 7*s.* 6*d.* per bond of $1,000 (200*l.*) The coupons are payable 1st April and 1st October, in the same manner as the above. The principal is to be repaid by means of an accumulative sinking fund in 1911. These bonds are also guaranteed by the Pennsylvania and Northern Central companies, and are secured on the main line of the company.

President—Hon. ODEN BOWIE, Annapolis, Maryland.

OFFICERS.—Gen. Man., Charles E. Pugh; Auditor, John Crowe; Treasurer, J. S. Leib; Eng., A. Feldpauche.

Offices—Baltimore, Maryland.

414.- CENTRAL PACIFIC.

The report for 1883 shows the following statement of earnings and disbursements:

Receipts.	1882. 3,041 miles.	1883. 2,998 miles.
Gross earnings from roads	$25,662,757	$24,744,421
Net earnings, river steamers	20,485	1,236
Dividends on investments	...	6,000
Interest earned on sinking funds	281,260	335,125
Land bonds redeemed with proceeds of land sales	711,000	574,000
Totals	$26,675,502	$25,660,782
Expenditure.	1882.	1883.
Operating expenses and rental	$16,067,183	$15,570,600
General and legal expenses, &c.	586,577	636,943
Taxes paid	448,005	442,727
Interest	3,443,418	3,546,591
	$20,545,180	$20,196,863
Amounts applied to reduction of debt:		
Land bonds redeemed	$711,000	$574,000
Paid into sinking funds of company	1,034,760	1,088,625
Paid United States on account of interest and sinking fund	792,920	671,381
	$2,538,680	$2,334,006
Totals	$23,083,860	$22,530,870
Balance available for dividends	$3,591,641	$3,129,912
Dividends, 6 per cent.	3,556,530	3,556,530
Surplus for 1882	35,111	...
Deficit for 1883	...	426,617

The figures above show a net decrease in the net profits for 1883 from the 1881 of $1,767,462, or in the past two years a net reduction of 36 per cent. The balance available for dividends on the business of 1883 amounts to 5½ per cent. on the capital stock.

CAPITAL.—The report for 1882 gave the paid-in capital stock of the road as $59,275,500, the funded debt, less sinking funds, $48,354,580, and the total capital stock and indebtedness, $159,776,290. The interest accrued on $27,885,680 in United States bonds is $24,285,183, of which $7,915,941 has been repaid in cash and transportation.

415.—CHICAGO AND NORTH WESTERN.

A consolidation of the Chicago and North Western, the Galena and Chicago Union, the Peninsular Railroad of Michigan, and some twenty other companies of Illinois, Wisconsin, Minnesota, Dakota, Michigan, and Iowa.

The total mileage owned and operated by the company at the end of the fiscal year, 31st May, 1884, was 3,719. In addition to this the company owns some 206 miles of road that has been added to its system since May, 1884. This makes a total mileage of 3,923. To this can properly be added the Chicago, St. Paul, Minneapolis, and Omaha, 1,304 miles; the Fremont, Elkhorn, and Missouri Valley, and the Sioux City and Pacific, 418 miles, which practically belong to the Chicago and North Western by purchase of the controlling interest in their stock. Marvin Hughitt is President, and M. L. Sykes Vice-President of these companies. The total system then may be said to embrace 5,645 miles of road in the States of Illinois, Iowa, Minnesota, Wisconsin, Michigan, and Nebraska and the territory of Dakota. Neither the stock, bonds, nor earnings of these last-named companies are included in the statements of the Chicago and North Western, as up to the present they are operated as independent corporations.

The capital stock of the Chicago, St. Paul, Minneapolis, and Omaha amounts to—

Common stock and scrip	$18,573,233
Preferred stock	10,759,933
Total	$29,333,166
To this is to be added an account of 50 miles of new road built this year	1,260,700
This makes the value of both classes of stock, after deducting a few hundred dollars cancelled under certain agreements	$30,593,626

The total bonded indebtedness on 31st December, 1883, was $21,161,620. Gross earnings for the calendar year 1883, $5,515,284; earnings per land department, $547,777. After deducting opening expenses, interest on bonds, taxes, rentals, &c., there was left $1,322,567 as net income. Dividends of 7 per cent are being paid on the preferred stock.

The capital stock of the Fremont, Elkhorn, and Missouri Valley, and the Sioux City and Pacific is $3,992,400, and bonded debt $6,689,402. The earnings in 1883 were $1,093,000. Seven per cent. dividends have been paid on the Sioux City and Pacific proportion of the preference stock. All saving 75 miles has been recently built, and was built to open up to settlement an unsettled but very fertile portion of the new State of Nebraska. The road is still being extended. About 140 miles are being prepared for the iron, and early in 1885 will be opened for business.

CAPITAL—The following figures show the company's financial position for the year ended 31st May, 1884:—

Amount of the preferred stock of the company	$22,333,900
Ditto common stock and scrip	16,608,004
Total	$38,933,300

Dividends at 8 per cent. on the preferred stock and 7 per cent on the common stock are being paid.

The directors have decided to pay dividends quarterly hereafter, instead of semi-annually.

President—ALBERT KEEP, Chicago.

Vice-President, Secretary, and Treasurer—M. L. SYKES, New York.

OFFICERS.—Asst. Sec. and Asst. Treasurer, S. O. Howe, New York; Second Vice-President and Gen. Man., Marvin Hughitt; Asst. Gen. Man., W. H. Stennett; Gen. Supt., C. C. Wheeler; Asst. Gen. Supt., S. Sanborn; Chief Eng., E. H. Johnson; Gen. Solicitor, B. C. Cook; Local Treas., M. M. Kirkman; Traffic Man., H. C. Wicker; Gen. Freight Agent, W. S. Mellon; Purchasing Agent, R. W. Hamer; Gen. Ticket Agent, W. A. Thrall; Gen. Passenger Agent, R. S. Hair; Auditor and Asst. Sec., J. B. Redfield; Land Commissioner, Charles E. Simmons.—All of Chicago.

Land Commissioner and General Agent for Great Britain, John Everitt, 11, Wood Street, Cheapside, E.C.

Offices—Chicago, Illinois; and 52, Wall Street, New York.

416.—CHICAGO, MILWAUKEE, AND ST. PAUL.

This is a consolidation of the Chicago and Milwaukee, Milwaukee and Prairie du Chien, and Milwaukee and St. Paul railroads. Total mileage, 4,740.

$3,000,000 of the 7 per cent. first mortgage bonds of the Milwaukee and St. Paul Company were issued in this country in 1872, by Messrs. Morton, Rose, and Co., at the price of 90*l.* per bond of $500 (100*l.*) The bonded debt of the Milwaukee and St. Paul at the time of its amalgamation in 1873 was $8,058,000, of which $5,527,000 were first mortgage bonds. The interest is payable 1st January and 1st July, in New York in gold, and in London in sterling. The principal is repayable in 1902, or holders may convert into gold dollar bonds, or into preferred stock of the consolidated company.

SOUTH WESTERN DIVISION.—In 1879 the Committee on Stock Lists, of the New York Stock Exchange, granted a quotation of the company's first mortgage, south-western division, 6 per cent. bonds. The official statement made by the company at the time contained the following information, viz.:—"The first mortgage, south-western division, 6 per cent bonds are issued upon the railroad and property of the Western Union Company as follows:—Length of road from Racine, Wis., to Rock Island, Ill., 212 miles. Equipment—Locomotives, 39; passenger cars, 14; baggage, mail, and express cars, 13; freight box cars, 410; stock cars, 60; platform cars, 50; coal cars, 82; service cars; 4; total 633.

Capital stock, all of which is now owned by the Chicago, Milwaukee, and St. Paul, except 66⅔ shares	$4,000,000
First mortgage 7 per cent. bonds	3,500,000
Other liabilities	238,224
	$7,738,224
Required for new equipment and permanent improvement	261,775
Total	$8,000,000

CHICAGO AND LAKE SUPERIOR DIVISION.—In May, 1882, Messrs. Borthwick, Wark, and Co., of Bartholomew House, Bartholomew Lane, E.C., invited subscriptions for $1,360,000 of 1st mortgage 40-year 5 per cent. gold bonds of the Chicago and Lake Superior Division. Price, 97 per cent., or 194*l.* per bond of $1,000. The bonds, which are of $1,000 each, are a direct obligation of the Chicago, Milwaukee, and St. Paul, and are further secured by a first mortgage of $20,000 per mile on the Chicago and Lake Superior Division. The bonds are to bearer, with coupons attached, but can be registered in the holder's name at the office of the company in New York. Dividends due half-yearly, 1st January and 1st July. Principal due 1st July, 1921. Principal and interest payable in New York in United States gold coin.

CHICAGO AND PACIFIC WESTERN DIVISION.—In July, 1882, the 5 per cent. first mortgage bonds of this division, to the extent of $3,000,000, were issued. Interest payable half-yearly, on 1st January and 1st July; principal payable 1st January, 1891, both payable in New York in United States gold coin. Agents, Messrs. Speyer Brothers, 1, Angel Court, E.C.

REVENUE.—According to the annual report for the year ended 31st Dec., 1883, the gross earnings were	$23,659,824
Operating expenses, including taxes	12,778,039
	$9,881,785

Being an increase of $1,661,139 over the net earnings for 1882. After paying interest on bonds for 1883, $5,573,926, two semi-annual dividends of 3½ per cent. on both common and preferred stock, $3,212,895, and operating expenses, a surplus of $5,079,086 for the year is shown including the 1882 surplus of $3,619,406.

CAPITAL.—The entire cost of the company's property, including rolling stock, depot grounds, cattle yards, elevators, machine shops, warehouses, docks, coal lands, and other property, together with five bridges across the Mississippi river, is represented by stock and bonds as follows:—

Common stock	$30,904,261
Preferred stock	16,540,983
Total stock	$47,445,244
Mortgage and land grant bonds, including all lines on purchased roads	96,272,000
Total capital, stock and bonds	$143,717,244

The Western Union Company has executed to the Chicago, Milwaukee, and St. Paul Company a lease of all its property for 999 years, from June 25th, 1879.

The Chicago, Milwaukee, and St. Paul Company has thereupon issued its 6 per cent. bonds of $1,000 each, dated July 1st, 1879, payable July 1st, 1909, interest at 6 per cent. per annum, payable January 1st and July 1st; numbered 1 to 4,000 inclusive, amounting to $4,000,000. These bonds are secured by a mortgage or deed of trust executed by the Chicago, Milwaukee, and St. Paul Company and the Western Union Company, upon the whole property of the Western Union Company, to John S. Kennedy and John S. Barnes as trustees.—For the purposes for which these bonds were issued see the MANUAL for 1881, page 500.

President—ALEXANDER MITCHELL, Milwaukee, Wisconsin.

Vice-President—JULIUS WADSWORTH, New York.

OFFICERS.—Sec., P. M. Myers; Treasurer, R. D. Jennings; Gen. Man., S.S. Merrill; Gen. Solicitor, John W. Cary; Auditor, J. P. Whaling; Chief Eng., D. J. Whittemore; Purchasing Agent, J. T. Crocker.

Chief Offices—Milwaukee; Transfer Office, 25, William Street, New York. London Agents—Morton, Rose, and Co., Bartholomew Lane, E.C.

417.—CLEVELAND, COLUMBUS, CINCINNATI, AND INDIANAPOLIS.

The annual report of President J. H. Devereux for 1883 shows:—

Earnings from freight	$3,068,717	
„ from passengers	965,693	
„ from mail	87,229	
„ from express	91,467	
„ from rents	58,811	
„ from interest and dividends	70,687	
Total earnings		$4,342,604
Expenses.		
Total operating expenses, 69·50 per cent	$3,018,383	
Taxes	125,144	
Interest on bonds	507,453	
Interest and exchange	26,890	
Total expenses, taxes, interest, &c.		3,677,870
Net earnings		$664,734

In a comparison with the results of the year 1882, there is shown:—A decrease in gross earnings of $98,997 or 02·23 per cent.; an increase in operating expenses of $54,604 or 01·84 per cent.; a decrease in net earnings of $153,601 or 10·39 per cent.; a decrease in tonnage of 227,874 tons or 08·27 per cent; a decrease in net freight earnings of $20,707 or 02·40 per cent.; an increase in net freight earnings per ton mile of ·013 cents or 06·73 per cent.; a decrease in passengers carried of 59,296 or 05·72 per cent.

418.—DENVER AND RIO GRANDE.

The report gives the following statement of the business of the year ended December 31, 1882:—

Average miles in operation	1,100
Gross earnings	$6,404,979
Operating expenses	3,821,124
Net earnings	2,583,855
Profits on Denver and Rio Grande Western lease	36,771
Total net income	2,620,627
Interest on first mortgage bonds	447,685
Interest on consolidated bonds	1,277,010
Interest on rolling stock trust	221,833
Balance of interest, discount, and exchange	47,348
Taxes and insurance	228.811
Sinking fund payment	22,146
Total charges of every nature, except principal of rolling stock trusts	2,244,834
Leaving surplus over all charges	375,792
Amount paid on principal of rolling stock trusts and charged to equipment account	338,000

The report says:—"The foregoing statement is made for the purpose of showing that after deducting all fixed and other charges of every nature (except principal of rolling stock trusts), there is a surplus of $375,792. Interest necessarily forms part of the cost of construction, and should properly for period of construction be so treated. It is customary, and was part of the original programme; hence, until the mileage has been put into operation, your board of trustees has considered it advisable to show on the books of the company, as chargeable against income account, only such an amount of interest pertained to the amount of bonds issued (viz., $15,000 per mile), in accordance with the consolidated mortgage, on the average mileage completed and in operation during the year, say 1,100 miles. The income account, as stated in the Comptroller's report, shows the manner in which this is arrived at—the difference between $1,277,010 interest, and $932,925=$344,085, being charged to cost of construction, leaving to the credit of income account, as result of years' operations, $719,877."—*Railway News.*

No recent returns have been received. At a meeting of Scotch bondholders, held in Dundee, in July, 1884, a committee was appointed to confer with the committees (already appointed to protect the interests of the bondholders and proprietary generally) in New York, Amsterdam, and London.

DENVER AND RIO GRAND WESTERN—This company is leased to the Denver and Rio Grand at 40 per cent. of the gross receipts as rental.

President—FREDERICK LOVEJOY, New York.

Vice-President—ADOLPH ENGLER, New York.

OFFICERS.—Sec., William Wagner, 47, William Street, New York; Treasurer, W. M. Spackman, New York; Gen. Man., D. C. Dodge; Gen. Supt., R. B. Cable; Chief Eng., J. A. McMurtrie; Auditor, E. R. Murphy.

419.—DETROIT, GRAND HAVEN, AND MILWAUKEE.

In 1855 the Oakland and Ottawa and the Detroit and Pontiac were consolidated under the title of the Detroit and Milwaukee. The latter company having failed to meet its bond interest in 1873, the road was placed in the hands of a receiver, by whom it was worked under the orders of the Courts of Michigan. Foreclosure suits were instituted by the first and second mortgage bondholders, and the railway was sold under a decree in September, 1878, and became the property of a purchasing committee representing about 95 per cent of the first and second mortgage bondholders.

The line has been reorganised under the title of the Detroit, Grand Haven, and Milwaukee, and is controlled by the Great Western of Canada (now united to the Grand Trunk of Canada) under a guarantee of bonds of the reorganised company, consisting of

Equipment 20 years' bonds (14th November, 1878), bearing interest at the rate of 6 per cent. per annum, "cumulative," and payable half-yearly 1st April and 1st October; redeemable 14th November, 1918, at par; first charge on all; principal and interest guaranteed by the Great Western of Canada (now Grand Trunk)	$2,000,000
Consolidated 20 years' bonds (15th November, 1878), bearing interest for the first five years at the rate of 5 per cent. per annum, and thereafter at 6 per cent. per annum; other conditions same as equipment bonds, except that these rank as a "second charge," and that they are redeemable on 15th instead of 14th November, 1918	3,200,000
	$5,200,000

Under the reorganisation $1,500,000 of ordinary stock was created, which is held entirely by the Great Western of Canada (now Grand Trunk), and upon which a dividend of 8 per cent. was earned for the year 1883.

The line extends in a north-westerly direction for 189 miles from Detroit, where it connects with the Great Western section of the Grand Trunk of Canada, to Grand Haven, a port on Lake Michigan, immediately opposite to Milwaukee, from which it is distant 84 miles. By this route, on which an improved passenger and freight service has been established, ready access is had not only to Milwaukee itself, but to the flour mills of Minneapolis, the great grain country of the west, and all the territory served by the Chicago, Milwaukee, and St. Paul and its connections.

The annual report for the year 1883 shows:—

	1883.	1882.
Gross earnings	$1,376,464	$1,354,671
Operating expenses	996,697	1,015,218
Net earnings	$379,767	$339,453
Gross earnings per mile	7,283	7,158
Net earnings per mile	2,009	1,796
Per cent. of expenses	72·41	74·94

The income account was as follows:—

Balance, January 1, 1883		$15,391
Net earnings		379,767
Interest received		16,75
Total		$411,912
Interest on bonds	$284,288	
Interest, exchange, &c.	5,571	
Dividends, 8 per cent.	120,000	=409,859
Balance, January 1, 1884		$2,053

President—JOSEPH HICKSON.

Offices—Detroit, Michigan; London Agent, Walter Lindley, 203, Dashwood House, E.C.

420.—GALVESTON, HARRISBURG, AND SAN ANTONIO.

Galveston, Texas, to San Antonio, Texas. Length of line, 215 miles; sidings, 20 miles; total, 235 miles. Completed to San Antonio, March 1st, 1877. The funded debt consists of first mortgage 6 per cent. gold sinking fund bonds, dated 1st February, 1871, due February 1st, 1910, amount $4,500,000. The bonds are further secured by the lands of the company, amounting to 1,500,000 acres, included in the mortgage deed, the proceeds from which are applicable to paying off the bonds through the trustees. The interest has always been regularly paid. The interest coupons are payable 1st February and 1st August in gold at Boston, and in sterling in London, at the rate of 6*l.* 5*s.* per cent., or say 12*l.* 10*s.* per annum per $1,000 bond.

DIRECTORS:

President—T. W. PEIRCE, Boston, Massachusetts.

Vice-President—H. B. ANDREWS, San Antonio, Texas.

Peter Butler, Boston, Massachusetts.
Andrew Peirce, Clifton Springs, New York.
George F. Stone, New York.
J. J. McComb, New York.
T. T. Buckley, New York.

OFFICERS.—Treas. and Asst. Sec., Charles Babbidge, Boston, Massachusetts; Sec. and Asst. Treas., J. E. Fisher, Houston, Texas; Gen. Supt. and Chief Eng., James Converse, Houston, Texas; Gen. Road Master and Supt. of Bridges, N. F. Bell, Columbus; Master Mechanic, J. G. Conlan, Harrisburg; Master of Transportation, E. G. Thompson, Columbus; General Ticket Agent, T. W. Peirce, jun., Houston; General Freight Agent, C. C. Gibbs, Harrisburg, Texas; Purchasing Agent, T. W. Peirce, Boston, Massachusetts; Transfer Agent, Charles Babbidge, Boston, Massachusetts.

Principal Office and Address—Houston, Texas.

Financial Agency and Transfer Office—58, Sears Buildings, Boston, Massachusetts.

421.—ILLINOIS CENTRAL.

Chartered on 10th February, 1851, with authority to construct a railroad from La Salle (at which point the Illinois and Michigan Canal has its South Western terminus) northwardly to the Mississippi River, opposite Dubuque, Iowa, and southward to Cairo, at the confluence of the Ohio with the Mississippi; and also a branch from this main line to Chicago, and another *vià* Galena to Dubuque, Iowa. The capital was fixed at $1,000,000, with power to increase to an amount equal to the money expended in the construction of the road and appurtenances. The company was authorised to establish its own rates of toll. The act of incorporation also surrendered to the company all the property acquired by the State of Illinois in the course of the previous efforts made by it to construct a railroad between the same points; and all the lands donated by the United States Government under the act of Congress, approved 20th September, 1850.

The two lines owned by this company extend from Cairo to Dunleith, 455¾ miles, and from Centralia to Chicago, 249¾ miles; total, 705½ miles. The company also leases the Dubuque and Sioux City, the Iowa Falls and Sioux City, and the Cedar Falls and Minnesota railroads, the combined length of which is 402¼ miles. The branch line running south-west from Otto has been extended nearly 19 miles; and another branch has been constructed, with iron rails running westerly from Otto towards the main line—length, about 12 miles. Of the 365 miles of line from Chicago to Cairo, 315 miles are laid with steel, and the remainder is to be completed in steel on an early date. The company have now 543 miles of steel rail north of the Ohio. Up to the close of 1881 the company's mileage had extended to 920 miles, and, in addition, 195 miles of sidings and double track.

The entire line of the Illinois Central proper, as well as that from Cairo to New Orleans, is now laid with steel rails, and the increased net result shown is largely owing to this fact. The expenditure for betterments in 1883, in Illinois, was not expected to exceed $500,000.

On January 1st, 1883, this company took formal possession as lessee of the Chicago, St. Louis, and New Orleans (which will be known in future as the "Southern Division"), thus increasing its mileage to 1,908·65 miles. During the past year $4,422,700 of the stock of the Chicago, St. Louis, and New Orleans has been exchanged for this company's leased line stock certificates, bearing four per cent. interest. Of this sum $1,100,000 was issued against stock formerly held by this company and sold, and the remaining $3,322,700 was exchanged by other holders, thus placing with this company all but $7,300 of the $10,000,000 of stock of the Chicago, St. Louis, and New Orleans, of which $4,422,700 is pledged against the leased line certificates, and $5,570,000 is the unencumbered property of this company.

There was expended during 1881 $108,000 upon the construction of a branch road running to the important manufacturing town of South Chicago. This, as well as the extension of the middle division to Bloomington, was expected to be opened for business in the spring of 1883.

Two important branch lines connecting with the Southern Division are also under construction, one from Jackson, the capital of Mississippi, to Yazoo City, 48 miles, which will be laid with selected iron taken from the track in 1882, and retained for that purpose; the other is a continuation of the Kosciusko Branch from that point to Aberdeen, 97 miles. It was estimated that about $2,000,000 would be required during 1883, in addition to the money already spent and material provided, for these branches.

CAPITAL.—The following figures will show the position of this account in 1880:—

Capital stock	$29,000,000
6 per cent. sterling bonds due 1895	2,500,000
6 per cent. currency bonds „ 1890	2,500,000
5 per cent. sterling bonds „ 1903	4,296,000
„ „ „ „ 1905	1,000,000
7 per cent. construction bonds outstanding	4,000
6 per cent. currency bonds of 1898 (on mortgage of Springfield Division)	1,600,000
6 per cent. registered currency bonds (secured on mortgage of Chatsworth Division)	200,000
Balance—Surplus account	504,529
Income account	2,072,840
Liabilities—Chicago office	117,229
Insurance fund	24,656
Total	$43,819,255

The outlays during the year 1883 on capital account, not provided from income, have been as follow:—

Middle division		$73,508
South Chicago		63,297
Canton, Aberdeen, and Nashville		1,463,314
Yazoo and Mississippi Valley		575,709
Iowa division		80,487
Total		$2,260,310
Since the directors' last report to the shareholders the company has sold Chicago, St. Louis, and New Orleans 5 per cent. bonds	$1,800,000	
And has issued middle division bonds	58,000=	1,858,000
Leaving		$402,310

The foregoing receipts have been absorbed in the cost of road, including supplies, cash assets, and bonds of the New Orleans Line, &c.

REVENUE.—The earnings for the year ended 31st December, 1883, after payment of all fixed charges, sufficed for dividends on the ordinary capital at the following rates, viz:—

$6, calculated at 24s. currency, payable 1st March, 1884.
$4, „ 16·2 „ „ 1st September, 1884.

The annual meeting is held at Chicago the last Wednesday in May. The coupons on all bonds issued in London (except those of 1875) are payable 1st April and 1st October. The coupons of the 1875 bonds are payable 1st June and 1st December.

President—W. K. ACKERMAN, Chicago.

OFFICERS.—Sec., L. A. Catlin, New York; Treasurer, L. V. F. Randolph, New York; Gen. Supt., E. T. Jeffery; Auditor, J. C. Welling; Master Mechanic, William Renshaw; Freight Agent, John J. Sproull, New York; Land Commissioner, Peter Daggy; Purchase Agent, O. Ott.—All at Chicago.

London Bankers—Consolidated Bank, and Glyn, Mills, Currie, and Co., 67, Lombard Street, E.C.

Offices—78, Michigan Avenue, Chicago, Illinois; 214, Broadway, New York; and 37, Carondelet Street, New Orleans.

London Agents—Morton, Rose, and Co., Bartholomew Lane, E.C.

422.—LAKE SHORE AND MICHIGAN SOUTHERN.

The president and directors of the Lake Shore and Michigan Southern submit to the stockholders the following report for the year ending 31st December, 1882:—

ROAD OPERATED:—

Main line—Buffalo, New York, to Chicago, Illinois	540·49 miles.
Five Lake Shore and Michigan Southern Branches	324·38 „
Total miles, Lake Shore and Michigan Southern proper	864·87 miles.
Three proprietary roads, owned wholly by Lake Shore and Michigan Southern, but under other organisations	160·07 „
Five leased roads	314·60 „
Total miles road operated	1,339·54 miles.

With 266·24 miles second track and 536·60 miles side tracks, making in all 2,142·38 miles of track, of which 1,351·49 miles are laid with steel, an increase of 124 miles in 1882. This company leased in perpetuity, as of 1st July, 1881, the Detroit, Hillsdale, and South Western, 64·89 miles, at a rental of $41,000 annually for two years, and after that $54,000 annually (4 per cent. upon its capital stock). Also as of 1st September, 1882, in perpetuity, the Fort Wayne and Jackson, 97·42 miles, at an annual rental of 5½ per cent. upon its preferred stock (rental, $126,027·88). These leases were made, after long and careful consideration, to protect the interests of the company.

CONSTRUCTION.—This account stands at $66,500,000, the same as at the end of 1881. Nothing was charged to this account in 1882.

EQUIPMENT.—This account was increased in 1882 from $16,150,000 to $17,169,000; increase $1,019,000 for the following increase in equipment:—

	31st Dec., 1882.	31st Dec., 1881.	Increase.
Locomotives	547	532	15
Cars	17,085	16,016	1,067

CAPITAL STOCK.—The capital stock of the company is $50,000,000, to wit—

Guaranteed (10 per cent.)	5,335 shares	—$100	$533,500
Ordinary	494,665 „	$100	$49,466,500
	500,000 shares	—$100	$50,000,000

Of the ordinary stock the company owns $268,200, as stated in the balance sheet.

FUNDED DEBT.—The usual annual contribution of $250,000 to the sinking fund reduces the first mortgage debt from $22,250,000 to $22,000,000.

The second mortgage debt was increased from $14,665,000 to $21,192,000 by the exchange of $6,527,000 second mortgage bonds for 140,500 shares preferred and 124,800 shares common stock in the New York, Chicago, and St. Louis, a controlling interest.

While this involves an increase in our fixed charges of $456,890 per annum, it is believed the results will confirm the wisdom of acquiring the control of that road.

Earnings for the year 1883.

	1883.	1882.
Freight	$12 480,093	$12,022,576
Passengers	4,736,088	4,897,185
Mails	683,867	713,240
Express	364,171	397,944
All other sources	249,435	194,691
Total	$18,513,656	$18,225,639
Operating expenses and taxes	11,001,853	11,057,807
Per cent.	59	60
Net earnings	$7,511,802	$7,167,831
Increase in gross earnings	$288,017	1·58 per cent.
Decrease in operating expenses	55,953	0·50 per cent.
Increase in net earnings	343,971	4·79 per cent.

Disposition of net earnings—1883.

Fixed charges	$3,498,806
Four quarterly dividends, 2 per cent. each—8 per cent.	3,957,320
Balance surplus for the year	55,676
Total net earnings	$7,511,802

The following is an estimated statement presented at a meeting of the directors in June, 1884:—

Earnings—First half-year.

	Jan. 1st. to June 30th, 1884.	Decrease.
Gross earnings	$7,330,900	$1,888,271
Operating extras and taxes	4,515,400	1,207,566
Net earnings	$2,815,500	$680,705
Deduct interest, rentals, &c.	1,800,000	Inc. 50,597
Balance for stock	$1,015,500	$731,302
Dividends—4 per cent. in 1883 and 3½ in 1884	1,731,327	247,233
Deficiency	$715,827	Inc. $484,069

Decrease in earnings	$1,888,271,	equals	20·48	per cent.
Do. expenses	1,207,566,	do.	21·07	do.
Do. net earnings	680,705,	do.	19·46	do.

The treasurer says:—"It will be seen from the foregoing statement that the earnings applicable to stock during the first half of the years 1882, 1883, and 1884 do not amount to the two quarterly dividends usually declared in that period, but the deficiency in 1882 and 1883 was made good in the second half. He has every reason to believe that the same will occur in 1884. Upon careful consideration of all the circumstances, however, it has been deemed expedient in the interest of the stock holders to reduce the dividends to a basis of 6 per cent. per annum."

DIRECTORS:

Chairman—WILLIAM K. VANDERBILT, New York.

President and General Manager—JOHN NEWELL.

OFFICERS.—Sec. and Treasurer, E. D. Worcester, New York; Gen. Supt., P. P. Wright; Chief Eng., L. H. Clarke; Purchasing Agent, A. C. Armstrong; Auditor, C. P. Leland.

Offices—New York, Cleveland, and Chicago.

423.—LEHIGH VALLEY.

This company owns a main line from Philipsburg, New Jersey, to Wilkes-Barre, Pennsylvania (101 miles), and has branches to Audenried (17¼ miles), to Mount Carmel (59¾ miles), to Tomhicken (35½ miles), and to Milnsville (17 miles); total owned, 230 miles. The share capital paid up is about $27,000,000. A consolidated mortgage for $40,000,000 was created in 1873, and of this $5,000,000 was issued in London in February, 1874, by Messrs. J. S. Morgan and Co., at the price of 90 per cent., or 180*l*. per bond of $1,000 (200*l*.) The interest, at 6 per cent., is payable half-yearly, free of all taxes, on the 1st June and 1st December, in Philadelphia in gold, and in London in sterling, at 4s. per dollar. The bonds are redeemable by annual drawings at par, by means of an accumulative sinking fund of 2 per cent. per annum, and the whole amount will be paid off by 1898. A further issue of $3,000,000 of these bonds was effected in this country in 1875, at the price of 88 per cent., or 176l. per bond of $1,000 (200l.) The interest is payable in gold in Philadelphia only, on the 1st June and 1st December, free from all taxes. The principal is repayable in 1923.

REVENUE.—The following is extracted from the company's report for the year ended 30th November, 1882, issued January 16th, 1883, viz.:—

Income from all sources, including interest received from investments, &c., amounted to		$11,239,313
Operating expenses of the road		5,833,677
Leaving		$5,405,636
Against which there has been charged—		
Interest on bonds (including interest and dividends on guaranteed bonds and stocks)	$2,019,734	
Dividends:—Four quarterly dividends amounting to 10 per cent. on "preferred" stock, and 6½ per cent. on common stock	2,850,516	
General expense, interest on floating debt, Pennsylvania and New Jersey State taxes, loss on Morris Canal lease, &c.	375,490	
Amount charged for estimated accumulated depreciations	554,349 =	5,300,089
Balance to be carried to the credit of our profit and loss account		$105,546

CAPITAL.—Year ended 30th November, 1882.—The following is copied from the company's report issued January 16th, 1883, viz.:—

At the close of the fiscal year this account was as follows:—

Preferred stock	$106,300	
Common stock, including scrip not yet converted	27,496,895 =	$27,603,195
First mortgage, 6 per cent. bonds (coupon and registered), due in 1898		5,000,000
Second mortgage, 7 per cent. bonds (registered), due in 1910		6,000,000
Consolidated mortgage 6 per cent. bonds, due in 1923, except sterling bonds:—		
Sterling	$4,013,000	
Coupon	1,952,000	
Registered	7,498,000	
Annuity	550,000 =	14,013,000
		$52,616,195

In addition to the above there are outstanding $2,500,000 of the 5 per cent. bonds of the Easton and Amboy, due in 1920, the interest upon which is charged in our accounts.

The second mortgage bonds of the Southern Central of New York, amounting to $400,000, endorsed and guranteed by this company, as approved by the stockholders in January, 1873, fell due on March 1st, 1882, and were taken up and paid for by us under an agreement with that company, and the holders of the greater part of its first mortgage bonds, under which both the existing mortgages were to be cancelled, and a new one created at a reduced rate of interest of sufficient amount to include all their indebtedness and provide means for additional business. This agreement is now being carried out, and will be completed as soon as it is assented to by the holders of a few of their first mortgage bonds.

One hundred and fifty-nine of the sterling bonds were drawn, payable 1st December, 1882, leaving $3,854,000, bearing interest from that date.

[No recent returns had been received up to the time of going to press.—ED.]

DIRECTORS:

President—HARRY E. PACKER, Philadelphia.

Vice-President—CHARLES HARTSHORNE, Pennsylvania.

William L. Conyngham.
Ario Pardee.
William A. Ingham.
George B. Markle.
Robert H. Sayre.
James I. Blakslee.
R. A. Packer.
Elisha P. Wilbur.
Joseph Patterson.
Garrett B. Linderman.
John R. Fell.

OFFICERS.—Sec., John R. Fanshawe; Treasurer, Lloyd Chamberlain; Gen. Supt. H. Stanley Goodwin, Bethlehem, Penn.; Chief Engineer, A. W. Stedman; Gen. Agent, W. H. Sayre, Bethlehem, Penn.

Offices—303, Walnut Street, Philadelphia.

London Agents—J. S. Morgan and Co., 22, Old Broad Street, E.C.

424.—LOUISVILLE AND NASHVILLE.

This important system, the outcome of many consolidations, had 2,028 miles in operation at the close of June, 1882, and in this general total the original main line from Louisville to Nashville only figured for 185 miles, to which the management has tacked on 1,393 miles of branches, while 450 miles of iron way are in addition leased and controlled. In April, 1883, two important connections were opened, viz.: the Knoxville Branch connecting with the East Tennessee, Virginia, and Georgia to Knoxville and the south west, and the Pensacola and Atlantic, giving a through route from Savannah to New Orleans. In 1880 the Louisville and Nashville paid a stock dividend of 100 per cent.; in July, 1881, it purchased the entire stock of the Louisville, Cincinnati, and Lexington (comprising 175 miles of line owned, and 73 miles leased); and in November, 1881, it issued a Louisville and Nashville mortgage, with a lien on this stock, of which $1,000,000 was common and $1,500,000 preferred. A general mortgage was also created, it should have been observed, in 1880, for $20,000,000, of which $9,716,000 was reserved to pay off prior liens. For the St. Louis and South Eastern lines $492,200 Trust Company certificates were issued, secured by $800,000 Evansville, Henderson, and Nashville bonds; the Trust Company certificates are redeemable in April and October in any year upon 30 days' notice being given to that effect. The South Eastern and St. Louis, which was reorganised after the foreclosure of the St. Louis and South Eastern in 1880, has been leased to the Louisville and Nashville for 49 years; and the latter issues its bonds secured on the line, which extends through Indiana and Illinois, and is about 210 miles in length. There is also $990,500 South Eastern and St. Louis stock in circulation. What are known as Louisville and Nashville (Lebanon and Knoxville) bonds, issued in 1881, cover 110 miles of line, subject to a prior lien; they are also a first lien on 62 miles of line building from Livingstone to the State Line. The Pensacola and Atlantic is a separate company, and its bonds are not a direct liability of the Louisville and Nashville. The bonds were sold to the latter stockholders upon the following terms:—$1,000 in bonds, $500 in bond scrip, and $400 in stock for $1,425 cash. The company also issued some third mortgage bonds in 1882; these bonds are secured by a special hypothecation of a large amount of other bonds and stock. In November, 1882, the company listed $3,213,513 of its stock, taken from the city of Louisville, and it further issued $3,786,487 of new stock to pay off its floating debt.

The annual report for the year ending June 30, 1883, shows the total mileage to be 2,065·27 miles, exclusive of the lines in which the company is interested as owner of a majority of the capital stock. These amount to 856 miles, including the Nashville, Chattanooga, and St. Louis, which makes the grand total 3,535·27 miles.

The mortgage debt as per last report, was	$58,117,778
Bonds issued during the year	50,000
Total	$58,167,778
Less bonds redeemed during the year	264,548
Outstanding June 30, 1883	$57,903,230

The capital stock of the company was stated in its last annual report, $18,133,513, not including certain stock held by the city of Louisville (as collateral for the loan of its $850,000 bonds to this company in 1856-57). This stock since the close of the last fiscal year was released, the company substituting therefor $850,000 United States bonds, bearing 3 per cent. interest. The stock thus released made the outstanding capital $21,213,513.

The stockholders, at the annual meeting held in Louisville, October 4, 1882, authorised the increase of the capital stock of the company to $30,000,000, an increase of $8,786,487. Of this new stock, $3,786,487 was listed at the New York stock exchange, making the total stock listed and outstanding $25,000,000. The remaining $5,000,000 of stock has not been listed, and is now in the treasury of the company. A considerable part of the stock resulting to the treasury from the release above mentioned, and of the increased stock so listed at the exchange, has been sold, realising $2,575,000 to the treasury.

In 1882 the stockholders also authorised an increase of the capital of the company to $30,000,000, the increase to be made as required. Of the stock thus authorised, $3,786,487 was at once listed, raising the amount of stock outstanding to $25,000,000.

In the latter part of the year 1884 the company announced the issue in London of $5,000,000 6 per cent. 10-40 adjustment bonds (coupons payable half-yearly, May 1st and November 1st), with the company's option of redemption in 10 or 40 years from date of issue, at par. Price of issue, 68 per cent., counting the $ at 4s., also $5,000,000 common stock in shares of $100 each, at $27 per share, counting the $ at 5s., both issues were allotted to the proprietory *pro rata*, the prospectus stating as follows:—

The stockholders are entitled in respect of every 50 shares or $5,000 stock held by them to claim the allotment of either or both of the following:—

$1,000 6 per cent. 10-40 adjustment bonds of the Louisville and Nashville, at 68 per cent., at 4s. per $.

Payable	18 per cent., or 36*l*. per bond, on application.		
	50 per cent., or 100*l*.	„	November 15th.
	136*l*. per bond or $1,000.		

10 shares or $1,000 common capital stock of the Louisville and Nashville, at 27 per cent., at 4s. per $.

Payable	7 per cent. or 14*l*. on application.
	20 per cent. or 40*l*. on November 15th.
	27 per cent. or 54*l*. for every 10 shares or $1,000 stock.

The mileage of roads owned by this company, on which its bonded debt and the issue of its stock are based, is as follows:—Owned absolutely, 976 miles; owned absolutely and not completed, 32 miles; roads in which the capital stock is owned entirely by the company, 720 miles; total, 1,728 miles.

		Per mile.
Total capital stock	$25,000,000	$14,467
Total mortgage debt	57,908,280	33,509
Total bonded debt and stock	$82,908,230	$47,976

REVENUE.—The dividends paid upon the stock between 1870 and 1882 were as follow:—In 1871, 1872, and 1873, 7 per cent. per annum; in 1874, 1875, and 1876, nil; in 1877, 1½ per cent.; in 1878, 3 per cent.; in 1879, 4 per cent.; in 1880, 8 per cent. (and 100 per cent. in stock); in 1881, 6 per cent.; and in 1882, 3 per cent.

The following is the report of this company for the fiscal year ending 30th June, 1884.—

Gross earnings	$14,351,093	
Operating expenses	8,823,783	
Net earnings from traffic	$5,527,310	
Other increase from investments, &c.	261,381 =	$5,788,691
Interest and rentals	$4,393,903	
Taxes	309,452 =	4,703,355
Net profit for year		$1,085,336
Sinking funds	$165,477	
Interest on P. and A. bonds	180,000	
Interest on O. and N. bonds	12,000	
Loss on lease Ga. railroad	11,000 =	368,477
Net balance		$716,859
Expended on capital account—construction	$367,263	
Car-trust bonds—former equipment	268,000 =	635,263
Surplus		$80,596

President—C. C. BALDWIN, 52, Wall Street, New York.

Vice-President and General Manager—MILTON H. SMITH.

OFFICERS.—Sec., Willis Ranney; Treas., C. B. Simmons; Con. Eng., F. W. Vaughan; Gen. Supt., D. W. C. Rowland; Purchasing Agent, P. P. Huston.

Offices—Louisville, Kentucky.

425.—NEW YORK CENTRAL AND HUDSON RIVER.

This is a consolidation (October 1st, 1869) of the New York Central and the Hudson River railroads. The main line then extended from New York to Albany (144 miles, opened 1851), and thence to Buffalo (297¾ miles, opened 1841), 441¾ miles. There were branch lines to Schenectady, Rochester, Attica, Suspension Bridge, Tonawanda, Charlotte, and Lewiston, measuring in all 292¼ miles. The company also leased the Spuyten Duyvil and Port Morris, 6 miles; the Troy and Greenbush, 6 miles; the Niagara Bridge and Canandaigua, 98½ miles; the Buffalo Junction, 7¾ miles; the New York and Harlem, 180¼ miles; the Dunkirk, Alleghany Valley, and Pittsburg, 104 miles. Other new lines and extensions have since been added, and the total owned, operated, and leased to 30th September, 1883, was 2,685 miles.

CAPITAL—30th September, 1883:—

Stock and Debts.

	September 30, 1882.	September 30, 1883.
Capital stock	*$89,428,300	†$89,428,300
Funded debt	48,473,033	49,997,233
Unfunded debt	5,254,369	4,[illegible]89,243
Total funded and unfunded debt	53,727,403	54,686,476
Average rate per annum of interest on funded debt	6½ per cent.	6½ per cent.
Number of shares of stock of par value of $100 per share	894,283	894,283
Number of stockholders	7,536	9,265

Funded Debt.

KIND OF BONDS.	When issued.	When due.	Rate of interest.	Amount issued Sept 30, 1882.	Amount issued Sept. 30, 1883.
New York Central and Hudson River Railroad first mortgage coupons	1873	1903	7 per cent.	$9,085,000	$9,545,000
New York Central and Hudson River Railroad first mortgage registered	1873	1903	7 per cent.	18,380,[illegible]00	20,455,000
New York Central and Hudson River Railroad first mortgage sterling	1873	1903	6 per cent.	9,733,333	9,733,333
Hudson River Railroad second mortgage and sinking fund ‡	1860	1885	7 per cent.	1,422,900	1,422,900
New York Central Railroad debt certificates	1853	1883	6 per cent.	6,632,300	6,450,000
New York Central Railroad to Buffalo and Niagara Falls Railroad	1854	1883	6 per cent.	74,500	Paid.
New York Central Railroad for real estate	1854	1883	6 per cent.	162,000	Paid.
New York Central Railroad for railroad stocks	1853	1883	6 per cent.	592,000	Paid.
New York Central Railroad six per cents., due 1887	1862	1887	6 per cent.	2,391,000	2,391,000
Totals				$48,473,033	$49,997,233

The cost of road and equipment to the same date amounted to $114,731,917.

The balance sheet to 30th September, 1884, was stated to be as under:—

Assets.

Cost of road and equipment	$145,959,142
Stocks and bonds of other companies	3,241,919
Other permanent investments	6,308,624
Due by agents and others	3,728,179
Supplies on hand	1,883,361
Cash on hand	1,491,220
Harlem construction account	6,720
Equipment Harlem Line	404,394
	$162,523,569

Liabilities.

Capital stock	$89,428,300
Bonds on real estate	109,320
Funded debt	56,497,233
Interest accrued	921,354
Dividends unpaid	51,522
Due for supplies, &c., September	1,757,835
Sundries due other R. R. companies, &c.	954,599
Profit and loss	12,803,404
	$162,523,569

* Includes $116,900 consolidation certificates not yet converted.
† Includes $16,900 consolidation certificates not yet converted.
‡ Balance after deducting sinking fund of $326,100.

New 5 Per Cent. Debenture Bonds.—In the latter part of 1884 there were issued 5 per cent. debenture bonds for $6,500,000, redeemable on the 1st September, 1904 (not before) at par, with interest payable half-yearly on the 1st March and September, the first coupon falling due 1st March, 1885. The prospectus inviting applications stated that these bonds were part of $10,000,000 authorised to be issued, and that it was provided that of these, $3,500,000 should be retained to restore $1,350,000 Hudson River second mortgage bonds, due June, 1885, and $2,150,000 New York Central bonds, due December, 1887, and also that any mortgage placed upon the company's property prior to 1st July, 1902, shall include the above issue, and further that each bond shall be countersigned by the Union Trust Company of New York as evidence of validity. They were issued either for $1,000 each to bearer, with interest coupons attached, or in registered certificates of $1,000, $5,000, and $10,000 each.—London Agents, J. S. Morgan and Co., 22, Old Broad Street, E.C.

Revenue.—This account for the year ending 30th September, 1884, compared with 1883, may be summarised as follows:—

	1884.	1883.	Decrease.
Freight earnings	$16,434,983	$20,142,433	$3 707,450
Passenger earnings	7,533,213	8,526,843	993,620
Miscellaneous earnings	4,180,472	5,101,445	920,973
Gross earnings	$28,148,669	$33,770,721	$5,622,052
Operating expenses, including taxes on property (63·46 per cent. in 1884 and 61·44 per cent. in 1883)	17,849,313	20,750,894	2,901,280
Net earnings	$10,299,355	$13,020,127	$2,720,771
Interest, rent of leased lines, and State taxes on capital and earnings	5,630,595	5,692,971	62,376
Profit (5·22 per cent. in 1884 and 8·19 per cent. in 1883)	$4,668,760	$7,327,155	$2,658,395
Dividends (8 per cent.)	7,169,643	7,141,131	11,511
	$2,490,883	$2,490,883	$2,669,907

The following is the statement for the quarter ending June 30th, 1884:—

Gross earnings	$6,361,070
Operating expenses	3,986,257
Net	$2,374,812
Interest, rentals, and taxes	1,641,000
Surplus	$733,812

BALANCE SHEET.—*Liabilities.*

Stock	$89,428,300
Bonds, mortgages on real estate	209,820
Funded debt	49,997,233
Loans	3,000,000
Interest due and unpaid	6,854
Dividends unpaid	45,391
Due for wages and supplies	3,035,050
Sundries	1,739,992
Profit and loss	14,692,613
Total	$162,154,756

Assets.

Cost, road and equipment	$145,997,478
Stock and bonds of other companies	3,241,919
Other investments	6,298,383
Due by agents and others	2,447,339
Supplies on hand	1,824,569
Cash on hand	1,252,075
Sundries	689,092
Harlem construction account	19,503
Equipment on Harlem	404,394
Total	$162,154,756

The dividends on the capital stock (which have been at the rate of 8 per cent. per annum for some time) are paid quarterly, viz., on the 15th of January, April, July, and October; the last two quarterly dividends were, however, at the reduced rate of 6 per cent. per annum, payable 15th October, 1884, and 15th January, 1885. The coupons on the bonds held in this country are paid by the Union Bank of London, on the 1st January and 1st July.

In the beginning of 1880, Messrs. J. S. Morgan & Co. gave notice that they were authorised by the company to authenticate and attest signatures of transfers of shares which may be presented at their offices (22, Old Broad Street), to be executed there by the registered holders, who must be satisfactorily identified.

President—J. H. RUTTER, New York.
First Vice-President—C. C. CLARKE.
Second Vice-President—C. M. DEPEW.
Third Vice-President—H. J. HAYDEN.
Chairman of Board of Directors—CORNELIUS VANDERBILT.

OFFICERS.—Sec., E. D. Worcester; Treasurer, E. V. W. Rossiter; Auditor, D. W. Tuthill; all at New York. Gen. Supt., John M. Toucey; Chief Eng., Charles H. Fisher; Loco. Supt., William Buchanan; all at Albany.

Chief Office—Grand Central Depôt, New York. Transfer Office—Duncan, Sherman, and Co., New York.

London Agents—J. S. Morgan and Co., 22, Old Broad Street, E.C.

426.—NEW YORK, CHICAGO, AND ST. LOUIS.

The following is an extract from the annual report of the President, W. K. Vanderbilt, for the year 1883:—

The road extends from Grand Crossing, near Chicago, to Buffalo, N.Y., a distance of 512·54 miles, 5·94 miles of which are double main track. There are 85·38 miles of sidings, including yard and shop tracks and Y connections with other roads, making a total of 603·86 miles; 561·8 miles of this are laid with steel and 41·99 miles with iron rails. 9·9) miles of main line used in Illinois; 152·56 miles of line used in Indiana; 239·53 miles of line used in Ohio; 43·98 miles of line used in Pennsylvania; 68·07 miles of line used in New York.

The road is divided into four working divisions, viz.:—Buffalo to Conneaut, 114 miles; Conneaut to Bellevue, 131 miles; Bellevue to Fort Wayne, 123 miles; Fort Wayne to Grand Crossing, 144 miles.

The equipment consists of 108 locomotives, 24 first class passenger cars, ten second class passenger cars, one officer's car, one pay car, ten baggage cars, four baggage and mail cars, 80 caboose cars, 1,200 flat cars, 210 gondola cars, four derrick cars, 700 stock cars, and 4,500 box cars.

The earnings and expenses are as follows:—

Earnings.

Freight	$2,000,562
Passengers	232,624
Express	7,802
Miscellaneous	86,696
Total	$2,327,584

Operating Expenses and Taxes.

Conducting of transportation	$608,756
Motive power	498,047
Maintenance of way	365,095
Maintenance of cars	87,656
General expenses	80,910
Total	$1,638,464
Taxes	56,839
Net earnings	$632,389

The operating expenses, exclusive of taxes, were 70·3 per cent. of the gross earnings.

Trains commenced running 23rd October, 1882, but on account of unsatisfactory arrangements for terminal facilities at Buffalo and Chicago, were practically limited to a car load exchange with connecting roads at those points, and prevented from transacting a merchandise business. This state of things remained unchanged until 1st May, 1883, when we were admitted to the premises of the Lake Shore, and the use of the tracks of the Illinois Central was then discontinued and trains run over the Lake Shore and Michigan Southern, between Grand Crossing and Chicago. The establishment of through line freight organisations *via* our different connections at Buffalo required time, and not until late in the season were satisfactory results realised. The net earnings in the last four months in 1883 were $467,827, being 73 per cent. of the net earnings of the entire year. The incomplete condition of the road rendered it necessary to make considerable expenditures for shops, shop machinery, station buildings, yard tracks, &c.

427.—NEW YORK, LAKE ERIE, AND WESTERN.

(LATE ERIE.)

This company is a reorganisation of the Erie Railroad Company (formerly the New York and Erie Railroad Company), which was incorporated by special act of the Legislature of New York, 24th April, 1832. Concurrent legislation was also obtained from the Assemblies of New Jersey and Pennsylvania relative to the portions of the system situated in those States. The Erie Company at one time made considerable payments on its open capital, but from 1865 to 1872 there was a total suspension of dividends on the ordinary capital and frequent partial defaults on the preference. A dividend of 1¾ per cent. was paid on the common stock for the year ended 31st December, 1872, and a further dividend of 1 per cent. for the six months ended 30th June, 1873. This was the last dividend paid on the common stock.

The certificate of incorporation of the new company is dated 26th April, 1878.

MILEAGE.—The official report for the year ended 30th September, 1884, gave the following figures (which include the New York, Pennsylvania, and Ohio from May 1st, 1883), viz.:—

Road and Equipment.

	1881-2.	1882-3.	1883-4.
Miles owned	580	592	594
Miles leased and controlled	480	1,028	1,028
Total operated	1,060	1,620	1,622

CAPITAL, &c.—30th September, 1884.—The total cost of road and equipment, and other expenditure on capital account to the above date, amounted to $179,815,587. The receipts amounted to $164,519,436. The balance was debited to profit and loss.

CAPITAL STOCK—30th September, 1884.—The total amount of stock upon which assessments have been paid is, as per last report, $85,240,500, and of this there has been issued in exchange therefor, to 30th September, 1884, the stock of this company, as follows, viz.:—

Common stock	$76,692,100	
Preferred stock	8,140,800	=$84,832,900
There is still held awaiting such exchange:—		
Common stock	$391,700	
Preferred stock	15,900	= 407,600
		$85,240,500

The total amount of capital stock issued to 30th September, 1884, is as follows:—

Amount exchanged as above	$84,832,900	
Common stock sold in fiscal year 1880-81 (5,000 shares)	500,000	=$85,332,900
Amount of assented stock awaiting exchange, as above		407,600
Amount on hand subject to sale—		
Common stock	4,162 shares	796,400
Preferred stock	3,802 "	
Total amount authorised		$86,536,900

Funded Debt, Year ended 30th September, 1884.

Bonds.	Principal.	Date of Maturity.	Rate.	Due.
First mortgage bonds............	$71,000	May 1, 1897	7¼ °/ₒ gold......	May & Nov.
" " "	2,411,000	"	7 " currency	"
Second " "	2,149,000	Sept. 1, 1919	5 " gold	Mar. & Sept.
Third " "	4,618,000	Mar. 1, 1923	4½ " "	"
Fourth " "	2,926,000	Oct. 1, 1920	5 " "	April & Oct.
Fifth " "	709,500	June 1, 1888	7 " currency	June & Dec.
Buffalo Branch mortgage bonds	182,600	July 1, 1891	7 " "	Jan. & July.
	$13,067,100	....	....	....
First consolidated mortgage bonds	16,890,000	Sept. 1, 1920	7 °/ₒ gold	Mar. & Sept.
First consolidated funded coupon bonds	3,705,977	"	7 " "	"
Second consolidated mortgage bonds	25,000,000	Dec. 1, 1969	6 " "	June & Dec.
Second consolidated funded coupon bonds......	8,597,400	"	6 " "	"
Reorganisation first lien bonds, from November 1, 1881	2,500,000	Dec. 1, 1908	6 " "	May & Nov.
Collateral trust bonds...........	5,000,000	Nov. 1, 1922	6 " "	"
Income bonds	508,008	June 1, 1977*	....	....
Total	$75,268,485	....	....	....

REVENUE.—The following official statement shows the result of the operations of this line for the year ended 30th September, 1884:—

The gross earnings and expenses of the road, including all branches and leased lines, have been as follow:—

Earnings.

General freight	$10,618,327	
Coal	5,154,678	
Passengers	4,675,871	
Mails	211,422	
Express	503,883	
Miscellaneous	258,408	
Car service—freight	59,982	
Passenger pool	30,217	
Freight pools	124,646=	$21,637,435

Working Expenses.

Conducting transportation	$7,059,155	
Motive power	4,749,570	
Maintenance of cars	1,247,324	
Maintenance of way	2,602,368	
General expenses	699,660=	16,358,078

Net earnings from traffic	$5,279,357
To which add earnings from other sources	1,077,626
Total	$6,356,983
From which deduct amount for interest on funded debt, rentals of leased lines, and other charges	5,375,736
Leaving	$981,247
The amount of coupon on the second consolidated mortgage bonds maturing 1st June, 1884, together with the amount of interest accruing on such bonds from 1st June to 30th September 1884, was.........	1,679,870
Leaving a deficit on the operations of the year of	$698,623

The earnings and expenses of the company (including the operations of the New York, Pennsylvania, and Ohio) for the year, as compared with those of 1883, show a decrease in gross earnings of $1,164,812, an increase in working expenses of $913,495, and a decrease in net earnings of $2,078,306, hence the increase in the

* Interest payable at the rate of 6 per cent. per annum, or at such lesser rate for any fiscal year as the net earnings of the company for that year, as declared by the board of directors and applicable for that purpose, shall be sufficient to satisfy.

working expenses is attributable to the fact that for 1883 there was but five months of the year for which this company was charged with such working expenses, while for 1884 it was charged with them for the entire year.

The working expenses have been 69$\frac{53}{100}$ per cent. of the earnings (including for this purpose the entire gross earnings of the New York, Pennsylvania, and Ohio), an increase over the previous year of 4$\frac{74}{100}$ per cent.

NEW YORK, LAKE ERIE, AND WESTERN PROPER.—The earnings and expenses for the year for the New York, Lake Erie, and Western proper, excluding those of the New York, Pennsylvania, and Ohio, as compared with those for 1883, show a decrease in gross earnings of $2,979,595, a decrease in working expenses of $1,509,362, and a decrease in net earnings of $1,470,233.

NEW YORK, PENNSYLVANIA, AND OHIO PROPER.—The gross earnings of this road accruing to the Erie under the lease (viz.: 68 per cent.) for the year were $4,018,459, and its entire working expenses were $4,288,740, resulting in a loss in in its operation of $270,281.

The result of operating this road from the commencement of the lease (May, 1883), to 30th September, 1884, is as follows:—

Net profit for the first five months, to 30th September, 1883	$199,540
Loss for the year 1884	270,281
Net loss to 30th September, 1884	$70,741

SCHEME OF RECONSTRUCTION.—The amended scheme of the Committee of Bond and Shareholders will be found in the *Appendix* to the MANUAL for 1877. The heads of such scheme may be thus briefly summarised:—

The 1st consolidated mortgage bonds (which were issued in 1872 for the conversion and extinction of the whole mortgage and bonded debts of the company) to bear the same rate of interest as heretofore, viz., at 7 per cent. per annum; and of the ten interest coupons, five overdue and five accruing up to and inclusive of 1st March, 1880, six to be funded and four paid off at various dates. Coupon bonds to be issued in exchange for the funded coupons, bearing interest at 7 per cent. per annum, and payable in gold on the 1st September, 1920.

The 6 per cent. sterling bonds to bear the same rights as though they were exchanged for 1st consolidated mortgage bonds as above, and to receive interest at 7 per cent. per annum after the 1st September, 1875—practically to form part of 1st consolidated mortgage bonds from that date.

The 2nd consolidated mortgage bonds and gold convertible bonds to be represented by new 2nd consolidated mortgage bonds, bearing interest at 6 per cent. per annum from 1st December, 1879, and maturing 1st December, 1969; the coupons up to 1st December, 1879, to be funded, and coupon bonds issued in lieu thereof, bearing interest at 5 per cent. per annum from 1st December, 1877, to 1st June, 1883, and thereafter at 6 per cent. per annum.

The ordinary and preference shareholders to be re-admitted to shares of equal amounts in the new organization, with voting powers as to one-half of the holdings vested in the trustees until the dividend on the preference shares has been paid for three successive years; the preference shares to carry dividends at the rate of 6 per cent. per annum, dependent upon the net earnings in any year. The admission of ordinary and preference shareholders into the scheme to be subject to the payment by them of an assessment of $6 per ordinary share and $3 per preference share, receiving in exchange for such payments non-accumulative income bonds without mortgage security, bearing interest at 6 per cent. per annum, and repayable in gold on 1st June, 1977; the interest on such income bonds to be dependent upon the profits of each year—the shareholders, however, to have the option of paying $4 and $2 per share respectively, without receiving income bonds.

[MEM.—The half-voting power vested in trustees expired in January, 1884, and the beneficiary certificates were therefore called in and exchanged for ordinary shares in the following April.]

The sale under foreclosure took place in New York on the 25th March, 1878.

FUNDED COUPON BONDS AND FRACTIONAL SCRIP.—Full particulars under this head were given in the MANUAL for 1879, while the funding of the respective coupons of 1st and 2nd mortgage bonds was in progress.

A concise summary showing the effect of the scheme, as finally passed, upon the different classes of bonds, together with other items of interest, will be found in the MANUAL for 1880, page 502.

The London office receives shares for registration free of expense to the owners.

The fiscal year ends 30th September; last year the annual meeting was held on the 30th November, the voting register of bonds held by unregistered owners being closed, at the London office of the company, from the 30th September to the 30th October previously.

NEW YORK, PENNSYLVANIA, AND OHIO.—Lease, &c., see GENERAL INDEX.

President—JOHN KING.

OFFICERS.—Sec., Agustus R. Macdonough; Gen. Man., Robt. Harris; Treasurer, B. W. Spencer; Gen. Supt., Edmund S. Bowen; Chief Eng., Octave Chanute; Auditor, A. J. M. Dowell; Auditor of Disbursements, J. N. Outwater; Supt. of Transportation, B. Thomas, Jersey City; Assistant Treasurer, H. H. Thompson, all at New York; Loco. Supt., F. M. Wilder, Susquehanna; Purchasing Agent, J. A. Hardenburgh, New York.

General Offices—Courtlandt Street, New York.

London Agent—J. D. Ayers.

London Offices—6, Old Jewry, E.C.

428.—NEW YORK, ONTARIO, AND WESTERN.

The report for the year ended 30th September, 1883, referred to the difficulties surmounted in connection with the Middleton and Weehawken Branch, opened in June last. The New York, West Shore, and Buffalo was opened for traffic between New York and Buffalo on the 1st day of January, 1884, and a large and profitable business is expected at an early date. The unfunded debt of the company, which is stated in the report to the Railroad Commissioners to be $2,311,898 on the 30th of September, 1883, has been reduced to $1,221,106, in which amount is included all sums due and claims for which the company may in any way be liable under its construction contracts. One-half (23,600 shares) of the capital stock of the West Shore and Ontario Terminal is owned by this company, and jointly with the New York, West Shore, and Buffalo it is lessee of all the terminal property at Weehawken and in New York.

The following are the principal figures given:—

	Earnings.		
Passenger	$180,152	$211,789	$354,777
Freight	469,156	605,478	754,279
Mail, express, &c.	275,737	219,297	248,722
Total gross earnings	$925,045	$1,036,564	$1,357,778
	Operating Expenses.		
Maintenance of road and real estate	$204,658	$250,740	$299,117
Maintenance of machinery and cars	141,388	171,877	265,770
Transportation expenses	361,455	425,656	633,189
Total	$707,501	$848,273	$1,198,076
Net earnings	217,544	188,291	159,702

The company owned $10,000,000 of the first mortgage bonds of the New York, West Shore, and Buffalo, $9,759,000 of which were offered to the stockholders of this company at 50 per cent. of their par value, and sold to them by subscription at that rate.

DIRECTORS:

President—E. F. WINSLOW.

Vice-President—T. HOUSTON.

OFFICERS.—Sec. and Asst. Treasurer, J. L. Nisbet; Treasurer, C. N. Jordan. Registrar of Stock—Third National Bank, 20, Nassau Street, New York.

429.—NEW YORK, PENNSYLVANIA, AND OHIO.

(LATE ATLANTIC AND GREAT WESTERN.)

The New York, Pennsylvania, and Ohio was organised on March 24th, 1880, having obtained by purchase all the property and franchises of the late Atlantic and Great Western, from purchasing trustees, who had bought the said property and franchises at a foreclosure sale on January 6th, 1880.

This company's main line extends from Salamanca, in the State of New York, a station on the New York, Lake Erie, and Western, through the north-western portion of the State of New York, through the north-western portion of the State of Pennsylvania, and crosses the State of Ohio in a south-westerly direction to the city of Dayton, in the last-mentioned State.

The property comprises 423¼ miles of railway, with the sidings and working stock, &c., appertaining thereto, and 144 miles of leased lines, together, say 567¼ miles owned or leased.

The lines owned consist of 388 miles of main line, Salamanca to Dayton; 35¼ miles of branches, viz., Franklin Branch, 33¾ miles; Silver Creek Branch, 1½ mile; together, 423¼ miles.

The lines held on lease consist of 125 miles of Cleveland and Mahoning Company's railways, viz., Cleveland and Mahoning, old lease, 81½ miles; and under the new lease, Niles and New Lisbon, 35¾ miles; and Vienna Junction to Vienna, 7¾ miles; 17 miles of Sharon Railway; and 2 miles of Westerman State Line to Sharon, together 144 miles.

The main line and branches belonging to this company were originally built of the exceptional gauge of six feet, but on 22nd June, 1881, the main line was narrowed to the standard gauge of the country, 4 feet 8½ inches. The Franklin Branch was narrowed to the same gauge on 29th September, 1881. All the lines owned and leased by the company are now of the standard gauge of the country, thus furnishing the means of a ready interchange of traffic with the numerous railroads which cross its line, a privilege which had not existed since the road was built.

368 miles of track are laid with steel rails.

The equipment consists of 220 locomotives; 101 passenger cars; 45 mail, baggage, and express cars; 4,543 freight cars; 15 tool and wrecking cars.

Lease to the "Erie."—It is stated from New York that the following are the securities lodged by the Erie Company as "guarantee" for due fulfilment of the terms of the lease of the Atlantic and Great Western property:—1st. First lien on all property Erie puts into New York, Pennsylvania, and Ohio. 2nd. Authority to collect from Erie all moneys in hands of agents along leased lines and branches. 3rd. $470,000 shares, capital stock, Suspension Bridge and Erie Junction. 4th. $35,000 first mortgage bonds of same company. 5th. $250,000 capital stock Paterson, Newark, and New York Railroad.

The following particulars are extracted from an official statement, showing the position, &c., of the various classes of securities of the reorganised company, viz.:—

Prior lien mortgage	$8,000,000	
First mortgage	36,154,000	
Second mortgage	14,500,000	
Third mortgage	30,000,000=	$87,500,000

PRIORITIES, DESCRIPTIONS, &c., OF MORTGAGES, STOCKS, &c.

No.	Year of Act	Full Description (to be observed in Transfer Deeds and all other Legal Documents).	Rate ₱ cent ₱ annum.
1	1880	Prior lien bonds	6
2	,,	First mortgage bonds	7
3	,,	Second ,, ,,	5
4	,,	Third ,, ,,	5
5	,,	Preferred stock ($10,000,000)	1
6	,,	Common ,, ($35,000,000)	1

For a statement containing the issue of bonds by the reorganisation trustees to 2nd November, 1882, see Manual for 1884, page 475.

General Balance Sheet.—30th September, 1884:—

Cost of property purchased		$139,854,710
Sharon stock, acquired at the time of purchase of property		141,319
New construction from capital		482,491
Additions—1880, 1881, 1882, and 1883	$290,765	
,, 1884	58,189=	348,954
Additions made by New York, Lake Erie, and Western		3,311
Sharon stock, acquired since the purchase of property	$36,076	
Additions on Sharon, to be paid in Sharon stock	38,847=	74,923
Chicago and Atlantic—advance account		66,926
Treasurer	$5,443	
Due by Agents—account of freight	234	
Due by Mansfield stock yards—capital account	400	
Due by New York, Lake Erie, and Western—rent account	327,605	
Due by sundry companies and individuals	26,852=	360,535
Deposited to meet interest on bonds.—See contra.		
Farmers' Loan and Trust Company, to pay prior lien coupons	$252,150	
Voting trustees, to pay 1st mortgage coupons	69,685=	321,835
		$141,655,034

CAPITAL, &c.—30th September, 1884:—Common stock ...	$34,999,350	$
Preferred stock	10,000,000=	44,999,350
Prior lien bonds	$8,000,000	
1st mortgage bonds	41,457,000	
2nd "	14,500,000	
3rd "	30,000,000=	93,957,000
Deferred warrants		1,408,920
Special fund for additions—1880, 1881, 1882, and 1883	$290,765	
Special fund for additions—1884	58,189=	348,954
Special fund to meet payments for Sharon stock		74,922
Special fund to meet interest on Chicago and Atlantic 1st mortgage bonds		75,000
Special fund to meet payments on account of capital		22,250
Surplus fund		185,802
Due for audited vouchers	$36,412	
Due for wages	298	
Due sundry companies and individuals	14,980	
Due New York, Lake Erie, and Western—permanent improvement account	88,331=	139,970
Interest on prior lien bonds—Series No. 10		40,000
Interest on bonds for which funds are deposited.—See contra:		
Prior lien bonds—Series No. 4	$270	
" " " " 5	150	
" " " " 6	120	
" " " " 7	450	
" " " " 8	11,160	
" " " " 9	240,000	
1st mortgage bonds " " 1	2,931	
" " " " 5	4,369	
" " " " 7	14,043	
" " " " 8	48,342=	321,835
		141,655,004
INCOME ACCOUNT for year ended 30th September, 1884:—		
Income from rental under the lease to New York, Lake Erie, and Western for the 12 months ended 30th September, 1884		$1,891,039
Income from business prior to 1st May, 1883		19,129
Income from other sources—dividend on Sharon stock		12,104
Total income from all sources		$1,922,272
Deductions from income:—		
Use of foreign cars and engines	$232	
Hire of cars under car trust—Clark, Post, and Martin	260,346	
Hire of cars under car trust—J. F. Clark	21,453	
Rent of Cleveland and Mahoning Valley	357,180	
Rent of Sharon	28,495	
Rent of Westerman	3,000	
Rent of water rights	292	
Rent of docks, lots, &c.	35,923	
General expenses	6,200	
Taxes	30,537	
Profit and loss	1,608	
London agency expenses	41,231	
Expenses of organisation	62,680	
Contingent liabilities	60,000	
	$919,178	
Less interest and exchange	11,033=	908,145
Net income for the 12 months		$1,014,128
Deduct:—Interest on prior lien bonds (due and accrued)	$480,000	
Special fund applicable to additions in the year 1884 on the company's lines, except the Sharon	58,189	
Special fund to meet payments of Sharon stock	74,922	
Special fund to meet payments on account of capital	22,250	
Dividend paid on account of coupon No. 8 of the 1st mortgage bonds, due 1st July, 1884	202,517=	838,880
		$175,248
Add surplus from period ending 30th September, 1883	$41,702	
Less correction on rental of five months ending 30th Sept., 1883	31,149=	10,553
Surplus carried to next year		$185,801

Payment of coupons on 1st mortgage bonds from 1st July, 1881:—

Due date.	Per cent. of $35 coupon in cash sterling.	Per cent. of $35 coupon in deferred warrants.	Sterling value of distribution per $1,000 bond or $35 coupons.
	£ s.	$.	£ s.
1881—July 1st	Nil.	35	3 17
1882—January 1st	Nil.	35.	3 0
1882—July 1st	Nil.	35	2 14
1883—January 1st	2 10	22¼	4 9
1883—July 1st	Nil.	35	3 2
1884—January 1st	3 5	18¾	5 0
1884—July 1st	1 0	30	2 16
1885—January 1st	Nil.	35	2 2

[MEM.—Full particulars of the manner in which the various securities of the old "Atlantic" Company were dealt with, under the reconstruction scheme given in preceding paragraphs, were inserted in the MANUAL for 1880, and previous editions, under the old heading of "Atlantic and Great Western."]

A description of the foregoing mortgages is as follows:—

All the bonds and their coupons are payable in gold coin of the United States of America, or in sterling at the rate of four shillings to the dollar.

Prior Lien Bonds.—Amount of issue $8,000,000, or 1,600,000*l.* sterling, all outstanding. Consisting of 5,500 bonds of $1,000, or 200*l.* sterling each, numbered consecutively from 1 to 5,500, both numbers inclusive, and 5,000 bonds of $500, or 100*l.* sterling each, numbered consecutively from 1 to 5,000, both numbers inclusive. Date of issue, May 5th, 1880; date of maturity, March 1st, 1895; rate of interest, 6 per cent. per annum, payable at the option of the holder, in New York or London, England, on March 1st and September 1st of each year. Stockholders in no event shall be personally liable for the interest or principal of these bonds. Name of trustee, Farmers' Loan and Trust Company of New York, New York City.

First Mortgage Bonds.—Amount authorised, $35,000,000, or 7,000,000*l.* sterling a large portion of which is outstanding. The total, consisting of 32,500 bonds of $1,000, or 200*l.* sterling each, numbered consecutively from 1 to 32,500, both numbers inclusive, and 5,000 bonds of $500, or 100*l.* sterling each, numbered consecutively from 1 to 5,000, both numbers inclusive. Date of issue, May 6th, 1880; date of maturity, July 1st, 1905; rate of interest, 5 per cent. per annum, from July 1st to December 31st, 1880, after which latter date 7 per cent. per annum, payable, at the option of the holder, at New York or London, England, on January 1st and July 1st of each year, if the net earnings or rental of the mortgaged premises shall be sufficient to pay the same. If part of the interest only be paid, deferred warrants will be issued for the part remaining unpaid, which warrants can be converted, in sums of $1,000, into bonds of the same class. Interest on these bonds does not become obligatory until after July 1st, 1895. No right of action or to foreclose the said mortgage shall exist until three months shall have elapsed after the prior lien bonds shall have become due and payable. The mortgagor reserves the right to lease the mortgaged premises. Stockholders are exempted from all personal or individual liability for, or in respect of, the interest or principal of these bonds. Trustees, Farmers' Loan and Trust Company of New York, New York.

Second Mortgage Bonds.—Amount authorised, $14,500,000, or 2,900,000*l.* sterling, a large portion of which is outstanding. The total, consisting of 13,000 bonds of $1,000, or 200*l.* sterling each, numbered consecutively from 1 to 13,000, both numbers inclusive, and 3,000 bonds of $500, or 100*l.* sterling each, numbered consecutively from 1 to 3,000, both numbers inclusive. Date of issue, May 7th, 1880; date of maturity, May 1st, 1910; rate of interest, 5 per cent. per annum, payable, at the option of the holder, at New York or London, England, on May 1st and November 1st of each year, the first coupon becoming due May 1st, 1881, if the net earnings or rental of the mortgaged premises shall be sufficient to pay the same. Interest non-accumulative. The mortgagor reserves the power of leasing the mortgaged premises. Stockholders are exempted from all personal and individual liability in respect of the interest or principal of this mortgage. Trustees, Herman Drisler and William Tell Niswanger, of New York.

Third Mortgage Bonds.—Amount authorised, $30,000,000, or 6,000,000*l.* sterling, a large portion of which is outstanding. The total, consisting of 28,500 bonds of $1,000, or 200*l.* sterling each, numbered consecutively from 1 to 28,500, both numbers inclusive, and 3,000 bonds of $500, or 100*l.* sterling each, numbered consecutively from 1 to 3,000, both numbers inclusive. Date of issue, May 7th, 1880; date of maturity, May 1st, 1915; rate of interest, 5 per cent. per annum, payable, at the option of the holder, at New York or London, England, on May 1st and November 1st of each year, the first coupon becoming due on May 1st, 1881, if the net earnings or rental of the mortgaged premises are sufficient to pay the same. Interest non-accumulative. The mortgagor reserves the power to lease the mortgaged premises. Stockholders are exempted from all personal or individual liability in respect of the interest or principal of this mortgage. Trustees, Herman Drisler and William Tell Niswanger, of New York.

The second and third mortgage bonds are included in the same mortgage. No right of action at law upon the bonds and coupons thereof, or of foreclosure, will accrue to the holders of these two classes of bonds.

In the event of a surplus remaining, after paying interest on all the foregoing described bonds as given, and of 1 per cent. per annum dividend on common and preferred stock, such surplus will be applied in increasing the interest on second and third mortgage bonds in succession to 7 per cent. in cash, and thereafter to 5 per cent. dividend on the preferred stock.

The company has no outstanding obligations other than its bonded debt.

The capital stock authorised is as follows:—

Common stock....................................	$35,000,000	
Preferred stock	10,000,000	= $45,000,000

None of which is issued, at the present writing, to the public.

The above stock is non-voting beneficiary stock, the holder possessing all the rights incident to the general ownership thereof, except the possession of the legal title and the right to vote thereon, which right is vested in voting trustees, during the existence of the voting trust, which will continue until the third mortgage bondholders receive 7 per cent. per annum during three years.

Deferred Warrants for First Mortgage Interest.—It may be well to state, for the information of those entitled to deferred warrants for the unpaid portion of each new first mortgage coupon, that such warrants will be exchangeable at the London agency of the company, in the months of May and November in every year, in sums of $1,000 (but not otherwise) for a first mortgage bond. Such bonds will carry the half-yearly coupon due next after the period of exchange, *ex. gr.*, a warrant presented in May will be exchanged for a bond carrying the half-year's coupon payable the 1st July following.

There will be two offices for the purpose of transferring stock, one in Cleveland, Ohio, with registrar at same place, and one at New York City, arrangements having been made with the Farmers' Loan and Trust Company of New York to transfer and register all stock dealt in, in that city, at the option of the owner.

ATLANTIC FIRST LEASED LINES RENTAL TRUST LIMITED.—See GENERAL INDEX.

LEASED LINES, &c.—For particulars of the Leased Lines Bonds of 1873, Western Extension Certificates, and Western Extensions, see the MANUAL for 1881, page 510, and for 1882, page 494, no further information having been received.

VOTING TRUST.—It will be recollected that an important part of the scheme of re-organization was the following:—"That the shares of the reconstructed company be deposited in trust, and the right to vote thereon be exercised by five trustees, elected annually at a meeting called for the purpose, three to be chosen by a majority in value of the first mortgage bondholders, one by a majority in value of the second mortgage bondholders, and one by a majority in value of the leased lines bondholders. This trust to continue until the third mortgage bondholders receive 7 per cent. interest in cash during three years. Certificates in exchange for and representing the deposited shares, and entitling to dividends when declared, will be issued by the trustees."

DIRECTORS:

President—JARVIS M. ADAMS, Cleveland, Ohio.

Vice-President—JOHN TOD, Cleveland, Ohio.

E. R. Perkins, Cleveland, Ohio.
Samuel L. Mather, Cleveland, Ohio.
W. J. McKinnie, Cleveland, Ohio.
J. M. Ferris, Cleveland, Ohio.
S. M. Felton, Jun., Cleveland, Ohio.
W. W. MacFarland, New York City.
Geo. Boyce, Sharon, Pennsylvania.
Henry B. Perkins, Warren, Ohio.
W. W. Scarborough, Cincinnati, Ohio.
C. C. Waite, Cincinnati, Ohio.
W. H Upson, Cincinnati, Ohio.

OFFICERS.—General Man., J. M. Ferris; Treasurer, F. E. Bittman; Auditor and Sec., Thomas Warnock; General Passenger and Ticket Agent, A. E. Clark; Chief Engineer, Chas. Latimer; General Freight Agent, G. G. Cochran.

General Office—Cleveland, Ohio.

TRUSTEES OF THE REORGANISATION:—

Chairman.—CHARLES E. LEWIS, Esq., M.P.

Gen. Sir George Balfour, K.C.B., M.P. | Rev. John Lockington Bates, M.A.

Secretary, Fred. W. Smith.

VOTING TRUSTEES:

Charles E. Lewis, Esq., M.P. | Rt. Hon. Henry Cecil Raikes, M.P.
Gen. Sir George Balfour, K.C.B., M.P. | Rev. John Lockington Bates, M.A.

London Agency, 20, Bucklersbury, E.C.

Secretary, London Agency, Fred. W. Smith.

430.—NORFOLK AND WESTERN.

(FORMERLY ATLANTIC, MISSISSIPPI, AND OHIO.)

This company was formed in February, 1881, for the purchase of the Atlantic, Mississippi, and Ohio, which was an amalgamation (authorised by act of the General Assembly of Virginia, 17th June, 1870) of the Norfolk and Petersburg, South Side, Virginia, and Tennessee, and Virginia and Kentucky railroads. The Norfolk and Petersburg Line runs between the two places named, and is 81 miles in length. The South Side Line extends from Petersburg to Lynchburg, 123 miles, and from Petersburg to City Point, 10 miles. The Virginia and Tennessee Line extends from Lynchburg to Bristol, 204 miles, and a branch line from Glade Springs to Salt Works, 10 miles. The number of miles of road owned is 296, and the number of miles operated is 373. The company now owns 1,933 cars.

The following information relates to the discharge of bonds, &c., of the old (Atlantic, &c.) Company, viz.:—The 7 per cent. consolidated mortgage bonds were the only securities of this railway quoted in this country. The railway was sold in February, 1881, under the foreclosure suit instituted by the committee appointed by the holders of the bonds in March, 1876, and realised $8,605,000. The United States Court ordered payment of the overdue interest on the bonds, and 95 per cent. of the principal, retaining the 5 per cent. for further order.

The committee paid in exchange for their certificates 134*l.* 2*s.* per cent., and at the same time issued a remnant warrant entitling the bearer to such further sum as may be divisible. In November, 1881, the United States Court decreed the payment of the 5 per cent. retained, and in January last the English Committee issued the following notice, viz.:—Notice is hereby given to the holders of remnant warrants (representing certificates for bonds) issued by the English Committee, appointed March 4th, 1876, that such remnant warrants are now payable at the Consolidated Bank Limited, 52, Threadneedle Street, E.C. The final amount payable in accordance with the committee's circular of 10th January, 1882, is 10*l.* 9*s.* 3*d.* for each certificate for a bond represented by remnant warrants. The remnant warrants must be left with the Consolidated Bank two clear days for examination, and may be presented between the hours of 11 and 3 on any week day. Forms of lists, which must be filled in on presenting the remnant warrants with forms of receipt annexed, can be obtained at the Consolidated Bank.

In April, 1881, the Norfolk and Western issued $5,000,000 general mortgage bonds, in 5,000 bonds to bearer of $1,000 each, forming part of a total of $11,000,000 general mortgage bonds, secured by a first mortgage on the property and franchises of the company made to the Fidelity Insurance Trust and Safe Deposit Company of Philadelphia. Principal payable in Philadelphia, and interest payable in New York and Philadelphia, in United States gold coin, without deduction for any United States or State tax. Principal payable May 1st, 1931, being fifty years from date. Interest payable May 1st and November 1st in each year.

Interest upon the bonds commenced to run from the date on which the final payment of 205*l.* 15*s.* was made, and the annual interest (calculating the dollar at 4*s.* 1*d.*) will be 12*l.* 5*s.* per $1,000 bond, equal to 5*l.* 13*s.* 6*d.* per cent. on the price of investment. The proceeds of this issue were made applicable to the purchase of the old undertaking, and for other purposes.

The third annual report (1883) of this company since its reorganisation, from the old Atlantic, Mississippi, and Ohio, in 1881, showed the earnings and expenses to be as follow:—

Gross earnings		$2,812,776
Operating expenses (53 7-10 per cent.)		1,509,573
Net earnings		$1,303,203
Interest charges:—		
Interest on funded debt	$780,635	
Other interest	30,157	
Total interest charges		810,792
Net income for the year		$492,411

The outstanding liabilities of the company as of date 31st December, 1883, were as follow:—

Divisional liens	$4,085,600
General mortgages	6,699,000
New River division, 1st mortgage	2,000,000
Improvement and extension mortgage bonds	1,500,000
Adjustment mortgage bonds	1,500,000
Convertible debenture bonds	525,000
Preferred capital stock	18,000,000
Common do.	7,000,000

There is no unfunded debt, it having been funded in October last into adjustment mortgage bonds. The outstanding car trust amounted to $1,600,000, and the surplus to credit of income account was about $500,000, and investments in other companies amounted to over $1,500,000.

The New River division was open to the Flat Top coal fields 21st May, 1883, since which time the length of the line in operation has been 503 miles:—

	Miles.
Main line, Norfolk to Bristol	408
Petersburg Branch	10
Saltville Branch	10
New River division	75
Total	503
Sidings	74

431.—NORTHERN CENTRAL.

This line extends from Baltimore, Maryland, to Sunbury, Pennsylvania, 138 miles, with branches as *follow*:—Baltimore Division, 91 miles; Susquehanna Division, 47 miles; and Green Spring Branch, 9 miles, making a total Northern Central mileage of 285 miles. The company leases the Shamokin Valley and Pottsville, 28 miles; the Elmira and Williamsport, 78 miles; the Chemung Railroad (Elmira to Watkins), 22 miles; and the Elmira and Canandaigua, 47 miles. The company have running powers over the Philadelphia and Erie, between Sunbury and Williamsport, a length of 40 miles, thereby obtaining connection with its northern leased lines. The company holds almost the whole of the capital stock of the Chemung, and the Elmira and Canandaigua roads, for which they paid seven per cent. income bonds, redeemable in 50 years, to the amount of $2,750,000.

$3,000,000 of 6 per cent. consolidated mortgage bonds of the company were issued in this country, $2,000,000 in 1874, and $1,000,000 in 1875, by Messrs. McCalmont Brothers and Co., at the price of 87½ per cent., or 175*l*. per bond of $1,000 (200*l*.) The coupons are payable in London, January 1st and July 1st, and the principal not later than 1904, by means of an accumulative sinking fund.

At the annual meeting, held in February, 1879, a committee of three stockholders was appointed to investigate thoroughly the affairs and condition of the company, and the sum of $6,000 was voted out of the gross revenues of the company to provide for the expenses of the investigation.

REVENUE.—The profits for the year 1880 sufficed for the payment of a dividend on the ordinary capital at the rate of 2½ per cent., payable on the 10th January, 1881; this is the first dividend on the ordinary capital since April 1st, 1876, when 3 per cent. was paid.

The annual report of this company for the year 1883, shows that the revenue of the main line, with its leased and controlled roads, was as follows:—

Passengers	$932,390	
Freight	4,749,929	
Express	75,494	
Mails	48,367	
Miscellaneous	257,466	
Miscellaneous passenger	24,695=	$6,088,131

The operating expenses were:—

Conducting transportation	$1,354,062	
Motive power	1,116,491	
Maintenance of way	826,014	
Maintenance of cars	472,060	
General expenses	63,067=	3,831,605
Net earnings		$2,256,526

In comparison with the year 1882, there was an increase in gross earnings of $287,955, equal to 4·96 per cent., and a decrease in expenses of $10,718, or ·28 per cent. The increase in net earnings was $298,673, or 15·26 per cent.

In addition to the net earnings as above stated	$2,256,526	
There was received from dividends and interest	241,914	
Net royalty on coal mined—Shamokin Division	4,929=	$2,503,369

Capital.—Up to 31st December, 1882, there had been expended on the main line and its equipment $18,029,911. The stock and bonds of the company are as follow, viz.:—

Capital stock, 130,000 shares		...	$6,500,000
Mortgage to State of Maryland to secure annuity of $90,000, irredeemable		...	1,500,000
Mortgage sinking fund 6 per cent. coupon bonds, due July 1st, 1885		$1,490,000	
Mortgage 6 per cent. coupon bonds, due April 1st, 1900		1,126,000	
Mortgage 6 per cent. gold bonds, due July 1st, 1900: coupons, $2,599,000; registered, $205,000		2,804,000	
Consolidated general mortgage 6 per cent. gold bonds, due July 1st, 1904:			
*Series "A" and "B," dollar or sterling sinking fund loans	$2,628,000		
Series "C," dollar loan	1,000,000		
1,000,000 dollar loan	930,000		
		4,558,000	
Second general mortgage 5 per cent. coupon bonds, series "A," due January 1st, 1926		2,901,000	
Second general mortgage 6 per cent. coupon convertible bonds, series "B," due January 1st, 1926		1,000,000	
			13,879,000
			$21,879,000

Elmira and Williamsport Bonds.—The president's report for the year ended 31st December, 1878, contains the following information, relating to the above-named bonds, which is inserted for future reference, viz.:—"Under the terms of the lease of the Elmira and Williamsport, it is made the duty of the Northern Central to provide for certain bonds of that company, amounting to $1,000,000, bearing interest at 7 per cent. per annum. These bonds mature on the 1st January, 1880. Arrangements have recently been made under which the bonds will be purchased at par and accrued interest on and after the 15th March, 1879, from such of the holders as may desire to sell; or the holders, if they so desire, may have the privilege of extending the same for a period of thirty years from maturity at 6 per cent. per annum, secured by the same mortgage and under the same guarantees, provided the option of extending is exercised before the 1st May, 1879."

*Agents for these loans—McCalmont Brothers and Co., 15, Philpot Lane, London, E.C.

DIRECTORS:

President—G. B. ROBERTS.

Vice-President—FRANK THOMSON.

Wistar Morris.	S. M. Shoemaker.
H. M. Phillips.	J. N. Hutchinson.
Edmund Smith.	Dell Noblit, Junr.
George Small.	H. Gilbert.
B. F. Newcomer.	H. Walters.

OFFICERS.—Sec., Stephen W. White; Asst. Sec., John W. Davis; Treas., John S. Leib; Gen. Man., Charles E. Pugh; Auditor, John Crowe; Gen. Counsel, Wayne MacVeagh.

Chief Office—Calvert Station, Baltimore, Maryland. Transfer Office—South Fourth Street, Philadelphia.

London Agents—London Joint Stock Bank Limited, Prince's Street, E.C.

432.—OHIO AND MISSISSIPPI.

At the annual meeting in Cincinnati, Ohio, October 11, 1883, the report submitted was substantially as follows:—The net earnings of the road for the past four years is as follows:—For the year ending June 30, 1880, $1,280,261; for the year ending June 30, 1881, $1,118,627: for the year ending June 30, 1882, $844,612; for the year ending June 30, 1883, $1,121,365. On account of the increase the directors have prepared bonds to take the road from the receiver, which are now ready for issue. The present financial status of the company may be stated thus:—

Liabilities.

First mortgage 7 per cent. bonds due January 1, 1898		$6,614,000
Second mortgage 7 per cent. bonds due April 1, 1911		3,829,000
Springfield division 7 per cent. bonds due November 1, 1905		2,009,000
		$12,452,000
In addition there are debts due as follows:—		
Income and funded debt bonds due October 1, 1882	$174,000	
Old western division bonds past due	97,000	
Debenture bonds due May 1, 1883	140,000	
Debts secured by pledge of Springfield division bonds	250,000	
Other debts about	100,000	
Arrears of interest on first, second, and Springfield division mortgage bonds at face	822,955	
Arrears of sinking funds, exclusive of interest on first mortgage bonds and first mortgage sinking fund	496,845=	2,080,800
Total debt		$14,532,800

The report stated there was a fair prospect of resuming the payment of dividends on preferred stock at an early day. Improvements made were noted, and the report concluded by referring to detailed statement of the earnings of the various divisions of the road.—*Railway Age.*

Capital, &c.—In 1884 this was stated to be as follows:—The capital consists of $4,030,000 preferred and $20,000,000 common stock. The preferred stock is entitled to 7 per cent. cumulative dividends, none of which have been paid since 1st March, 1875. The fixed charges are approximately: Interest on $13,000,000 7 per cents., $910,000; 5 per cent. on $3,000,000, $150,000; dividend on preferred stock, 7 per cent., $280,000; total fixed charges, $1,340,000.

Proposed Lease.—In 1884 it was reported in Baltimore that a lease had been effected of this company to the Baltimore and Ohio, which company had agreed to operate the leased road for 65 per cent. of the gross earnings.

At a meeting of the common stockholders held at the Cannon Street Hotel, on Tuesday, 3rd April, 1883, the following resolutions were passed:—1. That a permanent committee be formed to further the interests of the common stockholders. 2. That the committee representing the ordinary shareholders consist of the following gentlemen, with power to add to their number: F. A. Hankey, Esq.; Thomas C. Tatham, Esq.; E. Heinemann, Esq.; Dr. H. Clothier; F. P. Leon, Esq.; Captain F. Pavy. 3. That shareholders be requested to have their shares registered in their own names, or in the names of two members of this committee, in order that the committee may be able properly to represent the shareholders in any negotiations that may be entered into. 4. That shareholders be requested to pay to the secretary a subscription of 6*d.* per share towards defraying the expenses of the committee. No subscription to exceed 25*l.* Shareholders are requested to communicate with the secretary.

OFFICERS.—Sec., W. M. Walton, 54, William Street, New York; Receiver, J. M. Douglas, Cincinnati, Ohio; Treasurer, C. S. Cone; Gen. Man., W. W. Peabody; Auditor, A. Donaldson.

433.—OREGON AND CALIFORNIA.

This line extends from Portland, Oregon, to Roseburg and Junction, Oregon. and is in course of construction to the State Line of California, where it will meet the Oregon Branch of the Central Pacific.

In May, 1881, the position of the undertaking was thus defined:—The present Oregon and California is a reorganisation of the original Oregon and California, with which has been consolidated the Oregon Central, Western Oregon, and Albany and Lebanon, and it now owns all the railroads, lands, franchises, and property of those companies.

It derives its land grants and franchises from the Government of the United States:—

Firstly, from an act of Congress passed July 25th, 1866, for the construction of a railroad and telegraph line from the Central Pacific, in California, to Portland, in Oregon. Of this line the Oregon was to build the part in Oregon and the California (now consolidated with the Central Pacific) the part in California, each company, however, having the right to complete the line of the other company if the latter failed to do so within the specified time. 198 miles of road (East Portland to Roseburg) have been built under this act.

Secondly, from an act of Congress passed May 4th, 1870, for the construction of a line from Portland to Astoria, with a branch to McMinnville. About 47 miles of road (Portland to McMinnville) had been built under this act.

The grants of lands made by the acts mentioned were at the rate of 12,800 acres (= 20 square miles) per mile of road, subject to the ordinary reservations of existing rights. The amounts already earned are estimated in the last annual report of the manager, dated March 8th last, at 1,718,477 35-100 acres under the first act, and 237,000 57-100 under the second.

The portions of the lines completed and uncompleted are as follow:—

	Built.	Unbuilt.	Total Length.
Main Line—East Portland to California State Line, *via* Klamath Lake	198	167	365
West Side Division—Portland to Main Line at Junction, *via* McMinnville and Corvallis	97	25	122
Lebanon Branch	11½	—	12
Astoria Extension	—	96	96
	306½	288	595

In the beginning of 1881 a reorganisation of the undertaking was carried out under the terms given below; for this purpose $6,000,000 new bonds were issued (issue price 200*l.* per bond), which are quoted in London, New York, and Frankfort as Oregon and California first mortgage 6 per cent. gold bonds.

The loan was made in pursuance of the plan of reorganisation of the company adopted at the extraordinary general meeting of the Bondholders' Association, on the 5th of May, 1881, and adopted and ratified by the stockholders of the company on the 7th of May, 1881.

These bonds are to bearer, for $1,000 each, payable on the 1st of July, 1921, unless sooner drawn and redeemed, and will bear interest from January 1st, 1882, at six per cent. per annum, payable half-yearly, on the 1st of January and 1st of July, both principal and interest being payable in New York, in United States gold coin of the present standard. and free from tax.

The bonds contain an undertaking by the company to cash the bonds and interest coupons in London and Frankfort as they become due, at a fixed rate of exchange, viz., in London at 4*s.* 2*d.* per dollar, and in Frankfort of mark 4.25 per dollar.

A cumulative sinking fund of one per cent. per annum of the total amount of bonds issued is provided, commencing in 1866, and will be applied in redeeming annually the bonds drawn by lot for the purpose, at 110 per cent.

The bonds are secured by a first mortgage of the railroads of the company constructed and to be constructed, the lands granted by the United States Government, and all other its present and future property.

By the terms of the mortgage the amount of first mortgage bonds to be secured by it is limited to $20,000 per mile for each mile of road now or hereafter constructed, and the proceeds (deducting prior lien of $2,000,000 of German obligations, now paid off out of the bond proceeds) constitute a construction fund in the hands of the mortgage trustees exclusively applicable to the completion of the company's lines and the payment of interest, not exceeding four coupons per bond, during construction.

The mortgage provides that no further issue shall be made before January 1st, 1883.

In June, 1881, the conversion of old certificates under the reorganisation scheme took place, the following particulars being copied from the announcement of the trustees, viz.:—The original bonds and coupons represented by the Frankfort Committee certificates have, in accordance with the plan of reorganisation, been converted into "preferred" and common stock, and the mortgages securing the original bonds will be forthwith discharged. In pursuance, therefore, of the powers vested in them by the Bondholders' Association, the reorganisation trustees hereby declare the bond certificates issued by the Frankfort Committee withdrawn and annulled as from the 1st day of July, 1881, except for the purpose of conversion into stock in the manner provided in the plan of reorganisation. The rate of conversion is as follows:—Against each Frankfort Committee bond certificate for $1,000 will be issued ten shares of $100 each preferred stock, and five shares of $100 each common stock. Bond certificates of smaller amount receive "preferred" and common stock in the same ratio. A liquidation certificate, entitling the bearer to the dividend payable on the liquidation of the Bondholders' Association, is issued with the scrip. Deferred interest certificates are entitled to par in common stock. The scrip is prepared in units of ten shares, or $1,000 of preferred stock, and five shares, or $500 of common stock, and in fractions not exceeding nine shares, or $900 of preferred stock, and four shares, or $400 of common stock."

Both classes of stock are officially quoted in London and Frankfort, and listed in New York.

In December, 1881, the following further notice was issued:—"By the general meeting the liquidation dividend was fixed at 18*s.* 6*d.* per $1,000 as per proposition of the committee, and in accordance with the financial statement of account rendered by the latter. We, therefore, beg to give notice that the liquidation certificate can be cashed in London, at the London and San Francisco Bank Limited, 22, Old Broad Street, as follows:—A liquidation certificate for $1,000 (grey) with 18*s.* 6*d.*; a liquidation certificate for $500 (green) with 9*s.* 3*d.*; a liquidation certificate for $100 (red) with 1*s.* 10*d.* Copies of the committee's report to the meeting may be obtained at the bank. As per Article 13 of the Statutes, all overdue coupons on bond certificates are null and void on and after 31st December, 1884."

REVENUE.—The following particulars under this head were issued in March, 1883, viz.:—"The gross earnings for the year, amounting to $1,037,883, exceed the estimate. The net earnings, out of which 2½ per cent. dividend will be declared immediately, reach a total of $343,737. A considerable amount was paid out of revenue for renewals of plant. The net land sales for ten months ending February reached 25,482 acres, realising $59,869, being an average of $2·35 per acre. The funds at the disposal of the mortgage trustees for the completion of the southern extension to connect with the Central Pacific being exhausted, arrangements have been concluded for a lease of the Oregon and California to the Trans-Continental, the condition being that the amount requisite for finishing the line be raised by the lessee company, on an issue of bonds to be guaranteed by the latter, which also guarantees the rest of the bonded debt. It is expected that the route from Portland to San Francisco will be completed by Midsummer, 1884. The nominal capital of the guaranteeing company is $50,000,000, of which $40,000,000 have been paid up. A minimum interest of 2½ per cent. on the Oregon and California preference stock is assured by the Trans-Continental, 65 per cent. being allowed for working expenses."

The total gross earnings for the same period of 1881 were	$122,868
Total operating expenses	135,349
Showing a loss for first quarter of 1881 of	$12,481
As against a gain, in net earnings for first quarter of 1882, of	87,288
Increase, first quarter 1882 over that of 1881	$99,769

CAPITAL.—From the foregoing particulars the securities of the company, as reorganised, are as follow:—

First mortgage 6 per cent. gold bonds	$6,000,000
7 per cent. preferred stock	12,000,000
Common stock	7,000,000=$25,000,000

The reorganisation is now entirely closed, and the trust settled.

[MEM.—Up to the time of going to press no reports for 1884 had been received.—ED.]

President—H. VILLARD, New York.

OFFICERS.—Sec. and Treasurer, G. H. Andrews; Chief Eng., Charles A. F. Morris; Gen. Supt., J. Brandt.

Offices—Portland, Oregon.

434.—PENNSYLVANIA.

This railroad is a consolidation of the lines of various companies running between Philadelphia and Pittsburg. The charter which authorised the construction of the first line and branches, viz., from Harrisburg to Pittsburg, was granted on 13th April, 1846, and the construction was commenced in July, 1847, and with various extensions was completed in 1854, the last portion, from Altoona to the Portage Viaduct, having been opened on the 15th February of that year.

MILEAGE.—In April, 1883, this was stated to be as follows:—"The total length of lines owned, leased, and controlled by it east of Pittsburg and Erie is 3,859 miles, of which 406 miles comprise canals and ferries. The company owns 16 lines, consisting of the main line between Philadelphia and Pittsburgh and its direct branches and extensions; and it leases and controls 82 lines. Of the total length of main lines, 345·77 miles are owned and 2,255·25 miles are leased and controlled. Of branch lines, 88·75 miles are owned and 1,169·55 are leased and controlled. The total length of all the tracks owned, leased, and controlled, including sidings, is 5,906·22 miles, of which 4,531·51 miles are main lines, and 1,374·71 miles are branch lines. The mileage is located as follows:—Pennsylvania, 2,599·17; New Jersey, 644·23; Maryland, 328·39; Delaware, 164·05; New York, 70·50; Virginia, 33·60; West Virginia, 11·80; District of Columbia, 8·18."

WEST PENNSYLVANIA LEASE.—"At a meeting of the stockholders of the West Pennsylvania, in Philadelphia, May 29, a new lease to the Pennsylvania for a period of 30 years was approved, and an issue of $5,000,000 consolidated mortgage bonds was authorised. A notice has been received from the New Jersey Central terminating the contract which permits the Pennsylvania to use the tracks of the New York and Long Branch."

In 1878 a Trust was approved to provide for the gradual reduction of the company's liabilities, full particulars of which will be found on reference to MANUAL for 1884, page 485.

It was stated in February, 1882, that—"Since November, 1878, the company has put past $50,000 out of net earnings every month for use in buying up the securities of its leased and guaranteed lines. So far, the shareholders have received no distribution against this fund, for though it is true that this was once contemplated, the whole matter was in the end left in the hands of the Board."

The company paid 6 per cent. interest on all instalments of subscription to its capital stock up to October 30th, 1855, and since that date has declared and paid the following dividends, calculated at per cent. per annum:—

	Per cent.
1856—May, 4 per cent., November, 4 per cent	8
1857—May, 4 per cent., November, passed	4
1858—May, 3 per cent., November, 3 per cent	6
1859—May, 3 per cent., November, 3 per cent	6
1860—May, 3 per cent., November, 3 per cent	6
1861—May, 3 per cent., November, 3 per cent	6
1862—May, 4 per cent., November, 4 per cent	8
1863—May, 4 per cent., November, 5 per cent	9
1864—February, 30 per cent. in stock; May, 5 per cent. in cash; November, 5 per cent. in cash and 10 per cent. stock subscription privilege at par, making total pure dividend of	40
1865—May, 5 per cent., November, 5 per cent	10
1866—May, 5 per cent., November, 4 per cent	9

	Per cent.
1867—May, 5 per cent. in stock, and 3 per cent. in cash; November, 3 per cent. in cash	11
1868—May, 5 per cent. in stock, and 3 per cent. in cash; November, 5 per cent. in cash	13
1869—May, 5 per cent., November, 5 per cent	10
1870—May, 5 per cent., November, 5 per cent	10
1871—May, 5 per cent., November, 5 per cent	10
1872—May, 5 per cent., November, 5 per cent	10
1873—May, 5 per cent. in cash; November, 5 per cent. in scrip	10
1874—May, 5 per cent., November, 5 per cent	10
1875—May, 4 per cent.; August, 2 per cent.; November, 2 per cent.	8
1876—February, 2 per cent.; May, 2 per cent.; August, 2 per cent.; November, 2 per cent.	8
1877—February, 2 per cent., May, 1½ per cent	3½
1878—November, 2 per cent	2
1879—May, 2 per cent., November, 2½ per cent	4½
1880—May, 3 per cent., November, 4 per cent.	7
1881—May, 4 per cent., November, 4 per cent.	8
1882—May, 4 per cent., November, 2½ per cent. cash and 2 per cent. stock or cash	8½
1883—May, 4 per cent., November, 2½ per cent. cash and 2 per cent. scrip or cash	8½
1884—May, 4 per cent., November, 3 per cent.	7

Up to May, 1875, the dividends were half-yearly, but in August of that year they were made quarterly, and so continued up to the suspension in August, 1877. Since then the company has resolved to return to the half-yearly system. The dividends are usually made payable at the end of each May and November respectively.

Transfer Books.—The books do not close, but to be in time to receive dividend shareholders should be registered (in Philadelphia) for one clear calendar month before the date of its payment, thus:—For dividend payable 30th November, shareholders must be registered on the 30th October.

General Account.—The capital and debt of the company, as well as the cost of road and equipment, may be gathered from the following general account for 1882:—

Debit Side.

Capital stock		$85,301,300
First mortgage bonds, due 1880	$10,000	
General " " " 1910	19,999,760	
Consolidated " " 1905	28,041,250	
Consolidated " " 1909	5,000,000	
Navy Yard mortgage registered bonds, due 1881	1,000,000	
Lien of the State upon the public works between Philadelphia and Pittsburg	3,275,909	
Mortgages and ground rents at 6 per cent. remaining on real estate purchased	1,898,028 =	59,224,947
Accounts, profit and loss, trust fund, &c.		42,273,152
		$186,799,399

Credit Side.

Cost of road and equipment	$71,257,947	
Bonds and securities of other companies, mortgages, lands, and sundries	110,797,732 =	182,055,679
Cash balances		$4,743,720

In February, 1884, $3,000,000 in 4½ per cent. gold bonds were issued at 203*l.* per 200*l.*, or $1,000 bond. These bonds are to bearer, and are redeemable at par on the 1st June, 1913, and bear half-yearly interest; coupons payable 1st June and 1st December. Both principal and interest are payable in Philadelphia in American gold coin, free of all United State taxes. These bonds are the direct obligation of the Pennsylvania, and form part of $10,000,000 authorised to be issued upon the special collateral security of various mortgage bonds of subsidiary railroads, of the par value of $12,500,000, which are deposited in the hands of trustees, and bear an aggregate interest of $677,000 per annum. $3,000,000 are already in the hands of the public, and are officially quoted on the London Stock Exchange. They are not liable to be drawn or compulsorily redeemed before 1913; but a sinking fund of

1 per cent. per annum, defined in the deed of trust, is applicable to the purchase of the bonds if they can be obtained at or below $1,000 per bond and accrued interest.

Coupons on the bonds held in this country are payable as follows:—First mortgage bonds, 6 per cent., payable in Philadelphia, half-yearly, 1st January and 1st July. General mortgage bonds, and sterling consolidated bonds, 6 per cent., payable in London, half-yearly, 1st January and 1st July. Consolidated 6 per cent. currency bonds, payable in Philadelphia, half-yearly, 1st January and 1st July.

The general account of assets and liabilities to 31st December, 1883, shows the following totals:—

Liabilities.

Capital stock (being an increase over last year of $7,318,450)	$92,619,750
Mortgages, loans, ground rents, &c.	61,570,180
Insurance on lines and annuities, &c.	9,148,000
Accounts payable	16,749,602
Value securities and indebtedness transferred with leases	6,126,297
Fund for purchase of guaranteed securities	3,100,000
Redeemed and cancelled bonds	1,489,610
Balance to credit of profit and loss	13,616,184
Total liabilities	$204,411,625
Being a total increase over those of the previous year	$17,612,226

Assets.

Main line and branches, including wharves, warehouses, stations, &c.	$37,975,075
Equipment	23,585,950
Real estate and telegraph line	12,341,830
Bonds and stocks of other corporations	95,331,716
Other items, including trust and other funds, appraised value of securities not included above, and equipment of other leased lines	10,110,718
Fuel and materials on hand	3,963,457
Bills and accounts receivable	12,193,078
Cash balances	8,899,801
Total assets	$204,411,625

President—GEORGE B. ROBERTS, Philadelphia.

Vice-President—EDMUND SMITH, Philadelphia.

Second Vice-President—FRANK THOMSON, Philadelphia.

OFFICERS.—Sec., John C. Sims, junr.; Treasurer, John D. Taylor; General Manager, Charles E. Pugh; Solicitor, John Scott; Assistants to President, Strickland Kneass, J. P. Green, and J. N. Du Barry; Comptroller, Robert W. Downing; Auditor of Disbursements, T. R. Davis; Auditor of Passenger Report, Max Riebenack; Auditor of Freight Reports, George M. Taylor; Chief Engineer of Construction, W. H. Wilson; General Agent, L. P. Farmer; Purchasing Agent, Enoch Lewis; all at Philadelphia. Engineer of Permanent Way, William H. Brown, Philadelphia.

Offices—233, South Fourth Street, Philadelphia.

435.—PHILADELPHIA AND READING.

This company was working on the 30th November, 1879, 1,774 miles of road, viz.:—Roads owned, 801 miles; leased lines, 888 miles; lines controlled, 84 miles.

PERKIOMEN.—This line commences by a junction with the Philadelphia and Reading, 25 miles west of Philadelphia, and terminates at Emmaus. Length, 36½ miles. The consolidated mortgage bonds of this company were issued in London by Messrs. McCalmont Brothers and Co. in 1873, at the price of 90 per cent., or 180*l.* per bond of $1,000 (200*l.*) Interest at 6 per cent. per annum is payable 1st June and 1st December, in Philadelphia in gold, or in London in sterling. The principal is repayable not later than 1893, the bonds being redeemed by semi-annual drawings by means of an accumulative sinking fund of 2½ per cent. per annum. The principal and interest is guaranteed by the Philadelphia and Reading.

At a general meeting held in London on the 6th June, 1877, the following arrangement, to relieve the position of the company and give time for payment of its floating debt, was approved, viz.:—"1. The drawings on the improvement mortgage bonds and general mortgage bonds of the Philadelphia and Reading, and the consolidated mortgage bonds of the Perkiomen, to be suspended each for four years from and including the next drawing appointed to be made thereon, or such shorter time as may be necessary to pay off the floating debt. 2. One-half of the coupons upon the said Philadelphia and Reading general mortgage bonds and Perkiomen consolidated mortgage bonds for three years from the due date of and including the current coupon, to be paid in cash at maturity, the remaining half to be represented by five years' scrip now to be issued, bearing interest at 6 per cent., and convertible, at the holders' option, into 7 per cent. income mortgage bonds of the company, and payment of such remaining half to be deferred until the scrip becomes due. 3. Coupons, when the one-half is paid in cash, are to be deposited with trustees as security for holders until full payment. 4. Three persons to be named by the meeting to be trustees for bondholders. 5. Trustees to have power to terminate the suspension of drawings and of payment of second half of coupons, if circumstances in their judgment require it. 6. All other details, and the necessary deeds for carrying the plan into effect, to be settled by trustees according to their discretion."

In the early part of 1880 the company suspended payment, and receivers were appointed; subsequently the president arranged for an issue of deferred income bonds, with the object of paying off the floating debt of the company. The prospectus of this issue, dated 4th January, 1881, gave the following particulars relating to the deferred bonds, the position of the company, and the object for which the new capital was to be raised, viz.:—The capital of the company, even after the increase now proposed, will be less, in proportion to its traffic and earnings, than that of many of the great English railway companies. This issue of deferred bonds is simply a method of obtaining a voluntary contribution from the shareholders, by offering them, in lieu of an assessment, a reversionary interest in the earnings of the company, after payment of 6 per cent. per annum upon the common shares; and, though new in the United States, this system has been frequently adopted in Great Britain with great benefits both to the companies and to the subscribers. The vast estate of coal lands owned by the company gives to this reversionary interest great prospective value, irrespective of the large traffic receipts from the railroad. The net earnings of the Railroad Company and the Coal and Iron Company taken together, for the fiscal year ended 30th November last, were fully two and a quarter millions of dollars in excess of those of the preceding year, of which one-and-a-half million of dollars were gained during the last quarter, being the only three months of the year when the company worked at full time. The proceeds of this issue will be used by the receivers of the company, under the order of the court, for payment of the floating debt of the company. Receivers' certificates, deferred coupon scrip, income mortgage bonds, arrears of sinking funds (on improvement and general mortgage bonds), and of interest, all of which must be paid before resumption of dividends, will be provided for by the proceeds of an issue of 5 per cent. mortgage "consols" bonds already authorised by the managers of the company.

REVENUE—30th November, 1883.—The total net revenue of the railway amounted to $14,464,071, and of the coal company to $921,772, together $15,385,843, showing an increase over 1882 of $4,738,073.

The receivers' report for 1884 shows $13,519,201 net profit, after paying the working expenses, being $3,355,251 below the present fixed charges, also $2,000,000 below the net profit of 1883.

CAPITAL (Funded Liabilities and Stock)—30th November, 1883:—

Prior mortgage loans:—		
6 per cent. £ mortgage loan, 1843-1910, coupon..	$967,200	
6 " $ " 1843-1910, "	545,500	
6 " $ " 1844-80, "	1,000	
6 " $ " 1844-1910, "	795,000	
6 " $ " 1848-1910, "	92,000	
6 " $ " 1849-1910, "	67,000	
6 " $ mtg. conv. loan, 1857-86, "	79,000	
7 " $ mortgage " 1868-93, "	2,700,000	
		$5,246,700
Consolidated mortgage loan, 1871-1911:—		
6 per cent. gold $ or £ ....coupon	$6,999,000	
6 " " $ .... "	305,000	
6 " " $ .... registered	858,000	
7 " $ .... "	3,839,000	
7 " $ ....coupon	7,810,000	
		18,811,000
Carried forward...............		$24,057,700

Brought forward		$24,057,700	
Improvement mortgage loan, 1873-97:—			
6 per cent. gold $ or £ ....coupon		9,364,000	
		$33,421,700	
General mortgage loan, 1874-1908:—			
6 per cent. gold $ or £ ....coupon	$19,686,000		
7 „ $ .... „	5,000,000		
		24,686,000	
General mortgage, gold $ or £, scrip:—			
6 per cent., 1877-82 ....coupon	$226,170		
6 „ „ extended to July 1, 1885 „	1,468,080		
Perkiomen mort. guarantee, gold $ or £, scrip:—			
6 per cent., 1877-82 ....coupon	10,350		
„ „ extended to July 1, 1885 „	86,940		
		1,791,540	
Income mortgage loan, 1876-96:—			
7 per cent. $ ....coupon		2,454,000	
5 per cent. consols, mortgage loan, 1882-1922, 1st series:—			
5 per cent. gold $ ....coupon	$3,102,500		
5 „ „ $, fractional scrip........	30,564		
		3,133,064	
5 per cent. consols, mortgage loan, 1883-1933, 2nd series:—			
5 per cent. gold $ ....coupon	$1,683,500		
5 „ „ $, fractional scrip........	6,088		
		1,689,588	
		$67,175,892	
Bonds and mortgages on real estate		2,049,031	
Total mortgage loans........		$69,224,923	
Convertible adjustment scrip, 1883-88:—			
6 per cent. $ ....coupon		2,991,360	
Car-trust certificates, issue of Feb. 15, 1883 „		2,000,000	
Debenture loans:—			
6 per cent. $, 1868-93 ....coupon	$650,200		
6 „ $, 1878-98 .... „	20,300		
		670,500	
Debenture convertible loans:—			
7 per cent. $, 1870-90 ....coupon	$27,000		
7 „ $, 1873-93 .... „	10,389,900		
		10,416,900	
Debenture and guarantee scrip:—			
6 per cent., 1877-82	$317,090		
6 „ „ extended to July 1st, 1884...	292,890		
6 „ „ fractional	3,164		
		613,144	
Loans of Schuylkill Navigation:—			
Loan maturing 1895	$1,200,000		
„ „ 1913	756,650		
„ „ 1915	621,600		
		2,578,250	
Loan of East Pennsylvania, maturing 1888		495,900	
Common stock	$33,182,875		
Preferred stock	1,551,800		
		34,734,675	
Deferred income bonds:—			
Deferred income bonds (nominal par $23,795,650)	$7,138,695		
Scrip for deferred income bonds (nominal par $1,705,380)........	511,614		
		7,650,309	
Total carried forward........		$	131,375,961

Total brought forward				$ 131,875,961
Liabilities:—				
Bills payable and loans		$5,825,150		
Due on account of purchases of stocks and bonds		3.329,002		
Floating debt		9,154,162		
Debts due by the company:—				
Due to leased roads and canals, account rental	$1,648,492			
Due to connecting railroad companies	547,455			
Due on account current business	1,020,149			
Due for wages, materials, drawbacks, &c	1,587,503			
Unpaid interest and dividends	1,155,269			
State tax on capital stock and gross receipts	545,255			
Sundry credits..	514,472			
		6,963,695		
Insurance funds		493,992		
Sinking fund, loan 1836-82		166,070		
Sinking fund, Schuylkill Navigation improvement bonds, due November 1st 1880..............		228,000		
Materials received through lease of Central New Jersey lines		595,156		
			$17,601,065	
Income Accounts:—				
Profit of P. and R.:—				
Year ended November 30th, 1881		$142,589		
" " " " 1882		835,781		
		$978,370		
" " " " 1883		2,362,404		
		$3,340,774		
Less loss P. and R. C. and I. Co. for years ended November 30th, 1881, 1882, and 1883..............		117,343		
			3,223,431	20,824,496
			$	152,700,457

For the condition of coupon, scrip, and income mortgage bonds to 30th November, 1879, see MANUAL for 1883, page 492.

GENERAL MORTGAGE BONDS, COUPONS, &c.—Six coupons to January, 1880, have been paid, half in cash, and scrip issued for the other half bearing 6 per cent. interest, payable 1st January and 1st July, the principal to be paid July 1, 1882. Coupon due 1st July, 1880, was paid half in cash 9th November, 1880. These bonds are redeemable at par by annual drawings in May, for payment in July, by an accumulative sinking fund of 1 per cent. per annum. Loan to be extinguished by July 1, 1908.

On July 11th, 1881, second half of July, 1880, coupon paid. On 18th October the whole of the January, 1881, coupon was paid. All coupons since due have been paid, and there are, therefore, now no arrears.

FIVE PER CENT. CONSOLIDATED MORTGAGE BONDS *(issued for conversion of existing obligations)*.—For particulars under this head, see MANUAL for 1883, page 492.

NEW JERSEY CENTRAL.—In January, 1885, the "Reading" Committee of Bondholders, who have been engaged in framing a reorganisation scheme, stated as follows:—The New Jersey Central will be asked to accept 3 per cent. dividend for three years, with more if earned. These reductions are expected to decrease the fixed charges by $2,750,000 annually, while the saving of expenses now being enforced will aid in bringing the fixed charges below the net earnings. The floating debt is recommended to be funded into a new collateral trust loan of $20,000,000 at 5 per cent., for which all collaterals now held by lenders will be pledged. In order to aid in negotiating this plan the Reading shareholders will be asked to subscribe 25 per cent. of their stock, to be given to the company for use as a bonus to takers of the loan, or else to subscribe an equal amount to the loan.

Subsequently, the following explanation on this subject was supplied by the president of the company, viz.:—1. The committee proposes that both principal and interest of scrip issued for general mortgage half interest shall be paid before the junior securities receive interest, but no interest shall be payable on the scrip if its principal shall be redeemed before the maturity of the coupons which it represents. 2. It is intended that the interest shall be paid in full upon the sterling (general mortgage and Perkiomen mortgage) extended and unextended scrip. 3. The present recommendation of the committee is that the interest upon the income bonds proposed to be issued in respect of the consolidated mortgage bonds (first series) shall not be cumulative. 4 It is proposed that half the overdue general mortgage interest shall be paid, and that the overdue interest upon other securities of the company shall be funded into the same security as the principal. 5. The total floating debt of both companies amounts to $23,517,000, but there are included in this total $9,428,000 in respect of current liabilities for overdue coupons, rentals, wages, materials, &c., against which there are current assets.

Proposed Plan of Financial Reorganisation.—A committee of bondholders have prepared a scheme, with the above object, and it was stated in January, 1885, that their scheme "recognises the full liability for the principal and interest of the Reading general mortgage. also all prior mortgages. The general mortgage coupons for three years will be paid half in cash and half in scrip, bearing interest payable at maturity, the coupons being deposited with trustees as security until the scrip is paid. The bondholders will be asked to waive the sinking fund provision for a period. If before three years the earnings of the railway will warrant it, then the full general mortgage interest is to be paid, no junior security getting anything until the general mortgage be fully satisfied. All contracts are to be fully paid from income. The mortgage reduces the interest to 6 per cent., with 1 per cent. more if earned, all junior securities to be exchanged for 5 per cent. non-cumulative. The income is to be apportioned according to the standing of the security exchanged, but getting no interest till prior incumbrances are satisfied. All the leased line rentals earned will be paid." The full text of the scheme will be found in the *Appendix* to this Volume.

Registration of Voters.—The following instructions were contained in a circular issued by Mr. Gowen, in anticipation of the annual meeting on the 9th January, 1882, viz.:—"In order to avoid all objections as to the right of shareholders to vote, it is necessary that shares should be registered in the names of their owners on the books of the company in Philadelphia three full months before the election, say on or before October 8th next, and for this purpose the certificates should leave this country as soon as possible, and not later than by the steamers sailing September 24th. Shareholders whose certificates are made out in their own names are already properly registered and need take no further action, but those who hold certificates in the names of others should immediately have them exchanged for certificates in their own names, so that the latter will be properly entered on the books of the company. Proxies for the next election should not be executed until after October 9th, so as to be dated within three months of the election, and at the proper time a form for such proxies will be sent to each shareholder."

President—GEORGE DE B. KEIM, Philadelphia.
Receivers—George de B. Keim and Stephen A. Caldwell.

OFFICERS.—Sec., Albert Foster; Treasurer, W. A. Church; Chief Eng., William Lorenz; Canal Eng., James F. Smith; all at Philadelphia. Gen. Man., John E. Wootten, Reading.

Offices—227, South Fourth Street, Philadelphia.
London Agent—D. G. Bruce Gardyne.
London Office—43, Coleman Street, E.C.

436.—WABASH, ST. LOUIS, AND PACIFIC.

Total length of road, about 3,348 miles.

During the year 1882 the sum of $3,044,012 has been expended for new construction. Embraced in this charge is the sum of $377,827 for the St. Charles bridge over the Missouri river; $461,500 towards the completion of the Humeston and Shenandoah road; and $966,209 for car trust and other rolling stock obligations. These expenditures were rendered necessary in order to finish new lines commenced in the previous year, but the requirements of the current year will be comparatively small. The floating debt of the company is almost entirely the result of these construction payments, but the company owns securities, consisting mainly of bonds and stock, valued at $8,667,696, available for the liquidation of the floating debt and future requirements.

COMPARATIVE STATISTICS.

	1881.	1882.
Road and Equipment:—		
Total miles operated	3,348	3,518
Locomotives	*561	*598
Passenger, mail, and express cars	*372	*387
Freight and all other cars	*20,139	*19,660
Operations and Fiscal Results:—		
Passengers carried	3,215,200	4,251,393
Passenger mileage	137,114,727	166,198,560
Rate per passenger per mile	2·238*cts.*	2·373*cts.*
Freight (tons) moved	5,393,917	5,911,012
Freight (tons) mileage	1,149,774,547	1,247,611,320
Average rate per ton per mile	0·928*ct.*	0·951*ct.*
Earnings:—		
Passenger	$3,067,989	$3,944,520
Freight	10,667,906	11,885,226
Mail, express, &c.	731,894	1,021,943
Total gross earnings	$14,467,789	$16,851,689
Operating Expenses:—		
Conducting transportation	—	$4,294,713
Motive power	—	3,358,723
Maintenance of way	—	2,790,813
Maintenance of cars	—	897,142
General expenses	—	323,361
Total operating expenses	$10,792,943	$11,664,752
Net earnings	3,674,846	5,186,937
Per cent. of expenses to earn	74·59	69·22
Income Account—Receipts:—		
Net earnings	$3,674,846	$5,186,937
Other receipts	277,245	328,760
Total income	$3,952,091	$5,515,697
Disbursements:—		
Rentals paid	$1,009,079	$987,608
Interest on debt	3,447,627	4,302,006
Taxes, rent of cars, &c.	637,504	—
Dividends	1,329,918	809,105
Total disbursements	$6,424,128	$6,098,719
Deficit	2,472,037	583,022

GENERAL BALANCE-SHEET (CONDENSED) AT CLOSE OF EACH FISCAL YEAR.

	1881.	1882.
Assets:—		
Railroads, buildings, equipment, &c.	$107,658,815	$113,285,929
Securities and property on hand	435,862	8,667,697
Materials, fuel, &c.	1,212,245	700,404
Construction, &c., for year	11,578,866	3,044,013
Income account	1,452,858	2,035,881
Total	$122,338,646	$127,733,924
Liabilities:—		
Stock, common	$26,921,500	$27,140,500
Stock, preferred	23,033,200	23,034,200
Funded debt	66,291,858	70,937,854
Bills payable	355,466	239,057
Loans payable	1,500,000	3,037,000
Sundry balances†	4,236,622	3,345,313
Total liabilities	$122,338,646	$127,733,924

In 1884 Receivers were appointed to administer the affairs of this company, and a reorganisation scheme was proposed by a committee of directors. The *Appendix* to this Volume gives the full text of the order of the court appointing the Receivers, and a full copy of the circular and plan relating to the reorganisation scheme.

* Includes narrow gauge equipments.
† Includes audited vouchers, interest accrued, interest not due, unpaid taxes, &c.

President—JAY GOULD, New York.

First Vice-President—R. S. HAYES.

OFFICERS.—Sec., James F. How; Treasurer, A. H. Calef; Gen. Supt., Robert Andrews; Chief Eng., W. S. Lincoln; Solicitor, Wager Swayne; Auditor, D. B. Howard.

WEST INDIES.

437.—BARBADOS LIMITED.

Registered under "The Companies' Acts, 1862 and 1867," with the benefit of a guarantee of the Barbados Government, and authorised by acts of the Barbados Legislature, 34 and 35 Vic., cap. 38, and No. 11 of 1878.

This company was formed at the beginning of 1879, with capital—100,000*l.* in preference shares and 50,000*l.* in ordinary shares; of the last, 45,020*l.* only has been issued.

The construction of the line is authorised by an act of the Barbados Legislature, passed in 1873, amended by subsequent acts, of which the last was passed in 1882.

The railway (23 miles in length) is constructed on the narrow-gauge system, and starts from Bridgetown, the capital, crosses the best part of the island to its windward side, and thence runs northwards to the district called Scotland, affording railway communication to seven out of the eleven districts of the island.

The gauge of the railway is 3ft. 6in., and its total length, with sidings, 25 miles. This gauge will allow of the transit of wagons carrying two hogsheads of sugar side by side, six hogsheads in each wagon.

The Government has reserved to itself the right after the year 1898, if the divisible profits for five years prior thereto have exceeded 15 per cent. per annum on the authorised outlay, to revise the tolls in such manner as shall in the judgment of the Legislature be calculated to reduce the said profits to 10 per cent. per annum.

By the act of 1878 the Colonial Government guarantee to the Barbados Company, on the whole line being completed, and subject to its being duly maintained, a subsidy, not exceeding 6,000*l.* sterling per annum, for the period of twenty years from the opening of the railway throughout for public traffic. The net income is specially appropriated, under an express power given by the articles of association, to the 100,000*l.* 6 per cent. preference shares, and the articles also provide that no moneys shall be borrowed by the company without the consent of the holders of three-fourths of the preference shares. The act provides for recouping to the Colonial Treasury the payments made to the company under the guarantee out of net profits of the company exceeding the rate of 6 per cent. per annum.

The directors have been authorised, and the necessary consent obtained, to raise additional capital by the issue of mortgage bonds, not to exceed 50,000*l.*, bonds for which amount have been issued.

Upon the expiration of the twenty years for which the guarantee is given the preference shares will have a preferential charge on the net income of the railway up to 6 per cent. per annum.

After the year 1898, if the net rate of divisible profits amounts to 6 per cent. on the capital outlay, the Government have the right to purchase the railway at the price of not less than twenty years of the net annual divisible profits, such divisible profits to be calculated upon the average of three years preceding such purchase. Upon such right being exercised by the Government, the company will appropriate out of the amount so received a sum sufficient to redeem the 6 per cent. shares now offered for subscription, at the rate of 6*l.* for each 5*l.* share, being a bonus of 20 per cent. upon the price of subscription.

A statement of this company's capital, to 31st August, 1883, showed that there had been issued 6 per cent. preference shares, as before described; and 9,004 (part of 10,000) ordinary shares, which, after repayment of advances to the Colonial Government and interest at 6 per cent. on the preference shares, take earnings up to 6 per cent., after which earnings are divided between preference and ordinary shareholders up to 8 per cent., the remainder (if any) going to the ordinary shareholders.

Line completed and passed by the Government Engineer on 7th August, 1883. and fully opened for traffic on the 10th September, 1883.

DIRECTORS:

Chairman—Sir GEORGE H. CHAMBERS, 4, Mincing Lane, E.C.

Hon. H. Arden Adderley, Fillongley Hall, Coventry.

Forster M. Alleyne, Esq., 2, Stone Buildings, Lincoln's Inn, and 41, Cadogan Place, S.W.

Edward Chambers, Esq., 4, Mincing Lane, E.C.

David Campbell Da Costa, Esq., 47, Warrington Crescent, W.

Lieut.-Colonel H. M. Le Champion, 28, Cathcart Road, South Kensington, S.W.

OFFICERS.—Sec. in London, V. Perronet Sells; Auditors, Quilter, Ball, and Co., 5, Moorgate Street, E.C.; Solicitors, Freshfields and Williams, 5, Bank Buildings, E.C.; Bankers, Lloyds, Barnetts, and Bosanquet's Bank, 62, Lombard Street, E.C.

Offices—4, Mincing Lane, E.C.

438.—BAY OF HAVANA.

(LATE BAY OF HAVANA AND MATANZAS.)

Mileage (including the branch to Guamacaro), about 100 miles.

By an agreement of the 20th June, 1883, this railway has become the property of the Regla Warehouses Company and Bank of Commerce, in the Havana, in consideration of a sum in cash (paid to the bondholders on the 1st November, 1883) and 530,000*l.* of new consolidated 6 per cent. first mortgage bonds, to be issued in exchange for the old bonds. On delivery of the new bonds the original bonds will be cancelled, in accordance with the terms of the agreement of 20th June, 1883, made with the Regla Warehouses Company and Bank of Commerce. The new bonds are of 100*l.* each, and form the sole mortgage on the railway. They are to bearer with coupons attached, and are entitled to interest at the rate of 6 per cent. per annum, payable half-yearly, on the 1st January and 1st July, at Messrs. J. Henry Schröder and Co.'s, 145, Leadenhall Street, E.C. The first coupon was due and paid on the 1st January, 1884. The bonds are redeemable at par in 40 years by a cumulative sinking fund, by annual drawing, on 1st July, in London, at Messrs. J. Henry Schröder and Co.'s, 145, Leadenhall Street, E.C.

For particulars relating to the Bay of Havana and Matanzas, prior to the above vesting, see the MANUAL for 1883, page 494.

Representatives of the Bondholders—The Company of Bondholders of the Bay of Havana Limited, 1, Queen Victoria Street, E.C.

Secretary, Robert A. McLean.

IV.—CANALS.

439.—AIRE AND CALDER.

From Goole and Selby to Leeds and Wakefield.

The Calder and Hebble Navigation, from Wakefield to Sowerby Bridge, with a branch to Halifax, is under lease to the trustees for 21 years, from 1st February, 1865. The trustees also own the Barnsley Canal, and are joint owners, with the Leeds and Liverpool Canal Company, of the Bradford Canal.

The accounts are not published for general circulation.

OFFICERS.—Eng. and Gen. Man., William Hamond Bartholomew, C.E.; Sec and Chief Clerk, Marmaduke Storr Hodson.

Offices—Aire and Calder Navigation, Dock Street, Leeds.

440.—ASHTON AND OLDHAM.

From Manchester to Ashton-under-Lyne, with a branch from Openshaw to Heaton Norris. Length, 17½ miles.

Leased in perpetuity to the Manchester, Sheffield, and Lincolnshire Railway, under 11 and 12 Vic., cap. 86, subject to an annuity of 12,363*l*. 15*s*., which is equivalent to 7 per cent. interest on the existing 1,766½ shares of 100*l*. each.

By act 46 and 47 Vic., cap. 157, the Ashton and Oldham Canal was vested in the Manchester, Sheffield, and Lincolnshire Railway, and the annuities extinguished, the holders receiving in exchange therefor such an amount of the Sheffield Company's 4½ per cent. debenture stock as would produce an annual income equal to their interest in the annuities.

The interest is payable on the 1st January and 1st July. Transfer fee, 2s. 6*d*. each seller.

Secretary, Edward Ross, London Road Station, Manchester.

441.—BARNSLEY.

From the River Calder, near Wakefield, to Barnsley and Barnby Bridge, in the township of Cawthorn. Length, 16 miles.

This canal was leased to trustees of the Aire and Calder, and subsequently became their property under the Barnsley Canal Transfer Act of 1871.

Communications to be addressed to the Aire and Calder Offices, Dock Street, Leeds.

442.—BIRMINGHAM.

The London and North Western Railway, under the Arrangement Act 9 and 10 Vic., cap. 244, 1846, clause 15, enacts as follows, viz.:—"That as often as, in any year, ending 31st December, the net amount of the tolls and other income arising from the canal, and other property of the Birmingham Canal Company, after deducting all proper expenses and interest on the unallocated debt owing by the canal at the time of the passing of this act, shall be insufficient to produce a dividend of 4*l*. per share, clear of deduction (except property or income tax) upon each of the present shares of the canal company (and which shares amount to 17,600), and also upon each share into which the unallocated debt owing by the canal company shall, with the consent of the railway company, be converted, then, as often as the same shall happen: the railway company shall, within the time herein limited, pay unto the canal company, or their treasurer, such sum as with the sum (if any) which shall otherwise be applicable, shall be sufficient to make up the full dividend of 4*l*. per share, clear of deductions, &c. (except property or income tax), upon each share in the canal company." Clause 16 extends the above guarantee to 2,060 shares of the Dudley Canal Navigation. Clause 20 provides for a previous arrangement made by the canal company, whereby a reduction is made of 35*s*. 6*d*. from certain unallocated shares, on which the proportion of debt attaching thereto had not been paid; and of 19*s*. 6*d*. from certain unallocated Wyrley shares. Clause 22 provides that if the canal profits exceed the above minimum guarantee, no more shall be payable out of such profits than will be sufficient to pay 5*l*. per share, the remainder being set apart for a reserve fund, not to exceed 50,000*l*.; and out of any accumulation thereon (if any) a dividend of 5*l*. is to be maintained. The primary liability of the London and North Western to make up such dividend to 4*l*. per share remaining undisturbed. N.B.—Under this arrangement claims have been made upon the London and North Western revenue, and duly met.

CAPITAL.—The receipts on this account to 31st December, 1880, were as follow, viz.:—

Consolidated stock	£2,396,008
Four per cent. debenture stock	797,400
Loans (Canal)	82,074
Loans (B. W. and Stour Valley)	187,987
Land account	63,167
	£3,526,636

OFFICERS.—Clerk to the company, William Wakefield Pilcher; Auditor, William H. Thornbery, Chartered Accountant, Birmingham.

Transfers should be sent and communications addressed to the Clerk of the Company.

Address—Birmingham Canal Navigation, Paradise Street, Birmingham.

443.—BRIDGEWATER NAVIGATION LIMITED.

The canal owned by this company extends to a distance of 40 miles around Manchester, Leigh, and Runcorn. The company has a share capital of 100,000 ordinary 10*l.* shares, and 30,000 preference 5 per cent. shares of 10*l.* each; 3*l.* 10*s.* paid up on the ordinary shares, and 10*l.* on the 5 per cent. preference shares, to December, 1883; also debenture bonds, 200,000*l.*, at 4 per cent.

REVENUE.—The net earnings for the years ended 31st December, 1880, 1881, 1882, and 1883, admitted of the payment of dividends at the rate of 8 per cent. per annum upon the ordinary shares; and for 1883 an additional bonus of 1s. per share was paid.

The accounts are made up annually to 31st December, and the dividends have been paid in February. Transfer fee, 2*s.* 6*d.* per deed.

DIRECTORS:

Chairman—J. WAKEFIELD CROPPER, Esq., Dingle Bank, Liverpool.

Deputy Chairman—NATHANIEL BUCKLEY, Esq., Ryecroft, Ashton-under-Lyne.

John William Maclure, Esq., The Home, Whalley Range, and Cross Street, Manchester.
Thos. Roberts, Esq., The Hollies, Kersal.
Hugh Mason, Esq., M.P., Ashton-under-Lyne.
J. Arthur Kenrick, Esq., Berrow Court, Edgbaston, Birmingham.
Frederick Thorpe Mappin, Esq., M.P., Thornbury, Sheffield.
Peter Rylands, Esq., M.P., Massey Hall, Thelwall, Warrington.

OFFICERS.—Gen. Man., Henry Collier; Sec., John Oldfield.

Offices—Chester Road, Manchester.

444.—CALDER AND HEBBLE NAVIGATION.

(SEE AIRE AND CALDER.)

445.—DEARNE AND DOVE.

From Barnsley to Swinton, 15 miles.

By act 10 and 11 Vic., cap. 291, the Dearne and Dove Canal was vested in the South Yorkshire, Doncaster, and Goole Railway, and by subsequent amalgamations now forms part of the undertaking of the Manchester, Sheffield, and Lincolnshire Railway. The act transferring the canal to the South Yorkshire deferred the payment of the purchase money of 350*l.* for each share until the 2nd January, 1857, up to which date interest was payable at the rate of 4 per cent. An amount of purchase money still remains unclaimed, upon which the company continue to pay interest at the above rate. The interest is payable on 1st January and 1st July. Transfer fee, 2*s.* 6*d.* each seller.

Secretary, Edward Ross, M. S. & L. Railway, Manchester.

446.—DROITWICH.

This canal was leased in 1874 to the Sharpness New Docks and Gloucester and Birmingham Navigation, for 999 years, at an annual rental which suffices for the payment of dividends at 8*l.* per share, on a capital of 20,000*l.*, or 200 shares of 100*l.* each. The shares are real estate, entitling the holders to votes for both divisions of Worcestershire. Transfers exempt from stamp duty, fee, 2*s.* 6*d.* per ordinary transfer; other deeds and wills according to their length.

Clerk, J. Holyoake.

Offices—Droitwich.

447.—DROITWICH JUNCTION.

This canal is leased to the Sharpness New Docks. Rent, 1,200*l.* per annum. Capital, 24,000*l.* in 20*l.* shares. The dividends are equal to 5 per cent. per annum, less 6*d.* per share for expenses=half-yearly payments of 9*s.* 9*d.* per share, payable 1st March and September. Transfer fee, 6*d.* per share.

Secretary, W. D. George.

Offices—4, Gas Street, Birmingham.

448.—GRAND CANAL.

Incorporated in 1772. Length, 164 miles, from Dublin to Ballinasloe. Capital, 665,988*l*.

Accounts made up to 30th June and 31st December. Annual meeting, February and August. Ordinary transfer forms to be used; fee, 2*s*. 6*d*. per deed. The company have a reserve fund of 11,459*l*. invested in English Government stocks and stock of the Midland, Great Northern, and Great Southern and Western railways, and a fund retained under act 11 and 12 Vic., cap. 124, consists of 10,000*l*., which is invested in 3 per cent. consols. The dividends in February and August, 1884, were at the rate of 1¾ and 2 per cent. per annum respectively.

DIRECTORS:

Chairman—B. HONE, Esq.

Deputy-Chairman—E. H. KINAHAN, Esq.

J. J. Pim, Esq.
H. Hudson, Esq.
G. S. Warren, Esq.
W. J. Perry, Esq.
R. J. Corballis, Esq.

OFFICERS.—Sec., W. D. Cooke; Eng., Christopher Mulvany, C.E.; Auditors, W. J. Geoghegan and R. H. Scovill.

Offices—James's Street Harbour, Dublin.

449.—GRAND JUNCTION.

Incorporated 1793. From the Thames at Brentford and Paddington to Braunston, Northampton, Buckingham, Aylesbury, and Wendover. Length, with branches, 135 miles. Capital, 11,300 ordinary shares of 100*l*. each, all paid, 1,130,000*l*., and 9,370 6 per cent. preference shares of 10*l*. each, all paid, 93,700*l*.; total, 1,222,700*l*. Mortgages, 80,000*l*.

The dividends earned are at the rate of 4 per cent. per annum, and are payable half-yearly, about the middle of January and July. The preference dividends are payable half-yearly, on the 1st January and July. Meetings held in June and December. Accounts made up to 30th June and 31st December. Special transfer forms; fee, 5*s*. per deed.

SELECT COMMITTEE:

Chairman—The Hon. R. HOWE BROWNE.

Henry Pigeon, Esq.
Philip Henry Pepys, Esq.
Winthrop Mackworth Praed, Esq.
George Cavendish Taylor, Esq.
Edward Thornton, Esq.
John Stone Wigg, Esq.
Joseph Lloyd Gibbs, Esq.

Clerk, C. A. Mercer.

Offices—21, Surrey Street, Strand, W.C.

450.—LANCASTER.

This canal is leased to the London and North Western Railway for 999 years, at a rental equal to a dividend of 35*s*. per share per annum, payable half-yearly (less income tax) in April and October.

451.—LEEDS AND LIVERPOOL CANAL AND DOUGLAS NAVIGATION.

This company, after having been for many years a toll-taking undertaking, agreed to lease the tolls of the canal to the East Lancashire, Lancashire and Yorkshire, Midland, and London and North Western, for 21 years. This lease is said to have expired in 1874, and since then the company has been working on its own account.

The capital consists of 401,665*l*. in stock, upon which dividends have in the past been earned at rates ranging at from about 17*l*. to 21*l*. per share per annum, that for the year 1883 being at the latter rate, and on account of 1884 the sum of 10*l*. interim dividend was paid 1st November, 1884.

Transfers to be sent to the company's law clerk, Leeds. Form, special; fees, special.

Traffic Manager, J. Lee.

Offices—Old Hall Street, Liverpool.

452.—MACCLESFIELD.

From Marple to Hall Green. Length, 26½ miles.

Leased in perpetuity to the Manchester, Sheffield, and Lincolnshire Railway, under 9 and 10 Vic., cap. 267, subject to an annuity of 6,605*l*., which is equivalent to 2½ per cent. interest on the existing 2,642 shares of 100*l*. each.

By act 46 and 47 Vic., cap. 157, the Macclesfield Canal was vested in the Manchester, Sheffield, and Lincolnshire Railway, and the annuities extinguished, the holders receiving in exchange therefor such an amount of the Sheffield Company's 4½ per cent. debenture stock as would produce an annual income equal to their interest in the annuities.

The interest is payable on 1st January and 1st July. Transfer fee, 2*s*. 6*d* each seller.

OFFICERS.—Sec., Edward Ross, London Road Station, Manchester; Supt., R. Heathcott, 64, Dale Street, Manchester.

453.—OXFORD.

From Longford to Oxford, 91 miles. Communication with Grand Junction at Braunston, Warwick and Napton, at Napton, and the River Thames at Oxford. Capital, 178,648*l*. in 1,786 48-100th shares of 100*l* each, all paid. The dividends recently have been equal to 7½ per cent. The reports are not printed. A special form of transfer may be had, but the company do not refuse the ordinary form. Fee, 2*s*. 6*d*. per deed.

Secretary, Henry Robinson.

Offices—Oxford.

454.—PEAK FOREST.

From Dukinfield to Whaley. Length, 15 miles. Leased in perpetuity to the Manchester, Sheffield, and Lincolnshire Railway, under 9 and 10 Vic., cap. 267 (1846), subject to an annuity of 9,317*l*. 2*s*., which is equivalent to 3*l*. 18*s*. per share, or 5 per cent. interest on the existing 2,389 shares, of 78*l*. each.

By act 46 and 47 Vic., cap. 157, the Peak Forest Canal was vested in the Manchester, Sheffield, and Lincolnshire Railway, and the annuities extinguished, the holders receiving in exchange therefor such an amount of the Sheffield Company's 4½ per cent. debenture stock as would produce an annual income equal to their interest in the annuities.

Interest payable 1st July and 1st December. Transfer fee, 2*s*. 6*d*. each seller.

Secretary, Edward Ross, London Road Station, Manchester.

455.—REGENT'S.

Incorporated 1812. Length, 8½ miles from the Grand Junction Canal to the Thames at Limehouse, with a branch (Hertford Union) to the River Lee. Now the property of the Regent's Canal City and Docks Railway Company.

Offices—138, Leadenhall Street, E.C.

456.—ROCHDALE.

This canal was leased in 1854 to the Lancashire and Yorkshire, North Eastern, Manchester Sheffield and Lincolnshire, and London and North Western railways, but since the expiration of the lease in 1876, the company has worked independently, and hitherto paid a dividend on the 5,663 shares of 85*l*. each fully paid (which forms its share capital), of 2*l*. per share (less income tax), each half-year, in February and August.

OFFICERS.—Gen. Man., R. Eadson; Sec., C. R. Dykes.

Offices—Dale Street, Manchester.

457.—SHARPNESS NEW DOCKS AND GLOUCESTER AND BIRMINGHAM.

(ORIGINALLY GLOUCESTER AND BERKELEY.)

From the Droitwich and Droitwich Junction Canals (both of which are leased by this company) to Worcester and Birmingham. The company also purchased, in 1874, the Worcester and Birmingham Canal (see that company). The capital (at 25th September, 1882) consisted of 303,782*l*. of ordinary consolidated stock, 109,500*l*. "A" 5 per cent. preference stock, 100,000*l*. "B" 5½ per cent. preference stock, and 120,000*l*. "C" 5 per cent. preference stock; total stock and share capital, 633,282*l*.; debenture capital, 576,999*l*.

Accounts made up to 25th March and September. Annual meetings, May and November. Dividends have been earned at the rate of from 2 to 3 per cent. per annum. Transfers made on the common form; fee, 2*s.* 6*d.* per deed.

DIRECTORS:

Chairman—A. J. STANTON, Esq., M.P., The Thrupp, Stroud, Gloucestershire.

Deputy-Chairman—EDMUND VINER ELLIS, Esq., Gloucester.

Colonel R. Bourne, Grafton Manor, Bromsgrove.
John Corbett, Esq., M.P., Stoke Prior, Bromsgrove.
Thomas Nelson Foster, Esq., Alt Dinas, Cheltenham.
William Stedman Gillett, Esq., Harefield, Bittern, Southampton.
Robert Nathaniel Hooper, Esq., Stanshawes Court, Chipping Sodbury.
William Nicks, Esq., Greville House, Gloucester.
Thomas Parkinson, Esq., Southwell, Notts.
Wm. George Postans, Esq., Galton House, George Road, Edgbaston.
Major W. E. Price, Hillfield House, Gloucester.
Charles Sturge, Esq., The Summer House, Bewdley.
Joseph Marshall Sturge, Esq., Gloucester.
Charles B. Walker, Esq., Norton Court, Gloucester.

OFFICERS.—Sec., Henry Waddy; Eng., W. B. Clegram; Auditors, T. A. Washbourn and E. Sturge.

Offices—Gloucester.

458.—SHEFFIELD.

From Sheffield to Tinsley, length, 3½ miles.

By act of 11 and 12 Vic., cap. 94, the canal company was dissolved, and the canal vested in the Manchester, Sheffield, and Lincolnshire Railway. The capital of the canal company was 70,400*l.* in 704 shares of 100*l.* each, and under the powers of the above act the Sheffield Company issued an annuity of 2*l.* 10*s.* in exchange for each of the canal shares. The annuities are payable half-yearly on the 15th January and 15th July. In a transfer, annuities to be styled "one (or more) annuity of two pounds ten shillings, No.——, created by the Sheffield Canal Purchase Act, 1848." Transfer fee, 2*s.* 6*d.* each seller. No accounts are issued.

Secretary, Edward Ross, M. S. & L. Railway, Manchester.

459.—STAFFORDSHIRE AND WORCESTERSHIRE.

Length, 50 miles.

Capital, 210,000*l.* in ordinary stock, upon which dividends have been paid equal to about 5 per cent. per annum, and 180,594*l.* 4½ per cent. debenture stock.

Chairman—The Right Hon. Lord HATHERTON.

Manager, W. Jones.

Office—87, Darlington Street, Wolverhampton.

460.—STOURBRIDGE.

Capital, 43,500*l.* in 300 fully paid shares of 145*l.* each. The latest dividends were at the following rate, viz.:—2*l.* 10*s.* per share for the half-years ended 24th June and 25th December, 1884, the latter being made payable on the 1st March, 1885.

Address—The Secretary, Stourbridge Canal Co., Stourbridge.

461.—WARWICK AND BIRMINGHAM.

Length, 22½ miles. Opened throughout in 1799.

Capital, 150,000*l.*, in 1,000 shares of 100*l.* each and 1,000 shares of 50*l.* each, fully paid. The company's dividends have been at the rate of 3 per cent. per annum, payable half-yearly in May and November. Accounts are not published.

Secretary, E. J. Lloyd.

Offices—Lower Fazeley Street, Birmingham.

462.—WORCESTER AND BIRMINGHAM.

This company was purchased by the Gloucester and Berkeley (now Sharpness New Docks, &c.), under the powers of their act of 1874. The terms were the absorption by the purchasing company of the whole mortgage debt of this company, and an annual rent-charge of 1*l.* per share on the ordinary capital, which consists of 6,000 shares.

Communications to be addressed to the Sharpness New Docks, &c., Co.

V.—AUXILIARY ASSOCIATIONS.

463.—ASHBURY RAILWAY CARRIAGE AND IRON.

Incorporated under "The Limited Liability Acts," with a capital of 500,000*l.* in 3,000 shares of 100*l.* each, and 10,000 shares of 20*l.* each. By resolutions dated 21st March, and 11th April, 1882, the capital of this company was reduced from 500,000*l.* to 288,108*l.* in 3,000 shares of 60*l.* each (55*l* paid), and 9,828 shares of 11*l.* each (4½*l.* paid). The last dividend (2*l.* 15*s.* per old share, and 4*s.* 3*d.* per new share) was paid in November, 1884.

The company make and sell, or lend on hire, carriages and wagons, and all kinds of railway plant, fittings, machinery, and rolling stock; carry on the business of mechanical engineers and general contractors; and purchase, lease, work, and sell mines, minerals, land, and buildings; purchase and sell, as merchants, timber, coal, metals, or other materials, and buy and sell any such materials, on commission, or as agents. The accounts, which are made up annually to 31st August, are only issued to shareholders. The ordinary general meetings are held at Manchester, usually about the middle of November each year.

DIRECTORS:

Chairman—ROBERT PHILLIPS, Esq., Romiley, Cheshire.

Thomas Vickers, Esq., Wilton Polygon, Cheetham Hill, Manchester.
C. J. Schofield, Esq., J.P., Clayton, near Manchester.
T. J. Bolland, Esq., India Buildings, Cross Street, Manchester.
James Holden, Esq., 1, Marsden Street, Manchester.
Robert Boyd, Esq., 74a, Mosley Street, Manchester.

OFFICERS.—Sec., Wm. Charlton; Auditor, E. Collier (Chadwicks, Collier, & Co.), Manchester; Bankers, The Manchester and County Bank Limited, Manchester.

Offices and Works—Openshaw, Manchester.

London Office—28, Queen Street, E.C.

464.—BIRMINGHAM RAILWAY CARRIAGE AND WAGON LIMITED.

Established in 1855, and subsequently registered under "The Limited Liability Acts." The subscribed capital has amounted to 234,956*l.*, which is paid up as follows:—10,000 ordinary 10*l.* shares, fully paid up; 8,739 ordinary 10*l* shares, 4*l.* paid up; 10,000 preference 10*l.* shares, 6 per cent. preference shares, fully paid; 148,000*l.* debentures. Last yearly balance sheet issued 31st December, 1883.

The accounts are made up to 31st December, and the meetings held in Birmingham in the month of February. Interim dividends are paid in the month of August.

DIRECTORS:

Chairman—WILLIAM MIDDLEMORE, Esq., J.P., Holloway Head, Birmingham

R. L. Baker, Esq., Barham House, Leamington.
F. P. Broughton, Esq., Smethwick.
Thomas Pickard, Esq., Edgbaston.
John Ford, Esq., J.P., Portland Lawn, Leamington.

OFFICERS.—Managing Director, Edmund Fowler, Edgbaston; Sec., Walter Jefferies, Birmingham Railway Carriage and Wagon Works, Smethwick, near Birmingham; Auditors, Horatio N. Ashford, Shirley, and George Beech, Birmingham; Solicitors, Reece, Harris, and Harris, Birmingham.

465.—BRISTOL AND SOUTH WALES RAILWAY WAGON.

Incorporated under "The Limited Liability Acts." The company was established in 1860, and carries on the general business of a railway rolling stock company. Authorised capital, 330,000*l.*, in 10*l.* shares, all of which is subscribed, and 132,000*l.*, or 4*l.* per share, paid up. Debenture capital, 183,834*l.*

Revenue.—The accounts for the half-year ended 31st December, 1884, showed the receipts to have been 12,812*l*., including the balance brought from the previous half-year, and the expenses amounted to 944*l*., leaving a net profit of 11,868*l*., which, after the payment of interest charges, sufficed for a dividend of 10 per cent. per annum, placing 750*l*. to the credit of the contingent fund account, and carrying forward a balance of 436*l*.

Capital.—This account consists of 132,000*l*. in shares and 183,834*l*. in debentures; total, 315,834*l*.

The accounts are made up to 30th June and 31st December, and the meetings held in Bristol in February and August.

DIRECTORS:

Chairman—2 HENRY B. O. SAVILE, Esq., Clifton.

1 Thomas Gibson, Esq., Clifton.
3 Joseph Haynes Nash, Esq., Clifton.
2 Benjamin Spry Stock, Esq., Bristol.
1 John Hewitt, Esq., Bristol.
3 James Inskip, Esq., Bristol.

1, Retire in 1885; 2, in 1886; 3, in 1887. All are eligible for re-election.

OFFICERS.—Sec., John Curtis, Exchange Buildings, Bristol; Auditors, W. F. Brookman and Stephen Tryon; Solicitors, Murly, Sons, and Millard, Bristol.

466.—BRISTOL WAGON WORKS.

This is a limited liability company carrying on the ordinary business of like undertakings. The subscribed ordinary capital is 260,000*l*. in 20*l*. shares: on the first issue of 160,000*l*., 10*l*. per share, or 80,000*l*., is paid up, and on the new issue of 100,000*l*., 23,958*l*. has been received. Five per cent. 20*l*. preference shares for 40,000*l*. have been issued, and 20,000*l*., or 10*l*. per share, paid up. Debentures, 145,305*l*.

For the year ended 31st March, 1880, no dividend was paid. For the half-year ended 30th September, 1880, the arrears of dividend on the preference shares, at the guaranteed rate of 5 per cent., for the year ended March, 1880, was paid, and a dividend at the rate of 5 per cent. was paid on all the shares for the year ended March, 1881. A dividend of 5 per cent. was also paid on all the shares for the year ended March, 1882, and a like dividend was paid for the years ended March, 1883, and March, 1884. An *ad interim* dividend at the like rate was paid for the half-year ended 30th September last.

The accounts are made up to the end of March, and submitted to the shareholders in the following June. Interim dividends are paid in December.

DIRECTORS:

Chairman—1 JOSEPH D. WESTON, Esq., Bristol.

Managing Director—ALBERT FRY, Esq., Bristol.

3 John Chetwood Aiken, Esq., Bristol.
1 Francis Fry, Esq., Bristol.
2 Steuart Fripp, Esq., Bristol.

1, Retire in 1885; 2, in 1886; 3, in 1887. All are eligible for re-election.

OFFICERS.—Sec., Samuel Chappell; Auditors, Tribe, Clarke, and Co., Bristol; Solicitors, Fry, Abbot, Pope, and Brown, Bristol.

Offices and Works—Lawrence Hill, Bristol. London Offices—8, Victoria Chambers, Westminster, S.W. Show Rooms—Victoria Street, Bristol.

467.—BRITISH WAGON.

Incorporated under "The Companies' Acts, 1862 and 1867." This company lets on lease all kinds of railway wagons. Capital, 300,000*l*. in 20*l*. shares, of which 60,000*l*. is paid up as follows:—On 2,500 shares, 10*l*.; on 2,500 shares, 6*l*.; on 5,000 shares, 3*l*.; and on 5,000 shares, 1*l*. Debenture capital, 172,000*l*.

The dividend for the year 1875 was at the rate of 11¼ per cent., and for the first half of 1876 at the rate of 10 per cent. per annum; second half of 1876, 10 per cent. per annum; first half of 1877, 10 per cent.; second half of 1877, 10 per cent.; and first half of 1878, 10 per cent.; second half of 1878, 9 per cent.; first half of 1879, 8 per cent.; second half of 1879, 6 per cent.; first half of 1880, 7 per cent.; second half of 1880, 7 per cent.; first half of 1881, and each subsequent half-year to and including first half of 1884, the dividends have been at the rate of 6 per cent. per annum.

The accounts are made up to 30th June and 31st December, and the meetings held in Rotherham in February and August.

DIRECTORS:

Chairman—FRED. L. HARROP, Esq., Swinton, Rotherham.

*John Gibbs, Esq., Rotherham.
*B. H. Dale, Esq., New Parks, Scarborough.
Thomas Cooper, Esq., Rose Hill, Rotherham.
F. Wheatley, Esq., Kimberworth Park, Rotherham.

*Retire next, but are eligible for re-election.

OFFICERS.—Sec., Henry Hart, College Street, Rotherham; Auditors, Barber Brothers and Wortley.

468.—BROWN, MARSHALLS, AND CO. LIMITED.

Capital, 80,000*l.* in 10,000 shares of 8*l.* each. This company is established for the manufacture of railway carriages, wagons, engines, wheels, railway rolling stock of every description, and the disposing of, leasing, or hiring of railway carriages, wagons, and railway rolling stock, to railway companies and others, upon deferred payments or otherwise.

DIRECTORS:

Chairman—Sir JAMES JOSEPH ALLPORT, Knt., Littleover, Derby.

Francis Seddon Bolton, Esq., J.P., Broad Street, Birmingham.
*Henry Edmunds, Esq., Carpenter Road, Edgbaston, Birmingham.
Maximilian Lindner, Esq., Broad Street, Birmingham.
William Lansdowne Beale, Esq., Waltham St. Lawrence, Twyford, Berkshire.
*Charles Wells, Esq., Tettenhall Road, Wolverhampton.

* Retiring directors; eligible for re-election.

OFFICERS.—Sec. and Acct., Joseph Oldham; Gen. Man., Arthur L. Shackleford; Auditor, W. H. Thornbery, Accountant, Birmingham; Solicitors, Beale, Marigold, and Co., Birmingham.

Office—Britannia Railway Carriage and Wagon Works, Birmingham.

469.—GLOUCESTER WAGON.

Incorporated under "The Companies' Acts, 1862 and 1867," with a capital of 500,000*l.* in 10*l.* shares, and borrowing powers to the extent of one-half the share capital. The carriage and wagon stock belonging to the company at 30th June, 1884, consisted of 9,331 vehicles. During the year, 329 wagons had been built for the company's stock, all of which had been sold on deferred payments.

REVENUE—Year ended 30th June, 1884.—For this year a dividend at 4 per cent. per annum was paid, and a balance of 1,259*l.* carried forward.

CAPITAL.—This account at 30th June, 1884, stood as follows:—

Authorised	£500,000
Less—Amount uncalled	81,250
	£418,750
Loans on debentures	89,753
	£508,503

The accounts are made up annually to 30th June, and the meetings held at Gloucester in August.

DIRECTORS:

Chairman—JOSEPH REYNOLDS, Esq., Gloucester.

Deputy-Chairman—HENRY WRIGHT, Esq., Smallheath, Birmingham.

Thomas Wilson, Esq., Edgbaston, Birmingham.
Robert Blinkhorn, Esq., Gloucester.
A. C. Wheeler, Esq., Gloucester.
W. H. Williams, Esq., Bishopsgate Street E.C.
William Knowles, Esq., Gloucester.

OFFICERS.—Gen. Man., Isaac Slater, Russian Vice-Consul at Gloucester; Sec., H. T. Simpson; Auditors, Hudson Smith, Williams, and Co., Bristol and Cardiff.

Works—Bristol Road, Gloucester.
London Offices—26, Parliament Street, S.W.

470.—LANCASTER WAGON.

Incorporated under the provisions of "The Companies' Act, 1862," whereby the liability of the shareholders is limited to the amount of their shares. Capital, 200,000*l*. in 5*l*. shares. Of the subscribed ordinary shares, 28,070 are fully paid up.

This company manufactures railway carriages and tram-cars of every description, either for sale, on hire, or on deferred payment lease. It also manufactures extensively wheels and axles and general ironwork.

At the last annual meeting a dividend at 4 per cent., free of income tax, was declared upon the shares of the company, 6,000*l*. added to the reserve, and the balance of 692*l*. carried forward to next account.

DIRECTORS:

Chairman—CHARLES BLADES, Esq., Lancaster.

Edward Clark, Esq., Queen Street, Lancaster.
Albert Greg, Esq., Escowbeck, Caton, near Lancaster.
Henry Welch, Esq., Queen Street, Lancaster.
Stephen Wright Wearing, Esq., Fleet Square, Lancaster.

Two directors retire every year in March, and are eligible for re-election.

OFFICERS.—Sec., Benjamin Gregson; Man., W. C. Shackleford; Solicitor, Lawrence Holden.

Offices—Lancaster.

471.—LINCOLN WAGON AND ENGINE LIMITED.

Incorporated under "The Companies' Acts, 1862 and 1867," with a capital of 250,000*l*. in 20*l*. shares, with power to issue debentures for a like amount. The shares have all been issued, and consist of 5,000 "A" and 7,500 "B" shares respectively, the latter in three issues of 2,500 each. The total amount received on the various issues is 37,500*l*., of which 15,000*l*. belongs to the "A" and 22,500*l*. to the "B" shares. Up to 1st February, 1884, there had also been received 2,710*l*. on loans and in advance of calls, and 156,945*l*. on debenture loans.

REVENUE.—The revenue on rents, &c., for the year ended 1st February, 1884, amounted to 12,167*l*., and the expenditure, including interest and preferential charges, to 8,500*l*., leaving a profit of 3,662*l*., which was appropriated to the payment of a dividend equal to 7 per cent. per annum on the ordinary capital, and 500*l*. added to reserve fund.

The accounts are made up to 1st February, and submitted to the shareholders early in March. Meetings held at Lincoln. Interim dividends of 5 per cent. are paid in August.

DIRECTORS:

Chairman—HENRY NEWSUM, Esq., Lincoln.

William J. Warrener, Esq., Lincoln.
William Spencer, Esq., Lincoln.
Charles K. Tomlinson, Esq., J.P., Lincoln
James Birch, Esq., Lincoln.

OFFICERS.—Sec., William Watson, City Chambers, High Street, Lincoln; Auditor, John Masterman, King Street Chambers, Wakefield; Solicitors, Toynbee, Larken, and Toynbee, Lincoln; Bankers, Smith, Ellison, and Co., Lincoln.

472.—METROPOLITAN RAILWAY CARRIAGE AND WAGON LIMITED.

This company was formed to purchase and carry on the business of Joseph Wright and Sons, at Saltley, near Birmingham. Capital, 300,000*l*., viz., 30,000 10*l*. ordinary shares; 5*l*. called up. Borrowing powers, 100,000*l*. The company manufactures railway carriages, tramway cars, wagons, and railway iron of every description, and lets on hire coal, ironstone, ballast, and other wagons.

REVENUE.—The profits for the year ended 30th June, 1884, including 4,311*l*. from previous account, amounted to 22,320*l*., out of which the directors paid a dividend of 10 per cent. upon the paid-up capital, and carried forward a balance of 4,414*l*. A dividend at the same rate was paid for the year ended 30th June, 1883. The reserve fund now amounts to 100,000*l*.

The accounts are made up to 30th June, and the meeting is held at Birmingham in August.

DIRECTORS:

Chairman—WILLIAM HOLLIDAY, Esq., Edgbaston, Birmingham.

Daniel S. Hasluck, Esq., The Austins, Handsworth, Birmingham.
Charles L. Browning, Esq., Edgbaston, Birmingham.
James Watson, Esq., Berwick, Shrewsbury.
Harry Heaton, Esq., Harborne, Birmingham.

OFFICERS.—Sec. and Acct., F. S. Taylor; Gen. Man., John Rawlins; Auditors, Laundy & Co., Chartered Accountants, Birmingham; Solicitors, Beale, Marigold, and Co., Birmingham.

CHIEF OFFICE—Saltley Works, Birmingham.

London Office—85, Gracechurch Street, E.C.

Branch Wagon Works—East Moors, Cardiff, South Wales; and Great Eastern Railway, Peterborough.

473.—MIDLAND RAILWAY-CARRIAGE AND WAGON LIMITED.

Established 1853. Under special resolutions passed on the 14th August, 1877, and confirmed on the 29th of the same month, the name of the company, viz., "Midland Wagon," was changed as above, and the shares reduced from 50*l.* to 10*l.* each.

On the 12th September, 1881, the company was registered with limited liability.

Under a special resolution passed on the 26th August, 1881, the nominal amount of the 20,000 ordinary and 10,000 preference shares was increased from 10*l.* to 20*l.* per share, but no part of such increased capital shall be capable of being called up, except in the event of, and for the purposes of, the company being wound up.

The authorised capital now stands as follows:—

20,000 ordinary shares of 20*l.*, all issued, 10*l.* paid	£400,000
10,000 six per cent. preference shares of 20*l.* each, 1*l.* paid, all issued	200,000
Power to borrow on debentures	300,000
10,000 ordinary shares of 10*l.* each not yet issued	100,000
Total	£1,000,000

This company manufactures and lets on hire railway carriages and wagons of every description, for cash, or on deferred payments extending over a period of years; undertakes repairs, by contract or otherwise, in any part of the kingdom; and purchases, sells, and lets on hire second-hand coal, coke, ironstone, and other wagons, and keeps the same in repair. Railway wheels and axles, axle-boxes, and wrought and cast iron work of every sort, made to any pattern, specification, or drawing.

REVENUE.—The dividend for the year ended 30th June, 1884, was at the rate of 6 per cent. on preference and 5 per cent. on ordinary shares, carrying 1,440*l.* to the reserve fund for renewal of wagons.

The accounts are made up to June 30th, and submitted to the shareholders about the middle of August. Meeting held at Birmingham. Interim dividends are paid in March.

DIRECTORS:

Chairman—JOSEPH SCRIVENER KEEP, Esq., Westmere, Edgbaston, Birmingham.

Henry Griffiths, Esq., Assoc.Inst.C.E., 252, Victoria Park Road, Hackney, E.
Henry Field James, Esq., Alvechurch.
J. Powell Williams, Esq., Barford House, Gough Road, Edgbaston.
Leonard Brierley, Esq., Holmwood, Edgbaston.
Samuel De La Grange Williams, Esq., Woodgate, Great Malvern.

OFFICERS.—Sec., Edward Jackson; Solicitors, Ryland, Martineau, and Co.; Bankers, Birmingham and Midland Bank Limited.

Midland Works, Birmingham, and Abbey Works, Shrewsbury.

Chief Offices—Midland Works, Birmingham.

London Offices—Suffolk House, Laurence Pountney Hill, E.C.

474.—NORTH CENTRAL WAGON.

Established 1861. Authorised share capital, 200 000*l.* in 20*l.* shares; borrowing powers, 500.000*l.* The subscribed capital is 197,040*l.*, of which 126,475*l.* is paid up as follows:—2,500 shares fully paid; 2,500 with 18*l.* paid; 2,500 with 8*l.* paid; and 2,500 with 4*l.* paid; calls paid in advance, 2,653*l.* Debentures issued for 310,772*l.* The dividend for the year 1875 was at the rate of 14 per cent., for 1876 at the rate of 12 per cent.; for 1877 and 1878, 10 per cent.; for the first half-year 1879, 7½ per cent.; for the half-years ended 31st December, 1881, and 30th June, 1882, 8 per cent. per annum, and 31st December, 7½ per cent.; 30th June and 31st December, 1883, 6 per cent. per annum; 30th June, 1884, 6 per cent. per annum.

The accounts are made up to 30th June and 31st December, and the meetings held at Rotherham in February and August.

DIRECTORS:

Chairman—GEORGE WILTON CHAMBERS, Esq., Rotherham.

Henry Wigfield, Esq., Rotherham.
Francis Ebenezer Smith, Esq., Sheffield.
Wilson Waterfall, Esq., Rotherham.
Thomas Wragg, Esq., Rotherham.
Robert George Chambers, Esq., Rotherham.

OFFICERS.—Sec., J. Barras, Howard Street, Rotherham; Assist. Sec., E. Ball, Rotherham; Auditors, Septimus Short and Co, Sheffield.

475.—PATENT SHAFT AND AXLE-TREE LIMITED.

Incorporated, with limited liability, under "The Companies' Act, 1862." The capital of the company was, by special resolution dated 24th November, 1879, reduced by 3*l.* on the paid-up value of each share, making the nominal value of the ordinary shares 17*l.*, and the paid-up value 7*l.* per share; and the total paid-up capital now stands at 216,962*l.* ordinary, and 350,000*l.* 5 per cent. preference fully paid. Debentures to the amount of 60,000*l.* have also been authorised, and are all placed. The dividend for the year ended 30th June, 1881, was at the rate of 2½ per cent. per annum, free of income tax, the same rate being paid for the year ending 30th June, 1882. No dividend was paid in June, 1883, but 5 per cent. per annum in June, 1884. A uniform dividend of 5 per cent., free of income tax, has been paid regularly, since their issue in 1872, on the preference shares. Reserve fund, 12,000*l.*

This company, which was formed in 1864, to purchase and carry on the business of Mr. Thomas Walker, acquired in 1867 the extensive works of Messrs. Lloyds, Foster, and Co., together with their collieries, steel works, &c. They are manufacturers of railway material of every description, including wheels, turntables, anchors, steel castings, pipes, bridges, roofs, tyres, axles, rails, &c., in steel or iron.

The accounts are made up to the 30th June, and the annual meeting is held at Birmingham in August.

DIRECTORS:

Chairman—THOMAS WALKER, Esq., Berkswell Hall, near Coventry.

Deputy-Chairman—THOMAS EADES WALKER, Esq., Studley Castle, Warwickshire.

Richard Williams, Esq., Wednesbury.
John Nurthall Brown, Esq., Perry Bar, Birmingham.
George Allen Everitt, Esq., Knowle Hall, Warwickshire.
James Watson, Esq., Birmingham.

OFFICERS.—Gen. Man., J. W. Walles; Sec., John F. Cay, Wednesbury, Staffordshire; Auditors, Howard Smith and Slocombe, Accountants, Birmingham; Bankers, Birmingham and Midland Bank Limited.

Head Offices—Brunswick Ironworks, Wednesbury, Staffordshire.

476.—RAILWAY CARRIAGE.

Incorporated under the "Limited Liability Acts," with a capital of 150,000*l.* in 15,000 ordinary shares of 10*l.* each, and 15,000 preference shares of 5*l.* each. The ordinary capital has since been reduced from 150,000*l.* to 75,000*l.*, the shares being now 5*l.* each, fully paid; debenture capital, 2,000*l.*

Established for the purpose of constructing, repairing, selling, hiring, and letting of plant, wagons, carriages, and rolling stock for railways, tramways, and ordinary roads. For the making, selling, and letting of girders, roofs, machinery, and all kinds of ironwork, and for the working of railways and tramways.

REVENUE.—The earnings of this company for the yeae ended 30th June, 1884, were sufficient to pay a twelve months' dividend on the preference shares, and also to pay the twelve months in arrear upon these shares, which together absorbed 9,000*l.*

The accounts are made up to June 30th, and submitted to the shareholders about the middle of August. Meetings are held at the company's offices. Interim dividends are paid in February.

DIRECTORS:

Chairman—JOHN UNDERHILL, Esq., Wolverhampton.

John Kershaw, Esq., M.Inst.C.E., 1, Arlington Street, Piccadilly, S.W.
John Brooks, Esq., Carpenter Road, Edgbaston.
Arthur Higginson, Esq., 3, Westminster Chambers, S.W.
Herbert Wheeler, Esq., Rotton Park Road, Edgbaston.

OFFICERS.—Sec., Herbert Wheeler; Auditors, H. H. Hewlings, Boyne Lodge, Uxbridge Road, Notting Hill, W., and Francis Aysom, Holly Park, Crouch Hill, N.; Solicitors, Newman, Stretton, and Hilliard, 75, Cornhill, E.C.

Offices—Oldbury, near Birmingham; and 7A, Laurence Pountney Hill, E.C.

477.—RAILWAY ROLLING STOCK.

Established 1853, for the purpose of sale or hire, on deferred payments, of all kinds of railway rolling stock. Capital, 170,000*l.* in 10*l.* shares, divided as follows:—7,000 ordinary shares, fully paid; 7,916 6 per cent. irredeemable preference shares, fully paid; 2,082 ditto, 4*l.* paid up; total paid-up capital, 157,508*l.* The dividend for the year 1875 was at the rate of 10 per cent. per annum; for 1877, at 7½ per cent.; for 1878, at 4½ per cent.; for 1879, at 3 per cent.; to June, 1880, at 3 per cent.; and to December, 1880, 3 per cent., free of income tax on the ordinary shares, and 3 per cent. each half-year since.

The accounts are made up to 30th June and 31st December, and the meetings held at Wolverhampton in January and July.

DIRECTORS:

Chairman—SAMUEL LOVERIDGE, Danes Court, Tettenhall.

Deputy-Chairman—HENRY WARD, Esq., Rodbaston, Penkridge.

J. W. Williams, Esq.
Henry Walker, Esq.
M. Ironmonger, Esq.
Haden Corser, Esq.
H. H. Fowler, Esq., M.P., Woodthorne, The Wergs, Wolverhampton.

Secretary, J. Underhill, Wolverhampton.

478.—SCOTTISH WAGON.

Established in 1861, for the purposes of selling and letting on hire all kinds of railway wagons and trucks. Capital, 360,000*l.* in 10*l.* shares. The receipts on capital account are divided as follow:—18,000 original shares, fully paid; 18,000 new shares, 4*l.* paid. Debenture and other loans, 180,684*l.* Calls paid in advance, 4,836*l.*

REVENUE.—For the two half-years ended 30th June, 1884, and 31st December, 1884, the earnings have sufficed for the declaration of dividends at the rate of 5½ per cent. per annum on the ordinary shares, free of income tax.

The last two half-yearly meetings were held on the 31st July, 1884, and 30th January, 1885, respectively.

DIRECTORS:

Chairman—1 Sir JAMES FALSHAW, Bart., 14, Belgrave Crescent, Edinburgh.

1 Walter Maclellan, Esq., 129, Trongate, Glasgow.
2 William Handyside, Esq., 11, Claremont Crescent, Edinburgh.
3 John Weir, Esq., 3, Minto Street, Edinburgh.
2 Hugh Rose, Esq., 3, Hillside Crescent, Edinburgh.
3 Thomas Gill, Esq., Dunstane, West Coates, Edinburgh.

1, Retire in 1885; 2, in 1886; 3, in 1887. All eligible for re-election.

OFFICERS.—Sec. and Man., J. H. H. Horsfield; Auditors, Macandrew and Blair, C.A., Edinburgh.

Offices—5, St. Andrew Square, Edinburgh.

479.—STAFFORDSHIRE WHEEL AND AXLE.

Incorporated under the "Limited Liability Acts," with a nominal capital of 200,000*l.* in 10*l.* shares; subscribed, 7,272 shares; paid up, 3*l.* per share. Borrowing powers, 10,000*l.* The company are manufacturers of all kinds of railway carriage, wagon, and contractors' wheels and axles, and other iron-work used in the construction of railway rolling stock; also of hammered uses, forgings, and smithwork of every description, either for marine, locomotive, stationary, or other engineering purposes.

The accounts are made up to 30th June, and submitted to the proprietors early in August. Interim dividends are payable in February.

DIRECTORS:

Chairman—RALPH HEATON, Esq., Courtlands, Edgbaston, Birmingham.

Charles Lloyd Browning, Esq., Chad Mont, Edgbaston, Birmingham.

John Underhill, Esq., Wombourne, Wolverhampton.

John Brooks, Esq., Bell Street, Birmingham.

OFFICERS.—Gen. Man. and Sec., J. Rotheray Hill: Auditors, Carter and Carter, Accountants, Birmingham; Solicitors, Sanders, Smith, and Parish, Birmingham and Dudley; Bankers, Birmingham Banking Co. Limited.

Offices and Works—Heath Street South, Spring Hill, Birmingham.

480.—STARBUCK CAR AND WAGON.

This company was formed in 1871, and registered under "The Companies' Acts, 1862 and 1867," with a capital of 50,000*l*. in 10*l*. shares. The subscribed capital is 43,760*l*., of which 2,376 shares are fully paid, and 2,000 have 7*l*. 10*s*. paid. Total paid up, 38,760*l*. The net revenue for the year ended December 31st, 1883, after writing off 500*l*. against goodwill account, sufficed for a dividend at the rate of 6 per cent. per annum, and left a balance of 511*l*. to next account. The accounts are made up annually to 31st December, and submitted to the shareholders at the end of March. The directors have power to declare interim dividends.

DIRECTORS:

Chairman—WILLIAM MARTINEAU, Esq., 6, Great Winchester Street, E.C.

Managing Director—GEORGE STARBUCK, Esq., Birkenhead.

Peter Swinton Boult, Esq., 31, Exchange Alley, Liverpool.

John Hockin, Esq., Tower Chambers, Moorgate Street, E.C.

OFFICERS.—Sec. and Man., George F. Milnes; Auditor, Joshua Ponton; Bankers, North and South Wales Bank Limited, Birkenhead.

Registered Offices and Works—Cleveland Street, Birkenhead.
London Office—6, Great Winchester Street, E.C.

481.—SWANSEA WAGON.

Incorporated in 1866 under the "Limited Liability Acts." The capital account has been lately and now is as follows:—Ordinary 4*l*. shares, fully paid, 38,900*l*.; 10 per cent preference 10*l*. shares, fully paid, 20,000*l*.; reserve and contingent funds, 6,188*l*.; revenue account credit balance, 372*l*.

REVENUE.—The report for the year ended 30th June, 1884, states as follows:—The gross profits for the year amounted to 5,023*l*., being 254*l*. in excess of expenses and interest on loans and debentures—this added to 118*l*. brought forward last year makes 372*l*. to be carried forward to the credit of the current year's trading account. During the year wagon rents have ruled exceedingly low, and very few safe and profitable orders for new wagons have been obtainable. The amount of the gross profits notwithstanding this, gives the directors encouragement with respect to the future immediately any revival in trade sets in. The endeavour to relieve the company of the 10 per cent. preference shares referred to in the last report has been continued, and it will be seen from the accounts that up to the 30th June last 907 shares had been purchased. Since then the number has been increased to 1,182, out of a total of 2,000.

The accounts are made up to 30th June, and submitted to the shareholders in August or September.

DIRECTORS:

Chairman—ISAAC JENKS, Esq., Morley House, Wolverhampton.

Managing Director—ROBERT D. BURNIE, Esq., Swansea.

Joseph Sturge Gilpin, Esq., Nottingham. | Marcus Moxham, Esq., Swansea.

OFFICERS.—Auditor, Robt. Mellors, Nottingham; Solicitors, Winterbotham, Bell, and Co., Cheltenham.

482.—WAKEFIELD ROLLING STOCK.

Incorporated, with limited liability, 30th November, 1872, with a capital of 150,000*l*., and borrowing powers of a like amount. The paid up capital amounts to 36,000*l*. (30,000 fully paid 1*l*. shares, and 6,000 5*l*. shares having 1*l*. paid); calls in advance, 4,096*l*.; debentures issued, 7,475*l*. For the years 1875, 1876, 1877, and the first half of 1878, the dividends paid were at the rate of 7 per cent. per annum. For the second half-year of 1878 and first half-year of 1879 the dividends were at the rate of 6 and 5 per cent. per annum respectively. For the half-years ended 30th June and 31st December, 1880, and 30th, June, 1881, the dividend was at the rate of 5 per cent. per annum (less income tax), and for the six half-years ended 30th June, 1884, the dividend was at the rate of 4 per cent. per annum (less tax).

The meetings are held at Wakefield, in February and August.

DIRECTORS:

Chairman—B. WATSON, Esq., Wakefield.

R. Aconley, Esq., Huddersfield.
G. F. Wild, Esq., Wakefield.
J. Ingram, Esq., Wakefield.

Manager, C. Hopkinson.

Offices—8, Old Corn Exchange, Wakefield.

483.—WESTERN WAGON AND PROPERTY LIMITED.

(LATE WESTERN WAGON.)

This company was established in 1860, and carries on the business of manufacturing, for sale or hire, all classes of railway wagons. Capital, 100,000*l.* in 10*l.* shares. Subscribed capital, 89,560*l.*, of which 69,780*l.* is paid up, viz.:—5,000 original shares, fully paid, and 3,956 new shares, 5*l.* paid. Debentures, 12,250*l.* The company was reconstructed under the above title in October, 1881. The capital is now as follows:—Nominal, 30,000 shares of 6*l.* each; subscribed, 5.000 shares fully paid, and 3,963 shares 2*l.* paid; debentures, 15,72*l.*; reserve fund, 8,000*l.*

REVENUE.—The available balance for the year ended 30th June, 1884, was 2,170*l.*, which sufficed for a dividend at the rate of 5 per cent. per annum, 400*l.* to the reserve fund, and left 23*l.* to next year.

The accounts are made up to the 30th June in each year, and the meetings are held in Bristol in August.

DIRECTORS:

Chairman—JOHN BARTLETT, Esq., Welsh Back, Bristol.

Deputy Chairman—HENRY G. GARDNER, Esq., Nelson Street, Bristol.

Wilberforce Tribe, Esq., Albion Chambers, Bristol.
William Franklin, Esq., Stoneleigh, Cotham Park, Bristol.

All eligible for re-election.

OFFICERS.—Sec., V. A. Williams, 2, Clare Street, Bristol; Auditor, Thomas Gillford, 26, Broad Street, Bristol; Solicitors, Fry, Abbot, Pope, and Brown, Shannon Court, Bristol.

Offices—2, Clare Street, Bristol. Works—East Moors, Cardiff.

484.—YORKSHIRE RAILWAY WAGON.

Incorporated, with limited liability, under "The Companies' Acts, 1862 and 1867." Authorised capital, 500,000*l.*, in 10*l.* shares; subscribed, 394,540*l.*, of which 94,454*l.* is paid up, as follows:—3,000 shares, fully paid; 7,000 shares, 5*l.* paid; 29,454 shares, 1*l.* paid. Calls paid in advance, 13,220*l.*; debentures issued, 160,413*l.*

REVENUE.—The balance of profit and loss for the half-years ended 30th June and 31st December, 1883, after deducting general charges, debenture interest, &c., and adding amounts received for interest and sundries, sufficed for a dividend at the rate of 5*l.* per cent. per annum, 500*l.* to reserve fund, and 738*l.* to be carried to next account.

The meetings are held at Wakefield on the first Thursday in February and August.

DIRECTORS:

Chairman—HENRY ROBINSON, Esq., Wakefield.

W. H. B. Tomlinson, Esq., Wakefield.
H. J. Morton, Esq., 2, Westbourne Villas, Scarborough.
Henry Lee, Esq., Wakefield.
George Padley, Esq., Scarborough.

OFFICERS.—Sec., W. H. Saville; Auditor, J. J. Dickinson; Solicitors, Gill and Plews.

Offices—Barstow Square, Wakefield.

APPENDIX.

I.—AGREEMENTS, CONSOLIDATIONS, AMALGAMATIONS, &c.

1.—BORROWING POWERS, LLOYD'S BONDS, &c.

The following Report from the Select Committee of the House of Lords, appointed to enquire into this subject, was issued on the 15th July, 1864:—

"The Committee having examined witnesses, and considered the subject referred to them, are of opinion that a compulsory public registration of railway debentures and debenture stock will afford means whereby the directors of railway companies may be restrained from exceeding the amount of their statutory borrowing powers.

"It is the custom of Parliament, when granting to railway companies the powers necessary for carrying out their undertakings, to limit the amount of money they should be permitted to borrow, and to prescribe the conditions under which such borrowing powers should be exercised; and it is evidently the intention of the Legislature that no bonds, or other negotiable securities, other than those created under such limited and conditional powers, should be issued by the directors of railway companies.

"This intention is, however, easily and commonly defeated by the issue of obligations (purporting to be for work done, or materials supplied for the purposes of the undertaking), commonly called 'Lloyd's Bonds.' The holders of these obligations can sue upon them, and recover judgment against the companies; and success in any conflict for priority of claim between them and the holders of statutory debentures would appear, from evidence given before the committee, to be only a question of more or less diligence.

"The directors of some railway companies are in the habit of issuing securities of this description without consulting their shareholders, and without the knowledge or consent of the statutory debenture holders; and the gross amount of them, which may be outstanding against a company, is unlimited.

"The committee are of opinion that holders of statutory debentures, duly registered as above recommended, should have a right to recover and secure the payment of all principal and interest due to them, by the appointment of a receiver in priority to the holders of 'Lloyd's Bonds,' or of any other obligations or acknowledgment of indebtedness not issued under the authority of Parliament.

"Such an arrangement may, however, be defeated, or at all events materially interfered with, if a creditor is allowed to seize the stock of the company, and thereby stop the traffic on the line, and the income derived therefrom. The property is of a different character to other property. The public have a right to the use of the railway, and would be seriously inconvenienced by the stoppage of even a short line. It appears, therefore, to the committee that this power ought not to be allowed to the creditors of railway companies.

"The committee see no reason why railway companies should continue altogether free from the adjusting process to which other trading companies are liable through proceedings in bankruptcy. On the contrary, they are of opinion that the present practice by which the affairs of companies practically bankrupt are patched up by successive acts of Parliament is injurious to the public, and too frequently of no real benefit to the shareholders. When a company pays little or no dividend on its original capital, the working expenses are often cut down injuriously, danger arises from insufficient service, and the risk of present loss attending any reduction of fares, even with the fairest expectation of future profit, is a bar to liberality of management. For the public advantage, it is desirable that a railway should yield reasonable terms to those under whose control it is placed; and when a company becomes seriously embarrassed, it is expedient that the concern should be passed to others, under whose management it may be efficiently conducted. The knowledge that such must be the result of mismanagement would probably have a most beneficial effect on the proceedings of directors, and subject the credit which they would be able to obtain to some useful restraint. With the present facilities for forming companies, there would be no difficulty in finding purchasers under sound and just regulations to be provided in a public act, whereby Parliament would be relieved from having to deal with a class of private bills which are very troublesome to settle, and are never of a satisfactory character. The rights of the holders of statutory securities, including the regular payment of their dividends, should of course be carefully secured throughout all these proceedings."

The class of security referred to in the foregoing report as "Lloyd's Bonds" is issued generally in the following form:—

THE ______________________ RAILWAY COMPANY.

PROVISIONAL BOND OF OBLIGATION.

No. £

The Railway Company do hereby acknowledge that they stand indebted to of in the sum of for works executed by the said for the said company, for the purpose of their railway, certified by the engineer of the said company. And the said company, for themselves, their successors, and assigns, hereby covenant with the said his executors and administrators, to pay to him, his executors, administrators, or assigns, the said sum of upon the day of one thousand eight hundred and ; also interest thereon at the rate of per cent. per annum, from the date thereof until payment.

Given under the common seal of the said company the day of in the year of our Lord one thousand eight hundred and } (L.S.)

REGISTERED ______________

______________ *Secretary.*

The issue of these bonds recently came before the Court of Queen's Bench, in the case of "Chambers *v.* the Manchester and Milford Companies," when, after due consideration, it was decided that the issue of this form of security for the purpose of increasing the capital—"borrowing on the credit of the company"—is illegal. The report of the judgment in the legal department of the *Times* was preceded by the following explanatory observations:—

"The case raised the question of the validity of a species of security which have come to be known in the mercantile world, from the name of an eminent counsel who devised them, as 'Lloyd's Bonds,' and which, it was stated, have been issued to the amount of many millions. It was stated by counsel that the issue of these bonds had become a usual means of raising money by companies whose capital had either not been fully subscribed or had proved insufficient, and whose borrowing powers, for some reason, could not be directly resorted to, or had become exhausted, and that they have been issued to contractors and other creditors of such companies to an enormous amount, which certainly may be measured by millions, and which, as we are informed, might not improbably amount to 30,000,000*l.* Happily, as will be seen, the court decided that they may legally be issued to actual creditors of the company; but the question here raised was whether they could be issued as a means of indirectly borrowing money, in evasion of the restrictions and prohibitions of the Companies' Acts. The court has decided that they cannot legally be so issued; and it was stated by counsel that the learned gentleman who devised them never intended that they should be, but intended them merely to be issued to actual creditors for existing debts, a purpose to which it will be seen the court has determined they may still be legally applied. The attempt here has been to use them as a means for borrowing money—beyond and without any statutable authority—in place of those 'loan notes,' and other negotiable securities, which, as the Railway Companies' Act of 1844 recites, had been issued largely by such companies, and led to the passing of that act, prohibiting them, unless authorised by the special act of the particular company."

After quoting the act of 1844, the writer continues thus:—

"It has, however, been considered that this enactment only applied to negotiable securities; the 'mischief' at which the act was aimed being, as was deemed, the issue of such securities; so that the act did not apply to the mere borrowing of money on instruments not assignable; and, at all events, not to the issue of such non-assignable securities to creditors; and hence, notwithstanding that act, such non-assignable securities, in a form devised by eminent counsel, have, in fact, been largely issued."

The following is a summary of the judgment:—

"Mr. Justice Crompton said the court felt no doubt upon the point, and would proceed to give judgment at once. The law had been laid down by Lord Wensleydale in the case of the 'South Yorkshire *v.* the Great Northern' (9, *Exchequer Reports*).

"'The question which arises in this case is one of great importance and some nicety, and depends upon the construction of the 'Companies' Clauses Act.' Generally speaking, all corporations are bound by instruments under their corporate seal; but where a corporation is created by an act of Parliament, under special powers, another question arises, and the seal, though regularly affixed, does not bind the company if it appears that by the express provisions of the act creating the corporation, or by necessary and reasonable inference from its enactments, to be *ultra vires*—that is, that the Legislature intended that such a deed should not be made.' Now, it is clear from this that the instrument does not bind the company where it is in that sense *ultra vires*—that is, such as Parliament did not intend to be issued.

or the company have no right to affix their seal to an instrument not within the scope of their powers. Then the question arises whether the powers of this company are limited in this respect by express or implied prohibition. The 'Companies' Clauses Act' recites that :—

"' Railway companies have borrowed money in a manner not authorised by their acts of incorporation on the security of loan-notes, or other instruments purporting to give security for the repayment of sums borrowed upon them, and such loan-notes, &c., unless issued under the authority of an act of Parliament, have no legal validity.'

"It appeared to be assumed and implied in the act that these loan-notes or securities were invalid. And could it be said that the borrowing of money without such securities would be valid? That, surely, would be inconsistent. Then the act went on to enact that if such securities were given for money so borrowed, the company should be liable to a penalty, unless they were authorised by their special act. It might be that the penalty would not be incurred if the securities were not made assignable; but the whole effect of the act appeared to be this, that there must be no borrowing by the company, except under the authority of their special act. Now, in this case, the special act only conferred authority to borrow money on mortgage when a certain amount of capital was raised, which had not been raised. If, then, there was power to borrow money in the way which had been resorted to in this case, the language of the 'Companies' Clauses Act' as to borrowing being 'authorised by the special act' would be idle and nugatory. There was, in his opinion, no power to borrow money in any way not authorised by the special act. In this case the instruments issued were called 'Lloyd's Bonds,' from the name of the very eminent and learned gentlemen by whom they were devised; and, no doubt, they might probably be legally issued to contractors or others actually creditors of the company in the way of payment. Supposing the company to be liable for legitimate purposes to a contractor or other creditor, they might probably give him these bonds instead of money in payment, and though they were not legally assignable or negotiable, yet, practically, they would enable him to raise money upon them. To that there might be no legal objection. But there was an implied prohibition against borrowing of money, unless authorised by the special act, and it could not be done by means of these bonds. Now, here there could be no doubt that originally there had been a borrowing by the company, and upon that borrowing they were not liable. It was urged in argument that they would have power to borrow to some extent, as in overdrawing an account at a bank. But if they might do so for 100*l.*, they might for 100,000*l.*, or for 1,000,000*l.*, and so, indirectly, increase their capital to any amount, contrary to the express provisions of their special act. That could not be, and it was clear, therefore, that the original borrowing was illegal. Then the subsequent transaction was tainted with the same illegality. In substance it was a borrowing by the company, though in a roundabout way. The transaction with these bonds was, in reality, a borrowing on the 'credit of the company.' The bonds, therefore, being tainted with the original illegality, were clearly illegal and void, and, therefore, the plaintiff, the holder, could not recover upon them."—*Slaughter's Railway Intelligence*, 1866.

2.—PHILADELPHIA AND READING.

REORGANISATION SCHEME.—The following is the report of the committee of bondholders, referred to at page 501:—

"*To the Board of Managers of The Philadelphia and Reading.*

"The undersigned, the committee of the board of managers to whom was referred the report of the committee on reorganisation which was submitted to the annual meeting of the stockholders held 12th January, 1885, and was by that meeting referred to the incoming board, have considered the said report, and have arrived at the following conclusions :—

"We agree with the three principles laid down at the beginning of that report, to wit:

"1. That the fixed charges must be brought within the limit of net earnings, and that no higher estimate of those earnings should be made than the earnings of last year.

"2. That the existing order of priorities must be maintained.

"3. That the floating debt must be funded, and that meantime it must be dealt with in detail, at the best discretion of the receivers.

"Proceeding to details, we agree to the full payment of all those obligations which the committee's plan proposes to pay in full.

"Concerning the divisional coal land mortgages, we agree with the committee's report, which, being based upon the character and productiveness of the several tracts, and upon the rates of payment by purchase of coupons found practicable by the receivers, may be accepted as safe and reasonable. Excepting for the precedent thus set, we should have thought it necessary to require greater concessions in this class.

"The same acquiescence applies generally to the rentals and guarantees specifically named in the report, and we agree to all its suggestions in respect to leases and guarantees.

"At this point we encounter a question deserving separate consideration, to wit, the lease of the Central of New Jersey, as to which we are led to believe that, even though no fixed obligation should rest upon our company beyond the fixed charges and the net earnings of the Central up to 6 per cent. per annum upon its stock, those net earnings will, within a short time, if the union of the two systems continues, amount to such 6 per cent. We consider it, however, indispensable that the lease be so modified as to make the rental, beyond fixed charges, equal to the net earnings of the Central up to a maximum of 6 per cent. per annum for a period not exceeding five years.

"*General Mortgage.*—We are fully aware of the policy as well as the obligation of meeting the general mortgage coupons in full as they mature, and in a normal condition of the coal trade we should recommend that this be done. At present we recommend that the general mortgage coupon due 1st January be paid in cash, even at the cost of an unusual effort, and that thereafter the January coupon be paid in full, while for the July coupon, for three years, there be given scrip secured by the coupon, one series of scrip for each year, redeemable, with interest at 6 per cent. from maturity of coupon until payment, out of first surplus earnings before any subsequent interest, not embraced in the proposed fixed charges, be paid. The surplus earnings of any one year to be applied in all cases to the series of a past year if any is left unpaid. Under this plan, if sufficient earnings are made, the scrip given for the July coupons will be paid at the date of the maturity of the coupon, provided, however, that all conditions of the general mortgage which establish or call for a sinking fund to extinguish the bonds issued under it, shall be suspended until the company shall give due notice of its readiness to resume the sinking fund stipulations, since those stipulations are of no utility to the bondholders, and are at present a peril both to the well-meaning creditor and to the company by reason of the power they give for serious embarrassment to all interests of the company and of its creditors. We recommend that no payment of general mortgage coupons now overdue be made except to such general mortgage bondholders as consent to have their bonds properly stamped with such suspension of sinking fund. We recommend further that, if it shall be found practicable and expedient, $1,000,000 of the future collateral trust loan shall be set apart as a specific pledge for the redemption of all unpaid general mortgage coupons.

"*Income Mortgage Bonds*, covering as they do considerable property outside of the general mortgage, have a value independent of the remnant of the proceeds of sale or of income left after satisfaction of the general mortgage bonds or their coupons, and we should wish to put them upon an equal footing with those, but find it impracticable to do so. We therefore recommend the adoption of the committee's report concerning income mortgage bonds. It will be understood that the new income mortgage bonds will hold the same independent security upon property not covered by the general mortgage as do the existing income mortgage bonds.

"*Convertible Adjustment Scrip*, being overdue as to principal, through default in payment of coupons, we recommend shall be converted, together with the coupon of 1st January, 1885, into the new income mortgage bonds, after payment in cash of the overdue scrip coupon of 1st July, 1884.

"*First Series Five per cent. Consolidated Mortgage Bonds.*—The great mass of these bonds, now held in reserve to be issued when an advantageous sale can be made, should not be changed in form, neither must the comparatively small number already issued be allowed to cause confusion by standing upon a different footing from the others. We therefore recommend that the overdue coupon of 1st November, 1884, and the coupon due 1st May, 1885, of those outstanding, be converted, at par, into first series 5 per cent. consols, ex May, 1885, coupon, and that upon the release of a sufficient number of the income mortgage bonds now pledged for the floating debt, the entire issue of the first series 5 per cent. consols then outstanding be retired, the holders thereof to receive in exchange, at par, the new 6 per cent. income mortgage bonds, bearing interest from 1st June, 1885.

"*Second Series Five per cent. Consolidated Mortgage Bonds.*—As to these we accept the views of the committee's report that they shall be converted into 5 per cent. income bonds as there stated.

"*Convertible Seven per cent. Bonds.*—We think these bonds entitled to advantage over the debenture bonds of the company, bearing 1 per cent. lower interest. We see no way, however, to give them preference to any greater extent than by capitalisation into the new 5 per cent. income bonds, the difference in interest between 7 per cent. and 6 per cent. during the life of the convertible bonds, with fair allowance for discount until maturity of coupons, [being capitalised into similar bonds, but*] while the new 5 per cent. bonds issued in exchange for principal and for interest coupons to 1st February, 1885, inclusive, will be so marked as to carry the right of conversion into stock at par, those issued in capitalisation of interest difference will have no such right of conversion. With this modification we recommend the adoption of the committee's report concerning the convertible bonds.

"*Debenture Bonds, Guaranteed Scrip, and Susquehanna Canal Obligations.*—As to these we agree with the committee's report, with capitalisation of difference between 7 and 6 per cent. interest, in favour of the coal and iron debenture bonds now bearing 7 per cent.

"*Preferred Stock of Philadelphia and Reading* we recommend shall be treated according to the committee's report, viz., for all valid claims for dividends out of past earnings, give common stock and change form of certificate, so as to provide that hereafter the 7 per cent. dividend shall not be cumulative.

"*The Floating Debt.*—This we agree should be treated substantially as proposed in the report; yet though no definite arrangement for funding that debt can be made while the question of foreclosure remains as a present menace, we recommend that, in view of the hope that foreclosure may be prevented by amicable arrangement, detail plans for such funding should be studied and prepared for putting into operation so soon as practicable. The volume of securities, other than its own obligations, which are owned by the Philadelphia and Reading, is so large, and their independent earning power so great, as probably to justify a sound collateral trust loan of amount approximating that of the floating debt. We do not,

* Words equivalent to those in brackets have, it is believed, been omitted from the report forwarded to London.—D.G.B.G.

however, feel called upon, at the present time, to append a statement or valuation of those securities or to indicate even in general terms a plan for making them available. The committee's report is obviously right in pointing out that the duty of providing the funds for retiring the floating debt and other liabilities, including several millions of receivers' obligations and overdue coupons, must largely devolve upon the junior security-holders, the floating debt-holders, the stock-holders, and the deferred income bondholders, all of whose interests are necessarily in jeopardy so long as the floating debt remains unpaid. In order to provide for the contingency that so many junior security-holders may refuse or neglect to accept, within the stipulated time, the modifications proposed for their several classes, as to defeat the carrying out of an amicable arrangement, thus rendering foreclosure inevitable, we recommend a prompt and careful study of the best method of reorganisation under foreclosure, with due protection of the interests of those junior creditors who shall within that time have assented to the terms proposed. We recommend that the written assent of all parties interested be asked, upon the condition that the assent so given shall become binding only when, in the judgment of the board of managers, a sufficient proportion shall have given such assent. We recommend that the time for giving assent to the settlement proposed be fixed to end on 31st March, 1885. We recommend that this report, with an elaborate plan of reorganisation embracing such details as will make its provisions clear to all concerned, be promptly made public. We suggest also that, since a careful husbanding of resources is well understood by the public to be a necessary condition for the successful carrying out of any plan of financial reorganisation, attention might properly be called to the fact that a resolution adopted by the board of managers, at their meeting on 14th January, directs that no new work shall be undertaken or contract made, involving the credit or policy of the company, unless first submitted to and approved by an appropriate committee. It is understood that no money arising from income shall be diverted to any capital account, or used for any other purpose than the payment of working expenses, renewals, including betterments necessary for economical working, fixed charges, or income obligations, so long as any of the income charges established in this plan remain unpaid or unprovided for. It is further understood that neither the 5 per cent. consols, herein provided to be temporarily retired, nor any other unissued bonds of the company shall hereafter be used as collateral security for any indebtedness to be created by the company, unless ordered by the board of managers. To conclude, we are satisfied that the large economies already in operation, with those which are still being introduced, should be regarded as a margin to meet adverse contingencies. We call attention to these points—1. That foreclosure is inevitable, and probably near, unless prevented by some such amicable reorganisation as is proposed. 2. That the revenue we reckon on, though reasonably certain under such reorganisation, will surely not be realised in case the property should be torn asunder by foreclosure sales. 3. That under this plan, each class of creditors gets at once, without dispute, delay, or cost, all that it could hope to get after suffering the vexations of even a perfectly successful litigation; each creditor, according to his present relative priority, is to receive everything the property can, under the best circumstances, be made to earn for him. 4. Supposing the plan to fail through refusal or neglect of junior creditors to accept it, they then lose by foreclosure all their rights, unless they can combine to supply from their own pockets an amount of money greatly in excess of that which, under this plan, can, it is believed, be obtained upon the credit of the company and pledge of its own securities. Even the general mortgage bondholders, in case they should, after the inevitable delay and cost, succeed in forming a solid combination and in acquiring by foreclosure the property covered by their mortgage, would be far from possessing the magnificent estate and enormous earning power of the great property now held together by the Philadelphia and Reading. Foreclosure would doubtless sacrifice the extremely valuable franchises of the company, and also various leases and tributary connections to an extent impossible to foresee. A large sum of money, estimated at $5,000,000 to $10,000,000, would have to be raised to discharge receivers' debts and other obligations, besides great sums for working capital and so forth, to enable the curtailed new organisation to carry on business.

"JOSEPH WHARTON.
"J. B. LIPPINCOTT.
"I. V. WILLIAMSON.

"Philadelphia, 26th January, 1885."

"General Office of Philadelphia and Reading,
"No. 227, South Fourth Street, Philadelphia.

"The above report was this day adopted by the board of managers, and ordered to be published.

"GEORGE DE B. KEIM, President.

"Philadelphia, 26th January, 1885."

"We approve of the foregoing report, and recommend its acceptance by the creditors and stockholders of the company.

"GEORGE DE B. KEIM.
"STEPHEN A. CALDWELL.
"Receivers Philadelphia and Reading.

"Philadelphia, 26th January, 1885."

"The president of the company advises that printed copies of the plan for the financial reorganisation of the company will be mailed, which will embrace details of the scheme too lengthy to be cabled.

"D. G. BRUCE-GARDYNE,
"Manager London Agency.

"43, Coleman Street, London, E.C.
"27th January 1885."

3.—WABASH, ST. LOUIS, AND PACIFIC.

Appointment of Receivers, and Plan of Reorganisation.

The following is a copy of the order of the Court appointing the receivers:—

"By order of court it is ordered, adjudged, and decreed that Solon Humphreys and Thomas E. Tutt be, and the same are hereby appointed, receivers of the said railroad and all property of said company, with power and instruction to take possession of the same, and to manage, control, and operate said railroad, preserve and protect all said property, and collect, as far as possible, all accounts, choses in action, and credits due to said company, acting in all things under the order of this court, or of such other courts as may entertain jurisdiction of parts of said property as ancillary to the jurisdiction of this court.

"That the receivers, before entering upon their duties, give their joint and several bond to the master in chancery of this court for the benefit of all whom it may concern, in the penal sum of $500,000, conditioned for the faithful performance by said receivers of their duties as such, and that they will in all things observe and perform the orders of this court now or hereafter to be made.

"It is further ordered that the said receivers, out of the income that shall come into their hands from the operation of said railroad, or otherwise, proceed to pay all balances due or to become due to other railroads or transportation companies on balances growing out of the exchange of traffic, accruing during six months prior hereto.

"That said receivers also in like manner pay all rentals accrued or which may hereafter accrue upon all leased lines of said complainant, and for the use of all terminals or track facilities, and all such rentals or instalments as may fall due from said complainant for the use of any portion of road or roads or terminal facilities of any other company or companies, and also for all rentals due or to become due, upon rolling stock heretofore sold to complainant, and partially paid for.

"That said receivers also pay in like manner out of any incomes or other available revenues which may come into their hands, all just claims and accounts for labor, supplies, professional services, salaries of officers and employes, that have been earned or have matured within six months before the making of this order.

"That said receivers present their said bond to this court, or any judge thereof, for approval, and that upon said presentation and approval of said bond, said receivers are entitled and required to proceed at once with the performance of their duties.

"It is further ordered that all parties herein, upon being informed of this order, and of the approval of said bond by this court, proceed to surrender all the lines of said railroad and all the property, choses in action, and accounts of said company, to said receivers; and the complainant is authorised to apply to any other United States circuit court of competent jurisdiction for such order or orders in aid of the primary jurisdiction vested in this court in said cause as may have auxilliary jurisdiction herein.

"It is further ordered that said receivers pay all current expenses in the operation of said roads, collect all the revenues thereof, and all choses in action, accounts and credits due and to become due to the company.

"That such receivers keep such accounts as may be necessary to show the source from which all such income and revenues shall be derived with reference to the interest of all parties herein and the expenditures by them made.

"That said receivers report to this court from time to time once in each three months their doings under this decree and that they apply for instructions to this court when necessary.

"In auxillary proceedings, the same receivers were appointed in the other States through which the lines of the company pass."

The following is a copy of the official circular accompanying the plan of reorganisation given below, dated August 6th, 1884:—

"At a meeting of the board of directors of the Wabash, St. Louis, and Pacific, held at its office, 195, Broadway, August 5th, the outlines of a plan of reorganisation were presented and referred to a committee of four directors, consisting of James F. Joy, Samuel Sloan, George L. Dunlap, and Charles Ridgeley. The report of this committee, approving the plan with slight modifications, was read at an adjourned meeting of the board, August 6th, and in accordance with the recommendation of the committee, adopted unanimously in the following preamble and resolution:—'Whereas a plan of reorganisation has been presented to this board, which not only provides a method of relieving the company of its financial difficulties, but arranges for the preservation of every interest, in its rank of priority, and adjusts the concessions equitably according to that rank; and whereas it is important for all concerned that measures should be undertaken as speedy as possible to restore the property to the management of its owners; therefore, resolved: That the plan of the sub-committee of directors be, and the same is hereby, adopted, and the executive officers of the company are instructed to take such action in carrying out its provisions as they may deem advisable, under the direction of counsel for the company.' After the adoption of the resolution, Mr. Jay Gould, the president of the company, stated his inability to devote the time and attention required by the reorganisation plan, and therefore asked to have his resignation of the office of president accepted, consenting, at the same time, to remain a member of the executive committee, and to aid in the carrying out of measures in support of the plan. He also expressed his confidence in the practicability of the plan and his belief in its success.

Mr. Gould's resignation having been accepted, Mr. James F. Joy was unanimously elected president of the company. The report of the committee, embracing the plan of reorganisation, is as under, and an agreement for the signatures of the bondholders who desire to assent to it will be ready at the office of the company, 195, Broadway; and as soon thereafter as counsel may advise, books will be opened for the signatures of the stockholders. At the same time, also, similar agreements will be prepared for the assent of bondholders and stockholders in Europe.

"*Report of the Committee of Directors on Plan of Reorganisation.*

"The undersigned, a committee of the board of directors of the Wabash, St. Louis, and Pacific, after a careful consideration of the financial position of the company, respectfully submit the following report:—By order of the court, the receivers appointed June 1st have undertaken payments of interest on all the mortgages upon the original main lines of the consolidated companies except the general and collateral trust mortgages, and the following mortgages on leased and acquired lines, viz.:—The Detroit and Eel River division; the Indianapolis division; the Iowa division; the Havana division; the Cario division; the Toledo, Peoria, and Western; the Quincy, Missouri, and Pacific; the Centreville, Moravia, and Albai; the Havana, Rantoul, and Eastern. Assuming interest payment on all the mortgages included in the order of court, it seems only necessary, at the present time, to deal with those which will remain in default. In regard to the leased and acquired lines, not included in the order of the court, it is evidently impracticable to form any plans or to make any definite propositions, until a reorganisation of the company has been accomplished. It is proposed, therefore, to leave the adjustment of these claims to the new corporation which the report of the committee contemplates. If the measures suggested can be carried into effect, the new company can treat with these various interests with a reasonable certainty of being able to carry out the obligations then assumed. Meanwhile if the receivers, who have been ordered to keep separate accounts by the court, can make satisfactory arrangements with the holders of these securities, by appropriating to each line the net earnings thereof, the interests of the latter would be fairly protected until a new company may be in a position to negotiate with them. Leaving these subordinate questions, therefore, to be met when the parties have acquired the legal right to make new engagements, it is proposed to accomplish a reorganisation by foreclosure of the general mortgage and collateral trust mortgage, under an agreement which may be embodied in the decree of sale, if practicable. If these preliminary measures can be carried out, it is proposed to reorganise on the following basis:—The new company, upon its acquisition of the property, subject to the liens prior to the general and collateral trust mortgages, will issue, in satisfaction thereof, the following securities:—

1. Debenture mortgage bonds, interest 6 per cent., dependent upon income and not cumulative		$20,000,000
2. First preferred stock six per cent.	about	4,000,000
3. Second " "	about	23,000,000
4. Common " "	about	27,000,000

"The second preferred and common stock, stated here in round numbers, should be issued to correspond with the amount of old stock.

"In order to show the proposed distribution of the new securities as above specified, the following statement of the debt to be provided for is presented:—

General mortgage bonds issued	$16,000,000
Collateral trust mortgage bonds issued	5,671,000
Of which $1,000,000 guaranteed at (90 per cent.) say $900,000.	
Receivers' and company's notes guaranteed and endorsed	2,383,666
St. Louis, Iron Mountain, and Southern advance as lessee, secured by $1,329,000.	
Collateral trust mortgage bonds	1,100,000
	$25,154,666

"The collateral trust mortgage bonds are held as follows:—

St. Louis, Iron Mountain, and Southern, purchased at 90 per cent. for advances under the lease	$4,000,000
St. Louis and Iron Mountain as collateral for $1,100	1,329,000
Individuals	671,000
Individuals, guaranteed at 90 per cent	1,000,000
Mercantile Trust to secure endorsers and guarantors of notes as above	2,750,000
Pledged as collateral for endorsed notes	250,000
Total	$10,000,000

"Foreclosure of the collateral trust mortgage will release the securities controlled by that mortgage, and render them available in settlement of the claims specified in the foregoing list, so far as the interests of the new company may admit of such an appropriation of the securities. Among these securities are the following, which it is proposed to turn over to the St. Louis, Iron Mountain, and Southern in part settlement:—

General mortgage bonds	$1,000,000
Humeston and Shenandoah first mortgage	1,342,000
Wabash mortgage 7 per cent. of 1879	400,000
Detroit division mortgage	199,000
1,160 shares St. Louis and Mississippi Valley Transatlantic	116,000
	$3,057,000

"In the agreement of foreclosure it is proposed to provide that the new stock, viz., second preferred stock, about $23,000,000; common preferred stock, about $27,000,000: shall be offered to the holders of preferred and common stock at not exceeding $8 per share, the subscribers also receiving for the money subscribed, first preferred stock entitled to 6 per cent. dividends after payment of interest on the debenture bonds. In round numbers, this will produce the sum of $4,000,000 in cash, and the purchasing agents will then control the debenture bonds and this sum to provide for the claims before specified. These claims it is proposed to settle as follows:—

1. Exchange debenture mortgage bonds for general mortgage bonds at par		$17,000,000
(This will include the $1,000,000 now in the collateral trust, to be turned over to the St. Louis, Iron Mountain, and Southern.)		
2. Settle the claims of the St. Louis, Iron Mountain, and Southern, as follows:—		
Turn-over bonds so released by foreclosure of the collateral trust, as before stated		3,057,000
And debenture bonds for balance		2,272,000

"Thus arranging for the entire amount of collateral trust bonds held by that company as follows:—

Amount purchased at 90	$4,000,000	
Amount held as collateral	1,329,000	
		$5,329,000
3. Settle for $1,000,000 collateral trust bonds guaranteed, by payment of amount in cash		900,000
4. Pay receivers' endorsed notes in cash		2,383,666
(Thus relieving $3,000,000 call trust bonds.)		
5. Pay individual holders of $671,000 call trust bonds, one-half in cash		335,500
One half in debenture bonds		335,500

"The debenture mortgage bonds required in the foregoing settlement would be as follows:—

General mortgage bonds issued	$16,000,000
General mortgage bonds Iron Mountain	1,000,000
Balance collateral trust bonds Iron Mountain	2,272,000
Collateral trust bonds held by individuals	335,500
	$19,607,500
Leaving a balance for other purposes of	392,500
	$20,000,000

"The cash required will be as follows:—

To pay for $1,000,000 guaranteed collateral trust mortgage bonds	$900,000
To pay receivers' and company notes guaranteed or endorsed	2,383,666
To pay individual holders of collateral trust bonds one-half of amount of $671,000 ..	335,500
Total cash requirements	$3,619,166

"Which would be provided in the cash subscription of the stockholders, and leave a balance of $380,833.

"A successful conclusion to this proposed foreclosure and reorganisation would relieve the new company of the following amount of fixed interest bearing claims, viz.:—

General mortgage bonds six per cent.	$16,000,000	Int.	$960,000
Collateral trust	5,671,000	,,	340,260
Floating debt, secured	3,483,666	,,	209,019
	$25,154,666	,,	$1,509,279

"The calculations of the committee, as to the necessary concessions have been based upon the earning capacity of the lines controlled by the company during the two years 1882 and 1883, and although it is more than probable that in the near future much better results will be shown, it is safer to found our expectations on the minimum capacity of the property rather than on hopes and anticipations.

"The earnings and expenses of the two years have been as follows:—

	1882.	1883.
Gross earnings	$16,851,690	$16,915,120
Operating expenses	11,664,752	13,330,926
Net earnings	$5,186,938	$3,584,194
Interest, rentals, and taxes	5,769,960	5,621,897
Deficit	$583,021	$2,037,703

Debit balance to income account, 1st January, 1882	$1,452,858
Add deficit in 1882	583,021
Do. 1883	2,037,703
Debit balance income account, 1st January, 1884	$4,073,583

"The average annual deficit of the two years has therefore been $1,310,362, and the proposed adjustment will cover that deficiency, and not only enable the new company to commence operations with a reasonable assurance of earning its fixed charges, but to progr as rapidly towards interest on the debenture mortgage bonds and dividends on the stock as the growth of the business and the prosperity of the company will permit. The plan now submitted for the approval of the board of directors contemplates the preservation of the most valuable part of the system under much more favourable conditions than heretofore, and offers the possibility of adjusting the relations of the parent company with its allied connections and extensions upon equitable terms. It contemplates, also, the protection of each interest in the order of priority, asking of each only such concessions as the financial circumstances of the company require, and so arranged as to add greatly to the future peace, security, and prospects of all concerned. It proposes a method of amicable adjustment of claims secured by mortgage and collaterals which, treated in a spirit of hostility, would involve the property in expensive and tedious litigation, interfere with its traffic facilities and operations, interrupt the payment of interest on senior mortgages, and result finally, perhaps, in the extinction of the junior interests. In view of these possible complications and disastrous consequences, it has been the design of the committee to present a scheme which, in its fair and just consideration of each interest, would commend itself to the calm judgment of the mortgage bondholders, creditors, and stockholders. In order to adjust the concessions and burdens as equitably as the conditions would permit, it has been necessary to examine the nature and origin of the claims as well as the legal status of the claimants, and this has been done with a conscientious desire to arrive at an impartial judgment. The general mortgage covers, as a junior mortgage, all the lines belonging to the company. In a foreclosure designed to exclude creditors secured by the collateral trust mortgage and to extinguish the stock, the general mortgage bondholders would encounter the hostile opposition of the stockholders and hazard the possession of a large portion of the rolling stock, as well as the control of terminal facilities. The struggle which would be the inevitable result would not only be prolonged and expensive, but might lead to default on important senior mortgages and threaten the value of the general mortgage bonds with a great and permanent depreciation. The plan offered embraces all the advantages now possessed by the general mortgage, except that its interest is made dependent upon the capacity of the property to produce more than the interest on senior mortgages. As a matter of fact, this is exactly the position of the general mortgage bondholders now, for unless the property earns more than the fixed charges on prior liens, they can neither receive interest on their bonds nor dividends on any stock into which the bonds might be converted, in case of successful foreclosure, and as an equivalent for the concession stipulated—possession of rolling stock and terminal facilities is surrendered, and a troublesome claim removed by a cash contribution from the stockholders. The only disadvantage which could be urged by the bondholders is the increase in the amount of the debenture bonds by the sum of $3,000,000 over the amount of general mortgage bonds outstanding; but as this extinguishes a secured debt to that extent and removes a very serious and threatening complication, it is a matter of secondary importance to the owners of general mortgage bonds. The holders of collateral trust mortgage bonds, and the endorsers and guarantors of notes secured by them, are asked to surrender about $6,400,000 of the bonds in exchange, partly for bonds held in the collateral trust, while the endorsed paper and secured claims, amounting to about $3,600,000, are to be paid in cash. To arrive at a fair understanding of the nature of these claims, a brief retrospect of the history of the Wabash, St. Louis, and Pacific is essential. At near the close of the year 1881 the company found itself unable to meet the heavy interest payments which matured in December and in January and February of the ensuing year. The causes which led to this unfortunate result it is unnecessary to discuss in this paper, but it is only just to the managers to say that it was as unexpected to them as to the bondholders and stockholders. Having great faith, however, in the capacity of the consolidated system of roads to work out of its critical position, four of its directors advanced at once the sum of $605,000 to meet the interest payments of December. This money is represented by $671,000 of collateral trust bonds. To meet interest and car-trust payments of the year 1882, and to pay for the completion of roads in process of construction, these four directors also endorsed the paper of the company and guaranteed some of the collateral trust bonds to an aggregate amount of about $3,300,000. Every dollar of this money advanced by the four directors, or obtained on paper endorsed by them, has been appropriated to pay the interest on mortgage bonds, instalments on equipment, the almost entire reconstruction of the St. Charles Bridge, and the completion of roads in process of construction, as aforesaid. In the spring of 1883 the lines of the Wabash were leased to the St. Louis, Iron Mountain, and Southern, and the bonds held by that company simply represent the amount advanced by it as lessee to maintain the interest and car-trust payments. For these bonds the St. Louis, Iron Mountain, and Southern paid 90 per cent. in cash. For two years and a half, therefore, four directors of the company, and the Iron Mountain as lessee, have sustained the Wabash with their means and credit without the slightest compensation or profit. But for this assistance the company must have defaulted in 1881, and the general mortgage bondholders, as well as some of the senior bonds, would have been in a much more unfortunate position than at the present time. The troubles of the Wabash have resulted from the meagreness of the profits of a large business, due partly to crop failures and heavy disasters by flood, and partly to severe competition, while at the same time the company had assumed heavy burdens of interest on leased and acquired lines which have shared in the decline of profitable traffic. The records of the company furnish incontrovertible proof of the accuracy of all these statements. The stockholders are to be reinstated in the new organisation, and preferred and common stock as now held by them is to be issued to them share for share, subject, however, to the contribution of a sum not exceeding $8 per share, but for which each subscriber shall be entitled to a first preferred stock for the exact amount subscribed. The advantages acquired by the stockholders in this arrangement are obvious. They are, in the first place, relieved of all present danger of extinction by foreclosure in the exchange of a mortgage debt of about $20,000,000 for debenture bonds, and by the payment of a secured floating debt, which would be, otherwise, a constant and intolerable danger. The property, of which they will hold the fee, is preserved to them with a much lighter burden, with a great source of embarrassment removed, and with a good chance of outgrowing the difficulties of competition which excessive railway construction has brought upon so many of the western lines. Finally, this plan commends itself to the judgment of the committee, because it contemplates the peaceful and amicable solution of a complex and difficult problem by harmonising the different interests, and in preserving them as nearly as possible in their relative positions. Not a dollar is unrepresented in the reorganisation, and not a share is extinguished. Whatever the road can earn is to be applied precisely as before, and throughout the whole web of the plan the threads of adjustment are equally and evenly woven. No device, however ingenious, can give to the bondholders more interest than the road can earn, and no amount of litigation can place them in as safe and promising a position as they will occupy in a successful reorganisation according to the provisions herein detailed. The salient points of the proposed reorganisation are the just and equitable recognition of all claims, the impartial distribution of the necessary concessions, and the peaceful solution of very difficult and embarrassing questions. Deeply impressed with the importance of conciliating bondholders and stockholders, and holding it to be wise and intelligent for them to unite in fair measures of preservation, the committee have adopted as a fundamental principle the just consideration of each interest. If they have succeeded so far as to show the way out of the labyrinth of financial trouble presented by the affairs of the Wabash it will be very gratifying to all concerned.

(Signed) "JAMES F. JOY. GEORGE L. DUNLAP.
"SAMUEL SLOAN. CHARLES RIDGELEY.
"New York, 6th August, 1884." "Committee.

II.—UNITED STATES.

1.—STATE RAILROAD COMMISSION, &c.

THIRD ANNUAL CONVENTION—FORM FOR REPORTS AND RETURNS ADOPTED.

The Third Annual Convention of Railroad Commisioners of the several States was held at Saratoga Springs, N. Y., June 10th and 11th, 1879. The following Commissioners were present:—Charles F. Adams, Jr., E. W. Kinsley, and A. D. Briggs, of Mass.; George M. Woodruff and John W. Bacon, of Connecticut; Milton L. Bonham, of South Carolina; Thomas H. Carter, of Virginia; A. J. Turner, of Wisconsin; W. B. Williams, of Michigan; George M. Bogue and J. H. Oberly, of Illinois; G. P. Conn, Wm. A. Pierce, and D. E. Willard, of New Hampshire. There were also present, S. F. Cooke, deputy commissioner, of Michigan; George T. Utley, clerk, of Connecticut; George H. Goodspeed, accountant, of Massachusetts; Commissioner George T. Towne, of the Boston, Clinton, and Fitchburg Road; and C. P. Leyland, auditor, of the Lake Shore Road. W. B. Williams was appointed chairman, and Messrs. Utley and Goodspeed clerks.

Details of the form of reports and returns adopted at this convention will be found on reference to the MANUAL for 1884, pages 514 to 517, and also in previous editions, and for list of legal decisions, &c., see MANUAL for 1881, pages 547 to 549.

III.—GENERAL INFORMATION.

1.—RAILWAY COMMISSION.

(36 and 37 Vic., cap. 48, continued by 42 and 43 Vic., cap. 56/ Came into operation 1st September, 1873.)

OFFICES—Railway Commission Office, House of Lords. Hours, 10 to 5. Saturday, 10 to 2.

COMMISSIONERS:

The Right Hon. Sir FREDERICK PEEL, K.C.M.G.

W. P. PRICE, Esq.

ALEXANDER E. MILLER, Esq., Q.C.

Registrar—W. H. MACNAMARA, Esq.

Clerk—Mr. WHITTALL.

The Act of Parliament defining the powers of the Commissioners will be found in the *Appendix* to the MANUAL for 1874, and the General Orders made by the Commissioners for the regulation of proceedings before them in the APPENDIX to the Volume for 1880 and previous editions.

The Commissioners have issued the following report, summing up the work done by them during the year 1883:—

We, the Railway Commissioners, humbly present to Your Majesty a report of our proceedings under the Regulation of Railways Act, 1873, during the past year.

The decisions we gave in the principal cases heard by us in 1883, of undue preference or prejudice, are those we will first notice. In the Broughton and Plas Power Coal Company and others *v.* the Great Western Railway Company, the question was, whether the railway rates for the conveyance of coal from South Wales to Birkenhead, and from North Wales to Birkenhead, differed to an extent proportionate to the difference in distance, and in other circumstances, the colliery owners in North Wales maintaining that they did not, and that the rates for the South Wales coal were preferential rates, and prejudicial to their traffic. The distance from North Wales to Birkenhead varied from 27 to 36 miles, and the rate from 2*s.* to 2*s.* 5*d.* a ton; the average distance from South Wales was 156 miles, and the rate a uniform one of 6*s.* a ton. The respondents denied that the Traffic Act applied at all to a case in which the rates compared were one for a long and the other for a short distance, and where there was such a difference in their amounts as that between 6*s.* and 2*s.* 3*d.* But according to the construction given to the act from the first, it does not free a railway company from responsibility for unequal charges, that the charges are for different lengths of transit over either the same line or different lines belonging to the same company, distinct from each other. That was the construction the act received from the Court of Common Pleas in the case of Nicholson *v.* Great Western. There the complaint was that the railway company charged more per ton per mile for carrying coal from the Forest of Dean than from Ruabon in Denbighshire; and the court said, in giving judgment, "If we could see that a scale of rates with reference to distance had been framed with a view to, and having the effect of favouring the Ruabon coal traffic, and prejudicing the Forest of Dean coal traffic, we should hold it to be an undue preference within the act." Nor does it dispose of a complaint of inequality of charge, that the lower rate per ton per mile makes a higher aggregate charge. It is enough to bring a company within the act, that there is a competition of interests between the respective railway customers, and that the lower rate is not justified by considerations of cost of carriage, or profit, or the fair pecuniary interests generally of the company carrying. In this case the coal was competitive, and the earnings, less terminals, worked out per ton per mile, at about ·43*d.* of a penny South Wales, and ·74*d.* North Wales. It was not contended that there was a corresponding difference in the cost. The circumstances governing the cost were on the whole more favourable for the North Wales coal. The centres for marshalling trucks, and making them up into main line trains were for South Wales, Pontypool, for North Wales, Ruabon; and the difference in the gradients was shown by the maximum train loads, which were from Pontypool to Hereford 212 tons, from Hereford to Ruabon 190, and from Ruabon to Birkenhead 250 tons. The collection between the collieries and the centres was also part of the service, and the greater nearness of the North Wales collieries to their centre at Ruabon was another point in their favour, tending to economy in working. In short, the working cost per ton per mile was more for South Wales than North Wales coal, owing to the difference in the train load; but still the margin over cost upon the earning of ·43*d.* was sufficient, when multiplied by the longer distance, to make the profit at the lower rate exceed the profit at the greater rate, the profit as calculated being in the one case 1*s.* 9*d.*, and on the other 1*s.* 3*d.*, or 6*d.* per ton more on the South Wales coal, and the contention was, that as the extra sum charged for the longer distance sufficed to pay expenses and leave a profit, there was no *primâ facie* case of undue preference against the railway company, and that it devolved upon the applicants to show that the rates actually operated to their disadvantage, and that there was no due degree of pecuniary gain on the extra work done in the conveyance of South Wales coal. As to this, we said, that the decision of the Court of Appeal in the Denaby case, established beyond doubt, that if goods of the same kind are carried to the same destination over the same railway for distances that are not the same, and the gross charge from the intermediate point is as great as from the more distant one, there is a preference of one traffic over the other which is *primâ facie* an undue preference within the meaning of the act of 1854, and that it is not sufficient to rebut this presumption to show that the charge for the longer distance has been reduced to meet a competition from another route. We remarked also that the same presumption would obviously arise if the charge for the longer distance, though actually more, was not so to an amount sufficient to cover the cost of the extra services, because there would in that case, as in the other, remain a portion of the service rendered to the long distance traffic, which was altogether unpaid for, the amount, namely, by which the cost of the extra service exceeded the extra charge; neither would it, we considered, be sufficient, that these two items should exactly balance each other, for it would be as improper for the company to work without profit for one customer, while refusing to do so for another, as it would be unreasonable to expect them to do so at all; but where, as in the case we were dealing with, the larger rate yields also the larger profit, it was not necessary in our opinion, that these should be proportional; what would be a due degree of increase would depend in each case upon its particular circumstances, and the burden of proof would rest on those who impugned the rate, to show that the difference of charge operated to their injury, whereas in the other case it rested on the company to defend the inequality if they could. In the present case we were not satisfied upon the evidence, that the interests of the applicants had suffered by the inequality complained of, and the application therefore was refused.

In McFarlane and Co. *v.* the North British, it appeared that the applicants, a firm of iron-founders, sent castings in large quantities from Possil Park Station, Glasgow, to St. Pancras, London, by the North British, and they complained of the company for carrying the similar traffic of Geo. Smith and Co., another firm in Glasgow, from Sighthill Station, Glasgow, to St. Pancras, London, on more favourable terms. The railway company had a special rate for particular kinds of iron castings carried in quantities of not less than four tons, and the complaint was that the company's agents at the two stations in Glasgow had for many years applied the special rate in a different way, both as regards the articles deemed to be included in it, and also as to the condition of a four tons load. The rate was applied at Sighthill to all Smith and Co.'s iron castings indiscriminately, while at Possil Park it was restricted to iron castings of the kinds named in the rate, other kinds being charged according to their class. At the latter station also the condition as to weight was interpreted to mean consignments in one day and to one consignee amounting to four tons, while at Sighthill the minimum weight was allowed to be composed of the consignments on different days and to different consignees, the charges not being made out, till in the aggregate there was a full weight. The Midland were interested in traffic sent to London by their route being properly charged, and at their instance, the North British agents at the two stations were directed in 1881 to revert to the usual practice, and to treat the condition as to weight to mean that a consignor's goods in one day to one or more consignees should make up a load of four tons. Somewhat later the same company declined to support the extended application given to the special rate at the Sighthill Station, and a question they raised upon it led presently to an order being issued that traffic at Sighthill for London not coming strictly within the special rate should in future be charged, as at the other station, at the rate belonging to its class. The matter had gone on for a long time without the North British superintending officers knowing anything about it; and when their attention was at last called to it, and the applicants had also made formal complaint to them of the manner in which their competitors had been preferred, instead of frankly acknowledging that there had been a mistake and offering full reparation for it, they would not admit that there was a case against them for compensation, and insisted upon it that the trade had been on the same terms and footing all round, and that their company had not given Geo. Smith & Co. any advantage over the applicants. The applicants had therefore no choice but to submit the matters to a detailed investigation, and although when their application came to be heard it was urged on behalf of the respondents that it was not necessary that an injunction should issue, because the differential rates and treatment complained of were no longer existing, we had to consider whether the applicants might not reasonably decline to rely in the future on the voluntary action of the company, and not be content without the additional security of our injunction. And as it appeared to us under all the circumstances that they would not otherwise be adequately protected, we granted the injunction for which they applied.

In Girardot, Flinn, and Co. *v.* the Midland, the respondents were charged with a breach of the Traffic Act in having higher rates for grain to Derby than to Burton. A list of stations was given, from which barley was sent to both places, and it appeared that the charge from these stations to Derby averaged 6*s.* 11*d.* per ton, and that had it been regulated by the scale for carriage to Burton, had it, that is, been made out at the same rate per mile, it would have averaged 5*s.*, or 1*s.* 11*d.* per ton less. The answer of the company was that grain could not be carried to Derby as profitably as to Burton at any lower rate than was represented by the 6*s.* 11*d.*, and that there was no greater inequality in the rates than there was in the cost of carriage. Much stress was laid on the total traffic of Burton being 800,000 tons per annum, and that of Derby 220,000 only, but as the Burton rates were given not only to the large brewers and maltsters, but to all inhabitants of the place, however small might be the quantity of their traffic, and there was nothing exceptional in the natural position of Burton to affect the rate at which goods could be carried, we did not think that a difference of charge could be sustained on the general ground that the aggregate traffic of the one town exceeded that of the other. But the case turned principally upon the sufficiency of the special grounds alleged for the inequality in the rates for the inwards grain traffic of the two places. First, the truck loads conveyed to Derby did not weigh as much per truck as to Burton. The average extra weight of the truck load to Burton was from 8 to 10 cwt., and the earnings on the extra weight were claimed to be all clear profit, on the ground that half a ton more of paying load did not increase the cost of hauling the truck. Next a portion of the trucks received loaded with barley at Derby could not be reloaded there with any other traffic, and came away empty on the outward journey: whereas loaded wagons into Burton were practically certain of a back load; and lastly, station expenses, meaning the cost of the goods station staff, were, it was said, as much as *5d.* more per ton at Derby than at Burton. We found, however, that neither the applicants at Derby, nor the maltsters at Burton, used the goods station at those places for their barley traffic, and that the cost of the goods' staff was no part of the expense incurred in working such traffic. We declined, therefore, to recognise station expenses, as far as the present case was concerned, as a valid reason for a difference in the rates for a competitive traffic; but we allowed to a certain extent the claim in respect of the average weight of truck loads, and of the certainty of back loads. As to the larger part, however, of the excess in the Derby rate, we thought the applicants were subjected to an undue disadvantage, and our judgment in the case was substantially in their favour.

The Central Wales and Carmarthen Junction *v.* the London and North Western and Great Western was an application for through rates. The railway of the applicants, 13 miles long, and used and run over by the London and North Western, connects the London and North Western at Llandilo with the Great Western near Carmarthen, and for traffic between places west of Carmarthen, and places north or east of Craven Arms on the Shrewsbury and Hereford, the route *via* Craven Arms and the applicants' railway is shorter than the alternative route *via* Neath. All traffic, however, not ordered to go by the applicants' railway was carried *via* Hereford, and so much of this traffic as the London and North Western as well as the Great Western were interested in was exchanged between those companies at Hereford. Such traffic was carried by the two companies at agreed through rates, but neither of them would book through traffic by the other route except at local rates, nor further than to Carmarthen, where there was the junction of their lines, and the consequence was that little or no through traffic was consigned by this, though the shorter, route. We had held in a previous case, and our decision was confirmed on appeal, that the Central Wales and Carmarthen Junction were a company entitled to apply for through rates under sec. 11 of the act of 1873, and their present application was for through rates for all traffic between Haverfordwest and Chester, Liverpool, Manchester, Leeds, Burton, Birmingham, and Wolverhampton, required to be forwarded by their line. The distance saved by their line was for Chester, Liverpool, Manchester, and Leeds, 57 miles, for Burton 32, Wolverhampton 22, and Birmingham 7, but the Great Western attempted to show that the granting of the rates would be no facility in the interests of the public, because the traffic, whether by the long or the short distance, would occupy the same time in reaching its destination, and because there was no necessity in the amount of the traffic for more than one route. It appeared to us, however, that it could not be otherwise than an advantage to the public to have a second line of communication between the same places, and that it was wrong that the shorter route should not be able to be used because the companies working the traffic had no agreed through rates that way, and would take no steps to obtain them adversely to each other. But the amounts at which it was proposed to fix the rates were not in all cases such as we were able to approve. Some of them were, we thought, lower than was reasonable. The proposed Chester rates, for example, were one-third less than the existing through rates *vid* Hereford, although the distance was not more than one-fourth less, and as the mileage of the applicants' was only 13 miles out of 176, the question of the sufficiency of the rates proposed by them turned mainly upon whether the amounts would be fairly remunerative to the companies which owned the larger proportion of the route. Under the act of 1873, we have no power to increase or diminish a proposed through rate; we must either allow it or refuse it altogether and the result in this case was that the rates for Chester, Manchester, and Burton were refused, and the others allowed. Since then we have been empowered by a special act to settle through rates and fares for this line, both as to amount and apportionment, in such manner as we may think proper. The Central Wales and Carmarthen Junction Act, 1883 (46 & 47 Vic., c. 155), requires the companies, whose railways connect with it, to afford all due facilities for its being used as a through route, and of what kind these facilities shall be, and upon what terms and conditions they shall be afforded, and the amount and apportionment of the through rates and fares and other questions are, where not agreed, to be determined by us, in the manner provided for cases under section 8 of the Regulation of Railways Act, 1873.

Cairns *v.* the North Eastern, and Coxon *v.* the same, were two of several cases of their kind, where persons interested in ascertaining whether any terminal charge was included in a rate applied for an order against a company to distinguish in its rate book how much of such and such rates was for conveyance, and how much for other expenses. In the cases cited, the applicants had tried to get the company to give the information voluntarily, and had been refused, and the question was whether they were not only entitled to an order, but to an order with costs. If there was no general duty to furnish such information on request and the object of not requiring companies to publish it, except under an order, was merely to confine publication to cases where the information was of sufficient importance to be o public interest, we should not give costs, but it would be otherwise if the section proceeded upon the view that every railway customer or person interested was entitled to know how a rate was made up, and if to enforce the performance of that duty was the object aimed at in making companies in default liable to be required to set out all the details in their rate book for everyone to inspect. The latter is the sense in which we have always taken the section, and the applicants having in vain asked for the information, and having consequently been obliged to resort to their remedy under the statute, the order made was made with costs.

We come next to cases in which the matter in dispute was the amount that might reasonably be charged for terminal services performed by a railway company. In Young *v.* the Gwendraeth Valleys the railway belonging to the respondents commenced at Mynyddygarreg, near to the applicant's works, and ended in junctions at Kidwelly and Tycock with the Great Western and the Burry Port railways. It was 2¼ miles long, but there was power to charge as for a distance of 4 miles. The maximum rate for the conveyance of lime and coal in owner's wagons was 1*d*. per ton per mile, but a reasonable terminal charge for special services was also authorised. The company charged the applicant 9*d*. a ton for the carriage of lime and coals, and the 5*d*. excess over the mileage portion of this charge was the subject of the complaint. The excess was partly for terminal expenses at the Kidwelly and Tycock Junction, for which the company charged 2*d*. per ton, and partly for services at Mynyddygarreg. As to the 2*d*. for the Kidwelly Junction it was admitted during the inquiry that there were no such services performed there as would justify the company in imposing it, and we held the same to be the case in regard to Tycock Junction, as an incline at that junction, the two railways not being on the same level, was its only special circumstance, and for that incline or the working over it, we did not think any terminal charge was warranted under the special act. As to the 3d. at Mynyddygarreg, the applicant's quarries were about 200 yards from the end of the company's railway, and the continuation of the railway to the quarries was by a line belonging to the applicant, and laid upon land which, originally property of the railway company, had been sold by them to a lime company. The lime company charged a wayleave of 2*d*. a ton for traffic passing over their land, and the 3*d*. in question consisted of this wayleave and of a 1*d*. charged by the railway company for running over and maintaining the 200 yards of private line. As to the wayleave, the applicant contended that the railway company had no power to sell land acquired for the purposes of their railway so as to subject him to a wayleave for crossing it, and that if it was part of the contract of sale that the lime company should receive a transit toll on traffic, the toll ought to be paid by the railway company and not by its customers. But the fact was that he had made his line with the consent of the lime company on the terms of paying them the 2*d*. toll, and we declined to enter into his reasons for disputing the validity of that agreement, and for alleging that the lime company was only the railway company in disguise. The toll was a payment demanded by the lime company, and we had no jurisdiction to decide a question which concerned them principally, but in a case to which they had not been made a party. As respects the other part of the 3*d*., we were agreed, though somewhat differing in our reasons for thinking so, that the railway company could not under the circumstances charge extra for working over the lime company's land, and we held also that the maintenance of way could not, except by agreement, form the basis of a traffic charge, although the railway company were certainly not bound to maintain a line not their own. If the owner failed to keep it in repair he would be liable to the company if his negligence put them to expense, but a tonnage charge was not the proper means to secure them against loss.

This case was followed by the Neston Colliery Company *v.* the London and North Western and the Great Western. Here the railway companies had power by their act to make charges for the conveyance of goods not exceeding certain sums, and these charges included every expense incidental to conveyance, except the loading and unloading of goods. The charges, however, might be increased if certain extra duties were performed, and the clause which conferred the power to charge the additional sum, and specified the services for which it might be demanded was in the same form as in the last case, the terms being "a reasonable sum for the loading, unloading, and covering, and for the delivery and collection of goods and other services incidental to the business of a carrier, where such services respectively shall be performed by the company, and a further reasonable sum for warehousing and wharfage, and for other extraordinary services which may be reasonably and properly performed by the said company, in relation to such goods." The companies carried coal for the applicants from Parkgate Station to Birkenhead and other places, and they claim to be paid their full rate per ton per mile, and a further sum besides; and as regards this further sum, their right to which was the matter in dispute with the colliery company, they set out various services which they performed, some at the sending station, and others at the receiving station, and contended that the extra charge was no more than a reasonable remuneration for them. They also contended that the dispute did not come within sec. 15 of our act, but it seemed to us that it did, as it was a dispute about a terminal charge or charge for terminal expenses. For the applicants it was said that the services upon which the charge in question was founded were not of the kind mentioned in the terminal clause, and that they were incidental to conveyance and therefore covered by the mileage rate. The charge was mainly for signalling, shunting, invoicing, clerkage, use of sidings, return of empty wagons, and the like. No service falling within the terminal clause was performed or alleged to be performed, and the services that were rendered could not in our opinion be distinguished from conveyance or expenses incidental to conveyance, nor be held not to be comprised under those terms. We examined them one by one, and on the whole we determined that the claim to increase the rates by additions for terminals was not made out.

In Coxon *v* the North Eastern the railway company had power to charge, in addition to the prescribed rates for conveyance, "a reasonable sum for loading, unloading, collecting, receiving or delivering, and for providing covers for minerals, goods, articles or animals," and in this case the question for decision under section 15 of the 1873 act, was the amount that would be a reasonable sum to be paid to the company for admitted terminal services. The traffic was hay, sent to Newcastle from various other stations on the company's railways, and the charge exceeded the maximum for conveyance, the excess varying from 6*d*. to 3*s*. a ton. The company assisted in loading, and provided covers for the loaded wagons, but they performed no other service coming within the terminal clause of their special act. They valued the service of assisting to load at 3*d.* a ton, and of supplying covers and covering and uncovering at 2*s.* a ton, and they claimed also in case of need to be allowed 2*s.* 2*d.* a ton for use of sidings and wagons for the longer time than necessary taken by consignees to unload. Twenty-four hours, in their opinion, was a sufficient time to unload a hay and straw traffic, but three days was the customary time taken. The consignees incurred no demurrage for that time, and it was a convenience to them to keep the wagons in the sidings, but they had no right, it was said, to be so long in unloading; and the 2*s.* 2*d.* a ton was a sum which the company claimed to be entitled to charge for affording the accommodation, and to treat, if necessary, as one of the elements composing their hay and straw rates. But clearly no such charge could be made until a company had first given all due and reasonable facilities for the delivery of traffic, and what this would be, as respects time, would depend too much upon the varying circumstances of particular cases for any general rule to be laid down on the point. Twenty-four hours did not seem to us a sufficient average time, and in any case a special warehousing and wharfage charge, such as this, not due where traffic was not warehoused, formed, we thought, no proper part of a general rate for conveyance. As regards the other items, we fixed the reasonable terminal charges for assisting to load, and covering, and uncovering wagons at 2*d.* per ton respectively. And we allowed 9*d.* a ton for supplying sheets, for which the claim made was at the rate of 1*s.* 6*d.* a ton.

In the Halesowen *v.* the Great Western and Midland it was provided by agreement that the respondent companies should work the Halesowen Line conditionally on the Halesowen first doing certain things, and a question had arisen whether that company had done all that was requisite on their part to entitle them to call upon the respondent companies to work their line. Article 1 of the agreement was to the effect that the Halesowen should complete the railways and works authorised by the act (including proper sidings at the junction with the Midland for the convenient interchange of traffic) to the satisfaction of the engineers of the companies, the respondent companies being bound to work the railways from and after the time when so completed; and by article 18, all differences between the companies, and all questions as to the carrying into effect of the provisions of the agreement, were to be determined by arbitration under the Railway Companies Arbitration Act, 1859. The agreement was made before the passing of the Halesowen Act, and being only an agreement between the solicitors to the companies, it was by itself of no effect or validity as between the companies; but it was scheduled to the act, and by section 37 was confirmed and made binding on the companies respectively. The question in dispute was whether the Halesowen ought not to construct certain platforms at the junction, where they had to construct proper sidings for the interchange of traffic; and that company referred the question to us under section 8 of the act of 1873, which says that where any difference between railway companies is, under the provisions of any general or special act, required or authorised to be referred to arbitration, such difference shall, at the instance of any company party to the difference, be referred to the commissioners for their decision in lieu of being referred to arbitration. But our jurisdiction was objected to, on the ground first that the particular difference that had arisen was an engineering question under article 1 of the agreement, and did not come within article 18, and secondly, that section 37 of the Halesowen Act merely gave validity to the agreement, and that something more than that, some words requiring the companies to fulfil its provisions, were necessary to satisfy the condition on which our powers under section 8 of the act of 1873 depended, viz., that the difference should by general or special act be required or authorised to be referred to arbitration. We considered, however, that the words in section 37 "made binding on the companies" had that effect, and warranted us in holding that the reference to arbitration was authorised under the powers of an act, and as to the other ground, it seemed to us that the question was not as to the manner in which things required to be done by article 1 of the agreement should be done, or the completion of the works to the satisfaction of the engineers, but as to what works were to be done, and whether the meaning of the word "sidings," as used in article 1, extended to other requisite accommodation for the interchange of traffic; and that there was therefore a difference between the companies that they might refer to arbitration. On an application afterwards for a prohibition made by the Great Western to the Queen's Bench Division, the court gave no decision on the point as to section 8 of the act of 1873, but on the other point it held, contrary to our view, that the question as to what was meant by proper sidings was one to be determined under article 1 of the agreement, and not under article 18.

Another case was an arbitration under the North British, Dundee, and Arbroath Joint Line Act, 1879, the North British and the Caledonian mutually agreeing in the reference. Under that act the Caledonian from Dundee to Arbroath was in February, 1880, transferred from the Caledonian, and made joint property of the Caledonian and North British, on the terms that the North British should pay one-half of the value of the railway at the date of transfer. Some property which was North British was also made part of the joint line, and the terms on which the Caledonian were to share in this property were in like manner to be fixed by arbitration. The Caledonian had acquired the railway from Dundee to Arbroath in 1866, and were liable for about 26,000*l.* a year for guaranteed dividends and interest on debt in respect of its acquisition; and the Vesting Act imposed one-half of this liability on the North British, and directed that it should be paid as part of the value of their one-half share of the line, and that a capital sum of 30,000*l.* (the amount afterwards agreed on for this purpose) should be the minimum of what they should pay besides. We fixed this further sum after full inquiry at somewhat under 172,000*l.*, and the half value of the North British property at somewhat under 36,000*l.*, leaving a net capital sum of 136,000*l.* payable by the North British, with interest as from 1st February, 1880. This being a case between Scotch railway companies, we were prepared to hold the enquiry in Scotland, and if the parties had preferred a hearing in Scotland, we should have fixed the place of hearing accordingly. It was arranged, however, between them that the case should be heard in London.

In our last report we called attention to a clause in a bill then in Parliament entitled the Great Western Railway Act, 1883, by which it was proposed to confirm certain working agreements made in perpetuity under acts incorporating the Railway Clauses Act, 1863, Part 3, and to the effect which the clause, if passed as it was, would have in exempting such working agreements from being revised at the end of every ten years in the manner provided by section 27 of that act, as amended by the Regulation of Railways Act, 1873. The matter was considered by the committee on the bill, and the result was that the clause was amended, and a proviso added to it to secure the revision from time to time of the several working agreements, section 70 of the Great Western Act, 1883, having this proviso: "Provided always, that every such agreement shall be subject to revision by the Railway Commissioners in manner provided by section 27 of the Railway Clauses Act, 1863, as amended by the Regulation of Railways Act, 1873." There are two bills of the present session, "The Great Western, No. 1," and "The Caledonian, No. 2," which call for the same remarks that we made on the Great Western, 1883, in our last report. They respectively provide that statutory sanction shall be given to working agreements made in perpetuity under special acts incorporating the Railway Clauses Act, 1863, Part 3, and the operation of what is proposed to be enacted, if adopted, would be to exempt the agreements from the revision to which they would otherwise be subject under the general act. We would suggest that both these bills should be amended in this respect in accordance with the above view of the committee of last year, and that a proviso in the terms of that inserted in the Great Western Act, 1883, should be added to clause 64 of the Great Western, No. 1, as it respects the agreement in the second schedule of that bill, and to clause 51 of the Caledonian, No. 2.

All which is humbly submitted to Your Majesty.

Railway Commission, House of Lords. (Signed) FREDERICK PEEL.
March 18th, 1884. W. P. PRICE.
ALEX. EDW. MILLER.

2.—SHARE AND LOAN CAPITAL—TRAFFIC RECEIPTS—WORKING EXPENDITURE.

The following is the substance of Messrs. Calcraft and Giffen's report to the Board of Trade for the year 1883. The tables in the Appendix are of too extensive a nature for insertion in these pages, but the report itself shows the *results* of the formation of companies and the construction and working of their railways in a very clear and interesting manner:—

In submitting for the year 1883 the usual annual tables relating to the capital, traffic, and dividends of the railway companies of the United Kingdom, we have to remark the great similarity of the figures to those of the previous year. The changes are almost all of a minor character. As the final result, the dividends on the different descriptions of capital are maintained almost exactly at the previous year's level, that capital itself having increased by a small per-centage only, corresponding to the increase of traffic, working expenses, and net earnings. In 1882 and 1881 there was also very little change compared with the preceding year. For several years, therefore, the financial position of the railway companies of the United Kingdom has very little changed. Traffic and net earnings have steadily increased, so as to keep pace with a moderate increase of capital. The business is larger, but the rate of profit is no greater, although the improvement of 1880, as compared with the years immediately preceding, has been maintained.

Capital.—With regard to capital the increase in the twelve months is 17,000,000*l.*, equal to an increase of rather over 2 per cent. on the previously existing capital. This compares with an increase of 1·2 per cent. only in the mileage constructed, so that a considerable part of the expenditure of capital must have been on mileage already open for traffic, indicating a continually increasing capital cost per open mile. It is not suggested here that the expenditure of capital is not required; but the facts, taken in connection with the stationary rate of dividends, tend to show that the railway shareholders are not benefiting by an increasingly valuable monopoly, and are doing little more than holding their own. The public in various ways must get almost the whole benefit of the increasing capital expenditure, if that expenditure is at all judicious.

The increase of capital in the year is not so large as it was in 1882, but it is still much larger than the increase in the year 1880, when the new outlay of capital had sunk to a very small sum. The following table, which continues a similar table in previous reports, shows how this capital outlay increases, the increase in 10 years being more than 25 per cent., allowing for certain changes which involved an increase of nominal capital only:—

Year.	Amount of Capital.	Increase.
1873	£588,320,000	£19,273,000
1874	609,895,000	21,575,000
1875	630,223,000	20,328,000
1876	*658,214,000	27,991,000
1877	674,059,000	15,845,000
1878	*698,545,000	24,486,000
1879	717,003,000	18,458,000
1880	728,317,000	11,314,000
1881	745,528,000	17,211,000
1882	767,900,000	22,372,000
1883	784,921,000	17,021,000

* There were large nominal increases in these years from conversion of shares and stocks.

The proportions of the different descriptions of capital to each other have not appreciably changed in the year, and in fact have not done so for five years. These proportions now are—ordinary 37 per cent., guaranteed and preferential 38 per cent., and loans and debenture stock 25 per cent. The increase of ordinary capital is the largest in amount, but not sufficiently so to change the proportion. This steadiness in the proportions of the different kinds of capital is, of course, a means of keeping the rates of dividend steady so long as the proportion of net earnings to the whole capital remains unchanged. The English railway system, as far as capital is concerned, has become adjusted to the rule of having rather less than 40 per cent. of the capital in "open" stock.

Traffic Receipts.—The total increase of traffic corresponds very closely to the increase of capital, being 2·4 per cent. In passenger and goods respectively the increase is 2¼ per cent., but in "miscellaneous" only 0·4 per cent., this latter small percentage of increase contrasting with a somewhat large percentage of increase the previous year. The "miscellaneous" income is much smaller than the other sources of income of railway companies, and though liable apparently to much greater fluctuations in proportion, the effect is hardly perceived in the aggregate figures.

Analysing the changes in traffic income, we have to notice first with regard to goods that the improvement both in amount and proportion is mainly in the mineral traffic. The increase in receipts from minerals is from 15,606,000*l.* to 16,255,000*l.*, or 649,000*l.* equal to rather more than 4 per cent. In general merchandise, however, the increase is only from 20,836,000*l.* to 21,248,000*l.*, or 412,000*l.*, equal to about 2 per cent., while there is a decrease in the receipts from live-stock of 110,000*l.*, viz., from 1,282,000*l.* to 1,172,000*l.*, or about 9 per cent. The receipts from live stock, it may be noticed, fluctuate considerably from year to year, there having been a great increase in 1882 over the preceding year. From period to period, however, the receipts from this traffic do not increase. Ten years ago the average amount of income from this source was as large as it is now.

Large as the increase of income from mineral traffic is, it would appear that the business done has increased in rather greater proportion. The increase in the tonnage of minerals is from 181½ million tons to 189¼ million tons, or about 4¼ per cent., as compared with an increase of 4 per cent. only in the receipts. Unfortunately it is impossible to show what is the receipt per ton per mile, which would indicate decisively whether more business is being done at a cheaper rate, but the presumption would seem to be that more business is thus being done. The falling off in the total goods receipts per train mile from 73·05*d.* to 72·07*d.*, would seem to confirm the inference that such a change is going on in the conduct of business. It is much to be regetted, however, that the railway companies do not furnish *data* to show the average charge per ton per mile.

Coming to the passenger traffic, the change to notice is in the same direction as changes which have been noticed in previous years, viz., an increase in the third-class passenger traffic, while the first and second-class traffic is stationary or declining. In 1883, compared with 1882, it is a declining first and second-class traffic which has to be compared with an increasing third-class, viz.:—

Receipts from Passenger Traffic in 1883 and 1882 compared.

	1883.	1882.	Increase in 1883.	Decrease in 1883.
1st class	£3,670,000	£3,753,000	....	£83,000
2nd class	3,330,000	3,417,000	....	87,000
3rd class	17,050,000	16,380,000	£670,000	....
Season tickets, &c.	1,692,000	1,610,000	82,000	....
Excess luggage, &c.	3,766,000	3,636,000	130,000	....
Total	£29,508,000	£28,796,000	£712,000	....

As noticed last year, the receipt from third class traffic is now much more than double the receipts from first and second class traffic combined. At the present rate of progress it will be in a very few years thrice the combined receipts for first and second class traffic. The figures as to passenger journeys fully confirm these figures as to receipts, though, unfortunately, it is not possible to show the numbers of passengers conveyed one mile. In the year the receipts from passenger trains per train mile fell from 51·75*d.* to 50·73*d.* The presumption is that, as regards passengers in 1883, the railway companies were giving more service at a cheaper rate than they did in 1882.

To show how rapidly this change in the character of passenger traffic is proceeding, it may be useful to compare the figures of 10 years ago with the present time.

Receipts from Passenger Traffic in 1883 and 1873 compared, with other Particulars.

	1883.	1873.	Increase.	Decrease.
1st class receipts	£3,670,000	£4,373,000	....	£703,000
2nd class "	3,330,000	3,985,000	....	655,000
3rd class "	17,050,000	11,751,000	£5,299,000	....
Season tickets	1,692,000	979,000	713,000	....
Excess luggage, &c.	3,766,000	2,764,000	1,002,000	....
			£7,014,000	£1,358,000
Deduct	....	....	1,358,000	....
Total	£29,508,000	£23,852,000	£5,656,000	....

Passenger Journeys (in Millions).

	1883.	1873.	Increase.	Decrease.
1st class	36	38	..	2
2nd class	66	70	..	4
3rd class	581	347	234	..
			234	6
Deduct	..	..	6	..
Total	683	455	228	..

	1883.	1873.	Increase.	Decrease.
Passenger train mileage receipts	50·73*d.*	59·47*d.*	....	8·74*d.*

In all directions, therefore, the indications are that the railway companies are giving much more accommodation in proportion than they did 10 years ago. In consequence of the decline of first and second class traffic the increase in aggregate receipts is only 24 per cent., but the increase in passenger journeys is more than 50 per cent., being exclusively an increase in third class passenger journeys, while the receipt per train mile of passenger trains has declined about 15 per cent.

Working Expenditure.—On this head there is hardly anything to notice. The changes in 1883, compared with 1882, are not very great. Still the greater part of the increased receipt, viz., 1,685,000*l.*, is absorbed by the increase of expenditure, amounting to 1,198,000*l.*; so that the increase of net earnings is only 487,000*l.* It would appear, however, that the increase of expenditure is only in proportion to an increase in the work done, there being in fact a slight decrease of 0·3*d.* in the expenditure per train mile, as the following table, which is in the same form as a similar table in former reports, will show. The changes in the items of expenditure per train mile, it will be observed, call for little remark, the most significant, perhaps, being the diminution in traffic expenses, which have shown a marked tendency to increase permanently in the last decade:—

	Cost per train mile.		Increase and decrease in 1883.	
	1883.	1882.	Increase.	Decrease.
	d.	*d.*	*d.*	*d.*
Maintenance of way	6·01	6·14	..	0·13
Locomotive power	8·32	8·21	0·11	..
Rolling stock	2·95	2·95	..	..
Traffic expenses	9·99	10·12	..	0·13
General charges	1·45	1·47	..	0·02
Rates and taxes	1·66	1·65	0·01	..
Government duty	0·69	0·80	..	0·11
Compensation:				
Personal injuries	0·22	0·26	..	0·04
Damage to goods	0·18	0·19	..	0·01
Legal and Parliamentary expenses	0·33	0·31	0·02	..
Miscellaneous	0·41	0·42	..	0·01
Total	32·17	32·47	..	0·30

Net Earnings and Dividends.—The increase in net earnings, as already noticed, is inconsiderable, amounting only to 487,000*l.*, or 1¼ per cent. The increase of capital having been 2·2 per cent., a slight decrease in the proportion of net earnings to capital is to be noticed, but the decrease is very slight indeed, being from 4·32 per cent. to 4·29 per cent. For several years the proportion of net earnings to capital has been comparatively stationary, though it must always be remembered in this connection, of course, that the capital itself is steadily increasing. The limits of variation since 1876 have been from 4·15 per cent. (1879) to 4·38 per cent. (1880; and, excepting 1879, the limits have been 4·25 per cent. and 4·38 per cent. The percentage in 1883 is very near the average of the whole period.

The rate of dividend paid on the ordinary capital also slightly diminished last year, viz., from 4·73 to 4·68 per cent. As regards ordinary capital, the rate is still very nearly the highest which has been paid for nearly 10 years, the highest rates since 1873 having been 4·72 per cent. in 1875 and 1880, and 4·73 per cent. in 1882. In 1879 the dividend on the ordinary capital only averaged 4·02 per cent., so that the present state of matters is a considerable improvement on that minimum. It would seem that ordinary capital gained a little last year by a reduction in the rate of dividend on some guaranteed and preferential capital, in consequence of the date for such reduction provided for in the original issues having arrived.

While guaranteed and preferential capital has not changed in amount, the aggregate dividend paid on this description of capital has fallen from 12,625,000*l.* to 12,602,000*l.*, which arises from a reduction of the preferential capital at 4 to 5 per cent. interest from 96,000,000*l.* to 88,000,000*l.*, and an increase of the same capital at 3 to 4 per cent. rates from 89,000,000*l.* to 97,000,000*l.* But for this special windfall the return to ordinary capital would have farther diminished. As matters stands, however, the result to ordinary capital of the year's working is far from unsatisfactory.

The following summary of tables Nos. 3 and 4 in the Appendix shows the rates of interest and dividend paid on railway capital generally, and the amount of capital at each rate:—

Statement of the Rates of Interest and Dividend paid on the undermentioned Ordinary, Guaranteed, and Preferential Capitals, and Loans and Debenture Stocks, for the year 1883.

Rate of Interest or Dividend.	Ordinary.		Guaranteed.		Preferential.		Loans and Debenture Stock	
	Amount of Capital.	Per cent of Total	Amount of Capital.	Per cent. of Total	Amount of Capital.	Per cent. of Total	Amount of Capital.	Per cent. of Total
	£		£		£		£	
Nil	46,742,144	15·9	478,133	0·5	9,679,328	4·6	8,000	—
Not above 1 per cent.	1,826,613	0·6	—	—	360,000	0·2	—	—
Above 1 & not over 2 per cent.	15,223,068	5·2	101,180	0·1	328,829	0·2	151,320	0·1
" 2 " 3 "	6,975,487	2·4	—	—	625,750	0·3	1,032,521	0·5
" 3 " 4 "	14,841,704	5·0	52,673,451	55·6	97,364,719	48·5	132,038,010	67·4
" 4 " 5 "	67,741,099	23·1	37,234,412	39·3	87,896,017	43·7	59,301,935	30·3
" 5 " 6 "	54,263,835	19·2	4,119,580	4·4	3,929,555	2·0	3,385,999	1·7
" 6 " 7 "	19,067,471	6·5	—	—	500,000	0·2	—	—
" 7 " 8 "	38,357,288	13·1	—	—	—	—	5,400	—
" 8 " 9 "	23,031,613	7·8	—	—	—	—	—	—
" 9 " 10 "	1,955,248	0·7	52,000	0·1	40,000	—	—	—
" 10 " 12 "	—	—	14,067	—	—	—	—	—
" 12 " 13 "	30,000	—	—	—	—	—	—	—
At 17 per cent.	1,381,436	0·5	—	—	165,000	0·1	—	—
Total ...... £	293,437,106	100·0	94,672,823	100·0	200,888,198	100·0	195,923,185	100·0

As regards ordinary capital there is no important change in the per-centage of that capital at particular rates of dividend. A special change as regards preferential capital has already been noted: but the proportions of total capital at different rates are still without much change. About 70 per cent. of railway capital receives dividends ranging from 3 to 5 per cent., or very nearly the average proportion of net earnings to capital, which is rather over 4 per cent.

***Summary Statement.*—It will be convenient to bring the main changes between 1882 and 1883 into the following summary statement, which is in the same form as in previous reports:—**

Summary of the Mileage, Capital, Traffic Receipts, Working Expenses, and Net Earnings of the Railways of the United Kingdom in 1883 and 1882 compared.

	1883.	1882.	Increase in 1883.		Decrease in 1883.	
			Amount.	Per cent.	Amount.	Per cent.
Mileage	18,681	18,457	224	1·0	..	..
Double or more mileage.	10,105	10,044	61	0·6	..	..
Capital	£784,921,312	£767,899,570	£17,021,742	2·2	..	..
Capital per mile open	42,017	41,605	412	1·0	..	..
Ordinary capital	293,437,106	283,574,028	9,863,078	3·5	..	..
Receipts—Passenger	£29,508,733	£28,796,813	£711,920	2·5	..	..
Goods	38,701,319	37,740,315	961,004	2·5	..	..
Miscellaneous	2,852,218	2,839,996	12,222	0·4	..	..
Total	£71,062,270	£69,377,124	£1,685,146	2·4	..	..
Working expenditure	37,368,562	36,170,436	1,198,126	3·3	..	..
Net earnings	£33,693,708	£33,206,688	£487,020	1·5	..	..
	d.	*d.*			*d.*	*d.*
Receipts per train mile from passenger and goods traffic	60·88	61·90	..	..	1·02	1·7
Expenditure per train mile, exclusive of harbour, &c., expenses	32·17	32·47	..	..	0·30	0·9
Net earnings per train mile	28·71	29·43	..	..	0·72	2·4
Per centage of net earnings on capital	4·29	4·32	..	..	0·03	0·69
Dividend paid on ordinary capital	*4·68	*4·73	..	..	0·05	1·06

The reading of this summary statement is very clear. In every particular there is moderate increase, traffic and net earnings especially both showing improvement. Finally there is only a slight diminution in the rate of net earnings and dividends paid on a larger amount of capital, while the falling off in the receipts per train mile, coupled with an increase in the aggregate receipts, indicates an increase in the service rendered to the public. These results may be regarded by the public and the railway shareholder with some satisfaction. The public have obtained increased advantages in the year from the railway service, while the capitalist has lost nothing in dividends, and has gained by being able to invest additional capital, which receives the former rate. It does not appear that the results for the current year will be quite so satisfactory, but it is premature as yet to speculate on the out-turn of the year.

*** These percentages are calculated on amounts a little in excess of the true totals.**

3.—SESSION 1884—ITS RESULTS.

The following bills received the royal assent last session on the dates mentioned:—

Ballyclare, Ligoniel, and Belfast Junction, 14th July.
Barrmill and Kilwinning, 28th July.
Belfast Central (Western Extensions), 19th May.
Belfast, Holywood, and Bangor, 14th July.
Belfast and Northern Counties, 14th July.
Belfast, Strandtown, and High Holywood, 28th April.
Bishop's Castle Extension to Montgomery, 7th August.
Blackpool, 7th August.
Buenos Ayres and Ensenada Port, 3rd July.
Burry Port and North Western Junction, 28th July.
Caledonian (No. 1), 14th July.
Caledonian (No. 2), 28th July.
Cleveland Extension (Mineral), 28th July.
Cork and Bandon and Clonakilty Extension, 14th July.
Cranbrook and Paddock Wood, 14th July.
Dore and Chinley, 28th July.
Dublin, Wicklow, and Wexford, 28th July.
Dundee Suburban, 28th July.
East London, 14th July.
Eastern Bengal, 28th July.
Eastern and Midlands, 3rd July.
Easton and Church Hope, 14th August.
Golden Valley (Hay Extension), 14th August.
Great Northern, 19th May.
Great North of Scotland, 28th July.
Great Southern and Western (Additional Powers), 14th July.
Great Southern and Western (Tullow Extension), 14th July.
Great Western (No. 1), 7th August.
Great Western (No. 2), 28th July.
Great Western and Bristol and Portishead Pier and Railway, 14th August.
Halifax High Level and North and South Junction, 7th August.
Hendon, 7th August.
Henley-in-Arden and Great Western Junction, 23rd June.
Highland (New Lines), 28th July.
Highland (Northern Lines Amalgamation), 28th July.
Hull, Barnsley, and West Riding Junction Railway and Dock, 23rd June.
Hull, Barnsley, and West Riding Junction Railway and Dock (Money), 14th August.
Kenmare Junction, 14th July.
Kilrush and Kilkee (Light) and Poulnasherry Reclamation (No. 2), 7th August.
Lancashire and Yorkshire, 14th July.
Lancashire and Yorkshire and London and North Western (Preston and Wyre), 14th July.
Leominster and Bromyard, 7th August.
Limerick and Kerry, 3rd July.
Liskeard and Caradon, 28th July.
Liverpool, Southport, and Preston Junction, 7th August.
London, Brighton, and South Coast, 3rd July.
London, Chatham, and Dover, (Further Powers), 14th July.
London and North Western, 28th July.
London and South Western, 7th August.
London and South Western and Metropolitan District, 14th August.
London, Tilbury, and Southend, 14th July.
Manchester, Sheffield, and Lincolnshire (Additional Powers), 14th July.
Manchester, Sheffield, and Lincolnshire. (Chester to Connah's Quay), 28th July.
Mersey, 7th August.
Metropolitan (Various Powers), 28th July.
Metropolitan Board of Works (District Railway Ventilators), 3rd July.
Metropolitan District, 7th August.
Midland, 3rd July.
North Cornwall, 28th July.
North Eastern, 23rd June
North Pembrokeshire and Fishguard, 7th August.
Plymouth, Devonport, and South Western Junction, and Devon and Cornwall Central, 7th August.
Porthdinlleyn, 7th August.
Rotherham and Bawtry, 7th August.
Ruthin and Cerrig-y-Druidion, 23rd June.
Scarborough and Whitby, 3rd July.
Severn Bridge and Forest of Dean Central, 19th May.
South Eastern (Various Powers), 28th July
Sutton and Willoughby, 28th July.
Swindon and Cheltenham Extension, 23rd June.
Swindon, Marlborough, and Andover, and Swindon and Cheltenham Extension Amalgamation, 23rd June.
Taff Vale, 28th July.
Teign Valley, 14th July.
Totnes, Paignton, and Torquay District, 23rd June.
Treferig Valley, 14th July.
Upwell, Outwell, and Wisbech (Abandonment), 19th May.
Uxbridge and Rickmansworth, 28th July.
West Lancashire (Capital) 19th May.
West Lancashire (Extension), 7th August.
Wirral, 14th August.

4.—NOTICES FOR BILLS—SESSION 1885.

The following is a list of the companies who are seeking various powers in the coming Parliamentary session, with a short summary of those powers, viz.:—

Alexandra (Newport and South Wales) Docks and Railway.—Railway from Alexandra Dock to Newport Dock; junctions with railways at Newport; widening of portion of Inkerman street, in Newport; purchase of land; interference with streets, roads, and railways; tolls and charges; further money powers; running powers to company and Great Western, and Brecon and Merthyr Tydfil Junction; agreements with Great Western, Pontypridd, Caerphilly and Newport, and Brecon and Merthyr Tydfil Junction, Lord Tredegar, and the Newport (Alexandra) Dock Company, limited.

Avonmouth and South Wales Junction.—Incorporation of company; construction of railways in county of Gloucester, compulsory purchase of lands, tolls, &c., running powers over railway of Bristol Port Railway and Pier Company, working and other agreements with and transfer of powers or of undertaking of company to corporation of Bristol and various railway companies, and powers to that corporation and those companies; payment of interest out of capital.

Barry Dock and Railways.—New railways from Cadoxton, near Barry, to Cogan Pill, and in the parishes of Llantrissant, Llanwonno, and Ystradyfodwg; extension of limits of deviation for dock works, in the parishes of Sully, and Cadoxton-Juxta-Barry; compulsory purchase of land, tolls, and charges; additional capital and money powers; conversion of shares into preference shares or stock; provisions for the suppression of drunkenness and disorder; rules, regulations, and bylaws; additions of members to the pilotage board for the port of Cardiff; representation of the Barry Dock and Railways Company thereon; licensing pilots for Barry Dock; running powers over parts of the railway of the Penarth extension, the Penarth Harbour, Dock, and Railway, the Taff Vale and Great Western; agreements with railway companies.

Belfast Central (Abandonment).—Abandonment of works authorised by acts of 1880 and 1884, and return of money deposited in respect thereof.

Belfast Central (Sale).—Sale of undertaking of Belfast Central to Great Northern (Ireland); agreements between these companies; capital and other powers to Great Northern (Ireland); agreements between that company and the Belfast and Northern Counties and Belfast and County Down, and powers to last mentioned companies.

Bexley Heath.—New railway near Blackheath; construction of new road and sewer in parish of Eltham; compulsory purchase of lands; confirmation of working and other agreements with South-Eastern, and power to that company to contribute funds; power to sell or lease undertaking to the South-Eastern, and power to that company to purchase or lease the same; running powers over portion of South-Eastern.

Blackpool (Extension to Rossall and Fleetwood).—Construction of railways from Blackpool to Rossall and Fleetwood; compulsory purchase of lands; tolls; additional capital; agreements with Manchester, Sheffield, and Lincolnshire, London and North Western, Lancashire and Yorkshire, and the Preston and Wyre; running powers over portion of Preston and Wyre.

Canterbury and Kent Coast.—Incorporation of company; construction of railway between Grove Ferry and Reculver and new road and station at Beltinge and Herne Bay in the county of Kent; compulsory purchase of lands; power to levy tolls and rates; working, traffic, and other arrangements with the London, Chatham, and Dover and South Eastern; running powers over portions of railways of London, Chatham, and Dover and South Eastern; power to the said companies to subscribe.

Cardiff and Monmouthshire Valleys.—Incorporation of company; construction of railways in counties of Glamorgan and Monmouth; compulsory purchase of land; tolls and charges; traffic agreements; running powers and traffic facilities over other railways; payment of interest out of capital.

Cardiff, Penarth, and Barry Junction.—Incorporation of company; new railways between Cardiff and Penarth and Barry and other places; agreements with Taff Vale and Barry Dock and Railway Company; powers affecting the Barry Dock and Railways.

Central Argentine.—Amendment of memorandum and articles of association and additional powers as to execution of works and other matters.

Channel Tunnel (Experimental Works).—Powers to the South Eastern and the Submarine Continental, limited, or one of them, either alone or jointly with any other company, association, government, body or person, to maintain, vary, and enlarge existing works, and execute further experimental and other works for a tunnel beneath the straits of Dover; appropriation of soil and bed of the straits of Dover; application of capital of South Eastern to purposes of bill; agreements with the Submarine Continental, limited, the Channel Tunnel Company, limited, and other companies, &c.; amendment of section 14 of South Eastern Act, 1874; amendment or repeal of section 17 of the Railways Clauses Consolidation Act, 1845; amendment and repeal of acts; memorandum of association and other purposes.

Charing Cross and Euston.—Incorporation of company; construction of railways from the South Eastern to the London and North Western; new street and other works and stopping up of streets; agreements between the company and the Metropolitan Board of Works and other authorities; powers for purchase and sale of lands; power to levy tolls and rates.

Charing Cross and Waterloo Electric.—Abandonment of railway; release of deposit; winding up and dissolution of company.

Charing Cross and Waterloo Electric.—Extension of railway to Cockspur street; compulsory purchase of lands; tolls, rates, and charges; underpinning; repeal of 92nd section of Lands Clauses Consolidation Act, 1845; extension of time for the compulsory purchase of lands and buildings, and construction and completion of the railway authorised by the Charing Cross and Waterloo and Electric Railway Act, 1882.

Colne Valley and Halstead.—Reconstitution of the board of directors; qualification and powers of new board; suspension of proceedings; discharge of receiver; standing arbitrator; regulation of rights and priorities of bondholders; judgment and other creditors and shareholders; future government of the company; adjustment, consolidation, and conversion of existing capital; additional capital; powers to trustees, &c.; payment of costs.

Columbia Market and Railways.—New railways; new street, and street widening and stopping up streets in St. Leonard, Shoreditch, and St. Matthew, Bethnal Green; purchase of lands, compulsory and by agreement; additional lands; underpinning; powers to North London for construction or acquisition of intended railways and working agreements; traffic facilities; agreements with North London, Great Eastern, Great Western, Great Northern, London and North Western, Midland, London, Tilbury, and Southend, London and South Western, London, Brighton, and South Coast, North and South Western Junction, London, Chatham, and Dover, and East London as to traffic rates; markets; levying tolls, rates, and charges.

Croydon Direct.—Incorporation of company; powers to construct railway from London, Chatham, and Dover at Dulwich to Croydon and new road in Croydon; dedication to, and repair by public, of new road, and power to Borough of Croydon to subscribe towards cost of making and maintaining same; compulsory purchase of lands; tolls; running powers over railways, of agreements with, and provisions affecting the London, Chatham, and Dover.

Crystal Palace (High Level), Beulah, and Beckenham.—Incorporation of company, construction of railways between Camberwell, Norwood, Beckenham, and the Crystal Palace; compulsory purchase of Lands; power to take part only of certain property, underpinning, &c., tolls, rates, and charges; running powers; working and traffic agreements with the London, Chatham, and Dover, and provisions affecting that company; payment of interest or dividend out of the capital or other funds of the company.

Crystal Palace, South Eastern, and Metropolitan.—Construction of railways from or near New Cross to the Crystal Palace; compulsory purchase of lands; tolls; alteration of tolls; working and other agreements with the South Eastern, London, Brighton, and South Coast, London, Chatham, and Dover, East London, Metropolitan, Metropolitan District, Great Eastern, and Crystal Palace; contributions by those companies respectively, and powers to each of them to apply funds and capital to the purposes of the undertaking, and to raise further moneys, and to guarantee interest or dividends; powers to the London, Brighton, and South Coast to become joint owners of intended railways, and incidental powers; running powers over parts of railways of the East London; special powers to the Crystal Palace and to other companies specified to appropriate revenue and receipts on behalf of Crystal Palace as guarantee on capital, &c.; agreements with the Crystal Palace respecting sale, &c., of lands; to confer, vary, and extinguish rights and privileges.

Didcot, Newbury, and Southampton.—Extension of time for compulsory purchase of lands and completion of railways and works authorised by the Didcot, Newbury, and Southampton Junction Act, 1882; confirmation or alteration or variation of existing agreements with Great Western.

East London.—Road and lands at St. Mary's Station, Whitechapel; confirmation of scheme and other provisions as to rearrangement of capital and arrears of dividend on debenture stocks, and as to Whitechapel Junction capital; provisions as to superfluous lands over railways; reduction of directors.

Elham Valley Light.—Deviation of authorised Elham Valley Light; compulsory purchase of lands and construction of railway and works; additional capital; tolls.

Felixstowe, Ipswich, and Midlands.—Incorporation of company; power to make a railway between Cambridge and the Ipswich and Felixstowe at Westerfield with all necessary works; running powers to company over portions of railways of other companies, and to other companies over railways of company; working and other arrangements; compulsory facilities.

Great Eastern.—Widenings and improvements of railways from Loughton to Epping; from Colchester north station to Hythe, and of parts of the Tendring Hundred; from Kennett to Newmarket; of main line near Globe Road, Mile End Old Town; diversion of road at Thetford; alteration of bridges at West Ham and Cambridge; diversion of footpath at Dereham Station; stopping up of level crossings in the parish of Birchanger, Essex; compulsory purchase of lands; additional lands in various places; tolls; extension and revival of powers for compulsory purchase of lands for the completion of certain railways and works authorised by the Great Eastern Acts, 1876, 1877, 1879, 1881, 1882; abandonment of certain railways authorised by the Great Eastern Act, 1879, and East Norfolk Act, 1879, and tramways authorised by the Great Eastern Act, 1882; additional capital and borrowing powers; provisions as to separate capital for Parkeston Quay, Harwich; redemption of preference stocks.

Great Northern (Rates and Charges).—Consolidation of rates and charges; classification of traffic; alteration of existing rates and charges; provisions as to terminal and special charges, and other matters.

Great Northern (Various Powers).—New railways and works in Lincolnshire, Leicestershire, Derbyshire, Nottinghamshire, West Riding of Yorkshire, Middlesex, and Hertfordshire; stopping up of roads and level crossings; additional lands; confirmation of sale of lands of Duchy of Lancaster; abandonment of Shipley branch; extension of time for construction of roads and footway authorised by the Great Northern Act, 1882; extension of time for compulsory purchase (under the same act) of lands in West Riding of Yorkshire, and for sale of superfluous lands; agreements.

Great Western.—Railways in counties of Devon and Glamorgan; widening of bridge near Bristol; conversion into open cutting of tunnel near Bristol; roads, footpaths, bridges, and rights of way in the counties of Warwick, Somerset, Monmouth, Glamorgan, and Carmarthen; alterations of levels at Briton Ferry of South Wales and South Wales Mineral railways and sidings; additional lands in the counties of Wilts, Gloucester, Somerset, Monmouth, Glamorgan, and Carmarthen; amendment of section 92 of the Lands Clauses Consolidation Act, 1845; provisions as to the repair and construction of roads; tolls; provisions as to superfluous lands on the railways of the company; extension of time for the purchase of lands for and for construction of railways Nos. 1, 2, and 3, authorised by the Great Western No. 2 Act, 1882; revival of powers for the purchase of certain lands on the Helston, and extension of time for the construction of that railway; power to the company to subscribe to the capital and debenture debt of the Staines and West Drayton, Newent, and Abbotsbury companies, and to appoint Directors; agreements with these companies and other railway companies; release of the deposit made in respect of the Tiverton and North Devon; provisions as to cancellation of capital representing the debenture debt of the Vale of Towy; company may issue stocks in lieu of the Bristol and Portishead rent charge authorised by the Great Western and Portishead Act, 1884, and may establish savings banks; further provisions with reference to the superannuation funds of the company; extending certain provisions of the Companies' Clauses Act, 1845, to the debenture stock of the company, and altering the times for the payment of dividends thereon; authorising agreements between the company and other companies as to the guarantee fund of the company and enlargement of powers in relation thereto; power to company and the Helston company to apply corporate funds; capital.

Great Western (Merchandise, Rates, and Charges).—Consolidation and revision of tolls, rates, and charges; adoption of uniform classification of traffic; limitation and declaration of terminal charges.

Hadlow Valley.—Incorporation of company; powers to construct railways from the London, Chatham, and Dover at Boro' Green to the South Eastern at Tunbridge; compulsory purchase of lands; tolls, &c.; running powers over railways of the South Eastern and London, Chatham, and Dover; agreements with, and provisions affecting those companies; payment of interest or dividend out of the capital or other funds of the company.

Hassop and Padley.—Incorporation of company; railways from Rowsley to Buxton; extension of Midland to the Dore and Chinley; compulsory purchase of lands; tolls; running powers over railways; of agreements with and other provisions affecting Midland and Dore and Chinley; payment of interest out of capital.

Hull, Barnsley, and West Riding Junction Railway and Dock.—Abandonment of railway No. 1A authorised by the company's act, 1880; construction of substituted railway; compulsory purchase of lands; tolls; extending powers of deviation of and additional lands for railway No. 4, authorised by the company's act of 1882; extension of time for compulsory purchase of lands for, and for completion of railways and roads authorised by the said act of 1882; application of funds.

Ilfracombe.—Incorporation of company; construction of railway to Ilfracombe; power to the Great Western to subscribe or to guarantee interest on debentures or debenture stock and dividends on capital, and to enter into working and traffic agreements.

International Communication.—Incorporation of company; new and enlarged steam vessels between England and the Continent; water station, wharves, walls, and jetties at Dover; railways, stations, and road at Dover; levying tolls, rates, and dues; traffic and other arrangements with London, Chatham, and Dover and South Eastern; agreements with the corporation and local authorities of Dover and with the Dover Harbour Board; agreements and arrangements with Her Majesty's Government; exemption from town, harbour, and other dues and rates.

Isle of Wight.—Amalgamation of Isle of Wight, Isle of Wight (Newport Junction), Ryde and Newport, and Cowes and Newport; working arrangements between the companies; powers to London and South Western, London, Brighton, and South Coast, and Great Western, or any of them, to purchase or work the said Isle of Wight railways or any of them.

Lancashire and Yorkshire.—Connecting line at Agecroft near Manchester; loop line Pendlebury to Pendleton; loop line Pemberton to Hindley; short line at Horwich; connecting lines at Farrington, near Preston; alteration of levels of portion of authorised Hindley to Pendleton and diversion of footpath; widening lines at Hindley, and at Miles Platting, and of viaduct in Manchester; diversion of roads, &c., on Hindley to Pendleton and connecting line at Westhoughton: works and lands at Formby near Liverpool and repeal of provisions of former act relating thereto: diversion of Wango Lane, Fazakerley near Liverpool; subways in Liverpool; widening bridge Mill Hill, Blackburn; works at Heckmondwike; abandonment of authorised street and provision as to streets in Liverpool; repeal of provision as to road at Atherton; additional lands, &c.; superfluous lands; commonable lands; further provisions as to provident society; widening the Preston and Wyre at Kirkham and new line to Blackpool and works; powers to London and North Western; agreements.

Latimer Road and Acton.—Revival and extension of powers for compulsory purchase of land and construction and completion of works authorised by the Latimer Road and Acton Act.

Limerick and Kerry.—Vesting in the Limerick and Kerry the undertakings of the Rathkeale and Newcastle Junction and the Tralee and Fenit; dissolution of those companies; confirmation of agreements between the companies; creation of new debenture stock; transfer of guarantee of Barony of Trughenachmy to stock to be exchanged for Tralee and Fenit railway shares to which guarantee is now attached; provisions as to members of the joint committee of the Rathkeale and the Waterford and Limerick.

Listowel and Ballybunion.—Incorporation of company; construction of light railway from Listowel to Ballybunion, in the county of Kerry; purchase of land, compulsory or by agreement; breaking up and interference with streets and roads; levying tolls; power to Limerick and Kerry, Waterford and Limerick, and Great Southern and Western to subscribe and appoint directors; working agreements with the Limerick and Kerry and Waterford and Limerick; power to run over and use the railways of the Limerick and Kerry, Rathkeale and Newcastle Junction, and Waterford and Limerick; reciprocal running powers to those companies; power to make agreements to purchase, lease, or otherwise acquire sand hills and foreshore.

Llangammarch and Neath and Brecon Junction.—Extension of time for purchase of lands and completion of railway, working and traffic agreements.

London and Blackwall.—Widening and improvement of the London and Blackwall from near Fenchurch Street Station to Stepney Junction; extension of bridges over Leman Street, Mill Yard Lane, and Back Church Lane; stopping up of streets, &c.: compulsory purchase of lands; tolls; power to the London and Blackwall to apply existing funds and raise additional capital; agreements as to joint exercise by Great Eastern and London and Blackwall of powers of bill; agreements between Great Eastern and London, Tilbury, and Southend as to construction, &c., of widenings; applying sec. 33 of London, Tilbury, and Southend Act, 1882; extension of time for the sale of surplus lands.

London, Brighton, and South Coast.—Uniformity of tolls, rates, and charges; new classification of goods, &c.; fixing tolls, rates, terminals, and charges.

London, Brighton, and South Coast.—Abandonment of Keymer junction 1879 and 1882, and railway at Shoreham authorised by act of 1882; extension of time for compulsory purchase of land and completion of railway at Croydon authorised by act of 1882; extension of time for purchase of land at Croydon under act of 1882—abolition of level crossings at Lindfield and Chailey: stopping footpath at Streatham Park; guarantee of Brighton and Dyke loan capital; incorporating joint committee under East London Act, 1882; repeal or alteration of section 45 of that act; provision as to maintenance and manning of that railway.

London, Chatham, and Dover.—Construction of railways from Shortlands to Nunhead, and branch railways; constitution of separate undertaking; tolls, &c.; consolidation and alteration of existing tolls, rates, and charges: and provisions as to terminal charges; additional capital; additional lands; power to divert and stop up footpath at Ashford.

London, Chatham, and Dover.—Regulation and arrangement of company's capital; additional capital; power to attach preference to such capital, and to capital already authorised; conversion by agreement of company's second preference stock; conversion of Sheerness rent charge stock into company's arbitration debenture stock.

London and North Western.—Additional powers to company with reference to new railway and deviation and widening of railways and other works, footpaths, and lands in the counties of Northampton, York (West Riding), Lancaster, Middlesex, Stafford, Chester, and Brecon; new dock and works at Garston; powers to company and the Lancashire and Yorkshire as to junction at Bootle, and to company and the Great Western as to West Kirby extension and additional land and works; power to levy rates, &c., for railway dock and other works and alteration of existing dock rates; agreement between company and the before-mentioned companies respectively; further provisions as to superfluous lands of company and of company and the Furness and as to purchase of lands by company by agreement and amendment of London and North Western (Additional Powers) Act, 1879, and of London and North Western (New Railways) Act, 1881; agreements with the Duke of Bedford and amendment of 5 and 6 William IV., cap. 56, and 9 and 10 Vic., cap. 152; agreements with the corporation of Walsall: supply of gas at Wolverhampton; passage across railways of traction engines, &c.; confirmation of agreements between company and the Lancashire and Yorkshire and between company and the Brecon and Merthyr Tydfil Junction; vesting in company of undertaking of Lancaster Canal Navigation and dissolution of that company; further capital powers to Manchester, South Junction, and Altrincham, and subscription thereto by company and the Manchester, Sheffield, and Lincolnshire; additional capital and application of funds by the last mentioned companies and by Lancashire and Yorkshire and Great Western.

London and North Western.—Consolidation of tolls, rates and charges; classification of traffic; alteration of existing tolls, rates, and charges; provision as to terminal and special charges and other matters.

London and South Western (Rates, &c.)—Consolidation and revision of tolls, rates, and charges, on London and South Western and other railways leased, worked, &c., by the company; new classification of merchandise, &c., applicable thereto declaration and prescribing of terminal and other special charges.

London and South Western (Various Powers).—Extension of Thames Valley from Shepperton to Chertsey; extension of bridge over Latchmere Road, near Clapham Junction; alteration of road at Boldre, county of Southampton; purchase of additional lands in the parishes of St. Mary, Lambeth, St. Mary, Battersea, Wandsworth, Windlesham, Byfleet, Woking, and Farnham, in the county of Surrey, Sunninghill and Old Windsor, in the county of Berks, and Wootton St. Lawrence, in the county of Hants, and East Morden, St. Martin's, and Lady St. Mary, in the county of Dorset; taking of parts of commons and commonable lands; vesting in company lands in the parish of Barnes, in the county of Surrey, referred to in agreement confirmed by section 43 of the South Western Railway Act, 1884; extension of time or revival of powers for compulsory purchase of lands for and for the completion of works and station at South Kensington, and certain railways authorised by the South Western Act, 1882; special powers to verderers of New Forest to convey, &c., to company estates, &c., not vested in crown; agreements with verderers; dedication, &c., of new road, &c.; powers to highway authorities; further money powers; tolls, &c.; compulsory purchase of lands.

Lydd (Various Powers).—Extension of time for construction of railways and works authorised by the Lydd (Extensions) Act, 1882, and the Lydd (Extensions) Act, 1883; deviation from line and levels of portion of Loose and Headcorn Line authorised by Lydd (Extensions) Act, 1883; abandonment of portion between points of deviation; compulsory purchase of lands; tolls; confirmation of agreements with the South Eastern; power for the South Eastern to subscribe to the Lydd; transfer to company of Loose Valley undertaking; money powers.

Manchester, Sheffield, and Lincolnshire (Additional Powers).—New railway in the counties of York (West Riding) and Derby; new railway and deviation railway, in the county of Lancaster; consequential abandonment of railway No. 1 authorised by the Manchester, Sheffield, and Lincolnshire (New Works) Act, 1881; stopping up of level crossing at Gainsborough, and substitution of underbridge or subway therefor; compulsory purchase of lands, tolls, &c.; additional lands in the counties of Lancaster, Lincoln, and Chester; confirmation of purchases; stopping up of streets in Manchester; subscription to undertaking of Blackpool Company; purchase of the Sheffield Victoria Hotel and dissolution of the Sheffield Victoria Hotel Company; extension of time for sale of superfluous lands of the company, the Cheshire Lines, and the Sheffield and Midland; extension of time for the completion of certain works authorised by the Wigan Junction Act, 1874, and the Wigan Junction Act, 1875; extension of time for acquisition of lands and completion of certain works authorised by the Manchester, Sheffield, and Lincolnshire and Cheshire Lines Act, 1882; power to constitute railways authorised by the Manchester, Sheffield, and Linolnshire (Chester to Connah's Quay) Act, 1884, a separate undertaking with separate capital to be guaranteed by the company's additional capital.

Mersey.—New railways and subways in Liverpool and Birkenhead; additional lands; purchase of parts of properties only; stopping up streets and appropriation of sites; underpinning; ventilating shafts; tolls, rates, and charges; additional capital; agreements with corporations of Liverpool and Birkenhead and Mersey Docks and Harbour Board.

Metropolitan.—Construction of branch railway of Chesham; extension of time for construction, deviation of portion of Aylesbury and Rickmansworth, and to constitute same a separate undertaking; extension of time for completion of Rickmansworth Extension; new station in King's Cross Road; compulsory purchase of land and buildings; authorising works at New Cross, and arrangements with the South-Eastern; further provision for working the Inner Circle; to authorise agreements with Metropolitan Board of Works and others as to artisans' dwellings; power to deal with the capital stocks of the company; and to levy tolls.

Metropolitan (Bow Extension).—New railways between the Whitechapel branch of the East London at Whitechapel and the London, Tilbury, and Southend at Bow; provisions as to separate undertaking; powers to stop up and divert streets; amendment of section 92 of the Lands Clauses Consolidation Act, 1845; provisions as to superfluous lands on the railways; running powers over London, Tilbury, and Southend; agreements with that company; levying of tolls; powers to the company to borrow or raise additional capital and to apply funds.

Metropolitan, Notting Hill and Shepherd's Bush Extension.—Incorporation of company; railway from Notting Hill to Shepherd's Bush and other railways; running powers over portions of the railways of the Metropolitan, Great Western, London and North Western, and the London and South Western; agreements with those companies; compulsory purchase of lands and easements; exemption from some of the provisions of the Lands Clauses Consolidation Act, 1845; underpinning; temporary shafts.

Metropolitan Outer Circle.—Abandonment of undertaking; release of deposit; dissolution of the company's repeal of acts.

Midland.—Consolidation and equalisation of tolls, rates, and charges; classification of traffic; alteration of existing tolls, rates, and charges; provisions as to terminal and special charges, and other matters.

Midland.—New railway and other works and additional lands in the counties of Lancaster, Worcester, Bedford, Derby, Nottingham, Warwick, and Middlesex; further provisions as to superfluous lands and as to buildings in Bradford; vesting in company of undertaking of Bedford and Northampton; consolidation of shares and stocks; additional capital.

North British.—New railway commencing by a junction with their Edinburgh, Leith, and Granton Branch, and terminating by a junction with their railway from Easter Road Junction to Piershill Junction; a railway commencing at Thornton Loop, and terminating by a junction with the Edinburgh, Perth, and Dundee; a railway commencing by a junction with the Stobcross Branch, and terminating at or near the western boundary fence of Hyndland drive or road; a railway commencing by a junction with the Edinburgh and Glasgow, and terminating by a junction with the City of Glasgow Union; deviations of the Sighthill Branch and of the company's railway; a railway commencing by a junction in the company's goods station yard at Montrose, and terminating by a junction close to the south-west wall of the wet dock at Montrose; and two railways connected with the last-mentioned line; extension of time for the compulsory purchase of land and completion of works authorised by acts of 1881 and 1882, and the Austruther and St. Andrew Act 1880; improving hotel and general offices at Edinburgh; raising new capital for Perth Station and other purposes; repealing or altering the provisions of section 43 of the (Amalgamations, &c.) Act of 1880, authorising them to advance 100,000*l.* on loan to the Forth Bridge, and to apply this money to the purposes of their own undertaking; and amalgamating with the company the Edinburgh Suburban and South Side and the Kelvin Valley.

North Cornwall.—Extension of time for the compulsory purchase of lands and buildings and construction and completion of railways Nos. 1 and 3, and part of railway No. 2, and deviation railways 1, 2, 3, 4, 5, 6, and 7, and for the alterations and improvements of the Bodmin and Wadebridge, authorised by the North Cornwall Act, 1882.

North Eastern (Rates and Charges).—Consolidation and revision of tolls, rates, and charges; classification of traffic; provisions as to terminal and other special charges and other matters.

Plymouth, Devonport, and South Western Junction.—Extension of time for compulsory purchase of land and construction and completion of works of part of railway No. 3 and railway No. 4, and remainder of works and alterations of levels authorised by the Devon and Cornwall Central Act, 1882.

Portpatrick and Wigtownshire.—Transfer of undertakings to the London and North Western, Midland, Caledonian, and the Glasgow and South Western; vesting undertakings in those companies, or in a joint company or joint committee to be incorporated and appointed for the purposes of the act; defining rights and powers of joint company or committee; guarantee of dividends to shareholders of the Portpatrick and of the Wigtownshire; provision for dissolution of Portpatrick and Wigtownshire railway companies; additional money and other powers to the London and North Western, Midland, Caledonian, and Glasgow and South Western; money powers to the joint company or joint committee; tolls, rates, and duties; running powers to the four companies and the joint company or joint committee over portions of Caledonian, and Glasgow and South Western, and over Portpatrick and Wigtownshire; powers to contribute to steamboats; powers to compound as to town dues or petty customs at Stranraer; and terminating working agreement with Caledonian.

Regent's Canal City and Docks.—Repeal or amendment of section 201 of the Companies' Act of 1882; payment of interest or dividend out of capital; further borrowing powers; constitution of separate undertakings; fusion or amalgamation of separate undertakings; special provisions as to capital and borrowing powers, &c., and as to exercise of compulsory powers of purchase of land, &c.; provisions as to unauthorised taking of water from canals, &c.

Rhondda and Swansea Bay.—Construction of new railways in the county of Glamorgan; compulsory purchase of lands, tolls, &c.; additional lands in the parishes of Ystradyfodwg, Meshaelstone Super Avon, and Argam; further capital and borrowing powers; extension of time for compulsory purchase of lands not already purchased; agreements with and powers to Neath Harbour Commissioners.

Rhymney.—New railway in the county of Glamorgan; widening of bridge carrying Crwys-road over railway; compulsory purchase of land; power to levy tolls, and rates; additional lands; running powers over portions of the Taff Vale and traffic facilities; sidings to be made by Pontypridd, Caerphilly, and Newport at Pontypridd; stopping up of level crossing; abandonment of railway No. 4, described in section 5 of the Rhymney Act, 1882, and amendment of section 9 of that act; extension of time for purchase of certain lands and acquisition or use of occupation road for the purposes of that act; periodical closing of debenture transfer books; additional capital; application of capital; confirmation of agreement between the Marquis of Bute and the company.

Scarborough, Bridlington, and West Riding Junction.—Incorporation of company, with powers to make and maintain railways in the North and East Ridings of the county of York, with junctions with other railways; compulsory purchase of lands and houses, and interference with public roads, &c.; working and other agreements with North Eastern; tolls; payment of interest out of capital.

Scinde, Punjaub, and Delhi.—Modification or enlargement of existing agreements with the Secretary of State in Council of India or with the East India Company; power to make further agreements; definition and regulation of capital and borrowing powers; creation of additional capital; modification of existing leases of lands; new or substituted leases; purchase of undertaking by Secretary of State in Council; provision for distribution of purchase money; power to make arrangements with steam and other shipping companies.

Selbury and Mid-Yorkshire Union.—Extension of time for compulsory purchase of lands and for completion of railways.

Skipton and Kettlewell.—Abandonment of railway; release of deposit winding up and dissolution of the company.

South Eastern.—New railways, widenings of railways, and works in Kent and Surrey; new pier and extension of pier and harbour works at Folkestone and extension of limits of harbour; deviation of the East London at New Cross; alteration of levels of roads at Beckenham and Reigate; diversion of the river Ravensbourne and New Cut; diversion of streets in Lewisham, and St. Paul, Deptford, in the county of Kent; additional lands in city of London, and in Kent and Surrey; agreement with landowners and others for widening the Caterham Branch; compulsory purchase of lands; extension of time for purchase of lands and completion of railways and works under various acts relating to the South Eastern in the counties of Kent, Surrey, and Middlesex, and in the city of London; extension of time for purchase of lands for and completion of Caterham and Godstone Valley; extension of time for completion of works of Woodside and South Croydon; extension of time for purchase of lands for and completion of Loose Valley and Godstone Village Extension; to amend sections 27 and 46 of the South Eastern (Various Powers) Act, 1884, and section 39 of the Local and Personal Act, 9 and 10 Vic., cap. 305; agreements with company or urban sanitary authority, Folkestone; agreements with reference to the works and traffic at Port Victoria, and the tolls, &c., arising therefrom; agreements with owners, &c., for widening the Caterham; power to contribute, &c., to the Bexley Heath and Lydd, and to winter garden at Tunbridge Wells; amendment of exemption from provisions of section 92 of Lands Clauses Consolidation Act, 1845; power to take part only of certain properties in the parish of St. Mary, Lambeth, in the county of Surrey, authorised to be taken by South Eastern (New Lines and Widenings) Act, 1882, and of certain properties in the parishes of Frindsbury and Strood, in the county of Kent, authorised to be taken by the South Eastern Act, 1881; agreements with the Metropolitan and with the Metropolitan Board of Works, vestries, and district boards; levying of tolls, &c.; money powers.

South Eastern, and London, Chatham, and Dover (Arbitration).—Adjustment and settlement of claims, disputes, and differences, &c., between the South Eastern, and London, Chatham, and Dover under continental traffic agreements; provisions for compulsory reference to arbitration; constitution of court of arbitration; power to court to make and enforce award, &c., and amend or rescind agreements.

Stratford-upon-Avon, Towcester, and Midland Junction.—Deviation of portion of authorised railway; compulsory purchase of lands; tolls, rates, and charges; application of funds; additional capital; power to use Bedford and Northampton; confirmation of agreement, and deed of covenant with the East and West Junction; definition of rent-charge or preferential interest payable by East and West Junction; regulation of subsidy payable to company by East and West Junction.

Taff Vale.—New railways; diversions of roads; additional lands; extension of time for completing authorised works; amendment of section 24 of Taff Vale Act, 1879; provisions as to traction engines; additional capital.

Taff Vale.—New railway (No. 1) commencing in the parish of Whitchurch by a junction with the company's main line, at or near the bridge carrying the public road from College Ironworks to Gwauntreoda Common over the railway, and terminating by a junction with the railway No. 1 authorised by the Bute Docks Act, 1882, at or near the termination thereof; a railway (No. 2) commencing by a junction with the intended railway No. 1, and terminating by a junction with the railway No. 2 authorised by the Bute Docks Act, 1882; a railway (No. 3) commencing by a junction with the intended railway No. 1 and terminating by a junction with the Great Western; and a railway, No. 4, commencing in Llanwonno, by a junction with the company's Rhondda Fach Branch, and terminating in Ystradyfodwg, on the western side of the river Rhondda Fach. Authority is also sought to extend the time for purchasing land and for completing the railway described in the Company's Act of 1883.

Tilbury and Gravesend Tunnel Junction.—Abandonment of railways; release and deposit; winding up and dissolution of company.

Tilbury and Gravesend Tunnel Junction.—Alteration of levels of the railways Nos. 1 and 3 authorised by the Tilbury and Gravesend Tunnel Junction Act 1882; railways to be constructed as single lines; provision for single lines; extension of time for compulsory purchase of lands and completion of works; release of deposit made in respect of the application for the act of 1882; provisions for new deposit; further provisions as to capital; agreements with South Eastern, London, Chatham, and Dover, and London, Tilbury, and Southend.

Westerham and Oxted.—Incorporation of company; construction of railway between Westerham in the county of Kent and Oxted in the county of Surrey: compulsory purchase of lands, &c. tolls; running powers and facilities over portions of railways of London, Brighton, and South Coast and South Eastern, and by those companies over intended railways; working and other agreements with those companies; payment of interest out of capital and other alterations or amendments for the purposes of the bill of the Companies' Clauses Consolidation Act 1845.

Worcester and Broom.—Incorporation of company; construction of railways from Worcester to Broom; compulsory purchase of lands; tolls; running powers over the Evesham, Redditch, and Stratford-upon-Avon Junction, the East and West Junction, the Stratford-upon-Avon, Towcester, and Midland Junction, and portions of the Northampton and Banbury Junction, and of the Great Western, and use of stations on those railways; working and other agreements with the Great Western, the Midland, the Evesham, Redditch, and Stratford-upon-Avon Junction, the East and West Junction, the Stratford-upon-Avon, Towcester, and Midland Junction, and the Northampton and Banbury Junction.

5.—BILLS DEPOSITED—SESSION 1886.

The following is a complete list of bills for the construction, &c., of railways, &c., for which application will be made in the ensuing session of Parliament, in respect of which plans have been deposited at the railway department or the harbour department of the Board of Trade. The total number of bills is 73, as against 166 last year:—

Alexandra (Newport and South Wales) Docks and Railways.
Avonmouth and South Wales Junction.
Ballymena and Larne.
Bann Navigation and Railway.
Barry Dock and Railways.
Beckenham, South Norwood Park, and Crystal Palace.
Bexhill Direct.
Bexley Heath.
Canterbury and Kent Coast.
Cardiff and Monmouthshire Valleys.
Cardiff, Penarth, and Barry Junction.
Charing Cross and Euston.
Charing Cross and Waterloo Electric.
Columbia Market and Railways.
Cork and Fermoy Direct.
Croydon Direct.
Crystal Palace (High Level), Beulah, and Beckenham.
Crystal Palace, South Eastern, and Metropolitan
Dore and Chinley.
Dublin Grand Junctions.
Ealing, Harrow, and Edgware.
Eastern and Midlands.
East Usk.
East London.
Elham Valley, Light (Deviation, &c.)
Felixstowe, Ipswich, and Midland.
Filleigh and Blackmore Gate.
Great Eastern (General Powers).
Great Northern (Various Powers).
Great Western.
Giant's Causeway, Portrush, and Bush Valley Railway and Tramways.
Guiseley, Yeadon, and Rawdon.
Hadlow Valley.
Hassop and Padley.
Hull, Barnsley, and West Riding Junction Railway and Dock.
International Communications, Railways, &c.
Isle of Axholme.
Lancashire and Yorkshire.
Listowel and Ballybunion.
London and Blackwall.
London, Brighton, and South Coast (Various Powers).
London, Chatham, and Dover (Further Powers).
London and North Western.
London and South Western (Various Powers).
London, Tilbury, and Southend.
Lydd (Various Powers).
Manchester, Sheffield, and Lincolnshire (Additional Powers).
Merionethshire.
Mersey.
Metropolitan, Notting Hill, and Shepherd's Bush (Extension).
Metropolitan (Various Powers).
Midland (Additional Powers).
Northampton and Banbury and Metropolitan Junction.
Northampton, Daventry, and Leamington.
North British.
North London.
North Wales Narrow Gauge (Extension).
Rhondda and Swansea Bay.
Rhondda Heath.
Rhymney.
Scarborough and Bridlington and West Riding Junction.
Shanklin and Chale.
South Eastern (Various Powers).
St. Helens and Wigan Junction.
Stourbridge Western.
Stratford-upon-Avon, Towcester, and Midland Junction.
Taff Vale.
Tilbury and Gravesend Tunnel Junction.
Westerham and Oxted.
Wimborne and Christchurch.
Wirral.
Worcester and Broom.
Wrexham and Ellesmere.

6.—DIVIDENDS OF PRINCIPAL COMPANIES FROM THE EARLIEST PERIODS.

BELFAST AND NORTHERN COUNTIES.

	£	s.	d.		£	s.	d.		£	s.	d.
1849—Nov.	£0	18	0	1861—Dec.	£2	5	0	1873—Dec.	£3	15	0
1850—May	1	0	0	1862—June	2	5	0	1874—June	3	15	0
Nov.	1	10	0	Dec.	2	5	0	Dec.	3	10	0
1851—May	1	0	0	1863—June	2	0	0	1875—June	3	10	0
Nov.	1	2	0	Dec.	2	0	0	Dec.	3	15	0
1852—May	1	2	0	1864—June	1	10	0	1876—June	3	15	0
Nov.	1	7	0	Dec.	2	0	0	Dec.	3	15	0
1853—May	1	16	3	1865—June	1	15	0	1877—June	3	15	0
Nov.	2	4	0	Dec.	2	5	0	Dec	3	15	0
1854—May	2	4	0	1866—June	2	0	0	1878—June	3	10	0
Nov.	2	0	0	Dec.	2	10	0	Dec.	2	15	0
1855—May	2	10	0	1867—June	2	10	0	1879—June	1	15	0
Nov.	2	15	0	Dec.	2	10	0	Dec.	2	10	0
1856—May	3	10	0	1868—June	2	10	0	1880—June	2	2	0
Nov.	3	10	0	Dec.	2	10	0	Dec.	2	0	0
1857—May	2	10	0	1869—June	2	10	0	1881—June	1	5	0
Nov.	2	10	0	Dec.	2	10	0	Dec.	1	15	0
1858—May	2	5	0	1870—June	2	10	0	1882—June	2	0	0
Nov.	2	0	0	Dec.	2	10	0	Dec.	2	0	0
1859—May	2	5	0	1871—June	3	0	0	1883—June	1	15	0
Nov.	2	0	0	Dec.	3	10	0	Dec.	2	0	0
1860—May	2	0	0	1872—June	3	10	0	1884—June	1	5	0
Nov.	2	5	0	Dec.	3	15	0	Dec.	1	15	0
1861—June	2	5	0	1873—June	3	15	0				

CALEDONIAN.

1849	Jan.	£1	10	0
	July	Nil.		
1850	Jan.	Nil.		
	July	Nil.		
1851	Jan.	Nil.		
	July	Nil.		
1852	Jan.	0	5	0
	July	0	6	0
1853	Jan.	1	5	0
	July	1	0	0
1854	Jan.	1	10	0
	July	1	10	0
1855	Jan.	1	10	0
	July	1	10	0
1856	Jan.	1	0	0
	July	0	10	0
1857	Jan.	1	15	0
	July	1	15	0
1858	Jan.	2	10	0
	July	1	15	0
1859	Jan.	2	0	0
	July	1	17	6
1860	Jan.	2	10	0
	July	2	2	6
1861	Jan.	£2	15	0
	July	2	10	0
1862	Jan.	2	15	0
	July	2	10	0
1863	Jan.	3	0	0
	July	2	12	6
1864	Jan.	3	2	6
	July	3	5	0
1865	Jan.	3	12	6
	July	4	7	6
1866	Jan.	3	15	0
	July	3	12	6
1867	Jan.	3	5	0
	July	2	12	6
1868	Jan.	1	5	0
	July	0	15	0
1869	Jan.	1	17	6
	July	1	15	0
1870	Jan.	1	17	6
	July	1	15	6
1871	Jan.	2	2	6
	July	2	7	6
1872	Jan.	2	17	6
	July	2	10	0
1873	Jan.	£1	15	0
	July	1	15	0
1874	Jan.	2	2	6
	July	1	0	0
1875	Jan.	2	15	0
	July	3	2	6
1876	Jan.	3	12	6
	July	3	2	6
1877	Jan.	3	10	0
	July	3	2	6
1878	Jan.	3	0	0
	July	2	5	0
1879	Jan	2	2	6
	July	1	5	0
1880	Jan.	1	10	0
	July	1	17	6
1881	Jan.	1	5	0
	July	1	15	0
1882	Jan	2	7	6
	July	2	0	0
1883	Jan.	2	10	0
	July	2	0	0
1884	Jan.	2	10	0
	July	2	0	0

FURNESS.

1847	Feb.	£2	0	0
	Aug.	2	0	0
1848	March	1	0	0
	Aug.	Nil.		
1849	Feb.	Nil.		
	Aug.	1	0	0
1850	Feb.	1	0	0
	June	1	0	0
	Dec.	1	5	0
1851	June	1	10	0
	Dec.	1	10	0
1852	June	1	15	0
	Dec.	1	15	0
1853	June	2	0	0
	Dec.	2	10	0
1854	June	3	0	0
	Dec.	3	0	0
1855	June	3	0	0
	Dec.	3	0	0
1856	June	4	0	0
	Dec.	4	0	0
1857	June	4	0	0
	Dec.	4	0	0
1858	June	3	10	0
	Dec.	3	0	0
1859	June	3	10	0
1859	Dec.	£3	0	0
1860	June	3	10	0
	Dec.	4	0	0
1861	June	4	0	0
	Dec.	4	0	0
1862	June	4	0	0
	Dec.	4	0	0
1863	June	4	0	0
	Dec.	4	10	0
1864	June	5	0	0
	Dec.	5	0	0
1865	June	5	0	0
	Dec.	5	0	0
1866	June	5	0	0
	Dec.	5	0	0
1867	June	4	0	0
	Dec.	4	0	0
1868	June	4	0	0
	Dec.	3	0	0
1869	June	3	0	0
	Dec.	3	10	0
1870	June	4	0	0
	Dec.	4	10	0
1871	June	5	0	0
	Dec.	5	0	0
1872	June	5	0	0
1872	Dec.	£5	0	0
1873	June	5	0	0
	Dec.	4	10	0
1874	June	3	5	0
	Dec.	3	10	0
1875	June	3	5	0
	Dec	3	5	0
1876	June	3	0	0
	Dec.	3	5	0
1877	June	4	0	0
	Dec.	4	0	0
1878	June	3	10	0
	Dec.	2	10	0
1879	June	1	10	0
	Dec.	2	0	0
1880	June	3	5	0
	Dec.	3	10	0
1881	June	2	15	0
	Dec.	3	10	0
1882	June	3	15	0
	Dec.	3	5	0
1883	June	2	5	0
	Dec.	2	10	0
1884	June	1	10	0
	Dec.	3	10	0

GLASGOW AND SOUTH WESTERN.

Glasgow, Paisley, and Ayr.

1841	Jan.	£1	5	0
	July	1	5	0
1842	Jan.	1	15	0
	July	1	15	0
1843	Jan.	1	5	0
	July	1	5	0
1844	Jan.	2	0	0
	July	2	5	0
1845	Jan.	2	10	0
	July	3	0	0
1846	Jan.	3	10	0
	July	3	10	0
1847	Jan.	3	10	0
	July	3	10	0

Glasgow & South Western.

1848	Jan.	3	0	0
	July	2	0	0
1849	Jan.	£1	0	0
	July	Nil.		
1850	Jan.	1	5	0
	July	1	5	0
1851	Jan.	1	2	6
	July	1	0	0
1852	Jan.	1	0	0
	July	1	0	0
1853	Jan.	1	0	0
	July	1	10	0
1854	Jan.	1	5	0
	July	1	15	0
1855	Jan.	1	12	6
	July	1	17	6
1856	Jan.	1	15	0
	July	2	0	0
1857	Jan.	2	10	0
	July	2	10	0
1858	Jan.	2	5	0
1858	July	£2	0	0
1859	Jan.	2	5	0
	July	2	10	0
1860	Jan.	2	10	0
	July	2	12	6
1861	Jan.	2	15	0
	July	2	10	0
1862	Jan.	2	15	0
	July	2	10	0
1863	Jan.	2	10	0
	July	2	10	0
1864	Jan.	2	10	0
	July	2	17	6
1865	Jan.	2	17	6
	July	3	0	0
1866	Jan.	3	10	0
	July	3	10	0
1867	Jan.	3	2	6
	July	2	15	0

GLASGOW AND SOUTH WESTERN—*Continued.*

1868—Jan.	£2 10 0
July	2 5 0
1869—Jan.	2 5 0
July	2 10 0
1870—Jan.	2 15 0
July	2 15 0
1871—Jan.	2 15 0
July	2 10 0
1872—Jan.	2 17 6
July	3 0 0
1873—Jan.	3 5 0
July	2 10 0
1874—Jan	£2 0 0
July	1 5 0
1875—Jan.	1 15 0
July	2 0 0
1876—Jan.	1 17 6
July	2 0 0
1877—Jan.	2 2 6
July	2 2 6
1878—Jan.	2 0 0
July	1 15 0
1879—Jan.	1 10 0
1879—July	£1 7 6
1880—Jan.	2 0 0
July	2 10 0
1881—Jan.	2 10 0
July	2 10 0
1882—Jan.	2 15 0
July	2 15 0
1883—Jan.	2 15 0
July	2 12 6
1884—Jan.	2 12 6
July	2 7 6

GREAT EASTERN.

Eastern Counties.	
1841—Dec.	£0 17 0
1842—June	0 17 6
Dec.	0 12 0
1843—June	0 17 6
Dec.	0 12 6
1844—June	0 12 6
Dec.	1 5 0
1845—June	1 0 0
Dec.	3 0 0
1846—June	3 0 0
Dec.	3 5 0
1847—June	2 10 0
Dec.	2 0 0
1848—June	2 0 0
Dec.	Nil.
1849—June	0 10 0
Dec.	0 15 0
1850—June	0 10 0
Dec.	Nil.
1851—June	Nil.
Dec.	1 0 0
1852—June	1 0 0
Dec.	1 10 0
1853—June	1 5 0
Dec.	1 15 0
1854—June	0 17 6
Dec.	1 15 0
1855—June	1 2 6
Dec.	1 2 6
1856—June	0 10 0
Dec.	1 5 0
1857—June	1 5 0
Dec.	1 17 6
1858—June	1 3 9
Dec.	1 12 6
1859—June	1 1 3
Dec.	1 13 9
1860—June	1 1 3
Dec.	1 3 9
1861—June	0 16 3
Dec.	1 10 0
1862—June	£1 0 0
Norfolk.	
1845—Dec.	2 10 0
1846—June	3 0 0
Dec.	3 10 0
1847—June	3 0 0
Dec.	2 10 0
1848—June	2 0 0
Dec.	Nil.
1849—June	0 10 0
Dec.	0 15 0
1850—June	0 10 0
Dec.	Nil.
1851—June	Nil.
Dec.	1 0 0
1852—June	1 0 0
Dec.	1 10 0
1853—June	1 5 0
Dec.	1 15 0
1854—June	1 0 0
Dec.	1 10 0
1855—June	1 5 0
Dec	1 15 0
1856—June	1 5 0
Dec.	2 0 0
1857—June	1 10 0
Dec.	2 0 0
1858—June	1 7 6
Dec.	1 16 6
1859—June	1 4 0
Dec.	1 17 6
1860—June	1 10 0
Dec.	1 17 6
1861—June	1 10 0
Dec.	3 0 0
1862—June	2 10 0
Dec.	1 5 0
Great Eastern.	
1863—June	0 12 6
Dec.	1 5 0
1864—June	£0 12 6
Dec.	1 5 0
1865—June	Nil.
Dec.	Nil.
1866—June	Nil.
Dec.	Nil.
1867—June	Nil.
Dec.	Nil.
1868—June	Nil.
Dec.	Nil.
1869—June	0 5 0
Dec.	0 10 0
1870—June	Nil.
Dec.	0 17 6
1871—June	Nil.
Dec.	1 5 0
1872—June	0 5 0
Dec.	Nil.
1873—June	Nil.
Dec.	0 10 0
1874—June	Nil.
Dec.	Nil.
1875—June	Nil.
Dec.	0 10 0
1876—June	Nil.
Dec.	0 15 0
1877—June	Nil.
Dec.	1 2 6
1878—June	Nil.
Dec.	1 7 6
1879—June	Nil.
Dec.	1 7 6
1880—June	Nil.
Dec.	1 10 0
1881—June	Nil.
Dec.	1 12 6
1882—June	0 5 0
Dec.	1 15 0
1883—June	Nil.
Dec.	1 7 6
1884—June	0 7 6
Dec.	1 12 6

GREAT NORTH OF SCOTLAND.

1855	£1 5 0
1856	1 5 0
1857	4 10 0
1858	4 11 0
1858—July	2 10 0
1859—Jan.	3 0 0
1860—July	3 10 0
1861—Jan.	3 5 0
July	3 10 0
1862—Jan.	3 15 0
July	3 10 0
1863—Jan.	3 10 0
July	3 10 0
1864—Jan.	2 10 0
July	2 10 0
1865—Jan	Nil.
July	Nil.
1866—Jan.	Nil.
July	Nil.
1867—Jan.	Nil.
July	Nil.
1868—Jan.	Nil.
July	Nil.
1869—Jan.	Nil.
July	Nil.
1870—Jan.	Nil.
July	Nil.
1871—Jan.	Nil.
July	Nil.
1872—Jan.	Nil.
July	Nil.
1873—Jan.	Nil.
July	Nil.
1874—Jan.	£0 5 0
July	1 5 0
1875—Jan.	0 2 6
July	1 10 0
1876—Jan.	£1 0 0
July	1 10 0
1877—Jan.	0 15 0
July	1 7 6
1878—Jan.	0 15 0
July	Nil.
1879—Jan.	Nil.
July	0 10 0
1880—Jan.	0 10 0
July	Nil.
1881—Jan.	Nil.
July	Nil.
1882—Jan.	Nil.
July	Nil.
1883—Jan.	Nil.
July	Nil.
1884—Jan.	0 10 0
July	0 10 0

GREAT NORTHERN.

1851—June	....	£0	15	0
	Dec.	1	5	0
1852—June	....	1	0	0
	Dec.	1	5	0
1853—June	....	1	5	0
	Dec.	2	7	6
1854—June	....	1	7	6
	Dec.	2	17	6
1855—June	....	1	2	6
	Dec.	3	0	0
1856—June	....	1	15	0
	Dec.		Nil.	
1857—June	....	0	6	0
	Dec.	2	15	3
1858—June	....	1	13	9
	Dec.	3	1	3
1859—June	....	1	13	9
	Dec.	3	10	0
1860—June	....	2	5	0
	Dec.	3	3	9
1861—June	....	1	17	6
	Dec.	3	17	6
1862—June	....	2	5	0
	Dec.	£4	5	0
1863—June	....	2	2	6
	Dec.	4	7	6
1864—June	....	2	15	0
	Dec.	4	7	6
1865—June	....	2	15	0
	Dec.	4	7	6
1866—June	....	2	10	0
	Dec.	4	0	0
1867—June	....	2	5	0
	Dec.	3	15	0
1868—June	....	2	2	6
	Dec.	3	15	0
1869—June	....	2	2	6
	Dec.	3	17	6
1870—June	....	2	10	0
	Dec.	4	2	6
1871—June	....	2	15	0
	Dec.	4	7	6
1872—June	....	3	0	0
	Dec.	4	2	6
1873—June	....	3	0	0
	Dec.	4	5	0
1874—June	....	£2	15	0
	Dec.	4	2	6
1875—June	....	2	15	0
	Dec.	3	15	0
1876—June	....	2	2	6
	Dec.	3	7	6
1877—June	....	2	0	0
	Dec.	3	5	0
1878—June	....	2	0	0
	Dec.	3	5	0
1879—June	....	2	0	0
	Dec.	3	2	6
1880—June	....	2	0	0
	Dec.	3	2	6
1881—June	....	2	0	0
	Dec.	3	5	0
1882—June	....	2	0	0
	Dec.	3	0	0
1883—June	....	1	12	6
	Dec.	3	0	0
1884—June	....	1	12	6
	Dec.	3	0	0

GREAT NORTHERN (IRELAND).

Dublin and Drogheda.

1850—June	....	£0	16	0
	Dec.	1	0	0
1851—June	....	0	15	0
	Dec.	1	0	0
1852—June	....	1	1	4
	Dec.	1	17	0
1853—June	....	1	13	4
	Dec.	2	5	0
1854—June	....	2	0	0
	Dec.	2	0	0
1855—June	....	2	0	0
	Dec.	2	5	0
1856—June	....	2	5	0
	Dec.	2	5	0
1857—June	....	2	5	0
	Dec.	2	5	0
1858—June	....	2	5	0
	Dec.	2	5	0
1859—June	....	2	7	6
	Dec.	2	10	0
1860—June	....	2	10	0
	Dec.	2	10	0
1861—June	....	2	10	0
	Dec.	2	10	0
1862—June	....	2	10	0
	Dec.	2	10	0
1863—June	....	2	0	0
	Dec.	2	0	0
1864—June	....	2	0	0
	Dec.	2	0	0
1865—June	....	2	5	0
	Dec.	2	10	0
1866—June	....	2	5	0
	Dec.	2	5	0
1867—June	....	2	7	6
	Dec.	2	7	6
1868—June	....	2	10	0
	Dec.	2	10	0
1869—June	....	2	10	0
	Dec.	2	10	0
1870—June	....	2	11	3
	Dec.	2	11	3
1871—June	....	2	15	0
	Dec.	2	17	6
1872—June	....	2	15	0
	Dec.	3	0	0
1873—June	....	3	0	0
	Dec.	£3	0	0
1874—June	....	3	0	0
	Dec.	3	0	0

Dublin and Belfast Junction.

1850—June	....	1	2	0
	Dec.	1	2	0
1851—June	....	1	2	0
	Dec.	1	13	4
1852—June	....	1	13	4
	Dec.	2	9	0
1853—June	....	2	10	0
	Dec.	2	10	0
1854—June	....	2	10	0
	Dec.	2	10	0
1855—June	....	2	10	0
	Dec.	2	10	0
1856—June	....	2	10	0
	Dec.	2	10	0
1857—June	....	2	0	0
	Dec.	2	0	0
1858—June	....	2	0	0
	Dec.	2	0	0
1859—June	....	2	0	0
	Dec.	2	2	6
1860—June	....	2	2	6
	Dec.	2	2	6
1861—June	....	2	2	6
	Dec.	2	2	6
1862—June	....	2	2	6
	Dec.	2	0	0
1863—June	....	2	0	0
	Dec.	2	0	0
1864—June	....	1	12	6
	Dec.	1	15	0
1865—June	....	1	15	0
	Dec.	2	5	0
1866—June	....	2	0	0
	Dec.	2	0	0
1867—June	....	2	0	0
	Dec.	2	0	0
1868—June	....	2	0	0
	Dec.	2	2	6
1869—June	....	1	17	6
	Dec.	2	0	0
1870—June	....	2	0	0
	Dec.	2	5	0
1871—June	....	2	5	0
	Dec.	£2	5	0
1872—June	....	2	5	0
	Dec.	2	5	0
1873—June	....	2	5	0
	Dec.	2	5	0
1874—June	....	2	5	0
	Dec.	2	5	0

Ulster.

1840—Feb.	....	0	12	6
	Aug.	0	17	6
1841—Feb.	....	0	13	4
	Aug.	0	18	0
1842—Feb.	....	0	16	0
	Aug.	1	16	0
1843—Feb.	....	1	16	0
	Aug.	2	1	7
1844—Feb.	....	2	10	4
	Aug.	2	10	8
1845—Feb.	....	2	15	0
	Aug.	2	16	3
1846—Feb.	....	2	11	6
	Aug.	2	10	0
1847—Feb.	....	2	10	0
	Aug.	3	0	0
1848—Feb.	....	2	4	1
	Aug.	1	8	9
1849—Feb.	....	1	5	4
	Aug.	1	6	9
1850—Feb.	....	1	4	3
	Aug.	1	18	6
1851—Feb.	....	2	0	7
	Aug.	2	2	10
1852—Feb.	....	2	5	0
	Aug.	2	3	0
1853—Feb.	....	2	11	0
	Aug.	2	13	0
1854—Feb.	....	2	16	6
	Aug.	3	1	0
1855—Feb.	....	2	7	6
	June	2	5	11
	Dec.	3	0	4
1856—June	....	2	13	0
	Dec.	3	0	0
1857—June	....	3	0	0
	Dec.	3	0	0
1858—June	....	2	15	0
	Dec.	2	15	0

GREAT NORTHERN (IRELAND)—*Continued.*

1859—June	£2	10	0
Dec.	2	15	0
1860—June	2	10	0
Dec.	2	15	0
1861—June	2	10	0
Dec.	2	15	0
1862—June	2	10	0
Dec.	2	10	0
1863—June	2	10	0
Dec.	2	10	0
1864—June	2	5	0
Dec.	2	5	0
1865—June	2	0	0
Dec.	2	5	0
1866—June	1	16	0
Dec.	2	0	0
1867—June	2	0	0
Dec.	2	0	0
1868—June	£2	5	0
Dec.	2	5	6
1869—June	2	5	0
Dec.	2	5	6
1870—June	2	10	0
Dec.	2	10	0
1871—June	3	0	0
Dec.	3	5	0
1872—June	3	5	0
Dec.	3	10	0
1873—June	3	15	0
Dec.	3	15	0
1874—June	3	5	6
Dec.	3	10	6
1875—June	3	5	0
Dec.	3	15	0
Great Northern (Ireland).			
1876—June	3	0	0
1876—Dec.	£3	0	0
1877—June	3	0	0
Dec.	3	0	0
1878—June	3	0	0
Dec.	2	15	0
1879—June	2	5	0
Dec.	2	5	0
1880—June	2	12	6
Dec.	2	7	6
1881—June	2	0	0
Dec.	2	7	6
1882—June	2	7	6
Dec.	2	12	6
1883—June	2	6	0
Dec.	2	10	0
1884—June	2	2	6
Dec.	2	7	6

GREAT SOUTHERN AND WESTERN (IRELAND).

1850—June	£1	10	0
Dec.	1	15	0
1851—June	1	12	6
Dec.	1	16	1
1852—June	2	0	0
Dec.	2	5	0
1853—June	2	5	0
Dec.	2	5	0
1854—June	2	0	0
Dec.	2	0	0
1855—June	2	10	0
Dec.	2	10	0
1856—June	3	0	0
Dec.	3	0	0
1857—June	2	10	0
Dec.	2	10	0
1858—June	2	10	0
Dec.	2	10	0
1859—June	2	10	0
Dec.	2	10	0
1860—June	2	10	0
Dec.	2	10	0
1861—June	2	10	0
Dec.	2	10	0
1862—June	£2	10	0
Dec.	2	10	0
1863—June	2	2	6
Dec.	2	5	0
1864—June	2	5	0
Dec.	2	5	0
1865—June	2	5	0
Dec.	2	10	0
1866—June	2	10	0
Dec.	2	5	0
1867—June	2	10	0
Dec.	2	5	0
1868—June	2	10	0
Dec.	2	5	0
1869—June	2	10	0
Dec.	2	10	0
1870—June	2	10	0
Dec.	2	10	0
1871—June	2	10	0
Dec.	2	15	0
1872—June	2	15	0
Dec.	3	0	0
1873—June	3	15	0
1873—Dec.	£3	15	0
1874—June	2	10	0
Dec.	2	10	0
1875—June	2	12	6
Dec.	2	15	0
1876—June	2	15	0
Dec.	3	0	0
1877—June	2	15	0
Dec.	2	15	0
1878—June	2	15	0
Dec.	2	10	0
1879—June	2	0	0
Dec.	2	0	0
1880—June	2	7	6
Dec.	2	2	6
1881—June	1	17	6
Dec.	2	2	6
1882—June	2	5	0
Dec.	2	10	0
1883—June	2	10	0
Dec.	2	10	0
1884—June	2	2	6
Dec.	2	7	6

GREAT WESTERN.

1840—Dec.	£1	10	0
1841—June	1	10	0
Dec.	3	0	0
1842—June	3	0	0
Dec.	3	10	0
1843—June	2	10	0
Dec.	3	0	0
1844—June	3	10	0
Dec.	4	0	0
1845—June	4	0	0
Dec.	4	0	0
1846—June	4	0	0
Dec.	4	0	0
1847—June	4	0	0
Dec.	3	10	0
1848—June	3	10	0
Dec.	3	0	0
1849—June	2	0	0
Dec.	2	0	0
1850—June	2	0	0
Dec.	2	0	0
1851—June	2	0	0
Dec.	2	10	0
1852—June	2	0	0
Dec.	2	0	0
1853—June	2	0	0
Dec.	2	0	0
1854—June	£1	10	0
Dec.	1	10	0
1855—June	1	0	0
Dec.	1	5	0
1856—June	1	5	0
Dec.	1	10	0
1857—June	0	10	0
Dec.	1	0	0
1858—June	Nil.		
Dec.	1	5	0
1859—June	1	0	0
Dec.	1	15	0
1860—June	1	10	0
Dec.	1	15	0
1861—June	1	2	6
Dec.	1	10	0
1862—June	0	5	0
Dec.	1	10	0
1863—July	1	0	0
1864—Jan.	1	10	0
July	1	10	0
1865—Jan.	1	12	6
July	1	0	0
1866—Jan.	1	0	0
July	1	0	0
1867—Jan.	0	10	0
July	0	12	6
1868—Jan.	£0	15	0
July	0	12	6
1869—Jan.	0	15	0
July	1	0	0
1870—Jan.	1	12	3
West Midland (Oxford).			
1861—Dec.	0	7	6
1862—June	Nil.		
Dec.	0	15	0
1863—June	0	2	6
1864—Jan.	0	17	6
July	1	2	6
1865—Jan.	1	0	0
July	0	13	3
1866—Jan.	0	9	3
July	0	17	0
1867—Jan.	0	2	6
July	0	2	6
1868—Jan.	0	6	3
July	0	2	6
1869—Jan.	0	7	6
July	0	10	0
1870—Jan.	0	18	0
West Midland (Newport).			
1861—Dec.	0	5	0
1862—June	Nil.		

GREAT WESTERN—*Continued.*

	£	s.	d.
1862—Dec.	£0	5	0
1863—June	Nil.		
1864—Jan.	0	15	0
July	0	12	6
1865—Jan.	0	17	6
July	0	8	9
1866—Jan.	0	8	9
July	0	17	0
1867—Jan.	0	3	9
July	0	5	0
1868—Jan.	0	7	6
July	0	5	0
1869—Jan.	0	8	9
July	0	10	0
1870—Jan.	0	16	6

South Wales.

	£	s.	d.
1851—Dec.	0	15	0
1852—June	Nil.		
Dec.	1	0	0
1853—June	1	0	0
Dec.	1	10	0
1854—June	Nil.		
Dec.	1	10	0
1855—June	1	10	0
Dec.	1	10	0
1856—June	1	15	0
Dec.	2	0	0
1857—June	1	12	6
Dec.	1	15	0
1858—June	1	10	0
Dec.	1	5	0
1859—June	1	2	6
Dec.	1	7	6
1860—June	1	0	0
Dec.	1	10	0
1861—June	1	7	6
Dec.	1	10	0
1862—June	1	12	6
Dec.	1	12	6
1863—June	1	15	0
1864—Jan.	1	10	0
July	1	12	6
1865—Jan.	1	12	6
July	1	12	6
1866—Jan.	1	12	6
July	1	12	6
1867—Jan.	1	12	6
July	1	12	6
1868—Jan.	1	12	6
July	1	15	0
1869—Jan.	1	12	6
July	1	12	6
1870—Jan.	1	12	9

Bristol and Exeter.

	£	s.	d.
1842—Dec.	2	0	0
1843—June	2	0	0
Dec.	2	0	0
1844—June	2	0	0
Dec.	2	0	0
1845—June	2	0	0
Dec.	2	0	0
1846—June	2	0	0
Dec.	2	5	0
1847—June	2	5	0
Dec.	2	5	0
1848—June	2	5	0
Dec.	1	17	6
1849—June	1	15	0
Dec.	1	15	0
1850—June	1	8	0
Dec.	1	15	0
1851—June	£2	0	0
Dec.	2	5	0
1852—June	2	5	0
Dec.	2	5	0
1853—June	2	5	0
Dec.	2	5	0
1854—June	2	5	0
Dec.	2	5	0
1855—June	2	5	0
Dec.	2	5	0
1856—June	2	5	0
Dec.	2	10	0
1857—June	2	10	0
Dec.	2	10	0
1858—June	2	10	0
Dec.	2	10	0
1859—June	2	15	0
Dec.	3	0	0
1860—June	3	0	0
Dec.	2	15	0
1861—June	2	2	6
Dec.	2	10	0
1862—June	1	10	0
Dec.	2	10	0
1863—June	2	0	0
Dec.	2	10	0
1864—June	2	5	0
Dec.	2	15	0
1865—June	2	5	0
Dec.	2	15	0
1866—June	2	5	0
Dec.	2	5	0
1867—June	2	0	0
Dec.	2	7	6
1868—June	1	17	6
Dec.	2	7	6
1869—June	1	10	0
Dec.	2	10	0
1870—June	2	0	0
Dec.	2	15	0
1871—June	2	5	0
Dec.	3	5	0
1872—June	2	15	0
Dec.	3	10	0
1873—June	2	17	6
Dec.	3	12	6
1874—June	2	12	6
Dec.	3	0	0
1875—June	2	0	0

Monmouthshire.

	£	s.	d.
1849—March	2	10	0
Sept.	2	10	0
1850—March	2	10	0
June	Nil.		
Dec.	2	10	0
1851—June	2	0	0
Dec.	2	0	0
1852—June	2	0	0
Dec.	2	10	0
1853—June	3	0	0
Dec.	3	0	0
1854—June	2	10	0
Dec.	2	0	0
1855—June	Nil.		
Dec.	1	10	0
1856—June	2	0	0
Dec.	2	10	0
1857—June	2	10	0
Dec.	2	10	0
1858—June	1	15	0
Dec.	2	10	0
1859—June	2	10	0
1859—Dec.	£2	10	0
1860—June	2	10	0
Dec.	3	0	0
1861—June	2	15	0
Dec.	3	0	0
1862—June	2	15	0
Dec.	2	15	0
1863—June	2	15	0
Dec.	3	0	0
1864—June	3	5	0
Dec.	3	5	0
1865—June	3	5	0
Dec.	3	5	0
1866—June	3	0	0
Dec.	2	15	0
1867—June	2	10	0
Dec.	2	10	0
1868—June	2	0	0
Dec.	2	0	0
1869—June	2	5	0
Dec.	2	10	0
1870—June	2	15	0
Dec.	3	0	0
1871—June	2	15	0
Dec.	3	10	0
1872—June	3	10	0
Dec.	3	0	0
1873—June	2	10	0
Dec.	4	0	0
1874—June	3	15	0
Dec.	3	5	0
1875—June	1	0	0
Dec.	3	5	0
1876—June	3	5	0
Dec.	3	5	0
1877—June	3	5	0
Dec.	3	5	0
1878—June	3	5	0
Dec.	3	5	0
1879—June	3	5	0
Dec.	3	5	0

Consols.

	£	s.	d.
1870—July	1	10	0
1871—Jan.	1	17	6
July	2	5	6
1872—Jan.	2	13	9
July	2	15	0
1873—Jan.	3	5	0
July	2	17	6
1874—Jan.	3	7	6
July	2	0	0
1875—Jan.	2	10	0
July	1	17	6
1876—Jan.	2	7	6
July	1	17	6
1877—Jan.	2	2	6
July	1	15	0
1878—Jan	2	2	6
July	1	15	0
1879—Jan.	2	0	0
July	1	15	0
1880—Jan.	2	7	6
July	2	12	6
1881—Jan.	2	10	0
June	1	17	6
Dec.	3	12	6
1882—June	2	12	6
Dec.	3	12	6
1883—June	2	12	6
Dec.	3	15	6
1884—June	2	10	0
Dec.	3	10	0

HIGHLAND.

Inverness and Aberdeen.

1859—May	£1	5	0
Nov.	1	15	0
1860—May	2	0	0
Nov.	2	0	0
1861—May	1	15	0
Nov.	2	2	6
1862—May	1	15	0
Nov.	2	10	0
1863—May	2	0	0
Nov.	2	10	6
1864—May	2	2	0
Nov.	2	0	0
1865—May	2	0	0

Inverness and Perth.

1864—May	1	10	0
Nov.	1	15	0
1865—May	2	0	0

Highland.

1865—Aug.	£1	0	0
1866—Feb.	0	10	0
Aug.	0	10	0
1867—Feb.	0	10	0
Aug.	1	0	0
1868—Feb.	1	10	0
Aug.	1	10	0
1869—Feb.	1	2	6
Aug.	1	12	6
1870—Feb.	1	0	0
Aug.	2	0	0
1871—Feb.	2	0	0
Aug.	2	10	0
1872—Feb.	3	0	0
Aug.	3	0	0
1873—Feb.	3	0	0
Aug.	2	10	0
1874—Feb.	2	0	0
Aug	2	10	0
1875—Feb.	£1	0	0
Aug.	2	10	0
1876—Feb.	2	7	6
Aug.	2	10	0
1877—Feb.	2	10	0
Aug.	2	10	0
1878—Feb.	2	10	0
Aug.	2	10	0
1879—Feb.	1	15	0
Aug.	2	2	6
1880—Feb.	1	15	0
Aug.	2	10	0
1881—Feb.	1	15	0
Aug.	2	10	0
1882—Feb.	1	15	0
Aug.	2	10	0
1883—Feb.	1	15	0
Aug.	2	12	6
1884—Feb.	1	15	0
Aug.	2	10	0

LANCASHIRE AND YORKSHIRE.

Manchester and Leeds.

1841—Dec.	£3	0	0
1842—June	2	15	0
Dec.	2	15	0
1843—June	2	15	0
Dec.	3	10	0
1844—June	3	10	0
Dec.	4	0	0
1845—June	4	0	0
Dec.	4	0	0
1846—June	3	10	0
Dec.	3	10	0

East Lancashire.

1849—Dec.	1	0	0
1850—June	0	10	0
Dec.	1	0	0
1851—June	1	0	0
Dec.	1	5	0
1852—June	1	0	0
Dec.	1	10	0
1853—June	1	10	0
Dec.	1	15	0
1854—June	1	15	0
Dec.	2	0	0
1855—June	1	15	0
Dec.	1	15	0
1856—June	2	0	0
Dec.	2	10	0
1857—June	2	10	0
Dec.	2	2	6
1858—June	1	17	6
Dec.	2	0	0

Lancashire and Yorkshire.

1847—June	3	10	0
Dec.	3	10	0
1848—June	£3	0	0
Dec.	2	10	0
1849—June	2	0	0
Dec.	1	10	0
1850—June	1	0	0
Dec.	1	0	0
1851—June	1	0	0
Dec.	1	10	0
1852—June	1	10	0
Dec.	1	10	0
1853—June	1	12	6
Dec.	1	15	0
1854—June	1	15	0
Dec.	2	0	0
1855—June	2	0	0
Dec.	2	2	6
1856—June	2	5	0
Dec.	2	10	0
1857—June	2	10	0
Dec.	2	2	6
1858—June	1	17	6
Dec.	2	0	0
1859—June	2	5	0
Dec.	2	10	0
1860—June	2	15	0
Dec.	3	0	0
1861—June	2	15	0
Dec.	2	10	0
1862—June	1	17	6
Dec.	2	0	0
1863—June	2	2	6
Dec.	2	7	6
1864—June	2	17	6
Dec.	3	0	0
1865—June	2	15	0
Dec.	3	2	6
1866—June	3	7	6
1866—Dec.	£3	7	6
1867—June	3	5	0
Dec.	3	5	0
1868—June	3	7	6
Dec.	3	7	6
1869—June	3	7	6
Dec.	3	7	6
1870—June	3	10	0
Dec.	3	10	0
1871—June	3	17	6
Dec.	4	0	0
1872—June	3	16	3
Dec.	4	11	3
1873—June	3	12	6
Dec	3	10	0
1874—June	3	0	0
Dec.	3	5	0
1875—June	3	0	0
Dec.	3	0	0
1876—June	2	15	0
Dec.	3	2	6
1877—June	2	17	6
Dec.	3	5	0
1878—June	2	7	6
Dec.	3	0	0
1879—June	2	0	0
Dec	2	12	6
1880—June	2	10	0
Dec.	2	17	6
1881 June	2	2	6
Dec.	2	17	6
1882—June	2	7	6
Dec.	2	10	0
1883—June	2	0	0
Dec.	2	7	6
1884—June	2	0	0
Dec.	2	5	0

LONDON, BRIGHTON, AND SOUTH COAST.

1842—June	£1	0	0
Dec.	2	0	0
1843—June	Nil.		
Dec.	2	0	0
1844—June	1	4	0
Dec.	3	0	0
1845—June	2	0	0
Dec.	3	10	0
1846—June	2	10	0
1846—Dec.	£3	10	0
1847—June	2	0	0
Dec.	2	0	0
1848—June	1	6	0
Dec.	2	6	0
1849—June	1	9	0
Dec.	2	8	0
1850—June	1	10	0
Dec.	2	17	0
1851—June	£1	16	0
Dec.	3	0	0
1852—June	1	17	0
Dec.	2	17	0
1853—June	1	16	0
Dec.	3	4	0
1854—June	2	6	0
Dec.	3	4	0
1855—June	2	2	0

LONDON, BRIGHTON, AND SOUTH COAST—*Continued.*

1855—	Dec.	£2	18	0
1856—	June	2	10	0
	Dec.	3	10	0
1857—	June	2	10	0
	Dec.	3	10	0
1858—	June	2	10	0
	Dec.	3	10	0
1859—	June	2	10	0
	Dec.	3	10	0
1860—	June	2	10	0
	Dec.	3	10	0
1861—	June	2	10	0
	Dec.	3	10	0
1862—	June	2	10	0
	Dec.	3	10	0
1863—	June	2	10	0
	Dec.	2	10	0
1864—	June	2	10	0
	Dec.	3	0	0
1865—	June	2	10	0
1865—	Dec.	£3	5	0
1866—	June	2	0	0
	Dec.	2	0	0
1867—	June	Nil.		
	Dec.	Nil.		
1868—	June	Nil.		
	Dec.	0	12	6
1869—	June	Nil.		
	Dec.	0	10	0
1870—	June	Nil.		
	Dec.	0	15	0
1871—	June	0	7	6
	Dec.	2	2	6
1872—	June	0	15	0
	Dec.	2	7	6
1873—	June	0	15	0
	Dec.	2	10	0
1874—	June	0	15	0
	Dec.	3	5	0
1875—	June	1	7	6
1875—	Dec.	£3	12	6
1876—	June	1	7	6
	Dec.	3	12	6
1877—	June	1	10	0
	Dec.	4	2	6
1878—	June	2	2	6
	Dec.	4	2	6
1879—	June	1	10	0
	Dec.	4	10	0
1880—	June	2	7	6
	Dec.	4	2	6
1881—	June	1	12	6
	Dec.	4	2	6
1882—	June	1	5	0
	Dec.	3	2	6
1883—	June	1	0	0
	Dec.	3	10	0
1884—	June	1	0	0
	Dec.	3	10	0

LONDON AND NORTH WESTERN.

London and Birmingham.

1838—	Dec.	£3	17	6
1839—	June	3	17	6
	Dec.	4	8	9
1840—	June	4	8	9
	Dec.	4	8	9
1841—	June	4	14	6
	Dec.	5	5	6
1842—	June	5	11	0
	Dec.	5	11	0
1843—	June	5	0	0
	Dec.	5	0	0
1844—	June	5	0	0
	Dec.	5	0	0
1845—	June	5	0	0
	Dec.	5	0	0

Liverpool and Manchester.

1841—	Dec.	5	0	0
1842—	June	5	0	0
	Dec.	5	0	0
1843—	June	5	0	0
	Dec.	5	0	0
1844—	June	5	0	0
	Dec.	4	10	0
1845—	June	5	0	0

Grand Junction.

1841—	Dec.	6	0	0
1842—	June	5	0	0
	Dec.	5	0	0
1843—	June	5	0	0
	Dec.	5	0	0
1844—	June	5	0	0
	Dec.	5	0	0
1845—	June	5	0	0
	Dec.	5	0	0

Manchester & Birmingham.

1842—	Dec.	2	10	0
1843—	June	1	17	6
	Dec.	2	5	0
1844—	June	2	10	0
	Dec.	2	10	0
1845—	June	2	10	0
	Dec.	4	0	0

Whitehaven, Cleator, and Egremont.

1857—	June	3	0	0
	Dec.	3	10	0
1858—	June	£3	10	0
	Dec.	3	10	0
1859—	June	4	0	0
	Dec.	4	0	0
1860—	June	5	0	0
	Dec.	5	0	0
1861—	June	5	0	0
	Dec.	5	0	0
1862—	June	5	0	0
	Dec.	5	0	0
1863—	June	7	10	0
	Dec.	6	0	0
1864—	June	7	0	0
	Dec.	6	0	0
1865—	June	5	0	0
	Dec.	5	0	0
1866—	June	5	0	0
	Dec.	4	0	0
1867—	June	4	10	0
	Dec.	5	0	0
1868—	June	5	0	0
	Dec.	4	0	0
1869—	June	5	0	0
	Dec.	5	0	0
1870—	June	5	10	0
	Dec.	7	0	0
1871—	June	6	10	0
	Dec.	6	10	0
1872—	June	6	0	0
	Dec.	6	0	0
1873—	June	5	15	0
	Dec.	5	10	0
1874—	June	4	5	0
	Dec.	4	10	0
1875—	June	6	0	0
	Dec.	5	5	0
1876—	June	5	10	0

London and North Western.

1846—	June	5	0	0
	Dec.	5	0	0
1847—	June	4	10	0
	Dec.	4	0	0
1848—	June	3	10	0
	Dec.	3	10	0
1849—	June	3	10	0
	Dec.	2	10	0
1850—	June	2	10	0
	Dec.	2	15	0
1851—	June	2	15	0
1851—	Dec.	£3	0	0
1852—	June	2	15	0
	Dec.	2	10	0
1853—	June	2	10	0
	Dec.	2	10	0
1854—	June	2	10	0
	Dec.	2	10	0
1855—	June	2	7	6
	Dec.	2	12	6
1856—	June	2	10	0
	Dec.	3	0	0
1857—	June	2	10	0
	Dec.	2	10	0
1858—	June	1	17	6
	Dec.	2	2	6
1859—	June	2	2	6
	Dec.	2	12	6
1860—	June	2	10	0
	Dec.	2	12	6
1861—	June	1	17	6
	Dec.	2	7	6
1862—	June	1	17	6
	Dec.	2	15	0
1863—	June	2	2	6
	Dec.	3	0	0
1864—	June	2	17	6
	Dec.	3	10	0
1865—	June	3	0	0
	Dec.	3	12	6
1866—	June	3	0	0
	Dec.	3	7	6
1867—	June	2	12	6
	Dec.	3	7	6
1868—	June	2	12	6
	Dec.	3	7	6
1869—	June	2	15	0
	Dec.	3	10	0
1870—	June	3	0	0
	Dec.	3	12	6
1871—	June	3	7	6
	Dec.	4	7	6
1872—	June	3	10	0
	Dec.	4	5	0
1873—	June	3	10	0
	Dec.	4	0	0
1874—	June	3	5	0
	Dec.	3	12	6
1875—	June	3	2	6
	Dec.	3	12	6
1876—	June	3	0	0

LONDON AND NORTH WESTERN—*Continued.*

	£	s.	d.
1876—Dec.	£3	12	6
1877—June	3	0	0
Dec.	3	12	6
1878—June	3	0	0
Dec.	3	10	0
1879—June	2	15	0
1879—Dec.	£2	15	0
1880—June	3	7	6
Dec.	4	0	0
1881—June	3	5	0
Dec.	4	0	0
1882—June	3	10	0
1882—Dec.	£4	0	0
1883—June	3	10	0
Dec.	4	0	0
1884—June	3	0	0
Dec.	3	15	0

LONDON AND SOUTH WESTERN.

	£	s.	d.
1839—June	£1	10	0
Dec.	1	10	6
1840—June	2	0	0
Dec.	3	0	0
1841—June	3	0	0
Dec.	3	0	0
1842—June	3	0	0
Dec.	3	5	0
1843—June	3	0	0
Dec.	3	10	0
1844—June	3	5	0
Dec.	4	0	0
1845—June	3	15	0
Dec.	4	5	0
1846—June	3	15	0
Dec.	4	5	3
1847—June	3	15	0
Dec.	4	0	0
1848—June	3	0	0
Dec.	2	10	0
1849—June	1	12	6
Dec.	1	12	6
1850—June	1	10	0
Dec.	2	0	0
1851—June	1	15	0
Dec.	2	12	6
1852—June	1	12	6
Dec.	2	0	0
1853—June	1	15	0
Dec.	2	10	0
1854—June	2	2	6
1854—Dec.	£2	10	0
1855—June	2	3	9
Dec.	2	16	3
1856—June	2	15	0
Dec.	3	5	0
1857—June	2	7	6
Dec.	2	12	6
1858—June	2	2	6
Dec.	2	17	6
1859—June	2	2	6
Dec.	2	12	6
1860—June	2	2	6
Dec.	2	12	6
1861—June	2	0	0
Dec.	2	15	0
1862—June	2	0	0
Dec.	3	0	0
1863—June	2	5	0
Dec.	2	15	0
1864—June	2	5	0
Dec.	2	15	0
1865—June	2	5	0
Dec.	2	15	0
1866—June	2	0	0
Dec.	2	5	0
1867—June	1	17	6
Dec.	2	12	6
1868—June	2	0	0
Dec.	2	12	6
1869—June	2	0	0
Dec.	2	12	6
1870—June	£2	5	0
Dec.	2	17	6
1871—June	2	7	6
Dec.	3	2	6
1872—June	2	7	6
Dec.	3	5	6
1873—June	2	7	6
Dec.	3	2	6
1874—June	2	7	6
Dec.	3	2	6
1875—June	2	7	6
Dec.	3	5	0
1876—June	2	7	6
Dec.	3	5	0
1877—June	2	7	6
Dec.	3	7	6
1878—June	2	7	6
Dec.	3	17	6
1879—June	2	5	0
Dec.	3	7	6
1880—June	2	7	6
Dec.	3	12	6
1881—June	2	3	9
Dec.	3	10	0
1882—June	2	5	0
Dec.	3	10	0
1883—June	2	2	6
Dec.	3	10	0
1884—June	2	2	6
Dec.	3	7	6

MANCHESTER, SHEFFIELD, AND LINCOLNSHIRE.

	£	s.	d.
1846—Dec.	£2	10	0
1847—June	2	10	0
Dec.	2	10	0
1848—June	2	10	0
Dec.	Nil.		
1849—June	Nil.		
Dec.	Nil.		
1850—June	Nil.		
Dec.	Nil.		
1851—June	Nil.		
Dec.	Nil.		
1852—June	Nil.		
Dec.	Nil.		
1853—June	Nil.		
Dec.	Nil.		
1854—June	Nil.		
Dec.	0	2	6
1855—June	Nil.		
Dec.	0	5	0
1856—June	0	5	0
Dec.	0	10	0
1857—June	0	10	0
Dec.	0	10	0
1858—June	Nil.		
Dec.	Nil.		
1859—June	0	4	0
1859—Dec.	£0	10	0
1860—June	0	10	0
Dec.	0	15	0
1861—June	0	7	6
Dec.	0	12	6
1862—June	Nil.		
Dec.	Nil.		
1863—June	Nil.		
Dec.	0	15	0
1864—June	1	7	6
Dec.	1	5	0
1865—June	0	10	0
Dec.	1	15	0
1866—June	1	0	0
Dec.	1	10	0
1867—June	0	10	0
Dec.	1	0	0
1868—June	Nil.		
Dec.	1	5	0
1869—June	1	0	0
Dec.	1	5	0
1870—June	0	10	0
Dec.	1	5	0
1871—June	0	15	0
Dec.	2	0	0
1872—June	1	5	0
1872—Dec.	£2	5	0
1873—June	0	15	0
Dec.	1	10	0
1874—June	0	5	0
Dec.	1	10	0
1875—June	0	10	0
Dec.	2	0	0
1876—June	0	7	6
Dec.	1	17	6
1877—June	0	10	0
Dec.	2	7	6
1878—June	0	12	6
Dec.	2	7	6
1879—June	0	7	6
Dec.	1	15	0
1880—June	1	0	0
Dec.	2	0	0
1881—June	Nil.		
Dec.	2	0	0
1882—June	0	10	0
Dec.	2	0	0
1883—June	0	12	6
Dec.	2	5	0
1884—June	0	5	0
Dec.	2	0	0

MARYPORT AND CARLISLE.

		£	s.	d.
1845	Dec.	£2	0	0
1846	June	Nil.		
	Dec.	Nil.		
1847	June	1	10	0
	Dec.	1	10	0
1848	June	Nil.		
	Dec.	Nil.		
1849	June	Nil.		
	Dec.	Nil.		
1850	June	Nil.		
	Dec.	1	10	0
1851	June	1	10	0
	Dec.	2	0	0
1852	June	1	10	0
	Dec.	2	0	0
1853	June	1	10	0
	Dec.	2	0	0
1854	June	1	10	0
	Dec.	2	0	0
1855	June	1	10	0
	Dec.	2	0	0
1856	June	2	0	0
	Dec.	2	10	0
1857	June	2	10	0
	Dec.	2	10	0
1858	June	2	0	0
	Dec.	2	5	0
1859	June	£3	10	0
	Dec.	3	5	0
1860	June	3	5	0
	Dec.	3	10	0
1861	June	3	10	0
	Dec.	3	10	0
1862	June	3	0	0
	Dec.	3	10	0
1863	June	4	0	0
	Dec.	4	10	0
1864	June	5	0	0
	Dec.	5	10	0
1865	June	4	10	0
	Dec.	5	0	0
1866	June	4	15	0
	Dec.	4	15	0
1867	June	3	15	0
	Dec.	3	15	0
1868	June	3	15	0
	Dec.	3	15	0
1869	June	4	0	0
	Dec.	4	10	0
1870	June	5	0	0
	Dec.	6	0	0
1871	June	6	5	0
	Dec.	6	10	0
1872	June	£6	0	0
	Dec.	6	10	0
1873	June	6	10	0
	Dec.	6	10	0
1874	June	5	10	0
	Dec.	6	0	0
1875	June	6	0	0
	Dec.	5	10	0
1876	June	5	10	0
	Dec.	5	0	0
1877	June	5	10	0
	Dec.	6	0	0
1878	June	5	0	0
	Dec.	5	0	0
1879	June	4	0	0
	Dec.	4	15	0
1880	June	5	0	0
	Dec.	5	10	0
1881	June	5	0	0
	Dec.	5	10	0
1882	June	5	10	0
	Dec.	5	0	0
1883	June	5	0	0
	Dec.	4	15	0
1884	June	4	7	6
	Dec.	4	10	0

METROPOLITAN.

		£	s.	d.
1863	June	£2	10	0
	Dec.	2	10	0
1864	June	2	15	0
	Dec.	3	10	0
1865	June	3	10	0
	Dec.	3	10	0
1866	June	3	10	0
	Dec.	3	10	0
1867	June	3	10	0
	Dec.	3	10	0
1868	June	3	10	0
	Dec.	2	5	0
1869	June	2	0	0
	Dec.	2	0	0
1870	June	1	12	6
1870	Dec.	£1	12	6
1871	June	1	17	6
	Dec.	1	7	6
1872	June	0	10	0
	Dec.	1	0	0
1873	June	1	5	6
	Dec.	1	0	0
1874	June	1	5	0
	Dec.	1	10	0
1875	June	1	17	6
	Dec.	2	0	0
1876	June	2	0	0
	Dec.	2	2	6
1877	June	2	5	0
	Dec.	2	0	0
1878	June	£2	0	0
	Dec.	2	10	0
1879	June	2	10	0
	Dec.	2	10	0
1880	June	2	10	0
	Dec.	2	10	0
1881	June	2	10	0
	Dec.	2	10	0
1882	June	2	10	0
	Dec.	2	10	0
1883	June	2	10	0
	Dec.	2	10	0
1884	June	2	10	0
	Dec.	2	10	0

MIDLAND.

Bristol and Gloucester.

		£	s.	d.
1838	June	£2	10	0
	Dec.	2	10	0
1839	June	1	5	0
	Dec.	1	5	0
1840	June	2	10	0
	Dec.	2	10	0
1841	June	2	10	0
	Dec.	2	10	0
1842	June	2	0	0
	Dec.	2	0	0
1843	June	2	10	0
	Dec.	2	10	0
1844	June	2	15	0
	Dec.	2	0	0
1845	June	1	14	0
	Dec.	3	0	0
1846	June	3	0	0

Merged into the Midland at 6 per cent.

Birmingham and Derby.

		£	s.	d.
1840	June	1	0	0
	Dec.	0	15	0
1841	June	1	2	6
	Dec.	1	2	6
1842	June	£0	12	0
	Dec.	1	0	0
1843	June	0	5	0
	Dec.	1	8	0
1844	June	1	6	8

Midland Counties.

		£	s.	d.
1841	June	2	10	0
	Dec.	2	0	0
1842	June	1	10	0
	Dec.	1	10	0
1843	June	1	4	0
	Dec.	2	4	0
1844	June	2	2	6

North Midland.

		£	s.	d.
1841	June	2	0	0
	Dec.	1	10	0
1842	June	1	0	0
	Dec.	1	12	6
1843	June	1	19	0
	Dec.	2	0	0
1844	June	2	2	0

Birmingham and Gloucester.

		£	s.	d.
1841	June	0	15	0
	Dec.	0	15	0
1842	June	£0	12	6
	Dec.	0	12	6
1843	June	0	12	0
	Dec.	1	10	0
1844	June	1	5	0
	Dec.	2	0	0
1845	June	2	0	0
	Dec.	3	0	0
1846	June	3	0	0

Merged into the Midland at 6 per cent.

Leeds and Bradford.

		£	s.	d.
1846	Dec.	2	10	0
1847	June	2	10	0
	Dec.	2	10	0
1848	June	2	10	0
	Dec.	2	10	0
1849	June	5	0	0

Leased to Mid. at 10 pr cent.

Midland.

		£	s.	d.
1844	Dec.	3	0	0
1845	June	3	0	0
	Dec.	3	13	0
1846	June	3	10	0
	Dec.	3	10	0

MIDLAND—*Continued.*

1847—June	£3	10	0
Dec.	3	10	0
1848—June	3	0	0
Dec.	2	10	0
1849—June	1	10	0
Dec.	1	5	0
1850—June	0	16	0
Dec.	1	5	0
1851—June	1	5	0
Dec.	1	7	6
1852—June	1	10	0
Dec.	1	12	6
1853—June	1	12	6
Dec.	1	12	6
1854—June	1	15	0
Dec.	1	17	6
1855—June	1	15	0
Dec.	1	17	6
1856—June	2	0	0
Dec.	2	2	6
1857—June	2	2	6
Dec.	2	10	0
1858—June	2	2	6
Dec.	2	15	0
1859—June	2	12	6
Dec.	3	0	0
1860—June	£3	5	0
Dec.	3	10	0
1861—June	3	2	6
Dec.	3	10	0
1862—June	2	15	0
Dec.	3	5	0
1863—June	2	17	6
Dec.	3	10	0
1864—June	3	10	0
Dec.	3	17	6
1865—June	3	5	0
Dec.	3	10	0
1866—June	3	0	0
Dec.	3	2	6
1867—June	2	15	0
Dec.	2	15	0
1868—June	2	10	0
Dec.	2	17	6
1869—June	2	17	0
Dec.	3	5	6
1870—June	3	2	6
Dec.	3	7	6
1871—June	3	5	0
Dec.	3	15	0
1872—June	3	10	0
1872—Dec.	£3	15	0
1873—June	3	5	0
Dec.	3	5	0
1874—June	2	15	0
Dec.	3	5	0
1875—June	3	0	0
Dec.	3	0	0
1876—June	2	10	0
Dec.	2	17	6
1877—June	2	10	0
Dec	2	17	6
1878—June	2	10	0
Dec.	2	17	6
1879—June	2	10	0
Dec.	3	2	6
1880—June	3	0	0
Dec.	3	2	6
1881—June	2	15	0
Dec.	3	2	6
1882—June	2	15	0
Dec.	3	2	6
1883—June	2	15	0
Dec.	3	2	6
1884—June	2	10	0
Dec.	2	17	6

MIDLAND GREAT WESTERN.

1847—Dec.	£2	0	0
1848—June	2	0	0
Dec.	2	0	0
1849—June	2	0	0
Dec.	2	0	0
1850—June	Nil.		
Dec.	Nil.		
1851—June	Nil.		
Dec.	2	0	0
1852—June	2	0	0
Dec.	2	10	0
1853—June	2	10	0
Dec.	2	10	0
1854—June	2	10	0
Dec.	2	10	0
1855—June	2	10	0
Dec.	2	10	0
1856—June	2	10	0
Dec.	2	10	0
1857—June	2	10	0
Dec.	2	10	0
1858—June	2	10	0
Dec.	2	10	0
1859—June	2	10	0
Dec.	2	10	0
1860—June	£2	10	
Dec.	2	10	0
1861—June	2	10	0
Dec.	2	10	0
1862—June	2	10	0
Dec.	2	10	0
1863—June	2	5	0
Dec.	2	5	0
1864—June	2	0	0
Dec.	1	0	0
1865—June	1	2	6
Dec.	1	5	0
1866—June	1	5	0
Dec.	1	5	0
1867—June	1	5	0
Dec.	1	7	6
1868—June	1	5	0
Dec.	1	10	0
1869—June	1	10	0
Dec.	1	15	0
1870—June	1	15	0
Dec.	2	0	0
1871—June	2	0	0
Dec.	2	2	6
1872—June	2	0	0
1872—Dec.	£2	5	0
1873—June	2	5	0
Dec.	2	5	0
1874—June	1	15	0
Dec.	2	5	0
1875—June	2	0	0
Dec.	2	10	0
1876—June	2	10	0
Dec.	2	10	0
1877—June	2	10	0
Dec	2	10	0
1878—June	2	10	0
Dec.	2	0	0
1879—June	1	0	0
Dec.	1	10	0
1880—June	2	0	0
Dec	1	10	0
1881—June	1	0	0
Dec.	1	10	0
1882—June	1	10	0
Dec.	2	0	0
1883—June	1	15	0
Dec.	1	12	6
1884—June	1	10	0
Dec.	1	10	0

NORTH BRITISH.

Monkland.			
1852—Dec.	£1	15	0
1853—June	1	15	0
Dec.	2	0	0
1854—June	2	5	0
Dec.	2	7	6
1855—June	2	15	0
Dec.	3	5	0
1856—June	3	5	0
Dec.	3	10	0
1857—June	4	0	0
Dec.	4	0	0
1858—June	3	10	0
Dec.	4	0	0
1859—June	4	0	0
Dec.	4	0	0
1860—June	3	0	0
Dec.	3	5	0
1861—June	£2	15	0
Dec.	2	15	0
1862—June	2	15	0
Dec.	2	15	0
1863—June	2	5	0
Dec.	2	5	0
1864—June	2	10	0
Dec.	2	10	0
1865—June	2	10	0
Merged in the North British at 6 per cent.			
Edinburgh and Glasgow.			
1842—July	2	10	0
1843—Jan.	2	10	0
July	2	5	0
1844—Jan.	2	10	0
July	2	5	0
1845—Jan.	2	10	0
1845—July	£3	0	0
1846—Jan.	3	0	0
July	3	0	0
1847—Jan.	4	0	0
July	3	0	0
1848—Jan.	Nil.		
July	3	0	0
1849—Jan.	3	0	0
July	2	0	0
1850—Jan.	1	10	0
July	1	5	0
1851—Jan.	1	10	0
July	1	10	0
1852—Jan.	1	10	0
July	1	10	0
1853—Jan.	1	10	0
July	1	10	0
1854—Jan.	1	10	0

NORTH BRITISH—*Continued.*

1854—July	£1 10 0
1855—Jan.	1 10 0
July	1 10 0
1856—Jan.	1 0 0
July	1 0 0
1857—Jan.	1 5 0
July	1 10 0
1858—Jan.	1 12 6
July	1 10 0
1859—Jan.	1 12 6
July	1 12 6
1860—Jan.	1 12 6
July	2 0 0
1861—Jan.	2 2 6
July	2 2 6
1862—Jan.	2 2 6
July	1 10 0
1863—Jan.	1 10 0
July	1 10 0
1864—Jan.	2 0 0
July	2 5 0
1865—Jan.	2 10 0
July	2 12 6
1866—Jan.	2 5 0
July	Nil.
1867—Jan.	Nil.
July	Nil.
1868—Jan.	Nil.
July	Nil.
1869—Jan.	0 6 0
July	0 8 6
1870—Jan.	0 18 9
July	0 1 3
1871—Jan.	1 2 6
July	0 12 6
1872—Jan.	2 5 0
July	2 5 0
1873—Jan.	2 5 0
July	2 5 0
1874—Jan.	0 12 6
July	1 0 0
1875—Jan.	£2 5 0
July	2 5 0
1876—Jan.	2 12 6
July	2 10 0

North British.

1847—July	2 10 0
1848—Jan.	2 10 0
July	2 10 0
1849—Jan.	2 0 0
July	1 10
1850—Jan.	1 0 0
July	Nil.
1851—Jan.	Nil.
July	Nil.
1852—Jan.	Nil.
July	Nil.
1853—Jan.	Nil.
July	Nil.
1854—Jan.	0 7 6
July	Nil.
1855—Jan.	Nil.
July	Nil.
1856—Jan.	Nil.
July	1 5 0
1857—Jan.	1 5 0
July	1 7 6
1858—Jan.	1 7 6
July	1 7 6
1859—Jan.	1 7 6
July	1 10 0
1860—Jan.	1 10 0
July	1 10 0
1861—Jan.	1 12 6
July	1 10 0
1862—Jan.	1 10 0
July	0 10 0
1863—Jan.	0 7 6
July	0 12 0
1864—Jan.	0 17 6
July	1 0 0
1865—Jan.	£1 6 3
July	1 10 0
1866—Jan.	1 10 0
July	Nil.
1867—Jan.	Nil.
July	Nil.
1868—Jan.	Nil.
July	Nil.
1869—Jan.	Nil.
July	Nil.
1870—Jan.	Nil.
July	Nil.
1871—Jan.	Nil.
July	Nil.
1872—Jan.	0 12 6
July	0 15 0
1873—Jan.	0 6 3
July	Nil.
1874—Jan.	Nil.
July	Nil.
1875—Jan.	0 15 0
July	2 0 0
1876—Jan.	2 2 6
July	1 15 0
1877—Jan.	2 0 0
July	1 0 0
1878—Jan.	1 5 0
July	1 2 6
1879—Jan.	1 12 6
July	Nil.
1880—Jan	Nil.
July	0 10 0
1881—Jan.	1 0 0
July	1 0 0
1882—Jan.	2 2 6
July	1 5 0
1883—Jan.	2 10 0
July	1 10 0
1884—Jan.	2 15 0
July	1 15 0

NORTH EASTERN.

York and North Midland.

1839—Dec.	£3 10 0
1840—June	3 10 0
Dec.	3 10 0
1841—June	4 10 0
Dec.	5 0 0
1842—June	5 0 0
Dec.	5 0 0
1843—June	5 0 0
Dec.	5 0 0
1844—June	5 0 0
Dec.	5 0 0
1845—June	5 0 0
Dec.	5 0 0
1846—June	5 0 0
Dec.	5 0 0
1847—June	5 0 0
Dec.	5 0 0
1848—June	4 0 0
Dec.	6 0 0
1849—June	Nil.
Dec.	1 0 0
1850—June	0 5 0
Dec.	1 0 0
1851—June	0 10 0
Dec.	1 0 0
1852—June	0 10 0
Dec.	1 10 0
1853—June	0 15 0
Dec.	1 10 0
1854—June	£1 2 6
Dec.	1 7 6
1855—June	1 0 0
Dec.	1 12 6
1856—June	1 5 0
Dec.	1 17 6
1857—June	2 0 0
Dec.	2 0 0
1858—June	1 10 0
Dec.	2 0 0
1859—June	1 12 6
Dec.	2 5 0
1860—June	2 2 6
Dec.	2 10 0
1861—June	2 5 0
Dec.	2 5 0
1862—June	1 10 0
Dec.	2 5 0
1863—June	1 10 0
Dec.	2 10 0
1864—June	2 7 6
Dec.	2 17 6
1865—June	2 10 0
Dec.	3 2 6
1866—June	2 10 0
Dec.	2 15 0
1867—June	2 2 6
Dec.	2 15 0
1868—June	1 17 6
Dec.	2 15 0
1869—June	£2 12 6
Dec.	3 12 6

Great North of England.

1841—June	1 0 6
Dec.	2 10 0
1842—June	1 5 0
Dec.	1 5 0
1843—June	1 5 0
Dec.	1 12 6
1844—June	1 12 6
Dec.	3 0 0
1845—June	3 0 0
Dec.	5 0 0

Leased to York, Newcastle, and Berwick, at 10 per cent.

Newcastle and Darlington.

1844—Dec.	4 0 0
1845—June	4 0 0
Dec.	4 10 0
1846—June	4 10 0
Dec.	4 10 0
1847—June	4 10 0

York, Newcastle, & Berwick.

1847—Dec.	4 10 0
1848—June	4 0 0
Dec.	3 0 0
1849—June	Nil.
Dec.	1 7 6

NORTH EASTERN—*Continued*.

1850—June	£1	5	0
Dec.	1	15	9
1851—June	1	10	0
Dec.	1	10	0
1852—June	1	7	6
Dec.	1	10	0
1853—June	1	10	0
Dec.	2	0	0
1854—June	1	17	6
Dec.	2	0	0
1855—June	1	15	0
Dec.	2	5	0
1856—June	2	0	0
Dec.	2	7	6
1857—June	2	10	0
Dec.	2	10	0
1858—June	2	2	6
Dec.	2	7	6
1859—June	2	2	6
Dec.	2	12	6
1860—June	2	12	6
Dec.	2	17	6
1861—June	2	12	6
Dec.	2	10	0
1862—June	2	2	6
Dec.	2	10	0
1863—June	2	2	6
Dec.	2	15	0
1864—June	2	15	0
Dec.	3	2	6
1865—June	2	15	0
Dec.	3	5	0
1866—June	2	15	0
Dec.	3	0	0
1867—June	2	10	0
Dec.	3	0	0
1868—June	2	5	0
Dec.	3	0	0
1869—June	2	17	6
Dec.	3	12	6

Leeds Northern.

1857—June	1	0	0
Dec.	1	5	0
1858—June	0	16	3
Dec.	1	3	9
1859—June	0	17	6
Dec.	1	7	6
1860—June	1	7	6
Dec.	1	10	0
1861—June	1	8	9
Dec.	1	7	6
1862—June	0	18	9
Dec.	1	7	6
1863—June	0	18	9
Dec.	1	10	0
1864—June	1	11	3
Dec.	1	18	9
1865—June	1	12	6
Dec.	2	1	3
1866—June	1	12	6
Dec.	1	15	0
1867—June	1	5	0
Dec.	1	15	0
1868—June	1	1	3
Dec.	1	15	0
1869—June	1	13	9
Dec.	2	10	0

Newcastle and Carlisle.

1839—June	3	0	0
Dec.	3	0	0
1840—June	3	0	0
Dec.	3	0	0
1841—June	£2	10	0
Dec.	2	10	0
1842—June	2	0	0
Dec.	2	0	0
1843—June	2	0	0
Dec.	2	0	0
1844—June	2	10	0
Dec.	2	10	0
1845—June	2	10	0
Dec.	2	10	0
1846—June	2	15	0
Dec.	2	15	0
1847—June	3	0	0
Dec.	3	0	0
1848—June	3	0	0
Dec.	3	0	0
1849—June	2	5	0
Dec.	2	5	0
1850—June	2	0	0
Dec.	2	0	0
1851—June	2	0	0
Dec.	2	0	0
1852—June	2	0	0
Dec.	2	0	0
1853—June	2	0	0
Dec.	2	0	0
1854—June	2	5	0
Dec.	2	15	0
1855—June	2	10	0
Dec.	2	10	0
1856—June	2	10	0
Dec.	3	0	0
1857—June	2	10	0
Dec.	5	0	0
1858—June	2	7	6
Dec.	3	0	0
1859—June	2	15	0
Dec.	3	10	0
1860—June	3	2	6
Dec.	3	17	6
1861—June	3	2	6
Dec.	3	10	0
1862—June	3	0	0
Dec.	3	10	0
1863—June	3	0	0
Dec.	3	12	6
1864—June	3	10	0
Dec.	4	0	0
1865—June	3	15	0
Dec.	4	5	0
1866—June	3	15	0
Dec.	3	17	6
1867—June	3	7	6
Dec.	4	0	0
1868—June	3	2	6
Dec.	4	0	0
1869—June	3	15	0
Dec.	4	10	0

Stockton and Darlington.

1854—June	3	15	0
Dec.	4	10	0
1855—June	4	10	0
Dec.	4	10	0
1856—June	4	10	0
Dec.	5	0	0
1857—June	5	0	0
Dec.	5	0	0
1858—June	4	5	0
Dec.	4	15	0
1859—June	4	15	0
Dec.	4	10	0
1860—June	4	10	0
1860—Dec.	£4	15	0
1861—June	4	10	0
Dec.	4	5	0
1862—June	3	15	0
Dec.	4	0	0
1863—June	3	15	0
Dec.	4	0	0
1864—June	4	0	0
Dec.	4	10	0
1865—June	4	2	6
Dec.	4	12	6
1866—June	4	2	6
Dec.	4	5	0
1867—June	3	12	6
Dec.	4	2	6
1868—June	3	5	0
Dec.	4	2	6
1869—June	4	0	0
Dec.	5	0	0

Blyth and Tyne.

1853—Dec.	4	0	0
1854—June	4	10	0
Dec.	4	10	0
1855—June	4	10	0
Dec.	4	10	0
1856—June	4	10	0
Dec.	4	0	0
1857—June	3	5	0
Dec.	3	10	0
1858—June	4	0	0
Dec.	4	5	0
1859—June	4	10	0
Dec.	4	15	0
1860—June	4	15	0
Dec.	5	0	0
1861—June	4	15	0
Dec.	4	15	0
1862—June	4	15	0
Dec.	4	15	0
1863—June	4	15	0
Dec.	4	15	0
1864—June	4	15	0
Dec.	4	15	0
1865—June	4	15	0
Dec.	5	0	0
1866—June	5	0	0
Dec.	5	0	0
1867—June	5	0	0
Dec.	5	0	0
1868—June	5	0	0
Dec.	5	0	0
1869—June	4	10	0
Dec.	5	0	0
1870—June	5	0	0
Dec.	5	0	0
1871—June	5	0	0
Dec.	6	5	0
1872—June	6	5	0
Dec.	6	5	0
1873—June	5	0	0

Consols.

1870—June	£3	12	6
Dec.	4	5	0
1871—June	4	2	6
Dec.	5	0	0
1872—June	4	5	0
Dec.	4	15	0
1873—June	4	5	0
Dec.	5	0	0
1874—June	3	12	6
Dec.	4	12	6
1875—June	4	2	6

NORTH EASTERN—*Continued.*

Year	Half	£	s.	d.
1875	Dec.	£4	7	6
1876	June	3	10	0
	Dec.	3	17	6
1877	June	3	5	0
	Dec.	3	12	6
1878	June	3	0	0
	Dec.	3	10	0
1879	June	£2	10	0
	Dec.	3	7	6
1880	June	4	0	0
	Dec.	4	5	0
1881	June	3	15	0
	Dec.	4	5	0
1882	June	£3	15	0
	Dec.	4	7	6
1883	June	3	17	6
	Dec.	4	7	6
1884	June	3	7	6
	Dec.	3	10	0

NORTH LONDON.

Year	Half	£	s.	d.
1851	Dec.	£1	1	0
1852	June	1	0	0
	Dec.	1	10	0
1853	June	1	15	0
	Dec.	2	10	0
1854	June	2	10	0
	Dec.	2	0	0
1855	June	2	0	0
	Dec.	2	0	0
1856	June	2	5	0
	Dec.	2	10	0
1857	June	2	5	0
	Dec.	2	5	0
1858	June	2	10	0
	Dec.	2	10	0
1859	June	2	10	0
	Dec.	2	15	0
1860	June	2	10	0
	Dec.	2	15	0
1861	June	2	10	0
	Dec.	2	15	0
1862	June	2	10	0
	Dec.	3	0	0
1863	June	£3	0	0
	Dec.	3	10	0
1864	June	3	0	0
	Dec.	3	0	0
1865	June	3	0	0
	Dec.	3	0	0
1866	June	3	0	0
	Dec.	2	15	0
1867	June	2	15	0
	Dec.	3	0	0
1868	June	3	0	0
	Dec.	3	0	0
1869	June	3	5	0
	Dec.	3	5	0
1870	June	3	5	0
	Dec.	3	0	0
1871	June	3	0	6
	Dec.	3	0	0
1872	June	3	0	0
	Dec.	3	0	3
1873	June	2	15	0
	Dec.	2	15	0
1874	June	£2	10	6
	Dec.	2	10	0
1875	June	3	0	0
	Dec.	3	0	0
1876	June	3	0	0
	Dec.	3	5	0
1877	June	3	5	0
	Dec.	3	7	6
1878	June	3	12	6
	Dec.	3	12	6
1879	June	3	12	6
	Dec.	3	15	0
1880	June	3	15	0
	Dec.	3	15	0
1881	June	3	15	0
	Dec.	3	15	0
1882	June	3	15	0
	Dec.	3	15	0
1883	June	3	15	0
	Dec.	3	15	0
1884	June	3	15	0
	Dec.	3	15	0

NORTH STAFFORDSHIRE.

Year	Half	£	s.	d.
1848	June	£1	16	3
	Dec.	Nil.		
1849	June	0	17	6
	Dec.	Nil.		
1850	June	Nil.		
	Dec.	1	0	0
1851	June	0	14	3
	Dec.	0	17	6
1852	June	0	17	6
1853	June	1	10	0
	Dec.	1	10	0
1854	June	1	12	6
	Dec.	1	15	0
1855	June	Nil.		
	Dec.	2	0	0
1856	June	1	15	0
	Dec.	1	15	0
1857	June	2	0	0
	Dec.	2	0	0
1858	June	1	0	0
	Dec.	1	5	0
1859	June	1	10	0
	Dec.	2	0	0
1860	June	2	0	0
	Dec.	2	0	0
1861	June	£1	15	0
	Dec.	1	10	0
1862	June	1	10	0
	Dec.	1	15	0
1863	June	1	15	0
	Dec.	2	0	0
1864	June	2	0	0
	Dec.	2	5	0
1865	June	1	15	0
	Dec.	2	2	6
1866	June	2	0	0
	Dec.	2	0	0
1867	June	1	10	0
	Dec.	1	15	0
1868	June	1	5	0
	Dec.	1	7	6
1869	June	1	5	0
	Dec.	1	10	0
1870	June	1	5	0
	Dec.	1	10	0
1871	June	1	10	0
	Dec.	2	0	0
1872	June	1	15	0
	Dec.	1	15	0
1873	June	£1	5	0
	Dec.	1	7	6
1874	June	0	10	0
	Dec.	1	5	0
1875	June	0	17	6
	Dec.	1	5	0
1876	June	0	15	0
	Dec.	1	2	6
1877	June	0	17	6
	Dec.	1	2	6
1878	June	0	12	6
	Dec.	1	0	0
1879	June	0	15	0
	Dec.	1	5	0
1880	June	1	12	6
	Dec.	1	10	0
1881	June	1	0	0
	Dec.	1	10	0
1882	June	1	7	6
	Dec.	1	17	6
1883	June	1	15	0
	Dec.	2	5	0
1884	June	1	15	0
	Dec.	2	0	0

SOUTH EASTERN.

Year	Half	£	s.	d.
1844	July	£1	11	3
1845	Jan.	2	6	3
	July	2	10	0
1846	Jan.	2	12	6
	July	2	12	6
1847	Jan.	3	3	0
	July	3	3	0
1848	Jan.	3	3	0
	July	3	3	0
1849	Jan.	2	8	0
	July	1	11	0
1850	Jan.	1	10	0
	July	1	10	0
1851	Jan.	£1	13	4
	July	1	6	8
1852	Jan.	1	15	0
	July	1	5	0
1853	Jan.	1	16	8
	July	1	6	8
1854	Jan.	2	0	0
	July	1	8	4
1855	Jan.	1	13	4
	July	1	8	4
1856	Jan.	2	4	2
	July	1	11	8
1857	Jan.	2	10	0
1857	July	£1	10	0
1858	Jan.	2	6	8
	July	1	10	0
1859	Jan.	2	10	0
	July	2	0	0
1860	Jan.	3	0	0
	July	2	6	8
1861	Jan.	3	0	0
	July	2	1	8
1862	Jan.	2	10	0
	July	2	2	6
1863	Jan.	3	0	0
	July	2	5	0

SOUTH EASTERN—*Continued.*

1864—Jan.	£3	18	4
July	2	2	6
1865—Jan.	2	17	6
July	1	5	0
1866—Jan.	2	5	0
July	1	8	9
1867—Jan.	1	10	0
July	1	0	0
1868—Jan.	2	0	0
July	1	2	6
1869—Jan.	2	0	0
July	1	5	0
1870—Jan.	2	0	0
July	1	5	0
1871—Jan.	2	0	9
1871—July	£1	6	3
Dec.	3	0	0
1872—June	1	15	0
Dec.	3	5	0
1873—June	1	15	0
Dec.	3	5	0
1874—June	1	15	0
Dec.	3	5	0
1875—June	1	17	6
Dec.	3	15	0
1876—June	1	17	6
Dec.	3	15	0
1877—June	1	15	0
Dec.	3	15	0
1878—June	£2	0	0
Dec.	4	0	0
1879—June	1	10	0
Dec.	3	12	6
1880—June	2	0	0
Dec.	4	0	0
1881—June	1	15	0
Dec.	4	0	0
1882—June	1	15	0
Dec	3	10	0
1883—June	1	10	0
Dec.	3	12	6
1884—June	1	15	0
Dec.	3	2	6

TAFF VALE.

1850—June	£3	0	0
Dec.	3	4	0
1851—June	3	12	0
Dec.	3	12	0
1852—June	3	12	0
Dec.	3	12	0
1853—June	3	12	6
Dec.	3	15	0
1854—June	3	15	0
Dec.	3	15	0
1855—June	3	15	0
Dec.	3	15	0
1856—June	4	0	0
Dec.	4	0	0
1857—June	4	0	0
Dec.	4	0	0
1858—June	3	15	0
Dec.	3	15	0
1859—June	4	0	0
Dec.	4	0	0
1860—June	4	0	0
Dec.	4	10	0
1861—June	4	5	0
Dec.	4	5	0
1862—June	£4	10	0
Dec.	4	10	0
1863—June	4	10	0
Dec.	5	0	0
1864—June	5	0	0
Dec.	5	0	0
1865—June	5	0	0
Dec.	4	10	0
1866—June	4	10	0
Dec.	5	0	0
1867—June	4	0	0
Dec.	4	10	0
1868—June	4	5	0
Dec.	4	10	0
1869—June	4	15	0
Dec.	5	0	0
1870—June	5	0	0
Dec	5	0	0
1871—June	5	0	0
Dec.	5	0	0
1872—June	5	0	0
Dec.	5	0	0
1873—June	6	0	0
1873—Dec.	£6	0	0
1874—June	5	0	0
Dec	6	0	0
1875—June	2	10	0
Dec.	6	0	0
1876—June	6	0	0
Dec.	6	0	0
1877—June	6	0	0
Dec.	6	0	0
1878—June	6	0	0
Dec.	6	0	0
1879—June	5	10	0
Dec.	6	0	0
1880—June	7	0	0
Dec	8	0	0
1881—June	8	0	0
Dec.	8	10	0
1882—June	9	0	0
Dec.	8	10	0
1883—June	9	0	0
Dec.	8	0	0
1884—June	8	0	0
Dec.	7	0	0

WATERFORD AND LIMERICK.

1856—June	Nil.		
Dec.	£0	10	0
1857—June	Nil.		
Dec.	Nil.		
1858—June	Nil.		
Dec.	0	10	0
1859—June	0	10	0
Dec.	1	0	0
1860—June	0	10	0
Dec.	1	0	0
1861—June	0	10	0
Dec.	1	0	0
1862—June	0	10	0
Dec.	0	15	0
1863—June	0	10	0
Dec.	0	10	0
1864—June	0	5	0
Dec.	0	10	6
1865—June	0	2	6
Dec.	0	10	0
1866—June	£0	2	6
Dec.	0	10	0
1867—June	0	5	0
Dec.	Nil.		
1868—June	Nil.		
Dec.	Nil.		
1869—June	Nil.		
Dec.	0	10	0
1870—June	0	10	0
Dec.	1	10	0
1871—June	1	5	0
Dec.	1	10	0
1872—June	1	10	0
Dec.	0	17	6
1873—June	1	5	0
Dec.	1	10	0
1874—June	1	10	0
Dec.	1	5	0
1875—June	Nil.		
1875—Dec.	£1	15	0
1876—June	0	10	0
Dec.	1	15	0
1877—June	1	5	0
Dec.	3	10	0
1878—June	2	0	0
Dec.	1	15	0
1879—June	1	0	0
Dec.	1	10	0
1880—June	1	10	0
Dec.	1	5	0
1881—June	0	10	0
Dec.	1	0	0
1882—June	Nil.		
Dec.	1	0	0
1883—June	Nil.		
Dec.	Nil.		
1884—June	Nil.		
Dec.	Nil.		

7.—MILES OPENED IN THE UNITED KINGDOM IN 1884.

		When Opened	Mls.
Ballymena and Larne	Ballyclare to Doagh	May 1st.	2
Belfast and Northern Counties	Kingsbog Junction to Ballyclare	Nov. 3rd.	3¼
Bridport	Bridport to Bridport (West Bay)	March 31st.	2
Clara and Banagher	Clara to Banagher	May 29th.	18¾
Eastern and Midlands	Melton Constable to Holt	Oct. 1st.	5
East London	(See Metropolitan and Metropolitan District).		
Edinburgh Suburban and Southside Junction	Haymarket to Portobello	Dec. 1st.	8¼
Great Eastern	Fordham to Cambridge	June 2nd.	12
Great Northern	Denholme to Ingrow	April 7th.	4¾
Do.	Ingrow to Keighley	Nov. 1st.	1¼
Great North of Scotland	Portsoy to Tochineal	April 1st.	4¼
Do.	Elgin to Garmouth	Aug. 12th.	8½
Great Western	Weston-Super-Mare Loop	March 1st.	4
Do.	West Drayton to Colnbrook	Aug. 9th.	2¾
Highland	Keith to Portessie	Aug. 1st.	13⅛
Hounslow and Metropolitan	(See Metropolitan District)		
Jersey	St. Aubin to La Corbeire	Sept. 1st.	3¾
Leominster and Bromyard	Leominster to Steens Bridge	March 1st.	4
London, Brighton, and South Coast	Croydon to East Grinstead	March 10th.	19⅛
London, Brighton, and South Coast, & South Eastern Joint	Oxted to Crowhurst	Aug.	¾
London, Chatham, and Dover	Maidstone to Ashford	July 1st.	18¾
London and North Western	Penclawd to Llanmorlais	March 1st.	1¾
Do.	Kenilworth to Berkswell	June 2nd.	4⅛
Do.	Bangor to Bethesda	July 1st.	4¼
Do.	Sutton Coldfield to Lichfield	Dec.	8¼
London and South Western	Lymington to Lymington Pier	June	⅛
London, Tilbury, & Southend.	Southend to Shoeburyness	Feb. 1st.	3¾
Lydd	Lydd to New Romney	June 19th.	3
Manchester, Sheffield, and Lincolnshire	Glossop Loop	March 23rd	½
Metropolitan	Minories Junction to Whitechapel Extension	Oct. 6th.	⅓
Do.	North Curve Junction to Whitechapel Extension	" "	⅛
Metropolitan and Metropolitan District Joint	Inner Circle—Aldgate to Mansion House	" "	1
Do. (Leased)	St. Mary's, Whitechapel, to East London Main Line	March 3rd.	¼
Metropolitan District	Osterley to Hounslow Barracks	July 21st.	1⅛
Do.	St. Mary's, whitechapel, to Whitechapel, Mile End	Oct. 6th.	⅛
Midland	Brownhills to Aldridge	July 1st.	4
Do.	Woodville to Ashby	Sept. 1st.	2
Oldbury		Nov. 7th.	1¼
Southport and Cheshire Lines Extension	Aintree to Southport	Sept.	14½
Tiverton and North Devon	Tiverton to Morebath Junction	Aug. 1st	8⅛
Wigan Junction	Glazebrook to Wigan	April 1st.	11¼
Total Mileage		....	208⅞

8.—RAILWAY TELEGRAPH SUPERINTENDENTS, 1885.

Railway.	Telegraph Superintendent.
Brecon and Merthyr	Mr. J. B. Saunders, Cardiff.
Bristol and Exeter	Mr. F. Haynes, Taunton.
Bute Docks and Railway	Mr. J. B. Saunders, Cardiff.
Caledonian	Mr. A. S. Dunn, 25, Killermont Street, Glasgow.
Cambrian	Mr. J. B. Saunders, Cardiff.
Central Wales	Mr. J. B. Saunders, Cardiff.
Festiniog	Mr. J. B. Saunders, Cardiff.
Glasgow and South Western	Mr. James Reid, Glasgow.
Great Eastern	Mr. Henry Sach, Liverpool Street, E.C.
Great Northern	Mr. J. Radcliffe, Retford.
Great Western	Mr. C. E. Spagnoletti, Paddington, W.
Lancashire and Yorkshire	Mr. E. C. Warburton, Manchester.
Llanelly	Mr. Lloyd, Llanelly.
London, Brighton, and South Coast	Mr. E. J. Houghton, London Bridge, S.E.
London, Chatham, and Dover	Mr. F. Rudall, Victoria Station, S.W.
London and North Western	Mr. J. W. Fletcher, London Road, Manchester.
London and South Western	Mr. C. Goldstone, Southampton.
Manchester, Sheffield, & Lincolnshire	Mr. Scatcherd, Godley Junc., near Manchester.
Metropolitan	Mr. Spagnoletti, Gt. Western, Paddington, W.
Midland	Mr. W. Langdon, Derby.
Midland and South Western Junction	Mr. J. B. Saunders, Cardift.
Mid Wales	Mr. J. B. Saunders, Cardiff.
North British	Mr. A. F. Clement, North Bridge, Edinburgh.
North Eastern	Mr. A. Graves, York.
North Staffordshire	Mr. J. Neale, Stoke-on-Trent.
Pontypridd, Caerphilly, and Newport	Mr. J. B. Saunders, Cardiff.
Rhymney	Mr. J. B. Saunders, Cardiff.
Shrewsbury and Hereford	Mr. Spagnoletti, Gt. Western, Paddington, W.
Somerset and Dorset	Mr. J. B. Saunders, Cardiff.
South Eastern	Mr. W. Leonard, Tunbridge.
Stamford and Essendine	Mr. Radcliffe, Great Northern, Retford.
Taff Vale	Mr. J. B. Saunders, Cardiff.
West Lancashire	Mr. J. Lavender, 11, Todd Street, Manchester.
Wrexham, Mold, and Connah's Quay	Mr. J. B. Saunders, Cardiff.

9.—POWER OF ATTORNEY FOR RECEIPT OF DIVIDENDS.

The following is an extract from Schedule C to the Act 27 Vic., cap. 18 (passed 13th May, 1864), referring to the above subject:—

Letters or Powers of Attorney, Proxies, &c. (that is to say), for or upon any Letter or Power of Attorney:

For the Sale, Transfer, or Acceptance of any of the Government or Parliamentary Stocks or Funds:

If the value of such Stocks or Funds shall exceed £20	£1 0 0
And if such value shall not exceed £20	0 5 0

For the receipts of Dividends or Interest on any of the Government or Parliamentary Stocks or Funds, or of the Stocks, Funds, or Shares of or in any Joint Stock Company, or other Company or Society, whose Stocks or Funds are divided into Shares and transferable

If the same shall be for the receipts of one payment only	£0 1 0
And if the same shall be for a continuous receipt, or for the receipt of more than one payment	0 5 0

10.—TRAFFIC RECEIPTS IN THE UNITED KINGDOM.

The subjoined Table shows the traffic receipts of the principal lines in the United Kingdom for the half-year ended 31st December, 1884, compared with the corresponding period of 1883.

Company.	Weeks.	1884. Receipts.	1884. Miles open.	Weeks.	1883. Receipts.	1883. Miles open.
Belfast and County Down *e*	26	38,547	68	26	37,239	68
Belfast and Northern Counties	26	96,460	136	26	93,733	136½
Brecon and Merthyr *h*	26	33,129	61½	26	38,339	61
Caledonian	26	1,501,408	772	26	1,530,045	766¾
Cambrian	26	96,626	180½	26	95,907	180¾
Cheshire Lines	26	102,781	121¾	26	101,304	121
Cockermouth, Keswick, and Penrith	26	19,414	31	26	21,645	31½
Cornwall *a*	26	74,922	65½	26	74,702	65½
Eastern and Midlands *a g*	26	32,512	101½	26	29,892	96
Furness	26	242,561	139	26	278,201	139
Glasgow and South Western *a*	26	559,805	329	26	578,910	329
Great Eastern *a c*	26	1,751,653	919¾	26	1,750,824	907
Great Northern *a d*	26	1,944,550	943	26	1,949,060	928
Great Northern (Ireland)	26	330,711	467	26	319,163	467
Great North of Scotland	21	136,431	301	21	133,112	289
Great Southern and Western	26	337,739	474	26	356,625	474
Great Western *a*	26	3,900,991	2301	26	4,093,560	2282
Highland	21	150,372	423	21	154,022	409½
Isle of Wight	26	15,733	12	26	15,884	12
Kilkenny Junction	8	2,020	28	8	1,948	28½
Lancashire and Yorkshire	26	1,951,712	496½	26	1,941,618	496½
London, Brighton, and South Coast *a*	26	1,130,106	455½	26	1,131,759	435½
London, Chatham, and Dover *a b*	26	658,258	175	26	661,124	166½
London and North Western	26	5,270,087	1792¼	26	5,322,142	1774
London and South Western	26	1,406,947	798	26	1,304,029	798½
London, Tilbury, and Southend	26	55,039	49½	26	76,721	45½
Manchester, Sheffield, and Lincolnshire, and South Yorkshire *a f*	26	976,312	290¾	26	988,054	290¾
Maryport and Carlisle	26	61,079	41¾	26	65,833	41¾
Metropolitan *a*	26	317,639	19¾	26	318,652	18¾
Metropolitan District *a*	26	207,624	14	26	196,840	12¾
Midland *a*	26	3,765,500	1264	26	3,829,058	1260
Midland Great Western	26	228,837	370	26	230,592	370
Mid Wales	26	18,901	48½	26	18,052	48½
North British	26	1,353,886	984¼	26	1,378,354	984¼
North Eastern *a*	26	3,264,662	1536	26	3,553,204	1536
North London	26	217,747	12	26	221,386	12
North Staffordshire	26	331,422	193	26	344,076	193
Pembroke and Tenby	26	14,917	27	26	14,656	27
Rhymney	26	63,261	63¾	26	79,093	63¾
South Eastern *b*	26	1,064,068	385	26	1,113,976	382
Taff Vale	26	374,248	90	26	375,625	90
Waterford and Central Ireland	13	8,694	31	13	8,941	31
Waterford and Limerick *i*	26	100,237	272	26	104,333	272
Wrexham, Mold, and Connah's Quay	26	17,126	16	26	16,271	16

a The 1883 receipts are adjusted to the actual figures. *b* Includes the receipts of steam boats. *c* Includes 116¾ miles of joint line. *d* Includes 165 miles of foreign lines worked, and 156 miles of joint line—Great Northern proportion. *e* Includes receipts of the Belfast, Holywood, and Bangor from September 1st, 1884, and corresponding period. *f* Exclusive of the earnings of joint lines. *g* Exclusive of Midland and Eastern, and Peterborough, Wisbech, and Sutton sections. *h* Includes net tollage in 1883 on traffic from Pontypridd. *i* Includes 131 miles of joint lines.

11.—BANK RATES OF DISCOUNT.

The dates and duration of minimum rates of discount, from 1836 to 1894, inclusive, have been as follow:—

Year.	Date.	⅌ cent.	Year.	Date.	⅌ cent.
1836	July 21	4½	1858	February 4	3½
,,	September 1	5	,,	February 11	3
1838	February 15	4	,,	December 9	2½
1839	May 16	5	1859	April 28	3½
,,	June 20	5½	,,	May 5	4½
,,	August 1	6	,,	June 2	3½
1840	January 23	5	,,	June 9	3
1841	June 3	5	,,	July 14	2½
1842	April 7	4	1860	January 19	3
1845	March 13	2½	,,	January 31	4
,,	October 16	3	,,	March 29	4½
,,	November 6	3½	,,	April 12	5
1846	August 27	3	,,	May 10	4½
1847	January 14	3½	,,	May 24	4
,,	January 21	4	,,	November 8	4½
,,	April 8	5	,,	November 13	5
,,	August 2	6	,,	November 15	6
,,	August 5	5½	,,	November 29	5
,,	October 1	6	,,	December 31	6
,,	October 25	8	1861	January 7	7
,,	November 22	7	,,	February 14	8
,,	December 2	6	,,	March 21	7
,,	December 23	5	,,	April 4	6
1848	January 27	4	,,	April 11	5
,,	June 15	3½	,,	April 16	6
,,	November 22	3	,,	August 1	5
1849	November 22	2½	,,	August 14	4½
1850	December 26	3	,,	August 29	4
1852	January 1	2½	,,	September 19	3½
,,	April 22	2	,,	November 7	3
1853	January 6	2½	1862	January 9	2½
,,	January 20	3	,,	May 22	3
,,	June 2	3½	,,	July 10	2½
,,	September 1	4	,,	July 24	2
,,	September 15	4½	,,	October 30	3
,,	September 29	5	1863	January 15	4
1854	May 11	5½	,,	January 28	5
,,	August 3	5	,,	February 19	4
1855	April 5	4½	,,	April 23	3½
,,	May 3	4	,,	April 30	3
,,	June 14	3½	,,	May 16	3½
,,	September 6	4	,,	May 21	4
,,	September 13	4½	,,	Novembe 2	5
,,	September 27	5	,,	November 5	6
,,	October 4	5½	,,	December 2	7
,,	October 18	7	,,	December 3	8
1856	May 22	6	,,	December 24	7
,,	May 29	5	1864	January 20	8
,,	June 26	4½	,,	February 11	7
,,	October 1	5	,,	February 25	6
,,	October 6	7	,,	April 16	7
,,	November 13	7	,,	May 2	8
,,	December 4	6½	,,	May 5	9
,,	December 18	6	,,	May 19	8
1857	August 2	6½	,,	May 26	7
,,	June 18	6	,,	June 16	6
,,	July 16	5½	,,	July 25	7
,,	October 8	6	,,	August 4	8
,,	October 12	7	,,	September 8	9
,,	October 19	8	,,	November 10	8
,,	November 5	9	,,	November 24	7
,,	November 9	10	,,	December 15	6
,,	December 24	8	1865	January 12	5½
1858	January 7	6	,,	January 26	5
,,	January 14	5	,,	March 2	4½
,,	January 8	4	,,	March 30	4

BANK RATES OF DISCOUNT—*Continued.*

Year.	Date.	℔ cent.
1865	May 4	4½
,,	May 25	4
,,	June 1	3½
,,	June 15	3
,,	July 27	3½
,,	August 3	4
,,	September 27	4½
,,	October 2	5
,,	October 5	6
,,	October 7	7
,,	November 23	6
,,	December 28	7
1866	January 4	8
,,	January 6	8
,,	February 22	7
,,	March 15	6
,,	May 3	7
,,	May 8	8
,,	May 11	9
,,	May 12	10
,,	August 16	8
,,	August 23	7
,,	August 30	6
,,	September 6	5
,,	September 27	4½
,,	November 8	4
,,	December 20	3½
1867	January 7	3
,,	May 29	2½
,,	July 24	2
1868	November 19	2½
,,	December 3	3
1869	April 8	4
,,	May 6	4½
,,	June 10	4
,,	June 24	3½
,,	July 15	3
,,	August 19	2½
,,	November 4	3
1870	July 21	3½
,,	July 23	4
,,	July 28	5
,,	August 4	6
,,	August 11	5½
,,	August 18	4½
,,	August 25	4
,,	September 1	3½
,,	September 15	3
,,	September 29	2½
1871	March 2	3
,,	April 13	2½
,,	June 15	2½
,,	July 13	2
,,	September 21	3
,,	September 28	4
,,	October 7	5
,,	November 16	4
,,	November 30	3½
,,	December 14	3
1872	April 4	3½
,,	April 11	4
,,	May 9	5
,,	May 30	4
,,	June 13	3½
,,	June 20	3
,,	July 18	3½
,,	September 18	4
,,	September 26	4½
,,	October 3	5
1872	October 10	6
,,	November 9	7
,,	November 28	6
,,	December 12	5
1873	January 9	4½
,,	January 23	4
,,	January 30	3½
,,	March 26	4
,,	May 7	4½
,,	May 10	5
,,	May 17	6
,,	June 4	7
,,	June 12	6
,,	July 10	5
,,	July 17	4½
,,	July 24	4
,,	July 31	3½
,,	August 21	3
,,	September 25	4
,,	September 29	5
,,	October 14	6
,,	October 18	7
,,	November 1	8
,,	November 7	9
,,	November 20	8
,,	November 27	6
,,	December 4	5
,,	December 11	4½
1874	January 8	4
,,	January 15	3½
,,	April 30	4
,,	May 28	3½
,,	June 4	3
,,	June 19	2½
,,	July 30	3
,,	August 6	4
,,	August 20	3½
,,	August 27	3
,,	October 15	4
,,	November 16	
,,	November 30	6
1875	January 7	5
,,	January 14	4
,,	January 28	3
,,	February 18	3½
,,	July 8	3
,,	July 29	2½
,,	August 12	2
,,	October 7	2½
,,	October 14	3½
,,	October 21	4
,,	November 18	3
,,	December 30	4
1876	January 6	5
,,	January 27	4
,,	March 23	3½
,,	April 6	3
,,	April 20	2
1877	May 3	3
,,	July 5	2½
,,	July 12	2
,,	August 28	3
,,	October 4	4
,,	October 11	5
,,	November 29	4
1878	January 10	3
,,	January 31	2
,,	March 23	3
,,	May 30	2½

BANK RATES OF DISCOUNT—*Continued.*

Year.	Date.	℔ cent.	Year.	Date.	℔ cent.
1878	June 27	3	1882	February 23	5
,,	July 5	3½	,,	March 9	4
,,	August 1	4	,,	March 23	3
,,	August 12	5	,,	August 17	4
,,	October 14	6	,,	September 14	5
,,	November 21	5	1883	January 25	4
1879	January 16	4	,,	February 15	3½
,,	January 30	3	,,	March 1	3
,,	March 13	2½	,,	May 10	4
,,	April 10	2	,,	September 13	3½
,,	November 6	3	,,	September 27	3
1880	June 17	2½	1884	February 7	3½
,,	Dec-mber 9	3	,,	March 13	3
1881	January 13	3½	,,	April 3	2½
,,	February 17	3	,,	June 19	2
,,	April 28	2½	,,	October 9	3
,,	August 18	3	,,	October 30	4
,,	August 25	4	,,	November 6	5
,,	October 6	5	1885	January 29	4
1882	January 30	6			

12.—METHOD OF CALCULATING INTEREST AT FIVE PER CENT.

Multiply the principal by the number of days, and divide by 7,300. Example: To find the interest at 5 per cent. on £312 for 260 days

$$\frac{312 \times 260}{7{,}300} = £11\ 2s.\ 3d.$$

The interest at 5 per cent. being found as above, interest at 3 per cent. is found by multiplying the interest so found by 3, and dividing by 5; at 3½, 4, or 4½ per cent., by multiplying by the rate required, and dividing by 5; and at 2½, by taking half the interest at 5 per cent.

IV.—RAILWAY DIRECTORY, &c., 1885.

1.—LIST OF DIRECTORS AND OFFICERS.

NOTE.—The figures in this list refer to the numbers attached to each Railway, and *not* to the folios of the "*Manual*."

***** All are *Directors* when not otherwise specified.**

Abbott, Major-General Saunders A., 362, 404
Abbott Samuel, Esq , C.E., 347
Abbotts R. W., Esq.. 276
Aberdeen, The Rt. Hon. the Earl of, 121; Trustee, 594
Abernethy James, Esq., F.R.S.E., M.Inst.-C.E., Eng., 136
Acton William, Esq., 79
Adam, Mons. Achille, 267
Adam J. S., Esq., Sec.. 3
Adam Thomas, Esq., 121
Adams B. H., Esq., Auditor, 400
Adamson William Rushton, Esq., 241
Adams T., Esq., Auditor, 63
Adams Thomas, Esq., 295; Auditor, 174, 371
Adams William, Esq., Loco. and Car. Supt., 172
Adderley, The Hon. H. Arden, 437
Addison John, Esq., M.Inst.C.E., 185
Adler M. N., Esq , Auditor, 356
Adorno, Señor Don Juan N., 400
Affleck James, Esq.. Auditor, 218
Agar Samuel H., Esq., 131
Agnew, Sir Andrew, Bart., 238
Agnew Robert Vans, Esq., 313
Ailesbury, The Marquis of, 184, 198, 212
Ainslie Daniel, Esq., 40, 41
Ainsworth David, Esq., M.P., 185
Ainsworth John S., Esq., 52
Aitken William, Esq., 93, 206
Akers Henry Esq., 315
Albright Arthur, Esq., 225
Aldin Charles, Esq., 117
Alexander, Gen. Sir James, K.C.B., 364
Alexander J., Esq., 212
Alexander J., Esq., Asst. Supt., 117
Alexander James D., Esq., 379
Alexander John, Esq., 251
Alexander John S., Esq., Auditor, 15
Alexander Robert Jackson, Esq., D.L., 15
Alexander Samuel Maxwell, Esq., D.L., J.P., 22, 158
Alington Julius, Esq., 291
Alison John W., Esq., Sec., 65
Allan Thomas Henry, Esq., Auditor, 359
Allen George, Esq., Auditor, 245
Allen George Wm., Esq.. C.I.E., 354
Alleyne Forster M., Esq., 437
Allison Robert Andrew, Esq., 193
Allmand John, Esq., Auditor, 317
Allport, Sir James Joseph, Knt., 49, 193, 259, 285
Allsopp Samuel Charles, Esq., M.P., 101, 117, 119
Altham Thomas, Esq., 55
Amey David, Esq., Sec., 83
Anderson David, Esq., Audit Acct., 213
Anderson John, Esq., 23
Anderson John, Esq., Sec., 41
Anderson John, jun., Esq., 102
Anderton E. D., Esq., 63
Andrew, Sir William Patrick, C.I.E., 362
Andrews Thomas, Esq., 21
Annes W. L., Esq., 148
Anyon George H., Esq., Acct., 52
Appleby Henry, Esq., Loco. Supt., 297
Archer Henry, Esq., Auditor, 23, 45
Argyle, His Grace the Duke of, 41
Armstrong G. A., Esq., Eng., 118
Armstrong Henry, Esq., 274
Armstrong John Chinnery, Esq., B.L., 60
Armstrong Richard Owen, Esq., 80, 196
Armstrong Robert Clifton, Esq., Auditor, 134
Armstrong Wm. C. Heaton, Esq., 142
Armytage George John, Esq., 127, 153
Arnott, Sir John, Knt., D.L., 62
Ashton Arthur, Esq., 368
Ashton, Major Howarth, 155
Ashton Robert How, Esq., 75
Ashworth Edward, Esq., 386
Ashworth Howard H., Esq., Auditor, 83
Aslett Alfred, Esq., Traff. Man. and Accountant, 86
Aspinall John A. F., Esq., Loco. Supt., 122
Astell John Harvey, Esq., 117, 252, 4?5
Aston William, Esq., Loco. Supt., 43
Atcherley J. R., Esq., Auditor, 310
Athole, His Grace the Duke of, 1?3
Atkinson Charles R., Esq., M.Inst.C.E., 106; Eng., 118
Atock Martin, Esq., Loco. Supt., 196
Atwool Josiah, Esq., 384
Auckland, The Rt. Hon. Lord, 49, 181, 259, 305
Audus Thomas, Esq., Mineral Traff. Man., 215
Austin Thomas K., Esq., J.P., 59
Austin William, Esq., 247, 339
Avery W. H., Esq., Goods Man., 63
Awdry West, Esq., 42
Ayers J. D., Esq., Sec., 427
Aylmer Hugh, Esq., 76
Ayres Edmund, Esq., 336

Babbage James, Esq., 256
Bacon John E., Esq., Sec., 232
Badham R. L., Esq., Transfer Officer, 196
Bagshawe Wm. Henry Greaves, Esq., 75
Bailey Crawshay, Esq., 18, 232
Bailey R. W., Esq., Min. Traff. Man., 215
Bailey Wm. George, Esq., Sec., 58
Baily Laurence R., Esq., 49, 117, 368
Bain David Wise, Esq., 129
Bain J. R., Esq., 58
Baker J. B., Esq., Auditor, 66, 166

2.—CANALS.

3.—AUXILIARY ASSOCIATIONS.

4.—THE RAILWAY INTEREST IN PARLIAMENT.

HOUSE OF LORDS.

Aberdeen, Earl.—Great North of Scotland

Ailesbury, Marquis. — Marlborough; Midland and South Western Junction; Northampton and Banbury Junction.

Argyle, Duke.—Callander and Oban.

Athole, Duke.—Highland.

Auckland, Lord.—Cheshire Lines; Manchester, Sheffield, and Lincolnshire; Sheffield and Midland; West Riding and Grimsby.

Beaumont, Lord.—East and West Yorkshire Union; Hull, Barnsley, and West Riding Junction.

Bedford, Duke.—Plymouth, Devonport, and South Western Junction.

Bessborough, Earl.—Birkenhead; Great Western; Waterford and Limerick; West London.

Borthwick, Lord.—Wigtownshire.

Brabourne Lord.—Cranbrook and Paddock Wood; East London; Metropolitan; South Eastern; Metaurense Valley; Grahams Town and Port Alfred Limited (Cape of Good Hope).

Breadalbane, Earl.—Caledonian; Callander and Oban.

HOUSE OF LORDS—*Continued.*

Buckingham and Chandos, Duke.—Oxford, Aylesbury, and Metropolitan Junction.
Colville, Lord.—Cheshire Lines; Forth Bridge; Great Northern; Great Northern and London and North Western Joint; Royston and Hitchin.
Derwent, Lord.—North Eastern.
Devon, Earl.—Kingsbridge and Salcombe; Limerick and Kerry; Rathkeale and Newcastle Junction; Ravenglass and Eskdale; Tralee and Fenit.
Devonshire, Duke.—Fermoy and Lismore; Furness.
Eglinton and Winton, Earl.—Lanarkshire and Ayrshire.
Erne, Earl.—Great Northern (Ireland)
Fife, Earl.—Highland.
Forester, Lord.—Much Wenlock and Severn Junction.
Galloway, Earl.—Portpatrick; Wigtownshire.
Gough, Viscount.—Midland Great Western.
Glasgow, Earl.—Lanarkshire and Ayrshire.
Hardinge, Viscount.—Great Northern and Western.
Hawke, Lord. — Buenos Ayres Great Southern
Henniker, Lord.—Mellis and Eye.
Hothfield, Lord.—South Eastern.
Houghton, Lord.—Lancashire & Yorkshire.
Jersey, Earl.—Rhondda and Swansea Bay.
Kilmorey, Earl.—Dundalk, Newry, and Greenore.
Kintore, Earl.—Great North of Scotland.
Lifford, Viscount.—Finn Valley; West Donegal.
Lovat, Lord.—Highland.
Lucan, Earl.—Great Northern & Western.
Lyttelton, Lord.—Birkenhead; Great Western; Oldbury; West London.
Powis, Earl.—Shropshire Union.
Robartes, Lord.—Cornwall
Stair, Earl.—Portpatrick.
Sutherland, Duke.—Highland; London and North Western; Shropshire Union.
Templetown, Viscount.—Belfast & Northern Counties; Carrickfergus and Larne.
Thurlow, Lord. — Highland; Metaurense Valley.
Tredegar, Lord.—Alexandra (Newport and South Wales) Docks and Railway.
Tweeddale, Marquis.—North British.
Wharncliffe, Earl.—Cheshire Lines; Manchester, Sheffield, and Lincolnshire; North Cornwall; Sheffield and Midland; West Riding and Grimsby.
Windsor, Lord.—Barry Dock and Railways; Penarth Extension.

HOUSE OF COMMONS.

Ainsworth D. (West Cumberland).—Maryport and Carlisle.
Allsop S. C. (Taunton)—Forth Bridge; Great Northern; Great Northern and London and North Western Joint.
Balfour, Sir G. (Kincardineshire).—New York, Pennsylvania, and Ohio.
Baring T. C. (South Essex).—Russia.
Baring, Viscount (Winchester).—Didcot, Newbury, and Southampton.
Bass, Sir M. A., Bart. (East Staffordshire). Midland.
Beach W. W. B. (North Hants).—Bodmin and Wadebridge; Kingston and London; London and South Western.
Biddulph M. (Herefordshire).—Midland.
Bolton J. C. (Stirlingshire).—Caledonian; Callander and Oban.
Brassey H. A. (Sandwich). — Central Argentine.
Brassey, Sir T., K.C.B. (Hastings).—Wenlock; Dutch Rhenish.
Bruce, Sir H. H., Bart. (Coleraine).—Derry Central.
Bruce, Hon. T. C. (Portsmouth).—Highland; London and North Western; Portpatrick.
Carden, Sir R. W. (Barnstaple).—Royston and Hitchin.
Cavendish, Lord E. (North Derbyshire).—Furness.
Cecil, Lord E. H. B. G. (West Essex).—Northern and Eastern.
Chaine J. (Antrim Co.)—Ballymena and Larne; Ballymena and Portglenone; Carrickfergus and Larne.
Clarke J. C. (Abingdon). — Abingdon; Blackpool.
Clive, Lieut.-Col. G. H. W. W. (Ludlow).—Penarth Extension; Penarth Harbour, Dock, and Railway.
Cochran-Patrick R. W. (North Ayrshire).—City of Glasgow Union; Glasgow and South Western.
Collins E. (Kinsale).—Ilen Valley.
Cotton, Alderman W. J. R. (London).—Staines and West Drayton.
Cropper J. (Kendal).—Cockermouth, Keswick, and Penrith.
Cross, Sir R. A., G.C.B. (South West Lancashire).—Manchester, Sheffield, and Lincolnshire.
Crum A. (Renfrewshire).—Caledonian.
Davies D. (Cardigan Borough). — Barry Dock and Railways; Van.
Dickson, Major A. G. (Dover).—East and West Junction; Hounslow and Metropolitan; London, Chatham, and Dover; Grand Trunk of Canada.
Dick-Peddie J. (Kilmarnock).—Metaurense Valley.
Dillwyn L. L. (Swansea).—Great Western; West London Extension; Whitland and Cardigan.
Eckersley N. (Wigan).—Blackpool; Wigan Junction.
Elliot, Sir G., Bart. (North Durham).—Alexandra (Newport and South Wales) Docks and Railway.
Elliot G. W. (Northallerton).—Alexandra (Newport and South Wales) Docks and Railway.
Fairbairn, Sir A. (York, West Riding, East).—Great Northern; Halifax and Ovenden; Royston and Hitchin; West Riding and Grimsby.
Fellowes W. H. (Huntingdonshire).—Great Northern.
Findlater W. (Monaghan).—Dublin and Meath.
Fremantle, Hon. T. F. (Bucks).—London, Brighton, and South Coast; West London Extension.

HOUSE OF COMMONS—*Continued.*

Freshfield C. K. (Dover). — Ottoman-Smyrna to Aidin; East Indian.
Gladstone W. H. (East Worcestershire).—Wirral Limited.
Glyn, Hon. S. C. (Shaftesbury).—North London.
Goldney, Sir G., Bart. (Chippenham).—Buenos Ayres and Pacific Limited.
Gooch, Sir D. (Cricklade).—Bala and Festiniog; Birkenhead; Great Western; Llanelly; Newent; Oldbury; Princetown; Ross and Ledbury; Tiverton and North Devon; West London.
Gourley E. T. (Sunderland).—Corris.
Grosvenor, Rt. Hon. Lord R. (Flintshire).—London and North Western; Shropshire Union.
Gurdon R. T. (South Norfolk).—Northern and Eastern.
Hamilton, Lord Claud John (Liverpool).—Downham and Stoke Ferry; Great Eastern; King's Lynn Docks (with Railways); Tottenham and Hampstead Junction; Chicago and Grand Trunk; Grand Trunk Junction; Grand Trunk of Canada.
Hardy, Hon. J. S. G. (Mid Kent).—Cranbrook and Paddock Wood.
Hastings G. W. (East Worcestershire).—Worcester, Bromyard, and Leominster.
Hay, Rt. Hon. Sir J. C. D. (Wigtown).—Portpatrick.
Heathcoat-Amory, Sir J. H. (Tiverton).—Tiverton and North Devon.
Hicks-Beach, Rt. Hon. Sir M. E. (East Gloucestershire).—East Gloucestershire.
Hill T. R. (Worcester).—Worcester, Bromyard, and Leominster.
Holland S. (Merioneth).—Bala and Festiniog; Merionethshire.
Howard J. (Bedfordshire).—Bedford and Northampton.
Jackson W. L. (Leeds).—Great Northern; Halifax and Ovenden; West Riding and Grimsby.
Jenkins, Sir J. J., Knt. (Carmarthen)—Llanelly and Mynydd Mawr; Rhondda and Swansea Bay.
Kennard C. J. (Salisbury).—Arica and Tacna (Peru).
Kennaway, Sir J. H. (East Devon).—Sidmouth.
Laing S. (Orkney and Shetland).—London, Brighton, and South Coast.
Lawson, Sir W., Bart. (Carlisle).—Maryport and Carlisle.
Lee H. (Southampton).—Didcot, Newbury, and Southampton.
Lennox, Lord H. G. C. G. (Chichester).—Uruguay Central and Hygueritas.
Lewis C. E. (Londonderry).—Atlantic First Leased Lines Rental Trust Limited; New York, Pennsylvania, and Ohio.
Lloyd M. (Beaumaris).—Merionethshire; Minas Central of Brazil Limited.
Lopes, Sir Massey (South Devon).—Cornwall; Great Western; Princetown.
Lowther, Hon. W. (Westmorland).—Dundalk, Newry, and Greenore; London and North Western; Shropshire Union.
Loyd-Lindsay, Lieut.-Colonel R. J. (Berkshire).—Didcot, Newbury, and Southampton.
MacIver D. (Birkenhead).—Bala and Festiniog; Great Western.
Macpherson-Grant, Sir G., Bart. (Elgin and Nairn).—Highland.
Maitland W. F. (Brecknock).—Northern and Eastern.
Makins, Col. W. T. (South Essex).—Great Eastern.
Mappin F. T. (East Retford).—Midland; Midland and North Eastern Joint.
Martin P., Q.C. (Co. Kilkenny).—Waterford and Limerick.
Mason H. (Ashton).—Midland.
Nolan, Colonel J. P. (Co. Galway).—Athenry and Tuam.
Northcote H. S. (Exeter).—St Lawrence and Ottawa.
Otway, Sir A. J., Bart. (Rochester).—Ottoman-Smyrna to Aidin.
Palmer G. (Reading).—Didcot, Newbury, and Southampton.
Pease, Sir J. W. Bart (South Durham).—North Eastern.
Pemberton E. L. (East Kent).—London, Chatham, and Dover.
Pender J. (Wick).—Isle of Man; Oude and Rohilkund.
Plunket D. R. (Dublin University).—Dundalk, Newry, and Greenore; London and North Western; Chicago and Grand Trunk; Grand Trunk Junction; Grand Trunk of Canada.
Price Sir R. G., Bart. (Radnorshire).—Kington and Eardisley.
Pulley J. (Hereford)—Buenos Ayres Great Southern; Buenos Ayres and Rosaric.
Raikes, Rt. Hon. H. C. (Cambridge University).—Mersey; New York, Pennsylvania, and Ohio.
Rankin J. (Leominster).—Leominster and Bromyard.
Ridley, Sir M. W., Bart. (North Northumberland).—Forth Bridge; North Eastern.
Robertson H. (Shrewsbury).—Llangollen and Corwen; Seacombe, Hoylake, and Deeside; Vale of Llangollen; Wellington & Severn Junction; Wirral Limited.
Rothschild, Sir N. M. de (Aylesbury).—Northern of France; South Austrian.
St. Aubyn W. N. M. (Helston).—Helston.
Salt T. (Stafford).—North Staffordshire.
Shaw W. (Co. Cork).—Cork and Bandon.
Smith, Lieut.-Col. G. (Wycombe).—Hull, Barnsley, and West Riding Junction.
Stafford, Marquis of (Sutherland).—Great Northern and London and North Western Joint; London and North Western.
Talbot C. R. M. (Glamorganshire).—Great Western.
Thornhill T. (West Suffolk).—Northern and Eastern.
Tremayne J. (S. Devon).—North Cornwall.
Tyler, Sir H. W. (Harwich).—Great Eastern; Chicago and Grand Trunk; Grand Trunk Junction; Grand Trunk of Canada.
Verney, Sir H., Bart. (Buckingham).—Aylesbury and Buckingham; Oxford, Aylesbury, and Metropolitan Junction.
Vivian, Sir H. H., Bart. (Glamorgan).—Rhondda and Swansea Bay.
Walter J. (Berkshire).—Didcot, Newbury, and Southampton.
Waterlow, Sir S. H., Bart. (Gravesend).—London, Chatham, and Dover.

HOUSE OF COMMONS—*Continued.*

Watkin, Sir E. W., Bart. (Hythe).—Blackpool; Cheshire Lines; East London; Manchester, Sheffield, and Lincolnshire; Manchester, South Junction, and Altrincham; Metropolitan; Oldham, Ashton-under-Lyne, and Guide Bridge; Sheffield and Midland Joint; South Eastern; Wigan Junc

Waugh E. (Cockermouth).—Cockermouth, Keswick, and Penrith.

Whitworth B. (Drogheda).—Metropolitan.

Wiggin H. (East Staffordshire).—Midland.

Williamson S. (St. Andrews).—Copiapo (Chili).

Willyams E. W. B. (Truro).—Newquay and Cornwall Junction.

Wynn, Sir W. W., Bart. (Denbighshire).—Great Western; Llangollen and Corwen.

SUMMARY.

Directors in the House of Lords 45
,, in the House of Commons ... . 108=153

AUXILIARY ASSOCIATIONS.

HOUSE OF LORDS.

Hatherton, Lord—Staffordshire and Worcestershire Canal.

HOUSE OF COMMONS.

Corbett J. (Droitwich)—Sharpness New Docks and Gloucester and Birmingham Canal.

Fowler H. H. (Wolverhampton)—Railway Rolling Stock.

Mappin F. T. (East Retford)—Bridgewater Navigation Limited.

Mason H. (Ashton)—Bridgewater Navigation Limited.

Rylands P. (Burnley)—Bridgewater Navigation Limited.

Stanton A. J. (Stroud)—Sharpness New Docks, and Gloucester and Birmingham Canal.

SUMMARY.

Directors in the House of Lords 1
,, in the House of Commons .... 6=7

5.—COMMITTEE OF PRIVY COUNCIL FOR TRADE.

WHITEHALL GARDENS, S.W.

President—The Right Hon. JOSEPH CHAMBERLAIN, M.P.
Parliamentary Secretary—John Holms, Esq., M.P.
Permanent Secretary—Sir Thomas Henry Farrer, Bart.
Assistant Secretaries (Harbour Department)—C. Cecil Trevor, Esq., C.B.
,, (Marine ,,)—Thomas Gray, Esq.
,, (Railway ,,)—Henry G. Calcraft, Esq.
,, (Finance ,,)—Allen Stoneham, Esq.
Commercial Department (and Comptroller of Corn Returns)—Robert Giffen, Esq.
Junior Assistant Secretary—G. J. Swanston, Esq.
Private Secretary to the President—I. B. Walker, Esq.
Private Secretary to the Parliamentary and Permanent Secretaries—R. C. Heron Maxwell, Esq.
Principals—C. L. Bell, W. C. Monkhouse, H. A. Dobson, W. D. W. Lyons, E. Roscoe, A. E. Bateman, Esqrs.
Clerks—Alexander E. Pearson, R. P. P. Bingham, Ingram B. Walker, T. E. Price, J. W. Martyn, Henry R. Bence-Jones, Arthur H. Emberson, R. C. Heron Maxwell, Samuel Waddington, John Taylor, W. H. F. Hardinge, G. J. Stanley, W. J. Howell, G. S. Fry, Esqrs.
Professional Member of Marine Department—Sir Digby Murray, Bart.
Professional Member of Harbour Department—Captain Sir George S. Nares, R.N., K.C.B.
Solicitor—Walter Murton, Esq.
Chief Law Clerk—F. Hargrave Hamel, Esq.
Assistant Law Clerk—R. N. Somers Smith, Esq.
Clerk for Railway Works—Finlay McKenzie, Esq.
Inspector of Life Saving Apparatus—Captain J. F. Prowse, R.N.
Solicitor's Clerks—A. H. Strong, K. E. K. Gough, Esqrs.
Solicitor's Assistant Clerks—E. Gillett, G. C. Vaux, J. Hutchins, Esqrs.
Translator—E. W. Gosse, Esq.
Chief Book-keeper and Actuary—William Vaughan, Esq.
Superintendent of Statistics—G. H. Simmonds, Esq.
Clerk in charge of work under Electric Lighting Act—Sir T. W. Blomefield, Bart.
Assistant Book-keeper—J. M. Bamford, Esq.
Superintendent of Registry and Copying—Thomas Anderson, Esq.
First Class Assistant Clerks—W. W. Leaker, Samuel Bullock, J. Manger Nicolle, J. J. Dilley, Esqrs.

COMMITTEE OF PRIVY COUNCIL FOR TRADE—*Continued.*

Second Class Assistant Clerks—J. J. F. Croker, F. W. Haine. F. C. Pike. G. S. Tovey. Henry Jolliffe. Frank Hardy, Lewis Browne, John Peake, E. Portch, J. Milsted Spencer J. J. Mill, Thomas Thorpe, A. Barnes, P. H. Thomas, Esqrs.

Third Class Assistant Clerks—Arthur Hill, G. W. Sellar, James Quick. D. A. Pollard, G. E. Norman, A. Neeves, F. A. Fahy, P. J. Descours, J. G. Hargreaves, W. Greig, Esqrs.

Lower Division Clerks—J. L. Bendall, S. R. Miles, O. Jones, A. C. W. Gey, C. Thornton, E. Andrews, C. F. Baker, F. Barley, L. Goldie, G. W. Irons, R. J. Lister, J. Nicholls, J. C. Toovey, R. S. Lendrum, A. Mills, W. P. Scogings, R. E. Martyr, T. A Inch, F. H. McLeod, T. Hester, W. A Clark, W. Stanley, C. J. Young, H. C. Watson, E. C. Stoneham, S. G. Spencer, H. L. Tigar, F. W. Freeman, E. J. McDos Santos. G. R. Maskall, J. K. Grubby, H. T. Perry, H. C. Heney, W. H. Thomas, F. L Bamford, F. Briant. H. T. Holmes, B. C. Page, H. Cook, N. Stanger, A. A. Wetzel. N. R Bamford. H. Booth, H. J. Beard, R. F. G. Heatley, M. J. Collins, F. W. Perrett, J. Duffy, C. Jones, H. M. Bennell, A. S. Sudbury, D. Hughes, Esqrs.

Office Keeper and Clerk of Stationery—Henry T. Burgess.

Assistant Office Keeper—Kenneth Macdonald.

First Class Messengers—F. Quelch, T. Simmons, C. Eltenton, H. Turner.

Supernumerary Messenger—W. Johnson.

Second Class Messengers—S. Pace. R. Fish, F. Lloyd, W. J. Ensum, W. Horsfield.

Supernumerary Messenger—P. Horsfield.

Third Class Messengers—W. S. Bennett, J. Patstone, R. Day, T. Pike. F. Welch, C. Mulcock, T. Williams, F. Cook, M. Heeley, W. D. Jones, H. L. Rosser.

Hall Porter—F. Hill.

Firelighter—J. Eastland.

Assistant Firelighter—G. Sayer.

CONSULTATIVE BRANCH OF THE MARINE DEPARTMENT.—82, Basinghall Street, E.C. Engineer Surveyor-in-Chief and Inspector of Chain Cable and Anchor Proving Establishments under Chain Cable and Anchor Acts—T. W. Traill, Esq. C.E., R.N. Assistants—J. Ramsey, P. Samson, and D. G. Watson, Esqrs. Principal Shipwright Surveyor for Iron Ships—J. Winshurst, Esq. Principal Shipwright Surveyor for Wooden Ships—W. H. Turner, Esq. Principal Surveyor for Tonnage—W. Moore, Esq. Draughtsmen—A. Rushton and H. E. Brown, Esqrs. Chief Examiner of Engineers—J. McFarlane Gray, Esq. Principal Examiner in Navigation and Seamanship—G. Beall, Esq. Clerks—F. Harris, W. Kent, T. H. Gurrin, A. D. Samuel, and A. V. Doust, Esqrs.

INSPECTORS OF RAILWAYS.—1, Whitehall, S.W. Chief Inspector—Colonel W. Yolland, R.E., C.B. Inspectors—Colonel F. H. Rich, R.E., Major-Gen. C. S. Hutchinson, R.E., Major F. A Marindin, R.E.

STANDARD WEIGHTS AND MEASURES DEPARTMENT—Supt. H. J. Chaney, Esq.

GENERAL REGISTER AND RECORD OFFICE OF SHIPPING AND SEAMEN.—82, Basinghall Street, E.C. Registrar General of Shipping and Seamen—Robert Jackson, Esq.

BANKRUPTCY OFFICE.—31, Great George Street, S.W. Inspector General—John Smith, Esq. Inspectors—F. Wreford and Edwin Hough, Esqrs.

PATENTS DESIGNS AND TRADE MARKS OFFICE.—25, Southampton Buildings, Chancery Lane, W.C. Comptroller General—H. Reader Lack, Esq.

6.—RAILWAY CLEARING HOUSE.

Seymour Street, Euston Square, N.W.

Chairman—LORD WOLVERTON.

Secretary—P. W. DAWSON, Esq.

Auditors—HARRY CHUBB, Esq., and JOHN CLEGHORN, Esq.

7.—IRISH RAILWAY CLEARING HOUSE.

(23 Vic., cap. 29.)

5, Kildare Street, Dublin.

Chairman—J. W. MURLAND, Esq.

Treasurer—THE BANK OF IRELAND. Secretary—C. A. CLARKE, Esq

8.—THE CORPORATION OF FOREIGN BONDHOLDERS.

(Incorporated 1st August, 1873.)

Chairman of the Council—The Right Hon. E. PLEYDELL-BOUVERIE.

Secretary—CHARLES O'LEARY.

Council House—17, Moorgate Street, E.C.

9.—THE UNITED KINGDOM RAILWAY OFFICERS' AND SERVANTS' ASSOCIATION, AND RAILWAY PROVIDENT SOCIETY.

(Enrolled under Act of Parliament.)

For Pensions, Relief in Sickness, Sum in case of Death of Member or Wife, and for support of Orphans of Railway Servants.

To 31st December, 1884, upwards of **£45,000** were paid for Accidents, and Accidental and Ordinary Deaths, and 69 annuitants have been elected to **£20** each.

TRUSTEES:

The Right Hon. the EARL OF LEVEN and MELVILLE.

The Right Hon. the EARL OF LATHOM.

Major-Gen. LORD ALFRED PAGET, 56, Queen Anne Street, Cavendish Square, W.

Treasurer—JAMES RANKIN, Esq., M.P.

Bankers—NATIONAL PROVINCIAL BANK OF ENGLAND.

Secretary—Mr. JAMES SALMON, F.S.S.

Offices—21, Finsbury Pavement, E.C.

10.—RAILWAY BENEVOLENT INSTITUTION.

For the Relief of Railway Officers and Servants, their Widows, and Orphan Children, when in distressed circumstances.

Established 1858.

Under the Patronage of Her Most Gracious Majesty the Queen, and His Royal Highness the Prince of Wales, K.G.

Invested Fund, £186,000.

President—His Grace the DUKE OF SUTHERLAND, K.G.

TRUSTEES:

The EARL OF BESSBOROUGH, the EARL OF DEVON, and the EARL OF ABERDEEN.

Chairman of Board of Management:

HENRY OAKLEY, Esq., General Manager, Great Northern Railway Company.

Chairman of Committee in Scotland:

W. J. WAINWRIGHT, Esq., General Manager, Glasgow and South Western Railway.

Chairman of Orphanage Committee—JOHN BAILEY, Esq., Derby.

Treasurer—Sir JAMES ALLPORT, Derby.

AUDITORS:

P. W. DAWSON, Esq............R. C. H.
R. SAVILL, Esq. ......Late L. & N. W.
JOHN MORGAN, Esq. ......L. C. & D.
A. FITCH, Esq. ....G. N.
G. HOPWOOD, Esq.................Metropolitan District.

Treasurer—LORD WOLVERTON.

Secretary in Scotland—JOS. TATLOW, St. Enoch Station, Glasgow.

Secretary of the Orphanage—THOS. HALL, Ashbourne Road, Derby.

General Secretary—WILLIAM FREDERICK MILLS.

Offices—57 Drummond Street, Euston Square, London, N.W.

JOHN E. WILLIAMS & CO.,

PAINT MANUFACTURERS

AND

CONTRACTORS FOR PAINTING.

VICTORIA PAINT WORKS, OPENSHAW, MANCHESTER.

OFFICE—6 and 8, FAIRFIELD STREET, MANCHESTER. | **LONDON—2, GRESHAM BUILDINGS, GUILDHALL, E.C.**

TRADE MARK

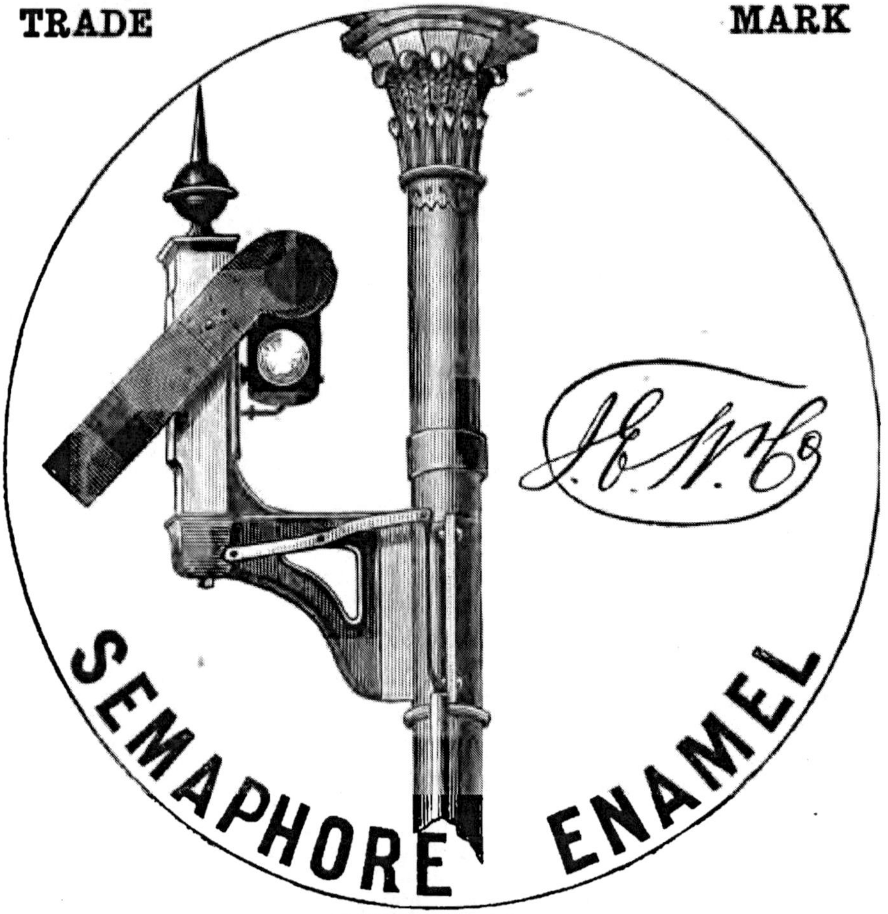

REGISTERED.

Original Manufacturers of the METALLIC OXIDE PAINTS, for Railway Stations, Bridges, Iron Ships, Steel Ships, Machinists, and Agricultural Implement Makers.

SEMAPHORE ENAMELS,

FOR RAILWAY SIGNALS.

Has Hard, Tough, and Glassy Surface; does not Crack, Blister, or Scale off.

JOHN E. WILLIAMS & CO., Manchester.

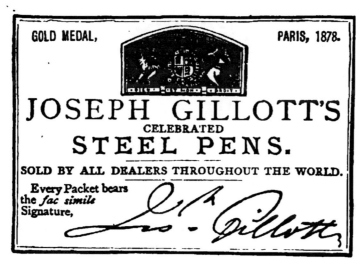

WHITE AND SOUND TEETH.

(Established by sixty years' experience as the best preservative for Teeth and Gums.)

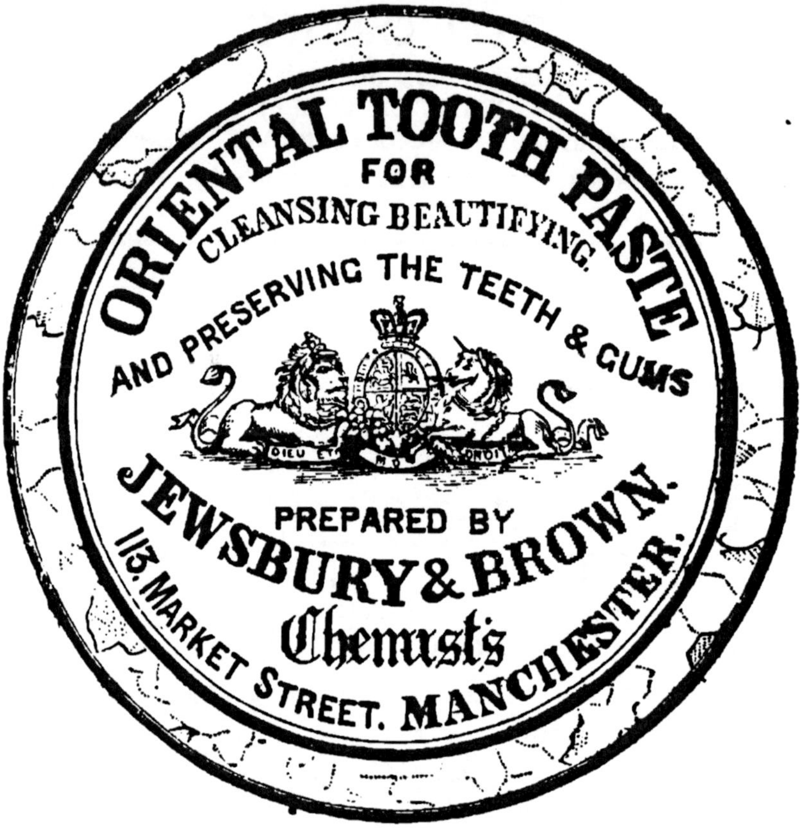

THE ORIGINAL AND ONLY GENUINE IS PREPARED SOLELY BY JEWSBURY AND BROWN, CHEMISTS, MANCHESTER, AND BEARS THE SIGNATURE AND TRADE MARK OF THE PROPRIETORS,

Retailed at 1s. 6d. and 2s. 6d. per Pot by the principal Perfumers, Chemists, &c., throughout the United Kingdom, America, and the Colonies. Warranted to keep in any climate, and supplied by all the leading wholesale houses.

16-B-34

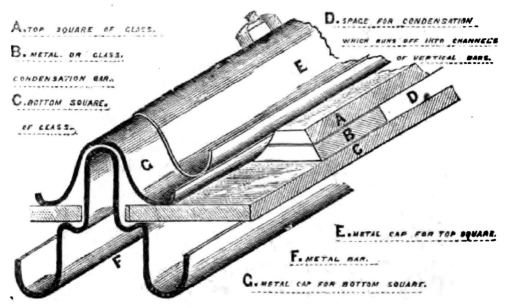

DENTON & JUTSUM,

MANUFACTURERS OF THE

FINEST VARNISHES & JAPANS

DENTON & JUTSUM'S VARNISHES AND JAPANS

Are unrivalled for Brilliancy, Durability, and General Excellence, and are specially prepared for Hot and Cold Climates. See Pamphlet for Testimonials from the largest consumers.

DENTON & JUTSUM'S CELEBRATED MIXED PAINTS,

Ready for use, in Tins of 3lbs. and upwards,

Are of GUARANTEED SUPERIORITY, dry well, and offer many advantages to the general public.

DENTON & JUTSUM'S
METALLIC OXIDE, SILICATE, & ANTI-CORROSIVE PAINTS & COLOURS.

These Paints are manufactured in every shade of colour, and are applicable to every description of exposed work.

DENTON & JUTSUM'S ZINC WHITES.

These whites are for many purposes much superior to White Lead, they are not so liable to turn yellow, and work equally well in oil-flatting or distemper.

DENTON & JUTSUM'S SUPERIOR LUBRICATING OILS

Are in the highest repute for Railway Locomotive, Marine, and Stationary Engines, Railway Carriage Axles, and Machinery generally.

DENTON & JUTSUM'S CELEBRATED GREASES

For Railway Carriages, Collieries, Contractors' Wagons, Carts, &c., &c. Are specially adapted to Railway, Mining, Agricultural, and all Lubricating purposes.

DENTON & JUTSUM'S "EXCELSIOR" CONCENTRATED GREASE

Is unsurpassed for durability and economy for Railways, Tram Cars, Cylinders, and Heavy Machinery.

DENTON & JUTSUM'S GLOBE AND CYLINDER OILS

Are selected from best brands and qualities.

Special Makes of Lardine and Sweet Rosin Oils.

Works: Bow Common, E. | Warehouses: Albert Embankment, S.E.
Offices: Dashwood House, 9, New Broad Street, E.C., LONDON.

Shippers offered UNUSUAL ADVANTAGES and IMMEDIATE ATTENTION given to their Indents. [Lo.-25.

Lightning Source UK Ltd.
Milton Keynes UK
176656UK00007B/103/P

9 781145 791190